CANADA

W9-CNB-017

MINNESOTA
St. Paul
Minneapolis

WISCONSIN
Milwaukee
Madison

Lake Superior

MICHIGAN
Lansing
Detroit
Chicago

Lake Huron

Lake Michigan

Lake Erie

Lake Ontario

VERMONT
Burlington

MAINE

NEW
HAMPSHIRE
Concord
Manchester

St. Lawrence River

NEW
YORK
Buffalo

Albany

Boston
MASS.
Providence
RHODE ISLAND
CONNECTICUT

Hartford

IOWA
Des Moines

ILLINOIS
Springfield
Indianapolis

INDIANA

OHIO
Columbus
Cincinnati

Cleveland
Wheeling

PENNSYLVANIA
Pittsburgh
Harrisburg

Philadelphia

Trenton
New York

NEW JERSEY

Dover
DELAWARE

Kansas City
peka

St. Louis

Jefferson
City

MISSOURI

shita

Frankfort
Louisville

KENTUCKY

Ohio River

Cumberland
River

WEST
VIRGINIA
Charleston

Baltimore
Annapolis

WASHINGTON, D.C.
MARYLAND

Potomac
River

Chesapeake
Bay

Richmond
Norfolk

APPALACHIAN MOUNTAINS

VIRGINIA

Raleigh

Knoxville

NORTH CAROLINA

Charlotte

ATLANTIC
OCEAN

Tulsa

AHOMA
homa City

ARKANSAS
Little Rock

Nashville
TENNESSEE

Memphis

Tennessee River

Mississippi River

Mt. Mitchell
(6,684 ft.; 2,037 m)

SOUTH CAROLINA
Columbia

Charleston

River

Dallas
rt Worth

LOUISIANA

MISSISSIPPI

Jackson

ALABAMA

Birmingham

Alabama River

Montgomery

GEORGIA

Atlanta

TIDEWATER

THE
UNITED STATES
OF AMERICA

Elevation

| Feet | Meters |
|---|---|
| Over 13,001 | Over 3,001 |
| 6,561-13,000 | 2,001-3,000 |
| 3,281-6,560 | 1,001-2,000 |
| 1,641-3,280 | 501-1,000 |
| 661-1,640 | 201-500 |
| 0-660 | 0-200 |
| Below sea level | Below sea level |

in

Houston

Baton Rouge

New Orleans

Gulf of Mexico

Jacksonville

Tallahassee

FLORIDA

Orlando

Lake
Okeechobee

BAHAMAS

ATLANTIC
OCEAN

VIRGIN
ISLANDS

San Juan

PUERTO RICO

Caribbean Sea

0        50        100 miles

0     50     100 kilometers

Miami

CUBA

# THE AMERICAN PROMISE

## A HISTORY OF THE UNITED STATES

### Compact Edition

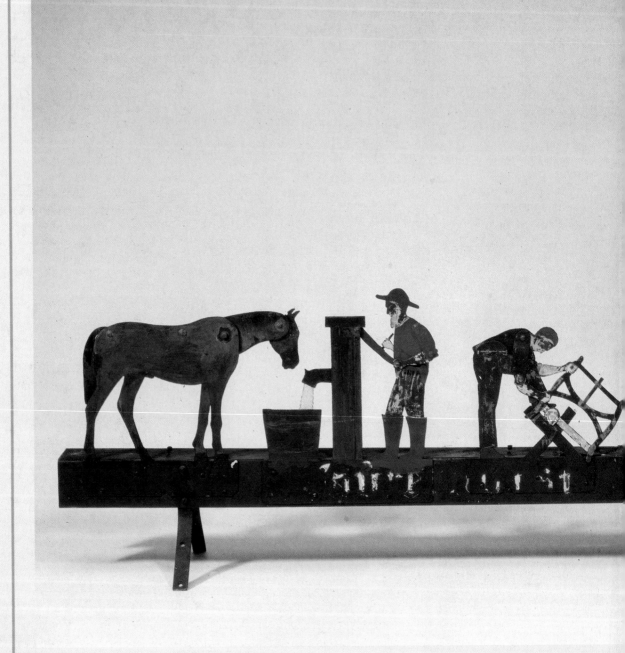

**FARM VIGNETTE.** *Artist unknown, early twentieth century. The Museum of American Folk Art, New York.*

# THE AMERICAN PROMISE

## A HISTORY OF THE UNITED STATES

### Compact Edition

JAMES L. ROARK
Emory University

MICHAEL P. JOHNSON
Johns Hopkins University

PATRICIA CLINE COHEN
University of California at Santa Barbara

SARAH STAGE
Arizona State University, West

ALAN LAWSON
Boston College

SUSAN M. HARTMANN
The Ohio State University

**BEDFORD/ST. MARTIN'S**

Boston • New York

*For Bedford/St. Martin's*
*Executive Editor:* Katherine E. Kurzman
*Senior Developmental Editor:* Elizabeth M. Welch
*Senior Production Editor:* Sherri Frank
*Production Supervisor:* Catherine Hetmansky
*Senior Marketing Manager:* Charles Cavaliere
*Editorial Assistants:* Becky Anderson and Gretchen Boger
*Production Assistants:* Helaine Denenberg and Coleen O'Hanley
*Copyeditor:* Barbara G. Flanagan
*Proofreaders:* Janet Cocker and Mary Lou Wilshaw
*Text Design:* Wanda Kossak
*Photo Researcher:* Pembroke Herbert/Sandi Rygiel, Picture Research Consultants & Archives, Inc.
*Cartography:* Mapping Specialists Limited
*Page Layout:* DeNee Reiton Skipper
*Indexer:* Anne Holmes/Rob Rudnick, EdIndex
*Cover Design:* Wanda Kossak
*Cover Art:* Collection of the Museum of American Folk Art, New York: promised bequest of
   Dorothea and Leo Rabkin
*Composition:* York Graphic Services, Inc.
*Printing and Binding:* R.R. Donnelley & Sons Company

*President:* Charles H. Christensen
*Editorial Director:* Joan E. Feinberg
*Director of Editing, Design, and Production:* Marcia Cohen
*Managing Editor:* Elizabeth M. Schaaf

Library of Congress Catalog Card Number: 99-71851

Manufactured in the United States of America.

4   3   2   1   0   9
f   e   d   c   b   a

*For information, write:* Bedford/St. Martin's, 75 Arlington Street, Boston, MA 02116
(617-426-7440)

ISBN: 0–312–19199–5 (hardcover)
ISBN: 0–312–19206–1 (paperback Vol. I)
ISBN: 0–312–19207–X (paperback Vol. II)

**Cover art:** *Uncle Sam Riding a Bicycle,* artist unknown, c. 1880–1920.

# BRIEF CONTENTS

# CONTENTS

# ABOUT THE AUTHORS

## James L. Roark

Born in Eunice, Louisiana, and raised in the West, James L. Roark received his B.A. from the University of California, Davis, in 1963 and his Ph.D. from Stanford University in 1973. His dissertation won the Allan Nevins Prize. He has taught at the University of Nigeria, Nsukka; the University of Nairobi, Kenya; the University of Missouri, St. Louis; and, since 1983, Emory University, where he is Samuel Candler Dobbs Professor of American History. In 1993, he received the Emory Williams Distinguished Teaching Award. He has written *Masters without Slaves: Southern Planters in the Civil War and Reconstruction* (1977). With Michael P. Johnson, he is author of *Black Masters: A Free Family of Color in the Old South* (1984) and editor of *No Chariot Let Down: Charleston's Free People of Color on the Eve of the Civil War* (1984). He has received research assistance from the American Philosophical Society and the National Endowment for the Humanities. Active in the Organization of American Historians and the Southern Historical Association, he is also a fellow of the Society of American Historians.

## Michael P. Johnson

Born and raised in Ponca City, Oklahoma, Michael P. Johnson studied at Knox College in Galesburg, Illinois, where he received a B.A. in 1963, and at Stanford University in Palo Alto, California, earning a Ph.D. in 1973. He is currently professor of history at Johns Hopkins University in Baltimore, having previously taught at the University of California, Irvine, San Jose State University, and LeMoyne (now LeMoyne-Owen) College in Memphis. He is the author, co-author, or editor of *Toward a Patriarchal Republic: The Secession of Georgia* (1977); *Black Masters: A Free Family of Color in the Old South* (1984); *No Chariot Let Down: Charleston's Free People of Color on the Eve of the Civil War* (1984); *Reading the American Past: Selected Historical Documents* (1998); and *Abraham Lincoln, Slavery, and the Civil War: Selected Speeches and Writings* (2000); and articles that have appeared in the *William and Mary Quarterly*, the *Journal of Southern History*, *Labor History*, the *New York Review of Books*, the *New Republic*, the *Nation*, and other journals. Johnson has been awarded research fellowships by the American Council of Learned Societies, the National Endowment for the Humanities, and the Center for Advanced Study in the Behavioral Sciences. He directed a National Endowment for the Humanities Summer Seminar for College Teachers and has been honored with the University of California, Irvine, Academic Senate Distinguished Teaching Award and the University of California, Irvine, Alumni Association Outstanding Teaching Award. He is an active member of the American Historical Association, the Organization of American Historians, and the Southern Historical Association.

## Patricia Cline Cohen

Born in Ann Arbor, Michigan, and raised in Palo Alto, California, Patricia Cline Cohen earned a B.A. at the University of Chicago in 1968 and a Ph.D. at the University of California, Berkeley in 1977. In 1976, she joined the history faculty at the University of California at Santa Barbara. Cohen has written *A Calculating People: The Spread of Numeracy in Early America* (1982) and *The Murder of Helen Jewett: The Life and Death of a Prostitute in Nineteenth-Century New York* (1998). She has also published articles on numeracy, prostitution, sexual crime, and murder in journals including the *Journal of Women's History*, *Radical History Review*, the *William and Mary Quarterly*, and the *NWSA Journal*. Her scholarly work has received assistance from the National Endowment for the Humanities, the National Humanities Center, the American Antiquarian Society, the Schlesinger Library, and the Newberry Library. She has served as chair of the Women's Studies Program and as dean of the humanities and fine arts at the University of California at Santa Barbara.

## Sarah Stage

Sarah Stage was born in Davenport, Iowa, and received a B.A. from the University of Iowa in 1966 and a Ph.D. in American studies from Yale University in 1975. She has taught U.S. history for more than twenty-five years at Williams College and the University of California, Riverside. Currently she is professor of Women's Studies at Arizona State University, West, in Phoenix. Her books include *Female*

*Complaints: Lydia Pinkham and the Business of Women's Medicine* (1979) and *Rethinking Home Economics: Women and the History of a Profession* (1997). Among the fellowships she has received are the Rockefeller Foundation Humanities Fellowship, the American Association of University Women dissertation fellowship, a fellowship from the Charles Warren Center for the Study of History at Harvard University, and the University of California President's Fellowship in the Humanities. She is at work on a book entitled *Women and the Progressive Impulse in American Politics, 1890–1914.*

## Alan Lawson

Born in Providence, Rhode Island, Alan Lawson received his B.A. from Brown University in 1955 and his Ph.D. from the University of Michigan in 1967. Since winning the Allan Nevins Prize for his dissertation, Lawson has served on the faculties of the University of California, Irvine, Smith College, and, currently, Boston College. He has written *The Failure of Independent Liberalism* (1971) and coedited *From Revolution to Republic* (1976). While completing the forthcoming *The New Deal and the Mobilization of Progressive Experience,* he has published book chapters and essays on political economy and the cultural legacy of the New Deal. He has served as editor of the *Review of Education* and the *Intellectual History Newsletter* and contributed articles to those journals as well as to the *History Education Quarterly.* He has been active in the field of American studies as director of the Boston College American studies program and as a contributor to the *American Quarterly.*

Under the auspices of the United States Information Agency, Lawson has been coordinator and lecturer for programs to instruct faculty from foreign nations in the state of American historical scholarship and teaching.

## Susan M. Hartmann

Professor of history and women's studies at Ohio State University, Susan M. Hartmann received her B.A. from Washington University in 1961 and her Ph.D. from the University of Missouri in 1966. After specializing in the political economy of the post–World War II period and publishing *Truman and the 80th Congress* (1971), she expanded her interests to the field of women's history, publishing many articles and three books: *The Home Front and Beyond: American Women in the 1940s* (1982); *From Margin to Mainstream: American Women and Politics since 1960* (1989); and *The Other Feminists: Activists in the Liberal Establishment* (1998). She has won research fellowships from the Rockefeller Foundation, the National Endowment for the Humanities, and the American Council of Learned Societies. Hartmann has taught at the University of Missouri, St. Louis, and Boston University, and she has lectured on American history in Greece, France, Austria, Germany, Australia, and New Zealand. She has served on book and article award committees of the American Historical Association, the Organization of American Historians, and the American Studies Association. At Ohio State she has served as director of women's studies, and in 1995 she won the Exemplary Faculty Award in the College of Humanities.

# PREFACE FOR INSTRUCTORS

*The American Promise* began as an outgrowth of our experience as longtime teachers of the survey course. Other texts simply did not work well in our classrooms. Most survey texts emphasized either a social or political approach to history; by focusing on one, they inevitably slighted the other. To write a comprehensive, balanced account of American history, we focused on the public arena—the place where politics intersects social and cultural developments—to show how Americans confronted the major issues of their times and created far-reaching historical change.

In our effort to write the most teachable text available, we also thought hard about the concerns most frequently voiced by instructors: that students often find history boring, unfocused, and difficult. How could we help introductory students see and remember the "big picture" of America's history, its main events and developments? We decided to explore fully the political, social, economic, and cultural changes that students need to understand and remember, at the same time avoiding unnecessary detail that threatened to daunt rather than inform them.

*The American Promise*, Compact Edition, represents our further attempt to provide teachers of the survey course greater options and opportunities for success. We wanted to offer a core text that teachers could assign alone with confidence or supplement easily with outside readings. To achieve our goal, we reduced the original text by one-third but retained all the color, pedagogy, and features of a full-length text. To preserve the narrative strengths of our book, all the authors revised their own chapters to make them more concise while preserving and even highlighting the qualities that have made *The American Promise* so successful in the classroom.

Abridgment allowed us to sharpen our focus on the "big picture"—the main events and themes of America's past. Maps and pictures accompany the extended discussions of major historical developments, giving these "big picture" topics greater visibility. This Compact Edition also answers even more clearly students' perennial complaint that they have difficulty figuring out what they need to know and why they need to know it.

An abridgment risks lapsing into dense "textbook prose," choppy, flattened writing shorn of real people and colorful detail. As we shortened the book, we worked hard to keep the narrative lively and coherent. To maintain the strong story line and balanced coverage, we reorganized material and combined thematically related sections throughout the text. To portray the power of human agency and the diversity of the American experience, we continued to stitch into the narrative the voices of hundreds of contemporaries from all walks of life—from presidents to pipefitters—who confronted the issues of their day. Illustrated vignettes open every chapter, spotlighting people who worked for change in their day and whose efforts still affect our lives. In short, we did not make *The American Promise* briefer simply by cutting; we also reimagined, reorganized, and rewrote.

## Features

To make American history as accessible as possible for students, the Compact Edition retains all the pedagogy of the full-length text. Each chapter is clearly structured to reinforce the essential people, events, and themes of the period. Innovative **call-outs**—key points pulled from the main narrative and set in larger type—help students focus and review. Two-tiered **running heads** on every page remind students where the reading falls chronologically. At the close of each chapter, **conclusions** summarize the main themes and topics and provide a bridge to the next chapter; **chronologies** provide a handy review of significant events and dates; and annotated **suggested readings** provide an up-to-date bibliography for students who want to learn more. We have largely retained the innovative **appendices** of the full-length text, expanding the section on research resources to include more information on Internet sites.

Because students learn best when they find a subject engaging, we have made a special effort to incorporate features that bring American history to life. **Chapter-opening vignettes** invite students into the narrative with a vivid account of a person or event that introduces the chapter's main themes. To help students understand that history is both a body of knowledge and an ongoing process of investigation, each chapter offers a two-page special feature that grows out of the narrative and prompts critical thinking. **Historical Questions** pose and investigate specific questions of continuing interest to demonstrate the depth and variety of possible answers, thereby countering the belief of many beginning students that historians simply gather facts and string them together into a chronological narrative. Our second special feature, **Texts in Historical Context**, combines three or four primary documents that dramatize the human dimension of major events and issues with interpretive commentary.

Finally, we are especially proud of our full-color design and art program. To achieve our goal of a complete text that can be assigned alone or with outside readings, we have preserved the **award-winning design** and over two-thirds of the **illustrations** that make *The American Promise* a visual feast. Over 300 images, many in full color, reinforce and extend the narrative. The images are large enough to study in detail, and they carry **comprehensive captions** that draw students into active engagement with the pictures and help them unpack the layers of meaning. Full-page **chapter-opening artifacts** combine with many in-text illustrations of artifacts to emphasize the importance of material culture in the study of the past. Over 100 full-color **maps** help students visualize the material and increase their knowledge of geography.

Our title, *The American Promise,* reflects our conviction that American history is an unfinished story. For millions, the nation held out the promise of a better life, unfettered worship, representative government, democratic politics, and other freedoms seldom found elsewhere on the globe. But none of these promises came with guarantees. And promises fulfilled for some meant promises denied to others. As we see it, much of American history is a continuing struggle over the definition and realization of the nation's promise. Abraham Lincoln, in the midst of what he termed the "fiery trial" of the Civil War, pronounced the nation "the last best hope of Earth." That hope, kept alive by countless sacrifices, has been marred by compromises, disappointments, and denials, but it lives still. Ideally, *The American Promise,* Compact Edition, will help students become aware of the legacy of hope bequeathed to them by previous generations of Americans stretching back nearly four centuries, a legacy that is theirs to preserve and to build upon.

# Supplements

All the print and electronic supplements available with the full-length text are offered with the Compact Edition, to assist students and teachers alike.

## For Students

*Reading the American Past: Selected Historical Documents.* This affordable two-volume collection of primary sources, selected and edited by text author Michael P. Johnson (Johns Hopkins University), permits students to go beyond the textbook narrative and puzzle out the meanings of historical documents. Paralleling the organization of the text, each chapter includes substantial passages from several documents—including presidential speeches, court records, estate inventories, private diaries, personal letters, and oral histories. Each document is introduced by a brief headnote and followed by questions that help students understand the document and its historical significance.

*Making the Most of* THE AMERICAN PROMISE: *A Study Guide.* This essential supplement for students, prepared by John Moretta and David Wilcox (both of Houston Community College), provides practice opportunities to reinforce the main themes and ideas of the text. For each chapter in *The American Promise,* Compact Edition, a corresponding chapter in the study guide includes learning objectives, a brief summary, a timeline with questions on important dates, a glossary of terms, map exercises, multiple-choice questions, and essay questions. An answer key allows students to test themselves.

*Mapping* THE AMERICAN PROMISE: *Historical Geography Workbook.* Prepared by Mark Newman (University of Illinois, Chicago), this stand-alone supplement provides additional exercises using maps drawn from *The American Promise.* Each exercise asks students to label landmarks on the American continent and then analyze the significance of geography in the unfolding of historical events. Working to suggest the implications of geography for history, these exercises also reinforce basic place names in a way that helps students remember them and understand why they should.

*The Bedford Series in History and Culture.* Any of the volumes from this highly acclaimed series of brief, inexpensive, document-based supplements can be packaged with *The American Promise,* Compact Edition, at a reduced price. More than forty titles include *The Sovereignty and Goodness of God, The Interesting Narrative of Olaudah Equiano, The Autobiography of Benjamin Franklin, Narrative of the Life of Frederick Douglass, The Souls of Black Folk, Plunkitt of Tammany Hall,* and many more.

**The Bedford/St. Martin's History Web Site.** Developed by a group of scholars and Ph.D. candidates from Columbia University and New York University, the Bedford History Site allows students both to crystallize their knowledge of the "big picture" of American history and to develop their own critical-thinking skills through a technological medium. Interactive chapter quizzes, map exercises, and primary-source research modules give students a means of reviewing what they have learned in *The American Promise,* Compact Edition, and of making meaningful connections between individual events in American history and larger trends. A prominently placed Research Room provides students with a collection of important documents from American history; an organized and annotated set of links to major libraries, history research centers, and U.S. history sites; and a tutorial to help students read historical sources critically for content and reliability. An online version of Scott Hovey's *Using the Bedford Series in History and Culture in the United States History Survey* can also help instructors integrate primary documents into their course syllabi, lectures, and class discussions.

## For Instructors

*Teaching* THE AMERICAN PROMISE, COMPACT EDITION: *A Hands-On Guide for Instructors.* Written by Sarah E. Gardner (Mercer University), this practical two-volume guide provides myriad suggestions and resources for teaching *The American Promise,* Compact Edition. Each chapter includes an outline of the text's narrative in question form, three lecture strategies, and multiple-choice questions, while suggested essay questions help tie together material from several chapters. A section called "Lecture Supplements and Classroom Activities" offers suggestions for classroom debates and activities, thought-provoking questions about historical contingencies, and suggestions for using both documentary and popular films in the classroom. For the first-time teacher, the manual offers a set of sample syllabi and anticipates common misconceptions that undergraduates bring to each chapter's topics.

Finally, a set of blank maps allows for easy photocopying for quizzes and tests.

*Testbank to Accompany* THE AMERICAN PROMISE. Written by two longtime teachers of the American history survey, John Moretta and David Wilcox (both of Houston Community College), this set provides 70–80 multiple-choice, true/false, short-answer, identification, and essay questions for each of the thirty-two chapters in *The American Promise.* The testbank is available either on disk (Macintosh and Windows), with a function that allows users to customize the exams, or in booklet form.

*Discussing* THE AMERICAN PROMISE: *A Survival Guide for First-Time Teaching Assistants.* This unique resource provides a wealth of practical suggestions to help first-time teaching assistants develop their skills and succeed in the classroom. Written by experienced TA adviser Michael A. Bellesiles (Emory University), this brief supplement offers concrete advice on teaching from *The American Promise,* working with professors, dealing with difficult students, running discussion sections, designing assignments, grading tests and papers, relating research to classroom experience, and more.

*Transparencies to Accompany* THE AMERICAN PROMISE *(with Teaching Suggestions).* More than 150 images are available as full-color acetates to adopters of *The American Promise,* including all the maps that appear in the textbook, the textbook's chapter-opening artifacts, and many of its striking illustrations. To assist instructors in presenting these images, a guide provides background and elaborates on teaching possibilities.

**CD-ROM for *The American Promise,* with Presentation Manager Pro.** This new CD-ROM for instructors offers full-color illustrations from *The American Promise,* Compact Edition, in an electronic format to enhance class presentations. Included as well are additional art and artifact images to supplement the collection in the book. Instructors can choose among the clearly labeled set of images for each chapter and can also incorporate their own images and figures from PowerPoint to design a customized visual presentation for lectures and discussions.

*Using the Bedford Series in History and Culture in the United States History Survey.* Recognizing that many instructors use a compact text in conjunction with an array of supplements, Bedford/St. Martin's has made the Bedford series volumes available at a discount to adopters of *The American Promise,* Compact Edition. This short guide by Scott Hovey gives practical suggestions for using more than forty volumes from the Bedford Series in History and Culture with a core text. The guide not only supplies links between the text and the supplements, but also provides ideas for starting discussions focused on a single primary-source volume.

## Acknowledgments

It is a pleasure to thank the many instructors who offered their expert advice and assistance during preparation of *The American Promise,* Compact Edition, and its parent text:

Katherine G. Aiken, University of Idaho
Kathleen Christine Berkeley, University of North Carolina—Wilmington
Elizabeth Brickley, Hudson High School, Hudson, Ohio
John C. Burnham, The Ohio State University
Vernon Burton, University of Illinois at Urbana-Champaign
Peter Coclanis, University of North Carolina at Chapel Hill
Matthew Ware Colter, Collin County Community College
Leonard Dinnerstein, University of Arizona, Tucson
Jonathan Earle, University of Kansas
Laura F. Edwards, University of South Florida
Joseph J. Ellis, Mount Holyoke College
Elizabeth Feder, Rhodes College
Dan Feller, University of New Mexico
Alan Gallay, Western Washington University
Mark Gelfand, Boston College
William Graebner, State University of New York, Buffalo at Fredonia
Michael D. Green, University of Kentucky
Jack Greene, Johns Hopkins University
Christopher J. Gurry, Phillips Academy, Andover
Michael J. Haridopolos, Brevard Community College
Thomas Hartshorne, Cleveland State University
Ronald Howard, Mississippi College
George Juergens, Indiana University
Wilma King, Michigan State University
Barbara Loomis, San Francisco State University
George McJimsey, Iowa State University
Melinda McMahon, University of California, Santa Barbara

John Moon, Fitchburg State University
Roger L. Nichols, University of Arizona, Tucson
Donald K. Pickens, University of North Texas
Theda Perdue, University of Kentucky
David Rankin, University of California, Irvine
Marguerite Renner, Glendale Community College
Herbert Rissler, Indiana State University
Dave Roediger, University of Minnesota
Nancy J. Rosenbloom, Canisius College
Bryant Simon, University of Georgia
Carole Srole, California State University, Los Angeles
April R. Summitt, Andrew University
Thomas Terrill, University of South Carolina
Daniel H. Usner Jr., Cornell University
Cynthia Wilkey, Tennessee State University
Walter Woodward, University of Connecticut
Jeffrey R. Young, Georgia Southern University

A project as complex as this requires the talents of many individuals. The authors would like to thank Pembroke Herbert and Sandi Rygiel of Picture Research Consultants, Inc., whose research and imagination are responsible for the fine illustrations. Thanks are also due to Louise Townsend, whose accomplished editing greatly improved the manuscript, and to Gerry McCauley, who represents us as literary agent.

We would also like to thank the many people at Bedford/St. Martin's who have been crucial to this project. No one has carried more of the burden than our Senior Editor, Elizabeth M. Welch, whose intelligence, knowledge of American history, commitment to excellence, and unfailing good judgment guided our every step. We thank as well Katherine Kurzman, Executive Editor, and Charles Cavaliere, Senior Marketing Manager, for their tireless efforts marketing the book. With great skill and professionalism, Sherri Frank, our Senior Production Editor, pulled all the pieces together with the assistance of Helaine Denenberg and Coleen O'Hanley as well as the invaluable guidance of Project Consultant Tina Samaha. Managing Editor Elizabeth Schaaf and Production Supervisor Catherine Hetmansky oversaw production of the book, and Becky Anderson and Gretchen Boger helped out on myriad editorial tasks. Our original copyeditor, Barbara Flanagan, returned to the project, and her sharp eye improved our best efforts. Charles H. Christensen, President, and Joan E. Feinberg, Editorial Director, have taken a personal interest in *The American Promise* from the start and have guided both the Compact Edition and its parent text through every stage of development.

# Presenting *The American Promise,* Compact Edition

*The American Promise,* Compact Edition, offers teachers and students of American history a fresh alternative: a book with all the color, pedagogy, and narrative strength of a full-length text but with fewer pages and a lower price. Condensed by the authors themselves, the Compact Edition replaces extraneous facts with full, vivid discussions of major political, social, economic, and cultural changes. This concentration on the "big picture" captures the interest of students and ensures understanding of the main events and themes of America's past. At two-thirds the length of the original text, the Compact Edition can be used alone or supplemented with outside readings to suit the needs of a particular course. It retains the number and order of chapters in the full-length text, allowing instructors to shift easily between the two.

The next few pages offer an overview of the book and introduce its student-centered features. We urge you to take a few minutes to examine its organization and design, evaluating this unique approach to the American history textbook.

## THE "BIG PICTURE" APPROACH

In shortening the book by one-third, the authors strengthened their focus on major historical events and developments, providing students with all the information they need to know in a dynamic narrative they will remember. Examples of the text's "big picture" approach include concentration on the Chesapeake in treatment of the southern colonies; a richly detailed account of the Homestead lockout and strike to represent the labor wars of the late nineteenth century; and focus on Cuba in discussion of U.S. involvement in Latin America and the Caribbean. In the Compact Edition, a picture or map accompanies nearly all discussions of major historical developments, to spotlight the text's "big picture" approach and to enhance student learning.

At the center of *The American Promise*, Compact Edition, are the actions of individuals: Written by social historians expert in their periods, the book makes clear how people of all classes and groups shape their own history. But as teachers with extensive experience, the authors also recognize that students need the framework a political narrative provides as well as the insights of social and cultural history. Integrating and balancing these perspectives, the Compact Edition explores major changes over time within a structure students can negotiate.

(The complete example can be found on pages 530–531.)

## The Homestead Lockout and Strike

At first glance it seemed ironic that Carnegie Steel's Homestead mill became the storm center of labor's fight for the right to unionize. Andrew Carnegie was unique among industrialists as a self-styled friend of labor. In 1886 he had written, "The right of the workingmen to combine and to form trades unions is no less sacred than the right of the manufacturer to enter into associations and conferences with his fellows." Yet six years later at Homestead, Carnegie set out to crush a union in on legendary confrontations.

Carnegie cherished his profits more. Labor had worked well for him during the years was building his empire. Labor strife at Ho during the 1870s had enabled Carnegie to plant from his competitors at cost and to ta the steel industry. And during the 1880s, str tional craft unions ensured that competir could not undercut his labor costs. But by th Carnegie held nearly total control of the st ing business. Standing in his way was the / mated Association of Iron and Steel Worker:

**THE BATTLE AT THE HOMESTEAD STEEL MILL**
*This contemporary lithograph portrays scenes from the battle between workers and strikebreakers in July 1892: the workers attacking the barges, the cannonading of the barges, the surrender of the Pinkertons, the captives being led to prison, and, finally, the arrival of the militia and the soldiers in camp. The lithograph also shows (lower right) the revenge the strikers took on the hated "Pinks." Of the 316 Pinkertons, not one escaped injury as the angry crowd, armed with clubs, hoes, and brickbats, forced them to run a bloody gauntlet.*
Carnegie Library, Pittsburgh.

# INNOVATIVE PEDAGOGY

Common to each chapter is a set of learning aids—opening vignette, two-tiered running heads, call-outs, conclusion, chronology, and suggested readings—that provide useful guides to the narrative.

## Opening vignettes

Illustrated chapter-opening vignettes invite students into the narrative with a compelling account of a person or event that embodies some of the chapter's main themes.

(See page 185 for the complete example.)

CHAPTER

# BUILDING A REPUBLIC
## 1775–1789

# 8

I N 1781, MERCY OTIS WARREN AND HER HUSBAND, JAMES, moved from Plymouth, Massachusetts, into an elegant residence that had once belonged to Thomas Hutchinson in Milton, six miles south of Boston. The ex-royal governor, in exile in England, would not have been pleased to know that his archenemies the Otis and Warren families entertained in his parlor and slept in his bedroom. Now that the war was finally over, James and Mercy had moved closer to the Boston capital to devote themselves to the political work of building the new Republic. James resumed his seat in the state's assembly, where he had served repeatedly in the 1760s and 1770s. Mercy turned to her ambitious project of the 1780s, the writing of a substantial history of the American Revolution.

Mercy Otis Warren, then fifty-three, was the foremost female political commentator and intellectual of her day. She had grown up in a household that lived and breathed politics and ideas. Her father, the lawyer James Otis, represented his town of Barnstable for fifteen years in the Massachusetts House. Otis provided his

## Two-tiered running heads

Double bars at the top of every page quickly orient students to their place in the book and in the chronology of American history.

762    CHAPTER 28 • A DECADE OF REBELLION AND REFORM

1960-1968

JOHNSON AND THE GREAT SOCIETY    763

1960-1968

## Call-outs

Highlighted passages in each chapter alert students to key points in the narrative, serving as a review aid while conveying the liveliness of the story.

*The North ground out the victory, bloody battle by bloody battle. The balance tipped in the Union's favor in 1863, but if the Confederacy was beaten, Southerners clearly did not know it.*

## Conclusions

Each chapter ends with a brief conclusion that summarizes the narrative's main points, analyzes their significance, and discusses their consequences.

(The complete example is found on page 378.)

### Conclusion: The Failure of Compromise

Northerners and Southerners had clashed as early as the writing of the Constitution. As their economies, societies, and cultures diverged in the nineteenth century, friction increased. But sectionalism shifted into a new gear in 1846 when David Wilmot proposed banning slavery in any Mexican territory won in the war. During the extended crisis of the Union

## Chronologies

A chronology at the end of each chapter provides a streamlined review of the most important dates and events.

(For the complete chronology, see page 702)

### CHRONOLOGY

| | |
|---|---|
| 1933 | Adolf Hitler becomes chancellor of Germany. United States recognizes Soviet Union. |
| 1935–1937 | Congress seeks to shield America from world conflicts with neutrality acts. |
| 1936 | Nazi Germany occupies Rhineland. Mussolini's fascist Italian regime conquers Ethiopia. Civil war breaks out in Spain. |
| 1937 | Japanese troops capture Nanking. Roosevelt delivers speech urging "quarantine" against aggressor nations. |
| 1938 | Hitler annexes Austria. British Prime Minister Chamberlain |

**December 7.** Japanese prise attack on Pearl States declares war on

1942  Japan captures Philip Civil rights activists f of Racial Equality (CC U.S. navy scores its fi ries in Battle of Coral Midway. Roosevelt authorizes hattan Project. **November.** U.S. force Africa. Roosevelt authorizes

## Suggested Readings

Each chapter includes an annotated list of recommended works to guide students to further reading on the subjects covered in the chapter.

(For the complete Suggested Readings list, turn to page 441.)

### SUGGESTED READINGS

Michael Les Benedict, *A Compromise of Principle: Congressional Republicans and Reconstruction* (1974). Explains the evolution of the reconstruction policies of Congress.

Michael Les Benedict, *The Impeachment of Andrew Johnson* (1973), and Hans L. Trefousse, *Impeachment of a President: Andrew Johnson, the Blacks, and Reconstruction* (1975). Investigations of the Johnson impeachment.

Ira Berlin, et al., eds., *Freedom: A Documentary History of Emancipation, 1861–1867* (1982–). Vividly documents the aspirations of ex-slaves.

Dan T. Carter, *When the War Was Over: The Failure of Self Reconstruction in the South, 1865–1867* (1985). Analyzes Johnson's conservative regimes in the South.

Eric Foner, *Reconstruction: America's Unfinished Revolution* (1988). A thoroughly researched, comprehensive interpretation that views the Africa as central to the era.

Michael Perman, *Reunion Without and Reconstruction, 1865–1868* ( *Redemption: Southern Politics, 18 ses of the South's political resp

George C. Rable, *But There Was N lence in the Politics of Reconstruc the pervasiveness of political vi

Brooks D. Simpson, *The Reconstruc lively examination of the recons coln, Johnson, Grant, and Haye

C. Vann Woodward, *Reunion and F of 1877 and the End of Reconstru and still valuable analysis of the aftermath.

# STRIKING VISUAL FEATURES

The Compact Edition of *The American Promise* retains the award-winning, full-color design of the original text and over two-thirds of its highly acclaimed illustration program. Every image has been chosen for its ability to enhance an understanding of the past.

## Chapter-opening artifacts

To emphasize the importance of material culture in studying the past, each chapter opens with a full-page reproduction of a contemporary cultural artifact, such as a household object, musical instrument, book, or political emblem. Full captions provide background information and invite readers to consider the artifact's historical implications.

(For the complete example of a chapter-opening artifact, turn to page 642.)

## Comprehensive illustration program with extensive captions

Over three hundred contemporary images, many in full color, reinforce and extend the narrative. All illustrations are reproduced large enough to study in detail, and each carries a comprehensive caption that draws students into active engagement with the picture.

(This illustration can be found on page 238.)

**SOUVENIR SEWING NEEDLE BOOK**
*Borrowing the current popular tune "Happy Days Are Here Again" as the theme song for Roosevelt's 1932 campaign was an inspired act of wishful thinking in those dark days. By 1936, conditions had improved enough that this souvenir needle book could celebrate "Happiness Restored" a bit more realistically. The major places where economic recovery was to be created— farm, factory, and office—are shown operating in full swing on the cover of this little container that held sewing needles. But in accord with the New Deal emphasis on security at home, the figure of domestic happiness looms largest in the center under the arch of prosperity.*
Collection of Janice L. and David J. Frent.

**JEFFERSON'S RED WAISTCOAT**
*During his presidency, Jefferson often wore this red silk waistcoat as informal daywear. The garment had a velvet collar, woolen sleeves, and a thick lining made from recycled cotton and wool stockings. The thrifty Jefferson preferred to conserve firewood by wearing layers of warm clothes. A New Hampshire senator visited in December 1802 and reported in dismay that the president was "dressed, or rather undressed, with an old brown coat, red waistcoat, old corduroy small clothes, much soiled, woolen hose, and slippers without heels." Another guest in 1804 found him in the red waistcoat, green velveteen breeches with pearl buttons, and "slippers down at the heels" and concluded*

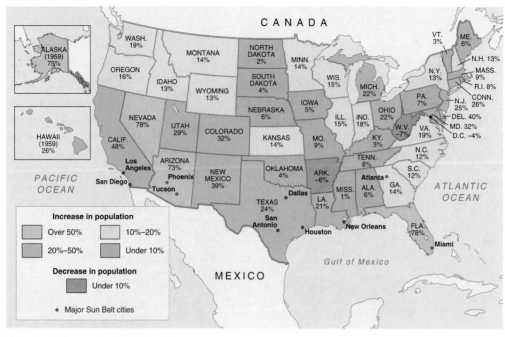

**MAP 27.1**
*The Rise of the Sun Belt, 1940–1980*
*The growth of defense industries, a nonunionized labor force, and the spread of air conditioning all helped spur economic development and population growth, which made the Sun Belt the fastest-growing region of the nation between 1940 and 1980.*

*Extensive map program*

Over one hundred full-color maps help students visualize the information presented and increase their knowledge of geography. A customized workbook that draws on maps from the text for analytical work is available at a minimal additional cost.

(This map is found on page 742.)

# ENGAGING SPECIAL FEATURES

Each chapter offers a two-page special feature intended to extend the narrative, engage the student, and prompt critical thinking.

## Historical Question

These interpretive essays investigate issues of ongoing debate and interest. Among the topics discussed are: Why Did Cortés Win?, What Did the War Mean to African Americans?, and What Happened to Rosie the Riveter?

(For this complete Historical Question, turn to pages 598–599.)

## What Did the War Mean to African Americans?

WHEN THE UNITED STATES ENTERED the First World War, some black leaders remembered the crucial role of African American soldiers in the Civil War. They rejoiced that military service would again offer blacks a chance to prove their wor[...] Robert Moton, president of the nation's forer[...] black college, Tuskegee Institute, recollected cle[...] when that thought had come to him. He was sit[...] in the midst of "dignified bankers [and] mercha[...] gathered in the Waldorf-Astoria Hotel in New [...] City to promote the sale of Liberty Bonds. At [...] moment of patriotic inclusion, Moton "could [...] but feel that m[...] people b[...]ir contribution, t[...]

even facilities for bathing. On[...] disease and exposure move[...] make conditions barely tolera[...]

When black soldiers bega[...] white commanders made a [...] racial distinctions. A special [...] quarters of the American com[...] J. Pershing, advised the Fren[...] draw the color line threatene[...] lations. They should resist th[...]

**AFRICAN AMERICAN MACHINE GUN COMPANY**
*This company from the 370th Regiment of the Illinois National Guard, shown early in their training, exemplifies the proud determination of black soldiers to prove their worth in battle. Once in France, the 370th encountered resistance from American commanders reluctant to use [...] that read [...] thing but hard labor behind the lines. When desperation [...]*

## Texts in Historical Context

A variety of primary documents—letters, diaries, speeches, memoirs, and testimony—bring students into direct contact with the human impact of major historical events and issues. Headnotes link the documents and provide interpretive commentary.

(For this complete Texts in Historical Context, see pages 282–283.)

## The Panic of 1837

*T*he panic of 1837 brought fright and hysteria to city after city. Crowds of hundreds thronged the banks during the spring to remove their money. Business came to a standstill and many merchants appeared to be ruined overnight. Whig leaders were certain that the crisis could be traced to President Jackson's antibank and hard-money policies, but others blamed it on what they saw as an immoral frenzy of greed and speculation that had gripped the nation in the preceding few years.

*H*arriet Martineau traveled throughout the United States and described booming land sales in the infant city of Chicago in 1836.

**DOCUMENT 1. An English Visitor Describes the "Mania" for Speculation**

some reasonable conjecture [...] of the lots, by calculating th[...] risks from accident, from th[...] from other places, &c., and fi[...] its, under the most favo[...] within so many years' purcl[...] would serve as some sort of [...] of purchase-money to be risl[...] on the banks of a canal, no [...] was selling at Chicago for m[...] improved, in the finest pa[...] Mohawk, on the banks of a [...] is already the medium of [...] amount of traffic. If sharper [...] be the sufferers by the impe[...] no one would feel much c[...] fortunately, are the people w[...] sion, in order to profit by i[...] but inexperienced, young n[...] tler, will be ruined for the a[...]

# COMPREHENSIVE APPENDICES

A three-part appendix offers a convenient compilation of important documents, historical data, and resources for student research.

## Documents

In addition to the complete texts of the Declaration of Independence and the Constitution, this section features annotations that provide historical background for the twenty-seven Constitutional amendments and for six significant amendments that were never ratified.

(The annotated amendments are on pages A-9–A-22.)

### Amendment XXVII
**[Adopted 1992]**

No law, varying the compensation for the services of the Senators and Representatives, shall take effect, until an election of Representatives shall have intervened.

1

*While the Twenty-Sixth Amendment was the most rapidly ratified amendment in U.S. history, the Twenty-Seventh Amendment had the longest journey to ratification. First proposed by James Madison in 1789 as part of the package that included the Bill of Rights, this amendment had been ratified by only six states by 1791. In 1873, however, it was ratified by Ohio to protest a massive retroactive salary increase by the federal government. Unlike later proposed amendments, this one came with no time limit on ratification. In the early 1980s, Gregory D. Watson, a University of Texas economics major, discovered the "lost" amendment and began a single-handed campaign to get state legislators to introduce it for ratification. In 1983, it was accepted by Maine. In 1984, it*

## Facts and Figures

This wide-ranging collection of political, economic, and demographic information supplements the statistical data in the text on subjects ranging from presidential elections to population and immigration patterns. It also includes summaries of twenty-four significant Supreme Court cases.

(For Facts and Figures, see pages A-23–A-46.)

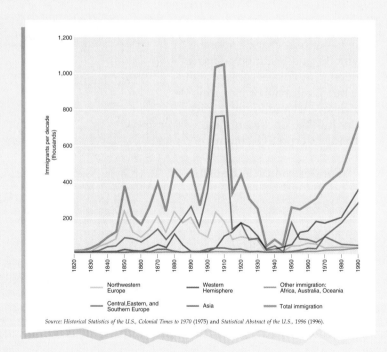

Source: *Historical Statistics of the U.S., Colonial Times to 1970* (1975) and *Statistical Abstract of the U.S., 1996* (1996).

## Research Resources in U. S. History

This annotated list of reference materials provides a valuable starting point for research papers, with extensive suggestions for locating a variety of primary and secondary sources. The section on the Internet features sites that are main gateways to extensive online information about American history.

(For the complete listing of Research Resources, see pages A-47–A-50.)

*American Memory: Historical Collection from the National Digital Library Program.* <http://rs6.loc.gov/amhome .html> An Internet site that features digitized primary source materials from the Library of Congress, among them African American pamphlets, Civil War photographs, documents from the Continental Congress and the Constitutional Convention of 1774–1790, materials on woman suffrage, and oral histories.

*Decisions of the U.S. Supreme Court.* <http://supct.law .cornell.edu/supct> This database can be used to search for information on various Supreme Court cases. Although the site primarily covers cases that occurred after 1990, there is information on some earlier historic cases. The justices' opinions, as originally written, are also included.

*Directory of Scholarly and Professional Electronic Conferences.* <http://n2h2.com/KOVAKS> A good place to find out what electronic conversations are going on in a scholarly discipline. Includes a good search facility and instructions on how to connect to e-mail discussion lists, newsgroups, and interactive chat sites with academic content. Once identified, these conferences are good places to raise questions, find out what controversies are currently stirring the profession, and even find out about grants and jobs.

*Douglass Archives of American Public Address.* <http://douglass.speech.nwu.edu> An electronic archive of American speeches and documents by a variety of
~~~am J~~ ~~Addams~~ to Jon~~~~~ Edwar~~~~

index of Native
category. Within t
nized under subc
tory, geographical
and photographic
in the search for
history.

*Index of Resources*
.ukans.edu/histor
links to sites of i
phabetically by
sources for gener
are on historical t
ploration of Inter

*Internet Archives o*
history.hanover.e
home page, the p
mary sources av
Arranged chrono
subject, the site
primary-documer
ondary sources or

*Internet Resources for*
<http://www.libr
/afrores.htm>A g
ics in African-Am
and linked to a v
primary docume
sources on Afric
do~~~~ments such a

## Index

The index offers a complete listing of people, events, topics, and concepts covered in the book, in a clear, easy-to-navigate format. Page numbers for a topic's main coverage are indicated in boldface; dates are included in entries for significant people and events; all images, maps, and graphics are listed; and related subjects are cross-referenced.

# COMPLETE SET OF SUPPLEMENTS

All the supplements available with the full-length text are offered with the Compact Edition to assist students and teachers alike. Please refer to the Preface for Instructors or to the Web site, <www.bedfordstmartins.com/history>, for details.

# MAPS AND CHARTS

## Maps

## Charts

# SPECIAL FEATURES

## Historical Questions

## Texts in Historical Context

# THE
# AMERICAN
# PROMISE

## A HISTORY OF THE UNITED STATES

### Compact Edition

**SALADO RITUAL FIGURES**

*About 1350—more than a century before Columbus arrived in the New World—these figures were carefully wrapped in the reed mat (shown in the back, on the right) and stored in a cave in a mountainous region of New Mexico by people of the Salado culture, descendants of the Mimbres, who had flourished three centuries earlier. Presumably used for sacred rituals, the effigies display the high artistry of ancient Americans. The haunting human figures are as close to self-portraits of ancient Americans as we are ever likely to have. Adorned with vivid pigments, cotton string, bright feathers, and stones, the effigies hint at the objects the Salado and other ancient Americans used and valued in their daily lives.*

The Art Institute of Chicago.

# ANCIENT AMERICA
## Before 1492

GEORGE MCJUNKIN WAS AN AFRICAN AMERICAN COWBOY who worked on a ranch near Folsom, New Mexico. Born a slave in Texas in 1851, McJunkin learned to ride wild horses as a boy, and soon after he obtained his freedom in 1865 at the end of the Civil War, he punched cows for ranchers in Colorado and New Mexico. In 1891, he became manager of the Crowfoot Ranch outside Folsom.

In August 1908, a violent storm ripped through Folsom, causing a devastating flood. Afterward, McJunkin rode out to mend fences and to look for missing cattle. As he rode along he noticed that the floodwaters had exposed a deposit of stark white bones in the bank of a dry gulch. Curious, he chipped away at the deposit until he had exposed an entire fossilized bone. This bone fossil was far larger than the parched skeletons of range cattle and buffalo familiar to McJunkin. He took the fossil back to the ranch for further study.

In 1912, McJunkin met Carl Schwachheim, a white blacksmith in Raton, New Mexico, who shared his curiosity about fossils. McJunkin told Schwachheim about what he called the "Bone Pit," but Schwachheim could not get out to the Crowfoot Ranch to take a look for himself. Ten years later, a few months after McJunkin's death, Schwachheim and some friends finally drove to the Bone Pit, dug out enough bones to fill a gunnysack, and brought them back to Raton. But they could not identify animals that had such huge bones.

In 1926, when Schwachheim delivered cattle to the stockyards in Denver, he took some of the old bones to the Denver Museum of Natural History and showed them to J. D. Figgins, a paleontologist who was an expert on fossils of ancient animals. Figgins immediately recognized the significance of the fossils and a few months later began an excavation of the Folsom Bone Pit that revolutionized knowledge about the first Americans.

When Figgins began his dig at Folsom, archaeologists (individuals who study the artifacts of prehistoric peoples) believed that Native Americans had arrived relatively recently in the Western Hemisphere, probably no more than three or four thousand years earlier when, the experts assumed, they had crossed the icy waters of the Bering Strait from what is now Russia in small boats. At Folsom, however, Figgins unearthed the bones of twenty-three giant bison, a species known to have been extinct for at least 10,000 years. McJunkin had been right that these were no ordinary bones. Far more startling were nineteen flint projectile points (Folsom points, they have since been called) associated with the bones, proof that human beings had been alive at the same time as the giant bison. One flint point remained stuck between two ribs of a giant bison, just where a Stone Age hunter had plunged it more than 10,000 years earlier. No longer could anyone doubt that human beings had inhabited the New World for at least ten millennia.

**GEORGE McJUNKIN**
*This photo of McJunkin was taken a few years after he discovered the Folsom site, but about fifteen years before the significance of his discovery was understood by anyone. He appears here on horseback in his work clothes, as he probably was when he made the discovery. The fossilized bones he discovered belonged to an extinct bison species that was much larger than modern bison; the horns of the ancient animal often spanned six feet, wide enough for McJunkin's horse to have stood sideways, as it appears in the photo, between the tips of the horns.*
Eastern New Mexico University, Blackwater Draw Site, Portales, New Mexico 88130.

The Folsom discovery sparked other major finds of ancient artifacts that, taken together, make clear that 95 percent of human history in the Americas occurred before the arrival of Columbus in 1492. Since the 1930s, scholars have tried to reconstruct this ancient history, making connections between the hunters who killed giant bison with flint points, their descendants who built southwestern pueblos and eastern burial mounds, and *their* descendants encountered by Columbus. The story they have assembled is, of course, incomplete. Much of what is known about ancient America remains controversial. Nonetheless, scholars have learned enough about ancient Americans to bring into focus who they were, where they came from, and some basic features of their history in the thousands of years before that moment in 1492 when Columbus stepped ashore on a small island in the Caribbean.

## The First Americans

Human beings existed elsewhere in the world long before they reached the Western Hemisphere. The first human beings (*Homo erectus*) evolved in Africa about 1.5 million years ago. Modern humans (*Homo sapiens*) appeared later still, within the last 350,000 years. Archaeologists have found fossil remains of these ancient humans in Africa, Europe, and Asia, but not in the Americas.

The basic reason for the prolonged absence of humans from the Western Hemisphere is that millions of years before human beings came into existence the American landmass became detached from Africa, Europe, and Asia. About 240 million years ago, North and South America were attached to Europe, Asia, and Africa in a gigantic continent scientists now call Pangaea (Map 1.1). Slowly over the next 150 million years, powerful forces deep within the earth pushed the continents apart to approximately their present positions. This process of continental drift encircled the land of the Western Hemisphere with large oceans and isolated it from the other continents. Millions of years after continental drift had disrupted Pangaea, human beings evolved in Africa and eventually migrated throughout Europe and Asia. For almost 95 percent of the time *Homo sapiens* have existed on the face of the globe, no one set foot in the Western Hemisphere.

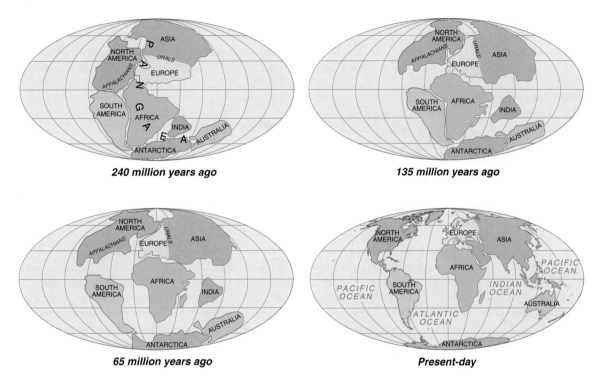

**240 million years ago**

**135 million years ago**

**65 million years ago**

**Present-day**

MAP 1.1
*Continental Drift*
*Massive geological forces separated North and South America from other continents eons be-*
*fore human beings evolved in Africa in the last 1.5 million years. This continental drift ex-*
*plains why human life developed elsewhere on the planet for hundreds of thousands of years*
*before the first person entered the Western Hemisphere during the last fifteen thousand years.*

## Asian Origins

Two major developments made it possible for human beings to migrate to the Western Hemisphere. First, humans successfully adapted to the frigid environment near the Arctic Circle. Second, the earth's climate changed and reconnected the New World to the Old World.

By about 25,000 years ago, humans had learned to use bone needles to sew animal skins into warm clothing that permitted humans to become permanent residents of extremely cold regions like northeastern Siberia. Today the Bering Strait, a body of water about sixty miles wide, separates easternmost Siberia from westernmost Alaska. Conditions now, however, are much different than they were when humans first came to America.

We live in a relatively warm period of the earth's climatic history. The last great cold spell—which scientists call the Wisconsin glaciation—endured from about 80,000 years ago to about 10,000

years ago. The colder temperatures during this era meant that snow piled up in glaciers that did not melt, causing the sea level to drop as much as 350 feet below its current level. The seafloor that is now submerged 120 feet below the surface of the Bering Strait was then dry land. It formed what is often called a "land bridge" between Asian Siberia and American Alaska. However, the exposed land was not a narrow passageway. Instead, it was about a thousand miles wide, roughly the distance from New Orleans to Minneapolis. Scientists refer to it as Beringia.

Periodically, Beringia sank beneath the waves when a global warm snap began to melt glaciers. But for most of the Wisconsin glacial period, Beringia stood above sea level. Grasses and small shrubs covered much of the land and supported herds of mammoth, bison, and horses. Smaller animals like seals, birds, and fish could also be found.

Siberian hunters presumably roamed into Beringia for thousands of years in search of game animals. Archaeologists speculate that hunters traveled in small bands of perhaps twenty-five people. How many such bands arrived in the New World before water once again covered Beringia will never be known. It may have been as few as one or two or three. When they arrived in the Western Hemisphere is hotly debated by experts. The first migrants probably arrived sometime after 15,000 years ago.

Archaeologists refer to these people and their descendants for the next few millennia as Paleo-Indians. Their Asian origins seem beyond dispute. Siberians hunted mammoths, and Beringia provided a mammoth-hunting ground that reached all the way to the Western Hemisphere, a wide avenue that existed for no other humans at the time. Furthermore, Native Americans today still share certain obvious physical characteristics of Asians, including straight black hair, light brown skin, relatively sparse facial and body hair, and incisor teeth that often have shovel-shaped indentations on their inner surface. Detailed analyses of Native American languages and of certain blood proteins provide additional compelling evidence of Asian origins.

### Paleo-Indian Mammoth Hunters

When humans first arrived in Alaska, massive glaciers covered most of Canada. A narrow corridor not entirely obstructed by ice ran along the eastern side of the Canadian Rockies, and most archaeologists believe that Paleo-Indians migrated through it in pursuit of game. At the southern edge of the glaciers, Paleo-Indians entered a hunters' paradise. North, Central, and South America teemed with wildlife that had never before confronted wily two-legged predators armed with razor-sharp spears. The abundance of big game presumably made hunting relatively easy. Ample food permitted the Paleo-Indian population to grow. Within a thousand years, Paleo-Indians had reached the southern tip of South America and virtually everywhere else in the Western Hemisphere.

Paleo-Indians used a distinctively shaped spearhead known as a Clovis point, named for the place in New Mexico where it was first excavated. The discovery of Clovis points throughout North and Central America in sites dated between 11,500 and 11,000 years ago (9500–9000 B.C.) is powerful evidence that these nomadic hunters shared a common ancestry and way of life. Clovis hunters prob-

ably staked out a watering hole, watched for an opportunity to isolate a mammoth from a herd, and then attacked it by repeatedly stabbing it with their spears. Typically, excavation of a Clovis mammoth kill uncovers one or two points, suggesting that the hunters worked in small groups of two or three.

*Archaeologists refer to the first Americans and their descendants for the next few millennia as Paleo-Indians. Their Asian origins seem beyond dispute.*

The Paleo-Indians who used Clovis points to kill big animals probably also hunted smaller animals, but the artifacts that have survived the millennia indicate that they specialized in big mammals. One mammoth kill supplied meat for weeks or, if dried, for months. In addition, the hide could

**CLOVIS POINTS**
*These Clovis points were found in a fossilized mammoth carcass discovered at Naco, Arizona. The large number of points hints that the mammoth may have escaped from its hunters, who then failed to recover their points when the animal died. Although the points are different sizes, note the similarity in shape and workmanship, the telltale characteristics of Clovis points. The size of the Clovis points also suggests the danger Paleo-Indian hunters encountered when they attacked a mammoth, using weapons tipped with these small flakes of stone against an animal almost as big as a modern African elephant.*
Arizona State Museum/University of Arizona.

be used for clothing and shelter. Bones and tusks could be used to erect a framework for small, hide-covered dwellings, fashioned into a variety of useful tools, or even burned for fuel.

About 11,000 years ago (9000 B.C.) Paleo-Indians confronted a major crisis. The big-game animals they hunted for food became extinct. Scientists are not completely certain why the extinction occurred, although the changing environment probably triggered it. About this time the Wisconsin glacial period came to an end, glaciers melted, and sea levels rose. Large mammals presumably had difficulty adapting to the warmer climate. Many archaeologists also believe that Paleo-Indian hunters contributed to the New World extinctions by killing animals more rapidly than they could reproduce.

Paleo-Indians adapted to the big-game extinctions by making at least two important changes in their way of life. First, throughout the hemisphere hunters focused their attention on smaller animals. Second, Paleo-Indians devoted more energy to foraging, that is, to collecting wild plant foods such as roots, seeds, nuts, berries, and fruits. When Paleo-Indians made these changes, the apparent uniformity of the mammoth-oriented Clovis culture* was replaced by great cultural diversity. Paleo-Indians adapted to the many natural environments throughout the hemisphere, ranging from icy tundra to steamy jungles. Compelling evidence of these adaptations to local environments is that about 11,000 years ago archaeological artifacts began to display great variety rather than Clovis-like uniformity.

Post-Clovis adaptations to local environments led to the astounding variety of Native American cultures that existed when Columbus arrived in 1492 (Map 1.2). By then, more than three hundred major tribes and hundreds of lesser groups inhabited North America alone; hundreds more lived in Central and South America. These people spoke different languages, practiced different religions, lived in different dwellings, followed different subsistence strategies, and observed different rules of kinship and inheritance. Hundreds of other ancient American cultures had disappeared or transformed themselves as their members constantly adapted to changing environmental conditions.

> About 11,000 years ago Paleo-Indians confronted a major crisis. The big-game animals they hunted for food became extinct.

A full account of those changes and the cultural diversity they created is beyond the scope of this textbook. But we cannot ignore the most important changes and adaptations made by ancient Americans in the centuries between 9000 B.C. (that is, 11,000 years ago) and A.D. 1492. The absence of written records makes oversimplification of these complex changes unavoidable. Nonetheless, the remarkable creativity demonstrated by the variety and longevity of ancient American cultures makes it far preferable to oversimplify their history than to overlook it.

## Archaic Hunters and Gatherers

Archaeologists use the term *Archaic* to describe the many different hunting and gathering cultures that descended from Paleo-Indians. *Archaic* also refers to the long period of time when those cultures dominated the history of ancient America, roughly from 8000 B.C. to somewhere between 2000 and 1000 B.C. Although the cultural and the chronological boundaries of the Archaic are not sharply defined, the term *Archaic* is still meaningful. It describes the important era in the history of ancient America that followed the Paleo-Indian mammoth hunters and preceded the development of agriculture. It also denotes a hunter-gatherer way of life that persisted throughout most of North America into the era of European settlement.

Like their Paleo-Indian ancestors, Archaic Indians hunted with spears; but they also took smaller game with traps, nets, and hooks. Unlike Paleo-Indians, most Archaic peoples used a variety of stone

---

*The word *culture* is used here to connote what is commonly called "way of life." It refers not only to how a group of people supplied themselves with food and shelter but also to their family relationships, social groupings, religious ideas, and other features of their way of life. For most prehistoric cultures—as for the Clovis people—more is known about food and shelter because of the artifacts that have survived. Ancient Americans' ideas, assumptions, hopes, dreams, and fantasies were undoubtedly important, but we know very little about them.

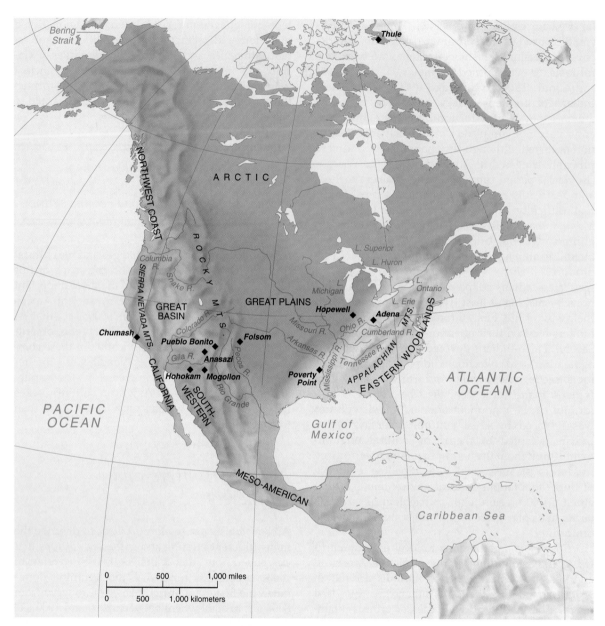

# MAP 1.2
## Native North American Cultures

*Environmental conditions defined the boundaries of the broad zones of cultural similarity among ancient North Americans. Using the map, try to specify the crucial environmental features that set the boundaries of each cultural region. The topography indicated on Map 1.3 may be helpful.*

tools to prepare food from wild plants. A characteristic Archaic artifact is a grinding stone used to pulverize seeds into edible form. Most Archaic Indians migrated from place to place to harvest plants and hunt animals. They usually did not establish permanent villages, although they often returned to the same river valley or fertile meadow from year to year to take advantage of abundant food resources. In certain regions where resources were especially rich—such as California and the Pacific Northwest—permanent settlements developed. Many Archaic groups became highly proficient basket makers in order to collect and store plant food. Above all, Archaic folk did not depend on agriculture for food. Instead, they gathered wild plants and hunted wild animals. These general traits of Archaic peoples were expressed in distinctive ways in the major environmental regions of North America.

## Great Plains Bison Hunters

Big-game hunting did not end with the extinction of mammoths. Instead, hunters began to concentrate on huge herds of bison grazing the grassy, arid plains that stretched for hundreds of miles east of the Rocky Mountains. For almost a thousand years after 9000 B.C., Archaic Indians hunted bison with Folsom points.

Like their predecessors, Folsom hunters were nomads who moved constantly to maintain contact with their prey. Often two or three hunters from a band of several families would single out a few bison from a herd and creep up close enough to spear them. Always the hunters were on foot. The ancient horses that had once existed in the New World were extinct; from 9000 B.C. to after A.D. 1500, bison hunters walked to work. They developed techniques of trapping that made it easier to kill groups of bison. At the original Folsom site, careful study of the bones McJunkin found suggests that early one winter hunters drove bison into the arroyo and speared twenty-three of them. Most likely such kills involved cooperation by hunters from several bands. At many other sites, hunters stampeded large numbers of bison over a cliff, killing some and injuring others, which could then be readily dispatched by waiting hunters.

Bows and arrows reached the Great Plains from the north by about A.D. 500 and largely replaced spears, which had been the hunters' weapon for more than 10,000 years. Bows permitted hunters to

**BISON KILL SITE**
*About 8,500 years ago at this kill site near Kit Carson, Colorado, hunters stampeded a bison herd into an arroyo. By carefully studying the jumbled animal bones, archaeologists have been able to reconstruct numerous details about the hunt. Many of the carcasses lay where the animals fell, facing south, suggesting that the wind blew from the south on the day of the hunt, as the hunters stayed downwind and maneuvered the herd toward the arroyo. Absolute cooperation among the hunters was necessary for the stampede and for the subsequent heavy labor of butchering. In all, the hunters butchered about three-fourths of these bison, probably feasting on bison tongues as they worked. From this hunt they obtained many valuable hides and enough meat to sustain more than one hundred people for at least a month.*
Joe Ben Wheat Photo, University of Colorado Museum.

strike an animal from farther away, and arrows made it easy to shoot repeatedly. These new weapons did not much alter the age-old techniques of bison hunting that had been developing since the Folsom era. The Archaic bison hunters demonstrate the continuity between the Paleo-Indians who first inhabited the continent and the numerous Native American peoples in A.D. 1492.

## Arctic Hunters

Arctic peoples had to subsist by hunting because the bitterly cold climate of most of Alaska and northern Canada prohibited gathering plants for most of the year. They preyed on caribou as well as seals, walruses, whales, and other sea mammals.

Archaic descendants of Paleo-Indians probably inhabited Alaska until around 4000 B.C. A new group appears to have migrated into Alaska around 2000 B.C., probably from Siberia. Although the archaeological evidence is sketchy, these new migrants were probably the ancestors of the Inuit (or Eskimos), whose culture came to dominate the entire Arctic. These newcomers were the earliest ancient Americans to use bows and arrows, which are found in Archaic Arctic sites dating to roughly 1500 B.C. Apparently they brought bows and arrows with them from Siberia; those weapons did not appear in other North American cultures until about A.D. 500, evidently the result of slow diffusion southward.

---

*The term* Archaic *describes the important era in the history of ancient America that followed the Paleo-Indian mammoth hunters and preceded the development of agriculture.*

---

About A.D. 1000, Thule people began to spread east from Alaska to the Atlantic coast. They crafted bone harpoons and sturdy kayaks of animal hides to hunt sea mammals far from shore. They also developed dogsleds for long-distance travel across snow and ice. Thule people were probably the first ancient Americans to encounter Europeans. At a Thule site on Ellesmere Island in far northeastern Canada, archaeologists have excavated chain-mail and armor that demonstrate contact with Viking seafarers who briefly settled in Greenland a few years before A.D. 1000.

## Great Basin Cultures

Unlike Arctic cultures, Archaic peoples in the Great Basin between the Rocky Mountains and the Sierra Nevada inhabited a region of great environmental diversity. Some Great Basin Indians lived along the shores of large marshes and lakes that formed during rainy periods. Other cultures survived in the foothills of mountains between the blistering heat on the desert floor and the cold, treeless mountain heights. These broadly defined zones of habitation changed constantly depending largely on the amount of rainfall.

Great Basin hunters took deer, antelope, and sometimes bison, as well as smaller game like rabbits, rodents, and snakes. At sites near water, Great Basin peoples hunted waterfowl with well-crafted decoys made of reeds. When unsuspecting ducks approached a group of decoys, lurking hunters grabbed their feet underwater or tossed a net over them before they could fly away. These people also ate fish of every available size and type, taking them with bone hooks as well as with nets.

Despite the variety and occasional abundance of animals, plants were the most important source of food for Great Basin Archaic people. Unlike animal food, plant food could be collected in large quantities and stored in baskets for long periods to protect against shortages caused by the fickle rainfall. Piñon nuts became a dietary staple for many Great Basin peoples, who used grinding stones to pulverize the nuts and wild seeds into a coarse flour. By diversifying their food sources and migrating to favorable locations, Great Basin peoples adapted to environmental challenges and, like Great Plains and Arctic cultures, maintained their basic hunter-gatherer way of life until long after A.D. 1492.

## Pacific Coast Cultures

The richness of the natural environment made California the most densely settled area in all of ancient North America. The abundant resources of both land and ocean offered such ample food that California groups remained hunters and gatherers for hundreds of years after A.D. 1492. The diversity of California's environment encouraged corresponding diversity among native peoples. By A.D. 1492, the mosaic of settlements in California included about five hundred separate tribes speaking some ninety languages, each with many local dialects. No other region of comparable size in North America exhibited such cultural variety.

The Chumash, one of the many California cultures, emerged near Santa Barbara about 3000 B.C. Chumash peoples hunted land animals like deer and bears, but they also preyed on sea mammals like seals, usually clubbing them while they were asleep on the shore. Chumash groups built large canoes from wooden planks and used them to fish in coastal waters and to travel along the coast. They also collected plant foods, especially acorns. After about 1000 B.C., the Chumash and other California cultures devoted increasing attention to gathering acorns, probably in response to the growing population and the greater need for food. Plentiful food resources permitted Chumash peoples to establish relatively permanent villages. Conflict frequently broke out among Chumash villages, and skeletons from prehistoric burials document a notable proportion of violent deaths. Archaeologists believe that such conflicts arose in part from efforts by Chumash villages to restrict access to their valuable acorn-gathering territory. Although few other California cultures achieved the population density and cultural complexity of the Chumash, all shared the hunter-gatherer way of life and reliance on acorns as a major food source.

Another rich natural environment lay along the Pacific Northwest coast. Abundant fish and marine life permitted the ancient Americans in this region to devote substantial time and energy to activities other than hunting and gathering. Especially after about 3500 B.C. they concentrated on catching large quantities of salmon, halibut, and other fish, which they dried to last throughout the year. With time free from the demands of food gathering, Northwest peoples developed sophisticated woodworking skills. They fashioned huge canoes, some big enough to hold fifty people, which they used to fish, hunt, and conduct warfare against neighboring tribes. Much of the conflict among Archaic northwesterners seems to have arisen from attempts to defend good fishing sites from incursions by outsiders.

Like the Chumash, the Northwest peoples built more or less permanent villages. They constructed large, multifamily houses from cedar planks. Beginning around A.D. 500 they often adorned their houses with totems, elaborately carved images of animals, supernatural beings, or their own ancestors (it is quite possible that similar carvings were made much earlier but disintegrated in the damp climate). These carvings, some of which Europeans later called "totem poles," honored the lineage of the family clan in a dwelling and displayed the clan's wealth and status. Maintaining such social distinctions was probably a principal function of the many artistic carvings that have survived.

## Eastern Woodlands Cultures

East of the Mississippi River, Archaic peoples adapted to a forest environment that included many local variants, such as the major river valleys of the Mississippi, Ohio, Tennessee, and Cumberland; the Great Lakes region; and the Atlantic coast (see Map 1.2). Throughout the diverse locales of the Eastern Woodlands, Archaic peoples adopted certain basic survival strategies.

**GREAT BASIN DUCK DECOYS**
*These decoys were crafted about two to three thousand years ago by observant ancient Americans who resided in the Great Basin. Discovered in a cave in the arid environment of west-central Nevada, the decoys show that the ancient Great Basin environment was sometimes marshy. The decoys, skillfully constructed of shoreline plants, were presumably used to attract waterfowl toward hunters hiding among reeds in what amounted to an ancient duck blind.*
Courtesy of the National Museum of the American Indian, Smithsonian Institution.

Deer were the most important prey of nearly all Woodlands hunters. At one Archaic dwelling site in Tennessee dating from 5000 to 3500 B.C., deer accounted for 90 percent of the excavated remains. In addition to food, deer supplied hides and bones that were crafted into useful items such as clothing, weapons, needles, and other tools. Like Archaic peoples elsewhere, Woodlands Indians gathered edible plants, seeds, and especially nuts. Hickory nuts were the most commonly gathered plant food, but pecans, walnuts, acorns, and hazelnuts were also collected. Woodlands groups migrated with the seasons to favorable hunting and gathering locations. After about 4000 B.C., some Woodlands peoples established more or less permanent settlements in locations that offered a wide variety of plant and animal resources. These Woodlands settlements were usually near a river or lake and typically included from 25 up to about 150 people. Woodlands folk at a site in southern Illinois built rectangular houses roughly twenty-five feet by fifteen feet. They placed large wooden poles in the ground around the perimeter of each house and filled in the space between the poles with sticks and mud. These houses were the earliest to be constructed in all of North America, experts believe. Woodlands people used similar building techniques for millennia afterward.

The existence of semipermanent settlements has permitted archaeologists to locate numerous Archaic burial sites that provide fascinating insights into the character of Woodlands cultures. At one site in western Kentucky, which dates to about 2500 to 2000 B.C., archaeologists found eleven hundred burials that allowed them to calculate that the life expectancy at birth for these Woodlands people was slightly over eighteen years. Some burials contain evidence of violent death; one skeleton, for example, had a spear point embedded in the rib cage. Archaeologists speculate that Woodlands groups sometimes fought over desirable hunting and gathering grounds. Some experts also believe that burials were a way to claim territory by making it literally the land of one's ancestors.

Around 2000 B.C., two important changes occurred among Woodlands cultures: Agriculture and pottery became incorporated into their basic hunter-gatherer lifestyles. First, some groups began to cultivate plants for food. Gourds and pumpkins that originated in Mexico were grown in parts of Missouri and Kentucky before 2000 B.C. After the introduction of these Mexican crops, Woodlands peoples began to cultivate local species such as sunflowers and other seed-bearing plants. It is likely that Woodlands folk also grew tobacco, an import from South America, since stone pipes for smoking appeared by 1500 B.C. and became common by 500 B.C. Corn, the most important plant food in Mexico, did not begin to be cultivated by Woodlands groups until about 300 B.C. and did not become a significant food crop until more than a thousand years later. Cultivated crops added to the quantity, variety, and predictability of Woodlands food sources, but they did not fundamentally alter the hunter-gatherer way of life.

Techniques for making ceramic pots probably also originated in Mexico and may have been brought north along with Mexican seeds. Pots were more durable than baskets for food preparation and storage, but they were also much heavier, probably an outgrowth of more permanent settlements. Neither pottery nor agriculture caused Woodlands peoples to turn away from their basic hunter-gatherer cultures, which persisted in most areas to A.D. 1492 and beyond.

*Around 2000 B.C., two important changes occurred among Woodlands cultures: Agriculture and pottery became incorporated into their basic hunter-gatherer lifestyles.*

Perhaps the most spectacular Archaic Woodlands site was Poverty Point near the Mississippi River in northeastern Louisiana. The Poverty Point culture existed from about 1700 B.C. to 700 B.C. These ancient Americans constructed an enormous earthworks consisting of six concentric half-circles more than a half-mile in diameter; each ring was built of dirt piled nine feet high and twenty-five feet wide. The purpose of this huge earthworks is unknown. It may have been used for astronomical observations since it seems aligned to view the spring and fall equinoxes. The labor and organization required to build such massive earthworks suggest that important ceremonies were conducted at the site. The complex may also have served as a meeting place for traders. At least a thousand people lived in dwellings near the earthworks and almost one hundred villages clustered nearby.

## Agricultural Settlements and Chiefdoms

Among Eastern Woodlands peoples and other Archaic cultures, agriculture supplemented rather than replaced hunter-gatherer subsistence strategies. Reliance on wild animals and plants required most Archaic groups to remain small and mobile. But in the centuries after 2000 B.C., distinctive Southwestern cultures slowly came to rely upon agriculture and to build permanent settlements. Later, around 500 B.C., Woodlands peoples in the vast Mississippi valley began to construct burial mounds and other earthworks that, like Poverty Point, suggest the existence of social and political hierarchies that archaeologists term *chiefdoms*. Although the hunter-gatherer lifestyle never entirely disappeared, the development of agricultural settlements and chiefdoms represented important innovations to the Archaic way of life that had endured since the Paleo-Indians.

## Southwestern Cultures

Ancient Americans in Arizona, New Mexico, and southern portions of Utah and Colorado developed southwestern cultures characterized by agriculture and eventually by multiunit dwellings called *pueblos*. All southwestern cultures confronted the challenge of a dry climate and unpredictable fluctuations in rainfall that made the supply of wild-plant food very unreliable for subsistence. These ancient Americans probably adopted agriculture in response to this basic environmental condition.

Until about 3000 B.C. the population of the Southwest appears to have been extremely sparse. Sometime within a few centuries of 1500 B.C., southwestern hunters and gatherers began to cultivate their signature food crop, corn (as it is called in North America; elsewhere it is called maize). Over the next three thousand years, corn became the basic cultivated food crop for Native American peoples throughout North America (and it remains one of the most productive food crops in the world today).

Central and South American peoples grew corn for millennia before the crop made its way to southwestern America. Corn, supplemented by squash and beans (which also traveled north from Mexico), became the staff of life of ancient southwesterners. The demands of corn cultivation encouraged southwestern hunter-gatherers to restrict their migratory habits in order to tend the crop. A vital consideration was access to water. Southwestern Indians became irrigation experts, conserving water from streams, springs, and rainfall and distributing it to thirsty crops. The adoption of agriculture and of more or less permanent settlements did not occur overnight. The long-term trend, however, clearly pointed toward sedentary villages that depended on growing corn.

Between about A.D. 200 and 900, small farming settlements appeared throughout southern New Mexico marking the emergence of the Mogollon culture. Typically a Mogollon settlement included about a dozen pit houses, made by digging out a rounded pit about fifteen feet in diameter and a foot or two deep and then erecting poles to support a roof of branches or dirt. Larger villages usually had one or two bigger pit houses that may have been the predecessors of the circular kivas, the ceremonial rooms that became a characteristic of nearly all southwestern settlements. Mogollon peoples began to make pottery about A.D. 200, and they also engaged in trade: Seashells, turquoise, and other luxuries from far away

appear in these sites. About A.D. 1000, Mogollon culture began to decline, for reasons that remain obscure. Among the descendants were the Mimbres peoples in southwestern New Mexico, who produced spectacular pottery with characteristic designs that often portrayed human and animal forms. By about A.D. 1150, the Mimbres culture also disappeared.

About A.D. 500, people who appear to have emigrated from Mexico established the distinctive Hohokam culture in southern Arizona. Hohokam peoples made extensive use of irrigation to plant and harvest twice a year. The comparatively high crop yields made possible by irrigation allowed the Hohokam population to grow and seek out more land to irrigate and settle. Hohokam culture continued to be strongly influenced by Mexican cultures. The people built sizable platform mounds and ball courts characteristic of cultures to the south. The Hohokam culture declined about A.D. 1400, for unknown reasons.

*Corn, supplemented by squash and beans, became the staff of life of ancient southwesterners.*

North of the Hohokam and Mogollon cultures, in a region that encompassed southern Utah and Colorado and northern Arizona and New Mexico, the Anasazi culture began to flourish during the first century A.D. The early Anasazi built pit houses and used irrigation much like their neighbors to the south. However, since many Anasazi settlements were on broad, flat mesas high above riverbeds, the people built reservoirs to capture rainwater and melted snow for irrigation. Beginning around A.D. 1000, for reasons that remain unclear, the Anasazi began to move their dwellings off the mesa tops. They built large, multistory cliff dwellings whose spectacular ruins can still be seen at Mesa Verde, Colorado, and Canyon de Chelly, Arizona. Other Anasazi communities, like the one whose impressive ruins can be visited at Chaco Canyon, New Mexico, erected huge, stone-walled pueblos with enough rooms to house the entire population of the settlement. Pueblo Bonito at Chaco Canyon, for example, contained more than eight hundred rooms. Anasazi pueblos and cliff dwellings typically contained one or more kivas used for secret ceremonies, restricted to men, that sought to communicate with the supernatural world.

**MIMBRES BOWLS**
*Mimbres peoples left a vivid record of their culture on bowls like these,*
*which were found in their graves. They punched a hole in the bottom of*
*a decorated bowl and then placed the inverted bowl over the face of the corpse.*
*The hole was obviously quite important in the burial ritual, but exactly what it meant is unknown.*
*The bowls shown here, made between A.D. 1000 and 1150, illustrate the hunting activities of Mimbres*
*men and the heavy lifting done by Mimbres women to haul deer back home. Mimbres women probably*
*made and decorated both bowls.*

Al Ligrani Photograph, Museum of Western Colorado; Transfer, Department of Anthropology, University of
Minnesota.

Pueblo Bonito stood at the center of a dozen large pueblos in or near Chaco Canyon. Scattered over 25,000 square miles were scores of smaller pueblos that were linked to Chaco Canyon and to the central site of Pueblo Bonito by a system of roads unprecedented in North America. The inhabitants of Chaco Canyon engaged in an extensive trade network involving turquoise, pottery, seashells, baskets, ritual items of many sorts, and even macaws—tropical birds valued for their brightly colored feathers. Around A.D. 1130, drought began to plague the region; it lasted for half a century and triggered the disappearance of the Chaco culture.

By A.D. 1200, the large Anasazi pueblos had been abandoned. The prolonged drought may have intensified conflict among pueblos and rendered ineffective the agricultural methods that had been developed in earlier centuries. Some Anasazi migrated toward regions with more reliable rainfall and settled in Hopi, Zuñi, and Acoma pueblos that their descendants in Arizona and New Mexico have occupied ever since.

## Burial Mounds and Chiefdoms

No other ancient Americans created dwellings similar to pueblos, but around 500 B.C., Woodlands cultures throughout the vast drainage of the Mississippi River began to build burial mounds that indicate the existence of chiefdoms. The size of the mounds, the labor and organization required to erect them, and the differences in the artifacts buried with certain individuals suggest the existence of a social and political hierarchy that archaeologists term a *chiefdom.*

Between about 500 B.C. and 100 B.C., Adena people built hundreds of burial mounds radiating from central Ohio (see Map 1.2). The Adena lived in small settlements and migrated to obtain food, as did previous Woodlands cultures. But when an important person died, small Adena groups coalesced into large gatherings that performed burial ceremonies involving the construction of mounds. In the burial mounds the Adena usually deposited a wide variety of grave goods, including spear points and stone pipes as well as decorative and ritualistic items such as thin sheets of mica (a glasslike mineral) crafted into naturalistic shapes. Men, evidently of high status, sometimes were buried with a skull, perhaps of an enemy or an ancestor. Women's and children's burials also often included grave goods. Once the body and grave goods were in place, dirt was piled into a mound one basketful at a time. Sometimes mounds were constructed all at once, but often they were built up over many years.

*The size of the burial mounds, the labor and organization required to erect them, and the differences in the artifacts buried with certain individuals suggest the existence of a social and political hierarchy that archaeologists term a* chiefdom.

About 100 B.C., Adena culture evolved into the more elaborate Hopewell culture, which lasted until about A.D. 400. It too was centered in Ohio but extended throughout the Ohio and Mississippi valleys. Hopewell people built larger mounds and filled them with more magnificent grave goods than had their Adena predecessors. Burial was probably reserved for the most important members of Hopewell groups. Most people were cremated. Careful analysis of skeletons in one Hopewell mound suggests that the more important graves contained men who were hunters; they tended to have arthritis of the elbow associated with stress to the elbow joint from using spear-throwers. These men were also taller than others, suggesting that high status may have been related to stature.

Grave goods at Hopewell sites were often lavish. In one burial a young man and woman lay side by side, each wearing many items of copper jewelry, necklaces of grizzly bear teeth, and artificial copper noses; the woman was surrounded with thousands of buttons and pearl beads. Hopewell sites testify not only to the high quality of their crafts but also to the existence of a wide-ranging trade network. Sites in Ohio contain obsidian from

the Yellowstone Park region of Wyoming; other stones originating in Missouri, Illinois, North Dakota, and Canada; shells and alligator teeth from the Florida and Gulf coasts; mica and minerals from North Carolina; and copper from near Lake Superior. Likewise, artifacts evidently exported from Hopewell centers appear at faraway sites in the Southeast, Northeast, and Midwest. After about A.D. 400, Hopewell culture declined, for reasons that are obscure. Some archaeologists believe that the adoption of the bow and arrow and of increasing reliance on agriculture may have made small settlements more self-sufficient and weakened their dependence on central chiefs responsible for the burial mounds.

**HOPEWELL EFFIGY PIPE**
*Hopewell burial mounds often contain effigy pipes in the shape of animals. This coyote pipe was carved from pipestone between about 200 B.C. and A.D. 100. To smoke the pipe, a Hopewell person would tamp tobacco into a bowl hollowed from the back of the coyote (not visible in the photo) and then light the pipe, perhaps with a flaming splinter. Facing the effigy, the smoker would inhale through the hole at the right end of the curved platform, under the coyote's nose. The coyote was probably more than simply an attractive decoration for a pipe, but what it signified remains unknown.*
Photograph © 1996 The Detroit Institute of Arts, Dirk Bakker Collection of Ohio Historical Society, Columbus.

Four hundred years later, another mound-building culture flourished. The Mississippian culture emerged in the floodplains of the major southeastern river systems about A.D. 800 and lasted until about A.D. 1500. Major Mississippian sites included huge mounds with platforms on top for ceremonies and for the residences of great chiefs. The largest Mississippian site was Cahokia, Illinois, just across the Mississippi River from St. Louis, Missouri.

At Cahokia, more than one hundred mounds of different sizes and shapes were grouped around large open plazas. Monk's Mound, the largest, covered sixteen acres at its base and was one hundred feet tall. Dwellings at one time covered five square miles and may have housed as many as thirty thousand inhabitants, easily qualifying Cahokia as the largest settlement in North America. At Cahokia and other Mississippian sites, people evidently worshiped a sun god; perhaps the mounds were a way to elevate elites nearer to the sun.

One Cahokia burial mound suggests the authority a great chief exercised. One man—presumably the chief—was buried with the dismembered bodies of several people, perhaps enemies or slaves; three men and three women of high status, perhaps the chief's relatives; four men, perhaps servants or guards, whose heads and hands had been cut off; and fifty young women between the ages of eighteen and twenty-three who had evidently been strangled. Such a mass sacrifice suggests the power a Cahokian chief wielded and the obedience he commanded.

Cahokia and other Mississippian sites had dwindled by 1500. By the time of European contact, most of the descendants of Mississippian cultures lived in small dispersed villages supported by agriculture, hunting, and gathering.

## Native Americans in 1492

By the time Europeans first arrived, North American tribes had incorporated and adapted many of the cultural achievements of their ancestors. The rigors of the continent's natural environments required that they maintain time-tested adaptations.

Eastern Woodlands peoples clustered into three major groups. Algonquian tribes inhabited the Atlantic seaboard, the Great Lakes region, and much of the upper Midwest (Map 1.3). The relatively mild climate along the Atlantic permitted the coastal Algonquians to grow corn and other crops as well as to hunt and fish. Around the Great Lakes and in northern New England, however, cool summers and severe winters made agriculture impractical.

Instead, the Abenaki, Penobscot, Chippewa, and other tribes hunted and fished, using canoes both for transportation and for gathering wild rice.

Inland from the Algonquians were the territories of the Iroquoian tribes, centered in Pennsylvania and upstate New York, as well as the hilly upland regions of the Carolinas and Georgia. Several features distinguished Iroquoian tribes from their neighbors. First, their success in cultivating corn and other crops allowed them to build permanent settlements, usually consisting of several bark-covered longhouses up to one hundred feet long and housing five to ten families. Second, Iroquoian societies were thoroughly matriarchal. Property of all sorts, including land, children, and inheritance, belonged to women. Women headed family clans and even selected the chiefs (normally men) who governed tribes. Third, for purposes of war and diplomacy, the Seneca, Onondaga, Mohawk, Oneida, and Cayuga tribes formed the League of Five Nations, an Iroquoian confederation that remained powerful well into the eighteenth century.

*North American cultures developed as adaptations to the natural environment local to each tribe. That great similarity underlay all the cultural diversity among native North Americans.*

Muskogean peoples spread throughout the Southeast, south of the Ohio River and east of the Mississippi. Including Creek, Choctaw, Chickasaw, and Natchez tribes, Muskogeans inhabited a bountiful natural environment that provided abundant food both from agriculture and from hunting and gathering. Remnants of the Mississippian culture existed in the religious rites common among the Muskogean. They practiced a form of sun worship, and the Natchez even built temple mounds modeled after those of their Mississippian ancestors.

West of the Mississippi River, Great Plains peoples straddled the boundary between the Eastern Woodlands and the western tribes. Many of the tribes had migrated to the plains within the century or two before 1500, forced out of the Eastern Woodlands by Iroquoian and Algonquian tribes. They were in the process of increasing their reliance on buffalo, although some tribes—especially the Mandan and Pawnee—were successful farmers, growing both corn and sunflowers as major food crops. The Teton Sioux, Blackfeet, Comanche, Cheyenne, and Crow on the northern plains and the Apache

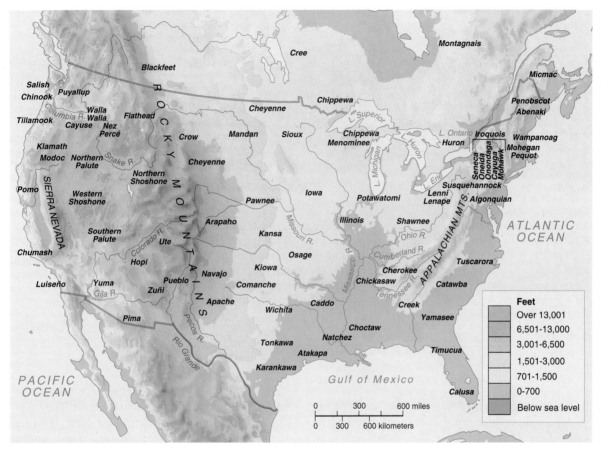

**M A P  1.3**
*Native North Americans about 1500*
*Distinctive Native American peoples resided throughout the area that, centuries later, would*
*become the United States. This map indicates the approximate location of some of the larger*
*tribes about 1500. In the interest of legibility, many other peoples who inhabited North Amer-*
*ica at the time are omitted from the map.*

and other nomadic tribes on the southern plains depended on buffalo. Tribes in the Great Basin region,
such as the Comanche and Shoshone, also continued to follow earlier subsistence practices, as did
Pacific coast cultures.

In the Southwest, descendants of the Mogollon, Hohokam, and Anasazi cultures lived in
settled agricultural communities, many of them
pueblos. However, a large number of warlike
Athapascan tribes had invaded the area within the
two hundred years before 1500. The Athapascans—
principally Apache and Navajo—were skillful warriors who preyed on the sedentary pueblo Indians,
reaping the fruits of agriculture without the work
of farming.

By the time Columbus arrived, the comparatively small Native American settlements in North

America supported a population estimated to be
about 4.5 million, slightly less than the population
of the British Isles at the time. All of them depended
on hunting and gathering for a major portion of
their food. Most of them also practiced agriculture,
some far more than others. All of them used bows
and arrows, as well as other weapons, for hunting
and warfare. None of them employed writing, but
they expressed themselves in many other ways.
They made drawings on stones, wood, and animal
skins; wove patterns in baskets and textiles; painted
designs on pottery; and crafted beadwork, pipes,
and other decorative items. They danced, sang, and
played music. They performed elaborate burial ceremonies and other religious rites.

Although they had rich and varied cultural resources, they lacked certain common features of life

**MEXICAN CALENDAR**

*The Mexican system of writing used glyphs, pictorial representations of gods, objects, and ideas. Some of the writing from before the arrival of Europeans has survived in the form of books, called codices. (Soon after the conquest, Spaniards burned all the codices they could find.) This precon-quest codex is a calendar of the 260-day religious year. The central figure on each page is Tlaloc, the rain god. The glyphs along the bottom of each page represent specific days; the symbols along the top indicate the sky and rain. Tlaloc priests used the calendar for many purposes, including setting the dates of major religious rituals.*
Lee Boltin.

in late-fifteenth-century Europe: They did not use wheels; sailing ships were unknown; they had no large domesticated animals like horses, cows, or oxen; their use of metals was restricted to copper; and metallurgy did not exist in North America. However, the absence of these European conveniences was profoundly irrelevant to ancient North Americans. Their cultures had developed as adaptations to the natural environment local to each tribe. That great similarity underlay all the cultural diversity among native North Americans.

## The Mexica: A Meso-American Culture

By 1492, the indigenous population of the New World numbered roughly 80 to 100 million, about the same as the population of Europe. All but about 4 million of these people lived in Central and South America. Like their North American counterparts, they too lived in a natural environment of tremendous diversity. They too developed hundreds of cultures, far too numerous to catalog here. But among all the Central and South American cultures the Mexica (often called Aztecs by Europeans, a

name the Mexica did not use) stood out. They were the most powerful Indians in the New World at the moment of European contact. Their empire stretched from coast to coast across central Mexico, encompassing as many as 25 million people. We know more about the fifteenth-century Mexica than about any other Native American society of the time. Their significance in the history of the New World after 1492 dictates a brief consideration of their culture and society.

*Despite pockets of resistance, by 1500 the Mexica ruled an empire that covered more land than Spain and Portugal combined and contained almost three times as many people.*

The Mexica began their rise to prominence about A.D. 1325 when small bands settled on a marshy island in Lake Texcoco, the site of the future city of Tenochtitlán. Resourceful, courageous, cold-blooded warriors, the Mexica were often hired as mercenaries by richer, more settled tribes. By 1430, the Mexica succeeded in asserting their dominance over their former allies and leading their own military campaigns in an ever-widening arc of empire building. Certain tribes battled the Mexica to a standoff and managed to preserve their independence. The Tlaxcalans, the most notable of these holdouts, eventually became allies of the European conquerors. Despite these pockets of resistance, by 1500 the Mexica ruled an empire that covered more land than Spain and Portugal combined and contained almost three times as many people.

The empire exemplified the central values of Mexican society. The Mexica worshiped the war god Huitzilopochtli. Warriors held the most exalted positions in the Mexican social hierarchy, even above the priests who performed the sacred ceremonies that won Huitzilopochtli's favor. In the almost constant battles necessary to defend and extend the empire, young Mexican men exhibited the courage and daring that would allow them to rise in the carefully graduated ranks of warriors. The Mexica considered capturing prisoners the ultimate act of bravery. The captives were usually turned over to the priests, who sacrificed them to Huitzilopochtli by cutting out their hearts. (See the Historical Question on page 20.)

The empire contributed far more to Mexican society than victims for sacrifice. At the most basic level, the empire was a military and political system for collecting tribute from subject peoples. The Mexica forced conquered tribes to pay tribute in goods, not money. Tribute included everything from candidates for human sacrifice to basic food products like corn and beans as well as exotic luxury items like gold or turquoise jewelry and rare bird feathers.

Tribute redistributed to the Mexica as much as a third of the goods produced by conquered tribes. The Mexica employed a sizable army of tribute collectors who made certain that each conquered settlement paid in full. On the whole, the Mexica did not much interfere with the internal government of conquered regions. Instead, they usually permitted the traditional ruling elite to stay in power—so long as they paid tribute. For their efforts, the conquered provinces received very little from the Mexica, except immunity from punitive raids by the dreaded Mexican warriors.

Tribute reflected the fundamental relations of power and wealth that pervaded the Mexican empire. The relatively small nobility of Mexican warriors, supported by a still smaller priesthood, possessed the military and religious power to command the obedience of thousands of nonnoble Mexica and of millions of other non-Mexica in subjugated provinces. The Mexican elite exercised their power to obtain tribute and thereby to redistribute wealth from the conquered to the conquerors, from the commoners to the nobility, from the poor to the rich. This redistribution of wealth made possible the achievements of Mexican society that eventually amazed Europeans: the temples,

**HUMAN SACRIFICE**

*Many ancient American peoples practiced human sacrifice as a sacred rite of communion with the gods. The Inca, a powerful people whose empire stretched down the west coast of South America, required each village to send one or two especially beautiful children to the capital, where they were honored in religious ceremonies and then taken back to their homes in a procession of priests and villagers. After joyous festivities, the children chosen for sacrifice were given an intoxicating drink and then buried in a prepared tomb, where they died. This mummy was probably a child sacrificed in such a ritual sometime around A.D. 1500. Discovered in Chile at an altitude of about 20,000 feet, where the dry, intense cold preserved the body, the mummy was accompanied by a female votive figure wrapped in finely woven cloth and capped with a bright feather headdress, a llama figurine, a bag of coca leaves, and other objects.*

Loren McIntyre.

# Why Did Mexicans Practice Human Sacrifice?

T HE MEXICA PRACTICED human sacrifice on a scale unequaled in human history. That does not mean, of course, that they intentionally killed more people than any other society. Plenty of other societies, both before and since, have systematically killed other human beings. Only a partial accounting of the years from 1930 to 1945, for example, would include millions of Jews murdered by the Nazis, millions of Russians killed by the Soviet leader Joseph Stalin, hundreds of thousands of Chinese slaughtered by the Japanese, and hundreds of thousands of Japanese annihilated by the atomic bombs dropped by the United States on Hiroshima and Nagasaki. Warfare of any kind involves intentional sacrifice of human life. However, the human sacrifice practiced by the Mexica was different. For them, human sacrifice was an act of worship—in fact, the ultimate act of worship.

Looking back from our vantage point five hundred years later, it is difficult for us to understand why the Mexica accepted human sacrifice as a normal and reasonable activity. Yet it is perfectly clear that they did. Although the precise number of victims is unknown, experts estimate that roughly 20,000 people were sacrificed each year throughout the Mexican empire. Celebration of an important victory or the appointment of a new emperor often involved the sacrifice of hundreds, sometimes thousands.

Most of the victims were prisoners captured in battle or rendered in tribute. Nonetheless, ordinary Mexican citizens—especially young men, women, and children—were often sacrificed in religious rituals. Every eighteen months, for example, a greatly honored young man was sacrificed to Tezcatlipoca, the god of human fate. From time to time, all Mexicans practiced sacrificial bloodletting, piercing themselves with stingray spines or cactus thorns to demonstrate their religious devotion. Both as symbol and reality, human sacrifice was an integral part of daily life in Mexican communities.

Mexicans employed several different techniques of sacrifice, all of them supervised and carried out by priests. By far the most common sacrifice was performed at an altar on the top of a temple where a priest cut out the still-beating heart of a victim and offered it to the gods. The victim's head and limbs were then severed and the torso fed to wild animals kept in cages in and near the temple. The heads were displayed on large racks at the base of the temples, while the limbs were cooked and eaten in sacred rituals. It is likely that participation in this ritualistic cannibalism was restricted to a minority of Mexicans, principally warriors, priests, and wealthier merchants. However, every Mexican participated in symbolic cannibalism by eating small cakes made of flour mixed with blood and shaped into human forms.

To us, these rituals seem ghoulish and disgusting, as they did to Europeans who eventually witnessed them. Yet the Mexica devoted so much time, energy, and resources to such rituals that it is impossible to doubt their importance to them. But why was human sacrifice so important?

In recent times, some scholars have argued that the Mexica practiced human sacrifice and cannibalism to remedy protein deficiencies in their diet. However, Mexicans' diet contained many sources of protein, including turkeys, chickens, fish, turtles, and eggs as well as corn and beans. For most Mexicans, dietary protein was adequate or better. Protein deficiency interprets human sacrifice as a solution to a problem that, evidently, did not actually exist.

Mexican religious beliefs offer a far more persuasive explanation for human sacrifice. Scholars know a good deal about Mexican religion because, in the years immediately following European conquest, Catholic priests studied Mexican religion in order to convert the people more readily to Christianity. These sources make clear that Mexica inhabited a world suffused with the power of supernatural beings. A special deity oversaw nearly every important activity. Mexicans believed that their gods communicated with human beings through omens, signs that the gods were either happy or displeased. In turn, the people communicated their own reverence for the gods by observing appropriate rituals. Bad omens such as an unexplained fire or a lightning bolt striking a temple meant that a god was angry and needed to be appeased with the proper rituals. Since almost every occurrence could be interpreted as an omen that revealed the will of a god, the routine events of daily life had a profound, supernatural dimension.

Mexicans' most powerful gods were Huitzilopochtli, the war god, and Quetzalcoatl, the god who gave sustenance to human beings. Mexicans believed that these two gods had created the world, the sun, the moon, the first human beings, the whole array of lesser deities, and everything else in the universe. Since the moment of creation, the earth had passed through four different epochs, which Mexicans called the Four Suns, each of which had ended in catastrophe. It fell to Quetzalcoatl and other potent deities to begin the Fifth Sun by re-creating human beings and all the other features of the universe. After years of work, Quetzalcoatl and the other gods had accomplished everything except the creation of the sun. Finally, two gods agreed to sacrifice themselves by jumping into a fire. Thereby they became the sun and moon, and other gods quickly followed them into the fire to keep the sun burning. But the sacrifice of the gods was sufficient only to ignite the sun. To maintain the light of the sun and keep it moving across the sky every day required human beings to follow the example of the gods and to feed the sun with human blood. Without the sacrificial blood, the world would go dark and time would stop. Mexicans considered the Fifth Sun the final stage of the universe, which would end when cataclysmic earthquakes destroyed the earth and supernatural monsters ravaged human life. By feeding the sun with human sacrifices, Mexicans believed they could delay that horrible final reckoning.

For the Mexica, human sacrifice was absolutely necessary for the maintenance of life on earth. Victims of sacrifice fulfilled the most sacred of duties. Through the sacrifice of their own lives they fed the sun and permitted others to live. The living demonstrated their respect and reverence for victims of sacrifice by eating their flesh. As one sixteenth-

**MEXICAN CEREMONIAL SKULL**
*This human skull, decorated by Mexican artisans with a mosaic of turquoise, jet, and shell, represented Tezcatlipoca, the Mexican deity who governed human fate. A handsome young man was selected for the great honor of impersonating Tezcatlipoca for the next eighteen months. The Mexican emperor gave the impersonator riches and privileges of all sorts, including allowing him to rule Tenochtitlán for the last five days of his life. On the last day, the impersonator climbed the steps of a temple where priests cut out his heart and decapitated him. This skull from the Tezcatlipoca ceremony presumably belonged to one of the impersonators. The skull is said to have been a gift from the emperor Montezuma to Cortés, leader of the Spanish conquest of Mexico.*
British Museum.

century Catholic priest explained, "The flesh of all those who died in sacrifice was held truly to be consecrated and blessed. It was eaten with reverence, ritual, and fastidiousness—as if it were something from heaven." From the Mexica's perspective, it was not wrong to engage in human sacrifice; it was wrong not to.

markets, bridges, waterworks, gardens, and zoos, not to mention the storehouses stuffed with gold and other treasures.

Subjugated communities felt exploited by the constant payment of tribute to the Mexica. By depending on military conquest and constant collection of tribute, the Mexica failed to create among their subjects a belief that Mexican domination was, at some level, legitimate and equitable. The high level of discontent among subject peoples constituted the soft, vulnerable underbelly of the Mexican empire. Instead of making friends for the Mexica, the empire created many bitter and resentful opponents, a fact Spanish conquerors eventually discovered.

## Conclusion: The Legacy of Ancient America

Ancient Americans shaped the history of human beings in the New World for more than twelve thousand years. They established continuous human habitation in the hemisphere from the time the first big-game hunters crossed Beringia until 1492 and beyond. Much of their history remains irretrievably lost. But much can be pieced together from artifacts they left behind, like the bones discovered at Folsom by George McJunkin. Ancient Americans achieved their success through resourceful adaptation to the hemisphere's many ever-changing natural environments. They also adapted to social and cultural changes caused by human beings—such as marriages, deaths, political struggles, and warfare—but the sparse evidence that has survived renders those adaptations almost entirely unknowable. Their creativity and artistry are unmistakably documented in the artifacts they left behind at kill sites, camps, and burial mounds. Those artifacts sketch the only likenesses of ancient Americans we will ever have—blurred, shadowy images that are indisputably human but forever silent.

In the five hundred years after 1492—barely 4 percent of the time human beings have inhabited the Western Hemisphere—Europeans and their descendants began to shape and eventually to dominate American history. Native American peoples continued to influence major developments of American history after 1492. But the new wave of immigrants that at first trickled and then flooded into the New World from Europe and from Africa forever transformed the peoples and places of ancient America.

## CHRONOLOGY

| | |
|---|---|
| c. 80,000–10,000 B.C. | Wisconsin glaciation exposes Beringia, "land bridge" between Siberia and Alaska. |
| c. 13,000–10,000 B.C. | First humans arrive in North America. |
| c. 9500–9000 B.C. | Paleo-Indians in North and Central America use Clovis points to hunt big game. |
| c. 9000 B.C. | Mammoths and many other big-game prey of Paleo-Indians become extinct. |
| c. 8000–1000 B.C. | Archaic hunter-gatherer cultures dominate ancient America. |

| | |
|---|---|
| c. 5000 B.C. | Corn cultivation begins in Central and South America. |
| c. 2000 B.C. | Some Eastern Woodlands people grow gourds and pumpkins and begin making pottery. |
| c. 1700–700 B.C. | Poverty Point culture flourishes in Louisiana. |
| c. 1500 B.C. | Southwestern cultures begin corn cultivation. |
| | Bows and arrows appear among Arctic peoples. |
| | Stone pipes for tobacco smoking appear in Eastern Woodlands. |

| | |
|---|---|
| c. 500 B.C. | Eastern Woodlands cultures start to build burial mounds. |
| c. 500–100 B.C. | Adena culture develops in Ohio. |
| c. 300 B.C. | Some Eastern Woodlands peoples begin to cultivate corn. |
| c. 100 B.C.–A.D. 400 | Hopewell culture emerges in Ohio and Mississippi valleys. |
| c. A.D. 200–900 | Mogollon culture emerges in New Mexico. |
| c. A.D. 500 | Bows and arrows appear in North America south of Arctic. Pacific Northwest cultures denote wealth and status with elaborate wood carvings. |
| c. A.D. 500–1400 | Hohokam culture develops in Arizona. |
| c. A.D. 800–1500 | Mississippian culture flourishes in Southeast. |
| c. A.D. 1000 | Thule peoples contact Vikings in northeastern Canada. |
| c. A.D. 1000–1150 | Anasazi peoples build cliff dwellings at Mesa Verde, Colorado, and pueblos at Chaco Canyon, New Mexico. Mimbres culture thrives in New Mexico. |
| c. A.D. 1325–1500 | Mexica conquer neighboring peoples and establish Mexican empire. |
| A.D. 1492 | Columbus arrives, beginning European conquest of New World. |

# SUGGESTED READINGS

Inga Clendinnen, *Aztecs: An Interpretation* (1991). A penetrating analysis of ancient Mexican society, emphasizing the coherence of religious belief and social behavior.

Michael Coe, Dean Snow, and Elizabeth Benson, *Atlas of Ancient America* (1986). A beautiful collection of detailed maps and authoritative commentary about ancient American peoples by leading scholars.

Brian M. Fagan, *Ancient North America: The Archaeology of a Continent* (1991). A readable survey of ancient North American cultures by a major interpreter of prehistoric life.

Brian M. Fagan, *Kingdoms of Gold, Kingdoms of Jade: The Americas before Columbus* (1991). A useful overview of ancient Americans throughout the Western Hemisphere.

Stuart J. Fiedel, *Prehistory of the Americas* (2nd ed., 1992). A somewhat technical but extremely valuable synthesis of current knowledge about ancient Americans.

Franklin Folsom and Mary Elting Folsom, *America's Ancient Treasure: A Guide to Archaeological Sites and Museums in the United States and Canada* (4th ed., 1993). An invaluable guide to the location of important archaeological sites that can be visited today.

Kendrick Frazier, *People of Chaco: A Canyon and Its Cultures* (1986). An accessible survey of the complex Anasazi culture responsible for the impressive prehistoric ruins in Chaco Canyon, New Mexico.

Alvin M. Josephy Jr., *America in 1492: The World of the Indian Peoples before the Arrival of Columbus* (1992). An informative overview of North American cultures on the eve of European arrival.

Timothy R. Pauketat, *The Ascent of Chiefs: Cahokia and Mississippian Politics in Native North America* (1994). A fascinating analysis of the power of chiefs in Mississippian culture as exemplified by Cahokia.

Lynda Shaffer, *Native Americans before 1492: The Moundbuilding Centers of the Eastern Woodlands* (1992). An informative examination of the cultures responsible for the many North American burial mounds that survive.

Bruce G. Trigger and Wilcomb E. Washburn, eds., *The Cambridge History of the Native Peoples of the Americas*, vol. 1, *North America* (1996). A comprehensive synthesis of the state of archaeological and historical knowledge about native North Americans from the time of first settlement to the present.

**TAINO ZEMI BASKET**

*This basket is an example of the effigies Tainos made to represent zemis, their deities. The effigy illustrates not only the artistry of the basket maker—probably a Taino woman—but also the basket maker's incorporation of European mirrors into a sacred object. Crafted sometime between 1492 and about 1520, the effigy suggests that Tainos readily adopted goods obtained in contacts with Europeans without altering their own traditional beliefs.*

Archivio Fotografico del Museo Preistorico Etnografico L. Pigorini, Roma.

# EUROPEANS AND THE NEW WORLD

## 1492–1600

A HALF HOUR BEFORE SUNRISE ON AUGUST 3, 1492, Christopher Columbus commanded three ships to catch the tide out of a harbor in southern Spain and sail west. Just over two months later, in the predawn moonlight of October 12, 1492, Columbus glimpsed an island on the western horizon. At last, he believed, he had found what he had been looking for, the western end of a route across the Atlantic Ocean to Japan, China, and India. At daybreak, Columbus could see people on the shore who had spotted his ships. He rowed ashore and, as the curious islanders crowded around, he claimed possession of the land for Ferdinand and Isabella, king and queen of Spain, who had sponsored his voyage. He named the island San Salvador, in honor of the Savior, Jesus Christ.

A day or two afterward, Columbus described that first encounter with the inhabitants of San Salvador in an extensive diary he kept during his voyage. He called these people Indians, assuming that their island lay somewhere in the East Indies near Japan or China. The Indians were not dressed in the finery Columbus expected. "All of them go around as naked as their mothers bore them; and the women also," he observed. Their skin color was "neither black nor white." They were not familiar with the Spaniards' weapons. "I showed them swords," Columbus wrote, "and they took them by the edge and through ignorance cut themselves." This first encounter led Columbus to conclude, "They should be good and intelligent servants, for I see that they say very quickly everything that is said to them; and I believe that they would become Christians very easily, for it seemed to me that they had no religion."

The people Columbus called Indians called themselves Tainos. They inhabited most of the islands Columbus visited on his first voyage, as had their ancestors for more than two centuries. Tainos were an agricultural people who grew cassava, a nutritious root, and other crops. Tainos worshiped gods they called zemis, the spirits of ancestors and of natural objects like trees and stones. Of utmost interest to Columbus, Tainos mined gold in small quantities.

What the Tainos thought about Columbus and his men we can only surmise. At first, Columbus believed that Tainos thought the Spaniards came from heaven. After six weeks of contact, Columbus was no longer confident that he understood them. Late in November 1492, he wrote that "the people of these lands do not understand me nor do I, nor anyone else that I have with me, them. And many times I understand one thing said by these Indians . . . for another, its contrary."

Columbus's perceptions of Tainos were shaped by European ideas, attitudes, and expectations, just as Tainos' perceptions of Europeans must have been colored

**COLUMBUS'S LETTER ANNOUNCING "THE DISCOVERED ISLANDS"**
*As soon as Columbus returned to Europe in 1493, he rushed a letter—written in Latin—to Ferdinand and Isabella with the good news of his startling discoveries across the Atlantic. In less than three months, by the time Columbus had traveled to Barcelona and reported personally to the Spanish monarchs, his letter had already been published in Spain and was soon reprinted in other countries. In the edition shown here, published in Switzerland in 1493, the ship under the Latin heading "Ocean Fleet" is the Santa María, which had in fact run aground in the Caribbean on Christmas Eve 1492. Columbus dismantled it and used its timbers to build a fort for the sailors he did not have room to take back to Spain on the remaining two ships.*
Special Collections, New York Public Library.

by their own culture. Yet the word that Columbus coined for the Tainos—*Indians,* a word that originated in a colossal misunderstanding—hinted at the direction of the future. To Europeans, *Indians* came to mean all native inhabitants of the New World, a name they gave to the lands in the Western Hemisphere.

Long before 1492, certain Europeans restlessly expanded the limits of the world known to them. Their efforts made possible Columbus's encounter with the Tainos. In turn, Columbus's landfall in the Caribbean changed the history not only of the Tainos, but also of Europe and the rest of the world.

## Europe in the Age of Exploration

Historically, the East—not the West—attracted Europeans. Wealthy Europeans developed a taste for luxury goods from Asia and Africa, and merchants competed to satisfy that taste. As Europeans traded with the East and with one another, they developed new information about the world they inhabited. Some learned that the known world was not all there was to know. A few people—sailors, merchants, aristocrats—took the risks of venturing beyond the limits of what was known. Those risks were genuine and could be deadly. But sometimes they paid off in new information, new opportunities, and eventually in the discovery of a New World.

## Mediterranean Trade and European Expansion

From the twelfth through the fifteenth century, spices, silk, carpets, ivory, gold, and other exotic goods traveled overland from Persia, Asia Minor, India, and Africa and then funneled into continental Europe through Mediterranean trade routes (Map 2.1). Dominated primarily by the Italian cities

of Venice, Genoa, and Pisa, this lucrative trade enriched Italian merchants and bankers. Rival merchants and financiers in other European cities coveted a share of the Mediterranean trade, but the Italians battled to protect their near-monopoly of access to eastern goods. Instead of trying to displace the Italians, merchants in other European countries chose the far safer alternative of trading with them.

Late in the thirteenth century, a fleet of Genoese ships ventured out of the western Mediterranean through the narrow Strait of Gibraltar into the stormy waters of the North Atlantic, for the first time bringing goods from southern Europe to markets in northern Europe. Ocean-borne access to North Atlantic ports allowed Mediterranean traders

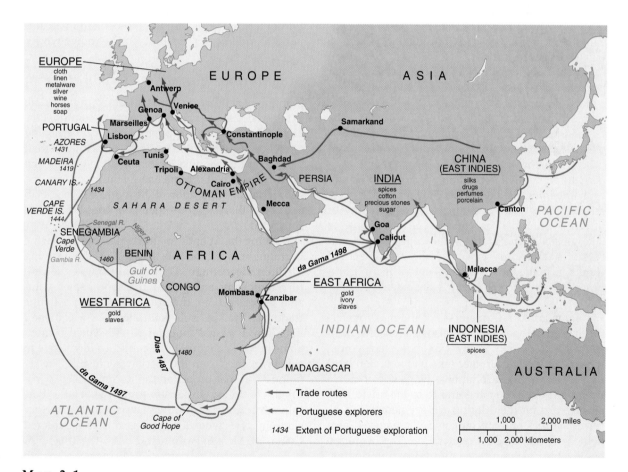

**MAP 2.1**
*European Trade Routes and Portuguese Exploration in the Fifteenth Century*
*The strategic geographic position of Italian cities as a conduit for overland trade from Asia was slowly undermined during the fifteenth century by Portuguese explorers who hopscotched along the coast of Africa and eventually found a sea route that opened the rich trade of the East to Portuguese merchants.*

to carry much larger quantities much less expensively than in the old overland trade. The vitality of the Mediterranean trade in the fourteenth and fifteenth centuries gave merchants and governments few reasons to look for alternatives. New routes to the East and the discovery of new lands were the stuff of fantasy.

Preconditions for turning fantasy into reality developed in fifteenth-century Europe. In the mid-fourteenth century, Europeans suffered a catastrophic epidemic of bubonic plague. The Black Death, as it was called, killed about a third of the European population. This devastating pestilence had repercussions that lasted for decades. So many people died that the pressure of population on Europe's food resources was significantly eased. Survivors, many of whom had inherited property from those who died, had greater opportunities for advancement. Many peasants moved from village to village and even to cities.

Most Europeans did not view these changes in positive terms. Instead, they perceived the world as a place of alarming risks where the delicate balance of health, harvests, and peace could quickly be tipped toward disaster by epidemics, famine, and violence. Most Europeans protected themselves from the constant threat of calamity by worshiping the supernatural, by living amid kinfolk and friends, and by maintaining good relations with the rich and powerful. Curiously, the insecurity and uncertainty of fifteenth-century life encouraged a few people to take greater chances. A sailor's willingness to embark on a dangerous sea voyage through uncharted waters to points unknown was one of many European responses to the hazards of fifteenth-century life.

Some aristocrats, members of the most powerful class in European society, also had reasons to engage in exploration. Many explorers were young sons of aristocratic families who had fallen on hard times. Others, like Columbus, were not of noble birth but hoped to gain entrance to the aristocracy as a reward for their daring achievements.

Scientific and technological advances also helped set the stage for exploration. The invention of movable type stimulated diffusion of information among literate Europeans. By 1400, the crucial navigational aids employed by marine explorers like Columbus were already available. Compasses were in widespread use. Hourglasses allowed fairly precise determination of elapsed time, useful in estimating speed. The astrolabe and the quadrant, devices for determining latitude, were beginning to be adopted by sailors. Charts called *portulanos* included detailed drawings of the shoreline and compass settings for sailing from one point to another.

*The insecurity and uncertainty of fifteenth-century life encouraged a few people to take great chances. A sailor's willingness to embark on a dangerous sea voyage through uncharted waters to points unknown was one of many European responses to the hazards of fifteenth-century life.*

These and other technological advances were known to many people throughout fifteenth-century Europe. Only the Portuguese used them in a campaign to sail beyond the limits of the known world.

## A Century of Portuguese Exploration

In many ways, Portugal was an unlikely candidate to take the lead in exploration. A small country, Portugal was populated by poor peasants governed by a tiny minority of noble families. Yet with less than 2 percent of the population of Christian Europe, the country devoted far more energy and wealth to the geographical exploration of the world between 1415 and 1460 than all the other countries of Europe combined.

Facing the Atlantic on the Iberian peninsula, the Portuguese lived on the fringes of the thriving Mediterranean trade. During the fourteenth century, merchants and sailors in Lisbon gained valuable experience in the extensive North Atlantic trade that Italians still controlled. As a Christian kingdom, Portugal cooperated with Spanish monarchs in the Reconquest, the centuries-long drive to expel Muslims from the Iberian peninsula. The religious zeal that propelled the Reconquest also justified continued expansion into what the Portuguese considered heathen lands. The key victory came in 1415 when Portuguese forces conquered Ceuta, the Muslim bastion at the mouth of the Strait of Gibraltar that had blocked Portugal's access to the Atlantic coast of Africa (see Map 2.1).

The most influential advocate of Portuguese exploration was Prince Henry the Navigator, son of the Portuguese king. From 1415 until his death in 1460, Henry collected the latest information about sailing techniques and geography, advocated new crusades against the Muslims, encouraged fresh sources of trade to fatten Portuguese pocketbooks, and pushed explorers to go farther still. Henry had the backing of the king and the pope to extend the Reconquest down the African coast. Economic motives also fueled Portuguese exploration. African conquests promised to wrest wheat fields from their Moroccan owners and to obtain gold, the currency of European trade. Gold was scarce in Europe where the accelerating pace of commerce increased the need for currency, while purchases in the East drained gold away from European markets.

Neither the Portuguese nor anybody else in Europe knew how big Africa was. At first, Portuguese mariners cautiously hugged the west coast of Africa, seldom venturing beyond sight of land. By 1434, they had reached the northern edge of the Sahara Desert, where strong westerly currents swept them out to sea. They soon learned how to ride those currents far away from the coast before sailing back toward land, a technique that allowed them to reach Cape Verde by 1444 (see Map 2.1).

To stow the supplies necessary for long periods at sea and to withstand the battering of ocean waves, the Portuguese developed the caravel, a sturdy ship that became the workhorse of exploration. The caravel enabled Portuguese sailors to round Cape Verde by first sailing hundreds of miles west into the Atlantic before catching favorable trade winds and currents that swung them back along the African coast. Navigating these huge westward loops into the Atlantic, Portuguese caravels sailed into and around the Gulf of Guinea and as far south as the Congo by 1480.

Portuguese explorations paid off handsomely in trade with Africans. Fierce African resistance confined the Portuguese to coastal trading posts where they bartered successfully for gold, slaves, and ivory. Portuguese merchants learned that relatively peaceful trading posts on the coast were far more profitable than violent conquests and attempts at colonization inland. In the 1460s, the Portuguese employed African slaves to develop sugar plantations on the Cape Verde Islands, inaugurating an association between African slaves and plantation labor that would be transplanted to the New World in the centuries to come.

In 1488, Bartolomeu Dias sailed around the Cape of Good Hope at the southern tip of Africa and hurried back to Lisbon with the exciting news that it appeared to be possible to sail on to India and China. In 1498, after ten years of careful preparation, Vasco da Gama commanded the first Portuguese fleet to sail to India. Portugal quickly

**BENIN BRONZE**
*This bronze was crafted in the sixteenth century by a highly skilled artist of the Benin people of western Africa. The bronze shows a Benin chief flanked by two of his warriors (lower left and right) and a Portuguese man (upper right). The Portuguese figure holds a gold spiral in his hand, presumably obtained in trade with Africans. In turn, the chief wears coral beads obtained in trade with the Portuguese on the African coast. The heavily armed chief and warriors suggest one reason why the Portuguese confined their activities to the coast. Note that the Portuguese figure does not have a weapon, clearly indicating the artist's sense of who had the upper hand.*
British Museum.

capitalized on the commercial potential of da Gama's new sea route. By the early sixteenth century, the Portuguese controlled a far-flung commercial empire in India, Indonesia, and China (collectively referred to as the East Indies). Their new sea route to the East eliminated overland travel and the numerous intermediate merchants and markups, integral parts of the old Mediterranean trade routes controlled by the Italians. As a result, Portuguese merchants could charge lower prices that allowed Europeans to purchase more eastern spices and other goods than ever before, to the great profit of Portugal.

# A Surprising New World in the Western Atlantic

In retrospect, the Portuguese seemed ideally qualified to discover America. They had pioneered the frontiers of seafaring, exploration, and geography for almost a century. However, the knowledge and experience that led them around Africa discouraged them from trying to sail across the Atlantic. They knew better than to undertake such a risky venture. The discovery of America required someone bold enough to believe that the experts were wrong, that despite the best available scientific knowledge the East Indies could be reached by sailing west. That person was Christopher Columbus.

## The Explorations of Columbus

Born in 1451 into the family of an obscure master weaver in Genoa, Italy, Columbus went to sea when he was about fourteen. About 1476, he moved to Lisbon and two or three years later married Felipa Moniz. Felipa's father, Bartolomeu, had been raised in the household of Prince Henry the Navigator and had retained close ties to the prince. Although Bartolomeu had died before Felipa's marriage, Columbus inherited his maps and papers, which were crammed with information about the currents and winds of the Atlantic. Columbus himself sailed frequently to the Madeira Islands and at least twice all the way to the coast of central Africa.

Like other Europeans, Columbus believed that the earth was a sphere. Theoretically, it was possible to reach the East Indies by sailing west. But according to Ptolemy, an ancient geographer whose writings were considered the final authority by most fifteenth-century Europeans, the earth was simply too big to make it feasible to sail west from Europe to Asia. Sailors would die of thirst and starvation long before they reached Asia.

Columbus rejected this conventional Ptolemaic wisdom. With flawed calculations, Columbus estimated the circumference of the earth to be 25 percent smaller than it really is. Columbus reasoned that Asia lay about 2,500 miles from the westernmost boundary of the known world, a shorter distance than Portuguese ships routinely sailed between Lisbon and the African Congo. In fact, the shortest distance to Japan from Europe's jumping off point in the Canary Islands was almost 11,000 miles. Convinced by his erroneous calculations, Columbus became obsessed with a scheme to prove he was right.

Columbus tried to convince the Portuguese king to sponsor an expedition west. But his peculiar notions about geography did not divert the Portuguese monarchy from its lucrative African explorations. Disappointed, Columbus moved to Spain in 1485 where he lobbied for his plan and even tried to interest the royal courts of England and France. He obtained a few modest but encouraging grants until 1492, when Spain's King Ferdinand and Queen Isabella finally agreed to finance most of the journey. The monarchs saw Columbus's venture as an inexpensive gamble: If it failed, not much was lost; if it succeeded, a great deal might be gained.

After barely three months of hurried preparation, Columbus and his small fleet—the *Niña* and *Pinta,* both caravels, and the *Santa María,* a larger merchant vessel—embarked for the Canary Islands. When he cast off from the Canaries, however, he did not head for the coast of Africa; instead he kept sailing west. Six weeks later, he landed on a tiny Caribbean island located about three hundred miles north of the eastern tip of Cuba, which he named San Salvador (Map 2.2).

Columbus and his men understood that they had made a momentous discovery. Yet they found it frustrating. Although the Tainos proved friendly and accommodating, they possessed little gold and none of the riches Columbus expected to find in the East. For three months Columbus cruised from island to island, looking for the king of Japan. In mid-January 1493, he started back, taking seven Tainos with him. When he reached Isabella and Ferdinand, they were overjoyed by his news. With a voyage that had lasted barely eight months, Columbus appeared to have catapulted Spain from a secondary position in the race for a sea route to Asia into that of a serious challenger to Portugal, whose explorers had not yet sailed to India or China. Columbus and his Taino companions became the toast of the royal court.

The Spanish monarchs, following Portuguese precedent, rushed to the pope to obtain confirmation of their claim to Columbus's discoveries. Pope Alexander VI, a Spaniard, complied. In May 1493, he granted to Spain all land discovered west of an imaginary line lying three hundred miles west of the Azores. The decree alarmed the Portuguese, who believed that it violated their rights under previous papal grants. To protect their African claims, the Portuguese negotiated the Treaty of Tordesillas with Spain in 1494, shifting the imaginary line eleven hundred miles west of the Canary Islands (see Map 2.2). Land discovered west of the line belonged

**MAP 2.2**
*European Explorations in Sixteenth-Century America*
*This map illustrates the approximate routes of early European explorations of the New World. Note that—with the exception of the voyage of John Cabot—English, French, and Dutch explorers were latecomers. What accounts for Spain's head start?*

to Spain, while Portugal claimed land to the east. In effect, the treaty reassured Portugal and allowed Spain to follow up Columbus's discovery without being threatened by the menacing Portuguese.

*With a voyage that had lasted barely eight months, Columbus appeared to have catapulted Spain from a secondary position in the race for a sea route to Asia into that of a serious challenger to Portugal, whose explorers had not yet sailed to India or China.*

In the fall of 1493, Isabella and Ferdinand sent Columbus west again to locate the Asian mainland. This time he commanded a fleet of seventeen ships and more than one thousand men, who planned to settle, explore, find gold, and get rich. Near the end of his first voyage, a shipwreck had forced Columbus

to leave behind thirty-nine of his sailors on the island of Hispaniola. When Columbus returned in 1493, he learned that his men had terrorized the Tainos, kidnapped local women, and held them in harems; in retaliation, Taino chiefs had killed all of the Spaniards. The brief history of that first group of Spaniards to reside in the New World prefigured much of what was to happen in the years ahead.

Before Columbus died in 1506, he returned to the New World two more times (1498–1500 and 1502–1504) without relinquishing his belief that the East Indies were there, someplace. Explorers continued to search for a passage to the East or some other source of profit. Before long, prospects of beating the Portuguese to Asia began to dim along with the hope of finding vast hoards of gold. For a generation after 1492, the yield from New World discoveries disappointed the Spanish crown. Nonetheless, Columbus's discoveries forced sixteenth-century Europeans to think about the world in new ways. Columbus proved that it was possible to sail from Europe to the western rim of the Atlantic and return to Europe. Most important, Columbus made clear that beyond the western shores of the Atlantic lay lands entirely unknown to Europeans.

## The Geographic Revolution and the Columbian Exchange

Within thirty years of Columbus's initial discovery, Europeans' understanding of world geography underwent a revolution. An elite of perhaps twenty thousand people surrounding the royal courts and trading centers of western Europe had access to information about the new geography of the world. It took a generation of additional exploration before they could comprehend the general contours of what Columbus had found.

In 1497, King Henry VII of England, who had spurned Columbus's request for sponsorship a decade earlier, sent another Genoese sailor, John Cabot, to look for a passage to the Indies across the North Atlantic, referred to as a "Northwest Passage" (see Map 2.2). Cabot managed to reach the tip of Newfoundland, which he too believed was part of Asia. Cabot hurried back to England, assembled a small fleet to follow up his discovery, and returned in 1498. But he was never heard from again. Three thousand miles to the south, in 1498 Columbus touched the mainland of Venezuela, near the mouth of the Orinoco River. A year later, another Spanish expedition landed about six hundred miles farther south, accompanied by Amerigo Vespucci, an Italian businessman whose avocation was geography. In 1500, Pedro Alvars Cabral commanded a Portuguese fleet bound for the Indian Ocean that accidentally made landfall on the coast of Brazil as it looped westward into the Atlantic. The next year the Portuguese sent Vespucci to learn whether Cabral's discovery lay on their side of the Tordesillas line, as in fact it did.

By 1500, it was clear that several large chunks of land cluttered the western Atlantic. A few cartographers speculated that these chunks were connected to one another in a landmass that was not Asia. In 1507, Martin Waldseemüller, a German cartographer, published the first map that showed the New World separate from Asia; he named the land America, in honor of Amerigo Vespucci.

Two additional discoveries confirmed Waldseemüller's speculation. In 1513, Vasco Núñez de Balboa crossed the isthmus of Panama and reached the Pacific Ocean. Clearly, more water lay between the New World and Asia. How much water Ferdinand Magellan discovered when he set out to circumnavigate the globe in 1519. Sponsored by King Charles I of Spain, Magellan's voyage took him first to the New World, around Cape Horn at the southern tip of South America through what became known as the Straits of Magellan, and into the Pacific late in November 1520. Crossing the Pacific took almost four months. When he reached the Philippines, his crew had been decimated by extreme hunger and thirst. Magellan himself was killed by Philippine tribesmen. A remnant of his expedition continued into the Indian Ocean and managed to transport a cargo of spices back to Spain in 1522.

In most ways Magellan's voyage was a disaster. One ship and 18 men crawled back from an expedition that had begun with five ships and more than 250 men. But the geographic information it provided left no doubt that America was a continent separated from Asia by the enormous Pacific Ocean. The voyage made clear that Columbus was dead wrong about the identity of what he had discovered. It was possible to sail west to reach the East Indies, but Magellan's voyage demonstrated that that was a terrible way to go. After Magellan, most Europeans who sailed west had their sights set on the New World, not on Asia.

---

*Magellan's voyage left no doubt that America was a continent separated from Asia by the enormous Pacific Ocean. The voyage made clear that Columbus was dead wrong about the identity of what he had discovered.*

---

Columbus's arrival in the Caribbean anchored the western end of what might be imagined as a sea bridge spanning the Atlantic and connecting the New World to Europe. That sea bridge ended the age-old separation of the hemispheres and initiated the Columbian exchange, a transatlantic exchange of goods, people, and ideas that has continued ever since. Spaniards brought things that were novelties in the New World but commonplace in Europe, including Christianity, iron technology, sailing ships, firearms, wheeled vehicles, and horses and other domesticated animals. Smuggled along unknowingly were also Old World mi-

### COLUMBIAN EXCHANGE

*The arrival of Columbus in the New World initiated an unending transatlantic exchange of goods, people, and ideas. Spaniards brought domesticated animals common in the Old World, including horses, cattle, goats, chickens, cats, and sheep. The novelty of such animals is demonstrated by the Nahua words the Mexican people initially used to refer to these strange new beasts: for horses, they used the Nahua word for deer; a cow was "one with horns"; a goat was "a bearded one with horns"; a chicken was a "Spanish turkey hen"; a cat was a "little cougar"; a sheep was referred to with the word for cotton, linking the animal with its fibrous woolen coat. Spaniards brought many other alien items such as cannon, which the Nahua at first termed "fat fire trumpets," and guitars, which the Nahua called "rope drums." Spaniards also carried Old World microorganisms that caused devastating epidemics of smallpox, measles, and other diseases. Ancient American people, goods, and ideas made the return trip across the Atlantic. Columbus's sailors quickly learned to use Indian hammocks and became infected with syphilis in sexual encounters with Indian women; then they carried both hammocks and syphilis back to Europe. Smoking tobacco, like the cigar puffed by the ancient Mayan lord, became such a fashion in Europe that some came to believe, as a print of two men relaxing with their pipes was captioned, "Life Is Smoke." The strangeness of New World peoples and cultures also reinforced Europeans' notions of their own superiority. Although the Columbian exchange went in both directions, it was not a relationship of equality. Europeans retained the upper hand.*

The Bancroft Library; Arxiv Mas; Francis Robicey.

croorganisms that caused epidemics of smallpox, measles, and other diseases that devastated Indian peoples.

Ancient American goods, people, and ideas made the return trip across the Atlantic. Europeans were introduced to such vital New World crops as corn and potatoes as well as exotic items like the pineapple, which they named for its resemblance to the pinecone. Columbus's sailors became infected with syphilis in sexual encounters with New World women and then unwittingly carried the deadly parasite back to Europe. New World tobacco created a European rage for smoking that has yet to abate. For almost a generation after 1492, the Columbian exchange did not reward Spaniards with the riches they longed to find.

# Spanish Exploration and Conquest

During the sixteenth century, the New World helped Spain become the most powerful country in both Europe and the Americas. Initially, Spanish expeditions reconnoitered the Caribbean, scouted stretches of the mainland coast, and established settlements on the large islands of Hispaniola, Puerto Rico, Jamaica, and Cuba. Spaniards enslaved Caribbean tribes and put them to work growing crops and mining gold. But the profits from these early ventures barely covered the costs of maintaining the settlers. After almost thirty years of exploration, the promise of Columbus's discovery seemed illusory.

Soon after 1519, however, that promise was fulfilled, spectacularly. The mainland phase of exploration began in 1519 with Hernán Cortés's march into Mexico and lasted until about 1545, when Spanish conquests extended from northern Mexico to southern Chile, and New World riches filled Spanish treasure chests. Cortés's expedition served as the model for all the rest.

## The Conquest of Mexico

Hernán Cortés, who would become the richest and most famous conquistador (conqueror) of all, arrived in the New World in 1504, an obscure nineteen-year-old Spaniard seeking adventure and the chance to make a name for himself. He fought in the conquest of Cuba and elsewhere in the Caribbean. In 1519, the governor of Cuba authorized Cortés to organize an expedition to investigate rumors of a fabulously wealthy kingdom somewhere in the interior of the mainland. A charming, charismatic leader, Cortés quickly assembled a force of about six hundred men. The Cuban governor soon had second thoughts about entrusting the expedition to an unpredictable man like Cortés, and he withdrew permission for the campaign. Characteristically, Cortés ignored the governor, loaded his ragtag army aboard eleven ships, and set out on his freelance crusade.

Cortés's confidence that he could talk his way out of most situations and fight his way out of the rest fortified the small band of Spaniards. Landing first on the Yucatán peninsula, Cortés had the good fortune to receive a gift from a Mayan chief: a young woman named Malinali who spoke both Mayan and Nahuatl, the language of most people in Mexico and Central America. Malinali, whom the Spaniards called Marina, soon learned Spanish and became Cortés's interpreter. (She also became one of Cortés's mistresses and bore him a son.) Marina served as the essential conduit of communication between the Spaniards and the Indians. With her help, Cortés talked and fought with Indians along the Gulf coast of Mexico, trying to discover the location of the fabled kingdom (see Map 2.2).

In Tenochtitlán, the capital of the Mexican empire, the emperor Montezuma heard about some strange creatures along the coast. (Montezuma and his people are often called Aztecs, but they called themselves Mexica.) He feared that the strangers were led by the god Quetzalcoatl, who was returning to Tenochtitlán as predicted by the Mexican religion. Montezuma sent emissaries, carrying gifts appropriate for a god, to meet with the intruders. When the emissaries arrived, Cortés obliged the visitors and donned the regalia they had brought, almost certain proof to the Mexica that he was indeed Quetzalcoatl. For their part, the Spaniards astounded the emissaries by blasting their cannon, showing off their iron swords and armor, and exhibiting their horses, which the Mexica considered a species of supernatural deer.

The emissaries hurried back to Montezuma with their amazing news. Montezuma arranged for large quantities of food to be brought to the coast to welcome the strangers and also to postpone (and perhaps prevent) Quetzalcoatl's arrival in Tenochtitlán. In addition, since Quetzalcoatl presumably hungered for blood, Montezuma sent numerous hostages for sacrifice. Before the food was served to the Spaniards, the Mexica sacrificed the hostages and soaked the food in their blood. This fare sickened the Spaniards and might have been enough to turn them back to Cuba. However, the Mexica also brought a gift, a "disk in the shape of the sun, as big as a cartwheel and made of very fine gold," as one Mexica recalled. Here was conclusive evidence that the rumors heard by Cortés and his army had some basis in fact.

In August 1519, Cortés embarked on a march to find Montezuma. Leading about 350 men armed with swords, lances, and muskets and supported by ten cannon, four smaller guns, and sixteen horses, Cortés had to live off the land, making friends with the indigenous tribes when he could and killing them when he thought necessary. On November 8, 1519, Montezuma came out to meet Cortés on a causeway leading into Tenochtitlán. After presenting Cortés with gifts, Montezuma welcomed the Spaniards to the royal palace and showered them with lavish hospitality. Quickly, Cortés took Montezuma hostage and held him under house arrest, hoping to make him a puppet through which the Spaniards could rule the Mexican empire. This uneasy peace existed for several months until, after a brutal massacre of many Mexican nobles by one of Cortés's subordinates, the population of Tenochtitlán revolted, murdered Montezuma, and mounted a ferocious assault on the Spaniards. On June 30, 1520, Cortés and about a hundred other Spaniards fought their way out of Tenochtitlán and retreated toward the coast about one hundred miles to Tlaxcala, a stronghold of bitter enemies of the Mexicas. The friendly Tlaxcalans allowed Cortés to regroup, obtain reinforcements, and plan a strategy to conquer Tenochtitlán.

In the spring of 1521, Cortés mounted a complex campaign against the Mexican capital. The Spaniards and tens of thousands of Indian allies laid siege to the city. With a relentless, scorched-earth strategy, Cortés finally defeated the last Mexican defenders on August 13, 1521. (See the Historical Question on page 36.) The great capital of the Mexican empire "looked as if it had been ploughed up,"

## Why Did Cortés Win?

B<small>Y CONQUERING MEXICO</small>, Hernán Cortés demonstrated that Columbus had in fact discovered a New World of enormous value to the Old. But why did a few hundred Spaniards so far away from home defeat millions of Indians fighting on their home turf?

First, several military factors favored the Spaniards. They possessed superior military technology, which largely offset the Mexica's numerical superiority. They fought with weapons of iron and steel against the Mexica's stone, wood, and copper; they charged on horseback against Mexican warriors on foot; they ignited gunpowder to fire cannon and muskets toward the attacking Mexica, whose only source of power was human muscle.

The Spaniards also enjoyed superior military organization, although they were far from a highly disciplined, professional fighting force. Cortés's army was composed of soldiers of fortune, young men who hoped to fight for God and king and get rich. The unsteady discipline among the Spaniards is suggested by Cortés's decision to beach and dismantle the ships that had brought his small army to the Mexican mainland—after that, the only way for his men to go was forward.

Nonetheless, the Spaniards were a well-oiled military machine compared with the Mexica, who tended to attack from ambush or in waves of frontal assaults, with great courage but little organization or discipline. They seldom sustained attacks, even when they had the Spaniards on the run. In the siege of Tenochtitlán, for example, the Mexica often paused to sacrifice any Spanish soldiers they had captured, taking time to skin "their faces," one Spaniard recalled, "which they afterward prepared like leather gloves, with their beards on." Spanish tactics, in contrast, emphasized concentrating their soldiers to magnify the effect of their firepower and to maintain communication during the thick of battle.

But perhaps the Spaniards' most fundamental military advantage was their concept of war. The Mexican concept of war was shaped by the nature of the empire. The Mexica fought to impose their tribute system on others and to take captives for sacrifices. From their viewpoint, war made their adversaries realize the high cost of continuing to fight and gave them a big incentive to surrender and pay tribute. For the Spaniards, war meant destroying the enemy's ability to fight. In short, the Spaniards sought total victory; the Mexica sought surrender. All these military factors weakened the Mexica's resistance, but they were insufficient to explain Cortés's victory.

Disease played a major part in the Mexica's defeat. When the Mexica confronted Cortés, they were not at full strength. An epidemic of smallpox and measles had struck the Caribbean in 1519, arrived in Mexico with Cortés and his men, and lasted through 1522. Thousands of Indians died, and many others became too sick to fight. When the Spaniards were regrouping in Tlaxcala, after their disastrous evacuation of Tenochtitlán, a great plague broke out in the Mexican capital. As one Mexica explained to a Spaniard shortly after the conquest, the plague lasted for seventy days, "striking everywhere in the city and killing a vast number of our people. Sores erupted on our faces, our breasts, our bellies. . . . The illness was so dreadful that no one could walk or move. . . . They could not get up to search for food, and everybody else was too sick to care for them, so they starved to death in their beds."

Religion also contributed to the Mexica's defeat. Mexican religious doctrine led Montezuma to be hesitant and uncertain in confronting the Spaniards during the months when they were most vulnerable. While Cortés marched toward Tenochtitlán, the Indians thought that the Spaniards and their horses were immortal deities. Cortés worked hard to maintain the illusion, hiding Spaniards who died. But by the time Cortés retreated from Tenochtitlán, the Mexica knew that the Spaniards could be killed, and their resistance stiffened accordingly.

While the Mexica's religion reduced their initial resistance to the conquistadors, Christianity strengthened the Spaniards. The Spaniards' Christianity was a confident and militant faith that commanded its followers to destroy idolatry, root out heresy, slay infidels, and subjugate nonbelievers. Their religious zeal had been honed for centuries in

**CONQUEST WARFARE**

*This postconquest painting by a sixteenth-century Mexican artist is one of a series illustrating crucial battles in the ultimate defeat of the Mexica. Here Mexican warriors are attacking the conquistadors shortly before the Spaniards retreated from Tenochtitlán and prepared for the final siege. The distinctive shields and costumes of the Mexica signify their military status, which was based on their battlefield prowess. The Spaniards, in contrast, wear gray armor, their crossbows and guns pitted against the Mexica's spears. The Mexica won this battle, a point the artist suggests by making the Mexican warriors appear bigger while the massed conquistadors lean slightly backward.*

Oronoz.

the battles of the Reconquest. Christianity was as much a part of the conquistadors' armory as swords and gunpowder.

Mexican military commanders often turned to their priests for military guidance. Spaniards routinely celebrated mass and prayed before battles, but their military and diplomatic decisions were made by Cortés and his subordinates, tough, practical, wily men. When the Spaniards suffered defeats, they did not worry that God had abandoned them. However, when the Mexica lost battles advised by their priests, they confronted the distressing fear that their gods no longer seemed to listen to them. The deadly sickness sweeping through the countryside also seemed to show that their gods had abandoned them. "Cut us loose," one Mexican pleaded, "because the gods have died."

Finally, political factors proved decisive in the Mexica's defeat. Cortés shrewdly exploited the tensions between the Mexica and their subjects. With skillful diplomacy, Cortés obtained cooperation from thousands of Indian soldiers, porters, and food suppliers who were the crucial ingredient in the Spaniards' success. Besides fighting alongside Cortés, the Spaniards' Indian allies provided the invaders with a fairly secure base from which to maneuver against the Mexica's stronghold. Cortés's small army was reinforced by thousands of Indians who were eager to seek revenge against the Mexica. Hundreds of thousands of other Indians helped the Spaniards by not contributing to the Mexica's defense. These passive allies of the Spaniards prevented the Mexica from fully capitalizing on their overwhelming numerical superiority. In the end, although many factors contributed to the conquest, Cortés won because the Mexican empire—the source of the Mexica's impressive wealth and power—was also their crippling weakness.

one of Cortés's soldiers remembered. A few years later, one of the Mexica described the utter despair of the defeated:

> Broken spears lie in the roads;
> we have torn our hair in grief.
> The houses are roofless now, and their walls
> are red with blood. . . .
>
> We have pounded our hands in despair
> against the adobe walls,
> for our inheritance, our city, is lost and dead.

## The Search for Other Mexicos

Lured by their insatiable appetite for gold, conquistadors quickly fanned out from Tenochtitlán in search of other Mexicos. To the south, Guatemala, El Salvador, and Nicaragua came under Spanish control by 1524. The Mayan tribes of the Yucatán peninsula did not succumb for another twenty years. The most spectacular prize fell to Francisco Pizarro, who conquered the Incan empire in Peru. The Incas controlled a vast, complex region that contained more than nine million people and stretched along the western coast of South America for more than two thousand miles. In 1532, Pizarro and his army of fewer than two hundred men captured the Incan emperor Atahualpa and held him hostage. As ransom, the Incas gave Pizarro the largest treasure yet produced by the conquests: gold and silver equivalent to half a century's worth of precious-metal production in Europe. With the ransom safely in their hands, the Spaniards executed Atahualpa. The Incan treasure proved that at least one other Mexico did exist.

---

*Lured by their insatiable appetite for gold, conquistadors quickly fanned out from Tenochtitlán in search of other Mexicos.*

---

In the north, Juan Ponce de León, who had sailed around the Florida peninsula in 1513, was encouraged by Cortés's success to return to Florida in 1521, where he was killed in a battle with Calusa Indians. In 1525, Lucas Vázquez de Ayllón explored the Atlantic coast north of Florida to South Carolina. A year later, he established a small settlement on the Georgia coast that he named San Miguel de Gualdape, the first Spanish attempt to create a town

in what is now the United States. Within a few months most of the settlers, including Ayllón, became sick and died, and the few survivors retreated to the Caribbean. In 1528, Pánfilo de Narváez surveyed the Gulf coast from Florida to Texas. The Narváez expedition ended disastrously on the Texas coast, near Galveston, where Indians enslaved the few survivors. After several years, four Spaniards managed to escape and were ultimately rescued by Spanish slave hunters in northern Mexico.

In 1539, Hernando de Soto, a seasoned conquistador who had taken part in the conquest of Peru, set out with nine ships and more than six hundred companions to find another Peru in North America. Landing in Florida, de Soto literally slashed his way through much of the southeastern United States for three years, searching for the rich, majestic civilizations he thought were there. After many brutal battles and much hardship, de Soto became sick and died in 1542, and his men buried him in the Mississippi River before turning back to Mexico, disappointed.

Tales of the fabulous wealth of the mythical Seven Cities of Cíbola also lured Francisco Vásquez de Coronado to search the Southwest and Great Plains of North America. In 1540, Coronado left northern Mexico with more than three hundred Spaniards, a thousand Indians, fifteen hundred horses, and a priest named Marcos de Niza who claimed to know the way to what he called "the greatest and best of the discoveries." Cíbola turned out to be a small Zuñi pueblo of about a hundred families. When the Zuñi shot arrows at the Spaniards, Coronado attacked the pueblo and routed the defenders after a hard battle. Convinced that the rich cities must lie somewhere over the horizon, Coronado kept moving all the way to central Kansas before deciding in 1542 that the rumors he had pursued were just that, nothing more.

Juan Rodríguez Cabrillo led an expedition in 1542 that sailed along the coast of California. Cabrillo died on Santa Catalina Island, offshore from present-day Los Angeles, but his men sailed on to the border of Oregon, where a ferocious storm forced them to turn back toward Mexico.

These probes into North America by de Soto, Coronado, and Cabrillo persuaded Spaniards that enormous territories stretched northward, yet their inhabitants had little to loot or exploit. After a generation of vigorous exploration, Spaniards concluded that there was only one Mexico and one Peru.

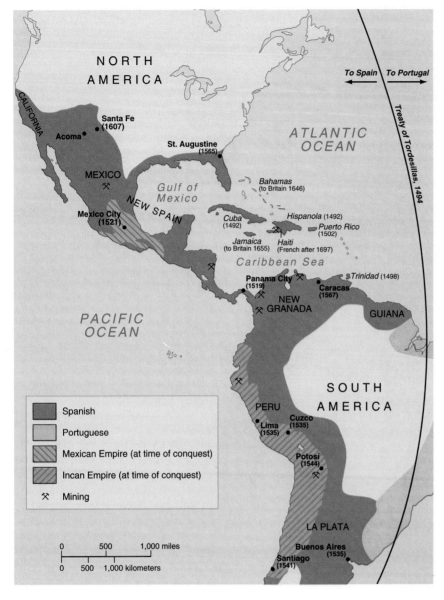

**MAP 2.3**
*New Spain in the Sixteenth Century*
*Spanish control spread throughout Central and South America during the sixteenth century, with the important exception of Portuguese Brazil. North America, although claimed by Spain under the Treaty of Tordesillas, remained peripheral to Spain's New World empire.*

## New Spain in the Sixteenth Century

For all practical purposes, Spain dominated the New World in the sixteenth century (Map 2.3). Portugal claimed the giant territory of Brazil under the Tordesillas treaty, but was far more concerned with exploiting its hard-won trade with the East Indies than in colonizing the New World. England and France were absorbed in the affairs of Europe and largely lost interest in America until late in the century. In the decades after 1519, Spaniards created the distinctive colonial society of New Spain that gave other Europeans a striking illustration of how the New World could be made to serve the purposes of the Old.

The Spanish monarchy claimed ownership of most of the land in the Western Hemisphere and gave the conquistadors permission to explore and plunder. The crown took one-fifth, called the "royal fifth," of any loot confiscated by the conquerors and allowed the conquerors to divide the rest. In the end, the conquistadors themselves received very little. After the conquest of Tenochtitlán, Cortés decided to compensate his disappointed, battle-hardened men by giving them the towns the Spaniards had subdued.

## MEXICAN TRIBUTE ACCOUNT

*This page from the* Codex Mendoza *records the tribute paid to the Mexican capital by the Xoconochco province, a tropical region along the Pacific coast near the Guatemalan border (present-day Chiapas). Prepared by a Mexican artist around 1540 for the viceroy of New Spain, the* Codex Mendoza *provides an inventory of the tribute exacted by the Mexican empire. Most Mexican provinces paid tribute in food or textiles, but Xoconochco contributed, as this account specifies, "first, two large strings of green stones, rich stones; also one thousand four hundred bundles of rich feathers of blue, red, green, turquoise-blue, . . . which are drawn in six bundles; also eighty complete bird skins, of*

Bodleian Library, Oxford, U.K. MS.Arch.Seld.A1.Fol.47r.

*rich turquoise-blue feathers and purple breasts, of the colors drawn; also another eighty complete skins of said birds; also eight hundred bundles of rich feathers; also eight hundred bundles of rich long green feathers . . . ; also two lip plugs of clear amber decorated with gold; also two hundred loads of cacao; also forty jaguar skins . . . ; also eight hundred rich bowls for drinking cacao; also two large pieces of clear amber of the size of a brick — all of which they gave in tribute every six months." In the Mexican capital, artists crafted the exotic feathers and skins into elaborate cloaks and the stones and amber into fashionable jewelry. The cacao was brewed into a mildly intoxicating beverage.*

The distribution of conquered towns institutionalized the system of *encomienda*, which empowered conquistadors to rule the Indians and the lands in and around their towns. The concept of encomienda was familiar to the Spaniards, who had used it to govern regions recaptured from the Muslims during the Reconquest. In New Spain, encomienda transferred to the Spanish *encomendero* (the man who "owned" the town) the tribute that the town had previously paid to the Mexican empire.

---

*In the decades after 1519, Spaniards created the distinctive colonial society of New Spain that gave other Europeans a striking illustration of how the New World could be made to serve the purposes of the Old.*

---

In theory, encomienda involved a reciprocal relationship between the encomendero and "his" Indians. In return for the tribute and labor of the Indians, the encomendero was supposed to encourage the Indians to convert to Christianity, to be responsible for their material well-being, and to guarantee order and justice in the town. Catholic missionaries labored earnestly to convert the Indians to Christianity. At first, the missionaries enjoyed great success, baptizing tens of thousands of Indians. However, missionaries soon discovered that the Indians continued to worship their own gods along with the Christian God. Some friars began to realize that authentic conversions could take place only if the Spaniards first learned about the Indians' religion. One friar, Fray Bernardino de Sahagún, conducted extensive interviews with the Mexica and, over forty years, compiled a systematic firsthand account of Mexican society, *General History of the Things of New Spain*. Most friars, however, came to believe that the Indians were lesser beings inherently incapable of fully understanding the Christian faith.

In practice, encomenderos were far more interested in what the Indians could do for them than in what they or missionaries could do for the Indians. Encomenderos subjected Indians to chronic overwork, mistreatment, and abuse without recompense. As one Spaniard remarked, "Everything [the Indians] do is slowly done and by compulsion. They are malicious, lying, thievish. . . . They are very ungrateful. . . . They are capital enemies of the Spaniards." Economically, however, encomienda recognized a fundamental reality of New Spain: The

most important treasure the Spaniards could plunder from the New World was not gold, but Indian labor. To exploit Indian labor, the hemisphere's richest natural resource, encomienda gave encomenderos the right to force Indians to work when, where, and how the Spaniards pleased.

Encomienda engendered two groups of influential critics. A few of the missionaries were horrified at the brutal mistreatment of the Indians. The cruelty of the encomenderos made it difficult for priests to persuade Indians of the tender mercies of the Spaniards' God. "What will [the Indians] think about the God of the Christians," Fray Bartolomé de Las Casas asked, when they see their friends "with their heads split, their hands amputated, their intestines torn open? . . . Would they want to come to Christ's sheepfold after their homes had been destroyed, their children imprisoned, their wives raped, their cities devastated, their maidens deflowered, and their provinces laid waste?" Las Casas and other outspoken missionaries softened few hearts among the encomenderos, but they did win some sympathy for the Indians from the Spanish monarchy and royal bureaucracy. Royal officials, however, interpreted the encomenderos' brutal treatment of the Indians as part of a larger general problem: the autonomy of the encomenderos. The Spanish monarchy sought to abolish encomienda in an effort to take the government of New Spain away from swashbuckling old conquistadors and to put it in the hands of royal bureaucrats.

One of the most important blows against encomienda was the imposition in 1549 of a reform called the *repartimiento*, which limited the labor an encomendero could command from his Indians to forty-five days per year from each adult male. The repartimiento, however, did not challenge the principle of forced labor nor did it prevent encomenderos from continuing to cheat, mistreat, and overwork their Indians. Enforcement was haphazard. Slowly, as the old encomenderos died, repartimiento replaced encomienda as the basic system of exploiting Indian labor.

The system of coerced labor in New Spain grew directly out of the Spaniards' assumption that they were superior to the Indians. As one missionary put it, the Indians "are incapable of learning. . . . The older they get, the worse they behave. . . . The Indians are more stupid than asses and refuse to improve in anything." Therefore, most Spaniards assumed, Indians' labor should be organized by and for their conquerors.

From the viewpoint of Spain, the single most important economic activity in New Spain after 1540 was silver mining. Spain imported more New World gold than silver in the early decades of the century, but that changed with the discovery of major silver deposits at Potosí, Bolivia, in 1545 and Zacatecas, Mexico, in 1546. As the mines swung into large-scale production during the 1540s, an ever-growing stream of silver flowed from New Spain to Old. Overall, exports of precious metals from New Spain during the sixteenth century were worth about twenty-five times more than hides, the next most important export (Figure 2.1). The silver mines required large capital investments and numerous workers. Typically, a mine was supervised by a handful of Spaniards, and the miners were mostly Indians, with some African slaves later in the sixteenth century. The mines exemplified the fundamental relationship between the colonists and Spain. The Indian miners worked for local Spanish bosses to produce silver for export to Spain. The mines and their products were valuable principally for their contribution to the wealth of Spain, not to that of the colony.

For Spaniards, life in New Spain was relatively easy. Only a few thousand Spaniards actually fought during the conquests. Although the riches the survivors won fell far short of their expectations, the benefits of encomienda provided a comfortable, leisurely existence that was the envy of many poorer noblemen in Spain. As one colonist wrote his brother back in Spain, "Don't hesitate [to come]. . . .

This land [New Spain] is as good as ours [Spain], for God has given us more here than there, and we shall be better off."

*Encomienda recognized a fundamental reality of New Spain: The most important treasure the Spaniards could plunder from the New World was not gold, but Indian labor.*

During the century after 1492, about 225,000 Spaniards settled in the colonies. Virtually all of them were poor young men of common (nonnoble) lineage who came directly from Spain. Laborers and artisans made up the largest proportion, but soldiers and sailors were also numerous. Throughout the sixteenth century, men vastly outnumbered women, although the proportion of women grew from about one in twenty before 1519 to nearly one in three by the 1580s. The gender and number of Spanish settlers shaped two fundamental features of the society of New Spain. First, despite the thousands of immigrants, Europeans never made up more than 1 or 2 percent of the total population. Although Spaniards ruled New Spain, the population was almost wholly Indian. Second, the shortage of Spanish women meant that a great deal of concubinage and inter-

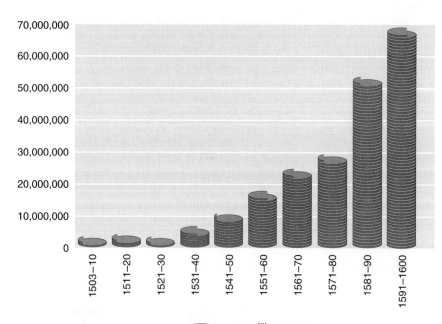

FIGURE 2.1
*New World Gold and Silver Imported into Spain during the Sixteenth Century, in Pesos*
Spain imported more gold than silver during the first three decades of the sixteenth century, but the total value of this treasure was quickly eclipsed during the 1530s and 1540s when rich silver mines were developed. Silver accounted for most of the enormous growth in Spain's precious metal imports from the New World.

= one million pesos

## MIXED RACES

*Residents of New Spain maintained a lively interest in each person's racial lineage. These eighteenth-century paintings illustrate forms of racial mixture common in the sixteenth century. In the first painting, a Spanish man and an Indian woman have a mestizo son; in the fourth, a Spanish man and a woman of African descent have a mulatto son; in the fifth, a Spanish woman and a mulatto man have a morisco daughter. The many racial permutations of parents led residents of New Spain to develop an elaborate vocabulary of ancestry. The child of a morisco and a Spaniard was a chino; the child of a chino and an Indian was a salta abas; the child of a salta abas and a mulatto was a lobo; and so on. Can you detect hints of some of the meanings of racial categories in the clothing depicted in these paintings?*
Bob Schalkwijk/INAH.

Español con India, Mestizo.

Mestizo con Españolo Castizo.

Castizo con Española Español.

Español con Mora Mulato.

5

6

Mulato con Española, Morisco.

Morisco con Española Chino.

7

Chino con India. Salta abas.

Salta abas con Mulata. Lobo.

marriage took place between Spanish men and Indian women.

The highest social status in New Spain was reserved for natives of Spain, *peninsulares* (people born on the Iberian peninsula). Below them but still within the elite were creoles (from the Spanish word for "native," *criollo*), the children born in the New World to Spanish men and women. Together, peninsulares and creoles made up barely 1 or 2 percent of the population, and, unlike all the others, they were whites of European ancestry. Below them on the social pyramid was a larger group of *mestizos,* the offspring of Spanish men and Indian women, who made up 4 or 5 percent of the population. So many of the mestizos were illegitimate that the term *mestizo* (from the Spanish word for "mixed") was almost synonymous with *bastard* in the sixteenth century. Some mestizos worked as artisans and labor overseers and lived well, and a few rose into the ranks of the elite, especially if their Indian ancestry was not obvious from their skin color. Most mestizos, however, were lumped with the Indians, the enormous bottom mass of the population.

The society of New Spain established the precedent for what would become a pronounced pattern in the European colonies of the New World: a society stratified sharply by social origin and race. All Europeans of whatever social origin considered themselves superior to the Native Americans; in New Spain, they were a dominant minority in both power and status.

The Spanish monarchy administered New Spain for its own purposes, mostly to provide a large and growing source of revenue for the royal treasury. The principles of royal government were simple: Tax economic transactions and retain monopolies on essential goods. The result in New Spain was that competition was stifled, incentive was thwarted, and economic development was rigidly controlled for the benefit of Spain rather than the colonists.

Conquest and colonization of New Spain devastated Indian cultures and stripped the Indians of their leaders. By 1560, the major centers of Indian civilization had been conquered, their leaders overthrown, their religion held in contempt, and their people forced to work for the Spaniards. Profound demoralization pervaded Indian society. As a Mexican poet wrote:

> Nothing but flowers and songs of sorrow
> are left in Mexico . . .
> where once we saw warriors and wise men. . . .
>
> We are crushed to the ground;
> we lie in ruins.
> There is nothing but grief and suffering
> in Mexico.

Adding to the culture shock of conquest and colonization was the deadly toll of European diseases. As conquest spread throughout New Spain, Indians were struck by virulent epidemics of measles, smallpox, and respiratory illnesses, diseases unknown to them before the arrival of the Europeans. By 1570, only a half century after Cortés entered Tenochtitlán, the Indian population of New Spain had fallen to about 10 percent of what it had been when Columbus arrived. The destruction of the Indian population was a catastrophe unequaled in human history. A Mayan Indian recalled that when sickness struck his village, "Great was the stench of the dead. . . . The dogs and vultures devoured the bodies. The mortality was terrible. . . . So it was that we became orphans. . . . We were born to die!" For most Indians, New Spain was a graveyard.

For the Spaniards, the deaths meant that the most valuable resource of New Spain—Indian labor—dwindled rapidly. By the last quarter of the sixteenth century, Spanish colonists felt the pinch of a genuine labor shortage. To help redress the need for laborers, colonists began to import African slaves. Some Africans had come to Mexico with the conquistadors; one Mexica recalled that among Cortés's men were "some black-skinned ones with kinky hair." But in the years before 1550, while Indian labor was still ample, only 15,000 slaves were imported from Africa. Even after Indian labor began to decline, the relatively high cost of African slaves kept imports

low, approximately 36,000 after 1550. During the sixteenth century, New Spain continued to rely primarily on a diminishing number of Indians.

## Northern Outposts in Florida and New Mexico

After the explorations of de Soto, Coronado, and Cabrillo, North America did not much interest officials in New Spain. The monarchy assumed that Spain owned North America as part of the grant made by the pope in 1493. By the mid-sixteenth century, however, France openly challenged Spain's claim and the papacy began to backpedal, pointing out that Spain did not have exclusive rights to North America since it had not yet been discovered in 1493. The Spanish monarchy insisted that a few settlements be established in North America to give some tangible reality to its legalistic claims. Settlements in Florida would have the additional benefit of protecting Spanish ships from pirates and privateers who lurked along the South Atlantic coast, waiting for the Spanish treasure fleet on its return to Spain.

In 1565, the Spanish king sent Pedro Menéndez de Avilés to create settlements along the Atlantic coast. In early September, Menéndez founded St. Augustine in Florida and within a few weeks mounted a deadly attack that eliminated a nearby French settlement. In addition to St. Augustine, the first permanent European settlement within what became the United States, Menéndez established a series of small outposts along the Florida coast. In 1567, he founded the town of St. Elena, on what is now Parris Island, South Carolina. In 1570, Menéndez sent an expedition to settle on the Chesapeake Bay, but within a few months the settlers were killed by local Indians.

Antagonisms between Spaniards and native peoples also plagued the earlier settlements. In 1576, an Indian attack forced evacuation of St. Elena. Spanish officials destroyed St. Elena themselves in 1587 and fell back to St. Augustine, where they dug in. By 1600, the garrison town had a population of about five hundred, mostly men (although women and children lived there too), mostly soldiers, and mostly there because military orders kept them from leaving. The small town was a token Spanish presence on the vast Atlantic shoreline of North America (see Map 2.3).

More than 1,600 miles west of St. Augustine, another Spanish outpost was founded, in 1598. During the 1580s, the Mexican mining frontier extended far into northern Mexico, and rumors of fabulous riches to be found just over the northern horizon still circulated, as they had in Coronado's time forty years earlier. In 1598, Juan de Oñate led an expedition of about five hundred people to settle New Mexico and claim the booty that supposedly awaited. Oñate had impeccable credentials for both conquest and mining. His father had helped discover the bonanza silver mines of Zacatecas and his wife was Isabel Tolosa Cortés Montezuma, the granddaughter of Cortés—the conqueror of Mexico—and the great-granddaughter of the Mexican emperor Montezuma.

Oñate and his companions set out from Mexico and after two months reached a pueblo near present-day Albuquerque, where Oñate solemnly convened the pueblo's leaders and, to his satisfaction, received their oath of loyalty to the Spanish king and the Christian God. Oñate repeated these ceremonies at additional pueblos as he made his way to a pueblo that he named San Gabriel, north of present-day Santa Fe. He soon sent out scouting parties to find the legendary treasures of the region and to locate the ocean, which he reasoned had to be nearby. Meanwhile, a large contingent of his soldiers planned to mutiny, and relations with the pueblo Indians deteriorated. When the Acoma pueblo revolted, Oñate ruthlessly suppressed the uprising, killing some eight hundred men, women, and children. Although Oñate reconfirmed the Spaniards' military superiority, he did not bring peace or stability to San Gabriel. Another pueblo revolted in 1599, and many of Oñate's settlers returned to Mexico, disillusioned. A few held on, deserting San Gabriel early in the seventeenth century for the greater security of Santa Fe. New Mexico was so marginal to New Spain that officials talked repeatedly of abandoning it, but they did not. Instead, New Mexico lingered as a small, dusty token of Spanish claims to the North American Southwest.

# The New World and Europe

The riches of New Spain helped make the sixteenth century Spain's Golden Age. After the deaths of Queen Isabella and King Ferdinand, their sixteen-year-old grandson became King Charles I of Spain in 1516. Charles used the wealth of New Spain to pursue his vast ambitions in the fierce dynastic and religious battles of sixteenth-century Europe. Through the power of Spain, the New World had a major impact on Europeans.

In 1519, Charles I used judicious bribes to secure his selection as the Holy Roman Emperor Charles V. His empire encompassed more than that of any other European monarch. With ambitions that matched his sprawling territories, Charles V confronted an unexpected challenge from Martin Luther, an obscure Catholic priest in central Germany.

## The Protestant Reformation and the European Order

In 1517, Martin Luther initiated the Protestant Reformation by publicizing his criticisms of the Catholic Church. Luther's ideas, although shared by many other Catholics, were considered extremely dangerous by church officials and by many monarchs like Charles V who believed firmly that, just as the church spoke for God, they ruled for God. Although a full account of Luther's doctrines and the complex history of the Reformation is beyond the scope of this book, it is easy to understand why the church and monarchs were alarmed.

Luther preached a doctrine known as justification by faith: Individual Christians could obtain salvation and life everlasting only by faith that God would save them. Giving offerings to the church, following the orders of the priest, or participating in church rituals did not get believers one step closer to heaven. The only true source of information about God's will was the Bible, not the church. By reading the Bible, any Christian could learn as much about God's commandments as any priest. Indeed, Luther called for a priesthood of all believers.

*Although Martin Luther hoped his ideas would reform the Catholic Church, instead they ruptured forever the unity of Christianity in western Europe.*

In effect, Luther charged that the Catholic Church was in many respects fraudulent. Contrary to the church's claims, priests were unnecessary for salvation; they even hindered it by engaging in religious practices not specifically commanded by the Bible. The church had neglected its proper role—to help individual Christians to understand the realm of faith revealed to them in the Bible—and instead had wasted its resources in the worldly realm of wars and politics. Although Luther hoped his ideas would reform the Catholic Church, instead they ruptured forever the unity of Christianity in western Europe.

Charles V pledged to exterminate the Protestant heresies. The wealth pouring into Spain from the New World fueled his efforts to defend the Catholic faith against Protestants, Muslims in eastern Europe, and any nation bold or foolhardy enough to contest Spain's supremacy. As the wealthiest and most powerful monarch in Europe, Charles V and his son and successor Philip II assumed responsibility for upholding the existing order of sixteenth-century Europe.

## New World Treasure and Spanish Ambitions

Both Charles V and Philip II fought wars throughout the world during the sixteenth century. Mexican silver funneled through the royal treasury into the hands of military suppliers, soldiers, and sailors wherever in the world Spain's forces happened to be fighting. New World treasure was dissipated in military adventures that served the goals of the monarchy but did little to benefit most Spaniards.

In a sense, American wealth made the Spanish monarchy too rich and too powerful among the states of Europe. The ambitions of Charles V and Philip II were so great that the expenses of constant warfare far outstripped the revenues arriving from New Spain. To help maintain military expenditures, both kings continually raised taxes in Spain. Between 1527 and 1598, taxes levied on Spaniards increased more than fivefold. In accordance with the principle of privilege, the nobility—by far the wealthiest class in Spain—was completely exempt from direct taxation, so the increasing tax burden was collected mostly from the peasantry. Not only did the ambitions of the monarchy impoverish the vast majority of Spain's population, but they also brought Spain to the brink of economic bankruptcy. When even taxes did not provide enough funds to fight its wars, the monarchy was forced to borrow, principally from Italian, German, and Flemish bankers. By the end of the century, paying interest on debts swallowed two-thirds of the crown's annual revenues. For Spain, the riches from New Spain proved a short-term blessing but a long-term curse.

But sixteenth-century Spaniards did not see it that way. As they looked at their accomplishments in the New World, they saw unmistakable signs of progress. They had added enormously to their knowledge and wealth. They had built mines, cities, churches, and even universities on the other side of the Atlantic. Their military, religious, and economic achievements gave them great pride and confidence.

## Europe and the Spanish Example

The lessons of sixteenth-century Spain were not lost on Spain's European rivals. Spain proudly displayed the fruits of its New World conquests. In 1520, for instance, Charles V exhibited some of the gifts Montezuma had presented to Cortés. After seeing the objects, the German artist Albrecht Dürer wrote in his diary of his amazement at "the things which were brought to the King from the New Golden Land: a sun entirely of gold, a whole fathom [six feet] broad; likewise a moon, entirely of silver, just as big. . . . I have never seen in all my days what so rejoiced my heart, as these things. For I saw among them amazing objects, and I marvelled over the subtle ingenuity of the men in these distant lands." Dürer's reaction illustrates the intellectual excitement the New World generated among some Europeans. But the most exciting news about "the men in these distant lands" was that they could serve the interests of Europeans, as Spain had shown. With a few notable exceptions, Europeans saw the New World as a place for the expansion of European influence, a place where, as one Spaniard wrote, Europeans could "give to those strange lands the form of our own."

Spain's example proved that an empire in the New World could make a major contribution to a nation's power and prestige in Europe. It also illustrated the profits that could be made in a new arena for commerce across the Atlantic. France and England tried to follow Spain's lead. Both nations warred with Spain in Europe, preyed on Spanish treasure fleets, and ventured to the New World, where they too hoped to find an undiscovered passageway to the East Indies or another Mexico or Peru.

In 1524, France sent Giovanni da Verrazano to scout the Atlantic coast of North America from North Carolina to Canada, looking for a Northwest Passage to the East Indies (see Map 2.2). Eleven years later, France probed farther north with Jacques Cartier's voyage up the St. Lawrence River. Encouraged, Cartier returned to the region with a group of settlers in 1541, but the colony they established—like the search for a Northwest Passage—came to nothing. In 1564, a group of French Huguenots (Protestants fleeing from persecution in Catholic France) established a settlement near present-day Jacksonville, Florida, that was soon eliminated by Spaniards led by Pedro Menéndez de Avilés. French interest in North America did not revive until the seventeenth century.

English attempts to mimic Spain were slower but equally ill-fated. Not until 1576, almost eighty years after John Cabot's voyages, did the English try again to find a Northwest Passage to the East Indies. This time Martin Frobisher sailed into the frigid waters of northern Canada; his sponsor was the Cathay Company, which hoped to open trade with China (see Map 2.2). Like many other explorers who preceded and followed him, Frobisher was mesmerized by the Spanish example and was sure he had found gold. But the tons of "ore" he hauled back to England proved worthless, the Cathay Company collapsed, and English interests shifted southward.

English attempts to establish North American settlements were no more fruitful than their search for a northern route to China. Sir Humphrey Gilbert led expeditions in 1578 and 1583 that made feeble efforts to found colonies in Newfoundland, until Gilbert himself vanished at sea. In 1585, Sir Walter Raleigh organized an expedition to settle Roanoke Island off the coast of present-day North Carolina. The first group of explorers left no colonists on the island, but two years later Raleigh sent a contingent of more than a hundred settlers to Roanoke under John White's leadership. White returned to England for supplies and when he came back in 1590, the Roanoke colonists had disappeared, leaving only the word *Croatoan* (whose meaning is unknown) carved on a tree. The Roanoke colonists most likely died from a combination of natural causes and unfriendly Indians. By the end of the century, England had failed to secure a New World beachhead.

## Conclusion: The Legacy of the Sixteenth Century

The sixteenth century in the New World belonged to the Spanish, who employed Columbus, and the Indians, who greeted him as he stepped ashore. Spanish explorers, conquistadors, and colonists forced the Indians to serve the interests of Spanish settlers and the Spanish monarchy. Spaniards initiated the Columbian exchange between the New World and the Old that continues to this day.

The exchange illustrated one of the most important legacies of the sixteenth century: After millions of years, the Atlantic no longer was an impermeable barrier separating the Eastern and Western Hemispheres. After the voyages of Columbus, European sailing ships regularly bridged the Atlantic and carried people, products, and ideas from one shore to the other.

**CAROLINA ALGONQUIAN MOTHER AND DAUGHTER**
*When the English artist John White visited the coast of present-day North Carolina in 1585 as part of Raleigh's Roanoke expedition, he painted this watercolor portrait of the wife and daughter of a local Algonquian chief. This and White's other portraits are the only surviving likenesses of sixteenth-century North American Indians that were drawn from direct observation in the New World. The young girl holds a doll and copies her mother by suspending her right wrist from her necklace. The mother's clothing and body paint or tattoos may signify her status as a mature woman and a chief's wife.*
British Museum.

No European monarch could forget the seductive lesson taught by Spain's example: The New World could vastly enrich the Old. Spain remained a New World power for almost four centuries, and its language, culture, and institutions left a permanent imprint. By the end of the sixteenth century, however, other European monarchies began to contest Spain's dominion in Europe and to make forays into the northern fringes of Spain's New World preserve. To reap some of the benefits the Spaniards enjoyed from their New World domain, they had to learn a difficult lesson: how to deviate from Spain's example. That discovery lay ahead.

## CHRONOLOGY

**1415**   Portugal conquers Ceuta at Strait of Gibraltar, gaining access to western coast of Africa.

**1444**   Portuguese explorers reach Cape Verde.

**1451**   Columbus born in Genoa, Italy.

**1480**   Portuguese ships reach Congo.

**1488**   Bartolomeu Dias rounds Cape of Good Hope.

**1492**   Columbus lands on Caribbean island that he names San Salvador.

**1493**   Columbus makes second voyage to New World.

**1494**   Portugal and Spain negotiate Treaty of Tordesillas to divide New World between them.

**1497**   John Cabot searches for Northwest Passage.

**1498**   Columbus makes third voyage to New World and reaches Venezuela.
Vasco da Gama sails to India.

**1500**   Pedro Alvars Cabral makes landfall in Brazil.

**1507**   German mapmaker Waldseemüller names New World America.

**1513**   Vasco Nuñez de Balboa crosses isthmus of Panama.

**1517**   Protestant Reformation begins in Europe.

**1519**   Hernán Cortés leads expedition to find and conquer Mexico.
Ferdinand Magellan sets out to sail around world.
Charles I of Spain becomes Holy Roman Emperor Charles V.

**1521**   Cortés conquers Mexica at Tenochtitlán.
Juan Ponce de León lands in Florida.

**1524**   Guatemala, El Salvador, and Nicaragua come under Spanish control.
Franciscan missionaries arrive in Mexico.

**1526**   Lucas Vázquez de Ayllón establishes San Miguel de Gualdape on Georgia coast.

**1528**   Pánfilo de Narváez leads expedition to survey Gulf coast from Florida to Texas.

**1532**   Francisco Pizarro begins conquest of Peru.

**1539**   Hernando de Soto launches exploration of Southeast.

**1540**   Francisco Vásquez de Coronado starts to explore Southwest and Great Plains.

**1542**   Juan Rodríguez Cabrillo explores California coast.

**1549**   Repartimiento reforms begin to replace encomienda.

**1565**   Pedro Menéndez de Avilés establishes St. Augustine, Florida.

**1587**   English colonists settle Roanoke Island.

**1598**   Juan de Oñate leads expedition into New Mexico.

# SUGGESTED READINGS

Cyclone Covey, trans., *Cabeza de Vaca's Adventures in the Unknown Interior of America* (1961). A rare firsthand memoir of a shipwrecked Spanish explorer who was enslaved by Indians and lived to publish this account in 1542.

Bernal Díaz, *The Conquest of New Spain,* trans. J. M. Cohen (1963). A riveting eyewitness story of the conquest of Mexico by one of Cortés's foot soldiers.

Ramon A. Gutiérrez, *When Jesus Came, the Corn Mothers Went Away: Marriage, Sexuality, and Power in New Mexico, 1500–1846* (1991). A revealing study of the impact of European culture on native peoples in New Mexico.

Paul Hulton, *America, 1585: The Complete Drawings of John White* (1984). Superb reproductions of the only images that survive of the people of sixteenth-century North America.

James Lockhart, *The Nahuas after Conquest: A Social and Cultural History of the Indians of Central Mexico, Sixteenth through Eighteenth Centuries* (1992). A monumental account of the impact of conquest on Mexican society, based on detailed analysis of Nahua documents.

James Lockhart, ed., *We People Here: Nahuatl Accounts of the Conquest of Mexico* (1993). Fascinating Mexican perspectives on conquest newly translated from original sixteenth-century sources.

John Lynch, *Spain, 1516–1598: From Nation State to World Empire* (1992). An informative survey of sixteenth-century Spain and the influence of its New World colonies.

William D. Phillips and Carla Rahn Phillips, *The Worlds of Christopher Columbus* (1992). An authoritative guide to Columbus and his social and intellectual world.

A. J. R. Russell-Wood, *A World on the Move: The Portuguese in Africa, Asia, and America, 1415–1808* (1992). An expert survey of the restless activity of the Portuguese throughout the world.

Hugh Thomas, *Conquest: Montezuma, Cortés, and the Fall of Old Mexico* (1993). A fascinating narrative of the conquest of Mexico attentive to the complexities of both Spanish and Mexican societies.

David J. Weber, *The Spanish Frontier in North America* (1992). A comprehensive, deeply informed overview of New Spain's northern frontier.

**VIRGINIA ALGONQUIAN TOTEM**

*This object was made by one of Powhatan's people, probably a woman skilled in sewing small shell beads into intricate patterns. Soon after it appeared in England about 1630, it was called "Powhatan's mantle," a name still used for it. It is more than six feet long and four feet wide, constructed of four deer hides sewn together. The hides and the decorative shells conclusively establish its Virginia Algonquian origins, although there is no firm evidence that it actually belonged to Powhatan or that it was used as a mantle or cloak. What looks like a neck opening is simply an unfinished seam between two deerskins. Furthermore, there is no record of a Virginia Algonquian wearing a cloak suspended from the neck. Cloaks worn by Powhatan, described by Captain John Smith and other settlers, evidently had fringe or animal tails dangling from them, unlike this object. A modern expert has concluded that this object was probably a totem kept in a treasure house where chiefs stored their valuables. The large human figure, the deer on the right, the mountain lion on the left, and the thirty-four concentric circles probably served as what Smith called "sentinels," standing guard on behalf of the chief over the valuable objects in the treasure house.*

Ashmolean Museum, Oxford.

# THE SOUTHERN COLONIES IN THE SEVENTEENTH CENTURY

3

## 1601–1700

EARLY IN 1607, POWHATAN RULED an Algonquian chiefdom on the brink of a strange new world in which white people from England would become a permanent and growing presence in North America. Explorers, missionaries, fishermen, pirates, and others cruised along the Atlantic coast from time to time before 1607 and made an occasional landing. But they did not stay or, if they tried to stay—as at Roanoke—they did not survive. In 1607, all that was about to change. The Powhatan chiefdom was the first Native American group in North America to encounter the new English world that would eventually engulf them all.

Powhatan was the supreme chief—in his language, the *mamanatowick*—of about fourteen thousand Algonquian people who inhabited the coastal plain of present-day Virginia, near the Chesapeake Bay. Powhatan's people belonged to more than thirty subordinate chiefdoms, each headed by its own chief, called a *werowance*. Hostile tribes surrounded Powhatan's chiefdom, and intertribal warfare occurred constantly. The arts of war were similar in many ways to the skills of hunting, the basic subsistence activity of Powhatan's men. Deer were their most important prey, supplying not only meat but also hides, bones, and antlers that were crafted into clothing, tools, weapons, and decorative objects. Successful hunters who kept their families well supplied with meat were accorded high status. Men hunted not only for food but also because Powhatan required each of his werowances to pay him an annual tribute in the form of deer hides. Powhatan collected many other forms of tribute, including turkeys, fish, beads, copper, and especially corn. Powhatan stored these tribute goods in huge storehouses and used them to reward favorites and to provide gifts to the parents of the young virgins he took as wives. He had well over fifty wives in all; at any one time, a dozen or more lived with him. Women's responsibility to gather the essential food that came from foraging and agriculture underscored their importance and status in Powhatan's communities. They also wove baskets and mats, fashioned various bone utensils, and kept the home fires burning.

By 1607, Powhatan had heard about white men who appeared from time to time. Confident of his formidable power, Powhatan was not afraid of these intruders. Yet in the century after 1607, Powhatan's people were decimated by English settlers and diseases. The newcomers had different ideas about what crops to plant, what rulers to obey, what labor to perform, and why. They built a new world of permanent colonies in North America, initiating the sporadic, long-term decline of Powhatan's chiefdom and others like it. A world of Stone Age hunters and gatherers began to be replaced by immigrant farmers with tools, weapons, and ideas unknown to Powhatan.

**SECOTAN VILLAGE**
*This engraving, published in 1612, was copied from an original drawing John White made in 1585 when he visited the village of Secotan on the coast of North Carolina (see page 47). The drawing provides a schematic view of daily life in the village, which may have resembled one of Powhatan's settlements. White noted on the original that the fire burning behind the line of crouching men was "the place of solemne prayer." The large building in the lower left was a tomb where the bodies of important leaders were kept. Dwellings similar to those illustrated on Smith's map of Virginia (see page 55) lined a central space, where men and women ate. Corn is growing in the fields along the right side of the village. The engraver has included hunters shooting deer at the upper left; hunting was probably never so convenient—no such hunters or deer appear in White's original drawing. This portrait conveys the message that Secotan was orderly, settled, religious, harmonious, and peaceful (note the absence of fortifications), and very different from English villages.*
Princeton University Libraries.

## An English Colony on the Chesapeake

By 1600, King James I of England eyed North America as a possible location for English colonies. England's defeat of the Spanish Armada in 1588 made it seem likely that England could also prevail against Spain in North America, a distant hinterland of Spain's colonial heartland in Mexico and South America. Maybe England could encroach on the outskirts of Spain's New World empire, start colonies, and dare Spain to intervene.

English merchants had used joint stock companies for many years to pool capital and share risks in trading voyages to Europe, Africa, and Asia. In 1606, a number of "knightes, gentlemen, merchauntes, and other adventurers of our cittie of London" organized the Virginia Company of London and petitioned King James to grant them permission to establish a colony in North America. The king gave the company a charter authorizing the group to settle a colony on the coast of Virginia and to possess all that lay within fifty miles north and south of the coastal settlement and one hundred miles inland (later extended to the Pacific). James boldly granted the Virginia Company over six million acres and everything they might contain, in large measure because they were not his to grant. In effect, the charter was a royal license to poach on Spanish claims and on Powhatan's chiefdom.

The adventurers in the Virginia Company hoped to found an empire that would strengthen England not only overseas but also at home. Richard Hakluyt, a strong proponent of colonization, argued that a colony would provide a convenient outlet for the swarms of poor "valiant youthes rusting and hurtfull by lacke of employement" in England. As colonial settlers, these jobless Englishmen would be put to work, producing goods that England currently had to import from other nations. They would also provide a ready market in the colony for English woolens. But the main reason the Virginia Company adventurers were willing to risk (or "adventure") their capital in Virginia was not to reduce unemployment in England or provide overseas markets for English textiles. Instead, they fervently hoped for quick profits. One way or another, Virginia promised to reward the adventurers. Or so they thought.

## The Fragile Jamestown Settlement

In December 1606, the *Susan Constant, Discovery,* and *Godspeed* carried 144 Englishmen toward Virginia. Delayed by storms and a stopover in the West Indies, they arrived at the mouth of the Chesapeake Bay on April 26, 1607. That night while the colonists rested onshore, one of them later recalled, a band of Indians "creeping upon all foure, from the Hills like Beares, with their Bowes in their mouthes," attacked and dangerously wounded two men. The attack gave the colonists an early warning that the North American wilderness was not quite the paradise described by the Virginia Company's publications in England. For the next three weeks, the 105 colonists (39 had died at sea) explored the bay for a suitable place to settle. On May 14, they put ashore on a small peninsula in the midst of Powhatan's chiefdom. With the memory of their first night in America fresh in their minds, they quickly built a fort, the first building in the settlement they named Jamestown (Map 3.1).

The Jamestown fort showed that, despite Spanish claims, English ambitions, and the king's charter, the colonists knew that native peoples were prepared to defend Virginia as their own. During May and June 1607, the settlers and Powhatan's warriors skirmished repeatedly. English muskets and cannon repelled Indian attacks on Jamestown, but the Indians' superior numbers and knowledge of the Virginia wilderness made it risky for the settlers to venture far beyond the Jamestown peninsula. Late in June, Powhatan sensed a stalemate and made peace overtures.

*The main reason the Virginia Company adventurers were willing to risk their capital in Virginia was quick profits.*

The settlers soon confronted far more dangerous, invisible threats: disease and starvation. By September, fifty of the colonists had died. "Our men were destroyed with [such] cruell diseases as Swellings, Fluxes, Burning Fevers," George Percy recalled. The colonists increased their misery by constant bickering and plotting. While real and imaginary conspiracies occupied Jamestown's leaders, crops went unplanted and food supplies dwindled, causing some to die "of meere famine," according to Percy. Powhatan's people came to the rescue of the weakened and distracted colonists. Early in September 1607, they began to bring corn to the colony for barter. When that was insufficient to keep the colonists fed, the settlers sent Captain John Smith to trade for corn with tribes upriver from Jamestown. More soldier than merchant, Smith did not hesitate to take hostages and shoot to kill when Indians were reluctant to trade. His efforts managed to keep 38 of the original settlers alive until a fresh supply of food and 120 more colonists arrived from England in January 1608.

Smith himself barely managed to survive that first year. Late in December, during one of his trading forays, Powhatan's warriors captured him and brought him before the powerful chief. Smith wrote that Powhatan "feasted him after their best barbarous manner." Then, after the chief had consulted with his men, "two great stones were brought before Powhatan: then as many [Indians] as could layd hands on [Smith], dragged him to [the stones], and thereon laid his head, and being ready with their clubs, to beate out his braines." At that moment, Pocahontas, Powhatan's young daughter, rushed forward and "got [Smith's] head in her

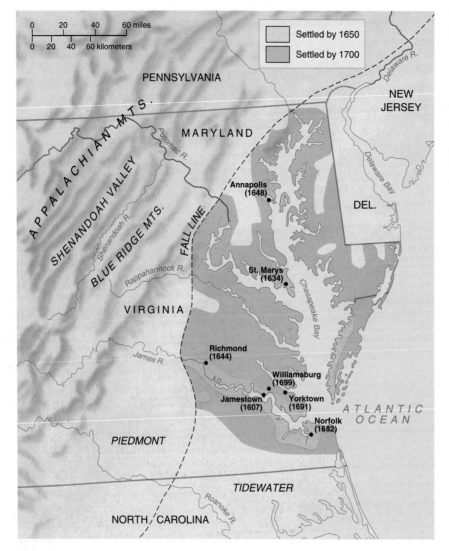

MAP 3.1
*The Chesapeake Colonies in the Seventeenth Century*
*The intimate association of land and water in the settlement of the Chesapeake in the seventeenth century is illustrated by this map. Why was access to navigable water so important?*

armes, and laid her owne upon his to save him from death." Powhatan spared Smith and, with a promise of friendship, released him to return to Jamestown. Smith's famous Pocahontas story probably happened about as he claimed. Certainly he was captured and released by Powhatan; and certainly Pocahontas was friendly with the colonists—she eventually married the Englishman John Rolfe and moved to England, where she died in 1617.

It is difficult to exaggerate the precarious state of the early Jamestown settlement. Although the Virginia Company sent hundreds of new settlers to Jamestown each year, few survived. During the "starving time" winter of 1609–10, food was so short that one or two famished settlers resorted to eating their recently deceased neighbors.

## Encounters between Natives and Newcomers

In retrospect, the weakened condition of the settlers raises the question of why Powhatan did not strike to eliminate them. Of course, we cannot be certain about Powhatan's motives. Since Indians relied on spoken rather than written language, they left no documents that record their ideas. All our information about them comes filtered through the dis-

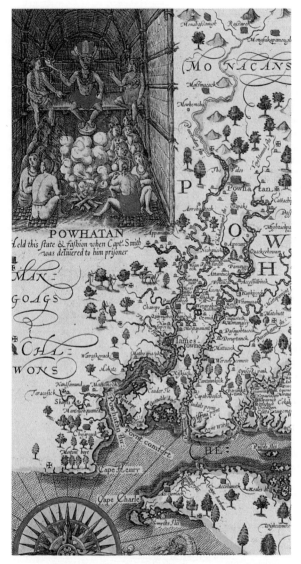

**JOHN SMITH'S MAP OF VIRGINIA**
*In 1612, John Smith published a detailed map of early Virginia that showed not only geographic features but also the limits of exploration (indicated by small crosses), the locations of the houses of the Indian "kings" (indicated by dwellings that look like Quonset huts), and "ordinary houses" of indigenous people (indicated by dots). The map shows the early settlers' intense interest in knowing where the Indians were—and were not. Note the location of Jamestown (upriver from Point Comfort) and of Powhatan's residence at the falls (just to the right of the large P outside the hut portrayed in the upper left corner). The drawing of Powhatan surrounded by some of his many wives (upper left corner) was almost certainly made by an English artist who had never been to Virginia or seen Powhatan but who tried to imagine the scene as described by John Smith.*
Princeton University Libraries.

torting lenses of English eyes. However, we can be certain what the Indians did. They maintained contact with the English settlers, and most of the time the contact was peaceful. But they also kept their distance.

The Virginia Company boasted that the settlers bought from the Indians "the pearles of earth [corn] and [sold] to them the pearles of heaven [Christianity]." In fact, few Indians converted to Christianity, and the English devoted scant effort to proselytizing. Marriage between Indian women and English men was also rare, despite the acute shortage of English women in Virginia in the early years. One of the few settlers who troubled to learn the Indians' language was John Smith. From his notes on Indian vocabulary, we know that the settlers quickly adopted several Virginia Algonquian words. But since Smith's writings contain almost all we know about the Algonquian language (which is now extinct), we remain ignorant of English words that may have entered the Indians' vocabulary. It is safe to speculate that such words were few, given the cultural distance the Indians maintained.

Powhatan's people regarded the English with suspicion, and for good reason. While the settlers often exhibited friendship toward the Indians, they did not hesitate to use their superior weapons— muskets, swords, and cannon—to enforce English notions of proper Indian behavior. More than once the Indians refused to trade corn to the settlers, evidently hoping to starve them out. But each time, the English broke the boycott by pillaging uncooperative villages and confiscating their corn. The Indians retaliated against English violence, but for fifteen years they did not organize an all-out assault on the European intruders, probably for several reasons. Although the Indians felt no attraction to Christianity, they were impressed by the power of the settlers' God. One chief told John Smith that "he did believe that our God as much exceeded theirs as our guns did their bows and arrows." Powhatan and his werowances probably concluded that these powerful strangers would make better allies than enemies. As allies, the English not only strengthened Powhatan's dominance over the tribes in the region; they also supplied his people with European goods, usually in exchange for corn. Although the native Virginians possessed copper before the English arrived, they immediately recognized the superiority of the settlers' iron and steel weapons and tools, and they could not get enough of them.

## Becauſe many doe deſire to know the manner
of their Language, I haue inſerted theſe few words.

KA katorawincs yowo. What call you this.
Nemarough, a man.
Crenepo, a woman.
Marowancheſſo, a boy.
Yehawkans, Houſes.
Matchcores, Skins, or garments.
Mockaſins, Shooes.
Tuſſan, Beds. Pokatawer, Fire.
Attawp, A bow. Attonce, Arrowes.
Monacookes, Swords.
Aumouhhowgh, A Target.
Pawcuſſacks, Gunnes.
Tomahacks, Axes.
Tockahacks, Pickaxes.
Pameſacks, Kniues.
Accowprets, Sheares.
Pawpecones, Pipes. Mattaſſin, Copper
Vſſawaſſin, Iron, Braſſe, Silver, or any
    white mettall. Muſſes, Woods.
Attaſſkuſſ, Leaues, weeds, or graſſe.
Chepſin, Land. Shacquohocan. A ſtone.
Wepenter, A cookold.
Suckahanna, Water. Noughmaſſ, Fiſh.
Copotone, Sturgeon.
Weghſhaughes, Fleſh.
Sawwehone, Bloud.
Netoppew, Friends.
Marrapough, Enemies.
Maskapow, the worſt of the enemies.
Mawchick chammay, The beſt of
    friends
Caſacunnakack, peya quagh acquintan
    vttaſantaſough, In how many daies
    will there come hither any more
    Engliſh Ships.
        Their Numbers.
Necut, 1. Ningh, 2. Nuſſ, 3. Yowgh, 4.
Paranske, 5. Comotinch, 6. Toppawoſſ, 7
Nuſſwaſh, 8. Kekatawgh, 9. Kaskeke 10
They count no more but by tennes
    as followeth.
Caſe, how many.
Ninghſapooeksku, 20.
Nuſſapooeksku, 30.

Yowghapooeksku, 40.
Parankeſtaſſapoockſku, 50.
Comatinchtaſſapoockſku, 60.
Nuſſwaſhtaſſapooekſku, 70.
Kekataughtaſſapooekſku, 90.
Necuttoughtyſinough, 100.
Necuttwevnquaough, 1000.
Rawcoſowghs, Dayes.
Keſkowghes, Sunnes:
Toppquough. Nights.
Nepawweſhowghs, Moones.
Pawpaxſoughes, Yeares.
Pummahumps, Starres.
Oſies, Heavens.
Okees, Gods.
Quiyoughcoſoughs, Pettie Gods, and
    their affinities.
Righcomoughes, Deaths.
Kekughes, Liues.
Mowchick woyawgh tawgh noeragh
    kaquere mecher, I am very hungry?
    what ſhall I eate?
Tawnor nehiegh Powhatan, Where
    dwels Powhatan.
Mache, nehiegh yourowgh, Orapaks.
    Now he dwelsa great way hence
    at Orapaks.
Vittapitchewayne anpechitchs nehaw-
    per Werowacomoco, You lie, he ſtaid
    ever at Werowacomoco.
Kator nehiegh mattagh neer vttapit-
    chewayne, Truely he is there I doe
    not lie.
Spaughtynere keragh werowance maw-
    marinough kekatē wawgh peyaquaugh.
    Run you then to the King Mawma-
    rynough and bid him come hither.
Vtteke, e peya weyack wighwhip, Get
    you gone, & come againe quickly.
Kekaten Pokahontas patiaquagh ningh
    tanks manotyens neer mowchick raw-
    renock audowgh, Bid Pokahontas
    bring hither two little Baskets, and
    I will giue her white Beads to make
    her a Chaine.    FINIS.

JOHN SMITH'S DICTIONARY OF POWHATAN'S LANGUAGE

In 1612, John Smith published this list of the English equivalents of words used by Powhatan's people, almost the only record of the coastal Algonquian language that exists. Smith probably compiled this list by pointing and listening carefully. Can you find any of Powhatan's words that made their way into common English usage? What do the words in the list suggest about Smith's encounters with Powhatan's people? What interested Smith? What compelled the interest of his informants?

Princeton University Libraries.

The trade that supplied Indians with European conveniences provided the English settlers with a prime necessity: food. But why did the settlers prove unable to feed themselves for more than a decade? First, as the staggering death rate suggests, many settlers were too sick to be productive members of the colony. Second, very few farmers came to Virginia in the early years. Instead, the largest group of newcomers was gentlemen and their servants, men who, in John Smith's words, "never did know what a day's work was." In fact, the proportion of gentlemen in Virginia in the early years was six times greater than in England, a reflection of the Virginia Company's urgent need for both investors and settlers. Instead of seeing gentlemen as a liability to the colony, the company tried to attract them. In a 1610 pamphlet, the company declared that nobody should believe that Virginia "excludeth Gentlemen . . . for though they cannot digge, use the square, nor practise the axe and chizell, yet [they know] . . . how to employ the force of knowledge, the exercise of counsell, the operation and power of their best breeding and qualities." In Virginia, however, breeding and quality were worthless for growing corn, catching fish, or even hunting deer. Nevertheless, for more than a decade, the colonists clung to English notions that gentlemen were not supposed to work with their hands and tradesmen were not supposed to work at trades for which they had not been trained, ideas about labor that made more sense in labor-rich England than in labor-poor Virginia. In the meantime, the colonists depended on the Indians' corn for food.

---

*Powhatan's people regarded the English with suspicion, and for good reason. While the settlers often exhibited friendship toward the Indians, they did not hesitate to use their superior weapons to enforce English notions of proper Indian behavior.*

---

The persistence of the Virginia colony, precarious as it was, created difficulties for Powhatan's chiefdom. The steady contact between natives and newcomers spread European viruses among the Indians, who suffered deadly epidemics in 1608 and between 1617 and 1619. While epidemics devastated the Indian population, trade with the settlers distorted Indian culture. If the Indians produced only enough corn for self-sufficiency, as they had for centuries, they risked famine when the English commandeered it to feed the settlers. The need to produce corn both for their own survival and for trade probably introduced tensions within Powhatan's villages, increasing the significance of agriculture and women's work. But from the Indians' viewpoint, the most important fact about the Virginia colony was that it was surviving. Instead

of a temporary outpost, it was proving to be a permanent settlement.

Powhatan died in 1618, and his brother Opechancanough replaced him as mamanatowick. In 1622, Opechancanough organized an all-out assault on the English settlers. Striking on March 22, the Indians killed 347 settlers, nearly a third of the English population. But the attack failed to dislodge the Virginia colonists. In the aftermath, the settlers unleashed a murderous campaign of Indian extermination that in a few years pushed Indians beyond the small circumference of white settlement. Before 1622, the settlers knew that the Indians, though dangerous, were necessary to keep the colony alive. After 1622, the settlers concluded that the life of the colony required the death of the Indians, at least in the vicinity of white settlement. After 1622, most colonists considered Indians their perpetual enemies.

## From Private Company to Royal Government

The 1622 uprising came close to achieving Opechancanough's goal of pushing the colonists back into the Atlantic—so close that it prompted a royal investigation of affairs in Virginia. The investigators discovered that the appalling mortality among the colonists was caused by disease and mismanagement more than by Indian raids. In 1624, King James revoked the charter of the Virginia Company and made Virginia a royal colony, subject to the direction of the royal government rather than to the company's private investors, an arrangement that lasted until 1776.

The king now appointed the governor of Virginia and his council, but most other features of local government established under the Virginia Company remained intact. In 1619, for example, the company had inaugurated the House of Burgesses, an assembly of representatives (called burgesses) elected by the colony's inhabitants. (Historians do not know which settlers were considered inhabitants and were thus qualified to vote for burgesses.) The company authorized the burgesses to propose laws that, when approved by company officials in London, would become enforceable. Under the new royal government, laws had to be approved by the king's bureaucrats in England rather than by the company. Otherwise, the House of Burgesses continued as before, acquiring distinction as the oldest representative legislative assembly in the British colonies. In addition, under the royal government in Virginia, all free adult men could vote for burgesses, giving the House of Burgesses a far broader and more representative constituency than the English House of Commons.

The demise of the Virginia Company marked the end of the first phase of colonization of the Chesapeake. From the 105 adventurers who had landed in 1607 and the hundreds more who followed, the population had grown to about 1,200 by 1624. Mortality rates among newcomers continued at levels higher than those in the worst epidemics in London, but new settlers still arrived. Their arrival and King James's willingness to take over the struggling colony signaled a fundamental change in Virginia. After years of fruitless experimentation, it was becoming clear that English settlers could make a fortune in Virginia by growing tobacco.

## A Tobacco Society

Tobacco did not figure in the plans of the Virginia Company. "As for tobacco," John Smith wrote later, "we never then dreamt of it." John Rolfe began to plant West Indian tobacco seeds in 1612. His experiments showed that the plant could be grown successfully in Virginia. The first commercial shipment of tobacco to England left the colony in 1617. When it sold for a high price, the same Virginia colonists who had difficulty growing enough corn to feed themselves quickly tried to learn how to grow as much tobacco as possible. In a sense, that first commercial cargo was a pivot on which Virginia turned from a colony of rather aimless adventurers into a society of dedicated tobacco planters.

Dedicated they were. In 1620, with fewer than a thousand colonists, Virginia shipped 60,000 pounds of tobacco to England. By 1700, tobacco exports from the Chesapeake region (encompassing Virginia and Maryland) topped 35 million pounds and over 98,000 colonists lived in the region. Per capita tobacco exports grew fivefold, demonstrating that Chesapeake colonists had mastered the demands of tobacco agriculture. Tobacco planters' endless need for labor attracted droves of indentured servants from England to work in tobacco fields and settle the Chesapeake.

## Tobacco Agriculture

Tobacco was a demanding crop. It required close attention and a great deal of hand labor year-round. By the time one year's crop was being readied for market, the next year's crop was already in the ground. Work on food crops had to be done in the

**TOBACCO ADVERTISEMENT**
*This ad for "Kositzky's Best Virginia" tobacco illustrates a colonial planter and tobacco merchant examining the quality of a sample of leaves from an open cask waiting to be shipped to London, while an onlooker samples the leaves more thoroughly, by smoking. To smooth the transaction, an African—presumably a slave—offers a glass of wine. One way the English artist emphasized the differences between the African and the other men was giving the African a skirt of leaves; it is doubtful that any slave in the Chesapeake wore such a skirt. How else did the artist highlight differences? Kositzky must have traded in other goods; the insignia at the top features scythes used for cutting grain but useless in harvesting tobacco, perhaps a hint of ignorance common in London about how tobacco was produced in the Chesapeake.*
Arents Collection, New York Public Library.

midst of the tobacco crop cycle, leaving little time for idleness. But in spare moments colonists enjoyed the fruits of their labor. As a traveler observed, "Everyone smokes while working or idling . . . men, women, girls, and boys from the age of seven years."

---

*The first commercial shipment of tobacco to England in 1617 was a pivot on which Virginia turned from a colony of rather aimless adventurers into a society of dedicated tobacco planters.*

---

English settlers were willing to work hard because they could expect to do much better in the Chesapeake than in England. One colonist declared that "the dirt of this Province affords as great a profit to the general Inhabitant, as the Gold of Peru doth to . . . the Spaniard." Although that observation was exaggerated, it was true that a hired man would have to work two or three years in England to earn as much as he could in just one year in Chesapeake tobacco fields. Better still, in Virginia land was so abundant that, by English standards, it was extremely cheap. In the mid-seventeenth century Chesapeake, even common laborers could buy one hundred acres of land for less than their annual wages—an utter impossibility in England. New settlers who paid their own transportation to the Chesapeake received a grant of fifty acres of free land (a headright), a policy begun by the Virginia Company and continued by the royal government to encourage settlement.

## A Servant Labor System

Headrights, cheap land, and high wages gave poor English folk powerful incentives to immigrate to the New World. Despite the incentives, many potential immigrants could not scrape together the fare to sail across the Atlantic. Their poverty and the colonists' crying need for labor formed the basic context for the creation of a servant labor system.

Today, people tend to think of the colonial South as a slave society. The seventeenth-century Chesapeake, however, was fundamentally a servant society. Twenty Africans arrived in Virginia in 1619, but until the last quarter of the seventeenth century, only a small number of slaves labored in Chesapeake tobacco fields. (Large numbers of slaves

came later, as Chapter 5 explains.) About 80 percent of the immigrants to the Chesapeake during the seventeenth century were indentured servants. Along with tobacco, the servant labor system profoundly influenced nearly every feature of Chesapeake society.

To buy passage aboard a ship bound for the Chesapeake, an English immigrant had to come up with about £5, roughly a year's wages for an English servant or laborer. Saving a year's wages was no easier at that time than it is now. Opportunities for work were shrinking in seventeenth-century England. Many country gentlemen fenced fields they had formerly planted with crops and began to pasture sheep in the enclosures, which required fewer farmhands. Even the employed found the purchasing power of their wages slowly deteriorating as prices rose.

Lacking the money to get across the Atlantic, poor immigrants signed a contract, called an indenture, with a local shopkeeper, mariner, or merchant specifying that the local merchant would pay for the immigrant's transportation to the Chesapeake. In return, the immigrant agreed to work for a period—usually four to seven years—without pay. During this period of indentured servitude, the immigrant received food and shelter from the employer in the colonies. When the indenture expired, the employer was required to give the former servant "freedom dues," usually three barrels of corn and a suit of clothes. In effect, indentures allowed poor immigrants to trade their most valuable asset—their ability to work—for a trip to the New World.

Most planters were willing to pay about twice the cost of transportation for the right to four to seven years of an immigrant's labor. Most of the planter's payment was returned as a handsome profit to the English merchant who had indentured the immigrant. And the planters profited as well. As one Virginia planter noted, "our principall wealth . . . consisteth in servants." More servants meant more hands to grow more tobacco. More servants also meant more land. For every servant purchased, a planter received from the colonial government a headright of another fifty acres of land. Even without the land, a servant was a good investment. A servant was expected to grow enough tobacco in one year to cover the cost of the indenture plus enough corn to feed himself or herself. The servant's labor for the rest of the indenture gave the planter a substantial return on investment.

At least it did if all went well. Bad weather, crop disease, or insects could ruin a harvest. But the biggest risk to both the planter and the servant was that the servant would get sick and die before serving out the term of the indenture. Life expectancy had improved so little by 1687 that a thirty-six-year-old planter remarked, "Now I look upon myself to be in my declining age." Among one group of 275 servant men who arrived in Maryland before midcentury, 40 percent died before their servitude ended. Less than a third of the original group remained in the colony for ten years after their indentures expired. Eight out of ten of these men managed to acquire small farms, and a few possessed servants of their own.

---

*The seventeenth-century Chesapeake was fundamentally a servant society, not a slave society.*

---

For the most part, servants were simply poor young English men seeking work. More than two-thirds of them were between fifteen and twenty-five when they came to the Chesapeake. Many were orphans. Most indentured servants had no special training or skills, although the majority had some experience with agricultural work. "Hunger and fear of prisons bring to us onely such servants as have been brought up to no Art or Trade," a Virginia planter complained in 1662. A skilled craftsman could obtain a shorter indenture, but few risked coming to the colonies since their prospects were better at home.

Women were almost as rare as skilled craftsmen in the Chesapeake and more ardently desired. In the early days of the tobacco boom, the Virginia Company shipped unattached young women to the colony as prospective wives for male settlers willing to pay "120 weight [pounds] of the best leaf tobacco for each of them." The company reasoned that, as one official wrote in 1622, "the plantation can never flourish till families be planted, and the respect of wives and children fix the people on the soil." The company's efforts as a marriage broker proved no more successful than its other ventures. Men continued to outnumber women by a wide margin until late in the seventeenth century. The servant labor system perpetuated the gender imbalance. Although female servants cost about the same as males and generally served for the same length of time, only about one indentured servant in four was a woman. Planters preferred male ser-

vants for field work, although many women also hoed tobacco fields. Most women servants, however, did household chores such as cooking, washing, cleaning, gardening, and milking.

Servant life was harsh by the standards of seventeenth-century England and even by the rougher frontier standards of the Chesapeake. Unlike their English counterparts, Chesapeake servants had virtually no control over who purchased their labor—and thus them—for the period of the indenture. A servant might be bought and sold several times before the indenture expired. One servant wrote from Virginia in 1623 that his master "hath sold me for £150 sterling like a damnd slave." The colonial practice of treating servants as property alarmed some Englishmen. But the colonists' need for labor and the profits to be made in supplying it quickly muffled such qualms.

Some former servants argued that indentured servitude had advantages, despite its rigors. But most found otherwise. James Revel, an eighteen-year-old thief who was punished by being indentured to a Virginia tobacco planter, described experiences common to most servants. In verse, Revel chronicled what happened when he arrived at his new master's plantation:

My Europian clothes were took from me,
Which never after I again could see.
    A canvas shirt and trowsers then they gave,
With a hop-sack frock in which I was to slave:
No shoes nor stockings had I for to wear,
Nor hat, nor cap, both head and feet were bare.
    Thus dress'd into the Field I next must go,
Amongst tobacco plants all day to hoe,
At day break in the morn our work began,
And so held to the setting of the Sun. . . .

Severe laws were designed to keep servants in their place in more ways than one. Punishments for petty crimes like running away or stealing a pig stretched servitude far beyond the original terms of indenture. Servant Christopher Adams, for example, had to serve three extra years for running away for six months; Richard Higby received six extra years of servitude for killing three hogs. Just after midcentury, the Virginia legislature added at least three years to the servitude of most servants by requiring them to serve until they were twenty-four years old.

Women servants were subject to special restrictions and risks. They were prohibited from marrying until their servitude had expired. A servant woman, the law assumed, could not serve two masters at the same time: one who owned her indentured labor and another who was her husband. However, the overwhelming predominance of men in the Chesapeake population inevitably pressured women to engage in sexual relations. The pressure was strong enough that about a third of immigrant women were pregnant when they got married. Pregnancy and childbirth sapped a woman's strength, and a new child diverted her attention, reducing her usefulness to her master. As a rule, if a woman servant gave birth to a child, she had to serve two extra years and pay a fine.

Such punishments reflected four fundamental realities of the servant labor system. First, masters' hunger for labor led them to demand as much work from their servants as possible, and they did not hesitate to devise legal ways to extend the period of servitude. Second, servants hoped to survive their period of servitude and then use their freedom to start a family and obtain land. They worked as hard as they had to rather than—as their masters wanted—as hard as they could. Third, servants saw themselves as free people in a temporary status of servitude, and they frequently resisted their masters' orders. Fourth, both servants and masters put up with this contentious arrangement because the alternatives were less desirable. Masters could not easily hire free men and women because land was so readily available that those who were free preferred to work on their own land for themselves. Furthermore, most masters could not depend on much labor from family members. The preponderance of men meant that families were few, were started late, and thus had few children. And, until the 1680s and 1690s, slaves were expensive and hard to come by. Before then, masters who wanted to expand their labor force and grow more tobacco had few alternatives to buying indentured servants.

# The Evolution of Chesapeake Society

The colonists' incessant desire to grow more tobacco propelled the evolution of Chesapeake society. The requirements of tobacco agriculture shaped patterns of settlement, making the landscape of the English colonies in the Chesapeake quite different from that of rural England. English colonists professed the Protestant and Catholic faiths, but they governed their daily lives less by the dictates of religious doctrine than by the demands of tobacco cultivation.

The system of indentured servitude sharpened inequality in Chesapeake society by the mid-seventeenth century. Social and political polarization culminated in 1676 with Bacon's Rebellion. The rebellion ultimately prompted reforms that stabilized relations between elite planters and their lesser neighbors and paved the way for a social hierarchy based less overtly on land and wealth than on race. (See the Historical Question on page 62.) Amidst this social and political evolution, one thing did not change: the dedication of Chesapeake colonists to growing tobacco.

## Life, Faith, and Labor

Villages and small towns dotted the rural landscape of seventeenth-century England, but colonists did not reproduce that English pattern in the Chesapeake. Instead, acres of wilderness were interrupted here and there by tobacco farms. This landscape arose from the settlers' determination to profit from tobacco, even at the expense of patterns of community life they had been accustomed to in England.

*English colonists professed the Protestant and Catholic faiths, but they governed their daily lives less by the dictates of religious doctrine than by the demands of tobacco cultivation.*

Tobacco was such a labor-intensive crop that one field worker could tend only about two acres of the plants in a year (an acre is slightly smaller than a football field). A family farmer needed to devote a few more acres to food crops, but a total of five or ten acres under cultivation sufficed to make a working tobacco farm. However, a successful farmer needed a great deal more land because tobacco quickly exhausted the fertility of the soil. Since each farmer cultivated only 5 or 10 percent of his land at any one time, a "settled" area comprised pockets of cultivated land surrounded by virgin forest.

Arrangements for marketing tobacco also contributed to the dispersion of settlements. Ideally, tobacco planters sought land that fronted a navigable river. Oceangoing ships could then dock at the planter's doorstep, minimizing the work of transporting and loading the heavy hogsheads of tobacco

## Why Did English Colonists Consider Themselves Superior to Indians and Africans?

**A YOUNG VIRGINIAN**

*In 1645, the Dutch artist Wenceslaus Hollar drew this portrait of a twenty-three-year-old Indian from Virginia. The young man had evidently been brought to London, where he posed for this likeness. Hollar portrayed his exotic adornment—the animal claw headband, shell earrings, and necklace, facial markings, Mohawk haircut, and bare-chested torso. Yet these distinctly non-European features did not cause Hollar to compromise his humane, dignified depiction of this man whose gaze seems to be fixed steadily and shamelessly upon the observer. If this young Virginian had been back in the Chesapeake rather than in London, he probably would have been engaged in the deadly warfare triggered by Opechancanough's 1644 uprising. One might imagine how this portrait would be different if it were drawn by a Virginia colonist in 1645.* British Museum.

WERE SEEDS OF THE RACIAL prejudice that has been such a powerful force in American history planted in the seventeenth-century Chesapeake? To answer that question, historians have paid close attention to the words the colonists used to describe Indians, Africans, and themselves.

In the mid-1500s, the English adopted the words *Indian* and *Negro* from Spanish, where they had come to mean, respectively, an aboriginal inhabitant of the New World and a black person of African ancestry. Both terms were generic, homogenizing an enormous diversity of tribal affiliations, languages, and cultures. Neither term originated with the people to whom it referred. The New England clergyman Roger Williams, who published a book on Indian languages in 1643, reported, "They have often asked mee, why we call them *Indians*," a poignant question that reveals the European origins of the term.

After *Indians*, the word the settlers used most frequently to describe Native Americans was *savages*. The Indians were savages, in the colonists' eyes, because they lacked the traits of English civilization. As one Englishman put it in 1625, the natives of Virginia were "so bad a people, having little of humanitie but shape, ignorant of Civilitie, of Arts, of Religion; more brutish than the beasts they hunt, more wild and unmanly than that unmanned wild countrey, which they range rather than inhabite; captivated also to Satans tyranny in foolish pieties, mad impieties, wicked idlenesse, busie and bloudy wickednesse." Some English colonists counterbalanced this harsh indictment with admiration for certain features of Indian behavior. They praised Indians' calm dignity and poise, their tender love and care for family members, and their simple, independent way of life in apparent harmony with nature.

Color was not a feature of the Indians' savagery. During the seventeenth century colonists never referred to Indians as "red." Instead, they saw Indians' skin color as tawny or tanned, the "Sun's livery," as one settler wrote. Many settlers held the view that Indians were innately white like the English but in every other way woefully un-English.

**AFRICAN MAN AND WOMAN**

*Albrecht Dürer, the foremost German artist of the Renaissance, drew these portraits early in the sixteenth century. They are among the first portraits of Africans to be made in Europe. Dürer drew Katarina, who was the servant of a Portuguese merchant Dürer visited in the Netherlands, in the spring of 1521. The portrait of the unidentified man was done several years earlier, but exactly when is unknown; the date 1508 was added after the portrait was completed. In any case, both portraits were completed before the Atlantic slave trade had begun to boom but well after Portuguese merchants had brought thousands of African slaves to Europe. Dürer's meticulously observed portraits betray no trace of racial prejudice. Both Katarina and the man appear to wear European clothing and to be depicted with the same respect and dignity Dürer accorded his European subjects. One might imagine how these portraits would be different if they had been executed by an artist in the southern colonies of North America in the late seventeenth century.*

Foto Marburg/Art Resource, NY.

In effect, the English colonists defined the Indians as "them," not "us." The colonists assumed that this distinction expressed a hierarchy of power and status: "We" are superior and should be dominant; "they" are inferior and should be subordinate. They enforced the distinction ferociously. In the early years of settlement, the colonists allowed a few young men to live for a while in Indian villages to learn native languages and then serve as interpreters. However, settlers who deserted English settlements in preference for Indian society were punished with a vengeance. *(Continued)*

The colonists identified Africans quite differently. Only a few Africans lived in the Chesapeake early in the seventeenth century. The first recorded arrival of Africans occurred in 1619, when a Dutch man-of-war brought to Virginia "20. and odd Negroes," as John Rolfe wrote. Rolfe's usage illustrates the colonists' most common term for Africans: *Negroes*. But the other word the colonists frequently used to refer to Africans was not *savage* or *heathen*, but *black*. What struck English colonists most forcefully about Africans was not their un-English ways but their un-English skin color.

Black was not a neutral color to the colonists. According to the *Oxford English Dictionary* (which catalogs the changing meaning of words), *black* meant to the English people who settled the Chesapeake "deeply stained with dirt; soiled, dirty, foul . . . having dark or deadly purposes, malignant; pertaining to or involving death, deadly; baneful, disastrous, sinister . . . foul, iniquitous, atrocious, horrible, wicked." Black was the opposite of white, which connoted purity, beauty, and goodness—attributes the colonists identified with themselves. In fact, by the middle of the seventeenth century, the colonists referred to themselves not only as English but also as free, implying that people who were not English were not free. After about 1680, the colonists stated that implication in racial terms by referring to themselves as white. By the end of the seventeenth century, blacks were "them"—un-English, unwhite, and unfree.

A few of the English dissented from such views. Thomas Phillips, a slave-ship captain, declared in 1694 that he could not "imagine why they [blacks] should be despis'd for their colour, being what they cannot help, and the effect of the climate it has pleas'd God to appoint them. I can't think there is any intrinsick value in one colour more than another, nor that white is better than black, only we think it so because we are so, and are prone to judge favourably in our own case, as well as the blacks, who in odium of the colour, say, the devil is white, and so paint him."

Virginians did not legally define slavery until 1660, but the sparse surviving evidence demonstrates that they practiced slavery long before that. Although there is no way to be certain, it is likely that the "20. and odd Negroes" who arrived in 1619 were slaves. And the punishments handed out to blacks who broke the law usually took for granted that their servitude could not be extended, presumably because they were already in bondage for life, rather than—like servants—for several years.

The debased status of slavery strengthened the colonists' prejudice toward blacks, just as racial prejudice buttressed slavery. A Virginia law of 1662, for instance, provided that "if any christian shall committ Fornication with a negro man or woman, hee or shee soe offending" had to pay a double fine. The law also demonstrates that, despite racial prejudice, sexual relations between white and black settlers were prevalent enough to attract the attention of the legislature.

For most of the seventeenth century, possession of a black skin did not automatically and necessarily condemn one to the status of slave in the eyes of whites. Some Africans in the Chesapeake served for limited periods of time like white servants, became free like white servants, and even acquired land, reared families, and participated in local affairs like former white servants. In fact, white colonists' prejudice against blacks represented an extreme form of wealthy colonists' attitudes toward servants and other poor white people. White servants, like blacks, were often considered "the vile and brutish part of mankind" by their masters.

The colonists hardened and exaggerated English attitudes about social hierarchy, about "us" and "them." Part of the reason is that, when colonists left England, they worried that they were separating themselves from "us"—the English—and risking becoming "them"—those uncivilized people found in the colonial wilds. To temper those fears and reduce those risks, colonists defined "us" and "them" in terms that emphasized their own Englishness in both color and civilization, providing a fertile seedbed for the growth of racial prejudice.

**TOBACCO PLANTATION**

*This print illustrates the tobacco harvest on a seventeenth-century plantation. Workers cut the mature plants and put the leaves in piles to wilt (left foreground and center background). After the leaves had dried somewhat, they were suspended from poles in a drying barn (right foreground), where they were seasoned before being packed in casks for shipping (see page 58). Sometimes they were also dried in the fields (center background). The print suggests the labor demands of tobacco by showing twenty-two individuals, all but two of them actively at work with the crop. The one woman depicted (hand in hand with a man in the left foreground) may be on her way to work in the harvest, but it appears more likely that she and the man are overseeing the labor of their servants or employees.*
From "About Tobacco," Lehman Brothers.

leaves. A settled region resembled a lacework of farms stitched around waterways.

On individual farmsteads, farmers built their houses from beams and planks hewn from felled timber. Although serviceable, the houses were by no means grand, or even particularly sturdy. A typical seventeenth-century tobacco farmer lived with his family and servants (if he had them) in a one- or two-room box of about four hundred square feet.

Most Chesapeake colonists were nominally Protestants. Attendance at Sunday services and conformity to the doctrines of the Church of England were required of all English men and women. However, clergymen were difficult to attract to the Chesapeake, and many of those who came were no more pious or righteous than their parishioners. Certainly some colonists took their religion seriously. Church courts punished fornicators, censured

blasphemers, and served notice on those who spent Sundays "goeing a fishing." But on the whole, religion did not awaken the zeal of Chesapeake settlers, certainly not as it did their counterparts who settled New England in these same years (see Chapter 4). What quickened the pulse of most Chesapeake folk was a close-run horse race, a bloody cock fight, or—most of all—an exceptionally fine tobacco crop. The religion of the Chesapeake colonists was Anglican, but their faith lay in the turbulent, competitive, high-stakes gamble of survival as tobacco planters.

The situation was the same in the Catholic colony of Maryland. In 1632, King Charles I (who had succeeded James I in 1625) granted his Catholic friend Lord Baltimore about six and a half million acres in the Chesapeake. Lord Baltimore intended to create a refuge for Catholics, who suffered severe discrimination in England. He fitted out two ships, the *Ark* and the *Dove,* gathered about 150 settlers, and sent them to the new colony, where they arrived on March 25, 1634. However, the population of Maryland grew very slowly for the next twenty years, and most settlers were Protestants rather than Catholics. The religious turmoil of the Puritan Revolution in England (discussed in Chapter 4) spilled across the Atlantic, creating conflict between Maryland's few Catholics—most of them wealthy and prominent—and the Protestant majority, few of whom were either wealthy or prominent. During the 1660s, Maryland began to attract settlers as readily as Virginia, most of them Protestants. Although Catholics and the Catholic faith continued to exert influence in Maryland, the colony's society, economy, politics, and culture became virtually indistinguishable from Virginia's. Both colonies shared a devotion to tobacco, the true faith of the Chesapeake.

One historian has aptly termed this the era of the yeoman planter—that is, a farmer who owned a small plot of land sufficient to support a family and tilled largely by family members and perhaps a few servants. A few elite planters had larger estates and commanded ten or more servants. But for the first thirty or forty years, few men lived long enough to accumulate a fortune sufficient to set them much apart from their neighbors. Until mid-century, the principal division in Chesapeake society was less between rich and poor planters than between free farmers and unfree servants. While these two groups contrasted sharply in their legal and economic status, their daily lives had many similarities: Most of them worked at the same tasks in the same fields, ate the same food, often at the same table, and slept in the same house. Although servants were required to be subordinate, they nonetheless looked forward to the time when their indentures would expire and they would be free. Once free, they usually had to work several more years as hired hands or tenant farmers to earn enough to buy land. Nonetheless, they readily assimilated into free society. On the whole, a rough, frontier equality characterized free families in the Chesapeake until about 1650.

Three major developments splintered that equality during the third quarter of the century. First, as tobacco production increased, prices declined. Cheap tobacco reduced planters' profits and made it more difficult for freed servants to save enough to become landowners. Second, because the

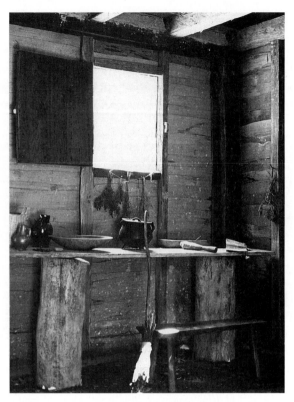

**INSIDE A POOR PLANTER'S HOUSE**
*The houses of seventeenth-century Chesapeake settlers were typically "earth-fast"—that is, the structural timbers that framed the house were simply placed in holes in the ground and the floor was packed dirt. No seventeenth-century house was substantial enough to survive until today. This photo shows a carefully documented historical reconstruction of the interior of a poor planter's house at St. Mary's City, Maryland. The wall of this one-room dwelling with a loft features a window with a shutter, but no glass; when the shutter was closed, the only source of light would be a candle or a fire. Note the rustic, unfinished bench, table, and walls. These meager furnishings were usually accompanied by a storage chest and some bedding, but not a bed. If and when the planters became more prosperous, they often made a bed their first acquisition, suggesting that the lack of a good night's sleep was one of their major discomforts.*
Paul Leibe, Historic St. Mary's City.

mortality rate dropped, more and more servants survived their indentures. As landless freemen became more numerous, they grew more discontent. Third, declining mortality also encouraged the formation of a planter elite. By living longer, the most successful planters compounded their success. The wealthiest planters also began to serve as merchants, marketing crops for their less successful neighbors, importing English goods for sale, and above all giving credit to hard-pressed customers.

*Until midcentury, the principal division in Chesapeake society was less between rich and poor planters than between free farmers and unfree servants.*

By the 1670s, the social structure of the Chesapeake had become polarized. Landowners—the planter elite and the more numerous yeoman planters—clustered around one pole. Landless colonists, mainly freed servants, gathered at the other. Each group eyed the other with suspicion and mistrust. For the most part, planters saw landless freemen as a dangerous rabble rather than as fellow colonists with legitimate grievances.

## Government, Politics, and Polarization

In general, government and politics amplified the inequality in Chesapeake society. The most vital distinction separated servants and masters, and the colonial government enforced it with an iron fist. Quick to prosecute critics, the governor's council hesitated to censure masters who brutalized their servants. No wonder poor men like William Tyler complained that "nether the Governor nor Counsell could or would doe any poore men right, but that they would shew favor to great men and wronge the poore." The poor had plenty of ammunition for such views. After 1640, no former servant ever served in either the governor's council or the House of Burgesses. Until 1670, all freemen could vote, and they routinely elected prosperous planters to the legislature. Most Chesapeake colonists, like most Europeans, assumed that the responsibilities of government were best borne by men of wealth and status.

In the 1660s and 1670s, colonial officials began to seek additional security as discontent mounted among the poor. Beginning in 1661, for example, Governor Berkeley did not call an election for the House of Burgesses for fifteen years. In 1670, the House of Burgesses limited voting rights to landowners and householders. Poor men with neither land nor homes were prohibited from voting.

The governor and other colonial officials also exploited their powers to squeeze colonists for personal gain. Tax agents, for example, received a slice of the revenues they collected. During his seven years as governor of Virginia, Lord Thomas Culpepper lived in England for all but nine months, pocketed the governor's annual salary, and hired a substitute to do the dirty work of governing the colony. Other governors spent more time in the colony, but they too expected to make their office pay.

In 1660, the king himself began to tighten the royal government's control of trade and to collect substantial revenue from the Chesapeake. The Navigation Act passed that year required all tobacco and other colonial products to be sent only to English ports. The act supplemented laws of 1650 and 1651 that specified that colonial goods had to be transported in English ships with predominantly English crews. A 1663 law stipulated that all goods sent to the colonies must pass through English ports and be carried in English ships by English sailors. Together, these navigation acts were designed to funnel the colonial import trade exclusively into the hands of English merchants, shippers, and seamen and reflected the English government's mercantilist assumptions about the colonies: What was good for England should determine policies toward the colonies.

These mercantilist assumptions underlay the import duty on tobacco inaugurated by the 1660 Navigation Act. The law assessed a duty of two pence on every pound of colonial tobacco imported into England, about the price a Chesapeake tobacco farmer received at the time. The duty gave the king a major financial interest in the size of the tobacco crop. In the 1660s, tobacco revenues amounted to about one-quarter of all English customs duties, and they continued to grow.

Hierarchy and inequality permeated all levels of government and politics, from the relation between king and colonies to that between master and servant. At every level, rulers expected to rule and to be obeyed; subjects expected to be ruled and to be punished for disobeying. To our ears, these expectations sound like a recipe for tyranny. In the seventeenth century, however, they were counterbalanced by other expectations that moderated their severity. Both rulers and subjects expected government to be administered for the good of the society as a whole. However, if rulers violated this precept, subjects might justifiably rebel, not so much to contest the principles of inequality and hierarchy but to protest their rulers' failure to govern for the general good.

## Bacon's Rebellion

In 1676, Bacon's Rebellion erupted as a dispute over Indian policy in the Chesapeake. Before it was over, the rebellion convulsed Chesapeake politics and society, leaving in its wake death, destruction, and a legacy of hostility between the great planters and their poorer neighbors.

Opechancanough, the old chief who had led the Indian uprising of 1622 in Virginia, mounted another surprise attack in 1644 and killed about five hundred colonists in two days. During the next two years of bitter fighting, the colonists captured and murdered Opechancanough, eventually gaining the upper hand. The treaty that concluded the war established policies toward the Indians that the government tried to maintain for the next thirty years. The Indians relinquished all claims to land already settled by the English. Wilderness land beyond the fringe of English settlement was supposed to be reserved exclusively for Indian use. The government hoped to minimize contact between settlers and Indians and thereby maintain the peace.

Had the Chesapeake population remained constant, the policy might have worked. But the number of land-hungry colonists, especially poor, recently freed servants, continued to multiply. In their quest for land, they pushed beyond the treaty limits of English settlement and encroached steadily on Indian land. During the 1660s and 1670s, violence between colonists and Indians repeatedly flared along the advancing frontier. The government, headquartered in the tidewater region near the coast, far from the danger of Indian raids, took steps to calm the disputes and reestablish the peace. Frontier settlers thirsted for revenge against what their leader, Nathaniel Bacon, termed "the protected and Darling Indians." Bacon minced no words about his intention: "Our Design [is] not only to ruine and extirpate all Indians in Generall but all Manner of Trade and Commerce with them."

Indians were not the only enemies Bacon and his men singled out. Bacon also urged colonists to "see what spounges have suckt up the Publique Treasure." He charged that "Grandees," or elite planters, operated the government for their private gain, a charge that made sense to many colonists.

By most measures, Bacon himself was one of the grandees. The son of an English country gentleman, Bacon came to Virginia in 1674 at the age of twenty-seven to make his fortune. A cousin of Governor Berkeley and a relative of other colonial officials, Bacon remained outside the inner circle of established planters who ran things in Jamestown and in local government. Within two years, he had crystallized the grievances of the small planters and poor farmers against both the Indians and the colonial rulers in Jamestown.

At first, Bacon insisted that Governor Berkeley appoint him to lead a small army against the Indians. Berkeley refused, hoping to maintain the fragile peace on the frontier. To put Bacon in his place, Berkeley pronounced him a rebel, threatened to punish him for treason, and called for new elections of burgesses that—Berkeley believed—would endorse his get-tough policy toward Bacon and his followers.

The elections backfired. To Berkeley's surprise, almost all the old burgesses were voted out of office and their places taken by local leaders, including Bacon. The legislature was now in the hands of minor grandees who, like Bacon, chafed at the rule of the elite planters.

In June 1676, the new legislature passed a series of reform measures known as Bacon's Laws. Among other changes, the laws gave local settlers a voice in setting tax levies, forbade officeholders from demanding bribes or other extra fees for carrying out their duties, placed limits on holding multiple offices, required officials to be native-born or resident for at least three years, and restored the vote to all freemen. When Bacon marched into Jamestown at the head of five hundred armed men demanding a commission to fight the Indians, Berkeley sensed that it was time to compromise. He pardoned Bacon and authorized his campaign of frontier warfare.

After Bacon trekked off to fight Indians, elite planters convinced Berkeley that it was extremely dangerous to have hundreds of armed men marauding through the countryside. What if they should decide to attack the grandees as well as Indians? What if they should call for servants, about half the population, to join them? Bacon's followers were desperate men, the secretary of the colony pointed out. Berkeley agreed that Bacon and his men were a greater threat than Indians.

When Bacon learned that Berkeley had once again branded him a traitor, he declared war against Berkeley and the other grandees. For three months, Bacon's forces fought Indians and sacked the grandees' plantations. Berkeley's loyalists retaliated by plundering the homes of Bacon's supporters. To obtain fresh recruits, both Bacon and Berkeley promised freedom to servants and slaves who would aid their cause. In mid-September, Bacon marched on Jamestown, routed Berkeley's forces, and burned the town. The fighting continued until late October, when Bacon unexpectedly died, most likely from dysentery, and several English ships arrived to bolster Berkeley's strength. Back in power, Berkeley hanged several of Bacon's allies and destroyed farms that belonged to Bacon's supporters.

The crucial distinction between Bacon's rebels and Berkeley's loyalists was less between poor and rich than between outsiders and insiders. Bacon's supporters generally were less wealthy than Berkeley's allies, but they included planters and small farmers as well as landless freemen. Bacon did not intend to overturn the hierarchy of Chesapeake politics and society. Instead, he challenged the ruthless and callous exploitation of the many outsiders by the few insiders. The rebellion did not dislodge the grandees from their seats of power. If anything, it strengthened their position. When the king learned of the turmoil in the Chesapeake and its devastating effect on tobacco exports and customs duties, he ordered an investigation. The royal officials replaced Berkeley with a governor more attentive to the king's interests, nullified Bacon's Laws, and instituted an export tax on every hogshead of tobacco as a way of paying the expenses of government without having to obtain the consent of the tightfisted House of Burgesses. In a sense, the grandees of the Chesapeake were put in their place by still grander royal officials.

---

*Bacon challenged the ruthless and callous exploitation of the many outsiders by the few insiders.*

---

In the aftermath of Bacon's Rebellion, tensions between great planters and small farmers gradually lessened. By 1700, the new export duty on tobacco allowed the government to cut other taxes to just one-fourth what they had been in 1660, a move welcomed by all freemen. In the long run, however, the most important contribution to political stability was the declining importance of the servant labor system. During the 1680s and 1690s, fewer servants arrived in the Chesapeake, partly because of im-

proving economic conditions in England. Accordingly, the number of poor, newly freed servants also declined, reducing the size of the lowest stratum of free society. In 1700, as many as one-third of the free colonists still worked as tenants on land owned by others, but the social and political distance between them and the great planters, enormous as it was, did not seem as profound as it had been in 1660. The main reason was that by 1700 the Chesapeake was in the midst of transition to a slave labor system that minimized the differences between poor farmers and rich planters and magnified the differences between whites and blacks.

# Toward a Slave Labor System

Spaniards and Portuguese engaged in an extensive African slave trade in the sixteenth century, and they established slavery as a major form of coerced labor in the New World. In the seventeenth century, British colonies in the West Indies followed the Spanish and Portuguese examples and developed sugar plantations with slave labor. In the British North American colonies, however, a slave labor system did not develop until the last quarter of the seventeenth century. During the 1670s, settlers from Barbados brought slavery to the new English mainland colony of Carolina, where the imprint of the West Indies remained strong for decades. In Chesapeake tobacco fields at about the same time, slave labor began to replace servant labor, marking the transition toward a society of freedom for whites and slavery for Africans.

## The West Indies: Sugar and Slavery

The most profitable part of the British New World empire in the seventeenth century lay in the Caribbean (Map 3.2). The tiny island of Barbados, colonized in the 1630s, was the jewel of the British West Indies. During the 1640s, Barbadian planters began to grow sugarcane, with such success that a colonial official proclaimed Barbados "the most flourishing Island in all those American parts, and I verily beleive in all the world for the production of sugar." Sugar commanded high prices in England, and planters rushed to grow as much as they could. By midcentury, annual sugar exports from the British Caribbean totaled about 150,000 pounds; by 1700, exports nearly reached 50 million pounds.

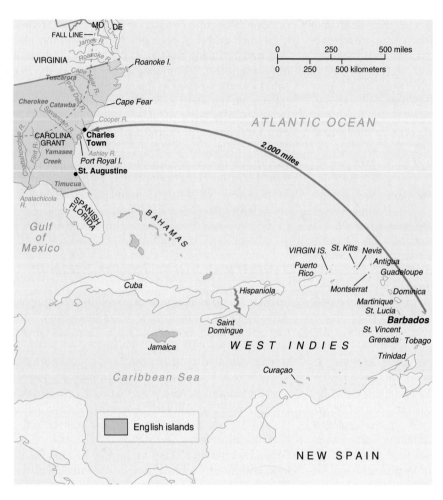

MAP 3.2
*The West Indies and Carolina in the Seventeenth Century*
*Although Carolina was geographically closer to the Chesapeake colonies, it was culturally closer to the West Indies in the seventeenth century since its early settlers—both blacks and whites—came from Barbados. South Carolina retained close ties to the West Indies for more than a century, long after many of its subsequent settlers came from England, Ireland, France, and elsewhere.*

Sugar transformed Barbados and other West Indian islands. Poor farmers could not afford the expensive machinery that extracted and refined the sugarcane juice. So many farmers left Barbados in quest of better opportunities that the white population in 1700 was only half what it had been in 1650. Planters who remained and had the necessary capital to grow sugar got rich. By 1680, the wealthiest Barbadian sugar planters were, on average, four times richer than tobacco grandees in the Chesapeake. The sugar grandees differed from their Chesapeake counterparts in another crucial way: The average sugar baron in Barbados in 1680 owned 115 slaves.

African slaves planted, cultivated, and harvested the sugarcane that made planters wealthy. Beginning in the 1640s, Barbadian planters purchased thousands of slaves to work their plantations, and the African population on the island mushroomed. During the 1650s, when blacks made up only 3 percent of the Chesapeake population, they had already become the majority on Barbados. By 1700, slaves constituted more than three-fourths of the island's population. Barbados was literally a slave society that belonged to white men.

*During the 1670s, settlers from Barbados brought slavery to the new English mainland colony of Carolina and slave labor began to replace servant labor in Chesapeake tobacco fields, marking the transition toward a society of freedom for whites and slavery for Africans.*

For slaves, work on a sugar plantation was a life sentence to brutal, unremitting labor. Slaves' life expectancy was short and their death rate high.

Furthermore, since slave men outnumbered slave women two to one, the vast majority of slaves could not form a family and have children. These grim realities meant that in Barbados and elsewhere in the West Indies, the slave population did not grow by natural reproduction. Instead, planters continually purchased slaves from Africa who tended to be bitter, unruly, and hostile, and sugar planters became all the more ruthless in enforcing obedience.

As the sugar boom moved from island to island in the Caribbean, this distinctively West Indian colonial society was reproduced repeatedly. Although sugar plantations did not gain a foothold in North America in the seventeenth century, the West Indies nonetheless exerted a powerful influence on the development of slavery in the mainland colonies.

## Carolina: A West Indian Frontier

The early settlers of what became South Carolina were emigrants from Barbados. In 1663, a Barbadian planter named John Colleton and a group of seven other men obtained a charter from King Charles II to establish a colony south of the Chesapeake and north of the Spanish territories in Florida. Colleton and his colleagues, known as the "proprietors," hoped to siphon settlers from Barbados and other colonies and encourage them to develop a profitable export crop comparable to West Indian sugar and Chesapeake tobacco.

Following the Chesapeake example, the proprietors offered headrights of up to 150 acres of land for each settler. In 1670, they established the first

**SUGAR MILL**

*This seventeenth-century drawing of a Brazilian sugar mill highlights the heavy equipment needed to extract the juice from sugarcane. A vertical waterwheel turns a large horizontal gear that exerts force on the jaws of a press, which squeezes the cane. Workers constantly remove crushed cane from the press and replenish it with freshly harvested cane as it is unloaded from an oxcart. Note that except for the overseer (just to the right of the waterwheel), all of the workers are black, presumably slaves from Africa, as suggested by their clothing. All of the mill workers appear to be men, a hint of the predominance of men among newly imported African slaves.*
Musées Royaux des Beaux-Arts de Belgique.

permanent English beachhead in the colony, on the west bank of the Ashley River just across from the peninsula where the king's namesake city, Charles Towne (later spelled Charleston), was founded (see Map 3.2).

As the proprietors had planned, most of the settlers were from Barbados. In fact, Carolina was the only seventeenth-century English colony to be settled principally by colonists from other colonies rather than from England. The Barbadian immigrants brought their slaves with them. More than a fourth of the early settlers were black, and, as the colony continued to attract settlers from Barbados, the black population multiplied. By 1700, blacks made up about half of the population of Carolina. English officials associated the colony so closely with Barbados that as late as 1700 they referred to "Carolina in ye West Indies."

The Carolinians experimented with tobacco, cotton, indigo, olives, and rice as potentially profitable export crops. But until the end of the seventeenth century, the experiments proved disappointing. Finally, in the mid-1690s, colonists identified a hardy strain of rice and worked out successful methods of cultivation that inaugurated a flourishing rice industry. During the first generation of settlement in the seventeenth century, however, Carolina remained an economic colony of Barbados. Settlers sold livestock and timber to the West Indies. They also exploited another "natural resource": They captured and enslaved several thousand local Indians and sold them to Caribbean planters. Both economically and socially, seventeenth-century Carolina was a frontier outpost of the West Indian sugar economy.

### The Chesapeake: Tobacco and Slaves

By 1700, more than eight out of ten people in the southern colonies of British North America lived in the Chesapeake. Until the 1670s, almost all Chesapeake colonists were white people from England. In 1700, however, one out of eight people in the region was a black person from Africa. Although a few blacks had lived in the Chesapeake since the 1620s, the black population increased fivefold between 1670 and 1700 as tobacco planters made the transition from servant to slave labor (Figure 3.1).

At bottom, the shift to slave labor occurred because hundreds of individual Chesapeake planters began to purchase slaves rather than servants to work in their tobacco fields. For planters, slaves had several obvious advantages over servants. Although

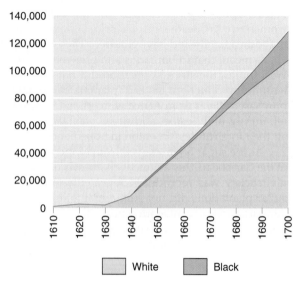

FIGURE 3.1
**White and Black Populations in the Southern Colonies in the Seventeenth Century**
*Although the first Africans arrived in the southern colonies in 1619, Africans and their descendants remained a small fraction of the population throughout the seventeenth century. What features of this chart reflect the servant labor system, the transition to slave labor, and the settlement of Carolina?*

slaves cost three to five times more than servants, slaves never became free. Since the mortality rate had declined by the 1680s, planters could reasonably expect slaves to live longer than a servant's period of indenture. Slaves also promised to be a perpetual labor force. Children of slave mothers inherited the status of slavery. As William Fitzhugh, a wealthy Chesapeake planter, pointed out to a friend, his "Negroes increase being all young, & a considerable parcel of breeders, will keep that Stock [of slaves] good for ever."

For planters like Fitzhugh, slaves had another important advantage over servants: They could be controlled politically. Servants came to the Chesapeake expecting to become free, obtain land, and participate in colonial society. Bacon's Rebellion had demonstrated how disruptive former servants could be when their expectations were not met. A slave labor system promised to avoid the political problems caused by the servant labor system. Slavery kept discontented laborers in permanent servitude, and their color was a badge of their bondage.

Slaves were even prohibited from defending themselves. A 1680 Virginia law provided that "any negroe or other slave [who] shall presume to lift up his hand in opposition against any [white] christian" would be punished with "thirty lashes on his bare back well laid on."

The slave labor system polarized Chesapeake society along lines of race and status: All slaves were black and nearly all blacks were slaves; almost all free people were white and all whites were free or only temporarily bound in indentured servitude. Unlike Barbados, however, the Chesapeake retained a vast white majority. Among whites, huge differences of wealth and status still existed. In fact, the emerging slave labor system sharpened the economic differences among whites since only prosperous planters could afford to buy slaves. By 1700, more than three-quarters of white families had neither servants nor slaves. Nonetheless, poorer white farmers enjoyed the privileges of free status. They could own property of all sorts; they could marry, have families, and bequeath their property and free status to their descendants; they could move when and where they wanted; they could associate freely with other people; they could serve on juries, vote, and even hold political office; they could work, loaf, or sleep as they chose. All these privileges and more were prohibited to slaves. These distinctions between slaves and free people made lesser white folk feel they had a genuine stake in the existence of slavery, even if they did not own a single slave. By emphasizing the privileges of freedom shared by all white people, the slave labor system reduced the tensions between poor folk and grandees that had plagued the Chesapeake in the 1670s.

The slaves purchased by Chesapeake planters in the seventeenth century came mostly from the West Indies. Chesapeake planters made a leisurely transition to slave labor with Africans who had already been "seasoned," that is, acclimated to the natural environment of the New World and the repressive confines of slavery. Many of the slaves probably had already learned some English. The transition was still under way in 1700, but by then the majority of laborers found in Chesapeake tobacco fields were slaves.

In contrast to Barbados, most slaves in the seventeenth-century Chesapeake colonies had frequent and close contact with white people. Slaves and white servants performed the same tasks on tobacco plantations, often working side by side in the fields. For slaves, work on a tobacco plantation was less onerous than on a sugar plantation. But slaves' constant exposure to white surveillance made Chesapeake slavery especially confining. Slaves took advantage of every opportunity to slip away from white supervision and seek out the company of other slaves, "going abroad" to visit slaves on neighboring plantations. Planters did not like such visiting, but they often permitted it. More than once, slaves turned such seemingly innocent social pleasures to political ends, either to run away or to conspire to strike against their masters. In 1680, for example, Virginia planters uncovered a "Negro Plott, formed . . . for the Distroying and killing his Majesties Subjects . . . with a designe of Carrying it through the whole Collony of Virginia." An investigation concluded that masters were at fault for allowing slaves to travel between plantations and to meet for funerals and admonished masters to be more vigilant.

---

*The slave labor system polarized Chesapeake society along lines of race and status: All slaves were black and nearly all blacks were slaves; almost all free people were white and all whites were free or only temporarily bound in indentured servitude.*

---

While slavery resolved the political unrest caused by the servant labor system, it created new political problems. By 1700, the bedrock political issue in the Chesapeake was keeping slaves in their place, at the business end of a hoe in a tobacco field. The Chesapeake was well on its way to developing a slave labor system that stood midway—both geographically and socially—between the sugar plantations and black majority of Barbados to the south and the small farms and homogeneous villages that developed in seventeenth-century New England to the north.

## Conclusion: Status and Race in the Southern Economy

By 1700, the colonies of Virginia, Maryland, and Carolina were firmly established. The staple crops they grew for export provided a livelihood for many, a fortune for a few, and valuable revenues for shippers, merchants, and the English monarchy. Their societies differed markedly from English society in most respects, yet the colonists considered themselves English people who happened to live in North America. They claimed the same rights and privileges of English men and women while they denied those rights and privileges to Native Americans and African slaves.

The English colonies also differed from the sixteenth-century example of New Spain. Large quantities of gold and silver never materialized in the Chesapeake. The system of encomienda was never adopted because Indians were too few and too hostile and their communities too small and decentralized, compared with those of the Mexica. Yet forms of coerced labor and racial distinction that developed in New Spain had North American counterparts, as English colonists employed servants and slaves and defined themselves as superior to Indians and Africans.

By 1700, only the remnants of Powhatan's people survived. As English settlement pushed north, west, and south of the Chesapeake, the various Indian peoples were faced with the new English world that Powhatan encountered in 1607. By 1700, few in North America—whether colonists or Native Americans—doubted that the English had come to stay.

## CHRONOLOGY

| | |
|---|---|
| **1588** | England defeats Spanish Armada. |
| **1606** | Virginia Company of London receives royal charter to establish colony in North America. |
| **1607** | English colonists found Jamestown settlement. |
| **1609** | Starvation plagues Jamestown. |
| **1612** | John Rolfe begins to plant tobacco in Virginia. |
| **1617** | First commercial tobacco shipment leaves Virginia for England. Pocahontas dies in England. |
| **1618** | Powhatan dies and Opechancanough becomes supreme chief. |
| **1619** | First Africans arrive in Virginia. House of Burgesses begins to meet in Virginia. |
| **1622** | Opechancanough leads Indian uprising against Virginia colonists. |

| | |
|---|---|
| **1624** | Virginia becomes royal colony. |
| **1632** | King Charles I grants Lord Baltimore land for colony of Maryland. |
| **1634** | Colonists begin to arrive in Maryland. |
| **1644** | Opechancanough leads Indian uprising against Virginia colonists. |
| **1660** | Navigation Act requires colonial tobacco to be shipped to English ports and to be assessed customs tax. |
| **1663** | Carolina proprietors receive charter from King Charles II for Carolina colony. |
| **1670** | Charles Towne, South Carolina, founded. Slave labor system emerges first in Carolina and more gradually in Chesapeake colonies. |
| **1676** | Bacon's Rebellion convulses Virginia. |

# SUGGESTED READINGS

Lois Green Carr, Russell R. Menard, and Lorena S. Walsh, *Robert Cole's World: Agriculture and Society in Early Maryland* (1991). A readable account of the life of a common tobacco planter in the Chesapeake, based on an unusually rich collection of documents.

Richard S. Dunn, *Sugar and Slaves: The Rise of the Planter Class in the English West Indies, 1624–1713* (1972). A major study of the emergence of the class of sugar planters who dominated the Caribbean world.

James Horn, *Adapting to a New World: English Society in the Seventeenth-Century Chesapeake* (1994). A study of English settlers' adaptation to the environment of the Chesapeake during the seventeenth century.

Winthrop D. Jordan, *White over Black: American Attitudes towards the Negro, 1550–1812* (1968). A landmark examination of the origins and evolution of white racial attitudes in North America.

James H. Merrell, *The Indians' New World: Catawbas and Their Neighbors from European Contact through the Era of Removal* (1989). A compelling account of the shifting encounters between Carolina colonists and a major Native American society.

Sidney W. Mintz, *Sweetness and Power: The Place of Sugar in Modern History* (1985). An insightful analysis of the far-reaching influence of sugar in the modern world in shaping patterns of both production and consumption.

Edmund S. Morgan, *American Slavery, American Freedom: The Ordeal of Colonial Virginia* (1975). A classic account of the social and economic history of the servant labor system in seventeenth-century Virginia, including Bacon's Rebellion, and the long-term consequences for American ideas of freedom and race.

James Perry, *The Formation of a Society on Virginia's Eastern Shore, 1615–1655* (1990). A thorough study of the first generation of settlement in a Chesapeake community.

Helen C. Rountree, *Pocahontas's People: The Powhatan Indians of Virginia through Four Centuries* (1990). A readable survey of historical and archaeological knowledge of Powhatan's people by a leading expert.

Hugh Thomas, *The Slave Trade* (1997). An encyclopedic survey of the transatlantic African slave trade that examines the involvement of Portuguese, Spanish, French, British, North American, Arabic, and African peoples.

Peter H. Wood, *Black Majority: Negroes in Colonial South Carolina from 1670 through the Stono Rebellion* (1974). A fascinating account of the origins of slavery in South Carolina, emphasizing the distinctive contributions of slaves to the colonial economy.

**GREAT CHAIR**

*This thronelike chair belonged to Michael Metcalf, a teacher in seventeenth-century Dedham, Massachusetts. The oldest known piece of New England furniture inscribed with a date, 1652, the chair was made in Dedham specifically for Metcalf (note the initials flanking the date), who turned sixty-six that year. Metcalf stored books, presumably including a well-thumbed Bible, in the enclosed compartment under the seat. No overstuffed recliner, the chair is suited less for a relaxing snooze than for alert concentration. The panels under the arms served to block chilly drafts. Otherwise, the chair shows few concessions to comfort or ease. The carved back—rigidly upright—displays motifs often found on Puritan tombstones. The grand austerity of the chair hints at the importance of serious Bible study and unflinching introspection in Puritan New England.*

Dedham Historical Society/photo by Forrest Frazier.

# THE NORTHERN COLONIES IN THE SEVENTEENTH CENTURY

4

## 1601–1700

I N 1630, AN OFFICIAL OF THE CHURCH OF ENGLAND FILED CHARGES against Reverend Charles Chauncy, a minister in the small village of Ware, a few miles north of London. Chauncy had sworn obedience to the doctrines of the Church of England, or Anglican Church, but church officials found him alarmingly disobedient.

The list of Chauncy's transgressions was long and detailed. During worship services, he announced that "people have been deluded" by the Book of Common Prayer and sinned by following the Church of England. He refused to make the sign of the cross in baptisms and marriage ceremonies. He refused to hold worship services on the special holy days appointed by the Church of England. He preached, for example, that the celebration of Christmas was sinful because it was not mentioned in the Bible. The church also accused Chauncy of creating "much strife, heart-burning, and dissension . . . amongst the inhabitants in Ware" by preaching that "the Sabbath doth begin every Saturday at sunset." If Chauncy was correct, then Saturday night was for worship rather than for such pleasures as singing, dancing, or drinking. Not surprisingly, the Church of England charged that Chauncy acted "under a false pretence of zeal and purity in religion," claiming "to be more precise than other men, and . . . [to] affect the name of Puritan."

Chauncy was indeed a Puritan, and proud of it. He warned his parishioners that "the preaching of the Gospel would be suppressed, and that some families are preparing to go for New England." Chauncy's warnings, the Church of England asserted, "caused a great distraction and fear amongst the people, . . . making them believe that there would forthwith ensue some alteration of religion."

The charges against Chauncy illustrate the religious, social, and political turmoil that pervaded England in the first decades of the seventeenth century. Puritans like Chauncy both responded to that turmoil and helped create it. Most Puritans and their followers stayed in England where, in the 1640s, they fought the battles of the Puritan Revolution. In the years before the revolution, however, thousands of other Puritans like Chauncy immigrated to New England. In the wilderness on the western shores of the Atlantic, they aspired to build a new, godly society purged of the idolatry, heresy, and corruption of England.

Experiences in New England tempered Puritan zeal during the seventeenth century, and the goal of founding a holy new England faded. Late in the century, new colonies—New York, New Jersey, and Pennsylvania—were founded that differed sharply from New England. Despite these differences, by 1700 all the North American colonies—the new middle colonies as well as New England and the southern colonies—were tied more firmly to the English empire.

## Puritan Origins: The English Reformation

In 1500, the church in England, like the church in other European countries, owed allegiance to the pope in Rome. The Roman church was a catholic, or universal, church. It was also a unified church. But when the Protestant Reformation arose in Germany in 1517 and spread to other countries soon afterward, that unity shattered forever.

During the early years of the Reformation, the English church remained within the Catholic fold. King Henry VIII, who reigned from 1509 to 1547, was such a loyal Catholic that the pope bestowed on him the honorific title Defender of the Faith. Henry's faith, like that of other European monarchs, was strongly influenced by political considerations. He witnessed the bitter religious disputes and popular unrest the Reformation brought to the European continent and hoped to prevent both from spreading to England. He also understood that the Reformation offered him an opportunity to break with Rome and take control of the church in England.

The pretext for a breach with Rome was Henry's desire for a divorce from his wife, Catherine of Aragon, the daughter of Ferdinand and Isabella of Spain. Their marriage had cemented a close relationship between the monarchies of England and Spain, but by the mid-1520s Henry was becoming alarmed at the increasing power of the Spanish crown, fueled in part by New World treasure. After the pope refused Henry's request for an annulment of the marriage, Henry arranged in 1533 for the archbishop of Canterbury, the top official in the English church, to dissolve the marriage. Henry then secretly married Anne Boleyn—who was already pregnant with their daughter, Elizabeth—and he was quickly excommunicated by the pope.

In 1534, Henry completed the break with Rome and formally initiated the English Reformation. At his insistence, Parliament passed the Act of Supremacy, which outlawed the Catholic Church and proclaimed the king "the only supreme head on earth of the Church of England." The vast properties of the Catholic Church in England were now the king's, as was the privilege of appointing bishops and other members of the church hierarchy. But Protestant doctrines advocated by Martin Luther and his followers held no attraction for Henry. In almost all matters of theology and religious practice, he remained an orthodox Catholic.

In the short run, the English Reformation allowed Henry VIII to achieve his political goal of controlling the church. In the long run, however, the English Reformation brought to England the political and religious turmoil that Henry had hoped to avoid. Henry himself sought no more than a halfway Reformation. Many English Catholics wanted no Reformation at all; they hoped to return the Church of England to the pope and to maintain Catholic doctrines and ceremonies. But many other English people insisted on a genuine, thoroughgoing Reformation; these people came to be called Puritans.

*In the short run, the English Reformation allowed Henry VIII to achieve his political goal of bringing the church under the dominion of the monarchy. In the long run, however, the English Reformation brought to England the political and religious turmoil that Henry had hoped to avoid.*

During the sixteenth century, Puritanism was less an organized movement than a set of ideas and religious principles that appealed strongly to many dissenting members of the Church of England. Puritans adhered to the doctrines of Protestantism developed by Martin Luther, John Calvin, and others on the European continent. They sought to purify the Church of England by eliminating what they considered the offensive features of Catholicism. For example, they demanded that the church hierarchy be abolished and that ordinary Christians be given greater control over religious life. They wanted to eliminate the rituals of Catholic worship and instead emphasize an individual's relationship with God developed through Bible study, prayer, and introspection. Although there were many varieties and degrees of Puritanism, all Puritans shared a desire to carry the Reformation to its logical Protestant conclusion.

When Henry VIII died in 1547, the advisers of the new king, Edward VI—Henry's nine-year-old son—initiated religious reforms that moved in a Protestant direction. The tide of reform reversed in 1553 when Edward died and was succeeded by Mary I, the daughter of Henry and Catherine of Aragon. Mary had remained a steadfast Catholic, and shortly after she became queen she married Europe's most powerful guardian of Catholicism, Philip II of Spain. Mary attempted to return England to a pre-Reformation Catholic Church. She

You shall be led before Princes and rulers for my names sake. *Math.*10.

**PERSECUTION OF ENGLISH PROTESTANTS**

*This sixteenth-century drawing shows the persecution of Protestants in England during the reign of Queen Mary, a staunch Catholic. Here Protestant prisoners are being marched to London to be tried for heresy. This pro-Protestant drawing emphasizes the severity of royal tyranny by depicting four well-armed guards, two of them mounted, escorting some fifteen prisoners, including at least five women, who are roped together, although they do not appear to be menacing or likely to run away. The guards seem to be necessary less to maintain order among the prisoners than to prevent sympathetic citizens from rushing toward the marchers and freeing them. The drawing assumes that most citizens opposed the queen's persecution of Protestants. The Bible verse from the book of Matthew underscores Protestants' fealty to Christ rather than mere "Princes and Rulers" like Queen Mary.*
Folger Shakespeare Library.

outlawed Protestantism and persecuted those who refused to conform, sentencing almost three hundred to burn at the stake.

The tide turned again in 1558 when Mary died and was succeeded by Elizabeth I, the daughter of Henry and Anne Boleyn. Elizabeth tried to consolidate the English Reformation midway between the extremes of Catholicism and Puritanism. She legalized Protestantism, reaffirmed the breach with Rome, and asserted her control over the Church of England. Like her father, she was less concerned with theology than with politics. Above all, she desired a church that would strengthen the monarchy and the nation. By the time Elizabeth died in 1603, many people in England looked on Protestantism as a defining feature of national identity.

Shortly after Elizabeth's successor, James I, came to the throne, English Puritans petitioned for further reform of the Church of England. The king authorized a new translation of the Bible, known ever since as the King James version. However, neither James I nor his son Charles I, who became king in 1625, was receptive to the ideas of Puritan reformers. James and Charles moved the Church of England away from Puritanism rather than toward it. They enforced conformity to the Church of England and punished dissenters, both ordinary Christians and ministers like Charles Chauncy. In 1629, Charles I dissolved Parliament—where Puritans were well represented—and initiated aggressive anti-Puritan policies. Many Puritans despaired about continuing to defend their faith in England

and began to make plans to emigrate. Some left for Europe, others for the West Indies. The largest number set out for America.

## Puritans and the Settlement of New England

Puritans who emigrated aspired to escape the turmoil of England and to build a new, orderly society that looked like a Puritan version of England. Their faith shaped the colonies they established in New England in virtually every way. Although some colonists were not Puritans, Puritanism remained the paramount influence in New England's religion, politics, and community life.

### The Pilgrims and Plymouth Colony

One of the earliest groups to emigrate, known subsequently as Pilgrims, espoused a heresy known as separatism: They sought to withdraw and separate from the Church of England, actions that would be punished severely in England. They moved first to Holland, in 1608, but by 1620 they found they could not establish the life they envisioned. William Bradford, a leading member of the group, recalled that "many of their children, by . . . the great licentiousness of youth in [Holland], and the manifold temptations of the place, were drawn away by evil examples." Determining that America was a place where they might protect their children's piety and preserve their community, the Pilgrims obtained permission to settle in the extensive lands granted to the Virginia Company. To finance their journey, they formed a joint stock company with London investors. The investors provided the capital; the Pilgrims, their labor, lives, and a share in all profits for seven years. Following months of delay in Holland and England, 102 prospective settlers finally boarded the *Mayflower* in August 1620. After eleven weeks at sea, all but one of them arrived at the outermost tip of Cape Cod, in present-day Massachusetts.

The Pilgrims realized immediately that they had landed far north of the Virginia grant and had no legal authority from the king to settle in the area. On the day they arrived, the Pilgrims drew up the Mayflower Compact. They agreed to "covenant and combine ourselves together into a civil Body Politick, for our better Ordering and Preservation." The signers (all men) agreed to enact and obey necessary and just laws. With this pact, the Pilgrims hoped to provide order and security as well as a claim to legitimacy until the king granted them legal rights.

Early in December, the Pilgrims settled at Plymouth and elected William Bradford as their governor, a position he held almost continuously until his death in 1657. That first winter "was most sad and lamentable," Bradford wrote later. "In two or three months' time half of [our] company [including Bradford's wife] died . . . being the depth of winter, and wanting houses and other comforts [and] being infected with scurvy and other diseases."

*Although some colonists were not Puritans, Puritanism remained the paramount influence in New England's religion, politics, and community life.*

In the spring, Indians rescued the floundering Plymouth settlement. First Samoset, then Squanto—both of whom understood English—befriended the settlers. Samoset arranged for the Pilgrims to meet and establish good relations with Massasoit, the chief of the Wampanoags, whose territory included Plymouth. Squanto, Bradford recalled, "was a special instrument sent of God for their [the Pilgrims'] good beyond their expectation. He directed them how to set their corn, where to take fish, and to procure other commodities, and was also their pilot to bring them to unknown places." With Squanto's help and their own hard labor, the Pilgrims managed to store enough food to guarantee their survival through the coming winter, an occasion they celebrated in the fall of 1621 with a thanksgiving feast attended by Massasoit and many of his warriors. Yet, the colony's status remained precarious. Only seven dwellings had been erected that first year, half the original colonists had died, and a new group of thirty-six threadbare, sickly settlers arrived in November 1621, requiring the colony to adopt stringent food rationing. The colonists quarreled with their London investors, who became frustrated when the colony failed to produce the expected profits. But the Pilgrims lived quietly and simply, coexisting in relative peace with the Indians, paying Massasoit when settlers gradually encroached on Wampanoag territory. By 1630, Plymouth had become a permanent settlement.

Having succeeded in founding a small Puritan haven, the Plymouth colonists failed to attract many

**PLYMOUTH FORT AND MEETINGHOUSE**

*This building is a careful historical reconstruction of a fort built by the Plymouth settlers in 1622, shortly after hearing of Powhatan's uprising against English colonists in Virginia (discussed in Chapter 3). It is adapted from the traditional design of a seventeenth-century granary, but the ports lining the second story are not for stacking sheaves of grain but for firing on attacking Indians or on hostile Spaniards or Frenchmen. In fact, no attack ever came. The Pilgrims nonetheless made good use of the fort as a meetinghouse. Sermons, prayers, and worldly testimony—not cannon—echoed through the fort. Colonists gathered on the first floor for church services and court sessions. The building evokes the Plymouth colonists' military vulnerability and religious security.*

Courtesy of Plimoth Plantation, Inc., Plymouth, MA USA/Ted Curtin.

---

other English Puritans. That did not alarm the Pilgrims. They had given up on reforming the English church and simply wanted to live godly lives as they saw fit.

## The Founding of Massachusetts Bay Colony

In 1629, shortly before Charles I dissolved Parliament, a group of Puritan merchants and country gentlemen obtained a royal charter for the Massachusetts Bay Company. The charter provided the usual privileges granted to joint stock companies. It granted land for colonization from sea to sea, including the present-day states of Massachusetts, New Hampshire, Vermont, Maine, and upstate New York. In addition, the charter contained a unique provision that allowed the government of the company to be located in the colony rather than in England. Exactly how the Massachusetts Bay Company slipped this innovation past the king's

advisers remains unknown. But the Puritans understood its significance. With royal permission, the Puritans could exchange their position as a harassed minority in England for self-government in Massachusetts—which, in practice, meant Puritan government.

To lead the emigrants, the stockholders of the Massachusetts Bay Company elected John Winthrop—a prosperous, respected lawyer and landowner—to serve as governor. In March 1630, eleven ships crammed with seven hundred (mostly Puritan) passengers and assorted livestock, tools, and food sailed for Massachusetts; six more ships and another five hundred emigrants followed a few months later.

Winthrop's fleet arrived in Massachusetts Bay in early June. The new arrivals did not want to be associated with the heretical separatism of the struggling colony at Plymouth. Unlike the Pilgrims, Winthrop's Puritans aspired to reform the corrupt Church of England (rather than separate from it) by setting an example of godliness in the New World. Winthrop and a small group chose to settle on the peninsula that became Boston, and other settlers clustered at promising locations nearby.

In a sermon to his companions aboard the *Arbella* while they were still at sea—probably the most famous sermon in American history—Winthrop explained the cosmic significance of their journey. The Puritans had "entered into a covenant" with God to "work out our salvation under the power and purity of his holy ordinances," Winthrop proclaimed. This sanctified agreement with God meant that "the Lord will [not] bear with such failings at our hands as he doth from those among whom we have lived" in England. The Puritans had to make "extraordinary" efforts to "bring into familiar and constant practice" religious principles that most people in England merely preached. They had to subordinate their individual interests to the common good. "We must be knit together in this work as one man," Winthrop declared. "We must delight in each other, make others' conditions our own, rejoice together, mourn together, labor and suffer together, always having before our eyes . . . our community as members of the same body." To do otherwise discredited God in the eyes of humankind, jeopardized God's plan for the world, and would surely cause him to "break out in wrath against us." The stakes could not be higher, Winthrop told his listeners. "We must consider that we shall be as a city upon a hill. The eyes of all people are upon us."

That belief shaped seventeenth-century New England as profoundly as tobacco shaped the Chesapeake. The vision of a city on a hill announced the Puritans' fierce determination to keep their covenant and live according to God's laws, unlike the backsliders and compromisers who accommodated to the Church of England. The Puritans believed that God had one perfect plan, and they resolved to do their best to discover it through prayer, Bible study, and church attendance. Their determination to adhere strictly to God's plan charged nearly every feature of life in seventeenth-century New England with a distinctive, high-voltage piety.

The new colonists, as Winthrop's son John wrote later, had "all things to do, as in the beginning of the world." Unlike the early Chesapeake settlers, the first Massachusetts Bay colonists encountered few Indians because the local population had been almost exterminated by an epidemic more than a decade earlier. Still, as in the Chesapeake, the colonists fell victim to deadly ailments. More than

**SEAL OF MASSACHUSETTS BAY COLONY**
*In 1629, the Massachusetts Bay Company designed this seal depicting an Indian man inviting English settlers to "Come Over and Help Us." Of course, such an invitation was never issued. Instead, the seal attempted to lend an aura of altruism to the Massachusetts Bay Company's colonization efforts. In English eyes, the Indian man obviously needed help. The only signs that he was more civilized than the pine trees flanking him were his girdle of leaves, his bow and arrow, and his miraculous use of English. In reality, colonists in Massachusetts and elsewhere were far less interested in helping Indians than in helping themselves. For the most part, that suited Indians just fine, since they did not want the colonists' "help."*
Courtesy of Massachusetts Archives.

two hundred settlers died during the first year, including one of Winthrop's sons and eleven of his servants. About the same number decided by the spring of 1631 that they had had enough and returned to England. But Winthrop maintained a confidence that proved infectious. Each year from 1630 to 1640, ship after ship followed in the wake of Winthrop's fleet. In all, more than twenty thousand new settlers came, their eyes fixed on the Puritans' city on a hill. Often, when the Anglican Church cracked down on a Puritan minister in England, he and many of his followers uprooted and moved together to New England. By 1640, New England had one of the highest ratios of preachers to population in all of Christendom: 129 preachers had settled in New England, among them such eminences of Puritanism as John Cotton, Richard Mather, Thomas Shepard, and Thomas Hooker. But the ratio was still not high enough to provide a trained minister for every band of settlers who hungered for religious instruction; one colonist complained that ordinary "fellowes which keepe hogges all weeke preach on the Saboth."

The occupations of the New England immigrants reflected the social origins of English Puritans. On the whole, the immigrants came from the middle ranks of English society. Few representatives of the nobility or the landed gentry came to Massachusetts; Winthrop was an exception. Instead, the vast majority of immigrants were either farmers or tradesmen, including carpenters, tailors, textile workers, and many others. Servants, whose numbers dominated the Chesapeake settlers, accounted for only about a fifth of those headed for New England. Most of the New England immigrants had paid their way to Massachusetts, even though the journey often took their life savings. To such people, reports like the one Winthrop sent his son must have been encouraging: "Here is as good land as I have seen there [in England]. . . . Here can be no want of anything to those who bring means to raise out of the earth and sea."

---

*The Puritans' determination to adhere strictly to God's plan charged nearly every feature of life in seventeenth-century New England with a distinctive, high-voltage piety.*

---

In contrast to the Chesapeake—where immigrant women and children were nearly as rare as atheists in Boston—New England immigrants usually arrived as a family. In fact, more Puritans came with family members than did any other group of immigrants in all of American history. A ship that left Weymouth, England, in 1635 carried 106 passengers, 98 of whom belonged to one of the 14 families aboard,

typically a husband, wife, and children, sometimes accompanied by a servant or two. In this group, women and children made up a solid majority.

These families were not democracies, of course. As Winthrop reminded the first settlers in his *Arbella* sermon, each family was a "little commonwealth" that mirrored the hierarchy among all God's creatures. Just as humankind was subordinate to God, so young people were subordinate to their elders, children to their parents, and wives to their husbands. The immigrants' family ties reinforced their religious beliefs with an effective and universally understood form of government. While immigrants to the Chesapeake were disciplined mostly by the coercions of servitude and the caprices of the tobacco market, immigrants to New England entered a social order defined by the interlocking institutions of family, church, and community.

## The Evolution of New England Society

The New England colonists, unlike their counterparts in the Chesapeake, settled in small towns, usually located on the coast or a river. Massachusetts Bay colonists founded 133 towns during the seventeenth century, each with one or more churches (Map 4.1). Church members' fervent piety, buttressed by the institutions of local government, enforced remarkable religious and social conformity in the small New England settlements. During the century, tensions within the Puritan faith and changes in New England communities splintered religious orthodoxy and weakened Puritan zeal. By 1700, however, Puritanism still maintained a distinctive influence in New England.

### Church, Covenant, and Conformity

The church stood at the center of each Puritan community. Typically, it was a simple meeting room with wooden benches for fifty or one hundred or more. Church buildings had no stained glass, no organs, not even any heat. At the front stood a table and a lectern or an elevated pulpit. To our eyes, the building would appear to be a plain lecture hall. That was precisely what the Puritans intended. God's word—not music or art—was the focus of religious services. Nothing about the meeting room

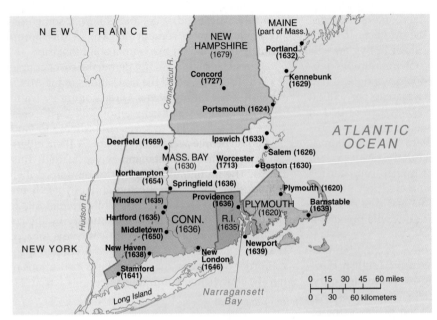

**M A P   4 . 1**
*New England Colonies in the Seventeenth Century*
New Englanders spread across the landscape town by town during the seventeenth century. (For the sake of legibility, only a few of the more important towns are shown on the map.) Why were towns so much more a feature of seventeenth-century New England than of the Chesapeake?

should interfere with the congregation's concentration on the sermon. And it took concentration. Each Sunday, ministers preached for five or six hours, interrupted by a noontime break. A minister's prayer alone often lasted an hour. During the frigid New England winter, fingers, toes, and cheeks grew numb while the communion bread and baptismal water froze solid. Whatever the weather, each town required every inhabitant to attend sermons on Sundays and usually on Thursdays too. They came, and they listened.

---

*Church members' fervent piety, buttressed by the institutions of local government, enforced remarkable religious and social conformity in the small New England settlements.*

---

To the Puritans, however, the church was not the building where the services were held. Instead, the church was composed of men and women who had entered a solemn covenant with one another and with God. Winthrop and three other men signed the original covenant of the first Boston church in 1630, agreeing to "Promisse, and bind our selves, to walke in all our wayes according to the Rule of the Gospell, and in all sincere Conformity to His holy Ordinaunces, and in mutuall love, and

respect to each other, so neere as God shall give us grace." A new member of the covenant also had to persuade existing members that she or he had fully experienced conversion. The fervent Puritans among the early colonists, whose faith had been tempered by persecution in England and by the journey to Massachusetts, had little difficulty meeting the test of covenant membership. By 1635, the Boston church had added more than 250 names to the four original subscribers to the covenant.

Puritan views on church membership derived from John Calvin, a sixteenth-century Swiss Protestant theologian. Calvin stressed the doctrine of predestination, which held that before the creation of the world, God exercised his divine grace and chose a few human beings to receive eternal life. Only God knew who these fortunate individuals—the "elect" or "invisible saints"—were. Nothing a person did could change God's inscrutable choice.

Puritans, however, believed that if one were among the elect, then one would surely act like it. To a certain extent, one's sainthood would become visible in one's behavior, especially if one were privileged to know God's Word as revealed in the Bible. However, the connection between sainthood and saintly behavior was far from firm. Some members of the elect, for example, had never heard God's Word and did not know how to manifest their sainthood in their behavior. One reason the Puritans required all town residents to attend church services was to enlighten invisible saints who remained ignorant of God's Truth. Other people might act as if they were saints, yet in fact not be one of the chosen few. But the Puritans thought that passing the demanding test of membership in one of their churches was a promising clue that one was in fact among God's elect.

Members of Puritan churches ardently hoped that they were visible saints and tried to act that way. Their covenant bound them to help each other attain this lofty goal and to discipline the entire community by saintly standards. Church members kept an eye on the behavior of everybody in town. Infractions of morality, order, or propriety were reported to the elders, who summoned the wayward to a church inquiry. The watchfulness that set the tone of life in Puritan communities is suggested by a minister's note that "the church was satisfied with Mrs. Carlton as to the weight of her butter." By saintly surveillance of everything, including Mrs. Carlton's butter, church members enforced a remarkable degree of righteous conformity in Puritan communities.

Despite their centrality, churches had no direct role in the civil government of New England communities. The Puritans did not want to emulate the Church of England, which they considered a puppet of the king rather than an independent body that served the Lord. They were determined to insulate New England churches from the contaminating influence of the civil state and its merely human laws. Although ministers were the most highly respected figures in New England towns, they were prohibited from holding government office.

Puritans had no qualms about their own beliefs influencing New England governments, however. As much as possible, the Puritans brought public life into conformity with their view of God's law. Most Puritans agreed that the Sabbath began at sunset on Saturday evening, as Charles Chauncy was censured for preaching in England, and enforcement of proper Sabbath behavior was taken seriously. After the Sabbath began, townsfolk could not work, play, or travel. Fines for Sabbath breaking were issued for transgressions such as playing a flute, smoking a pipe, and visiting neighbors. The Puritans mandated other purifications of what they considered corrupt English practices. They refused to celebrate either Christmas or Easter. They outlawed religious wedding ceremonies; couples were married by a magistrate in a civil ceremony—the first Massachusetts wedding to be performed by a

minister did not occur until 1686. They prohibited elaborate, colorful clothing, censuring such fineries as lace trim, short sleeves ("whereby the nakedness of the arm may be discovered"), and long hair. Cards, dice, shuffleboard, and other games of chance were banned, as were music and dancing. The distinguished minister Increase Mather insisted

**THE PURITAN CHALLENGE TO THE STATUS QUO**
*This title page of* The World Turn'd Upside Down *satirizes the Puritan notion that the contemporary world was deeply flawed. Printed in London in 1647, the pamphlet refers to the "distracted Times" of the Puritan Revolution in England. The drawing ridicules criticisms of English society that were also common among New England Puritans. The drawing shows at least a dozen examples of the conventional world of seventeenth-century England turned upside down. Can you identify them? Puritans, of course, would claim that the drawing had it wrong, that instead the conventional world turned God's order upside down. How might the drawing have been different if a devout Puritan had drawn it?*
British Library.

that "Mixt or Promiscuous Dancing . . . of Men and Women" could not be tolerated since "the unchaste Touches and Gesticulations used by Dancers have a palpable tendency to that which is evil." On special occasions, Puritans proclaimed days of fasting and humiliation, which, as one preacher boasted, amounted to "so many Sabbaths more."

## Government by Puritans for Puritanism

It is only a slight exaggeration to say that seventeenth-century New England was governed by Puritans for Puritanism. The charter of the Massachusetts Bay Company empowered the company's stockholders (freemen) to meet as a body known as the General Court and make the laws to govern the company's affairs. The colonists transformed this arrangement for running a joint stock company into a structure for governing the colony. In 1631, the General Court expanded the small number of original stockholders by admitting almost 120 settlers to the status of freemen. At the same time, the court ruled that freemen must be male church members, hoping to ensure that godly men would decide government policies. Only freemen had the right to vote for governor, deputy governor, and other colonial officials. When new settlers continued to be admitted as freemen, the number became too large to meet conveniently. In 1634, the freemen in each town agreed to send two deputies to the General Court to act as the colony's legislative assembly.

All other men were classified as "inhabitants," and they had the right to vote, hold office, and participate fully in town government. A "town meeting," composed of all the town's inhabitants and freemen, chose the selectmen and other officials who administered local affairs. New England town meetings routinely practiced a level of popular participation in political life that was unprecedented elsewhere during the seventeenth century. Almost every adult man could speak out in town meetings and fortify his voice with a vote. However, town meetings were far from democratic. All women—even church members—were prohibited from voting, and towns did not permit "contrary-minded" men to become or remain inhabitants. Although town meetings wrangled from time to time, widespread political participation reinforced conformity to Puritan ideals.

One of the most important functions of New England government was land distribution. Settlers who desired to establish a new town entered a covenant and petitioned the General Court for a grant of land. The court granted town sites to suitably pious petitioners but did not allow settlement until the Indians who inhabited a grant agreed to relinquish their claim to the land, usually in exchange for manufactured goods. For instance, William Pynchon purchased the site of Springfield, Massachusetts, from the Agawam Indians for "eighteen fathams [arm's lengths] of Wampam, eighteen coates, 18 hatchets, 18 hoes, [and] 18 knives."

Having obtained their grant, town founders apportioned land among themselves and any newcomers they permitted to join them. Normally, each family received a house lot large enough for an adjacent garden as well as one or more strips of agricultural land on the perimeter of the town. Although there was a considerable difference between the largest and smallest grants, most allocations clustered in the middle—typically 50, 100, or 150 acres—giving New England a more homogeneous distribution of wealth than the Chesapeake. Towns usually allotted only a fraction of their total grant. They reserved some common land, which all inhabitants could use for grazing livestock and cutting wood, and saved the rest for new settlers and the descendants of the founders.

The physical layout of the towns encouraged settlers to look inward toward their neighbors, multiplying the opportunities for godly vigilance. Most people considered the forest that lay just beyond every settler's house an alien environment that was interrupted here and there by those oases of civilization, towns. The footpaths connecting one town to another were so rudimentary that even John Winthrop once got lost within a half mile of his house and spent a sleepless night in the forest, circling the light of his small campfire and singing psalms.

## The Splintering of Puritanism

Almost from the beginning, John Winthrop and other leaders discovered that Puritans sang with more than one voice. In England, persecution as a dissenting minority unified Puritan voices in opposition to the Church of England. But in New England, Puritanism's emphasis on individual Bible study led the faithful to discover not God's Way but God's Ways. Yet Puritan leaders interpreted dissent as an error caused either by a misguided believer or by the malevolent power of Satan. Whatever the

**TOWN PLAN OF NEW HAVEN**

*This drawing shows the distribution of land in New Haven, Connecticut, in 1641. Although the church was the spiritual center of each New England town, the New Haven church (indicated by the small square) was carefully located at the geographical center as well. New Haven was founded in 1638 by the wealthy Puritan merchant Theophilus Eaton and the Puritan minister John Davenport. The town plan contains clear evidence of their leadership. Can you locate it? In New Haven as in other New England towns, land was distributed according to status and need. The town plan therefore provides a revealing map of New Haven's social structure. Try to identify the lots of the leading families and of the lesser folk. What does the town plan suggest about the character of New Haven society?*

New York Public Library.

cause, errors could not be tolerated. As one Puritan minister proclaimed, "God doth no where in his word tolerate Christian States, to give Tolerations to . . . adversaries of his Truth, if they have power in their hands to suppress them. The Scripture saith . . . there is no Truth but one."

Among the immigrants who arrived in Massachusetts in 1630 was Roger Williams, a lively young minister who counted Winthrop and other Puritan elders among his friends. From the start, Williams needled the colony's leadership with his outspoken views that their church was fatally impure. He pronounced that requiring people who were not full church members to attend sermons was a policy that "stinks in God's nostrils." Worse from the viewpoint of Winthrop and other leaders, Williams de-

clared that the government of Massachusetts contaminated the purity of the church, which had to be kept absolutely separate from civil influence. For these opinions and others, Massachusetts banished Williams in 1635. He helped found the colony of Rhode Island as a refuge for dissenters from Puritan orthodoxies.

Another early immigrant pushed Puritan doctrines in a different direction. In 1634, Anne Hutchinson arrived in Massachusetts with her husband and their family. A brilliant woman, Hutchinson had received an excellent education from her father. The mother of fourteen children, she also served her neighbors as a skilled midwife. Most of all, she was an ardent Puritan, steeped in Scripture and absorbed by sermons, especially those of John

Cotton. After she settled into her home in Boston, women gathered there to hear her Thursday lectures on Cotton's most recent sermons. As the months passed, the meetings increased to twice a week and the crowds grew to sixty or eighty women and men.

In his sermons, Cotton emphasized that individuals could be saved only by God's grace in choosing them to be members of the elect, a doctrine Cotton termed the "covenant of grace." Cotton contrasted this familiar Puritan tenet with the "covenant of works," the erroneous belief that one's behavior—one's works—could win God's favor and, ultimately, salvation. Belief in the covenant of works was a heresy known as Arminianism. Cotton's sermons strongly hinted that many Puritans, even ministers, leaned toward Arminianism, and Anne Hutchinson agreed. In effect, Hutchinson amplified Cotton's somewhat muted message that the leaders of the colony were repudiating the basis of Puritan faith, and she did so without the protection of Cotton's status as a minister and a man.

The meetings at Hutchinson's house alarmed her nearest neighbor, John Winthrop, who believed that she was subverting the good order of the colony. In 1637, Winthrop had formal charges brought against Hutchinson and confronted her in court as her chief accuser. Winthrop denounced Hutchinson's lectures as "not tolerable nor comely in the sight of God nor fitting for your sex." Winthrop was no match for Hutchinson's learning, wit, and insight. Hutchinson pointed to passages in the Bible that instructed women to meet and teach one another. When Winthrop claimed those Scriptures did not apply to her, she asked him, if it is "not lawful for me to teach women . . . why do you call me to teach the court?" Outsmarted and off-balance, Winthrop pressed forward with the investigation, fishing for some heresy that he could pin on Hutchinson.

Winthrop and other elders referred to Hutchinson and her followers as "Antinomians," that is, people who opposed the law. Hutchinson's opponents charged that she believed that Christians could be saved by faith alone, that they did not need to act according to God's law in the Bible as interpreted by the colony's leaders. Hutchinson nimbly defended herself against this accusation. Yes, she believed that men and women were saved by faith alone; but no, she did not deny the need to obey God's law. "The Lord hath let me see which was the clear ministry and which the wrong," she said.

Finally, her interrogators cornered her. How could she tell which was which? "By an immediate revelation," she replied, "by the voice of [God's] own spirit to my soul." Here was the crime Winthrop had been searching for, the heresy of prophecy, the erroneous claim that God revealed his will directly to a believer instead of exclusively through the Bible, as every good Puritan knew.

In 1638, the Boston church formally excommunicated Hutchinson. The minister decreed, "I doe cast you out and . . . deliver you up to Satan that you may learne no more to blaspheme to seduce and to lye. . . . I command you . . . as a Leper to withdraw your selfe out of the Congregation." Banished, Hutchinson and her family moved first to Rhode Island and then to Long Island, where all but her ten-year-old daughter were killed by Indians.

Hutchinson's admission of divine revelation was a departure from standard Puritan belief. Yet by directing believers to search for evidence of God's grace, Puritanism encouraged the faithful to listen for a whisper from God that they were among the elect. Puritanism was a volatile combination of rigid insistence on conformity to God's law and aching uncertainty about how to identify and act upon it. Despite the best efforts of Winthrop and other leaders to render God's instructions in no uncertain terms, Puritanism inspired believers to draw their own conclusions and stick to them. In this sense, Anne Hutchinson was more a product of Puritanism than a dissenter from it.

Such strains within Puritanism caused it to splinter repeatedly during the seventeenth century. The prominent minister Thomas Hooker, for example, clashed with Winthrop and Cotton over the composition of the church. Hooker argued that men and women who lived godly lives should be admitted to church membership, even if they had not experienced conversion. This question, like most others in New England, had both religious and political dimensions, since only church members could vote in Massachusetts. In 1636, Hooker led an exodus of more than eight hundred colonists from Massachusetts to the Connecticut River valley, where they founded Hartford and neighboring towns. In 1639, the towns adopted the Fundamental Orders of Connecticut, a quasi-constitution that could be altered by vote of the freemen, who did not have to be church members, although nearly all of them were.

Puritan churches divided and subdivided throughout the seventeenth century as acrimony developed over doctrine and church government.

Sometimes churches split over the appointment of a controversial minister. Sometimes families who had a long walk to the meeting house simply decided to form their own church nearer their houses. The schism of Puritan churches arose from the ambiguities and tensions within Puritan belief. As the colonies matured, other tensions developed as well.

## Growth, Change, and Controversy

In England, disputes between King Charles I and Parliament escalated in 1642 to civil war, known as the Puritan Revolution. The king and his supporters were defeated both politically and militarily by the parliamentary forces led by the staunch Puritan Oliver Cromwell. In 1649, Cromwell's forces crowned their victories by executing Charles I and proclaiming a Puritan Republic. From 1649 to 1660, England's rulers were not monarchs who tried to suppress Puritanism but believers who tried to champion it. In a half century, English Puritans rose from a harassed group of religious dissenters to a dominant power in English government.

Such a revolutionary transformation in the fortunes of English Puritans had profound consequences in New England. When the Puritan Revolution began, the stream of immigrants to New England dwindled to a trickle, creating hard times for the colonists. They could no longer consider themselves a city on a hill setting a godly example for humankind. English society was being reformed by Puritans in England, not New England. Furthermore, the steady current of immigrants during the 1630s had stimulated the New England economy. Newcomers brought money and English goods to exchange for the food, supplies, and services they needed to put down roots in New England. When that immigrant trade came to a halt, the colonists faced sky-high prices for scarce English goods and few customers for their plentiful colonial products. As they searched to find a substitute for the immigrant trade, they marked out the basic patterns of the New England economy.

New England's rocky soil and short growing season ruled out cultivating the southern colonies' crops of tobacco and rice that found a ready market in Atlantic ports. Exports that New Englanders could not get from the soil they took instead from the forest and the sea. During the first decade of settlement, colonists traded with Indians for animal pelts in demand in Europe. By the 1640s, fur-bearing animals were scarce unless traders ventured far beyond the frontiers of English settlement. Trees from the seemingly limitless forests of New England proved a longer-lasting resource. Masts for ships and staves for barrels of Spanish wine and West Indian sugar were crafted from New England timber.

But the most important New England export was fish. During the religious and political turmoil of the 1640s, English ships withdrew from the rich North Atlantic fishing grounds and New England fishermen quickly took their place. Dried, salted codfish found markets in southern Europe and the West Indies. The fish trade also stimulated colonial shipbuilding and trained generations of fishermen, sailors, and merchants. New England fishermen and merchants built a commercial network that endured for more than a century. But the export economy remained peripheral to most New England colonists. Their lives revolved around their farms, their churches, and their families.

Families were the source of one of the most important long-term changes in seventeenth-century New England. Although immigration came to a

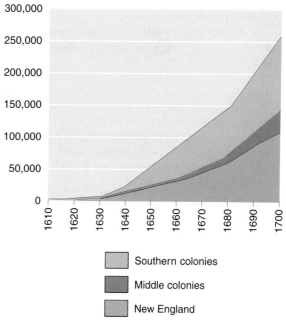

**FIGURE 4.1**
**Population of British North American Colonies in the Seventeenth Century**
*The colonial population grew at a steadily accelerating rate during the seventeenth century. On the whole, New England and the southern colonies each comprised about half the total colonial population until after 1680, when the growth in Pennsylvania and New York contributed to a surge in the population of the middle colonies.*

standstill in the 1640s, the population continued to boom, doubling every twenty years. In New England, universal marriage and frequent births (a woman often had eight or nine children) created an ever-growing population. Long, cold winters eliminated the warm-weather ailments that plagued the southern colonies, reducing mortality. New England children survived the hazards of infancy and childhood at a higher rate than children elsewhere. Thus the descendants of the immigrants of the 1630s multiplied and remultiplied, boosting the New England population to roughly equal that of the southern colonies (Figure 4.1).

Under the pressures of steady population growth and integration into the Atlantic economy, the white-hot piety of the founders cooled during the last half of the seventeenth century. After 1640, the population grew faster than church membership. All residents attended sermons on pain of fines and punishment, but many could not find seats in the meeting houses. Boston's two churches in 1650 could house only about a third of the population. By the 1680s, women were the majority among full church members throughout New England. In some towns, only 15 percent of the adult men were church members. Puritan minister Michael Wigglesworth asked:

How is it that I find
    In stead of holiness Carnality,
In stead of heavenly frames an Earthly mind,
    For burning zeal luke-warm Indifferency,
For flaming love, key-cold Dead-heartedness,
    For temperance (in meat, and drinke, and
        cloaths) excess?

Whence cometh it, that Pride, and Luxurie
    Debate, Deceit, Contention, and Strife,
False-dealing, Covetousness, Hypocrisie
    (With such Crimes) amongst them are so rife,
That one of them doth over-reach another?
    And that an honest man can hardly trust his
        Brother?

Most alarming to Puritan leaders, the children of visible saints often failed to experience conversion and attain full church membership. Puritans tended to assume that sainthood was inherited—that the children of the elect were probably also among the elect. Acting on this premise, churches permitted saints to baptize their babies, symbolically cleansing the infants of their contamination with original sin. Yet during the 1640s and 1650s, children of visible saints seldom experienced the

**A NEW ENGLAND CHILD**
*Young Alice Mason, who appears to be five or six years old in this 1668 painting, shows little of the lightheartedness or endearing vulnerability we might expect in a child today. Instead, she fixes the viewer with a confident, steady gaze. The painting illustrates the drift away from the intense piety and plain dress of New England's founding generation. The elaborately decorated dress, especially the slashed sleeves, reflects the prosperity that some New Englanders had achieved by the 1660s, prosperity they displayed in their clothing and homes in ways the founders would have deemed profane. By pointing to an apple, Alice—the portrait hints—has already grasped the temptation Eve succumbed to in the biblical account of the Garden of Eden, but she has not yet surrendered to it.*
Adams National Historic Site.

inward transformation that signaled conversion and qualification for church membership. The problem became urgent during the 1650s when the children of saints—people who had grown to adulthood in New England—began to have children themselves. These babies, the grandchildren of visible saints, could not receive baptism and the protection it afforded against the terrors of an early death.

Puritan churches debated what to do. To allow anyone, even the child of a saint, to become a church member without conversion was an unthinkable retreat from the most fundamental Puritan doctrine. In 1662, a synod of Massachusetts ministers reached a compromise known as the Halfway Covenant. The unconverted children of saints were permitted to become halfway church members. They could baptize their infants, but they could not participate in communion or have the voting privileges of church membership. The Halfway Covenant generated a controversy that sputtered through Puritan churches for the remainder of the century. Opponents protested the "many chaffy hypocrites" the compromise brought into the covenant, if only halfway. Defenders argued that the Halfway Covenant permitted the church to *nurse up* still successively *another Generation* of Subjects to Christ." With the Halfway Covenant, Puritan churches came to terms with the replacement of "burning zeal" by "luke-warm Indifferency."

---

*Under the pressures of steady population growth and integration into the Atlantic economy, the white-hot piety common among Winthrop and the founders cooled.*

---

During the last half of the seventeenth century, Puritan communities continued to enforce piety with holy rigor. Beginning in 1656, small bands of Quakers began to arrive in Massachusetts determined to bear witness for their faith. Quakers—or members of the Society of Friends, as they called themselves—believed that God spoke directly to each individual through an "inner light." Neither a preacher nor the Bible was necessary to discover God's Word. Furthermore, since all human beings were equal in God's eyes, subordination to mere temporal authority should be refused unless God, speaking through each person's inner light, requested otherwise. Quakers affronted Puritan doctrines of faith and social order. They refused to observe the Sabbath, for example, because they insisted that God did not set aside any special day for worship but instead expected the faithful to worship every day.

Puritan communities treated Quakers with ruthless severity. Some Quakers were branded on the face "with a red-hot iron with [an] H. for heresie." Several Quaker women were stripped to the waist, tied

to the back of a cart, and whipped as they were paraded through towns. When Quakers refused to leave Massachusetts, the Boston magistrates sentenced two men and a woman to be hanged in 1659. The three Quakers walked to the gallows "Hand in Hand, all three of them, as to a Weding-day, with great cheerfulness of Heart," one colonist observed.

The Puritans' success in building a godly society ultimately undermined the intense appeal of Puritanism. In the pious communities of New England, leaders did everything possible to eliminate sin. In the process, they diminished the sense of utter human depravity that was the wellspring of Puritanism. By 1700, New Englanders did not doubt that human beings sinned, but they were far more concerned with the sins of others than with their own, as the Salem witch trials demonstrated. (See the Historical Question on page 92.) The Brattle Street Church, founded in Boston in 1699, symbolized the change in Puritanism. Any person who contributed money to the Brattle Street Church could participate in the selection of a minister. The contrast between the financial contributors to the Brattle Street Church and the members of the covenant John Winthrop described in his *Arbella* sermon was one measure of the change in Puritanism during the seventeenth century.

# The Founding of the Middle Colonies

The English colonies of New York, New Jersey, and Pennsylvania originated as proprietary colonies—that is, colonies granted by the crown to one or more proprietors, who then possessed both the land and extensive, almost monarchical, powers of government. Before the 1670s, few Europeans settled in any of these middle colonies (Map 4.2). For the first two-thirds of the seventeenth century, the most important European outpost in the region north of the Chesapeake and south of New England was the relatively small Dutch colony of New Netherland. By 1700, however, the English monarchy had seized New Netherland, renamed it New York, and encouraged the creation of a Quaker colony led by William Penn.

## From New Netherland to New York

In 1609, the Dutch East India Company dispatched Henry Hudson to search for a Northwest Passage to the Orient. Hudson sailed along the Atlantic coast

# Why Were Some New Englanders Accused of Being Witches?

ALMOST EVERYBODY IN seventeenth-century North America—whether Native American, slave, or colonist—believed that supernatural spirits could cause harm and misfortune. Outside New England, however, few colonists were legally accused of being witches, persons who had become possessed by evil spirits. More than 95 percent of all legal accusations of witchcraft in the North American colonies occurred in New England. In 1691 and 1692, an epidemic of witchcraft accusations broke out in Salem, Massachusetts, and more than one hundred individuals were formally accused, although many other New Englanders may have been called witches privately. To charge a person with witchcraft was a serious matter. As a 1641 Massachusetts law stated, "If any man or woman be a witch . . . they shall be put to death." The other New England colonies had identical laws. During the seventeenth century, courts carried out the letter of the law: Thirty-four accused witches were executed, nineteen of them during the Salem outbreak.

To understand the peculiar New England preoccupation with witchcraft, historians have gathered a great deal of information about accused witches and the dark deeds their accusers attributed to them. Almost anyone could be accused of being a witch, but 80 percent of the accusations were leveled against women. About two-thirds of the accused women were over forty years old, past the normal age of childbearing. About half the men who were accused as witches were relatives of accused women. Normally one family member did not accuse another. Nor did accusers single out a stranger as a witch. Instead, accusers pointed to a neighbor they knew well.

Almost always the accused witch denied the charge. Occasionally, the accused confessed. A confession could sometimes win sympathy and a reduced punishment from officials. During the Salem witch-hunt, those who confessed usually saved their own skins by naming other people as witches. The testimony of the confessed witch was then used to accuse others.

Accusers of all descriptions stepped forward to testify against alleged witches. Witchcraft investigations often stretched over weeks, months, or even years as courts accumulated evidence against (and sometimes in favor of) the accused. About 90 percent of accusers were adults, about six out of ten of them men. Young women between the ages of sixteen and twenty-five made up almost all of the remaining 10 percent of accusers; they claimed to be tortured by the accused witches.

At Salem, for example, afflicted young girls shrieked in pain, their limbs twisted into strange, involuntary contortions as they pointed out the witches who tortured them. At the trial of accused witch Bridget Bishop in Salem, the court record noted that if Bishop "but cast her eyes on them [the afflicted], they were presently struck down. . . . But upon the touch of her hand upon them, when they lay in their swoons, they would immediately revive." The bewitched girls testified that "the shape of the prisoner did oftentimes very grievously pinch them, choke them, bite them, and afflict them; urging them to write their names in a book," the devil's book.

Such sensational evidence of torture by a witch was relatively rare in witch-hunts and trials. Usually, accusers attributed some inexplicable misfortune they had suffered to the evil influence of an accused witch. One woman testified against a witch who had bewitched her cow, causing it to give discolored milk. A man was accused as a witch because his "spirit bewitched the pudding," which was inexplicably "cut lengthwise . . . as smooth as any knife could cut it." Mary Parsons testified that she suspected her husband, Hugh, of being a witch "because almost all that he sells to anybody does not prosper."

From our present-day perspective, the accusers seem to have been victims not of witches but of

**WITCHES SHOW THEIR LOVE FOR SATAN**
*Mocking pious Christians' humble obeisance to God, witches hideously debased themselves by standing in line to kneel and kiss Satan's butt—or so it was popularly believed. This seventeenth-century print portrays Satan with hands, feet, and tail of a rodent, wings of a bat, and head of a lustful ram attached to the torso of a man. Note that women predominate among the witches eager to express their devotion to Satan.*
The Library and Center for Knowledge Management, University of California, San Francisco.

simple accidents, of overheated imaginations, or—in the case of the possessed young women—of emotional distress. But why did seventeenth-century New Englanders find the testimony of accusers persuasive?

Seventeenth-century New Englanders believed that almost nothing happened by chance. Supernatural power—whether God's or Satan's—suffused the world and influenced the smallest event, even the color of a cow's milk. When something bad happened, an unhappy God may have caused it to show his displeasure with the victim, who had perhaps sinned in some way. But maybe the victim was not in fact responsible for the misfortune; maybe Satan, acting through a witch, had caused it. If misfortunes could be pinned on a witch in thrall to Satan, the accuser was absolved from responsibility; the accuser became a helpless victim rather than a guilty party. Witches were an explanation for the disorder that continually crept into New England communities, an explanation that attributed the disorder not to chance or to the faults of individuals but to the witches' evil purposes.

Accusers usually targeted a vulnerable neighbor, such as an older, often poor woman. Historians have noted that accusers often complained that accused witches were quarrelsome, grumbled about being mistreated, muttered vague threats about getting even, and seemed to be dissatisfied with their lives. Researchers have pointed out that many New Englanders had such feelings after about 1650, but most people did not express them openly or, if they did, felt guilty about doing so. Accused witches often expressed and acted on feelings that other people shared but considered inappropriate, shameful, or sinful in their zeal to lead the saintly lives prescribed by their Puritan religion. Witches made it somewhat easier for New Englanders to consider themselves saints rather than sinners.

MAP 4.2
*Middle Colonies in the Seventeenth Century*
For the most part, the middle colonies in the seventeenth
century were inhabited by settlers who clustered along the
Hudson or Delaware River. The vast geographic extent of
the colonies shown in this map represented land grants
authorized in England but still inhabited by Native
Americans rather than settled by colonists.

and settle them as serflike tenants on their huge domains. Only one patroonship succeeded; the others
failed to attract settlers and much of the land was
sold back to the company. Like New England and
the Chesapeake colonies, New Netherland never realized the profits of its sponsors' dreams.

Although few in number, the New Netherlan-
ders were remarkably diverse, especially compared
with the homogeneous English settlers to the north
and south. Religious dissenters and immigrants
from Holland, Sweden, France, Germany, and elsewhere made their way to the colony. A minister of
the Dutch Reformed Church complained to his superiors in Holland that several groups of Jews had
recently arrived, adding to the religious mixture of
"Papists, Mennonites and Lutherans among the
Dutch . . . [and] many Puritans . . . and many other
atheists . . . who conceal themselves under the name
of Christians."

The West India Company struggled to govern
the motley colonists for its own purposes. Under
the stern leadership of Peter Stuyvesant, governor
from 1647 to 1664, the population slowly grew, but
it remained intractable. Stuyvesant tried to enforce
conformity to the Dutch Reformed Church, but the
company declared that "the consciences of men
should be free and unshackled," making a virtue of
New Netherland necessity. The company never permitted the colony's settlers to form a representative
government. Instead, the company appointed government officials who set policies, including taxes,
which many colonists deeply resented.

*The English colonies of New York, New
Jersey, and Pennsylvania originated as proprietary colonies—that is, colonies granted
by the crown to one or more proprietors who
then possessed both the land and extensive,
almost monarchical, powers of government.*

and ventured up the large river that now bears his
name until it dwindled to a stream that obviously
did not lead to China.

A decade later, the Dutch government granted
the West India Company—a group of Dutch merchants and shippers seeking to mimic the success
of the East India Company—exclusive rights to
trade with the Western Hemisphere. In 1624, the
West India Company established fur trading posts
on the Hudson River as well as along the Connecticut and Delaware Rivers. Two years later, Peter
Minuit, the resident director of the company, purchased Manhattan Island from the Manhate Indians
for trade goods worth sixty florins, the equivalent
of a dozen beaver pelts. New Amsterdam, the small
settlement established at the southern tip of Manhattan island, became the principal trading center
in New Netherland and the colony's headquarters.

Unlike the English colonies, New Netherland
did not attract many European immigrants. The
company tried to stimulate immigration by granting patroonships—allotments of eighteen miles of
land along the Hudson River—to wealthy stockholders who would bring fifty families to the colony

In 1664, New Netherland became New York.
Charles II, who became king of England in 1660,
gave his brother James, the Duke of York, an enormous grant of land that included New Netherland.
Of course, the Dutch colony did not belong to the
king of England. But that legal technicality did not
impede the king or his brother. The duke quickly
organized a small fleet of warships, which soon
appeared off Manhattan island in late summer

1664, and demanded that Stuyvesant surrender. With little choice, he did.

As the new proprietor of the colony, the Duke of York exercised almost the same unlimited authority over the colony as had the West India Company. The duke himself never set foot in New York, but his governors struggled to impose order on the unruly colonists. Like the Dutch, the duke permitted "all persons of what Religion soever, quietly to inhabit . . . provided they give no disturbance to the publique peace, nor doe molest or disquiet others in the free exercise of their religion." This policy of religious toleration was less an affirmation of liberty of conscience and more a recognition of the reality of the most heterogeneous colony in seventeenth-century North America.

## New Jersey and Pennsylvania

The creation of New York led indirectly to the founding of two other middle colonies, New Jersey and Pennsylvania (see Map 4.2). In 1664, the Duke of York subdivided his grant and gave the portion between the Hudson and Delaware Rivers to two of his friends. The proprietors of this new colony, New Jersey, soon discovered that Puritan and Dutch settlers already in the region stubbornly resisted the new government. The continuing strife persuaded one of the proprietors to sell his share to two Quakers. When the Quaker proprietors began to quarrel, they called in a prominent English Quaker, William Penn, to arbitrate their dispute. Penn eventually worked out a settlement that continued New Jersey's proprietary government but did little to end the conflict with the settlers. In the process, Penn became intensely interested in what he termed a "holy experiment" of establishing a genuinely Quaker colony in America.

Unlike most Quakers, William Penn came from an eminent family. His father served both Cromwell and Charles II and had been knighted. Born in 1644, the younger Penn trained for a military career, but the ideas of dissenters from the reestablished Anglican Church appealed to him, and he became a devout Quaker. By 1680, he had published fifty books and pamphlets and spoken at countless public meetings, although he had not won official toleration for Quakers in England.

The Quakers' concept of an open, generous God who made his love equally available to all people manifested itself in unusually egalitarian worship services and in social behavior that continually brought Quakers into conflict with the English

government. Quaker leaders were ordinary men and women, not specially trained preachers. More than any other seventeenth-century sect, Quakers allowed women to assume positions of religious leadership. "In souls there is no sex," they said. Since all people were equal in the spiritual realm, Quakers considered social hierarchy false and evil. They called everyone "friend" and shook hands instead of curtsying or removing their hats—even when meeting the king. These customs enraged many non-Quakers and provoked innumerable beatings and worse. Penn himself was jailed four times, once for nine months.

Despite his many run-ins with the government, Penn remained on good terms with Charles II, who granted him land to found a Quaker colony in America. Partly to rid England of the troublesome Quakers, in 1681 Charles made Penn the proprietor of 45,000 square miles for his new colony of Pennsylvania.

## Toleration and Diversity in Pennsylvania

When Penn announced the creation of his colony, Quakers flocked to English ports in numbers exceeded only by the great Puritan migration to New England fifty years earlier. Between 1682 and 1685, nearly eight thousand immigrants came to Pennsylvania, most of them Quakers from England, Ireland, and Wales. They represented a cross section of the artisans, farmers, and laborers who predominated among English Quakers. Quaker missionaries also encouraged immigrants from the European continent, and many came, giving Pennsylvania greater ethnic diversity than any other English colony except New York.

Penn was determined to live in peace with the Indians who inhabited the region. His Indian policy expressed his Quaker ideals and contrasted sharply with the hostile policies of the other English colonies. On the eve of colonization, he explained to the chief of the Lenni Lenape (or Delaware) Indians that "God has written his law in our hearts, by which we are taught and commanded to love and help and do good to one another . . . [and] this great God has been pleased to make me concerned in your parts of the world, and the king of the country where I live has given unto me a great province therein, but I desire to enjoy it with your love and consent." Penn instructed his agents to obtain the Indians' consent by purchasing their land, respecting their claims, and dealing with them fairly.

**WILLIAM PENN**
*This portrait of William Penn was drawn about a decade after the founding of Pennsylvania. At a time when extravagant clothing and fancy wigs proclaimed that their wearer was an important person, Penn is portrayed informally, lacking even a coat, his natural hair neat but undressed—all a reflection of his Quaker faith. Penn's full face and double chin show that his faith did not make him a stranger to the pleasures of the table. No hollow-cheeked ascetic or wild-eyed enthusiast, Penn appears sober and observant, as if sizing up the viewer and reserving judgment. The portrait captures the calm determination, anchored in his faith, that inspired Penn's hopes for his new colony.*
Historical Society of Pennsylvania.

Penn declared that the first principle of government was that every settler would "enjoy the free possession of his or her faith and exercise of worship towards God." Accordingly, Pennsylvania tolerated Protestant sects of all kinds as well as Roman Catholics. All voters and officeholders had to be Christians, but the government did not compel settlers to attend religious services or to pay taxes to maintain a state-supported church.

Despite its toleration and diversity, Pennsylvania was as much a Quaker colony as New England was a stronghold of Puritanism. Penn had no hesitation about using civil government to enforce

religious morality. One of the colony's first laws provided severe punishment for "all such offenses against God, as swearing, cursing, lying, profane talking, drunkenness, drinking of healths, obscene words . . . all prizes, stage plays, cards, dice, May games, gamesters, masques, revels, bull-baitings, cock-fightings, bear-baitings, and the like, which excite the people to rudeness, cruelty, looseness, and irreligion." The ethnic and religious diversity of Pennsylvania prevented strict enforcement of these prohibitions, but the Quaker expectations of godly order and sobriety set the tone of Pennsylvania society.

> *Despite its toleration and diversity, Pennsylvania was as much a Quaker colony as New England was a strong-hold of Puritanism.*

Pennsylvania prospered and the capital city, Philadelphia, soon rivaled New York—though not yet Boston—as a center of commerce. By 1700, the city's five thousand inhabitants participated in a thriving trade exporting flour and other food products to the West Indies and importing textiles and manufactured goods. In less than two decades, Philadelphia had become one of the most important cities in British North America.

As proprietor, Penn had extensive powers, subject only to review by the king. But he did not want a proprietary government in which "the will of one man may . . . hinder the good of an whole country." Penn proposed instead to appoint a governor who would maintain the proprietor's power to veto any laws passed by the colonial council, which was elected by property owners who possessed at least one hundred acres of land or who paid taxes. The council had the power to originate laws and administer all the affairs of government. An elected assembly served as a check on the council; its members had the authority to reject or approve laws framed by the council.

Penn stressed that the exact form of government mattered less than the men who served in it. In Penn's eyes, "good men" staffed Pennsylvania's government since Quakers dominated elective and appointive offices. Quakers, of course, differed among themselves. Members of the assembly struggled to win the right to debate and amend laws, especially tax laws. They finally won the battle in 1701 when a new Charter of Privileges gave the proprietor the power to appoint the council and in turn stripped the council of all its former powers and gave them to the assembly, which became the only unicameral legislature in all the British colonies.

# The Colonies and the British Empire

The creation of proprietary colonies permitted the king to reward his friends with faraway lands to which he had tenuous claims and over which he exercised almost no real control. From the king's point of view, the proprietary grants were, in a sense, cheap gifts. As the colonies grew, however, the gifts became more valuable. After 1660, the king took initiatives to channel colonial trade through English hands and to consolidate royal authority over colonial governments. These initiatives defined the basic relationship between the colonies and England that endured until the American Revolution.

## Royal Regulation of Colonial Trade

English economic policies toward the colonies were designed to yield customs revenues for the monarchy and profitable business for English merchants and shippers. In addition, the policies were intended to divert the colonies' trade from England's enemies, the Dutch and the French.

*After 1660, the king took initiatives to channel colonial trade through English hands and to consolidate royal authority over colonial governments. These initiatives defined the basic relationship between the colonies and England that endured until the American Revolution.*

The Navigation Acts of 1650, 1651, and 1660 set forth two fundamental regulations governing colonial trade. First, all colonial goods imported into England had to be transported in English ships. Second, the Navigation Acts "enumerated" (listed) specific colonial products that could be shipped only to England or to other English colonies. While enumeration prevented Chesapeake planters from shipping their tobacco directly to the European continent, it did not interfere with the commerce of New England and the middle colonies. Their principal exports—fish, lumber, and flour—were not enumerated and could still be shipped to their most important market in the West Indies.

The Staple Act of 1663 imposed a third regulation on colonial trade. It required all goods imported into the colonies to pass through England. Goods manufactured in France or Italy, for example, had to be shipped first to England, unloaded and taxed, and then reloaded in English ships before they could be sent to the colonies. The Staple Act gave English merchants a monopoly on exports to the colonies and, by raising the prices of non-English goods, gave English manufacturers a competitive edge in colonial markets.

By the end of the seventeenth century, colonial commerce was defined by regulations that subjected merchants and shippers to royal supervision and gave them access to markets throughout the British Empire on the same terms as residents of England. In addition, colonial commerce came under the protection of the British navy, the world's strongest. By 1700, colonial goods (including those from the West Indies) accounted for one-fifth of all British imports and for two-thirds of all goods re-exported from England to the continent. In turn, the colonies absorbed more than one-tenth of British exports. The commercial regulations gave economic meaning to England's proprietorship of American colonies.

## Consolidation of Royal Authority

The monarchy also took steps to exercise greater control over colonial governments. Virginia had been a royal colony since 1624; Maryland, South Carolina, and the middle colonies were proprietary colonies with close ties to the crown. The New England colonies possessed royal charters, but they had developed their own distinctively Puritan governments. Charles II, whose father, Charles I, had been executed by Puritans in England, took a particular interest in harnessing the New England colonies more firmly to the British Empire. The occasion was a royal investigation following King Philip's War between colonists and Indians.

In 1675, warfare between Indians and colonists erupted in the Chesapeake and in New England.

**PINE TREE SHILLING**

*Currency was in short supply in the colonies. Since England prohibited the export of its coins, the precious currency circulating in the North American colonies tended to be Spanish, Dutch, French, or Portuguese. In violation of English rules that forbade colonies from issuing their own currency, John Hull, a wealthy Boston merchant and shipowner, began to mint coins in 1652. Shown here is one of his pine tree shillings, boldly announcing its Massachusetts origins. A shilling was worth twelve pennies; twenty shillings equaled a pound sterling. Despite Hull's attempt to ease the currency shortage, the legal tender most colonists used consisted of such commonly available items as bushels of corn or wheat, skins of beaver or deer, or—following the Native American practice—wampum.*

Courtesy of the Museum of the American Numismatic Association.

Almost a half century earlier, in 1637, Massachusetts settlers had massacred hundreds of Pequot Indians, establishing relatively peaceful relations with the more potent Wampanoags. Afterward, New Englanders encroached steadily on Indian lands and, in 1675, the Wampanoags struck back with attacks on settlements in western Massachusetts. Metacomet—whom the colonists called King Philip—was the chief of the Wampanoags and the son of Massasoit, who had befriended William Bradford and his original band of Pilgrims. Metacomet probably neither planned the attacks nor masterminded a conspiracy with the Nipmucks and the Narragansetts, as the colonists feared. But when militias from Massachusetts and other New England colonies counterattacked all three tribes, a deadly sequence of battles killed over a thousand colonists and thousands more Indians. The Indians utterly destroyed thirteen English settlements and partially burned another half dozen. By the spring of 1676, Indian warriors ranged freely within seventeen miles of Boston. The colonists finally forced the Indians to stop fighting, principally with a scorched-earth policy of burning their food supplies.

The war left the New England colonists with an enduring hatred of Indians, a large war debt, and a devastated frontier. And in 1676, Edward Randolph, an agent of the king, arrived to investigate whether New England abided by English laws.

Not surprisingly, Randolph found all sorts of deviations from English rules, and the English government decided to govern New England more directly. In 1684, an English court revoked the Massachusetts charter, the foundation of the distinctive Puritan government. Two years later, royal officials incorporated Massachusetts and the other colonies north of Maryland into the Dominion of New England. To govern the dominion, the English sent Sir Edmund Andros to Boston. Some New England merchants cooperated with Andros, but most colonists were offended by his flagrant disregard of such Puritan traditions as keeping the Sabbath. Worst of all, the Dominion of New England invalidated all land titles, confronting every landowner in New England with the horrifying prospect of losing his or her land.

Events in England, however, permitted Massachusetts colonists to overthrow Andros and retain title to their property. When Charles II died in 1685, he was succeeded by his brother James II, a zealous Catholic. James's aggressive campaign to appoint Catholics to government posts engendered such unrest that in 1688 a group of Protestant noblemen invited the Dutch ruler William of Orange to claim the English throne. When William landed in England at the head of a large army, James fled to France and William became king in the bloodless Glorious Revolution. Rumors of the revolution raced across the Atlantic and emboldened colonial uprisings in Massachusetts, New York, and Maryland.

In Boston, colonists seized Andros and other English officials and tossed them in jail. The rebels reestablished the former charter government, destroying the Dominion of New England. New Yorkers followed the Massachusetts example. Under the leadership of Jacob Leisler, rebels seized the royal governor and ruled the colony for more than a year. When King William's new governor arrived in 1691, Leisler relinquished control of the government without violence, but the governor executed him for treason. In Maryland, the Protestant Association, led by John Coode, overthrew the colony's pro-Catholic government in 1689, fearing it would not recognize the new Protestant king. Coode's men ruled until the new royal governor arrived in 1692 and ended both Coode's rebellion and Lord Baltimore's proprietary government.

Much as they chafed under increasing royal control, the colonists still valued English protection from hostile neighbors. While the northern colonies were distracted by the Glorious Revolution, French forces from the fur trading regions along the Great Lakes and in Canada attacked villages in New England and New York. Known as King William's War, the conflict with the French was a colonial outgrowth of William's war against France in Europe. The war dragged on until 1697 and ended inconclusively in both Europe and the colonies. But it made clear to many colonists that along with English royal government came a welcome measure of military security.

In Massachusetts, John Winthrop's city on a hill became another royal colony in 1691, when a new charter was issued. Under the charter, the governor was appointed by the king rather than elected by the colonists' representatives. But perhaps the most unsettling change was the new qualification for voting. Possession of property replaced church membership as a prerequisite for voting in colony-wide elections. Wealth replaced God's grace as the defining characteristic of Massachusetts citizenship.

## Conclusion: The Seventeenth-Century Legacy of English North America

By 1700, the diverse English colonies in North America had developed along lines quite different from the example New Spain had set in 1600. In the North American colonies, English immigrants and their descendants created societies of settlers, unlike the largely Indian societies in New Spain ruled by a tiny group of Spaniards. Although many settlers came to North America from other parts of Europe and a growing number of Africans arrived in bondage, English laws, habits, ideas, and language dominated all the colonies.

Economically, the English colonies thrived on agriculture and trade instead of mining silver and exploiting Indian labor as in New Spain. Southern colonies grew huge crops of tobacco and rice with the labor of indentured servants and slaves, while farmers in the middle colonies planted wheat and New England fishermen harvested the sea. Although servants and slaves could be found throughout the North American colonies, many settlers depended principally on the labor of family members. Relations between settlers and Native Americans often exploded in bloody warfare, but Indians seldom served as an important source of labor for settlers, as they did in New Spain.

Protestantism prevailed in the North American settlements, relaxed in some colonies and straitlaced in others. The convictions of Puritanism motivated Charles Chauncy, John Winthrop, and others to build a new England in the colonies, but they became muted as the New England colonies matured. Catholics, Quakers, Anglicans, Jews, and others settled in the middle and southern colonies, creating considerable religious toleration, especially in Pennsylvania and New York.

Politics and government differed from colony to colony, although the imprint of English institutions and practices existed everywhere. And everywhere local settlers who were free, adult, white men had an extraordinary degree of political influence, far beyond that of colonists in New Spain or ordinary citizens in England. A new world of settlers that Columbus could not have imagined, that Powhatan only glimpsed, had been firmly established in English North America by 1700. During the next half century, that world would undergo surprising new developments built upon the legacies of the seventeenth-century colonies.

## CHRONOLOGY

**1534**   Henry VIII breaks with Roman Catholic Church and initiates English Reformation.

**1609**   Henry Hudson searches for Northwest Passage for Dutch East India Company.

**1620**   English Puritans found Plymouth colony.

**1626**   Peter Minuit purchases Manhattan island for Dutch West India Company and founds New Amsterdam.

**1629**   Massachusetts Bay Company receives royal charter for colony.

**1630**   John Winthrop leads Puritan settlers to Massachusetts Bay.

**1635**   Roger Williams, banished from Massachusetts, establishes Rhode Island colony.

**1636**   Thomas Hooker leaves Massachusetts and helps found Connecticut colony.

**1637**   Anne Hutchinson accused of Antinomianism, excommunicated from Boston church.

**1642**   Civil war inflames England, pitting Puritans against royalists.

**1649**   English Puritans win civil war and execute King Charles I.

**1656**   Quakers arrive in Massachusetts, persecuted there.

**1660**   Monarchy restored in England; Charles II becomes king.
Navigation Act requires colonial goods to be shipped in English vessels through English ports.

**1662**   Many Puritan congregations adopt Halfway Covenant.

**1663**   Staple Act requires all colonial imports to come from England.

**1664**   English seize New Netherland colony from Dutch, rename it New York.
Duke of York subdivides his colony, creating new colony of New Jersey.

**1675**   Indians and colonists clash in King Philip's War.

**1681**   King Charles II grants William Penn charter for colony of Pennsylvania.

**1686**   Royal officials create Dominion of New England.

**1688**   James II overthrown by Glorious Revolution; William III becomes king.

**1691**   Massachusetts becomes royal colony.

**1692**   Witch trials flourish at Salem.

## SUGGESTED READINGS

Francis J. Bremer, *Shaping New Englands: Puritan Clergymen in Seventeenth-Century England and New England* (1994). A careful analysis of the influence of Puritan ministers in both England and New England.

Jon Butler, *Awash in a Sea of Faith: Christianizing the American People* (1990). An authoritative survey of the growth of Christianity among Americans.

William Cronon, *Changes in the Land: Indians, Colonists, and the Ecology of New England* (1983). A landmark study of the ecological impact of settlement.

Bruce Colin Daniels, *Puritans at Play: Leisure and Recreation in Colonial New England* (1995). A refutation of the myth that the Puritans had no fun.

Philip J. Greven Jr., *Four Generations: Population, Land, and Family in Colonial Andover, Massachusetts* (1970). A meticulous social history of the growth and evolution of a New England town.

David D. Hall, *Worlds of Wonder, Days of Judgment: Popular Religious Belief in Early New England* (1989). A fascinating study of popular religious beliefs that coexisted with Puritanism and other variants of Christianity.

Stephen Innes, *Creating the Commonwealth: The Economic Culture of Puritan New England* (1995). An expert analysis of economic ideas and institutions in Puritan New England.

Carol F. Karlsen, *The Devil in the Shape of a Woman: Witchcraft in Colonial New England* (1987). A careful study of the connections between witchcraft and women in New England.

Kenneth A. Lockridge, *A New England Town: The First Hundred Years, Dedham, Massachusetts, 1636–1736* (1970). A study of the difficulty of maintaining the vision of the Puritan founders under the pressure of population growth and family dispersion.

Perry Miller, *The New England Mind: From Colony to Province* (1953). A classic examination of Puritan ideas and their evolution.

Edmund S. Morgan, *The Puritan Dilemma: The Story of John Winthrop* (1958). A penetrating brief biography that explores the social and intellectual tensions of Puritanism.

Daniel K. Richter, *The Ordeal of the Longhouse: The Peoples of the Iroquois League in the Era of European Colonization* (1992). An insightful account of colonists' encounters with the most powerful Native Americans in New England.

Allen Tully, *Forming American Politics: Ideals, Interests, and Institutions in Colonial New York and Pennsylvania* (1994). A valuable study of the emergence of political institutions and ideas in two major middle colonies.

Laurel Thatcher Ulrich, *Good Wives: Image and Reality in the Lives of Women in Northern New England, 1650–1750* (1982). A revealing investigation of the norms and activities of women in the New England colonies.

Alden T. Vaughan, *New England Frontier: Puritans and Indians, 1620–1675* (3rd ed., 1995). An informative survey of encounters between settlers and Native Americans in New England.

**"DUMMY BOARD" OF PHYLLIS,
A NEW ENGLAND SLAVE**

*This life-size portrait of a slave woman named Phyllis, a mulatto who worked as a domestic servant for her owner, Elizabeth Hunt Wendell, was painted sometime before 1753. Known as a "dummy board," it was evidently propped against a wall or placed in a doorway or window to suggest that the residence was occupied and to discourage thieves. Phyllis is portrayed as a demure, well-groomed woman whose dress and demeanor suggest that she was capable, orderly, and efficient. Although tens of thousands of slaves were brought from Africa to the British North American colonies during the eighteenth century, it does not appear that Phyllis was one of them. Instead, she was probably born in the colonies of mixed white and black parentage. Like thousands of other slave women who labored in the homes of prosperous white families, Phyllis illustrates the integration of the mundane tasks of housekeeping with the shifting currents of transatlantic commerce.*

Courtesy of the Society for the Preservation of New England Antiquities/photo by David Bohl.

# COLONIAL AMERICA IN THE EIGHTEENTH CENTURY

## 1701–1770

# 5

E ARLY ON A SUNDAY MORNING IN OCTOBER 1723, young Benjamin Franklin stepped from a wharf along the Delaware River onto the streets of Philadelphia. As he wrote later in his autobiography, "I was dirty from my Journey; my Pockets were stuff'd out with Shirts and Stockings; I knew no Soul, nor where to look for Lodging. I was fatigu'd with Travelling, Rowing and Want of Rest. I was very hungry."

Born in 1706, Benjamin Franklin grew up in Boston, where his father, Josiah, worked as a tallow chandler, making soap and candles. The father of seventeen children, Josiah apprenticed each of his sons to learn a trade. At the age of twelve, Benjamin signed an indenture to serve for nine years as an apprentice to his brother James, a printer. In James's shop Benjamin learned the printer's trade and had access to the latest books and pamphlets, which he read avidly. In 1721, James inaugurated the *New England Courant,* avowing to "expose the Vice and Follies of Persons of all Ranks and Degrees" with articles written "in a very easy and familiar manner, so that the meanest ploughman, the very meanest of God's people may understand them."

Benjamin's responsibilities in the print shop grew quickly, but he chafed under his brother's supervision. James "considered himself as my Master, and me as his Apprentice," Benjamin remembered; "I thought he demean'd me too much. . . . My Brother was passionate and had often beaten me, which I took extreamly amiss." Benjamin resolved to escape from his apprenticeship and "to assert my Freedom."

Benjamin secretly traveled to New York, nearly three hundred miles from anyone he knew. When he could not find work, he wandered to the Delaware River and then talked his way aboard a small boat heading toward Philadelphia. After rowing half the night, Franklin arrived in the city and went straight to a bakery where he purchased bread. After quenching his thirst with "a Draught of the River Water," Franklin followed "many clean dress'd People . . . to the great Meeting House of the Quakers. . . . I sat down among them, and . . . I fell fast asleep, and continu'd so till the Meeting broke up."

Franklin's account of his arrival in Philadelphia is probably the most well known portrait of life in eighteenth-century America. It illustrates everyday experiences that Franklin shared with many other colonists: a large family; long hours of labor subject to the authority of a parent, relative, or employer; and a restless quest for escape from the ties that bound, for freedom. Franklin's account hints at

**PHILADELPHIA WHARF**

*This early-nineteenth-century drawing of the Arch Street wharf in Philadelphia approximates the world Benjamin Franklin entered when he stepped ashore in 1723. The wharf was a center of industrious activity; almost everyone depicted appears to be working. The pulse of Atlantic commerce propels casks of products from the deck of the small local sailboat (right) toward the hold of large oceangoing ships (center) bound for England and Europe. The small rowboat carrying four people (just to the right of the large ships) is probably similar to the boat Franklin rowed to the city. Coordinating the complicated comings and goings of people and goods that moved through the wharf required individuals who combined intelligence, energy, and discipline with efficiency, reliability, and trustworthiness—traits Franklin and other eighteenth-century colonists sought to cultivate.*

Rare Book Department, The Free Library of Philadelphia.

other, less tangible trends: an eagerness to subvert orthodox opinion by publishing dissenting views; a confidence that, with a valued skill and a few coins, a young man could make his way in the world, a confidence few young women could dare assert; and a slackening of religious fervor.

Franklin's story introduces some of the major changes that affected all the colonies in eighteenth-century British North America. Social and economic changes tended to reinforce the differences among New England, the middle colonies, and the southern colonies, while important cultural and political developments tugged in the opposite direction, creating common experiences, aspirations, and identi-

ties. In 1776, when *E Pluribus Unum* (Latin meaning "From Many, One") was adopted as the motto for the Great Seal of the United States, the changes in eighteenth-century America that strengthened *Pluribus* also planted the seeds of *Unum*.

## A Growing Population and Expanding Economy

The most important fact about eighteenth-century colonial America was its phenomenal population growth. In 1700, colonists numbered about 250,000;

by 1770, they tallied well over 2 million. An index of the emerging significance of colonial America is that in 1700 there were 19 people in England for every American colonist, whereas by 1770 there were only 3. The eightfold growth of the colonial population signaled the maturation of a distinctive colonial society. That society was by no means homogeneous. Colonists of different ethnic groups, races, and religions lived in varied environments under thirteen different colonial governments, all of them part of the British Empire.

> *The eightfold growth of the colonial population signaled the maturation of a distinctive colonial society. That society was by no means homogeneous.*

In general, the growth and diversity of the eighteenth-century colonial population derived from two sources: immigration and natural increase (that is, growth through reproduction). Natural increase contributed about three-fourths of the population growth, immigration about one-fourth. Immigration shifted the ethnic and racial balance among the colonists, making them by 1770 less English and less white than ever before. Fewer than 10 percent of eighteenth-century immigrants came from England; about 36 percent were Scots-Irish, mostly from northern Ireland; 33 percent arrived from Africa, almost all of them slaves; nearly 15 percent left the many German principalities (the nation of Germany did not exist until 1871); and almost 10 percent came from Scotland. These new colonists profoundly altered the colonial population. In 1670, more than 9 out of 10 colonists were of English ancestry, and only 1 out of 25 was of African ancestry. By 1770, only about half the colonists were of English descent, while more than 20 percent descended from Africans. By 1770, the people of the colonies had a distinctive *colonial*—rather than English—profile (Map 5.1).

The booming population of the colonies hints at a second major feature of eighteenth-century colonial society: an expanding economy. Today, societies with rapidly growing populations often have more people than they can adequately feed; or, put another way, they have a high ratio of people to land. In the eighteenth-century colonies, very different conditions prevailed.

In 1700, after almost a century of settlement, nearly all the colonists lived within fifty miles of the

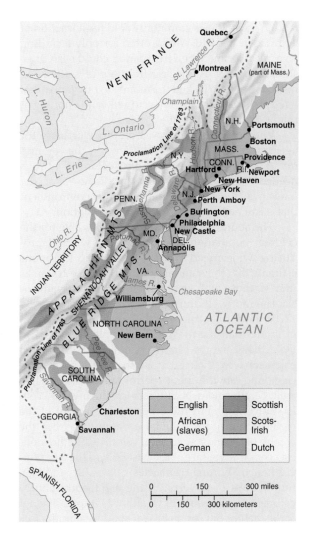

**Map 5.1**

***Europeans and Africans in the Eighteenth Century***
*This map illustrates regions where Africans and certain immigrant groups clustered. It is important to avoid misreading the map. Predominantly European regions, for example, also contained colonists from other places. Likewise, regions where African slaves resided in large numbers also included many whites, their masters among them. The map suggests the polyglot diversity of eighteenth-century colonial society.*

Atlantic coast, on the edge of a vast wilderness peopled by native Indians and a few trappers and traders. The almost limitless wilderness gave the colonies an extremely low ratio of people to land. Consequently, land was cheap. Of course, it was never so cheap that every colonist owned some. But land in the colonies commonly sold for a fraction of its price in the Old World, often for only a shilling an acre, at a time when a carpenter could earn three shillings a day. Along the frontiers of settlement, newcomers who lacked the money to buy land often lived as squatters on unoccupied land, hoping it might eventually become theirs.

Without labor, land was almost worthless for agriculture. The abundance of land in the colonies made labor precious, and the colonists always needed more. The colonists' insatiable labor demand was the fundamental economic environment that sustained the mushrooming population.

The abundance of land made it possible for the colonial population to grow rapidly without producing widespread poverty. Economic historians estimate that the standard of living of free colonists (that is, those who were not indentured servants or slaves) improved during the eighteenth century: By 1770, most free colonists had a higher standard of living than the majority of people elsewhere in the Atlantic world. That did not mean that most colonists were rich but that their rare social and economic environment permitted them to live well. Many colonists did get rich during the eighteenth century, but the unique achievement of the eighteenth-century colonial economy was not the wealth of the most successful colonists but the modest economic welfare of the vast bulk of the free population. In Europe, pinnacles of wealth stood on foundations of poverty; in the eighteenth-century colonies, the pyramid of wealth was impressive not for its height but for its broad, solid base in the free population.

## New England: From Puritan Settlers to Yankee Traders

The New England population grew sixfold during the eighteenth century, but it lagged behind the growth in the other colonies. The main reason New England failed to keep pace was that most immigrants chose other destinations, partly because Puritan orthodoxy made these colonies comparatively inhospitable for both religious dissenters and those indifferent to theology. But the most important reason immigrants avoided New England was that its growth of population produced a higher and less desirable ratio of people to land than in the other colonies. As the population grew, many settlers in search of farmland dispersed from towns, and Puritan communities lost much of their cohesion. Nonetheless, networks of economic exchange laced rural settlers to their neighbors, local market towns, Boston merchants, and the broad currents of Atlantic commerce. In many ways, trade became a faith that competed strongly with the traditions of Puritanism.

## Natural Increase and Land Distribution

The New England population grew mostly by natural increase, much as it had during the seventeenth century. Nearly every adult woman married. Most married women had children and, thanks to the relatively low New England mortality rate, often many children. The perils of childbirth gave wives a shorter life expectancy than husbands, but wives often lived to have six, seven, or eight babies. When a wife died, her husband usually remarried quickly. A wife's labor and companionship were too vital for a family to do without. Benjamin Franklin's father had seven children with his first wife and ten (including Benjamin) with his second.

---

*In many ways, trade became a faith that competed strongly with the traditions of Puritanism.*

---

The burgeoning New England population pressed against a limited amount of land. The interior of New England was smaller than that of colonies farther south (see Map 5.1). Moreover, as the northernmost group of colonies, New England had a contested northern and western frontier. Powerful Indian tribes—especially the Iroquois and Mahicans—jealously guarded their territories. When provoked by colonial or European disputes, the French (and Catholic) colony of Quebec also menaced the English (and Protestant) colonists of New England.

During the seventeenth century, New England towns parceled out land to individual families. In most cases, the original settlers practiced partible inheritance (that is, they subdivided the land more or less equally among sons). By the eighteenth century, the original land allotments had to be further subdivided to accommodate grandsons and great-grandsons, and many plots of land became too small for a family to make a living. Sons who could not hope to inherit sufficient land to farm had to move away from the town where they were born.

During the eighteenth century, colonial governments in New England abandoned the seventeenth-century policy of granting land to towns. Needing revenue, the governments of both Connecticut and Massachusetts sold land directly to individuals, including speculators. Now money, rather than membership in a community bound by a church covenant, determined whether a person could obtain land. The new land policy also caused the disintegration of the seventeenth-century pattern of settlement. As colonists moved into western Massachusetts and Connecticut and north into New Hampshire and Maine, they tended to settle on individual farms rather than in the towns and villages that characterized the seventeenth century. New Englanders still depended on their relatives and neighbors for help in clearing land, raising a house, worshiping God, and having a good time. But far more than in the seventeenth century, they regulated their behavior in newly settled areas by their own individual dictates.

## Farms, Fish, and Trade

The relative scarcity of land in New England encouraged agricultural diversification. New England farmers grew food for their families, but their fields did not produce a huge marketable surplus. Without one big crop, farmers grew many small ones and, if they had extra, sold to or traded with neighbors. Poor roads made travel difficult, time-consuming, and expensive, especially with bulky and heavy agricultural goods. The one major agricultural product the New England colonies exported—livestock—walked to market on its own legs. A New England farm was a place to get by, not to get rich. By 1770, for example, New Englanders had only one-fourth as much wealth as free colonists in the southern colonies.

As consumers, New England farmers made up the foundation of a diversified commercial economy that linked remote farms to markets throughout the world. Merchants large and small stocked imported goods—English textiles, ceramics, and metal goods; Chinese tea; West Indian sugar; and Chesapeake tobacco. Farmers' needs for sturdy shoes, a warm coat, a sound cart, or a solid building supported local shoemakers, tailors, wheelwrights, and carpenters. In the larger towns and especially in Boston, specialized artisans such as

cabinetmakers and silversmiths could be found, along with tallow chandlers and printers, like Benjamin Franklin's father and brother. Shipbuilders tended to do better than other artisans because they served the most dynamic sector of the New England economy.

---

*As consumers, New England farmers made up the foundation of a diversified commercial economy that linked remote farms to markets throughout the world.*

---

As they had since the seventeenth century, many New Englanders made their fortunes at sea. Fish accounted for more than a third of New England's eighteenth-century exports, with livestock and timber making up another third. The West Indies absorbed two-thirds of all New England's exports, while almost all the rest went to England and continental Europe (Map 5.2). This Atlantic commerce benefited the entire New England economy, providing jobs for laborers and tradesmen as well as for ship captains, clerks, and—especially—merchants.

Merchants dominated the commercial economy of New England. Whether in inland communities like Hartford, Connecticut, or seaports like Providence, Rhode Island, merchants stood at the hub of trade between local folk and the international market. The largest and most successful merchants lived in Boston, where they not only bought and sold imported goods but also owned and insured the ships that carried the merchandise. When John Adams, a Massachusetts lawyer who became a leader during the American Revolution and ultimately the second president of the United States, was invited to a wealthy Boston merchant's home, he was stunned by its magnificence. It was a house "for a noble Man, a Prince," he wrote: "The Turkey Carpets, the painted Hangings, the Marble Tables, the rich Beds with crimson Damask Curtains and Counterpins, the beautiful Chimney Clock, the Spacious Garden, are the most magnificent of any Thing I have ever seen." The contrast Adams noted between the luxurious home of this merchant prince and the lives of other New Englanders indicates the polarization of wealth that occurred in Boston and other seaports during the eighteenth century. In the late seventeenth century, the richest 5 percent of Bostonians owned about one-third of the city's wealth; by 1770,

**M A P   5.2**

*Atlantic Trade in the Eighteenth Century*

*This map illustrates the economic outlook of the colonies in the eighteenth century: that is, east toward the Atlantic world rather than west toward the interior of North America. The long distances involved in the Atlantic trade and the uncertainties of seaborne travel suggest the difficulties Britain experienced governing the colonies and regulating colonial commerce.*

---

they owned about half. At the other end of the spectrum, the share of the city's wealth possessed by the poorest two-thirds of the population declined from about one-sixth to less than one-tenth.

The rich got richer, and everybody else had a smaller share of the total wealth, but the incidence of genuine poverty did not change much. Roughly 5 or 6 percent of the New England population qualified for poor relief throughout the eighteenth century. The colony's growing population increased the sheer numbers of unemployed or sick, but compared with the poverty in England, the colonists were better off. As a Connecticut traveler wrote

from England in 1764, "We in New England know nothing of poverty and want, we have no idea of the thing, how much better do our poor people live than 7/8 of the people on this much famed island."

The contrast with English poverty had meaning since the overwhelming majority of New Englanders traced their ancestry to England, making the region more homogeneous than any other. The population of African ancestry (almost all slaves) in the region remained small. New Englanders had no hesitation about acquiring slaves, and many Puritan ministers, including Cotton Mather, owned one or two. But except for the Narragansett region of

Rhode Island, where numerous slaves worked raising livestock, New England's family farms were unsuited for slave labor. New England's slaves concentrated in towns, especially Boston, where most of them worked as domestic servants and laborers. Although the black population of New England grew to over 15,000 by 1770, it barely diluted the region's 97 percent white, mostly English, majority.

By 1770, the population, wealth, and commercial activity of New England differed from what they had been in 1700. Ministers still enjoyed high status in New England, but Yankee traders had replaced Puritan settlers as the symbolic New Englanders.

## The Middle Colonies: Immigrants, Wheat, and Work

In 1700, almost twice as many people lived in New England as in the middle colonies (Pennsylvania, New York, New Jersey, and Delaware). But by 1770, the population of the middle colonies had multiplied tenfold—mainly from an influx of German, Irish, Scotch, and other immigrants—and nearly equaled the population of New England. Immigrants made the middle colonies a uniquely diverse society. By the end of the eighteenth century, barely one-third of Pennsylvanians and less than half the total population of the middle colonies traced their ancestry to England.

### German and Scots-Irish Immigrants

Germans made up the largest contingent of migrants from the European continent to the middle colonies. By 1770, more than 100,000 Germans had arrived in the colonies. Their fellow colonists often referred to them as "Pennsylvania Dutch," an English corruption of *Deutsch*, the word the immigrants used to describe themselves.

Most German immigrants came from a region in southwestern Germany called the Palatinate, although some hailed from German-speaking parts of Switzerland, Austria, and the Netherlands. Throughout Europe, peasants suffered from exploitation by landowners and governments, and they had few opportunities to improve their lives. Palatine peasants in particular, one observer noted, were "not as well off as cattle elsewhere." Devas-

**NATHANIEL HURD, A BOSTON ARTISAN**
*Like Benjamin Franklin, Nathaniel Hurd was born into an artisan family in Boston. The descendant of a tailor great-grandfather, a joiner grandfather, and an accomplished silversmith father, Hurd apprenticed with his father and became an expert engraver, designing bookplates as well as various commercial and social notices, such as loan certificates and wedding invitations. This portrait was painted in 1765 by John Singleton Copley, the most accomplished American artist of the time. Hurd's fine clothing and dignified bearing illustrate the prosperity and security a highly skilled artisan in a good trade could achieve. His open collar and plain cuffs show that he was no idle gentleman; the prominence of his hands suggests their centrality in his life and work.*
John Singleton Copley, American, 1738–1815. *Nathaniel Hurd,* c. 1765. Oil on canvas, 76.2 × 64.8 cm. © The Cleveland Museum of Art, Gift of the John Huntington Art and Polytechnic Trust, 1915.534.

tating French invasions of the Palatinate during Queen Anne's War (1702–1713) made ordinarily bad conditions even worse and triggered the first large-scale migration. German immigrants to the middle colonies included numerous artisans and a few merchants, but the great majority were farmers and laborers. Economically, they represented "middling" folk, neither the poorest (who could not afford the trip) nor the better off (who did not want to leave).

By the 1720s, Germans who had established themselves in the colonies wrote back to their friends and relatives, as one reported, "of the civil and religious liberties [and] privileges, and of all the goodness I have heard and seen." Such letters prompted still more Germans to pull up stakes and embark for America, to exchange the miserable certainties of their lives in Germany for the uncertain attractions of life in the colonies.

*Immigrants made the middle colonies a uniquely diverse society. By the end of the eighteenth century, barely one-third of Pennsylvanians and less than half the total population of the middle colonies traced their ancestry to England.*

Similar motives propelled the Scots-Irish, who outnumbered German immigrants by more than two to one. The term *Scots-Irish,* like *Pennsylvania Dutch,* was a misleading label coined in the colonies. Immigrants labeled Scots-Irish actually hailed from the north of Ireland (Ulster Scots), Scotland, and northern England. Some of the Scots-Irish were Irish natives who had no personal or ancestral connection whatever with Scotland.

Like the Germans, the Scots-Irish were Protestants, but with a difference. Most German immigrants worshiped in Lutheran or German Reformed churches; many others belonged to dissenting sects like the Mennonites, Moravians, and Amish, whose adherents sought relief from persecution they had suffered in Europe for their refusal to bear arms and to swear oaths, beliefs they shared with Quakers. In contrast, the Scots-Irish tended to be militant Presbyterians who seldom hesitated to swear oaths or bear arms. Also, like German settlers, Scots-Irish immigrants were clannish, residing when they could among relatives or neighbors from the old country.

In the eighteenth century, wave after wave of Scots-Irish immigrants arrived, beginning in 1717, cresting every twelve or fifteen years thereafter and culminating in a flood of immigration in the years just before the American Revolution. Deteriorating economic conditions in northern Ireland, Scotland, and England pushed many toward America. Most of the immigrants were farm laborers or tenant farmers fleeing droughts, crop failures, high food prices, or rising rents. By 1773, British officials became so concerned about the drain of people to the colonies that they began to quiz prospective settlers about why they were leaving. The answers Scots-Irish gave echoed the motives of their predecessors: "out of work"; "poverty"; "tyranny of landlords"; and to "do better in America."

Both Scots-Irish and Germans probably heard the common saying that "Pennsylvania is heaven for farmers [and] paradise for artisans," but they almost certainly did not fully understand the risks of their decision to leave their native lands. Gottfried Mittelberger, a musician who traveled from Germany to Philadelphia in 1750, described the grueling passage to America commonly experienced by eighteenth-century emigrants. Mittelberger's trip from his home village in the interior to the port of Rotterdam took seven weeks and cost four times more than the trip from Rotterdam to Philadelphia. Nearly two-thirds of all German emigrants arrived at their port of departure with no money to stock up on extra provisions for the trip or even to buy a ticket. Likewise, they could not afford to go back home. Ship captains, aware of the hunger for labor in the colonies, eagerly signed up the penniless emigrants as "redemptioners," a variant of indentured servants. A captain would agree to provide transportation to Philadelphia, where redemptioners would obtain the money to pay for their passage from a friend or relative who was already in the colonies or, as most did, by selling themselves as servants. Impoverished Scots-Irish emigrants, especially the majority who traveled alone rather than with families, typically paid for their passage by contracting to become indentured servants before they sailed.

Mittelberger enjoyed the amenities reserved for passengers who paid their way to Pennsylvania, but he witnessed the distress among the four hundred other Germans aboard his ship, most of them redemptioners. They were packed, he wrote, "as closely as herring," in bunks two feet by six feet. Seasickness compounded by exhaustion, poverty, poor food, bad water, inadequate sanitation, and tight quarters encouraged the spread of disease. The dismal conditions on Mittelberger's ship were not unusual. One historian has noted that on the sixteen immigrant ships arriving in Philadelphia in 1738, over half of all passengers died en route.

When his ship finally approached land, Mittelberger explained, "everyone crawls from below to the deck . . . and people cry for joy, pray, and sing praises and thanks to God." Unfortunately, their troubles were far from over. Once the ship docked, passengers who had paid their fare could go ashore, as could redemptioners who provided the captain some collateral while they tried to raise the funds for their passage. All the other redemptioners and indentured servants—the majority of passengers— had to stay on board until someone came to purchase their labor. Unlike indentured servants, redemptioners negotiated independently with their purchasers about their period of servitude. Typically, a healthy adult redemptioner agreed to four years of servitude. Indentured servants commonly served five, six, or seven years, as did weaker, younger, and less skilled redemptioners. Children ten years old or younger usually had to become servants until they were twenty-one.

## Pennsylvania: "The Best Poor [White] Man's Country"

New settlers, whether free or in servitude, poured into the middle colonies because they perceived unparalleled opportunities, particularly in Pennsylvania, "the best poor Man's Country in the World," as indentured servant William Moraley wrote in 1743. Although Moraley reported that "the Condition of bought Servants is very hard" and masters often failed to live up to their promise to provide decent food and clothing, opportunity abounded because there was more work to be done than workers to do it.

Most servants toiled in Philadelphia, New York City, or one of the smaller towns or villages. Artisans, small manufacturers, and shopkeepers prized the labor of male servants. Female servants made valuable additions to households, where nearly all of them worked cleaning, washing, cooking, and minding children. From the masters' viewpoint, servants were a bargain. A master could purchase five or six years of a servant's labor for approximately the wages a common laborer would earn in four months. Wage workers could walk away from their jobs when they pleased, and they did so often enough to be troublesome to employers. Servants, however, were legally bound to work for their masters until their terms expired. The restrictions and confinements of bondage were genuine, and they were vigorously enforced.

A few black slaves worked in shops and homes in Philadelphia and New York City. For example, after Benjamin Franklin became prosperous, he purchased five slaves. Since a slave cost at least three times as much as a servant, only affluent colonists could afford the long-term investment in slave labor. While the population of African ancestry

**BENJAMIN FRANKLIN**
*This is the earliest known portrait of Benjamin Franklin. Painted by Robert Feke in about 1748 when Franklin was in his early forties, the portrait illustrates Franklin's status as an aspiring printer, merchant, and citizen of Philadelphia. To the present-day viewer, Franklin appears prim, foppish, and mannered, with an elaborately curled wig framing a composed, satisfied face. However, compare Franklin's demeanor and dress with that of Nathaniel Hurd (page 109) and of Mrs. Barnard Elliott (page 122). Franklin appears more pretentious than Hurd and less elegant than Elliott, a rough index of his in-progress social mobility from a hardworking printer to a prominent and wealthy thinker and statesman.*
Courtesy of the Harvard University Portrait Collection, Bequest, Dr. John C. Warren, 1856.

(almost all slaves) in the middle colonies grew to over 30,000 in 1770, it represented only about 7 percent of the total population, and in most of the region much less.

During the eighteenth century, most slaves came to the middle colonies as they did to New England, in ships returning from the West Indies. Enough arrived to prompt colonial assemblies to pass slave codes that punished slaves much more severely than servants for the same transgressions. "For the least trespass," servant Moraley reported, slaves "undergo the severest Punishment." In practice, both servants and slaves were governed more by their masters than by the laws. But in cases of abuse, servants could and did charge masters with violating the terms of their indenture contracts. The terms of a slave's bondage were set forth in a master's commands, not in a written contract.

Small numbers of slaves managed to obtain their freedom, but free African Americans did not escape whites' firm convictions about black inferiority and white supremacy. Whites' racism and blacks' lowly social status made African Americans scapegoats for European Americans' suspicions and anxieties. In 1741, when arson and several unexplained thefts plagued New York City, officials suspected a murderous slave conspiracy. On the basis of little more than evidence of slaves' "insolence" (that is, refusal to conform fully to whites' expectations of servile behavior), city authorities had thirteen slaves burned at the stake and eighteen others hanged. Although slaves were certifiably poor (they usually had no property whatever), they were not included among the poor for whom the middle colonies were reputed to be the best country in the world.

The reason more slaves were not brought to the middle colonies was that farmers, the vast majority of the population, had little use for them. Most farms operated with family labor. Wheat, the most widely grown crop, did not require more labor than farmers could typically muster from relatives, neighbors, and a hired hand or two.

Immigrants swarmed to the middle colonies because of the availability of land. The Penn family encouraged immigration to bring in potential buyers for their enormous tracts of land in Pennsylvania. From the beginning, Pennsylvania followed a policy of negotiating with Indian tribes to purchase additional land. This policy greatly reduced the violent frontier clashes elsewhere in the colonies. Yet the Penn family did not shrink from pushing its agreements with Indian tribes to the limit and beyond. In a dispute with tribes on the northern Delaware in 1737, the Penn family pulled out a deed that showed that local tribes had in 1686 granted the Penns land that stretched as far as a man could walk in a day and a half. Under the terms of this infamous "Walking Purchase," the Penns sent out three runners, two of whom collapsed before the thirty-six hours expired. The third runner managed to cover sixty miles of wilderness, approximately doubling the size of the Penns' claim.

Few colonists drifted beyond the northern boundaries of Pennsylvania. Owners of the huge estates in New York's Hudson valley preferred to rent rather than sell their land, and thus they attracted fewer immigrants. The Iroquois dominated the lucrative fur trade of the St. Lawrence valley and eastern Great Lakes, and they had the political and military strength to defend their territory from colonial encroachment. Few settlers wanted to risk having their scalps lifted by Iroquois warriors in northern New York when they could choose to settle instead in the comparatively safe environs of Pennsylvania.

The price of farmland varied depending on soil quality, access to water, distance from a market town, and the extent of improvements. One hundred acres of improved land that had been cleared, plowed, fenced, ditched, and perhaps had a house and barn built on it might cost three or four times more than the same acreage of uncleared, unimproved land. Since the cheapest unimproved land always lay at the margin of settlement, would-be farmers tended to migrate to promising areas just beyond already improved farms. From Philadelphia, settlers moved north along the Delaware River and west along the Schuylkill and Susquehanna Rivers (see Map 5.1). By midcentury, settlement had reached the eastern slopes of the Appalachian Mountains, and newcomers spilled down the fertile valley of the Shenandoah River into western Virginia and the Carolinas. Thousands of settlers migrated from the middle colonies through this back door to the South.

Farmers made the middle colonies the breadbasket of North America. They planted a wide variety of crops to feed their families, but they grew wheat in abundance. Flour milling was the number one industry and flour the number one export, constituting nearly three-fourths of all exports from the middle colonies. Pennsylvania flour fed residents in other colonies, in southern Europe, and—above all—in the West Indies (see Map 5.2). For farmers, the world grain market proved risky but profitable. Grain prices rose steadily after 1720; by 1770, a bushel of wheat was worth twice (in real terms, that is, adjusted for inflation) what it had been fifty years earlier.

The standard of living in rural Pennsylvania was probably higher than in any other agricultural region of the eighteenth-century world. The comparatively widespread prosperity of all the middle colonies permitted residents to indulge in a half-century shopping spree for English imports. The middle colonies' per capita consumption of imported goods from England more than doubled between 1720 and 1770, far outstripping the per capita consumption of English goods in New England and the southern colonies.

**BETHLEHEM, PENNSYLVANIA**

*This view of the small community of Bethlehem, Pennsylvania, in 1757 dramatizes the profound transformation of the natural landscape in the eighteenth century by highly motivated human labor. Founded by Moravian immigrants in 1740, Bethlehem must have appeared at first like the dense woods on the upper left horizon. In fewer than twenty years, precisely laid-out orchards and fields had replaced forests and glades. Carefully penned livestock (lower center right) and fenced fields (lower left) kept the handiwork of farmers separate from the risks and disorders of untamed nature. Not only individual farmsteads (lower center), but impressive multistory brick town buildings (upper center) combined the bounty of the land with the delights of community life. Few eighteenth-century communities were as orderly as Bethlehem, but many effected a comparable transformation of the environment.*

Miriam and Ira D. Walsh Division of Art, Prints, and Photographs, New York Public Library. Astor, Lenox, and Tilden Foundations.

---

At the crossroads of trade in wheat exports and English imports stood Philadelphia. By 1776, Philadelphia had a larger population than any other city in the entire British Empire except London. Merchants occupied the top stratum of Philadelphia society. They made fortunes in trade, shipping, insurance, land, and law. In a city where only 2 percent of the residents owned enough property (£50) to qualify to vote, merchants built grand homes and dominated local government. They sent their sons to Europe for education and refinement; their daughters learned enough at home, they believed.

Many of Philadelphia's wealthiest merchants were Quakers. Quaker traits of industry, thrift, honesty, and sobriety encouraged the accumulation of wealth. A colonist complained that a Quaker "prays for his neighbor on First Days [the Sabbath] and then preys on him the other six."

The ranks of merchants reached downward to aspiring tradesmen like Benjamin Franklin. After he started to publish the *Pennsylvania Gazette* in 1728, Franklin opened a shop, run mostly by his wife, Deborah, that sold a little bit of everything: cheese, codfish, coffee, goose feathers, sealing wax, soap, and now and then a slave. In 1733, Franklin began to publish *Poor Richard's Almanack,* a calendar of weather predictions, astrological alignments, and pithy epigrams. Poor Richard preached the likelihood of long-term rewards for tireless labor. The *Almanack* sold thousands of copies, quickly becoming Franklin's most profitable product.

The popularity of *Poor Richard's Almanack* suggests that many Pennsylvanians thought less about the pearly gates than about their pocketbooks. Where were the mysteries of divine providence in what might be considered Poor Richard's motto for the middle colonies, "God gives all Things to Industry"? The promise of a worldly payoff made work a secular faith in the middle colonies. Poor Richard advised, "Work as if you were to live 100 years, Pray as if you were to die Tomorrow."

---

*The promise of a worldly payoff made work a secular faith in the middle colonies.*

---

William Penn's Quaker utopia became a center of worldly affluence whose most famous citizen, Franklin, was neither a Quaker nor a utopian. Quakers remained influential, but Franklin spoke for most colonists with his aphorisms of work, discipline, and thrift that echoed Quaker rules for outward behavior. Franklin's maxims did not look to the Quakers' divine inner light for guidance. They depended instead on the spark of ambition and the glow of gain.

## The Southern Colonies: Land of Slavery

Between 1700 and 1770, the population of the southern colonies—Virginia, Maryland, North Carolina, South Carolina, and Georgia—grew almost ninefold. By 1770, about twice as many people lived in the South as in either the middle colonies or New England. As elsewhere, natural increase and immigration accounted for this rapid population growth. Many Scots-Irish and German immigrants funneled from the middle colonies into the southern backcountry. Other immigrants were indentured servants (mostly English and Scots-Irish) who followed their seventeenth-century predecessors.

But involuntary immigrants—slaves—made the most striking contribution to the booming population of the southern colonies, transforming the racial and ethnic composition of the population and shaping the region's economy, society, and politics.

## The Atlantic Slave Trade and the Growth of Slavery

The number of southerners of African ancestry (nearly all of them slaves) rocketed from just over 20,000 in 1700 to well over 400,000 in 1770. The black population increased nearly three times faster than the South's briskly growing white population. Consequently, the proportion of southerners who were black grew from 20 percent in 1700 to 40 percent in 1770. By then, the number of slaves in the South considerably exceeded the entire population (white and black) of New England in 1750 or the middle colonies in 1760. Slavery became the defining characteristic of the southern colonies during the eighteenth century.

Southern colonists clustered into two distinct geographic and agricultural zones. The colonies in the upper South, surrounding the Chesapeake Bay, specialized in growing tobacco, as they had since the early seventeenth century. Throughout the eighteenth century, nine out of ten southern whites and eight out of ten southern blacks lived in the Chesapeake region. The upper South retained a white majority during the eighteenth century, although it dwindled from four-fifths to two-thirds because the slave population grew so dramatically.

In the lower South, a much smaller cluster of colonists inhabited the coastal region and specialized in the production of rice and indigo (a plant used to make blue dye). Lower South colonists made up only 5 percent of the total population of the southern colonies in 1700 but inched upward to 15 percent by 1770. South Carolina was the sole British colony along the South Atlantic coast until 1732 when Georgia was founded. In contrast to every other British mainland colony, blacks in South Carolina outnumbered whites almost two to one; in some low country districts, the ratio of blacks to whites exceeded ten to one.

The enormous growth in the South's slave population occurred through natural increase and the flourishing Atlantic slave trade (Map 5.3). Slave ships brought almost 300,000 Africans to British North America between 1619 and 1780. Of those Africans, 95 percent arrived in the South and 96 percent arrived during the eighteenth century. Unlike indentured servants or redemptioners, the Africans did not choose to come to the colonies. They were imported. The word *imported*—a word normally used to describe the shipment of goods for sale—accurately conveys their status. Most of them had been born into free families in villages located within a few hundred miles of the West African coast. Captured in war, kidnapped, or sold into slavery by other Africans, they were brought to the coast, sold to African traders who assembled slaves for sale, and sold again to European or colonial slave traders or ship captains who bought them for shipment to the New World. Packed aboard a

slave ship with two to three hundred or more other slaves, they were subjected to the infamous Middle Passage—the crossing of the Atlantic in the hold of a slave ship—and then sold yet again by the ship captain to a colonial slave merchant or to a southern planter.

The voices of Africans who were swept up in the slave trade have been enveloped by a deafening historical silence, with one major exception. In 1789, Olaudah Equiano published *The Interesting Narrative,* an account of his own enslavement that hints at the stories that might have been told by the thousands of silenced Africans. Equiano was born in 1745 in the interior of what is now Nigeria. "I

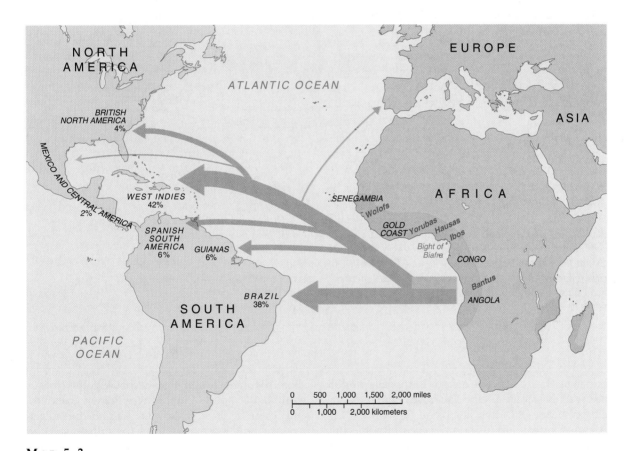

**M A P  5.3**
*The Atlantic Slave Trade*
*Although the Atlantic slave trade endured from about 1450 to 1870, its heyday occurred during the eighteenth century, when more than six million African slaves were imported to the New World. Only a small fraction of the African slaves imported to the Western Hemisphere were taken to British North America; most went to sugar plantations in Brazil and the Caribbean. Why were so many more African slaves sent to the West Indies and Brazil than to British North America?*

**SECTIONS OF A SLAVE SHIP.**

**SLAVE SHIP**

*Newly enslaved Africans endured the Middle Passage crammed belowdecks on a slave ship like this one, sitting upright in a space just over three feet high. Other ships installed an intermediate shelf, forcing slaves into a reclining position with barely enough vertical space to turn from side to side. Profit calculations dictated carrying as many slaves as possible to offset the fixed costs of the ship, insurance, supplies, and crew. But security precautions were the prime consideration in confining slaves to unhealthy, tight quarters belowdecks. Slaves vastly outnumbered the crew aboard the ship, and crew members justifiably feared a slave uprising. Note that the cannon on deck (pointing at one of the hatches over the slave quarters) swiveled to permit shooting at mutinous slaves as well as unfriendly ships.*

British Library.

had never heard of white men or Europeans, nor of the sea," he recalled. One day when Equiano was eleven years old, two men and a woman, all Africans, broke into his home, seized him and his sister, and carried them off. The kidnappers soon separated Equiano from his sister, leaving him "in a state of distraction not to be described. I cried and grieved continually, and for several days did not eat anything but what they forced into my mouth."

During the next six or seven months, Equiano was sold to several different African masters, each of whom moved him closer to the coast. When Equiano arrived at the coast, a slave ship waited off-shore. Equiano feared that he had "gotten into a world of bad spirits," that he was going to be killed and "eaten by those white men with horrible looks, red faces, and loose hair." Once the ship set sail, the slaves were confined to the hold, which "became absolutely pestilential." Many slaves died from sickness, crowded together in suffocating heat fouled by filth of all descriptions. "The shrieks of the women and the groans of the dying rendered the whole a scene of horror almost inconceivable," Equiano recalled. The ship finally arrived in Barbados, and merchants and planters came on board to examine the slaves. In a few days, white masters in

Barbados had purchased most of Equiano's ship-mates, but he was "not saleable," probably because he was so young. He and other leftovers "were shipped off in a sloop for North America." The sloop sailed to Virginia, where Equiano "saw few or none of our native Africans and not one soul who could talk to me." Soon all the other slaves had been sold "and only myself was left. I was now exceedingly miserable and thought myself worse off than any of the rest of my companions, for they could talk to each other, but I had no person to speak to that I could understand." Equiano finally was sold to a white man, the captain of a tobacco ship bound for England. Equiano remained a slave for ten years, traveling frequently from England to the West Indies and North America until he bought his freedom in 1766.

Some of the slaves brought into the southern colonies came as Equiano did, aboard ships from the West Indies. Merchants in the North American colonies often specialized in this trade; Equiano himself was owned for several years by a Quaker merchant from Philadelphia who traded extensively with the West Indies. But slaves arriving from the West Indies accounted for only about 15 percent of all the Africans brought into the southern colonies during the eighteenth century. All the rest came directly from Africa, and almost all the ships that brought them (roughly 90 percent) belonged to British merchants. Most slaves on board were young adults, men usually outnumbering women two to one. Children under the age of fourteen, like Equiano, were typically no more than 10 or 15 percent of a cargo.

Mortality during the Middle Passage varied considerably from ship to ship. On average, about 15 percent of the slaves died, but sometimes half or more perished. The average mortality among the white crew of slave ships was often nearly as bad. In general, the longer the voyage, the larger the number of deaths. Recent studies suggest that many slaves succumbed not only to virulent epidemic diseases such as smallpox and dysentery but also to acute dehydration caused by fluid loss from heavy perspiration, vomiting, and diarrhea combined with a severe shortage of drinking water to replace the lost fluids.

Normally an individual planter purchased at any one time a relatively small number of newly arrived Africans, or "new Negroes," as they were called. In the Chesapeake in 1735, for example, a healthy adult slave cost about the same as nineteen head of cattle. Slave prices escalated with surging

**OLAUDAH EQUIANO**
*This portrait of Olaudah Equiano was painted by an unknown English artist about 1780, when Equiano was in his mid-thirties, more than a decade after he had bought his freedom. The portrait evokes Equiano's successful acculturation to the customs of eighteenth-century England. His clothing and hairstyle reflect the fashions of respectable young Englishmen. In his* Interesting Narrative, *Equiano explained that he had learned to speak and understand English while he was a slave. He wrote that he "looked upon [the English] . . . as men superior to us [Africans], and therefore I had the stronger desire to resemble them, to imbibe their spirit and imitate their manners; I therefore embraced every occasion of improvement, and every new thing that I observed I treasured up in my memory." Equiano's embrace of English culture did not cause him to forsake his African roots. In fact, he honored his dual identity by campaigning against slavery. His* Narrative *was one of the most important and powerful antislavery documents of the time.*
Royal Albert Memorial Museum, Exeter, England.

demand for their labor; by 1770, a comparable slave cost as much as thirty head of cattle. Planters often bought slaves on credit, hoping to pay off their debt with the boost in production they anticipated from their new laborers.

Another reason planters preferred to purchase small groups of slaves was to permit the newcomers to be trained by the planters' other slaves. Like Equiano, newly arrived Africans were often profoundly depressed, demoralized, and disoriented. Planters counted on their other slaves—either those who had been born into slavery in the colonies (often called "country-born" or "creole" slaves) or Africans who had arrived earlier—to help new Negroes become accustomed to their strange new surroundings.

---

*Slaves made the most striking contribution to the booming population of the southern colonies, transforming the racial and ethnic composition of the population and shaping the region's economy, society, and politics.*

---

Planters' preferences for slaves from specific regions of Africa aided the process of acculturation (or "seasoning," as it was called) to the routines of slave life in the southern colonies. Chesapeake planters preferred slaves from Senegambia, the Gold Coast, or—like Equiano—the Bight of Biafra, the origin of 40 percent of all Africans imported to the Chesapeake. South Carolina planters favored slaves from the central African Congo and Angola regions, the origin of about 40 percent of the African slaves they imported. Although slaves within each of these regions spoke many different languages, enough linguistic and cultural similarities existed that they could communicate with other Africans from the same region.

Seasoning acclimated new Africans to the physical as well as the cultural environment of the southern colonies. Slaves who had just endured the Middle Passage were poorly nourished, weak, and sick. In this vulnerable state they encountered the alien diseases of North America without having developed a biological arsenal of acquired immunities. As many as 10 or 15 percent of newly arrived Africans, sometimes more, died during their first year in the southern colonies. New arrivals who survived for a year or two were considered seasoned.

While newly enslaved Africans poured into the southern colonies, slave women made an even greater contribution to the growth of the black population. Both country-born women and seasoned Africans gave birth to slave babies, which caused the slave population to mushroom. Slaveowners encouraged these births. Thomas Jefferson explained, "I consider the labor of a breeding [slave] woman as no object, that a [slave] child raised every 2 years is of more profit than the crop of the best laboring [slave] man." The growing number of slave babies set the southern colonies apart from other New World slave societies, which experienced natural *decrease*; that is, slave deaths exceeded births. The high rate of natural increase in the southern colonies meant that by the 1740s the majority of southern slaves were country-born. But the large numbers of newly enslaved Africans made the influence of African culture in the eighteenth-century South stronger than ever before—or since.

## Slave Labor and African American Culture

Planters expected slaves to work from sunup to sundown and beyond. George Washington wrote that his slaves should "be at their work as soon as it is light, work til it is dark, and be diligent while they are at it." The conflict between the masters' desire for maximum labor and the slaves' reluctance to do more than necessary made the threat of physical punishment a constant for eighteenth-century slaves. Masters preferred black slaves over white indentured servants not just because slaves served for life, but also because colonial laws did not limit the force masters could use against slaves. Masters often reached for their whips, or worse. As a traveler observed in 1740, "A new negro . . . will require more discipline than a young spaniel . . . let a hundred men show him how to hoe, or drive a wheelbarrow; he'll still take the one by the bottom and the other by the wheel and . . . often die before [he] . . . can be conquered." Slaves, the traveler noted, were not stupid or simply obstinate; despite the inevitable punishment, they resisted their masters' demands because of their "greatness of soul," their stubborn unwillingness to conform to their masters' definition of them as merely slaves.

Some slaves escalated their acts of resistance to direct physical confrontation with the master, mistress, or an overseer. But a hoe raised in anger, a punch in the face, or a desperate swipe with a knife led to swift and predictable retaliation by whites. Throughout the southern colonies, the balance of physical power rested securely in the hands of whites.

Rebellion occurred, however, at Stono, South Carolina, in 1739. Before dawn on a September Sunday, a group of about twenty slaves attacked a country store, killed the two storekeepers, confiscated the store's guns, ammunition, and powder, and set out toward Spanish Florida after pausing to set the severed heads of the storekeepers on the store's front steps. Enticing other rebel slaves to join the march south, the group plundered and burned more than a half dozen plantations and killed more than twenty white men, women, and children. As their numbers grew, the rebels stopped to rest, to beat drums to signal more slaves to join them, and to dance and sing in celebration. A mounted force of whites attacked the exultant slaves and killed many of them. They placed rebels' heads atop mileposts along the road, grim reminders of the consequences of rebellion. The Stono rebellion illustrated that eighteenth-century slaves, no matter how determined, had no chance of overturning slavery and very little chance of defending themselves in any bold strike for freedom. After the rebellion, South Carolina legislators enacted repressive laws designed to guarantee that whites would always have the upper hand. (See Texts in Historical Context on page 120.) No other similar uprising occurred during the colonial period.

Day-to-day experience convinced most slaves that survival lay within the boundaries of slavery. But slaves maneuvered constantly to protect themselves and to gain a measure of autonomy. In Chesapeake tobacco fields, most slaves were subject to close supervision by whites. In the lower South, the task system gave slaves some control over the pace of their work and some discretion in the use of the rest of their time. A task was typically defined as a certain area of ground to be planted, cultivated, and harvested or a specific job to be completed. A slave who completed the assigned task could use the remainder of the day to work in a garden, fish, hunt, spin, weave, sew, or cook. If a master sought to increase productivity by changing the definition of tasks, slaves did their best to defend customary practices.

Eighteenth-century slaves planted the roots of African American lineages that branch out to the present. Historians are only beginning to explore the kin networks slaves built; much remains unknown. But it is clear that slaves valued family ties and that, as in West African societies, kinship structured slaves' relations with one another. Slave parents often gave a child the name of a grandparent, aunt, or uncle. In selecting a husband or wife (when the master permitted a choice), slaves avoided first cousins or closer relatives, further evidence of their awareness of kin connections.

*Eighteenth-century slaves planted the roots of African American lineages that branch out to the present.*

In West Africa, kinship not only identified a person's place among living relatives; it also linked the person to ancestors among the dead and to descendants in the future. Kinship rooted people in both society and time. Newly imported African slaves usually arrived alone, without kin; like Equiano, they had been snatched away from their relatives in Africa. Often slaves who had traversed the Middle Passage on the same ship adopted one another as "brothers" and "sisters." Likewise, as new Negroes were seasoned and incorporated into existing slave communities, established families often adopted them as kin and recognized them as aunts or uncles. Through kin networks, slaves endowed their personal lives with relationships and meanings that they controlled, as much as the circumstances of slavery permitted.

## Tobacco, Rice, and Prosperity

Slaves' labor bestowed prosperity on their masters, British merchants, and the monarchy. The southern colonies supplied 90 percent of all North American exports to England. Rice exports from the lower South exploded from less than half a million pounds in 1700 to eighty million pounds in 1770, virtually all of it grown by slaves. Exports of indigo also boomed. Together, rice and indigo made up three-fourths of lower South exports, nearly two-thirds of them going to England and most of the rest to the West Indies, where sugar-growing slaves ate slave-grown rice. Tobacco exports from the Chesapeake did not accelerate as rapidly as rice exports, but they still leaped from about thirty million pounds in 1700 to a hundred million pounds in 1770. Tobacco was by far the most important export from British North America; by 1770, it represented almost one-third of *all* colonial exports and three-fourths of all Chesapeake exports. And under the provisions of the Navigation Acts (see Chapter 4), nearly all of it went to England, where the monarchy collected a lucrative tax on each pound. British merchants then re-exported more than 80 percent of the tobacco to the

# Regulating Slavery

*The slave rebellion at Stono, South Carolina, in 1739 alarmed white South Carolinians. The colony's legislators responded in the spring of 1740, only a few months after the rebellion had been suppressed, by enacting new regulations governing slavery. The laws disclosed widespread perceptions among whites of the dangers posed by slaves and of the remedies that would maintain order.*

### DOCUMENT 1. Excerpt of an Act Requiring White Men to Serve on Patrols

Forasmuch as many late horrible and barbarous massacres have been actually committed, and many more designed, on the white inhabitants of this Province, by negro slaves, who are generally prone to such cruel practices, which makes it highly necessary that constant patrols should be established . . . for the better preventing any future insurrections or cabals of said slaves; we therefore humbly pray his most sacred Majesty that it may be enacted. . . .

That every patrol shall go to and examine the several plantations in their districts . . . at least once in a fortnight, and may take up all slaves which they shall see without the fences or cleared ground of their owners' plantations, who have not a ticket or letter to shew the reasonableness of their absence, or who have not some white person in company to give an account of his, her, or their business, and such patrol may correct every such slave or slaves by whipping with a switch or cowskin, not exceeding twenty lashes; provided no patrol man shall beat or abuse any slave quietly and peaceably being in his master's plantation. . . . And the said patrols shall have full power to search and examine all negro houses for offensive weapons and ammunition . . . [and] to enter into any disorderly tipling houses or other houses suspected of harbouring, trafficking or dealing with negroes, either of white persons, free negroes or others, and to apprehend and correct all disorderly slaves there found, by whipping.

*Another act sought to increase the security of the white population by imposing a tax on purchasers of African slaves and using the revenue to attract white immigrants to settle in the colony.*

### DOCUMENT 2. Excerpt of an Act to Tax Imported Slaves

Whereas, the great importation of negroes from the coast of Africa, who are generally of a barbarous and savage disposition, may hereafter prove of very dangerous consequence to the peace and safety of this Province, and which we have now more reason to be apprehensive of from the late rising in rebellion of a great number of the negroes lately imported into this Province from the coast of Africa . . . and whereas, the best way to prevent those fatal mischiefs for the future, will be to establish a method . . . for the better settling . . . of this Province with white inhabitants, by which we may be the better enabled to suppress any future insurrection of negroes and slaves. . . . [T]here shall be imposed and paid by all and every [one of] the inhabitants of this Province . . . first purchasing any negro or other slave . . . , a certain tax or sum of ten pounds current money for every such negro and other slave of the height of four feet and two inches and upwards; and for every one under that height, and above

European continent, pocketing a nice markup for their troubles.

These products of slave labor made the southern colonies by far the richest in North America. The per capita wealth of free whites in the South was four times greater than that in New England and three times that in the middle colonies. At the top of the wealth pyramid stood the rice grandees of the lower South and the tobacco gentry of the Chesapeake. These elite families commonly resided on large estates adorned by handsome mansions and luxurious gardens, maintained and supported by slaves. The extravagant lifestyle of one gentry family astonished a young tutor from New Jersey who noted that during the winter months the family kept twenty-eight large fires roaring, requiring three feet two inches, the sum of five pounds like money; and for all under three feet two inches, (sucking children excepted) two pounds ten shillings like money. . . . And . . . that out of the said tax or duty on negroes and slaves . . . two-third parts . . . of the net sum arising by the tax . . . [be used] for defraying the charge of transportation or carriage of poor protestants from Charlestown to the townships or other place where they shall settle . . . and for purchasing tools necessary for planting and settling, and for provisions for one year for each of such poor protestants, (not being upwards of fifty years of age) and also for purchasing one cow and calf over and besides such provisions, for every five persons who shall actually become settlers.

*The legislators also enacted a comprehensive slave code containing fifty-eight separate provisions. All the regulations indirectly acknowledged the lesson whites took from the Stono rebels—namely, that slaves must be controlled and disciplined more rigorously.*

### Document 3. Excerpt from South Carolina Slave Code

XVI. Be it . . . enacted . . . That . . . if any slave, free negro, mulattoe, Indian or mustizoe [mestizo, a person of mixed white and Indian ancestry], shall wilfully and maliciously burn or destroy any stack of rice, corn, or other grain, of the product, growth or manufacture of this Province, or shall wilfully and maliciously set fire to, burn or destroy any tar kiln, barrels of pitch, tar, turpentine or rosin, or any other [of] the goods or commodities of the growth, produce or manufacture of this Province, or shall felo-

niously steal, take or carry away any slaves, being the property of another, with intent to carry such slave out of this Province, or shall wilfully or maliciously poison or administer any poison to any person, free man, woman, servant or slave, every such slave, free negro, mulattoe, Indian . . . and mustizoe, shall suffer death as a felon. . . .

XXIV. And be it further enacted . . . That if any slave shall presume to strike any white person, such slave, upon trial and conviction . . . shall for the first and second offence, suffer such punishment as the said justice [of the peace] and freeholders . . . shall, in their discretion think fit, not extending to life or limb; and for the third offence, shall suffer death. But in case any such slave shall grievously wound, maim or bruise any white person, though it be only the first offence, such slave shall suffer death. . . .

LVI. And whereas, several negroes did lately rise in rebellion, and did commit many barbarous murders at Stono and other parts adjacent thereto; and whereas, in suppressing the said rebels, several of them were killed and others taken alive and executed; and as the exigence and danger the inhabitants at that time were in and exposed to, would not admit of the formality of a legal trial of such rebellious negroes, but for their own security, the said inhabitants were obliged to put such negroes to immediate death. . . . Be it enacted . . . That all and every act . . . done, committed and executed, in and about the suppressing and putting all and every [one of] the said . . . negroes to death, is and are hereby declared lawful . . . as fully and amply as if such rebellious negroes had undergone a formal trial and condemnation.

**Documents 1, 2, and 3.** Cooper and McCord, eds., *Statutes at Large of South Carolina* (1840s), 556–63, 568–73, 397–417.

six oxen to haul in a heavy cartload of slave-cut wood four times a day. By contrast, yeoman families—who supported themselves on a small plot of land without slaves and cut their own wood—normally warmed themselves around one fire.

The vast differences in wealth among white southerners engendered envy and occasional tension between rich and poor, but remarkably little

open hostility. The gentry looked down upon the "meaner sort" and spoke of them disparagingly in private. In public, the planter elite acknowledged humble whites as their equals, at least in belonging to the superior—in their minds—white race. Looking upward, white yeomen and tenants (who owned neither land nor slaves) sensed the gentry's condescension and veiled contempt. But they also

**PLANTATION MISTRESS**
*The wife of a wealthy South Carolina rice planter,
Mrs. Barnard Elliott displays the opulence made possible
by the soil of plantations and the toil of untold slaves.
Mrs. Elliott appears to be a discriminating consumer.
Although she probably made most of her purchases in the
best Charleston shops, her custom-made fashions would
not have been out of place in the drawing rooms of the
English gentry. Sensuous textiles, billowing lace-
encrusted sleeves, a daring neckline, and dazzling jewels
demonstrate Mrs. Elliott's cosmopolitan tastes despite her
colonial residence. Her formal, almost regal pose evokes
the enormous distance between the luxurious refinements
of elite planters and the workaday plantation realities that
gilded their world. Contrast the appearance of Mrs. Elliott
with that of her approximate contemporary, the New England household slave Phyllis (page 102).*
The Gibbes Museum of Art, Carolina Art Association.

appreciated the gentry for granting favors, upholding white supremacy, and keeping slaves in their
place. While racial slavery made a few whites much
richer than others, it also gave those who did not
get rich a powerful reason to feel similar (in race)
to those who were so different (in wealth).

The slaveholding gentry dominated politics, the
economy, and the culture of the southern colonies.
In Virginia, only adult white men who owned at
least one hundred acres of unimproved land or
twenty-five acres of land with a house could vote.
This property-holding requirement prevented about
40 percent of white men in Virginia from voting for
representatives to the House of Burgesses. In South
Carolina, only fifty acres of land were required to
vote, and most adult white men qualified. But in
both colonies, voters elected members of the gentry
to serve in the colonial legislature. The gentry passed
elected political offices from generation to generation, almost as if they were hereditary. Politically, the
gentry built a self-perpetuating oligarchy—rule by
the elite few—with the votes of their many humble
neighbors. The gentry also set the cultural standard
in the southern colonies. They bought fine wines
from France and the latest fashions and books from
London. They entertained lavishly, gambled regularly, and attended Anglican church services more
for social than religious reasons. Above all they cultivated a life of leisurely pursuit of happiness. They
did not condone idleness, however. Their pleasures
and their responsibilities kept them busy. Thomas
Jefferson, a phenomenally productive member of the
gentry, recalled that his earliest childhood memory
was of being carried on a pillow by a family slave—
a powerful image of the slave hands beneath the
gentry's leisure and achievement.

## Unifying Experiences

While the societies of New England, the middle
colonies, and the southern colonies became more
sharply differentiated during the eighteenth century, colonists throughout British North America
shared certain unifying experiences. The first was
economic: The economies of all three regions had
their roots in agriculture. But the tempo of commerce quickened during the eighteenth century.
Colonists sold their distinctive products in markets
that, in turn, offered to consumers throughout the
colonies a more or less uniform array of goods. A
second unifying experience was a decline in the importance of religion. Throughout the colonies, although some settlers called for a revival of religious
intensity, for most people religion mattered less, the
affairs of the world more, than they did in the seventeenth century. Third, white inhabitants throughout North America became aware that they shared

a distinctive identity as British colonists. Thirteen different governments presided over the North American colonies, but all of them answered to the British monarchy. Royal officials who expected loyalty from the colonists often had difficulty obtaining obedience. The North American colonists asserted their prerogatives as British subjects to defend their special colonial interests.

## Commerce and Consumption

Eighteenth-century commerce whetted the appetite to consume. Colonial products spurred the development of mass markets throughout the Atlantic world. Huge increases in the supply of colonial tobacco and sugar brought the price of these small luxuries within reach of most free whites, at least from time to time. Colonial goods brought into focus an important lesson of eighteenth-century commerce. Ordinary people, not just the wealthy elite, would buy the things that they desired in addition to what they absolutely needed. With the appropriate stimulus to desire, markets seemed unlimited.

The Atlantic commerce that took colonial goods to markets in England brought objects of consumer desire back to the colonies. English merchants and manufacturers recognized that colonists made excellent customers, and the Navigation Acts gave English exporters privileged access to the colonial market. By midcentury, export-oriented industries in England were growing ten times faster than firms attuned to the home market. Most English exports went to the vast European market, where potential customers outnumbered those in the colonies by more than one hundred to one. But as European competition stiffened, colonial markets became increasingly important. English exports to North America multiplied eightfold between 1700 and 1770, outpacing the rate of population growth after midcentury. When the colonists' eagerness to consume exceeded their ability to pay, English exporters willingly extended credit, and colonial debts soared.

Imported mirrors, silver plate, spices, bed and table linens, clocks, tea services, wigs, books, and more infiltrated parlors, kitchens, and bedrooms throughout the colonies. Despite the many differences among the colonists, the consumption of English exports built a certain material uniformity across region, religion, class, and status. Consumption of English exports did not simply tie the colonists to the British economy. It also made the

colonists look and feel more British, even though they lived at the edge of a wilderness an ocean away from England.

*Colonial goods brought into focus an important lesson of eighteenth-century commerce. Ordinary people, not just the wealthy elite, would buy the things that they desired in addition to what they needed.*

The rising tide of colonial consumption had other less visible but no less important consequences. Because consumption so often arose from desire rather than necessity, it presented colonists—both women and men—with a novel array of choices. In many respects the choices were seemingly trivial: whether to buy knives and forks, teacups, or a clock. But such small choices confronted eighteenth-century consumers with a big question: "What do you want?" As colonial consumers defined and expressed their desires with greater frequency during the eighteenth century, they became accustomed to thinking of themselves as individuals who had the power to make decisions that influenced the quality of their lives—attitudes of considerable significance in the hierarchical world of eighteenth-century British North America.

## Religion, Enlightenment, and Revival

Eighteenth-century colonists could choose from almost as many religions as consumer goods. Virtually all of the bewildering variety of religious denominations represented some form of Christianity, almost all of them Protestant. Roman Catholics concentrated in Maryland as they had since the seventeenth century, but even there they were outnumbered by Protestants. Slaves made up the largest group of non-Christians. A few slaves converted to Christianity in Africa or after they arrived in North America, but most continued to embrace elements of indigenous African religions.

The varieties of Protestant faith and practice ranged across an extremely broad spectrum. Throughout the plantation South and in urban centers like Charleston, New York, and Philadelphia, prominent colonists attended the Anglican Church, conforming to the rituals and relaxed worldliness of the king's faith. In New England, old-style Puritanism splintered into strands of Congregationalism that differed over fine points of theological doctrine. The thousands of immigrants in the middle colonies and the southern backcountry included militant Baptists and Presbyterians. Huguenots who had fled persecution in Catholic France peopled congregations in several cities. In New England, the Congregational Church was the official established church and all residents paid taxes for its support. In the South, the Anglican Church enjoyed a similar status. But in both regions, dissenting faiths grew, and in most colonies adherents of other faiths won the right to worship publicly, although the established churches retained official sanction.

Rivalry and competition for converts often developed among Protestant churches. A faith that affirmed the "priesthood of all believers" (in Martin Luther's famous phrase) empowered Christians to look into their Bibles and their hearts to find God's Way. Not surprisingly, faithful and well-meaning Protestants identified different Ways, denouncing the Ways of others as misguided heresies. The strife engendered by the core of Protestant belief led many colonists to favor toleration of religious differences and peaceful coexistence among disputing churches.

Many educated colonists became deists, looking for God's plan in nature more than in the Bible. Deists shared the ideas of eighteenth-century European Enlightenment thinkers, who believed that science and reason could disclose God's laws in the natural order. During the seventeenth century, Isaac Newton, the brilliant English scientist, demonstrated that all physical objects obeyed precise mathematical laws, such as the law of gravity. Newton's ideas suggested a new vision of the universe and the place of human beings in it. In the Newtonian universe, order was maintained not by the constant intervention of God but by basic mathematical laws. God had presumably created those laws and set the universe in motion, but then he had stepped back, like a watchmaker who assembled a watch and then let it run. To eighteenth-century thinkers, a watchmaker God seemed more distant from the world, less interested in the minutiae of each person's vices and virtues. A watchmaker God was not arbitrary, capricious, or vengeful, plaguing the world with floods, famine, or fires to express his displeasure. Instead, God was orderly and predictable, although still mysterious because the deepest underlying principles of his order remained unknown.

Although human beings seemed to matter less to the Newtonian God, they had an important role

to play. First, they needed to study nature to discover the basic principles of God's order. Second, they must clear away any obstacles that impeded smooth functioning of the natural order. Some obstacles were false ideas, such as that the Bible or the church was the final authority on God's truth. Other obstacles were social or political institutions that violated natural laws. The underlying concept of equality in the Newtonian universe suggested that human beings should try to eliminate social distinctions that violated the principles of the divine order.

## The dominant faith overall was religious indifference.

The ideas associated with a Newtonian universe percolated through the Atlantic world during the eighteenth century, influencing devout Christians as well as skeptical deists. In the colonies as well as in Europe, Enlightenment ideas encouraged people to study the world around them, to think for themselves, and to ask whether the disorderly appearance of things masked the principles of a deeper, more profound order. From New England towns to southern drawing rooms, individuals met to discuss such matters. Philadelphia was the center of these conversations, especially after the formation of the American Philosophical Society in 1769, an outgrowth of an earlier discussion group organized by Benjamin Franklin, who was a deist. The American Philosophical Society fostered communication among leading colonial thinkers; Benjamin Franklin was its first president, Thomas Jefferson its third. Among the purposes of these discussions was to find ways to improve society. Franklin's interest in electricity, stoves, and eyeglasses exemplified the way Enlightenment ideas shifted the gaze of many eighteenth-century colonists from heaven to the here and now.

Most eighteenth-century colonists went to church seldom or not at all, although they probably considered themselves Christians. A minister in Charleston observed that on the Sabbath "the Taverns have more Visitants than the Churches." In the leading colonial cities, church members were a small minority of eligible adults, no more than 10 or 15 percent. Anglican parishes in the South rarely claimed more than one-fifth of eligible adults as members. In some regions of rural New England and the middle colonies, church membership embraced two-thirds of eligible adults, while in other

**GEORGE WHITEFIELD**
*An anonymous artist portrayed George Whitefield preaching, emphasizing the power of his sermons to transport his audience to a revived awareness of divine spirituality. Light from above gleams off Whitefield's forehead. His crossed eyes and faraway gaze suggest that he spoke in a semihypnotic trance. Note the absence of a Bible at the pulpit. Rather than elaborating on God's word as revealed in Scripture, Whitefield speaks from his own inner awareness. The young woman bathed in light below his hands appears transfixed, her focus not on Whitefield but on some inner realm illuminated by his words. Her eyes and Whitefield's do not meet, yet the artist's use of light suggests that she and Whitefield see the same core of holy Truth. The other people in Whitefield's audience appear not to have achieved this state. They remain intent on Whitefield's words, failing so far to be ignited by the divine spark.*
National Portrait Gallery, London.

areas only one-quarter of the residents belonged to a church. The dominant faith overall was religious indifference. As a late-eighteenth-century traveler observed, "Religious indifference is imperceptibly disseminated from one end of the continent to the other."

The spread of religious indifference, of deism, of denominational rivalry, and of comfortable backsliding profoundly concerned many ministers. A few despaired that, as one wrote, "religion . . . lay a-dying and ready to expire its last breath of life." To combat what one preacher called the "dead formality" of church services, some ministers set out to convert the unchurched and to revive the piety of the faithful with a new style of preaching that appealed more to the heart than the head. Historians have termed this wave of revivals the "Great Awak-

ening." In Massachusetts during the mid-1730s, the fiery Puritan minister Jonathan Edwards reaped a harvest of souls by reemphasizing traditional Puritan doctrines of humanity's utter depravity and God's vengeful omnipotence. The title of Edwards's most famous sermon, "Sinners in the Hands of an Angry God," conveys the flavor of his message. In Pennsylvania and New Jersey, Presbyterian William Tennent led revivals dramatizing conventional appeals for spiritual rebirth with accounts of God's miraculous powers—such as raising his son William Tennent Jr. from the dead.

The most famous revivalist in the eighteenth-century Atlantic world was George Whitefield. An Anglican, Whitefield preached well-worn messages of sin and salvation to large audiences in England using his spellbinding, unforgettable voice. Whitefield visited the North American colonies seven times, staying for more than three years during the mid-1740s and attracting tens of thousands in his travels. His sermons transported many in his audience to emotion-choked states of religious ecstasy. At one revival, he wrote, "the bitter cries and groans were enough to pierce the hardest heart. Some of the people were as pale as death; others were wringing their hands; others lying on the ground; others sinking into the arms of their friends; and most lifting their eyes to heaven, and crying to God for mercy. They seemed like persons . . . coming out of their graves to judgment."

Whitefield's successful revivals spawned many lesser imitations. Itinerant preachers, many of them poorly educated, toured the colonial backcountry after midcentury, echoing Whitefield's medium and message as best they could. Educated and established ministers often regarded them with disgust. But in fact, the revivals that they deplored awakened and refreshed the spiritual energies of thousands of colonists struggling with the uncertainties and anxieties of eighteenth-century America. The conversions at revivals did not substantially boost the total number of church members, however. After the revivalists moved on, the routines and pressures of everyday existence reasserted their primacy in the lives of many converts. But revivals imparted an important message to colonists, both converted and unconverted. They communicated that every soul mattered, that men and women could choose to be saved, that individuals had the power to make a decision for everlasting life or death. Colonial revivals expressed in religious terms many of the same democratic and egalitarian values expressed in economic terms by colonists' patterns of consumption. One colonist noted the analogy by referring to itinerant revivalists as "Pedlars in divinity." Like consumption, revivals contributed to a set of common experiences that bridged colonial divides of faith, region, class, and status.

## Bonds of Empire

The plurality of peoples, faiths, and communities that characterized the North American colonies arose from the somewhat haphazard policies of the eighteenth-century British Empire. Since the Puritan Revolution of the mid-seventeenth century, British monarchs had valued the colonies' contributions to trade and encouraged their growth and development. Unlike France—whose policy of excluding Protestants and foreigners kept the popu-

**HURON BONNET**
*This dazzling bonnet illustrates the trade between Native Americans and colonists. Beads of Venetian glass were one of the many items colonists imported from Europe specifically to exchange for animal skins offered by Indian hunters and trappers. Native American women in turn incorporated these European beads into designs they had previously wrought with porcupine quills, shells, bones, and other natural objects. European needle and thread were also used to craft this bonnet. Native American artistry transformed these simple trade goods into a beautiful bonnet useful and valuable among the Huron, who lived near the Great Lakes.*
Musée de l'Homme.

lation of its territory tiny—Britain kept the door to its colonies open to anyone, and tens of thousands of non-British immigrants settled in the North American colonies and raised families. The open door did not extend to trade, however, as the seventeenth-century Navigation Acts restricted colonial trade to British ships and traders. These policies evolved because they served the interests of the monarchy and of influential groups in England and the colonies. The policies of empire gave the colonists a common framework of political expectations and experiences.

At a minimum, British power defended the colonists from foreign enemies. Each colony organized a militia, and privateers sailed from every port to prey on foreign ships. But the British navy and army bore responsibility for colonial defense. Royal officials warily eyed the settlements of New France and New Spain for signs of threats to the colonies. Alone, neither New France nor Spanish Florida jeopardized British North America, but with Indian allies they became a potent force that kept colonists on their guard.

**BEAVER HAT**

*European colonists, like Native Americans, adapted items obtained in trade to their own purposes. The beaver hat shown here is a careful reproduction of a seventeenth-century design. Although a colonial hatmaker pressed and molded beaver skin in the process of manufacture, the animal origins of the hat were still evident in the finished product. A good-quality beaver hat like this one was sturdy, water-repellent, and warm. But compared to the Huron bonnet opposite, it was drab and utilitarian. Women colonists sewed garments of all kinds, but they did not create intricate designs of beadwork on hats or other items.*

Pilgrim Society.

All along the ragged edge of settlement, colonists encountered Indians. Indians' impulse to defend their territory from colonial incursions warred with their desire for trade, which tugged them toward the settlers. The fur trade was the principal medium of exchange between the two groups. To trade for goods manufactured largely by the British—knives, axes, blankets, guns, powder—Indians trapped animals throughout the interior and colonial traders competed for the furs. British officials monitored the trade to prevent French, Spanish, and Dutch competitors from deflecting the flow of hides toward their own markets. Indians took advantage of this competition to improve their own prospects, playing one trader off against another. And Indian tribes and confederacies competed for favored trading rights with one colony or another, a competition colonists encouraged.

The shifting alliances and complex dynamics of the fur trade struck a fragile balance along the frontier. The threat of violence from all sides was ever present, and the threat became reality often enough for all parties to be prepared for the worst.

In the Yamasee War of 1715, Yamasee and Creek Indians—with French encouragement—mounted a coordinated attack against colonial settlements in South Carolina and inflicted heavy casualties. The Cherokees, traditional enemies of the Creeks, refused to join the attack. Instead, they protected their access to British trade goods by allying with the colonists and turning the tide of battle, thus triggering a murderous rampage of revenge by the colonists against the Creeks and Yamasees.

Relations between Indians and the colonists differed from colony to colony and from year to year. But the colonists' nagging perception of menace on the frontier kept them continually hoping for help from the British in keeping the Indians at bay and in maintaining the essential flow of trade. In 1754, the colonists' endemic competition with the French flared into the French and Indian War, which would inflame the frontier for years. Before the 1760s, neither the colonists nor the British developed a coherent policy toward Indians. But both agreed that Indians made profitable trading partners, powerful allies, and deadly enemies.

British attempts to exercise their political power in colonial governments met with success so long as British officials were on or very near the sea. Colonists acknowledged—although they did not always readily comply with—British authority to collect customs duties, inspect cargoes, and enforce trade regulations. But when royal officials tried to wield their authority on land, in the internal affairs of colonies, they invariably encountered colonial resistance. A governor appointed by the king in each of the nine royal colonies (Rhode Island and Connecticut selected their own governors) or by the proprietors in Maryland and Pennsylvania headed the government of each colony. The British envisioned colonial governors as mini-monarchs able to exert influence in the colonies much as the king did in England. But colonial governors were not kings and the colonies were not England.

Eight out of ten colonial governors had been born in England, not in the colonies. Some governors—like the two men who served as governor of Virginia for the first half of the eighteenth century—stayed in England, close to the source of royal patronage, and delegated the grubby details of colonial affairs to subordinates. Even the best-intentioned colonial governors had difficulty developing relations of trust and respect with influential colonists because their terms of office averaged just five years and could be terminated at any time. Too, colonial governors did not have access to many patronage positions to secure political friendships. The officials who administered the colonial customs service, for example, received their positions through patronage networks centered in England rather than in the hands of colonial governors. In obedience to their instructions from England, colonial governors fought incessantly with representatives in the colonial assemblies. They battled over governors' vetoes of colonial legislation, removal of colonial judges, creation of new courts, dismissal of the representative assemblies themselves, and other local issues. Some governors developed a working relationship with the assemblies. But during the eighteenth century, the assemblies developed the upper hand.

British policies did not clearly define the powers and responsibilities of colonial assemblies. In effect, the assemblies made many of their own rules and established a strong tradition of representative government analogous—in their eyes—to the English Parliament. Voters often returned representatives to the assemblies year after year, building continuity in power and leadership that far exceeded that of the governor. By 1720, colonial assemblies had won the power to initiate legislation, including tax laws and authorizations to spend public funds. Although all laws passed by the assemblies (except in Maryland, Rhode Island, and Connecticut) had to be approved by the governor and then by the Board of Trade in England, the difficulties in communication about complex subjects over long distances effectively ratified the assemblies' decisions. Years often passed before laws were repealed, and in the meantime the assemblies' laws prevailed.

The heated political struggles between royal governors and colonial assemblies that occurred throughout the eighteenth century taught colonists a common set of political lessons. They learned to employ traditionally British ideas of representative government to defend their own interests. They learned that power in the British colonies rarely belonged to the British government.

## Conclusion: The Dual Identity of British North American Colonists

During the eighteenth century, a distinctive society emerged in British North America, a society that was both distinctively colonial and distinctively British. Tens of thousands of immigrants and slaves gave the colonies an unmistakably colonial complexion. People of different ethnicities and faiths sought their fortunes in the colonies, where land was cheap, labor was dear, and—as Benjamin Franklin preached— work promised to be rewarding. Indentured servants and redemptioners risked a temporary period of bondage for the potential reward of better opportunities than on the Atlantic's eastern shore. Slaves endured lifetime servitude that they neither chose nor desired, and their masters benefited.

Identifiably colonial products from New England, the middle colonies, and the southern colonies flowed across the Atlantic. Back came unquestionably British consumer goods along with fashions in ideas, faith, and politics. The bonds of the British Empire required colonists to think of themselves as British subjects and, at the same time, encouraged them to consider their status as colonists.

By the 1750s, colonists could not imagine that their distinctively dual identity—as British and as colonists—would soon become a source of intense conflict. But by 1776, colonists in British North America had to choose whether they were British or American.

## CHRONOLOGY

| | |
|---|---|
| **1702** | Queen Anne's War triggers large German immigration to American colonies. |
| **1715** | Yamasee War pits South Carolina colonists against Yamasee and Creek Indians. |

| | |
|---|---|
| **1717** | Scots-Irish immigration to American colonies begins to increase. |
| **1721** | *New England Courant* begins publication. |
| **1723** | Benjamin Franklin arrives in Philadelphia. |

| 1730s | Jonathan Edwards leads New England religious awakening. | | Majority of southern slaves born in the colonies rather than in Africa. |
| 1732 | Georgia founded. | 1741 | New York officials suspect slave conspiracy and execute thirty-one slaves. |
| 1733 | Benjamin Franklin begins to publish *Poor Richard's Almanack*. | 1745 | Olaudah Equiano born in present-day Nigeria. |
| 1737 | The Penn family takes advantage of "Walking Purchase" to claim twice as much land as originally agreed upon with Indians. | 1750s | Colonists begin to move down Shenandoah Valley from Pennsylvania into southern backcountry. Colonists increasingly become indebted to English merchants. |
| 1739 | Slave insurrection occurs at Stono, South Carolina. | 1769 | American Philosophical Society founded in Philadelphia. |
| 1740s | George Whitefield preaches revival of religion throughout colonies. | | |

# SUGGESTED READINGS

Bernard Bailyn, *The Peopling of British North America* (1986). A sweeping overview of immigration to the North American colonies.

Ira Berlin, *Many Thousands Gone: The First Two Centuries of Slavery in North America* (1998). A comprehensive synthesis of the history of slavery in North America during the seventeenth and eighteenth centuries.

Robin Blackburn, *The Making of New World Slavery: From the Baroque to the Modern, 1492–1800* (1997). An expert portrait of slavery in the New World, the hemispheric context of North American slavery.

Kathleen M. Brown, *Good Wives, Nasty Wenches, and Anxious Patriarchs: Gender, Race, and Power in Colonial Virginia* (1996). A fascinating exploration of the intersection of gender, race, and power in colonial Virginia.

Barbara De Wolfe, ed., *Discoveries of America: Personal Accounts of British Emigrants to North America during the Revolutionary Era* (1997). An invaluable collection of rare firsthand accounts of immigration to North America on the eve of the American Revolution.

Olaudah Equiano, *The Interesting Narrative of the Life of Olaudah Equiano Written by Himself,* ed. Robert Allison (1995). The most important autobiography of an eighteenth-century African, telling the spellbinding story of his enslavement and eventual freedom.

Benjamin Franklin, *The Autobiography of Benjamin Franklin,* ed. Leonard W. Labaree et al. (1964). The classic explanation of how to become a success in eighteenth-century America, by one who knew.

Jack P. Greene, *The Intellectual Construction of America: Exceptionalism and Identity from 1492–1800* (1993). A masterful analysis of what North American colonists thought about who they were.

Christine Leigh Heyrman, *Commerce and Culture: The Maritime Communities of Colonial Massachusetts, 1690–1750* (1984). An expertly crafted history of the broader social and cultural consequences of eighteenth-century commerce.

Susan E. Klepp and Billy G. Smith, eds., *The Infortunate: The Voyage and Adventures of William Moraley, an Indentured Servant* (1992). A rare firsthand account of the experiences of an indentured servant.

Philip D. Morgan, *Slave Counterpoint: Black Culture in the Eighteenth-Century Chesapeake and Low Country* (1998). A meticulous comparison of slavery in the Chesapeake and low country during the eighteenth century.

Robert Olwell, *Masters, Slaves, and Subjects: The Culture of Power in the South Carolina Low Country, 1740–1790* (1998). A valuable analysis of the larger cultural influence of slavery in the South Carolina low country.

A. G. Roeber, *Palatines, Liberty, and Property: German Lutherans in Colonial British America* (1993). An expert account of German immigration to the colonies.

Sharon V. Salinger, *"To Serve Well and Faithfully": Labor and Indentured Servitude in Pennsylvania, 1682–1800* (1987). A careful analysis of indentured servitude in the most important of the middle colonies.

Carole Shammas, *The Pre-Industrial Consumer in England and America* (1990). A revealing examination of the English and American worlds of eighteenth-century commerce.

**GILDED BRASS GORGET**

*George Washington wore this small brass* gorget *during the French and Indian War. It symbolized, in miniature, the throat piece of a medieval suit of armor. Eighteenth-century gorgets
probably did not stop many Indian arrows, but they reminded officers of their noble loyalty to
their monarch. The inscribed Latin motto,* En Dat Virginia Quartam, *boasts that Virginia
is fourth in importance in the British Empire, after England, Scotland, and Ireland—and
therefore first among the many American colonies.*

Courtesy of the Massachusetts Historical Society ©.

# THE BRITISH EMPIRE AND THE COLONIAL CRISIS

## 1754–1775

T HOMAS HUTCHINSON WAS A FIFTH-GENERATION DESCENDANT of Anne Hutchinson, the woman of conscience who so rattled the Puritan town of Boston in the 1630s. Thomas Hutchinson likewise was a man of conscience, but there the resemblance to his famous ancestor ended. A Harvard-educated member of the Massachusetts elite, from a family of successful merchants, Hutchinson was also a measured and cautious man. "My temper does not incline to enthusiasm," he once wrote, in a shrewd self-assessment.

After serving two decades in the Massachusetts general assembly, Hutchinson was appointed lieutenant governor in 1758. In 1771, with Boston politics a powderkeg, he agreed to become the royal governor, knowing full well the risks. Despite his family's deep roots in American soil, Hutchinson remained steadfastly loyal to England. His love of order and tradition inclined him to unconditional support of the British Empire, but loyalty was a dangerous choice in Boston after 1765. Hutchinson faced agitated crowds during demonstrations over the Stamp Act, the Townshend duties, the Boston Massacre, and the Boston Tea Party, all landmark events on the road to the American Revolution. Privately he lamented the stupidity of the British acts that provoked trouble, but his sense of duty required him to defend the king's policies, however misguided. Quickly, he became an inspiring villain to the emerging revolutionary movement. The man not inclined to enthusiasm unleashed popular enthusiasm all around him. He never appreciated that irony.

As early as anyone, Thomas Hutchinson recognized the difficulties of maintaining full rights and privileges for Americans so far from their supreme government, the king and Parliament in England. In 1769, soon after British troops had come to occupy Boston, he wrote privately to a friend in England, "There must be an abridgement of what are called English liberties. . . . I doubt whether it is possible to project a system of government in which a colony three thousand miles distant from the parent state shall enjoy all the liberty of the parent state." What he could not imagine was the possibility of giving up the parent state altogether and creating an independent government closer to home.

Thomas Hutchinson was a loyalist; in the 1750s, most English-speaking colonists were affectionately loyal to England. But the French and Indian War, which England and its colonies fought together as allies, shook that affection, and imperial policies in the decade following the war (1763–1773) shattered it completely. Over the course of that decade, serious questions about American liberties and rights were raised insistently and repeatedly, especially over the issues of taxation and

**THOMAS HUTCHINSON**
*The only formal portrait of Thomas Hutchinson still in existence shows an assured young man in ruffles and hair ribbons. Decades of turmoil in Boston failed to puncture his self-confidence. Doubtless he sat for other portraits, as did all the Boston leaders in the 1760s to 1780s, but no other likeness has survived. Hutchinson was hated; any portrait that fell into his enemies' hands would probably have been mutilated.*
Courtesy of the Massachusetts Historical Society ©.

# The French and Indian War

For twenty-two of the first fifty years of the eighteenth century, England was at war, with either France or Spain. Often the colonists in America felt friction from these conflicts, which pitted British colonists in New England against French colonists in Canada. In the 1750s, tensions mounted again, but this time over events originating in America. The French pushed their empire south from Canada into western lands that some British colonists desired for themselves. The result was the costly French and Indian War, which first brought the British and Americans together as allies but then began to split them over questions of war-related expenses.

## French-English Rivalry in the Ohio Valley

The French advanced from Canada into Indian territory in the western region of present-day Pennsylvania, hoping to establish a barrier to British-American expansion. But that same region was already claimed by a group of wealthy Virginians, including the brothers Lawrence and Augustine Washington, who had formed the Ohio Company in 1747 and obtained a grant from the English king to some 200,000 acres of forests. The Virginians were interested in profits from the eventual resale of the land; the British government was more interested in blocking the advances of the French. By 1753, the enterprising Virginians had blazed an eighty-mile road and set up a trading post near present-day Pittsburgh. The Virginia governor, Robert Dinwiddie, himself a major shareholder in the Ohio Company, sent a messenger to warn the French that they were trespassing on Virginia land.

The man who volunteered to be the messenger on this dangerous mission was George Washington, younger half-brother of the Ohio Company leaders. Although he was only twenty-one, Washington was an ambitious youth whose imposing height (six foot three) and air of silent competence convinced the governor he could do the job. The middle child in a family of eight, Washington did not stand to inherit much wealth; his path upward, he knew, required that he cultivate the Virginia elite, so he was eager to volunteer.

Washington returned from his mission with crucial intelligence about French military plans. Impressed, Dinwiddie appointed the youth to lead a small military force west to chase off the adver-

representation. Many on the American side came to believe what Thomas Hutchinson could never credit, that a tyrannical Britain had embarked on a course to enslave the colonists by depriving them of their traditional English liberty. The opposite of liberty was slavery, a condition of unfreedom and of coercion. Political rhetoric about liberty, tyranny, and slavery heated up emotions during the many crises of the 1760s and 1770s. But this rhetoric turned out to be a two-edged sword. The call for an end to tyrannical slavery meant one thing when sounded by Boston merchants whose commercial shipping rights had been revoked; the same call meant something quite different when sounded by black Americans in 1775, locked in the bondage of perpetual slavery.

saries. A skirmish with about forty French soldiers in May 1754 proved inconclusive. In defense, the Virginians erected a flimsy fortification, called Fort Necessity, but in early July a large contingent of French troops stormed and took it.

Thus began the French and Indian War. Unlike earlier French-British conflicts, this one started in America, and its battles would be centered there. By 1756, the war had escalated to include a half dozen European countries, with battles in the Caribbean and in Europe. To the Europeans, the war was known as the Seven Years' War, once it concluded in 1763. But for Americans, with their two-year head start, it actually lasted nine years.

## The Albany Congress and Intercolonial Defense

To succeed in even a limited war, the British needed help from the colonists as well as some prospect of Indian support, or at least neutrality. Colonies from Virginia northward were instructed to send delegates to a meeting in Albany, New York. One goal of the Albany Congress was to construct an intercolonial agency to provide for the mutual defense of the colonies. A second and perhaps more crucial goal was to woo with gifts and promises selected tribes of the powerful Iroquois Nation of western New York.

In June 1754, twenty-four delegates from seven colonies met in Albany, among them Benjamin Franklin of Pennsylvania and Thomas Hutchinson of Massachusetts. These two men, both rising political stars in their home colonies, coauthored a document called the Albany Plan of Union, which proposed a unified administration over all the colonies. A president general, appointed by the crown, together with a grand council, would have powers only over defense and Indian affairs. The Albany Plan humbly reaffirmed Parliament's authority over the colonies; this was no bid for enlarged autonomy of the colonies.

To Franklin's surprise, not a single colony approved the Albany Plan. One assembly feared it was "a Design of gaining power over the Colonies," especially the power of taxation (necessary to pay for defense). Others objected that it would be impossible to agree on unified policies toward hundreds of quite different Indian tribes. Oddly enough, the British government never backed the Albany Plan either, which perplexed both Franklin and Hutchinson, who were earnestly trying to solidify British authority. Many years later, after the Revolution, Franklin wistfully reflected that if the Albany Plan "had been adopted and carried into Execution, the subsequent Separation of the Colonies from the Mother Country might not so soon have happened."

Representatives of the Iroquois League, embracing the Seneca, Mohawk, Onondaga, Cayuga, Oneida, and Tuscarora tribes, also attended the Albany Congress. They collected thirty wagon loads of gifts and made ambiguous promises to the colonists but left without pledging support. The Iroquois preferred to stall and play off the English

**PORTRAIT OF GEORGE WASHINGTON, BY CHARLES WILLSON PEALE**

*In 1772, George Washington posed for the artist Charles Willson Peale in his splendid uniform from the French and Indian War. Note the ornamental gorget (see page 130), the graceful sash, and the brass vest buttons that still meet buttonholes over the Virginian's forty-year-old girth. Washington's pocket contains an "Order of March," implying that military duty still lies ahead. Peale captured Washington's grandeur in his clothes but not his face, which appears plain and simple. Washington wrote a friend that he was "in so grave—so sullen a mood" and often so sleepy "that I fancy the skill of this gentleman's pencil will be hard put to it, in describing to the world what manner of man I am."*

Washington and Lee University.

against the French, for their interests were best served by being on the winning side, which in 1754 looked to be the French.

## The War and Its Consequences

By 1755, Washington's frontier skirmish had turned into a major mobilization of British and American troops against the French. At first the British hoped for quick victory by throwing armies at the French in three strategic places. General Edward Braddock from England was to attack the French at Fort Duquesne in western Pennsylvania, accompanied by George Washington's Virginia militia. In Massachusetts, Governor William Shirley aimed his soldiers at Fort Niagara, critically located between Lakes Erie and Ontario. And finally, forces under William Johnson of New York moved north toward Lake Champlain to push the French back to Canada.

Unfortunately for the British, a French spy learned details of the plans. In July 1755, General Braddock's army of 2,000 British and Virginian troops were ambushed by a combined French and Indian force, leaving 976 killed or wounded. Washington was unhurt, though two horses in succession were shot from under him; Braddock was killed. Despite the humiliation of defeat, Washington's bravery in battle caused the governor to promote him to commander of the Virginia army. At age twenty-two, Washington was beginning to realize his ambitions.

News of Braddock's defeat alarmed the other two armies, then hacking their way through dense New York forests. Shirley's forces gave up their mission, and Johnson's troops were put on the run before reaching Lake Champlain. For the next two years, the British stumbled badly on the American front, with inadequate soldiers and supplies.

What finally turned the war around was the rise to power in 1757 of William Pitt, England's Secretary of State, a man willing to commit massive resources to an all-out war. Within two years, Pitt's strategy resulted in a string of resounding successes, including the capture of Fort Duquesne in 1758 and Fort Niagara and Fort Ticonderoga in 1759. With Niagara and Ticonderoga gone and the British navy now advancing up the St. Lawrence River, the French cities of Montreal and Quebec were isolated from help. The decisive victory was the capture of the seemingly invincible fortress city of Quebec in September 1759 by the young British general James Wolfe.

The backbone of the French in North America was broken by the fall of Quebec. The victory was completed by the surrender of the French at Montreal to Sir Jeffrey Amherst in late 1760. American colonists rejoiced, but the French and Indian War was not officially over yet. Battles continued in the Caribbean, where the French sugar islands Martinique and Guadeloupe fell to the English in 1762, and in Europe and India. France finally capitulated, and the Treaty of Paris was signed in 1763.

The triumph of victory was sweet but short-lived. Much of the territory England should have won in this costly war was given away at the peace negotiations, because of the inexperience of the minister who replaced William Pitt. England at least got Canada, which eliminated the French threat from the north and west. But all French territory west of the Mississippi River, including New Orleans, was transferred to Spain as compensation for its assistance to France during the war. Stranger still, Martinique and Guadeloupe, the Caribbean islands captured late in the war, were returned to France (Map 6.1).

In truth, the French islands in the Caribbean were hardly a threat to Americans, for they provided a profitable trade in smuggled molasses. The main threat to the safety of colonists came instead from Indians disheartened by England's victory. The Treaty of Paris completely ignored the Indians. Indian lands—dense with native populations—were assigned to English rule on the map. With the French gone, the Indians had lost the advantage of having two opponents to play off against each other, and they now had to cope with the westward-moving Americans. Indian policy would soon become a serious bone of contention between the British government and the colonists.

England's version of the victory of 1763 awarded all credit to the mighty British army. In this version, ungrateful colonists had provided inadequate support for a war fought to save them from the French. In defiance of British law, colonists had engaged in smuggling, especially a lively trade in beaver pelts with French fur traders and an illegal molasses trade in the Caribbean. American traders, grumbled the British leaders, were really traitors. William Pitt was convinced that the illegal trade "principally, if not alone, enabled France to sustain and protract this long and expensive war."

Colonists, of course, read the lessons of the war differently. American militia units turned out in force, they claimed, but the troops had been relegated to grunt work by arrogant British military leaders. General Braddock had foolishly bragged to

**MAP 6.1**
*North America before and after the French and Indian War, 1750–1763*
In the peace treaty of 1763, France ceded its interior lands but retained fishing rights and tiny islands in the far north and, more important, several sugar islands in the Caribbean. A large part of France's claim—to land called Louisiana west of the Mississippi River—went not to England but to Spain.

Benjamin Franklin that "these savages may, indeed, be a formidable enemy to your raw American militia, but upon the king's regular and disciplined troops, sir, it is impossible they should make any impression." Braddock's defeat "gave us Americans," Franklin wrote, "the first suspicion that our exalted ideas of the prowess of British regulars had not been well founded."

*The enormous expense of the French and Indian War cast another large shadow over the British victory. At the heart of the matter was disagreement about the relative responsibility the colonists should bear in helping to pay off that debt.*

The human costs of the war were also etched sharply in the minds of New England colonists, who had contributed most of the colonial troops. About one-third of all Massachusetts men between age fifteen and thirty had seen service. Many families lost loved ones, and this cost would not soon be forgotten.

The enormous expense of the war caused by Pitt's no-holds-barred military strategy cast another huge shadow over the victory. By 1763, England's national debt, double what it had been when Pitt took office, posed a formidable challenge to the next decade of leadership in England. At the heart of the matter was disagreement about the relative responsibility the colonists should bear in helping to pay off that debt.

## Tightening the Bonds of Empire

Throughout the 1760s, inconsistent leadership in England pursued a hodgepodge of policies toward the colonies. A new and inexperienced king gained the throne in 1760, and he spent the next ten years searching for a prime minister he could trust. Nearly half a dozen ministers in succession took their turns formulating policies designed to address one basic, underlying British reality: A huge war debt needed to be serviced, and the colonists, as British subjects, should expect to have to pay. From the American side, however, these policies deeply violated what colonists perceived to be their rights and liberties as British subjects.

## British Leadership and the Indian Question

In 1760, in the middle of the French and Indian War, George III, age twenty-two, came to the British throne, quite underprepared for his monarchical duties. The previous king, George II, was his grandfather; his father's death when young George was thirteen, thrust the boy suddenly into the role of heir-apparent. Timid and insecure, the new King George trusted only his tutor, John Stuart, earl of Bute, a Scotsman who was an outsider to power circles in London. George III immediately installed Bute as head of his cabinet of ministers.

Bute opposed Pitt's strategy on the war in America as "too bloody and expensive." He next squandered England's war victory by negotiating the unfavorable Treaty of Paris. Within two years, the best talents in the cabinet had resigned, leaving Bute isolated. In his short remaining time in office, Bute made one other significant decision—to keep a standing army in the colonies. In terms of money and political tension, this was a costly move.

The ostensible reason for keeping ten thousand British troops in America was to maintain the peace between the colonists and the Indians. This was not a misplaced concern. Three months after the Treaty of Paris was signed, Pontiac, chief of the Ottawa tribe in the northern Ohio region, seized the moment to attack the westernmost settlers. From spring until fall 1763, Pontiac's uprising visited destruction on isolated settlements in far western Pennsylvania, the Ohio country, and north into the Great Lakes region. Pontiac mobilized the Chippewa, Huron, Delaware, and Seneca tribes and captured all but three British forts in the region. More than two thousand colonists were killed or taken captive. Scots-Irish men in the town of Paxton, in western Lancaster County, decided that the Pennsylvania assembly was shirking its responsibility to defend against Pontiac's warriors, so they attacked two nearby Indian settlements—inhabited by friendly Conestoga Indians, as it happened— and murdered twenty of them. Several hundred Paxton men then marched on Philadelphia to demand better protection and a larger voice in the state assembly; they were never punished for their murderous vigilante injustice to the Conestoga.

**MOHAWK WARRIOR**
*This rear view of a Mohawk warrior highlights clothes*
*and body decoration: arm and ankle bracelets, earrings,*
*a hair ornament, and body paint. An important element*
*of frontal display is included by the English watercolor*
*artist—the warrior's tomahawk.*
Ville de la Rochelle.

Pontiac's uprising was quelled in December 1763 by
the combined efforts of British and colonial soldiers,
plus the news that French aid to the Indians would
not materialize. Pontiac later wrote to the British,
"All my young men have buried their hatchets."

The potential for continued and costly wars
with the Indians, so well illustrated by Pontiac's uprising, caused the British government to issue an
order, called the Proclamation of 1763, which forbade colonists to settle west of a line drawn from
Canada to Georgia along the crest of the Appalachian Mountains. The ten thousand British

troops were to police this line. Meant as a temporary expedient rather than a permanent boundary,
the line promised to protect not only the Indians but
also the lucrative fur trade, now in British rather
than French hands. But the pressure of frontier population meant that the proclamation line would be
very difficult to enforce. Settlers had already moved
west of the line, as had land speculators, such as
those of Virginia's Ohio Company, who stood to
lose opportunities for profitable resale of their
claims. Bute's decision to leave a standing army in
the colonies was thus cause for concern for western
settlers and eastern speculators alike.

## Growing Resentment of British Authority

The mission of George Grenville, the king's next
chief minister, was to tackle the problem of the war
debt, which in 1763 amounted to £123 million, a
shockingly high figure. The annual interest alone on
the debt was nearly £5 million, owed to anxious
London bankers.

To find increased revenue, Grenville first scru-
tinized the customs service, a division of the government responsible for monitoring the flow of
ships and collecting duties on specified trade items
in both England and America. Grenville found that
customs officers' salaries cost the government four
times what was collected in revenue. The revenue
shortfall was due in part to bribery and smuggling,
and so Grenville began to insist on rigorous attention to paperwork and a strict accounting of collected duties.

The hardest duty for Grenville to enforce was the
one imposed by the Molasses Act of 1733—a stiff tax
of six pence per gallon on any molasses purchased
from non-British sources. The purpose of the tax was
to discourage trade with French Caribbean islands
and redirect the molasses trade to British sugar islands. But it did not work: French molasses remained
cheap and abundant because French planters on
Martinique and Guadeloupe had no use for it. A byproduct of sugar production, molasses was a key ingredient in making rum, a drink the French scorned.
Rum-loving Americans were eager to buy French
molasses, and they flouted the tax law for decades.

Grenville's ingenious solution to this problem
was the Revenue Act of 1764, popularly dubbed the
Sugar Act. It lowered the duty on French molasses
to three pence, making it more attractive for shippers to obey the law, and at the same time raised

penalties for smuggling. The act appeared to be in the tradition of navigation acts, meant to regulate trade. But Grenville had added a new twist: His actual intent was to raise revenue, not redirect trade. He was using an established form of law for new ends, and he was doing it by the novel means of lowering a duty.

The Sugar Act set out tougher enforcement policies. From now on, Grenville announced, all British naval crews could act as impromptu customs officers, boarding ships suspected of smuggling and seizing cargoes found to be in violation. Smugglers caught without proper paperwork would be prosecuted, not in a friendly civil court with a local jury, but in a vice-admiralty court located in Halifax, Nova Scotia, where a single judge presided without a jury. The implication was that justice would be more sure and severe.

Grenville hoped that his tightening of the customs service and the lowered duties of the Sugar Act would reform American smugglers into law-abiding shippers and in turn generate income for the empire. Unfortunately, the decrease in duty was not sufficient to offset the attractions of smuggling, which continued unabated, and the vigilant enforcement of the act greatly annoyed American shippers. The increased numbers of customs officers made it harder for shippers to rely on the old smooth-working system of bribery, and several ugly confrontations occurred in key port cities such as Newport, Rhode Island, and New York City. Reaction to the Sugar Act foreshadowed questions about England's right to tax Americans, but in 1764 objections to the act came principally from Americans in the shipping trades inconvenienced by the law.

One other new act engineered by Grenville added to the growing resentment of British authority. The Currency Act of 1764 flatly prohibited the colonies from printing any paper money. During the French and Indian War, colonies had resorted to paper money to finance wartime expenses. In modest amounts, colonial currency lubricated the economy by increasing the volume of money in a society perpetually short of silver and gold coins. But London merchants squawked about not getting full value for their goods, and Grenville persuaded Parliament to ban new paper money. Colonies were left with no short-term financing flexibility and a reduced flow of money.

From the British point of view, the 1763 Proclamation Act, the Sugar Act, and the Currency Act all seemed to be reasonable efforts to administer the colonies. From the American point of view, however, the British supervision appeared to be a disturbing intrusion into colonial practices.

## The Stamp Act Crisis

By his second year in office, Grenville had made almost no dent in the national debt. Continued evasion prevented the Sugar Act from becoming the moneymaker he had hoped it would be. So in February 1765, he secured passage of the Stamp Act, which precipitated the first major conflict between England and the colonies over Parliament's right to tax.

### Taxation and Consent

The Stamp Act imposed a tax on various colonial documents—newspapers, pamphlets, contracts, court documents, licenses, deeds, wills, ships' bills of lading—and required that a special stamp be embossed on the documents proving that the tax had been paid. Unlike the Sugar Act, which was part of a trade regulation system, the Stamp Act broke new ground. It instituted a tax whose purpose was simply to raise money. Moreover, the tax had to be paid in sterling silver, a condition that made the Stamp Act even more unpopular, because hard money was in short supply.

Grenville was no fool; anticipating that the stamp tax would be unpopular, he delegated the administration of the act to Americans, to avoid the problem of hostility to British enforcers. In each colony, native stamp distributors would be hired at a handsome salary of 8 percent of the revenue collected.

*In February 1765, Grenville secured passage of the Stamp Act, which precipitated the first major conflict between England and the colonies over Parliament's right to tax.*

Grenville's forewarnings came partly from Thomas Hutchinson, lieutenant governor of Massachusetts, who privately lobbied against the tax. Hutchinson immediately appreciated the key legal issue at stake. Aside from the navigation acts, which were intended primarily to regulate trade,

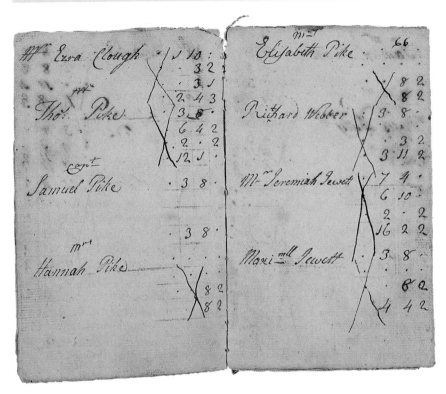

**TAX ASSESSMENT BOOK**
*American colonists routinely paid property taxes to local authorities. This 1772 tax book from Rowley, Massachusetts, records amounts due in pounds, shillings, and pence. The several entries for each name indicate assessments on real estate, personal property, and a poll (per head) tax. Notice that two women owe taxes. Since married women by law owned no property, we can conclude that these were widows. Several numbers are frequently repeated; what might that suggest?*
Chicago Historical Society.

Parliament had levied no taxes on the colonists before this. Hutchinson warned that the colonies could reasonably conclude that Parliament had conceded to them the right to tax themselves. On practical grounds, he also urged the British officials to consider whether trade disruptions caused by the Stamp Act might cost more than the revenue the act generated. But Hutchinson's warnings went unheeded.

The colonists, of course, paid taxes to support their local governments, but the taxing bodies were always the colonial assemblies, composed of elected representatives. A long English tradition held that taxation was a gift of the people to the king offered by the people's representatives. This view of taxes, as a freely given gift, preserved an essential concept of English political theory, the idea that citizens have the liberty to enjoy and use their property without fear of confiscation. The king could not simply demand money; only the House of Commons could grant it. Grenville, in agreement with the notion of taxation by consent, argued that the colonists were already "virtually" represented in Parliament; the House of Commons represented all British subjects, wherever they were. This British view of representation was emphatically rejected by colonial leaders. A Maryland lawyer named Daniel Dulany wrote a best-selling pamphlet explaining that virtual representation, while it might perhaps work within England, could not withstand the stretch across the Atlantic. The Stamp Act itself illustrated the problem: It was levied by a distant Parliament only on the colonies. Voters in Anne Arundel County, Maryland, denounced Grenville's reasoning as illusory: "The MINISTER'S *virtual Representation* in Support of the TAX on us is fantastical and frivolous."

## Resistance Strategies and Crowd Politics

The Stamp Act carried a November 1, 1765, start-up date. News of its passage arrived in the colonies in April 1765, leaving colonial leaders seven months to contemplate a response. Colonial governors were unlikely to challenge the law, since most of them owed their office to the king. Instead, the colonial assemblies took the lead; eight of them held discussions on objections to the Stamp Act.

Virginia's assembly, the House of Burgesses, waded into the implications of objecting to the Stamp Act and learned where that road led. At the very end of the May 1765 session, when two-thirds of the members had already gone home, a twenty-nine-year-old lawyer and political new-comer named Patrick Henry presented a series of resolutions on the Stamp Act that were de-bated and passed, one by one. They came to be called the Virginia Resolves.

The drift of Henry's successive resolutions inched the assembly toward radical opposition to the Stamp Act. The first three resolutions stated the obvious: that Virginians were British citizens, that they enjoyed the same rights and privileges as Britons, and that self-taxation was one of those rights. The fourth resolution noted that Virginians had always taxed themselves, via their representatives in the House of Burgesses. The fifth took the radical leap, by pushing the other four unexceptional statements to one logical conclusion—that the Virginia assembly alone had the sole right to tax Virginians. Henry persuaded the small group of burgesses present to endorse this declaration, but the ebbing numbers of positive votes indicated shrinking support.

Two more fiery resolutions were debated, but majority support eroded as Henry pressed the logic of his case to the extreme. The sixth resolution de-nied any legitimacy to a tax law originating outside Virginia, and a seventh boldly called anyone who disagreed with these propositions an enemy of Vir-ginia. This was too much for the burgesses. They backed away from resolutions six and seven and the following day, after Henry had left, retracted their vote on number five as well.

Their caution hardly mattered, however, be-cause newspapers in other colonies printed all seven Virginia Resolves, creating the impression that a daring first challenge to the Stamp Act had taken place in Virginia. This made it easier for other assemblies to consider more radical ques-tions, and a few finally debated the thorniest of all: By what authority could Parliament legislate for the colonies without also taxing them? No one dis-agreed, in 1765, that Parliament had legislative power over the colonists, who were, after all, British subjects. Several assemblies advanced the argument that there was a distinction between *ex-ternal* taxes, imposed to regulate trade, and *inter-nal* taxes, such as a stamp tax or a property tax, which could only be self-imposed.

By October 1765, delegates sent by nine colo-nial assemblies met in New York City. Calling their meeting the Stamp Act Congress, they petitioned Grenville for repeal of the Stamp Act, while politely affirming their subordination to Parliament. This particular congress was timid and cautious; but the very notion of having an intercolonial meeting held radical potential.

Reaction to the Stamp Act ran far deeper than the politicians in assemblies. Every person whose livelihood required the use of official paper had to decide whether to comply with the act. Hence, local communities strategized their response. Should they boycott all paper usage? Should they conduct business as usual and just ignore the law? A third strategy promised the safest, surest success: to de-stroy the stamped paper or prevent its distribution at the source, before the law took effect. This tactic would ensure universal noncompliance.

The first concerted effort to resist the Stamp Act began in Boston, capital of Massachusetts and port city of about seventeen thousand people packed into a square-mile peninsula. Virtually all of Boston's major occupational groups—lawyers and politi-cians, merchants and shipowners, tradesmen and artisans, dockworkers and sailors—depended on official papers to conduct business. In June 1765, the *Boston Gazette* offered its readers all seven Virginia Resolves as an example of a "spirited" response. The *Gazette* exuberantly appropriated the language of the seventh resolution, calling anyone who agreed that Parliament could tax Massachusetts "AN ENEMY TO THIS HIS MAJESTY'S COLONY."

Over the summer a plan took shape to head off the Boston stamp distribution at its source. The lead-ership behind the plan came from a small group of shopkeepers and master craftsmen, working closely with Samuel Adams, a forty-three-year-old town politician. They called themselves—and anyone who joined them—the Sons of Liberty. Adams, the Harvard-educated son of a prosperous brewer, de-voted himself to politics in the Boston town meeting and in the Massachusetts assembly. In distinct contrast to Thomas Hutchinson, he cared nothing for status, exalted office, or fine material goods. He was obliv-ious to his daily clothing, a matter that occasionally distressed his friends. Adams, however, did have shrewd political instincts and a gift for organizing.

The plan hatched by Samuel Adams and oth-ers called for a large street demonstration high-lighting a ritualized mock execution, designed to convince Andrew Oliver, the stamp distributor, that his personal safety would best be served by re-signing. With no stamp distributor, no stamps could be sold. On the morning of August 14, 1765, an ef-figy (stuffed dummy) of Oliver was found hanging from a tree. The royal governor of Massachusetts,

**SAMUEL ADAMS**

*Samuel Adams consented to pose for Boston artist John Singleton Copley in 1770. The portrait highlights Adams's face, which projects a dramatic intensity and dominates the bulky body, subdued by dark clothes. Adams stares thoughtfully and silently at the viewer and points to important legal documents before him, including the Massachusetts charter of 1689. Wealthy merchant John Hancock commissioned the portrait, which hung in his house. Copley painted scores of Boston's leaders in the 1760s, both loyalists and patriots. He maintained neutrality until 1773, when his father-in-law became an official East India tea distributor. Copley's home was threatened by a crowd, and he left for England in 1774.*

Deposited by the City of Boston, Museum of Fine Arts, Boston.

---

Francis Bernard, met with Hutchinson and the governor's council and decided to take no action, in an effort to keep tensions under control. By evening, a large crowd of two to three thousand people paraded the effigy around town, using it as a prop in short plays demonstrating the dangers of selling stamps. The crowd then pulled down a small building on Oliver's dock, reported to be the future stamp office. Next, at Oliver's house, they beheaded and burned the effigy and broke some windows. The flesh-and-blood Oliver was in hid-

ing; the next day he resigned his office in a well-publicized announcement.

There were lessons from the August 14 demonstration for everyone. Oliver learned that stamp distributors would be very unpopular people. Bernard and Hutchinson learned the limitations of their own powers to govern, with no police to call on. The demonstration's leaders learned that street action was very effective. And hundreds of laborers, sailors, and apprentices not only learned what the Stamp Act was all about but also gained pride in their ability to have a decisive impact on politics.

Twelve days later, a second crowd action, more properly termed a riot, showed just how well some of these lessons had been learned. On August 26, a crowd visited the houses of four detested officials. One was a customs officer and two others were officers of the admiralty courts, where smugglers were tried; windows were broken and wine cellars raided. The fourth house was the finest dwelling in Massachusetts, owned by the stiff-necked Thomas Hutchinson. Rumors abounded that Hutchinson had urged Grenville to adopt the Stamp Act. In fact, he had done the opposite, but he refused to set the record straight, saying curtly, "I am not obliged to give an answer to all the questions that may be put me by every lawless person." The crowd attacked his house, and by daybreak only the exterior walls were standing.

The destruction of Hutchinson's house brought a halt to crowd activities in Boston for a while. The Boston town meeting issued a statement of sympathy; but a reward of £300 for the arrest and conviction of riot organizers failed to produce a single lead. The emerging Sons of Liberty denied planning the event.

Essentially, the opponents of the Stamp Act in Boston had won the day; no one volunteered to replace Oliver as distributor. When November 1 arrived, the day the Stamp Act took effect, the customs officers allowed ships to pass through the harbor without properly stamped clearance papers. They had little choice; they simply did not have the staff to force the ships to halt.

## Liberty and Property

Boston's crowd actions of August sparked similar eruptions by groups calling themselves Sons of Liberty in virtually every colony, and stamp distributors everywhere hastened to resign. A New Hampshire distributor resigned three times in public places, to make sure that the word got out. A Connecticut distributor was forced by a crowd to throw his hat and powdered wig in the air while shouting a cheer of "Liberty and property!" This man fared better than another Connecticut stamp agent, who was nailed in a coffin and lowered in the ground by the local Sons of Liberty. Only when the thuds of dirt sounded on the box did he have a sudden change of heart, shouting out his resignation to the crowd above. In Charleston, South Carolina, the stamp distributor resigned in late October after crowds burned effigies and chanted "Liberty! Liberty!" But when a crowd of Charleston blacks paraded with similar shouts of "Liberty!" a few months later, the town militia turned out to break up the demonstration.

---

*In March 1766, the Stamp Act was repealed, but Parliament then passed the Declaratory Act, which asserted Britain's right to legislate for the colonies "in all cases whatsoever."*

---

The rallying cry of "Liberty and property" made perfect sense to many white Americans of all social ranks who feared that their traditional rights as English subjects were threatened by the Stamp Act. Englishmen claimed liberty as a birthright, meaning that they had a right to be free from interference by other people. The opposite of liberty was slavery, the condition of being under the total control of someone else. Civil society required some interference to perfect freedom in the form of laws, but Englishmen preserved liberty by making sure that only representative governments passed the laws. Up to 1765, Americans consented to accept Parliament as a body that in some way represented them, at least for purposes of legislation. But the right to own property was a special kind of liberty, requiring even stricter safeguards, given the possibility that a greedy ruler might try to deprive citizens of their property. This was why the tradition arose that only a representative body could tax British subjects.

To Americans, the Stamp Act violated this principle of liberty and property, and some Americans began to speak and write about a plot by British leaders to enslave them. A Maryland writer warned that if the colonies lost "the right of exemption from all taxes without their consent," that loss would "deprive them of every privilege distinguishing freemen from slaves." The oppositional meanings of *liberty* and *slavery* were utterly clear to white Americans, who stopped short of applying similar logic to the one million black Americans they held in bondage.

Politicians and merchants in England reacted with alarm to the American demonstrations. Merchants particularly feared trade disruptions and pressured Parliament to repeal the Stamp Act. In the summer of 1765, yet another new minister, Charles Watson-Wentworth, the marquess of Rockingham, headed the king's cabinet and his dilemma was to find a dignified way to repeal the act that did not yield to the Americans' claim that Parliament could not tax them.

Parliament debated repeal, and George Grenville, now a member of that body, seized the occasion to deliver an impassioned condemnation of American ingratitude, which also served to justify his own policy of the stamp tax. "When they want the protection of this kingdom, they are always ready to ask for it. . . . The nation has run itself into an immense debt to give them their protection; and now [when] they are called upon to contribute a small share towards the public expence, an expence arising from themselves, they renounce your authority, insult your officers, and break out, I might almost say, into open rebellion."

No doubt many in the British government shared Grenville's anger, but economic considerations won out. In March 1766, the Stamp Act was repealed, but Parliament at the same time passed the Declaratory Act, which asserted Parliament's right to legislate for the colonies "in all cases whatsoever." Perhaps the stamp tax had been inexpedient, but the power to tax—one prime case of a legislative power—was stoutly upheld.

## The Townshend Acts and Economic Retaliation

Rockingham did not last long as prime minister. By the summer of 1766, George III had persuaded William Pitt to resume that role. Pitt then appointed Charles Townshend to be chancellor of the exchequer, the chief financial minister. Townshend faced both the old war debt problem and the continuing cost of stationing the British army in America, and he turned again to taxation. But Townshend's knowledge of the developing political climate in the colonies was unfortunately limited; his simple idea to raise revenue turned into a major blunder.

## The Townshend Duties

Townshend proposed new taxes in the old form of a navigation act. Officially called the Revenue Act of 1767, it established new duties on tea, glass, lead, paper, and painters' colors imported into the colonies, to be paid by the importer but surely passed on to consumers in the retail price. A year before, the duty on French molasses had been reduced from three pence down to one pence per gallon, and finally the Sugar Act was pulling in a tidy revenue of about £45,000 annually. So it was not unreasonable to suppose that duties on additional trade goods might also improve the cash flow. Townshend assumed that external taxes—that is, duties levied on the transatlantic trade—would be more acceptable to Americans than internal taxes, such as the stamp tax. He also established an American Board of Customs Commissioners to be located in Boston, a decision that showed Townshend was not very shrewd about colonial protest politics.

The Townshend duties by themselves were not especially burdensome, but the principle they embodied—taxation extracted through trade duties—looked different to the colonists now, when seen against the backdrop of the Stamp Act crisis. If Americans once distinguished between external and internal taxes, that distinction was wiped out by an external tax meant only to raise money. John Dickinson, a Philadelphia lawyer, articulated this view in a series of articles titled *Letters from a Farmer in Pennsylvania,* widely reprinted in the winter of 1767–68. "We are taxed without our consent. . . . We are therefore—SLAVES," Dickinson wrote, calling for "a total denial of the power of Parliament to lay upon these colonies any 'tax' whatever."

A controversial provision of the Townshend duties directed that some of the revenue generated would be used to pay the salaries of royal governors. Before 1767, local assemblies set the salaries of their own officials, giving them significant influence over crown-appointed officeholders. But the assemblies seemed to Townshend to be getting out of hand, and he wanted to strengthen the independence of the governors.

In New York, for example, the assembly had refused to enforce a British rule of 1765 called the Quartering Act, which directed the colonies to furnish shelter and provisions for the British army, and the royal governor was unable to make them comply. The assembly argued that the Quartering Act was really a tax measure since it required New Yorkers to pay money by order of Parliament. Townshend came down hard on the New York assembly: He orchestrated a parliamentary order, the New York Suspending Act, which declared all of the assembly's acts null and void until it met its obligations to the army.

Both these measures—the new way to pay royal governors' salaries and the suspension of the governance functions of the New York assembly—struck a chill throughout the colonies. Many Americans wondered if their legislative government was at all secure.

The Massachusetts assembly quickly took the lead in protesting the Townshend duties. Samuel Adams, a member from Boston, argued that any form of parliamentary taxation was unjust because Americans were not represented in Parliament and that the new way to pay the governors' salaries subverted the proper relationship between the people and their rulers. The assembly circulated a letter with Adams's arguments to other colonial assemblies and urged their endorsement. Not since the Stamp Act Congress of 1765 had there been any similar attempt to coordinate the response of the colonies to British measures.

> *"We are taxed without our consent. . . . We are therefore—SLAVES," wrote Philadelphia lawyer John Dickinson, calling for "a total denial of the power of Parliament to lay upon these colonies any 'tax' whatever."*

In response to Adams's letter, the new man in charge of colonial affairs in Britain, Wills Hill, Lord Hillsborough, instructed the Massachusetts governor, Francis Bernard, to dissolve the assembly if it refused to rescind its statement. The assembly refused, by a vote of 92 to 17, and Governor Bernard carried out his instruction. In the summer of 1768, Boston was in an uproar.

## Nonconsumption and the Daughters of Liberty

The Boston town meeting had already passed resolutions, termed "nonconsumption agreements," calling for a boycott of British-made goods. Dozens of other towns passed similar resolutions in 1767 and 1768. For example, prohibited purchases in the town of New Haven, Connecticut, included carriages, furniture, hats, clothing, shoes, lace, iron plate, clocks, jewelry, toys, textiles, velvets, linseed oil, malt liquors, and cheese. The idea was to encourage home manufacture of such items and to hurt trade with Britain, causing London merchants to pressure Parliament for repeal of the duties.

But nonconsumption agreements were very hard to enforce. With the Stamp Act, there was one hated item, a stamp, and a limited number of official distributors. In contrast, an agreement to boycott all British goods required serious personal sacrifice from many individuals. Some merchants were wary of nonconsumption because it hurt their pocketbooks, and a few continued to import in readiness for the end of nonconsumption (or indeed to sell on the side to people choosing to ignore nonconsumption). In Boston, such merchants found themselves blacklisted in newspapers and broadsides.

A more direct blow to trade came from nonimportation agreements, but it proved even more difficult to get merchants to agree to these. There was always the risk that merchants in other colonies might continue to trade and thus receive handsome profits if neighboring colonies prohibited trade. Not until late 1768 could Boston merchants agree to suspend trade through nonimportation agreements. Sixty men signed the agreement, to be in effect exactly one year—from January 1, 1769, to January 1, 1770. New York merchants soon followed suit, as did Philadelphia and Charleston merchants in 1769.

Doing without British products, whether they were luxury goods or basics such as tea or textiles, no doubt was a hardship for the American population. But it also presented an opportunity, for many of the British goods specified in nonconsumption agreements were household items and goods traditionally under the control of women. By 1769, male leaders in the patriot cause clearly understood that women's cooperation in nonconsumption and home manufacture was essential. The Townshend duties thus provided an unparalleled opportunity for developing and showcasing female patriotism. During the Stamp Act crisis, Sons of Liberty took to the streets in protest. During the difficulties of 1768–1769, the Daughters of Liberty emerged and gave shape to a new idea—that women could play a role in public affairs.

Any individual woman could express affiliation with the colonial protest by complying with the nonconsumption agreements and by taking up home manufacture of items previously imported from England. One young Philadelphia woman inscribed some "patriotic poesy" in her commonplace book in 1768, the gist of which was that women can take up the patriotic cause even if men falter and stumble: "If the Sons (so degenerate) the Blessing despise, / Let the Daughters of Liberty nobly arise, / And tho' we've no Voice, but a negative here, / The use of the Taxables, let us forbear, / (Then Merchants import till yr. Stores are all full / May the Buyers be few and yr. Traffick be dull.) / Stand

**EDENTON TEA LADIES**
*American women in many communities renounced British apparel and tea during the early 1770s. Women in Edenton, North Carolina, publicized their pledge and drew hostile fire in the form of a British cartoon. The cartoon's message is that brazen women who meddle in politics will undermine their femininity. Neglected babies, urinating dogs, wanton sexuality, and mean-looking women are some of the dire consequences, according to the artist. The cartoon works as humor for the British because of the gender inversions it predicts and because of the insult it poses to American men.*
Library of Congress.

firmly resolved and bid Grenville to see / That rather than Freedom, we'll part with our Tea." Women in some towns met together formally to sign nonconsumption agreements.

Homespun cloth became a prominent symbol of patriotism. In the latter half of 1769, dozens of towns organized public spinning "frolicks" or bees where women staged competitions in spinning and weaving. Cloth making was no longer simply a chore of family service but a task invested with political content. A Connecticut girl who spun ten knots of wool in one day proclaimed in her diary that her work made her feel "Nationly."

On the whole, the year of boycotts was a success. British imports fell by more than 40 percent, and British merchants felt the pinch.

## Military Occupation and "Massacre" in Boston

By the summer of 1768, Boston's royal officials felt alarm. Townshend's new customs commissioners had fled to an island in Boston harbor for safety. On August 15, a rollicking celebration of the Stamp Act demonstration of 1765 put crowds in the street and apprehension in the hearts of Governor Bernard and Lieutenant Governor Hutchinson. With no police force and no reasonable hope of controlling the town militia, Bernard concluded that he needed British soldiers to keep the peace.

In the fall of 1768, three thousand uniformed troops arrived to occupy Boston. The soldiers conspicuously drilled on the Common, played loud music on the Sabbath, and in general grated on the nerves of Bostonians. To occupy their spare time, some soldiers took casual day-labor work, putting themselves in direct competition with laboring Bostonians for low-wage jobs.

Although the situation was frequently tense, there were no major troubles during that winter and through most of 1769. But as January 1 approached, marking the end of the nonimportation agreement, it was clear that some merchants could no longer be kept in line. Thomas Hutchinson's two sons, for example, were both importers hostile to the boycott, and they had already ordered new goods from England. The early months of 1770 were thus bound to be an eventful and conflict-ridden period in Boston.

Serious troubles began in January. The shop of the Hutchinson sons was visited by a crowd that smeared "Hillsborough paint," a potent mixture of human excrement and urine, on the door. In mid-February, a crowd surrounded the house of Ebenezer Richardson, a cranky, low-level customs official. Richardson panicked and pulled out his musket, but when he fired it, the shot struck an eleven-year-old boy on the fringes of the crowd; the boy died within hours. The Sons of Liberty mounted a massive funeral procession to mark this first instance of violent death in the struggle with England.

For the next week, heightened tensions gripped Boston, and frequent brawls occurred. The climax came on Monday evening, March 5, 1770, when a small crowd taunted a soldier guarding the customs house. Among other things, he was called a "damned rascally Scoundrel Lobster Son of a Bitch." (The red uniforms of the British were often likened to lobsters.) British Captain Thomas Preston decided to send a seven-man guard to join the lone sentry. Meanwhile, the hostile crowd grew, and the soldiers raised their loaded muskets in defense. Onlookers threw snowballs, daring the soldiers to fire. Preston restrained his men, but finally one of the soldiers, hit by a piece of ice, slipped to the ground and rose up with a blast from his gun. After a second's pause, the other soldiers fired as well. Eleven men in the crowd were hit, five of them fatally. The victims had funerals befitting martyrs, with elaborate orations by leaders of the Sons of Liberty about the threat to all Americans posed by the British army.

The Boston Massacre, as it quickly became called, was over in minutes, but its repercussions were serious and long-lasting. In the immediate aftermath, Hutchinson (now acting governor after Bernard's recall to England) showed courage in confronting the crowd personally, from the balcony of the customs house. By daybreak of March 6, he ordered the removal of the regiments to an island in the harbor to prevent further bloodshed. Hutchinson also jailed Preston and the eight soldiers, as much for their own protection as to appease the townspeople, and promised they would be held accountable for their actions.

Preston and the soldiers came to trial in the fall of 1770, defended by two young attorneys, Samuel Adams's cousin John Adams and Josiah Quincy. Because Adams and Quincy had direct ties to the leadership of the Boston Sons of Liberty, their decision to defend the British soldiers at first seems odd. But John Adams was deeply committed to the idea that even unpopular defendants deserve a fair trial. Samuel Adams respected his cousin's decision to take the case, for there was a tactical benefit as well.

***THE BLOODY MASSACRE PERPETRATED IN KING STREET, BOSTON, ON MARCH 5, 1770***
*This mass-produced engraving by Paul Revere sold for six pence per copy. In this patriot version, the soldiers fire on an unarmed crowd under orders of their captain. The tranquil dog is an artistic device to signal the crowd's peaceful intent; not even a deaf dog could actually hold that pose during the melee. Among the five killed was Crispus Attucks, a black dockworker, but Revere shows only whites among the casualties.*
Anne S. K. Brown Military Collection, Providence, R.I.

It showed that the Boston leadership was not lawless but could be seen as defenders of British liberty and law.

Preston was fully acquitted of all responsibility for the Boston Massacre, as were all but two of the soldiers; the two were convicted of manslaughter and then branded on the thumbs and released. John Adams and Samuel Adams were very satisfied with the outcome. Nothing materialized in the trial to fix blame for the massacre on anyone—not on the soldiers, or on any crowd participants, or on the leaders of the Sons of Liberty. The defense lawyers were no doubt men of integrity, but they were at the same time very sympathetic to the patriot side. They astutely chose to defend without pointing the finger of blame elsewhere. To this day, the question of who was responsible for the Boston Massacre remains obscure.

## The Tea Party and the Coercive Acts

In the same week as the Boston Massacre, the new British prime minister, Frederick North, contemplated the decrease in trade caused by the Townshend duties and recommended repeal. A skillful politician, Lord North took office in 1770 and kept it for twelve years; at last King George had stability at the helm. North sought peace with the colonies and prosperity for British merchants, so all the Townshend duties were removed, except the tax on tea, a pointed reminder of Parliament's ultimate power. North hoped to cool tensions without sacrificing principles.

Those few Americans who could not abide the symbolism of the tea tax turned to smuggled Dutch tea. The renewal of trade and the return of cooperation between England and the colonies gave men like Thomas Hutchinson hope that the worst of the crisis was behind them. For nearly two years, it looked as though Hutchinson's hope might be realized.

## The Calm before the Storm

With the repeal of the Townshend duties came an end to the nonimportation agreements, despite the tax on tea. Trade boomed in 1770 and 1771. Moreover, the leaders of the popular movement seemed to be losing their power. Samuel Adams, for example, ran for a minor local office in Boston and lost to a conservative merchant.

In 1772, however, several incidents brought the conflict with England into focus again. One was the burning of the *Gaspée*, a Royal Navy ship chasing down suspected smugglers off the coast of Rhode Island. Although a royal investigating commission failed to arrest anyone, it announced it would send suspects, if it found any, to England for trial for high treason.

This decision seemed to fly in the face of the traditional English right to a trial by a jury of one's peers. When the news of the *Gaspée* investigation spread, it was greeted with disbelief in other colonies. Patrick Henry, Thomas Jefferson, and Richard Henry Lee from the Virginia House of Burgesses proposed that a network of standing committees be established to link the colonies and pass along alarming news. By mid-1773, every colonial assembly except Pennsylvania had a "committee of correspondence." The British handling of the *Gaspée* incident had backfired, for it provoked the first serious effort to create semiofficial links among the American colonial governments.

Another British action in 1772 further spread the communications network of committees of correspondence. Lord North proposed to pay the salaries of superior court justices out of the tea revenue, in a move parallel to Townshend's earlier plan

for royal governors. The Boston town meeting, alarmed that judges would now be in the pockets of their new paymasters, established a committee of correspondence and urged other towns to do likewise. The first vital message, circulated far and wide in December 1772, attacked the judges' salary policy as the latest proof of a British plot to undermine traditional English "liberties": unjust taxation, military occupation, massacre, now capped by the subversion of justice.

By spring 1773, half of the towns in Massachusetts had set up their own committees of correspondence, providing local forums for debate stimulated by letters sent out by the more radical Boston group. Committees of correspondence politicized ordinary townspeople and bypassed the usual flow of political power and information through the colony's royal government.

The third and final incident that irrevocably shattered the relative calm of the early 1770s was the Tea Act of 1773. Americans had been drinking moderate amounts of English tea and paying the tea duty without objection, but they were also smuggling large quantities of Dutch tea, causing the British East India Company to experience sagging sales. So Lord North proposed special legislation giving favored status to the East India Company, allowing it to sell its tea through special agents, appointed by the government, rather than through public auction to independent merchants. The hope was that the price of the East India tea, even with the duty, would then fall below that of the smuggled Dutch tea, creating an incentive for Americans to obey the law as well as boosting sales for the East India Company.

## The Boston Tea Party

In the fall of 1773, news of the Tea Act reached the colonies. Parliamentary legislation to make tea inexpensive struck many colonists as a subtle and therefore evil plot to trick Americans into buying large quantities of the duties tea. The real goal, some argued, was the increased revenue, which would then be used to pay the royal governors and judges. The Tea Act was thus a sudden and painful reminder of Parliament's claim to the power to tax and legislate for the colonies.

As with the Stamp Act and the Townshend duties, the colonists' strategy was crucial. Nonimportation was not a viable option, because the trade was too lucrative to expect colonial merchants to give it up willingly. Consumer boycotts of tea had

## Who Got Tarred and Feathered, and Why?

Tarring and feathering as a form of vigilante brutality has long been associated with the American Revolution. British political cartoons gave wide currency to images of befeathered victims in humiliating postures. Boston loyalist Peter Oliver (brother-in-law of Thomas Hutchinson) claimed that tarring and feathering was an American invention and supplied shocked British friends with the "recipe," as he termed it:

> First, strip a Person naked, then heat the Tar until it is thin, & pour it upon the naked Flesh, or rub it over with a Tar Brush, *quantum sufficit*. After which, sprinkle decently upon the Tar, whilst it is yet warm, as many Feathers as will stick to it. Then hold a lighted Candle to the Feathers, & try to set it all on Fire; if it will burn so much the better.

Both the cartoon depictions and Oliver's recipe for this messy ritual must be taken cautiously, however, for they were promulgated by pro-British men who had a stake in portraying Americans as barbarians. How often did tarring and feathering really occur? Who were the victims? Was actual harm done? Answers to such questions allow historians to evaluate the role of violence and terrorism as tactics of revolutionary struggle.

Recorded incidents of tarring and feathering do not support Oliver's assertion that the practice was frequent. Probably fewer than a dozen instances occurred between 1765 and the outbreak of war in April 1775. The practice peaked in popularity in the turbulent year 1775, making a total of perhaps two to three dozen cases in all the colonies.

Tarred and feathered victims were *not* British officials. Instead, they were colonists who openly identified with British authority. Often, more moderate demonstrations of crowd displeasure prevailed, such as hanging or burning an effigy of the victim's body or conducting a mock funeral. Using a body substitute made a chilling point and released anger without doing any real physical harm.

Tarring and feathering pushed the boundaries of restraint, for the act involved considerable bodily discomfort. Victims of the sticky, feathery assault were usually community members suspected of being informers, violators of agreements to spurn British goods, or men conspicuous for their animosity toward the revolutionary point of view. They were men *of* the community who had to be

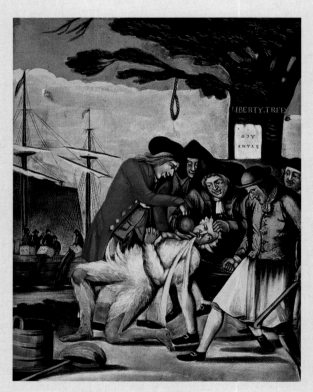

**TAR AND FEATHERING CARTOON**
*John Malcolm, a customs official in Boston, becomes a feathery chicken forced to drink tea. A tar bucket and brush are in the left foreground; the Boston Tea Party— in reality ten months before the cartoon was published— proceeds in the rear. The Liberty Tree has become a gallows; posted to it is the Stamp Act, upside down.*
Courtesy of John Carter Brown at Brown University.

ritually distanced from the community for breaking a moral code, not a law. The standard treatment for lawbreakers was a flogging, fine, or jail, imposed by a judge. Transgressors of the moral code, in contrast, got symbolic punishments from their neighbors on the local committee of public safety, without benefit of legal procedures.

Tarring and feathering was a severe variant in a long tradition of ritual humiliations for transgressive people. Typical humiliations imposed on fornicators, adulterers, or other deceivers included dressing victims in clothes of the opposite sex, riding them around town backward on an ass, or making them stand in public wrapped in white sheets. The object was to shame them into apologizing for their bad behavior as a condition of acceptance back into the community. Tarring and feathering introduced a new variation on the theme: A person was rendered into an animal—a fowl or chicken—and paraded around in a state of near nakedness, the better to garner public shame.

For example, in 1771 a Providence, Rhode Island, man suspected of informing on smugglers was stripped, tied up, painted with warm tar, and feathered, after which dirt was thrown in his face. A man in Charleston, South Carolina, snarled, "Damnation to the Committee and their proceedings" and was soon tarred and feathered for his outburst. A New Jersey artisan who reviled the Continental Congress in late 1775 was set upon by townsmen, stripped, tarred and feathered, and paraded in a wagon for a half hour until he begged pardon. Probably the most famous case occurred in 1774, involving the Bostonian John Malcolm, a dishonest customs collector who extorted extra money from shippers. Malcolm's horrid fate was immortalized in a London cartoon showing five cruelly gleeful Americans forcing tea into his mouth, yanking his hair, and terrorizing him with a noose about his neck.

Peter Oliver's assertion that feathers were set on fire was a serious exaggeration. Hot tar of course hurt, and the eventual removal of the suit of feathers posed the risk of additional pain. It mattered what feathers were used. Soft goose down was an expensive household item in the eighteenth century; few Revolutionary women would relinquish treasured quilts and pillows easily. A more prevalent source of feathers, scratchy ones at that, was the chicken coop. Powerful humiliation, not serious injury, was the goal. In one of the few known instances of a female-inspired sticky assault, girls at a quilting frolic in a small Hudson River village in fall 1775 reportedly stripped to the waist a young man of loyalist sympathies and adorned him with molasses and weeds.

In one unusual case, British soldiers in Boston in March 1775 turned the tables and attacked a rural man who had tried to buy a gun from a soldier. The man was stripped, tarred, feathered, and hauled around on a cart, with a sign affixed to his back proclaiming, "American Liberty, or a Specimen of Democracy"—meaning, a sorry specimen. A fife and drum accompanied him, playing "Yankee Doodle" to irritate the Bostonian onlookers, and twenty bayonet-bearing British soldiers surrounded him, to prevent a rescue attempt. The soldiers' inversion fundamentally changed the ritual: No longer community-confirming, the event became in their hands a mockery of the civilian population.

Tarring and feathering was not practiced often. Other tactics involving less personal violence were more frequently used: publishing offenders' names in the newspaper, boycotting businesses, intimidating their families, and breaking windows. Sometimes just the threat of a tar and feather treatment was sufficient, as when a Pennsylvania loyalist had his nose pushed up to a barrel of tar or when a warning directed at an individual mysteriously appeared in a newspaper, signed by a fictional "Committee for Tarring and Feathering."

Peter Oliver did not think so, but historians generally agree that the years of revolutionary turmoil from 1765 to the 1770s were remarkably free of serious personal violence, aside from organized warfare. The Boston Massacre of five people hardly qualifies as a massacre by twentieth-century war zone standards. Tarring and feathering was rough stuff, but it did not cause death. The American Revolution, even in its aspects that resemble a civil war, stopped short of the kind of massive bloodshed and torture of civilians against civilians that would characterize revolutions from the 1789 French Revolution onward.

proved ineffective since 1770, chiefly because it was impossible to distinguish between dutied tea (the object of the boycott) and smuggled tea (illegal but politically clean) once it was in the teapot. Like the Stamp Act, the Tea Act mandated special agents to handle the tea sales, and that requirement pointed to the solution for anti-tea activists. In nearly every port city, revived Sons of Liberty found ways to pressure tea agents to resign.

The Boston Sons of Liberty were slower to act than their compatriots in other cities, but their action—more direct and illegal than anywhere else—ultimately provoked the most alarming reprisals from England. Three ships bearing tea arrived in Boston in late November 1773. They cleared customs and unloaded their other cargoes, but not the tea. Sensing the extreme tension, the captains wished to return to England, but because the ships had already entered the harbor, they could not get clearance to leave without first paying the tea duty. On top of that, there was a twenty-day limit on the stay allowed in the harbor, by which time either the duty had to be paid or the tea would be confiscated and sold by the authorities. Governor Hutchinson refused to bend any rules.

For the full twenty days, pressure built in Boston. Daily mass meetings energized the citizenry not only from Boston but from surrounding towns, alerted by the committees of correspondence. On the final day, December 16, a large crowd gathered at Old South Church to hear Samuel Adams declare, "This meeting can do nothing more to save the country." This was a signal to initiate the end of the stalemate. The meeting adjourned to the harbor, where some five dozen men dressed as Indians destroyed the tea while a crowd of two thousand watched. It took three hours to dump 342 chests of tea—weighing ninety thousand pounds—into Boston harbor; its value was £10,000 sterling. Bostonians quickly dubbed the event the Boston Tea Party, a jolly name that blunted the massive illegal destruction of property.

## The Coercive Acts

Lord North's response was swift and stern. Within three months he persuaded Parliament to issue the first of the Coercive Acts, a series of four laws meant to punish Massachusetts for the Tea Party. The laws were soon known as the Intolerable Acts in America, along with a fifth one not aimed at Massachusetts alone, the Quebec Act.

The first, the Boston Port Act, closed Boston harbor to all shipping traffic as of June 1, 1774, for as long as the destroyed tea was not paid for. In effect, England was obliterating the commercial life of the city.

The second act, called the Massachusetts Government Act, altered the colony's charter (in itself an unprecedented step, underscoring Parliament's claim to supremacy over Massachusetts): The royal governor's powers were greatly augmented; the council became an appointive, not elective, body; and no town meeting beyond the annual spring election of town selectmen could be held unless the governor expressly permitted it. Not only Boston but every Massachusetts town felt the punitive sting.

The third of the Coercive Acts, the Impartial Administration of Justice Act, stipulated that any royal official accused of a capital crime—for example, Captain Preston and his soldiers at the Boston Massacre—would now be tried in a court in England. It did not matter that Preston in fact got a fair trial in Boston. What this act ominously suggested was that down the road, there might be more Captain Prestons and soldiers firing into crowds.

*If England could step on Massachusetts and change its charter, suspend government, inaugurate military rule, and on top of that give Ohio to Catholic Quebec, then what liberties were possibly secure?*

The fourth of the Coercive Acts was a new amendment to the 1765 Quartering Act, permitting military commanders to lodge soldiers wherever necessary, even in private households. For Boston this was no idle gesture, for in a related move Lord North appointed General Thomas Gage, commander of the Royal Army in New York, to be the new governor of Massachusetts. Thomas Hutchinson was out, relieved at long last of his duties, and military rule, including soldiers, returned once more to Boston.

The fifth Intolerable Act, the Quebec Act, had little to do with the first four but, ill-timed, it greatly fed the fear of Americans. It confirmed the continuation of French civil law, government form, and Catholicism for Quebec, all an affront to Protestant New Englanders denied their own representative government. The act also gave Quebec control of

**BOSTONIANS IN DISTRESS**
*This British cartoon portrays the effects of the closure of the port of Boston in 1774. Men in a cage, surrounded by cannons and British soldiers, act like animals eating raw fish. The three fishermen get a bundle labeled "promises" in return. Is this cartoon sympathetic to the distress of Boston, or is it scornful?*
Courtesy of the John Carter Brown Library at Brown University.

disputed lands (and hence control of the lucrative fur trade) throughout the Ohio River valley, lands claimed variously by Virginia, Pennsylvania, and Connecticut.

The Coercive Acts spread alarm to all the colonies. If England could step on Massachusetts and change its charter, suspend government, inaugurate military rule, and on top of that give Ohio to Catholic Quebec, then what liberties were possibly secure? Fearful royal governors in a half dozen colonies suspended sitting assemblies, adding to

the sense of urgency; some defiantly continued to meet in new locations. Via the committees of correspondence, the colonies agreed to meet in Philadelphia in the fall of 1774 to respond to the crisis.

## The First Continental Congress

Every colony except Georgia sent delegates to Philadelphia for the meeting of the First Continental Congress in September 1774. The gathering included the leading patriots, such as Samuel and John Adams from Massachusetts and George Washington and Patrick Henry from Virginia. A few colonies sent men who were cool to provoking a crisis with England, like Pennsylvania's Joseph Galloway. Whatever their views, most of the delegates were the leading statesmen of their localities. John Adams wrote to his wife, Abigail, that "the magnanimity and public spirit which I see here make me blush for the sordid, venal herd which I have seen in my own Province."

Two difficult tasks confronted the congress: The delegates wanted to agree on exactly what liberties they claimed as English subjects and what rights Parliament held over them, and they needed to make a unified response to the Coercive Acts. Some delegates wanted a total ban on trade with England, to force a repeal of the Coercive Acts, but others—especially from the southern colonies heavily dependent on the export of tobacco and rice—could not afford such a comprehensive stoppage. Samuel Adams and Patrick Henry were more than eager for a ringing denunciation of all parliamentary control, whereas the conservative Joseph Galloway proposed a plan (quickly defeated) to create a colonial miniparliament in America to assist the British Parliament in ruling the colonies.

The congress met for seven weeks in Carpenter's Hall, Philadelphia, and eventually hammered out a declaration of rights, couched in traditional language: "We ask only for peace, liberty and security. We wish no diminution of royal prerogatives, we demand no new rights." Yet the rights assumed already to exist were in fact radical, from England's point of view. Chief among them was the claim that Americans were not represented in Parliament and so each colonial government had the sole right to legislate for and tax its own people. The one slight concession to England was a carefully worded agreement that the colonists would "cheerfully consent" to trade regulations for the larger good of the empire—so long as trade regulation was not a covert means of raising revenue. By consenting to this one power, however, the patriots were implying their right to revoke consent at any time.

To put pressure on England, the delegates agreed to a staggered and limited boycott of trade—imports prohibited this year, exports the following year, and rice totally exempted, to keep South Carolinians happy. To enforce the boycott, they created a mechanism called the Continental Association, with chapters in each town. Local associations, variously called committees of public safety or of inspection, would monitor all commerce and confront suspected violators of the boycott. Its work done, the congress disbanded on October 26, 1774, with a vote to reconvene the following May in a Second Continental Congress.

The committees of public safety, the committees of correspondence, the regrouped colonial assemblies, and the Continental Congresses were all functioning political bodies without any formal constitutional authority. British officials did not recognize them as legitimate, but many Americans who supported the patriot cause instantly accepted them. A key reason for the stability of such unauthorized bodies throughout the Revolutionary period was that they were composed of the same men, by and large, who had composed the official bodies now disbanded.

## Domestic Insurrections

Before the Second Continental Congress could meet, war began in Massachusetts. General Thomas Gage, military commander and new governor, at first thought he faced a domestic insurrection that needed only a show of force to quiet it. The rebels saw things differently: They were defending their homes and liberties against an intrusive power bent on enslaving them. To the south, a different and inverted version of the same story began to unfold, as thousands of enslaved black men and women seized an unprecedented opportunity to mount a different kind of domestic insurrection, against planter-patriots who looked over their shoulders uneasily whenever they called out for liberty from the British.

### Lexington and Concord

Over the winter of 1774–1775 Americans pressed on with boycotts. Some hoped for the repeal of the Coercive Acts, while pessimists started accumulating arms and ammunition. In Massachusetts, gunpowder and shot were secretly stored, and militia units called "minutemen" prepared to respond on a minute's notice to any threat from the British in Boston.

Thomas Gage soon realized how desperate the British position was. The people, he wrote Lord North, were "numerous, worked up to a fury, and not a Boston rabble but the freeholders and farmers of the country." He strongly advised repeal of the

**MAP 6.2**
*Lexington and Concord, April 1775*
*Under pressure from England, British forces at Boston staged a raid on a suspected rebel arms supply in Concord, Massachusetts, starting the first battle of the Revolutionary War.*

Coercive Acts, but leaders in England could not admit failure. Instead Gage was ordered in mid-April 1775 to arrest the troublemakers immediately, before the Americans got better organized.

Gage quickly planned a surprise attack on a suspected ammunition storage site at Concord, a village about eighteen miles west of Boston (Map 6.2). Near midnight on April 18, 1775, British soldiers moved west across the Charles River. Boston silversmith Paul Revere raced ahead to alert the minutemen. When the British soldiers got to Lexington, a village five miles east of Concord, they met with some seventy armed American men, who at first backed down. But then someone fired; who it was has never been clear. In the next two minutes, more firing left eight Americans dead and ten wounded. One British soldier suffered a slight wound.

The British units then moved on to Concord, no longer under cover of dark or with any pretense of surprise. Three companies of minutemen nervously occupied the center of Concord but offered no challenge to the British troops as they searched in vain for the ammunition storage. Finally, at the Old North Bridge in Concord, shots were exchanged, killing two Americans and three British soldiers.

By now both sides were very apprehensive. The British had failed to find the expected arms storage, and the Americans had failed to stop their raid. As the British returned to Boston along a narrow road,

militia units attacked from the sides in the bloodiest fighting of the day. In the end, 273 British soldiers were wounded or dead; the toll for the Americans stood at about 95. It was April 19, 1775, and the war had begun.

## Another Rebellion against Slavery

News of the battles of Lexington and Concord spread rapidly. Within eight days, Virginians had heard of the fighting, and, as Thomas Jefferson reflected, "A phrenzy of revenge seems to have seized all ranks of people." The royal governor of Virginia, Lord Dunmore, had just removed a large quantity of gunpowder from the Williamsburg powder house and put it on a ship in the dead of night, out of reach of any frenzied Virginians. Next, Dunmore threatened to arm the slaves, if necessary, to ward off attacks by colonists.

This was clearly Dunmore's ace card, for he understood full well how to produce panic among the planters. Yet he did not play the card until November 1775, when he issued an official proclamation promising freedom to defecting, able-bodied slaves who would fight for the British. Dunmore's dilemma was that while he wanted to scare the planters, he had no intention of liberating all slaves or of starting a real slave rebellion. So his offer was limited to able-bodied men. Female, young, and elderly slaves were not welcome behind British lines, and many were sent back to face irate masters.

In the northern colonies as well, slaves clearly recognized the evolving political struggle with England as an ideal moment to bid for freedom. A twenty-one-year-old Boston domestic slave employed sarcasm in a 1774 newspaper essay to call attention to the hypocrisy of local slave owners: "How well the Cry for Liberty, and the reverse Disposition for exercise of oppressive Power over others agree,—I humbly think it does not require the Penetration of a Philosopher to Determine." This remarkable young woman, Phillis Wheatley, had already gained international recognition through a book of poems endorsed by Governor Thomas Hutchinson and Boston merchant John Hancock and published in London in 1773. Possibly neither man fully appreciated the irony of his endorsement, however, for Wheatley's poems spoke of "Fair Freedom" as the "Goddess long desir'd" by Africans enslaved in America. At the urging of his wife, Wheatley's master freed the young poet in 1775.

---

*Slaves clearly recognized the evolving political struggle with England as an ideal moment to bid for freedom.*

---

Wheatley's poetic ideas about freedom found concrete expression among other discontented groups. Some slaves in Boston petitioned Thomas Gage, promising to fight for the British if he would liberate them. Gage turned them down. In Ulster County, New York, along the Hudson River, two blacks were overheard discussing gunpowder, and thus a plot unraveled that involved at least twenty slaves in four villages discovered to have ammunition stashed away.

The numerical preponderance of black slaves in the southern colonies deepened white fears of rebellion. In Maryland, soon after the news of the Lexington battle arrived, slaves exhibited impatience with their status, in light of the revolutionary movement unfolding around them. One Maryland planter reported that "the insolence of the Negroes in this county is come to such a height, that we are under a necessity of disarming them. . . . We took about eighty guns, some bayonets, swords, etc." In

**LORD DUNMORE'S PROCLAMATION**
*In November 1775, Lord Dunmore of Virginia offered freedom to "all indented Servants, Negroes, or others (appertaining to Rebels)" who would help put down the rebellion. Dunmore issued multiple printed copies in broadside form from the safety of a ship anchored at Norfolk, Virginia.*
Special Collections, University of Virginia Library.

North Carolina, a planned uprising was uncovered and scores of slaves were arrested. No one seemed to see any irony in the fact that it was the revolutionary committee of public safety that dealt severely with this quest for liberty: Each conspiring slave suffered eighty lashes on the back and had both ears cropped.

Understandably, Lord Dunmore's proclamation to encourage slave defection was not reported in many southern newspapers. Blacks, however, did not depend on newspapers for their information. John Adams was assured by southern delegates to the Continental Congress that a proclamation like Dunmore's would quickly draw twenty thousand slaves in South Carolina because "the Negroes have a wonderful art of communicating Intelligence among themselves; it will run several hundreds of miles in a week or fortnight." The contagion of liberty spread quickly by newspaper, by word of mouth, and even by drumbeat.

In 1775, probably several thousand slaves in Virginia took Lord Dunmore up on his offer, and by 1778 the number had escalated to as many as thirty thousand. Possibly eighty thousand southern blacks over the course of the Revolutionary War voted against slavery with their feet. Some failed to achieve the liberation they were seeking. The British army generally used them for menial labor; and disease, especially smallpox, devastated encampments of runaways. But several thousand persisted through the war and later left America under the protection of the British army to start new lives in freedom in Nova Scotia, Canada, or Sierra Leone in Africa.

## Conclusion: How Far Does Liberty Go?

The French and Indian War set the stage for the imperial crisis of the 1760s and 1770s by creating distrust between England and its colonies and by running up a huge deficit in the British treasury. The years from 1763 to 1775 brought repeated attempts by the British government to subordinate the colonies into taxpaying partners.

American resistance grew slowly but steadily over those years. In 1765, Thomas Hutchinson shared with Samuel Adams the belief that it was exceedingly unwise for England to assert a right to taxation, because Parliament did not really represent Americans. But by temperament and office, Hutchinson had to uphold British policy; Adams, in contrast, protested the policy and made political activists out of thousands in the process.

By 1775, events propelled many Americans to the conclusion that a concerted effort was afoot to deprive them of all their liberties, the most important of which were the right to self-taxation, the right to live free of an occupying army, and finally their right to self-rule. Hundreds of minutemen converged on Concord, prepared to die for these American liberties. April 19 marked the start of their rebellion.

Another rebellion under way in 1775 was doomed to be short-circuited. Black Americans who had experienced actual slavery now listened to shouts of "Liberty!" from white crowds and appropriated the language of revolution swirling around them that spoke to their deepest needs and hopes. Defiance of authority was indeed contagious.

The emerging leaders of the patriot cause were mindful of a delicate balance they felt they had to strike. To energize the American public about the crisis with England, they had to politicize masses of men—and eventually women too—and infuse them with a keen sense of their rights and liberties. But in so doing, they became fearful of the unintended consequences of teaching a vocabulary of rights and liberties. They worried that the rhetoric of enslavement might go too far.

The question of how far the crisis could be stretched before something snapped was largely unexamined in 1765. Patriot leaders in that year wanted a correction, a restoration of an ancient liberty of self-taxation that Parliament seemed to be ignoring. But events from 1765 to 1775 convinced many that no return to the old ways was possible. A challenge to Parliament's right to tax had led, step by step, to a challenge to Parliament's right to legislate over the colonies in any matter. If Parliament's sovereignty was set aside, then who actually had authority over the American colonies? By 1775, with the outbreak of fighting and the specter of slave rebellions, American leaders turned to the king for the answer to that question.

## CHRONOLOGY

**1747**   Ohio Company of Virginia formed.

**1754**   French and Indian War begins in America.
Albany Congress proposes Plan of Union and courts Iroquois support.

**1755**   General Braddock defeated by French and Indians in Pennsylvania.

**1757**   William Pitt, prime minister in Britain, fully commits to war effort.

**1759**   Quebec falls to British.

**1760**   George III becomes king.

**1763**   Treaty of Paris ends French and Indian War.
Pontiac's uprising provokes fear and destruction in western frontier settlements.
Proclamation of 1763 prohibits settlement west of Appalachians.

**1764**   The Revenue (Sugar) Act lowers tax on foreign molasses to promote compliance with trade duty.

**1764**   Currency Act prohibits issuance of colonial paper money.

**1765**   Stamp Act imposes tax on documents.
**May.** Patrick Henry sponsors Virginia Resolves.
**August.** Crowd actions in Boston inaugurate Sons of Liberty.
**October.** Stamp Act Congress meets in New York City.

**1766**   Stamp Act repealed; Declaratory Act asserts Parliament's control over colonies.

**1767**   Townshend duties reinstate revenue-raising taxes.

**1768**   **Fall.** British troops stationed in Boston.

**1769**   Year of nonimportation agreements; Daughters of Liberty appear.

**1770**   **March 5.** Boston Massacre.
Townshend duties repealed; Lord North comes to power.

**1772**   **June.** *Gaspée* attacked off Rhode Island.
Committees of correspondence formed.

**1773**   Tea Act lowers price of tea to tempt American boycotters.
**December 16.** Boston Tea Party.

**1774**   Parliament passes Coercive Acts (Intolerable Acts): Boston Port Act, Massachusetts Government Act, Impartial Administration of Justice Act, Quartering Act, Quebec Act.
**September.** First Continental Congress meets. Continental Association formed.

**1775**   **April 19.** Battles of Lexington and Concord.
Virginia's Lord Dunmore promises freedom to defecting slaves.

## SUGGESTED READINGS

Bernard Bailyn, *The Ordeal of Thomas Hutchinson* (1974). A sympathetic and prize-winning biography of this much-vilified royal official.

Ira Berlin and Ronald Hoffman, *Slavery and Freedom in the Age of the American Revolution* (1983). A collection of local studies detailing blacks' involvement in the American Revolution.

Richard D. Brown, *Revolutionary Politics in Massachusetts: The Boston Committee of Correspondence and the Towns, 1772–1774* (1970). An important examination of the central role of committees of correspondence in spreading Revolutionary opinions and ideas.

Sylvia Frey, *Water from the Rock: Black Resistance in a Revolutionary Age* (1991). The author posits a three-sided struggle in the revolutionary South, involving the British, white Americans, and black slaves, who played a vital role in shaping the meaning of the Revolution.

Robert A. Gross, *The Minutemen and Their World* (1976). An absorbing local study of Concord, Massachusetts, exploring the meaning of the Revolution from the perspectives of individual inhabitants.

Linda Kerber, *Women of the Republic: Intellect and Ideology in Revolutionary America* (1980). A study of women's intellectual engagement with legal and political ideas of the Revolutionary era.

Pauline Maier, *The Old Revolutionaries: Political Lives in the Age of Samuel Adams* (1980). Revealing portraits of the 1760s generation of American leaders.

James Kirby Martin, *In the Course of Human Events: An Interpretive Exploration of the American Revolution* (1979). An excellent one-volume overview of the Revolutionary period.

Robert Middlekauff, *The Glorious Cause: The American Revolution, 1763–1789* (1982). A comprehensive history of the Revolution with attention to British politics, diplomacy, and military history.

Gary B. Nash, *The Urban Crucible: Social Change, Political Consciousness, and the Origins of the American Revolution* (1979). A detailed history of crowd actions and radical leaders in three cities.

Mary Beth Norton, *Liberty's Daughters: The Revolutionary Experience of American Women, 1750–1800* (1980). A social history of women's participation in the Revolution, based on extensive research in diaries and letters.

Ann Fairfax Withington, *Toward a More Perfect Union: Virtue and the Formation of American Republics* (1991). An exploration of community behaviors and rituals of patriotism that demonstrate how revolutionary ideas were embraced at the grassroots level.

Alfred F. Young, *The American Revolution: Explorations in the History of American Radicalism* (1976). A collection of essays focusing on ordinary Americans—blacks, women, Indians, workers—and their growing political engagement during the Revolution.

**PAINTED DRUM**

*Drums were essential military equipment in eighteenth-century wars. Small to carry but loud in use, they provided a percussive beat that penetrated the din of the battlefield to signal troop advances, retreats, or other field movements. Drummers often stood right behind soldiers in firing formation, regulating the timing of each volley of shots. The eagle painted on this Revolutionary-era drum from Fort Ticonderoga in New York holds a banner inscribed "Sons of Liberty," a name adopted in 1765 to distinguish protesters of British policies toward the colonies.*

Fort Ticonderoga Museum.

# THE WAR FOR AMERICA
## 1775–1783

ABIGAIL ADAMS WAS IMPATIENT for American independence. While her husband, John, was away in Philadelphia as a member of the Second Continental Congress, Abigail tended house and farm in Braintree, Massachusetts, just south of British-occupied Boston. She had four young children to look after, and in addition to her female duties, such as cooking, sewing, and making soap, she also had to shoulder male duties in her husband's absence—hiring farm help, managing rental property, selling the crop. John wrote to her often, approving of the fine "Farmeress" who was conducting his business so well. She replied, conveying news of the family along with shrewd commentary on revolutionary politics. In December 1775, she chastised the congress for being too timid and urged that independence be declared. A few months later, she astutely observed to John that southern slave owners might shrink from a war in the name of liberty: "I have sometimes been ready to think that the passion for Liberty cannot be Equally strong in the Breasts of those who have been accustomed to deprive their fellow Creatures of theirs."

"I long to hear that you have declared an independency," she wrote in March 1776. "And by the way in the new Code of Laws which I suppose it will be necessary for you to make I desire you would Remember the Ladies, and be more generous and favourable to them than your ancestors." If Abigail was politically precocious for being in favor of independence and for being suspicious of slave owners' devotion to liberty, she showed herself to be positively visionary in this extraordinary plea to her husband to "Remember the Ladies." "Do not put such unlimited power into the hands of the Husbands," she advised. "Remember all Men would be tyrants if they could." Abigail had put her finger on another form of tyranny that was rarely remarked on in her society: that of men over women. "If particular care and attention is not paid to the Ladies," she jokingly threatened, "we are determined to foment a Rebellion, and will not hold ourselves bound by any Laws in which we have no voice, or Representation."

John Adams dismissed his wife's provocative idea as a "saucy" suggestion: "As to your extraordinary Code of Laws, I cannot but Laugh." The Revolution had perhaps unleashed discontent among other dependent groups, he allowed; children, apprentices, students, Indians, and blacks had grown "disobedient" and "insolent." "But your Letter was the first Intimation that another Tribe more numerous and powerful than all the rest were grown discontented." Men were too smart to repeal their "Masculine Systems," John assured her, for otherwise they would find themselves living under a "despotism of the petticoat."

This clever exchange between husband and wife in 1776 says much about the cautious, limited radicalism of the American Revolution. Both John and Abigail Adams understood (Abigail probably far more than John) that ungluing the hier-

**ABIGAIL ADAMS**
*Abigail Smith Adams was twenty-two when she sat for this pastel portrait in 1766. A wife for two years and a mother for one, Adams exhibits a steady, intelligent gaze. Pearls and a lace collar anchor her femininity, while her facial expression projects a confidence and maturity not often credited to young women of the 1760s.*
Courtesy of the Massachusetts Historical Society ©.

archical bond between the king and his subjects potentially unglued other kinds of social inequalities. John was surely joking in listing the groups made unruly in the spirit of a challenge to authority, for children, apprentices, and students were hardly rebellious in the 1770s. But it would soon prove to be an uncomfortable joke, because Indians and blacks did take up the cause of their own liberty during the Revolution, and the great majority of them saw their liberty best served by joining the British side in the war.

Though Abigail Adams was impatient for independence, many other Americans feared separation from Britain. What kind of civilized country had no king? Who, if not Britain, would protect Americans from the French and Spanish? How could the colonies possibly win a war against the most powerful military machine on the globe? Reconciliation, not independence, was favored by many.

Members of the Continental Congress, whether they were pro-independence like John Adams or more cautiously hoping for reconciliation, had their hands full in 1775–1776. The war had already begun, and it fell to the congress to raise an army, finance it, and explore diplomatic alliances with foreign countries. For the next six years, the war for America engrossed everyone's attention. In part, it was a classic war with professional armies and textbook battles. But it was also a civil war in America, at times even a brutal guerrilla war, of committed rebels versus loyalists.

Only in one glorious moment did the congress issue a ringing statement about social hierarchy and how it would be rearranged in America after submission to the king was undone. That was on July 4, 1776, when the Declaration of Independence asserted in its preamble that "all men are created equal." This striking phrase went completely unremarked in the two days of congressional debate spent tinkering with the language of the Declaration. The solvent to dissolve social inequalities in America was created at that moment, but none of the men at the congress, or even Abigail Adams up in Braintree, fully realized it at the time.

## The Second Continental Congress

On May 10, 1775, nearly one month after the fighting at Lexington and Concord, the Second Continental Congress assembled in Philadelphia. The congress immediately set to work on two crucial and seemingly contradictory tasks: to raise and supply an army and to negotiate a reconciliation with England. But as the war progressed and hopes of reconciliation faded, delegates at the congress began to ponder the treasonous act of declaring independence.

### Assuming Political and Military Authority

Like the First Continental Congress, the second had no legal authority for existing. Neither did most of the legislatures that had selected the delegates to go to Philadelphia. The political leadership of one colony after another subverted British authority by simply assuming power on its own.

The same pattern was replicated in town after town as well: Men who had once been the selectmen or town councillors now called themselves the committee of public safety, of inspection, or of correspondence and took it upon themselves to be the ruling body of the town. The inspiration for such creative government came initially from the Coercive Acts that had crippled town government in Massachusetts in 1774. Government by committee spread to other colonies when the First Continental Congress implemented the Continental Association and recommended that local committees of public safety form to enforce economic boycotts of British goods.

Royal administrators found there was little they could do to stop such actions, with no police force and a militia of, at best, uncertain loyalty. For their own protection, most governors packed their bags and sailed for England. By the end of 1775, royal authority was virtually dead in the colonies, a feat accomplished with hardly a single act of violence.

The delegates to the Second Continental Congress were well-established political figures in their home colonies, but they still had to learn to know and trust each other, and they found they were not of similar minds about the political issues facing them. The Adams cousins John and Samuel defined the radical end of the spectrum, favoring independence from England. John Dickinson of Pennsylvania, no longer the eager revolutionary who had dashed off *Letters from a Farmer* back in 1767, was now a moderate, seeking reconciliation with England. George Washington showed up wearing his old military uniform from the French and Indian War, a conspicuous hawkish declaration. Benjamin Franklin, in contrast, was feared by some to be a British spy. He had returned from an eleven-year residence in England just five days before the congress met. His long sojourn abroad, plus his long silences in the congress in the first months, made his loyalty suspect. Mutual suspicions flourished easily when the undertaking was so dangerous, opinions were so varied, and a misstep could spell disaster.

Most of the delegates were not yet prepared to break with England. Total independence was an alarming idea to many, and some legislatures, chiefly those in the middle colonies such as New York and Pennsylvania, had instructed their delegates to oppose any such move. Some felt that government without a monarchical element was surely unworkable. Others feared that the colonies would always need the protection of England against their traditional enemies, France and Spain, and that independence would therefore be suicidal. Colonies that traded actively with England feared undermining their economies. Nor were the vast majority of ordinary Americans ready or able to envision independence from the British monarchy. From the Stamp Act to the Coercive Acts, the decade-long constitutional struggle with England had turned on the issue of parliamentary power. During that decade almost no one questioned the legitimacy of the monarchy.

The few men at the Continental Congress who did think that independence was desirable were, not surprisingly, the Massachusetts delegates. Their colony had been stripped of civil government under the Coercive Acts and their capital was occupied by the British army. Even so, those men knew that it was premature to push for a break with England. John Adams wrote to Abigail in June 1775: "America is a great, unwieldy body. Its progress must be slow. It is like a large fleet sailing under convoy. The fleetest sailors must wait for the dullest and slowest."

As slow as the American colonies were in sailing toward political independence, they needed to take swift action to coordinate a military defense, for the Massachusetts countryside was under the threat of further attack and the New England militias were clearly inadequate. Even the hesitant moderates in the congress agreed that a military buildup was necessary. Around the country, militia units from New York to Georgia collected arms and drilled on village greens in anticipation.

On June 14, the congress voted to create an army, which mainly meant proclaiming that the New England soldiers dug in around Boston *were* the American army, henceforth called the Continental army and directed and paid by the congress. The congress also called for ten companies of riflemen from Virginia, Maryland, and Pennsylvania to join the New England troops.

Choosing a commander in chief to lead the army presented the congress with an opportunity to demonstrate that this was no local war of a single rebellious colony. The most obvious candidate for the job was Artemus Ward, a Connecticut man and a veteran officer from the French and Indian War, who was already commanding the soldiers massed around Boston. But congress instead turned to a southerner, George Washington, a man not much known beyond his native Virginia. Washington was actually far less experienced leading troops than Ward, but he looked every bit the part of commander in his old military uniform. His leadership signaled England that there was widespread commitment to war beyond New England.

Next a committee of the congress drew up a declaration of war, called "A Declaration of the Causes and Necessity of Taking Up Arms," which rehearsed familiar arguments about the tyranny of Parliament and the need to defend traditional English liberties. This document was first drafted by a young Virginia planter, Thomas Jefferson, a newcomer to the congress and a radical on the question of independence. The moderate John Dickinson, fearing that the declaration would offend England and rule out reconciliation, was allowed to rewrite it; however, he still left much of Jefferson's highly charged language about choosing "to die freemen rather than to live slaves." Even a man as reluctant for independence as Dickinson acknowledged the necessity of military defense against an invading army.

> *In just two months, the Second Continental Congress had taken on the major functions of a legitimate government, both military and financial, without any legal basis for its authority.*

To pay for the military buildup, the congress authorized a currency issue of two million dollars. The Continental dollars were merely paper; they did not represent gold or silver, for the congress owned no precious metals. The delegates somewhat naively expected that the currency would be accepted as valuable on trust as it spread in the population through the hands of soldiers, farmers, munitions suppliers, and beyond.

In just two months, the Second Continental Congress had created an army, declared war, and issued its own currency. It had taken on the major functions of a legitimate government, both military and financial, without any legal basis for its authority, for it had not—and would not for a full year yet—declare independence from the legitimate authority of the king. Equally unnoticed, the congress's assumption of governance lacked any real power to compel compliance by Americans. Enthusiasm for the cause drew recruits to the army, and optimism kept the newly printed Continental dollars afloat at full value for a time. But when that initial enthusiasm waned, the congress and the war effort fell on hard times.

## Pursuing Both War and Peace

Three days after the congress voted to raise the Continental army, the bloodiest battle of the entire Revolution occurred. The British commander in Boston, Thomas Gage, had recently received troop reinforcements, three talented major generals (William Howe, John Burgoyne, and Henry Clinton), and new instructions to root out the rebels around Boston. But before Gage could take the offensive, Massachusetts and Connecticut militias fortified the hilly terrain of Charlestown, a peninsula just north of Boston, on the night of June 16, 1775.

The British generals could have nipped off the peninsula where it met the mainland, to box in the Americans. But General Howe insisted on a bold frontal assault, across the water and up the hill, more intimidating but potentially costly. The American troops, 1,400 strong, held their fire until the British were about twenty yards away. At that distance the musket volley was sure and deadly, and the British turned back. Twice more General Howe sent his men up the hill to receive the same blast of firepower; each time they had to step around the bodies felled in the previous attempts.

On the third assault, the British took the hill, mainly because the American ammunition supply gave out, and the defenders quickly retreated across the Charlestown neck. The Battle of Bunker Hill was thus a British victory, but an expensive one. The dead numbered 226 on the British side, with more than 800 wounded; the Americans suffered 140 dead, 271 wounded, and 30 captured. As General Clinton later remarked, "It was a dear bought victory; another such would have ruined us."

General Clinton wanted to pursue the fleeing Americans to their headquarters at Cambridge, a few miles away, but Howe overruled him and pulled the army back to Boston. There they sat, penned up, unwilling to risk more raids into the countryside. Their food had to be shipped in by British naval vessels. If the British had had any grasp of the basic instability of the American units gathered at Cambridge, they might have pushed westward and perhaps decisively defeated the core of the Continental army in its infancy. Instead they lingered in Boston, abandoning it without a fight nine months later.

A week after Bunker Hill, when General Washington arrived to take charge of the new Continental army, he found enthusiastic but undisciplined troops. Sanitation was an unknown concept, with inadequate latrines fouling the campground. Drunkenness on duty was common, and soldiers appeared to be free to come and go at will. The amazed general attributed the disarray to the New England custom of letting militia units elect their own officers, a custom he felt undermined deference and respect. Washington moved quickly to establish military discipline, staging whippings and frequent courts-martial to impress on the soldiers the importance of obedience to superiors. "Discipline is the soul of the army," he stated.

While military plans moved forward, the Second Continental Congress pursued its second, contradictory objective, reconciliation with England. Delegates from the middle colonies, especially Pennsylvania, Delaware, and New York, whose merchants depended on trade with England, urged that channels for negotiation remain open. Congressional moderates led by John Dickinson engineered an appeal to the king, called the Olive Branch Petition, in July 1775. The petition affirmed loyalty to the monarchy and resorted to a convenient fiction of blaming all the troubles on bad advice from the king's ministers and on Parliament. It proposed that the American colonial assemblies be recognized as individual parliaments, all under the umbrella of the monarchy. That Dickinson himself could write both the "Declaration on the Causes and Necessity of Taking Up Arms" and the Olive Branch Petition within a few days of each other shows how ambivalent the American position was in the summer of 1775.

By late fall 1775, however, reconciliation was out of the question. King George rejected the Olive Branch Petition and heatedly condemned the Americans, calling them rebels, traitors, and enemies. It was thereafter hard to maintain the illusion that ministers and not the king himself were to blame for the conflict. And while the Continental Congress still shied away from an official declaration of independence, moderates like Dickinson would not be able to keep a lid on revolutionary sentiments much longer.

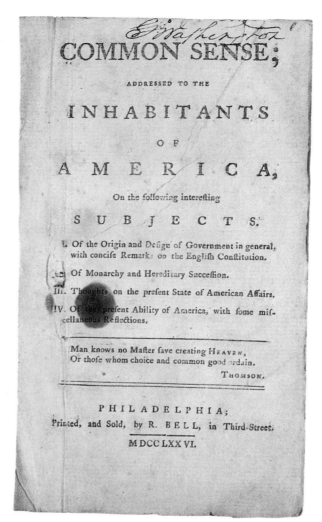

**WASHINGTON'S INSCRIBED COPY OF COMMON SENSE**
*Thomas Paine's incendiary pamphlet* Common Sense *was widely read after its publication in Philadelphia in January 1776. Copies were passed from hand to hand and read aloud in public. Virginian George Washington, a member of the Second Continental Congress, inscribed his name on the title page to declare his ownership of Paine's booklet.*
Boston Athenaeum.

## Thomas Paine and the Case for Independence

Pressure for independence was pushed into high gear starting in January of 1776, when a pamphlet titled *Common Sense* appeared in Philadelphia. Thomas Paine, its author, was an English artisan and coffeehouse intellectual who had come to America in the fall of 1774. He landed a job with the *Pennsylvania Magazine* and soon met delegates from the Second Continental Congress. With their encouragement, he wrote *Common Sense* to lay out a lively and compelling case for complete independence.

In simple yet forceful language, Paine elaborated on the absurdities of the British monarchy. Why should one man, by accident of birth, claim extensive power over others? he asked. A king might be foolish or wicked. "One of the strongest natural proofs of the folly of hereditary right in kings," Paine wrote, "is that nature disapproves it; otherwise she would not so frequently turn it into ridicule by giving mankind an *ass for a lion.*"

Calling the king of England an ass broke through the automatic deference most Americans still had for the monarchy. And by moving the focus from Parliament to the king, Paine succeeded in making a case for independence. To replace monarchy, he advocated republican government, based on the consent of the people. Rulers, according to Paine, were only representatives of the people, and the best form of government relied on frequent elections to achieve the most direct democracy possible.

---

*In simple yet forceful language, Paine elaborated on the absurdities of the British monarchy. Why should one man, by accident of birth, claim extensive power over others? he asked.*

---

Paine's pamphlet sold more than 150,000 copies in a matter of weeks. Newspapers reprinted it, men read it aloud in taverns and coffeehouses, John Adams sent a copy to Abigail Adams, who passed it around to neighbors. Another of John Adams's correspondents wrote him in late February that ninety-nine out of a hundred New Englanders desired an official declaration of independence. But of course New England had two armies on its doorstep to fire its spirit. The middle and southern colonies, under no immediate threat of violence, remained cautious.

One factor hastening official independence was the advantage of an alliance with France. France could provide military supplies as well as naval power, but not without firm assurance that the Americans would separate from England. By May, all but four colonies were agitating for a declaration. The exceptions were Pennsylvania, Maryland, New York, and South Carolina, the latter two containing large loyalist populations.

Finally on June 7, 1776, the Virginia delegation introduced a resolution calling for independence. Here was the assertion everyone had been anticipating, some with impatience, others with dread. (See Texts in Historical Context on page 166.) The

moderates still commanded enough support to postpone a vote on the measure until July, which allowed them time to go home and consult about this extreme step. In the meantime, the congress appointed a committee, with Thomas Jefferson and others, to draft a longer document setting out the justification for independence.

On July 1, the first vote was taken on the resolution of June 7. Pennsylvania and South Carolina voted against it, while the two-man Delaware delegation was split and the New Yorkers abstained. On July 2, after a night of politicking, a second vote shifted South Carolina and Pennsylvania into the pro-independence camp, and a newly elected delegate from Delaware rode all night to cast the deciding pro-independence vote. The New Yorkers still abstained, but since they had not voted negatively, the congress could truthfully claim that the resolution for independence had passed without a negative vote.

On July 2 and 3, the congress turned to the document drafted by Thomas Jefferson and his committee. Jefferson began with a preamble that articulated philosophical principles about natural rights, equality, the right of revolution, and the consent of the governed as the only true basis for government. He then listed more than two dozen specific grievances against King George. The congress merely glanced at the political philosophy, finding nothing exceptional in it; the ideas about natural rights and the consent of the governed were seen as "self-evident truths," just as the document claimed. In itself, this absence of comment showed a remarkable transformation in political thinking since the end of the French and Indian War. The single phrase declaring the natural equality of "all men" was also passed over without comment; no one elaborated on its radical implications.

What the congress did wrangle over were the specific grievances, especially the issue of slavery. Jefferson had included an impassioned statement blaming the king for slavery, which delegates from Georgia and South Carolina struck out. They had no intention of denouncing their labor system as an evil practice.

On July 4, the corrections to Jefferson's text were complete and the delegates formally affixed their signatures to it. Four men, including John Dickinson, declined to sign; several others "signed with regret . . . and with many doubts," according to John Adams. The document was then printed and distributed by the thousands. In New York, a crowd listened to a public reading of it and then toppled

**DECLARATION OF INDEPENDENCE READ TO A CROWD**
*Printed copies of the Declaration of Independence were
read aloud in public places throughout America in the
weeks after July 4, 1776, often accompanied by carefully
orchestrated celebrations.*
Historical Society of Pennsylvania.

a statue of George III on horseback. On July 15, the
New York delegation switched from abstention to
endorsement, making the vote on independence
truly unanimous.

## The First Two Years
## of War, 1775 – 1777

Both sides had cause to approach the war for America with uneasiness. The Americans opposed the
mightiest military power in the world, and many
thought it was foolhardy to expect victory. Further,
pockets of loyalism remained strong; the country

was not united. But the British faced serious obstacles as well. Their utter disdain for the fighting
abilities of the Americans had to be reevaluated in
light of their costly Bunker Hill victory. The logistics of supplying an army with food across three
thousand miles of water were daunting. And since
the British goal was to regain allegiance, not to destroy and conquer, the army was often constrained
in its actions.

### The American Military Forces

Americans claimed that the initial months of war
were purely defensive, triggered by the British
army's invasion. But quickly the war also became a
rebellion, an overthrowing of long-established authority. As both defenders and rebels, Americans
were generally highly motivated to fight, and the
potential manpower that could be mobilized was
in theory very great. The recruitment pool, able-
bodied men aged sixteen to sixty, already had some
military training arising out of the American tradition of militia service. From the earliest decades of
settlement, local defense rested with a militia requiring service from nearly every man. Militia units
engaged in regular practices, and men supplied
their own weapons.

The militia style of warfare was well suited to
American defensive needs; for two centuries the
main threat to public safety had come from occasional Indian attacks. In the mid-eighteenth century,
southern militias trained with potential slave rebellions in mind, and in cities militias became a police
force in rare times of civil disorder. Militias worked
well in limited circumstances, and they continued
to function in local theaters of war, but they were
not appropriate for extended wars requiring military campaigns far from home. In forming the Continental army, the congress set enlistment at one
year, but army leaders soon learned that that was
not enough time to carry out campaigns. A three-
year enlistment earned a new soldier a twenty-
dollar bonus, paid up front, while men who committed for the duration of the war were promised a
postwar land grant of one hundred acres. To make
this inducement effective, of course, recruits had to
believe that the Americans would win. By early
1777, the army was the largest it would ever be—
29,000 troops; it was still not enough.

The Continental Congress assigned troop quotas to each state; local committees of public safety
began to function like draft boards. Draftees tended
to be the marginal men in a community, such as

# The Issue of Independence

*In May and June 1776, talk of independence gripped Americans everywhere. When would it come? What would it mean? Why was the congress so slow to declare it? Town meetings all over Massachusetts were voting for immediate action; with war already on their doorstep, they saw no reason to delay. In contrast, political leaders in New York City were ambivalent and divided, and they did their best to avert calls for action. Independence-minded planters in Virginia worried that the common people might take a completely different meaning from the rush for independence. And merchants everywhere expressed anxiety that a declaration would kill all chances at reconciliation. While the congress no doubt hoped that the July 4 Declaration of Independence would help unite the country, the reality was that disunity was fearfully evident.*

political Artifice and Corruption, they have at length had a fatal Recourse to a Standing Army, so repugnant to the nature of a free Government, to fire and Sword, to Bloodshed and Devastation, calling in the aid of foreign Troops, as well as endeavouring to stir up the Savages of the wilderness to exercise their barbarities upon us, being determined, by all appearances, if practicable, to extirpate the Americans from the face of the Earth, unless they tamely resign the Rights of humanity, and to repeople this once happy Country with the ready Sons of Vassalage, if such can be found.

We therefor, Apprehending such a subjection utterly inconsistant with the just rights and blessings of Society, unanimously Instruct you to endeavour that our Delegates in Congress be informed, in case that Representative Body of the Continent should think fit to declare the Colonies Independant of Great Britain, of our readiness and determination to assist with our Lives and Fortunes in Support of that, we apprehend, necessary Measure.

*Men of Scituate debated independence on June 4, 1776, and conveyed their remarks to their town representative.*

*In New York, a group of craftsmen drafted their own document justifying independence. They delivered it to the assembly and encountered a chilly reception.*

### DOCUMENT 1. The Town Meeting of Scituate, Massachusetts, Pledges to Fight for Independence

The Inhabitants of this Town being called together on the recommendation of our General Assembly to Signify our minds on the great point of Independence on Great-Britain, think fit to Instruct you on that head.

The Ministry of that Kingdom, having formed a design of Subjecting the Colonies to a distant, external and absolute power in all Cases whatsoever, wherein the Colonies have not, nor in the nature of things can have any share by Representation, have, for a course of years past, exerted their utmost Art and Endeavours to put the same plan, so destructive to both Countries, into Execution. But finding it, through the noble and virtuous opposition of the Sons of Freedom, impracticable by means of mere

### DOCUMENT 2. Minutes of the New York Assembly, June 3, 1776

A number of citizens, who style themselves a Committee of Mechanicks, having come into the Congress-Chamber . . . and delivered at the Chair a paper which they style an Address, the House was ordered to be cleared, in order that the said paper may be inspected, to discover whether it is proper for this Congress to receive the same. . . . The door was opened, and the said citizens were desired to come into the Chamber, . . . the said paper being read by Lewis Thibou.

They therein set forth that they are devoted friends to their bleeding country; that they are afflicted by beholding her struggling under heavy loads of oppression and tyranny; . . . that their Prince is deaf to petitions for redressing our grievances; that one year has not sufficed to satisfy the rage of a cruel Ministry in their bloody pursuits, designed to reduce us to be slaves, and to be taxed by them without our consent; that, therefore, they rather wish to separate from such oppressors; and declare that, if this Congress should think proper to instruct their Delegates in Continental Congress to cause these United Colonies to become independent of Great Britain, it would give them the highest satisfaction.

We are of opinion that the Continental Congress alone have that enlarged view of our political circumstances which will enable them to decide upon those measures which are necessary for the general welfare. We cannot presume . . . to make or declare any resolutions upon so momentous a concern; but are determined patiently to await and firmly to abide by whatever a majority of that august body shall think needful.

*In Virginia, ordinary citizens circulated petitions pressing for a Declaration of Independence in May 1776. Landon Carter, a wealthy and worried planter, feared that what they meant by independence might be far more radical than he could accept. In a letter to George Washington on May 9, Carter expressed his concerns.*

### DOCUMENT 3. Virginian Landon Carter Warns Fellow Planter George Washington

I need only tell you of one definition that I heard of Independency: It was expected to be a form of Government that, by being independent of the rich men, every man would then be able to do as he pleased. . . . One of the Delegates [to the Virginia assembly] I heard exclaim against the Patrolling law, because a poor man was made to pay for keeping a rich man's slaves in order. I shamed the fool so much for it that he slunk away; but he got elected by it. . . . I know who I am writing to, and therefore I am not quite so confined in my expressions. . . . And from hence it is that our independency is to arise! Papers, it seems, are everywhere circulating about for poor ignorant creatures to sign, as directions to their Delegates to endeavour at an independency. In vain do we ask to let it be explained what is designed by it!

*Even after July 4, many merchants remained dubious about the wisdom of independence. The Philadelphia merchant Joseph Reed wrote to Robert Morris on July 18.*

### DOCUMENT 4. Merchants Joseph Reed and Robert Morris Exchange Fading Hopes for Reconciliation

I fear the die is irrevocably cast, and that we must play out the game, however doubtful and desperate. . . . My private judgment led me to think that if the two great cardinal points of exemption from British taxation and charge of internal government could have been secured, our happiness and prosperity would have been best promoted by preserving the dependence. The Declaration of Independence is a new and very strong objection to entering into any negotiation. . . . But I fancy there are numbers, and some of them firm in the interests of America, who would think an overture ought not to be rejected.

*Robert Morris replied to Reed on July 21.*

I am sorry to say there are some amongst us that cannot bear the thought of Reconciliation on any terms. I cannot help Condemning this disposition as it must be founded in keen Resentment or on interested Views. . . . I have uniformly voted against & opposed the declaration of Independance because in my poor oppinion it was an improper time and will neither promote the interest or redound to the honor of America, for it has caused division when we wanted Union.

**Document 1.** Henry S. Commager and Richard B. Morris, eds., *The Spirit of Seventy-Six* (1958; reprint, 1975), 298–99. Original in the Massachusetts Archives, CLVI, 103.

**Document 2.** Peter Force, *American Archives*, 4th ser., vol. 6 (1846), 1362–63.

**Document 3.** Peter Force, *American Archives*, 4th ser., vol. 6 (1846), 389–92.

**Document 4.** John H. Hazelton, *The Declaration of Independence: Its History* (1906), 226–28.

servants or the unemployed; thus the army had a very different look from the state militias. In some towns, suspected loyalists were drafted first, either as an effective way to smoke them out or as a way to punish them. Although it proved hard to get adequate numbers of men to enlist, the total number of individual enlistments over the course of the war totaled 231,950 men, or roughly one-quarter of the white male population over age sixteen.

Women also served in the Continental army. They were needed to do the daily cooking and washing, and after battle they nursed wounded men. The professional British army established a ratio of one woman to every ten men; in the Continental army, the ratio was set at one woman to fifteen men. Close to twenty thousand women served during the war, probably most of them wives of men in service. Children tagged along as well, and babies were born in the camps and on the road.

Black Americans were at first excluded from the Continental army, a rule that slave owner George Washington made on his fifth day as commander in chief. But as manpower needs increased, the northern states began to welcome free blacks into service; even slaves could serve in some states, with their masters' permission. About five thousand black men served in the Revolutionary War on the rebel side, mostly from the northern states. While some of these were draftees, others were clearly men inspired by the ideals of freedom being voiced in a war against tyranny. For example, five Connecticut blacks gave "Liberty" as their surname at the time of enlistment, and another eighteen said their name was "Freedom" or "Freeman."

Military service helped to politicize Americans during the early stages of the war. In early 1776, independence was a risky idea, potentially treasonous. But as the war heated up and leaders and recruiters demanded commitment, some apathetic Americans discovered that apathy had its dangers as well. Anyone who refused to serve ran the risk of being called a traitor to the cause. Military service established one's credentials as a patriot; it became a prime way of defining and demonstrating political allegiance.

The American army was at times raw and inexperienced and much of the time woefully undermanned. It never had the precision and discipline of European professional armies. But it was never as bad as the British continually assumed. The British were to learn that it was a serious mistake to underrate the enemy.

**BLACK REVOLUTIONARY WAR SAILOR**
*Thousands of black men served on the patriot side as soldiers and sailors, usually at the rank of private or ordinary seaman. Their names are preserved in regiment records and crew lists; rarely, however, were their faces preserved. This 1780 portrait by an unknown artist shows an unnamed man, sword and scabbard at hand, dressed in military finery with a ship in view to establish his naval connection.*
Collection of A. A. McBurney.

## The British Strategy

The American strategy was relatively straightforward—to repulse and defeat an invading army. The British strategy was not nearly so clear. England wanted to put down a rebellion and restore monarchical power in the colonies, but the question was how to accomplish this. A decisive defeat of the Continental army was essential but not sufficient to end the rebellion, for there were all those militiamen around the countryside to contend with. An armed and highly motivated insurgent population proved a tough enemy.

Furthermore, there was no single political nerve center whose capture would spell certain victory. The Continental Congress floated from place to place, staying just out of reach of the British. During the course of the war, the British captured and for a time occupied every major port city—Boston, New York, Newport, Philadelphia, and Charleston—but with no significant gain. The British needed these harbor cities for their constant caravan of supply ships, but capturing them brought no serious loss to the Americans, 95 percent of whom lived in the countryside.

England's delicate task was to restore the old governments, not to destroy an enemy country. Hence, the British generals were usually reluctant to ravage the countryside, confiscate food, or burn villages and towns. There were thirteen distinct political entities to capture, pacify, and then restore to the crown, and they were spread out in a very long line from New Hampshire to Georgia. Clearly a large land army was required for the job. Without the willingness to seize food from the locals, such an army needed hundreds of supply ships that could keep several months' worth of food in storage.

---

*England's delicate task was to restore the old governments, not to destroy an enemy country.*

---

Another ingredient of the British strategy was the assumption (quite untested) that large numbers of Americans remained loyal to the king and would come to the aid of the British army. Without substantial numbers of loyal subjects, the plan to restore old royal governments made no sense.

The overall British plan was a divide-and-conquer approach to recapturing the thirteen colonies. The plan focused first on New York, the state judged to harbor the greatest number of loyal subjects, perhaps as much as half the population. New York offered a geographic advantage as well: Control of the Hudson River would allow the British to isolate the most troublesome states, those in New England. Armies could descend from Canada and move up from New York City along the Hudson River into western Massachusetts. Between a naval blockade on the eastern coast and army raids in the west, Massachusetts would be driven to surrender. Or so the British hoped.

South of New York, in New Jersey and Pennsylvania, the British also expected to find large pockets of loyalist strength to secure their advances. Rebellious citizens would be pressured to sign loyalty oaths to the crown. Virginia was a problem, like Massachusetts, but the British were confident that the Carolinas contained many loyalists and that they could thus isolate and subdue Virginia.

## Quebec, New York, and New Jersey

While Washington disciplined his troops in Massachusetts, an American expedition was launched in late 1775 to capture the British cities Montreal and Quebec, a clear sign that the war was not merely a defensive reaction to the invasion of Massachusetts. The two cities were symbolic as well as strategic goals, having been sites of contest in the French-British wars of the 1740s and 1750s. American commanders moved swiftly north to attack before British reinforcements could arrive. A force of New York Continentals commanded by General Richard Montgomery took Montreal easily in September 1775 and then advanced on Quebec. Meanwhile, a second contingent of Continentals led by Colonel Benedict Arnold moved through Maine along the Kennebec River to Quebec, a punishing trek through freezing rain with woefully inadequate food and boats; many men died. Arnold's fierce determination to get to Quebec was heroic, but in human costs the campaign was a tragedy. Arnold and Montgomery jointly attacked Quebec in December but suffered heavy losses and failed to take the city (Map 7.1).

The main action of the first year of war came not in Canada, however, but in New York, the state deemed crucial to England. In August 1776, some 20,000 fresh British troops (including 8,000 German mercenary soldiers, called Hessians) landed on Staten Island, south of New York City. They were joined by regiments from Nova Scotia, bringing the total to nearly 45,000 soldiers, under the command of General Howe. General Washington had anticipated that New York would be Howe's target and had moved his army, numbering about 20,000, from Massachusetts to an area of fortified ground on Long Island.

The Battle of Long Island, in late August 1776, pitted the well-trained British redcoats against a very green Continental army. Howe attacked the American fortifications, inflicting many casualties (1,500 dead and wounded) and spreading panic

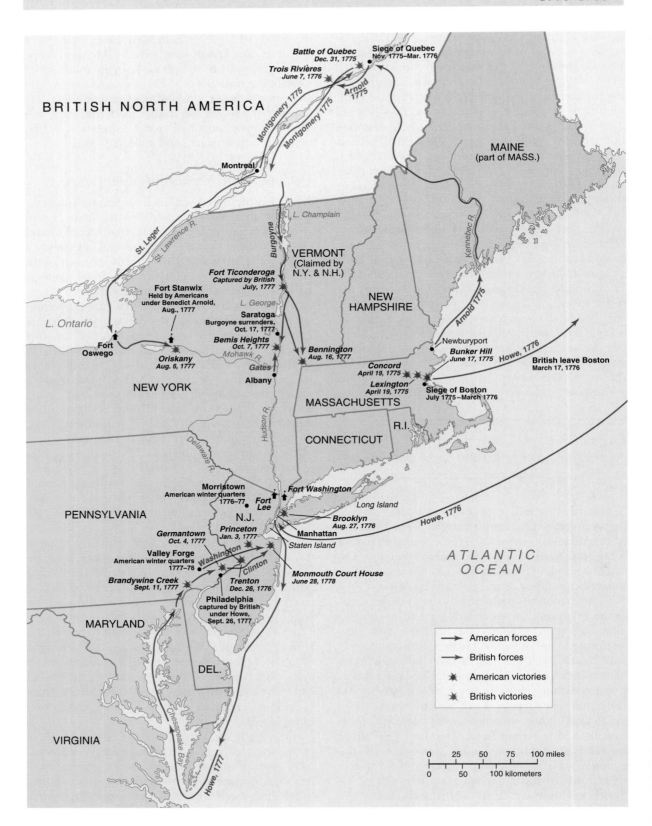

BRITISH NORTH AMERICA

**Battle of Quebec**
Dec. 31, 1775

**Siege of Quebec**
Nov. 1775–Mar. 1776

**Trois Rivières**
June 7, 1776

Arnold 1775

Montgomery 1775

Montgomery 1775

Montreal

St. Leger

St. Lawrence R.

L. Champlain

Burgoyne

MAINE
(part of MASS.)

Kennebec R.

VERMONT
(Claimed by
N.Y. & N.H.)

**Fort Ticonderoga**
Captured by British
July, 1777

**Fort Stanwix**
Held by Americans
under Benedict Arnold,
Aug., 1777

L. George

NEW
HAMPSHIRE

Arnold 1775

**Saratoga**
Burgoyne surrenders,
Oct. 17, 1777

L. Ontario

**Bemis Heights**
Oct. 7, 1777

Fort
Oswego

**Oriskany**
Aug. 6, 1777

Mohawk R.

Gates

**Bennington**
Aug. 16, 1777

Newburyport

**Bunker Hill**
June 17, 1775

Howe, 1776

**British leave Boston**
March 17, 1776

NEW YORK

Albany

**Concord**
April 19, 1775

**Lexington**
April 19, 1775

**Siege of Boston**
July 1775–March 1776

MASSACHUSETTS

Hudson R.

CONNECTICUT

R.I.

Delaware R.

**Morristown**
American winter quarters
1776–77

Fort
Lee

**Fort Washington**

Long Island

**Brooklyn**
Aug. 27, 1776

Howe, 1776

PENNSYLVANIA

N.J.

**Princeton**
Jan. 3, 1777

**Germantown**
Oct. 4, 1777

Washington

Manhattan

Staten Island

ATLANTIC
OCEAN

**Valley Forge**
American winter quarters
1777–78

Clinton

**Monmouth Court House**
June 28, 1778

**Brandywine Creek**
Sept. 11, 1777

**Trenton**
Dec. 26, 1776

**Philadelphia**
captured by British
under Howe,
Sept. 26, 1777

MARYLAND

DEL.

Chesapeake Bay

VIRGINIA

Howe, 1777

American forces

British forces

American victories

British victories

| 0 | 25 | 50 | 75 | 100 miles |

| 0 | | 50 | | 100 kilometers |

M A P 7.1
*The War in the North, 1775–1778*
*After the early battles in Massachusetts in 1775, rebel*
*forces invaded Canada but failed to capture Quebec. A*
*large British army landed in New York in August 1776,*
*turning New Jersey into a continual site of battle in 1777*
*and 1778. Burgoyne arrived to secure Canada and made*
*his attempt to pinch off New England along the Hudson*
*River line, but he was stopped at Saratoga in 1777 in the*
*key battle of the early war years.*

among the American soldiers, who fled under fire
to the eastern edge of Long Island. Howe failed to
press forward, however, perhaps remembering the
costly victory of Bunker Hill, and in the meantime
Washington evacuated his troops to Manhattan Island in the dead of night, under cover of an unusually thick fog.

From September to November, the two armies
juggled for position and engaged in limited fighting. In November, Howe finally attacked and captured two critical forts on either side of the Hudson
River, Fort Washington and Fort Lee, taking thousands of prisoners. Washington retreated quickly
across New Jersey into Pennsylvania. Yet again,
Howe unaccountably failed to take advantage of the
situation. Had he attacked Washington's army at
Philadelphia, he would probably have taken the
city. Instead he parked his German troops in winter quarters along the Delaware River. Perhaps he
knew that many of the Continental soldiers' enlistment periods ended on December 31, so he felt confident that the Americans would not attack him. But
he was wrong. On Christmas—a holiday Germans
celebrated with much more spirit (and spirits) than
did Americans—Washington recrossed the Delaware River at night with 2,400 men and made a
quick capture of the unsuspecting German soldiers
at Trenton. The victory was impressively executed,
and it did much to restore the sagging morale of the
patriot side. For the next two weeks, Washington
remained on the offensive, dancing just ahead of the
British army, capturing supplies in a clever attack
on British units at Princeton on January 3. Soon he
was safe in Morristown, in northern New Jersey,
settled in for the winter.

All in all, in the first year of declared war, the
rebellious Americans had a few isolated moments
to feel proud of but also much to worry about. The
very inexperienced Continental army had barely

hung on in the New York campaign. Washington
had shown exceptional daring as well as admirable
restraint, but what really saved the American army
may have been the repeated reluctance of the
British to follow through militarily when they had
the advantage.

## The Home Front

Battlefields alone did not determine the outcome of
the war. Struggles on the home front were equally
important. In 1776, each community contained
small numbers of highly committed people on both
sides and far larger numbers who were either apolitical or uncertain about whether independence
was worth a war. The contest for the allegiance of
the many neutrals thus figured as a major factor,
and both persuasion and force were used. Revolutionaries who took control of local government
often used it to punish loyalists and intimidate neutrals. On their side, loyalists worked to reestablish
British authority. The struggle to secure political allegiance was complicated greatly by the wartime instability of the economy. The creative financing of
the fledgling government brought hardships as well
as opportunities, forcing Americans to confront new
manifestations of virtue and corruption.

### Patriotism at the Local Level

Committees of correspondence, of public safety, and
of inspection dominated the political landscape in
patriot communities. These committees took on
more than customary local governance; they enforced boycotts, picked army draftees, and policed
suspected traitors. They sometimes invaded homes
to search for contraband goods.

Loyalists were dismayed by what seemed to
them to be excessive or arbitrary power taken on by
committees. On occasion, secret and resourceful
loyalists managed to win election to these committees in order to subvert them. Others were open
with their denunciations. A man in Westchester,
New York, described his response to intrusions by
committees: "Choose your committee or suffer it to
be chosen by a half dozen fools in your neighborhood—open your doors to them—let them examine your tea-cannisters and molasses-jugs, and your
wives' and daughters' petty coats—bow and cringe
and tremble and quake—fall down and worship

our sovereign lord the mob. . . . Should any prag-matical committee-gentleman come to my house and give himself airs, I shall show him the door, and if he does not soon take himself away, a good hick-ory cudgel shall teach him better manners." Exces-sive or not, the powers of the local committees were rarely challenged. Committees of safety and of cor-respondence became the local governing agencies, and their persuasive powers convinced many middle-of-the-road citizens that neutrality was not a comfortable option.

Another group new to political life—white women—increasingly demonstrated a capacity for patriotism at the local level as wartime hardships dramatically altered their own work routines. Like Abigail Adams on her Braintree farm, many wives with husbands away on military or political service found themselves taking on masculine duties. Their increased competence to tend farms and make busi-ness decisions appears to have encouraged some to assert competence in political matters as well. Eliza Wilkinson managed a plantation on the South Car-olina coast and talked revolutionary politics with her women friends. "None were greater politicians than the several knots of ladies who met together," she remarked, alert to the unusual turn female con-versations had taken. "We commenced perfect statesmen."

Women from prominent Philadelphia families went a step beyond political talk to action. In 1780, they formed the Ladies Association, going door to door collecting a substantial sum of money to help support the Continental soldiers. A pub-lished broadside, "The Sentiments of an American Woman," defended their female patriotism. "The time is arrived to display the same sentiments which animated us at the beginning of the Revolution, when we renounced the use of teas . . . [and] when our republican and laborious hands spun the flax."

### The Loyalists

Between 20 and 30 percent of the American popu-lation remained openly loyal to the British monar-chy in 1776, and another 20 to 40 percent could be described as neutral. Such a large population base could have sustained the British Empire in Amer-ica, if only the British army leaders had known how to use it (Map 7.2).

In general, loyalists were people who still found the idea of the British Empire, with all its historical, cultural, and economic ties, an appealing vision. They were convinced that American prosperity and stability depended on British rule and on a gov-ernment anchored by monarchy and aristocracy. Perhaps most of all, they feared democratic tyranny. Like Abigail Adams, they understood that dissolv-ing the automatic respect that submissive subjects had for their king could potentially lead to a soci-ety where all deference and hierarchy came un-glued. Adams welcomed this chance to identify tyranny in unequal power relations, as between men and women; loyalists feared it. Patriots seemed to them to be unscrupulous, violent, self-interested men who simply wanted power for themselves.

The most visible and dedicated loyalists (also called Tories by their enemies) were royal officials, not only top officeholders like Thomas Hutchinson in Massachusetts, but also local judges and customs officers. Wealthy merchants with commercial ties to England were made uneasy by the thought of aban-doning the trade protections of navigation acts and the British navy. Urban lawyers of a conservative temperament often found it impossible to imagine forgoing the stability of British law and order.

The early-eighteenth-century grants of reli-gious liberty to grateful groups like the Palatine Germans in upstate New York and the French Huguenots in the Carolinas influenced some of them to remain loyal to Britain. Two other religious enclaves, the Quakers and the Moravians, located in Pennsylvania and North Carolina, were pacifists by religious conviction and were therefore often treated as though they were loyalists.

Some were loyalists merely as a product of op-positional politics with leading patriot men. For ex-ample, backcountry farmers in the Carolinas grav-itated toward loyalism out of resentment over the political and economic power of the lowlands gen-try. Southern slaves had their own resentments against the white slave-owning class. Many thou-sands in Virginia responded to Lord Dunmore's promise of eventual freedom if they would defect and aid the British, and more still in South Carolina ran off to Charleston to seek refuge with the British army when it occupied the city.

Many, indeed most, Indians eventually sup-ported the British side, not only because they as-sumed that England would win the war. Some tribes, like the powerful Iroquois Nation in New York, had strong economic ties to the empire. One young Mohawk leader, Thayendanegea (known to Americans as Joseph Brant), traveled to England in 1775 to complain to King George about how the colonists repeatedly deceived the Mohawks. "It is very hard when we have let the King's subjects

**MAP 7.2**
*Loyalist Strength and Rebel Support*
The exact number of loyalists can never be known. No one could have made an accurate count at the time of the Revolution; political allegiance often shifted with the winds. This map shows the pockets of loyalist strength that the British relied on—the lower Hudson valley, the Carolina piedmont, and the areas most hotly contested by both sides: New Jersey and the Mohawk River valley, regions repeatedly torn by battles and skirmishes.

have so much of our lands for so little value," he wrote, "they should want to cheat us in this manner of the small spots we have left for our women and children to live on. We are tired out in making complaints & getting no redress." Thayendanegea negotiated Indian support for the king in exchange for protection from encroaching settlers, under a revived implementation of the Proclamation Act of 1763.

Pockets of loyalism thus existed everywhere. Most were in the middle colonies and the backcountry of the South. But even New England towns at the heart of turmoil, like Concord, Massachusetts, had a small and increasingly silenced core of loyalists who refused to countenance armed revolution.

The loyalists were most vocal between 1774 and 1776, when the possibility of a full-scale rebellion against England was still uncertain. Loyalists challenged the emerging patriot side using pamphlets, broadsides, and newspapers; every major city had

one or sometimes two loyalist printers. In New York City in 1776, some loyalists even circulated a broadside titled "A Declaration of Dependence," in rebuttal to the Congress's July 4 manifesto, denouncing this "most unnatural, unprovoked Rebellion that ever disgraced the annals of Time."

Speeches and rallies amplified the spread of loyalism in backcountry areas where print culture had not fully penetrated. Loyalist ministers used their pulpits, while other defenders of the empire staged rallies or disrupted patriot gatherings. At an open-air rally in backcountry South Carolina in 1775, a loyalist elbowed his way to the platform to remind the audience of the superior might of the British army and of the damage to trade independence would surely bring. But his winning argument was to invoke the backcountry's resentments of the coastal planters' wealth and political power: It is ironic, he said, that "the charge of our intending to enslave you should come oftenest from the

**JOSEPH BRANT**
*The Mohawk leader Thayendanegea, called Joseph Brant by Americans, had been educated in English ways at Eleazar Wheelock's New England school (which became Dartmouth College in 1769). In 1775, Brant traveled to England with another warrior to negotiate Mohawk support for the British. There he had his portrait painted by George Romney. The thirty-four-year-old Brant wears a feudal gorget around his neck over his English shirt (compare with Washington, page 133), along with Indian armbands and headdress.*
National Gallery of Canada, Ottawa.

mouths of those lawyers who in your southern provinces, at least, have long made you slaves to themselves."

## Who Is a Traitor?

The rough treatment that loyalists experienced at the hands of the revolutionaries seemed to substantiate their worst fears. In June 1775, the First Continental Congress passed a resolution declaring loyalists to be traitors. Over the next year, state after state wrote laws defining treasonable acts, such as joining the British army or providing it with food or ammunition. In some states, it was treason to discourage men from enlisting in the Continental army

or to say or print anything undermining patriot morale. Punishments ranged from house arrest and suspension of voting privileges to confiscation of property and deportation. And sometimes self-appointed committees of Tory hunters bypassed the judicial niceties and terrorized loyalists, raiding their houses or tarring and feathering them.

Tarring and feathering, property confiscation, deportation, terrorism—to the loyalists, such denials of liberty of conscience and of freedom to own private property proved that democratic tyranny was more to be feared than the monarchical variety. A Boston loyalist, Mather Byles, aptly expressed this point: "They call me a brainless Tory, but tell me . . . which is better—to be ruled by one tyrant three thousand miles away, or by three thousand tyrants not a mile away?" Byles, a minister, was soon sentenced to deportation.

> *"They call me a brainless Tory, but tell me . . . which is better—to be ruled by one tyrant three thousand miles away, or by three thousand tyrants not a mile away?"*

Throughout the war, probably 7,000–8,000 loyalists fled to England, while 28,000 found closer haven in Canada. But many chose to remain in the new United States and tried to swing with the changing political fortunes of their communities as best they could. In some places, that proved extremely hard to manage. In New Jersey, for example, 3,000 Jerseyites felt protected enough by the occupying British army in 1776 to swear an oath of allegiance to the king. Even a man who just months before had signed the Declaration of Independence, Richard Stockton, came forward to beg pardon for his action. What those 3,000 publicly sworn loyalists could not foresee was that General Howe would draw back to New York City and leave them at the mercy of local patriot committees. British strategy depended on using loyalists to hold occupied territory, but the New Jersey experience showed just how poorly that strategy was put into practice.

## Financial Instability and Corruption

Wars cost money—to pay soldiers; to pay suppliers for food, clothing, and housing; to pay manufacturers for muskets, cannon, and gunpowder. The Continental Congress printed money, but within a few short years its value had deteriorated, since the congress held no reserves of gold or silver to back the currency. In practice, the currency was worth only what a buyer and seller agreed it was worth. The dollar eventually bottomed out at one-fortieth of its face value; a loaf of bread that once sold for two and a half cents now sold for a dollar.

Soon the congress had to resort to other means to procure supplies and labor. One method was to borrow hard money (not paper) from wealthy men, who would get certificates of debt (also called public securities) promising repayment with interest. In effect, the wealthy men had bought government bonds. To pay soldiers, the congress offered land bounties, which amounted to a promise of a tangible form of wealth. Public securities and land bounties quickly became a form of negotiable currency. For example, a soldier with no paycheck or cash might sell his land bounty certificate to get food for his family. These certificates also fluctuated in value, mainly depreciating.

Depreciating currency inevitably led to rising prices, as sellers compensated for the falling value of the money. The wartime economy of the late 1770s, with its unreliable currency and price inflation, was unprecedented and extremely demoralizing to Americans everywhere. So local committees of public safety in 1778 began to fix prices on goods such as flour, bread, and other essentials for short periods in an effort to impose some brief stability. Such short-run expectations for holding down prices testify to the wild character of the economy.

Inevitably, some Americans turned this rollercoaster situation to their advantage. Money that fell fast in value needed to be spent quickly; being in debt was suddenly advantageous because the debt could be repaid weeks later in devalued currency. A brisk black market sprang up in prohibited luxury imports, such as tea, sugar, textiles, and wines. No matter that these items came from Britain. A New Hampshire delegate to the congress denounced the extravagance that flew in the face of the virtuous homespun association agreements of just a few years before: "We are a crooked and perverse generation, longing for the fineries and follies of those Egyptian task masters from whom we have so lately freed ourselves."

## The Campaigns of 1777: Highs and Lows

In early 1777, the Continental army had a bleak road ahead. Washington had shown considerable skill in avoiding outright military defeat, but the minor victories in New Jersey lent only faint optimism to the American side. The British moved large numbers of soldiers into Quebec, readying their plan to isolate New England by controlling the Hudson River.

## Burgoyne's Army and the Battle of Saratoga

In 1777, General John Burgoyne assumed command of an army of 7,800 soldiers in Canada and began the northern squeeze on the Hudson River valley. His goal was to capture Albany, a town 150 miles north of New York City near the intersection of the Hudson and Mohawk Rivers (see Map 7.1).

In addition to his soldiers, Burgoyne traveled with another 1,000 assorted "camp followers" (cooks, laundresses, musicians) and 400 Indian scouts. This very large army did not travel light, requiring food supplies not only for 9,000 people but also for the more than 400 horses needed to haul heavy artillery. Burgoyne, who was nicknamed "Gentleman Johnny," also carted thirty trunks of personal belongings, including fine wines and elegant clothing.

Burgoyne first captured Fort Ticonderoga with ease. Some 3,000 American troops stationed there spotted the approaching British and, low on food and supplies, abandoned the fort without a fight. The British continued to move south, but the large army moved slowly on primitive roads through forest land. Local farmers created obstacles by felling trees in the army's path. Burgoyne lost a critical month hacking his way down the road, and meanwhile his supply lines back to Canada were severely stretched. Soldiers sent out to forage food were beaten back by local militia units.

The logical second step in isolating New England should have been to advance troops up the Hudson from New York City to meet Burgoyne. American surveillance indicated that General Howe in Manhattan was readying his men for a major move in August 1777. George Washington, watching from New Jersey, was astonished to see Howe's men sail south; Howe had decided to try to capture Philadelphia.

The third prong of British strategy involved troops moving east from the Great Lakes down the Mohawk River, aided by Indians of Joseph Brant's Iroquois League. The British believed that the Palatine Germans of the Mohawk valley were heavily loyalist, so they expected little trouble getting to Albany. But a hundred miles west of their goal they encountered American soldiers at Fort Stanwix, reinforced by militia units composed of local Palatine Germans. Iroquois Indians ambushed the militia

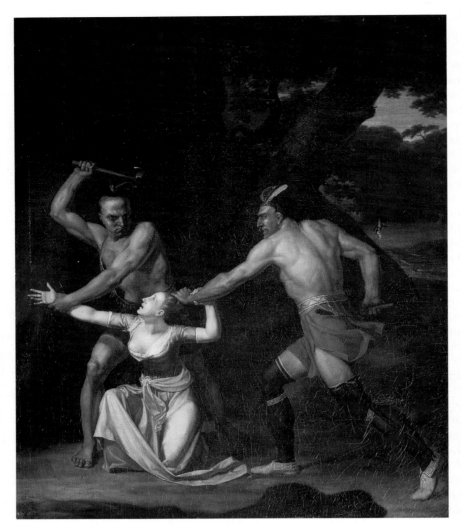

**DEATH OF JANE McCREA**
*This 1804 painting by John Vanderlyn memorializes the martyr legend of Jane McCrea. McCrea lived with her patriot family in upstate New York, but in July 1777 she fled to join her fiancé, a loyalist fighting with Burgoyne's army. She was murdered en route, allegedly by Iroquois allies of the British. The American general Horatio Gates sent Burgoyne an accusatory letter. "The miserable fate of Miss McCrea was particularly aggravated by her being dressed to meet her promised husband," Gates wrote, "but she met her murderers employed by you." Gates skillfully used the story of the vulnerable, innocent maiden dressed in alluring clothes as propaganda to inspire his soldiers' drive for victory at Saratoga. Vanderlyn's work, and other similar pictorial representations, emphasized McCrea's helplessness and sexuality. Yet had McCrea been a man, her flight would have been traitorous. Why this different treatment of a woman?*
Wadsworth Atheneum, Hartford.

units in a narrow ravine called Oriskany and inflicted heavy losses. But Fort Stanwix held back the British and Indians and eventually sent them into retreat (see Map 7.1).

Burgoyne thus did not have the additional troops he expected. Camped at a small village called Saratoga, he was isolated and stuck; his food supplies were dwindling, and his men were deserting. His adversary at Albany, General Horatio Gates, began moving 7,000 Continental soldiers north in search of the British. Burgoyne decided to attack first, since every day his army weakened. The first Battle of Saratoga was a British victory, but an expensive one, leaving 600 dead and wounded redcoats. Only three

weeks later, a second Battle of Saratoga cost Burgoyne another 600 men and most of his cannon as well. Burgoyne tried to retreat, but Gates's army blocked his path. With food running out and many of his men wounded and demoralized, Burgoyne finally officially surrendered to the Americans on October 17, 1777.

Americans on the side of the rebellion were jubilant. This was the first decisive victory for the Continental army. Practically overnight, a popular dance called "General Burgoyne's Surrender" swept through the country, and bookies in the major cities set odds at five to one that the war would be won in just six months.

General Howe, meanwhile, had succeeded in occupying Philadelphia in September 1777. Washington had moved his army south of the city to defend it, but he lost a crucial battle at Brandywine Creek. The British government figured that Burgoyne's surrender was evenly balanced by the capture of Philadelphia and thus proposed a negotiated settlement—not including independence—to end the war. But the American side refused.

Their optimism was not well founded, however, in the winter of 1777–78; spirits ran high, but finances and supplies ran precariously low. Washington moved his troops into winter quarters at Valley Forge, a day's march west of occupied Philadelphia. Quartered in drafty sheds, the men lacked blankets, boots, and stockings. Washington complained to the congress that nearly 3,000 of his men were "unfit for duty because they are bare foot and otherwise naked"; without blankets, large numbers were forced to "set up all Night by fires, instead of taking comfortable rest in a natural way." Food was also scarce. Standard rations dwindled for a time to "firecake," a tasteless pancake made of flour and water, and in one week in February there were no food rations at all. Local farms had produced adequate food that year, but Washington was sure that the farmers were selling their grain to the British, who could pay with the king's silver. His young aide-de-camp Alexander Hamilton openly wondered if the country was even worth fighting for, so corrupt did it seem.

The evidence of corruption indeed appeared abundant. Army suppliers too often provided defective food, clothing, and gunpowder. Washington's men unfolded a shipment of blankets only to discover that they were a quarter of their customary size. Teamsters who hauled barrels of preserved salted meat might drain out the brine to lighten their load and then refill the barrels later, allowing the meat to rot in transit. Selfishness and greed seemed to infect the American side. As one Continental officer said, "The people at home are destroying the Army by their conduct much faster than Howe and all his army can possibly do by fighting us."

### The French Alliance

On their own, the Americans could not have defeated England. Essential help arrived as a result of the victory at Saratoga, which convinced the French to enter the war, and a formal alliance was signed in February 1778. France recognized the United States as an independent nation and promised full military and commercial support throughout the war. The most crucial support was the French navy, which now could challenge England's transatlantic pipeline of supplies and troops.

Although France had been waiting for a promising American victory to justify a formal declaration of war, since 1776 the French had aided the Americans in many ways. They had provided military goods—cannons, muskets, gunpowder— and highly trained French military experts who had advised the American army in the field.

*On their own, the Americans could not have defeated England. Essential help arrived as a result of the victory at Saratoga, which convinced the French to enter the war.*

Still, monarchical France was understandably cautious about endorsing a democratic revolution that attacked the principles of kingship. The main attraction of an alliance for France was simply the opportunity to defeat England, its archrival. A victory would also open pathways to trade and perhaps result in France acquiring the coveted British West Indies. Even American defeat was not a full disaster for France, if the war took many years and drained England of men, money, and psychological energy.

The French navy arrived off the coast of Virginia in July 1778 and then sailed north to threaten (but not attack) the British in New York. In August, the allied ships went farther north to Newport, Rhode Island, also held by the British, and engaged in limited battle. By 1781, the French proved indispensable to the American victory, but the first months of the alliance brought no dramatic victories, inducing grumbling from some Americans that the partnership would prove worthless. Indeed, by late fall 1778, the French fleet had sailed off for the West Indies.

## The Southern Strategy and the End of the War

When France joined the war, some British officials paused to consider whether the fight was worth continuing. A troop commander, arguing for an immediate negotiated settlement, shrewdly observed that "we are far from an anticipated peace, because the bitterness of the rebels is too widespread, and in regions where we are masters the rebellious spirit is still in them. The land is too large, and there are too many people. The more land we win, the weaker our army gets in the field." The commander of the British navy argued for abandoning the war, and even Lord North, the prime minister of King George's cabinet, was believed to be in favor of ending it quickly. But the king was determined to crush the rebellion, the French notwithstanding, and he encouraged the development of a new strategy for victory. It was a brilliant but desperate plan.

## Georgia and South Carolina

The new strategy shelved the plan to isolate New England and instead focused on the South, thought to be easier to recapture for the crown. The southern region had valuable crops—tobacco, rice, and indigo—worth struggling to keep under the British flag. Further, the high slave population was a powerful destabilizing factor from which the British hoped to benefit. White southerners could ill afford the instability of all-out war, for it might unleash violence from two sides—from the British and from slaves seizing the moment to claim freedom themselves. Georgia and the Carolinas also looked promising for victory because of the large pockets of loyalism presumed to be prevalent and, most important, militant. The British hoped to recapture the southern colonies one by one, restore the loyalists to power, and then move north to the more problematic middle colonies, saving prickly New England for last.

Georgia, the first target, fell at the end of December 1778 (Map 7.3). A small army of British soldiers occupied Savannah and Augusta, and a new royal governor and loyalist assembly were quickly installed. Taking Georgia was easy because the bulk of the Continental army was in New York and New Jersey, keeping an eye on General Clinton, Howe's replacement as commander in chief, and the French were in the West Indies. The British in Georgia quickly organized twenty loyal militia units, and 1,400 Georgians swore an oath of allegiance to the king. So far, the plan looked as if it might work.

The next target was South Carolina. General Clinton moved British troops south from New York, while the Continental army put ten regiments into Charleston to defend the capital city. For five weeks in early 1780, the British laid siege to the city, which finally surrendered in mid-May 1780, sending 3,300 soldiers, a tremendous loss, into British captivity.

Again, the king's new strategy seemed to be working as planned.

Clinton returned to New York, leaving the task of pacifying South Carolina to General Charles Cornwallis and 4,000 troops. The boldest of all the British generals in the war for America, Lord Cornwallis quickly moved into action. He chased out the remaining Continental army units and established military control of the state by midsummer 1780. He purged rebels from government office and disarmed potential rebel militias. The export of South Carolina's main crop, rice, resumed, suggesting an easy normalization of relations between England and the colony. As in Georgia, pardons were offered to Carolinians who swore loyalty oaths to the crown.

In August 1780, the Continental army was ready to strike back at Cornwallis. General Gates, the hero of the Battle of Saratoga, arrived in South Carolina with more than 3,000 troops, some of them experienced army units and others green militiamen. They met Cornwallis's army at Camden, South Carolina, on August 16. Gates put the militiamen into the center of the battle, where a contagious panic gripped them at the sight of the approaching enemy cavalry. Men threw down unfired muskets and ran from the field of battle. When regiment leaders tried to regroup the next day, only 700 showed up. The rest were either dead, captured, or still in flight—including Gates, who traversed a speedy 180 miles in three days before he stopped to file a report on the battle. Camden was a devastating defeat; prospects now seemed very grim for the Americans.

The new British strategy succeeded in 1780 partly as a product of improved information about American troop movements and supplies that was secretly furnished to General Clinton in New York by General Benedict Arnold, the onetime American hero of several key battles. Arnold was a brilliant military talent but also a deeply insecure man who never felt he got his due, in either honor or financial reward. Sometime in 1779, he opened secret negotiations with the British commander in New York, Henry Clinton, trading information for money and hinting he could deliver far more of value. When he was assigned the command of West Point, a new fort sixty miles north of New York City on the Hudson River, his plan crystallized. West Point controlled the Hudson; its easy capture by the British might well have meant instant victory in the war.

Arnold's treasonous plot to sell West Point to the British was foiled by the capture of the messenger between Arnold and Clinton. News of the

**BENEDICT ARNOLD**
*Benedict Arnold in 1776, when he was the hero of the Quebec campaign. Probably the final straw for Arnold came when he failed to earn promotion, while men he considered inferior were elevated to higher rank.*
Anne S. K. Brown Military Collection, Providence, R.I.

treason created shock waves. Arnold represented all of the patriots' worst fears: greedy self-interest like that of the war profiteers, unprincipled abandonment of the war aims like that of the turncoat Tories of the South, panic like that of the terrified soldiers with Gates at Camden. But instead of symbolizing all that was troubling about the American side of the war, the treachery of Arnold became celebrated in a kind of displacement of the anxieties of the moment. Vilifying Arnold allowed Americans to stake out a wide distance between themselves and dastardly conduct. It inspired a renewal of patriotism at what had been a particularly low moment.

## The Other Southern War: Guerrillas

Shock over Gates's defeat at Camden and the treason of Benedict Arnold revitalized rebel support in western South Carolina, an area that Cornwallis had believed to be pacified and loyal. The backcountry of the South soon became the site of a guerrilla war. In hit-and-run attacks, both sides burned and ravaged not only opponents' property but the property of anyone claiming to be neutral. The loyalist militia units organized by the British were met by fierce rebel militia units who now figured they had little to lose. Guerrilla warfare soon spread to Georgia and North Carolina. Both sides murdered enemies, committed atrocities, and plundered property, clear deviations from standard military practice.

The British southern strategy counted on sufficient loyalist strength—in terms of both numbers of people and the respect and authority they could command—to hold reconquered territory as the army moved north. The backcountry civil war proved this assumption false. The Americans won few major battles in the South, but they ultimately succeeded by dogging the British forces, harassing them, and thus preventing them from foraging for food. Cornwallis boldly moved the war into North Carolina in late 1780, not because he thought South Carolina was secure—it was not—but because the North Carolinians were supplying the South Carolina rebels with arms and men. But news of a brutal defeat—a massacre, actually—of loyalist units in western South Carolina at Kings Mountain, at the hands of 1,400 frontier riflemen, sent him hurrying back. The British were stretched too thin to hold even two of their onetime colonies.

## Surrender at Yorktown

In the early months of 1781, Cornwallis set out to try his North Carolina plan again; if successful, it would isolate South Carolina and Georgia. For months, he moved his army around the state, taking land but not holding it. In February 1781, Cornwallis proclaimed, prematurely, that North Carolina was reconquered, a move calculated to increase loyalist support. But few loyalists could be found who were willing to take up arms against the energized rebel forces.

Cornwallis decided to push the war farther north, into Virginia. He captured Williamsburg, which had been the colony's seat of government until the previous year. Then he raided Charlottesville, where Virginia's revolutionary government was meeting, and seized members of the assembly; Governor Thomas Jefferson narrowly avoided capture. (More than a dozen of Jefferson's slaves chose this moment to seek refuge with the British army.) As late as the start of September,

**MAP 7.3**
*The War in the South, 1780–1781*
*After taking Charleston in 1780, the British advanced into South Carolina and the foothill region of North Carolina, leaving a bloody civil war in their wake. Cornwallis next invaded Virginia but was overpowered by American and French forces at Yorktown in 1781 in the final battle of the Revolutionary War.*

Cornwallis was not wrong to think he had the upper hand in Virginia.

What changed the picture dramatically was an infusion of French military support. A large French army under the command of the comte de Rochambeau had joined Washington in Rhode Island in mid-1780. News that a large fleet had sailed from France in the spring of 1781 set in motion Washington's plan to defeat the British. The fleet was bound for the Chesapeake Bay, so Washington and Rochambeau fixed their attention on Cornwallis's campaign in Virginia. Bypassing New York (where Clinton had been expecting an attack), thousands of American and French soldiers headed south in the last week of August 1781, traveling on four separate roads to confuse the British.

British intelligence about the French fleet movement had been delayed, and by the time British ships arrived at the mouth of the Chesapeake, the French had already taken control of it. A five-day naval battle in early September sent the British ships limping away and left the French in clear command of the bay and the Virginia and North Carolina coasts. This proved to be the decisive factor in ending the war, because it eliminated a water escape route for Cornwallis's land army, encamped at Yorktown, Virginia.

General Cornwallis and his 7,500 troops now faced a combined French and American army numbering over 16,000. For twelve days, the Americans and French bombarded the British fortifications at Yorktown; Cornwallis ran low on food and ammunition. An American observer keeping a diary noted that "the enemy, from want of forage, are killing off their horses in great numbers. Six or seven hundred of these valuable animals have been killed, and their carcasses are almost continually floating down the river." Realizing escape was impossible, Cornwallis signaled his intention to surrender, and on October 19, 1781, he formally capitulated.

What had begun as a promising southern strategy by the British in 1778 had turned into a discouraging defeat by 1781. British attacks in the South energized American resistance, as did the timely exposure of Benedict Arnold's treason. The arrival of the French fleet sealed the fate of Cornwallis at Yorktown, and the military war quickly came to a halt.

## The Losers and the Winners

The surrender at Yorktown proved to be the end of the war, but it took some time for the principals to realize that. The peace treaty was nearly two years in the making, and in the meantime both the American and the British armies remained in the field, in case the treaty fell through. Clinton continued to occupy New York; Charleston and Savannah, too, stayed under British control, although the British had been chased out of the rest of the South. King George tenaciously clung to the idea of pursuing the war, but the sentiment for a formal peace was growing in Parliament. The war had become unpopular among the British citizenry in general, and support for it dwindled until finally the king had to realize it was over.

It took six months for the three American commissioners, Benjamin Franklin, John Adams, and John Jay of New York, to negotiate the three-way settlement in Paris. The British tried to exploit differences between French and American interests. For example, the French had no problem with dividing up the colonies, giving New York, the Carolinas, and Georgia back to the British; the Americans wanted not only all thirteen colonies but Canada as well.

In late November 1782, eighty-two articles of peace were agreed to. The first article went to the heart of the matter: "His Britannic Majesty acknowledges the said United States to be free Sovereign and independent States." Other articles described the boundaries of the new country: a northern line separating Canada, which remained British, a western line along the Mississippi River, and a southern line sectioning off Florida, which England soon handed over to Spain in a separate treaty. Creditors on both sides were entitled to collect debts owed them, in sterling money; this was an important provision for British merchants, especially those in the southern trade, who claimed that commercial debts owed them had gone uncollected during the war. England agreed to withdraw its troops quickly; more than a decade later, this promise would still not be fully satisfied. The final, official peace treaty—the Treaty of Paris—was signed nearly a year later, on September 2, 1783.

At last, the British began their evacuation of New York, Charleston, and Savannah, a process made complicated by the sheer numbers involved—soldiers, fearful loyalists, and runaway blacks by the thousands. In New York City, more than 27,000 soldiers and 30,000 loyalists sailed on hundreds of ships for England in late fall 1783. In a final act of mischief, on the November day when the last ships left, the losing side raised the British flag at the southern tip of Manhattan, cut away the ropes used to hoist it, and greased the flagpole.

## Conclusion: Why the British Lost

The British began the war for America with a conviction that they could not lose. They had the strongest and best-trained army and navy in the world; they were familiar with the American landscape from the French and Indian War; and they outnumbered their opponents in uniform. They easily captured the capital and every other port city of consequence in America. Probably one-fifth of the population was loyalist, and another two-fifths were undecided. Why, then, did they lose?

One continuing problem the British faced was the uncertainty of food and supplies. Unwilling to ravage the countryside, the army depended on a steady stream of supply ships from home. Insecurity about food helps explain the repeated reluctance of Howe and Clinton to pursue the Continental army aggressively.

A second obstacle to British success was their continual misuse of loyalist energies. Any plan to repacify the colonies required the cooperation of the loyalists as well as new support from the many neutrals. But again and again, the British failed to back the loyalists, leaving them to the mercy of vengeful rebels. In the South, they allowed loyalist militias to engage in vicious guerrilla warfare that drove away potential converts among the rest of the population. There was no real program to court the neutrals and to show them that the stability of British rule was preferable to the rebel government. If the British had been more lenient and forgiving, they might have succeeded in retaking the South.

The French alliance looms large in any explanation of the British defeat. The artillery and ammunition the French supplied throughout the war, even before 1778, were critical necessities for the Continental army. In 1780, the French army brought a fresh infusion of troops to a war-weary America, and the French navy made the Yorktown victory possible. The symbolic impact of the major naval defeat in the Chesapeake, just before the Yorktown siege, dissolved the pro-war spirit in England and forced the king to admit it was over.

Finally, the British abdicated civil power in the colonies in 1775 and 1776, when royal officials were forced to flee to safety, and they never really regained it. For nearly seven years, the Americans of necessity created their own government structures, from the Continental Congress to local committees and militias. Staffed by many who before 1775 had been the political elites, these new government agencies had remarkably little trouble establishing their credentials and authority to rule. The single effort in Georgia to appoint a new royal governor was not successful, and the British did not try to repeat the experiment. The basic British goal in the war—to turn back the clock to imperial rule—receded into impossibility as the war dragged on.

The war for America had taken five and a half years to fight, from Lexington to Yorktown; negotiations and the evacuation took two more. It pro-

foundly disrupted the lives of Americans everywhere, from Canada to Georgia. It was a war for independence from England, but it was also much more. It was a war that required men and women to think about politics and the legitimacy of authority. New government structures had to be forged to fill the vacuum left by the departing British. The precise disagreement with England about representation and political participation had profound implications for the kinds of governance the Americans would choose to adopt, both in the short-run moment of emergency, as extralegal committees and bodies took charge, and in the longer run of the late 1770s and early 1780s when state constitutions began to be written and the Continental Congress pondered its own legitimacy. The rhetoric employed to justify the revolution against England put words like *liberty, tyranny, slavery, independence,* and *equality* into common usage. These words carried far deeper meanings than a mere complaint over taxation without representation. As Abigail Adams and others saw, the Revolution unleashed a dynamic of equality and liberty. That it was largely unintended and unwanted by the revolutionary leaders of 1776 made it all the more potent a force in American life in the decades to come.

## CHRONOLOGY

**1775**  **May 10.** Second Continental Congress convenes in Philadelphia.

**June 14.** Continental Congress creates Continental army.

**June 17.** Battle of Bunker Hill.

**July.** Congress offers the Olive Branch Petition in attempt at reconciliation with king.

American armies march on Montreal and Quebec.

**1776**  **January 1.** Americans lose assault on Quebec.

**January.** Thomas Paine's *Common Sense* published.

**March.** British evacuate Boston.

**July 4.** Declaration of Independence adopted.

**August 27.** Battle of Long Island.

**September 15.** British take Manhattan.

**November.** Americans retreat to Philadelphia.

**December 26.** Washington surprises British and Hessians at Trenton.

**1777**  **January.** Washington winters at Morristown, New Jersey.

**July.** Burgoyne takes Fort Ticonderoga for British.

**August 6.** Fort Stanwix ambush.

**September.** British occupy Philadelphia.

**October 17.** Burgoyne surrenders at Saratoga.

**December.** Washington goes into winter quarters at Valley Forge, Pennsylvania.

1778  **February.** France enters war on American side.

**July–August.** French fleet threatens New York and Newport, Rhode Island.

**December.** Savannah, Georgia, falls to British.

1779  **January–June.** Skirmishes in South Carolina and Georgia.

**October.** British evacuate Newport.

1780  Philadelphia Ladies Association raises money for soldiers.

**March–May.** British lay siege to Charleston, South Carolina.

**July.** Rochambeau and French army arrive at Newport.

**August 16.** Battle of Camden, South Carolina, dims hopes for Americans.

**September–October.** Benedict Arnold's treason exposed.

**September–December.** Guerrilla warfare in South.

**October 7.** Battle of Kings Mountain, South Carolina.

1781  **May–August.** Cornwallis in Virginia.

**August.** Cornwallis occupies Yorktown, Virginia.

**September 5.** French fleet takes Chesapeake Bay.

**September 28–October 19.** Siege of Yorktown.

**October 19.** Cornwallis surrenders.

1783  Treaty of Paris ends war.

# SUGGESTED READINGS

Clare Brandt, *The Man in the Mirror: A Life of Benedict Arnold* (1994). A fascinating psychological portrait of a talented but venal man.

E. Wayne Carp, *To Starve the Army at Pleasure: Continental Army Administration and American Political Culture, 1775–1783* (1984). Corruption, politics, and the Continental army: the ambivalence of revolutionary struggle.

Eric Foner, *Tom Paine and Revolutionary America* (1976). A detailed study of Thomas Paine's radicalism and his influence on American political thought.

Edith Gelles, *Portia: The World of Abigail Adams* (1992). A study of Adams through her voluminous correspondence, exploring her incipient awareness of gender questions and the balance she struck between that and her devotion to domestic duty.

Sidney Kaplan and Emma Nogrady Kaplan, *The Black Presence in the Era of the American Revolution* (1989). A richly illustrated volume that documents the experiences of many dozens of individual black Americans during the Revolution.

Piers Mackesy, *The War for America, 1775–1783* (1964). An older but lively account of the war from the British perspective.

Pauline Maier, *American Scripture: Making the Declaration of Independence* (1997). A deep and absorbing history of that famous document, exploring its antecedents in the states, its context, and its later sacralization.

Jack N. Rakove, *The Beginnings of National Politics: An Interpretive History of the Continental Congress* (1979). An authoritative account of the politics of the Continental Congress.

Charles Royster, *A Revolutionary People at War: The Continental Army and American Character, 1775–1783* (1979). A splendid social and military history of the men of the Continental army, exploring the roles of individual soldiers and officers and their contributions to the making of the new country.

John Shy, *A People Numerous and Armed: Reflections on the Military Struggle for American Independence* (rev. ed., 1990). Essays from a noted military historian on daily life in the army and militias and the meaning of the Revolution for men involved.

**REVOLUTIONARY WAR FLAG FROM NEW HAMPSHIRE**

*This cotton and linen flag from the early 1780s shows the final, official version of the Stars and Stripes. The earliest forms of the flag simply reconfigured the British Union Jack symbol of double red and white crosses on a field of blue. In January 1776, Washington's army in Massachusetts adopted a banner called the Grand Union Flag, which combined the Union Jack symbol with thirteen red and white stripes representing the thirteen colonies. Such a flag reflected genuine ambivalence about independence and a symbolic allegiance to British sovereignty. Worse still, it ran the risk of signaling capitulation in battle. In June 1777, the Continental Congress decreed a new American flag, carrying thirteen red and white stripes and a blue corner embellished with thirteen stars in no prescribed pattern.*

David A. Schorsch, NYC.

# BUILDING A REPUBLIC
## 1775–1789

I N 1781, MERCY OTIS WARREN AND HER HUSBAND, JAMES, moved from Plymouth, Massachusetts, into an elegant residence that had once belonged to Thomas Hutchinson in Milton, six miles south of Boston. The ex-royal governor, in exile in England, would not have been pleased to know that his archenemies the Otis and Warren families entertained in his parlor and slept in his bedroom. Now that the war was finally over, James and Mercy had moved closer to the Boston capital to devote themselves to the political work of building the new Republic. James resumed his seat in the state's assembly, where he had served repeatedly in the 1760s and 1770s. Mercy turned to her ambitious project of the 1780s, the writing of a substantial history of the American Revolution.

Mercy Otis Warren, then fifty-three, was the foremost female political commentator and intellectual of her day. She had grown up in a household that lived and breathed politics and ideas. Her father, the lawyer James Otis, represented his town of Barnstable for fifteen years in the Massachusetts House. Otis provided his sons with the extensive tutoring in Greek, Latin, history, and English literature required for entrance to Harvard College. In a virtually unprecedented move, Mercy, a bright and confident girl, was fully included in these private lessons.

Mercy married James Warren, a Harvard classmate of her brother James's, and the three men in her life—father, brother, and husband—immersed themselves in the tumultuous events of 1760s Boston. In the early 1770s, Mercy herself took up her pen in the cause of American liberty, producing poems and satirical plays with thinly disguised characters that made the royal officials look like corrupt buffoons. The plays were published in Boston, New York, and Philadelphia newspapers, anonymously of course. As antigovernment satires, they required protection for the author. But just as important, Mercy Warren needed to conceal her female authorship. A woman writing about politics violated a well-established gender boundary of the eighteenth century. Even in her letters to John Adams, a close personal friend in the 1770s, Mercy carefully prefaced her political opinions with apologies for stepping "so far beyond the line of my sex."

By the 1780s, Mercy Warren's confidence in her political judgment had grown. So had her anxiety about the direction of the newly independent Republic, which, she wrote, "resembled the conduct of a restless, vigorous youth, prematurely emancipated from the authority of a parent, but without the experience necessary to direct him to act with dignity or discretion." First came years of disagreement among the states over the ownership of western lands, followed by bickering over taxation and the war debt. To make matters worse, severe economic chaos clouded much of the 1780s. No currency could keep value for long; prices fluctuated wildly, and speculators grew rich while other people grew poor. Mercy Warren worried that the simplicity, virtue, and self-sacrifice cherished by the sturdy American

**MERCY OTIS WARREN**
*The Boston artist John Singleton Copley painted Mercy Otis Warren when she was thirty-six. The blue satin gown adorned with point lace sleeves and silk braid conveys a message of proper—and prosperous—femininity. Warren's warm and intelligent face bears a gentle yet appraising expression.*
Bequest of Winslow Warren, Courtesy, Museum of Fine Arts, Boston.

patriots of 1776 had vanished, replaced by a greed to profit from the uncertain economy and a selfish desire to indulge in luxury.

By the mid-1780s, the Massachusetts state government embarked on a course the Warrens condemned, taxing inhabitants at high rates to retire the state debt. But they equally disapproved of citizens' armed protests against taxes. Mercy Warren considered such protesters "incendiary and turbulent" and "too ignorant to distinguish between an opposition to regal despotism and a resistance to a government recently established by themselves."

When a group of American leaders responded to such protests by drafting a new constitution for the Republic, Mercy Warren, now thoroughly alarmed, took up her pen again to denounce the "many-headed monster" that threatened individual liberties. Her unsigned nineteen-page pamphlet gained wide circulation.

But by 1788, Mercy Warren's views had lost out and the Constitution was ratified. The Warrens also lost their own private indulgence, their new house; the financial instability of the 1780s forced them to sell it. Mercy spent the next fifteen years polishing her three-volume *History of the Rise, Progress, and Termination of the American Revolution.* Published in 1805, the work boldly credited its author, "Mrs. Mercy Warren," on the title page. The work's public reception, however, fell far short of its genuine merit. Her onetime mentor John Adams objected strongly to her treatment of him and the other proponents of the Constitution. "History is not the Province of the Ladies," he fumed. But Mercy Otis Warren's own life proved him wrong.

## The Articles of Confederation

For five years, from independence in 1776 until 1781, the Second Continental Congress continued to meet in Philadelphia and other cities. It existed without any formal constitutional basis, while its members groped to establish a government on principles congruent with the themes of the Revolution. With monarchy gone, where did sovereignty lie? If people could not be taxed except by their representatives, where did the power of taxation lie? What was the nature of representation? If distant governments inevitably lost sight of the interests of the people, what was the proper size for a political entity? And just who were "the people" anyway?

The initial answers to these questions took the form of a plan called the Articles of Confederation. The plan, however, proved to be controversial and difficult to implement.

### Congress and Confederation

The Second Continental Congress assumed power in May 1775, when the British attack on Lexington and Concord required a unified colonial response. Only as they fashioned the Declaration of Independence a year later did the delegates consider the need for a written document that would specify what powers the congress had, by what authority it existed, and how it was to be constituted. It finally fell to John Dickinson, the moderate conciliator from Pennsylvania, to chair the committee entrusted with the important task of drafting such a document.

Dickinson's draft of the Articles of Confederation reveals that the delegates, unified by their opposition to England, agreed that the congress should handle functions such as pursuing war and peace, conducting foreign relations, regulating trade, and running a postal service. The draft called for a congress with those powers plus the authority to issue bills of credit and to borrow money, to settle all disputes between states, and to administer the unsettled western lands. It was these final two points that proved to be the major sources of disagreement over the draft. Some states, such as Virginia and Connecticut, had very old colonial charters that located their western boundaries many hundreds of miles to the west. States without extensive land grants could not abide such grandiose claims. Dickinson's Articles granted the congress final authority on this and many other matters.

Off and on over the next sixteen months, the congress tinkered with the Articles. Its immediate attention, however, was focused on the war, and a final version of the Articles of Confederation emerged only in November 1777. This second draft departed from Dickinson's by identifying the union as a loose confederation of states. Gone was the provision giving the congress control of state boundaries and western lands. Also, each state retained all powers and rights not expressly delegated to the congress, and the union was characterized as "a firm league of friendship" existing mainly to foster a common defense. There was no national executive (that is, no president) and no national judiciary.

The structure of the government paralleled that of the existing Continental Congress. The confederation was embodied in a congress, composed of two to seven delegates from each state, selected annually by the state legislatures and prohibited from serving more than three years out of any six. The actual number of delegates was not critical, since each state delegation cast a single vote.

Routine decisions in the congress required a simple majority of seven states; for momentous powers, such as declaring war, nine states needed to agree. But to approve or amend the Articles required the unanimous consent both of the thirteen state delegations and of the thirteen state legislatures. The congressional delegates undoubtedly thought they were guaranteeing that no individual state could be railroaded by the other twelve in fundamental constitutional matters. But what this requirement really did was to hamstring the government. One renegade state could—and did—hold the rest of the country hostage to its demands.

On the delicate question of deriving revenue to run the government, specifically to finance the war, the Articles provided an ingenious but ultimately troublesome solution. Each state was to contribute to the common treasury in proportion to the current property value of the state's land. Large and populous states would contribute more than small or sparsely populated states whose land was not settled and improved. The actual taxes would be levied by the state legislatures, not by the congress, to preserve the Revolution's principle of taxation only by direct representation. However, no mechanism was created to compel states to contribute their fair share.

In general, the lack of centralized authority in the confederation government was exactly what many state leaders wanted in the late 1770s. A league of states with rotating personnel, no executive branch, no power of taxation, and a requirement of unanimity for any major change seemed to be a good way to avoid the potential tyranny of government. But soon the inherent weaknesses of these features became apparent.

## The Problem of Western Lands

Once approved by the congress in 1777, the Articles of Confederation had to be approved unanimously by the state legislatures. Newspapers published the plan, but there was little public discussion because the war monopolized the news.

*In general, the lack of centralized authority in the confederation government was exactly what many state leaders wanted in the late 1770s.*

The most important proposed change that occupied the delegates in the final debate over the Articles was a plea by five states to give the congress administrative control of the western lands up to the Mississippi River as a national domain that could eventually constitute new states. Not surprisingly, these five states were small, with boundaries at most a few hundred miles from the coast: Maryland, Delaware, New Jersey, Rhode Island, and Pennsylvania. Though Pennsylvania was much larger than the others, about one-fifth of its area was simultaneously claimed by Connecticut, whose charter set its western boundary unimaginably far west.

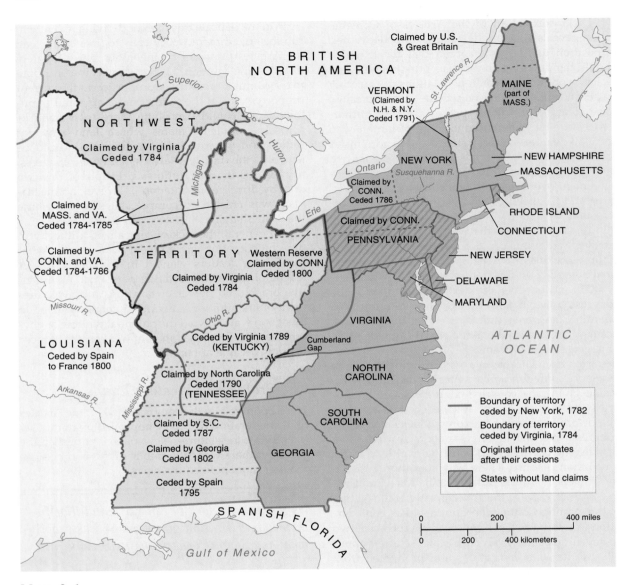

MAP 8.1
*Cession of Western Lands, 1782–1802*
*The thirteen new states found it hard to ratify the Articles of Confederation without settling their conflicting land claims in the West, an area larger than the original states and occupied by Indian tribes.*

The remaining eight states claimed boundaries extending far to the west on the basis of early colonial charters from the British government (Map 8.1). Virginia's view of the map put the name Virginia over territory stretching west to the Mississippi River and north to Lake Superior, taking in present-day West Virginia, Kentucky, Ohio, Indiana, Illinois, Michigan, and Wisconsin. Massachusetts claimed a strip of present-day New York, Michigan, and Wisconsin, while the Carolinas and Georgia drew their western boundaries at the Mississippi River. A great portion of the contested western lands actually fell under the control of another group which was not party to the disputes in the Continental Congress: the many thousands of Indians who inhabited that region.

The eight states with western land claims were ready to sign the Articles of Confederation as approved by the congress in 1777. Rhode Island, Pennsylvania, and New Jersey eventually capitulated and signed, "not from a Conviction of the Equality and Justness of it," said a New Jersey delegate, "but merely from an absolute Necessity there was of complying to save the Continent." But Delaware and Maryland continued to hold out for many months, insisting on a national domain policy. Compromise finally came near the end of 1779 when the congress agreed that any "unappropriated lands that may be ceded or relinquished to the United States, by any particular state, . . . shall be disposed of for the common benefit of the United States and be settled and formed into distinct Republican States, which shall become members of the federal union." But not until early 1781, when Virginia finally ceded much of its land to the confederation, did the Articles go into effect.

The western lands issue demonstrated that powerful interests divided the thirteen new states; the apparent unity of purpose inspired by fighting the war against England papered over sizable cracks in the new confederation.

## Running the New Government

No fanfare greeted the long-awaited inauguration of the new government. The congress continued to sputter along, its problems far from solved by the signing of the Articles. Day-to-day activities were often hampered by the lack of a quorum. The Articles required representation from seven states to conduct business, with a minimum of two men for each state's delegation. But some days fewer than fourteen men showed up.

State legislatures were slow to select delegates; those appointed were often reluctant to attend, especially those with wives and children at home. (James Warren of Massachusetts, Mercy's husband, was chosen twice by his state to be a delegate, yet he failed to show up for even one session.) The confederation congress at times seemed deadlocked or irrelevant, and so active politicians generally preferred to devote their energies to their state governments. It also did not help that the congress had no permanent home. During the war, when the

British army threatened Philadelphia, the congress relocated to small Pennsylvania towns like Lancaster and York and then to Baltimore. After hostilities ceased, the congress moved from Trenton to Princeton to Annapolis to New York City.

To address the inherent difficulties of an inefficient congress, executive departments of war, finance, and foreign affairs were created to handle the purely administrative functions. When the department heads were ambitious—as was Robert Morris, a wealthy Philadelphia merchant who served as superintendent of finance—they could exercise considerable executive power. The Articles of Confederation had deliberately refrained from setting up an executive branch, but a modest one was being invented by necessity.

Because of the pressing needs of running a war machine, the confederation government got a slow start on writing its justifying document, the Articles of Confederation. Then the difficulties over ownership of western lands slowed down ratification for years. By the time the Articles were fully functioning, yet another problem emerged. Much more exciting political work was going on at the state level, especially during the creative burst of state constitution writing in the late 1770s. Before 1776, the cream of political talent in the country was attracted to the Continental Congress, but between 1776 and 1780 the talent flowed instead to the state governments.

# The Sovereign States

In the first decade of independence, the states were sovereign and all-powerful. Only a few functions, like that of declaring war and peace, had been transferred to the confederation government. Familiar and close to home, state governments claimed the allegiance of their citizens. As Americans discarded their English identity, they thought of themselves instead as Virginians or New Yorkers or Rhode Islanders. State government was thus the arena where the Revolution's innovations would first be tried.

## The State Constitutions

In May 1776, the congress in Philadelphia recommended that all the states draw up constitutions based on "the authority of the people." By 1778, ten of the thirteen states had produced documents spelling out the liberties, rights, and obligations of citizens and rulers. Americans felt they had been injured by the unwritten nature of British political traditions. They wanted a written contract whose basic principles could not be easily altered by the government in power at the moment.

A shared feature of all the state constitutions was the conviction that government ultimately rests on the consent of the governed. Political writers in the late 1770s embraced the concept of republicanism as the underpinning of the new governments. Republicanism meant more than just the practice of popular elections and representative institutions. For some, republicanism invoked a way of thinking about who leaders should be—ideally autonomous, virtuous, public-minded citizens who placed civic values above private interests. For others, it suggested direct democracy, with not much of anything standing in the way of the will of the people. For all, it meant government that promoted the people's welfare.

Widespread agreement about the virtues of republicanism went hand in hand with the idea that republics could succeed only in relatively small units. A government run for and by the people had to be near at hand, so the people could make sure their interests were being served. Distant governments could easily become tyrannical; that was the lesson of the 1760s.

It followed, then, that the best form of government was one that allowed maximum voice to the people. Nearly every state continued the colonial practice of a two-chamber assembly but greatly augmented the powers of the lower house. Two states, Pennsylvania and Georgia, did away with the upper house altogether. Virtually all of the state constitutions severely limited the powers of the governor, identified in most people's minds with the royal governor of colonial days. Governors could no longer convene or dismiss legislatures at will, veto legislation, or buy loyalty through land grants or job patronage. Most states also restricted the governor's term to one year, with limited eligibility for reelection. Pennsylvania and Georgia abolished the office of governor altogether.

Most states made their lower houses very responsive to popular majorities. Annual elections and guaranteed rotation in office prevented anyone from monopolizing power; if a representative displeased his constituents, he could be out of office in a matter of months. Daily governance of the state rested with the lower house, whose most important decisions were economic: printing, borrowing, taxing, and spending money to finance each state's war effort.

Six of the state constitutions included bills of rights, lists of basic individual liberties that governments could not abridge. Virginia debated and passed the first bill of rights in June 1776, and many of the other states borrowed from it. Its language also bears a close resemblance to the wording of the Declaration of Independence, which Thomas Jefferson was composing that same June in Philadelphia: "That all men are by nature equally free and independent, and have certain inherent rights, of which, when they enter into a state of society, they cannot by any compact deprive or divest their posterity; namely, the enjoyment of life and liberty, with the means of acquiring and possessing property, and pursuing and obtaining happiness and safety." Along with these inherent rights went more specific rights to freedom of speech, freedom of the press, and trial by jury.

## Who Are "the People"?

When the Continental Congress called for state constitutions based on "the authority of the people," and when the Virginia bill of rights granted "all men" certain rights, who was meant by "the people"? Who exactly were the citizens of this new country, and how far did the principle of democratic government extend? Different people answered this question differently, but in the 1770s certain limits to full political participation by all Americans were widely agreed upon.

Every state set property qualifications for voters and candidates. The idea prevailed everywhere that the propertied classes were the only legitimate participants in government. In nearly every state, the highest offices—the governorship and membership in the upper house—drew only on the richest segment of the population. In Maryland, for example, a candidate for the governorship had to be worth £5,000, quite a large sum of money. Voters in Maryland had to own fifty acres of land or £30, a sum that would screen out perhaps one-third of adult white males.

The justification for restricting political participation to property owners was so widely accepted that it rarely needed to be explained. Only property owners were presumed to possess the necessary independence of mind to make wise political choices. Are not propertyless men, asked John Adams, "too little acquainted with public affairs to form a right judgment, and too dependent upon other men to have a will of their own?"

Probably one-quarter to one-half of all adult white males were disfranchised by property qualifications. Not all of them took their nonvoter status quietly. One Maryland man wondered what was so special about being worth £30: "Every poor man has a life, a personal liberty, and a right to his earnings; and is in danger of being injured by government in a variety of ways." Why then restrict such a man from voting for his representatives? Others pointed out that propertyless men were fighting and dying in the Revolutionary War; surely they were expressing an active concern about politics. Finally, a very few radical voices challenged the notion that owning property automatically transformed men into good citizens. Perhaps it did the opposite: The richest men might well be greedy and selfish, the worst kind of citizen.

But ideas like this were clearly outside the mainstream. The writers of the new constitutions were themselves men of property and often considerable wealth, and they viewed the Revolution as an effort to guarantee people the right to own property and to prevent unjust governments from appropriating it through taxation. John Adams urged the framers of the Massachusetts constitution not even to discuss the scope of suffrage but simply to adopt the traditional colonial property qualifications. If suffrage is brought up for debate, he warned, "there will be no end of it. New claims will arise; women will demand a vote; lads from twelve to twenty-one will think their rights not enough attended to; and every man who has not a farthing, will demand an equal voice with any other." Adams was astute enough to anticipate complaints about excluding women, youth, and poor men from political life, but it did not even occur to him to worry about another excluded group: slaves.

## Equality and Slavery

Restrictions on political participation did not mean that propertyless people enjoyed no civil rights and liberties. The various state bills of rights applied to all individuals who had, as the Virginia bill so carefully phrased it, "enter[ed] into a state of society."

No matter how poor, a free person was entitled to life, liberty, property, and freedom of conscience. Unfree people, however, were another matter.

*If suffrage is brought up for debate, John Adams warned, "there will be no end of it. New claims will arise; women will demand a vote . . . and every man who has not a farthing, will demand an equal voice with any other."*

The author of the Virginia bill of rights was George Mason, a plantation owner with 118 slaves. When he penned the sentence "all men are by nature equally free and independent," he did not have his slaves in mind. Other members of the Virginia legislature, however, feared that the words could be construed to apply to slaves. These aristocratic slaveholders were finally put at ease by the addition of the phrase specifying that rights belonged only to people who had entered civil society. As one wrote, with relief, "Slaves, not being constituent members of our society, could never pretend to any benefit from such a maxim."

One month later, the Declaration of Independence used essentially the same phrase about equality, this time without the modifying clause about entering society. Two state constitutions, for Pennsylvania and Massachusetts, also included the inspiring language about equality, again without limiting it as in Virginia. In Massachusetts, where the state constitution was sent around to be ratified town by town, one town suggested that the sentence on equality be reworded to read "All men, whites and blacks, are born free and equal." But the suggestion fell on deaf ears.

Nevertheless, after 1776, the ideals of the Revolution about natural equality and rights and liberty began to erode the institution of slavery. In some cases, enslaved blacks themselves challenged their legal status. In 1777, some Massachusetts slaves petitioned the state legislature, claiming a "natural & unalienable right to that freedom which the great Parent of the Universe hath bestowed equally on all mankind." They modestly asked for freedom for their children at age twenty-one and were turned down. In 1779, similar petitions in Connecticut and New Hampshire met with no success. Seven Massachusetts freemen, including the mariner brothers Paul and John Cuffe, refused to pay taxes for three years on the grounds that they could not vote and so were not represented. The Cuffe brothers landed in jail in 1780 for tax evasion, but their petition to the state legislature spurred the extension of suffrage to taxpaying free blacks in that state.

**PAUL CUFFE'S SILHOUETTE**
*Captain Paul Cuffe of Martha's Vineyard, off the Massachusetts coast, was the son of a Wampanoag Indian woman and an African father who had purchased his own freedom from a Quaker owner. Cuffe studied navigation and went to sea at age sixteen during the American Revolution (enduring several months of imprisonment by the British). After the war, he and his brother petitioned for tax relief, a move that foreshadowed Cuffe's life of dedication to racial issues. In his thirty-year career as a shipbuilder and master mariner; Cuffe traveled extensively. By 1812, when this engraving with silhouette was made, Cuffe had explored the African country of Sierra Leone as a possible site for resettlement of American blacks and had met with African kings, English dukes, and an American president.*
Library of Congress.

Another way to bring the issue before lawmakers was to sue in court. In 1781, a Massachusetts slave named Quok Walker charged his master with assault and battery. His lawyers argued in court that he was, under the Massachusetts constitution, a free man. Walker won and was set free. Several similar cases followed, and by 1789 judges agreed that slavery had been abolished by judicial decision in Massachusetts.

Pennsylvania was the first state to prohibit slavery by statute, in 1780. Gradual emancipation laws were passed in Rhode Island and Connecticut in 1784 and in New York and New Jersey in 1785 and 1786, respectively. Gradual emancipation illustrates the tension between radical and conservative implications of republican ideology. Republican government was designed to protect people's liberties and property; yet slaves were both people and property. Gradual emancipation balanced the civil rights of blacks and the property rights of their owners by delaying the promise of freedom. Most such laws declared that children born after a certain date would be free at a particular age, usually twenty-one or twenty-eight.

In the Upper South—Maryland and Virginia—general emancipation bills were debated and defeated. Slavery was too deeply entrenched and too important to the economy to abolish. However, in both states legal restrictions were eased on individual acts of emancipation, under new manumission laws. Virginia's law passed in 1782, and by 1790 close to ten thousand Virginia slaves had been freed. Most of these ex-slaves remained in Virginia and formed free black communities complete with schools and churches, a visible alternative to the system of slavery.

*Every state from Pennsylvania northward acknowledged that the enslavement of blacks was fundamentally inconsistent with revolutionary ideology; "all men are created equal" was beginning to acquire real force as a basic principle.*

In the Deep South—the Carolinas and Georgia—freedom for slaves was unthinkable for whites. Yet more than ten thousand slaves from South Carolina—more than in all the northern states combined—achieved immediate freedom in 1783 by leaving with the British army from

CUFFE'S PETITION
*This 1780 petition of Paul and John Cuffe and five others "of the African Extract" asked the Massachusetts state legislature for tax relief. The document explains that "by Reason of Long Bondag and hard Slavery we have been deprived of Injoying the Profits of our Labouer or the advantage of Inheriting Estates from our Parents as our neighbouers the white peopel do . . . & yet . . . we have been & now are Taxed both in our Polls and that small Pittance of Estate which through much hard Labour & Industry we have got together to Sustain our selves and families withal . . . we are not allowed the privilage of freemen of the State having no vote or Influence in the election of those that Tax us . . . yet many of our Colour (as is well known) have Cheerfully Entered the field of Battle in the defence of the Common cause and that (as we conceive) against a similar Exertion of Power (in regard to taxation) too well known to need a recital in this place." Paul Cuffe was twenty-one at the time.*
Courtesy of Massachusetts Archives.

Charleston, and another six thousand set sail under the British flag from Savannah, Georgia. In sheer numbers alone, this was by far the largest emancipation of blacks in the entire country. Some went to Canada, some to England, and a small number relocated in the 1790s to Sierra Leone, on the west coast of Africa.

Although emancipation affected fewer blacks in the North, simply because there were fewer of them to begin with, its symbolic importance was enormous. Every state from Pennsylvania northward acknowledged that the enslavement of blacks was fundamentally inconsistent with revolutionary ideology; "all men are created equal" was beginning to acquire real force as a basic principle. On some level, southerners also understood this, but their inability to imagine a free biracial society prevented them from taking action. From the 1780s on, the North was associated with freedom and the South with slavery. This geographical pattern would have profound consequences for the next two centuries of American history.

## The Critical Period

From 1781 to 1788, a sense of crisis gripped some of the revolutionary leaders who feared the Articles of Confederation were too weak. But others defended the Articles as the best guarantee of individual liberty, because real governance occurred at the state level, closer to the people. Political theorizing about the proper relation among citizen, state, and confederation remained active and controversial throughout the decade as Americans confronted questions of finance, territorial expansion, and civil disorder.

### Financial Chaos and Paper Money

Seven years of war produced a booming but chaotic economy in the 1780s. The confederation and the individual states had run up huge war debts, financed by printing paper money and borrowing from private sources. Some $400 to $500 million in paper currency had been injected into the economy, and prices and wages fluctuated wildly. Private debt and rapid expenditure flourished. Newspapers bemoaned the rampant spending on imported items—hats, silks, china, tea—indulged in even by ordinary people. Some political leaders warned that the economy was headed for disaster. Legal suits between debtors and creditors quadrupled in many localities over the prewar levels, and debtors' prisons became crowded. A serious postwar depression settled in by the mid-1780s and did not lift until the 1790s.

The confederation government was itself in a terrible financial fix in 1781. Continental dollars had lost almost all value: It took 146 of them to buy what a dollar had bought in 1775. Desperate times required desperate measures. The congress turned to Robert Morris, a merchant and newly reelected delegate from Pennsylvania, appointing him superintendent of finance for the confederation. Six years earlier, the wealthy Morris had procured from Europe much-needed muskets for the army which were shipped to his private firm in crates disguised as routine merchandise. Morris had resigned from the congress in 1778 under suspicion that he had unfairly profited from his public service efforts; indeed, he had left public life several million dollars richer than he had entered it. Nevertheless, the congress called on him from 1781 to 1784 to apply his considerable talent to the confederation's economic problems. Not everyone was pleased. Mercy Otis Warren's husband, James, wrote to John Adams:

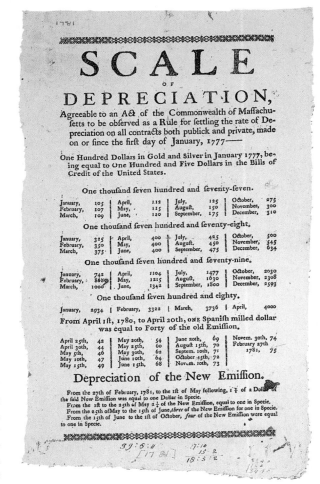

**SCALE OF DEPRECIATION**
*This complicated chart shows the monthly value of United States Continental dollars from 1777 to February 1781, as stipulated by the government of Massachusetts. For example, in March 1780, it took $3,736 Continental dollars to equal the buying power of $100 in gold or silver, up from $3,322 the month before. Such a chart was needed when debtors and creditors settled accounts contracted at one time and paid off later in greatly depreciated dollars.*
Courtesy, American Antiquarian Society.

"Morris is a King, and more than a King. He has the Keys of the Treasury at his Command, Appropriates Money as he pleases, and every Body must look up to him for Justice and for Favour."

To augment the revenue of the confederation government, Morris first proposed a 5 percent import tax (called an impost). Since there was no authority in the Articles of Confederation for any such tax, Morris's plan required a constitutional amendment approved unanimously by the thirteen states. But unanimous agreement was impossible. States with bustling ports already collected taxes on imports and were loath to share that income. Rhode Island, with its active wharves at Newport and Providence, absolutely refused. When Morris pushed the impost amendment again in 1783, it was New York (whose premier port had just been freed from British occupation) that refused.

Morris's next idea was the creation of a private bank, the Bank of North America, which would enjoy a special relationship with the confederation government. It would hold the government's hard-money deposits (insofar as there were any) as well as private deposits, and it would make short-term loans to the government. The bank's contribution to economic stability came in the form of banknotes, pieces of paper inscribed with a dollar value. Un-like paper money, banknotes were backed by hard money in the bank's vaults and thus would not de-preciate. Morris hoped that the new banknotes would perform the functions of paper money with-out its drawbacks. Congress agreed and voted to approve the bank in 1781.

The Bank of North America, located in Philadel-phia, had limited success curing the confederation's economic woes. In the short run, the bank supplied the government with a currency that held its value, but it issued so little that the impact was very small. It mainly enriched Morris and three close associates who owned 40 percent of the bank stock. When its charter expired in 1786, the Pennsylvania legislature refused to renew it.

If Morris could not resuscitate the economy in the 1780s, probably no one could have done it. Be-cause the Articles of Confederation reserved most economic functions to the states, congress was help-less to tax trade, control inflation, curb the flow of state-issued paper money, or pay the mounting public debt. But the confederation had acquired one source of potential enormous wealth: the huge ter-ritory ceded by Virginia, which in 1784 became the national domain.

## Land Ordinances and the Northwest Territory

The Continental Congress appointed Thomas Jeffer-son to draft a policy for handling the national do-main. Jefferson proposed dividing the territory north of the Ohio River and east of the Mississippi—called the Northwest Territory—into ten new states, with

**THOMAS JEFFERSON**
*This miniature shows Thomas Jefferson at age forty-five, during his years as a diplomat in Paris. The American artist John Trumbull visited France in 1788 and painted Jefferson's likeness in this five-by-four-inch format so he could later copy it into his planned large canvas depicting the signing of the Declaration of Independence. Jefferson requested three replicas of the miniature to bestow as gifts, a common and intimate item of exchange. One went to his daughter Martha, another to an American woman in Lon-don, and the third to Maria Cosway, a British artist of whom the widower Jefferson had grown very fond during his stay in France.*
Monticello.

each state divided into townships ten miles square. Jefferson advocated giving the land to settlers, rather than selling it, on the grounds that the improved lands would so enrich the country through property taxes over the years that there was no need to make the settlers contribute to the government twice. His aim was to encourage rapid and democratic settle-ment of the land, to build a nation of freeholders (as opposed to renters), and to avoid speculative frenzy.

**JEFFERSON'S MAP OF THE NORTHWEST TERRITORY**
*Thomas Jefferson sketched out borders for ten new states in his initial plan for the Northwest Territory in 1784. Straight lines and right angles held a strong appeal for him. But such regularity ignored inconvenient geographic features like rivers and even more inconvenient political features like Indian territorial claims, most unlikely to be ceded by treaty in orderly blocks. Jefferson also submitted ten distinctive names for the states. Number 9, for example, was Polypotamia, or "land of many rivers" in Greek.*
William L. Clements Library.

Jefferson also insisted that the new states have representative governments equal in status with the original states once they reached a certain population. This ensured that the new United States, so recently released from colonial dependency, would not itself become a colonial power. Finally, Jefferson's draft prohibited slavery and involuntary servitude in all of the ten new states.

The congress adopted parts of Jefferson's plan in the Ordinance of 1784: the rectangular grid, the

ten states, and the guarantee of self-government and eventual statehood. What the congress found too radical was the proposal to give away the land; the national domain was the confederation's only source of independent wealth. And the slavery prohibition failed to be included by only one state's vote.

A year later, the congress reconsidered the land act and passed a new version, the Ordinance of 1785 (Map 8.2). The new plan called for walkable townships six miles square, each containing thirty-six

**MAP 8.2**
*The Northwest Territory and Ordinance of 1785*
*Surveyors mapping the eastern edge of the Northwest Territory followed the Ordinance of 1785,
using the stars as well as poles and chains (standard surveying equipment) to run long boundary
lines. The result was a blanket of six-mile-square townships, further subdivided into one-mile
squares each containing sixteen forty-acre farms.*

sections; each section contained 640 acres, enough for four family farms. One lot in each township was set aside for educational purposes. The 1785 ordinance reduced Jefferson's plan for ten rectangular states down to three to five states, with boundaries conforming to natural geographic features like the Great Lakes and major rivers instead of abstractly drawn survey lines. Land sales would occur by public auction; the minimum price was set at $1 an acre, but market forces could drive up the prices of the most desirable land. Two further restrictions applied: Land was sold in minimum parcels of 640 acres each, and payment had to be in hard money or in certificates of debt issued by the confederation government.

To join in the land boom, a purchaser thus had to have at least 640 hard dollars or an equivalent amount in debt certificates. Like every other currency substitute in the war years, debt certificates had been circulated, depreciated, and purchased by speculators at a small fraction of their face value. The speculators tended to be wealthy easterners who could afford the risk that the certificates would become worthless—or suddenly be worth a handsome amount. The Land Ordinance of 1785 made good their bet.

Speculators purchasing the Northwest Territory acreage usually held the land for resale rather than settling on it. Thus they avoided direct contact with the most serious obstacle to settlement: the dozens of Indian tribes that occupied the land. Treaties signed at Fort Stanwix in 1784 and Fort McIntosh in 1785 coerced partial cessions of land from Iroquois, Delaware, Huron, and Miami tribes, but a united Indian meeting near Detroit in 1786 issued an ultimatum: No cession would be valid without unanimous consent. The Indians advised the United States to "prevent your surveyors and other people from coming upon our side of the Ohio river"—precisely the land claimed as the new national domain. For two more decades, violent and terrible Indian wars in Ohio and Indiana would continue to impede settlement.

In 1787, a third land act, called the Northwest Ordinance, promised eventual self-government for a territory when the white male population reached five thousand, but it devised an interim plan for sparsely settled territories with a congressionally appointed governor. The other landmark feature of the 1787 act was a prohibition on slavery in the entire region, which this time passed without any debate. Something less than a fervent antislavery sentiment was at work in the passage of this provision, as shown by an accompanying warning that fugitive southern slaves caught in the Northwest Territory would be returned to their owners. And the prohibition applied only to the area north of the Ohio River; plenty of territory south of the river and west of Georgia was still available for the spread of slavery. Still, the prohibition on slavery in the Northwest Territory perpetuated the dynamic of gradual emancipation in the North: A North-South sectionalism, based on slavery, was slowly taking shape.

## Shays's Rebellion

Without an impost amendment, the confederation turned to the states to contribute revenue voluntarily. The states were struggling with their own war debts, and most state legislatures were reluctant to tax their constituents too heavily. Massachusetts, however, had a tough-minded, fiscally conservative upper house with veto power over its lower house. The upper house, dominated by the commercial centers of eastern Massachusetts, wanted to retire the state debt by raising taxes; to make matters worse, it insisted that taxes be paid in hard money, not cheap paper. Farmers in the western half of the state found it difficult to comply, and by 1786 sheriffs frequently confiscated property and committed tax delinquents to jail.

However, the western farmers had learned from the American Revolution how to respond to oppressive taxation. They called conventions to discuss their grievances and circulated petitions demanding tax reductions and debt relief legislation. In the fall of 1786, about 2,500 armed men marched on the courthouses in three western Massachusetts counties. The leader of this tax revolt was a farmer and onetime captain in the Continental army, Daniel Shays.

---

*Shays's Rebellion caused leaders throughout the country to worry whether the confederation could handle problems of civil disorder.*

---

The governor of Massachusetts, James Bowdoin, who had once organized protests against British taxes, now characterized the Shaysites as illegal rebels and called out the militia. Another former rebel, Samuel Adams, defined the protest movement as a treasonous rebellion and took the extreme position that "the man who dares rebel against the laws of a republic ought to suffer death."

Why did the protesting farmers so upset the aging tax protesters of an earlier era? The Shaysites challenged the idea that popularly elected governments would always be fair and just. The revolutionary generation, and particularly its most democratically inclined members, had given little thought to the possibility that popular majorities, embodied in a state legislature, could be oppressive, just as monarchs could. The farmers now felt they

**SILVER BOWL FOR ANTI-SHAYS GENERAL**
*The militia of Springfield in western Massachusetts presented its leader, General William Shepard, with this silver bowl to honor his victory over the insurgents in Shays's Rebellion. Presentational silver conveyed a double message. It announced gratitude and praise in engraved words, and it transmitted considerable monetary value in the silver itself. General Shepard could display his trophy on a shelf, use it as a punch bowl, will it to descendants to keep his famous moment alive in memory, or melt it down in hard times. Not only is Shepard's name commemorated on the silver; SHAYS too appears in the last line, there for the ages to remember.*
Yale University Art Gallery, Mabel Brady Garvan Collection.

were an oppressed minority in Massachusetts with no hope of altering the composition of the state legislature, dominated by eastern counties.

Governor Bowdoin sent more than four thousand soldiers to quell the rebellion. The militia met the protesters at Springfield in January 1787 and dispersed the ragtag dissidents back to their homes. The leaders fled the state, but more than a thousand men were rounded up and jailed. The legislature passed the Disqualifying Act prohibiting the rebels from ever again voting, holding public office, working as schoolmasters, or operating taverns. The first two prohibitions denied the men a political voice, and the second two denied them occupations in which they could instruct or influence others.

Shays's Rebellion caused leaders throughout the country to worry whether the confederation could handle problems of civil disorder. Perhaps there were similar "combustibles" in other states, awaiting the spark that would set off a dreadful political conflagration. New York lawyer and diplomat John Jay wrote to George Washington, "Our affairs seem to lead to some crisis, some revolution—something I cannot foresee or conjecture. I am uneasy and ap-

prehensive; more so than during the war." Benjamin Franklin, in his eighties, shrewdly observed that in 1776 Americans had feared "an excess of power in the rulers," whereas now the problem was "a defect of obedience" in the subjects. To some, the sense of crisis in the confederation had greatly deepened.

## The Federal Constitution

Events in the fall of 1786 provoked an odd mixture of fear and hope that the government under the Articles of Confederation was losing its grip on power. A small circle of Virginians decided to try one last time to augment the powers granted to the government by the Articles. Their call for a meeting to discuss trade regulation led, more quickly than they could have imagined in 1786, to a total reworking of the national government.

### From Annapolis to Philadelphia

The Virginians took their lead from James Madison, thirty-five, the eldest son of a wealthy Virginia planter. A Princeton graduate, bookish and solitary by nature, the bachelor Madison was an avid student of politics. In 1776, he served in Virginia's assembly; from 1779 to 1782, he was a delegate in the Continental Congress and then returned to a seat in the state assembly.

Madison persuaded the Virginia assembly to call for a meeting of delegates at Annapolis, Maryland, to revise the trade regulation powers of the Articles. Delegates from only five states actually showed up in September 1786. Like Madison, the dozen men who attended were deeply troubled by a sense of impending crisis, and they rescheduled the meeting for Philadelphia in May 1787. The congress of the confederation government reluctantly endorsed the Philadelphia meeting and tried to limit its scope to "the sole and express purpose of revising the Articles of Confederation." But at least one representative at the Annapolis meeting had far more ambitious plans. Alexander Hamilton of New York hoped the Philadelphia meeting would do whatever was necessary to strengthen the federal government.

Alexander Hamilton by character was suited for such bold steps. The illegitimate son of a poor mother in the West Indies, Hamilton was taken up by an American trader and sent to college in New

**JAMES MADISON,**
**PORTRAIT BY CHARLES WILLSON PEALE**
*This miniature portrait was made of James Madison in*
*1783 when he was in his early thirties. The natural hair*
*and smooth face emphasize his youthful looks.*
Library of Congress.

York. He served at George Washington's side through much of the Revolution. After the war, he studied law, married into a wealthy New York mercantile family, and sat in the Continental Congress for two years. Despite his stigmatized childhood, the thirty-year-old Hamilton identified with the elite classes and their fear of democratic disorder.

The fifty-five men who assembled at Philadelphia in the spring of 1787 to consider the shortcomings of the Articles of Confederation were generally those most concerned about weaknesses in the present government. Few attended who were opposed to revising the Articles. Patrick Henry, author of the Virginia Resolves in 1765 and more recently the governor of his state, refused to go, saying he "smelled a rat." Rhode Island refused to send delegates. Two New York delegates, strongly op-

posed to revising the Articles, left in dismay in the middle of the convention, leaving Hamilton as the sole New York representative.

This gathering of white men included no artisans or day laborers or even farmers of middling wealth. Two-thirds of the delegates were lawyers. The majority had served in the Continental Congress and were intimately familiar with the workings of that government. Fully half had been officers in the Continental army, giving them a practical perspective on the financial difficulties faced by the confederation government. Seven men had been governors of their states and knew firsthand the frustrations of thwarted executive power. A few elder statesmen attended, such as Benjamin Franklin and George Washington, who was elected to preside over the meeting. But on the whole, the delegates were young, like Madison and Hamilton.

## The Virginia and New Jersey Plans

The convention pursued its work in secrecy, so the men could freely explore alternatives without fear that their honest opinions would come back to haunt them. With quiet understatement, Mercy Otis Warren evaluated the public reaction to the news blackout: "It was thought by some, that the greatest happiness of the greatest number was not the principal object of their contemplations, when they ordered their doors to be locked, their members inhibited from all communications abroad, and when proposals were made that their journals should be burnt, lest their consultations and debates be viewed by the scrutinizing eye of a free people."

The Virginia delegation first laid out a fifteen-point plan for a complete restructuring of the government. The Virginia Plan, as it became known, was a total repudiation of the principle of a confederation of states. Largely the work of Madison, the plan set out a three-branch government composed of a two-chamber legislature, a powerful executive, and a judiciary. It virtually eliminated the voices of the smaller states by pegging representation in both houses of the congress to population. The theory was that government operated directly on people, not on states. Among the breathtaking powers assigned to the congress were the rights to veto state legislation and to coerce states militarily to obey national laws. To prevent the congress from having absolute power, the executive and judiciary could jointly veto the actions of the congress.

In mid-June, delegates from New Jersey, Connecticut, Delaware, and New Hampshire, all small states, unveiled an alternative proposal. The New Jersey Plan, as it was called, resembled the existing Articles of Confederation in that it set out a single-house congress in which each state had one vote. Acknowledging the need for an executive, it created a plural presidency to be shared by three men elected by the congress from among its membership. Where it sharply departed from the existing government was in the sweeping powers it gave to the congress: the right to tax, to regulate trade, and to use force on unruly state governments. In favoring national power over states' rights, it aligned itself with the Virginia Plan. But the New Jersey Plan retained the confederation principle that the national government was to be an assembly of states, not of people.

For two weeks, delegates debated the two plans, focusing on the key issue of representation. The small-state delegates were willing to concede that one house in a two-house legislature could be apportioned by population, but they would never agree that both houses could be. Madison was equally vehement about bypassing representation by state, which he viewed as the fundamental flaw in the Articles.

The debate seemed deadlocked, and for a while the convention was "on the verge of dissolution, scarce held together by the strength of a hair," according to one delegate. Only in mid-July did the so-called Great Compromise break the logjam and produce the basic structural features of the emerging United States Constitution. Proponents of the competing plans agreed on a bicameral legislature; representation in the lower house, the House of Representatives, would be apportioned by population and representation in the upper house, the Senate, would come from all the states equally. But instead of one vote per state in the upper house, as in the New Jersey Plan, the compromise provided two senators who voted independently of each other.

Representation by population turned out to be an ambiguous concept once it was subjected to rigorous discussion. Who counted? Were slaves, for example, people or property? As people, they added weight to the southern delegations in the House of Representatives, but as property they added to the tax burdens of those states. What emerged was the compromise known as the three-fifths clause: All free persons plus "three-fifths of all other Persons" constituted the numerical base for the apportionment of representatives.

Using "all other Persons" as a substitute for "slaves" indicates the discomfort delegates felt in acknowledging the existence of slavery in a republican document. The words *slave* and *slavery* appear nowhere in the Constitution, but slavery figured in two other places besides the three-fifths clause. Trade regulation, for example, a power of the new Congress, naturally included regulation of the slave trade. In euphemistic language, a compromise between southern and northern states specified that "the Migration or Importation of such Persons as any of the States now shall think proper to admit, shall not be prohibited by the Congress prior to the Year one thousand eight hundred and eight." And a third provision guaranteed the return of fugitive slaves: "No person, held to Service or Labour in one State, under the Laws thereof, escaping into another, shall, in Consequence of any Law or Regulation therein, be discharged from such Service or Labour but shall be delivered up on Claim of the party to whom such Service or Labour may be due." Slavery was nowhere named, but it was recognized, guaranteed, and thereby perpetuated by the U.S. Constitution.

Plenty of fine-tuning followed the Great Compromise of mid-July, but the most difficult problem— that of representation—had been solved. The small states worked to consolidate power in the Senate, where their weight would be proportionately greater than in the lower house, and Madison slowly recovered from the crushing sense of defeat he experienced at first. He had entered the convention convinced that the major flaw in the old government was that it had relied on unreliable states, and he feared that the Great Compromise perpetuated that flaw. But as the respective powers of the House and Senate were hammered out, he lent his support to the package as the most reasonable of political outcomes.

## Democracy versus Republicanism

The delegates at the Philadelphia convention made a distinction between democracy and republicanism that had been absent from the political vocabulary a decade earlier. Pure democracy was now taken to be a dangerous thing. As a Massachusetts delegate put it, "the evils we experience flow from the excess of democracy." The delegates still claimed to favor republican institutions, but they created a government that gave direct voice to the people only in the House and that granted a check on that voice to the Senate, which would be composed of men more removed from the control of the people.

In the final document, senators would hold office for six years, with no limit on reelection. They were to be elected not by direct popular vote but by the state legislatures. In a country that was itself only eleven years old, a guaranteed six years in office was a very long time. Senators were protected from the whims of democratic majorities, and their long terms fostered experience and maturity in office.

---

*The framers had developed a far more complex form of a federal government than that provided by the Articles of Confederation. To curb the excesses of democracy, they devised a government with limits and checks on all branches.*

---

Similarly, the presidency evolved into a powerful office out of the reach of direct democracy. The delegates devised an electoral college whose only function was to elect the president and vice president. Each state's legislature would choose the electors, whose number was the sum of representatives and senators for the state, an interesting melding of the two principles of representation. The president thus would owe his office not to the Congress, the states, or the people, but to an ephemeral body of distinguished citizens who could vote their own judgment on the candidates.

The convention carefully listed the powers of Congress and of the president. The president could initiate policy and propose legislation; he could veto acts of Congress; he could command the military and direct foreign policy; and he could make appointments to numerous lesser executive offices and to the entire judiciary, subject only to the approval of the Senate. Congress held the purse strings: the power to levy taxes, to regulate trade, and to coin money and control the currency. States were expressly forbidden to issue paper money. Two further powers of Congress—to "provide for the common defence and general Welfare" of the country and "to make all laws which shall be necessary and proper" for carrying out its powers—provided elastic language that came closest to Madison's wish to grant sweeping powers to the new government.

The framers had developed a far more complex form of a federal government than that provided by the Articles of Confederation. To curb the excesses of democracy, they devised a government with limits and checks on all branches. They set forth a powerful president who could veto Congress but then gave Congress power to override presidential vetoes. They set up a national judiciary to settle disputes between states and citizens of different states. They made each branch of government as independent from the other branches as they could, by basing election on different universes of voters—voting citizens, state legislators, the electoral college.

The Constitution was a product of lengthy debate and compromise; no one was entirely satisfied with every line. Madison himself, who soon became its staunchest defender and has been called the Father of the Constitution, remained unsure that the most serious flaws of the Articles had been expunged. But when the final vote was taken at the Philadelphia convention in September 1787, only three dissenters refused to endorse the Constitution. The thirty-nine who signed it (thirteen others had gone home early) no doubt wondered how to sell this plan, with its powerful executive and Congress and its deliberate limits on pure democracy, to the American public. The Constitution specified a mechanism for ratification that avoided the dilemma faced earlier by the confederation government: Nine states, not all thirteen, had to ratify it, and special ratifying conventions, not state legislatures, would make the crucial decision. The innovation of debating the Constitution in special bodies elected only for that purpose drew attention to a major theme of the proposed plan: that the national government was no longer a league of states, but a government for all the people. But who could predict how the people, acting through the ratifying conventions, would react?

## Ratification of the Constitution

Had a popular vote been taken on the Constitution in the late fall of 1787, it would probably have been rejected. In the three most populous states—Virginia, Massachusetts, and New York—substantial majorities opposed a powerful new national government. North Carolina and Rhode Island refused to call ratifying conventions. In only a few of the eight remaining states could the proponents of the Constitution count on an easy victory. Securing the approval of nine states appeared to be a formidable task.

## The Federalists

The proponents of the Constitution plotted their course carefully and moved into action swiftly. To silence the charge that they had illegally bypassed the confederation government, they sent the new document to the Continental Congress for approval. The congress, at first reluctant, finally resolved to send the Constitution to the states for their consideration.

The pro-Constitution forces shrewdly secured another advantage by calling themselves Federalists. By all logic, this label was more suitable for the backers of the confederation concept, since the Latin root of the word *federal* means "league." The new Federalists, however, preempted the term and its positive Revolutionary-era associations and applied it to a comparatively nonfederalist plan that diminished the power of the states in a national government. Their opponents became known as Antifederalists, a label that made them sound defensive and negative, lacking a program of their own.

*Had a popular vote been taken on the Constitution in the late fall of 1787, it would probably have been rejected.*

The Federalists identified the states most likely to ratify quickly, and they immediately scheduled special local elections to select delegates to ratifying conventions in those states. Delaware managed to push through elections, a convention, and unanimous ratification by early December, before the Antifederalists had barely begun a campaign. Pennsylvania, New Jersey, and Georgia followed within a month. In the latter two states, voter turnout was extremely low; apathy favored the Federalists. Delaware and New Jersey were small states that lived in the shadows of more powerful neighbors; a government that would regulate trade and set taxes according to population was an at-

tractive proposition to them. Georgia had a different reason for ratifying: A powerful national government would afford greater protection against hostile Indians and Spanish Florida that bordered the state.

Another three states to ratify with relative ease were Connecticut, Maryland, and South Carolina. As in Pennsylvania, merchants, lawyers, and urban artisans in general favored the new Constitution, as did large landowners and slaveholders. This tendency for the established political elite to be Federalist enhanced the prospects of the Federalists' victory, for they already had power disproportionate to their numbers. Antifederalists in these states tended to be rural, western, and noncommercial, men whose access to news was limited and whose participation in state government was tenuous. (See the Historical Question on page 204.)

Massachusetts was the only early state in which the Federalists encountered difficulty. The popular vote for delegates gave a twenty-man advantage to the Antifederalists, whose strength came mainly from the western areas, home to Shays's Rebellion. Some easterners opposed the Constitution too: Mercy Otis Warren weighed in with her Antifederalist pamphlet, a sustained analysis of the dangers of corruption invited by the proposed government. One rural delegate from the town of Sutton voiced widely shared suspicions: "These lawyers and men of learning and money men that talk so finely, and gloss over matters so smoothly, to make us poor illiterate people swallow down the pill, expect to get into Congress themselves; they expect to be the managers of the Constitution and get all the power and all the money into their own hands, and then they will swallow up all us little folks." Nevertheless, the Antifederalist lead was slowly eroded by a vigorous newspaper campaign. In the final vote, the Federalists won by a very slim margin and only with promises that amendments to the Constitution suggested by the Massachusetts Antifederalists would be taken up at the first Congress.

By May 1788, eight states had ratified; only one more was needed. The Federalists knew that North Carolina and Rhode Island were hopeless, and New Hampshire looked nearly as bleak. More worrisome was their failure to win over the largest and most important states. In Virginia and New York, Antifederalists emerged distinctly and coherently as opponents of the Constitution.

# Was the New United States a Christian Country?

REBECCA SAMUEL, a Jewish resident of Virginia, conveyed her excitement about the new U.S. Constitution when she wrote her German parents in 1791 that finally "Jew and Gentile are as one" in the realm of politics and citizenship. Other voices were distinctly less approving. An Antifederalist pamphlet warned that the pope could become president; another feared that "a Turk, a Jew, a Roman Catholic, and what is worse than all, a Universalist, may be President."

The document that produced such wildly different readings was indeed remarkable in its handling of religion. The Constitution did not invoke Christianity as a state religion. It made no reference to an almighty being, and it specifically promised, in Article 6, section 3, that "no religious test shall ever be required as a qualification to any office or public trust under the United States." The six largest congregations of Jews—numbering about two thousand and located in Newport, New York, Philadelphia, Baltimore, Charleston, and Savannah—were delighted with this nearly unprecedented statement of political equality and wrote George Washington to express their hearty thanks.

But more than a few Christian leaders were stunned at the Constitution's near silence on religion. It seemed to represent a complete turnabout from the state constitutions of the 1770s and 1780s. A New Yorker warned that, "should the Citizens of America be as irreligious as her Constitution, we will have reason to tremble, lest the Governor of the universe . . . crush us to atoms." A delegate to North Carolina's ratifying convention played on anti-immigrant fears by predicting that the Constitution was "an invitation for Jews and pagans of every kind to come among us." A concerned Presbyterian minister asked Alexander Hamilton why religion was not in the Constitution, and Hamilton reportedly quipped, "Indeed, Doctor, we forgot it."

Measured against the practices of state governments, Hamilton's observation is hardly credible.

The men who wrote and debated the state and federal constitutions from 1775 to 1787 actively thought about principles of inclusion and exclusion when they defined citizenship, voting rights, and office-holding. They carefully considered property ownership, race, gender, and age in formulating rules about who could participate. And they also thought about religious qualifications.

Most leaders of the 1780s took for granted that Christianity was the one true faith and the essential foundation of morality. All but two state constitutions assumed the primacy of Protestantism, and a third of them collected public taxes to support Christian churches. Every state but New York required a Christian oath as a condition for office-holding. Every member of Pennsylvania's legislature swore to "acknowledge the Scripture of the Old and New Testament to be given by divine inspiration." North Carolina's rule was even more restrictive, since it omitted Catholics: "No person who shall deny the being of God or the truth of the Protestant religion, or the divine authority of the Old or New Testaments" could hold office. In South Carolina all *voters* had to be Protestants.

Other common political practices affirmed that the United States was a Christian country. Governors proclaimed days of public thanksgiving in the name of the Holy Trinity. Chaplains led legislatures in Christian prayer. Jurors and witnesses in court swore to Christian oaths. New England states passed Sabbath laws prohibiting all work or travel on Sunday. Blasphemy laws punished people who cursed the Christian God or Jesus.

Close to half the state constitutions included the right to freedom of religion as an explicit guarantee. But freedom of religion meant only that difference would be tolerated; it did not guarantee political equality.

How then did the U.S. Constitution come to be such a break from the immediate past? Had the framers really just forgotten about religion?

Not James Madison of Virginia. Madison arrived at the 1787 convention fresh from a hard-won victory in Virginia to establish religious liberty. At the end of 1786, he had finally secured passage of a bill written by Thomas Jefferson seven years earlier called the Virginia Statute of Religious Freedom. "All men shall be free to profess, and by argument to maintain, their opinions in matters of religion, and that the same shall in no wise diminish, enlarge, or affect their civil capacities," the bill read. Madison had convinced both the Episcopalians and the Baptist dissenters, at war with each other over state support, that to grant either or both churches tax money would be to concede to the state the authority to endorse one religion—and by implication to crush another. The statute separated church from state to protect religion. Further, it went beyond mere toleration to guarantee that religious choice was independent of civil rights.

In Madison's judgment, it was best for the U.S. Constitution to say as little as possible about religion, especially since state laws reflected a variety of positions. When Antifederalists demanded a bill of rights, Madison drew up a list for the First Congress to consider. Two items dealt with religion, but only one was approved. One became part of the First Amendment: "Congress shall make no law respecting an establishment of religion, or prohibiting the free exercise thereof." In a stroke, Madison set religious worship and the privileging of any one church beyond Congress's power. Significantly, his second proposal failed to pass: "No State shall violate the equal rights of conscience." Evidently, the states wanted to be able to keep their Christian-only rules without federal interference. Different faiths would be tolerated—but not guaranteed equal standing. And the very same session of Congress proceeded to hire Christian chaplains and proclaim days of thanksgiving.

Gradually, states deleted restrictive laws, but as late as 1840 Jews still could not hold public office in four states. Into the twentieth century, some states maintained Sunday laws that forced business closings on the Christian Sabbath, working enormous hardship on those whose religion required Saturday closings. The guarantee of freedom of religion was embedded in state and federal founding documents in the 1770s and 1780s, but it has taken many years to fulfill Jefferson's vision of what true religious liberty means: the freedom for religious belief to be independent of civil status.

## The Antifederalists

Antifederalists were a composite group, united mainly in their desire to block the Constitution. Much Antifederalist strength came from rural and backcountry areas with a long tradition of suspicion of the motives of eastern elites. Yet clearly many Antifederalist leaders came from the same social background as Federalist leaders; economic class alone did not differentiate them. Antifederalism also drew strength in states already on a sure economic footing, like New York, that could afford to remain independent. Probably the biggest appeal of antifederalism lay in the long-nurtured fear that distant power might infringe on people's liberties. The language of the 1760s and 1770s revolutionary movement was not easily forgotten.

But by the time eight states had ratified, the Antifederalists faced a far harder task than they had at first imagined. First, they were no longer defending the status quo, now that the momentum lay with the Federalists. Second, it was difficult to defend the confederation government with its admitted flaws. Even so, they remained genuinely fearful that the new government would be too distant from the people and could thus become corrupt or tyrannical.

The new government was indeed distant. In the House of Representatives, the only directly democratic element of the government, one member represented some thirty thousand people. How could such a representative really know or communicate with his constituency, the Antifederalists wondered. And how could the constituents judge their representative's service to them?

In addition, the Antifederalists were convinced that elected representatives would always be members of the elite. Such men "will be ignorant of the sentiments of the middling and much more of the lower class of citizens, strangers to their ability, unacquainted with their wants, difficulties, and distress," worried a Maryland man. None of this would be a problem under a confederation system, according to the Antifederalists, because real power would continue to reside in the state governments.

The Federalists generally agreed with the Antifederalist assumption that the elite would be favored for election to Congress, not to mention the Senate and the presidency. That was precisely what they hoped. The Federalists wanted power to flow to intelligent, virtuous, public-spirited leaders like themselves. They did not envision a government

constituted of every class of people. The Antifederalists challenged the notion that any class of men could be free of selfish interests. They feared that the Federalists were merely resurrecting rule by a wealthy aristocracy.

The most widespread objection to the Constitution was its lack of any guarantees of individual liberties. Unlike nearly half of the state constitutions, the proposed Constitution did not contain a bill of rights.

> *The Federalists generally agreed with the Antifederalist assumption that the elite would be favored for election to Congress, not to mention the Senate and the presidency.*

Despite the Federalists' campaigns in the large states, it was a small state—New Hampshire—that provided the decisive ninth vote for ratification, on June 21, 1788. Federalists there succeeded in getting the convention postponed from February to June and in the interim conducted an intense lobbying effort on specific delegates.

## The Big Holdouts: Virginia and New York

Four states still remained outside the new union, and a glance at a map demonstrated the necessity of pressing the Federalist case in the two largest, Virginia and New York. Though Virginia was home to Madison and Washington, an influential Antifederalist group led by Patrick Henry and George Mason made the outcome uncertain. Mason had been present throughout the Philadelphia convention and was one of the three delegates who refused to sign the Constitution; this made him an especially effective opponent. The Federalists finally won his support by including a resolution that certain individual rights and republican principles were inviolate in the new government and by proposing twenty specific amendments that the new government would promise to consider. By a 10-vote margin, out of 168 votes cast, the Federalists got their ratification.

In New York, Governor George Clinton represented agrarian interests in upstate New York, but more central to his antifederalism was a sense that a state as large and powerful as New York did not need to relinquish so much authority to the new federal government. New York was also home to some of the most persuasive and resourceful Federalists. Starting in October 1787, Alexander Hamilton collaborated with James Madison and New York lawyer John Jay on a series of essays on the political philosophy of the new Constitution. Ultimately numbering eighty-five, the essays were published in New York newspapers and later republished as *The Federalist Papers*. The essays brilliantly set out the failures of the Articles of Confederation and offered an analysis of the complex nature of federalism. In one of the most compelling essays, Madison argued for successful large-scale republican government, a direct challenge to one of the Antifederalists' most heartfelt convictions. Madison argued that a large and diverse population was itself a guarantee of liberty. In a national government, no single faction or self-interested group could ever be large enough to subvert the freedom of other groups. "Extend the sphere, and you take in a greater variety of parties and interests; you make it less probable that a majority of the whole will have a common motive to invade the rights of other citizens," Madison asserted.

New York's ratifying convention met at Poughkeepsie, a town halfway between New York City and Albany, deep in the heart of Antifederalist country. An unmistakable majority of the delegates were Antifederalist, but newspaper debate and heavy lobbying produced some switches in votes. The last-minute arrival of news that Virginia had ratified finally tipped the balance in favor of the Federalists.

New York's ratification assured the solidity and legitimacy of the new government. It took another year and a half for the Antifederalists in North Carolina to come around, and fiercely independent Rhode Island held out until May 1790, and even then ratified by only a two-vote margin.

In less than twelve months, the U.S. Constitution was both written and ratified. An amazingly short time by twentieth-century standards, it is equally remarkable for the late eighteenth century, with its horsepowered transportation and handprinted communications. The Federalists had faced a formidable task, but by building momentum and assuring a bill of rights, they did indeed carry the day.

## Conclusion: Decade of Decision

Thus ended one of the most intellectually tumultuous and creative decades in American history. Americans experimented with ideas and drew up plans to embody their evolving and conflicting notions of how a society and a government ought to be formulated. Widespread agreement supported the concept of a republican government in which the people are sovereign and government leaders derive their power and authority from the people. State constitutions, the Articles of Confederation, and finally the federal Constitution wrestled with different conceptions of the degree of democracy— of the amount of direct control of government by the people—that was truly workable in American society and that was consistent with the ideal of republicanism.

The decade began in 1776 with a confederation government that could barely be ratified because of its requirement of unanimity. There was no reaching unanimity on the western lands, on the impost amendment, or on the proper way to respond to unfair taxation in a republican state. The new Constitution offered one set of solutions to these problems, but it drew intense opposition from Antifederalists. Once it was ratified, the Antifederalists accepted it but continued to worry that the government might fail. Mercy Otis Warren expressed the view of many when writing to a correspondent in England, "We are too poor for Monarchy—too wise for Despotism, and too dissipated, selfish, and extravagant for Republicanism."

The Federalists still hoped for a society in which leaders of exceptional wisdom would discern the best path for public policy. They looked backward to a society of hierarchy, rank, and benevolent rule by an aristocracy of talent, but they created a government with forward-looking checks and balances as a guard against corruption, which they figured would most likely emanate from the people. The Antifederalists also looked backward, but to an old order of small-scale direct democracy and local control, where virtuous people kept a close eye on potentially corruptible rulers. Antifederalists feared a national government led by distant, heterogeneous, self-interested leaders who needed to be held in check. In the 1790s, these two conceptions of republicanism and of leadership would be tested in real life.

## CHRONOLOGY

**1775**  **May.** Second Continental Congress begins.

**1776**  Virginia adopts state bill of rights.

John Dickinson of Pennsylvania drafts Articles of Confederation.

**1777**  **November.** Final draft of Articles of Confederation approved by congress and sent to states.

**1778**  State constitutions completed.

**1780**  Pennsylvania abolishes slavery.

**1781**  Articles of Confederation ratified.

Creation of executive departments; Robert Morris appointed superintendent of finance.

Bank of North America formed.

Slave Quok Walker sues for freedom in Massachusetts.

**1782**  Virginia relaxes state manumission law.

**1783**  Treaty of Paris signed.

**1784**  Gradual emancipation laws passed in Rhode Island and Connecticut.

Treaty of Fort Stanwix with Iroquois.

**1785**  Gradual emancipation in New York.

**1786**  Gradual emancipation in New Jersey.

Bank of North America expires.

Virginia adopts Statute of Religious Freedom.

Farmer Shays leads rebellion in western Massachusetts.

Annapolis meeting proposes convention to revise Articles of Confederation.

**1787**  Northwest Ordinance allows self-government and prohibits slavery in Northwest Territory.

**May–September.** Constitutional convention meets in Philadelphia.

**1788**  United States Constitution ratified.

## SUGGESTED READINGS

Willi Paul Adams, *The First American Constitutions: Republican Ideology and the Making of the State Constitutions in the Revolutionary Era* (1980). A comprehensive analysis of the various state constitutions and the political thinking embedded in them.

Morton Borden, *Jews, Turks, and Infidels* (1984). A concise and lively survey of the relationship between church and state at the time of the Constitution.

Steven R. Boyd, *The Politics of Opposition: Antifederalists and the Acceptance of the Constitution* (1979). A close study of the Antifederalists' ideas and strategies in the ratification process.

Eric Foner, *Tom Paine and Revolutionary America* (1976). An engaging study of Paine's life and the impact of his pamphlet *Common Sense* in 1776.

Merrill Jensen, *The New Nation: A History of the United States During the Confederation, 1781–1789* (1950). The classic, detailed account of the Confederation period.

Ralph Ketcham, *James Madison* (1971). The standard biography of the Father of the Constitution.

Peter S. Onuf, *Statehood and Union: A History of the Northwest Ordinance* (1987). The best account of the evolving ideas about how the new nation should treat the Northwest Territory.

Jack N. Rakove, *The Beginnings of National Politics: An Interpretive History of the Continental Congress* (1979). A close and fascinating study of the daily work of Congress under the confederation government.

Jack N. Rakove, *Original Meanings: Politics and Ideas in the Making of the Constitution* (1996). A prize-winning, subtle analysis of the political philosophy behind the Constitution.

David P. Szatmary, *Shays' Rebellion: The Making of an Agrarian Insurrection* (1980). A full account of the thwarted tax rebellion and its role in bringing about the Constitution.

Gordon Wood, *The Creation of the American Republic, 1776–1787* (1969). A prize-winning intellectual history of the evolution of political thought about republicanism and democracy in the 1780s.

Rosemarie Zagarri, *A Women's Dilemma: Mercy Otis Warren and the American Revolution* (1995). A concise and readable account of Warren's life set against the momentous events of her adult years.

**MISS LIBERTY NEEDLEWORK**

*An unknown artist skillfully rendered Miss Liberty offering drink to an eagle, executed in a combination of needlework and watercolor. Liberty's cap—the symbol that always accompanied a female figure representing liberty—sits atop a flagpole. The pose of woman, eagle, and flagpole is borrowed exactly from a popular 1796 engraving by the American artist Edward Savage and was copied many times in needlework and watercolor by amateurs, many of them young women. Where Savage put Boston harbor in the background of his picture, this needleworker (perhaps a New Jersey resident) chose to paint the decorative arches at Trenton, New Jersey, erected to honor George Washington on his inaugural journey to New York City to assume the presidency.*

The Daughters of the American Revolution Museum, Washington, D.C. (Gift of the New Jersey State Society, honoring Mrs. John Kent Finley, State Regent 1962–1964).

# THE NEW NATION TAKES FORM

# 9

## 1789–1800

T HE ELECTION OF GEORGE WASHINGTON in February 1789 was quick work. Seven months earlier, right after Virginia and New Hampshire ratified the Constitution, many July 4 orators and newspaper editors considered the Virginia planter as good as president, and the tallying of the unanimous votes by the electoral college became a mere formality. Washington was everyone's first choice. He perfectly embodied the republican ideal of disinterested, public-spirited leadership; indeed, he cultivated that image. At the end of the Revolutionary War, he had dramatically surrendered his sword to the Continental Congress, symbolizing the subservience of military power to the law.

Although somewhat reluctant, Washington ultimately accepted the presidency. He journeyed from Virginia to the capital, New York City, in six days, encountering cheering crowds, large triumphal arches, and military parades at many villages en route. In New York City, Washington, on a white horse, headed a procession down Broadway while a crowd of thirty thousand applauded wildly. He took the oath of office at the newly built Federal Hall at Broad and Wall Streets; a cannon salute in the harbor signaled his inauguration.

The pageantry was a kind of hero worship for Washington as an individual. But the question, as yet unresolved, was whether the office of the presidency itself would be grandly heroic. The arches, the grand entry on a white horse, the gun salute—all this was an uneasy reminder of the trappings of monarchy. In its first month, Congress debated the proper form of address for the president, raising explicitly the issue of how kingly this new presidency was to be. Titles such as "His Highness, the President of the United States of America and Protector of Their Liberties" and "His Majesty, the President" were floated as possibilities, while Washington himself was known to favor "His High Mightiness." Several former Antifederalists sitting in Congress held out for a less exalted title. The final version was simply "President of the United States of America," and the established form of address became "Mr. President," a subdued yet dignified title in a society where only independent, property-owning adult white males could presume to be called "Mister."

Washington's genius in establishing the presidency lay in his capacity for implanting his own reputation for integrity into the office itself. He was not a particularly brilliant thinker, nor was he a shrewd political strategist. He was not even a very congenial man. In the political language of the day, he was virtuous. Washington was studiously aloof, resolute, and dignified, to the point of appearing wooden at times. He encouraged pomp and ceremony to create respect for the authority of his office, traveling with no fewer than six horses drawing his coach,

**GEORGE WASHINGTON BY JOSEPH WRIGHT**
*George Washington wears a laurel wreath, the traditional mark of honor in ancient times. Carved in beeswax in 1784, the work elevates Washington to the status of a Greek or Roman hero.*
Courtesy of the Mount Vernon Ladies Association.

in the political leadership of the 1790s. The disagreements were articulated around particular events and policies, but at heart they arose out of opposing ideological stances about the value of democracy, the nature of leadership, and the limits of federal power. By 1800, these divisions had crystallized into full-fledged political parties, the Federalists and the Republicans.

## The Search for Stability

Conventional wisdom today praises the development of a party system: Parties organize conflict, legitimize disagreement, and mediate among competing political strategies. Yet they were entirely unanticipated by the writers of the Constitution. James Madison had argued in *The Federalist Papers* in 1788 that a superior feature of the national government was precisely that its extensive size would prevent small, selfish factions from becoming dangerously dominant. No one was prepared for the intense and passionate polarization of the mid-1790s.

Instead, leaders in the early 1790s sought stability to heal divisions of the 1780s. Veneration for President Washington provided one powerful source of unity. People trusted him to initiate the untested and perhaps elastic powers of the presidency. Congress quickly agreed on passage of the Bill of Rights in 1791, which satisfied many Antifederalist critics. And the private virtue of women was mobilized to bolster the public virtue of male citizens; republicanism was forcing a rethinking of women's relation to the state.

hosting formal balls, and surrounding himself with servants in livery. But he always managed, perhaps just barely, to avoid the extreme of royal splendor.

The thirteen American states had just come through a difficult decade, swinging between a distrust of executive power on the one hand and a fear of turbulent factional politics on the other. Washington's reputation for integrity boosted confidence that executive power could be compatible with the public good. And his strong pronouncements about the evils of divisive factions raised hopes that at last America was on a steady course.

National harmony proved elusive, however. Political parties developed in the 1790s, despite the best intentions of the decade's statesmen. Even men who had worked together to ratify the Constitution found that the process of implementing it exposed serious disagreement. Economic policy and foreign affairs proved to be the two most significant fissures

### Washington's Cabinet

Congress immediately set up departments of war, treasury, and state, leaving to Washington the selection of secretaries over each. The president picked talented and experienced individuals for each post, regardless of their deep philosophical differences. For the Department of War, he chose ex-General Henry Knox, who had been secretary of war in the confederation government. For the Treasury, he turned to Alexander Hamilton of New York, known for his general brilliance and financial astuteness. Washington understood that heading the Treasury would be the hardest job; revenue problems excited discontent and had largely caused the confederation government to fail. To lead the

Department of State, the foreign policy arm of the executive branch, Washington chose Thomas Jefferson, who had just returned from a four-year stint as minister to France, a country now in the early stages of a democratic revolution. No one understood the intricacy of diplomatic relations better than Jefferson.

In addition, for attorney general Washington picked Edmund Randolph, a Virginian who had attended the Constitutional Convention but had turned Antifederalist during ratification. For chief justice of the Supreme Court, Washington designated John Jay, the New York lawyer who vigorously defended the Constitution along with Madison and Hamilton in *The Federalist Papers.*

---

*No one anticipated that fundamental disagreements leading to two decades of party turbulence would emerge from the brilliant but explosive mix of Washington's first cabinet.*

---

Washington liked and trusted all these men, and by 1793, in his second term, he was meeting regularly with them, thereby establishing the precedent of a presidential cabinet. (Vice President John Adams did not join these meetings; his only official duty was to preside over the Senate, a job he found "a punishment" because he could not actually participate in legislative debates.) No one anticipated that fundamental disagreements leading to two decades of party turbulence would emerge from the brilliant but explosive mix of Washington's first cabinet.

## The Bill of Rights

Many Antifederalists had complained about the absence of guarantees of individual liberties and limitations to federal power in the Constitution, and seven states had ratified on the condition that a bill of rights be swiftly incorporated. Many state constitutions already protected freedom of speech, press, religion, and peaceable assembly and the rights to petition and to have jury trials. In the final days of the 1787 Philadelphia convention, the delegates had decided that an enumeration of rights was unnecessary. But the complaint surfaced continually in the ratification process, and so in 1789, James Madison drew up a set of amendments.

Final agreement from both House and Senate on the first ten amendments to the Constitution, collectively known as the Bill of Rights, came in September 1789. Amendments 1–8 dealt with individual liberties, and 9 and 10 concerned the boundary between federal and state authority. The amendments had the immediate effect of cementing a sense of national unity. The process of state ratification of the amendments took another two years, but there was no serious doubt about the outcome.

Still, not everyone was entirely satisfied. Amendments that would change the structural details of the new government, ardently desired by some Antifederalists, were never considered by Congress. Madison had no intention of reopening debates settled at the Philadelphia convention about the length of term for the president or the power to levy excise taxes or the power of Congress to maintain a peacetime army.

Significantly, no one complained about another striking omission in the Bill of Rights: the right to vote. Only much later was voting seen as a fundamental liberty requiring protection by constitutional amendment—indeed, by four amendments. The 1788 Constitution deliberately left all decisions about defining voters to individual states, to promote stability in the new federal government. Any uniform federal voting law would run the double risk of excluding some who could already vote in state elections or including too many new voters deemed undesirable in the more restrictive states. Most states maintained property qualifications for voting, thus excluding slaves, servants, apprentices, tenants, wives, and a new and growing class of propertyless wage laborers at the lower end of the social scale.

The New Jersey state constitution of 1776, however, enfranchised all free inhabitants worth over £50, thereby including free blacks as well as unmarried women who met the property requirement. (Married women owned no property, for by law their husbands held title to everything.) Little fanfare accompanied this radical shift, and some historians have inferred that the inclusion of blacks and unmarried women was accidental, the result of an unstated assumption that the voters would be whites and men. Yet other parts of the suffrage clause pertaining to residency and property were extensively debated when it was put in the state constitution, and no objections were raised at that time to its gender- and race-free language. Other historians have concluded that the law was intentionally broad. By 1790, a revised election law used the words *he or she* in reference to voters, thus making woman suffrage explicit. As one legislator boasted, "Our Constitution gives this right to maids or widows *black or white.*" This highly unusual state of affairs lasted until 1807, when a new law specifically disfranchised both blacks and women in New Jersey. Henceforth, independence of mind, that essential precondition of voting, was now redefined to be sex- and race-specific. After 1807, free black men could not vote in New Jersey until 1870, with the passage of the Fifteenth Amendment; for women, white and black, it took until 1920, when the Nineteenth Amendment became law.

## The Republican Wife and Mother

The general exclusion of women from political activity did not mean that they had no civic role or responsibility. A flood of periodical articles of the 1790s by both male and female writers reevaluated courtship, marriage, and motherhood in light of republican ideals. Tyrannical power in the ruler, whether king or husband, was now declared a thing of the past. Affection, not duty, bound wives to their husbands and citizens to their government. In republican marriages, the writers claimed, women had the capacity to reform the morals and manners of men. One male author promised women that "the solidity and stability of the liberties of your country rest with you; since Liberty is never sure, 'till Virtue reigns triumphant." By upholding public virtue, women bolstered political liberty.

*Republican ideals cast motherhood in a new light, centering on the importance of mothers as the teachers of virtuous sons.*

Until the 1790s, public virtue was strictly a masculine quality. But another sort of virtue loomed in importance: sexual chastity, a private asset prized as a feminine quality. Essayists of the 1790s explicitly advised young women to use sexual virtue to produce more public virtue in men. "Love and courtship . . . invest a lady with more authority than in any other situation that falls to the lot of human beings," one male essayist proclaimed. If women spurned selfish suitors, they could promote good morals more than any social institution could, essayists promised.

**REPUBLICAN WOMANHOOD:**
**MRS. REUBEN HUMPHREY OF CONNECTICUT**
*This late-eighteenth-century American mother displayed her gentility by the objects she chose to grace her portrait: an intricate wood frame mirror, a silver tea service, a plumed hat incongruously worn indoors while tending the baby. Mrs. Reuben Humphrey of East Granby, Connecticut, was married to the superintendent of a state prison; this painting was done by a prisoner.*
The Connecticut Historical Society, Hartford.

Republican ideals also cast motherhood in a new light, centering on the importance of mothers as the teachers of virtuous sons. Benjamin Rush, a Pennsylvania physician and educator, called for female education because "our ladies should be qualified . . . to concur in instructing their sons in the principles of liberty and government." Throughout the 1790s, advocates legitimized female education, still a controversial proposition, through the claim of significant maternal influence on the future male citizenry. A series of essays by Judith Sargent Murray of Massachusetts, using the pen name Constantia, favored education that would remake women into self-confident, competent, rational beings, poised to become the equals of men. But even Murray had to dress her advanced ideas in the cloak of republican motherhood, justifying female education in the context of family duty.

Although women's domestic obligations as lovers, wives, and mothers were now infused with political meaning, traditional gender relations remained unaltered. The analogy between marriage and civil society worked precisely because of the self-subordination inherent in the term *virtue*. Men should put the public good first, before selfish desires, just as women must put their husbands and families first, before themselves. Women might gain literacy and knowledge, but only in the service of improved domestic duty.

## Sources of Economic Change

Following a decade of severe economic instability, the 1790s ushered in a period of prosperity and sustained economic growth. New agricultural opportunities, transportation improvements, and innovations in finance were beginning to transform not only the economy but the way ordinary men and women thought about their work and their chances for bettering their lives.

### Commercial Agriculture

From at least the mid-eighteenth century, most farmers had participated in market transactions at local stores and in nearby towns. Self-sufficiency was simply not possible in a society where a taste for some of the luxuries of life had taken hold. For example, a store in the village of Brookfield, in central Massachusetts, stocked fine cloth from England and India; watch chains and shoe buckles; teapots and dishware; and raisins, allspice, salt, sugar, and tea. Rarely was cash exchanged at the moment of purchase. Instead, the store owner recorded transactions in his account book, keeping a running total of each customer's debt, which was periodically paid off in either cash or, more likely, "country goods"—a surplus of cheese, butter, or grain from the farmer's production.

This pattern of local market exchange was altered in the 1790s, when dramatic increases in the international price of grain motivated farmers to step up their grain production. Food prices, driven by population growth, were generally rising in Europe in the late eighteenth century. After 1793, prices rose even more sharply, when France and England entered two decades of conflict known as the Napoleonic Wars. Soon all the major European powers were embroiled in war, leaving the United States, the only neutral shipper, with a near-monopoly on the Atlantic trade. American grain farmers from the Connecticut River valley to the Chesapeake responded by growing more wheat. The increase in overseas grain trade generated a host of new jobs in related areas as the number of millers, coopers, and ship and wagon builders expanded.

Cotton production also underwent a boom, spurred by market growth and a mechanical invention. Limited amounts of smooth-seed cotton had long been grown in the low-lying coastal areas of the South; but this variety of cotton did not prosper in the drier, inland regions. Green-seed cotton grew well inland, but it contained many rough seeds that adhered tenaciously to the cotton fibers. Typically, it took an entire day to clean a pound of cotton by hand. In 1793, a Yale graduate named Eli Whitney, visiting a Georgia plantation, turned his mechanical talents to the task of reducing the labor in cotton production. His invention, the cotton gin, could clean fifty pounds of cotton per day. The English textile industry provided a ready market for raw cotton; now the southern states could meet the increasing demand. The figures of cotton production tell the story: 138,228 pounds of cotton were grown in the South in 1792; two years later, the number was 1,601,000, eleven times as much, and by 1800, the figure was 35 million pounds of cotton. Cotton fever had gripped the South, with momentous and chilling consequences for the one million enslaved black Americans living there.

### Transportation

The prosperous cash economy made possible by grain exports and cotton culture was initially confined to areas within thirty miles of navigable waterways or the coast. The high cost of transporting goods over muddy or rutted paths barely wide enough for a wagon was the single biggest obstacle to the spread of commercial farming. The only major continuous road existing at the beginning of the 1790s was the Post Road, running near the East Coast for 1,600 miles from Maine to Georgia. It consisted of local country roads, linked together in the 1780s, and it carried an increasing load of passenger traffic in stagecoaches as well as freight and the U.S. mail.

In the 1790s, east-to-west road building commenced. In 1794, the Lancaster Turnpike, the first

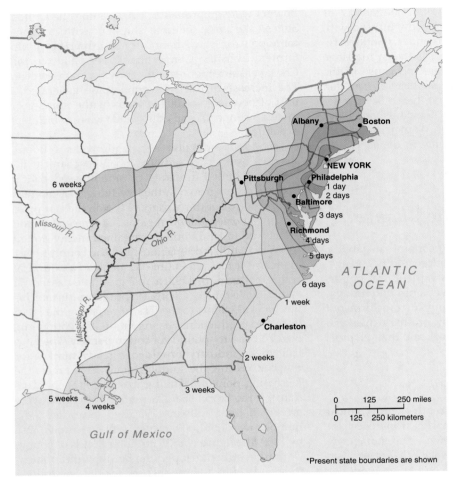

**MAP 9.1**
*Travel Times from New York City in 1800*
Notice that the first week of travel out of New York extends over a much greater distance than subsequent weeks because of poor or nonexistent roads in the west, mountain barriers, and Indian dangers. River corridors in the west and east speeded up travel—if one were going downriver. Also note that travel by sea (north and south along the coast) was much faster than land travel.

private toll road in the nation, connected Philadelphia with Lancaster, sixty-five miles west, and, later, with Pittsburgh in western Pennsylvania. Soon another turnpike connected Boston with Albany, New York. Private companies under charter by state governments financed these turnpikes; a company built the road and collected fees from all vehicles. In areas away from the coast, a major road extended southwest down the Shenandoah Valley, while a road called Zane's Trace moved across southern Ohio. A new road linked Richmond, Virginia, with the Tennessee towns of Knoxville and Nashville. An early Ohio law reveals the primitive character of the western roads compared with state-of-the-art gravel turnpikes in the East: The law prohibited stumps in the roadway higher than one foot.

By 1800, a dense network of dirt, gravel, or plank roadways connected cities and towns in southern New England and the Middle Atlantic states, while isolated roadways and old Indian trails fanned out to the west. Commercial stage lines connected major eastern cities, offering four-day travel time between New York and Boston and an exhausting but speedy one-and-one-half-day trip between New York and Philadelphia (Map 9.1). In 1790 only three stagecoach companies operated out of Boston, but in 1800 there were twenty-four. Western roads facilitated the migration of settlers—Vermont, Kentucky, Tennessee, and Ohio became sufficiently populated to join the Union by 1800—but the roads were generally too slow to allow an economical movement of heavy, bulky agricultural products like grain.

South of the Potomac River, road building and commercial stagecoach travel remained rudimentary, chiefly because of low passenger demand. Two-thirds of the southern population—the enslaved blacks and the poorer whites—could not travel, and the elite planters generally owned their own coaches and wagons. Growers of cotton and tobacco continued to rely on the many southern rivers to move produce to market, a practice that reinforced the economic dominance of property owners fronting on the eastern waterways.

## Merchants and Capital

The surge in the overseas grain and cotton trades stimulated the growth of the commercial classes in seacoast cities. At the pinnacle of the business community were the merchants, often men with multiple financial dealings in both wholesale and retail operations. The richest merchants not only bought and sold foreign goods, they typically owned some fraction of the ships that carried the goods.

In the 1780s, states could and did erect trade barriers, but the creation of the federal government finally removed all obstacles to interstate business alliances and guaranteed the free movement of goods across state borders. The horizons of the business community widened, and the volume of trade mushroomed. New investment opportunities beckoned in mercantile trades and in such areas as the chartering of turnpike companies and stagecoach lines and the development of textile mills.

These opportunities required a larger and longer commitment of capital than did a joint venture for a single cargo in a ship. The need for investment capital was met by the development of commercial banking, a financial innovation that had not existed in America before the Revolution. During the 1790s, the number of banks multiplied nearly tenfold, from three at the beginning of the decade to twenty-nine in 1800. Banks drew in money chiefly through the sale of stock. They then made loans in the form of banknotes, paper currency backed by the gold and silver paid in by stockholders. Because they issued two or three times as much money in banknotes as they held in hard money, banks were really creating new money for the economy.

# Hamilton's
# Political Economy

In late 1790, the government moved from New York City to Philadelphia, which was more centrally located. This too was a temporary home; the long-range plan entailed construction of the capital on the Potomac River between Maryland and Virginia, independent of any state. (See the Historical Question on page 218.) Serious economic choices faced the country, and the young secretary of the treasury, Alexander Hamilton, proposed a wide-ranging economic program as innovative as it was controversial.

## The Public Debt and Taxes

Hamilton first turned his attention to the very large public debt, nearly $52 million. About $11.7 million was owed to foreign creditors, while a tangled web of domestic IOUs and interest-bearing public securities amounted to a further $40.4 million. The debt dated from the difficult war years, when the government needed supplies and manpower but had no independent source of revenue. In the 1780s, the actual paper IOUs and certificates of debt had fallen in value, in some states to as little as one-twentieth of the original value; this drop reflected the widespread belief that the confederation government could never make good on them. The question now was open: What exactly should be done about the debt?

Hamilton's answer, elaborated in his *Report on Public Credit* in January 1790, was that the debt, both foreign and domestic, be funded at full value. This meant that an old IOU or a certificate of debt would be rolled over into a new bond, at the same value, with a schedule of regular interest payments from government to holder and a promise to retire the debt in forty years. Thus there would still be a public debt, but it would be secure, supported by the confidence of Americans in their new government. The new bonds would circulate as a stable medium of exchange, injecting new and more valuable money into the economy. "A national debt if not excessive will be to us a national blessing; it will be a powerfull cement of our union," Hamilton wrote to another financier.

Probably about 2 percent of the white population held the largest portions of the debt. Many of them were wealthy speculators who had bought up the IOUs cheaply, betting that they might rise in value in the long run. Now these influential men would have a direct stake in the new government, support that Hamilton regarded as essential to the country's stability. He was also providing those same few men with more than $40 million released for new investment, a distinct improvement over the old depreciated bonds, which had circulated in daily transactions at only a small fraction of their face value.

## How Did Washington, D.C., Become the Federal Capital?

WHY DIDN'T BOSTON, Philadelphia, or New York City become the capital of the United States? The great cities of London and Paris were great precisely because political power was situated at the heart of commerce and culture in those European countries. Although much smaller in scale, the several American cities boasted elegant houses, cultural institutions, lively economies, newspapers, food markets, taverns, coffeehouses, and stagecoach and shipping lines—nearly everything necessary to accommodate the political elites who would be running the new government. Instead, the infant United States chose marshy, vacant acreage along the Maryland shore of the Potomac River for its permanent capital.

While the choice of that particular site was by no means inevitable, the country's leaders agreed that there should be only one site. During the war years, the Continental Congress had jumped around many times, from Philadelphia, Lancaster, and York in Pennsylvania to Princeton and Trenton in New Jersey, and down to Baltimore, often on the run from the British army. Even after the war, the congress continued to circulate, meeting in Trenton, in Annapolis and Georgetown in Maryland, and finally in New York City. When the confederation government commissioned an equestrian statue of George Washington to inspire and dignify its meetings, a humorist suggested that the marble horse be fitted with wheels so it could be towed from place to place.

For some, a floating capital symbolized the precarious status of the confederation. But the alternative, a fixed location, put the federal government at the mercy of the particular state it sat in. If irate citizens stormed the congress, as had happened once in Philadelphia in 1783, could the local state's militia always be counted on to protect it? The writers of the Constitution thus came up with a novel solution. They decided to locate the capital on land not controlled by any state. The 1788 Constitution specified a square district, not exceeding ten miles on a side, where Congress would have sole jurisdiction; but they deferred the complicated choice of the exact site to the First Congress.

In 1790, more than forty cities and towns clamored for consideration, from Kingston and Newburgh in New York's Hudson River valley down to Richmond and Williamsburg in Virginia. Eleven contenders clustered along the Delaware River between New Jersey and Pennsylvania, roughly the demographic center of the country. Six more sites fell in the interior of Pennsylvania, along the Susquehanna River, each claiming to be the future geographic center as the country grew westward. Another eleven locations dotted the Potomac River from the Chesapeake to the Appalachians. Clearly, river transportation figured heavily in all these plans, and investors in canal and river navigation companies took special notice.

The First Congress struggled to reconcile private interests, regional jealousies, and genuine dilemmas of citizen access. A Pennsylvania proposal naming a Susquehanna River site finally passed the House but not the Senate. Virginians held out for the Potomac, drawing objections from New Englanders fearful of disease-laden southern swamps. Philadelphians insisted that their city, the premier cultural and economic center of America, was the only logical choice. In short, the situation was at a stalemate.

Another, unrelated stalemate obstructed Congress in early 1790. Alexander Hamilton presented Congress with his controversial plan to fund the public debt by assuming state debts. James Madison objected and wrested the necessary votes from Hamilton—at first.

Hamilton approached Robert Morris of Pennsylvania to propose a deal: If Morris would deliver votes for Hamilton's assumption plan, the influential Hamilton would back a capital site in Pennsylvania. But Morris could not command enough congressional votes, so Hamilton next approached Thomas Jefferson, secretary of state, who invited him to dinner with James Madison. There the three reached agreement: enough southern votes for assumption in exchange for a Potomac River site. Madison could not bring himself to vote for as-

**PLAN FOR WASHINGTON, D.C., ON A HANDKERCHIEF**
*In 1791 and 1792, the pressure was high to get a detailed map of the proposed capital city into circulation so that prospective land buyers could be lined up. Finally a Philadelphia engraving firm produced this plan of the future city with each block numbered. It was reproduced on large handkerchiefs in an early marketing strategy to entice buyers. The actual site in 1792 consisted of fields and marshes.*
Library of Congress.

sumption, but he rounded up the necessary votes from men representing districts along the river. In the final bill, Philadelphia was named the interim capital until 1800, by which time a site on the Potomac River, to be selected by President Washington, would be constructed and open for business. Robert Morris gloated that the Virginians had been tricked; he felt sure that Philadelphia's charms would ensnare the government permanently. Assumption quickly passed, by six votes.

Washington, drawing on his surveying expertise, took another year to select the hill-banked plain east of Georgetown, after scouting far up the river. For any location he chose, the Potomac Company—of which Washington himself was president and principal investor—stood to benefit, but this was not considered a conflict of interest in the 1790s. What made the Potomac advantageous both for a capital site and for investment in navigation was that it penetrated the farthest inland of any East Coast river, traversing the lowest point in the Appalachian Mountains. Washington's scouting trips convinced him that with short portages, water routes could connect the Chesapeake Bay to western Pennsylvania and beyond to the Ohio and Mississippi Rivers.

Next, the rural site had to be purchased from the Maryland farmers who owned it. Washington and Jefferson purposely deployed surveyors in widely scattered locations up and down the river, to keep local owners from guessing where the government center would finally rest within the district—and thus to keep a lid on land prices. The president also deputized friends to purchase the land, "as if for yourselves, and to conduct your propositions so as to excite no suspicion that they are on behalf of the public."

Washington then hired a French-born master designer to plan the capital. Pierre L'Enfant, an architect living in New York City, mapped out a grid of streets slashed dramatically by wide diagonal boulevards. L'Enfant envisioned a mall surrounded by grand government buildings. The rest of his map showed small lots intended for private buyers, who, it was hoped, would provide housing and services for the government population. The proceeds of the land sales would fund the government construction, so that a city could be built without having to draw on the U.S. Treasury at all.

In the end, the capital landed in the South because a major east–west river was there and because the South had crucial votes to trade on the assumption bill. Washington, D.C., represented the geographic but not the demographic center of the thirteen states. Its placement exerted a southern tug on the federal government, augmented by the fact that five of the first seven presidents were also southerners. In all the political horse trading over choosing the site, nobody thought it worthy to note that the capital of the Republic sat in the heart of a slave society. But it would turn out to be of major significance some sixty years later, when the capital of President Abraham Lincoln's Union was surrounded by slavery, with many of its inhabitants of doubtful loyalty to the Union.

**ALEXANDER HAMILTON**
*Alexander Hamilton in 1792 at age thirty-seven, painted by John Trumbull. Ever a prodigy, Hamilton, at age nineteen, became an indispensable wartime aide to George Washington. In his midtwenties he gained admission to the bar after only three months of study. In 1789, he became Washington's youngest cabinet member.*
Yale University Art Gallery.

If the *Report on Public Credit* had gone only this far, it would have been somewhat controversial. But Hamilton took a much bolder step by adding into the federal debt another $25 million still owed by some state governments to individuals. All the states had obtained supplies during the war by issuing IOUs to farmers, merchants, and moneylenders. Some states, such as Virginia and New York, had paid off these debts entirely, while others, like Massachusetts, had partially paid them through heavy and painful taxation of the inhabitants; about half the states had made little headway. Hamilton called for the federal government to assume these state debts and add them to the federal debt. His "assumption plan" in effect consolidated federal power over the states.

The assumption of state debts required the federal government to exercise even stronger powers of taxation. To meet the interest payments on a national debt swollen to some $77 million, Hamilton did not propose raising import duties, for that would have been unacceptable to the merchant class whose support he was seeking. Instead, he convinced Congress in 1791 to pass a 25 percent excise tax on distilled spirits, to be paid by the farmer when he brought his grain to the distillery. Members of Congress favored the tax, especially those from New England where the favorite drink was rum, an imported beverage already taxed under the import laws. A New Hampshire representative pointed out that the country would be "drinking down the national debt," an idea he evidently thought was good.

> Hamilton called for the federal government to assume these state debts and add them to the federal debt. His "assumption plan" in effect consolidated federal power over the states.

Congressman James Madison objected to Hamilton's funding plan, fearing that windfall profits would go mainly to speculators who had bought the original IOUs at bargain prices. He also strenuously objected to assumption of all the states' debts. A large debt was dangerous, Madison warned, especially because it would lead to high taxation. But he lost the vote in Congress. Madison and Hamilton, so recently allies in writing *The Federalist Papers*, were becoming opponents.

Secretary of State Jefferson also was fearful of Hamilton's proposals. Cabinet meetings had become disagreeable and uncomfortable, causing President Washington to rebuke them both. Hamilton misread the motives of Madison and Jefferson, thinking they were rivals for his power. Jefferson had a clearer picture of the problem: "No man is more ardently intent to see the public debt soon and sacredly paid off than I am. This exactly marks the difference between Colonel Hamilton's views and mine, that I would wish the debt paid tomorrow; he wishes it never to be paid, but always to be a thing where with to corrupt and manage the legislature."

## The First Bank of the United States

A second element of Hamilton's economic plan was his proposal for a national Bank of the United States, which he presented to Congress in December 1790. Believing that banks were the "nurseries of national wealth," Hamilton modeled his plan on the Bank of

England: a private corporation that worked primarily for the public good. In Hamilton's plan, 20 percent of the bank's stock would be bought by the federal government. In effect, the bank would become the fiscal agent of the new government, holding and handling its revenues derived from import duties, land sales, and the whiskey excise tax. The other 80 percent of the bank's capital would come from private investors, who could buy stock in the bank with either hard money (silver or gold) or federal securities. By its size and the privilege of being the only national bank, the bank would help stabilize the economy by exerting prudent control over credit, interest rates, and the value of the currency. Five of the twenty-five directors of the bank would be appointed by the government, to look out for the public interest. Hamilton had extraordinarily good faith in the virtue of the other twenty directors, who would be chosen from among the private stockholders, merchants from the world of commerce and high finance.

Madison, concerned that the bank gave a handful of rich men undue influence over the economy, tried but failed to stop the plan in Congress. An equally concerned Jefferson advised Washington that creating a national bank was unconstitutional because there was nothing about chartering banks in the specified powers granted to Congress by the Constitution. Hamilton, however, argued that the same list specified many powers to regulate commerce and ended with a broad grant of the right "To make all laws which shall be necessary and proper for carrying into execution the foregoing powers." Washington, who studied the arguments for two weeks, ultimately agreed with Hamilton and signed the bank into law in February 1791, providing it with a charter to operate for twenty years.

When the bank's privately held stock went on sale in New York City in July, it sold out in a few hours, touching off an immediate mania of speculation in resale. A discouraged Madison reported that "the Coffee House is an eternal buzz with the gamblers," some of them self-interested congressmen intent on "public plunder."

## The **Report on Manufactures**

The third component of Hamilton's plan was set out in December 1791 in the *Report on Manufactures,* a proposal to encourage the production of American-made goods. Manufacturing was in its infancy in 1790, the result of years of dependence on British imports. Hamilton recognized that a balanced and self-reliant economy required the United States to produce its own cloth and iron products. His plan mobilized the new powers of the federal government to impose tariffs and grant subsidies to encourage the growth of local manufacturing. Hamilton had to be careful not to undercut his important merchant allies who traded with England and generated over half the government's income. A high tariff would either seriously dampen that trade or would force merchants into smuggling. So Hamilton favored a moderate tariff, with extra bounties paid to American manufacturers to encourage production. The *Report on Manufactures* was the one Hamiltonian plan that was not approved by Congress.

## The Whiskey Rebellion

Hamilton's excise tax on whiskey showed that he could make serious political mistakes. Many more voters were grain farmers and whiskey drinkers than were merchants. Western farmers with an abundance of wheat and rye suddenly faced high taxes that had to be paid up front at the distillery. Cash-short farmers deeply resented their assigned role in Hamilton's plan for economic recovery.

In 1791, angry grain farmers in the western parts of Pennsylvania, Virginia, Maryland, and the Carolinas and throughout Kentucky conveyed to Congress their resentment of Hamilton's tax. Congress responded with modest modifications in the tax in 1792; but even so, discontent was rampant.

*At the core of the Whiskey Rebellion lay the question of what citizens can and cannot do when they think a law is unjust and what governments can and cannot do when groups of citizens resort to extralegal and even violent means to express their grievances.*

Simple evasion of the law was the most common response from the farmer. And indeed, the tax proved hard to collect. Federally appointed tax inspectors soon learned the unpleasant consequences, as crowds threatened to tar and feather them. Even in Philadelphia, the nation's capital, major distilleries right under Hamilton's nose were evading the tax by underreporting their production by nearly half. With embarrassment, Hamilton admitted to Congress that the revenue yield from the tax was far less than anticipated. But rather than abandon the law, he tightened up on the prosecution of tax evaders.

**WHISKEY REBELLION "FIRE COPPER"**
*This forty-gallon "fire copper" produced Monongahela rye whiskey in the 1790s in western*
*Pennsylvania. Mashed rye grain was mixed and heated with mash from a previously distilled*
*brew. The distiller next added yeast and water and let the mixture ferment for several days. The*
*mixture was then heated to 175 degrees, the boiling point of alcohol, in this three-foot copper ves-*
*sel (called a "still"). Alcohol-laden vapor from the boiling brew cooled and condensed in a spiral*
*copper tubing that dripped whiskey into a jug. High-proof, expensive whiskey required a second*
*processing in the still to concentrate the vapors. The owner of this fire copper was James Miller,*
*whose nephew Oliver Miller Jr. was an early fatality in the Whiskey Rebellion.*
Oliver Miller Homestead/Photo by Andrew Wagner; Courtesy of *American History* magazine.

In western Pennsylvania, Hamilton had one ally, a stubborn tax collector named John Neville who had refused to quit even after a group of spirited farmers had burned an effigy of him. In late May 1794, Neville filed charges against seventy-five farmers and distillers for tax evasion. In mid-July, he and a federal marshal were ambushed in Allegheny County by a group of forty men, and during the next two days Neville's house was burned to the ground by a crowd estimated at five hundred. At the end of July, seven thousand farmers staged a march on Pittsburgh to express their hostility to the hated tax.

An angry Hamilton convinced President Washington to respond with a show of force. Washington nationalized the Pennsylvania militia, donned his old military garb, and set out, with Hamilton at his side urging him on, at the head of fifteen thousand soldiers. By the time the military force arrived, in late September, the demonstrators had all gone home. No battles were fought, and no fire was exchanged. Twenty men were rounded up as rebels and charged with high treason, but only two were convicted, and both were soon pardoned by Washington.

Had the government overreacted? Or was Hamilton right to think that the whiskey rioters posed a serious threat to the stability of the federal government? At the core of the Whiskey Rebellion lay the question of what citizens can and cannot do when they think a law is unjust and what governments can and cannot do when groups of citizens resort to extralegal and even violent means to express their grievances.

The long colonial tradition of crowd action to protest unfair practices or to express public opinion had worked comfortably when colonial people had limited formal access to power. But in a republic, laws were passed by the supposed representatives of the people, not by tyrannical kings or distant parliaments. Burning effigies of stamp tax collectors in 1765 made sense as an effective contribution to the political process. Burning effigies of whiskey tax collectors in 1792 appeared to many to be an unlawful rejection of the will of the people as expressed through Congress.

The whiskey rebels, however, recognized oppressive taxes for what they were and felt entitled to resort to protest and demonstration. Representative government had not worked to their benefit. The Whiskey Rebellion was an early example of what would prove to be a long-term conflict, the tension between minority rights and majority rule.

## Conflicts West and East

Washington's second term began in 1793, after a smooth and again unanimous reelection. But as the Whiskey Rebellion demonstrated, the widespread admiration for the individual man did not translate to complete domestic tranquility. While the whiskey rebels challenged federal leadership from within the country, disorder threatened the United States from external sources as well. To the west, a powerful confederation of Indian tribes in the Ohio country resisted white encroachment. The result was a brutal war. At the same time, conflicts between the major European powers forced Americans to take sides and nearly thrust the country into another war, this time across the Atlantic.

### To the West: The Indians

By the Treaty of Paris of 1783, England had given up all land east of the Mississippi River to the United States. But this land was not entirely England's to give; the English neglected to consult their allies in the Revolutionary War, the Indian tribes who inhabited 25,000 square miles of that land. As recently as 1768, England had formally guaranteed the Indians their rights to all land north of the Ohio River, but the Treaty of Paris simply ignored that obligation.

When the British commanders at forts in North America finally told their Indian neighbors about the treaty terms, the Indians expressed astonishment. "They told me they never could believe that our king could pretend to cede to America what was not his own to give," the commander at Fort Niag-

ara wrote of the Iroquois. In southern Ohio, British Indian agents assured the Shawnees and Delawares that England had relinquished only political control to the United States but that Indians still had the right to occupy the land over the claims of American settlers. Such confusion and misrepresentation aggravated an already volatile situation.

A doubled American population, from 2 million in 1770 to nearly 4 million in 1790, created an insistent pressure for western land. Several thousand settlers a year moved down the Ohio River in the mid-1780s, some bound for Kentucky but many others eyeing the fresh forests and fields north of the Ohio River. By the late 1780s, government land sales in eastern Ohio commenced (Map 9.2).

Even western Ohio was not safe from American incursions. Downriver, at the site of present-day Cincinnati, an outpost named Fort Washington was constructed in 1789 and put under the command of General Arthur St. Clair, who was also named governor of the entire Northwest Territory. St. Clair's mission was to displace the Indians and clear the way for permanent American settlement in Ohio. He first tried peaceful tactics: He got an assortment of Indians to sign a treaty yielding land near the Muskingum River, in eastern Ohio. But the signing Indians were not chiefs authorized to undertake negotiations, so the dubious treaty did nothing to improve the chances for peace in the region.

Bloody frontier raids and skirmishes between settlers and Indians led the United States to expand its military force. Finally, St. Clair took direct action. In the fall of 1791, more than two thousand men (and two hundred women camp followers) marched north from Fort Washington to engage in battle with Miami and Shawnee Indians. The Indians attacked first, at daybreak on November 4, at the headwaters of the Wabash River in western Ohio. The ferocious battle was a total disaster for the Americans. Fifty-five percent of the force were dead or wounded before noon; only three of the women escaped alive. It was the worst American defeat in the entire history of the U.S.-Indian wars. The Indians captured valuable guns and artillery and scalped and dismembered the dead and dying. They pursued fleeing survivors for miles into the forest. The grisly tales of St. Clair's defeat became instantly infamous, increasing, if this were possible, the level of sheer terror that Americans brought to their confrontation with the Indians.

President Washington doubled the American military presence in Ohio and appointed a new commander, General Anthony Wayne of Pennsylvania.

**MAP 9.2**
*Western Expansion and Indian Land Cessions to 1810*
By the first decade of the nineteenth century, the period of intense Indian wars had resulted in significant cessions of land to the U.S. government by treaty. The battles of the 1790s concentrated in Ohio, and in 1803 the region was pacified sufficiently to become the seventeenth state in the Union.

An officer in the Continental army during the Revolution, Wayne had earned the nickname "Mad Anthony" for his headstrong and rambunctious style of leadership. With some 3,500 men, Wayne established two new military camps, Fort Greenville and Fort Recovery, deep in Indian territory in western Ohio.

In December 1793, Wayne was ready to seize the initiative, and by spring his army had engaged in several skirmishes with the Shawnees and Delawares. The decisive action came in August 1794 at the Battle of Fallen Timbers, near the Maumee River where a recent severe rainstorm had felled many trees. The confederated Indians— mainly Ottawas, Potawatomis, and Delawares,

numbering around 800—first ambushed the Americans, but they were underarmed, many having only tomahawks. Wayne's well-disciplined troops made effective use of their guns and bayonets, and in just over an hour the Indians had retreated and scattered.

Fallen Timbers was a major defeat for the Indians. The Americans had destroyed cornfields and villages on the march north, and with winter approaching, the Indians' confidence was sapped. They reentered negotiations in a much less powerful bargaining position. In 1795, about a thousand Indians representing a confederacy of nearly a dozen tribes met with Wayne and other American

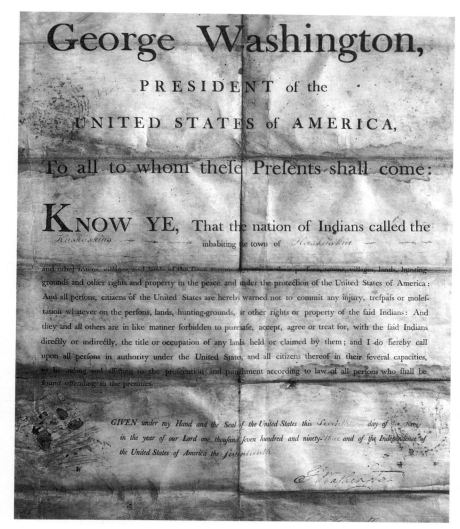

George Washington,

PRESIDENT of the

UNITED STATES of AMERICA,

To all to whom thefe Prefents shall come:

**K**NOW YE, That the nation of Indians called the _Kaskaskias_ inhabiting the town of _Kaskaskia_

and other towns, villages, and lands of that fame community... perfons, towns, villages, lands, hunting-grounds and other rights and property in the peace and under the protection of the United States of America: And all perfons, citizens of the United States are hereby warned not to commit any injury, trefpafs or molef-tation whatever on the perfons, lands, hunting-grounds, or other rights or property of the faid Indians: And they and all others are in like manner forbidden to purchafe, accept, agree or treat for, with the faid Indians directly or indirectly, the title or occupation of any lands held or claimed by them; and I do hereby call upon all perfons in authority under the United States, and all citizens thereof in their feveral capacities, to be aiding and affifting to the profecution and punifhment according to law of all perfons who fhall be found offending in the premifes.

GIVEN under my Hand and the Seal of the United States this _Seventh_ day of _January_ in the year of our Lord one thoufand feven hundred and ninety-_three_ and of the Independence of the United States of America the _feventeenth._

_G. Washington_

### WASHINGTON'S PROCLAMATION ABOUT THE KASKASKIA INDIANS' LAND

_The president's name, in bold print, prefaces a warning that American citizens were forbidden to injure Indians or trespass their lands in the Northwest Territory. When the federal government signed treaties with tribes ceding land, it often guaranteed protections for land not ceded. This poster of 1793 announced federal protection for the Kaskaskia Indians in central Illinois Territory. The warnings were not very effective, however. Washington wrote in 1796, "I believe scarcely any thing short of a Chinese Wall, or line of Troops will restrain Land Jobbers, and the Incroachment of Settlers, upon Indian Territory."_

Chicago Historical Society.

---

emissaries to work out the Treaty of Greenville. The Americans offered $25,000 worth of treaty goods (calico shirts, axes, knives, blankets, kettles, mirrors, ribbons, thimbles, and abundant wine and liquor casks) and promised additional shipments every year. The government's idea was to create a dependency on American goods to keep the Indians friendly. In exchange, the Indians ceded most of Ohio to the Americans; only the northwest region of the territory was reserved solely for the Indians (see Map 9.2).

The treaty brought peace to the region, but it did not bring back a peaceful life to the Indians. The annual allowance from the United States too often came in the form of liquor. "More of us have died since the Treaty of Greenville than we lost by the years of war before, and it is all owing to the introduction of liquor among us," said Little Turtle, chief of the Miami tribe, in 1800. "This liquor that they introduce into our country is more to be feared than the gun and tomahawk."

### Across the Atlantic: France and England

Since 1789, a violent revolution had been raging in France. At first, the general American reaction was positive, for it was flattering to think that the American Revolution had inspired imitation in France. Monarchy and privilege were overthrown in the name of republicanism; towns throughout America celebrated the victory of the French people with civic feasts and public festivities.

But news of the beheading of King Louis XVI quickly dampened the uncritical enthusiasm for everything French. Those who fondly remembered the excitement and risk of the American Revolution were still apt to regard France with the same kind of optimism. However, the reluctant revolutionaries of the 1770s and 1780s, who had worried about excessive democracy and social upheaval in America, deplored the far greater violence occurring in the name of republicanism as France moved into the Reign of Terror.

Support for the French Revolution could remain a matter of personal conviction until 1793, when England and France went to war, and French versus British loyalty became a very delicate and critical foreign policy question. France had helped America substantially during the American Revolution, and the confederated government had signed an alliance in 1778 promising aid if France were ever under attack. Americans still optimistic about the eventual outcome of the French Revolution wanted to deliver on that promise now. But others, including those shaken by the guillotining of thousands of French people as well as those with strong commercial ties to England, sought ways to stay neutral.

---

*Support for the French Revolution could remain a matter of personal conviction until 1793, when England and France went to war, and French versus British loyalty became a very delicate and critical foreign policy question.*

---

In May 1793, President Washington issued a Neutrality Proclamation, with friendly assurances to both sides. His aim was to cool the tensions abroad and protect American interests in both countries. But tensions at home flared in response to official neutrality. "The cause of France is the cause of man, and neutrality is desertion," wrote H. H. Brackenridge, a western Pennsylvanian, voicing the sentiments of thousands. Dozens of popular, pro-French political clubs sprang up around the country, called Democratic or Republican Societies. The societies mobilized farmers and mechanics, issued circular letters, injected pro-French and anti-British

feelings into local elections, and in general heightened popular participation and public interest in foreign policy. The activities of these societies made Washington and Hamilton intensely uncomfortable, for they vented opposition to the policies of the president.

The Neutrality Proclamation was in theory a fine idea, in view of Washington's goal of staying out of European wars. Yet American ships continued to trade between the French West Indies and France, carrying primarily grains, sugar, and other foodstuffs. In late 1793 and early 1794, England expressed displeasure with the limited American interpretation of neutrality by capturing more than three hundred of these ships near the West Indies. A crisis ensued, and even pro-British politicians like Hamilton agreed that it was necessary to make a formal agreement with England. Washington sent John Jay, the chief justice of the Supreme Court and a man known to have very strong pro-British sentiments, to negotiate a treaty.

### The Jay Treaty

John Jay's assignment was to secure agreement about general commercial ties between the two countries and to negotiate compensation for the seizure of American ships. In addition, he was supposed to resolve several long-standing problems dating from the end of the Revolution. Southern planters wanted reimbursement for the slaves lured away by the British army during the war, and western settlers wanted England to vacate the western forts still occupied for their strategic proximity to the Indian fur trade.

Jay returned from his diplomatic mission with a treaty that almost no one liked because of several major concessions to the British. First, the treaty made no direct provision for the captured ships or the lost property in slaves. Second, the treaty granted the British eighteen months to withdraw from the western forts while guaranteeing them continued rights in the fur trade. Finally, the Jay Treaty called for repayment with interest of the debts some American planters still owed to British firms dating from the Revolutionary War. In exchange for granting such generous terms to England, Jay secured some favorable commercial agreements for the United States, but even there the results were mixed. The treaty was widely regarded as exchanging the country's strong moral bargaining power (the outrage over the seized ships) for an improved trading status beneficial to only a handful of merchants in the overseas trade.

When newspapers published the terms of the treaty, powerful opposition emerged from Maine to Georgia. Nevertheless, the Jay Treaty passed the Senate in 1795 by a vote of twenty to ten. Some representatives in the House, led by Madison, tried to undermine the Senate's approval by insisting on a chance to vote on the funding provisions of the treaty, on the grounds that the House controlled all money bills. Finally, in 1796, the House approved funds to implement the various commissions mandated by the treaty, but by only a three-vote margin. The cleavage of votes in both houses of Congress divided along the same lines as the Hamilton-Jefferson split on economic policy.

## Federalists and Republicans

The assumption that a division into political parties was a sign of failure was soon put to a severe test. In Washington's second term, consistent voting blocs first appeared in Congress on economic issues. By the time of the Jay Treaty, party labels—Federalist and Republican—had come into use for rival politicians and rival newspapers. Washington's decision not to seek a third term opened the floodgates to serious partisan electioneering.

### The Election of 1796

Washington struggled to appear to be above party politics, and in his farewell address of September 1796 he stressed the need to maintain a "unity of government" reflecting a unified body politic. He also urged the country to "steer clear of permanent alliances with any portion of the foreign world." The leading contenders for his position, John Adams of Massachusetts and Thomas Jefferson of Virginia, in theory agreed with him: Political parties were deplorable, and neutrality toward England and France was essential. But around them raged a party contest split along pro-English versus pro-French lines.

Adams and Jefferson were not adept politicians in the modern sense, skilled in the arts of persuasion and intrigue. Bruised by his conflicts with Hamilton, Jefferson had resigned as secretary of state in 1793 and retreated to Monticello, his home in Virginia. Adams's job as vice president kept him closer to the political action, but his personality

**JOHN ADAMS BY JOHN TRUMBULL**
*John Adams in 1793 at age fifty-eight, when he was vice president. A friend once listed Adams's shortcomings as a politician: "He can't dance, drink, game, flatter, promise, dress, swear with gentlemen, and small talk and flirt with the ladies."*
National Portrait Gallery, Smithsonian Institution/Art Resources, N.Y.

often put people off. He was temperamental, thin-skinned, and quick to take offense.

The leading Federalists and Republicans informally caucused to choose candidates. To run with Adams, the Federalists picked Thomas Pinckney of South Carolina; the Republicans settled on Aaron Burr of New York to pair with Jefferson. The Constitution did not anticipate parties and tickets. Instead, each electoral college voter could cast two votes, on only one ballot; the top vote-getter became president and the next highest assumed the vice presidency. (This procedural flaw was corrected by the Eleventh Amendment, adopted in 1804.) With only one ballot, careful maneuvering was required to make sure the chief rivals for the presidency did not land in the top two spots.

Into that maneuverable moment stepped Alexander Hamilton. No longer in the cabinet, Hamilton had returned to his law practice in 1795, but he kept a firm hand on political developments. Hamilton did not trust Adams; he preferred Pinckney, and he tried to influence electors to throw their support to the South Carolinian. But his plan backfired: Adams was elected president with seventy-one electoral votes, and Jefferson came in second with sixty-eight votes and thus became vice president. Pinckney got fifty-nine votes, while Burr trailed with thirty.

Adams's inaugural speech before Congress emphasized his determination to rise above party strife. He promised to be neutral in foreign affairs and lifted Republican hopes by noting his great respect for the French people based on seven years' residence there. To solidify Federalist support, he retained the same three cabinet members from Washington's administration, the secretaries of state, treasury, and war, without fully realizing that all three were Hamilton loyalists. They wrote Hamilton for advice which they then passed on to the unwitting Adams as their own. Thus, private citizen Hamilton exercised a great deal of power in the Adams presidency.

Vice President Jefferson, a gracious loser to Adams after the electoral college balloting, extended a conciliatory arm when the two old friends met in Philadelphia, still the capital. They took temporary lodging in the same boardinghouse as if expecting to work closely together. But quickly the Hamiltonian cabinet ruined the honeymoon. Jefferson's advice was spurned, and he withdrew from active counsel of the president.

## The XYZ Affair

Foreign policy lay at the heart of the rift between Adams and Jefferson and between Federalists and Republicans. If the Jay Treaty heated American tempers initially, the French response in 1797 was like oil added to the fire.

France read the Jay Treaty as the Republicans did: as a document giving so many concessions to the British that it made America a British satellite. In retaliation, France abandoned the terms of the 1778 wartime alliance with the United States and allowed privateers—armed private vessels—to seize American ships carrying British goods. By March 1797, when Adams's inaugural address promised evenhanded neutrality, French privateers had already detained more than three hundred American vessels and seized the goods on board. In a related move, in the winter of 1796–97, France refused to recognize a new minister sent by President Washington, Charles Cotesworth Pinckney.

To avenge these insults, Federalists started murmuring openly about war with France. Adams preferred negotiations and dispatched a three-man commission to France in the fall of 1797. When the three arrived in Paris, French officials would not receive them. Finally the French minister of foreign affairs, Talleyrand, sent three French agents, unnamed and later known to the American public as X, Y, and Z, to the American commissioners with the suggestion that $250,000 might grease the wheels of diplomacy and that a $12 million loan to the French government would be the price of a peace treaty. The three Americans were incensed by the suggestion of a bribe, and they departed to inform the president.

*Foreign policy lay at the heart of the rift between Adams and Jefferson and between Federalists and Republicans. If the Jay Treaty heated American tempers initially, the French response in 1797 was like oil added to the fire.*

Americans reacted to the XYZ affair with shock and anger. Even staunch pro-French Republicans began to reevaluate their allegiance. The Federalists' demand for military action became more insistent. Congress voted to expand the navy with new frigates and men; it also repealed all prior treaties with France. In 1798, twenty naval warships launched the United States into its first undeclared war, called the Quasi War by historians to underscore its uncertain legal status. The main scene of action was the Caribbean, where more than one hundred French privateers were captured.

The Federalist-dominated Congress also appropriated funds to recruit an army of ten thousand men immediately, with a further plan for a provisional army of fifty thousand. Republicans feared that the Federalists' real aim might be to use the army to threaten domestic dissenters, since there seemed to be little chance of a land invasion by France. Some claimed that Hamilton had masterminded the army buildup and was lobbying to be second in command of the army, behind the aging Washington. President Adams was increasingly mistrustful, but his cabinet pressured for Hamilton, and Adams was too weak politically to prevail. He was, however, beginning to suspect that his cabinet was more loyal to Hamilton than to the presidency.

Antagonism intensified between Federalists and Republicans. Republican newspapers launched heated attacks on Adams: One denounced him as "a person without patriotism, without philosophy, and a mock monarch." On July 4, 1798, a pro-French mob roamed the streets in Philadelphia wearing hats with cockades, small ribbon florets that indicated solidarity with the radical revolutionaries of France. An alarmed Adams stocked guns and ammunition in his house, fearing attack by a Republican mob.

Federalists too were taking the offensive. In Newburyport, Massachusetts, they staged a huge bonfire, burning issues of the state's Republican newspapers. Officers in a New York militia unit drank a menacing toast on July 4, 1798: "One and but one party in the United States." A leading Federalist newspaper declared that "he who is not for us is against us."

## The Alien and Sedition Acts

If the United States had actually declared war on France, the pro-French Republicans could have been labeled traitors, subject to laws of treason. But without a declared war, Federalists had to invent another law to muffle opposition. In June and July 1798, Congress hammered out a Sedition Act that mandated a heavy fine or a jail sentence for anyone engaged in conspiracies or revolts against the government, or convicted of "speaking, writing, or publishing any false, scandalous, or malicious statement, with the intent to defame or bring into contempt or disrepute the President, the Congress, or the Government." In other words, spoken or written words that falsely criticized government leaders were now criminal utterances.

Congress also passed two Alien Acts. The first extended the waiting period required for an alien to

**CARTOON OF MATTHEW LYON FIGHT IN CONGRESS**
*The political tensions of 1798 were not merely intellectual. A February session in Congress degenerated from name-calling to a brawl. Roger Griswold, a Connecticut Federalist, called Matthew Lyon, a Vermont Republican, a coward. Lyon responded with some well-aimed spit, the first departure from the gentleman's code of honor. Griswold responded by raising his cane to Lyon, whereupon Lyon grabbed nearby fire tongs to beat back his assailant. Madison wrote to Jefferson that the two should have dueled: "No man ought to reproach another with cowardice, who is not ready to give proof of his own courage" by negotiating a duel, the honorable way to avenge insults.*
Library of Congress.

achieve status as a naturalized citizen from five to fourteen years and required all aliens to register with the federal government. The second empowered the president in time of war to deport or to imprison without trial any foreigner suspected of being a danger to the United States. The clear intent of the alien laws was to harass French immigrants in the United States and discourage others from coming.

The main targets of the Sedition Act were the Republican newspaper editors who were free and abusive in their criticism of the Adams administration. One Federalist in Congress justified his vote for the law with reference to the Republican press: "Let gentlemen look at certain papers printed in this city and elsewhere, and ask themselves whether an unwarrantable and dangerous combination does not exist to overturn and ruin the government by publishing the most shameless falsehoods against the representatives of the people." In all, twenty-five men, almost all newspaper editors, were charged with sedition; twelve were convicted by juries.

Jefferson, Madison, and other Republicans strongly opposed the Alien and Sedition Acts on the grounds that they were in conflict with the Bill of Rights, but they did not have the votes to revoke the acts in Congress, nor could the federal judiciary, dominated by Federalist judges, be counted on to challenge them. So Jefferson and Madison turned to the state legislatures, the only other competing political arena, to mount their opposition. They each drafted a set of resolutions condemning the acts and had the legislatures of Virginia and Kentucky present them to the federal government in late fall 1798. The Virginia and Kentucky Resolutions tested the novel argument that state legislatures have the right to judge the constitutionality of federal laws and to nullify laws that infringe on the liberties of the people as defined in the Bill of Rights. The resolutions made little dent in the application of the Alien and Sedition Acts, but the idea of a state's right to nullify federal law did not disappear; it surfaced again some thirty years later and played a role in the coming of the Civil War.

Amidst all the war hysteria, sedition fears, and party conflict in 1798, President Adams somehow managed to regain a measure of caution. Uncharacteristically, he was remarkably restrained in pursuing opponents under the Sedition Act, and he finally refused to be pushed into a hasty declaration of war by the extreme Federalists. No doubt he was beginning to realize how much he had been the dupe of Hamilton. He also shrewdly realized that France was in fact not eager for war and that a peaceful settlement might be close at hand. In January 1799, a peace initiative from France arrived, in the form of a letter assuring Adams that diplomatic channels were open again and that new commissioners would be welcomed in France. Adams accepted this overture and appointed a new negotiator; by late 1799, the Quasi War with France had subsided. But in responding to the French initiative, Adams lost the support of a significant part of his own party and sealed his fate as the first one-term president of the United States.

The election of 1800 was openly organized along party lines, with the self-designated national leaders of each group meeting to handpick their candidates for president and vice president. Adams ran again but was doomed to lose. When the election was over, the new president, Thomas Jefferson, mounted the inaugural platform to announce, "We are all republicans, we are all federalists," an appealing rhetoric of harmony appropriate to an inaugural address. But his formulation perpetuated a denial of the validity of party politics, a denial that ran deep in the founding generation of political leaders.

## Conclusion: Parties Nonetheless

The Federalists had dominated Congress and the presidency throughout the 1790s and persisted in thinking of themselves as the legitimate, disinterested rulers who could give the country enlightened leadership. President Washington sought unity for the new Union and deplored party strife, which in his view resulted from a vocal minority. Yet under Federalist presidencies, the issues that divided the country—Hamilton's economic program, the whiskey tax, the Jay Treaty, the Quasi War, and the Alien and Sedition Acts—engendered serious opposition.

The emerging Republicans were not a small minority. Many were onetime Federalists in Congress, like Madison, now in strenuous disagreement with Federalist policies and joined by politically active citizens. The Federalists were pro-British, pro-commerce, and ever alarmed about the potential excesses of democracy, while the Republicans celebrated, up to a point, the radical republicanism of France and feared a powerful federal government.

When Jefferson offered his conciliatory assurance that Americans were at the same time "all republicans" and "all federalists," he was possibly thinking of widely shared ideas that undergirded the country's political institutions. Certainly his listeners favored republican government, where power derived from the people, and likewise they favored the unique federal system of shared governance structured by the Constitution. But by 1800, these same two words, adapted to be the proper names of parties, had come to signify competing philosophies of government.

## CHRONOLOGY

| | |
|---|---|
| **1789** | Washington inaugurated president. French Revolution begins. First Congress meets in New York City. |
| **1790** | Hamilton's funding and assumption plans approved. Government moves from New York to Philadelphia. First federal census conducted. |
| **1791** | Bill of Rights ratified by states. Bank of the United States chartered by Congress. St. Clair's defeat by Ohio Indians. Congress passes whiskey tax. |
| **1793** | Washington's second term begins. War breaks out between France and England. |
| **1793** | Washington issues Neutrality Proclamation. Battle of Fallen Timbers; U.S. victory over Indians in Ohio. |
| **1794** | Whiskey Rebellion in western Pennsylvania. |
| **1795** | Treaty of Greenville with Indians. Jay Treaty with England. |
| **1796** | John Adams elected president, Thomas Jefferson vice president. |
| **1797** | XYZ affair with France. |
| **1798** | Quasi War with France. Alien and Sedition Acts. Virginia and Kentucky Resolutions. |
| **1801** | Jefferson elected president. |

# SUGGESTED READINGS

Joyce Appleby, *Capitalism and a New Social Order: The Republican Vision of the 1790s* (1984). A brief and lucid account of the emerging Republican views of the economy in the 1790s.

Stanley Elkins and Eric McKitrick, *The Age of Federalism: The Early American Republic, 1788–1800* (1993). A dense and comprehensive account of the politics of the 1790s.

John Fering, *John Adams: A Life* (1992). A balanced and probing narrative of the public life of Adams.

Drew McCoy, *The Last of the Fathers: James Madison and the Republican Legacy* (1989). An engaging and readable brief biography of Madison.

John R. Nelson, *Liberty and Property: Political Economy and Policymaking in the New Nation, 1789–1812* (1987). An excellent study of Hamilton's economic policies.

Robert A. Rutland, *The Birth of the Bill of Rights, 1776–1791* (1991). The standard account of the Constitution's first ten amendments.

James Rogers Sharp, *American Politics in the Early Republic: The New Nation in Crisis* (1993). A penetrating and lively account of the tumultuous origins of party politics in the 1790s.

Thomas P. Slaughter, *The Whiskey Rebellion: Frontier Epilogue to the American Revolution* (1986). A close-textured study of the western farmers' tax revolt.

James Morton Smith, *Freedom's Fetters: The Alien and Sedition Laws and American Civil Liberties* (1966). The standard account of the Federalists' efforts to stifle the Republican opposition.

Wiley Sword, *President Washington's Indian War: The Struggle for the Old Northwest, 1790–1795* (1985). A detailed and harrowing history of the bloody warfare in the Ohio Territory.

Richard White, *The Middle Ground: Indians, Empires, and Republics in the Great Lakes Region, 1650–1815* (1991). A richly textured synthesis of nearly two centuries of Indian-European interaction in the "middle ground," a concept denoting both a geographical place (the Ohio country) and a shared intercultural exchange.

**A JEFFERSON FAN**

*Ladies' fans became increasingly popular fashion accessories in the late eighteenth and early nineteenth centuries. This folding fan of vellum and carved ivory, made in the early 1800s, features a medallion portrait of President Thomas Jefferson. Carried by the ribbon on a woman's wrist, the fan could be flicked open to announce a partisan political statement. Fans and other hand-held articles such as parasols and handkerchiefs expanded the repertoire of nonverbal expression for women, who by the custom and training of the time were expected to be less assertive than men in mixed conversation. Many emotions and messages—including modesty, coyness, and flirtatiousness as well as anger, irritability, and boredom—could be communicated by the expert deployment of this delicate emblem of femininity.*

Collection of David J. and Janice L. Frent.

# REPUBLICAN ASCENDANCY

## 10

### 1800–1824

ERIWETHER LEWIS CAME UPON three Shoshone women near the Continental Divide in mid-August 1805; one ran off and the other two sank to their knees in fear. Lewis and three other white men were an advance party of the Lewis and Clark expedition, sent by President Thomas Jefferson to explore the vast continent from the Mississippi River to the Pacific Ocean. Lewis approached the women and gave them gifts of friendship. He also rolled up his sleeve to make a show of his whiteness, to demonstrate the "truth of the ascertion that I was a white man for my face and hands which have been constantly exposed to the sun were quite as dark as their own." He assumed that being white was less threatening than being an Indian from an unknown tribe.

For some time, President Jefferson had eyed the trans-Mississippi west with intense curiosity; in early 1803, he arranged congressional funding for a secret exploration into Spanish and Indian lands and appointed the twenty-eight-year-old Lewis to head it. Although he was already negotiating with the French to buy New Orleans, Jefferson did not realize that the very region Lewis was sent to explore would shortly become part of the United States, in a stupendous land deal known as the Louisiana Purchase.

Jefferson, ever the scientist, instructed Lewis to investigate Indian cultures, to collect plant and animal specimens, and to chart the geography of the West. Congress had more traditional goals in mind: The expedition was to scout out locations for military posts, open commercial agreements for the fur trade, and locate any possible waterway between the East and West Coasts.

For his co-leader, Lewis chose Kentuckian William Clark, a fellow veteran of the 1790s Indian wars. Together they handpicked a crew of forty-five, including expert rivermen, gunsmiths, fishermen, hunters, interpreters, a cook, and a slave in his thirties named York who belonged to Clark. The explorers left St. Louis in the spring of 1804, working their way northwest up the Missouri River. They camped for the winter at a Mandan village in what is now central North Dakota. The Mandan Indians were familiar with British and French traders from Canada, but the black man York created a sensation. As happened repeatedly on the expedition, Indians rubbed moistened fingers over the man's skin to see if the color was painted on.

The following spring, the explorers headed west, aided by a French trapper accompanied by his wife, a sixteen-year-old Indian woman named Sacajawea, who had just had a baby. Sacajawea's presence was to prove unexpectedly helpful. Indian tribes encountered en route withdrew their suspicion that the Americans were hostile because, as Lewis wrote in his journal, "no woman ever accompanies a war party of Indians in this quarter."

**SACAJAWEA**

*Sacajawea is pictured here with her baby, as imagined by mid-nineteenth century artist Edgar S. Paxson, who produced a series of paintings of grand moments on the Lewis and Clark expedition. The young Shoshone mother was also called Janey by the two explorers, who admired her courage and fortitude. Her baby, Jean Baptiste Charbonneau, was nicknamed Pompey. William Clark brought the boy to St. Louis when he was six years old to educate him. In the 1820s, the youth was taken to Germany by the prince of Württemberg; he returned six years later, fluent in several languages—German, French, Spanish, and English. Half Shoshone and half French, Charbonneau became a guide and interpreter for numerous trading expeditions throughout the West until his death in the 1860s.*

Sacajawea oil painting by Edgar S. Paxson. The University of Montana Museum of Fine Arts Collection.

The Lewis and Clark expedition reached the Pacific Ocean in November 1805. When they returned home the following year, they were greeted as national heroes. They had established favorable relations with dozens of Indian tribes; they had collected invaluable information on the people, soils, plants, animals, and geography of the West; and they had inspired a nation of restless explorers and solitary imitators.

The Lewis and Clark expedition marked a high point in Jefferson's early presidency. Other undertakings proved far more problematic. Serious Indian troubles in the Northwest Territory continued to plague his administration, and soon those Indians allied with the British, mounting pressures for war. Jefferson adopted experimental economic policies to forestall military conflict, but the War of 1812 came anyway and perilously divided the United States. Jefferson's successors in office, James Madison and James Monroe, continued his policies, only to find that the combination of slavery and westward movement created the first great constitutional crisis, over Missouri statehood in 1820.

The Lewis and Clark expedition turned out to be the high point in the explorers' lives as well. Sacajawea died of a fever about ten years later in the Dakota region. Meriwether Lewis met a violent end in 1809 under mysterious circumstances, ruled a suicide at the time. William Clark became governor of the Missouri Territory and embroiled himself in the Missouri crisis. And York, a courageous and valuable member of the explorers' team, was returned to slavery in Kentucky.

## Jefferson's Presidency

Thomas Jefferson later called his election the "revolution of 1800." Certainly the years 1799–1800, marked by conflict and instability, had many classic ingredients of a revolutionary moment. Pervasive discontent engulfed the country, touched off by the Alien and Sedition Acts and the Quasi War with France. Newspaper invective intensified, making it seem that the very survival of the United States was at stake. Jefferson's election ushered in a period of relative calm and peace in the federal government. The new president, wedded to notions of republican simplicity, aimed for a more limited government. Yet he found that circumstances sometimes required him to draw on the expansive powers of the presidency.

## The "Revolution of 1800"

Although John Adams had ensured his own defeat in 1800 by reopening diplomatic channels with France, it was by no means assured that Thomas Jefferson—both Adams's vice president and his Republican opponent—would therefore win the presidency. The electoral college produced a tie vote, surprisingly, between Jefferson and his running mate, Senator Aaron Burr of New York, both with seventy-three votes. The election was thus thrown to the House of Representatives, where a Federalist-dominated chamber would make the final choice. In the newly elected House, Jefferson's party had secured sixty-five seats, the Federalists, forty-one. But it was the existing House, not the new one, that would choose the new president.

In February 1801, the House met to consider its options. The choice was not at all obvious; for example, some wished to elect neither of the candidates who had tied in the electoral college but instead preferred Adams or his running mate, Charles Cotesworth Pinckney. It took thirty-six separate ballots and six days for Jefferson to secure the presidency. What finally determined the outcome was Alexander Hamilton's support of his enemy Jefferson. Hamilton recognized that Burr, who was known for his high-strung, ambitious, and arrogant character, would be more dangerous in the presidency than Jefferson, with his hated but steady habits of republicanism. (See the Historical Question on page 236.)

## The Jefferson Vision of Republican Simplicity

Once in office, Jefferson emphasized republican simplicity and frugality. He scaled back on Federalist building plans for Washington and cut the government budget. He wore plain clothes and presented an appearance that was "neglected but not slovenly," according to one onlooker. He cultivated a casual style, wearing slippers to greet important guests and seating them haphazardly at his table, avoiding the formality of state dinner parties or liveried servants like Washington's. Jefferson's studied carelessness was very deliberate.

Jefferson was no Antifederalist. At a distance, he had supported the Constitution in 1788 from his diplomatic post in France, although he had some qualms about the unrestricted reelection allowed to the president. But his political service of the 1790s,

first as Washington's secretary of state and then as Adams's vice president, caused him to fear what he regarded as an inappropriate stretching of governmental powers in the executive branch.

Jefferson had watched with mounting distrust as Hamilton led the Federalists to fund the public debt, establish a national bank, and secure commercial ties with England. The Hamiltonian program seemed to Jefferson to be wrongly promoting the interests of a small circle of money-hungry speculators at the expense of the rest of the country. Jefferson was not at all anticommerce. But financial schemes that seemed merely to allow rich men to become richer, without enhancing the vast and natural productivity of America, were corrupt and worthless, he believed, and their promotion had no authority under the Constitution.

In Jefferson's vision, the source of true freedom in America was the independent farmer, someone who owned and worked his land both for himself and for the market. Widespread landownership, which would support unsubservient and therefore virtuous citizens, was Jefferson's cornerstone of liberty. He had embedded the idea of easy access to land in the various land ordinances he designed in the 1780s for the Northwest Territory, even going so far as to suggest that western lands be given away free, in fifty-acre parcels, to any landless white man. Although his idea had been quickly dismissed, Jefferson remained committed to the idea of cheaply available land as the insurance policy that guaranteed American freedom.

> *In Jefferson's vision, the source of true freedom in America was the independent farmer, someone who owned and worked his land both for himself and for the market.*

Distrusting Hamiltonian plans, Jefferson as president set about to dismantle many Federalist innovations. He reduced the size of the army by a third, leaving only three thousand soldiers, and cut back the navy from twenty-five to seven ships. Peacetime defense, he felt, should rest with "a well-disciplined militia," not a standing army. With the consent of Congress, he abolished all federal internal taxes, including both those based on population and the hated whiskey tax; government revenue would now derive solely from customs duties and from the sale of western lands. By the end of his

# How Could a Vice President Get Away with Murder?

ON JULY 11, 1804, the vice president of the United States, Aaron Burr, shot Alexander Hamilton, the architect of the Federalist Party, in a duel on a narrow ledge below the cliffs of Weehawken, New Jersey, across the Hudson River from New York City. The pistol blast tore through a rib, demolished Hamilton's liver, and splintered his spine. The forty-seven-year-old Hamilton died the next day, in agonizing pain.

How could it happen that a sitting vice president and a prominent political leader could put themselves at such risk? Why did men who made their living by the legal system go outside the law and turn to the centuries-old ritual of the duel? Here were two eminent attorneys, skilled in the legalistic negotiations meant to substitute for violent dispute resolution, firing .54-caliber hair-trigger weapons at ten paces. Did anyone try to stop them? How did the public react? Was Hamilton's death a criminal act? How could Burr continue to fulfill his federal office, presiding over the U.S. Senate?

Burr challenged Hamilton in late June after learning about a newspaper report that Hamilton "looked upon Mr. Burr to be a dangerous man, and one who ought not be trusted with the reins of government." Burr knew that Hamilton had long held a very low opinion of him and had never hesitated to say so in private, but now his private disparagement had made its way into print. Compounding the insult were political consequences: Burr was sure that Hamilton's remark cost him election to the governorship of New York.

Quite possibly he was right. Knowing that Jefferson planned to dump him from the federal ticket in the 1804 election, Burr had chosen to run for New York's highest office. His opponent was an obscure Republican judge; Burr's success depended on the support of the old Federalist leadership in the state. Up to the eve of the election, he appeared to have it—until Hamilton's remark was circulated.

So on June 18, Burr challenged Hamilton to a duel if he did not disavow his comment. Over the next three weeks, the men exchanged several letters clarifying the nature of the insult that aggrieved Burr. Hamilton the lawyer evasively quibbled over

words, causing Burr finally to rail against his focus on syntax and grammar. At heart, Hamilton could not deny the insult, nor could he spurn the challenge without injury to his reputation for integrity and bravery. Both Burr and Hamilton were locked in a highly ritualized procedure meant to uphold a gentleman's code of honor.

Each man had a trusted "second," in accord with the code of dueling, who helped frame and deliver the letters and finally assisted at the duel site. Only a handful of close friends knew of the challenge, and no one tried to stop it. Hamilton did not tell his wife. He wrote her a tender farewell letter the night before, to be opened in the event of his death. He knew full well the pain dueling brought to loved ones, for his nineteen-year-old son Philip had been killed in a duel three years earlier, at the same ledge at Weehawken, as a result of hotheaded words exchanged at a New York theater. Even when

**AARON BURR BY JOHN VANDERLYN**
*Aaron Burr was fifty-three years old at the time of this portrait, painted in 1809 by the New York artist John Vanderlyn.*
Collection of The New-York Historical Society.

Hamilton's wife was called to her husband's deathbed, she was first told he had terrible spasms from an illness. Women were completely shut out of the masculine world of dueling.

News of Hamilton's death spread quickly in New York and then throughout the nation. On the day of the funeral, church bells tolled continuously and New York merchants shut down all business. Thousands joined the procession, and the city council declared a six-week mourning period. Burr fled to Philadelphia, fearing retribution by the crowd.

Northern newspapers expressed indignation over the illegal duel and the tragic death of so prominent a man. (Response in the South was more subdued. Dueling was fully accepted there as an extralegal remedy for insult, and Burr's grievance fit perfectly the sense of violated honor that legitimated duels. In addition, southerners had never been particularly fond of the Federalist Hamilton.) Many northern states had criminalized dueling recently, treating a challenge as a misdemeanor and a dueling death as a homicide. Even after death, the loser of an illegal duel could endure one final penalty—being buried without a coffin, having a stake driven through the body, being strung up in public until the body rotted, or, more horrible still for the time, being donated to medical students for dissection. Such prescribed mutilation of the dead showed that northern lawmakers themselves participated in the code of honor by using threats of postmortem humiliation to discourage dueling. Hamilton's body was spared such a fate. But two ministers in succession refused to administer Holy Communion to him in his dying hours because he was a duelist; finally, one relented.

The public demanded to know the reasons for the duel, so the seconds prepared the correspondence between the principals for publication. A coroner's jury in New York soon indicted Burr on misdemeanor charges for issuing a challenge; a grand jury in New Jersey indicted him for murder. By that time, Burr was a fugitive from justice hiding out with sympathetic friends in South Carolina.

But not for long. Amazingly, he returned to Washington, D.C., in November 1804 to resume presiding over sessions of the Senate, a role he continued to assume until his term ended in March 1805. Federalists snubbed him, but eleven Republican senators petitioned New Jersey to drop its indictment on the grounds that "civilized nations" do not treat dueling deaths as "common murders." New Jersey did not pursue the murder charge. Burr freely

**PISTOLS FROM THE BURR-HAMILTON DUEL**

*Hamilton's brother-in-law John B. Church purchased this pair of dueling pistols in London in 1797. He used them once in a duel with Aaron Burr, occasioned by Church's calling Burr a scoundrel in public; neither man was hurt. Hamilton's son Philip borrowed them for his fatal duel, fought at Weehawken. When Burr challenged Hamilton, the latter turned to John Church for the weapons. The guns stayed in the Church family until 1930, when they were given to the Chase Manhattan Bank in New York City, chartered in 1799 as the Manhattan Company. (Burr, Church, and Hamilton all served on the bank's board of directors.) When the pistols were cleaned in 1874, a hidden hair trigger came to light. It could be cocked by moving the trigger forward one-eighth inch. It then required only a half-pound pull, instead of ten pounds, to fire the gun. Hamilton gained no advantage from the hair trigger, if he knew of it.*

Courtesy of Chase Manhattan Archives.

visited New Jersey and New York for three more decades, paying no penalty for killing Hamilton.

Few would doubt that Burr was a scoundrel, albeit a brilliant one. A few years later, he was indicted for treason against the U.S. government in a presumed plot to break off part of the United States and start his own country in the Southwest. (He dodged that bullet too, in a spectacular trial presided over by John Marshall, chief justice of the Supreme Court.) Hamilton certainly thought Burr a scoundrel, and when that opinion reached print, Burr had cause to defend his honor under the etiquette of dueling. The accuracy of Hamilton's charge was of absolutely no account. Dueling redressed questions of honor, not questions of fact.

Dueling continued to be a feature of southern society for many more decades, but in the North the custom became extremely rare by the 1820s, helped along by the disrepute of Hamilton's death and by the rise of a legalistic society that now preferred evidence, interrogation, and monetary judgments to avenge injury.

**JEFFERSON'S RED WAISTCOAT**

*During his presidency, Jefferson often wore this red silk waistcoat as informal daywear. The garment had a velvet collar, woolen sleeves, and a thick lining made from recycled cotton and wool stockings. The thrifty Jefferson preferred to conserve firewood by wearing layers of warm clothes. A New Hampshire senator visited in December 1802 and reported in dismay that the president was "dressed, or rather undressed, with an old brown coat, red waistcoat, old corduroy small clothes, much soiled, woolen hose, and slippers without heels." Another guest in 1804 found him in the red waistcoat, green velveteen breeches with pearl buttons, and "slippers down at the heels" and concluded he looked like an ordinary farmer. Such colorful clothing in silk and velveteen carries dressy or feminine connotations in the twentieth century, but not in 1800. Jefferson did dress up in silken hose and clean linen for fancy dinner parties; and when he lived in Paris in the 1780s, he wore an elaborately embroidered silk waistcoat under a greatcoat trimmed with gold lace. But in the 1800s, he used his plain, colorful clothes to make a point about republican simplicity. Not until the 1830s did black suits become standard wear for men.*

Courtesy Monticello, photo by Colonial Williamsburg.

first term, he had deeply reduced Hamilton's cherished national debt.

A properly limited federal government, according to Jefferson, was responsible merely for running a postal system, maintaining the federal courts, staffing lighthouses, collecting customs duties, and conducting a census once every ten years. Government jobs were kept to a minimum. The president had just one private secretary to help with his correspondence, and Jefferson paid him out of his own pocket. The Department of State employed only 8 people: Secretary James Madison, 6 clerks, and a messenger. The Treasury Department was by far the largest unit, with 73 revenue commissioners, auditors, and clerks and 2 watchmen. The entire payroll of the executive branch amounted to a mere 130 people in 1801. In the hot summer months, it shrank to just a few dozen men.

## The Judiciary and the Midnight Judges

There was one set of government workers not under Jefferson's control to appoint. His predecessor, John Adams, seized the short time between his election defeat and Jefferson's assumption of office to appoint 217 Federalist men to various judicial, diplomatic, and military posts.

Some of this windfall of appointments came to Adams as a result of the Judiciary Act of 1801, passed in the final month of his presidency. The new law revised the first Judiciary Act of 1789, which had established a six-man Supreme Court and six circuit courts, each presided over by a Supreme Court justice. The new act set up sixteen circuit courts, each headed by a new judge. A fast-acting Adams could appoint sixteen new judges with lifetime tenure, plus dozens more state attorneys, marshals, and clerks for each court. The 1801 act also reduced the size of the Supreme Court, from six to five justices. Adams had recently appointed John Marshall, a Virginia lawyer and solid Federalist, to a vacant sixth seat, but once the Judiciary Act became law, the Republican president would not be able to fill the next empty seat.

Adams and Marshall worked feverishly in the last weeks of February to secure agreements from the new appointees. In view of the slowness of mail and travel, their getting 217 acceptances was astonishing. The two men were still at work until 9 P.M. on the last night Adams was president, signing and delivering commissions to the new officeholders.

The appointment of "midnight judges" infuriated the Republicans. Jefferson, upon taking office, immediately canceled the appointments of the non-tenured men. A few commissions had not yet been delivered, by Marshall's oversight, and Jefferson refused to send them out. One of them was addressed to William Marbury, who soon decided to sue the new secretary of state, James Madison, for failure to make good on the appointment. This action gave rise to a landmark Supreme Court case, *Marbury v. Madison,* decided in 1803. The Court, presided over by John Marshall, ruled that although Marbury's commission was valid and the new president should have delivered it, the Court could not compel him to do so. What made the case significant was little noted at the time: The Court found that the grounds of Marbury's suit, resting in the Judiciary Act of 1789, were in conflict with the Constitution. For the first time, the Court acted to disallow a law (part of the 1789 act) on the grounds that it was unconstitutional. John Marshall quietly established the concept of judicial review; the Supreme Court in effect assumed the legal authority to nullify acts of the other branches of the federal government.

*In* Marbury v. Madison, *John Marshall quietly established the concept of judicial review; the Supreme Court in effect assumed the legal authority to nullify acts of the other branches of the federal government.*

The reach of the *Marbury* decision went largely unnoticed in 1803 because the president and Congress were completely preoccupied with other major issues. One was a concerted effort to repeal via Congress the Judiciary Act of 1801. Republicans argued that so many new courts were expensive. Federalists argued that removing the judges was unconstitutional because they had been guaranteed lifetime tenure, and nothing but a criminal trial could unseat them. At issue was the power relation between Congress and the judiciary, with the Republicans claiming that if Congress could create courts, it could abolish them. The Judiciary Act was finally repealed in 1802.

## The Louisiana Purchase

Jefferson's vision of a limited federal government could be sustained as long as international affairs remained peaceful. The rise of Napoleon to power in France in 1799 soon brought France and England into open warfare again. And renewed European tensions created an unexpected opportunity for Jefferson's administration.

In 1800, the Mississippi River formed the western boundary of the United States; the expanse of land west of the river was under the flag of Spain. For a century before the French and Indian War, France had claimed and partly settled the territory, only to lose it to Spain in the 1763 Treaty of Paris. Spain never sent adequate forces to control or settle the land, however; Spanish power remained precarious everywhere outside New Orleans.

Meanwhile, American farming families were advancing west, to Kentucky and Tennessee, in the 1790s. They settled along rivers emptying into the upper Mississippi, on which they depended for shipping their agricultural produce. For a while the Spanish governor of New Orleans allowed free navigational rights on the lower Mississippi, and American farmers supplied the city with flour, whiskey, and other foodstuffs. The Spanish crown even encouraged Americans to settle across the river, in an effort to augment the population, and by 1801 Americans made up a sizable minority of present-day Louisiana.

In the same year, rumors reached Jefferson that Spain had struck a secret bargain with France to hand over Louisiana to Napoleon in exchange for a duchy in Italy. Spain had proved a weak western neighbor, but France was another story. Jefferson was sufficiently alarmed that he instructed Robert R. Livingston, America's minister in France, to try to buy New Orleans. At first the French denied they owned the city, but Livingston politely announced that he had seen the treaty with Spain. Livingston hinted that the United States might simply seize New Orleans if buying it was not an option. Finally, the French negotiator suddenly asked Livingston to name his price for the entire Louisiana Territory, stretching north to Canada. Livingston stalled, and the Frenchman floated prices ranging from $125 million to $60 million. Livingston, sensing an eagerness to sell, shrewdly stalled some more. Within a few days, the French sold the entire territory for the bargain price of $15 million (Map 10.1).

Jefferson and most of Congress were delighted with the outcome of the diplomatic mission. Congress quickly approved the purchase and voted for a bond issue to raise money for the price. However, all but one of New England's representatives voted against it. Federalist-dominated New England had been willing to consider war to seize New Orleans and control navigation rights on the river, but the

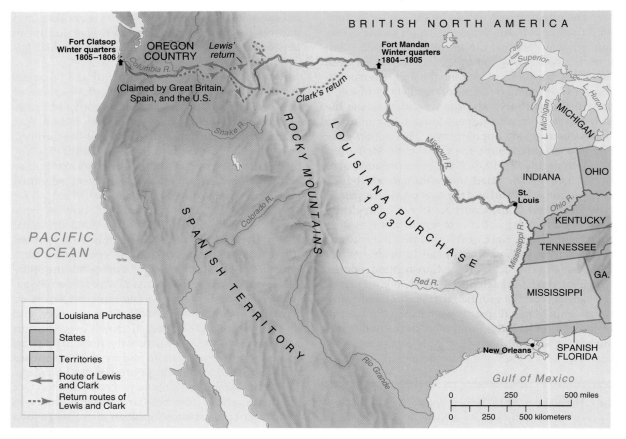

### MAP 10.1
***Lewis and Clark and the Louisiana Purchase***
*Lewis and Clark's expedition in 1804–1806 brought the Indians of the far Northwest their first look at Anglo-American and African American men. The huge dimensions of the Louisiana Purchase of 1803 were scarcely imaginable to East Coast Americans. Federalists of New England, worried that their own geographically based power in the federal government would someday be eclipsed by the West, voted against the purchase.*

unexpectedly huge territory raised anxiety about the ultimate geographic balance of power in the United States. So much land, sure to be carved into states one day, made some fear the eventual marginalization of New England.

Jefferson had his own reason to be reluctant about the Louisiana Purchase. The price was right, and the enormous territory fulfilled Jefferson's dream of abundant farmland for generations of Americans to come. But by what authority in the Constitution could he justify the purchase? His frequent criticism of the Hamiltonian stretching of the Constitution came back to haunt him. His legal reasoning told him he needed a constitutional amendment to fully authorize the addition of territory; more expedient minds told him the treaty-making

powers of the president could cover his action. Expediency won out. In late 1803, the American army took formal control of the Louisiana Territory, and the United States was now 828,000 square miles larger than it had been before.

## Republicans in a Dangerous World

The election of 1804 proved an easy triumph for the Republican Party. The Federalist candidate, Charles Cotesworth Pinckney of South Carolina, secured only 14 votes in the electoral college, in contrast to 162 for the president. Just months before the election, the Federalists had lost their shrewdest statesman: Alexander Hamilton, called by some "the brains of the Federalist Party," was tragically killed in a duel with Aaron Burr. Republicans would hold the presidency for another twenty years.

Jefferson's second term was dominated by the ongoing war between France and England, which continually threatened to involve the United States. As peaceful alternatives to war, the president experimented with economic sanctions and trade embargoes. Jefferson and his successors faced war threats not only across the Atlantic but also in the new states of the old Northwest Territory, where a powerful new Indian confederacy challenged the westward press of American settlement.

## Troubles at Sea and the Embargo Act of 1807

In the 1790s, American shipping had prospered when the two leading European powers, France and England, were at war, for they left trade routes and markets wide open. Determined not to make that mistake again when war broke out between them in 1803, the two countries established independent restrictions on American trade with the enemy, backed up by threats to blockade routes and seize ships.

British enforcement of their threats beginning in 1806 affected many hundreds of Americans. In addition to searching for prohibited goods, British naval patrols claimed the right to seize (and impress into service) sailors whom they accused of being deserters from the British navy. In fact, some of those captured in the impressment sweeps *were* deserters, but hundreds of native-born Americans were caught up as well. Between 1807 and 1812, about 2,500 men were taken captive and impressed into royal naval service. Jefferson and the American public were outraged.

One incident in particular made the usually cautious Jefferson nearly belligerent. In June 1807, an American ship, the *Chesapeake*, harboring some British deserters, was ordered to stop for inspection by a British frigate. The *Chesapeake* refused, and the British opened fire, killing three Americans. What was worse, this incident took place in Chesapeake Bay, well within U.S. territory. President Jefferson prepared a heated manifesto to send to Great Britain, demanding an end to impressment. But the United States was not actually prepared for war— the much-reduced army and navy presented a seri-

ous problem—and Jefferson's advisers toned down his challenge to England, limiting it to a ban on British warships in American waters.

Before the *Chesapeake* incident, Jefferson had convinced Congress to pass nonimportation laws banning a select list of British-made goods. But after the *Chesapeake* incident, Jefferson and Secretary of State James Madison pushed the idea of a total embargo, passed by Congress as the Embargo Act in December 1807. American ships were forbidden from engaging in trade with any foreign port. It was a drastic measure, but it was intended as economic coercion rather than the far more drastic possibility of war. The immediate goal was to make England suffer, and all foreign ports were included in the ban so as to discourage illegal trading through secondary ports. The two Republican leaders were convinced that England needed America's trade goods, mainly agricultural products, far more than America needed British goods.

The Embargo Act of 1807 was a total disaster. From 1790 to 1807, U.S. exports had increased fivefold, and in an instant the Embargo Act wiped out all commerce. Worse, it was ineffective; instead of suffering, England simply turned to South American countries for agricultural supplies, sailing on seas now empty of American vessels. In New England, the heart of the shipping industry, trade came to a standstill, and unemployment began to rise.

> *The Embargo Act of 1807 was a total disaster. From 1790 to 1807, U.S. exports had increased fivefold, and in an instant the Embargo Act wiped out all commerce.*

Protest petitions flooded Washington. Federalists in Barre, Massachusetts, pointed out that farmers were also hurt: "We consider the interest of Agriculture and Commerce as inseparable"; the "belief that the farmer can flourish, while [the merchant] is neglected and depressed" was a serious error, they warned. In the South, tobacco rotted on the docks and cotton went unpicked. The wheat crop of the central and western states plummeted in value, and river traffic came to a halt. The federal government itself suffered too, for import duties were a significant source of national revenue. Jefferson paid political costs as well. The Federalist Party, in danger of fading away after its very weak showing in the election of 1804, began to pick up strength from the anti-Jefferson protest.

**TWO CAPTAINS AT SEA**
*The captains of two sailing ships confer at sea, using horns to amplify their voices, in this watercolor*
*by Benjamin Latrobe (the architect of the Capitol). New England coastal towns like Salem, Newburyport,*
*Portsmouth, and Portland played a major role in the shipping trade and extended their routes to China*
*and India in the early nineteenth century, in addition to traversing the West Indies–Europe circuit. Some*
*schooners really were as small as these depicted, measuring fifteen to eighteen feet wide and as little as*
*forty feet long. Jefferson's embargo worked a great hardship on the New England shipping industry.*
Maryland Historical Society, Baltimore.

The embargo stayed in place until the last day of Jefferson's presidency, in March 1809, but it created a very rocky final year for the administration. Congress at last replaced it with the Non-Intercourse Act of 1809, which prohibited trade only with England and France and their colonial possessions. In effect, the new law opened the way for legal, indirect trade, so the economic anguish of New England shippers and southern planters was greatly diminished, for the moment.

## Madison Gets Entangled

In mid-1808, Jefferson indicated that he would not run for a third term. James Madison, the secretary of state for eight years and Jefferson's closest ally, was the clear heir apparent. Disgruntled Republicans

from hurting tobacco regions of the South made a move to support James Monroe, a Virginia planter with wide experience as a diplomat to England, but Madison was the favorite among the various state caucuses of Republicans. At this point, party politics, still held to be a bad thing by leading statesmen, operated through informal coalition building and statewide caucuses that orchestrated state and local elections. The Federalist caucuses, thinking they would gain strength from the unpopular Embargo Act, chose Charles Cotesworth Pinckney again to run against Madison. Pinckney did much better than in 1804; he received forty-seven electoral votes, nearly half the number Madison got. Support for the Federalists remained centered in the New England states, but Republicans still held the balance of power nationwide.

The attacks on American ships continued, by both the British and French. In 1810, the Non-Intercourse Act expired, and Congress replaced it with a law that permitted direct trade with either France or England, whichever first gave assurance that it would stop harassing American ships. Napoleon seized the initiative and declared that France would comply. Madison too hastily accepted Napoleon's offer, reopened trade with France, and notified England that he intended to reinstate the embargo in the spring of 1811 unless England rescinded its search and seizure policy.

Unfortunately for Madison, the duplicitous French leaders continued to seize American ships. Furthermore, the British made no move to stop impressments or to repeal trade restrictions, and Madison was forced to reactivate the embargo, much to the great displeasure of the New England shipping industry. In 1811, the country was seriously divided and in a deep quandary. To some, it seemed the United States must be on the verge of war; but was the enemy to be France or England? To others, war meant disaster, for it would surely finish off the grievously hurting shipping industry.

A new Congress, elected in the fall of 1810, arrived in Washington in March 1811 just as Madison's threatened embargo was to take effect. Some of the new and much younger members were eager to avenge the insults from abroad. In particular, Henry Clay, thirty-four, from Kentucky, and John C. Calhoun, twenty-nine, from South Carolina, became the center of a group informally called the War Hawks. Though calling themselves Republicans, like Madison, these younger men had much more expansive ideas of the way the United States should meet the challenge of enemies abroad.

## Indian Troubles in the West

In the atmosphere of indecision about war with European powers, news filtered east about renewed difficulties with Indian tribes in the old Northwest Territory. Since the mid-1790s, after the Battle of Fallen Timbers, a general peace had obtained in the Ohio valley. The Treaty of Greenville had established a boundary to Indian territory that had held until recent years. But by 1810, white settlement was again encroaching north and west, threatening Indian lands and driving the Indians back into the arms of British Indian agents and fur traders in Canada, who could supply them with food and weapons. While Madison contemplated war with England, he could be certain that part of the sting

of war would be felt on the frontier, as Indians and the British reinvigorated the alliance they had shared since the 1760s.

But this time a new element emerged in the Indian strategy. A powerful and charismatic Shawnee war chief named Tecumseh was building a confederacy among the many Indian tribes in the Indiana, Ohio, and Michigan region. Tecumseh's remarkable political talents were enhanced by the reputation of his visionary brother Tenskwatawa, known throughout the region as the "Prophet." Tenskwatawa urged Indians everywhere to return to the customs of their ancestors and to give up borrowed practices—using European dress, plows, firearms, bread, and alcohol—learned from the white invaders.

From 1805 to 1807, the Prophet's popularity spread and sparked a religious revival throughout the

**TENSKWATAWA**

*Tenskwatawa, the Shawnee Prophet, and his brother Tecumseh led the spiritual and political efforts of a number of Indian tribes to resist land-hungry Americans moving west in the decade before the War of 1812. The Prophet is shown in a portrait by George Catlin with necklaces, metal arm- and wristbands, earrings, and a necklace that looks very similar to George Washington's gorget (see page 130).*

National Museum of American Art, Washington, D.C./Art Resource, New York.

Ohio valley and as far as the Mississippi. He preached that the Americans were children of the Evil Spirit, destined to be destroyed. The Master of Life wished the Indians to stay forever where they were, and so the Prophet led his people to a site where Tippecanoe Creek joined the Wabash River in northern Indiana and established a village called Prophetstown. Tecumseh, too, inspired followers and denounced white Americans. "Once," he said, "there was not a white man in all this country. Then it all belonged to the redmen . . . now made miserable by the white people, who are never satisfied but always encroaching on our land. . . . The only way to stop this evil, is for all the redmen to unite in claiming a common right in the soil." The brothers' potent blend of spiritual regeneration and political unity proved very attractive to the many tribes of the Northwest.

The American governor of the Indiana Territory, William Henry Harrison, became alarmed by the brothers' growing influence. Although skeptical of the Prophet's powers, Harrison understood that in Tecumseh he faced a formidable opponent, "one of those uncommon geniuses which spring up occasionally to produce revolutions." Harrison moved quickly to undermine Tecumseh's goal of a united Indian confederacy by arranging to buy tribal lands from three tribes. The Treaty of Fort Wayne (1809) prompted Tecumseh to extend his alliances into the South in preparation for a pan-Indian war against the Americans.

In 1811, while Tecumseh was in Alabama enlisting the Creek and Chickasaw tribes, Harrison decided to march on Prophetstown. With one thousand armed men he approached Tippecanoe Creek, but the Indians attacked first. The two-hour battle resulted in about a hundred deaths—sixty-two Americans and forty Indians—before the Prophet's forces fled. Harrison burned the town and its food supplies. The November 1811 Battle of Tippecanoe was heralded as a glorious victory for the Americans; Harrison acquired the nickname "Tippecanoe" and used it as a patriotic rallying cry when he ran for the presidency in 1840. The Indians' faith in the Prophet's magical powers diminished sharply; Tenskwatawa never again enjoyed such influence. But Tecumseh was now more ready than ever to make war on the Americans.

# The War of 1812

The Indian conflicts in the Northwest Territory in 1811 soon merged into the wider conflict with England known as the War of 1812. The defeat at Tippecanoe propelled Tecumseh into a renewal of the old alliance with British military commanders stationed at outposts in lower Canada. If there had been doubt before about who should be the target of a declaration of war, France or England, it was now abundantly clear, especially to westerners living near the frontier, that the British should get the honor.

## The War Begins

The several dozen young War Hawks new to Congress saluted Harrison's Tippecanoe victory and continued to urge the country on to war. Mostly lawyers by profession, they came from the West and South, and they welcomed a war with England both to legitimize attacks on the Indians and to bring an end to impressment. Many were also expansionists, looking to occupy Florida and threaten Canada. And they captured prominent posts in Congress from which to wield influence. Henry Clay was elected Speaker of the House, an extraordinary honor for a young newcomer. John C. Calhoun won a seat on the Foreign Relations Committee. The War Hawks approved major defense expenditures; the army, for example, was quadrupled in size. New England Federalists in Congress staunchly refused to endorse any of these war preparations, just as they had opposed the embargo in 1807.

In June 1812, Congress declared war on Great Britain in a vote that divided on sectional lines: New England and some of the Middle Atlantic states opposed the war, while the South and West were strongly for it. Ironically, Great Britain had just formally decided to stop the search and seizure of American ships. News of that diplomatic breakthrough arrived too late, however; the war machine would not be stopped. The Foreign Relations Committee issued an elaborate justification titled *Report on the Causes and Reasons for War,* written mainly by Calhoun. The report went far beyond a condemnation of Britain's naval actions to assert that war was necessary to avenge British insults in treating the United States like a third-rate power. Extravagant language about Britain's "lust for power," "unbounded tyranny," and "mad ambition" suggested that America was actually engaged in a second revolution for independence. These were fighting words, in a war that was in large measure about insult and honor.

The War Hawks proposed an invasion of Canada, confidently predicting victory in four weeks, before the fall elections. Instead, the war

A BOXING MATCH, or Another Bloody Nose for JOHN BULL.

lasted two and a half years, and Canada never fell. The northern invasion turned out to be a series of strategic blunders that revealed the grave unpreparedness of the United States for war. The combined strength of British soldiers and Indian allies was unexpectedly powerful, and the United States made no attempt at the outset to create a naval presence on the Great Lakes. Detroit quickly fell to the British and Indian forces, as did Fort Dearborn (site of the future Chicago). By the fall of 1812, the war was in a dismal state.

Worse, the New England states dragged their feet in raising troops, while New England merchants carried on illegal trade with Great Britain. Britain encouraged friendly overtures with New England, hoping to divide and conquer the Americans. New Englanders drank India tea in Liverpool cups, while President Madison fumed in Washington about Federalist disloyalty.

The presidential election in 1812 solidified Federalist discontent with the war. Madison stood for a second term, opposed by DeWitt Clinton of New York. The nephew of Madison's first-term vice president, George Clinton, the younger Clinton was nominally Republican but able to attract the Federalist vote. He picked up all of New England's electoral votes, with the exception of Vermont's, and also took New York, New Jersey, and part of Maryland. Madison won in the electoral college, 128 to 89, but his margin of victory was considerably smaller than in the 1808 election.

In late 1812 and early 1813, the tide began to turn in the Americans' favor. First came some reassuring victories at sea, by the navy ships *Constitution, Wasp,* and *Hornet,* but little lasting gain. Americans attacked York (now Toronto), the capital of Upper Canada, and burned it in April 1813. A few months later, Commodore Oliver Hazard Perry defeated the British fleet at the western end of Lake Erie. Emboldened, General Harrison drove an army into Lower Canada from Detroit and in October 1813 defeated the British and Indians at the Battle of the Thames, where Tecumseh met his death (Map 10.2).

Indians also met defeat in the South, where a general named Andrew Jackson led 2,500 Tennessee militiamen in an attack on Creek Indians, who were fighting in solidarity with Tecumseh's confederacy. At the Battle of Horseshoe Bend in March 1814, Jackson's militia killed more than 550 Indians, including women and children.

## The British Offensives of 1814

In August 1814, British ships sailed into Chesapeake Bay toward Washington, D.C. For three days, Washington dwellers were thrown into a panic. Families evacuated their children and valuables, banks removed their money, and government clerks packed

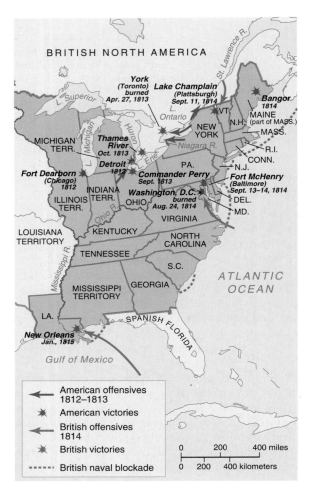

**M A P  1 0 . 2**
*The War of 1812*

*Battles in the War of 1812 were fought along the border of Canada and in the Chesapeake region. The most important American victory came in New Orleans, two weeks after peace had been agreed to in England.*

up boxes of important papers to be carted away. One clerk in the State Department quickly located the Declaration of Independence and removed it to safety.

When five thousand British troops landed and marched toward the city, the only defense came from inexperienced militia units from Maryland. President Madison and his cabinet mounted horses and vainly tried to inspire the militia, who fled in disorder as the British advanced. The British entered the city, set fire to the president's house, and

burned the Capitol building, a newspaper office, some dockyards, and a well-stocked arsenal. August 24 was a low moment for the American side.

Instead of trying to hold the city, the British headed north for the port of Baltimore. They attacked the city on September 11, 1814, but a fierce defense by the Maryland militia and a steady barrage of gunfire from Fort McHenry in the harbor kept them at bay. The firing continued until midnight, motivating Francis Scott Key to compose a poem he called "The Star-Spangled Banner" the next day. The British pulled back, unwilling to try to take the city.

September 1814 brought another powerful British offensive. Marching from Canada into New York State, the British seemed to have every advantage—trained soldiers, superior artillery, cavalry, professional leaders. But a series of blunders cost them a minor naval engagement at Plattsburgh on the northern end of Lake Champlain. It also cost them their nerve, for, without ever engaging the astonished American troops, the British general turned his huge army around and retreated to Canada. This nonbattle was in fact a decisive military event, for British leaders in England, hearing the news of the retreat, concluded that incursions by land into the United States would be costly, difficult, and perhaps ineffective.

This point was confirmed when a large British army landed in lower Louisiana in December 1814 and encountered General Andrew Jackson and his militiamen just outside New Orleans. Jackson's forces dramatically carried the day. The British suffered between two and three thousand casualties, the Americans less than eighty. Jackson became an instant hero, and the Battle of New Orleans was the most glorious and decisive victory the Americans had experienced. Ironically, negotiators in Europe had signed a peace agreement two weeks earlier.

### The War Ends

The Treaty of Ghent, signed in December 1814, settled few of the surface issues that had led to war. Neither country could claim the role of victor, and no land traded hands. Instead, the treaty reflected a mutual agreement to give up certain goals. The Americans yielded on impressment and gave up any claim to Canada; and the British agreed to evacuate western forts and abandoned their aid to Indians. Nothing was said about shipping rights, but both sides agreed to submit lingering trade disputes to arbitration at a future time. The most concrete result was an agreement to set up a commission to determine the exact boundary between the United States and Canada.

New England Federalists, united in opposition to the war, did not enjoy a sense of triumph over its ambiguous conclusion. Instead they felt a sting of disgrace because of an antiwar meeting convened by New England politicians in Hartford, Connecticut, in December 1814. Delegates to the Hartford Convention discussed but did not agree on secession from the Union. The main thrust of the convention was to protect New England's sectional interests by amending the Constitution. Proposed amendments would abolish the three-fifths clause as a basis of representation; specify that congressional powers to pass embargoes, admit states, or declare war should require a two-thirds vote instead of a simple majority; and limit the president to one term and prohibit successive presidents from the same state. The cumulative effect of these proposals was to reduce the South's political power and break the lock of the Virginia dynasty on national office. New England wanted to make sure that no sectional party or group could again lead the country into war against the clear interests of some other section.

Just as the Hartford Convention broke up, news came first of Jackson's victory at New Orleans and then of the formal peace treaty signed at Ghent. The combative list of amendments suddenly looked very unpatriotic and were dismissed by the U.S. Congress. The Federalist Party never recovered its grip, and within a few years its hold even in New England was reduced to a shadow.

*Perhaps the biggest winners in the War of 1812 were the young men, once called War Hawks, who took up the banner of the Republican Party and carried it in new, expansive directions.*

No one really won the War of 1812. Americans celebrated as though they had, however. The war gave rise to a new spirit of nationalism, even in New England. The paranoia over British tyranny evident in the 1812 declaration of war was laid to rest, replaced by pride in a more equal relationship with the old mother country.

Perhaps the biggest winners in the War of 1812 were the young men, once called War Hawks, who took up the banner of the Republican Party and car-

ried it in new, expansive directions. These younger politicians favored trade, western expansion, internal improvements, and the energetic development of new economic markets after the war. The biggest losers of the war were the Indians. Tecumseh was dead, the Prophet discredited, the prospects of an Indian confederacy dashed, and the British protectors vanished.

# Women's Status in the Early Republic

Unlike the American Revolution, the War of 1812 had little impact on the status of women. Developments in women's status in the early Republic came not as a result of wartime emergency but instead in incremental steps. As state legislatures and the courts grappled with the legal dependency of married white women in a country whose defining characteristic was independence, religious organizations struggled to redefine the role of women in church governance.

## Women and the Law

The Anglo-American view of women, implanted in British common law, was that wives had no independent legal or political personhood. The legal doctrine of *feme covert* held that a wife's civic life was completely subsumed by her husband's: A wife was obligated to obey her husband; her property was his; her domestic and sexual services were his; and even their children were legally his. If the husband died, the court assigned responsibility for children to a guardian, usually a near male relative. Women had no right to keep their wages, to make contracts, or to sue or be sued. Any crime committed by a wife in the presence of her husband was chargeable to him, with two exceptions: treason against the state and keeping a brothel. The fundamental assumption of coverture was that husbands did—and ought to—control their wives.

State legislatures, when codifying their laws, generally passed up the opportunity to rewrite the laws of domestic relations, even though they redrafted so much other British law in light of republican principles. The standard treatise on family law, published in 1816 in Connecticut, was titled *The Law of Baron and Feme* ("lord and woman"). Lawyers never paused even to defend, much less to challenge, the assumption that unequal power relations lay at the heart of marriage. The early Republic's conception of the "republican wife and mother" (see Chapter 9) in no way altered the basic legal framework inherited from British law.

The one aspect of family law that changed in the early Republic was divorce. Before the Revolution, only New England jurisdictions had recognized a right to divorce; by 1820, every state except South Carolina had set up divorce procedures. Divorce was uncommon and difficult, however. In many states, divorce could be obtained only by petition to the state's legislature, a daunting obstacle for many ordinary people. A mutual wish to terminate a marriage was never sufficient grounds for divorce. A New York judge affirmed that "it would be aiming a deadly blow at public morals to decree a dissolution of the marriage contract merely because the parties requested it. Divorces should never be allowed, except for the protection of the innocent party, and for the punishment of the guilty." States upheld the institution of marriage both to protect persons they thought of as naturally dependent (women and children) and to regulate the use and inheritance of property. The state's enforcement of marriage as an unequal relationship played a major role in maintaining gender inequality in the nineteenth century.

Single adult women could own and convey property, make contracts, initiate suits, and pay taxes. They could not vote (except in New Jersey until 1807; see Chapter 9), serve on juries, or practice law, so their civil status was limited. Single women's economic status was often limited as well: Unless a woman had inherited adequate property, being a single adult woman in the early Republic was highly correlated with poverty.

---

*The Anglo-American view of women, implanted in British common law, was that wives had no independent legal or political personhood. The legal doctrine of* feme covert *held that a wife's civic life was completely subsumed by her husband's.*

---

None of the legal institutions that structured white gender relations applied to black slaves in the South. As property themselves, slaves could not freely consent to any contractual obligations, including marriage. Husbands could not guarantee support, nor could wives guarantee exclusive services, because both were controlled by a more powerful authority, the slave owner. But this also meant that slave unions did not establish unequal power relations backed by the force of law, as did free marriages.

## Women and Church Governance

In most Protestant denominations around 1800, white women made up the majority of congregants, as they had for some time. Yet the church hierarchy—ordained ministers and elders—was exclusively male, and the governance of most denominations rested in men's hands.

There were some exceptions, however. In several small evangelical groups, notably Baptist congregations in New England that had been strongly affected by the Great Awakening, women served along with men on church governance committees, deciding admission of new members, voting on the hiring of ministers, participating in disciplinary proceedings, and even debating doctrinal points. Quakers, too, had a history of recognizing that women's spiritual talents could equal men's. Quaker women who felt a special call were accorded the status of ministers, which among Quakers meant they were capable of leading and speaking in religious meetings. Quaker governance, however, proceeded along sex-segregated lines: Separate men's and women's committees heard disciplinary cases and formulated church policy.

Between 1790 and 1820, a small and highly unusual set of women emerged who actively engaged in open preaching. Most were from the Freewill Baptist groups centered in Maine, New Hampshire, Vermont, and upstate New York. Others were from small Methodist sects, and yet others rejected any formal religious affiliation. Probably fewer than a hundred such women existed, most of them single or widowed, but several dozen became known beyond their local communities because they traveled, creating converts and controversy wherever they went. They spoke from the heart, without prepared speeches, often exhibiting trances and claiming to exhort (counsel or warn) rather than to preach.

Perhaps the most well known exhorting woman was Jemima Wilkinson, who called herself the "Publick Universal Friend." After a near-death experience in 1776, Wilkinson awoke to proclaim that her body was no longer female *or* male, but the incarnation of the "Spirit of Light." She dressed in men's clothes, wore her hair in a masculine style, shunned gender-specific pronouns, and preached openly in Rhode Island and Philadelphia. In the

**WOMEN AND THE CHURCH: JEMIMA WILKINSON**
*Jemima Wilkinson, the "Publick Universal Friend," in an early woodcut, wears a clerical collar and body-obscuring robe, in keeping with the claim that the former Jemima was now a person without sex or gender. Her hair is pulled back tight on her head and curled at the neck in a masculine style of the 1790s.*
Rhode Island Historical Society.

early nineteenth century, Wilkinson withdrew to a settlement called New Jerusalem in western New York with more than 250 followers.

As more women exhorters cropped up, their behavior came under increasing fire. A Baptist periodical in Massachusetts printed frequent reminders of the biblical prohibition "Let your women learn to keep silence in the churches" (1 Corinthians 14:34). Female preachers well knew such scriptural passages and were ready with biblical interpretations of their own, as in Deborah Pierce's 1817 book *A Scriptural Vindication of Female Preaching, Prophesying, and Exhortation.*

The decades from 1790 to the 1820s marked a period of unusual confusion, ferment, and creativity in American religion. New denominations blossomed, new styles of religiosity gripped adherents, and an extensive periodical press devoted to religion popularized all manner of theological and institutional innovations. In such a climate, the age-old tradition of gender subordination came into question here and there among the most radically democratic of the churches. Yet on balance, the presumption of male authority over women was deeply entrenched in American culture. Even denominations that had allowed women to participate in church governance began to pull back, and most churches reinstated patterns of dominance and subordination along gender lines.

## Madison's Successors

Through the elections of 1812, 1816, and 1820, Republican Virginians extended their lock on the presidency to twenty-four years. In 1816, James Monroe beat Federalist Rufus King of Massachusetts for the presidency by an electoral vote of 183 to 34. When Monroe stood for reelection in 1820, the national presence of the Federalists was fully eclipsed, with all but one electoral vote going to Monroe. The unanimity of the 1820 election did not reflect voter satisfaction with the status quo, however, for barely one-quarter of eligible voters bothered to vote.

Monroe's two terms were dubbed the "Era of Good Feelings" by a contemporary newspaper. Yet during Monroe's presidency, a major constitutional crisis emerged over the admission of Missouri to the Union. Foreign policy questions animated sharp disagreements as well. The election of 1824 brought forth an abundance of candidates, all claiming to be Republicans. A one-party political system was put to the test of practical circumstances; it failed and then fractured.

### The Missouri Compromise

In February 1819, Missouri applied for statehood. In the years since 1815, four other states had joined the Union (Indiana, Mississippi, Illinois, and Alabama), following the smooth pathway from territory to statehood that had operated since the 1790s. But Missouri's path was not smooth. While the northern part of Missouri lined up geographically with Illinois, Indiana, Ohio, and Pennsylvania, the territory already contained ten thousand slaves, brought by southern whites migrating from Virginia, Kentucky, and Tennessee. They constituted about one-sixth of the territory's population.

**A VIEW OF ST. LOUIS FROM AN ILLINOIS TOWN**
*Just fifteen years after the Missouri Compromise, St. Louis was already a booming city, having gotten its start in the eighteenth century as a French fur trading village. It was incorporated as a town in 1809 and chartered as a city in 1822. In this 1835 view, commercial buildings and steamships line the riverfront; a ferry on the Illinois shore pre-* *pares to transport travelers across the Mississippi River. Black laborers (in the foreground) handle loading tasks. The Illinois side is a free state; Missouri, where their ferry lands, is a slave state.*
The Saint Louis Art Museum. Private Collection of Dorothy Ziern Hanon and Joseph B. Hanon.

Missouri's unusual combination of geography and demography led a New York representative in Congress named James Tallmadge Jr. to propose two amendments to the Missouri statehood bill. The first stipulated that slaves born in Missouri after enactment of the law would be free at age twenty-five, and the second declared that no new slaves could be imported into the state. The combined effect of the two, if federally imposed, would be gradual emancipation—eventually slavery would disappear in Missouri. Southerners in Congress loudly protested Tallmadge's amendments. Although gradual emancipation protected slave owners from immediate financial loss, in the long run it made Missouri a free state, and southerners were increasingly sensitive to the national balance of power between free and slave states. Just as southern economic power rested on slave labor, southern political power also drew extra strength from the slave population, counted at three-fifths the weight of free persons. In 1820, the South as a region had seventeen more representatives in Congress than it would have had if only whites were counted.

Both of Tallmadge's amendments passed in the House of Representatives, but with a close and sharply sectional vote of North against South (with a few northern Republicans taking the side of the South). The debate was ferocious and explosive, nearly a complete dress rehearsal of the arguments that would surface a generation later in the struggle leading to civil war. A Georgia representative predicted that the Missouri slavery question had started

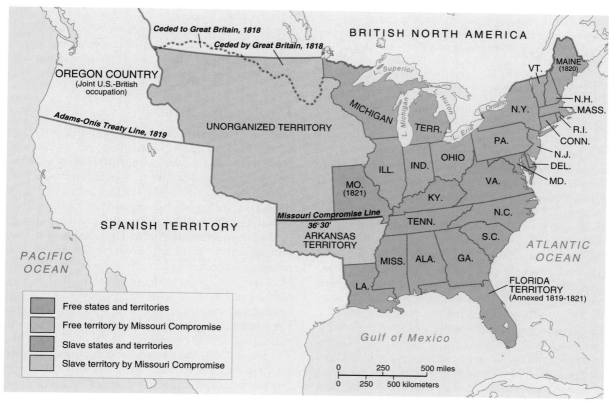

**M A P  10.3**

*The Missouri Compromise, 1820*

*After a difficult battle in Congress, Missouri entered the Union in 1821 as part of a package*
*of compromises. Maine was admitted as a free state to balance slavery in Missouri; and*
*a line drawn at latitude 36°30' put most of the rest of the Louisiana Territory off limits*
*to slavery in the future.*

"a fire which all the waters of the ocean could not extinguish. It can be extinguished only in blood." The Senate, with an even number of slave and free states, voted down the amendments, with some border states joining the proslavery line. The deadlock meant that determination of Missouri statehood was set aside for the next congressional term.

In 1820, the components of a compromise slowly took shape in the Senate debate. Maine, once a part of Massachusetts, applied for statehood as a free state; it would balance Missouri as a slave state in the Senate. To quiet northern fears about the slave state Missouri reaching so far into the North, the Senate agreed that the southern boundary of Missouri, latitude 36°30', extended west would become the permanent line dividing slave from free.

All of the Louisiana Territory north of the line—except Missouri—would be closed to slavery. The compromise plan passed in the Senate and, after vigorous debate, also passed in the House (Map 10.3).

President Monroe and Thomas Jefferson, retired to his home in Charlottesville, Virginia, at first worried that the Missouri crisis would reinvigorate the Federalist Party as the party of the North. But even ex-Federalists agreed that the division of free versus slave states was too dangerous a fault line to let shape national politics. When new parties did develop in the 1830s, they took pains to bridge geography, each party developing a presence in both North and South. Monroe and Jefferson also worried about the future of slavery. Each understood slavery to be deeply problematic, but, as Jefferson said, "We have the wolf by the ears, and we can neither hold him, nor safely let him go. Justice is in one scale, and self-preservation in the other."

## The Monroe Doctrine

New foreign policy challenges arose even as Congress struggled with the slavery issue. In 1816, American troops led by General Andrew Jackson invaded the northern part of Spanish Florida in search of Seminole Indians who had been welcoming and harboring escaped slaves. Once there, Jackson declared himself the commander of northern Florida, demonstrating his power in 1818 by executing two British men who he claimed were dangerous enemies. In asserting rule over the territory, and surely in executing the two British subjects on Spanish land, Jackson had gone too far. Privately, President Monroe was grievously distressed and pondered court-martialing Jackson. But Jackson's immense popularity as a war hero dissuaded the president. Instead, John Quincy Adams, the secretary of state, opened negotiations with Spain to acquire the territory. The result was a treaty that delivered Florida to the United States in 1819. In exchange, the Americans agreed to abandon any claim to Texas or Cuba. The South took this as a large concession, since southerners had eyed both places as potential slave states. Adams's treaty also established a boundary between New Spain to the west and the Louisiana Territory.

Spain at that moment was preoccupied with its colonies in South America, several of which were on the verge of breaking away. One after another—Chile, Colombia, Peru, and finally Mexico—declared itself independent in the early 1820s. For a time, it appeared that Spain, perhaps joined by France and Prussia, might try to regain the lost colonies. In response to this possibility, Monroe formulated a declaration of principles on South America, incorporated into his annual message to Congress in December 1823. It would be known in decades to come as the Monroe Doctrine. He asserted that "the American Continents, by the free and independent condition which they have assumed and maintain, are henceforth not to be considered as subjects for future colonization by any European power." Any new attempt to interfere in the Western Hemisphere would be regarded as "the manifestation of an unfriendly disposition towards the United States." In exchange for noninterference by Europeans, Monroe pledged that the United States would stay out of European struggles. Monroe articulated these policy goals without any real

force to back them up. The American navy could not defend Chile or Peru against Spain or France. Monroe did not even have the backing of Congress for his statement; it was merely his idea of a sound policy laid out in a public message.

## The Election of 1824

Monroe's nonpartisan administration was the last of its kind, a fitting throwback to eighteenth-century ideals, led by a president who was the last in that office to wear a powdered wig and knee breeches. Monroe's cabinet contained men of sharply different philosophies, all calling themselves Republicans. Secretary of State John Quincy Adams represented the urban Northeast, South Carolinian John C. Calhoun spoke for the commercial planter aristocracy as secretary of war, and William H. Crawford of Georgia, secretary of the treasury, was a proponent of Jeffersonian states' rights and limited federal power. Well before the end of Monroe's second term, these men and others began to maneuver for the presidency.

Since 1800, the congressional caucus of each party had met to identify and lend its considerable but still informal support to its party's leading candidate. In 1824, with only one party, the caucus system splintered. Some New York and Virginia representatives met and endorsed Crawford, but the fifty-one-year-old planter had just suffered a serious stroke, which left him largely incapacitated.

John Quincy Adams had headed the State Department for eight years; since 1800, every secretary of state had become the next president, and so Adams felt he had a claim on the office. Henry Clay, Speaker of the House, also was a declared candidate. The Kentuckian put forth a set of policies he called the American System, a package of protective tariffs to promote manufacturing and federal expenditures for extensive internal improvements, many of them roads and canals in the western states. Secretary of War Calhoun, who combined the riches of a well-off Carolina planter with the agile mind of a bright Yale-trained lawyer, was another serious contender. Like Clay, he favored internal improvements, protective tariffs, and banking measures, which he figured would gain him support in northern states.

The final candidate was an outsider: General Andrew Jackson of Tennessee. Jackson had much less political experience than the others. His fame rested completely on his reputation as a military leader, but that was sufficient to give him a huge surge of support, much to the surprise of the experienced politicians. Calhoun soon dropped out of the race and shifted his attention to winning the vice presidency.

The 1824 election was the first presidential contest in which popularity with ordinary voters could be measured. Recent changes in state constitutions gave voters in all but six states the power to choose electors for the electoral college. (Before, state legislatures had held this power.) Jackson was by far the most popular candidate with voters. He won more than 153,000 votes, while Adams was second with 109,000; Clay won 47,000 votes and the incapacitated Crawford garnered 46,600.

Translated to the electoral college, Jackson had 99 votes, Adams 84, Crawford 41, and Clay 37. Jackson did not have a majority, so the election was thrown to the House of Representatives, for the second (and last) time in American history. Each state delegation voted as one vote, and only the top three candidates could enter the runoff, under the terms of the Twelfth Amendment to the Constitution, passed in 1804. Thus Henry Clay, Speaker of the House, was out of the race and in a position now to throw his support to another candidate.

The election of 1824 came to be characterized as the "corrupt bargain" in the eyes of Jackson's supporters. Clay backed Adams, and Adams won by one vote in the House (Map 10.4). Clay's support made sense on many levels. He and Adams were close on many issues, particularly on Clay's American System and Adams's backing of internal improvements. Clay was uneasy with Jackson's volatile temperament and unstated political views and with Crawford's diminished capacity. But Clay's choice still was not easy because of a strong personal animosity he felt for Adams.

What made Clay's decision look unseemly was that three days after the election, Adams offered to appoint Clay secretary of state—and Clay accepted. There probably was no actual bargain; Adams's subsequent cabinet appointments abundantly demonstrated that he was incapable of making appointments for purely political reasons. But the Clay appointment looked bad, and a storm of public protest greeted it. Andrew Jackson felt that the election had been stolen from him and wrote bitterly that "the Judas of the West has closed the contract and will receive the thirty pieces of silver."

## The Adams Administration

John Quincy Adams, like his father before him, was a one-term president. His career had been built on diplomacy, not electoral politics, and his political horse sense was not well developed. His choices for cabinet posts drew his opposition into his inner circle. He asked Crawford to stay on in the Treasury, and he retained the postmaster general, an openly pro-Jackson man, even though that position controlled thousands of patronage appointments all over the country. Most amazingly, he asked Jackson to become secretary of war. With Calhoun as vice president (elected without opposition by the electoral college) and Clay at State, the whole argumentative crew was thrust into the executive branch. Crawford and Jackson had the good sense to decline appointments.

Adams had lofty ideas for federal action during his presidency, and the plan he put before Congress was so sweeping that it took Henry Clay aback. Adams called for federally built roads, canals, and harbors. He proposed a national university in Washington as well as government-sponsored scientific research. He wanted to build observatories to advance astronomical knowledge and to promote precision in timekeeping. He issued a massive report on a decimal-based system of

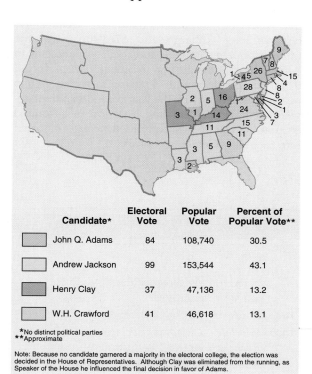

| Candidate* | Electoral Vote | Popular Vote | Percent of Popular Vote** |
|---|---|---|---|
| John Q. Adams | 84 | 108,740 | 30.5 |
| Andrew Jackson | 99 | 153,544 | 43.1 |
| Henry Clay | 37 | 47,136 | 13.2 |
| W.H. Crawford | 41 | 46,618 | 13.1 |

*No distinct political parties
**Approximate

Note: Because no candidate garnered a majority in the electoral college, the election was decided in the House of Representatives. Although Clay was eliminated from the running, as Speaker of the House he influenced the final decision in favor of Adams.

**MAP 10.4**
*The Election of 1824*

weights and measures, written when he was secretary of state. In all these endeavors, Adams believed he was picking up where both Jefferson and Madison had left off, using the powers of government to advance knowledge. But his opponents feared he was taking too much from Hamilton's legacy, using federal power inappropriately to advance commercial interests.

Whether he was more truly Federalist or Republican was a moot point, however. Lacking political skills, Adams was unable to implement much of his program. He scorned the idea of courting voters to gain support. He also scorned the use of the patronage system to enhance his power. He often used his appointive powers (to posts like customs house collectors) to placate enemies rather than reward friends. A story of a toast offered to the president may well have been mythical, but as humorous folklore it made the rounds during his term and came to summarize Adams's precarious hold on leadership. A dignitary raised a glass and pledged, "May he strike confusion to his foes . . . ," to which another voice scornfully chimed in, "as he has already done to his friends."

## Conclusion: From Jefferson to Adams

The nineteenth century opened with the Jeffersonian Republicans in power, trying to undo much of the Federalist structure created in the 1790s. But Jefferson's desire for a more limited government, in size, scope, and power, finally gave way to the realities of increasing interaction with foreign powers as well as steady expansion westward. Jefferson had sent Lewis and Clark to explore for scientific knowledge the far reaches of the continent, and then unexpectedly that region dropped into his hands as the Louisiana Purchase. Jefferson and Madison tried valiantly to avoid war with England and France, experimenting with high-minded but costly trade embargoes, but nonetheless the War of 1812 came, caused less by concrete economic or political issues than by questions of honor. Its conclusion at the Battle of New Orleans allowed Americans to feel they had fought a second war of independence.

The war elevated to national prominence General Andrew Jackson, whose sudden popularity with voters in the 1824 election surprised traditional politicians and threw the one-party rule of Republicans into a tailspin. John Quincy Adams barely secured the presidency in the early months of 1825 before the election campaign of 1828 was off and running. Appeals to the people—the mass of white male voters—would be the hallmark of all elections after 1824.

The War of 1812 started another chain of events that would prove momentous in later decades. Jefferson's long embargo and Madison's wartime trade stoppages gave strong encouragement to American manufacturing, momentarily protected from competition with English factories. When peace resumed in 1815, the years of independent development burst forth into a period of sustained economic growth that continued nearly unabated into the mid-nineteenth century.

## CHRONOLOGY

| | |
|---|---|
| **1789** | Judiciary Act establishes six Supreme Court justices who preside over circuit courts. |
| **1800** | Thomas Jefferson and Aaron Burr tie in electoral college. |
| **1801** | Judiciary Act reduces Supreme Court justices to five and allows for sixteen circuit judges. |

|  |  |
|---|---|
|  | Jefferson elected president by House of Representatives. |
| **1802** | Judiciary Act of 1801 repealed. |
| **1803** | *Marbury v. Madison* declares part of Judiciary Act of 1789 unconstitutional. |
|  | Embargoes on American shipping by England and France. |
|  | Louisiana Purchase from France. |

| | | | | |
|---|---|---|---|---|
| **1804** | Jefferson reelected president. Burr-Hamilton duel. | | **1814** | British attack Washington, D.C., burning several buildings. Treaty of Ghent ends War of 1812. Hartford Convention. |
| **1804–1806** | Lewis and Clark expedition. | | **1815** | Battle of New Orleans won by Andrew Jackson's forces. |
| **1807** | **June.** *Chesapeake* attacked and searched by British in Chesapeake Bay. **December.** Embargo Act forbids all American trade with England and France and their colonies. | | **1816** | James Monroe elected president. |
| | | | **1819** | Spain cedes Florida to United States. |
| | | | **1820** | Missouri Compromise admits Missouri as slave state and Maine as free state. Monroe reelected president. |
| **1808** | James Madison elected president. | | | |
| **1809** | Treaty of Fort Wayne with Indians in Indiana Territory. Non-Intercourse Act. | | **1823** | Monroe Doctrine asserts independence of Western Hemisphere from European intervention. |
| **1811** | Battle of Tippecanoe won by William Henry Harrison's troops. | | **1824** | "Corrupt bargain" election of John Quincy Adams. |
| **1812** | **June.** War declared on Great Britain. Madison reelected president. | | | |

# SUGGESTED READINGS

Stephen E. Ambrose, *Undaunted Courage: Meriwether Lewis, Thomas Jefferson, and the Opening of the American West* (1996). A gripping account of the epic story of Lewis and Clark, one that restores Lewis to his leadership role and gives due credit for the expedition's scientific findings along with their exciting adventure saga.

Norma Basch, *Framing American Divorce: From the Revolutionary Generation to the Victorians* (1999). A richly detailed study of early divorce laws that illuminates intimate gender relations in the early republic.

R. David Edmunds, *Tecumseh and the Quest for Indian Leadership* (1984). A fascinating biography of the Shawnee chief and his brother, the Prophet.

Joseph J. Ellis, *American Sphinx: The Character of Thomas Jefferson* (1997). A prize-winning exploration of the many contradictory facets of Jefferson.

Mary W. M. Hargreaves, *The Presidency of John Quincy Adams* (1986). The best concise history of Adams's one-term administration.

Donald R. Hickey, *The War of 1812: A Forgotten Conflict* (1989). A stimulating and controversial study of the War of 1812 that takes a pro-Federalist line, condemning Jefferson and Madison for taking America into a needless war.

Susan Juster, *Disorderly Women: Sexual Politics and Evangelicalism in Revolutionary New England* (1994). The definitive study of women and gender in evangelical denominations in the early national period.

Drew R. McCoy, *The Elusive Republic: Political Economy in Jeffersonian America* (1980). An ambitious and subtle history of the intellectual ideas about economics differentiating the Republicans and the Federalists.

Robert V. Remini, *Andrew Jackson and the Course of American Empire, 1767–1821* (1977). An older but classic history of Jackson's early career.

Donald L. Robinson, *Slavery in the Structure of American Politics, 1765–1820* (1971). A study of the impact of slavery on politics, including detailed coverage of the Missouri Compromise.

Robert A. Rutland, *The Presidency of James Madison* (1990). A vivid and provocative study of Madison as chief executive, the first president to lead the United States in a declared war.

Stephen Watts, *The Republic Reborn: War and the Making of Liberal America, 1790–1820* (1987). A provocative intellectual history that identifies the War of 1812 as a crucial moment in the transformation of America from republicanism to liberalism.

## SHIP'S FIGUREHEAD OF ANDREW JACKSON

*Carved in 1834 and affixed to the bow
of the revered navy frigate* Constitution, *this figurehead of Andrew Jackson
symbolized national pride by putting
"the image of the most popular man of
the West upon the favorite ship of the
East," according to the commodore who
commissioned it. But when Jackson introduced a
new, strict banking policy, his popularity in the
urban East quickly evaporated. In Boston, where
the* Constitution *was docked, protesters complained that the figurehead of a tyrant corrupted their ship. On
the night of July 3, 1834, the eve of the national holiday, an eighteen-year-old youth stole on
board and decapitated the figurehead, sawing it through just below the ears. The commodore,
himself alert to symbolic statements, wrapped the headless statue in a flag and sent it to New
York City where woodworkers fashioned a new head in 1835. It was reattached to the ship in
another port: Jackson's banking policies still rankled in urban financial centers, and naval
authorities did not want to risk a second mutilation of the president's image.*

Museum of the City of New York.

# ANDREW JACKSON'S AMERICA

## 11

### 1815–1840

PRESIDENT ANDREW JACKSON WAS THE DOMINANT FIGURE of his age, yet his precarious childhood little foretold the fame, fortune, and influence he would enjoy in the years after 1815. Jackson was born in the Carolina backcountry in 1767. His Scots-Irish father had recently died, leaving a poor, struggling mother to support three small boys. During the Revolution, young Andrew followed his brothers into the militia, where both died of disease, as did his mother. Orphaned at fourteen, Jackson drifted, drinking, gambling, and brawling.

But at seventeen, his prospects improved. He studied law for three years with a North Carolina lawyer, and then moved west to Nashville, a frontier community full of opportunities for a young man of legal training and aggressive temperament. He became a public prosecutor, married into a leading family, and acquired land and slaves. When Tennessee became a state in 1796, Jackson, then twenty-nine, was elected to Congress for a single term.

Jackson captured national attention in 1815 by leading the victory at the Battle of New Orleans. Songs, broadsides, and an admiring biography set him up as the original self-made man, the parentless child magically responsible for his own destiny. Jackson seemed to have created himself, a gritty, forceful personality extracting opportunities from the dynamic, turbulent frontier.

Jackson was more than a man of action. He was also strong-willed, reckless, and quick to anger, impulsively challenging men to duels on slight pretexts. In one legendary fight, in 1806, Jackson deliberately let his opponent, an expert marksman, shoot first. The bullet hit him in a rib, but Jackson masked all sign of injury under a loose cloak and immobile face. He then took careful aim at the astonished man and killed him. Such steely courage chilled his political opponents.

Jackson's image as a frontier action hero set him apart from the learned and privileged gentlemen from Virginia and Massachusetts who had monopolized the presidency up to 1828. When he lost the 1824 election to John Quincy Adams, an infuriated Jackson vowed to fight a rematch and started running for the office immediately. He won in 1828 and again in 1832, capturing large majorities of voters. His appeal stretched across the urban working classes of the East, frontier voters of the West, and slaveholders in the South, who all saw something of themselves in Jackson.

The confidence and even recklessness of Jackson's personality mirrored the new confidence of American society in the years after 1815. An entrepreneurial spirit gripped the country, producing a market revolution of unprecedented scale. Old social hierarchies eroded; the most ordinary of men could dream of moving high on the wheel of fortune, just as Jackson had done. Stunning advances in transportation and economic productivity fueled such dreams and propelled thousands to move west and many thousands more to move to cities. Urban growth and technological change fostered the diffusion of a distinctive and vibrant public culture, spread through newspapers and the spoken word. The development of rapid print allowed popular opinions to coalesce and intensify; Jackson's sudden nationwide celebrity was a case in point.

Expanded communication transformed politics dramatically. Sharp disagreements over the best way to promote individual liberty, economic opportunity, and national prosperity in the new market economy defined key differences between Jackson and Adams and the parties they gave rise to in the 1830s. The process of party formation brought new habits of political participation and party loyalty to many thousands more adult white males. Religion became democratized as well: An evangelical revival of national proportions brought its adherents the confidence that salvation and perfection were now available to all.

As president from 1828 to 1836, Jackson presided over all these changes, fighting some and supporting others in his vigorous and volatile way. And as with his own stubborn personality, there was a dark underside to the confidence and expansiveness of American society. Steamboats blew up, banks and businesses periodically collapsed, alcoholism rates soared, Indians were killed or relocated farther west, and slavery continued to expand. The brash confidence that turned some people into Jackson-like, rugged, self-promoting individuals inspired others to think about the human costs of rapid economic expansion and thus about reforming society in dramatic ways. The common denominator was a faith that people and societies can shape their own destinies.

# The Market Revolution

The return of peace in 1815 unleashed powerful economic and social forces that revolutionized the organization of the market. Spectacular changes in transportation facilitated the movement of commodities, information, and people, while textile mills and other factories created many new jobs, especially for young unmarried women. Innovations in banking functions, legal practices, and tariff policies promoted swift economic growth.

This was not yet an industrial revolution, but a market revolution. The energy to fuel development still came from ancient sources—water, wood, beasts of burden, and human muscle. What was new was the accelerated pace of economic activity and the scale of distribution of goods. Men and women were drawn out of old patterns of rural self-sufficiency and into the wider realm of national market relations. At the same time, the nation's money supply enlarged considerably, leading to speculative investments in commerce, manufacturing, transportation, and land. The new nature and scale of production and consumption changed behavior, attitudes, and expectations.

## Improvements in Transportation

Before 1815, transportation in the United States was slow, difficult, and expensive; it cost as much to ship freight over thirty miles of domestic roads as it did to send the same weight of cargo across the Atlantic Ocean. A stagecoach trip from Boston to New York took an uncomfortable four days. But between 1815 and 1840, networks of roads, canals, steamboats, and finally railroads dramatically raised the speed and lowered the cost of travel (Map 11.1). Migrants like Andrew Jackson went west to Nashville in the 1790s by walking or riding horseback for weeks along old Indian trails. But when he returned east in 1829 for his inauguration, the newly elected President Jackson traveled by steamboat and turnpike to the capital city in a matter of days.

The benefits of improved transportation to economic development were abundantly clear: Products could be sold more cheaply in a wider market. Equally important, transportation facilitated the flow of political information; traffic in newspapers had profound consequences for Jacksonian-era elections. Travel encouraged cultural change as well. Easily accessible passenger travel lifted men and women out of their local communities, brought country merchants on buying trips to urban centers, and pulled adolescents of both sexes into employment opportunities in cities or factory towns, often far from home.

Enhanced public transport was very expensive to build, and it produced uneven economic benefits. The federal government was therefore reluctant to undertake federally sponsored transportation. During Jefferson's presidency, Congress approved start-up funding for the National Road, to connect Baltimore with the heart of Ohio, provided that the money came from the sale of Ohio public lands, the area that would ultimately and directly benefit. Laying the roadbed went slowly; by 1818, the National

**MAP 11.1**
*Routes of Transportation in 1840*

*Transportation advances by the 1830s had cut travel times significantly. Goods and people could move from New York City to Buffalo, New York, in four days via the Erie Canal, a trip that took two weeks by road in 1800. A trip from New York to New Orleans that took four weeks in 1800 could now be accomplished in less than half that time on steamboats on the western rivers.*

Road extended to Wheeling, West Virginia, reaching Ohio only in the 1830s. President John Quincy Adams was willing to spend federal money on transportation, but Congress would not agree.

Instead, private investors sponsored transportation improvements. They pooled resources and chartered stagecoach, canal, and railroad companies, with significant aid from state governments in the form of subsidies and guarantees of monopoly rights. Turnpike and roadway mileage dramatically increased after 1815, reducing the cost of land shipment of goods. Stagecoach lines proliferated in an extensive network of passenger corridors dense in the populated East and fanning out to the Mississippi River. Travel time on main routes was cut in half; Boston to New York now took two days.

Steamboats signaled an important advance in the technology of transportation. In 1807, Robert Fulton adapted a steam engine to propel a 133-foot boat, the *Clermont*. Its first voyage, up the Hudson River from New York City to Albany, took thirty-two hours against a head wind, compared with two days for the land route. Soon a steamboat craze was in full swing, and by 1820 a dozen steamboats left New York City daily, churning up the Hudson to Albany in half a day or moving east on the Long Island Sound to Providence, Rhode Island. Traffic soon spread to the western rivers and the Great Lakes. A voyager on one of the first steamboats to go down the Mississippi reported that the Chickasaw Indians called the vessel a "fire canoe" and considered it "an omen of evil . . . the sparks from the chimney of the boat being likened to the train of the celestial visitant"—that is, a comet, also feared as an evil omen. By the early 1830s, more than seven hundred steamboats had been swiftly launched into

**EARLY STEAMBOATS**

*Steamboats revolutionized travel in the 1820s and 1830s. The basic technology consisted of a steam engine, powered by the steam from a furnace-heated boiler, that propelled a boat by turning a wooden paddlewheel. In concept, steam-powered travel was ingenious, but it took years of trial-and-error improvements to reduce risks. Boiler explosions and fires loomed large as a deadly hazard; in the 1830s alone, there were eighty-nine such accidents. This lithograph shows the explosion of the* Lexington, *whose boiler blew up on Long Island Sound in January 1840, causing great loss of life from scalding steam, flying wreckage, fire, and icy waters.*
Library of Congress.

operation on the Ohio and Mississippi Rivers. A journey upriver from New Orleans to Louisville, Kentucky, took only one week.

Such speed came with costs, however. Repeatedly, boiler explosions revealed the risks of steam transport; by 1830, close to eighty vessels had been blasted out of the water, killing hundreds of passengers. Despite such horrors, the public remained excited over fast travel.

Canals were another major innovation of the transportation revolution. These two-way highways of water could be shallow; usually four feet of water sufficed to float a flat-bottomed barge, which was powered by horses or mules trudging along a towpath beside the canal. Travel speed was slow, under two miles per hour, but the economy came from increased loads: The low-friction water allowed one horse to pull a fifty-ton barge. In winter, canals froze over and became smooth, stump- and rock-free highways for sleighs.

Pennsylvania in 1815 and New York in 1817 commenced major state-sponsored canal enterprises intended to create large regional markets for goods. Pennsylvania's Schuylkill Canal stretched 108 miles west into the state when it was completed in 1826. It was overshadowed by the impressive Erie Canal in New York, begun in 1817 and finished in 1825, connecting the 350 miles between Albany on the Hudson River with Buffalo on Lake Erie. In effect, the Erie Canal linked the port of New York City with the inland region of New York State and, via the Great Lakes, the entire Northwest Territory.

Wheat and flour moved east, while textiles and books moved west, joined by heavy passenger traffic in both directions. By the 1830s, the cost of shipping by canal fell to less than a tenth of the cost of overland transport, and New York City quickly blossomed into the premier city of trade and commerce in the United States.

In the 1830s, private railroad companies began to give canals stiff competition, and by the mid-1840s the canal-building era was over. (However, use of the canals for freight continued well into the twentieth century.) Rail lines in the 1830s were generally short, on the order of twenty to one hundred miles; they were not yet an efficient distribution system for goods. But passengers flocked to experience the marvelous travel speeds of fifteen to twenty miles per hour, enduring the frightful noise and cascades of ashes and cinders that rained on them.

## Factories, Workingwomen, and Wage Labor

Transportation advances promoted a rapid expansion of manufacturing after 1815. Teamsters, wagoners, and bargemen hauled products like shoes, textiles, clocks, guns, and books into nationwide distribution. Some of the gain in manufacturing, especially in the textile industry, came from the development of water-driven machinery, built near fast-coursing rivers. (The steam power harnessed for steamboats and railroads had limited application in industry until the 1840s.) But much of the new manufacturing involved only a reorganization of production, still using the power and skill of human hands. Both mechanized and manual manufacturing pulled young women into the labor market for the first time and greatly enlarged the segment of the population earning a living by selling labor for hourly wages.

The earliest factory, built by British immigrant Samuel Slater in Pawtucket, Rhode Island, in the 1790s, featured a mechanical spinning machine that produced thread and yarn. By 1815, nearly 170 spinning mills dotted lower New England. Unlike English manufacturing cities, where entire families worked in low-wage, health-threatening factories, American spinning and textile factories targeted young women as employees. The assumption was that adolescent girls would gladly work for minimal wages in view of their limited options for paid employment. After a few years, they would retire to marriage, their jobs taken by fresh recruits from the countryside earning a beginner's wage. There would thus be no class of permanent poor clustered around factories, and factory labor would remain cheap.

A female labor force came to be called the "Waltham system" after 1814, when a group of Boston entrepreneurs headed by Francis Cabot Lowell consolidated and mechanized all aspects of cloth production—carding, fulling, spinning, weaving, and dyeing—in one location, in Waltham, Massachusetts, and hired young women. A decade later, the Waltham system was improved on at Lowell, Massachusetts, a new manufacturing town built by Lowell and his associates along the Merrimack River. By 1830, the eight mills in Lowell employed more than six thousand young women. A key innovation was the close moral supervision of the female workers, who lived in company-owned boardinghouses run by middle-aged women. Both parents and mill owners alike gained assurance that the mill workers were watched, guarded, and disciplined to be an industrious and orderly group. Soon the Waltham system was replicated in many towns in New Hampshire and Maine.

---

*The mill workers welcomed the unprecedented if still limited personal freedom of living in an all-female social space, away from parents, excused from domestic tasks, and with the exhilarating bonus of a little pocket money.*

---

The vast majority of mill workers were women age sixteen to twenty-three who worked for a year or two before leaving. Pay averaged two to three dollars a week, more than what a seamstress or domestic servant could earn but less than a young man's wages. The hours were long, typically eleven to thirteen hours a day, six days a week. The mill workers tended noisy machines in large rooms kept hot and humid (ideal for yarn, not so comfortable for people). The boardinghouses were often crowded, sometimes with six to a bedroom.

Despite the discomforts, young women flocked to obtain textile jobs. Animated by the same energy that moved Andrew Jackson westward—the faith that people can shape their own destinies—the mill workers left rural farms behind and traveled to new factory towns in the hope of becoming more autonomous individuals. They welcomed the unprecedented if still limited personal freedom of living in an all-female social space, away from parents, excused from domestic tasks, and with the exhilarating bonus of a little pocket money. In Lowell, the women workers could engage in evening self-improvement activities, like lectures, and the company established a newspaper, *The Lowell Offering,* written and edited by some of the working-women.

In the mid-1830s, worldwide changes in the cotton market impelled the mill owners to increase productivity from their labor force by adding more machines per worker and by lowering wages. The workers protested, emboldened by their communal living arrangements and by their relative independence from the job, being only temporary, not lifelong, employees. In 1834 and again in 1836, several hundred women at Lowell went out on strike. Their assertiveness surprised many; but ultimately their easy replaceability undermined their bargaining power. Still, the owners gradually realized that an all-female labor force could not be counted on to be compliant and submissive. In the 1840s, mill owners began to shift to immigrant families as their labor source, and factory towns came to resemble European industrial sites with their permanent working class.

Other manufacturing enterprises of the 1820s and 1830s, such as shoemaking, employed women in ever larger numbers. No new machinery transformed the actual work, but new modes of organizing the work allowed the manufacturers to step up production, control wastage and quality, and lower wages by subdividing the tasks and by hiring women. Male workers cut leather and made soles, while the stitching of the upper part of the shoe, called shoebinding, became women's work, performed at home so that it could mesh with women's domestic chores. Women shoebinders earned piecework wages—that is, a payment per item completed. Women's wages were much smaller than men's, but their contribution to family income was now tangible, in cash. By 1830, there were more women shoebinders in Massachusetts than mill workers.

The new shoe entrepreneurs who had reorganized the industry moved to cut shoebinder wages in the economically turbulent 1830s. Unlike the mill workers, women shoebinders worked in relative isolation, a serious hindrance to organized protest. In Lynn, Massachusetts, a major shoemaking center, women turned to other female networks, mainly churches as sites for meetings and religious

**FANCY WEDDING SHOES MADE IN LYNN, MASSACHUSETTS**
*These shoes were part of the wedding outfit of Emily Lucinda Alden when she married Addison Davis in 1840. The soles are flat, with no heel, and the upper shoe is hand-stitched of white satin. Nothing except the ankle lacing distinguishes right from left shoe. (All footwear from the period was made with identical rights and lefts; only usage over time differentiated the shoes.) An extraordinary clue about women and marriage is revealed in the bride's name-to-be affixed to the shoe box. Etiquette books of the 1840s uniformly decreed that the correct public name should be Mrs. Addison Davis. We might surmise that Emily, on the verge of marriage, had not entirely internalized the eclipse of her own public and legal personage that marriage would soon impose on her. When Elizabeth Cady married Henry Stanton in 1840, she had to do battle to be called Mrs. Elizabeth Cady Stanton when she became a leader of the emerging women's rights movement in 1848 (see Chapter 13).*
Lynn Historical Society/photo by Lightstream.

newspapers as forums for communication. The Lynn shoebinders who demanded higher wages in 1834 built on a collective sense of themselves as women even though they did not share daily work lives. "Equal rights should be extended to all—to the weaker sex as well as the stronger," they wrote in a document forming the Female Society of Lynn.

Yet ultimately, the Lynn shoebinders' protests of the 1830s failed to achieve wage increases. Isolated workers all over New England continued to accept low wages, undercutting attempts to establish a minimum rate. And even within the town of

Lynn, many shoebinders shied away from organized protest, preferring to situate their work in the context of family duty instead of market relations.

## Bankers and Lawyers

Entrepreneurs like the Lowell factory owners relied on innovations in the banking system to finance their ventures. The number of state-chartered banks in the country more than doubled in the boom years 1814–1816, from fewer than 90 to 208; by 1830, there were 330, and hundreds more by 1840. Banks stimulated the economy both by making loans to merchants, manufacturers, and real estate purchasers and by enlarging the country's money supply. Borrowers were issued loans in the form of banknotes, certificates unique to each bank. The borrowers then used the notes exactly like money, good for all transactions. Neither federal nor state governments issued paper money, so banknotes became the currency of the country.

In theory, a note could always be traded in at the bank for its equivalent in gold or silver (in a transaction known as "specie payment"). A note from a solid local bank might be worth exactly what it was written for, but if the note came from a distant or questionable bank, its value would be discounted by some fraction. The money market of Jacksonian America definitely required knowledge, caution, and trust.

Bankers exercised great power over the economy in their decisions about who would get loans and what the discount rates would be. The most powerful bankers sat on the board of directors for the second Bank of the United States, headquartered in Philadelphia. (The first Bank of the United States, chartered in 1791 for twenty years, had lapsed in 1811.) The second bank opened for business in 1816 under a twenty-year charter with eighteen branches throughout the country. The rechartering of this second bank would prove to be a major issue in Andrew Jackson's reelection campaign in 1832.

Accompanying the market revolution was a revolution in commercial law. In the decades after 1815, lawyers fashioned a legal system that advanced the interests of commercial activity and enhanced the prospects of private investment. Of particular significance was the changing practice of legal incorporation, the chartering of businesses by states. Earlier, charters were generally limited to businesses formed to serve the public good, such as to build a bridge. Under new state laws dating from 1811 on, corporations could be formed for any reasonable purpose; a key value of incorporation was legal protections for individual investors. In 1800, there were perhaps twenty corporations in the United States; by 1817, there were eighteen hundred.

The legal revolution of these decades reformulated older concepts of contract to reflect the burgeoning entrepreneurial marketplace. Courts had enforced business contracts in the eighteenth century in light of notions of fairness. If a seller foolishly contracted to sell a barrel of wheat for half its true or accepted value and then had regrets, he could rely on the courts to declare the agreement void. In the nineteenth century, courts moved toward an interpretation of contracts as freely negotiated, legally binding agreements, regardless of the fairness of the outcome; the law now presumed that a price was, simply, what a buyer and seller agreed it should be.

Ever-increasing numbers of young men were drawn to legal training in the years after the War of 1812. By 1820, most representatives in the U.S. Congress were lawyers, and a similar wave of legal professionals moved into state politics. Articulate and legalistic, lawyers brought formidable skills to the job of writing and enforcing the new laws governing commerce.

Working through legislatures and courts, lawyers established rights to contract without state interference and designed the model of the business corporation that would carry the United States through the commercial and industrial transformation of the nineteenth century. Lawyers outlawed the use of strikes by aggrieved employees on the grounds that strikes constituted illegal conspiracies. They wrote the laws of eminent domain, empowering states to buy land for roads and canals, even from unwilling sellers. They drafted legislation on contributory negligence, relieving employers from responsibility for workplace injuries if it could be shown that the employees exercised inadequate caution and thus contributed to the injuries. In these ways and many others, entrepreneurial lawyers of the 1820s and 1830s created the legal foundation for an economy that gave priority to ambitious individuals interested in maximizing their own wealth.

Not everyone applauded these developments. Andrew Jackson, himself a skillful lawyer-turned-politician, spoke for a large and mistrustful segment of the population when he warned about the abuses of power "which the moneyed interest derives from a paper currency which they are able to control, from the multitude of corporations with exclusive privileges which they have succeeded in obtaining in the different states, and which are employed altogether for their benefit." Jacksonians believed that ending government-granted privileges was the way to maximize individual liberty and economic opportunity.

### Booms and Busts

One aspect of the economy that the lawyer-politicians could not control was the threat of financial collapse. The boom years from 1815 to 1818 exhibited an energy and volatility that resulted in the first large-scale economic panic in U.S. history; the pattern was repeated in the 1830s. Rapidly rising consumer demand stimulated rising prices for goods, and speculative investment opportunities with high payoffs abounded—in bank stocks, western land sales, urban real estate, and commodities markets. Steep inflation made some people wealthy but created hardships for workers on fixed incomes.

When the bubble first burst in 1819, the overnight rich suddenly became the overnight poor. Some suspected that a precipitating cause of the panic of 1819 was the second Bank of the United States. For too long, the bank had neglected to exercise control over state banks, many of which had suspended specie payments—the exchange of gold or silver for banknotes—in their eagerness to make loans and expand the economic bubble. Then, in mid-1818, the Bank of the United States started to call in its loans and insisted that state banks do likewise. The contraction of the money supply created tremors throughout the economy, a foretaste of the catastrophe to come.

What made the crunch worse was a parallel financial crisis in Europe in the spring of 1819. Overseas prices of agricultural products plummeted; cotton, tobacco, and wheat suddenly fell in value by more than 50 percent. Now when the Bank of the United States and state banks tried to call in their outstanding loans, debtors involved in the commodities trade could not pay. The number of business and personal bankruptcies skyrocketed.

The intricate web of credit and debt relationships meant that almost everyone with even a toe in the new commercial economy was affected by the panic of 1819. Thousands of Americans lost their savings and property. Estimates of unemployment suggest that a half million people lost their livelihoods nationwide.

It took several years for the country to recover from the panic of 1819. Unemployment rates slowly improved, but the emotional shock and bitterness lasted a long time. A powerful resentment against banks lingered, ready to be mobilized by politicians in the decades to come. The dangers of a system that depended on extensive credit were now clear: In one memorable, folksy formulation that gained circulation around 1820, a farmer was said to compare credit to "a man pissing in his breeches on a cold day to keep his arse warm—very comfortable at first but I dare say . . . you know how it feels afterwards."

*The intricate web of credit and debt relationships meant that almost everyone with even a toe in the new commercial economy was affected by the panic of 1819.*

By the mid-1820s, the booming economy was back on track, driven by high productivity, a resumed consumer demand for goods, a greatly accelerating volume of international trade, and a restless and calculating people moving goods, human labor, and investment capital in ever larger and expanding circles of commerce. But an undercurrent of fear and anxiety about rapid economic change continued to shape the political views of many Americans.

### The Spread of Democracy

Just as the market revolution held out the promise, if not the reality, of economic opportunity for anyone who worked hard, the political transformation of the 1830s held out the promise of political opportunity for hundreds of thousands of new voters. Between 1828 and 1836, the years of Andrew Jackson's presidency, the second American party system took shape, although not until 1836 would the parties have distinct names and consistent programs that transcended the particular personalities running for office. Over those years, more men could and did vote, responding to new methods of arousing voter interest. In 1828, Jackson's charismatic personality defined his party. By 1836, both parties had institutionalized one of his most successful themes: that politicians had to appear to have the common touch in an era when popularity with voters drove the electoral process.

## Popular Politics and Partisan Identity

The election of 1828 was the first presidential contest in which popular votes determined the outcome; in twenty-two out of twenty-four states, voters—and not state legislatures—now designated electors committed to a particular candidate. More than a million voters participated, nearly three times the number in 1824, reflecting the high stakes voters perceived in the Adams-Jackson rematch. Throughout the 1830s, the number of voters rose to all-time highs. Partly this increase resulted from relaxed voting restrictions; by the mid-1830s, all but three states allowed universal white male suffrage, without property qualifications. But the higher turnout also indicated increased political interest. In contrast to the sleepy Monroe elections of 1816 and 1820, more than half the electorate voted in 1828, and in some states the turnout ran as high as 70 percent. By 1840, national elections generated unprecedented voter turnouts.

The 1828 election inaugurated new campaign styles as well. State-level candidates routinely gave speeches to woo the voters, appearing at picnics and public banquets. (Adams and Jackson still declined such activities in 1828 as too undignified; but Henry Clay of Kentucky, campaigning for Adams, earned the nicknames the "Barbecue Orator" and the "Gastronomic Cicero.") Campaign rhetoric, under the necessity to create popular appeal, became more informal and often blunt.

As party rivalry evolved, political leaders in the 1830s orchestrated public events such as rallies and parades. The Jackson camp established many Hickory Clubs, trading on Jackson's popular nickname, "Old Hickory," from a common Tennessee tree suggesting resilience and toughness. (Jackson was the first presidential candidate to have an affectionate and widely used nickname.) Political committees made sure their supporters got to the polls, which could be a day's ride or more away for some voters.

Partisan newspapers defined issues and publicized political personalities as never before. Party leaders cultivated editors and judiciously dispensed subsidies and other favors to secure the loyalties of papers, even in remote towns and villages. In New York State, where party development was most advanced, a pro-Jackson group called the Bucktails had fifty weekly publications under its control. Stories from the leading Jacksonian paper in Washington, D.C., would be reprinted two days later in a Boston or Cincinnati paper, as fast as the mail stage could carry them. Presidential campaigns were now coordinated in a national arena.

Parties declined to adopt official names in 1828, still honoring the fiction of Republican Party unity. Instead, they called themselves the Jackson party or the Adams party. By the 1832 election, labels began to appear; Adams's political heir, Henry Clay, represented the National Republicans, while Jackson's supporters called themselves Democratic Republicans. Both parties were still claiming the mantle of the Jefferson-to-Monroe heritage by keeping "Republican" in the name, but the National Republicans favored national action to promote commercial development, while the Democratic Republicans promised to be responsive to the will of the majority. By 1834, a few state-level National Republicans shortened their name to the Whig Party, a term that was gradually accepted and in common use by 1836, the same year that Jackson's party became simply the Democrats. Thus, Whig and Democrat crystallized as names only at the end of an eight-year evolutionary process.

## The Election of 1828 and the Character Issue

The campaign of 1828 was modern in more ways than just the drawn-out electioneering and the importance of popular votes. It was also the first national election in which scandal and character questions reigned supreme.

John Quincy Adams was vilified by his opponents as a hopeless elitist, a bookish academic, and perhaps even a monarchist. Critics pointed to a billiard table and an ivory chess set in Adams's White House as symbols of his aristocratic degeneracy along with the "corrupt bargain" of 1824, the alleged election deal between Adams and Henry Clay. Jackson men were especially happy to malign Clay because they viewed him as the chief architect of anti-Jackson propaganda as well as the most credible threat in future elections.

The Adams men returned fire with fire. They portrayed Jackson as the bastard son of a prostitute, a story made remotely plausible by his fatherless childhood. Worse, the cloudy, undocumented circumstances around his marriage to Rachel Donelson Robards gave rise to the story that Jackson was a seducer and an adulterer, having married a woman in 1791 whose divorce from her first husband was not entirely legal. Pro-Adams newspapers howled that Jackson was a sinful and impulsive man, while Adams was portrayed as a man of restraint, piety, learning, and virtue.

*Parties mobilized and delivered voters, sharpened the focus of differences in candidates, and created loyalty to the party.*

Editors in favor of Adams played up Jackson's notorious violent temper, evidenced by the many duels, brawls, and canings they could recount. Jackson men, of course, used the same stories to project the old man as a tough frontier hero who knew how to command obedience. As for learning, Jackson's rough frontier education gave him a "natural sense," wrote a Boston editor, which "can never be acquired by reading books—it can only be acquired, in perfection, by reading men."

These stories were not smoke screens to obscure the "real" issues in the election. They became real issues themselves because voters used them to comprehend the kind of public officer each man would make. Character issues conveyed in shorthand larger questions about morality, honor, discipline, and the sanctity of contracts. Jackson and Adams presented two radically different styles of masculinity, and the voters, all men, concluded that the behavior of these candidates foreshadowed their presidential styles and policies.

Throughout the campaign, Jackson was vague on economic and political issues; he was famous for his support of a "judicious tariff," a position that could be endorsed by proponents of both higher and lower taxes on imports. His supporters were thus a diverse group who could be sure only that Jackson favored western expansion and more limited federal powers than Adams. As the incumbent, Adams stood by his record, mainly his promise to promote commerce through federal action, which brought him strength in New England and parts of New York.

Jackson won a sweeping victory, with 56 percent of the popular vote and 178 electoral votes (compared with Adams's 83). The victor took most of the South and West and carried Pennsylvania and New York as well. Jackson's vice president was John C. Calhoun, who had just served as vice president under Adams but had broken with Adams's policies.

After 1828, national politicians no longer deplored the existence of political parties. They were coming to see that parties mobilized and delivered voters, sharpened the focus of differences in candidates, and created loyalty to the party that surpassed that to individual candidates and elections. Jackson was an especially charismatic man, and his election did much to solidify voter loyalty to what would soon be called the Democratic Party. An election over personalities went far to create a party system that could withstand and override personality contests. This apparent contradiction makes sense because the personalities of Jackson and Adams clearly symbolized and defined for voters the competing ideas of the emerging parties: a moralistic, top-down party ready to make major decisions to promote economic growth competing against a contentious, energetic party ready to embrace liberty-loving individualism.

## Jackson's Democratic Agenda

Between the November election and the inauguration in March 1829, Rachel Jackson died. An embittered Andrew Jackson, certain that the ugly campaign had hastened her death, went into deep mourning. His depression was worsened by constant pain from the 1806 bullet still lodged in his chest and by lead and mercury poisoning unwittingly caused by the medicines he took constantly. Sixty-two years old, he carried only 140 pounds on his six-foot-one frame. His adversaries doubted he would make it to a second term.

His supporters, however, went wild at the inauguration. Thousands cheered his ten-minute inaugural address, the shortest in history. An open reception at the White House turned into a near-riot as well-wishers jammed the premises, used windows as doors, stood on furniture for a better view of the great man, and broke thousands of dollars' worth of china and glasses.

During his presidency, Jackson continued this hospitality to the throngs that arrived daily to see him. Some visitors came without invitation to seek jobs in the new administration. Others were tourists just calling to chat. The courteous Jackson, committed to his image as the president of the "common man," held audience with unannounced visitors throughout his two terms.

Jackson's cabinet appointments marked a departure. Whereas past presidents had tried to lessen party conflict by including men of different factions in their cabinets, Jackson would have only Jackson loyalists, a reasonable tactic followed by most later presidents. The most important position, secretary of state, he offered to Martin Van Buren, one of the shrewdest politicians of the day and newly elected governor of New York.

Jackson's agenda quickly came into focus once he was in office. He favored a Jeffersonian limited federal government, fearing that intervention in the economy inevitably favored some groups at the expense of others. He therefore opposed federal support of transportation and grants of monopolies and charters that privileged wealthy investors. Like Jefferson, he anticipated rapid settlement of the interior of the country, where land sales would spread economic democracy to settlers. Establishing a federal Indian policy thus had high priority.

Unlike Jefferson, however, Jackson exercised full presidential powers over Congress. In 1830, he vetoed a highway project in Kentucky that Congress voted to support with federal dollars. In addition to his principled objection that it was unconstitutional, Jackson took satisfaction from the fact that the project was centered in the home state of Henry Clay, who was fast becoming the center of the opposition party. Jackson used the veto twelve times during his tenure in office; all previous presidents had exercised that right a total of nine times.

## Cultural Shifts

Despite differences about the best or fairest way to enhance commercial development, Jackson's Democratic Republicans and Henry Clay's National Republicans shared enthusiasm for the outcome—a growing, booming economy. For increasing numbers of families, especially in the highly commercialized Northeast, the standard of living rose, consumption patterns changed, and the nature and location of work altered.

All of these changes had a direct impact on the roles and duties of men and women in families and on the training of youth for the economy of the future. New ideas about gender relations in a commercial economy surfaced in printed material and in public behavior. In Jacksonian America, a widely shared public culture came into being, originating within the new commercial classes and spreading rapidly through rising levels of literacy, an explosion of print, and an increase in all of the performance arts.

### The Family and Separate Spheres

The centerpiece of new ideas about gender relations held that husbands found their status and authority in the new world of work, leaving wives to tend the hearth and home. Sermons, advice books, periodical articles, and novels reinforced the idea that men and women inhabited separate spheres with separate duties. "To woman it belongs . . . to elevate the intellectual character of her household [and] to kindle the fires of mental activity in childhood," wrote Mrs. A. J. Graves in a popular book titled *Advice to American Women.* For men, in contrast, "the absorbing passion for gain, and the pressing demands of business, engross their whole attention." In particular, the private home, which was now the exclusive domain of women, was sentimentalized as the source of intimacy, love, and safety, an island of refuge from the cruel and competitive world of market relations.

---

*The private home, now the exclusive domain of women, was sentimentalized as the source of intimacy, love, and safety, an island of refuge from the cruel and competitive world of market relations.*

---

Some new aspects of society gave substance to this formulation of separate spheres. Men's work, especially in the manufacturing and urban Northeast, was undergoing profound change after 1815. Increasingly, men's jobs brought cash to the household. Farmers and tradesmen sold products in a market, and bankers, bookkeepers, shoemakers, and canal diggers got pay envelopes. Furthermore, many men's jobs were performed outside of the home, at an office or store. For men who were not farmers, work indeed seemed newly disconnected from the home.

**CELESTIA BULL'S DOMESTIC SCENE**
*Celestia Bull of Winchester, Connecticut, painted this do-*
*mestic scene as part of a "friendship book" for her friend*
*Sarah Sawyer in 1826. The garlanded inscription at the*
*top notes that "Lord Charles is fiddling . . . Lady Sarah is*
*sewing." The billing doves identify this as a scene of mar-*
*ital bliss. Charles has the leisure to play music to his lady*
*while she intently sews; sheet music and books lie open on*
*the table.*
Private collection. Photograph courtesy Walters-Benisek Art &
Antiques, Northampton, Mass. David Stanbury Photography,
Springfield, Mass.

A woman's role in the home was more complicated than the cultural prescriptions indicated. Although the vast majority of married white women
did not hold paying jobs, the home continued to be
a site of time-consuming labor. But the advice books
treated household tasks as loving familial duties;
housework as *work* was thereby rendered invisible
in an economy that evaluated work by how much
cash it generated.

These ideas about the sentimental, noncommercial, feminine home and the masculine world
of work gained acceptance in the 1830s (and well
beyond) because of the cultural dominance of the
middle and upper classes of the Northeast. The doc-

trine of separate spheres unambiguously defined
masculinity and femininity. Men achieved a sense
of manhood through work and pay; women established a sense of femininity through duty to the
home and family and service to others. The convenient fiction of this formulation of gender difference
helped smooth the path for the first generation of
Americans experiencing the market revolution. The
doctrine of separate spheres ordained that men
would absorb and display the values appropriate to
the market economy—competition, acquisitiveness—
while women would exemplify and foster older,
noncommercial values of loving service to family and community. Both men and women of the
middle classes benefited from this bargain; men
were set free to pursue wealth, while women
gained moral authority within the home. Beyond the
middle and upper classes, these new gender ideals
had limited applicability. Despite their apparent
dominance in printed material of the period, they
were never monolithic.

## The Education and Training of Youth

The market economy with its new expectations for
men and women required fresh methods of training youth of both sexes. The generation that came
of age in the 1820s and 1830s had opportunities for
education and work unparalleled in previous generations. Northern states adopted public schooling
between 1790 and the 1820s, and within another
decade southern states began to provide "common
schools" for white children. The curriculum produced pupils who were able, by age twelve or fourteen, to read and to participate in marketplace calculations. Remarkably, girls usually received the
same basic education as boys. Literacy rates for
white females climbed dramatically, rivaling white
male rates for the first time.

The fact that taxpayers paid for children's education created an incentive to seek an inexpensive
teaching force. By the 1830s, northeastern school
districts had replaced male teachers with young females. Like mill workers, teachers were in their late
teens and regarded the work as temporary. Some
had acquired education in private girls' academies
that were springing up to meet the middle-class ambition for polished daughters. In the 1840s, several
states opened teacher training schools ("normal"
schools) for women students. With the exception of

Oberlin College in Ohio, no other colleges admitted women until after the Civil War, but a handful of private "female seminaries" established a rigorous curriculum that rivaled that of the best men's colleges. The three most prominent were the Troy Seminary in New York, founded by Emma Willard in 1821; the Hartford Seminary in Connecticut, founded by Catharine Beecher in 1822; and Mount Holyoke in Massachusetts, founded by Mary Lyon in 1837.

Male youths leaving the common school faced two paths. A small percentage continued at private boys' academies (numbering in the several hundreds nationwide), and a far smaller number matriculated at the country's two dozen colleges. More typically, boys left school at fourteen to apprentice to a specific trade or to seek business careers in entry-level clerkships, abundant in the growing urban centers. Young girls also headed for mill towns or for the cities in unprecedented numbers, seeking work in the expanding service sector as seamstresses and domestic servants.

Changes in patterns of youth employment and training meant that large numbers of youngsters in the 1830s and later escaped the watchful eyes of their families. Moralists fretted about the dangers of unsupervised youth, and, following the lead of the Lowell mill owners, some established apprentices' libraries and uplifting lecture series to keep young people honorably occupied. Advice books published by the hundreds instructed youth in the virtues of hard work and delayed gratification.

## Public Life, the Press, and Popular Amusements

Many new forms of inexpensive reading matter and public entertainments competed with the moralistic messages for youth. Innovations in printing technology as well as rising literacy rates created a brisk market in the 1830s for publications appealing to popular tastes: adventure and mystery pamphlets, dime novels, and penny press newspapers. In cities, theaters were nightly magnets for audiences in the thousands.

In the 1790s, fewer than ninety newspapers, each printing a few thousand copies per issue, provided the knowledge base of current events. By 1830, there were eight hundred papers, sixty-five of them urban dailies, and in the 1830s the most successful of these, the new penny press papers, gained

circulations of ten to twenty thousand copies daily. Six-cent papers covered politics, banking, and shipping news; the one-cent papers featured breezy political coverage, irreverent editorializing on current events, racetrack results, and crime reporting.

New York had three penny papers by 1835, and Philadelphia, Boston, and Baltimore each had one or two. Their influence extended throughout the

**MARY JANE PATTERSON, OBERLIN'S FIRST BLACK WOMAN GRADUATE**
*Mary Jane Patterson was the first black woman to earn a bachelor's degree in the United States. Oberlin College was founded in Ohio by evangelical and abolitionist activists in the 1830s; it admitted white and black men and women, although in the early years the black students were all male and the women students were all white. Patterson, the daughter of slaves, earned her degree in 1862. She taught school in Philadelphia and Washington for the next three decades, until her death in 1894.*
Oberlin College Archives, Oberlin, Ohio.

**LURID COVER OF A CRIME PAMPHLET, NEW YORK**

*Cheap and easy printing in the early nineteenth century gave rise to new genres of popular reading matter, including large pamphlet literature detailing horrific murder stories that invited readers to contemplate the nature of evil. This woodcut cover from 1836 promises to reveal the "interesting particulars" of the murder of Ellen Jewett, a New York City prostitute axed to death in her brothel bed. The pamphlet claims to constitute "an impressive warning" to youth about the tragedies of "dens of infamy." But the crude picture of the female corpse, with bare legs and breasts fully exposed, suggests that alternative, less moralistic readings of the same material were certainly possible for the purchasers.*

William L. Clements Library.

nation, facilitated by a regular system of newspaper exchange via the postal system. Town and village papers reprinted the snappy political editorials and sensationalized crime stories, putting very undeferential ideas into the heads of readers new to politics.

Newspapers were not the only new medium for spreading a shared American culture. Starting in the 1830s, traveling lecturers crisscrossed the country, bringing entertainment and instruction to small-town audiences. Speakers gave dramatic readings of plays or poetry or lectured on history, current events, popular science, or controversial topics like advanced female education.

Theater blossomed in the 1830s, providing Americans with their most common form of shared entertainment. An increase in the number and size of theaters along with a drop in ticket prices, put theatergoing within the reach of many ordinary Americans. The major cities each had a half dozen or more theaters, with as many as three thousand seats apiece. Audiences mostly comprised white men of all classes, but women and blacks attended as well, in smaller numbers and in segregated seating.

Shakespeare's plays were an all-round favorite. In 1835 in Philadelphia, no less than sixty-five separate Shakespeare productions were staged. Other English and American productions of tragedies, comedies, and melodramas rotated nightly. Before and after plays, theaters provided short acts featuring singers, dancers, and, increasingly, minstrelsy, a blackface musical comedy first performed in New York City in 1831. White performers with blackened faces parodied everything from romance to Shakespeare, trading on and reinforcing racist stereotypes about African Americans' speech, dress, and conduct.

The public culture of the theater demonstrates a fluidity of cultural styles in the 1830s. In the era of the "common man," ordinary men and women had a surprisingly well-honed acquaintance with Shakespeare. Not until the 1840s and beyond would a kind of market segmentation appear in public amusements, with some theaters targeting the cultural elite and others the working classes.

The popularity of theaters also exemplified a general cultural turn toward the celebration of brilliant public speech. In this golden age of oration, actors, lawyers, politicians, and ministers could hold crowds spellbound with their flawless elocution and elegant turns of phrase. Criminal trials, for example, were very short by modern standards, but the lawyers' closing arguments might consume many hours, with crowds of spectators hanging on every word. Senator Daniel Webster of Massachusetts was the acknowledged genius of political oration, putting grown men into raptures. Ministers with gifted tongues could in the space of hours transform crowds of skeptics into deeply moved believers.

## Democracy and Religion

An unprecedented revival of evangelical religion peaked in the early 1830s, after gathering three decades of momentum in states across the North and the upper South. Known as the Second Great Awakening, the outpouring of religious fervor changed the shape of American Protestantism. The heart of the evangelical message was that salvation was available to anyone willing to eradicate individual sin and accept faith in God's grace. Just as universal male suffrage allowed all white men to vote, democratized religion offered salvation to all who chose to embrace it.

Among the most serious adherents of evangelical Protestantism were men and women of the new mercantile classes whose self-discipline in pursuing market ambitions meshed well with the message of self-discipline in pursuit of spiritual perfection. Not content with individual perfection, many of these men and women sought to perfect society as well.

### The Second Great Awakening

The earliest manifestations of an unusual outbreak of fervent piety appeared in 1801 in Kentucky. A crowd estimated from ten to twenty thousand people camped out on a hillside at Cane Ridge for an evangelical revival meeting that lasted several weeks. By the 1810s and 1820s, camp meetings had spread to the Atlantic seaboard states, finding especially enthusiastic audiences in western New York and Pennsylvania.

The gatherings attracted women and men hungry for a more immediate access to spiritual peace, one not requiring years of soul-searching preparation. Ministers adopted an emotional style and invited an immediate experience of conversion and salvation. One eyewitness at a revival reported that "some of the people were singing, others praying, some crying for mercy in the most piteous accents.

. . . At one time I saw at least 500 swept down in a moment as if a battery of a thousand guns had been opened upon them, and then immediately followed shrieks and shouts that rent the very heavens."

From 1800 to 1820, church membership doubled in the United States, much of it among the evangelical groups. Methodists, Baptists, and Presbyterians formed the core of the new movement, while Episcopalians, Congregationalists, Unitarians, Dutch Reformed, Lutherans, and Catholics maintained strong skepticism about the emotional enthusiasm. Women more than men were attracted to the evangelical movement, and wives and mothers typically recruited husbands and sons to join them.

*Just as universal male suffrage allowed all white men to vote, democratized religion offered salvation to all who chose to embrace it.*

The leading exemplar of the Second Great Awakening was a lawyer-turned-minister named Charles Grandison Finney. Finney lived in western New York, where the completion of the Erie Canal in 1825 fundamentally altered the social and economic landscape overnight. Towns swelled with new inhabitants who brought in remarkable prosperity along with other, less admirable aspects of urban growth, such as prostitution, drinking, and gaming. Finney saw New York canal towns like Utica, Rome, and Buffalo as ripe for evangelical awakening. In Rochester, New York, he sustained a six-month revival through the long winter of 1830–31, generating thousands of new converts.

The message that Finney preached was directed primarily at women and men of the business classes, and, true to his training, Finney couched his message in legal metaphors. "The world is divided into two great political parties," he announced in a sermon—the party of Satan and the party of Jehovah. "Ministers should labor with sinners, as a lawyer does with a jury . . . ; and the sinner should weigh his arguments, and make up his mind as upon oath and for his life, and give a verdict upon the spot." Finney urged his listeners to take control of their own salvation, arguing that a reign of Christian perfection loomed. The promise of perfection required a public-spirited outreach to the less than perfect to foster their salvation. Christian benevolence, or do-good action, was demanded of all believers. Evangelicals promoted Sunday schools to

THE BROADWAY TABERNACLE.

**CHARLES G. FINNEY'S BROADWAY TABERNACLE**
*The Reverend Charles G. Finney took his evangelical movement to New York City in the early
1830s, operating out of existing Presbyterian churches. In 1836, the Broadway Tabernacle was
built for his pastorate. In its use of space the Tabernacle resembled a theater more than a traditional church, but in one respect it departed radically from one very theaterlike tradition of
churches — the custom of charging pew rents. In effect, most churches required worshipers to
purchase their seats. In contrast, Finney insisted that all seats in his house were free, unreserved,
and open to all.*
Oberlin College Archives, Oberlin, Ohio.

bring piety to children; they battled to end mail delivery, stop public transport, and close shops on
Sundays to honor the Sabbath. Many women
formed missionary societies, which printed and distributed millions of Bibles and religious tracts. Maternal associations sprang up to promote a new style
of moral mothering. Through such avenues, evangelical religion offered women expanded spheres of
influence.

By 1832, Finney had moved to New York City
and adopted tactics of Jacksonian-era politicians to
sell his cause: publicity, argumentation, rallies, and
dramatic speeches. His object, he said, was to get
Americans to "vote in the Lord Jesus Christ as the
governor of the Universe."

## The Temperance Movement and the Campaign for Moral Reform

The evangelical disposition—a combination of
righteousness, energy, self-discipline, and faith—
animated vigorous campaigns to eliminate alcohol

abuse and eradicate sexual sins. Millions of Americans took the temperance pledge to abstain from strong drink, and hundreds became involved in efforts to end prostitution.

Alcohol consumption had steadily risen in the decades up to 1830, when historians estimate the per capita annual consumption of alcohol for people over age thirteen amounted to an astonishing 9.5 gallons of hard liquor plus 30.3 gallons of hard cider, beer, and wine. To a degree, consumption of bottled, fermented drinks made a certain amount of sense, in view of unsafe urban water sources and the lack of reliable refrigeration. However, alcohol abuse was on the rise.

And all classes imbibed. Leisure-time drinking flourished in urban streets in saloons, barbershops, and groceries selling liquor by the glass. A lively saloon culture fostered masculine camaraderie among laborers along with extensive alcohol consumption and a new style of binge drinking that alarmed older proponents of moderate drinking. In elite homes, the after-dinner whiskey or sherry was commonplace. Colleges before 1820 routinely served students a pint of ale with meals, and the army and navy included rum in the standard daily ration.

Organized opposition to drinking first surfaced in the 1810s among health reformers in New England. In 1826, Lyman Beecher, a Connecticut minister of an "awakened" church, founded the American Temperance Society, which condemned drinking as a moral vice leading to poverty, idleness, crime, and family violence. Adopting the methods of evangelical ministers, temperance lecturers traveled the country expounding the damage of drink; by 1833, some six thousand local affiliates of the American Temperance Society boasted more than a million members. Middle-class drinking began a steep decline. One powerful tool of persuasion was the temperance pledge, which many manufacturers and business owners began to require of employees.

In 1836, the temperance leaders regrouped into a new society, the American Temperance Union, which demanded total abstinence of its adherents; even sacramental wine was condemned. The intensified war against alcohol moved beyond individual moral suasion into the realm of politics, as reformers sought to deny taverns liquor licenses and to wipe out the dram shops selling liquor by the glass. By 1845, temperance advocates had put an impressive dent in alcohol consumption, which had diminished to one-quarter of the per capita con-

sumption of 1830. In 1851, Maine became the first state to ban entirely the sale or manufacture of all alcoholic beverages.

More controversial than evangelical temperance was a social movement called "moral reform," which first aimed at public morals in general but quickly narrowed to a campaign to eradicate sexual sin, especially prostitution. In 1833, a group of Finneyite women started the New York Female Moral Reform Society. Its members insisted that male sexual expression, which they considered the ultimate in lack of self-control, posed a serious threat to society in general and to women in particular.

The women reformers published a newspaper, *The Advocate of Moral Reform,* that quickly established a national circulation. It was the first major woman-edited, woman-written, and woman-typeset paper in the country. Columns were devoted to first-person tales of woe and to advice about curbing sexual sin. The reformers condemned clerks who visited brothels and traveling businessmen who befriended and then allegedly seduced girls away from home. Within five years, more than four thousand auxiliary groups had sprung up, mostly in New England, New York, Pennsylvania, and Ohio, all areas where evangelical religion was strong. Not content merely to publicize sin, the New York group engaged in direct action, stationing women outside brothels to intimidate the patrons. They urged chaste women to sign pledges, like the pledges of the temperance movement, promising to accept only virtuous men in courtship.

The Female Moral Reform Society drew on the evangelicals' familiar themes of self-control and suppression of sin. But in its analysis of the causes of licentiousness and its conviction that women had a duty to speak out about unspeakable things, it pushed the limits of what even the men in the evangelical movement could tolerate. Yet the moral reformers did not regard themselves as radicals of any kind. They were simply pursuing the logic of a gender system that defined home protection and morality as their special sphere and a religious conviction that called for the eradication of sin.

## Organizing against Slavery

Even more radical than moral reform was the evangelicals' effort to eradicate the sin of slavery in the 1830s. The abolition movement was also far more radical than the only previous antislavery organization, the American Colonization Society. A group of Maryland and Virginia planters in 1817 had promoted gradual emancipation by individual owners followed by colonization of African Americans in Africa, and by the early 1820s several thousand ex-slaves had been transported to Liberia on the West African coast. But not surprisingly, newly freed men and women were often not eager to move to Liberia; their African roots were three or more generations in the past. Emigration to Africa proved to be so gradual (and expensive) as to have a negligible impact on American slavery.

A more insistent attention to the evils of slavery emerged in 1831, spurred by the perfectionist impulse of the Second Great Awakening. Charles Finney's religious campaigns in Rochester and New York City identified slavery as a major obstacle to America's progress toward perfection. Both of those cities quickly became centers of antislavery agitation.

In Boston, an antislavery movement developed around William Lloyd Garrison, who started publishing a weekly newspaper called the *Liberator* in 1831. Garrison, then twenty-six, launched a drive for immediate abolition, promising that his paper would be "as harsh as truth, and as uncompromising as justice. On this subject, I do not wish to think, or speak, or write, with moderation. No! No! Tell a man whose house is on fire to give a moderate alarm; tell him to moderately rescue his wife from the hands of the ravisher; tell the mother to gradually extricate her babe from the fire into which it has fallen;—but urge me not to use moderation in a cause like the present." No gradualist plan could ever be acceptable to Garrison.

Garrison's visibility in Boston built on several years of growing local antislavery sentiment. In 1829, a black printer named David Walker published *An Appeal to the Colored Citizens of the World,* which condemned racism, invoked the egalitarian language of the Declaration of Independence, and hinted at racial violence if whites did not change their prejudiced ways. Walker's fervent *Appeal* electrified Garrison, pushing him into a more radical stance on slavery. It electrified the South as well, and several southern states prohibited the circulation of both Walker's *Appeal* and the *Liberator.*

In 1831, a young black woman, Maria Stewart, began a series of public lectures for black audiences in Boston on slavery and racial prejudice. While her arguments against slavery were welcomed, her voice—that of a woman—created problems. Few American-born women had yet engaged in public speaking beyond ceremonial or theatrical performance; Stewart was breaking a social taboo.

Boston's elite black men in the audience discouraged her career, and she retired from the platform in 1833. Garrison published her lectures, giving them wider circulation.

In 1832 and 1833, the antislavery movement got organized. The New England Anti-Slavery Society coalesced in 1832 around Garrison, and New York and Philadelphia Anti-Slavery Societies became active in 1833. The print media were fully enlisted with a dozen antislavery newspapers as well as pamphlets and books in circulation. Effective antislavery speakers embarked on lecture tours and inspired the formation of new societies. By 1837, thirteen hundred local antislavery societies had sprung up all over the North with a membership totaling a quarter of a million men and women. This was a significant number but by no means a large one in relation to the North's population.

---

*By 1837, thirteen hundred local antislavery societies had sprung up all over the North, with a membership totaling a quarter of a million men and women.*

---

Many northerners were not prepared to embrace the abolitionist call for emancipation, immediate or gradual. They might oppose slavery as a blot on the country's ideals or as a rival to the free-labor system of the North, but at the same time most white northerners remained antiblack and therefore antiabolition. From 1834 to 1838, there were more than a hundred eruptions of serious mob violence against abolitionists or free blacks. On one occasion, antislavery headquarters in Philadelphia and a black church and orphanage were burned to the ground, and in another incident, Illinois abolitionist editor Elijah Lovejoy was killed by a rioting crowd that tried to destroy his printing press.

Women played a prominent role in abolition, just as they did in moral reform and evangelical religion. They formed women's auxiliaries and engaged in fundraising to support agents in the field and the expenses of pamphlet publication. In the political realm, women circulated antislavery petitions, which they presented to the U.S. Congress with tens of thousands of signatures.

Garrison particularly welcomed women's activity. When a southern plantation daughter named Angelina Grimké wrote him about her personal repugnance for slavery, Garrison published the letter

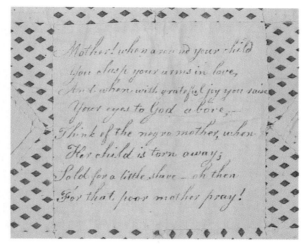

**ABOLITIONIST CRIB QUILT**
*This crib quilt (left) was sewn by women of the Boston Female Anti-Slavery Society in 1836.*
*Many abolitionist women produced handcrafted items for sale at antislavery fairs to raise money*
*to support antislavery activity. The central square of this quilt (detail) reminds mothers hugging*
*their own free babies to "Think of the negro mother, when / Her child is torn away; / Sold for a*
*little slave — oh then / For that poor mother pray!"*
Courtesy of Society for Preservation of New England Antiquities/photo by David Bohl.

in the *Liberator* and brought her overnight fame. Grimké and her older sister Sarah, now living in Philadelphia, quickly became lecturers for the anti-slavery movement and started a speaking tour to women's groups in Massachusetts in 1837. Grimké's powerful eyewitness speeches attracted men as well, causing the Congregational church leadership of Massachusetts to issue a warning to all its ministers not to let the Grimké sisters use their pulpits. As with Maria Stewart, the Grimkés had violated a gender norm by presuming to instruct men.

In the late 1830s, the cause of abolition divided the nation as no other issue did. Even among the abolitionists significant divisions emerged. The Grimké sisters, radicalized by the public reaction to their speaking tour, began to write and speak about women's rights. They were opposed by moderate abolitionists who were unwilling to mix a new and controversial issue about women with their first cause, the rights of blacks. A few radical men, like Garrison, embraced women's rights fully, working to get women leadership positions in the national antislavery group. Out of the New England antislavery movement came the first organized women's rights movement in U.S. history, in the 1840s.

The many men and women active in reform movements in the 1830s found their initial inspiration in evangelical Protestantism's dual message: Salvation was open to all and society needed to be perfected. Their activist mentality squared well with the interventionist tendencies of the party forming in opposition to Andrew Jackson's Democrats. On the whole, reformers gravitated to the Whig Party.

## Jackson Defines the Democratic Party

In his eight years in office, Jackson worked to implement his vision of a politics of opportunity for all white men. He also greatly enhanced the power of the presidency. He favored rapid western land settlement, which led to conflict with Indian tribes. He had a dramatic confrontation with John C. Calhoun and South Carolina when that state tried to nullify the tariff of 1828. Disapproving of all government-granted privilege, Jackson challenged what he called the "monster" Bank of the United States and took it down to defeat. Jackson's legacy

**CHEROKEE PHOENIX**

*Around 1820, Sequoyah, about forty-five years old and nephew of a Cherokee chief, invented written symbols to convey the Cherokee language. Each symbol represented a syllable of sound. In 1828, the Cherokee in New Echota, Georgia, ordered custom-made type embodying the new symbols and began printing a newspaper, the* Cherokee Phoenix, *the first newspaper published by Native Americans, printed in both English and Cherokee.*

Special Collections Division, Georgetown University Library, Washington, D.C.

to his successor, Martin Van Buren, was a Democratic Party strong enough to withstand the passing of the powerful old man.

## Indian Policy and the Trail of Tears

Improved transportation after 1815 greatly accelerated the westward flow of white settlers, and states containing Indian tribes rapidly joined the Union. But fundamental questions remained unresolved: What was the legal status of the quarter of a million Indians now resident in the United States? Were they subject to state and federal law?

From the 1790s to the 1820s, the federal government negotiated treaties with tribes on the assumption that the tribes were foreign nations. The

Indians, though within state borders, asserted their sovereignty and communal rights to their land. Treaty making, however, proved a precarious practice. American negotiators found it hard to strike terms that whole tribes would accept, and all too often a few Indians with no legitimacy to speak for their tribes signed treaties ceding vast acreage.

As an army general, Andrew Jackson had negotiated many such treaties, but he privately thought it was "absurd" to call the Indians foreigners. In his view, they were now subjects of the United States, entitled perhaps to keep their improved land but not their large hunting grounds. When he became president in 1829, Jackson moved to implement his idea.

Others in the period from 1790 to the 1820s proposed assimilation as a more peaceable solution. Various missionary associations tried to "civilize" native peoples by converting them to Christianity. In 1819, Congress authorized $10,000 a year for interdenominational missions to instruct Indians in religion, reading and writing, and agricultural practices. Missionaries also tried to get Indians to adopt white gender customs, but Indian women were reluctant to adopt practices that accorded them less power than their tribal system did. The general failure of assimilation moved Jackson to a more drastic policy.

In his first message to Congress in 1829, Jackson declared that Indians within the United States borders could not remain independent and in sovereign control of tribal lands. Congress agreed and passed the Removal Act of 1830, appropriating $500,000 to relocate tribes west of the Mississippi River (Map 11.2).

For northern tribes, their numbers greatly diminished by years of war, gradual removal was well under way. But not all the Indians went quietly. In 1832 in western Illinois, Black Hawk, a leader of the Sac and Fox Indians, resisted removal. Federal troops attacked and chased the Indians into southern Wisconsin, where, after several skirmishes and battles, Black Hawk was captured and many of his two thousand people massacred.

Southern tribes proved to be even more resistant to removal. The powerful Creek, Chickasaw, Choctaw, and Cherokee, whose lands encompassed parts of North Carolina, Tennessee, and northern Georgia, Alabama, and Mississippi, at first refused to relocate. But their land attracted cotton-hungry white settlers, and a rumor of gold on Cherokee land in Georgia in 1829 only intensified the pressure.

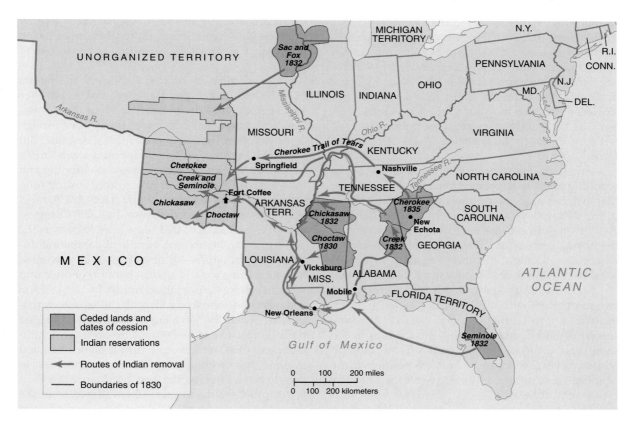

**M A P  11.2**
*Indian Removal and the Trail of Tears*
*The federal government under President Andrew Jackson pursued a vigorous policy of Indian removal in the 1830s. Southern tribes were forcibly moved west to land known as the Indian Territory (in present-day Oklahoma). As many as a quarter of the Cherokee Indians died in 1838 on their route, known as the Trail of Tears.*

Ironically, the seventeen thousand members of the Cherokee tribe had "assimilated" most successfully, spurred by dedicated missionaries living with them. Starting in 1808, they had adopted written laws, culminating in 1827 in a constitution with a bicameral legislature, an executive office, and a court system modeled on that of the United States. More than two hundred of the wealthiest Cherokee had intermarried with whites and had adopted white styles of housing, dress, and cotton agriculture, including the ownership of more than a thousand African American slaves. They had developed a written alphabet and published a newspaper as well as Christian prayerbooks in their language.

In 1831, after Georgia announced it would subject the Indians to state law, the Cherokee responded by suing Georgia before the U.S. Supreme Court. Chief Justice John Marshall set aside the suit on technicalities but encouraged the Cherokee to seek further legal redress. When Georgia jailed two missionaries under an 1830 law forbidding missionary aid to Indians without state permission, the Cherokee brought suit again. In the 1832 case, *Worcester v. Georgia*, the Supreme Court found for the missionaries and also recognized the Cherokees' existence as "a distinct community, occupying its own territory, in which the laws of Georgia can have no force."

An angry President Jackson announced that he would ignore the Supreme Court's decision. "John Marshall has made his opinion, now let him enforce it," he declared, proceeding to enforce the Removal Act. "If they [the Cherokee] now refuse to accept the liberal terms offered, they can only be liable for whatever evils and difficulties may arise. I feel conscious of having done my duty to my red children."

Still, the Cherokee remained in Georgia for two more years without significant violence. Then, in 1835, a small, unauthorized part of the tribe signed a treaty ceding all the tribal lands to the state, and Georgia rapidly sold off the land to whites. Several thousand Cherokee petitioned the U.S. Congress to ignore the bogus treaty, but their pleas went unheard.

The disputed treaty relinquished a large piece of northern Georgia in exchange for $5 million and equal acreage west of Arkansas, in present-day Oklahoma. But most of the Cherokee refused to move, and in May 1838, the deadline for voluntary evacuation, federal troops arrived to deport them. Under armed guard, the Cherokee embarked on a twelve-hundred-mile journey that came to be called the Trail of Tears. A newspaperman in Kentucky described the forced march: "Even aged females, apparently, nearly ready to drop into the grave, were traveling with heavy burdens attached to the back. . . . they buried fourteen to fifteen at every stopping place." Nearly a quarter of the Cherokee died en route, from hardship and starvation. They joined fifteen thousand Creek, twelve thousand Choctaw, and five thousand Chickasaw Indians also forcibly relocated to what is now Oklahoma.

## The Tariff of Abominations and Nullification

Jackson's Indian policy happened to harmonize with the principle of states' rights: The president supported Georgia's right to ignore the Supreme Court decision in *Worcester v. Georgia*. But in another pressing question of states' rights, Jackson trounced on South Carolina's claim to ignore federal tariff policy.

Federal tariffs as high as 33 percent on imports like textiles and iron goods had been passed in 1816 and again in 1824, in an effort to favor new American manufactures and shelter them from foreign competition as well as to raise federal revenue. But some southern congressmen opposed steep tariffs, fearing they would decrease overseas shipping and hurt the South's export of raw cotton. During John Quincy Adams's administration (1825–1829), tariff policy generated heated debate. In 1828, Congress passed a revised tariff that came to be known as the Tariff of Abominations. A bundle of conflicting duties, the set of tariffs—some as high as 50 percent—had something for *and* against every economic and sectional interest. Assembled mostly by pro-Jackson congressmen, who loaded it with duties on raw materials needed by New England, it also contained protectionist elements favored by northern manufacturers. One wealthy cotton mill owner laughed that the tariff would "keep the South and West in debt to New England the next hundred years."

South Carolina in particular suffered from the Tariff of Abominations. Worldwide prices for cotton were already in sharp decline in the late 1820s and early 1830s, and the further depression of shipping caused by the high tariffs hurt the South's export market. In 1828, a group of South Carolina politicians headed by John C. Calhoun drew up a statement outlining a doctrine of nullification. The Union, they argued, was a confederation of states that had yielded some but not all power to the federal government. When Congress overstepped its powers, states had the right to nullify its acts; as precedents they pointed to the Virginia and Kentucky Resolutions of 1798, which had attempted to invalidate the Alien and Sedition Acts (see Chapter 9). Congress had erred in using tariff policy as an instrument to benefit specific industries, the South Carolinians claimed; tariffs should be used only to raise revenue.

On assuming the presidency in 1829, Jackson ignored the South Carolina statement of nullification and proceeded to shut out Calhoun, his new vice president, from influence or power. Tariff revisions in early 1832 brought little relief to the South. Sensing futility, Calhoun resigned from the vice presidency in 1832 and accepted election by the South Carolina legislature to a seat in the U.S. Senate, where he could better protect his state's anti-tariff stance. Strained to their limit, the South Carolina leaders took the radical step of declaring the federal tariffs to be null and void in their state as of February 1, 1833.

Finally, the constitutional crisis was out in the open. Opting for a dramatic confrontation, Jackson sent armed ships to Charleston's harbor and threatened to invade the state. He pushed through Congress a bill, called the Force Bill, defining the Carolina stance as treason and authorizing military action to collect federal tariffs.

At the same time, Congress moved quickly to pass a revised tariff more acceptable to the South. The astute Senator Henry Clay rallied support for a moderate bill that gradually lowered tariffs by half, back to the level prevailing in 1816. Both the new tariff and the Force Bill were passed by Congress on March 1, 1833. South Carolina responded by withdrawing its nullification of the old tariff—and then nullifying the Force Bill. It was a symbolic gesture, since Jackson's show of muscle was no longer necessary. Both sides took a measure of satisfaction in the immediate outcome. Federal power had prevailed over a dangerous assertion of states' rights; and South Carolina got the lower tariff it wanted.

Yet the question of federal power versus states' rights was far from settled. The implied threat behind nullification was secession, a position articulated in 1832 by some South Carolinians whose concerns went beyond tariff policy. The growing voice of antislavery activism in the North threatened the South's economic system. If and when a

northern-dominated federal government decided to end slavery, the South Carolinians thought, the South must have the right to remove itself from the Union.

## The Bank War and the Panic of 1837

Along with the tariff and nullification, President Jackson had another political battle on his hands over the Bank of the United States. After riding out the panic of 1819, the bank had prospered under the leadership of Philadelphian Nicholas Biddle. It handled the federal government's deposits, extended credit and loans, and issued banknotes—by 1830 the most secure and steady circulating currency in the country. With twenty-nine branches, it spread its stabilizing benefits to the whole nation. Jackson, however, did not find the bank's temperate functions sufficiently valuable to offset his criticism of the concept of a national bank. In his first and second messages to Congress, in 1829 and 1830, Jackson claimed that the bank concentrated undue economic power in the hands of a few. His Democratic allies privately hoped he would be content with antibank rhetoric, without taking concrete action.

National Republican Senators Daniel Webster and Henry Clay decided to force the issue. They convinced Biddle to apply for renewal of the bank's federal charter in 1832, well before the fall election, even though the bank's twenty-year charter ran until 1836. They fully expected that Congress's renewal would force Jackson to follow through on his rhetoric with a veto. The unpopular veto would then cause Jackson to lose the election, while the bank would survive on an override vote from a new Congress swept into power in the anti-Jackson tide.

At first the plan seemed to work. Biddle applied for recharter, Congress voted to renew, and Jackson, angry over being manipulated, issued his veto. But it was a brilliantly written veto, full of fierce language about privileges of the moneyed elite who oppress the liberties of the democratic masses in order to concentrate wealth in their own hands. Jackson had translated the bank controversy into a language of class antagonism and egalitarian ideals that strongly resonated with many Americans. Old Hickory won the election easily over his Republican opponent, Henry Clay, gaining 55 percent of the popular vote and a lopsided electoral college vote

**FISTFIGHT BETWEEN OLD HICKORY AND BULLY NICK**
*This 1834 cartoon represents President Andrew Jackson squaring off to fight Nicholas Biddle, the director of the Bank of the United States. Pugilism as a semiprofessional sport gained great popularity in the 1830s; the joke here is that the aged Jackson and the aristocratic Biddle would strip to such revealing tight pants and engage in open combat. To Biddle's left are his seconds, Daniel Webster and Henry Clay; behind the president is his vice president, Martin Van Buren. Whiskey and port lubricate the action.*
The Library Company of Philadelphia.

of 219 to 49. The Jackson party still controlled Congress, so no override was possible. The bank's fate was sealed; it would cease to exist after 1836.

But Jackson took his reelection as a mandate to destroy the bank sooner. Calling the bank a "monster," he ordered the secretary of the treasury to remove the federal deposits from Biddle's vaults, ignoring the opposition of nearly his entire cabinet. The money was redeposited into "pet banks," Democratic-leaning institutions throughout the country; because of the high tariffs and high-volume sales of public lands, this government nest egg was quite sizable. In retaliation, Biddle raised interest rates and called in loans, claiming the bank's dangerously low deposits forced him to do so. This action caused a minor recession in 1833 and actually enhanced Jackson's claim that the bank was too powerful for the good of the country.

Unleashed and unregulated, the economy went into high gear, to Jackson's dismay. Perhaps only a small part of the problem arose from irresponsible banking practices; just at this moment, an excess of silver from Mexican mines had made its way into American banks, giving bankers license to print ever more banknotes. Inflation soared from 1834 to 1837; prices of basic goods rose more than 50 percent. Southern planters bought land and slaves fast, paying as much as 30 percent interest on bank loans

for their purchases. Many hundreds of new private banks were quickly chartered by the states, each bank issuing its own banknotes and setting interest rates as high as the market would bear. Entrepreneurs borrowed and invested money, much of it funneled into privately financed railroads and canals.

The market in western land sales heated up. In 1834, about 4.5 million acres of the public domain had been sold, the highest annual volume since the peak year 1819, and by 1836 the total reached an astonishing 20 million acres. What was most disturbing to the Jackson administration was that the purchasers were overwhelmingly eastern capitalists, not individual yeoman farmers who intended to settle on the land.

In one respect, the economy attained an admirable goal: The national debt disappeared, and, for the first and only time in American history, from 1835 to 1837 the government had a surplus of money. But much of it consisted of questionable bank currencies—"bloated, diseased" currencies, in Jackson's vivid terminology.

Jackson decided to restrain the economy. In 1836, the Treasury Department issued the Specie Circular, an order that public land could be purchased only with hard money, federally coined gold and silver. In response, bankers started to reduce their loans, fearing a general contraction of the economy. Compounding the difficulty, the Bank of England also now insisted on hard-money payments for American loans, which had grown large in the years since 1831 because of a trade imbalance. Some short-run failures in various crop markets, a downturn in the price of cotton on the international market, and the silver glut, all unrelated to Jackson's fiscal policies, fed the growing economic crisis.

The familiar events of the panic of 1819 unfolded again, with terrifying rapidity. In April 1837, a wave of bank and business failures ensued, and the credit market tumbled like a house of cards. (See Texts in Historical Context on page 282.) The Specie Circular was only one precipitating cause, but the Whig Party held it and Jackson responsible for the depression. For more than five years after the panic of 1837, the United States suffered from economic hard times.

## Van Buren's One-Term Presidency

The election of 1836, which preceded the panic by six months, demonstrated the transformation of the Democrats from coalition to party. The personality of Jackson had stamped the elections of 1824, 1828, and 1832, but now the party apparatus was sufficiently developed to support itself. Local and state committees existed throughout the country. Democratic candidates ran in every state election, succeeding even in old Federalist states like Maine and New Hampshire. More than four hundred newspapers declared themselves Democratic. In 1836, the Democrats repeated an innovation begun in 1832, holding a national convention that nominated Vice President Martin Van Buren of New York for president, balanced by running mate Richard M. Johnson, a slave owner from Kentucky.

Van Buren was a backroom politician, not a popular public figure, and the Whigs hoped that he might be defeatable. In many states, Whigs had captured high office in 1834, shedding the awkward National Republican label and developing statewide organizations to rival those of the Democrats. However, no figure at the national level could command support in all regions; Massachusetts Senator Daniel Webster, for example, had no following in the South, a heavily pro-Jackson region. The result was that three candidates opposed Van Buren in 1836, each with a solid popular regional base. Webster could deliver New England; Tennessee Senator Hugh Lawson White attracted

proslavery, pro-Jackson, but anti–Van Buren voters in the South; and the aging General William Henry Harrison of Indiana, memorable for his Indian war heroics in 1811, pulled in the western, anti-Indian vote. Not one of the three candidates could have won the presidency, but together they came close to denying Van Buren a majority vote. Their combined strength pulled many Whigs into office at the state level and laid the groundwork for an alternative to the Democrats in the South, an area that had been solidly pro-Jackson until 1836. In the end, Van Buren had 170 electoral votes, while the other three received a total of 113.

Van Buren took office in March 1837, and a month later the panic hit. The new president called a special session of Congress to consider creating an independent treasury system to fulfill some of the functions of the defunct Bank of the United States. Such a system, funded by the government's deposits, would deal only in hard money, and gold and silver would flow out of commercial banks, with restrictions on their issuance of paper currency. Equally important, the new system would not make loans and would thus avoid the danger of speculative meddling in the economy. In short, an independent treasury system could exert a powerful moderating influence on inflation and the credit market without itself being directly involved in the market. But Van Buren encountered strong resistance in Congress, even from Democrats. The treasury system finally won approval in 1840, but by then Van Buren's chances of a second term in office were virtually nil.

In 1840, the Whigs settled on William Henry Harrison, aged sixty-seven, as their single candidate to oppose Van Buren. The campaign drew on voter involvement as no other presidential campaign ever had. The Whigs took tricks out of the Democrats' book: Harrison was touted as a common man, born in a log cabin, although a Virginia plantation was the real site. His Indian-fighting days, now thirty years behind him, were played up to give him an aura like that of Jackson. Whigs staged festive rallies all over the country, drumming up mass appeal with candlelight parades and song shows. Women participated in campaign rallies as never before. Some 78 percent of eligible voters cast ballots—the highest percentage ever in American history. Even so, the campaign was not really close. Harrison took 53 percent of the popular vote and won a resounding 234 electoral college votes, to Van Buren's 60. A Democratic editor lamented, "We have taught them how to conquer us!"

# The Panic of 1837

*The panic of 1837 brought fright and hysteria to city after city. Crowds of hundreds thronged the banks during the spring to remove their money. Business came to a standstill and many merchants appeared to be ruined overnight. Whig leaders were certain that the crisis could be traced to President Jackson's antibank and hard-money policies, but others blamed it on what they saw as an immoral frenzy of greed and speculation that had gripped the nation in the preceding few years.*

*Harriet Martineau traveled throughout the United States and described booming land sales in the infant city of Chicago in 1836.*

### DOCUMENT 1. An English Visitor Describes the "Mania" for Speculation

I never saw a busier place than Chicago was at the time of our arrival. The streets were crowded with land speculators, hurrying from one sale to another. A negro, dressed up in scarlet, bearing a scarlet flag, and riding a white horse with housings of scarlet, announced the times of sale. At every street-corner where he stopped, the crowd flocked round him; and it seemed as if some prevalent mania infected the whole people. The rage for speculation might fairly be so regarded. As the gentlemen of our party walked the streets, store-keepers hailed them from their doors, with offers of farms, and all manner of land-lots, advising them to speculate before the price of land rose higher. A young lawyer of my acquaintance there, had realised five hundred dollars per day, the five preceding days, by merely making out titles to land. . . . Of course, this rapid money-making is a merely temporary evil. A bursting of the bubble must come soon. The absurdity of the speculation is so striking, that the wonder is that the fever should have attained such a height as I witnessed. The immediate occasion of the bustle which prevailed, the week we were at Chicago, was the sale of lots . . . along the course of a projected canal. . . . Persons not intending to game, and not infected with mania, would endeavour to form some reasonable conjecture as to the ultimate value of the lots, by calculating the cost of the canal, the risks from accident, from the possible competition from other places, &c., and finally, the possible profits, under the most favourable circumstances, within so many years' purchase. Such a calculation would serve as some sort of guide as to the amount of purchase-money to be risked. Whereas, wild land on the banks of a canal, not yet even marked out, was selling at Chicago for more than rich land, well improved, in the finest part of the valley of the Mohawk, on the banks of a canal [the Erie] which is already the medium of an almost inestimable amount of traffic. If sharpers and gamblers were to be the sufferers by the impending crash at Chicago, no one would feel much concerned: but they, unfortunately, are the people who encourage the delusion, in order to profit by it. Many a high-spirited, but inexperienced, young man; many a simple settler, will be ruined for the advantage of knaves.

*Philip Hone, a wealthy New York Whig, had an early taste of the crash to come when his son's business failed in March, on the last day of President Jackson's term.*

### DOCUMENT 2. The Diary of Philip Hone, 1837

Saturday, March 4.—This is the end of Gen. Jackson's administration—the most disastrous in the annals of the country. . . .

This is a dark and melancholy day in the annals of my family. Brown & Hone stopped payment to-day, and called a meeting of their creditors. My eldest son has lost the capital I gave him, and I am implicated as endorser for them to a fearful amount. The pressure of the times, the immense amount they have paid of extra interest, and the almost total failure of remittances have been the causes of their ruin. . . .

Friday, March 17.—The great crisis is near at hand, if it has not already arrived. The banking house of I. and L. Joseph . . . stopped payment to-day, and occasioned great consternation in Wall Street, for their business has been enormous. . . . The immediate cause of this disaster was the intelligence received from New Orleans by this day's mail of the stoppage of the House of Hermann & Co. and others connected with them, for whom the Josephs are under acceptances to the amount of two millions of dollars. This is another evidence of the reckless manner in which business has been conducted, or rather, to speak more charitably, of the straits to which men have been driven by the wicked interference of the government with the currency of the country. . . .

Wednesday, May 10.— . . . The volcano has burst and overwhelmed New York; the glory of her merchants is departed. After a day of unexampled excitement, and a ruthless run upon all the banks, which drew from their vaults $600,000 in specie yesterday, nearly as much having been drawn on Monday, the officers held a meeting last evening and resolved to *suspend specie payments*. . . .

Thursday, May 11.—A dead calm has succeeded the stormy weather of Wall Street and the other places of active business. All is still as death. No business is transacted, no bargains made, no negotiations entered into; men's spirits are better because the danger of universal ruin is thought to be less imminent. A slight ray of hope is to be seen in countenances where despair only dwelt for the last fortnight, but all is wrapped up in uncertainty. Nobody can foretell the course matters will take. The fever is broken, but the patient lies in a sort of syncope, exhausted by the violence of the disease and the severity of the remedies.

*T*he July 1837 issue of the Christian Examiner, *a Boston monthly, counseled that some good would come from the catastrophe.*

## DOCUMENT 3. A Religious View of "Existing Commercial Embarrassments"

There will be then much individual improvement of character. . . . One of the first and most valuable . . . will be a check upon that extravagant estimate and overstrained pursuit of wealth, which are marked features in the character of the nation and the times. That such a check was needed and will be a blessing to the social and moral condition of the community, cannot be doubted. We were get-

ting to be almost insane upon the subject of wealth. The lust of accumulation has ever been the root of much evil among men, but in this country several causes have naturally operated to give a strong impulse to this passion. Our political organization is that which offers the widest scope to enterprise, and applies the strongest stimulus to ambition and exertion, while, at the same time, it produces a state of society in which wealth is necessarily the principal distinction, the surest and readiest of attainment, and therefore the first and most eagerly sought. . . . A new country like ours, of almost unbounded extent, rich beyond comparison in resources, . . . naturally awakens in its inhabitants earnest and insatiable desires. . . .

. . . Great benefits have . . . flowed from . . . enterprise. . . . Towns have been built and cities reared, mountains levelled, and valleys filled, and distant places brought near, and the wide wilderness of nature changed to a garden of human civilization, comfort, and luxury. . . .

But the moral influence of these causes has not all been good. They were making us proud, presumptuous, extravagant, luxurious, visionary. We were getting to think that there was no end to the wealth, and could be no check to the progress of our country; that economy was not needed, that prudence was weakness, that moderation was a sinful neglect of the golden chances by which many were winning fortunes. The tardy gains of honorable enterprise were spurned, that the lucky speculation of an hour might bestow a fortune. We needed a check, a restraint, a rebuke. Many felt that it was needed and foresaw that it must come, and he who ruleth over the nations has at length sent it. As in other general calamities, the evil in many individual cases falls on those who may not themselves have been guilty, but the benefit will be reaped by all. The fever which has raged in society will abate.

**Document 1.** Harriet Martineau, *Society in America* (London, 1837), 350–52, reprinted in David Brion Davis, *Antebellum American Culture: An Interpretive Anthology* (Lexington, Mass.: D. C. Heath, 1979), 121–22.

**Document 2.** Allan Nevins, ed., *The Diary of Philip Hone, 1828–1851* (New York: Dodd Mead, 1936), 244, 248–49, 257, 259.

**Document 3.** "Existing Commercial Embarrassments," *Christian Examiner and General Review* 22, 3rd ser., vol. 4 (1837): 395–96.

## Conclusion: Democrats and Whigs

From 1828 to 1840, the Democrats put together an unlikely, tenuous, but ultimately workable coalition of rural western farmers, urban laborers, pro-state bank commercial men, and wealthy southern slave owners. These groups embraced personal liberty, free competition, and egalitarian opportunity open to all white men, all values perfectly symbolized by Andrew Jackson. Jacksonian Democrats accepted drinking and tolerated Sabbath violations, preferring not to legislate morality. And they avoided debating the wisdom of slavery at all costs.

In contrast, the Whigs were the party of activist moralism and state-sponsored entrepreneurship. Wealthy merchants from Boston to Savannah who appreciated a national bank and protective tariffs tended to be Whigs, as did the evangelical middle classes. Personal liberty was a fine thing, Whigs thought, but it had to be tempered by self-discipline and backed by government controls over moral issues.

National politics in the 1830s were more heated and divisive than at any other time since the 1790s.

The party system of Democrats versus Whigs cut far deeper into the electorate than had the system of Federalists and Republicans. Innovations in transportation and communication disseminated political information from the city to the backwoods, politicizing voters who were now part of a national economy. Politics acquired immediacy and excitement, causing nearly four out of five white men to cast a ballot in 1840.

Yet slavery, the source of one of the deepest divisions in American society, was almost completely ignored by 1830s politics. Indeed, coalition politics required the parties to remain silent on this issue to build strength in the South. Whigs found this silence harder to maintain than Democrats, since Whigs diverged more widely on the issue, stretching from ex-president John Quincy Adams, now sponsoring antislavery petitions from his Whig seat in the House of Representatives, to John C. Calhoun, nullifier, slaveholder, and Whig cabinet member in Harrison's new administration.

Slavery, however, was the defining difference in American social, economic, and political life in the nineteenth century. It could not be ignored for long by either Whigs or Democrats.

## CHRONOLOGY

| | |
|---|---|
| **1807** | Robert Fulton develops first commercially successful steamboat, *Clermont*. |
| **1816** | Second Bank of the United States chartered for twenty years. <br> Import tariff imposed on foreign textiles. |
| **1817** | American Colonization Society founded to promote gradual emancipation and removal of African Americans to Liberia. |
| **1818** | National Road links Baltimore and Wheeling, West Virginia. |
| **1819** | Economic collapse and panic nationwide. |
| **1824** | Congress passes expanded tariff bill. |
| **1825** | Erie Canal spans 350 miles in New York State. |
| **1826** | Schuylkill Canal—108 miles long—opens in Pennsylvania. |
| **1828** | Tariff of Abominations passed. <br> Andrew Jackson elected president. |
| **1829** | David Walker's *Appeal to the Colored Citizens of the World* published. |
| **1830** | Indian Removal Act appropriates money to relocate Indian tribes west of Mississippi River. |
| **1831** | William Lloyd Garrison begins publishing abolitionist newspaper *Liberator*. <br> Charles G. Finney stages evangelical revival in Rochester, New York. <br> Supreme Court allows Georgia to continue to subject Indians to state laws. |
| **1832** | Supreme Court in *Worcester v. Georgia* recognizes Cherokee as distinct community outside legal jurisdiction of Georgia. |

| | |
|---|---|
| **1832** Jackson vetoes renewal of Bank of United States charter.<br><br>New England Anti-Slavery Society founded.<br><br>Andrew Jackson reelected president. | **1834, 1836** Female mill workers strike in Lowell, Massachusetts. |
| | **1836** Jackson issues Specie Circular.<br><br>Martin Van Buren elected president. |
| | **1837** Economic panic. |
| **1833** Nullification crisis: South Carolina declares federal tariffs void in state.<br><br>New York and Philadelphia Anti-Slavery Societies founded. | **1838** Trail of Tears—Cherokee forced to relocate west. |
| | **1840** Congress approves independent treasury system. |

# SUGGESTED READINGS

Robert Abzug, *Cosmos Crumbling: American Reform and the Religious Imagination* (1994). A compelling exploration of the cosmological views and religious motives of a variety of leading Christian activists who translated their spiritual evangelism into moralistic social reform in the 1830s.

Jeanne Boydston, *Home and Work: Housework, Wages, and the Ideology of Labor in the Early Republic* (1990). A well-crafted study of women's unpaid labor in the antebellum home which describes the actual activity and cash value of domestic work and explores the process by which it came to be conceptualized as something other than work.

Thomas Dublin, *Women at Work: The Transformation of Work and Community in Lowell, Massachusetts, 1826–1860* (1979). The classic social history of the Lowell mill girls which covers their social origins, work experience, pioneering living and social arrangements, and politicization into strikers.

William W. Freehling, *Prelude to Civil War: The Nullification Controversy in South Carolina, 1816–1836* (1965). The classic study of the nullification episode of 1832–1833.

Lori D. Ginzberg, *Women and the Work of Benevolence: Morality, Politics, and Class in the Nineteenth-Century United States* (1990). An examination of the rhetoric of early charitable and reform movements and its relation to women's alleged special nature as the keepers of morality.

Karen Halttunen, *Confidence Men and Painted Women: A Study of Middle-Class Culture in America, 1830–1870*

(1982). A fascinating cultural history of gentility and sentimentalized sincerity, as manifested in the prescribed etiquette rituals of the self-made men and women of the emerging middle classes.

Theda Perdue and Michael D. Green, eds., *The Cherokee Removal: A Brief History with Documents* (1995). The essentials of the complicated story of the Cherokee's struggle to retain their southeastern homelands, with primary source documents.

Merrill D. Peterson, *The Great Triumvirate: Webster, Clay, and Calhoun* (1987). An authoritative biography of three of the nineteenth century's most prominent political leaders, men whose long-term influence on American politics equaled or even exceeded others who held the presidency.

Charles G. Sellers, *The Market Revolution: Jacksonian America, 1815–1846* (1991). A provocative and masterful synthesis of social, cultural, economic, and political history that identifies competing forces—both pro- and anti-capitalist—that struggled over the emergence and eventual triumph of antebellum capitalism.

Christine Stansell, *City of Women: Sex and Class in New York, 1789–1860* (1986). A rich and innovative recovery of the social history of working-class women in the country's largest urban center, New York City.

Harry L. Watson, *Liberty and Power: The Politics of Jacksonian America* (1990). A concise narrative synthesis of the Jacksonian era that places the market revolution and the hopes and fears it generated at the center of political party developments.

**GOURD FIDDLE**

*Found in St. Mary's County, Maryland, this slave-made gourd fiddle is an example of the many musical instruments that African Americans crafted and played throughout the South. Henry Wright, an ex-slave from Georgia, remembered: "I made a fiddle out of a large sized gourd—a long wooden handle was used as a neck, and the hair from a horse's tail was used for the bow. The strings were made of catgut." A hybrid of African and European elements, this fiddle offers material evidence of the cultural transformation of African slaves. While Africans lost much in their forced journey to the Americas, Africa remained in their cultural memory. Black men and women drew on the traditions of their homeland and the South to create something new—an African American culture. Music, a crucial component of that sustaining culture, provided slaves with a creative outlet and relief from the rigors of slavery.* Smithsonian Institution/Aldo Tutino/Folio.

# THE SLAVE SOUTH
## 1820–1860

I N 1822, IN THE BEAUTIFUL CITY OF CHARLESTON, SOUTH CAROLINA, with its white steeples, shaded gardens, and elegant mansions, a free black man named Denmark Vesey plotted a bloody slave rebellion. Until the year 1800, Vesey had been a slave, as were more than nine of every ten African Americans in the South. He had worked as a seaman in the Caribbean trade on the ship of his master, Captain Joseph Vesey.

In 1800, in Captain Vesey's home port of Charleston, Denmark Vesey won $1,500 in a lottery, bought his freedom, and set up a carpentry shop. Vesey prospered, and in time he owned a home on Bull Street and became a respected leader of the African Church of Charleston, founded in 1818 when thousands of the city's black Methodists withdrew from the white-led Methodist Church. But despite his own free status and considerable wealth, he continued to identify with the humiliation and oppression of slaves. At the age of fifty-five, one year after Charleston's white authorities had closed Vesey's beloved church, he decided to take his people out of the land of bondage or die trying.

He quietly began gathering his lieutenants. All were slaves, most belonged to the banned African Church, and some were African-born, as Vesey himself might have been. The conspirators' plan was evidently quite simple. At midnight on July 14, 1822, they would storm Charleston's arsenal, capture its weapons, kill any white who stood in their way, and set fire to the city. The flames would signal rebels in the countryside to rush in and complete the victory. Vesey may have planned to crowd as many slaves as he could on a ship and sail away to Haiti.

But the revolt never occurred. Before the conspiracy could become a full-blown insurrection, it was betrayed by other blacks, both slave and free. The first arrests came in May. One arrest led to another as suspects, prodded by torture and the threat of death, implicated others. Shaken badly by the disclosures, whites feverishly tracked down every conspirator. After three months, the authorities had banished thirty-seven blacks from the state and executed thirty-five others, including Denmark Vesey.

The Vesey affair not only reveals the complex calculation of blacks about how best to defend themselves—join Vesey or betray him—but also illustrates the determination of whites to beat back any challenge to their supremacy. Slave revolts were whites' worst nightmare. The Vesey affair was doubly terrifying because it occurred in the wake of the Missouri controversy of 1819–1820, with its display of powerful antislavery, antisouthern political forces. By the 1820s, the northern states had either abolished slavery or put it on the road to extinction while the southern states aggressively built the largest slave society in the New World. The division of the nation generally coincided with the "Mason-Dixon line"—the line drawn in 1763 by the English surveyors Charles Mason and Jeremiah Dixon to decide the boundary between the bickering colonies of Maryland and Pennsylvania. Half a

## CLASS No. 1.

*Comprises those prisoners who were found guilty and executed.*

| Prisoners Names. | Owners' Names. | Time of Commit. | How Disposed of. |
|---|---|---|---|
| Peter | James Poyas | June 18 | |
| Ned | Gov. T. Bennett, | do. | Hanged on Tuesday |
| Rolla | do. | do | the 2d July, 1822, |
| Batteau | do. | do. | on Blake's lands, |
| Denmark Vesey | A free black man | 22 | near Charleston. |
| Jessy | Thos. Blackwood | 23 | |
| John | Elias Horry | July 5 | Do on the Lines near |
| Gullah Jack | Paul Pritchard | do. | Ch.; Friday July 12. |
| Mingo | Wm. Harth | June 21 | |
| Lot | Forrester | 27 | |
| Joe | P. L. Jore | July 6 | |
| Julius | Thos. Forrest | 8 | |
| Tom | Mrs. Russell | 10 | |
| Smart | Robt. Anderson | do. | |
| John | John Robertson | 11 | |
| Robert | do. | do. | |
| Adam | do. | do. | |
| Polydore | Mrs. Faber | do. | Hanged on the Lines |
| Bacchus | Benj. Hammet | do. | near Charleston, |
| Dick | Wm. Sims | 13 | on Friday, 26th |
| Pharaoh | — Thompson | do. | July. |
| Jemmy | Mrs. Clement | 18 | |
| Mauidore | Mordecai Cohen | 19 | |
| Dean | — Mitchell | do. | |
| Jack | Mrs. Purcell | 12 | |
| Bellisle | Est. of Jos. Yates | 18 | |
| Naphur | do. | do. | |
| Adam | do. | do. | |
| Jacob | John S. Glen | 16 | |
| Charles | John Billings | 18 | |
| Jack | N. McNeill | 22 | |
| Cæsar | Miss Smith | do. | |
| Jacob Stagg | Jacob Lankester | 23 | Do. Tues. July 30. |
| Tom | Wm. M. Scott | 24 | |
| William | Mrs. Garner | Aug. 2 | Do. Friday, Aug. 9. |

**THE PRICE OF CONSPIRACY**
*This official account from 1822 gives the names of the one free black man and thirty-four slaves Charleston officials hanged for taking part in a conspiracy to overthrow slavery. We know little about most of the men. One exception is Gullah Jack, an Angolan. He hoped to draw upon the African traditions of the slaves, thousands of whom had been brought to South Carolina when the state reopened the African slave trade from 1804 to 1807. A conjurer, Gullah Jack empowered parched corn, ground nuts, and crab claws to protect those who joined the revolution.*
Rare Books, Manuscript, and Special Collections Library, Duke University.

century later, the English surveyors' mark divided the free North and slave South.

Black slavery dominated southern society and shaped the South into a distinctive region. Antebellum (pre–Civil War) Southerners included diverse peoples who at times found themselves at odds with one another—not only slaves and free people, but also women and men; Indians, Africans, and Europeans; aristocrats and common folk; merchants and mule drivers; and politicians and

thinkers. Nevertheless, beneath this diversity of Southerners there was also "a South," with features that arose from slavery and that distinguished it from the North. Increasingly, a sectional self-consciousness spread among most white Southerners. The South was a slave society, and most white Southerners were proud of it.

In the decades after 1820, Southerners raced westward, spreading slavery, cotton, and plantations halfway to the Pacific. Geographic expansion meant that slavery became more vigorous and profitable than ever, embraced more people, and increased the South's political power. In the end, the South's identification with slavery and insistence on its preservation culminated in the creation of a separate Confederacy that ultimately brought about what Denmark Vesey had tried in vain to achieve in 1822: the end of slavery. Some of the white Charlestonians who witnessed Vesey's execution lived to see slavery's death in 1865. But from 1820 through 1860, most white Southerners simply assumed that slavery was a permanent and valuable feature of their society, as it had been since colonial days. In their eyes, slavery made the South the South—and always would.

## The Southern Difference

When the Frenchman Alexis de Tocqueville visited the United States in the early 1830s, he observed that the inhabitants "constitute a single people . . . more truly a united society than some nations of Europe which lived under the same legislation and the same prince." Tocqueville identified an important truth about the young nation. Southerners and Northerners were all Americans.

From the earliest settlements, inhabitants of southern colonies had shared a great deal with northern colonists. Most whites in both sections were British and Protestant, and they spoke a common language, even if a regional twang or drawl flavored their speech. They shared an exuberant pride in their victorious revolution against British rule. The creation of the new nation under the Constitution in 1789 forged strong political ties that bound all Americans. And by the mid-nineteenth century, an incipient national economy was fostering economic interdependence and communication across sectional boundaries. White Americans everywhere celebrated the achievements of the prosperous young nation, and they looked forward to its seemingly boundless future.

Despite these national similarities, Southerners and Northerners were different. Tocqueville believed he knew why. "I could easily prove," he asserted in 1831, "that almost all the differences which may be noticed between the character of the Americans in the Southern and Northern states have originated in slavery." A quarter century later, most Americans agreed with the Frenchman. And neither Northerners nor Southerners liked what they saw on the other side of the Mason-Dixon line. "On the subject of slavery," the Charleston *Mercury* declared, "the North and South . . . are not only two Peoples, but they are rival, hostile Peoples." Slavery made the South different, and it was the differences between the North and the South, not the similarities, that came to shape antebellum American history.

## Cotton Kingdom, Slave Empire

In the first half of the nineteenth century, legions of Southerners migrated west. Eager slaveholders seeking virgin acreage for new plantations, struggling yeomen looking for patches of good land for small farms, herders and drovers pushing their hogs and cattle toward fresh pastures—anyone who was restless and ambitious felt the pull. Southerners pushed into the territories of Alabama, Mississippi, Louisiana, Texas, and Arkansas, until by midcentury the South encompassed nearly a million square miles, much of it planted in cotton (Map 12.1).

*Slavery made the South different, and it was the differences between the North and the South, not the similarities, that came to shape antebellum American history.*

The South's climate and geography were ideally suited for the cultivation of cotton. As Southerners advanced a thousand miles west from the Atlantic, they encountered a variety of terrain, soil, and weather, but the cotton seeds they carried with them were very adaptable. They grew in sandy plains and red clay, as well as in rich soil. Cotton requires two hundred frost-free days from planting to picking and prefers rains that are plentiful in spring and lighter in fall, conditions found in much of the South. In less than a half century, cotton fields stretched from southern Virginia to central Texas. Production soared, and by 1860 the South produced three-fourths of the world's supply. The South—especially that tier of states from South Carolina west to Texas known as the Lower South—had become the cotton kingdom.

The cotton kingdom was also a slave empire. The South's cotton boom rested on the backs of slaves, who grew 75 percent of the crop on plantations, toiling in gangs in broad fields under the direct supervision of whites. As cotton agriculture expanded westward, hundreds of thousands of slaves moved away from the old seaboard states. Some accompanied masters who were leaving behind worn-out, eroded plantations in the East. Most, however, were victims of a brutal but thriving domestic slave trade. Traders advertised for slaves who were "hearty and well made" and marched black men, women, and children hundreds of miles to the new plantation regions of the Lower South. Cotton, slaves, and plantations moved west together.

The slave population also grew enormously. Southern slaves numbered fewer than 700,000 in 1790, about 2 million in 1830, and about 4 million by 1860, an increase of almost 600 percent in seven decades. The South contained more slaves than all the other slave societies in the New World combined. The extraordinary growth was not the result of huge purchases in the international slave trade. The United States outlawed the importation of slaves in 1808. The main reason for the growth in the slave population was natural reproduction. By the nineteenth century, most slaves were southern-born. They were black Southerners.

## The South in Black and White

In 1860, the South contained 95 percent of the nation's African American population (Figure 12.1). One in every three Southerners was black (about 4 million blacks and 8 million whites). In the Lower South, the proportion was higher, for whites and blacks lived there in almost equal numbers. In Mississippi and South Carolina, blacks were the majority. The contrast with the North was striking. In 1860, only one Northerner in 76 was black (about 250,000 blacks to 19 million whites).

The presence of large numbers of African Americans had profound consequences for the South. Southern culture—language, food, music, religion, and even accents—was shaped by blacks.

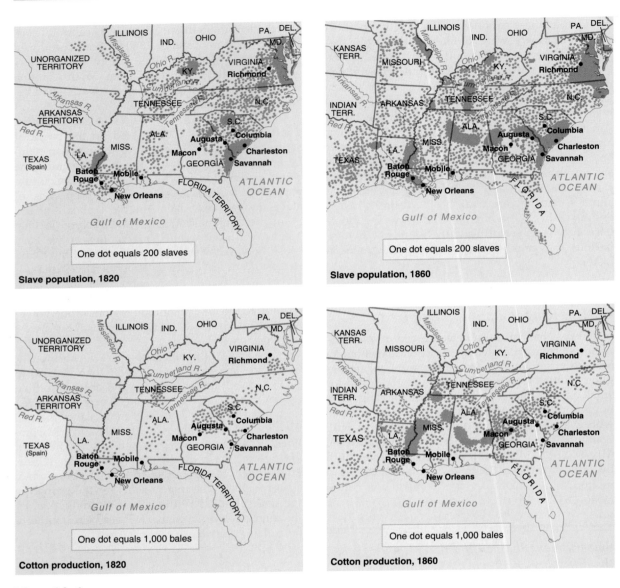

**MAP 12.1**
*Cotton Kingdom, Slave Empire: 1820 and 1860*
*As the production of cotton soared, the slave population increased dramatically. Slaves continued to toil in tobacco and rice fields along the Atlantic seaboard, but increasingly they worked on cotton plantations in Alabama, Mississippi, and Louisiana.*

But the most direct consequence of the South's biracialism was the response it stimulated in the region's white majority. Southern whites were dedicated to white supremacy. Northern whites were, too, but they lived in a society in which blacks made up barely more than 1 percent of the population.

By contrast, white Southerners lived among millions of blacks, whom they simultaneously despised and feared. They despised blacks because they considered them members of an inferior race, further degraded by their status as slaves. They feared blacks because they realized that slaves had

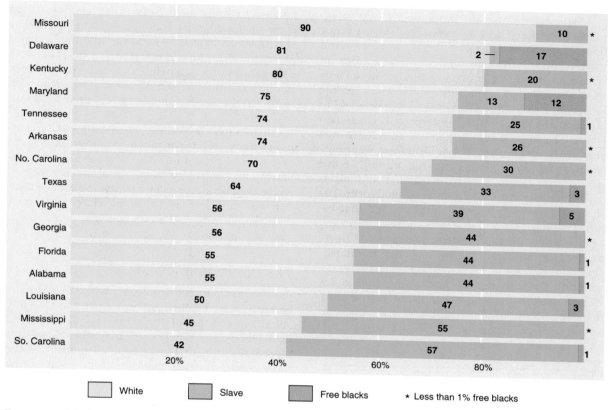

| State | White | Slave | Free blacks |
|---|---|---|---|
| Missouri | 90 | 10 | * |
| Delaware | 81 | 2 | 17 |
| Kentucky | 80 | 20 | * |
| Maryland | 75 | 13 | 12 |
| Tennessee | 74 | 25 | 1 |
| Arkansas | 74 | 26 | * |
| No. Carolina | 70 | 30 | * |
| Texas | 64 | 33 | 3 |
| Virginia | 56 | 39 | 5 |
| Georgia | 56 | 44 | * |
| Florida | 55 | 44 | 1 |
| Alabama | 55 | 44 | 1 |
| Louisiana | 50 | 47 | 3 |
| Mississippi | 45 | 55 | * |
| So. Carolina | 42 | 57 | 1 |

White   Slave   Free blacks   * Less than 1% free blacks

FIGURE 12.1
*Black and White Population in the South, 1860*
*Blacks represented a much larger fraction of the population in the South than in the North, but considerable variation existed from state to state. Only one Missourian in ten, for example, was black, while Mississippi and South Carolina had black majorities. States in the Upper South were "whiter" than in the Lower South, despite the Upper South's greater number of free blacks.*

every reason to hate their oppressors and to seek to end their oppression, as Denmark Vesey had, by any means necessary.

Attacks on slavery—from blacks within and from abolitionists without—jolted southern slaveholders into a distressing awareness that they lived in a dangerous world. In response, southern leaders in the 1820s and 1830s initiated fresh efforts to strengthen slavery and ward off threats. State legislatures constructed elaborate slave codes that required the total submission of slaves to their masters and to white society in general. As the Louisiana code stated, a slave "owes his master . . . a respect without bounds, and an absolute obedience." The laws underlined the authority of all whites, not just masters. Any white could stop a slave on a road and demand to see the slave's written permission to be away from home. Any white could "correct" slaves who did not stay "in their place" and show the proper deference.

Intellectuals joined legislators in the campaign to strengthen slavery. The South's academics, writers, and clergy constructed a proslavery argument that sought to unify the region's whites around slavery and provide ammunition for the emerging war of words with northern abolitionists. Under the intellectuals' tutelage, the white South gradually moved away from defending slavery as a "necessary evil"—the halfhearted argument popular in Jefferson's day—and toward a full-throated, aggressive defense of slavery as a "positive good."

Slavery's champions employed every imaginable defense. The law protected slavery, they observed, for slaves were legal property. And wasn't the security of property the bedrock of American liberty? History also endorsed slavery. Weren't the great civilizations—like those of the Hebrews, Greeks, and Romans—slave societies? In addition, the Bible, properly interpreted, sanctioned slavery. Didn't the Old Testament patriarchs own slaves? Didn't Paul in the New Testament return the runaway slave Onesimus to his master? Some proslavery spokesmen went on the offensive and attacked the economy and society of the North. The Virginian writer George Fitzhugh argued that behind the North's grand slogans—individualism and egalitarianism—lay a heartless philosophy: "Every man for himself, and the devil take the hindmost." Gouging capitalists exploited wage workers unmercifully, Fitzhugh said, and he contrasted the vicious capitalist-laborer relationship with the humane relations that prevailed between masters and slaves because slaves were valuable capital that masters sought to protect.

---

*The presence of large numbers of African Americans had profound consequences for the South. Southern culture—language, food, music, religion, and even accents—was shaped by blacks.*

---

Since slavery was a condition Southerners reserved exclusively for African Americans, at bottom the white defense of slavery rested on claims of black inferiority. Black enslavement was both necessary and proper, defenders argued, because Africans were inferior beings. Rather than exploitative, slavery was a mass civilizing effort that lifted lowly blacks from barbarism and savagery, taught them disciplined work, and converted them to soul-saving Christianity. Freeing blacks, the Charleston *Mercury* declared, would mean their destruction as well as the destruction of southern "civilization, society, and government."

Black slavery encouraged whites to unify around race rather than to divide by class. The grubbiest, most tobacco-stained white man could proudly proclaim his superiority to blacks and his equality with the most refined southern patrician. Because slaves were not recognized as citizens in the South, Georgia attorney Thomas R. R. Cobb observed, everyone who was a citizen "feels that he belongs to an elevated class. It matters not that he is no slaveholder; he is not of the inferior race; he is a freeborn citizen." Consequently, the "poorest meets the richest as an equal; sits at his table with him; salutes him as a neighbor; meets him in every public assembly, and stands on the same social platform." In the South, Cobb boasted, "there is no war of classes."

In reality, slavery did not create perfect harmony among whites or ease every strain along class lines. But by providing every white symbolic membership in the ruling class, racial slavery helped whites bridge differences in class, wealth, education, and culture. Slavery meant white dominance, white superiority, and white equality.

## The Plantation Economy

Race was important in unifying white Southerners because most whites did not own slaves. Only about one-quarter of the white population lived in slaveholding families. A majority of masters owned fewer than five. About 12 percent of the slave owners owned twenty or more slaves, the number historians consider necessary to distinguish a planter from a farmer. Fewer than 1 percent of slaveholders owned one hundred or more slaves and thus could be considered "great planters." Although greatly outnumbered by nonslaveholders and small slaveholders, planters dominated the southern economy. Fifty-two percent of the South's slaves lived and worked on plantations. Plantation slaves produced more than 75 percent of the South's export crops, the backbone of the region's economy.

Patterns of plantation slavery established along the Atlantic seaboard persisted as Southerners raced westward in the nineteenth century. The dominant crops of southern agriculture were the four major staples grown on plantations: tobacco, sugar, rice, and cotton. All plantations had similar features, but they differed depending on the staple crop they produced (Map 12.2).

Tobacco was the original plantation crop in North America. By the nineteenth century, however, most planters around the Chesapeake had shifted to wheat and other crops, and tobacco had moved to western Virginia and to Tennessee and Kentucky. Work in the tobacco fields was labor-intensive. Most phases of the process—planting, transplanting, thinning, picking off caterpillars, cutting, drying, packing—required field hands to stoop or bend down in painful labor over the tobacco plants.

ATTENTION PAID A POOR SICK WHITE MAN.

ATTENTION PAID A POOR SICK NEGRO.

**PROSLAVERY WOODCUTS**

*As antislavery critics accelerated their verbal attacks, white Southerners fought back. These 1853 woodcuts contrast the callousness of free labor with the benefits of slavery. The message was clear: While free laborers ("wage slaves") were carted directly from the factory to the poorhouse, aged and infirm slaves were made comfortable by their masters and mistresses. Slavery's advocates asked: Which society was brutally exploitative and which cared for its laborers from cradle to grave?*

Josiah Priest's *In Defense of Slavery,* Rare Book and Manuscript Department, Boston Public Library.

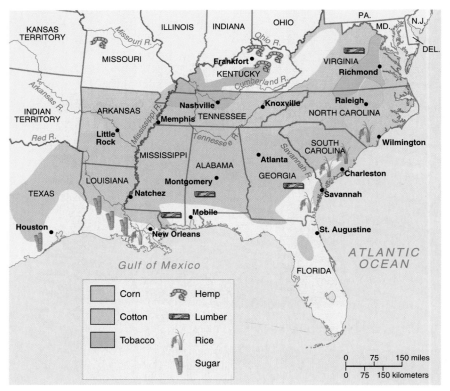

**M A P  1 2 . 2**
*The Agricultural Economy of the South, 1860*
Cotton dominated the South's agricultural economy, but the region grew a diversity of crops and was largely self-sufficient in foodstuffs.

Large-scale sugar production began in 1795, when Etienne de Boré built a modern sugar mill in what is today New Orleans. Labor on sugarcane plantations was reputed to be the most physically demanding in the antebellum South. Masters elsewhere would attempt to frighten obstinate slaves with the threat of selling them "down the river"—down the Mississippi River to sugar planters. During the fall, slaves worked eighteen hours a day to cut the cane and haul it to the sugar mill, where they would grind and boil it. Sugar plantations, which were confined almost entirely to Louisiana, required large sums for expensive refining equipment to turn cane juice into sugar and for large gangs of slaves.

Commercial rice production began in seventeenth-century South Carolina. Like sugar, rice was confined to a small geographic area, a narrow strip of the tidewater stretching from the Carolinas into northern Georgia. Because of the need for canals, dikes, and gates to flood rice fields with water and then drain them and to protect the ripening plant from saltwater, rice planting was an expensive undertaking. Since rice plantations required huge numbers of slaves, blacks accounted for 90 percent of the population in the coastal rice districts. For slaves, rice meant danger and extreme discomfort. Working in water and mud in the heat of a Carolina summer regularly threatened slaves with malaria, yellow fever, and other diseases.

If tobacco, sugar, and rice were princes of plantation agriculture, cotton was king. Cotton became commercially significant after the invention of the cotton gin by Eli Whitney in 1793. By the early years of the nineteenth century, cotton had displaced tobacco and had begun to dominate the southern economy. The white fluffy stuff was grown almost everywhere in the South and by almost everyone, small farmer and planter alike. It was relatively easy to grow and took little capital to get started—just enough for land, seed, and simple tools. Nonetheless, plantations produced three-quarters of the South's cotton, and planters received a disproportionate slice of the region's income. While hardscrabble farmer Jessup Snopes grew half a bale, Mississippian Frederick Stanton, who owned more than fifteen thousand prime acres, produced 3,054 bales of cotton worth $122,000 in 1859. With a record-breaking crop of 4,861,000 bales in 1859, the South's planters were, as they liked to put it, in "high cotton."

For slaveholders, then, the Old South's economy was productive and profitable. Further, plantation slavery benefited the national economy. Throughout the antebellum years, the products of southern plantations made up the greatest part of America's exports. By 1840, cotton alone accounted for more than 60 percent of the nation's sales abroad. Much of the profit from sales of cotton overseas returned to planters, but some did not. Cotton had to be bought, sold, insured, warehoused, and shipped before it reached the mills in Great Britain and elsewhere. Increasingly, these services were in the hands of northern middlemen, each of whom made a profit from slave-grown southern crops. As these profits were invested in the burgeoning northern economy, industrial development there received much-needed capital. Furthermore, planters provided an important market for northern textiles, agricultural tools, and other manufactured goods. Without cotton, one economist has estimated, American industrial development would have been retarded a generation.

*Although greatly outnumbered by nonslaveholders and small slaveholders, planters dominated the southern economy.*

The economies of North and South steadily diverged. While the North developed a mixed economy—agriculture, commerce, and manufacturing—the South remained overwhelmingly agricultural. Since planters were earning healthy profits, they saw little reason to diversify. Moreover, economic change could threaten plantation slavery, the key to the social and economic order that planters dominated. Planters knew that if the southern economy followed the path blazed by the North, then manufacturing in the South would mean the rise of an urban, industrial working class without direct ties to slavery and the plantation. Would city-dwelling factory workers accept rural planter rule and give their hearty support to slavery, or would they favor free labor, as northern workers did? Planters did not want to find out. Year after year, they funneled the profits they earned from land and slaves back into more land and slaves.

**THE COTTON GIN**
*By the 1790s, the English had succeeded in mechanizing the manufacture of cotton cloth, but they were unable to get enough raw cotton. The South could grow cotton in unimaginable quantities, but cotton that was stuck to seeds was useless in English textile mills. In 1793, Eli Whitney, a Northerner who was serving as a tutor on a Savannah River plantation, built a simple device for separating the cotton from the seed—just wire teeth set in a wooden cylinder that, when rotated, reached through narrow slats to pull cotton fibers away from seeds, while the brush swept the fibers from the revolving teeth. Widespread use of the cotton gin (the word* gin *is simply short for* engine*) broke the bottleneck in the commercial production of cotton and eventually bound millions of African Americans to slavery.*
Smithsonian Institution.

With its capital flowing into agriculture, the Old South did not develop many factories. By 1860, only 10 percent of the nation's industrial workers were in the South. Indiana and Illinois—two midwestern states known for agriculture—had more capital invested in industry than the seven Lower South states, including Louisiana with its sugar mills. Southern factories usually processed agricultural products and raw materials produced in the region. Cotton mills, for example, developed where cotton, water power, and cheap labor existed. Still, in 1860 the region that produced 100 percent of the nation's cotton manufactured less than 7 percent of its cotton textiles.

Without significant economic diversification, the South developed fewer cities than the North. In 1860, it was the least urban region in the country. While nearly 37 percent of New England's population lived in towns, less than 12 percent of Southerners were urban dwellers. That figure would have been dramatically smaller without Maryland's 34 percent urban population (because of Baltimore) and Louisiana's 26 percent (because of New Orleans). In fact, nine southern states had 5 percent or fewer of their people in towns.

Not only were cities less common in the South, but they were also different from those in the North. They were mostly port cities on the periphery of the region and busy principally with exporting the agricultural products of plantations in the interior. The region's urban merchants provided agriculture with indispensable economic services, such as hauling, insuring, and selling the South's cotton, rice, and sugar. But as the tail of the plantation dog, southern cities did not become significant manufacturing centers or important independent centers of social and economic innovation.

Because the South had so few cities and industrial jobs, it attracted relatively small numbers of European immigrants. Seeking economic opportunity, not competition with slaves, immigrants steered well north of the South's slave-dominated, agricultural economy. In 1860, 13 percent of all Americans were foreign-born. But in nine of the fifteen slave states, only 2 percent or fewer were born abroad. Immigrants who did venture below the Mason-Dixon line concentrated in cities, as they did in the North.

Not every Southerner celebrated the region's plantation economy. Critics railed against the excessive commitment to cotton and slaves and bemoaned the "deplorable scarcity" of factories. Diversification, they promised, would make the South not only economically independent but more prosperous and healthy as well. State governments encouraged economic development by helping to create banking systems that supplied credit for a wide range of projects, industrial as well as agricultural. Government joined private investors in building an extensive railroad network. Alabama constructed its first railroad in 1830, just five years after the first modern railroad in the world was constructed in England and only three years after the inauguration of the first railroad in America. Thirty years later, 9,280 miles of track spanned the South.

But encouragement of a diversified economy had clear limits. State governments failed to create some of the essential services modern economies require. By midcentury, for example, no southern legislature had created a statewide public school system. Consequently, the South's illiteracy rate for whites topped 20 percent. Dominant slaveholders failed to see any benefit in educating the region's

labor force. Indeed, after the 1830s it was illegal in the South to teach slaves to read. Despite the flurry of railroad building, the South's mileage in 1860 was less than half that of the North. Moreover, northern railroads crisscrossed the region connecting towns and cities and carrying manufactured goods as well as agricultural products. In the South, most rail lines ran from port cities back into farming areas and were built to export staple crops.

Northerners claimed that slavery was outmoded and doomed, but few Southerners perceived economic weakness in their region. In fact, the planters' pockets were never fuller than at the end of the antebellum period. But planters' individual profits did not automatically translate into longterm regional economic health. When the South bet on plantation agriculture, especially cotton, it not only committed itself to slavery but also left itself vulnerable to the fickle world market. Compared with antebellum Northerners, Southerners committed less of their capital to investment in industry, transportation, and public education. Planters' decisions to reinvest in staple agriculture ensured the momentum of the plantation economy and the social and political relationships that were rooted in it.

## Masters, Mistresses, and the Big House

Nowhere was the contrast between northern and southern life more vivid than in the plantations of the South. Located on a patchwork of cleared fields and dense forests, a plantation typically included a "big house" and slave quarters. Scattered about were numerous outbuildings, each with a special function. Near the big house were the kitchen, storehouse, smokehouse (for curing and preserving meat), and hen coop. More distant were the barns, toolsheds, artisans' workshops, and overseer's house. Large plantations sometimes had separate buildings for an infirmary, nursery, and chapel for the slaves. Depending on the crop, there was a tobacco shed, a rice mill, a sugar refinery, or a cotton gin house. Lavish or plain, plantations everywhere had an underlying similarity (Figure 12.2).

The plantation was the home of masters, mistresses, and slaves. Slavery shaped the lives of all the plantation's inhabitants, but it affected each differently. A hierarchy of rigid roles and duties governed relationships. Presiding was the master, who ruled his wife, children, and slaves, none of whom had many legal rights and all of whom were designated by the state as dependents under his dominion and protection.

## Plantation Masters

Plantations were usually organized quite simply. Smaller planters supervised the labor of their slaves themselves. Larger planters usually hired an overseer. Overseers were either ambitious young white men—perhaps relatives of the planter or poor men from the neighborhood—or professionals who made a career of supervising slaves. Because overseers went to the fields with the slaves, planters could concentrate instead on marketing, finance, and general plantation affairs. Planters also found time to escape to town to discuss the weather, to the courthouse and legislature to debate politics, and to the woods to hunt and fish.

Increasingly in the nineteenth century, planters characterized the master-slave relationship in terms of what historians have called "paternalism." The concept of paternalism denied that the form of slavery practiced in the South was brutal and exploitative. Instead, it defined slavery as a set of reciprocal obligations between masters and slaves. In exchange for the slaves' labor and obedience, masters provided basic care and necessary guidance. To northern claims that they were tyrants and exploiters, slaveholders responded that they were stewards and guardians. As owners of blacks, masters argued, they had the heavy responsibility of caring for a childlike, dependent people. In 1814, Thomas Jefferson captured the essence of the ideal: "We should endeavor, with those whom fortune has thrown on our hands, to feed & clothe them well, protect them from ill usage, require such reasonable labor only as is performed voluntarily by freemen, and be led by no repugnancies to abdicate them, and our duties to them."

Paternalism was part propaganda and part self-delusion. But it was more. Indeed, there was some truth in the assertion that master-slave relationships in the South were unique. Unlike planters elsewhere in the New World, most southern planters lived year-round where their slaves worked, which meant that the relationship between master and slave was face to face, direct, and personal. In addition, slavery in the South reached its prime in the nineteenth century, after the nation had closed its external slave trade in 1808. Masters realized that the expansion of the slave labor force could come only from natural reproduction. Thus,

**FIGURE 12.2**

*A Southern Plantation*

*Slavery determined how masters laid out their plantations, where they situated their "big houses" and the quarters, and what kinds of buildings they constructed. This model of the "Hermitage," the mansion built for Georgia rice planter Henry McAlpin in 1830, shows the overseer's house poised in the grove of oak trees halfway between the owner's mansion and the houses of his slaves. The mansion at the end of the extended road underscored McAlpin's great affluence and authority.*

Adapted from *Back of the Big House: The Architecture of Plantation Slavery* by John Michael Vlach. Copyright © 1993 by the University of North Carolina Press. Original illustration property of the Historic American Buildings Survey, a division of the National Park Service.

SAVANNAH RIVER

7

5
6
4
3
2

1

BRICK WALL

9    8

PLOT
PLAN

10    10

LEGEND

1  MANSION          6  LOT
2  KITCHEN          7  SUNKEN GARDEN
3  SMOKE HOUSE      8  OVERSEER'S HOUSE
4  STABLES          9  HOSPITAL
5  COACH HOUSE     10  SLAVE HUTS

masters had to provide slaves with a certain minimum level of physical welfare if they wanted more slaves, and they certainly did want more slaves.

One consequence was a relative improvement in slaves' material welfare. The nineteenth-century slaves' diet still consisted mainly of fatty pork and cornmeal. The cabins still had cracks large enough, slaves said, for cats to slip through. Slaves' clothing seldom amounted to much more than two crude outfits a year. Nevertheless, conditions in the quarters got better. In the fields, workdays remained sunup to sundown, but planters often provided a rest period in the heat of the day. And most owners ceased the eighteenth-century practices of punishing slaves by branding, castrating, and other forms of mutilation.

---

*The plantation was the home of masters, mistresses, and slaves. Presiding was the master, who ruled his wife, children, and slaves.*

---

Paternalism should not be mistaken for "Ol' Massa's" kindness and goodwill. It had nothing to do with gentleness and niceness. It encouraged better treatment, but it was essentially self-interested and self-serving. It made economic sense to provide at least minimal care for valuable slaves. Nor did paternalism require that planters put aside their whips. They could lay on the leather and claim that they were only fulfilling their responsibilities as guardians of their naturally lazy and at times insubordinate dependents. Paternalism gave slaves some protection against the most brutal punishments, but whipping remained the planters' essential coercion. (See the Historical Question on page 300.)

The Virginia statesman Edmund Randolph argued that slavery created in white southern men a "quick and acute sense of personal liberty" and a "disdain for every abridgement of personal independence." Indeed, prickly individualism and aggressive independence became crucial features of the southern concept of honor. Social standing, political advancement, and even self-esteem rested on a reputation of honor. Defending honor became a male passion. Andrew Jackson's mother reportedly told her son, "Never tell a lie, nor take what is not your own, nor sue anybody for slander or assault and battery. *Always settle them cases yourself.*" Southern boys were expected to master the "manly" arts, and among planters such advice sometimes led to

duels. Dueling arrived from Europe in the eighteenth century. It died out in the North, but in the South, even after legislatures banned it, gentlemen continued to defend their honor with pistols at ten paces.

Southerners also expected an honorable gentleman to be a proper patriarch. Nowhere in America was patriarchy more accentuated. In the South, slavery buttressed the power of husbands and fathers. Planters described the plantation as a single social unit, incorporating their "white and black families"—their personal households and the slave quarters. Attempts by family members to assert themselves against the patriarch—the head of the family, the master of slaves—threatened slavery itself. The master's absolute dominion sometimes led to miscegenation, the sexual mixing of the races. Laws prohibited interracial sex, and some masters condemned sex with slaves as immoral and practiced self-restraint. Others merely urged discretion. How many trips masters and their sons made to slave cabins is impossible to tell, but as long as slavery gave white men extraordinary power over black women, liaisons occurred.

Individualistic impulses were strong among planters, but duty to family was paramount. In time, as the children of one elite family married the children of another, ties of blood and kinship as well as ideology and economic interest linked planters to one another. Conscious of what they shared as slaveholders, planters worked together to defend their common interests. The values of the big house—slavery, honor, male domination—washed over the boundaries of plantations and flooded all of southern life.

## Plantation Mistresses

Like their northern counterparts, southern ladies were expected to possess feminine virtues of piety, purity, chastity, and obedience within the context of marriage, motherhood, and domesticity. Southerners also expected ladies to exemplify all that was best in plantation society. Countless toasts praised the southern lady as the perfect complement to her husband, the patriarch. She was physically weak, "formed only for the less laborious occupations," and thus dependent on male protection. To gain this protection, she was modest and delicate, beautiful and graceful, cultured and charming. The lady, southern men said proudly, was an "ornament."

But for women, the image of the lady, which rigidly prescribed proper character and behavior, was

**THE PRICE OF BLOOD**
*This 1868 painting by T. S. Noble depicts a transaction between a slave trader and a rich planter.
The trader nervously pretends to study the contract, while the planter waits impatiently for the
completion of the sale. The planter's mulatto son, who is being sold, looks away. The children
of white men and slave women were property and could be sold by the father/master. But the
tragedy of miscegenation extended beyond the son shown here. Who is absent from the painting?
Whose marriage has been betrayed? Who else's son is being sold away?*
Morris Museum of Art, Augusta, Ga.

no blessing. Chivalry—the South's romantic ideal of
male-female relationships—glorified the lady while
it subordinated her. Chivalry's underlying assumptions about the weakness of women and the protective authority of men resembled the paternalistic
defense of slavery. Indeed, the most articulate
proslavery advocates also eloquently defended the
subordination of women. Just as the slaveholder's
mastery was written into law, so too were the paramount rights of husbands. Once married, antebellum
southern women found divorce almost impossible.

Daughters of planters confronted chivalry's demands at an early age. Their educations aimed at
fitting them to become southern ladies. At their private boarding schools they read literature, learned

languages, and struggled to master the requisite
drawing-room arts. Elite women married early, usually before they were twenty. Kate Carney exaggerated only slightly when she wrote in her diary:
"Today, I am seventeen, getting quite old, and am
not married." Elizabeth Ruffin, who was about the
same age, complained of being pushed into a wedding. Everyone, she said, seemed determined to
"deter me from all the anticipated horrors of *old-
maidenhood.*" When they married, elite women usually made enormous efforts to live up to their region's
lofty ideal.

In fact, they faced an impossible task. The ideal
of the southern lady clashed with the daily reality
of the plantation mistress. Rather than being freed

# How Often Were Slaves Whipped?

AS IMPORTANT AS THIS QUESTION IS to historians, and obviously was to slaves, we have very little reliable evidence on the frequency of whipping. We know from white sources that whipping was the prescribed method of physical punishment on most antebellum plantations. Masters' instructions to overseers authorized whippings and often set limits on the number of strokes an overseer could administer. Some planters allowed fifteen lashes, some fifty, and some one hundred. But slave owners' instructions, as revealing as they are, tell us more about the severity of beatings than their frequency.

Remembrances of former slaves confirm that whipping was widespread and frequent. In the 1930s, a government program gathered testimony from more than 2,300 elderly African Americans about their experiences as slaves. Their accounts offered grisly evidence of the cruelty of slavery. "You say how did our Master treat his slaves?" asked one woman. "Scandalous, they treated them just like dogs." She was herself whipped "till the blood dripped to the ground." A few slaves remembered kind masters and never personally felt the sting of the lash. Bert Strong was one such slave, but he also recalled hearing slaves on other farms "hollering when they get beat." He said, "They beat them till it a pity." Beatings occurred often, but how often?

A remarkably systematic record of whippings over a sustained period of time comes from the diary of Bennet H. Barrow, the master of Highland plantation in West Feliciana Parish, Louisiana. For a twenty-three-month period in 1840–1841, Barrow meticulously recorded every whipping he administered or ordered. On most large plantations, overseers handled the business of day-to-day management, but in 1838, Barrow concluded that overseers were "good for nothing" and "a perfect nuisance." He dismissed his white overseer and, assisted only by a black driver, began managing his own plantation.

What does the Barrow evidence show? In 1840, according to the federal census, Barrow owned 129 slaves. In the twenty-three-month period, Barrow recorded 160 whippings. That means that, on the average, a slave was whipped every four and one-half days. Sixty of the seventy-seven slaves who worked in the fields were whipped at least once. Most of the seventeen field slaves who escaped being beaten were children and pregnant women. Eighty percent of male cotton pickers and 70 percent of the female cotton pickers were whipped at least once in this period. Dave Barley received eight floggings, more than any other Barrow slave, and Patience received six whippings, more than any other female slave.

In most instances, Barrow recorded not only the fact of a whipping but also its cause. All sorts of "misconduct," "rascallity," and "disorderly acts" made Barrow reach for his whip. The provocations included family quarrels in the slave quarters, impudence, running away, and failure to keep curfew. But nearly 80 percent of the acts recorded related to poor work. Barrow gave beatings for "not picking as well as he can," for picking "very trashy cotton," and for failing to pick the prescribed weight of cotton. One slave claimed to have lost his eyesight and for months refused to work until Barrow "gave him 25 cuts yesterday morning & ordered him to work Blind or not."

Whippings should not be mistaken for spankings. Some planters used whips that raised welts, caused blisters, and bruised. Others resorted to rawhide and cowhide whips that broke the skin, caused scarring, and sometimes permanently maimed. Occasionally, slaves were beaten to death. Whipping was not Barrow's only means of inflicting pain. He was inventive. His diary mentions confining slaves to a plantation jail, putting them in chains, shooting them, breaking a "sword cane" over one slave's head, having slaves mauled by dogs, placing them in stocks, "staking down" slaves for hours, "hand sawing" them, holding their heads under water, and a variety of punishments intending to ridicule and to shame, including making men wear women's clothing and do "women's work," such as the laundry. Still, Barrow's preferred instrument of punishment was the whip.

**GORDON**

*This photograph of Gordon, a runaway slave from Baton Rouge, Louisiana, was taken on April 2, 1863, and sent home from the Civil War by Frederick W. Mercer, an assistant surgeon with the Forty-seventh Massachusetts Regiment. Mercer examined four hundred other runaways and found many "to be as badly lacerated." Masters claimed that they whipped only when they had to and only as hard as they had to, but slave testimony and photographic evidence refute their defense of slavery as a benign institution.*

Courtesy of the Massachusetts Historical Society.

On the Barrow plantation, as on many others, whipping was public. Victims were often tied to a stake in the quarters, and the other slaves were made to watch. In a real sense the entire slave population on the plantation experienced a whipping every four and one-half days. Even though some never felt the lash personally, all were familiar with its terror and agony.

Was whipping effective? Did it produce a hard-working, efficient, and conscientious labor force? Not according to Barrow's own record. No evidence indicates that whipping changed the slaves' behavior. What Barrow considered bad work continued. Unabated whipping is itself evidence of the failure of punishment to achieve the master's will. Slaves knew the rules. Yet they continued to act "badly." And they continued to suffer. It was a gruesome drama—the master seeking from his slaves hard labor and slaves denying their master what he most wanted—day after day.

Did Barrow whip with the same frequency as other planters? We simply do not know. Because of the lack of quantifiable evidence, we will never know precisely how often whippings occurred. But the Barrow evidence allows us to speculate profitably on the frequency of whipping by large planters. We do know that Barrow did not consider himself a cruel man. He bitterly denounced his neighbor as "the most cruel Master i ever knew of" for castrating three of his slaves. Moreover, Barrow had dispensed with the overseers in part because of their "brutal feelings" toward slaves. Like most whites, he believed that the lash was essential to get work done. He used it no more than he believed absolutely necessary.

Most masters, including Barrow, tried to encourage work with promises of small gifts and brief holidays, but punishment was their most important motivator. We will never know if the typical slave was beaten once a year as on the Barrow plantation, but the admittedly scanty evidence suggests that on large plantations the whip fell on someone's back every few days.

And former slaves remembered. More than half a century after emancipation, their sharpest recollections usually involved punishment. They remembered the pain, the injustice, and their bitter resentment. They evaluated their former masters according to how frequently they reached for the whip. According to one former slave, "some was good and some was bad, and about the most of them was bad."

from labor by servants, she discovered that having servants required her to work long hours. Like her husband, the mistress had managerial responsibilities. She managed the big house, often supervising anywhere from two or three to more than a dozen servants. But unlike her husband, who was often insulated from the aggravations of direct supervision of slaves, the mistress had no overseer. All the house servants answered to her. She assigned them tasks each morning, directed their work throughout the day, and punished them when she found fault. In addition to supervising a complex household, she had responsibility for the henhouse and dairy. And on some plantations, she directed the slave hospital and nursery and rationed supplies for the slave quarters. In addition, she bore the burdens of childbearing and child rearing. Southern ladies did not lead lives of leisure.

The mistress's life was circumscribed by the plantation, as was the slave's life. Masters used their status as slaveholders as a springboard into public affairs, but their wives served the family, not the community. Masters left the plantation when they pleased, but plantation mistresses needed chaperones to travel. When they could find the time, they went to church, for their faith was important to them. But women spent most days on the plantation, where they often became lonely. In 1853, Mary Kendall wrote how much she enjoyed her sister's letter: "For about three weeks I did not have the pleasure of seeing *one white female face,* there being no white family except our own upon the plantation." When a parade of family, friends, and strangers broke the isolation, the burden of hospitality fell on the mistress and the house slaves, not the master.

As members of slaveholding families, mistresses lived privileged lives. But they also had significant grounds for discontent, and a few independent-minded women protested. Some complained of their exhausting burdens as mistresses. Others protested their tiring and dangerous cycle of childbearing. Two decades of childbearing could mean ten or eleven children. And some women denounced slavery itself. In the early 1820s, Sarah and Angelina Grimké, daughters of a Charleston planter, fled their home for the North, where they wrote blistering attacks on slavery. Sarah's *Letters on the Equality of the Sexes* also protested the South's "image of women."

No feature of plantation life generated more rage and anguish among mistresses than miscegenation. Mary Boykin Chesnut of Camden, South Carolina, wrote in her diary, "God forgive us, but ours is a monstrous system, a wrong and iniquity. Like the patriarchs of old, our men live all in one house with their wives and their concubines; and the mulattos one sees in every family partly resemble the white children. Any lady is ready to tell you who is the father of all the mulatto children in everybody's household but her own. Those, she seems to think drop from the clouds."

But the mistress's world rested on slavery, just as the master's did. Most planters' wives—including Mary Boykin Chesnut—found ways to accept slavery. They raised their children, read their Bibles, and lived busy and responsible lives. But they were not considered equal to men.

## Slaves and the Quarters

On most plantations, only a few hundred yards separated the big house and the slave quarters. The distance was short enough to assure whites easy access to the labor of blacks. Yet the distance was great enough to provide slaves with some privacy, despite increased paternalistic intrusion. Out of eyesight and earshot of the big house, slaves drew together and built lives of their own.

The rise of plantations still left a substantial minority of slaves living and working elsewhere. Most worked on small farms, where they wielded a hoe alongside another slave or two and perhaps their master. But by 1850, as many as half a million slaves (one in eight) did not work in agriculture at all. Some were employed in towns and cities as domestics, day laborers, bakers, barbers, tailors, and more. Others, far from urban centers, toiled as fishermen, lumbermen, railroad workers, and deckhands and stokers on riverboats. Slavery was a flexible labor system, and slaves could be found in virtually every skilled and unskilled occupation throughout the South, including the region's few factories. Nevertheless, a majority of slaves (52 percent) counted plantations as their homes and workplaces.

### Work

Above all, what masters wanted from slaves was work. The desire for exploitable labor was the chief explanation of slavery's origin in the New World and the principal reason it persisted into the nineteenth century. Slaves understood clearly the motive for their enslavement. As ex-slave Albert Todd recalled, "Work was a religion we was taught."

All slaves who were capable of productive labor worked. Young children were introduced to the world of work as early as age five or six. Ex-slave Carrie Hudson recalled that children who were "knee high to a duck" had to work. Some were sent to the fields to carry water to thirsty workers or to protect ripening crops from hungry birds. Others helped in the slave nursery, caring for children even younger than themselves, or in the big house, where they did simple chores, such as sweeping floors or shooing flies in the dining room. When slave boys and girls reached the age of eleven or twelve, masters sent most of them to the fields, where they learned farmwork by laboring along-side their parents. After a lifetime of labor, old women left the fields to care for the small children and spin yarn and old men to mind livestock and clean stables.

---

*Slaves understood clearly the motive for their enslavement. As ex-slave Albert Todd recalled, "Work was a religion we was taught."*

---

The overwhelming majority of slaves in 1860 were field hands. Planters sometimes assigned men and women to separate gangs, the women working at lighter tasks and the men doing the heavy work of clearing and breaking the land. But women also did heavy work. "I had to work hard," Nancy Boudry remembered, "plow and go and split wood just like a man." Although the daily tasks of slaves working in tobacco, rice, and sugar fields differed from those of slaves laboring in cotton fields, the backbreaking labor and the monotonous year-round routines made for grim similarity. As one ex-slave observed, on the plantation the "history of one day is the history of every day."

A few slaves (only one or two in every ten) became house servants. And virtually all of those who did (nine of ten) were women. There, under the critical eye of the white mistress, they cooked the white family's food, cleaned their house, babysat their infants, washed their clothes, and did the dozens of other tasks the master and mistress required. House servants enjoyed certain advantages over field hands, such as somewhat less physically demanding work, better food, and more comfortable quarters. But working in the big house had significant drawbacks. House servants were constantly on call, with no time that was entirely their own. Since no servant could please constantly, most bore the brunt of white frustration and rage. Ex-slave Jacob Branch of Texas remembered, "My poor mama! Every washday old Missy give her a beating." No wonder

some house servants wished they could trade places with field hands.

Even rarer than house servants were skilled artisans. In the cotton South, no more than one slave in twenty (almost all men) worked in a skilled trade. Most were blacksmiths and carpenters, but slaves also worked as masons, mechanics, millers, and shoemakers. Slave craftsmen took pride in their skills and often exhibited an independence of spirit that caused slaveholder James H. Hammond of South Carolina to declare in disgust that when a slave became a skilled artisan, "he is more than half freed." Skilled slave fathers often taught their crafts to their sons. "My pappy was one of the black smiths and worked in the shop," John Mathews remembered. "I had to help my pappy in the shop when I was a child and I learnt how to beat out the iron and make wagon tires, and make plows."

Rarest of all slave occupations was that of driver. Probably no more than one slave in a hundred—all men—worked in this capacity. These men were well named, for their primary task was driving other slaves to greater efforts in the fields. In some drivers' hands, the whip never rested. Ex-slave Jane Johnson of South Carolina called her driver the "meanest man, white or black, I ever see." But other drivers showed all the restraint they could. "Ole Gabe didn't like that whippin' business," West Turner of Virginia remembered. "When Marsa was there, he would lay it on 'cause he had to. But when old Marsa wasn't lookin', he never would beat them slaves."

Work dominated the slaves' daylight hours. Normally, slaves worked from what they called "can to can't," from "can see" in the morning to "can't see" at night. Even with a break at noon for a meal and rest, it made for a long day. For slaves, Lewis Young recalled, "work, work, work, 'twas all they do."

## Family, Religion, and Community

From dawn to dusk, slaves worked for the master. But from dusk to dawn, when the labor was done, and all day Sundays and usually Saturday afternoons, slaves were left largely to themselves. Bone tired perhaps, they nonetheless used the time and space to develop and enjoy what mattered most: family, religion, and community.

In the quarters, slaves lived lives that their masters were hardly aware of. Temporarily leaving the master-slave relationship at their cabin doors, slaves became husbands and wives, mothers and fathers, sons and daughters, preachers and singers, storytellers and conjurers. Over the generations, they created a community and a culture of their own that

**NANCY FORT, HOUSE SERVANT**

*This rare portrait of a slave woman at the turn of the nineteenth century depicts a strong and dignified person. Some who worked in domestic service took pride in their superior status and identified more with the master than with the slaves. "Honey, I wan't no common eve'day slave," one former servant recalled proudly. "I [helped] de white folks in de big house." But intense interaction with whites did not necessarily breed affection. Most domestic servants remained bound by ties of kinship and friendship, as well as by common oppression, to the slave quarters.*
Courtesy of Georgia Department of Archives and History.

**SLAVE CARPENTER**

*Haywood Dixon (1826–c. 1889) was a slave carpenter who worked in Greene County, North Carolina. In this 1854 daguerreotype, he is posed with a symbol of his craft, the carpenter's square. When work was slow on the home plantation, masters could hire out their skilled artisans to neighbors who needed a carpenter, blacksmith, or mason.*
Collection of William L. Murphy.

buoyed them up during long hours in the fields and brought them joy and hope in the few hours they had to themselves.

One of the most important consequences of the slaves' limited autonomy was the preservation and persistence of the family. Perhaps the most serious charge abolitionists leveled against slavery was that it wrecked black family life, a telling indictment in a society that put family at the heart of decent society. Slaveholders sometimes agreed that blacks had no family life, but they placed the blame on the slaves themselves, claiming that blacks chose to lead licentious, promiscuous lives.

Contrary to both abolitionists' and slaveholders' claims, the black family survived slavery. Indeed,

family was the chief fact of life in the quarters. Owners sometimes encouraged the creation and maintenance of families, but as often they were indifferent to the living arrangements of their slaves, as long as the quarters were quiet. Slave family life grew primarily from black commitment. While no laws recognized slave marriage, and therefore no master or slave was legally obligated to honor the bond, plantation records show that slave marriages were often long lasting. Young men and women in the slave quarters fell in love, married, and set up housekeeping in cabins of their own. The primary cause of the ending of slave marriages was death, just as it was in white families. But the second most frequent cause of the end of slave marriages was the sale of the husband or wife, something no white family ever had to fear. Precise figures are unavailable, but one scholar estimates that in the years 1820–1860, sales destroyed 300,000 slave marriages. Years after Moses Grandy was parted from his slave wife, he said, "I have never seen or heard of her from that day to this." And he added, "I loved her as I love my life."

Plantation records also reveal the importance of slave fathers. Not all fathers could live with their children—some men had been sold away and others had married women on neighboring plantations—but most fathers were present. Despite their inability to fulfill the traditional roles of provider and protector, slave fathers gained status by doing what they could to provide for their families: hunting, raising hogs, cultivating a garden, making furniture. In the eyes of slaves, an ex-bondsman recalled, "the man who does this is a great man amongst them." Although patri-

archal masters sharply circumscribed the authority of slave husbands, ex-slaves held both their mothers and fathers in high esteem, grateful for the refuge they had provided from the rigors of slavery.

Like families, religion also provided slaves with a refuge and a reason for living. In the seventeenth century and for most of the eighteenth, masters cared little about the spiritual lives of their slaves, and most blacks clung to their African beliefs. Beginning about the time of the American Revolution, however, Protestant evangelical sects, particularly the Baptists and Methodists, began trying to convert slaves. Evangelicals offered an emotional "religion of the heart" to which blacks (and many whites as well) responded enthusiastically. By the mid-nineteenth century, perhaps as many as one-quarter of all slaves claimed church membership, and many of the rest would not have objected to being called Christians.

**SLAVE CABIN**
*Other than the well-built brick chimney, this one-room, dirt-floored cabin on a small Georgia plantation had little to recommend it. Still, it no doubt housed a family. The six children in the photograph probably lived there with their mother and perhaps with their father. It may be Sunday—the oldest children are working about the cabin rather than in the fields, while the youngest children are playing in the bare yard. "The first seven or eight years of the slave-boy's life are about as full of sweet content as those of the most favored and petted white children," recalled the ex-slave and leading abolitionist Frederick Douglass. The two boys in straw hats are about the age when childhood ended and "light" chores began, chores that would grow increasingly heavy over the slave's lifetime.*
Collection of the New-York Historical Society.

Planters began promoting Christianity in the quarters because they came to see the slaves' salvation as part of their obligation and to believe that religion made slaves more obedient. Certainly, the Christianity that masters broadcast to slaves emphasized the meeker virtues. White preachers admonished their black congregants to love God and to obey their owners. Many slaves laughed up their sleeves at the message. "That old white preacher just was telling us slaves to be good to our masters," a Virginia ex-slave chuckled. "We ain't cared a bit about that stuff he was telling us 'cause we wanted to sing, pray, and serve God in our own way."

Meeting in their cabins or secretly in the woods, slaves created an African American Christianity that served their needs, not the masters'. Despite laws prohibiting teaching slaves to read, some could read enough to struggle with the Bible. With the help of black preachers, they interpreted the Christian message themselves. Rather than obedience, their faith emphasized justice. God kept score, and accounts of this world would be settled in the next. "God is punishing some of them old suckers and their children right now for the way they use to treat us poor colored folks," an ex-slave declared. But the slaves' faith involved more than retribution. It also spoke to their experiences in this world. In the Old Testament they discovered Moses, who delivered his people from slavery, and in the New Testament they found Jesus, who offered salvation to all and thereby established the equality of all people. Jesus' message of equality provided a potent antidote to the planters' claim that blacks were an inferior people whom God condemned to slavery and a crucial buttress to the slaves' self-esteem.

Christianity did not entirely drive out traditional African beliefs. Some slaves saw no contradiction between their faith in Christianity and their belief in conjurers, witches, and spirits. Christian music, preaching, and rituals showed the influence of Africa, as did much of the slaves' secular activities, such as wood carving, quilt making, and storytelling.

## Resistance and Rebellion

Slaves did not suffer slavery passively. They were, as whites said, "troublesome property." Slaves understood that accommodation to what they could not change was the price of survival, but in a hundred ways they protested their bondage. Theoretically, the master was all-powerful and the slave powerless. But sustained by their culture and emboldened by the slave community, slaves engaged in day-to-day resistance against their enslavers.

The spectrum of slave resistance ranged from mild to extreme. Telling a pointed story by the fireside in a slave cabin was probably the mildest form of protest. But when the weak got the better of the strong, as they did in tales of Brer Rabbit and Brer Fox ("Brer" is a contraction of "Brother"), listeners could enjoy the thrill of a vicarious victory over their masters. Protest in the fields was more active than that around firesides. Slaves were particularly inventive in resisting their master's demand that they work. They dragged their feet getting to the fields, put rocks in their cotton bags before putting them on the scale to be weighed, feigned illness, and pretended to be so thickheaded that they could not understand the simplest instruction. Slaves broke so many hoe handles that owners outfitted the hoes with oversized handles. Slaves so mistreated the work animals that masters switched from horses to mules, which could absorb more abuse. While slaves worked hard in the master's fields, they also sabotaged his interests.

Running away, a widespread form of protest, particularly angered masters. By escaping the plantation, runaways denied masters what they wanted most from their slaves—work. Sometimes runaways sought the ultimate prize: freedom in the North or in Canada. Over the decades, thousands of slaves, mostly from the Upper South, made it. But from the Lower South, escape to freedom was almost impossible. At most, runaways could hope to escape for a few weeks. They usually stayed close to the plantation, keeping to the deep woods or swamps and slipping back into the quarters at night to get food. "Lying out," as it was known, usually ended when the runaway, worn out and ragged, gave up or was finally chased down by slave-hunting dogs.

While resistance was common, outright rebellion—a violent assault on slavery by large numbers of slaves—was rare. The scarcity of revolts in the antebellum South is not evidence of the slaves' contentedness. Rather, existing conditions gave rebels virtually no chance of success. Whites outnumbered blacks two to one and were heavily armed. Moreover, communication between plantations was difficult, and the South provided little protective wilderness into which rebels could retreat and defend themselves. Organized rebellion in the American South was virtual suicide.

Given the odds, it is perhaps surprising to find any organized rebellion. But slaves in the antebellum

South did rise up. The best-known slave revolt, led by Nat Turner, occurred in 1831 in Southampton County, Virginia. Turner worked as a field hand, but he also preached to the slaves. "Ol' Prophet Nat," the slaves called him. In time, Turner became convinced that God had appointed him an instrument of divine vengeance. He set out to punish sinful white slaveholders and free their suffering slaves. Following an eclipse of the sun, which he took as a sign from the Lord, Turner and a few followers murdered his master and his family. By the next day, some sixty other slaves, armed with axes, had joined the insurrection. White militiamen crushed the revolt in less than two days, but by then the rebels had killed about sixty white men, women, and children. In retaliation, whites killed about 120 blacks, many of them innocent bystanders. Turner managed to escape to the woods, but the authorities captured him nine weeks later. Tried on November 5, 1831, Nat Turner was hanged six days later.

Although masters often boasted that their slaves were "instinctively contented," steady resistance and occasional rebellion proved otherwise. Slaves did not have the power to end their bondage, but by asserting themselves, they affirmed their humanity and worth. By resisting their masters' will, slaves also helped shape their own destiny. They became actors in the plantation drama, helping to establish limits beyond which planters and overseers hesitated to go.

It would be false to the historical record to minimize what the lack of freedom meant to slaves. Because the essence of slavery was the inability to shape one's own life, slavery blunted and thwarted African Americans' hopes and aspirations. Slavery broke some and crippled others. But slavery's destructive power had to contend with the resiliency of the human spirit. Slaves fought back physically, culturally, and spiritually. They not only survived bondage but created in the slave quarter a vibrant African American culture and community that would sustain them through more than two centuries of slavery and after.

## Black and Free: On the Middle Ground

Not every black Southerner was a slave. In 1860, some 260,000 (approximately 6 percent) of the region's 4.1 million African Americans were free (see Figure 12.1). What is surprising is not that their numbers were small but that they existed at all. "Free black" seemed a contradiction to most white Southerners. According to the dominant racial thinking, blacks were supposed to be slaves; free people were supposed to be white. Blacks who were free did not fit neatly into the South's idealized social order. They stood out, and whites made them objects of special scrutiny. Free blacks realized that they stood precariously between slavery and full freedom, on what a young free black artisan in Charleston characterized in 1848 as "a middle ground."

## Free Blacks and the White Response

Free blacks were rare in the colonial era, but their numbers swelled after the Revolution, when the natural rights philosophy of the Declaration of Independence and the egalitarian message of evangelical Protestantism joined to challenge slavery. Although probably not more than one slaveholder in a hundred freed his slaves, a brief flurry of emancipation visited the Upper South, where the ideological assault on slavery coincided with a deep depression in the tobacco economy. Other planters permitted favorite slaves to work after hours to accumulate money with which to buy their freedom. By 1810, free blacks numbered more than 100,000 and had become the fastest-growing element of the southern population. Burgeoning numbers of free blacks worried white Southerners, who, because of the cotton boom, wanted desperately to see more slaves, not more free blacks.

In the 1820s and 1830s, state legislatures acted to stem the growth of the free black population and to shrink the liberty of those blacks who had already gained their freedom. Laws denied masters the right to free their slaves. Other laws humiliated and restricted free blacks by subjecting them to special taxes, requiring them to register annually with the state or to choose a white guardian, prohibiting them from interstate travel, denying them the right to have schools and to participate in politics, and requiring them to carry "freedom papers" to prove they were not slaves. Increasingly, whites subjected free blacks to many of the same laws as slaves. They could not testify under oath in a court of law or serve on juries. They were liable to punishment meted out to slaves such as whipping and the treadmill. Like slaves, free blacks were forbidden to strike whites, even to defend themselves. "Free negroes belong to a degraded caste of society," a South Carolina judge summed up in 1848. "They are in no respect on a perfect equality with the white man. . . . They ought, by law, to be compelled to demean themselves as inferiors."

The elaborate system of regulations confined most free African Americans to a constricted life of poverty and dependence, which led most whites to despise them as degraded parasites. Typically, free blacks were rural, uneducated, unskilled agricultural laborers and domestic servants, scrambling to find work and eke out a living. Opportunities of all kinds—for work, education, community—were slim. Planters looked upon free blacks as worthless rascals, likely to set a bad example for slaves. They believed that free blacks subverted the racial subordination that was the essence of slavery.

### Achievement Despite Restrictions

Despite increasingly harsh laws and stepped-up persecution, free African Americans made the most of the advantages their status offered. Unlike slaves, free blacks could legally marry. They could protect their families from arbitrary disruption by whites and pass on their heritage of freedom to their children. Freedom also meant that they could choose occupations and own property. For most, however, these economic rights proved only theoretical, for whites allowed most free blacks few opportunities. Unlike whites, a majority of the antebellum South's free blacks remained propertyless.

---

*The elaborate system of regulations confined most free African Americans to a constricted life of poverty and dependence, which led most whites to despise them as degraded parasites.*

---

Still, some free blacks escaped the poverty and degradation whites thrust upon them. Particularly in urban areas—especially the cities of Charleston, Mobile, and New Orleans—a small elite of free blacks developed and even flourished. Urban whites enforced many of the restrictive laws only sporadically, allowing free blacks room to maneuver. The elite consisted overwhelmingly of light-skinned African Americans who worked at skilled trades, as tailors, carpenters, mechanics, and the like. Their customers were prominent whites—planters, merchants, and judges—who appreciated their able, respectful service. The free black elite operated schools for their children and traveled in and

out of their states, despite the laws. They worshiped with whites (in separate seating) in the finest churches and lived scattered about in white neighborhoods, not in separate ghettos. And like elite whites, some owned slaves. Blacks could own blacks because, despite all of the restrictions whites placed on free African Americans, whites did not deny them the right to own property, which in the South included human property. Of the 3,200 black slaveholders (barely 1 percent of the free black population), most owned only a few, who were sometimes family members whom they could not legally free. But others owned slaves in large numbers, none of whom were family and all of whom were exploited for labor.

One such free black slave owner was William Ellison of South Carolina. Ellison was himself born a slave in 1790, but in 1816 he bought his freedom from his white master (who may have been his father) and moved to a thriving plantation district about one hundred miles north of Charleston. He set up business as a cotton gin maker, a trade he had learned as a slave. Ellison's gin business grew with the cotton boom until by 1835 he was prosperous enough to purchase the home of a former governor of the state. Ellison lived in the house until his death in 1861. By then he had become the wealthiest free black in his state, a big planter who made a hundred bales of cotton a year with sixty-three slaves on an eight-hundred-acre plantation.

Not every free black was willing to accommodate to whites and enslave other blacks. At the very time Ellison was building his slave empire, Denmark Vesey was plotting slavery's destruction. Most free blacks followed a middle course. They neither became slaveholders nor sought to raise a slave rebellion. Rather, they simply tried to preserve their freedom. Increasingly under attack from planters who wanted to eliminate or enslave them and from white artisans who coveted their jobs, they sought to impress whites with their reliability, their economic progress, and their good behavior.

## The Plain Folk

Most whites in the South did not own slaves, not even one. In 1860, more than six million of the South's eight million whites lived in slaveless families. Most "plain folk" were small farmers. Perhaps three out of four were yeomen, small farmers who owned their own land. As in the North, farm ownership provided a family with an economic foundation, social respectability, and political standing. Unlike their northern counterparts, however, southern yeomen lived in a region whose economy and society were dominated by unfree labor. By no means did the nonslaveholding white majority escape the influence of slavery.

## Yeomen Societies

In an important sense, the South had more than one white yeomanry. The huge southern landscape provided space enough for two yeoman societies, separated roughly along geographical lines. Yeomen throughout the South had a good deal in common, but the life of a small farm family in the plantation belt—the flatlands that included the richest soils—differed from the life of one in the upcountry—the area of hills and mountains.

Plantation belt yeomen lived within the orbit of the planter class. Small landholdings actually outnumbered the larger plantations in that great arc of fertile land that spread from South Carolina to east Texas, but they were dwarfed in importance. Like planters, yeomen devoted a significant portion of their land to growing cotton. But with only family labor to draw upon, they produced only a couple of four-hundred-pound bales each year, whereas large planters measured their crop in hundreds of bales. The small farmers' cotton tied them to planters. Unable to afford cotton gins or baling presses of their own, they relied on helpful neighborhood slave owners to gin and bale their small crops. With no link to merchants in the port cities, yeomen turned to better-connected planters to ship and sell their cotton.

A dense network of personal relationships laced small farmers and planters together in patterns of reciprocity and mutual obligation. A planter

**GATHERING CORN**
*In this 1865 drawing, two white men, perhaps kinfolk or neighbors, join in harvesting corn. While one cuts and gathers the stalks, the other shucks the corn. A black man, who was probably a slave either owned or hired by one of the white men, loads the corn into a wagon. Corn was a primary crop of most antebellum yeoman farmers, even those who grew considerable cotton. Yeomen usually grew about twice the corn needed for their families and livestock and marketed the rest.*
Library of Congress.

might send his slaves to help a newcomer build a house or a sick farmer get in his crop. He hired out surplus slaves to ambitious yeomen who wanted to expand cotton production. He sometimes chose his overseers from among the sons of local farm families. Plantation mistresses sometimes nursed ailing neighbors. Family ties could span class lines, making rich and poor kin as well as neighbors. Yeomen shared the planters' commitment to white supremacy and actively defended black subordination. Rural counties required adult white males to ride in slave patrols, which nightly scoured country roads to make certain that no slaves were moving about without permission. On Sundays, plantation dwellers and plain folk came together in church to worship and afterward lingered to gossip and to transact small business.

---

*Yeomen throughout the South had a good deal in common, but the life of a small farm family in the plantation belt—the flatlands that included the richest soils—differed from the life of one in the upcountry—the area of hills and mountains.*

---

By contrast, the hills and mountains of the South resisted the penetration of slavery and plantations. While increasing participation in the market was a trend everywhere in the South, the western parts of Virginia, North Carolina, and South Carolina, northern Georgia and Alabama, and eastern Tennessee and Kentucky retained a quite different economy and society (see Map 12.2). The higher elevation, colder climate, rugged terrain, and poor transportation made it difficult for commercial agriculture to make headway. For yeomen who lived in the hills and mountains, planters and slaves were not everyday acquaintances. Geographically isolated, the upcountry was a yeoman stronghold.

At the core of the distinctive upcountry culture was the independent farm family working its own patch of land; raising a considerable number of hogs, cattle, and sheep; and seeking self-sufficiency and independence. Toward that end, all members of the family worked, their tasks depending on their sex and age. Husbands labored in the fields, and with their sons they cleared, plowed, planted, and cultivated primarily food crops—corn, wheat,

sweet potatoes, and perhaps some fruit. Although pressed into field labor at harvest time, wives and daughters worked in and about the cabin most of the year. One upcountry farmer remembered that his mother "worked in the house cooking, spinning, weaving [and doing] patchwork." Women also tended the vegetable garden, kept a cow and some chickens, preserved foods, cleaned their homes, fed their families, and cared for their children. Male and female tasks were equally crucial to the farm's success, but as in other white southern households, the female domestic sphere was subordinated to the will of the male patriarch.

The typical upcountry yeoman also grew a little cotton or tobacco, but production for home consumption was more important than production for the market. Not much currency changed hands in the upcountry. Credit was common, as was direct barter. A yeoman might trade his small commercial crop to a country store owner for a little salt, lead shot, needles, and nails. Networks of exchange and mutual assistance tied individual homesteads to the larger community. Farm families swapped goods and work and joined together in logrolling, house- or barn-raising, and cornhusking. Strong communal ties made the yeoman's goal of maintaining his family's independence realistic.

Yeomen did not have the upcountry entirely to themselves. Even the hills had some plantations and slaves. But they existed in much smaller numbers than in the plantation belt. Farmers and farms, not planters and plantations, dominated upcountry culture. Yeoman domination did not mean that the upcountry opposed slavery. As long as they were free to lead their own lives, upcountry plain folk defended slavery and white supremacy just as staunchly as did other white Southerners.

Whether plain folk lived in the hills or in the flatlands, they did not usually associate "book learning" with the basic needs of life. In any case, the children of yeomen had limited opportunity for schooling. A northern woman visiting the South in the 1850s observed, "Education is not extended to the masses here as at the North." Even where public schools existed, terms were short, only about 50 or 60 days a year in the South compared with 100 to 150 days in the North. Although most people managed to pick up a basic knowledge of the "three R's," approximately one southern white man in five was illiterate in 1860, and the rate for white women was even higher. "People here prefer talking to reading," a Virginian remarked. Telling stories, reciting ballads, and singing hymns were important activities in yeoman folk culture.

Plain folk everywhere spent more hours in revival tents than in classrooms. The greatest of the early-nineteenth-century revivals occurred in 1801 at Cane Ridge, Kentucky, where some twenty thousand people gathered to listen to a host of evangelical preachers who spoke day and night for a week. Ministers sought to convert and save souls by bringing individuals to a personal conviction of sin. Revivalism crossed denominational lines, but Baptists and Methodists adopted it wholeheartedly and by midcentury had become the South's largest religious groups. By emphasizing free choice and individual worth, the plain folk's religion was hopeful and affirming. Hymns and spirituals provided guides to right and wrong—praising modesty and steadfastness, condemning drinking and devilish activity like dancing. Above all, hymns spoke of eventual release from worldly sorrows and the assurance of eternal salvation.

## Poor Whites

Northerners denied the claim that the South's white majority constituted a sturdy yeomanry—hardworking, landholding small farmers. Instead, they charged that the institution of slavery had pushed slaveless whites so far down the social and economic ladder that they had lost heart, ambition, and energy. The majority of the South's whites, according to northern critics, were landless, shiftless, and degraded. Contemporaries called these Southerners a variety of derogatory names: hillbillies, crackers, rednecks, and poor white trash. Even slaves were known to chant: "I'd rather be a nigger an' plow ol' Beck, / Than a white hill-billy with a long red neck." Poor whites were not just whites who were poor. The label carried a moral as well as a material meaning. Poor whites were ignorant and inbred, sick in body and degenerate in culture.

Significant numbers of Southerners were poor, as the critics claimed. Perhaps one in four farmers was landless. Landless farm families lived as tenants, renting rather than owning land. Other poor rural Southerners worked as unskilled day laborers, hunters, herders, and fishermen. Living on the periphery of the southern economy, some barely made a go of it. Wits could declare that "poor whites were born lazy and had a relapse." In fact, poor whites subsisted on unhealthy diets, lived in miserable housing, spent summers going barefooted around animals, and, consequently, suffered high incidences of hookworm, pellagra, and other debilitating diseases that thrived in the South's warm, wet climate. Although impoverished, most of these Southerners were not degenerate. Instead, they were ambitious people scratching to survive and aspiring to climb into the yeomanry.

Poor whites were sometimes poor only temporarily. The Lipscomb family illustrates the possibility of upward mobility. In 1845, Smith and Sally Lipscomb and their children abandoned tired land in South Carolina for Benton County, Alabama. "Benton is a mountainous country but ther is a heep of good levil land to tend in it," Smith wrote back to his brother. All of the Lipscombs fell ill, but all recovered, and the entire family went to work. Because they had no money to buy land, they squatted on seven acres. With the help of neighbors, they built a twenty-two-foot-by-twenty-four-foot cabin, a detached kitchen, and two stables. From daylight to dark, Smith and his sons worked the land. Nature cooperated, and they produced enough food for the table and several bales of cotton. The women worked as hard in the cabin, and Sally contributed to the family's income by selling homemade shirts and socks. In time, the Lipscombs bought land of their own. They joined Hebron Baptist Church and completed their transformation from landless poor whites to respectable yeomen.

The upward mobility demonstrated by the Lipscombs became rarer in the 1850s. The prosperity of the cotton economy encouraged planters to expand their operations, driving the price of land beyond the reach of poor families. Squeezed by competition with plantation slavery and pushed to the least fertile regions of the South, such as the pine barrens along the Atlantic coast, poor whites were likely to remain poor.

## The Politics of Slavery

Like every other significant feature of southern society, politics showed the impress of slavery. Even after the South's politics became democratic in form for the white male population, political power remained unevenly distributed. The nonslaveholding white majority wielded less political power than their numbers indicated. The slaveholding white minority wielded more. Self-conscious, cohesive, and with a well-developed sense of class interest, slaveholders busied themselves with party politics, campaigns, and officeholding and made demands of state governments. As a result, they received significant benefits. But nonslaveholding whites were concerned mainly with preserving their liberties and keeping their taxes low. Collectively, they asked government for little of an economic nature, and they received little.

Slaveholders worried about nonslaveholders' political loyalty to slavery. Ultimately, they need not have fretted. Since the eighteenth century, the mass of whites had accepted the planters' argument that the existing social order served all Southerners' interests. Slavery compensated every white man—no matter how poor—with membership in the South's white ruling class. It also provided the means by which nonslaveholders might someday advance into the ranks of the planters. White men in the South fought furiously about many things, but they agreed that they should take land from Indians, promote agriculture, uphold white supremacy, and defend slavery from its enemies.

## The Democratization of the Political Arena

The political reforms that swept the nation in the first half of the nineteenth century reached deeply into the South. Southern politics became democratic politics—for white men. State by state, Southerners eliminated the wealth and property requirements that had restricted political participation. By the early 1850s, every state had extended suffrage to all white males who were at least twenty-one years of age. Most southern states also removed the property requirements for holding state offices. To be sure, undemocratic features lingered. Plantation districts still wielded disproportionate power in several state legislatures. Nevertheless, southern politics increasingly took place within a democratic political structure.

White male suffrage ushered in an era of vigorous electoral competition. Eager voters rushed to the polls to exercise their new rights. In South Carolina, for example, in the 1810 election—the last election with voting restrictions in place—only 43 percent of white men cast ballots. By 1824, the number of white men voting had climbed to a remarkable 76 percent. High turnouts became hallmarks of southern electoral politics. Voters displayed considerable political savvy and expected solid argument

as well as stirring oratory. They also demanded good entertainment—barbecues and bands, rum and races. The candidates competed in producing extravaganzas, hoping to attract attention as well as votes.

As politics became aggressively democratic, it also grew fiercely partisan. From the 1830s to the 1850s, Whigs and Democrats battled for the electorate's favor. Whigs and Democrats both presented themselves as the plain white folk's best friend. All candidates declared their fervent commitment to republican equality and pledged themselves to defend the people's liberty. Each party sought to portray the other as a collection of rich, snobbish, selfish men who had antidemocratic designs up their silk sleeves. Each, in turn, claimed for itself the mantle of humble "servant of the people."

*By the early 1850s, southern politics became democratic politics—for white men.*

The Whig and Democratic Parties sought to serve the people differently, however. Southern Whigs tended, as Whigs did elsewhere in the nation, to favor government intervention in the economy, and Democrats tended to oppose it. Whigs generally backed state support of banks, railroads, and corporations, arguing that government aid would stimulate the economy, enlarge opportunity, and thus increase the general welfare. Democrats emphasized the threat to individual liberty that government intervention posed, claiming that granting favors to special economic interests would result in concentrated power, which would in turn jeopardize the common man's opportunity and equality. Beginning with the Panic of 1837, the parties clashed repeatedly on concrete economic and financial issues.

## Planter Power

Whether Whig or Democrat, southern officeholders were likely to be slave owners. The power slaveholders exerted over slaves did not translate directly into political authority over whites, however. In the nineteenth century, political power could be won only at the ballot box, and almost everywhere nonslaveholders were in the majority. Yet year after year, proud and noisily egalitarian common men elected wealthy slaveholders (Table 12.1).

TABLE 12.1
SLAVEHOLDERS AND PLANTERS IN
LEGISLATURES, 1860

| Legislature | Percent of Slaveholders | Percent of Planters* |
|---|---|---|
| Virginia | 67.3 | 24.2 |
| Maryland | 53.4 | 19.3 |
| North Carolina | 85.8 | 36.6 |
| Kentucky | 60.6 | 8.4 |
| Tennessee | 66.0 | 14.0 |
| Missouri | 41.2 | 5.3 |
| Arkansas | 42.0 | 13.0 |
| South Carolina | 81.7 | 55.4 |
| Georgia | 71.6 | 29.0 |
| Florida | 55.4 | 20.0 |
| Alabama | 76.3 | 40.8 |
| Mississippi | 73.4 | 49.5 |
| Louisiana | 63.8 | 23.5 |
| Texas | 54.1 | 18.1 |

*Planters: Owned 20 or more slaves.

Source: Adapted from Ralph A. Wooster, *The People in Power: Courthouse and Statehouse in the Lower South, 1850–1860* (1969), 41; *Politicians, Planters, and Plain Folks: Courthouse and Statehouse in the Upper South* (1975), 40.

Courtesy of the University of Tennessee Press.

In 1860, the percentage of slave owners in state legislatures ranged from 41 percent in Missouri to nearly 86 percent in North Carolina. Legislators not only tended to own slaves—they often owned large numbers. The percentage of planters (individuals with twenty or more slaves) in southern legislatures in 1860 ranged from 5.3 percent in Missouri to 55.4 percent in South Carolina. In North Carolina, where only 3 percent of the state's white families belonged to the planter class, 36.6 percent of the legislature were planters. The democratization of politics in the nineteenth century meant that more ordinary citizens served in government than in the eighteenth century, but yeomen and artisans remained rare sights in the halls of southern legislatures.

Upper-class dominance of southern politics reflected, in part, the strength of the rural folk culture, which valued tradition and stability. In the colonial era, yeomen had looked to the upper class for political leadership. Large planters possessed great wealth, education, oratorical gifts, experience in public affairs, the habit of command, and eagerness to serve. Notions of hierarchy and habits of deference declined in the nineteenth century as democracy rose, but planter status remained important in the South and the surest ticket to political advancement.

But tradition was not enough to ensure planter rule. Slaveholders had to persuade the white majority that what was good for slaveholders was also good for them. Slaveless whites proved to be receptive to the planters' argument. The South had, on the whole, done well by them. Most had farms of their own. They participated as equals in a democratic political system. As white men, they enjoyed an elevated social status, above all blacks and in theory equal to all other whites. As long as slavery existed, they could dream of joining the planter class, of rising above the drudgery of field labor.

Most slaveholders took pains to win the plain folk's trust and to nurture their respect. In the plantation districts especially, where slaveholders and nonslaveholders lived side by side, planters learned that flexing their economic muscle was a poor way to win the political allegiance of common men. Instead, they developed a lighter touch, fully attentive to their own interests but aware of the personal feelings of poorer whites. One South Carolinian told his wealthy neighbor that he had a bright political future because he never thought himself "too good to sit down & talk to a poor man."

While not all of the gentry behaved astutely, smart candidates found ways to convince wary yeomen of their democratic convictions and egalitarian sentiments, whether they were genuine or not. When young John A. Quitman ran for a seat in the Mississippi legislature, he amazed a boisterous crowd of small farmers at one campaign stop by not only entering but winning contests in jumping, boxing, wrestling, and sprinting. For his finale he outshot the area's champion marksman. Then, demonstrating his deft political touch, he gave his prize, a fat ox, to the defeated rifleman. The electorate showed its approval by sending Quitman to the state capital.

The massive representation of slaveholders ensured that southern legislatures would make every effort to preserve slavery. Georgia politics show how well the planters protected themselves in the political struggle. In 1850, about half of the state's revenues came from taxes on slave property, the characteristic form of planter wealth. However, the tax rate on slaves was trifling, only about one-fifth the rate on land. Moreover, planters benefited far more than other social groups from public spending, for financing railroads—which carried cotton to market—was the largest state expenditure in the late antebellum period. The legislature established low tax rates on land, the characteristic form of yeoman wealth, which meant that the typical yeomen's annual tax bill was small. Still, relative to their wealth, large slaveholders paid less than did other whites. Relative to their numbers, they got more. A sympathetic slaveholding legislature protected planters' interests and gave the impression of protecting the small farmers' interests as well.

In the antebellum South, therefore, the rise of the common man occurred alongside the continuing, even growing, power of the planter class. Rather than pitting slaveholders against nonslaveholders, elections remained an effective means of binding the region's whites together. Elections affirmed the sovereignty of white men, whether genteel planter or plain folk, and the subordination of African Americans. Those twin themes played well among white women as well. Although unable to vote, white women supported equality for whites and slavery for blacks.

## Conclusion: A Slave Society

Southerners and Northerners came to see the South as fundamentally different from the rest of the nation. It was a rural region with a biracial population that reflected the dominance of plantation slavery. Regional differences generally increased over time, not merely because the South became more and more dominated by slavery, but also because developments in the North rapidly propelled it in a very different direction.

In 1860, nearly four million black Southerners, one-third of the South's population, were enslaved. Bondage saddled blacks with enormous physical and spiritual burdens: hard labor, poor treatment, broken families, and, most important, the denial of freedom itself. Although degraded and exploited, they were not defeated. Out of African memories and New World realities, blacks created a life-affirming African American culture that sustained and strengthened them. Their families, religion, and community provided antidotes to white racist ideas and even to white power. Defined as property, they refused to be reduced to things. Perceived as inferior beings, they rejected the notion that they were natural slaves. The imbalance of power made Denmark Vesey's path of outright rebellion suicidal, but most slaves rebelled inwardly. They engaged in a war of wills with masters who sought their labor while they sought to live dignified, autonomous lives.

Much more than racial slavery contributed to the South's distinctiveness and to the loyalty and regional identification of its whites. White Southerners felt strong attachments to local communities, to extended families, to personal, face-to-face relationships, to rural life, to evangelical Protestantism, and to codes of honor and chivalry, among other things. But slavery was crucial to the South's economy, society, and culture, as well as to its developing sectional consciousness. After the 1830s, little disturbed the white consensus south of the Mason-Dixon line that racial slavery was necessary and just. By making all blacks a pariah class, all whites gained a measure of equality and harmony.

Racism did not erase all stress along class lines. Nor did the other features of southern life that helped confine class tensions: the wide availability of land, rapid economic mobility, the democratic nature of political life, the shrewd behavior of slaveholders toward poorer whites, kinship ties between rich and poor, and rural traditions. Anxious slaveholders continued to worry that yeomen would defect from the proslavery consensus. But during the 1850s a far more ominous division emerged between the "slave states" and the "free states."

## CHRONOLOGY

| | | | | |
|---|---|---|---|---|
| **1808** | External slave trade outlawed. | | **1820–** | Cotton production soars from about |
| **1810s–** | Suffrage gradually extended | | **1860** | 300,000 bales to nearly 5 million |
| **1850s** | throughout South to white males | | | bales. |
| | over twenty-one years of age. | | **1822** | Denmark Vesey's slave rebellion |
| **1820s–** | Southern legislatures enact slave | | | thwarted in South Carolina. |
| **1830s** | codes to strengthen slavery. | | **1831** | Nat Turner's slave rebellion occurs |
| | | | | in Virginia. |

**1808** External slave trade outlawed.

**1810s–1850s** Suffrage gradually extended throughout South to white males over twenty-one years of age.

**1820s–1830s** Southern legislatures enact slave codes to strengthen slavery.

Southern legislatures enact laws to restrict growth of free black population and to hem in freedom of free blacks.

Southern intellectuals begin to fashion systematic defense of slavery.

**1820–1860** Cotton production soars from about 300,000 bales to nearly 5 million bales.

**1822** Denmark Vesey's slave rebellion thwarted in South Carolina.

**1831** Nat Turner's slave rebellion occurs in Virginia.

**1860** The slave population of the South approaches 4 million, an increase of 600 percent in seven decades.

# SUGGESTED READINGS

Ira Berlin, *Slaves without Masters: The Free Negro in the Antebellum South.* An impressive interpretive survey of free people of color.

William J. Cooper Jr., *In Liberty and Slavery: Southern Politics to 1860* (1983). A solid survey of antebellum southern political life.

Drew G. Faust, *James Henry Hammond and the Old South* (1982). A fine biography that reveals the character and values of masters.

Eugene D. Genovese, *Roll, Jordan, Roll: The World the Slaves Made* (1974). A classic study that remains the starting point for understanding life in slave quarters.

Stephanie McCurry, *Masters of Small Worlds* (1995), Steven Hahn, *The Roots of Southern Populism* (1983), and Christine Leigh Heyrman, *Southern Cross* (1997). Three studies that illuminate the world of yeoman whites.

Peter Wallenstein, *From the Slave South to New South* (1987). An analysis of politics and power in Georgia.

Marli F. Weiner, *Mistresses and Slaves* (1998). A balanced, recent interpretation of mistresses.

Harold D. Woodman, *King Cotton and His Retainers* (1968), and Gavin Wright, *Old South, New South* (1986). Two studies that demonstrate the centrality of plantation slavery in the southern economy.

**HOME INDUSTRIES
POLITICAL EMBLEM**

*Common trades practiced by American workers are represented on this political emblem designed in Pennsylvania to be carried in political parades in 1840 by supporters of presidential candidate William Henry Harrison. Like most northern Whigs, Harrison favored a tariff to protect home industries. Carpenters, tanners, shoemakers, blacksmiths, masons, butchers, bakers, tailors, and farmers were represented by their tools. Try to identify the tool each might use. Note that the emblem identifies industries with hand tools rather than with complex machinery, illustrating that the transition to industrial production was still at an early stage in the 1840s and 1850s. The emblem also engages in a kind of political misrepresentation. Tariffs mostly protected domestic manufacturers of machine-made goods like textiles that already were produced in factories. Whigs used the symbols of handwork in this emblem to provide an appealing apple-pie image for the manufacturing industries that were protected by the tariffs. One cannot imagine, for example, a Whig enthusiast parading around with an emblem of a textile mill. Also notice that the emblem does not illustrate the skilled work done by women in homes throughout the nation such as cooking, dairying, and cleaning. What tools might be portrayed if the emblem featured women's work?*

# ABRAHAM LINCOLN'S AMERICA

# 13

## 1840–1860

EARLY IN NOVEMBER 1842, Abraham Lincoln and his new wife, Mary, moved into their first home in Springfield, Illinois, a rented room on the second floor of the Globe Tavern measuring eight by fourteen feet, the nicest place Lincoln had ever lived. Fewer than twenty years later, in March 1861, the Lincolns moved into what would prove to be their last home, the presidential mansion in Washington, D.C. Lincoln climbed from the Globe Tavern to the White House by relentless work, unslaked ambition, and immense talent, traits he had honed since boyhood.

Born in a Kentucky log cabin in 1809, Lincoln grew up on small, struggling farms. His father, Thomas, never learned to read and, Abraham explained, "never did more in the way of writing than to bunglingly sign his own name." Lincoln's mother, Nancy, could neither read nor write. In December 1816, Thomas Lincoln moved his young family out of Kentucky, crossing the Ohio River to the Indiana wilderness. They lived for two frozen months in a crude lean-to only partially enclosed by limbs and bushes while Thomas, a skilled carpenter, built a new cabin. There Abraham learned the arts of farming practiced by families throughout the nation. Although only eight years old, Abraham "had an axe put into his hands at once" and used it "almost constantly" for the next fifteen years, he recalled. In 1830, Thomas Lincoln decided to start over once again. With Abraham astraddle one of the family's oxen, the Lincolns moved two hundred miles west to central Illinois. The next spring Abraham set out on his own, a "friendless, uneducated, penniless boy," as he described himself.

By dogged striving, Lincoln gained an education and the respect of his Illinois neighbors, although a steady income eluded him for years. He eventually built a prosperous law practice in Springfield and served in the Illinois legislature and in Congress. Even though he did not hold office during the 1850s, his ceaseless political activity and hard-driving ambition won him a large and admiring following that ultimately catapulted him into the White House.

Like Lincoln, millions of Americans believed they could make something of themselves, whatever their origins, so long as they were willing to work. Individuals who refused to work—who were lazy, improvident, or foolish—had only themselves to blame if they failed. Work was a prerequisite for success, not a guarantee. The promise of rewards from hard work spurred efforts that shaped the contours of Lincoln's America, pushing the boundaries of the nation south to the Rio Grande and west to the Pacific Ocean. That expansion—economic, political, and geographic—also raised anew the question of slavery that Lincoln confronted as president.

**ABRAHAM LINCOLN'S HAT**

*Abraham Lincoln wore this stovepipe hat, made of beaver pelt, during his years as president of the United States. Stovepipe hats were worn by established, respectable, middle-class men in the 1850s. Workingmen and farmers would have felt out of place wearing such a hat, except perhaps on special occasions like weddings or funerals. Growing up in Kentucky, Indiana, and Illinois, Lincoln may have seen stovepipe hats on the leading men of his community, but he probably never owned one until he became an aspiring Illinois lawyer and politician. Wearing such a hat was a mark that one had achieved a certain success in life, in Lincoln's case the enormous social distance he had traveled from his backwoods origins to the White House. But even as president he continued a backwoods practice he had begun as a young postmaster in New Salem, Illinois, using his hat as a place to store letters and papers. Lincoln's law partner, William Herndon, termed Lincoln's hat "an extraordinary receptacle [that] served as his desk and memorandum book."*

Smithsonian Institution.

## Economic and Industrial Evolution

During the 1840s and 1850s, Lincoln and other Americans lived amidst profound economic transformation that had been under way since the start of the nineteenth century. (Economic changes in the early nineteenth century are discussed in Chapter 11.) By 1860, Americans' per capita income was twice what it had been in 1800. At first glance that may not seem impressive evidence of economic change. But consider that during those same years the nation's population grew sixfold, to over 31 million. For the per capita income to double, the total output of the American economy had to multiply twelvefold in sixty years. Four fundamental changes in American society fueled this phenomenal economic growth.

First, Americans began to move from farms to cities, a long-term shift that would continue well into the twentieth century. In 1860, farmers still made up 80 percent of the nation's population. But Abraham Lincoln and millions of other Americans left farms behind, boosting the urban population. By 1860, the nation had 186 towns about the size of Springfield, Illinois (9,500 people), and 16 cities with 50,000 or more.

A second major change, closely related to the movement away from farms, was that a growing number of Americans worked in factories, by 1860 almost 20 percent of the labor force. This trend contributed to the nation's economic growth because, in general, factory workers were twice as productive (in output per unit of labor input) as agricultural workers.

A third fundamental change—from water to steam as a source of energy—permitted factories to be brought to the labor force in cities. The first American factories had to be situated on streams that supplied water power, and workers had to be attracted to the factory site. Steam power freed business owners to locate their factories in cities where workers and materials could be readily brought together. Beginning around 1840, steam became harnessed to manufacturing, but the transition was slow, delayed by the continued effectiveness of water power and muscles. By 1850, for example, animal and human muscles still provided thirty-three times more energy for manufacturing than steam.

The shortage of cheap, plentiful fuel had prevented earlier use of steam in factories. But during the 1830s, extensive mining began in Pennsylvania coal fields and massive quantities of coal became available for industrial fuel. Heat from coal not only powered steam engines in factories. It also permitted new methods of iron production and metalworking required for the full-scale mechanization of production. In addition, those methods made it possible to couple steam power to land transportation in the building of railroads.

This cascade of interrelated developments—steam, coal, iron, mechanization, railroads—had begun to transform the character of the American economy by the 1850s. Historians have often referred to this transformation as an industrial revolution. Certainly the profound changes in the American economy in these years pushed the nation toward industrialization. Yet those changes did not cause a revolutionary discontinuity in the economy or society. The United States remained overwhelmingly agricultural. Old methods of production continued alongside the new. Changes in production tended to be evolutionary and cumulative. In the long term—by the early twentieth century—the consequences of these and other changes were indeed revolutionary. Before 1860, however, the American economy underwent a process that might best be termed "industrial evolution."

That evolution was made possible by a fourth fundamental development that propelled American economic growth. Agricultural productivity (defined as crop output per unit of labor input) nearly doubled during Lincoln's lifetime. This dramatic increase contributed more than any other single factor to the economic growth of Lincoln's America. While cities, factories, and steam engines blossomed throughout the nation—especially outside the South—the roots of American economic growth lay in agriculture.

## Agriculture and Land Policy

It may seem odd to consider an ax a basic agricultural tool, like a hoe or a shovel. Yet farmers in Lincoln's America needed axes. A French traveler observed that Americans had "a general feeling of hatred against trees" and taught their children "at an early age to use the axe against the trees, their enemies." Although the traveler exaggerated, his observation contained an important truth. Forests impeded agriculture. With axes—which Lincoln termed "that most useful instrument"—farmers leveled trees, cleared land for planting, and built cabins, fences, and barns.

The sheer physical labor required to convert forest to field limited agricultural productivity. Energy that might have gone to growing crops went instead to felling trees. But as farmers pushed westward, they encountered thinner forests and eventually the Midwest's comparatively treeless prairie, where they could spend less time with an ax and more time at the plow or hoe, significantly boosting agricultural productivity. Rich prairie soils also gave somewhat higher crop yields than eastern farms, and farmers migrated to the Midwest by the tens of thousands between 1830 and 1860. The population of Indiana, Illinois, Michigan, Wisconsin, and Iowa exploded tenfold, growing from 500,000 in 1830 to more than 5 million by 1860, four times

faster than the growth of the nation as a whole. During the 1850s, Illinois added more people than any other state in the Union.

Labor-saving improvements in other farm implements also hiked agricultural productivity. Frontier farmers commonly planted their first crop by chopping a hole in the ground with an ax or hoe and then dropping in a few kernels of corn. If they plowed at all, they used wooden plows that tended to stick to the soil and break easily. In 1819, Jethro Wood patented a plow that used replaceable cast-iron parts to cut and scour the soil. Wood's cast-iron plow required only half as much labor as a wooden plow, and farmers throughout the Northeast quickly adopted it or one of the many variations crafted by local blacksmiths.

---

*The dramatic increase in agricultural productivity contributed more than any other single factor to the economic growth of Lincoln's America.*

---

But cast-iron plows proved too weak and sticky for the thick turf and dense soil of the midwestern prairie. In 1837, John Deere patented a strong, smooth steel plow that sliced through prairie soil so cleanly that farmers called it the "singing plow." Deere's steel plow underwent many improvements that made plowing less work, prairie farmers more productive, and Deere's company the leading plow manufacturer in the Midwest, turning out more than ten thousand plows a year by the late 1850s. By 1860, the energy for plowing still came from animal and human muscles, but better plows permitted that energy to break more ground and plant more crops.

Improvements in wheat harvesting also multiplied farmers' productivity. Although corn rather than wheat was the basic dietary staple of most farmers and their animals, all the corn was harvested by hand. Outside the South, most farmers planted some wheat, and in the Midwest—where soil and climate conditions were nearly ideal—many planted mostly wheat. Wheat was more difficult than corn to grow and harvest, but it was also more desirable. More dense and less bulky than corn, wheat was more readily transported to market and sold for a much higher price.

The crucial point in wheat production came at harvest time. Once ripe, wheat had to be cut quickly

**HARVESTING GRAIN WITH CRADLES**

*This late-nineteenth-century painting shows the grain harvest during the mid-nineteenth century at Bishop Hill, Illinois, a Swedish community where the artist, Olof Krans, and his parents settled in 1850. The men swing cradles, slowly cutting a swath through the grain; the women gather the cut grain into sheaves to be hauled away later for threshing. As a well-organized community, Bishop Hill could call upon the labor of a large number of men and women at harvest time. Most farmers had only a few family members and a hired hand or two to help with the harvest. Note that although the grain field appears level enough to be ideal for a mechanical reaper, all the work is done by hand; no machine is in sight.*

Bishop Hill State Historic Site, Illinois Historic Preservation Agency.

before rain or wind ruined the crop or overripe grains scattered uselessly on the ground. Early in the nineteenth century, farmers harvested wheat by cutting the stalks with a sharp-bladed scythe. Working hard, a farmer could scythe three-fourths of an acre of wheat a day. By 1850, most farmers had adopted scythes with cradles (a frame that projected above the scythe). Their long wooden fingers were able to gather more grain stalks to be cut by each stroke of the attached blade. A cradle allowed a farmer to harvest two or three acres of wheat a day, but it remained backbreaking work.

Tinkerers throughout the nation tried to fashion a mechanical reaper that would make the wheat harvest easier and quicker. Cyrus McCormick and others experimented with designs and methods of manufacturing until the late 1840s, when mechanical reapers began to appear in American wheat fields. A McCormick reaper that cost between $100 and $150 allowed a farmer to harvest up to twelve acres a day, at least when it worked. During the 1850s, reapers became more reliable and more readily repaired, and thousands of farmers decided to buy them. By 1860, about 80,000 reapers had been sold. Although reapers represented the cutting edge of agricultural technology, they still had to be powered by the muscles of a horse or an ox. Most farmers had not yet shifted their wheat harvest to animal power, so they continued to muscle the heavy cradle through their grain.

Mechanical reapers and better plows permitted farmers to produce more wheat and corn only because the labor farmers saved could be used to plow and plant more land. Neither reapers nor plows increased the yield of a given acre of cultivated land. Instead, they allowed more land to be brought into cultivation. Without access to fresh, uncultivated land, farmers could not have doubled the corn and wheat harvests between 1840 and 1860, as they in fact did. In the end, the agricultural productivity that fueled the nation's economy was an outgrowth of federal land policy.

Up to 1860, the United States continued to be land rich and labor poor. During the nineteenth century, the nation became a great deal richer in land, acquiring more than a billion acres with the Louisiana Purchase and the annexation of Florida, Oregon, and vast territories following the Mexican War (discussed later in this chapter). The federal government made the land available for purchase to attract settlers and to generate revenues. Although federal land only cost $1.25 an acre, millions of Americans could not afford to pay $50 for a forty-acre farm. They squatted on unclaimed federal land and carved out a farm they neither rented nor owned. Many poor farmers never accumulated enough money to purchase the land on which they squatted, and eventually they moved elsewhere, often to squat again on unclaimed federal land.

Government land policy not only aided small farmers. It also enriched wily speculators who found ways to claim large tracts of the most desirable plots and sell them to settlers at a generous markup. Nonetheless, by making land available to millions of ordinary people, the federal government achieved the goal of attracting settlers to the new territories, which in due course joined the Union as new states. Above all, federal land policy created the basic precondition for the increase in agricultural productivity that underlay the nation's impressive economic growth.

## Manufacturing and Mechanization

Changes in manufacturing arose in the context of the nation's land-rich, labor-poor economy. England and other European countries had land-poor, labor-rich economies; there, meager opportunities in agriculture kept factory laborers plentiful and wages low. In the United States, geographical expansion and government land policies buoyed agriculture, keeping millions of people on the farm and thereby limiting the supply of workers for manufacturing and elevating wages. Because of this shortage of workers, manufacturers searched constantly for ways to save labor. Mechanization offered the best prospects. But it was easier to say "mechanize" than it was actually to build a machine to do a task previously done by human hands—and to do it better, faster, cheaper, and with tireless repetition.

*Because of the shortage of workers, manufacturers searched constantly for ways to save labor. Mechanization offered the best prospects.*

Consider the seemingly simple process of making axes. The ax market was a manufacturer's dream since Americans needed as many axes as they could get. In the early 1830s, however, each ax still had to be handcrafted by a skilled metalworker. Between 1836 and 1849, Elisha K. Root, a machinist who worked at the Collins ax factory in Connecticut, invented a series of sophisticated machines that produced axes more quickly, safely, and cheaply and that did not require skilled operators. Root's machines turned out twenty-five times as many axes as skilled craftsmen did, and the machine-made axes were of better quality.

Manufacturers had such a strong incentive to save labor that mechanization marched forward as quickly as innovative ideas like Root's could be fashioned into workable combinations of gears, levers, screws, and pulleys. Outside the textile industry (see Chapter 11), homegrown machines set the pace. Early in the nineteenth century, the manufacture of firearms was mechanized, led by gun makers at the federal armories who had to keep the army supplied with rifles and pistols. The desire to make each gun as much as possible like every other encouraged gun makers to devise uniform parts that could be interchanged from one gun to another. The practice of manufacturing and then assembling interchangeable parts spread from industry to industry and became known as the "American system." Clock makers used it; sewing machine makers used it; even ax makers used it.

Mechanization became so integral to American manufacturing that some machinists specialized in what came to be called the machine tool industry. That is, they built machines that made parts for other machines that in turn produced goods for general consumption. Nothing better illustrated the transformation in American manufacturing than this mechanization of machine making.

Manufacturing and agriculture meshed into a dynamic national economy. New England led the nation in manufacturing, shipping products like clocks, guns, and axes west and south, while commodities like wheat, pork, whiskey, tobacco, and cotton flowed north and east. Manufacturers specialized in producing for the gigantic domestic market rather than for export. British goods dominated the international market and, on the whole, they were cheaper and better than American-made products. U.S. manufacturers supported tariffs to minimize British competition. But their best protection from British competitors was to be more eager to please their American customers, the vast majority of whom were farmers. From their side, farmers were only too happy to buy American manufactured goods, if they were affordable and especially if they saved labor that could be redirected to plow more furrows and plant more seeds.

Throughout American manufacturing, hand labor continued to be an essential component of production, despite the advances in mechanization. Even in heavily mechanized industries, factories remained fairly small, few having more than twenty or thirty employees. A measure of the distinctive character of manufacturing in this predominantly agricultural economy is that by 1860 iron manufacturing—so important in virtually all phases of mechanization—was only the sixth largest industry (in value), following cotton goods, lumber, boots and shoes, flour and meal, and men's clothing, in that order. The industrial evolution under way before 1860 would quicken later in the nineteenth century; railroads were a harbinger of that future.

## Railroads: Breaking the Bonds of Nature

To a degree unequaled by any other industry, railroads incorporated the most advanced developments of the age: steam energy; massive locomotives; mile after mile of iron rails; boldly engineered bridges vaulting rivers and chasms; unprecedented sums of money to undertake these tasks; and large, complex organizations to keep the trains running efficiently, safely, and on time. No wonder a Swedish visitor in 1849 noticed that American schoolboys constantly doodled sketches of locomotives, always smoking, always in motion.

Railroads captured Americans' imaginations in part because they seemed to break the bonds of nature. When canals and rivers froze in winter or became impassable during summer droughts, trains steamed ahead. When becalmed sailing ships went nowhere, locomotives kept on chugging, averaging over twenty miles an hour during the 1850s. Above all, railroads offered cities not blessed with canals or navigable rivers a way to compete for the trade of the countryside.

On July 4, 1828, Charles Carroll, the last surviving signer of the Declaration of Independence, broke ground for the Baltimore and Ohio Railroad. By connecting Baltimore to the Ohio River, the B&O promised to short-circuit western trade away from New Orleans, Philadelphia, and New York. Building the roadbed and laying track went slowly; by 1830, the B&O had 13 miles of track; by 1842, the route consisted of 125 miles; and finally, by 1852, the 379 miles that connected Baltimore to Ohio were completed.

Despite the slow pace of construction, the B&O motivated leading citizens in other American cities to undertake railroad projects to bring western commerce to their own shops, markets, and wharves. In 1830, the entire nation had fewer than 100 miles of railroad track. By 1850, trains steamed along 9,000 miles of track, almost two-thirds of it in New England and the Middle Atlantic states. By 1860, several railroads had crossed the Mississippi River to link frontier farmers to the nation's 30,000 miles of track, approximately as much as all the rest of the world combined. (In 1857, for example, France had 3,700 miles of track; England and Wales had a total of 6,400 miles.) Chicago stood at the hub of eleven railroads, including the Illinois Central, the longest railroad in the world (Map 13.1). The massive expansion of railroads in Lincoln's America helped the United States catapult into position as the world's second leading industrial power, behind Great Britain.

In addition to speeding transportation, railroads also fostered the growth of other industries. Iron production grew five times faster than the population during the decades up to 1860, in part to meet the demand for rails, wheels, axles, locomotives, and heavy, gravity-defying iron bridges. Likewise, coal production more than doubled during the 1850s to provide fuel for iron furnaces and locomotive boilers.

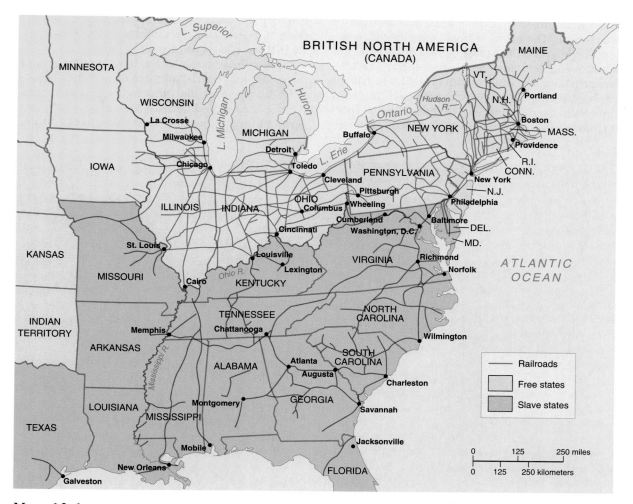

**M A P  13.1**
*Railroads in 1860*
*Railroads were a crucial component of the revolutions in transportation and communications that transformed nineteenth-century America. The railroad system reflected the differences that had developed in the economies of the North and South.*

Railroads also stimulated the fledgling telegraph industry. In 1844, Samuel F. B. Morse persuasively demonstrated the potential of his telegraph by transmitting a series of dots and dashes that instantly conveyed an electronic message along forty miles of wire between Washington and Baltimore. By 1861, more than 50,000 miles of wire stretched across the continent to the Pacific. Often telegraph lines ran alongside railroad tracks, and railroad managers soon discovered the advantages of instantaneous communication. Since most railroads had only one set of tracks, careful scheduling

was required to avoid disastrous head-on collisions. Telegraph messages permitted managers to speed trains on their way when a track was clear and hold them when it was not. By 1860, nearly every railroad station had a clattering telegraph.

Almost all railroads were built and owned by private corporations rather than by local, state, or federal governments. Undergirding these private investments was massive government aid, especially federal land grants. Up to 1850, the federal government had granted a total of seven million acres of federal land to various turnpike, highway, and canal projects. In that year, Illinois senator Stephen A. Douglas obtained congressional approval for a precedent-setting grant of federal land to railroads, including the Illinois Central. The 1850 law provided a grant of six square miles of federal land for each mile of track constructed. Railroad companies quickly lined up congressional support for other lucrative land deals. By 1860, Congress had granted railroads more than twenty million acres of federal lands, establishing a generous policy that would last for decades.

The railroad boom of the 1850s was a signal of the growing industrial might of the American economy. But railroads, like other industries, succeeded because they served farms as well as cities. Passengers and freight routinely sped along tracks during

**RAILROAD TRAVEL**

*In addition to carrying people and goods more quickly and reliably than ever before, railroads also brought many Americans face to face for the first time with machinery that was much larger and more powerful than any human being. (Compare, for example, the locomotives in this painting with the handtools in the illustration on page 316.) This painting of a train leaving Rochester, New York, in 1852 contrasts the size and power of human beings and machines. The huge, lovingly portrayed, steam-belching locomotive is barely held back by some unseen brake against which the massive engine strains, ready to pull the long train through the columns of the station, out of the past and into the future. The people, in contrast, appear indistinct, passive, and dependent. They are waiting for the train rather than vice versa. Except for the two women and child in the foreground, the people face backward, and all of them avoid looking directly at the locomotive. The painting evokes the way the almost incomprehensible power of the railroads dwarfed human effort.*

Rochester Historical Society.

the 1850s, but the continued significance of older forms of transportation is suggested by the operation of the federal postal system, which reached into every village and hamlet. By 1857, trains carried about one-third of the mail; most of the rest still went by stagecoach or horseback. In 1860, most Americans were still far more familiar with horses than with iron horses.

The economy of Lincoln's America linked axes, muscles, animals, and farms to machines, steam, railroads, and cities. Abraham Lincoln split rails as a young man and defended railroad corporations as a successful attorney. His legendary upward mobility illustrated the direction of economic change and the opportunities that change offered to enterprising individuals.

## Free Labor: Promise and Reality

The impressive performance of the antebellum economy did not reward all Americans equally. With few exceptions, women were excluded from the opportunities open to men. Although tens of thousands of women worked as seamstresses, laundresses, domestic servants, factory hands, and teachers, both men and women tended to think of the economy of Lincoln's America as a man's world, in particular a white man's world. Outside the South, slavery was slowly eliminated in the half century after the American Revolution, but free African Americans in the North found themselves relegated, on the whole, to dead-end jobs as laborers and servants. This discrimination against women and free blacks did not trouble most white men. With certain notable exceptions, they considered it proper and just. Instead, the varied experiences of white men—the presence of poverty in the midst of prosperity, of failure alongside success, of the bust that seemed to follow every boom—caught the attention of influential spokesmen.

### The Free-Labor Ideal: Freedom plus Labor

During the decades before the Civil War, leaders throughout the North emphasized a set of ideas that seemed to explain why the changes under way in their society benefited some more than others. They referred again and again to the advantages of what they termed "free labor." (The word "free" referred to laborers who were not slaves; it did not mean laborers who worked for nothing.) By the 1850s, "free labor" identified the basic character of the economy and society taking shape in the North. Free-labor ideas contrasted northern society with the South, whose slave economy also prospered during these years. Free-labor ideas proposed a social and economic ideal that accounted for both the successes and the shortcomings of northern society.

Free-labor spokesmen celebrated hard work, self-reliance, and independence. They proclaimed that the door to success was open not just to those who inherited wealth or status but also to self-made men like Abraham Lincoln. Lincoln himself declared, "Free labor—the just and generous, and prosperous system, which opens the way for all— gives hope to all, and energy, and progress, and improvement of condition to all." The free-labor system permitted farmers and artisans to enjoy the products of their own labor. Free labor also benefited individuals who worked for wages, Lincoln and others pointed out. Unlike slaves, wage laborers were not fixed in perpetual bondage, and they received compensation for their labor.

*By the 1850s, "free labor" identified the basic character of the economy and society taking shape in the North.*

Ultimately, the free-labor system made it possible for hired laborers to become independent property owners, proponents argued. "The prudent, penniless beginner in the world," Lincoln asserted, "labors for wages awhile, saves a surplus with which to buy tools or land, for himself; then labors on his own account another while, and at length hires another new beginner to help him." Wage labor was the first rung on the ladder that reached upward toward self-employment and, eventually, to hiring others.

The free-labor ideal affirmed an egalitarian vision of human potential. Lincoln and other spokesmen stressed the importance of universal education to permit "heads and hands . . . [to] cooperate as friends." Throughout the North, communities supported public schools to make the rudiments of learning available to young children. By 1860, many cities and towns boasted that up to 80 percent of children aged seven to thirteen attended school, at least for a few days each year. In rural areas, where the labor of children was more difficult to spare, schools typically enrolled no more than half the school-age children. Lessons included more than arithmetic, penmanship, and a smattering of other subjects. Textbooks and teachers—most of whom were young women—drummed into students the virtues of the free-labor system: self-reliance, discipline, and above all hard work. "Remember that all the ignorance, degradation, and misery in the world is the result of indolence and vice," one textbook intoned. Free-labor ideology, whether in school or out, emphasized labor as much as freedom.

## Economic Inequality

The free-labor ideal made sense to many Americans, especially in the North, because it seemed to describe their own experience. Lincoln frequently referred to his humble beginnings as a hired laborer and silently invited his listeners to consider how far he had come. In 1860, his wealth of $17,000 easily placed him in the top 5 percent of the population. The opportunities presented by the expanding economy made a few men much, much richer. In 1860, the nation had about forty millionaires, including Cyrus McCormick, whose wealth exceeded $2 million. Most Americans, however, measured success in far more modest terms. The average wealth of adult white men in the North in 1860 barely topped $2,000. Only about a quarter of American men possessed that much. Nearly one-half had no wealth at all; almost 60 percent owned no land. It is difficult to estimate the wealth of adult white women since property possessed by married women was normally considered to belong to their husbands, but certainly women had less wealth than men. Free African Americans had still less; 90 percent were propertyless.

Free-labor spokesmen considered these economic inequalities a natural outgrowth of freedom, the inevitable result of some individuals being more able, more willing to work, and luckier. These inequalities suggest, however, the gap between the promise and the performance of the free-labor ideal in Lincoln's America. Economic growth permitted many men to move from landless squatters to landowning farmers and from hired laborers to independent, self-employed producers. But many more Americans remained behind, landless and working for wages. Even those who had realized their aspirations had a precarious hold on their independence; bad debts, crop failure, sickness, or death could quickly eliminate a family's gains.

Since the free-labor ideal pointed to individuals as the source of both success and failure, many Americans felt anxious about their prospects. Seeking out new opportunities in pursuit of free-labor ideals created restless social and geographic mobility. Commonly up to two-thirds of the residents of a rural area moved every decade, and the population turnover in cities was even greater. Such constant coming and going weakened community ties to neighbors and friends and threw individuals even more upon their own resources for help in times of trouble. The stress on individual achievement encouraged personal introspection that often turned into intense self-doubt. Abraham Lincoln managed to get out of the log cabin in which he grew up, but that log cabin—with its economic insecurities, educational deficiencies, an illiterate mother, and a semiliterate father—remained with him, reminding him how far he had come and how few had come so far.

## Immigrants and the Free-Labor Ladder

The risks and uncertainties of free labor did not deter millions of immigrants from entering the United States, especially during the 1840s and 1850s. Almost four and a half million immigrants arrived between 1840 and 1860, six times more than had come during the previous two decades (Figure 13.1). The half million immigrants who came in 1854 accounted for nearly 2 percent of the entire population, a higher proportion than in any other single year of the nation's history. By 1860, foreign-born residents made up about one-eighth of the American population, a fraction that held steady well into the twentieth century.

Nearly three out of four of the immigrants who arrived between 1840 and 1860 came from either Germany or Ireland. The vast majority of the 1.4 million Germans who entered the United States during these years were skilled tradesmen and their families. They left Germany to escape deteriorating economic conditions and to seize opportunities offered by the expanding economy of Lincoln's America, where skilled artisans had little difficulty finding work. German butchers, bakers, beer makers, carpenters, shopkeepers, machinists, and others tended to congregate in cities, particularly in the Midwest. Roughly a quarter of German immigrants were farmers, most of whom scattered throughout the Midwest, although some settled in Texas. On the whole, German Americans settled into that middle stratum of sturdy independent producers celebrated by free-labor spokesmen; relatively few Germans occupied the bottom rung of the free-labor ladder as wage laborers or domestic servants.

Irish immigrants, in contrast, entered at the bottom of the free-labor ladder and had difficulty

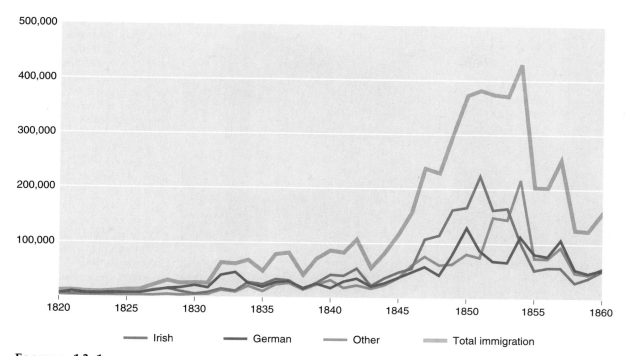

FIGURE **13.1**
*Antebellum Immigration, 1820–1860*
*After increasing gradually for several decades, immigration shot up in the mid-1840s. Between 1848–1860, nearly 3.5 million immigrants entered the United States.*

climbing up. Nearly 1.7 million Irish immigrants arrived between 1840 and 1860, nearly all of them desperately poor and often weakened by hunger and disease. Potato blight struck Ireland in 1845 and returned repeatedly in subsequent years, spreading a catastrophic famine throughout the island. Millions of poor farmers and hired hands depended on potatoes as their principal source of food. When the blight ruined the potatoes, tens of thousands literally starved to death. The lucky ones, half-starved, crowded into the holds of ships and set out for America. As one immigrant group declared, "All we want is to get out of Ireland; we must be better anywhere than here." Death trailed after them. So many died crossing the Atlantic that ships from Ireland were often termed "coffin ships." But enough survived to make the Irish the largest single immigrant group in Lincoln's America.

Roughly three out of four Irish immigrants worked as laborers or domestic servants. Irish men dug canals, loaded ships, built railroad tracks, and took what other work they could find. Irish women hired out to cook, wash and iron, mind children, and clean house. Slaveholders often preferred to

hire Irish laborers for heavy, dangerous jobs rather than risk injury to their valuable slaves. Most Irish immigrants, however, congregated in northeastern cities. Almost all Irish immigrants were Catholics, a fact that set them apart from the overwhelmingly Protestant native-born residents. Many natives regarded the Irish as hard-drinking, obstreperous, half-civilized folk. Such views lay behind the discrimination that often excluded Irish immigrants from better jobs; job announcements commonly stated, "No Irish need apply." Despite these prejudices, native residents hired Irish immigrants because they accepted low pay and worked hard.

In the labor-poor economy of Lincoln's America, Irish laborers could earn in one day wages that would require several weeks' work in Ireland, if work could be found there. In America, one immigrant explained in 1853, there was "plenty of work and plenty of wages plenty to eat and no land lords thats enough what more does a man want." But some immigrants wanted more, especially respect and decent working conditions. One immigrant prayed, "May heaven save me from ever again being compelled to labour so severely . . . driven

**EVICTION OF IRISH TENANT**
*An Irish tenant (the seated man with crossed arms) and his family (two barefoot boys are shown) are evicted; their few pieces of furniture have been piled outside the cottage. The landlord or his agent (the man near the doorway) has brought four armed police to force the tenant to leave. Evictions like this were common in Ireland in the mid-nineteenth century, an example of the poverty and human suffering that pushed many Irish immigrants to the United States.* Lawrence Collection, National Library of Ireland.

like horses . . . a slave for the Americans as the generality of the Irish . . . are."

Such testimony illustrates that the free-labor system, whether for immigrants or native-born laborers, often did not live up to the optimistic vision outlined by Abraham Lincoln and others. If wage laborers could not realistically aspire to become independent, self-sufficient property holders—if wage laborers became a permanent rather than a temporary working class—what would become of the free-labor ideal? By 1860, a few workingmen asked such questions, but the continuing economic expansion muted their voices.

## Reforming Self and Society

The emphasis on self-discipline and individual effort at the core of the free-labor ideal pervaded Lincoln's America. Many Americans believed that insufficient self-control caused the most important social problems of the era. Evangelical Protestants struggled to control individuals' propensity to sin, and temperance advocates exhorted drinkers to control their urge for alcohol. In the midst of the worldly disruptions of geographic expansion and economic change, evangelicals brought more Americans than ever before into churches. Historians estimate that church members accounted for about one-third of the American population by midcentury. Most Americans remained outside churches,

as did Abraham Lincoln. But the influence of evangelical religion reached far beyond those who belonged to churches. The evangelical temperament—a conviction of righteousness coupled with energy, self-discipline, and faith that the world could be improved—animated most reformers to one degree or another.

A few activists pointed out that certain fundamental injustices lay beyond the reach of self-control. Transcendentalists and utopians believed that perfection could be attained only by rejecting the competitive values of the larger society. Women's rights activists and abolitionists sought to reverse the subordination of women and to eliminate the enslavement of blacks by changing society. They confronted the daunting challenge of repudiating widespread assumptions about male supremacy and white supremacy and somehow subverting the entrenched institutions that reinforced those assumptions: the family and slavery.

### The Pursuit of Perfection: Transcendentalists and Utopians

A group of New England writers that came to be known as transcendentalists believed that individuals should not conform to the materialistic world or to some abstract notion of religion. Instead, people should look within themselves for truth and guidance. The leading transcendentalist, Ralph Waldo Emerson—an essayist, poet, and lecturer—

proclaimed that most Americans failed to lift their eyes from the mundane task of making a living. "We hear . . . too much of the results of machinery, commerce, and the useful arts," Emerson wrote. The power of the solitary individual was nearly limitless. Henry David Thoreau, Margaret Fuller, and other transcendentalists agreed with Emerson that "if the single man plant himself indomitably on his instincts, and there abide, the huge world will come round to him." In many ways, transcendentalism represented less an alternative to the values of mainstream society than an exaggerated form of the rampant individualism of the age.

---

*The evangelical temperament—a conviction of righteousness coupled with energy, self-discipline, and faith that the world could be improved—animated most reformers.*

---

Unlike transcendentalists, a few reformers tried to change the world by organizing utopian communities. Although these communities never involved more than a few thousand people, their activities demonstrated both their dissatisfactions with the larger society and their efforts to realize their visions of perfection. Some communities functioned essentially as retreats for those who did not want to sever their ties with the larger society. Brook Farm, organized in 1841 in West Roxbury, Massachusetts, provided a short-lived haven for literary and artistic New Englanders who agreed to balance bookish pursuits with manual labor. Novelists and essayists often weeded the garden while others read poetry to them. Emerson, who declined to join, described Brook Farm as "a perpetual picnic."

Other communities set out to become models of perfection that they hoped would point the way toward a better life for everyone. During the 1840s, more than two dozen communities—principally in New York, New Jersey, Pennsylvania, and Ohio—organized around the ideas of Charles Fourier, a French critic of contemporary society. Members of these Fourierist communities (or phalanxes, as they were called) believed that individualism and competition were evils that denied the basic truth that "men . . . are brothers and not competitors." Fourierist phalanxes tried to replace competition with harmonious cooperation based on communal ownership of property. In addition, members were supposed to work not because they had to but because their work was satisfying and fulfilling. One former

member complained that "there was plenty of discussion, and an abundance of variety, which is called the spice of life. This spice however constituted the greater part of the fare, as we sometimes had scarcely anything to eat." Such complaints signaled the failure of the Fourierist communities to achieve their ambitious goals. Few survived more than two or three years.

The Oneida community went beyond the Fourierist notion of communalism. John Humphrey Noyes, the charismatic leader of Oneida, believed that individuals who had achieved salvation were literally without sin. The larger society's commitment to private property, however, made even saints greedy and selfish. Noyes believed that the root of the evil of private property lay in marriage, in men's conviction that their wives were their exclusive property. With a substantial inheritance, Noyes organized the Oneida community in New York in 1848 to practice what Noyes called "complex marriage." Sexual intercourse was permissible between any man and woman in the community who had been saved; in effect, every saved man in the community was married to every saved woman. Noyes usually reserved for himself the duties of "first husband," namely introducing sanctified young virgins to complex marriage. To prevent a population explosion and to promote health and self-control, Noyes insisted that Oneida men practice "male continence," that is, sexual intercourse without ejaculation. Noyes also required all members to relinquish their economic property to the community, which developed a lucrative business manufacturing animal traps. Oneida's sexual and economic communalism attracted several hundred members, but most of their neighbors considered Oneidans adulterers, blasphemers, and worse. Yet the practices that set Oneida apart from its mainstream neighbors also strengthened the community, and it survived long after the Civil War.

## Women's Rights Activists

Women participated in the many reform activities that grew out of evangelical churches. Women church members outnumbered men two to one, and they worked to put their religious ideas into practice by joining peace, temperance, antislavery, and other societies. Although women supplied much energy and membership in these societies, men normally headed the groups. Assumptions of male supremacy were so strong and pervasive that even women's rights activists feared the consequences of

**MARY CRAGIN, ONEIDA WOMAN**

*Mary Cragin, one of the founding members of the Oneida community, had a passionate sexual relationship with John Humphrey Noyes even before the community was organized. Within the bounds of complex marriage as practiced by the Oneidans, Cragin's magnetic sexuality made her a favorite partner of many men. In her journal, Cragin confessed that "every evil passion was very strong in me from my childhood, sexual desire, love of dress and admiration, deceit, anger, pride." Oneida, however, transformed evil passion to holy piety. Cragin wrote, "In view of [God's] goodness to me and of his desire that I should let him fill me with himself, I yield and offer myself, to be penetrated by his spirit, and desire that love and gratitude may inspire my heart so that I shall sympathize with his pleasure in the thing, before my personal pleasure begins, knowing that it will increase my capability for happiness." After she accidentally drowned in 1851, a eulogist proclaimed, "Her only ambition was to be the servant of love and she was beautifully and wonderfully made for the office." Oneida's sexual practices were considered outrageous and sinful by almost all other Americans. Even Oneidans did not agree with all of Noyes's ideas about sex. "There is no reason why [sex] should not be done in public as much as music and dancing," he declared. It would display the art of sex, he explained, and watching "would give pleasure to a great many of the older people who now have nothing to do with the matter." Nonetheless, public sex never caught on among Oneidans.* Oneida Community Mansion House/James Demarest.

openly confronting them. Involvement in reform organizations gave a few women activists practical experience in such political arts as speaking in public, running a meeting, drafting resolutions, and circulating petitions. Along with such experience came confidence. Abolitionist Lydia Maria Child pointed out in 1841 that "those who urged women to become missionaries and form tract societies . . . have changed the household utensil to a living energetic being and they have no spell to turn it into a broom again."

In 1848, about one hundred living energetic beings, led by reformers Elizabeth Cady Stanton and Lucretia Mott, gathered at Seneca Falls, New York, for the first women's rights convention in the United States. The Seneca Falls Declaration of Sentiments proclaimed that "the history of mankind is a history of repeated injuries and usurpations on the part of man toward woman, having in direct object the establishment of an absolute tyranny over her." In the style of the Declaration of Independence, the Seneca Falls Declaration listed the ways women had been discriminated against. Through the tyranny of male supremacy, men "endeavored in every way that [they] could to destroy her confidence in her own powers, to lessen her self-respect, and to make her willing to lead a dependent and abject life." The Seneca Falls Declaration insisted that women "have immediate admission to all the rights and privileges which belong to them as citizens of the United States," particularly the "inalienable right to the elective franchise."

Nearly two dozen other women's rights conventions assembled before 1860, repeatedly calling for suffrage. But they had difficulty receiving a respectful hearing, much less obtaining legislative action. No state came close to permitting women to vote. Politicians and editorialists hooted at the idea. Everyone knew, they sneered, that a woman's place was in the home, rearing her children and civilizing her man. Nonetheless, the Seneca Falls Declaration served as a path-breaking manifesto of dissent against male supremacy and of support for woman suffrage, which would become the focus of the women's rights movement during the next seventy years.

## Abolitionists and the American Ideal

During the 1840s and 1850s, abolitionists continued to struggle to draw the nation's attention to the plight of slaves and the need for emancipation. Former slaves like Frederick Douglass, Henry Bibb, and Sojourner Truth lectured to reform audiences

**ABOLITIONIST MEETING**
*This rare daguerreotype was made by Ezra Greenleaf Weld in August 1850 at an abolitionist meeting in Cazenovia, New York. Frederick Douglass, who had escaped from slavery in Maryland twelve years earlier, is seated on the platform next to the woman at the table. One of the nation's most brilliant and eloquent abolitionists, Douglass also supported equal rights for women. The man immediately behind Douglass gesturing with his outstretched arm is Gerrit Smith, a wealthy New Yorker and militant abolitionist whose funds supported many reform activities. Note the two black women in similar clothing on either side of Smith and the white woman next to Douglass. Most mid-nineteenth-century white Americans considered such voluntary racial proximity scandalous and promiscuous. Clearly, what scandalized these respectable-appearing Americans was slavery, not biracial protest meetings.*
Collection of the J. Paul Getty Museum, Malibu, Calif.

throughout the North about the cruelties, horrors, and indignities of slavery. Abolitionists published newspapers, held conventions, and petitioned Congress. But they never attracted a mass following among white Americans. Many white Northerners became convinced that slavery was wrong, but they still believed that blacks were inferior. Many other white Northerners shared the common view of white Southerners that because blacks were inferior, slavery was necessary and even desirable. The geographic expansion of the nation during the 1840s offered abolitionists an opportunity to link their unpopular ideal to a goal that many white Northerners found much more attractive—limiting the geographic expansion of slavery, an issue that moved to the center of national politics during the 1850s (see Chapter 14).

Black leaders rose to prominence in the abolitionist movement during the 1840s and 1850s. African Americans had actively opposed slavery for decades, but a new generation of leaders came to the forefront in these years. Men like Douglass, Henry Highland Garnet, William Wells Brown, and Martin R. Delany became impatient with white abolitionists' appeals to the conscience of the white majority. Garnet, for example, proclaimed in 1843 that slaves should rise in insurrection against their masters, an idea that alienated almost all white people. To express their own uncompromising ideas, black abolitionists founded their own newspapers and held their own antislavery conventions, although they still cooperated with sympathetic whites.

The commitment of black abolitionists to battling slavery grew out of their own experiences with white supremacy. The 250,000 free African Americans in the North constituted less than 2 percent of the total population. They confronted the humiliations of racial discrimination in virtually every arena of daily life: at work, at school, at church, in shops, in the streets, on trains, in hotels, and elsewhere. Only four northern states (Maine, Massachusetts, New Hampshire, and Vermont) permitted black men to vote; New York imposed a special property-holding requirement on black—but not white—voters, effectively excluding most black men from the franchise. All other states prohibited black voting. The pervasive racial discrimination in the North both handicapped and energized black abolitionists. Garnet said, as if he were speaking to slaves, "While you have been oppressed, we have also been partakers; nor can we be free while you are enslaved. We . . . [are] bound with you." African American leaders organized campaigns against segregation in northern communities, particularly in transportation and education. Their most notable success came in 1855 when Massachusetts integrated public schools. Elsewhere white supremacy continued unabated.

Outside the public spotlight, many free African Americans in the North contributed to the antislavery cause by quietly aiding fugitive slaves. Harriet Tubman escaped from slavery in Maryland in 1849 and repeatedly risked her freedom and her life to return to the South and escort scores of slaves to freedom. Few matched Tubman's heroic courage, but when the opportunity arose, many free blacks in the North provided fugitive slaves with food, a safe place to rest, and a helping hand. This "underground railroad" ran mainly through black neighborhoods, black churches, and black homes, an outgrowth of the antislavery sentiment and opposition to white supremacy that unified virtually all African Americans in the North. While thousands of southern slaves rode the underground railroad to freedom in the North, millions of other Americans uprooted their families and headed west.

## The Westward Movement

The 1840s ushered in an era of rapid westward movement. Until then, the overwhelming majority of Americans lived east of the Mississippi River. To the west, Native Americans inhabited the plains, prairies, and deserts to the rugged coasts of the Pacific. The British claimed the Oregon Country, and the Mexican flag flew over the vast expanse of the Southwest. But by 1850, the boundaries of the United States stretched to the Pacific, and the nation had more than doubled its size. By 1860, the great migration had carried four million Americans west of the Mississippi River.

Thomas Jefferson, John Quincy Adams, and other government officials had helped clear the way for the march across the continent. The nation's revolution in transportation and communication, its swelling population, and its booming economy propelled the westward surge. But the emigrants themselves conquered the continent. Farmer-settlers craved land and stubbornly shoved ahead. Shock troops of the American empire, frontier settlers took the soil and then lobbied their government to follow them with the flag. The human cost of westward expansion was high. Two centuries of Indian wars east of the Mississippi ended during the 1830s, but the old, fierce struggle between native inhabitant and invader continued for another half century in the West.

### Manifest Destiny

Most Americans believed that the superiority of their institutions and white culture bestowed on them a God-given right to spread their civilization across the continent. They imagined the West as a howling wilderness, empty and undeveloped. If they recognized Indians and Mexicans at all, they dismissed them as primitive drags on progress who would have to be redeemed, shoved aside and isolated, or exterminated. The sense of uniqueness and mission was as old as the Puritans, but by the 1840s the conviction of superiority had been bolstered by the young nation's amazing success. What right had Americans, they asked, to keep the blessings of liberty, democracy, and prosperity to themselves? The West needed the civilizing power of the hammer and plow, the ballot box and pulpit, that had transformed the East.

In the summer of 1845, New York journalist John L. O'Sullivan coined the term *manifest destiny* as the latest justification for white settlers to take the land they coveted. O'Sullivan was an armchair expansionist, but he took second place to no one in his passion for conquest of the West. O'Sullivan called on Americans to resist any foreign power—British, French, or Mexican—that attempted to thwart "the fulfillment of our manifest destiny to overspread the continent allotted by Providence for the free development of our yearly multiplying millions . . . [and] for the development of the great experiment of liberty and federative self-government entrusted to us." Almost overnight, the magic phrase "manifest destiny" swept the nation and provided an ideological shield for conquering the West.

As important as national pride and racial arrogance were to manifest destiny, economic gain made up its core. Land hunger drew hundreds of thousands of average Americans westward. Some politicians, moreover, had become convinced that national prosperity depended on capturing the rich trade of the Far East. To trade with Asia, the United States needed the Pacific ports that stretched from San Francisco to Puget Sound. No one was more eager to extend American trade in the Pacific than Missouri senator Thomas Hart Benton. "The sun of civilization must shine across the sea: socially and commercially," he declared. The United States and Asia must "talk together, and trade together. Commerce is a great civilizer." In the 1840s, American economic expansion came wrapped in the rhetoric of uplift and civilization.

## "Oregon Fever" and the Overland Trail

Oregon Country, that vast region bounded on the west by the Pacific, on the east by the Rockies, on the south by the forty-second parallel, and on the north by Russian Alaska, caused the pulse of American expansionists to race (Map 13.2). But Americans were not alone in hungrily eyeing the Pacific Northwest. The British traced their interest (and their rights) to the voyage of Sir Francis Drake, who, they argued, discovered the Oregon coast in 1579. Americans matched the British assertion with historic claims of their own. Unable to agree on ownership, the United States and Great Britain decided in 1818 on a "joint occupation" that would leave Oregon "free and open" to settlement by both countries. A handful of American fur traders and "mountain men" roamed the region in the 1820s, but in the 1830s and 1840s, expansionists made Oregon Country an early target of manifest destiny.

"Oregon fever" broke out in 1833 when a Methodist journal published a fictitious letter from an Indian in the Northwest begging for the Bible. Pulpits across the East broadcast the plea, and soon earnest missionaries responded to the call. The Indians they encountered displayed a decided lack of enthusiasm for Christianity, but the missionaries' letters home glowed with astonishment at the

bounty nature had bestowed on Oregon. By the late 1830s, settlers began to trickle along the Oregon Trail, following a path blazed by the mountain men. The first Oregon wagon trains hit the trail in 1841, and by 1843 about 1,000 emigrants a year set out from Independence, Missouri. By 1869, when the first transcontinental railroad was completed, something like 350,000 migrants had traveled west to the Pacific over the Oregon Trail (see Map 13.2).

---

*As important as national pride and racial arrogance were to manifest destiny, economic gain made up its core. Land hunger drew hundreds of thousands of average Americans westward.*

---

Emigrants encountered Plains Indians, whose cultures differed markedly from those of the Eastern Woodlands tribes. The quarter of a million Native Americans who populated the area between the Rocky Mountains and the Mississippi River defy easy generalization. Some were farmers who lived peaceful, sedentary lives, but a majority of Plains Indians—the Sioux, Cheyenne, Shoshoni, and Arapaho of the Central Plains and the Kiowa, Wichita, Apache, and Comanche in the Southwest—were horse-mounted, nomadic, nonagricultural peoples whose warriors symbolized the "savage Indian" in the minds of whites.

Horses, which had been brought to the continent by Spaniards in the sixteenth century, permitted the Plains tribes to become highly mobile hunters of buffalo. In time they came to depend on buffalo for most of their food, clothing, shelter, and fuel. As they followed the huge herds over the Plains, these peoples bumped into one another. Competition and warfare became a crucial component of their way of life. Young men were introduced to the art of war early, learning to ride ponies at breakneck speed while firing off arrows and, later, rifles with astounding accuracy.

Plains Indians struck fear in the hearts of whites who rode on the wagon trains. But Native Americans had far more to fear from whites. Indians killed fewer than four hundred emigrants on the trail between 1840 and 1860, while whites proved to be deadly to the Indians. Even though they were usually just passing through on their way to the Pacific slope, whites brought alcohol and disease, especially destructive epidemics of smallpox, measles, cholera, and scarlet fever. Moreover, whites killed the buffalo, slaughtering hundreds of thousands for fun and leaving their carcasses to rot in the sun. Buffalo still numbered some twelve million in 1860, but the herds were shrinking rapidly, intensifying conflict among the Plains Indians. Intertribal warfare weakened the Indians and made them more vulnerable to conquest.

As the number of wagon trains increased, emigrants insisted that the federal government provide them more protection. The government responded by constructing a chain of forts along the trail. More

important, the United States adopted a new Indian policy of "concentration." To clear the way, the government rescinded the "permanent" frontier it had granted the Indians west of the ninety-fifth meridian, which was only a few miles west of the Mississippi River. Then, in 1851, it called the Plains tribes to a conference at Fort Laramie, Wyoming. Some ten thousand Dakota, Sioux, Arapaho, Cheyenne, Crow, and other Indians showed up, hopeful that something could be done to protect them from the ravages of the wagon trains. Instead, government negotiators persuaded the chiefs to sign agreements restricting their people to specific

**MAP 13.2**
*Trails to the West*
*In the 1830s, wagon trains began snaking their way to the Southwest and the Pacific coast. Deep ruts, some of which can still be seen today, soon marked the most popular routes.*

**WI-JUN-JON, AN ASSINIBOIN CHIEF**

*Pennsylvania-born artist George Catlin, the painter of this 1845 dual portrait, was present in the Assiniboin village when Wi-Jun-Jon returned from Washington, D.C., wearing the military uniform that President Andrew Jackson had presented to him. His uniform and ceaseless boasting bred so much dislike and distrust that a young warrior from a nearby tribe murdered him. Catlin was convinced that the western Indian cultures that he had begun observing in the 1830s would soon disappear, and he sought to document Indian life through hundreds of paintings and prints.*
Library of Congress.

areas that whites promised they would never violate. This policy of isolation became the seedbed for the subsequent policy of reservations. But whites would not keep out of Indian territory, and Indians would not easily give up their traditional way of life. Competition meant warfare for decades to come.

Still, Indians threatened emigrants less than life on the trail did. The men, women, and children who headed west each spring could count on four to six months of grueling travel. Until 1860, maps labeled the vast area between the Rockies and the Mississippi River as the "Great American Desert." With nearly two thousand miles to go and traveling no more than fifteen miles a day, the pioneers endured parching heat, drought, treacherous rivers, disease, physical and emotional exhaustion, and, if the snows closed the mountain passes before they got through, freezing and starvation. Women sometimes faced the dangers of trailside childbirth. It was said that one could walk from Missouri to the Pacific stepping only on the graves of those who had failed to make it.

Everyone experienced hardships on the trail, but no one felt the burden quite as much as the women who made the trip. Since husbands usually decided to pull up stakes and go west, many wives went involuntarily. Men viewed the privation as a necessary step to a new, better life; women tended to judge it by the homes, kin, and friends they had left behind to take up what one called "this wild goose chase."

When women reached Oregon, they confronted a wilderness, not new homes. "I had all I could do to keep from asking George to turn around and bring me back home," one woman wrote to her mother in Missouri. Neighbors were few and far between, and the isolation weighed heavily. Moreover, things were in a "primitive state." One young wife set up housekeeping with her new husband with only one stew kettle and three knives. Necessity blurred the traditional division between men's and women's work. "I am maid of all traids," one busy woman remarked in 1853. Work seemed unending. "I am a very old woman," remarked twenty-nine-year-old Sarah Everett. "My face is thin sunken and wrinkled, my hands bony withered and hard." Pioneer life left little room for leisure or refinement. As one wife observed, "A woman that can not endure almost as much as a horse has no business here."

Despite the ordeal of the trail and the difficulties of starting from scratch, emigrants kept coming. By 1845, Oregon counted five thousand American settlers. And from the beginning, they clamored for the protection of the U.S. government.

## The Mormon Migration

Not every wagon train heading west had the Pacific slope as its destination. One remarkable group of religious emigrants chose to settle in the heart of the arid West. Halting near the Great Salt Lake in what was then Mexican territory, the Mormons deliberately chose the remote site as a refuge. After years of persecution in the East, they sought religious freedom and communal security in the West. Protected by mountains and deserts, Deseret, as they called their kingdom, lay a thousand miles from the Kansas frontier.

In 1830, Joseph Smith Jr., who was only twenty-four, published *The Book of Mormon* and founded the Church of Jesus Christ of Latter-Day Saints (the Mormons). A decade earlier, the upstate New York farm boy had begun to have uncommon religious experiences. His visions and revelations were followed, he said, by a visit from an angel who led him to golden tablets buried near his home. With the aid of magic stones, he translated the mysterious language on the tablets. What was revealed was *The Book of Mormon*. It told the story of an ancient Christian civilization in the New World and predicted the appearance of an American prophet who would reestablish Jesus Christ's undefiled kingdom in America. Converts, attracted to the promise of a pure faith in the midst of antebellum America's social turmoil and rampant materialism, flocked to the new church.

"Gentile" neighbors branded Mormons heretics and resented their close-knit community, what they considered the Mormons' religious self-righteousness, and their sympathy toward abolitionists and Indians. Persecution drove Smith and his followers from New York to Ohio, then to Missouri, and finally in 1839 to Nauvoo, Illinois. But the Mormons had not outrun trouble. Dissenters within the church accused Smith of advocating plural marriage (polygamy) and published an exposé of the practice. Non-Mormons caught wind of the controversy and eventually arrested Smith and his brother. On June 27, 1844, a mob stormed the jail and shot both men dead.

The embattled church turned to an extraordinary new leader, Brigham Young, who immediately began to plan the exodus of his people from Illinois. In 1846, traveling in 3,700 wagons, twelve thousand Mormons made their way to eastern Iowa, where they established refugee camps. In 1847, Young led an advance party to their new home beside the Great Salt Lake. Young described it as a barren waste, "the paradise of the lizard, the cricket and the rattlesnake." Within ten years, however, the Mormons developed an efficient irrigation system and made the desert bloom. They accomplished the feat through cooperative labor, not the individualistic and competitive enterprise common among most emigrants. Under the stern leadership of Young and other church leaders, the Mormons built a thriving community.

In 1850, only three years after its founding, Deseret became annexed to the United States as Utah Territory. But what focused the nation's attention on

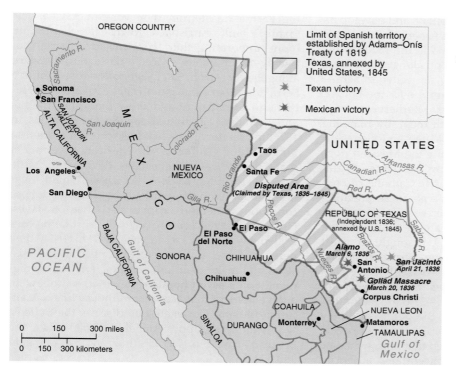

**M A P   13.3**
*Texas and Mexico in the 1830s*
As Americans spilled into lightly populated and loosely governed northern Mexico, Texas and then other Mexican provinces became contested territory.

the Latter-Day Saints was the announcement by Brigham Young in 1852 that many Mormons practiced polygamy. Although only one Mormon man in five had more than one wife (Young had twenty-three), Young's public statement caused an outcry that forced the government to establish its authority in Utah. In 1857, 2,500 U.S. troops invaded Salt Lake City in what was known as the Mormon War. The bloodless occupation illustrates that most Americans viewed the Mormons as a threat to American morality, law, and institutions. The invasion did not dislodge the Mormon Church from its central place in Utah, however, and for years to come, most Americans perceived the Mormon settlement as a strange, and suitably isolated, place.

## The Mexican Borderlands

In the Mexican Southwest, westward-moving Anglo-American pioneers confronted northern-moving Spanish-speaking frontiersmen. On this frontier as elsewhere, cultures, interests, and aspirations collided. Since 1821, when Mexico won its independence from Spain, the Mexican flag had flown over the vast expanse that stretched from the Gulf of Mexico to the Pacific and from Oregon Country to Guatemala. Mexico's borders remained ill-defined, and its northern provinces were sparsely populated. Moreover, severe problems plagued the young nation: civil wars, economic crises, quarrels between the Roman Catholic Church and the state, and devastating raids by the Comanche, Apache, and Kiowa. Mexico found it increasingly difficult to defend its borderlands, especially when faced with a northern neighbor that was convinced of its superiority and bent on territorial acquisition.

The American assault began quietly. In the 1820s, when Anglo-American trappers, traders, and settlers began drifting into Mexico's far northern provinces, they discovered that their newly independent neighbor was eager for American business. Santa Fe, a remote outpost in the province of New Mexico, became a magnet for American enterprise. American traders gathered each spring at Independence, Missouri, for the long trek southwest along the Santa Fe Trail. They crammed their wagons with inexpensive American manufactured goods and returned with Mexican silver, furs, and mules.

The Mexican province of Texas attracted a flood of Americans who had settlement, not long-distance trade, on their minds (Map 13.3). The Mexican government, which wanted to populate and develop its northern territory, granted the American Stephen F. Austin a huge tract of land, and in the 1820s he established a thriving settlement along the Brazos River. Land was cheap—only ten cents an acre—and thousands of farmers poured over the border. Most of the migrants were Southerners, who brought cotton and slaves with them. By 1835, the number of American settlers—free and slave—in Texas had reached 30,000, while the Mexican population was less than 8,000. By and large, Anglo-American settlers were not Roman Catholic, did not speak Spanish, and cared little about assimilating into a culture that was so different from their own. The Mexican government realized that it had a problem on its hands. In 1829, it sought to arrest further immigration with an emancipation proclamation, which it hoped would make Texas less attractive. The settlers sidestepped the decree by calling their slaves servants, but settlers had other grievances, most significantly the puny voice they had in local government. General Antonio López de Santa Anna all but extinguished that voice when he seized political power and concentrated authority in Mexico City.

Faced with what they considered tyranny, the Texan settlers rebelled and declared the independent Republic of Texas. Santa Anna took the field and in March 1836 arrived at the outskirts of San Antonio with 6,000 troops. The rebels, who included the Tennessee frontiersman Davy Crockett and the Louisiana adventurer Jim Bowie, took refuge in the old Franciscan mission the Alamo. Wave after wave of Mexicans crashed against the walls until the attackers finally broke through and killed all 187 defenders. A few weeks later in the small town of Goliad, Mexican forces surrounded and captured a garrison of 365 Texans. Following orders from Santa Anna, Mexican firing squads executed the men as pirates. But in April 1836 at San Jacinto, Santa Anna suffered a crushing defeat at the hands of forces under General Sam Houston. Texans had succeeded in establishing their Lone Star Republic, and the following year the United States recognized the independence of Texas from Mexico.

The distant Mexican province of California also caught the eye of a few Anglo-Americans. Spain had first extended its influence into California in 1769, when it sent a naval expedition north from Mexico to San Francisco Bay in an effort to block Russian fur traders who were moving south along the Pacific Coast from their base in Alaska. The Spanish built garrisoned towns (*presidios*), but, more important, they constructed a string of twenty-one missions, spaced a day's journey apart, along the coast from San Diego to Sonoma. Junípero Serra and other Franciscan friars converted the Indians to Christianity and drew them into the life and often hard agricultural labor of the missions. In 1824, in an effort to increase Mexican migration to thinly settled California, the Mexican government granted *ranchos*—huge estates devoted to cattle raising—to new settlers. *Rancheros* ruled over near-feudal empires worked by Indians whose condition sometimes approached that of slaves. Not satisfied, *rancheros* coveted the vast lands controlled by the Franciscan missions. In 1834, they persuaded the government to confiscate the missions and make their lands available to new settlement. Some seven hundred new *ranchos* followed, a development that accelerated the decline of California Indians. Devastated by disease, the Indians, who numbered approximately 300,000 when the Spanish arrived in 1769, declined by 1846 to barely 150,000.

Despite the efforts of the Mexican government, California in 1840 counted a population of only 7,000 Mexican settlers. Non-Mexican settlers numbered only 380, but among them were Americans who championed manifest destiny. Thomas O. Larkin, a prosperous merchant, John Marsh, a successful *ranchero* in the San Joaquin Valley, and others became boosters who sought to attract Americans from Oregon Country to California. The first overland party arrived in California in 1841. Thereafter, wagon after wagon followed the California Trail. As the trickle of Americans became a river, Mexican officials grew alarmed. California, they feared, would go the way of Texas. As a New York newspaper put it in 1845, "Let the tide of emigration flow toward California and the American population will soon be sufficiently numerous to play the Texas game." Indeed, many Americans in California continued to live apart, unassimilated, and to view themselves as superior to their Mexican neighbors. Not all Americans in California wanted to play the "Texas game," but many dreamed of living again under the American flag.

The U.S. government made no secret of its desire to acquire California. In 1835, President Andrew Jackson tried to purchase it. In 1842, Commodore Thomas Catesby Jones, hearing a rumor that the

United States and Mexico were at war, seized the port of Monterey and ran up the American flag. The red-faced officer promptly ran it down again when he learned of his error. But his actions left no doubt about Washington's intentions. In 1846, American settlers in the Sacramento Valley took matters into their own hands. Prodded by John C. Frémont, a former army captain and explorer who had arrived in December 1845 with a party of sixty buckskin-clad frontiersmen spoiling for a fight, the Californians raised an independence movement known as the Bear Flag Revolt. By then, James K. Polk, a champion of expansion, sat in the White House.

## The Politics of Expansion

Although emigrants were the advance guard of American empire, there was nothing automatic about the U.S. annexation of territory in the West. Acquiring territory required political action, and in the 1840s the difficult problems of Texas, Oregon, and the Mexican borderlands intruded into national politics. The politics of expansion thrust the United States into dangerous diplomatic crises with Great Britain and Mexico. Even more ominous, expansion became hopelessly entangled with sectionalism and the slavery question.

### Tyler and the Whig Fiasco

The complicated issues of westward expansion and the nation's boundaries ended up on the desk of John Tyler when he became president in April 1841. William Henry Harrison, a Whig, had been elected president in 1840, but one month after he took office, he died, the victim of pneumonia caught as he delivered his long inaugural address. For the first time in American history, a president had died in office, and it was not clear whether Vice President Tyler—"His Accidency," as his opponents called him—could legally exercise the full powers of an elected president.

Worse for the Whigs, Tyler was really a Democrat in Whig clothing. The fifty-one-year-old Virginian was a Whig only because he had fallen out with Andrew Jackson during the South Carolina nullification crisis. Tyler had consistently opposed all the measures of the Whig Henry Clay's American System: protective tariffs, the national bank, and internal improvements at federal expense. Tyler fa-

vored strict construction and states' rights, positions closer to those of the Democrats than of the Whigs. Whigs had placed Tyler on the ballot to appeal to Southerners, but they never expected that Tyler would wield power. Even after Tyler moved into the White House, they assumed that he would bow to the party's leader, Kentucky senator Henry Clay.

*The politics of expansion became hopelessly entangled with sectionalism and the slavery question.*

Clay viewed the Whig victory in 1840 as "a great civil revolution." After twelve years of Democratic rule, he could hardly wait to translate Whig programs and principles into law. Clay guided a raft of legislation through Congress. Tyler accepted the repeal of the Democrats' independent treasury and grudgingly approved a slightly higher tariff, but he vetoed a bill for internal improvements. Clay pressed on, emerging from Congress with a bill for a new national bank. The president promptly rejected it with a Jackson-like argument that it was "unconstitutional."

With his second veto, Tyler forfeited all claim to Whig leadership. His opposition left Clay's economic plan in shambles. The Whigs formally expelled Tyler from the party, and, in an unprecedented move, most of the cabinet resigned. Secretary of State Daniel Webster, however, stayed on to settle the boundary between Canada and the United States, still undetermined after fifty-six years. Observers dubbed the negotiations with Britain the "battle of the maps," but the Webster-Ashburton Treaty of 1842 settled all border issues with Canada, except Oregon.

Even Webster's success could not redeem the Tyler administration. Tyler betrayed the economic principles of his supposed party, and Clay did not hesitate to compare John Tyler to Benedict Arnold. "Tyler is on his way to the Democratic camp," Clay declared. "They will give him lodgings in some outhouse, but they will never trust him. He will stand here, like Arnold in England, a monument of his own perfidy and disgrace." Writing off Tyler, Clay's followers hoisted Clay's banner for the presidency in 1844. Tyler dove into a quest for the Democratic nomination, but he needed an issue that could provide a bridge back to his former party.

## Texas, Oregon, and the Election of 1844

The issue that stirred John Tyler's blood, and that of much of the nation, was Texas. Texans had sought admission to the Union almost since their independence from Mexico in 1836, and Tyler, an ardent expansionist, knew that the acquisition of Texas would appeal strongly to southern and western Democrats. He also understood that Texas was a dangerous issue. Any suggestion of adding another slave state to the Union brought many Northerners to a boil. Annexing Texas also risked precipitating war because Mexico had never relinquished its claim to its lost province.

Inhabitants of the Lone Star Republic lived a precarious existence. They often exchanged shots with Mexicans along the border, and they worried that Mexico would launch an invasion. Cold-shouldered by the United States, Texans explored Great Britain's interest in recognition and trade. They discovered that the British were eager to keep Texas independent. In Britain's eyes, Texas provided a buffer against American expansion and a new market for English manufactured goods. Moreover, Britain hoped to persuade Texas to adopt gradual emancipation. Americans worried that Britain's real object was adding Texas to the British Empire. This fluid mix of threat, fear, and opportunity convinced Tyler to risk negotiations with Texas, and he worked vigorously to annex the republic before his term expired. His efforts pushed Texas and the slavery issue to the center of national politics.

In April 1844, after months of secret negotiations between Texas and the Tyler administration, the new secretary of state, South Carolinian John C. Calhoun, laid an annexation treaty before the Senate. But when Calhoun publicly linked annexation to the defense of slavery, he doomed the treaty. His statement strengthened the abolitionist claim that annexation was merely a proslavery plot, and howls of protest against annexation erupted everywhere north of the Mason-Dixon line. When the Senate soundly rejected the treaty, it appeared that Tyler had succeeded only in inflaming sectional conflict.

The issue of Texas had not died down by the 1844 elections. Henry Clay looked forward to waging his campaign on the old Whig economic principles that Tyler had frustrated. But everywhere he spoke, he confronted a barrage of questions about Texas. Finally, to appeal to northern voters, he came out against the immediate annexation of Texas. "Annexation and war with Mexico are identical," Clay declared. When news of Clay's statement reached Andrew Jackson at his plantation in Tennessee, he chuckled, "Clay [is] a dead political Duck." In Jackson's shrewd judgment, no man who opposed annexation could be elected president. But the Whig Party paid no attention, nominated Clay, and adopted a platform that proclaimed the principles of Clay's American System while remaining silent on Texas.

Among Democrats, Martin Van Buren expected to receive the party's nomination, but when he announced his opposition to Texas annexation, his candidacy collapsed in the South. Van Buren's demise opened the door at the Democratic convention. After John Tyler generated little support, James K. Polk of Tennessee gained his party's presidential nomination. Polk was as strong for the annexation of Texas as Clay was against it.

In the 1844 election, Democrats sought to champion Texas annexation without splitting their party or the nation. They succeeded by yoking Texas to

**A POLK SNUFFBOX**
*The use of political paraphernalia to appeal to the electorate is not a new phenomenon. James K. Polk, the Democratic presidential candidate in 1844, was portrayed on this fine snuffbox. In a time when almost every adult male used tobacco in one form or another, this handsome political object was sure to attract attention.*
Collection of Janice L. and David J. Frent.

Oregon, thus tapping the desire for expansion in the free states of the North as well as in the slave states of the South. The Democratic platform pulled out all the stops on behalf of manifest destiny. It called for the "reannexation of Texas" and the "reoccupation of Oregon." The suggestion that the United States was merely reasserting its existing rights was poor history but good politics. According to the Democratic formula, Texas annexation did not give an advantage to slavery and the South. Linked to Oregon, Texas expanded America to the advantage of the entire nation.

Much to Henry Clay's discomfort, Texas, not the tariff, emerged as the dominant issue of the 1844 campaign. When Clay finally recognized the groundswell for expansion, he lost his nerve. He waffled on Texas, hinting that he might accept annexation under certain circumstances. His retreat won little support in the South and only succeeded in alienating antislavery opinion in the North. James G. Birney, the candidate of the fledgling Liberty Party, picked up the votes of thousands of disillusioned Clay supporters. In the November election, Polk received 170 electoral votes and Clay 105. New York's 35 electoral votes proved critical to Clay's defeat. Birney received 15,000 votes in New York, but since Clay lost the state by only 5,000, a shift of just one-third of Birney's votes to Clay would have given him the state and the presidency.

The nation did not have to wait for Polk's inauguration to see results from his victory. One month after the election, President Tyler announced that the Democratic triumph provided a mandate for the annexation of Texas "promptly and immediately." After a fierce debate between antislavery and proslavery forces, Congress approved a joint resolution offering the Republic of Texas admission to the United States. On March 1, 1845, three days before Polk took office, Texas entered the Union as a slave state.

Tyler had seen to Texas, but James Polk had promised Oregon, too. Settlers in the West and expansionists elsewhere demanded that the new president make good on the Democrats' campaign slogan—"Fifty-four Forty or Fight"—that is, all of Oregon, right up to Alaska ("fifty-four forty" being the southern latitude of Russian Alaska). But Polk was close to war with Mexico and could not afford a simultaneous war with Britain over its claims to Canada. After the initial bluster, therefore, Polk buried the Democrats' campaign promise and renewed an old offer to divide Oregon along the forty-ninth parallel. After some hesitation, the British accepted the compromise. Westerners cried betrayal,

but most Americans celebrated the agreement that gave the nation an enormous territory peacefully. Besides, when the Senate finally approved the treaty in June 1846, the United States and Mexico were already at war.

## The Mexican War

From its independence in 1821, Mexico realized that its security and success in nation building depended on harmonious relations with its northern neighbor. The United States, however, exhibited expansionist tendencies from the beginning. Aggravation between the two nations escalated to open antagonism in 1845 when the United States annexed Texas. Absorbing territory still claimed by Mexico ruptured diplomatic relations between the United States and Mexico and set the stage for war. But it was President James K. Polk's insistence on having Mexico's other northern provinces that made war certain. The war was not as easy as Polk anticipated, but it ended in American victory and acquisition of a new American West. Mexicans could only lament, "Poor Mexico, so far from God, so near the United States."

### "Mr. Polk's War"

From the day he entered the White House, Polk craved Mexico's remaining northern provinces: California and New Mexico, land that today makes up California, Nevada, and Utah, most of New Mexico and Arizona, and parts of Wyoming and Colorado. Polk hoped to buy the territory. But the Mexicans refused to sell off their country, and in March 1846 they sent Polk's envoy, John Slidell, packing. A furious Polk concluded that it would take military force to realize the United States' manifest destiny.

Polk had already ordered General Zachary Taylor to march his 4,000-man Army of Occupation of Texas from its position on the Nueces River, the southern boundary of Texas according to the Mexicans, to the banks of the Rio Grande 150 miles south, the boundary claimed by Texans. The Mexican general in Matamoros viewed the American advance as aggression and ordered Taylor back to the Nueces. Taylor refused, and on April 25, Mexican cavalry attacked a party of American soldiers, killing or wounding 16 and capturing the rest. Even before news of the battle arrived in Washington,

Polk had already obtained his cabinet's approval of a war message.

On May 11, 1846, the president told Congress, "Mexico has passed the boundary of the United States, has invaded our territory, and shed American blood upon American soil." Thus "war exists, and, notwithstanding all our efforts to avoid it, exists by the act of Mexico herself." Two days later, Congress passed a declaration of war and began raising an army. Despite years of saber rattling toward Mexico and Britain, the American army was pitifully small, only 7,400 soldiers. Faced with the nation's first foreign war, up against a Mexican army that numbered more than 30,000, Polk called for volunteers who would serve for six to twelve months. Men everywhere rushed to the colors. More than 30,000 Tennesseans competed for the state's 3,000 allotted positions. Even Massachusetts, where many citizens denounced the war as a plot to extend slavery, filled its quota within a month. Eventually, more than 112,000 white Americans (blacks were banned) joined the army to fight in Mexico.

Despite the outpouring of support, the war divided the nation. Northerners were not nearly as hot-blooded about the war as Southerners. Although some Northerners kept their opposition to themselves because they did not want to appear unpatriotic or unwilling to support American soldiers in the field, a hard core of northern Whigs loudly condemned the war as the unwarranted bullying of a weak nation by its greedy expansionist neighbor.

On January 12, 1848, a gangly freshman representative from Illinois rose from his back-row seat in the House of Representatives to deliver his first important speech in Congress. Abraham Lincoln took direct aim at the president and his war. Polk's defense of the war, Lincoln declared, was from beginning to end the "sheerest deception." He challenged the president's version of the incident that precipitated war and sought to disprove Polk's claim that the territory between the Nueces and the Rio Grande was indisputably American soil. He likened the president's views to "the half-insane mumbling of a fever dream" and proclaimed Polk "a bewildered, confounded, and miserably perplexed man." Before he sat down, Lincoln had questioned the president's intelligence, honesty, and sanity. President Polk simply ignored the upstart representative, but antislavery, antiwar Whigs kept up the attack throughout the conflict. In their effort to undercut national support, they labeled it "Mr. Polk's War."

Since most Americans backed the war, it was not really Polk's war, but the president acted as if it were. Although he had no military experience, he directed the war personally. Working eighteen hours a day, Polk established overall strategy and oversaw the details of military campaigns. He planned a short war in which American armies would occupy Mexico's northern provinces and defeat the Mexican army in a decisive battle or two, after which Mexico would sue for peace and the United States would keep the territory its armies occupied.

*The war was not as easy as Polk anticipated, but it ended in American victory and acquisition of a new American West. Mexicans could only lament, "Poor Mexico, so far from God, so near the United States."*

And, indeed, Polk's strategy seemed to work at first. In May 1846, Zachary Taylor's troops drove south from the Rio Grande and routed the Mexican army, first on the plain of Palo Alto and then in a palm-filled ravine known as Resaca de la Palma (Map 13.4). Taylor became an instant war hero. Sixty-two years old, "Old Rough and Ready," as he was affectionately known, had an undistinguished career behind him. But his simplicity and informality, as well as his cool behavior under fire, endeared him to his men. Polk rewarded Taylor for his victories by making him commander for the conquest of Mexico.

A second prong of the campaign to occupy Mexico's northern provinces centered on Colonel Stephen Watts Kearny, who led a 1,700-man army from Missouri into New Mexico. Without firing a shot, American forces took Santa Fe in August 1846. Kearny promptly proclaimed New Mexico American territory and with 300 troops headed for California. In January 1847, after several clashes, the American forces occupied Los Angeles. California and New Mexico were in American hands.

By then, Taylor had driven deep into the interior of Mexico. In September 1846, after a five-day siege and house-to-house fighting, he took the fortified city of Monterrey. With reinforcements and fresh supplies, Taylor pushed his 5,000 troops southwest, where the Mexican hero of the Alamo, General Antonio López de Santa Anna, was concentrating a huge army of 21,000, which he hoped

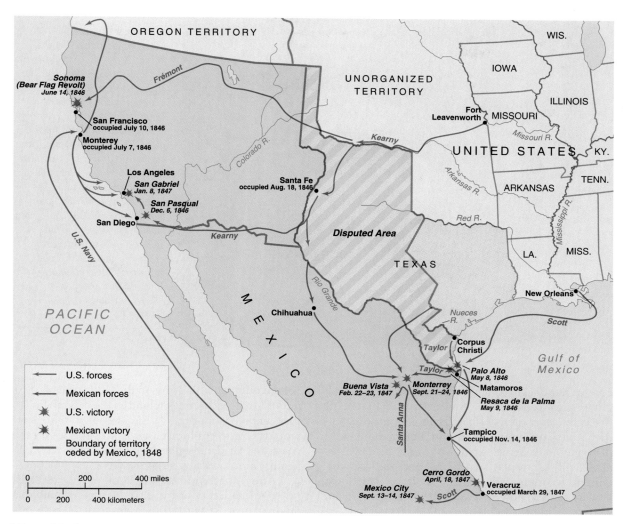

**M A P   1 3 . 4**
*The Mexican War, 1846–1848*
*American and Mexican soldiers skirmished across much of northern Mexico, but the major battles took place between the Rio Grande and Mexico City.*

would strike a decisive blow against the invaders from the north.

On Washington's birthday 1847, Taylor's troops met Santa Anna's at Buena Vista. Superior American artillery and accurate musket fire won the day, but the Americans suffered heavy casualties, including Henry Clay Jr., the son of the man who had opposed Texas annexation for fear it would precipitate war. But the Mexicans suffered even greater losses, and during the night Santa Anna removed his battered army from the battlefield, much to the

"profound disgust of the troops," one Mexican officer remembered. "They are filled with grief that they were going to lose the benefit of all the sacrifices that they had made; that the conquered field would be abandoned, and that the victory would be given to the enemy."

The series of uninterrupted victories in northern Mexico fed the American troops' sense of superiority and very nearly led to a feeling of invincibility. "No American force has ever thought of being defeated by any amount of Mexican troops,"

**MEXICAN FAMILY**
*Mexican civilians, like this family in 1847, were vulnerable to atrocities committed by an invading army. Volunteers, a large portion of American troops, received little training and resisted military discipline. The "lawless Volunteers stop at no outrage," Brigadier General William Worth declared. "Innocent blood has been basely, cowardly, and barbarously shed in cold blood." Generals Zachary Taylor and Winfield Scott gradually tamed the "wild volunteers" by employing stern military justice.*
Courtesy Amon Carter Museum, Fort Worth.

one soldier declared. The Americans worried about other hazards, however. "I can assure you that fighting is the least dangerous & arduous part of a soldier's life," one young man said. Letters home told of torturous marches across burning, arid wastes alive with tarantulas, scorpions, and rattlesnakes. Others recounted dysentery, malaria, smallpox, cholera, and yellow fever. Of the 13,000 American soldiers who died in Mexico, only 2,000 fell to Mexican bullets and shells. Disease killed most of the others. Medicine was so primitive and conditions so harsh that army doctors could do little. As a Tennessee man observed, "nearly all who take sick die."

### Victory in Mexico

Although Americans won battle after battle, President Polk's strategy misfired. Despite its loss of territory and men, Mexico determinedly refused to trade land for peace. One American soldier captured the Mexican mood: "They cannot submit to be deprived of California after the loss of Texas, and nothing but the conquest of their Capital will force them to such a humiliation." Polk had arrived at the same conclusion. Zachary Taylor had not proven decisive enough for Polk, and the president tapped another general to carry the war to Mexico City. While Taylor occupied the north, General Winfield

Scott would land his army on the Gulf coast of Mexico and march 250 miles inland to the capital. Polk's plan entailed enormous risk; it meant that Scott would have to cut himself off from supplies on the coast and lead his men deep into enemy country against a numerically superior foe.

After months of careful planning and the skillful coordination of army and navy, an amphibious landing near Veracruz put 8,600 American troops ashore in five hours without the loss of a single life. The Americans encircled the city, and after eighty-eight hours of furious shelling, Veracruz surrendered. Scott immediately began preparations for the march west.

Meanwhile, after the frightful defeat at Buena Vista, Santa Anna had returned to Mexico City. He rallied his ragged troops and marched them east to set a trap for Scott in the mountain pass at Cerro Gordo. But the Americans knifed through Mexican lines, almost capturing Santa Anna, who fled the field on foot. Ever resilient, Santa Anna again rallied the Mexican army. Some 30,000 troops took up defensive positions on the outskirts of Mexico City, where they hurriedly began melting down church bells to cast new cannon.

In August, Scott began his assault on the Mexican capital. The fighting proved the most brutal of the war. Santa Anna backed his army into the city, fighting each step of the way. At the battle of

Churubusco, the Mexicans took 4,000 casualties in a single day and the Americans more than 1,000. At the castle of Chapultepec, American troops scaled the walls and fought the Mexican defenders hand to hand. After Chapultepec, Santa Anna evacuated Mexico City, and on September 14, 1847, General Winfield Scott rode in triumphantly. The ancient capital of the Aztecs had fallen once again to an invading army.

With Mexico City in American hands, Polk sent Nicholas P. Trist, the chief clerk in the State Department, to Mexico to negotiate the peace. When Trist arrived, he found that Santa Anna had resigned as president and had fled the country. But Trist began talks with commissioners appointed by a new Mexican president and on February 2, 1848, signed the Treaty of Guadalupe Hidalgo. Mexico agreed to give up all claims to Texas above the Rio Grande and to cede the huge provinces of New Mexico and California to the United States. The United States agreed to pay Mexico $15 million and

to assume $3.25 million in claims that American citizens had against Mexico. Some Americans clamored for all of Mexico, but the treaty gave the president what he wanted. Polk sent the treaty to the Senate, which ratified it by a vote of thirty-eight to fourteen in March 1848. The last American soldiers left Mexico a few months later.

The American triumph in the Mexican War had enormous consequences. Less than three-quarters of a century after its founding, the United States achieved its self-proclaimed manifest destiny to stretch from the Atlantic to the Pacific (Map 13.5). With the northern half of Mexico in American hands, California gold, which was discovered almost simultaneously with the transfer of territory, neither made Mexicans rich nor bankrolled Mexico's economic development. Instead, the West became an enclave for Anglo-American enterprise and wealth. (See the Historical Question on page 346.) The war also reinforced the worst stereotypes Mexicans and Americans had of each other. A virulent

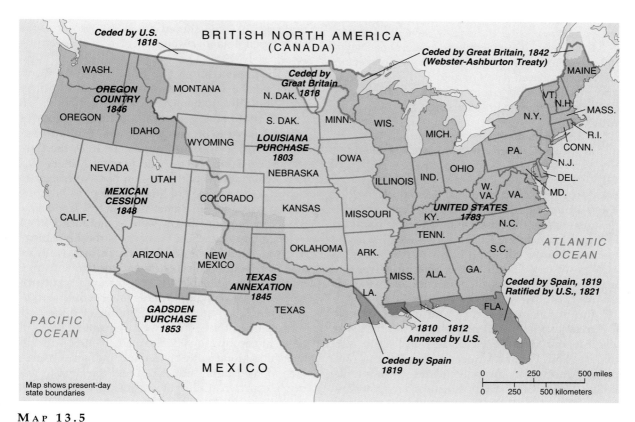

**MAP 13.5**

*Territorial Expansion by 1860*

*Less than a century after its founding, the United States had spread from the Atlantic seaboard to the Pacific Ocean. War, purchase, and diplomacy had gained a continent.*

# What Was the Impact of the California Gold Rush?

On a cold January morning in 1848, while James Marshall was walking along the American River in the foothills of the Sierra Nevada, he detected the glint of yellow metal in the stream. The nuggets he found set off the California gold rush, one of the wildest mining stampedes in the world's history. Between 1849 and 1852, more than 250,000 forty-niners, as the would-be miners were known, descended on the Golden State.

Marshall discovered gold in the same year that the Treaty of Guadalupe Hidalgo transferred California and other northern provinces of Mexico to the United States. Americans did not find it surprising that the discovery coincided with American acquisition. "God kept that coast for a people of the Pilgrim blood," one minister intoned. "He would not permit any other to be fully developed there."

Gold proved irresistible to easterners. Newspapers went crazy with stories about prospectors who extracted half a pan of gold from every pan of gravel they scooped from western streams. Soon, cities reverberated with men singing:

> Oh Susannah, don't you cry for me;
> I'm gone to California with my wash-bowl on
> my knee.

Scores of ships sailed from East Coast ports, headed either around South America to San Francisco or to Panama, where the passengers made their way by foot and canoe to the Pacific and waited for a ship to carry them north. Even larger numbers of gold seekers took riverboats to the Missouri River and then set out in wagons, on horseback, or by foot for the West.

But young men everywhere contracted gold fever. As stories of California gold circled the globe, Chinese and Germans, Mexicans and Irish, Australians and French, Chileans and Italians, and people of dozens of other nationalities set out to strike it rich. Louisa Knapp Clappe, wife of a minister and one of the few women in gold country, remarked that when she walked through Indian Bar, the little mining town where she lived, she heard English, French, Spanish, German, Italian, Kanaka (Hawaiian), Asian Indian, and American Indian languages. Hangtown, Hell's Delight, Gouge Eye, and a hundred other crude mining camps became temporary home to a diverse throng of nationalities and peoples.

One of the largest groups of new arrivals was the Chinese. Between 1848 and 1854, Chinese men numbering 45,000 (but almost no Chinese women) arrived in California. Most considered themselves "sojourners," temporary residents who planned to return home as soon as their savings allowed. The majority came under a Chinese-controlled contract labor system in which the immigrant worked out the cost of his transportation. In the early years, most worked as wage laborers in mining. By the 1860s, they dominated railroad construction in the West. Ninety percent of the Central Pacific Railroad's 10,000 workers were Chinese. The Chinese also made up nearly one-half of San Francisco's labor force, working in the shoe, tobacco, woolen, laundry, and sewing trades. By 1870, the Chinese population had grown to 63,200, including 4,500 women. They constituted nearly 10 percent of the state's people and 25 percent of its wage-earning force.

The presence of peoples from around the world shattered the Anglo-American dream of a racially and ethnically homogeneous West, but ethnic diversity did nothing to increase the tolerance of Anglo-American prospectors. In their eyes, no "foreigner" had a right to dig gold. In 1850, the California legislature passed the Foreign Miners' Tax Law, which levied high taxes on non-Americans to drive them from the gold fields, except as hired laborers working on claims owned by Americans. Stubborn foreign miners were sometimes hauled before "Judge Lynch." One of the earliest lynchings in the gold fields was of a Frenchman and a Chilean.

Anglo-Americans considered the Chinese devious and unassimilable. They also feared that hardworking, self-denying Chinese labor would undercut white labor and drive it from the country. As a consequence, the Chinese were segregated residentially and occupationally and made ineligible for citizenship. Along with blacks and Indians, Chinese were denied public education and the right to testify in court. In addition to exclusion, they suffered from violence. Mobs drove them from Eureka, Truckee, and other mining towns.

American prospectors swamped the *Californios,* the Spanish and Mexican settlers who had lived in California for generations. On the eve of the American takeover, *Californios* included *rancheros,* professionals, merchants, artisans, and laborers. Raging prejudice and discriminatory laws increasingly pushed Hispanics into the ranks of unskilled labor. Americans took their land, even though the federal government had pledged to protect Mexican and Spanish land titles after the cession of 1848. Anglo forty-niners branded Spanish-speaking miners, even native-born *Californios,* "foreigners" and drove them from the diggings. Mariano Vallejo, a leading *Californio,* said of the forty-niners: "The good ones were few and the wicked many."

For Native Americans, the gold rush was a catastrophe. Numbering about 150,000 in 1848, the Indian population fell to 25,000 in 1856. *Californios* had exploited the native peoples, but the forty-niners wanted to eradicate them. Starvation, disease, and a declining birthrate took a heavy toll. Indians also fell victim to wholesale murder. "That a war of extermination will continue to be waged between the two races until the Indian race becomes extinct must be expected," declared California governor Peter W.

Burnett in 1851. Nineteenth-century historian Hubert Howe Bancroft described white behavior toward Indians during the gold rush as "one of the last human hunts of civilization, and the basest and most brutal of them all." To survive, Indians moved to the most remote areas of the state and tried to stay out of the way.

The forty-niners created dazzling wealth—in 1852, eighty-one million ounces of gold, nearly one-half of the world's production. But because Anglo-Americans made the rules, not everyone shared equally. And only a few prospectors—of whatever race and nationality—struck it rich. The era of the individual prospector panning in streams quickly gave way to corporate-owned deep-shaft mining. Most forty-niners eventually took up farming or went to work for the corporations that pushed them out. But because of gold, an avalanche of people had roared across California. Anglo-Americans were most numerous, and Anglo dominance developed early. But the gold rush also brought a rainbow of nationalities. Anglo-American dominance and ethnic and racial diversity in the West both count among the most significant legacies of the gold rush.

anti-Yankee sentiment took root in Mexico, while deeply prejudiced views of Mexicans and Mexican culture flourished in the fertile soil of American victory. For Mexico, defeat meant national humiliation, but it also had a positive effect. It generated for the first time a genuine nationalism, no small thing in a country still trying to build a nation. In America, victory increased the sense of superiority that was already deeply ingrained.

## Conclusion: Free Labor, Free Men

In the 1840s, diplomacy and war handed the United States 1.2 million square miles and more than 1,000 miles of Pacific coastline. To most Americans, vast geographical expansion seemed to be the natural companion of a stunning economic transformation. A cluster of interrelated developments—steam power, railroads, and the growing mechanization of agriculture and manufacturing—resulted in greater productivity, a burst of output from farms and factories, and prosperity for many.

To Northerners, their industrial evolution confirmed the choice they had made to put slavery on the road to extinction and to promote free labor as the key to independence, equality, and prosperity. Millions of Northerners, like Abraham Lincoln, could point to personal experience as evidence of the practical truth of the free-labor ideal. But millions of others had different stories to tell. Rather than producing economic equality, the free-labor system saw wealth and poverty continue to rub shoulders. Instead of social independence, more than half of the nation's free-labor workforce toiled for someone else by 1860. Free-labor enthusiasts denied that the problems were built into the system. They argued that most social ills—including poverty and dependency—sprang from individual deficiencies. Consequently, reformers usually focused on the lack of self-control and discipline, on sin and alcohol. They denied that free labor meant exploitation. Slaves, not free workers, suffered, they argued.

Differences between North and South had appeared early in the nation's history, but by midcentury the distinctive ways in which North and South organized their labor systems left their mark on all aspects of regional life. Each region was increasingly animated by economic interests, cultural values, and political aims that were antithetical to those of the other. In the midst of deepening differences between the regions, Mexican land thrust the fundamental issue of slave or free labor into the center of national life. Now that Americans had half of Mexico, they had to decide what to do with it. Would the new American West, like the United States, be half slave and half free, or would it be all one or the other? The debate about the territory taken from Mexico became a struggle over the nation's future.

## CHRONOLOGY

| | | | |
|---|---|---|---|
| **1828** | America's first railroad, the Baltimore and Ohio, breaks ground. | | Vice President John Tyler becomes president of the United States when William Henry Harrison dies in office after one month. |
| **1836** | Texas declares independence from Mexico. | | |
| **1837** | John Deere patents his steel plow. | **1842** | Webster-Ashburton Treaty settles all border issues with British Canada except Oregon. |
| **1840s** | Americans begin harnessing steam power to manufacturing. | | |
| | Cyrus McCormick and others create practical mechanical reapers. | **1844** | Democrat James K. Polk elected president on platform calling for annexation of Texas and Oregon. |
| **1841** | First wagon trains set out for West on Oregon Trail. | | Samuel F. B. Morse invents telegraph. |

| 1845 | Term "manifest destiny" coined by New York journalist John L. O'Sullivan; used as justification for Anglo-American settlers to take land in West. |
| | United States annexes Texas, which enters Union as slave state. |
| 1846 | Bear Flag Revolt, independence movement to secede from Mexico, takes place in California. |
| | **May 13.** Congress declares war on Mexico. |
| | United States and Great Britain agree to divide Oregon Country at forty-ninth parallel. |
| 1847 | Brigham Young leads advance party of Mormons to Great Salt Lake in Utah. |
| 1848 | Treaty of Guadalupe Hidalgo ends Mexican War. Mexico gives up all claims to Texas north of Rio Grande and cedes provinces of New Mexico and California to United States. |
| | Oneida community organized in New York. |
| | First women's rights convention in United States takes place at Seneca Falls, New York. |
| 1849 | California gold rush begins. |
| | Harriet Tubman escapes from slavery in Maryland. |
| 1850 | Mormon community of Deseret annexed to United States as Utah Territory. |
| 1851 | Conference in Laramie, Wyoming, between U.S. government and Plains tribes marks beginning of government policy of forcing Indians onto reservations. |
| 1855 | Massachusetts integrates public schools as result of campaigns led by African American leaders. |

# SUGGESTED READINGS

Stuart Bruchey, *Enterprise: The Dynamic Economy of a Free People* (1990). A readable synthesis of economic trends with broader social and cultural developments.

David Brion Davis, ed., *Antebellum American Culture: An Intrepretive Anthology* (1979). An outstanding collection of primary sources that reveal the cross-currents of American society and thought.

David Herbert Donald, *Lincoln* (1995). A comprehensive, up-to-date biography by a master historian.

John S. C. Eisenhower, *So Far from God: The U.S. War with Mexico, 1845–1848* (1989), and James M. McCaffrey, *Army of Manifest Destiny: The American Soldiers in the Mexican War, 1846–1848* (1992). Useful analyses of the American war with Mexico.

John Mack Faragher, *Sugar Creek: Life on the Illinois Frontier* (1986). A fine-grained account of rural life familiar to Lincoln and his contemporaries.

Patricia Nelson Limerick, *The Legacy of Conquest: The Unbroken Past of the American West* (1987), and Richard White, *"It's Your Misfortune and None of My Own": A New History of the American West* (1991). Fresh syntheses of the social and cultural history of the American West.

Charles J. McClain, *In Search of Equality: The Chinese Struggle against Discrimination in Nineteenth-Century America* (1994), and Robert M. Utley, *The Indian Frontier of the American West, 1846–1890* (1984). Valuable analyses of the experiences of two major groups in the West.

Frederick Merk, *Manifest Destiny and Mission in American History* (1963), and David M. Pletcher, *The Diplomacy of Annexation: Texas, Oregon, and the Mexican War* (1973). Important analyses of the ideology and politics of expansion.

Steven Mintz, *Moralists and Modernizers: America's Pre-Civil War Reformers* (1995). A useful survey of reformers and their ideas.

C. Peter Ripley et al., eds., *Witness for Freedom: African American Voices on Race, Slavery, and Emancipation* (1993). A wide-ranging set of historical documents that illustrate the dilemmas confronting African Americans.

Malcolm Rohrbough, *Days of Gold: The California Gold Rush and the American Nation* (1997). A lively new interpretation of the meaning and consequences of the gold rush.

Jean Fagan Yellin and John C. Van Horne, eds., *The Abolitionist Sisterhood: Women's Political Culture in Antebellum America* (1994). A valuable collection of essays that detail women's political activities.

**FREDERICK DOUGLASS DOLLS**
*These dolls were made in the late 1850s by Cynthia Hill of New Bedford, Massachusetts, where Frederick Douglass had first settled after he escaped from slavery. They celebrate Douglass's transformation from barefoot, tattered slave to dignified, respectable man of substance. They also announce more generally that African Americans were held back by their enslavement, not by their race.*
Old Dartmouth Historical Society, New Bedford Whaling Museum.

# THE HOUSE DIVIDED

## 1846–1861

ALREADY KNOWN AS THE "GATEWAY TO THE WEST," St. Louis, Missouri, in 1830 was a thriving river port. Among the newcomers arriving that year was Dred Scott, a slave. Scott had been born in Virginia at the turn of the century and in 1818 had moved with his master Peter Blow to a cotton plantation in Alabama. Twelve years later, the Blow family and their six slaves moved to St. Louis. St. Louis's population of six thousand included some twelve hundred African Americans, both slave and free. Free blacks lived hard lives—crammed into rotten shacks in dismal alleys, employed in the meanest jobs, excluded from much of the city's activities, harassed on account of their race. Details of Dred Scott's life are scarce, but we know that freedom—even the severely restricted freedom of St. Louis's free blacks—became Dred Scott's dream.

In 1833, Scott was sold to Dr. John Emerson, an army doctor who took Scott with him as his personal servant to Fort Armstrong, Illinois. Two years later, Scott accompanied Emerson when he was transferred to Fort Snelling on the Minnesota River in Wisconsin Territory. Other moves followed, but in a few years Emerson returned Scott to St. Louis. In 1842, Emerson quit the army and died a year later. On April 6, 1846, Dred Scott sued to prove that he, his wife Harriet, and their two daughters, Eliza and Lizzie, were legally entitled to their freedom.

Dred Scott's claim was based on his travels and residences. He argued that living in Illinois, a free state, and in Wisconsin Territory, a free territory according to the Missouri Compromise of 1820, had made him and his family free; and once free they remained free, even after returning to Missouri, a slave state. The Scotts had a strong claim. Missouri had freed a dozen slaves on similar grounds, and in January 1850 a jury of twelve white men sided with the Scotts. But Dr. Emerson's widow was determined to keep them as her slaves. On appeal, the Missouri Supreme Court overturned three decades of precedents and reversed the lower court.

But Dred and Harriet Scott and their supporters (white friends, several sympathetic lawyers, and probably some of St. Louis's free blacks) were not easily discouraged. In 1854, Dred Scott turned to the federal courts in Missouri, but lost. Scott then appealed to the U.S. Supreme Court. Although proslavery and antislavery forces had begun to see the potential opportunity (and danger) in the *Dred Scott* case, no one could have anticipated the sweeping decision that came down from the Supreme Court in 1857. It left the Scotts slaves, and it brought the nation closer to civil war.

What had begun as the straightforward effort of one black family to gain freedom had become entangled in the national debate about slavery. Victory over Mexico and the acquisition of Mexican land thrust the issue of the expansion of

### THE DRED SCOTT FAMILY

*The* Dred Scott *case in 1857 produced a fierce political storm, but it also fueled an enormous curiosity about the family suing for freedom. Popular magazines rushed to supply the demand with images and interviews. The correspondent for the popular* Frank Leslie's Illustrated *met Dred Scott in St. Louis and reported: "We found him on examination to be a pure-blooded African, perhaps fifty years of age, with a shrewd, intelligent, good-natured face, of rather light frame, being not more than five feet six inches high." But as this illustration makes clear, Northerners who had been introduced to slavery through Harriet Beecher Stowe's powerful family drama wanted to see all of the Scotts: Harriet, who was a slave when Dred Scott married her in Wisconsin Territory in about 1836; daughter Eliza, who was born in 1838 on board a ship traveling in free territory north of Missouri; and daughter Lizzie, born after the Scotts returned to St. Louis.*
Library of Congress.

slavery into national politics. The principle of excluding slavery from western territories would set the course for the next decade and a half. The debate over slavery would transform party politics into sectional politics. And sectional politics worked like a blacksmith's hammer on the South's separatist impulses. A fitful tendency before the Mexican War, southern separatism gained strength with each blow. Year by year, the constituency for conciliation and compromise wore away. The era ended as it began—with a crisis of the Union.

## Fruits of War

South Carolina Senator John C. Calhoun saw the sad truth of Mexican land earlier than most. "Mexico is to us the forbidden fruit," he declared in May 1846. "The penalty of eating it [is] to subject our institutions to political death." When the Mexican War ended in 1848, Congress had made no headway in solving the question of slavery in the national territories. Nor did the presidential election that year produce an answer. Instead, the territorial issue ripped apart the Whig and Democratic Parties, spawned a third party, and raised the political temperature of the nation to a boil. In 1850, after four years of strife, Congress patched together a settlement, one that most Americans hoped would be permanent.

### The Wilmot Proviso and the Expansion of Slavery

Curiously, between 1846 and 1861, Americans did not focus on slavery where it existed but on the possibility that it might expand into areas where it did not exist. The Constitution confined the sectional controversy to these narrow limits. Except for a few abolitionists who strove to uproot slavery wherever they found it, most of the nation agreed that the Constitution had left the issue of slavery to the individual states to decide. One by one, northern states had done away with slavery, while southern states had retained it. But what about slavery in the nation's territories? The Constitution stated that "Congress shall have power to . . . make all needful rules and regulations respecting the territory . . . belonging to the United States." The debate between the North and South about slavery, then, turned toward Congress and the definition of its authority over western lands.

The spark for the national debate was provided in August 1846 by a young Democratic representative from Pennsylvania, David Wilmot, who proposed that Congress bar slavery from all lands acquired in the war with Mexico. He modeled his proposal, which became known as the Wilmot Proviso, after the Northwest Ordinance of 1787, which banned slavery in territory north of the Ohio River. Wilmot explained that the Mexicans had already abolished slavery in all of their territory. "God forbid," he declared, "that we should be the means of planting this institution upon it."

The Wilmot Proviso rallied an interesting assortment of antislavery Northerners. Abolitionists supported "free soil," that is, territory from which slavery was prohibited. Many Whigs also stepped forward on the basis of principle. They often denounced slavery as a sin and emphasized Congress's authority to ban it from the territories. But not all Northerners who opposed slavery's extension did so out of sympathy for slaves. Some Democratic politicians feared that the Whigs would pick up voters by claiming that the Mexican War was a land-grab for slaveholders. By denying slavery a place in the territory the United States took from Mexico, Democrats could support territorial expansion without offending antislavery constituents. One Northerner declared that the "adoption of the principle of the 'Wilmot proviso' is the only way to save the Democratic party in the free states." Without coming out against slavery's expansion, Democrats "are destined to defeat and doomed . . . from Iowa to Maine."

Support for blocking slavery's expansion also came from Northerners who were not so much antislavery as they were anti-South. New slave territories would eventually mean new slave states, and they wanted nothing to do with magnifying the power of Southerners, who often brought to Congress economic policies radically different from their own, especially in banking, internal improvements, and the tariff. Further support came from Northerners who were hostile to African Americans and wanted to reserve new lands for whites. Wilmot himself had blatantly encouraged racist support when he declared, "I would preserve for free white labor a fair country, a rich inheritance, where the sons of toil, of my own race and own color, can live without the disgrace which association with negro slavery brings upon free labor." Hundreds of thousands of white men dreamed of land in the West, and few wanted to work shoulder to shoulder with blacks. It is no wonder that some called the Wilmot Proviso the White Man's Proviso.

While the specter of new slave territory alarmed diverse Northerners, the thought that slavery might be excluded outraged diverse Southerners. From the colonial era, yeoman and planter alike regarded the West as a ladder for economic and social opportunity. Although they knew that the arid West was not ideal plantation country, some Southerners still agreed that the exclusion of slavery was a slap in the face. An Alabaman pointed out that at least half of the American soldiers in Mexico were Southerners. "When the war-worn soldier returns home," he asked, "is he to be told that he cannot carry his property to the country won by his blood?" But beyond economic opportunity, social mobility, and honor, southern leaders understood the need for political parity with the North to protect the South's interests, especially slavery. The need never seemed more urgent than in the 1840s, when the North's population and wealth were booming. James Henry Hammond of South Carolina predicted that ten new states would be carved from the acquired Mexican land. If free soil won, the North would "ride over us rough shod" in Congress, he claimed. "Our only safety is in *equality* of POWER."

In the nation's capital, the two sides squared off. Because Northerners had a majority in the House, they easily passed the Wilmot Proviso over the united opposition of Southerners. In the Senate, John C. Calhoun denied that Congress had constitutional authority to exclude slavery from the nation's territories. He reasoned that the territories were the "joint and common property" of all the states, that Congress could not justly deprive any state of equal rights in the territories, and that Congress therefore could not bar citizens of one state from migrating with their property (including slaves) to the territories. Where Wilmot demanded that Congress slam shut the door to slavery, Calhoun required that Congress hold the door wide open. Because slave states outnumbered free states fifteen to fourteen, southern senators stopped the proviso.

Between these extremes there appeared to be little middle ground. One plan proposed by President Polk and others—to extend the Missouri Compromise line to the Pacific—generated no significant enthusiasm. But Senator Lewis Cass of Michigan offered a compromise that he hoped would find support among moderates everywhere. He proposed the doctrine of "popular sovereignty": letting the people who actually settled the territories decide for themselves slavery's fate. The most attractive feature of this plan was its ambiguity

about the precise moment when settlers could determine slavery's fate. Northern advocates told their constituents that the decision on slavery could be made as soon as the first territorial legislature assembled. With free-soil majorities likely, they would shut the door to slavery almost before the first slave arrived. Southern supporters declared that popular sovereignty guaranteed that slavery would be unrestricted throughout the entire settlement period. Only at the very end, when settlers drew up a constitution and applied for statehood, could they decide the issue of slavery or freedom. By then, slavery would have sunk deep roots.

*Northerners who demanded no new slave territory anywhere, ever, and Southerners who demanded free entry for their slave property into all territories, or else, staked out their extreme positions.*

But when Congress ended its session in 1848, no plan had won a majority in both houses. Northerners who demanded no new slave territory anywhere, ever, and Southerners who demanded free entry for their slave property into all territories, or else, staked out their extreme positions. Unresolved in Congress, the territorial question naturally intruded into the presidential election of 1848.

## The Election of 1848

The Democratic and Whig Parties were both hurting in 1848. The territorial debate revealed free-soil factions in both parties. Antislavery northern Democrats challenged Democratic President Polk and the dominant southern element of their party. Northern Whigs split between an antislavery faction called Conscience Whigs and a more conservative group, Cotton Whigs (because many of them were textile mill owners), who sought compromise to hold the party together. Conscience Whigs denounced the evil alliance of northern "lords of the loom" and southern "lords of the lash" and threatened to bolt the party.

Polk—worn out, ailing, and unable to unite the Democratic Party—chose not to seek reelection. The Democratic convention nominated Cass, the man most closely associated with popular sovereignty, but the party platform avoided a firm position on slavery in the territories. The Whigs passed over

"Mr. Whig"—Henry Clay, the seventy-one-year-old founder of the party and chief spokesman for its American System—and nominated the hero of Buena Vista, "Old Rough and Ready," General Zachary Taylor. They declined to adopt any party platform, no matter how vague.

Taylor, who owned more than one hundred slaves on plantations in Mississippi and Louisiana, was hailed by Georgian Robert Toombs as a "Southern man, a slaveholder, a cotton planter." Conscience Whigs balked and looked for an alternative. As old party allegiances unraveled, the time seemed ripe for a major political realignment. Senator Charles Sumner called for "one grand Northern party of Freedom," and in the summer of 1848 antislavery Democrats and antislavery Whigs founded the Free-Soil Party. Nearly fifteen thousand noisy Free-Soilers gathered in Buffalo, New York, where they welded the factions together by nominating a dissident Democrat, Martin Van Buren, for president and a Conscience Whig, Charles Francis Adams, for vice president. The platform boldly proclaimed, "Free soil, free speech, free labor, and free men."

The November election dashed the hopes of the Free-Soilers. Although they succeeded in making slavery the campaign's central issue, they did not carry a single state. The major parties went through contortions to present their candidates favorably in both the North and the South, and their evasions succeeded. Taylor won the all-important electoral vote, 163 to 127, carrying eight of the fifteen slave states and seven of fifteen free states (see Map 14.3). (Wisconsin had entered the Union earlier in 1848, making fifteen slave states and fifteen free states.) Northern voters proved they were not yet ready for Sumner's new party, but the struggle between freedom and slavery in the territories had shaken the major parties badly.

## Debate and Compromise

Zachary Taylor was very much a mystery when he entered the White House in March 1849. He surprised almost everyone—and he infuriated Southerners. Who among them had imagined that the slaveholding father-in-law of Mississippi Senator Jefferson Davis would champion a free-soil solution to the problem of western land? But he did. The discovery of gold in California and the rush of 1849 made the existing military rule of California and New Mexico pitifully inadequate and the need for competent civil government urgent. Taylor sent agents west to persuade settlers to frame constitutions and apply immediately for admission to the Union as states. Predominantly antislavery, the settlers began writing free-state constitutions. "For the first time," Jefferson Davis declared, "we are about permanently to destroy the balance of power between the sections."

When Congress convened in December 1849, anxious citizens packed the galleries, eager for the "Great Debate." They witnessed what proved to be one of the longest, most contentious, and most significant sessions in the history of Congress. For seven months, politicians orated, debated, buttonholed, cajoled, and threatened in efforts to fashion a solution to the problems that divided the nation.

Foremost was the territorial issue. In January 1850, President Taylor urged Congress to admit California as a free state immediately and to admit New Mexico, which lagged behind by a few months, as soon as it applied. Southerners exploded. In their eyes, Taylor had betrayed his region. Southerners who would "consent to be thus degraded and enslaved," a North Carolinian declared, "ought to be whipped through their fields by their own negroes." Into this rancorous scene stepped Henry Clay, recently returned to the Senate by his home state of Kentucky. His reputation preceded him: the "Great Pacificator," master of accommodation, architect of Union-saving compromises in the Missouri and nullification crises. At seventy-two, Clay remained a powerful public speaker, and he had no doubt that the South's desperate mood threatened the Union.

"Mr. President," Clay declared when he took the floor on January 29, 1850, "I hold in my hand a series of resolutions which I desire to submit to the consideration of this body. Taken together, in combination, they propose an amicable arrangement of all questions in controversy between the free and slave states, growing out of the subject of slavery." His comprehensive plan sought to balance the interests of the slave and free states. Admit California as a free state, he proposed, but organize the rest of the Southwest without restrictions on slavery. Require Texas to abandon its claim to parts of New Mexico, but compensate it by assuming its preannexation debt. Abolish the slave trade in Washington, D.C., but confirm slavery itself in the nation's capital. Reassert Congress's lack of authority to interfere with the interstate slave trade. And enact a more effective fugitive slave law.

Abolitionists and "fire-eaters" (as radical southern secessionists were called) stumbled over one another in their rush to condemn Clay's plan. Senator Salmon Chase of Ohio ridiculed it as "sentiment for the North, substance for the South." Senator Henry S. Foote of Mississippi denounced it as more offensive to the South than the speeches of abolitionists William Lloyd Garrison, Wendell Phillips, and Frederick Douglass combined. The most ominous response came from the mighty Calhoun. Too weakened by consumption to deliver his own speech, he slumped in his Senate chair, wrapped his black cloak around him, and listened as a colleague read his gloomy words concluding that the time for compromise had passed. Unending northern agitation on the slavery question, Calhoun said, had "snapped" many of the "cords which bind these states together in one common Union . . . and has greatly weakened all the others." The fragile political equilibrium between North and South depended on continued equal representation in the Senate, which Clay's plan for a free California destroyed. Without equality, Calhoun declared, Southerners could not remain in the Union.

After Clay and Calhoun had spoken, it was time for the third member of the "great triumvirate," Daniel Webster of Massachusetts. Like Clay, Webster sought to balance the grievances of the North and South and build a constituency for compromise among moderates. Admitting that the South had complaints that required attention, he argued forcefully that secession from the Union would mean civil war. He appealed for an end to reckless proposals and, to the dismay of many Northerners, mentioned by name the Wilmot Proviso. A legal ban on slavery in the territories was unnecessary, he said, because nature prohibited the expansion of cotton and slaves into the Southwest. Why, then, "taunt" or "reproach" Southerners with the proviso?

Free-soil forces recoiled from Webster's desertion. Theodore Parker, a Boston clergyman and abolitionist, could only conclude that "the Southern men" must have offered Webster the presidency. Senator William H. Seward of New York responded that Webster's and Clay's compromise with slavery was "radically wrong and essentially vicious." He flatly rejected Calhoun's argument that Congress lacked constitutional authority to exclude slavery from the territories. In any case, Seward said, in the most sensational moment in his address, there was a "higher law than the Constitution"—the law of God—to ensure freedom in all the public domain. Claiming that God was a Free-Soiler did nothing to cool the superheated atmosphere of Washington.

**JOHN C. CALHOUN**
*Hollow-cheeked and dark-eyed in this 1850 daguerreotype by Mathew Brady, Calhoun had only months to live. Still, his passion and indomitable will come through. British writer Harriet Martineau once described the champion of southern rights as "the cast-iron man who looks as if he had never been born and could never be extinguished."*
National Portrait Gallery, Smithsonian Institution/Art Resource, N.Y.

In May, a Senate committee (with the tireless Clay at its head) reported a bill that joined Clay's resolutions into a single comprehensive package, known as the Omnibus Bill because it was a vehicle on which "every sort of passenger" could ride. Clay bet that a majority of Congress wanted compromise and that while the omnibus contained items individuals disliked, each would vote for the package to gain an overall settlement of sectional issues. But the omnibus strategy backfired. Free-Soilers, Conscience Whigs, and proslavery Southerners would support separate parts of Clay's bill, but they would not endorse the whole. After seventy speeches defending his plan, Clay saw it go down to defeat.

Fortunately for those who favored a settlement, Senator Stephen A. Douglas, a rising Democratic star from Illinois, stepped into Clay's shoes. Rejecting the omnibus strategy, he broke the bill into its various parts and skillfully ushered each through Congress by fashioning a different coalition for its support. The agreement Douglas won in September 1850 was very much the one Clay had proposed in February. California entered the Union as a free state. New Mexico and Utah became territories in which the question of slavery would be decided by popular sovereignty. Congress enacted a more stringent fugitive slave law and ended the slave trade in the District of Columbia. Texas accepted its present-day boundary with New Mexico and received $10 million from the federal government. In September, Millard Fillmore, who had become president upon the death of Zachary Taylor in July, signed each bill, collectively known as the Compromise of 1850, into law (Map 14.1).

Actually, the Compromise of 1850 was not a true compromise at all. Douglas's parliamentary skill, not a spirit of conciliation, led to legislative success. Nor was the Compromise the "final settlement," as President Fillmore announced. The settlement resolved certain pesky conflicts, and it preserved the Union and peace for the moment, no small feat given the severity of the threats. But it scarcely touched the deeper conflict over slavery.

Free-Soiler Salmon Chase was correct when he told Congress, "The question of slavery in the territories has been avoided. It has not been settled."

## The Sectional Balance Undone

The words "final settlement" echoed through the halls of Congress like a magical phrase, but in reality the Compromise of 1850 began to come apart almost immediately. The thread that unraveled the Compromise was not slavery in the Southwest, the crux of the disagreement, but runaway slaves in New England, a component of the settlement that had received relatively little attention. Rather than restore calm, the Compromise brought the horrors of slavery into the North.

Millions of Northerners who never saw a runaway slave also discovered slavery in the early 1850s. Harriet Beecher Stowe's *Uncle Tom's Cabin*, a novel that vividly depicted the brutality and heartlessness of the South's "peculiar institution," aroused passions so deep that many found goodwill toward white Southerners nearly impossible. But no popular uprising forced Congress to reopen the slavery controversy. Politicians did it themselves. Four years after Congress delicately stitched the sectional compromise together, it

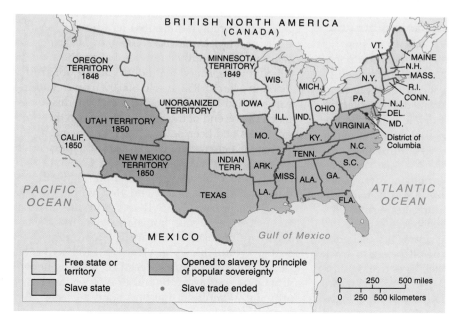

**MAP 14.1**
*The Compromise of 1850*
*The patched-together sectional agreement was both clumsy and unstable. Few Americans—in either the North or the South—supported all five parts of the Compromise.*

ripped the threads out. It reopened the question of slavery in the territories, the most deadly of all sectional issues.

### The Fugitive Slave Act

The Fugitive Slave Act proved the most explosive of the Compromise measures. The issue of runaways was as old as the Constitution, which contained a provision for the return of any "person held to service or labor in one state" who escaped to another. In 1793, a federal law gave muscle to the provision by authorizing slave owners to enter other states to recapture their slave property. Proclaiming the 1793 law a license to kidnap free blacks, northern states in the 1830s began passing "personal liberty laws" that provided fugitives with some protection. Many northern communities also formed vigilance committees to help runaways and to obstruct white Southerners who came north to reclaim them. Each year, a few hundred slaves escaped into free states and found friendly northern "conductors" who put them aboard the "underground railroad," which was not a railroad at all but a series of secret "stations" (hideouts) on the way to Canada.

---

*The words "final settlement" echoed through the halls of Congress like a magical phrase, but in reality the Compromise of 1850 began to come apart almost immediately.*

---

Furious about northern interference, Southerners in 1850 insisted that any comprehensive settlement of sectional differences include an effective fugitive slave law. They got what they wanted in the stricter law passed as part of the Compromise. To seize an alleged slave, a slaveholder or his agent simply had to appear before a commissioner appointed by the court and swear that the runaway was his. The commissioner earned ten dollars for every black returned to slavery but only five dollars for those set free. Most galling to Northerners, the law stipulated that all citizens were expected to assist officials in apprehending runaways. Sickened by the prospect, thousands vowed never to track down people who had risked their lives fleeing slavery. Others actively resisted the law. Theodore Parker, the clergyman and abolitionist, denounced the law as "a hateful statute of kidnappers" and

headed a Boston vigilance committee that openly violated it. In February 1851, an angry crowd in Boston overpowered federal marshals and snatched a runaway named Shadrach from a courtroom, put him on the underground railroad, and whisked him off to Montreal, Canada.

Southerners viewed the Fugitive Slave Act as the one true concession they received in the Compromise. Now it seemed that the "fanatics of the 'higher law' creed" had whipped Northerners into a frenzy of massive resistance. Actually, the overwhelming majority of fugitives claimed before federal commissioners were reenslaved and shipped south peacefully. Spectacular rescues such as the one that saved Shadrach were rare. Still, brutal enforcement of the unpopular law had a radicalizing effect in the North, particularly in New England. And as a Tennessee man warned in November 1850, "If the fugitive slave bill is not enforced in the north, the moderate men of the South . . . will be overwhelmed by the 'fire-eaters.'"

## Uncle Tom's Cabin

The spectacle of shackled African Americans being herded south seared the conscience of every Northerner who witnessed such a scene. But even more Northerners were turned against slavery by a fictional account, a novel. Harriet Beecher Stowe, a Northerner who had never seen a plantation, made the South's slaves into flesh-and-blood human beings more real than life. The daughter of evangelist Lyman Beecher and a member of the famous clan of preachers, teachers, and reformers, Stowe wrote to expose the sin of slavery. Beginning in June 1851 as a serial in an antislavery weekly, *Uncle Tom's Cabin, or Life among the Lowly* made the author famous before the final installment was printed ten months later. Published as a book in March 1852, it sold 300,000 copies within a year and had become America's first literary blockbuster. By the end of the decade, more than three million copies had been sold at home and overseas.

Stowe's characters leaped from the page. Here was the gentle slave Uncle Tom, a Christian saint who forgave those who beat him to death; the courageous slave Eliza, who fled with her child across the frozen Ohio River; and the fiendish Simon Legree, whose Louisiana plantation was a nightmare of torture and death. Stowe aimed her most powerful blows at slavery's destructive impact on the family. Eliza succeeds in keeping her son from being sold away, but other mothers are not so fortunate. When told that her infant has been sold, Lucy drowns herself. Driven half mad by the sale

## PRACTICAL ILLUSTRATION OF THE FUGITIVE SLAVE LAW.

**FUGITIVE SLAVE CARTOON**
*In this scathing attack on the Fugitive Slave Act of 1850, a brutal southern slave catcher rides
Daniel Webster, who counseled compliance with the act. With a chain in one hand and a rope in
the other, the slave catcher attempts to capture a woman and take her south. The slave catchers
parade the fact that they have the law on their side, but the woman's black and white defenders
take up arms nevertheless. "Every slave-hunter," Frederick Douglass declared, "who meets a
bloody death in this infernal business, is an argument in favor of the manhood of our race."*
Library of Congress.

of a son and daughter, Cassy decides "never again
[to] let a child live to grow up!" She gives her third
child an opiate and watches as "he slept to death."

Responses to the novel depended on geography. In the North, common people and literary giants alike shed tears and sang its praises. The poet
John Greenleaf Whittier sent "ten thousand thanks
for thy immortal book," and poet Henry Wadsworth
Longfellow judged it "one of the greatest triumphs
recorded in literary history." What Northerners accepted as truth, Southerners denounced as slander.
Virginian George F. Holmes proclaimed Stowe a

member of the "Woman's Rights" and "Higher
Law" schools and dismissed the novel as a work of
"intense fanaticism." Unfortunately, he said, this
"maze of misinterpretation" had filled those who
knew nothing about slavery "with hatred for that
institution and those who uphold it." Holmes found
only one character convincing: Simon Legree. Stowe
had made Legree a transplanted Yankee.

As Legree's northern origins suggest, the novel
did not indict just the South. Stowe rebuked the entire nation for tolerating slavery. Although it is impossible to measure precisely the impact of a novel

on public opinion, *Uncle Tom's Cabin* clearly helped to crystallize northern sentiment against slavery and to confirm white Southerners' suspicion that they no longer had any sympathy in the free states. (See Texts in Historical Context on page 362.) A decade after its publication, when Stowe visited Abraham Lincoln at the White House, he reportedly said, "So you are the little woman who wrote the book that made this great war."

## The Election of 1852

As national elections approached in 1852, Democrats and Whigs sought to close the sectional rifts that had opened within their parties. For their presidential nominee, the Democrats turned to Franklin Pierce of New Hampshire. Pierce was an amiable

veteran of the Mexican War and a former senator, but his most valuable asset was his well-known sympathy with southern views on public issues. His leanings caused northern critics to include him among the "doughfaces," northern men with principles that were malleable enough to champion southern causes. The Whigs were less successful in compromising differences. They agreed to reject the incumbent, Millard Fillmore, but disagreed for fifty-two ballots on someone else. Finally, adopting the formula that had proved successful in 1848, they chose another Mexican War hero, General Winfield Scott of Virginia.

Hopelessly divided between Conscience and Cotton factions, the Whigs suffered a humiliating defeat in 1852. Pierce carried twenty-seven states to Scott's four, 254 electoral votes to 42 (see Map 14.3).

**THEATER POSTER**
*During the 1850s, at least ten individuals, including Harriet Beecher Stowe herself, dramatized the novel* Uncle Tom's Cabin. *These plays, known as "Tom Shows," drew crowds in America and Britain. Stowe's moral indictment of slavery translated well to the stage. Scenes of Eliza crossing the ice with bloodhounds in pursuit, the cruelty of Legree, and Little Eva borne to heaven on puffy clouds gripped the imagination of audiences and fueled the growing antislavery crusade.*
Smithsonian Institution.

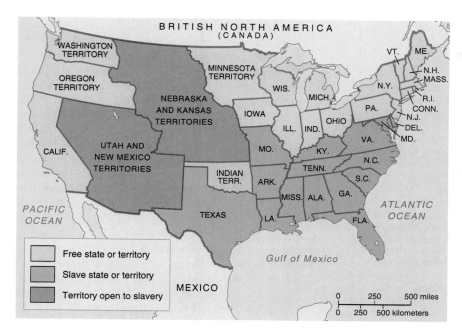

**MAP 14.2**
*The Kansas-Nebraska Act, 1854*
*Americans hardly thought twice about dispossessing the Indians of lands guaranteed them by treaty, but many worried about the outcome of repealing the Missouri Compromise and opening up lands to slavery.*

In the afterglow of the Compromise, the Free-Soil Party lost almost half of the voters who had turned to it in the tumultuous atmosphere of 1848.

Eager to leave the sectional controversy behind, the new president turned swiftly to foreign expansion. Manifest Destiny remained robust. Pierce's major objective was Cuba, which was owned by Spain and in which slavery flourished. Earlier efforts by President Polk to purchase the island had failed. Pierce's clumsy efforts to acquire Cuba galvanized antislavery Northerners, who denounced the administration for promoting expansion on behalf of slavery and blocked Cuba's acquisition. Although Pierce's foray in Cuba ended badly, his fortunes improved in Mexico. In 1853, he sent James Gadsden to negotiate a $15 million purchase of some 45,000 square miles of territory south of the Gila River in present-day Arizona and New Mexico. The Gadsden Purchase stemmed from the dream of a transcontinental railroad to California. The burgeoning population of the Pacific coast made it obvious that the vast, loose-jointed republic needed a railroad to bind it together. Talk of a railroad ignited rivalries in cities from New Orleans to Chicago as they maneuvered to become the eastern terminus. Thus the railroad became a sectional contest, which by the 1850s inevitably involved slavery.

## The Kansas-Nebraska Act

No one played the railroad game more enthusiastically than Senator Stephen A. Douglas. The "Little Giant," as he was called, was a "steam engine in britches," an energetic spokesman for western economic development. He badly wanted the transcontinental railroad for Chicago and his home state, Illinois. His chairmanship of the Senate Committee on Territories provided him with an opportunity. Any railroad that ran west from Chicago would pass through a region that Congress in 1830 had designated a "permanent" Indian reserve. Douglas proposed giving this vast area between the Missouri River and the Rocky Mountains an Indian name, Nebraska, and then nullifying Indian titles and throwing the Indians out. Once the region achieved territorial status, whites could survey and sell the land, establish civil government, and build a railroad.

Congress's promise to the Indians did not cause Douglas to hesitate, but another of its promises did. Nebraska lay within the Louisiana Purchase north of 36°30′, which, according to the Missouri Compromise of 1820, closed it to slavery. Since Douglas could not count on New England to back western economic development, he needed southern votes to pass his Nebraska legislation. But Southerners

# Women's Politics

*A*lthough women could not vote before the Civil War, many women nevertheless participated in public political activity. Uncle Tom's Cabin, Harriet Beecher Stowe's searing indictment of slavery, galvanized support for the Republican Party's campaign against the extension of slavery. The novel's moral power stemmed from its author's vivid description of how slavery assaulted cherished American institutions and values—Christian duty, female domesticity, and the family. Some political women challenged what Stowe found sacred, however, arguing that women's equality depended on their liberation from tradition. These women not only attended women's rights conventions but also signed petitions asking legislators to change laws that discriminated against women and worked to put the ideas of equal rights into practice in their personal lives.

In 1852, for example, Harriot K. Hunt protested having to pay taxes when she was prohibited from voting. A physician who had practiced medicine in Boston since 1835, Hunt had been refused admission to Harvard Medical School before she finally received her medical degree in 1853 from the Female Medical College of Philadelphia.

### DOCUMENT 1. Harriot K. Hunt's Letter "to . . . [the] Treasurer, and the Assessors, and other Authorities of the city of Boston, and the Citizens generally"

Harriot K. Hunt, physician, a native and permanent resident of the city of Boston, and for many years a taxpayer therein, in making payment of her city taxes for the coming year, begs leave to protest against the injustice and inequality of levying taxes upon women, and at the same time refusing them any voice or vote in the imposition and expenditure

of the same. The only classes of male persons required to pay taxes, and not at the same time allowed the privilege of voting, are aliens and minors. The objection in the case of aliens is their supposed want of interest in our institutions and knowledge of them. The objection in the case of minors, is the want of sufficient understanding. These objections can not apply to women, natives of the city, all of whose property interests are here, and who have accumulated, by their own sagacity and industry, the very property on which they are taxed. But this is not all; the alien, by going through the forms of naturalization, the minor on coming of age, obtain the right of voting; and so long as they continue to pay a mere poll-tax of a dollar and a half, they may continue to exercise it, though so ignorant as not to be able to sign their names, or read the very votes they put into the ballot-boxes. Even drunkards, felons, idiots, and lunatics, if men, may still enjoy that right of voting to which no woman, however large the amount of taxes she pays, however respectable her character, or useful her life, can ever attain. Wherein, your remonstrant would inquire, is the justice, equality, or wisdom of this?

*S*tymied by male politicians' indifference to petitions like Hunt's, women's rights activists pondered how to translate their dedication to equality into arenas of life more directly under their personal control. In an 1855 letter to a friend, suffragist leader Elizabeth Cady Stanton explained how women's fashions could be tailored to promote equality.

### DOCUMENT 2. Elizabeth Cady Stanton's Letter on Women's Fashions

I fully agree with you that woman is terribly cramped and crippled in her present style of dress. I have not one word to utter in its defense; but to

had no incentive to create another free territory or to help a northern city win the Pacific railroad. Douglas learned, however, that Southerners might agree to organize Nebraska—for a price: nothing less than the repeal of the Missouri Compromise. Southerners insisted that Congress organize Nebraska

according to popular sovereignty, the formula it had used in 1850 in New Mexico and Utah. It meant reopening the dangerous issue of slavery expansion that Douglas himself had so ably helped to resolve only four years earlier. A politician with presidential ambitions, a champion of his state's economic me, it seems that if she would enjoy entire freedom, she should dress just like a man. Why proclaim our sex on the house-tops, seeing that it is a badge of degradation, and deprives us of so many rights and privileges wherever we go? . . . In male attire, we could travel by land or sea; go through all the streets and lanes of our cities and towns by night and day, without a protector; get seven hundred dollars a year for teaching, instead of three, and ten dollars for making a coat, instead of two or three, as we now do. All this we could do without fear of insult, or the least sacrifice of decency or virtue. If nature has not made the sex so clearly defined as to be seen through any disguise, why should we make the difference so striking? Depend upon it, when men and women in their every-day life see and think less of sex and more of mind, we shall all lead far purer and higher lives.

*Marriage typically consigned women to a legal status inferior to their husbands, but women's rights activists refashioned marriage vows to honor equality rather than subordination. When women's rights leader Lucy Stone married Henry B. Blackwell in 1855, both signed the following statement.*

### DOCUMENT 3. Lucy Stone–Henry B. Blackwell Marriage Agreement

While acknowledging our mutual affection by publicly assuming the relationship of husband and wife, yet in justice to ourselves and a great principle, we deem it a duty to declare that this act on our part implies no sanction of, nor promise of voluntary obedience to such of the present laws of marriage, as refuse to recognize the wife as an independent, rational being, while they confer upon the husband an injurious and unnatural superiority, investing him with legal powers which no honorable

man would exercise, and which no man should possess. We protest especially against the laws which give to the husband:

1. The custody of the wife's person.
2. The exclusive control and guardianship of their children.
3. The sole ownership of her personal [property], and use of her real estate. . . .
4. The absolute right to the product of her industry.
5. Also against laws which give to the widower so much larger and more permanent an interest in the property of his deceased wife, than they give to the widow in that of the deceased husband.
6. Finally, against the whole system by which "the legal existence of the wife is suspended during marriage," so that in most States, she neither has a legal part in the choice of her residence, nor can she make a will, nor sue or be sued in her own name, nor inherit property.

We believe that personal independence and equal human rights can never be forfeited, except for crime; that marriage should be an equal and permanent partnership, and so recognized by law; that until it is so recognized, married partners should provide against the radical injustice of present laws, by every means in their power. . . .

Thus reverencing law, we enter our protest against rules and customs which are unworthy of the name, since they violate justice, the essence of law.

(signed) Henry B. Blackwell
Lucy Stone

---

Document 1. Elizabeth Cady Stanton, Susan B. Anthony, and Matilda Josyln Gage, eds., *History of Woman Suffrage* (New York: Fowler & Wells, 1881), 1:259.
　Document 2. Ibid., 841.
　Document 3. Ibid., 260–61.

interests, a defender of western development, and a believer in popular sovereignty, Douglas persuaded himself that Nebraska was worth the price.

In January 1854, Douglas introduced his bill to organize the Nebraska Territory, leaving to the settlers themselves the decision about slavery. At

southern insistence, and even though he knew it would "raise a hell of a storm," Douglas added an explicit repeal of the Missouri Compromise. Indeed, the Nebraska bill raised a storm of controversy. Antislavery Northerners wanted no part of a proposal that offered slavery a chance to expand. They branded Douglas's plan "a gross violation of a sacred pledge" and an "atrocious plot" to transform free land into a "dreary region of despotism, inhabited by masters and slaves."

As Douglas said later, he could have traveled from Washington back to Chicago by the light of his own burning effigies. But instead, he skillfully shepherded the bill through Congress in May 1854 (Map 14.2). It passed because nine-tenths of all southern members (Whigs and Democrats) and half of the northern Democrats cast votes in favor. In its final form, the Kansas-Nebraska Act divided the huge territory in two: Nebraska west of the free state of Iowa and Kansas west of the slave state of Missouri.

## The Realignment of the Party System

The Kansas-Nebraska Act marked a fateful escalation of the sectional conflict. Douglas's ill-advised measure had several consequences, none more crucial than the realignment of the nation's political parties. Since the rise of the Whigs in the early 1830s, Whigs and Democrats had organized and channeled political conflict in the nation. This party system dampened sectionalism and strengthened the Union. To achieve national political power, Whigs and Democrats had to retain strength in both the North and the South. Strong northern and southern wings required that the party compromise and find positions acceptable to both.

The Kansas-Nebraska controversy shattered this conservative political system. In place of two national parties with bisectional strength, the mid-1850s witnessed the development of one party heavily dominated by one section and another party entirely limited to the other section. Parties now had the advantage of sharpening ideological and policy differences between the sections and no longer muffling moral issues, like slavery. But the new party system also thwarted political compromise. Instead, it promoted political polarization. The breakup of the old party system of the 1830s and 1840s snapped one of what John C. Calhoun called the "cords of Union."

### The Old Parties: Whigs and Democrats

Distress signals could be heard from the Whig camp as early as the Mexican War, when members clashed over the future of slavery in annexed Mexican lands.

But the disintegration of the party dated from 1849–1850, when southern Whigs watched in stunned amazement as Whig President Zachary Taylor sponsored a plan for a free California. And the strains of the slavery issue split northern Whigs. The Conscience Whigs, who responded to slavery as a moral blight, gained a majority by 1852. The party could please the southern wing or the northern wing but not both. The Whigs' miserable showing in the election of 1852 made clear that they were no longer a strong national party. By 1856, after more than two decades of contesting the Democrats, they were hardly a party at all (Map 14.3).

The decline and eventual collapse of the Whig Party left the Democrats as the country's only national party. Although the Democrats were not immune to the disruptive pressures of the territorial question, they discovered in popular sovereignty a doctrine that many Democrats could support. But popular sovereignty very nearly undid the party as well. When Stephen Douglas applied the doctrine to that part of the Louisiana Purchase where slavery had been barred, he destroyed the dominance of the Democratic Party in the free states. Most of the northern Democrats in the House who had cast ballots in support of Douglas's Kansas-Nebraska bill were not reelected the following year. As a result, northern Democratic representation in the House fell sharply, and after 1854 the Democrats became a southern-dominated party.

---

*In place of two national parties with bisectional strength, the mid-1850s witnessed the development of one party heavily dominated by one section and another party entirely limited to the other section.*

---

Nevertheless, Democrats remained the dominant party throughout the 1850s. Gains in the South more than balanced losses in the North. During the decade, Democrats elected two presidents and won majorities in Congress in almost every election. But national power required that the party maintain a northern and a southern wing, which in turn required that they avoid the issue of the expansion of slavery.

The breakup of the Whigs and the disaffection of significant numbers of northern Democrats set many Americans politically adrift. As they searched

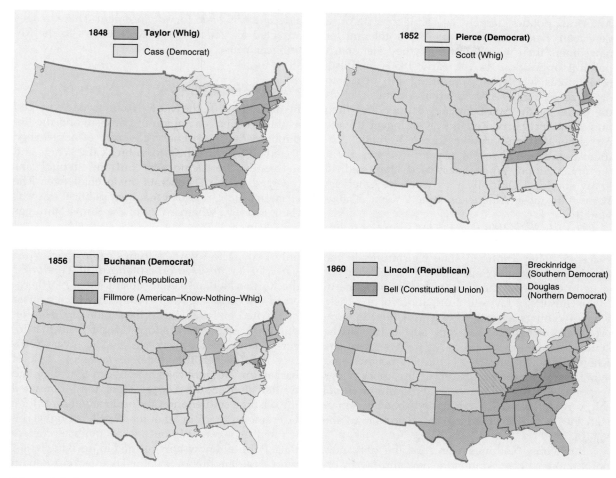

**MAP 14.3**
*Political Realignment, 1848–1860*
*In 1848, slavery and sectionalism began hammering the country's party system. The Whig Party was an early casualty. By 1860, national parties—those that contended for votes in both the North and the South—had been replaced by regional parties.*

for new political harbors, they found that the death of the old party system created a multitude of fresh political alternatives. The question was which party would attract the drifters.

## The New Parties: Know-Nothings and Republicans

Among the new organizations that vied to replace the Whigs were splinter groups with such odd names as Anti-Nebraskaites, Fusionists, Rum Democrats, Hard Shell Democrats, Soft Shells, and others. Out of

this confusion, two organizations emerged as true contenders. One grew out of the slavery controversy, a spontaneous coalition of indignant antislavery Northerners. The other arose from an entirely different split in American society, that between Roman Catholic immigrants and native Protestants.

The tidal wave of immigrants that broke over America in the decade from 1845 to 1855 produced a nasty backlash among Protestant Americans, who believed they were about to drown in a sea of Irish and German Roman Catholics. The new arrivals encountered economic prejudice, ethnic hostility, and religious antagonism. When the immigrants entered

American politics, largely as Democrats because they perceived that party as more tolerant of newcomers than were the Whigs, they met sharp political opposition. In the early 1850s, nativists (individuals who were anti-immigrant) began to organize, first into secret fraternal societies such as the Order of the Star-Spangled Banner, and then into a political party. Recruits swore never to vote for either foreign-born or Roman Catholic candidates and not to reveal any information about the organization. When questioned, they said: "I know nothing." Officially, they were the American Party, but most Americans called them Know-Nothings.

The Know-Nothings exploded onto the political stage in 1854 and 1855 with a series of dazzling successes. They captured state legislatures in the Northeast, West, and South and claimed dozens of seats in Congress. Their greatest triumph came in Massachusetts, a favorite destination for the Irish. Know-Nothings elected the Massachusetts governor, all of the state senators, all but two of the state representatives, and all of the congressmen. Know-Nothings attracted both Democrats and Whigs, but with their party crumbling, more Whigs responded to the attraction. In 1855, an individual might reasonably have concluded that the American Party had emerged as the successor to the Whigs.

But Know-Nothings were not the only new party making noise. Among the new antislavery organizations provoked by the Kansas-Nebraska Act, one called itself Republican. Republicans attempted to unite under their banner all the dissidents and political orphans—Whigs, Free-Soilers, even Know-Nothings—who opposed the extension of slavery into any territory of the United States. The Republican creed tapped basic beliefs and values of the northern public. Slave labor and free labor, Republicans argued, had spawned two incompatible civilizations. In the South, they said, slavery degraded the dignity of white labor by associating work with blacks and servility. Repression and tyranny laid heavily on every Southerner, except planter aristocrats. Those insatiable slave lords, whom antislavery Northerners called the Slave Power, now conspired to expand slavery, subvert liberty, and undermine the Constitution through the Democratic Party. Only by restricting slavery to the South, Republicans believed, could free labor flourish elsewhere. Free labor respected the dignity of work and provided anyone willing to toil an opportunity for a decent living and for advancement. These images attracted a wide range of Northerners to the Republican cause.

## The Election of 1856

By the mid-1850s, the Know-Nothings had emerged as the principal champion of nativism and the Republicans as the primary advocate of antislavery. Together, they had helped to break the Whigs and to bloody the Democrats. But the Republicans emerged as the Democrats' main challenger. The election of 1856 revealed that their political star was rising sharply, whereas that of the Know-Nothings was dead.

Slavery in the territories became the election's only issue. The Know-Nothings came apart when party leaders insisted on a platform that endorsed the Kansas-Nebraska Act, causing most Northerners to walk out. The Know-Nothings who remained nominated ex-President Millard Fillmore. The Republicans, in contrast, adopted a platform that focused almost exclusively on "making every territory free." When they labeled slavery a "relic of barbarism," Republicans announced that they had written off the South. For president, they nominated the dashing soldier and California adventurer John C. Frémont, "Pathfinder of the West." Though a celebrated explorer, Frémont lacked political credentials. Political know-how resided in his wife, Jessie, who, as a daughter of Senator Thomas Hart Benton of Missouri, knew the political map as well as her husband knew western trails. The Democrats, successful in 1852 in bridging sectional differences by nominating a northern man with southern principles, chose another "doughface," James Buchanan of Pennsylvania. The Democrats took refuge in the ambiguity of popular sovereignty and portrayed Republicans as extremists whose support for the Wilmot Proviso risked pushing the South out of the Union.

The Democratic strategy helped carry the day for Buchanan, but Frémont did astonishingly well. Buchanan won 174 electoral votes against Frémont's 114 and Fillmore's 8. Frémont carried all but five of the states north of the Mason-Dixon line. The election made clear that the Whigs had disintegrated, that the Know-Nothings would not ride nativism to national power, and that the Democrats were badly strained. But the big news was the "glorious defeat" of the Republicans. Despite being a brand-new party and purely sectional, they challenged other

**JOHN C. AND JESSIE BENTON FRÉMONT**
*The election of 1856 was the first time a candidate's wife appeared on campaign items. The woman who made the breakthrough was Jessie Benton Frémont, seen here on a silk ribbon with her husband, John C. Frémont, Republican Party presidential nominee. Jessie proved a valuable asset, helping to plan her husband's campaign, coauthoring his election biography, and drawing northern women into political activity as never before. Jessie Frémont was, as Abraham Lincoln observed ambivalently, "quite a female politician."*
Collection of Janice L. and David J. Frent.

parties for national power. Sectionalism had fashioned a new party system, one that spelled danger for the Republic (see Map 14.3).

## Freedom under Siege

The "triumph" of the Republicans meant that the second party in the new two-party system was entirely sectional. It felt no compelling need to compromise, to conciliate, to keep a southern wing happy. Indeed, the Republican Party organized around the premise that the slaveholding South provided a profound threat to "free soil, free labor, and free men."

Events in distant Kansas Territory provided the young Republican organization with an enormous boost. Kansas reeled with violence between pro-slavery and antislavery settlers, which Republicans argued was southern in origin and not restricted to the Kansas frontier. Republicans pointed to the brutal beating by a Southerner of a respected northern senator on the floor of Congress. Even the Supreme Court, in the Republicans' view, reflected the South's drive toward tyranny and minority rule. Then in 1858, the issues dividing North and South received an extraordinary airing in a senatorial contest in Illinois, when the nation's foremost Democrat debated a resourceful Republican.

### "Bleeding Kansas"

Three days after the House of Representatives approved the Kansas-Nebraska Act, Senator William H. Seward of New York boldly challenged the South. "Come on then, Gentlemen of the Slave States," he cried, "since there is no escaping your challenge, I accept it in behalf of the cause of freedom. We will engage in competition for the virgin soil of Kansas, and God give the victory to the side which is stronger in numbers as it is in right." Because of Stephen Douglas, popular sovereignty would determine whether Kansas became slave or free. No one really expected New Mexico and Utah to become slave states when Congress instituted popular sovereignty there in 1850. But Kansas was different. Kansas sat on the borderline, and everyone believed it could go either way. Free-state and slave-state settlers each sought majorities at the ballot box, claimed God's blessing, and kept their rifles ready.

In the North, emigrant aid societies sprang up to promote settlement from the free states. The most famous, the New England Emigrant Aid Company, sponsored some 1,240 settlers in 1854 and 1855. In the South, proslavery expansionists eagerly took up Seward's challenge. Tiny rural communities from Virginia to Texas raised money to support proslavery settlers. Missourians, already bordered on the east by the free state of Illinois and on the north by the free state of Iowa, especially thought it important to secure Kansas for slavery.

In theory, popular sovereignty meant an orderly tallying of ballots. In Kansas, however, elections became circuses. Thousands of Missourians, egged on by Missouri Senator David Rice Atchison, invaded Kansas. "There are eleven hundred coming over from Platte County to vote," Atchison reported, "and if that ain't enough we can send five thousand—enough to kill every God-damned abolitionist in the Territory." Not surprisingly, proslavery candidates swept the early elections. When the first territorial legislature met, it enacted laws that

made the Missouri slave law look tame. For example, it became a felony merely to argue that slavery did not legally exist in Kansas. Ever-pliant President Pierce endorsed the work of the fraudulently elected proslavery legislature. Free-state men did not. They elected their own legislature, which promptly banned both slaves and free blacks from the territory and applied for admission to the Union as a free state. Organized into two rival governments and armed to the teeth, Kansans verged on civil war.

Fighting broke out on the morning of May 21, 1856, when a mob of several hundred proslavery men entered the town of Lawrence, the center of free-state settlement. Only one man died—a proslavery raider who was killed when a burning wall collapsed—but the "Sack of Lawrence," as free-soil forces called it, inflamed northern opinion. In Kansas, news of Lawrence provoked one free-soil settler, John Brown, to "fight fire with fire." Announcing that "it was better that a score of bad men should die than that one man who came here to

**FRAUDULENT VOTING IN KANSAS**
*In this northern indictment of the corruption of popular sovereignty by Missourians, rough frontier types, with pistols and knives tucked into their belts, rush to get free whiskey and then line up at the polling place, where next to a sign, "DOWN WITH THE ABOLITIONISTS," they doubtlessly voted the proslavery ticket.*
The Kansas State Historical Society, Topeka, Kansas.

make Kansas a Free State should be driven out," he led a posse that massacred five allegedly proslavery settlers along the Pottawatomie Creek. After that, guerrilla war engulfed the territory.

By providing graphic evidence of a dangerously aggressive Slave Power, "Bleeding Kansas" gave the fledgling Republican Party fresh ammunition. The Republicans received additional encouragement from an event that occurred in the national capital. On May 19 and 20, 1856, Senator Charles Sumner of Massachusetts delivered a scathing speech entitled "The Crime against Kansas." He damned the administration, the South, and proslavery Kansans. He also indulged in a scalding personal attack on South Carolina's elderly Senator Andrew P. Butler, whom Sumner described as a "Don Quixote" who had taken as his mistress "the harlot, slavery."

Preston Brooks, a young South Carolina member of the House and a kinsman of Butler, felt compelled to defend the honor of his aged relative and of his state. On May 22, armed with a walking cane, Brooks entered the Senate, where he found Sumner working at his desk. After accusing him of libel, Brooks began beating Sumner over the head with his cane. After about a minute, Sumner lay bleeding and unconscious on the Senate floor. Brooks resigned his seat in the House, only to be promptly reelected. In the North, the southern hero became the archvillain. Like Bleeding Kansas, "Bleeding Sumner" provided the Republican Party with a potent symbol of the South's twisted and violent "civilization."

## The Dred Scott Decision

As the French visitor Alexis de Tocqueville observed in the 1830s, "Scarcely any question arises in the United States that is not resolved, sooner or later, into a judicial question." Because the Constitution lacked precision on the issue of slavery in the territories, political debate reflected sectional interests and party politics. Only the Supreme Court spoke definitively about the meaning of the Constitution. In 1857, in the *Dred Scott* case, the Court proved that it enjoyed no special immunity from the sectional and partisan passions that convulsed the land.

Eleven years after Dred and Harriet Scott first sued for freedom, the Supreme Court ruled in the case. The justices could have simply settled the immediate issue of Scott's status as a free man or slave, but they saw the case as an opportunity to settle once and for all the vexing question of slavery in

the territories. On the morning of March 6, 1857, seventy-nine-year-old Chief Justice Roger B. Taney read the majority decision of the Court. Taney hated Republicans and detested racial equality, and the Court's decision reflected those prejudices. First, the Court ruled that Dred Scott could not legally claim that his constitutional rights had been violated because he was not a citizen of the United States. At the time of the Constitution, Taney said, blacks "had for more than a century before been regarded as beings of an inferior order . . . so far inferior, that they had no rights which the white man was bound to respect." Second, the laws of Dred Scott's home state, Missouri, determined his status, and thus his travels in free areas did not make him free. Third, Congress's power to make "all needful rules and regulations" for the territories did not include the right to prohibit slavery. The Court then explicitly declared the Missouri Compromise unconstitutional, even though it had already been voided by the Kansas-Nebraska Act.

Republicans exploded in outrage. Taney's extreme proslavery decision ranged far beyond a determination of Dred Scott's freedom. By declaring unconstitutional the Republican program of federal exclusion of slavery in the territories, the Court had cut the ground from beneath the party. Moreover, as the *New York Tribune* lamented, the decision cleared the way for "all our Territories . . . to be ripened into Slave States." Particularly frightening to African Americans in the North was the Court's declaration that blacks were not citizens and had "no rights which the white man was bound to respect."

The Republican rebuttal to Taney's decision relied heavily on the brilliant dissenting opinion of Justice Benjamin R. Curtis. Scott *was* a citizen of the United States, Curtis argued. At the time of the writing of the Constitution, free black men could vote in five states and participated in the ratification process. Scott *was* free: Because slavery was prohibited in Wisconsin, the "involuntary servitude of a slave, coming into the Territory with his master, should cease to exist." And the Missouri Compromise *was* constitutional. The Founders meant exactly what they said: Congress had the power to make "*all* needful rules and regulations" for the territories, including barring slavery.

Unswayed by Curtis's dissent, the Court's seven-to-two majority had validated the most extreme statement of the South's territorial rights. John C. Calhoun's claim that Congress had no authority to exclude slavery now became the law of the land. But what southern Democrats cheered, northern Democrats found profoundly disturbing. They feared that the *Dred Scott* decision annihilated not just the Wilmot Proviso but popular sovereignty as well. If Congress did not have the authority to exclude slavery, how could Congress's creation, a territorial government, assume that right? No one was in a tighter bind than Stephen A. Douglas. Civil war raged in Kansas at that very moment because Douglas's Kansas-Nebraska Act had opened the territory to popular sovereignty. Now, contrary to Douglas's promise, it appeared that a free-soil majority could not keep slavery out. No one could exclude slavery until the moment of statehood. By draining the last drop of ambiguity out of popular sovereignty, the *Dred Scott* decision jeopardized not only Douglas's presidential ambition but the ability of the Democratic Party to hold its northern and southern wings together.

Ironically, the *Dred Scott* decision strengthened the young Republican Party by giving credence to its claim that a hostile Slave Power conspired against northern liberties. Only the capture of the Supreme Court by the "slavocracy," Republicans argued, could explain the tortured and historically inaccurate *Dred Scott* decision. As for Dred Scott, although the Court rejected his suit, he did in the end gain his freedom. White friends, the sons of his first owner, Peter Blow, purchased and freed Scott and his family. Dred Scott died less than a year later.

## Prairie Republican: Abraham Lincoln

The reigniting of sectional flames provided Republican politicians with fresh challenges and fresh opportunities. None proved more eager for them than Abraham Lincoln of Illinois. Lincoln had long since put behind him his hardscrabble, log cabin beginnings in Kentucky and Indiana. At the time of the *Dred Scott* decision, he lived in a fine two-story house in Springfield, had enough business from the Illinois Central Railroad to be known as the "railroad lawyer," and by virtue of his marriage and successful practice associated with men and women of reputation and standing.

The law provided Lincoln's living, but politics was his life. "His ambition was a little engine that knew no rest," observed his law partner William Herndon. At age twenty-six, he served his first term in the Illinois state legislature. Between 1847 and 1849, he enjoyed his only term in the House of Representatives, where he fired away at "Mr. Polk's War" and cast dozens of votes for free soil but otherwise served inconspicuously. When he returned to Springfield, he pitched into his law practice but kept his eye fixed on public office. As a young man, he had chosen as his political hero the Whig Henry Clay. On the vexing issues of Union, slavery, and race, Clay exemplified for Lincoln the reasonable moderate, the realistic pragmatist, and the effective compromiser.

> *Just as Lincoln staked out the middle ground on antislavery, he also held what were, for his times, moderate racial views.*

But, like Whigs everywhere in the mid-1850s, Lincoln had no political home. With their party in shambles, a good many Illinois Whigs gravitated to the Know-Nothings. Mary Todd Lincoln, Lincoln's Kentucky-born wife, sympathized with the nativists, for she knew, she said, the burdens of "wild Irish" servants. But Lincoln was not a Know-Nothing. "How could I be?" he asked. "How can any one who abhors the oppression of negroes be in favor of degrading classes of white people?" Lincoln's credo—opposition to "the *extension* of slavery"—made the Democrats an impossible choice. But the Republicans made free soil their principal tenet, and in 1856 Lincoln joined the party.

Just as Lincoln staked out the middle ground on antislavery, he also held what were, for his times, moderate racial views. Like a majority of Republicans, he defended black humanity without challenging white supremacy. He denounced slavery as immoral and believed that it should end, but he also viewed black equality as impractical and unachievable. "Negroes have natural rights . . . as other men have," he said, "although they cannot enjoy them here." Insurmountable white prejudice made it impossible to extend full citizenship and equality to blacks in America. Freeing blacks and allowing them to remain in this country would lead to race war. In Lincoln's mind, social stability and black progress required that slavery end and that blacks leave the country.

Lincoln realized that because most Northerners lacked sympathy for blacks, humanitarian concern would not mobilize them to fight for free soil. Instead, he appealed to northern labor's self-interest. He described the territories as "places for poor people to go to, and better their conditions." He spoke

**DISCUSSING THE NEWS**

*Newspapers permitted midwesterners to keep up-to-date. Here a farmer takes a break from his task of cutting firewood to debate the latest news with his friends. He is so engrossed that he ignores the little girl tugging at his pants leg and trying to get him to notice the woman waving in the doorway. Men like these increasingly accepted Lincoln's portrait of the Republican Party as the guardian of the common people's liberty and economic opportunity. When Lincoln claimed that southern slaveholders threatened free labor and democracy, they listened.*

Copyright © 1971, The R.W. Norton Art Gallery, Shreveport, La. Used by permission. Painting by Arthur F. Tait.

to those millions of white Americans who wanted to make something of themselves: farmhands who wanted to become farm owners, clerks who aspired to be merchants, rail-splitters who dreamed of being lawyers. "The *free* labor system," he said, "opens the way for all—gives hope to all, and energy, and progress, and improvement of condition to all." In Lincoln's view, slavery's expansion threatened this freedom to succeed.

Lincoln became persuaded that slaveholders formed an aggressive and dangerous conspiracy to nationalize slavery. Evidence abounded. The Kansas-Nebraska Act repealed the restriction on slavery's advance in the territories. The *Dred Scott* decision denied Congress the right to impose fresh restrictions. The next step, Lincoln warned, would be "another Supreme Court decision, declaring that the Constitution of the United States does not permit a *State* to exclude slavery from its limits." Unless its citizens woke up, he warned, the Supreme Court would make "Illinois a slave State."

In his memorable 1858 "House Divided" speech, Lincoln declared that the nation could not "endure, permanently half slave and half free." Either opponents of slavery would arrest its spread and place it on the "course of ultimate extinction" or its advocates would push it forward until it became legal in *"all* the States, *old* as well as *new— North* as well as *South."* Lincoln's convictions that slavery was wrong, that Congress must stop its spread, and that it must be put on the road to extinction formed the core of the Republican ideology. By 1858, he had so impressed his fellow Republicans in Illinois that they put him forward to challenge the nation's premier Democrat who was seeking reelection to the Senate.

### The Lincoln-Douglas Debates

When Stephen Douglas learned that Abraham Lincoln would be his opponent for the Senate, he confided in a fellow Democrat: "He is the strong man of the party—full of wit, facts, dates—and the best stump speaker, with his droll ways and dry jokes, in the West. He is as honest as he is shrewd, and if I beat him my victory will be hardly won."

Not only did Douglas have to contend with a formidable foe, but he also carried the weight of a burden not of his own making. The previous year, the nation's economy experienced a sharp downturn, a depression that antebellum Americans called a "panic." Prices plummeted, thousands of businesses failed, and unemployment rose. The causes of the panic of 1857 lay in the international economy, but Americans reflexively interpreted the panic in sectional terms. Northeastern businesses and industries suffered most, and Northerners blamed the southern-dominated Congress, which had just months before reduced tariff duties to their lowest levels in the nineteenth century. Given this invitation, Northerners believed, foreign competition ravaged the northern economy. Southerners, in contrast, had largely escaped hardship because cotton prices remained high. Although Illinois suffered less than the Northeast, Douglas had to go before the voters in 1858 as a member of the freshly accused, southern-dominated Democratic Party.

Douglas's response to another crisis in 1857, however, helped shore up his standing with his constituents. During the previous winter, proslavery forces in Kansas met in Lecompton, drafted a proslavery constitution, and applied for statehood. President Buchanan blessed the Lecompton constitution and instructed Congress to admit Kansas as the sixteenth slave state. Everyone knew that free-soilers outnumbered proslavery settlers two or three to one, and Republicans denounced the "Lecompton swindle." Douglas broke with the Democratic administration and came out against the proslavery constitution, not because it accepted slavery but because it violated the democratic requirement of popular sovereignty. In March 1858, despite Douglas's vigorous opposition, the Senate passed the Kansas statehood bill, but the northern majority in the House killed it. (When Kansans would reconsider the Lecompton constitution in an honest election, they would reject it six to one, and Kansas would enter the Union in 1861 as a free state.)

A relative unknown and a decided underdog in the Illinois election, Lincoln challenged the incumbent Douglas to debate him face to face. Douglas agreed, and the two met in seven communities for what became a legendary series of debates. To the thousands who stood straining to see and hear, they must have seemed an odd pair. Douglas was five feet four inches tall, broad, and stocky; Lincoln was six feet four inches tall, angular, and lean. Douglas was in perpetual motion, darting across the platform, shouting, and jabbing the air. Lincoln stood still and spoke deliberately. Douglas wore the latest fashion and dazzled audiences with his flashy vests. Lincoln wore good suits but managed to look rumpled anyway. But their differences in physical appearance and style were of least importance. They showed the citizens of Illinois (and much of the nation because of national press coverage) the difference between an anti-Lecompton Democrat and a true Republican. They debated, often brilliantly, the central issue before the country: slavery and freedom.

Lincoln badgered Douglas with the question of whether he favored the spread of slavery. He tried to force Douglas into the damaging admission that the Supreme Court had repudiated his territorial solution, popular sovereignty. In the debate at Freeport, Illinois, Douglas admitted that settlers could not now pass legislation barring slavery, but he argued that they could ban slavery just as effectively by not passing protective laws. Without "appropriate police regulations and local legislation," such as those found in slave states, he explained, slavery could not live a day, an hour. Southerners condemned Douglas's "Freeport Doctrine" and charged him with trying to steal the victory they had gained with the *Dred Scott* decision. Lincoln chastised his opponent for his "don't care" attitude about slavery, for "blowing out the moral lights around us."

For his part, Douglas worked the racial issue. He called Lincoln an abolitionist and a color-blind egalitarian enamored with "our colored brethren." Put on the defensive, Lincoln came close to staking out positions on abolition and race that were as conservative as Douglas's. Lincoln reiterated his belief that slavery enjoyed constitutional protection where it existed. He also reaffirmed his faith in white rule. "I will say, then, that I am not, nor ever have been, in favor of bringing about in any way the social and political equality of the white and black race." But Lincoln was no negrophobe like Douglas, who told racist jokes and spit out racial epithets. Lincoln always tried to steer the debate back to what he considered the true issue: the morality and future of slavery. "Slavery is wrong," he repeated, because "a man has the right to the fruits of his own labor."

As Douglas predicted, the election was hard-fought. It was also closely contested. In the nineteenth century, citizens voted for state legislators, who in turn selected the U.S. senator. Since Democrats won a slight majority in the legislature, the new legislature chose to return Douglas to the Senate. But the debates thrust Lincoln, the prairie Republican, into the national spotlight.

## The Union Collapses

Lincoln's thesis that the "slavocracy" conspired to make slavery a national institution now seems exaggerated. But from the northern perspective, the Kansas-Nebraska Act, the Brooks-Sumner affair, the *Dred Scott* decision, the panic of 1857, and the Lecompton constitution seemed irrefutable evidence of the South's aggressiveness. Southerners, of course, saw things differently. They were the ones who were under siege and had grievances, they declared. Which was the minority section? they asked. In a democracy, how could a minority hope to control the government?

Threats of secession increasingly laced the sectional debate, for the 1850s delivered powerful blows to Southerners' confidence that they could remain Americans and protect slavery and their way of life. When the Republican Party won the White House in 1860, many Southerners concluded that national power had shifted permanently.

## John Brown's Raid

Three years after the 1856 Pottawatomie massacre in Kansas, John Brown reemerged. Time had not dampened his zeal for abolition. More than ever, he was a man on fire. He had spent thirty months begging money from New England abolitionists to support his vague plan for military operations against slavery, perhaps in Kansas, perhaps in the South itself. Although he won more hearts than pocketbooks, Brown received enough in gifts to gather a small band of antislavery warriors.

---

*The 1850s delivered powerful blows to Southerners' confidence that they could remain Americans and protect slavery and their way of life.*

---

On the night of October 16, 1859, John Brown took his war against slavery into the South. With only twenty-two men, including five African Americans, he crossed the Potomac River and occupied a federal arsenal at Harpers Ferry, Virginia. The invaders were quickly surrounded, first by local militia and then by a contingent of U.S. Marines commanded by Colonel Robert E. Lee. When Brown refused to surrender, federal troops charged with bayonets. It was all over in less than thirty-six hours. Seventeen men, including two slaves, lost their lives. Ten of Brown's raiders, including two of his sons, died. Although a few of Brown's troops escaped, federal forces captured seven men, including Brown himself.

If Brown had been killed during his raid, his impact on history would probably have been minor. But he lived, was tried by the state of Virginia for treason and conspiracy to incite insurrection, and on December 2, 1859, was hanged. In life, "Old Brown" was a ne'er-do-well who failed at nearly everything he tried. He died, however, with courage, dignity, and composure. With his "piercing eyes" and "resolute countenance," he uttered some of the most stirring words ever to issue from a courtroom: "If it is deemed necessary that I should forfeit my life for the furtherance of the ends of justice, and mingle my blood further with the blood of . . . millions in this slave country whose rights are disregarded by wicked, cruel, and unjust enactments, I say, let it be done."

Some Northerners grieved for John Brown. One abolitionist proclaimed Brown the "bravest and humanest man in all the country." In Boston, the essayist Ralph Waldo Emerson dubbed him "that new saint" who "will make the gallows glorious like the cross." Generally, however, abolitionists did not condone violence, and northern opinion did not celebrate bloody slave insurrection. Lincoln spoke for the majority when he endorsed Brown's antislavery stance but concluded that noble ideals could not "excuse violence, bloodshed, and treason."

In the South, Lincoln's sober voice did not still a gathering fury. Many white Southerners lost the capacity to distinguish between Northerners who opposed slavery, like Lincoln, and those who were willing to see it washed away in a river of blood, like Brown. They contemplated what they had in common with people who "regard John Brown as a martyr and a Christian hero, rather than a murderer and robber." Robert Toombs of Georgia announced solemnly that Southerners must "never permit this Federal government to pass into the traitorous hands of the black Republican party." At that moment, the presidential election was only months away.

### Republican Victory in 1860

Anxieties provoked by John Brown's raid flared for months as southern whites feverishly searched for abolitionists and tarred and feathered (or treated even worse) those they suspected. Moreover, other events in the eleven months between Brown's hanging and the presidential election heightened sectional hostility. The most important of these was the demand of Jefferson Davis that the Senate adopt a federal slave code for the territories, a goal of extreme proslavery Southerners for several years. Not only could Congress not block slavery's spread, he argued, but it must offer it all "needful protection."

When Democrats converged on Charleston for their convention in April 1860, Southerners gave notice that they intended to make their extreme position binding doctrine. Proud to be meeting only blocks from the grave of John C. Calhoun, southern fire-eaters denounced Stephen Douglas and demanded a platform that included federal protection of slavery in the territories. But northern Democrats needed a platform that they could take home, and northern voters would not stomach a federal slave code. When two platforms—one with a federal slave code and one with popular sovereignty—came before the delegates, popular sovereignty

won. Representatives from the entire lower South and Arkansas stomped out of the convention. The remaining delegates adjourned to meet a few weeks later in Baltimore, where they nominated Douglas for president and adopted a platform that required nothing more than congressional noninterference in the territories.

When southern Democrats met, they nominated Vice President John C. Breckinridge of Tennessee for president and approved a platform with a federal slave code. But southern moderates refused to hand over their section to Breckinridge and the fire-eaters. Senator John J. Crittenden of Kentucky and others formed a new party that would provide voters a Unionist choice. Instead of adopting a platform—which inevitably fanned controversy—the new Constitutional Union Party merely approved a vague resolution pledging "to recognize no political principle other than *the Constitution . . . the Union . . . and the Enforcement of the Laws.*" For president they picked former Senator John Bell of Tennessee. Southern Democrats accused the new party of "insulting the intelligence of the American people" when it ignored "the slavery question. That issue must be met and settled."

The Republicans smelled victory. Four years earlier they had enjoyed a "glorious defeat." Now the Democratic Party had broken up. Still, Republicans estimated that they needed to carry nearly all the free states to win and that they must therefore broaden their appeal. In 1856, opponents had charged that the Republicans were a one-idea party. In 1860, the Republicans built a platform with more than a single antislavery plank. Free homesteads, a protective tariff, a Pacific railroad, and a guarantee of immigrant political rights defined an economic and social agenda broad enough to unify the North. While recommitting themselves to stopping the spread of slavery, they also denounced John Brown's raid as "among the gravest of crimes" and confirmed the security of slavery in the South.

Republicans cast about for a moderate candidate to go with their evenhanded platform. Since bursting onto the national scene in 1858, Lincoln had demonstrated his clear purpose, good judgment, and solid Republican credentials on a speaking tour through the Midwest and East. That, combined with his rock-solid reputation for integrity and his residence in Illinois, a crucial state, made him attractive to the party. Masterful maneuvering by Lincoln's managers converted his status as the second choice of many delegates into a majority on

**ABRAHAM LINCOLN**
*Lincoln actively sought the Republican presidential nomination in 1860. When in New York City to give a political address, he had his photograph taken by Mathew Brady. "While I was there I was taken to one of the places where they get up such things," Lincoln explained, sounding more innocent than he was, "and I suppose they got my shaddow, and can multiply copies indefinitely." Multiply they did. Copies of the dignified photograph of Lincoln soon replaced the less flattering drawings. Later, Lincoln credited his victory to his New York speech and to Mathew Brady.*
The Lincoln Museum, Fort Wayne, Indiana. Photo: #0-17; drawing: #2024.

the third ballot. Defeated by Douglas in a state contest less than two years earlier, Lincoln now stood ready to take Douglas on for the presidency.

The election of 1860 was like none other in American politics. It took place in the midst of the nation's severest crisis. Moreover, four major candidates crowded the presidential field. Rather than a four-cornered contest, however, the election broke into two contests, each with two candidates. In the North, Lincoln faced Douglas, and in the South, Breckinridge confronted Bell. Southerners did not even permit Lincoln's name to appear on the ballot in ten of the fifteen slave states, so outrageous did they consider the Republican Party.

An unprecedented number of voters cast ballots on November 6, 1860. Approximately 82 percent of eligible northern men and nearly 70 percent of eligible southern men went to the polls. The Republican platform succeeded in attracting a broad coalition of northern interests, and Lincoln swept all of the eighteen free states except New Jersey, which split its votes between him and Douglas. While Lincoln received only 39 percent of the popular vote, he won easily in the electoral balloting, gaining 180 votes, 28 more than he needed for victory. Lincoln did not win because his opposition was splintered. Even if the votes of his three opponents were combined, Lincoln would still have won.

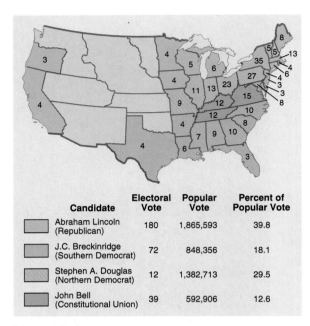

| Candidate | Electoral Vote | Popular Vote | Percent of Popular Vote |
|---|---|---|---|
| Abraham Lincoln (Republican) | 180 | 1,865,593 | 39.8 |
| J.C. Breckinridge (Southern Democrat) | 72 | 848,356 | 18.1 |
| Stephen A. Douglas (Northern Democrat) | 12 | 1,382,713 | 29.5 |
| John Bell (Constitutional Union) | 39 | 592,906 | 12.6 |

**MAP 14.4**
*The Election of 1860*

Ominously, however, Breckinridge, running on a southern-rights platform, won the entire Lower South plus Delaware, Maryland, and North Carolina. Two fully sectionalized parties swept their regions, but the northern one won the presidency (Map 14.4).

## Secession Winter

The telegraphs had barely stopped tapping out the news of Lincoln's victory when anxious Southerners began reappraising the value of the Union. Although Breckinridge had carried the South, a vote for "southern rights" was not necessarily a vote for secession. In fact, Breckinridge steadfastly denied that he was a secession candidate. Besides, slightly more than half of the Southerners who voted cast ballots for Douglas and Bell, two stout defenders of the Union. During the winter of 1860–61, Southerners debated what to do.

Southern Unionists tried to calm the fears that Lincoln's election triggered. Extremists in both sections, they argued, had created the crisis. Former Congressman Alexander Stephens of Georgia eloquently defended the Union. He asked what Lincoln had done to justify something as extreme as secession. Had he not promised to respect slavery where it existed? In Stephens's judgment, secession

might lead to war, which would loosen the hinges of southern society, possibly even open the door to slave insurrection or a revolt by nonslaveholding whites. "Revolutions are much easier started than controlled," Stephens warned. "I consider slavery much more secure in the Union than out of it."

Secessionists emphasized the urgency of the moment and the dangers of delay. No Southerner should mistake Republican intentions, they argued. "Mr. Lincoln and his party assert that this doctrine of equality applies to the negro," Howell Cobb of Georgia asserted, "and necessarily there can exist no such thing as property in our equals." Why wait for Lincoln to appoint Republicans to federal posts throughout the South? Each one would become an abolitionist emissary spreading dangerous ideas among blacks and attempting to turn nonslaveholding whites against slaveholders. As for war, there would be none. The Union was a voluntary compact, and coerced patriotism was alien to America. If Northerners did resist secession with force, the conflict would be brief, for one southern woodsman could whip five of Lincoln's greasy mechanics.

For all their differences, southern whites were generally united in their determination to defend slavery, to take slave property into the territories, and to squeeze from the North an admission that they were good and decent people. They disagreed about whether the mere presence of a Republican in the White House made it necessary to exercise what they considered a legitimate right to secede.

The debate about what to do was briefest in South Carolina. It seceded from the Union on December 20, 1860. By February, the six other Deep South states marched in South Carolina's footsteps. Only South Carolinians voted overwhelmingly in favor of secession, however; elsewhere, the vote was close. In general, the nonslaveholding inhabitants of the pine barrens and mountain counties displayed the greatest attachment to the Union. Slaveholders spearheaded secession. On February 4, 1861, representatives from South Carolina, Georgia, Florida, Alabama, Mississippi, Louisiana, and Texas met in Montgomery, Alabama, where three days later they celebrated the birth of the Confederate States of America. Jefferson Davis became president and Alexander Stephens, who had spoken so eloquently about the dangers of revolution, became vice president.

Lincoln's election had split the Union. Now secession split the South. Seven slave states seceded during the winter, but eight did not. The fact was that the Upper South had a smaller stake in slavery.

Only about half as many white families in the Upper South held slaves (21 percent) as did those in the Lower South (37 percent). Slaves represented twice as large a percentage of the population in the Lower South (48 percent) as in the Upper South (23 percent). Consequently, whites in the Upper South had fewer fears that Republican ascendancy meant economic catastrophe, racial war, and social chaos. Lincoln would have to do more than just be elected to provoke them into secession.

*For all their differences, southern whites were generally united in their determination to defend slavery, to take slave property into the territories, and to squeeze from the North an admission that they were good and decent people.*

The nation had to wait until March 4, 1861, to see what Lincoln would do. (Presidents-elect waited four months to take office until the Twentieth Amendment to the Constitution shifted the inauguration forward to January 20.) Throughout the winter, while Southerners debated the fate of the Union, Lincoln watched from Springfield. "Lame duck" President James Buchanan watched from Washington. Buchanan firmly denied the constitutionality of secession but also denied that he had power to resist it. Without leadership from the White House, the search for a peace-saving compromise shifted to Congress. To allay southern fears, a Senate committee hastily recommended a series of constitutional amendments, the most important of which revived the Missouri Compromise. Slavery would be prohibited in territories north of 36°30′ and protected south of it. Republicans blocked the measure, but the Confederate states showed little interest in the proposal because they no longer focused on the territorial issue. Since the election of a Republican president, they had independence on their minds.

Finally, Lincoln arrived in Washington, forced to sneak in at night because of an assassination plot. His entrance did nothing to build confidence in a nation that doubted that this odd-looking man with almost no national political experience would be up to the task before him. The frantic search for a sectional compromise had failed, and the Confederate States of America acted as if they were independent and assumed that the price of secession would be censure, nothing more.

**"THE UNION IS DISSOLVED!"**
*On December 20, 1860, the Charleston* Mercury *put out this special edition of the paper to celebrate South Carolina's secession from the Union. Six weeks earlier, upon hearing the news that Lincoln had won the presidency, it had predicted as much. "The tea has been thrown overboard," the* Mercury *announced. "The revolution of 1860 has been initiated."*
Chicago Historical Society.

In his inaugural address, Lincoln began with reassurances to the South. He had "no lawful right" to interfere with slavery where it existed, he said again, adding for emphasis that he had "no inclination to do so." There would be "no invasion—no using of force against or among the people anywhere." In filling federal posts, he would not "force obnoxious strangers" on the South. Conciliatory toward Southerners, he proved inflexible about the

Union. The Union, he declared, is "perpetual." Secession was "anarchy" and "legally void." The Constitution required him to execute the law "in all the States." He would hold federal property, collect federal duties, and deliver the mails.

The decision for civil war or peace rested in the South's hands, he said. "You can have no conflict, without being yourselves the aggressors. You have no oath registered in Heaven to destroy the government, while I shall have the most solemn one to 'preserve, protect, and defend' it." What Southerners in Charleston held in their hands at that very moment were the cords for firing the cannons that they aimed at the federal garrison at Fort Sumter.

## Conclusion: The Failure of Compromise

Northerners and Southerners had clashed as early as the writing of the Constitution. As their economies, societies, and cultures diverged in the nineteenth century, friction increased. But sectionalism shifted into a new gear in 1846 when David Wilmot proposed banning slavery in any Mexican territory won in the war. During the extended crisis of the Union

that stretched from 1846 to 1861, the nation's attention fixed on the expansion of slavery. But from the beginning, both Northerners and Southerners recognized that the controversy had less to do with the expansion of slavery than with the future of slavery in America. The territories, then, were "merely the skirmish line of a larger and more fundamental conflict."

Lincoln doubted that the nation could "endure, permanently half slave and half free." But for more than seventy years, imaginative statesmen had found compromises that, while making no improvement in the condition of millions of slaves in the South, did preserve the Union. The *Dred Scott* decision, which proclaimed that the Scott family were slaves, aimed at ending once and for all dangerous slavery controversy among whites. Citizens on both sides of the Mason-Dixon line took enormous pride in the national experiment in republican democracy, and few gave up the experiment easily. But accommodation had limits. Whites in the Deep South took Lincoln's election in 1860 as a signal that slavery and the society they had built on it were at risk in the Union, and they seceded. In his inaugural, Lincoln pleaded, "We are not enemies but friends. We must not be enemies." But by then, the Deep South had ceased to sing what he called "the chorus of the Union." It remained to be seen whether disunion would mean war.

## CHRONOLOGY

| | |
|---|---|
| **1846** | Wilmot Proviso proposes barring slavery from all lands acquired in Mexican War. |
| **1847** | John C. Calhoun challenges Wilmot Proviso on constitutional grounds, stating that Congress has no power to exclude slavery from territories. |
| | Senator Lewis Cass offers compromise of "popular sovereignty," allowing people of territories to determine fate of slavery. |
| **1848** | Opponents of expansion of slavery found Free-Soil Party. |
| | Whig General Zachary Taylor elected president of United States, defeating |

| | |
|---|---|
| | Democrat Lewis Cass and Free-Soil candidate Martin Van Buren. |
| **1850s** | Vigilance committees in North challenge and sometimes thwart Fugitive Slave Act. |
| **1850** | **July 9.** President Zachary Taylor dies; succeeded by Vice President Millard Fillmore. |
| | Senator Henry Clay proposes Omnibus Bill to avert territorial crisis over slavery; bill ultimately defeated. |
| | Senator Stephen Douglas's compromise bills (Compromise of 1850) pass Congress, signed into law by President Fillmore. |
| **1852** | Harriet Beecher Stowe's *Uncle Tom's Cabin* published. |

| | | | |
|---|---|---|---|
| **1852** | Democrat Franklin Pierce elected president of United States, defeating Whig Winfield Scott. | **1857** | *Dred Scott* decision declares that African Americans have no constitutional rights, that Congress cannot exclude slavery in territories, and that the Missouri Compromise is unconstitutional. |

**1852** Democrat Franklin Pierce elected president of United States, defeating Whig Winfield Scott.

**1853** Gadsden Purchase adds 45,000 square miles of territory in present-day Arizona and New Mexico.

**1854** American (Know-Nothing) Party emerges, advocating nativist positions.

Kansas-Nebraska Act opens Kansas and Nebraska Territories to popular sovereignty.

Republican Party emerges on platform opposing extension of slavery in territories.

**1856** Armed conflict between proslavery and antislavery forces erupts in Kansas.

Preston Brooks of South Carolina brutally assaults Charles Sumner of Massachusetts on Senate floor.

Democrat James Buchanan elected president of United States, defeating Republican John C. Frémont.

**1857** *Dred Scott* decision declares that African Americans have no constitutional rights, that Congress cannot exclude slavery in territories, and that the Missouri Compromise is unconstitutional.

Nation experiences economic downturn, panic of 1857.

**1858** In Illinois senatorial campaign, Abraham Lincoln and Stephen A. Douglas debate slavery; Douglas defeats Lincoln for Senate seat.

**1859** **October 16.** John Brown's attempt to foment slave uprising in Harpers Ferry, Virginia, further alienates South and moves nation toward war.

**1860** Republican Abraham Lincoln elected president in four-way race that divides electorate along sectional lines.

**December 20.** South Carolina secedes from Union.

**1861** Representatives of seven southern states, meeting in Montgomery, Alabama, form Confederate States of America.

# SUGGESTED READINGS

Gary Collison, *Shadrach Minkins: From Fugitive Slave to Citizen* (1997), and Albert J. Von Frank, *The Trials of Anthony Burns: Freedom and Slavery in Emerson's Boston* (1998). Lively examinations of two famous fugitive-slave cases in New England.

William J. Cooper Jr., *Liberty and Slavery: Southern Politics to 1860* (1983). An effective survey of the South's response to the gathering storm.

Don E. Fehrenbacher, *Prelude to Greatness: Lincoln in the 1850s* (1962). An important examination of Lincoln's response to and impact on the major events of the 1850s.

Don E. Fehrenbacher, *Slavery, Law, and Politics* (1981). An effective abridgment of the author's magisterial study of the *Dred Scott* case.

Eric Foner, *Free Soil, Free Labor, Free Men* (1970). A persuasive analysis of the free-labor ideology.

Michael F. Holt, *The Political Crisis of the 1850s* (1978). An important interpretation of the death of the second party system.

Robert W. Johannsen, *Stephen A. Douglas* (1973). A rich biography that also explores the concept of popular sovereignty.

Bruce Levine, *Half Slave and Half Free: The Roots of Civil War* (1992). A lively survey of the contrasts and conflicts between North and South.

Stephen B. Oates, *To Purge This Land with Blood: A Biography of John Brown* (2nd ed., 1984). A powerful analysis of the man and his role in the sectional conflict.

Merrill D. Peterson, *The Great Triumvirate: Webster, Clay, and Calhoun* (1987). An eloquent consideration of the braided political careers of three great statesmen.

David Potter, *The Impending Crisis, 1848–1861* (1976). A classic study that remains the best analysis of the politics that led to war.

Richard H. Sewell, *Ballots for Freedom: Antislavery Politics in the United States, 1837–1860* (1976). A useful survey of the rise of antislavery in northern politics.

**DAGUERREOTYPE OF UNION DRUMMER BOY**

*The Civil War is often called a "brother's war." Families sometimes split and offered up soldiers for both the Union and the Confederate armies. But the war was also a children's war, as this daguerreotype of the twelve-year-old Johnny Clem, a Union drummer boy, reminds us. Clem ran away from his Ohio home when he was ten, joined the Twenty-second Michigan Regiment, and fought with it in all its major battles from Shiloh to Atlanta. He became a hero in the North when during the retreat of Union soldiers at Chickamauga he shot and wounded a Confederate officer with a sawed-off musket cut down to his small size. When he retired from the U.S. Army in 1915, Major General John L. Clem was the last federal soldier who had fought in the Civil War. Clem's childlike face shows no trace of the horrors he had seen, but even children who stayed at home often experienced the heartbreak of youth destroyed and innocence lost.*
Library of Congress.

# THE CRUCIBLE OF WAR

## 15

### 1861–1865

I N 1838, A TWENTY-YEAR-OLD MARYLAND SLAVE by the name of Frederick Bailey fled north to freedom. The young runaway took a new name, Frederick Douglass, and might understandably have settled into obscurity, content just to avoid the slave catchers and to live quietly as a free man. Instead, he chose to wage war against slavery. An agent for the Massachusetts Anti-Slavery Society observed in 1841 that "the public have itching ears to hear a colored man speak, and particularly a slave." Dozens of fugitive slaves brought to northern audiences the authority of hard personal experience. None stripped away the myth of the contented slave more eloquently than Frederick Douglass. In 1845, he published his immensely popular autobiography. In 1847, he began the *North Star,* an antislavery newspaper that reached thousands. Douglass's powerful denunciations of slavery and moving pleas for emancipation made him the most famous African American in the English-speaking world.

During the secession winter of 1860–61, Douglass found himself torn between hope and despair. Abraham Lincoln's election in November had revived his optimism in the wake of the *Dred Scott* decision. "The slaveholders know that the day of their power is over," Douglass exulted. But he realized that the Republican Party's free-soil principles fell short of abolition. Republicans opposed slavery's right to expand into the national territories, not slavery's right to exist in the South. Indeed, Douglass feared that the Republicans would become "the best protectors of slavery where it now is."

When news came from Charleston in April 1861 that Southerners had fired on the American flag, Douglass celebrated the outbreak of fighting. Much earlier than most, he understood that a war to save the Union would inevitably affect slavery. The South had initiated a "war for slavery," Douglass said, and it followed that a war to crush southern independence must become a war *against* slavery. Even though "the Government is not yet on the side of the oppressed, events mightier than the Government are bringing about that result," Douglass declared. *"Friends of freedom!"* he cried, *"be up and doing;—now is your time."* Few Northerners, certainly not Abraham Lincoln, agreed that the outbreak of fighting marked the beginning of the end of slavery. For eighteen months, Union soldiers fought solely to uphold the Constitution and preserve the nation. But in 1863, as Douglass foresaw, the Union war effort took on a dual purpose: to save the Union and to free the slaves.

Even if the Civil War had not touched slavery, the war still would have transformed America. The war proved to be the first modern war, a "total war" that mobilized entire populations, harnessed the productive capacities of entire economies, and enlisted millions of troops, with single battles pitting 200,000 soldiers and

**FREDERICK DOUGLASS**
*The North's antebellum black community was avidly abo-
litionist. Like Frederick Douglass (seen here in an 1847
photograph), black crusaders sometimes lost heart. "The
time has gone by for colored people to talk of patriotism,"
Charles L. Remond said in the wake of the 1857 Dred Scott
decision. "We owe no allegiance to a country which grinds
us under its iron heel and treats us like dogs." Yet, like
Douglass, the black community stayed the course and helped
transform a war against rebellion into a war for freedom.*
Chester County Historical Society, West Chester, Pa.

casualties mounting into the tens of thousands. The
carnage lasted four years and cost the nation 633,000
lives, nearly as many as in all of its other wars before and after. The war became a crucible that
molded the modern American nation-state. The federal government emerged with new power and responsibility over national life. War furthered the
emergence of a modern industrializing nation. But
because the war to preserve the Union also became
a war to destroy slavery, the northern victory had
truly revolutionary meaning. Defeat and emancipation destroyed the slave society of the Old South
and gave birth to a different society.

Years later, remembering the Civil War years,
Douglass said, "It is something to couple one's
name with great occasions." It *was* something—for

millions of Americans. Whether they battled or defended the Confederacy, whether they labored behind the lines to produce goods for northern or
southern soldiers, whether they kept the home fires
burning for Yankees or rebels, all Americans experienced the crucible of war. But the war affected no
group more than the four million African Americans who began the war in 1861 as slaves and
emerged in 1865 as free people.

## "And the War Came"

New to high office, Abraham Lincoln faced the
worst crisis in the history of the nation, the threat
of disunion. Lincoln revealed his strategy on March
4, 1861, in his inaugural address, which was carefully crafted to combine firmness and conciliation.
First, he would try to stop the contagion of secession. Eight of the fifteen slave states had said no to
disunion, but they remained suspicious and skit-
tish. Lincoln was determined to do nothing that
would push the Upper South (North Carolina, Virginia, Maryland, Delaware, Kentucky, Tennessee,
Missouri, and Arkansas) into leaving. Second, he
would buy time so that emotions could cool. By reassuring the Deep South (South Carolina, Georgia,
Florida, Alabama, Mississippi, Louisiana, and
Texas) about the safety of slavery, he would provide
Unionists there the opportunity to reassert themselves and to overturn the secession decision. Always, Lincoln expressed his uncompromising will
to oppose secession and to uphold the Union.

His counterpart, Jefferson Davis, fully intended
to establish the Confederate States of America as an
independent republic. To achieve permanence, he
had to sustain the secession fever that had carried the
Deep South out of the Union and to dampen reunion
sentiment. Even if the Deep South held firm, however,
the Confederacy remained weak without additional
states from the Upper South. Davis watched for opportunities to add new stars to the Confederate flag.

Neither man sought war. Both wanted to
achieve their objectives peacefully. But as Lincoln
later observed, "Both parties deprecated war, but
one of them would make war rather than let the nation survive, and the other would accept war rather
than let it perish. And the war came."

### Attack on Fort Sumter

Fort Sumter's thick brick walls rose forty feet above
the tiny island on which it perched at the entrance
to Charleston harbor. Only four miles from the city,

the fortress with its Union flag was a sight that infuriated Confederates. Major Robert Anderson and some eighty U.S. soldiers occupied what Charlestonians claimed as Confederate property. The fort became a hateful symbol of the nation they had abandoned, and Southerners wanted federal troops out. But Sumter was also a symbol to Northerners, a beacon affirming federal sovereignty in the seceded states.

*Always, Lincoln expressed his uncompromising will to oppose secession and to uphold the Union.*

The situation at Fort Sumter presented the new president with hard choices. Ordering the fort's evacuation would play well in the Upper South, whose edgy slave states threatened to bolt to the Confederacy if Lincoln resorted to military force. But yielding the fort would make it appear that Lincoln accepted the Confederacy's existence. Abandonment would divide the North, batter the new Republican administration, and magnify the rebel nation's status in the eyes of the world. Lincoln decided to hold Fort Sumter. But to do so, he had to provision it, for Anderson was running dangerously short of food. In the first week in April, Lincoln authorized a peaceful expedition to bring supplies, but not military reinforcements, to the fort. Lincoln understood that he risked war, but his plan honored his inaugural promises to defend federal property and to avoid using military force unless first attacked. Masterfully, Lincoln had shifted the fateful decision of war or peace to Jefferson Davis.

On April 9, 1861, Jefferson Davis and his cabinet met to consider the situation in Charleston harbor. The territorial integrity of the Confederacy demanded the end of the federal presence, Davis argued. But his secretary of state, Robert Toombs of Georgia, pleaded against military action. "Mr. President," he declared, "at this time it is suicide, murder, and will lose us every friend at the North." Davis rejected Toombs's prophecy and sent word to General Pierre Gustave T. Beauregard, the Louisianan commanding Confederate troops in Charleston, to take the fort before the relief expedition arrived. Thirty-three hours of bombardment reduced the fort to rubble, but, miraculously, not a single Union soldier died. On April 14, with the fort ablaze, Anderson offered his surrender. The Confederates had Fort Sumter, but they also had a war.

The response of the free states was thunderous. When Lincoln called for 75,000 troops to put down the rebellion, several times that many rushed to defend the flag. Lincoln asked Indiana for six regiments, and the governor wired that "without seriously repressing the ardor of the people, I can hardly stop short of twenty." Democrats responded as fervently as Republicans. Stephen A. Douglas, the recently defeated Democratic candidate for president, pledged his support. "There are only two sides to the question," he told a massive crowd in Chicago. "Every man must be for the United States or against it. There can be no neutrals in this war, only patriots—or traitors." No one faced more acutely the issue of loyalty than the men and women of the Upper South.

## The Upper South Chooses Sides

Lincoln's call for troops confronted the Upper South with a horrendous choice: either to fight against the Lower South or to fight against the North. Many who had only months earlier rejected secession now embraced the Confederacy. To oppose southern independence was one thing, to fight fellow Southerners was another. Thousands felt betrayed, believing that Lincoln had promised to achieve reunion peacefully by waiting patiently for Unionists to reassert themselves in the seceding states. One man furiously denounced the conflict as a "politician's war," conceding that "this is no time now to discuss the causes, but it is the duty of all who regard Southern institutions of value to side with the South."

Some found the choice excruciating. Robert E. Lee, a career military officer and the son of one of Virginia's oldest families, denounced the Lower South's separation as the work of cotton state hotheads. "I can anticipate no greater calamity for the country than a dissolution of the Union," he told his son in January 1861. Still, he said, "a Union that can only be maintained by swords and bayonets . . . has no charm for me." Following the bombardment of Fort Sumter, Lee was summoned from his white-columned mansion in Arlington, Virginia, to the nation's capital, where he was offered command of federal military forces. But Lee could not fight against the South. When he returned home, he learned that Virginia had left the Union. He quickly penned his resignation from the United States army and declared, "Save in defense of my native State, I never desire again to draw my sword."

One by one the other states of the Upper South jumped off the fence. Within weeks, Arkansas, North Carolina, and Tennessee followed Virginia's

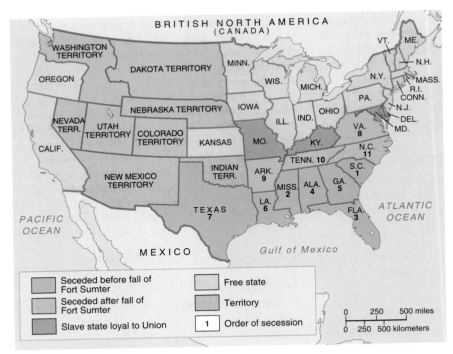

**MAP 15.1**
*Secession, 1860–1861*
*After Lincoln's election, the fifteen slave states debated what to do. Seven states quickly left the Union, four left after the firing on Fort Sumter, and four refused to go.*

lead (Map 15.1). But in the border states of Delaware, Maryland, Kentucky, and Missouri, Unionism triumphed. Only in Delaware, where slaves accounted for less than 2 percent of the population, was the victory easy. In Maryland, Unionism needed a helping hand. Rather than allow the state to secede and make Washington, D.C., a federal island in a Confederate sea, Lincoln suspended the writ of habeas corpus, essentially setting aside normal constitutional guarantees such as trial before a jury of peers, and marched troops into Baltimore. Maryland's legislature, frightened by the federal invasion and aware of the strength of Union sentiment in the western counties, rejected secession.

The struggle turned violent in the West. In Missouri, Unionists won a narrow victory, but southern-sympathizing guerrilla bands roamed the state for the duration of the conflict, waging bloody war on civilians and soldiers alike. In Kentucky, Unionists narrowly defeated secession, but, as in Missouri, a prosouthern minority claimed that the state had severed its ties with the Union. The Richmond government, not particularly fastidious in counting votes, eagerly made Missouri and Kentucky the twelfth and thirteenth Confederate states.

Throughout the border states, but especially in Kentucky, the Civil War was truly a "brother's war."

Seven of Henry Clay's grandsons fought in the Civil War: four for the Confederacy and three for the Union. Lincoln understood that the border states—particularly Kentucky—contained indispensable resources, population, and wealth, and they controlled major rivers and railroads. "I think to lose Kentucky is nearly the same as to lose the whole game," Lincoln said. "Kentucky gone, we can not hold Missouri, nor, as I think, Maryland. These all against us, and . . . we would as well consent to separation at once."

In the end, only eleven of the fifteen slave states joined the Confederate States of America. Moreover, the four seceding Upper South states contained significant populations that felt little affection for the Confederacy. Dissatisfaction was so rife in the western counties of Virginia that citizens there voted to create the separate state of West Virginia in 1863 and to remain loyal to the Union. Still, the acquisition of four new Confederate states greatly strengthened the cause of southern independence.

## The Combatants

Although fierce struggle continued in the border states and in some areas within the seceding states of the Upper South, most whites in the South chose to defend the Confederacy. For them, Yankee "aggression" was no longer a secessionist's abstraction; it was real, and it was at their door. For Northerners, rebel "treason" threatened to destroy the noble experiment of republican self-government. Men rallied behind their separate battle flags, fully convinced that they were in the right and that God was on their side.

While both sides claimed the lion's share of virtue, only fools argued that the South's resources and forces equaled the North's. A glance at the census figures contradicted such a notion. Yankees took heart at their superior power, but the rebels believed they had advantages that nullified every northern strength. Both sides mobilized swiftly in the spring and summer of 1861, and each devised what it believed would be a winning military and diplomatic strategy.

## What They Fought For

Across the South, planters, yeomen, and artisans raced to enlist and to fight Yankees. Only slaveholders, of course, had a direct economic stake (estimated at some $3 billion in 1860) in preserving slavery. But all white Southerners—slaveholders and nonslaveholders alike—united in the defense of the institution. Slavery controlled blacks, whom they thought an inferior and potentially dangerous race. Moreover, the degraded and subjugated status of blacks was the basis of an elevated status for even the most humble whites. "It matters not whether slaves be actually owned by many or by few," one observer declared. "It is enough that one simply belongs to the superior and ruling race, to secure consideration and respect."

---

*While both sides claimed the lion's share of virtue, only fools argued that the South's resources and forces equaled the North's.*

---

Rather than explicitly naming slavery as their reason for fighting, however, ordinary whites emphasized defending a special southern civilization from "subjugation" and protecting hearth and home from northern hordes bent on plunder and domination. In 1861, white Southerners equated their position with that of American patriots in 1776. In both cases, they argued, a freedom-loving minority waged war to protect its liberty against the encroachments of a tyrannical central government.

As one Georgia woman observed, Southerners wanted "nothing from the North but—*to be let alone*—and *they,* a people like ourselves whose republican independence was won by a rebellion, whose liberty was achieved by a secession, to think that they should attempt to coerce us—the idea is preposterous."

Northerners saw secession as an unconscionable attack on the best government on earth. The South's failure to accept the lawful election of a president and its firing on the nation's flag challenged the rule of law, the authority of the Constitution, and the ability of the people to govern themselves. Northerners believed that the South's effort to wreck the Republic threatened them in a personal way. Lincoln captured the Union's special magnetism. "This is essentially a People's contest," he declared on the first Fourth of July after the war began. The Union's cause, he said, was the preservation of the government "whose leading object is, to elevate the condition of man—to lift artificial weights from all shoulders—to clear the paths of laudable pursuit for all—to afford all, an unfettered start, and a fair chance, in the race of life." In short, secession menaced the life chances of millions of eager and aspiring individuals. Self-interest as well as patriotic fervor welded Northerners to the preservation of the nation.

## How They Expected to Win

The balance sheet of northern and southern resources reveals enormous advantages for the Union (Figure 15.1). The twenty-three states remaining in the Union had a population of 22,300,000, while the eleven Confederate states had a population of only 9,100,000, of whom 3,670,000 (40 percent) were slaves. The North had 22,000 miles of railroads; the South, only 9,280. The North manufactured more than 90 percent of the nation's industrial goods. It produced 17 times as much textiles; 21 times as much coal; 24 times as many locomotives; and 32 times as many firearms. The list is nearly endless. So overwhelming were the North's advantages that the question becomes why the South made war at all. Was not the South's cause lost before Confederates lobbed the first rounds at Fort Sumter? The answer quite simply is no. Southerners expected to win—and for some good reasons. They came very close to doing it.

Southerners believed that they would triumph because of their region's lofty cause, superior civilization, and unsurpassed character. Southerners

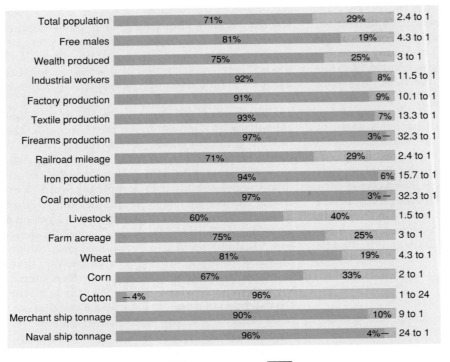

| | | |
|---|---|---|
| Total population | 71% | 29% | 2.4 to 1 |
| Free males | 81% | 19% | 4.3 to 1 |
| Wealth produced | 75% | 25% | 3 to 1 |
| Industrial workers | 92% | 8% | 11.5 to 1 |
| Factory production | 91% | 9% | 10.1 to 1 |
| Textile production | 93% | 7% | 13.3 to 1 |
| Firearms production | 97% | 3%— | 32.3 to 1 |
| Railroad mileage | 71% | 29% | 2.4 to 1 |
| Iron production | 94% | 6% | 15.7 to 1 |
| Coal production | 97% | 3%— | 32.3 to 1 |
| Livestock | 60% | 40% | 1.5 to 1 |
| Farm acreage | 75% | 25% | 3 to 1 |
| Wheat | 81% | 19% | 4.3 to 1 |
| Corn | 67% | 33% | 2 to 1 |
| Cotton | —4% | 96% | 1 to 24 |
| Merchant ship tonnage | 90% | 10% | 9 to 1 |
| Naval ship tonnage | 96% | 4%— | 24 to 1 |

☐ Union   ☐ Confederacy

FIGURE 15.1
*Resources of the Union and Confederacy*
The Union's enormous statistical advantages failed to convince Confederates that their cause was doomed.

bucked the military odds, but hadn't the liberty-loving colonists, too? How could anyone doubt the outcome of a contest between lean, hard, country-born rebel warriors defending family, property, and liberty, and soft, flabby, citified Yankee mechanics waging an unconstitutional war of aggression and subjugation?

The South's confidence also rested on its estimation of the economic clout of cotton. A war correspondent for the London *Times* found that "King Cotton" was "the fixed idea everywhere." For years, Southerners had argued that northern prosperity depended on the South's cotton. Without southern cotton, New England textile mills would stand idle. Without southern planters purchasing northern manufactured goods, northern factories would drown in their own surpluses. Without the foreign exchange earned by the overseas sales of cotton, the financial structure of the entire Yankee nation would collapse. One Virginian spoke for most Confederates when he declared that in the South's ability to "withhold the benefits of our trade, we hold a power over the North more powerful than a powerful army in the field."

King Cotton also could make Europe a powerful ally of the Confederacy. After all, Southerners said, England's economy (and to a lesser degree, France's) also depended on cotton. Of the 900 million pounds of cotton England imported annually, more than 700 million came from the South. If the supply were interrupted, sheer necessity would make England (and perhaps France) a Confederate ally. And because the British navy ruled the seas, the North would find Britain a formidable foe.

Southerners' faith in their ability to win seems naive today because that faith turned out to have been misplaced. But even hard-eyed European military observers picked the South. Offsetting the North's power was the South's expanse. The North, Europeans predicted, could not conquer the vast territory (750,000 square miles) from the Potomac to the Rio Grande, with its rugged terrain and bad roads. It would require raising a massive invading army, supplying it with huge quantities of provisions and arms, and protecting supply lines that would stretch farther than any in modern history.

Indeed, the South enjoyed major advantages, and the Confederacy devised a military strategy to exploit them. Jefferson Davis called it an "offensive-defensive" strategy. It recognized that a Union victory required the North to defeat and subjugate the South. A Confederate victory required only that the South stay at home, blunt invasions, avoid battles that risked annihilating its army, and outlast the northern will to fight. When an opportunity presented itself, the South would strike the invaders. Like the American colonists, the South could win independence by not losing the war.

If the North did nothing, the South would by default establish its independence. The Lincoln administration therefore adopted an offensive strat-egy. Four days after the president issued the proclamation calling for 75,000 volunteers to put down the rebellion, he issued another proclamation declaring a naval blockade of the Confederacy. He sought to deny the Confederacy the use of its most valuable commodity—cotton. Without the sale of cotton abroad, the South would have far fewer dollars to pay for war goods. Even before the North could mount an effective blockade, however, Jefferson Davis decided voluntarily to cease exporting cotton. He wanted to create a cotton "famine" that would enfeeble the northern economy and precipitate European intervention.

**BRIDGE ON THE ORANGE AND ALEXANDRIA RAILROAD**
*Confederate forces burned southern railroads and bridges to slow Union advances, cut federal supply lines, and protect Confederate retreats. West Point–trained Herman Haupt, seen here inspecting a rebuilt bridge, was in charge of the Union's efforts at railroad construction and repair. While the railroad had been used as an instrument of war in the Crimea in the 1850s, it was during the Civil War that the railroad took on revolutionary importance. Railroads helped set new standards of overland mobility, rapid maneuver, and concentration of forces.*
Library of Congress.

Southerners were not the only ones with illusions. Lincoln's call for 75,000 men for ninety days illustrates his failure to predict the magnitude and duration of the war. He was not alone. Most Americans thought of war in terms of their most recent experience, the Mexican War in the 1840s. In Mexico, fighting had taken place between relatively small armies, had taken relatively small numbers of lives, and had inflicted only light damage on the countryside.

Americans on the eve of the Civil War could not know that four ghastly years of bloodletting lay ahead. Early theories and strategies, however, like the expectations of military glory and fame, quickly confronted harsh reality.

## Lincoln and Davis Mobilize

Mobilization required effective political leadership, and at first glance it appeared that the South had the decided advantage. An aristocrat from a Mississippi planter family, Jefferson Davis brought to the Confederate presidency a distinguished political career, including a stint in the U.S. Senate. He was also a West Point graduate, a combat veteran of the Mexican War, and a former secretary of war. Dignified and erect, with "a jaw sawed in steel," Davis appeared to be everything a nation could want in a wartime leader.

In contrast, an Illinois lawyer-politician occupied the White House. He brought with him one undistinguished term in the House of Representatives, where he had opposed the Mexican War in which Davis had served gallantly. He had almost no administrative experience, and his sole brush with anything military was as a captain in the militia in the Black Hawk War, a brief struggle in Illinois in 1832 in which whites expelled the last Indians from the state. The lanky, disheveled Westerner looked anything but military or presidential in his bearing, and even his friends feared that he was in over his head.

Davis, however, proved to be less than he appeared. Possessing little capacity for broad military strategy and yet vain about what he regarded as his own superior judgment, he intervened constantly in military affairs. He was an even less able political leader. Quarrelsome and proud, he had an acid tongue that made enemies the Confederacy could ill afford. It is true that Davis faced a daunting task. For example, state sovereignty, which was enshrined in the Confederate constitution, made Davis's task of organizing a new nation and fighting a war difficult in the extreme. The Confederacy's intimidating problems might have defeated an even more talented leader.

In Lincoln, however, the North got far more than met the eye. He proved himself a master politician and a superb leader. He never allowed personal feelings to get in the way of his objectives. When forming his cabinet, for example, Lincoln shrewdly appointed representatives of every Republican faction, men who were often his chief rivals and critics. He made Salmon P. Chase secretary of the treasury, knowing that Chase had presidential ambitions. As secretary of state, he chose his chief opponent for the Republican nomination in 1860, William Seward, who expected to twist Lincoln around his little finger and formulate policy himself. Despite his civilian background, Lincoln displayed an innate understanding of military strategy. In time, no one was more crucial in mapping the Union war plan. Moreover, Lincoln was an enormously eloquent man who reached out to the North's people, galvanizing them in defense of the nation he called "the last best hope of earth."

Guided by Lincoln and Davis, the North and South began gathering their armies. Southerners had the task of building almost everything from scratch, and Northerners had to mobilize their superior numbers and industrial resources for war. The puny federal army numbered only 16,000 men in 1861, and most of those who wore Union blue were scattered over the West subjugating Indians. One-third of the officers followed Robert E. Lee's example, resigning their commissions and heading south. The navy was in better shape. Forty-two ships were in service, and a large merchant marine would in time provide more ships and sailors. Most of the officers and men were Northerners and loyal to the Union. Though it had strong leadership in its secretary of the navy, Stephen R. Mallory, the Confederate navy was never a match for the Union fleet, and the South pinned its hopes on its armies. Military companies sprang up everywhere. Since soldiers at first supplied their own uniforms, Confederate gray was just one of a rainbow of colors. Moreover, volunteers brought their own weapons, as often Bowie knives and shotguns as rifles and pistols.

From the beginning, the South exhibited more enthusiasm than ability to provide its soldiers with supplies and transportation. The Confederacy made prodigious efforts to build new factories to produce tents, blankets, shoes, and uniforms, but many soldiers slept in the open air without proper clothes and sometimes without shoes. Even when factories managed to produce what soldiers needed, southern railroads—constructed to connect plantations with ports—often could not deliver the goods. And before long, most railroads were captured, destroyed, or in disrepair. Food production proved less of a problem, but food sometimes rotted before it reached the soldiers. The one bright spot was the Confederacy's Ordnance Bureau, headed by Josiah Gorgas. In April 1864, Gorgas observed: "Where three years ago we were not making a gun, a pistol nor a sabre, no shot nor shell . . . —a pound of powder—we now make all these in quantities to meet the demands of our large armies."

Recruiting and supplying huge armies required enormous public spending. Before the war, the federal government's tiny income had come primarily from tariff duties and the sale of public lands. Massive wartime expenditures made new revenues imperative. At first, both the North and the South resorted to selling war bonds, which essentially were loans from patriotic citizens. In time, both North and South began printing paper money. Inflation soared, but the South suffered more because it financed a greater part of its wartime costs through the printing press. Prices in the North rose about 80 percent during the war, while in the South inflation topped 9,000 percent. Eventually, the Union and the Confederacy turned to taxes, but the North raised one-fifth of its wartime revenue from taxes, the South only one-twentieth.

Within months of the bombardment of Fort Sumter, both sides had found men to fight and people to supply and support them. But the underlying strength of the northern economy gave the Union the decided advantage. With their military and industrial muscles beginning to ripple, Northerners became itchy for action. Northerners wanted an invasion that would once and for all smash the rebellion. Horace Greeley's *New York Tribune* began the chant: "Forward to Richmond! Forward to Richmond!"

# The Battlefields, 1861–1862

During the first year and a half of the war, armies fought major campaigns in two theaters: in Virginia-Maryland in the East and in Tennessee-Kentucky in the West. With rival capitals of Richmond and Washington, D.C., only ninety miles apart and each threatened more than once with capture, the eastern campaign was more dramatic and commanded public attention. But the battles in the West proved more decisive. And as Yankee and rebel armies pounded each other on land, their navies fought it out on the seas and their diplomats sought advantage in the corridors of power in Europe. All the while, casualty lists reached appalling lengths.

## Stalemate in the Eastern Theater

As commander in chief, Lincoln appointed Irvin McDowell commanding general of the army assembling outside Washington. McDowell had no thought of taking his raw recruits into battle during the summer of 1861, but Lincoln ordered McDowell to prepare his 30,000 men for an attack on the Confederate army gathered at Manassas, a railroad junction in Virginia about thirty miles southwest of Washington. When McDowell complained, Lincoln replied, "You are green, it is true, but they are green, also; you are all green."

Repeating to the last that he did not want to go, McDowell moved his greenhorn troops out on July 16. Five days later, the Union army forded Bull Run, a branch of the Potomac, and engaged the southern forces effectively (Map 15.2). But fast-moving southern reinforcements blunted the Union attack and then counterattacked. What began as an orderly retreat turned into a panicky stampede. Demoralized soldiers ran over shocked civilians as they raced back to Washington.

By Civil War standards, casualties at Manassas (or Bull Run, as Northerners called the battle) were light, but the significance of the battle lay in the lessons Northerners and Southerners drew from it. For Southerners, it confirmed the superiority of rebel fighting men and the inevitability of Confederate nationhood. Manassas was *"one of the decisive battles of the world,"* a Georgian proclaimed. It "has secured our independence." While victory lifted southern pride to new levels, defeat sobered Northerners. It was a major reversal, admitted the *New York Tribune,* but, the writer added, "Let us go to work, then, with a will." Manassas taught Lincoln that victory would be neither quick nor easy. Within four days of the disaster, the president signed bills authorizing the enlistment of one million men.

Lincoln also found a new general, replacing McDowell with the arrogant young George B. McClellan. Born in Philadelphia of well-to-do parents, educated in the best schools before graduating from

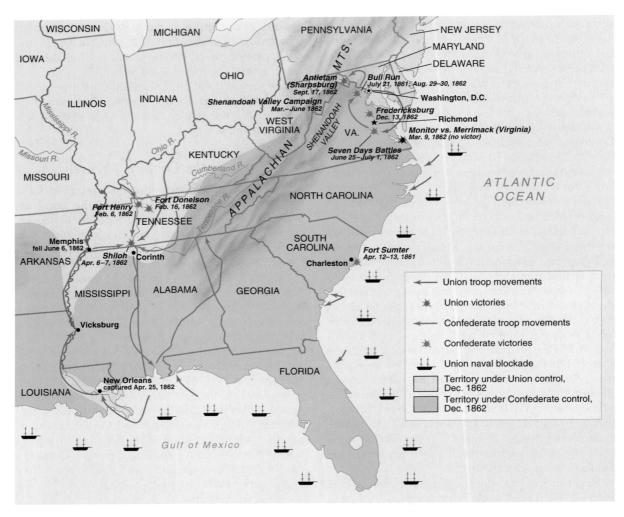

MAP 15.2
*The Civil War, 1861–1862*
*While eyes focused on the eastern theater, especially the tiny geography between the two*
*capitals of Washington and Richmond, strategic victories were being won by Union troops*
*in the West.*

West Point second in his class, the thirty-four-year-old McClellan believed that he was a great soldier and that Lincoln was the "original Gorilla." A superb administrator and organizer, McClellan was brought to Washington as commander of the newly named Army of the Potomac. In the months following his appointment, McClellan energetically whipped his army of dispirited veterans and fresh recruits into shape. The troops cheered their boyish general when he rode among them, in part no doubt because of his reluctance to send them into battle.

Lincoln said McClellan had a bad case of "the slows," and, indeed, McClellan lacked decisiveness and the will to act. Lincoln wanted a general who would advance, take risks, and fight, but McClellan went into winter quarters without budging from the Potomac. "If General McClellan does not want to use the army I would like to *borrow* it," Lincoln declared in frustration.

Finally, in the spring of 1862, McClellan launched his long-awaited offensive. He transported his highly polished army, now 130,000 strong, down the Chesapeake Bay to the mouth of the James River and began moving up the peninsula toward Richmond. McClellan took two and a half months to advance sixty-five miles. When he was within six miles of the Confederate capital, Confederate General Joseph Johnston hit him like a hammer. In the assault, Johnston was wounded and was replaced by Robert E. Lee, the reluctant Confederate who would become the Confederacy's most celebrated general. Lee named his command the Army of Northern Virginia.

The contrast between Lee and McClellan could hardly have been greater. McClellan overflowed with conceit and braggadocio, while Lee was courteous and reserved. But on the battlefield, where McClellan grew timid and irresolute, Lee became audaciously, even recklessly, aggressive. And Lee had at his side in the peninsula campaign military men of real talent: General Thomas J. ("Stonewall") Jackson, so nicknamed for holding the line at Manassas, and James E. B. ("Jeb") Stuart, the twenty-nine-year-old cavalry commander who wore a red-lined cape, yellow sash, and hat with ostrich feather plume and rode circles around Yankee troops. Lee's assault initiated the Battle of Seven Days and began McClellan's backward march down the peninsula. By the time McClellan reached the water and the safety of the Union navy, 30,000 men had died or been wounded. Although Southerners suffered twice the casualties of Northerners, Lee had saved Richmond and achieved a strategic success. Lincoln wired McClellan to abandon the peninsula campaign and replaced him with General John Pope.

In August, just north of Richmond, Pope had his own rendezvous with Lee. At the Second Battle of Bull Run, Lee's smaller army battered Pope's forces and sent them scurrying back to Washington. Lincoln ordered Pope to Minnesota to pacify Indians and again put McClellan in command. Lincoln had not changed his mind about McClellan's capacity as a warrior. Instead, he reluctantly concluded, "If he can't fight himself, he excels in making others ready to fight."

Lee could fight. Sensing that he had his enemy on the ropes, he sought to land the knockout punch. Lee pushed the Army of Northern Virginia across the Potomac and invaded Maryland. A victory on northern soil would dislodge Maryland from the Union, Lee reasoned, and might even cause Lincoln to sue for peace. On September 17, 1862, McClellan's forces finally engaged Lee's army at Antietam Creek (see Map 15.2). Earlier, a Union soldier had found a copy of Lee's orders to his army wrapped around some cigars, dropped by a careless Confederate officer. McClellan had a clear picture of Lee's position, but his characteristic slowness meant that he missed a great opportunity to destroy the opposing army. Still, he did it great damage. With "solid shot . . . cracking skulls like egg-shells," the armies threw everything they had at each other. By nightfall the battlefield lay littered with 6,000 men dead or dying and 17,000 more wounded, making the Battle of Antietam the bloodiest day of the war. Badly damaged and deeply disappointed, Lee headed back to Virginia.

But Lee remained alert for an opportunity to punish his enemy. In December, General Ambrose Burnside, yet another replacement for the ineffectual McClellan, provided the Virginian a fresh chance. At Fredericksburg, Virginia, Burnside's 122,000 Union troops faced 78,500 Confederates dug in behind a stone wall on the heights above the Rappahannock River. Half a mile of open ground lay between the armies. A Confederate artillery officer predicted that "a chicken could not live on that field when we open on it." Yet Burnside ordered a frontal assault. Wave after wave of bluecoats crashed against impregnable defenses. When the guns finally ceased, the federals counted nearly 13,000 casualties while the Confederates suffered fewer than 5,000. It was one of the Union's worst defeats.

At the end of 1862, the North seemed no nearer to taking Richmond, to whipping Lee, or to ending the rebellion than it had been when the war began. Rather than checkmate, military struggle in the East had reached a stalemate.

## Union Victories in the Western Theater

While most eyes focused on the East, the decisive early encounters of the war took place between the Appalachians and the Ozarks. The West's rivers—the Mississippi, the Tennessee, and the Cumberland—became the keys to the military situation. Southerners looked northward along the rivers and spied Missouri and Kentucky, states they claimed but did not control. Looking southward, Northerners knew that by taking the Mississippi they would split Arkansas, Louisiana, and Texas from the Confederacy. And the Cumberland and Tennessee penetrated one of the Confederacy's main producers of food, mules, and iron—all vital resources.

Ulysses S. Grant became the key northern figure on the western battlefields. Although Grant had graduated from West Point, when war broke out he was a thirty-nine-year-old dry goods clerk in Galena, Illinois. Gentle at home, he became pugnacious on the battlefield. "The art of war is simple," he said. "Find out where your enemy is, get at him as soon as you can and strike him as hard as you can, and keep moving on." Grant's philosophy of war as annihilation took a huge toll in human life, but it played to the North's strength: superior manpower.

In February 1862, operating in tandem with navy gunboats, Grant captured Fort Henry on the Tennessee and Fort Donelson on the Cumberland (see Map 15.2). Defeat forced the Confederates to withdraw from all of Kentucky and most of Tennessee. Grant pushed after the retreating rebels until, on April 6, General Albert Sidney Johnston's army surprised him at Shiloh Church in Tennessee. Although his troops were badly mauled the first day, Grant remained cool and brought up reinforcements throughout the night. The next morning, the Union army counterattacked, driving the Confederates before it. The battle was terribly costly; there were 20,000 casualties, including the death of Johnston. Manassas disabused Lincoln of the illusion of a short war, and, after Shiloh, Grant "gave up all idea of saving the Union except by complete conquest."

> Manassas disabused Lincoln of the illusion of a short war, and, after Shiloh, Grant "gave up all idea of saving the Union except by complete conquest."

Although no one knew it at the time, Shiloh inflicted a mortal wound to the Confederacy's bid to control the Mississippi valley. In short order, the Yankees captured the strategic town of Corinth, Mississippi, the river city of Memphis, and New Orleans, the South's largest city. By the end of 1862, most—but not all—of the Mississippi valley lay in Union hands.

## War and Diplomacy in the Atlantic Theater

With a blockade fleet of only about three dozen ships at the beginning of the war and more than 3,500 miles of southern coastline to patrol, the U.S.

navy faced an impossible task. At first, rebel ships slipped in and out of port nearly at will. But with the U.S. navy commissioning a new blockader almost weekly, the fleet eventually reached 150 ships on duty, and the Union navy dramatically improved its score.

Unable to build a conventional navy equal to the expanding federal fleet, the Confederates experimented with a radical new maritime design: the ironclad warship. At Norfolk, Virginia, they layered the wooden hull of the frigate *Merrimack* with two-inch-thick armor plate. Rechristened *Virginia*, it steamed out in March 1862 to engage the federal blockade. Within a few hours, it sank two large federal ships, killing at least 240 sailors. But when the *Virginia* returned the following morning to finish its work, it found the *Monitor*, a federal ironclad that had arrived from Brooklyn during the night. The *Monitor*, a ship of even more radical design, including a revolving turret containing two eleven-inch guns, and the *Virginia* hurled shells at each other for two hours, but because neither could penetrate the other's armor, the duel ended in a draw.

The Confederacy never found a way to break the blockade. Each month the blockade grew tighter until by 1865 the Union fleet intercepted about half of the southern ships that attempted to break through. Even more significant than the ships the Union fleet captured (about 1,500 in total) were the ships that never sailed for fear of being captured. By 1863, the South had abandoned its embargo policy and desperately wanted to ship cotton to pay for imports it needed to fight the war. But the growing effectiveness of the federal blockade, a southern naval officer observed, "shut the Confederacy out from the world, deprived it of supplies, weakened its military and naval strength."

What they could not achieve on saltwater, Confederates sought through foreign policy. According to the theory of King Cotton, cotton-starved European nations had no choice but to break the blockade and recognize the Confederacy. The British and French briefly discussed joint action to lift the blockade, but it came to nothing. Although European nations granted the Confederacy "belligerent" status, which enabled it to buy goods and build ships in European ports, none recognized Confederate nationhood.

King Cotton diplomacy failed for several reasons. A bumper cotton crop in 1860 meant that the warehouses of British textile manufacturers bulged with surplus cotton throughout 1861. In 1862, when Europe began to feel the pinch of the cotton famine, manufacturers found new sources of cotton in Egypt and India. In addition, a brisk trade developed between the Union and Britain—British war materiel for American grain and flour—which helped offset the decline in textiles and encouraged Britain to remain neutral. Even when the Union stepped hard on tender British toes, the British remained tolerant. In November 1861, a Union warship intercepted a British mail packet, the *Trent,* and illegally removed James Mason and John Slidell, Confederate diplomats on their way to Europe. Sentiment for war flared briefly in Britain, but when Lincoln ordered the Southerners' release, the British allowed the affair to end peacefully.

Europe's temptation to intervene disappeared for good in 1862. Union military successes on the rivers of the West made Britain and France think twice about linking their fates to the Confederacy. And in the fall of 1862, Lincoln announced a new policy that made an alliance with the Confederacy an alliance with slavery. The president finally acknowledged that it was impossible to fight for union without fighting against slavery.

# Union **and** Freedom

Slavery and freedom had coexisted in North America for more than two centuries when the Civil War erupted. In his inaugural address in March 1861, Abraham Lincoln solemnly announced to the nation that the war would not disturb that ancient relationship. He had "no legal right" and "no inclination" to interfere with slavery. For a year and a half Lincoln insisted that emancipation was not a goal; the war was strictly to save the Union.

Despite Lincoln's pronouncements, the war for union became a war for African American freedom. Each month the war dragged on, it became clearer that the Confederate war machine depended heavily on slavery. Rebel armies used slaves to build fortifications, haul materiel, tend horses, and perform camp chores. On the home front, slaves labored in ironworks and shipyards, and they grew the food that fed both soldiers and civilians. Slavery undergirded the Confederacy as certainly as it had the Old South. In the field among military commanders, in the halls of Congress, and in the White House, the truth gradually came into focus: To defeat the Confederacy, the North would have to destroy slavery. "I am a slow walker," Lincoln said, "but I never walk back."

## *From Slaves to Contraband*

Personally, Lincoln detested human bondage, but as president he felt compelled to act prudently in the interests of the Union. An astute politician, he worked within the limits of public opinion, and in 1861 Lincoln believed those limits were tight. The issue of black freedom was particularly explosive in the loyal border states, where slaveholders threatened to jump into the arms of the Confederacy at even the hint of emancipation. Black freedom also attracted attention in the free states. The Democratic Party gave notice that emancipation would kill the bipartisan alliance and make the war strictly a Republican affair. Democrats were as ardent for union as Republicans, but they fought against treason—period. They marched under the banner "The Constitution As It Is, the Union As It Was."

*In the field among military commanders, in the halls of Congress, and in the White House, the truth gradually came into focus: To defeat the Confederacy, the North would have to destroy slavery.*

Moreover, most white Northerners were not about to risk their lives to satisfy abolitionist "fanaticism." "We Won't Fight to Free the Nigger," one popular banner read. They feared that emancipation would propel "two or three million semisavages" northward, where they would crowd into white neighborhoods, compete for white jobs, and mix with white "sons and daughters." An antiemancipation backlash, then, threatened to dislodge the loyal slave states from the Union, alienate the Democratic Party, deplete the armies, and perhaps even spark race warfare.

Proponents of emancipation pressed Lincoln as relentlessly as the anti-emancipation forces. Abolitionists argued that by seceding, Southerners had forfeited their right to the protection of the Constitution. Lincoln could now—as the price of treason—legally confiscate their property in slaves.

**CONTRABANDS**

*These refugees from slavery crossed the Rappahannock River in Virginia in August 1862 to seek the sanctuary of a federal army. Most slaves fled with little more than the clothes on their backs, but not all escaped slavery empty-handed. The oxen, wagon, and goods seen here could have been procured by a number of means—purchased during slavery, "borrowed" from the former master, or gathered during flight. Refugees who possessed draft animals and a wagon had much more economic opportunity than those who had only their labor to sell.*
Library of Congress.

When Lincoln refused, abolitionists scalded him. Frederick Douglass labeled Lincoln "the miserable tool of traitors and rebels." Abolitionists won increasing numbers of converts during the war, especially among the radical faction of the Republican Party, which came to believe that restoring the Union with the moral evil of slavery intact would make a mockery of the sacrifices of Union soldiers.

The Republican-dominated Congress refused to leave slavery policy entirely in Lincoln's hands. In August 1861, Congress approved the Confiscation Act, which allowed the seizure of any slave who was employed directly by the Confederate military. It also fulfilled the free-soil dream of prohibiting slavery in the territories and abolished slavery in Washington, D.C. Democrats and border state representatives voted against even these mild measures, but little by little, Congress displayed a stiffening of attitude as it cast about for a just and practical slavery policy.

But slaves, not politicians, became the most insistent force for emancipation. By escaping their masters by the tens of thousands and running away to Union lines, they placed slavery on the North's wartime agenda. Union officials could not ignore the flood of fugitives, and runaways precipitated a series of momentous decisions on the part of the military, Congress, and the president. Were the runaways now free, or were they still slaves who, according to the fugitive slave law, had to be returned to their masters? At first, most Yankee military commanders believed that administration policy required them to send the fugitives back. But Union armies needed laborers, and some officers accepted the runaways and put them to work. At Fort Monroe, Virginia, General Benjamin F. Butler not only refused to turn them over to their owners but also provided them with a new status. He called them "contraband of war," meaning "confiscated property." Congress established national policy in March 1862 when it forbade the practice of returning fugitive slaves to their masters. Slaves were still not legally free, but there was a tilt toward emancipation.

## From Contraband to Free People

On August 22, 1862, Lincoln replied to an angry abolitionist who demanded that he go after slavery. "My paramount objective in this struggle is to save the Union," Lincoln said deliberately, "and is not either to save or destroy slavery. If I could save the Union without freeing any slave I would do it, and if I could save it by freeing all the slaves I would do it; and if I could save it by freeing some and leaving others alone I would also do that." At first glance, it seemed a restatement of his old position: that union was the North's sole objective. But what marked it as a radical departure was Lincoln's refusal to say that slavery was safe. Instead, he said that he would emancipate every slave if it would preserve the Union.

By the summer of 1862, events were tumbling rapidly toward emancipation. On July 17, Congress adopted a second Confiscation Act. The first had confiscated slaves employed by the Confederate military, the second declared all slaves of rebel masters "forever free of their servitude." In theory, this breathtaking measure freed most of the slaves in the Confederacy, for slaveholders formed the backbone of the rebellion. Congress had traveled far since the war began. Lincoln had too, but he wanted to blaze his own path. On July 21, the president informed his cabinet that he was ready "to take some definitive steps in respect to military action and slavery." The next day, he read a draft of a preliminary emancipation proclamation that promised to free all slaves in the seceding states on January 1, 1863.

Lincoln described emancipation as an "act of justice," but it was not the abolitionists' appeal to conscience that finally brought him around. It was the lengthening casualty lists. The duration and difficulty of the war eroded and then ended Lincoln's policy of noninterference. Emancipation, he declared, was "a military necessity, absolutely essential to the preservation of the Union." Only freeing the slaves would "strike at the heart of the rebellion." His cabinet approved Lincoln's plan but advised him to wait for a military victory before announcing it so that critics would not call it an act of desperation. On September 22, five days after the battle at Antietam, Lincoln served notice that if the rebel states did not lay down their arms and return to the Union by January 1, 1863, their slaves "shall be then, thenceforward, and forever free."

By presenting emancipation as a "military necessity," Lincoln hoped he had disarmed his conservative critics. Emancipation would shorten the war and thus save lives. Instead, Democrats exploded with rage. They charged that the "shrieking and howling abolitionist faction" had captured the White House and made it "a nigger war." The fall elections were only weeks away, and Democrats sought to make political hay out of Lincoln's action. War-weariness probably had as much to do with the results as emancipation, but Democrats gained thirty-four congressional seats in 1862. When House Democrats proposed a resolution branding emancipation "a high crime against the Constitution," the Republicans, who maintained narrow majorities in both houses, beat it back. As promised, on New Year's Day, Lincoln issued the final Emancipation Proclamation. In addition to freeing the slaves in the states that were in rebellion, the edict also committed the federal government to the fullest use of African Americans to defeat the Confederate enemy.

## War of Black Liberation

Even before Lincoln proclaimed freedom a Union war aim, African Americans in the North had volunteered to fight. But the War Department, doubtful of their abilities and fearful of white reaction to serving shoulder to shoulder with them, refused to make black men soldiers. Instead, the army employed black men as manual laborers; black women sometimes found employment—usually as laundresses and cooks—but less often. The navy, however, from the outset accepted blacks as sailors. They usually served in noncombatant roles, but within months a few blacks served on gun crews.

As the Union experienced manpower shortages, Northerners gradually and reluctantly turned to African Americans to fill blue uniforms. With the Militia Act of July 1862, Congress authorized enrolling blacks in "any military or naval service for which they may be found competent." Lingering resistance to black military service largely disappeared in 1863. After the Emancipation Proclamation, whites—like it or not—were fighting and dying for black freedom, and few were likely to insist that blacks remain out of harm's way behind the lines. Indeed, rather than resist black military participation, whites insisted that blacks share the danger, especially after March 1863, when Congress resorted to the draft to fill the Union army.

Black soldiers discovered that the military was far from colorblind. The Union army established segregated black regiments, paid black soldiers $10 per month rather than the $13 it paid to whites, refused blacks the opportunity to become commissioned officers, punished blacks as if they were slaves, and assigned blacks to labor battalions rather than to combat units. But nothing deterred black recruits. When the war ended, 179,000 African American men had served in the Union army, approximately 10 percent of the army total. An astounding 71 percent of black men age eighteen to forty-five in the free states wore blue, a participation rate that was substantially higher than that of white men. More than 130,000 black soldiers came from the slave states, perhaps 100,000 of them ex-slaves. Blacks played a crucial role in the triumph of the Union and the destruction of slavery.

From the beginning, African Americans viewed the Civil War as a revolutionary struggle for black liberation. They fought to overthrow slavery and to gain equality for their entire race. "Once let the black man get upon his person the brass letters, U.S.; let him get an eagle on his button, and a musket on his shoulder and bullets in his pocket," Frederick Douglass declared, "and there is no power on earth which can deny that he has earned the right of citizenship." As Douglass predicted, when black men became liberators, they and their families gained new confidence, pride, and self-esteem. Military service taught them new skills, showed them more of the world, and introduced them to political struggle as they battled for their rights within the army. War's experiences and lessons stood African Americans in good stead when the war of liberation was over and the battle for equality began. But first, there was the matter of the rebellion. Victory depended as much on what happened behind the lines as on the battlefields.

**DRESS PARADE FOR THE FIRST SOUTH CAROLINA INFANTRY**
*The first regiment of black troops mustered in the South, the First South Carolina was made up overwhelmingly of ex-slaves and led by Colonel Thomas W. Higginson, a white Massachusetts clergyman and abolitionist. After the regiment's first skirmish with Confederate soldiers, Higginson celebrated his men's courage: "No officer in this regiment now doubts that the key to the successful prosecution of this war lies in the unlimited employment of black troops. . . . Instead of leaving their homes and families to fight they are fighting for their homes and families."*
National Archives.

# The South at War

During the secession winter of 1860–61, a Louisiana planter had declared confidently that the creation of the Confederate States of America would "guarantee order, security, tranquility, as well as liberty." The irony was staggering. By seceding, Southerners brought on themselves a firestorm of unimaginable fury. Monstrous losses on the battlefields nearly bled the Confederacy to death. But white Southerners also perceived themselves as under attack on the home front.

The most surprising thrust came from their own government. Richmond's efforts to centralize power to fight the war more effectively convinced many that the Confederacy had betrayed them. Southerners also endured severe deprivation. Wartime economic changes hurt some more than others, and by 1863, planters and yeomen no longer stood shoulder to shoulder. Most disturbing of all, slaves became open participants in the destruction of slavery and the Confederacy.

## Revolution from Above

When Jefferson Davis arrived in Richmond in 1861, he faced the gargantuan task of building an army and navy from scratch, supplying them from factories that were scarce and anemic, and paying for it all from a treasury that did not exist. The president agreed with one of his generals who observed that Southerners were engaged in a total war "in which the whole population and the whole production . . . are to be put on a war footing, where every institution is to be made auxiliary to war." Building the army proved easiest. Hundreds of officers defected from the federal army, and hundreds of thousands of eager young rebels volunteered to join them. Very quickly, the Confederacy developed formidable striking power.

The Confederacy's economy and finances proved tougher. Because of the Union blockade, the government had no choice but to build an industrial sector itself. Government-owned clothing and shoe factories, mines, arsenals, and powder works "sprung up almost like magic," according to one Mississippian. In addition, the government harnessed private companies, such as the huge Trede-gar Iron Works in Richmond, to the war effort. The financial task proved most difficult because Southerners had invested their capital in land and slaves, which were not easily tapped for the war. Richmond

**REBEL SOLDIER**
*Treasvant "Tris" D. Childers was twenty-seven years old in March 1862 when he enlisted as a private in Phelan's Battery, Alabama Light Artillery. He fought at Chicka-mauga, Missionary Ridge, Franklin, and Nashville and survived. His older brothers William and Thomas died while fighting in Virginia. After the war, Childers moved to Arkansas and became a farmer. When he died in 1910, his widow, Emma McShan Childers, collected a state pension for her husband's service in the Civil War.*
Private Collection.

came up with a mix of bonds, taxes, and paper money to finance the war effort.

Despite its bold measures, however, the Davis administration failed to transform the slave-labor, staple-producing agricultural economy into a modern industrial one. The Confederacy manufactured much more than many people imagined possible, but it never produced all that the South needed. Each month, the gap between the North's and the South's production widened. The flood of paper money caused debilitating inflation. By 1863, Charlestonians paid ten times more for food than they had at the start of the war. By Christmas 1864, a Confederate soldier's monthly pay no longer bought a pair of socks.

Richmond's war-making effort meant that government intruded in unprecedented ways into the private lives of Confederate citizens. In April 1862, the Confederate Congress passed the first conscription (draft) law in American history. All able-bodied white males between the ages of eighteen and thirty-five (later seventeen and fifty) were liable to serve in the rebel army for three years. The Confederate government adopted a policy of impressment, which allowed officials to confiscate food, horses, wagons, or whatever they wanted from private citizens and to pay for them at below-market rates. After March 1863, they also legally impressed slaves, employing them as government military laborers. In addition, Richmond took control of the South's railroads and shipping. The war necessitated much of the government's unprecedented behavior, but citizens found it arbitrary and inequitable. In time, Jefferson Davis became the South's most hated politician, after Lincoln.

## Resistance from Below

Richmond's centralizing efforts ran head-on into the South's traditional values of states' rights and unfettered individualism. The states lashed out at what Georgia Governor Joseph E. Brown denounced as the "dangerous usurpation by Congress of the reserved right of the States." A tug-of-war between Richmond and the states ensued for control of money, supplies, and soldiers, with damaging consequences for the war effort. Individual citizens also remembered that Davis had promised to defend southern "liberty" against Republican "despotism." Luckily for Davis, the Confederate constitution provided for a single, six-year term for the president, which meant he did not have to face the voters during the war.

Hardships were widespread, but they fell most heavily on the poor. Inflation, for example, threatened the poor with starvation. Salt—necessary for preserving meat—shot up from $2 to $60 a bag during the first year of the war. Flour that cost three or four cents a pound in 1861 cost thirty-five cents in 1863. The draft depopulated yeomen farms of men, leaving the women and children to grow what they ate. A rampaging army, a drought, a sickness, a lame mule—any one calamity could cost a family a crop. When farm wives succeeded in bringing in a harvest, government agents took 10 percent of it as a "tax-in-kind" on agriculture. Shortages, like inflation, also afflicted the entire population, but the rich lost luxuries while the poor lost necessities. In the spring of 1863, bread riots broke out in a dozen cities and villages across the South. In Richmond, a mob of nearly a thousand hungry women broke into shops and took what they needed.

Severe deprivation had powerful consequences. As one southern leader observed in November 1862, "men cannot be expected to fight for the Government that permits their wives & children to starve." By some estimates, when the war ended, one-third of the soldiers had already gone home. A Mississippi deserter explained, "We are poor men and are willing to defend our country but our families [come] first."

The Confederacy also failed to persuade the suffering white majority that the war's burdens were being shared equally. Instead, yeomen saw a profound inequality of sacrifice. They called it "a rich man's war and a poor man's fight," and they had evidence. The original draft law permitted a man who had money to hire a substitute to take his place. Moreover, the "twenty-Negro law" exempted one white man on every plantation with twenty or more slaves. The government intended to provide protection for white women and to see that slaves tended the crops. But yeomen perceived rich men evading military service.

*Yeomen saw a profound inequality of sacrifice. They called it "a rich man's war and a poor man's fight," and they had evidence.*

Government officials hoped that the crucible of war would mold a region into a nation. Instead, the long, grueling war increased discord among whites and widened divisions. War also threatened to rip the southern social fabric along its racial seam.

## The Disintegration of Slavery

The legal destruction of slavery was the product of presidential proclamation, congressional legislation, and eventually constitutional amendment, but the practical destruction of slavery was the product of war, what Lincoln called war's "friction and abrasion." When the war ended in 1865, the institution had taken a heavy pounding, especially from within. More than 100,000 men fled bondage, took up arms, and attacked slavery directly. Other men and women stayed in the slave quarters, and as the slaveholders' grip loosened, they staked a claim to more freedom.

**SOUTHERN WOMEN**
*Women such as these North Carolinians were expected to shift their energies from family to the southern cause. Most served by sewing uniforms, knitting socks, and rolling bandages at home. Some founded hospitals, while others worked in them nursing the sick and wounded. Sarah Morgan Dawson of Baton Rouge, Louisiana, declared that she would be a soldier if she had been born a man, but "as I was unfortunately born a woman, I stay home and pray with heart and soul."*
Museum of the Confederacy.

In dozens of ways, the war disrupted the routine, organization, and discipline of bondage. Almost immediately, it called the master away, leaving white women to assume managerial responsibilities. As one plantation mistress wrote to a newspaper, "Do impress upon the soldiers . . . that we are *working* for them, while they are *fighting* for us—and that their wants shall be supplied, as long as there is a *woman* or a *dollar* in the 'Southern Confederacy.'" But plantation mistresses could not maintain traditional standards of slave discipline. By stifling the production of cotton, war had divorced slaves from their principal work. Also, the impressment of slaves severed the personal relationship between masters and slaves. Moreover, military action increasingly sliced through the South's farms and plantations. Sometimes slaveholders fled, leaving behind their slaves. More often, they took their slaves with them. But flight meant additional chaos and offered slaves more opportunities to resist bondage. In large parts of the South, the balance of power between master and slave gradually shifted. Slaves got to the fields late, worked indifferently, and quit early. Some slaveholders responded violently, but most saw no alternative but to strike bargains—offering gifts or part of the crop—to keep slaves at home and at work. The changes in slave behavior shocked slaveholders. They had prided themselves on "knowing" their slaves, and they learned that they did not know them at all. When the war began, a North Carolina woman praised her slaves as "diligent and respectful." When it ended, she said, "As to the idea of a *faithful servant, it is all a fiction.*"

## The North at War

Because rebel armies generally remained within the Confederate borders, the North remained untouched by fighting. But Northerners could not avoid being touched by war. Almost every family had a son, a husband, a brother in uniform. Moreover, this war—a total war—blurred the distinction between home front and battlefield. As in the South, men marched off to fight, but preserving the country, either Union or Confederacy, was also women's work. For civilians as well as soldiers, for women as well as men, war was transforming.

The need to build and fuel the Union war machine caused the northern economy to boom. The North sent nearly two million men into the military and still increased production in almost every area. But because the rewards and burdens of patriotism were not evenly distributed, the North experienced sharp, even violent, divisions. Workers confronted employers, whites confronted blacks, and Republicans confronted Democrats. Still, Northerners on the home front remained fervently attached to the ideals of free labor and the Union.

## The Government and the Economy

Democrats and Republicans traditionally disagreed about the best way to encourage economic growth. Democrats generally argued that in economic matters, the less government intrusion the better, while Republicans advocated government support to develop economic resources. Democratic domination of national politics for two decades before the war meant that the Republicans inherited a financial and economic structure that restricted government direction of the economy. There were no national banking system, no national currency, and no federal income or excise taxes.

---

*For civilians as well as soldiers, for women as well as men, war was transforming.*

---

The secession of eleven slave states cut the Democrats' strength in Congress in half and destroyed their capacity to resist the Republican steamroller. The Republican platform of 1860 advocated an array of federal programs to encourage economic growth, and during the war Republicans had little trouble enacting their philosophy into law. In May 1862, Congress approved the Homestead Act, which offered 160 acres of public land to settlers who would live and labor on it. In time, the Homestead Act resulted in more than a million new farms in the West. Two months later, Congress passed the Pacific Railroad Act, which provided massive federal assistance for the building of a transcontinental railroad. When completed in 1869, the railroad ran from Omaha to San Francisco. Congress also enacted a higher tariff. Republicans defended the legislation by arguing that additional economic muscle meant increased military might.

The Legal Tender Act of February 1862 created a national currency, paper money that Northerners called "greenbacks." With passage of the National Banking Act in February 1863, Congress created a system of national banks. Congress also enacted a series of sweeping tax laws that taxed everything from incomes to liquor to billiard tables. The Internal Revenue Act created the Bureau of Internal Revenue to collect taxes. By revolutionizing the country's banking, monetary, and tax structures, the Republicans generated enormous economic power.

Two additional initiatives had long-term consequences for agriculture and industry. Congress created a Department of Agriculture and passed the Land-Grant College Act (also known as the Morrill Act after its sponsor, Representative Justin Morrill of Vermont), which set aside public lands to support universities that emphasized "agriculture and mechanical arts." The first task of Lincoln's administration was winning the war, but initiatives from Washington were permanently changing the nation.

## Women and Work on the Home Front

With more than a million farm men called to the military, farm women added men's chores to their own. "I met more women driving teams on the road and saw more at work in the fields than men," a visitor to Iowa reported in the fall of 1862. Rising production figures testified to their success in plowing, planting, and harvesting. Rapid mechanization assisted farm women in their new roles. Cyrus McCormick sold 165,000 of his reapers during the war years. The combination of high prices and increased production ensured that war and prosperity walked hand in hand in the rural North.

While a few industries, such as textiles (which depended on southern cotton), declined during the war, many more grew. Huge profits prompted one Pennsylvania ironmaster to remark, "I am in no hurry for peace." The boom proved friendlier to owners than to workers, however. In industry, as in agriculture, prewar trends continued to accelerate: specialization, mechanization, growth in the size of the workplace, and loss of worker control. With orders pouring in and a million workers siphoned off into the military, unemployment declined and wages often rose. But inflation and taxes cut so deeply that workers' standard of living actually fell.

As on the farm, women in cities stepped into jobs vacated by men, particularly in manufacturing, and also into essentially new occupations, such as government civil service. Often, they had no choice because they could not make ends meet on their

**UNION ORDNANCE, YORKTOWN, VIRGINIA**
*As the North successfully harnessed its enormous industrial capacity to the needs of war, cannon, mortars, and shells poured out of its factories. A fraction of that abundance is seen here in 1862 at Yorktown, ready for transportation to Union troops in the field. Two years later, Abraham Lincoln observed that the Union was "gaining strength, and may if need be maintain the contest indefinitely. . . . Material resources are now more complete and abundant than ever. . . . The national resources are unexhausted, and, as we believe, inexhaustible."* Library of Congress.

husbands' army pay. Women made up about one-quarter of the manufacturing workforce when the war began and one-third when it ended. But as more women entered the workforce, employers cut wages. By 1864, fourteen-hour days earned New York seamstresses only an average of $1.54 per week. As Cincinnati seamstresses explained to Abraham Lincoln, their wages were not enough "to sustain life." However, tough times failed to undermine the patriotism of most workers, who took pride in their contribution to northern victory.

Middle-class white women were supposed to be homebodies, and hundreds of thousands contributed to the war effort in traditional ways. Like many southern white women, they labored long hours in sewing circles, wrapped bandages, and sold homemade goods at local fairs to raise money to aid the soldiers. Unpaid labor by "lady volunteers" proved crucial in supplying the opposing war machines. But other women expressed their patriotism in an untraditional way—as wartime nurses.

Thousands of women on both sides defied prejudices about female delicacy and volunteered to nurse the wounded. Many of the northern female volunteers worked through the U.S. Sanitary Commission, a civilian organization that bought and distributed clothing, food, and medicine and recruited doctors and nurses. Nursing meant working in the midst of unspeakable sights, sounds, and smells, but it brought the profound satisfaction of displaying competence and serving well. Katherine Wormeley of Rhode Island, who served three months as a volunteer nurse on a hospital ship in 1862, recorded in her diary, "We all know in our hearts that it is thorough enjoyment to be here,—it is life."

Some volunteer nurses went on to become paid military nurses. In April 1861, Dorothea Dix, well known for her efforts to reform insane asylums, was named Superintendent of Female Nurses, and eventually some three thousand women served under her. Most nurses worked in hospitals behind the battle lines, but some, like Clara Barton, who later founded the American Red Cross, worked in battlefield units. At Antietam, as Barton was giving a wounded man a drink, a bullet ripped through her sleeve and struck him in the chest, killing him instantly.

## Politics and Dissent

At first, the bustle of economic and military mobilization seemed to silence politics, with Democrats supporting the Union as fervently as Republicans. But bipartisan unity did not last. Within a year, Democrats were labeling the Republican administration a "reign of terror," and Republicans were calling Democrats the party of "Dixie, Davis, and the Devil." As bruising as the political struggle became, the North's two-party system actually strengthened government. In the Confederacy, which had no well-organized parties, political disagreement spiraled down into fruitless bickering, but in the Union, parties helped to discipline and legitimize political debate. Fear of being driven from office by their rival's victory served to unify each party and to strengthen the political structure.

Nevertheless, Republican policy pushed the Democrats toward a dangerous alienation. Under Lincoln, the Republicans emancipated the slaves, subsidized private business, and expanded federal power at every turn. The Lincoln administration argued that the war required a loose interpretation of the Constitution, to which the Democrats countered, "The Constitution is as binding in war as in peace." Democrats had good evidence that Lincoln did not always reach first for a copy of the Constitution when he confronted a problem. In September 1862, in an effort to stifle opposition to the war, Lincoln placed under martial law any person who discouraged enlistments, resisted the draft, or engaged in "disloyal" practices. Before the war ended, his administration had imprisoned nearly fourteen thousand individuals, most in the border states. The campaign fell short of a reign of terror, for most were not northern Democratic opponents but Confederate citizens, blockade runners, and foreign nationals, and most of the arrested gained quick release. But the administration's heavy-handed tactics did suppress free speech.

One Democratic dissenter, ex-Congressman Clement L. Vallandigham of Ohio, proved indefatigable. He lambasted every Republican innovation, which meant most of Lincoln's conduct of the war.

After the Emancipation Proclamation, Vallandigham came out against the war itself. He denounced this "wicked, cruel and unnecessary war" waged "for the purpose of crushing out liberty and erecting a despotism . . . a war for the freedom of the blacks and the enslavement of the whites."

Was such talk protected by the right of free speech, or was it treason? In April 1863, General Ambrose Burnside decided that "the habit of declaring sympathy for the enemy will not be allowed" and arrested Vallandigham for treason. Lincoln had not ordered the arrest but decided to back his general, arguing that the Constitution permitted the military arrest of civilians during rebellions. "Must I shoot a simple-minded soldier boy who deserts, while I must not touch a hair of a wily agitator who induces him to desert?" Lincoln asked. Vallandigham's arrest and conviction in a military court sparked Democratic protest throughout the North. In 1866, a year after the war ended, the Supreme Court in *Ex parte Milligan* declared unconstitutional military trials of civilians where civil courts were still able to operate.

When the Republican-dominated Congress enacted the draft law in March 1863, Democrats had another grievance. The act required that all men between the ages of twenty and forty-five enroll and make themselves available for a lottery, which would decide who went to war. What poor men found particularly galling were provisions that allowed a draftee to hire a substitute or simply to pay a $300 fee and get out of his military obligation. As in the South, common folk could be heard chanting, "A rich man's war and a poor man's fight."

Democrats linked the draft and emancipation, arguing that Republicans employed an unconstitutional means (the draft) to achieve an unconstitutional end (emancipation). In the summer of 1863, antidraft, antiblack mobs went on rampages in northern cities. New York experienced an explosion of unprecedented proportions. Solidly Democratic Irish workingmen, crowded into stinking, disease-ridden tenements, gouged by inflation, enraged by the inequities of the draft, and dead set against fighting to free blacks, erupted in four days of rioting. By the time police and soldiers restored order, at least 105 people, most of them black, lay dead.

The riots stunned black Northerners, but the racist mobs failed to achieve their purpose: the subordination of African Americans. Free black leaders had lobbied aggressively for emancipation, and after Lincoln's proclamation they fanned out over the North agitating for equality. They won some small wartime successes. Illinois and Iowa overturned laws that excluded blacks from entering the states. Illinois and Ohio began permitting blacks to testify in court. But defeat was more common. Indiana, for example, continued to forbid blacks to vote, testify, and attend public schools, and additional blacks were not allowed to enter the state.

# Grinding out Victory, 1863–1865

In the early months of 1863, the Union's prospects looked bleak, while the Confederate cause stood at high tide. But in July 1863, the tide receded. The military man who was most responsible for seeing that it never rose again was Ulysses S. Grant. Lifted from obscurity by brilliant successes in the West in 1862 and 1863, Grant became *"the great man of the day,"* one man observed in July 1864, "perhaps of the age." Elevated to supreme command, Grant knit together a powerful war machine that integrated a sophisticated command structure, modern technology, and complex logistics and supply systems. But the arithmetic of this plain man remained unchanged: Killing more of the enemy than he kills of you equaled "the complete overthrow of the rebellion."

The North ground out the victory, bloody battle by bloody battle. The balance tipped in the Union's favor in 1863, but if the Confederacy was beaten, Southerners clearly did not know it. The fighting reached new levels of ferocity in the last two years of the war. As national elections approached in the fall of 1864, a discouraged Lincoln expected a war-weary North to make him a one-term president. Instead, northern voters declared their willingness to continue the war in the defense of the ideals of union and freedom.

## Vicksburg and Gettysburg

Perched on the bluffs above the eastern bank of the Mississippi River, Vicksburg, Mississippi, bristled with cannon and dared Yankee ships to try to pass (Map 15.3). This Confederate stronghold stood between Union forces and complete control of the river. Grant attacked from the south and east, and when the Confederates beat back the assault, he

began siege operations to starve out the enemy. Civilian inhabitants took to living in caves to escape incessant Union cannon bombardment, and to survive they soon began eating mules and rats.

Eventually, the siege succeeded. On July 4, 1863, nearly thirty thousand rebels marched out of Vicksburg, stacked their arms, and surrendered unconditionally. A Yankee captain wrote home to his wife: "The backbone of the Rebellion is this day broken. The Confederacy is divided. . . . Vicksburg is ours. The Mississippi River is opened, and Gen. Grant is to be our next President."

On the same Fourth of July that a grateful nation received the news of Vicksburg, word arrived that Union forces had crushed General Lee at Gettysburg, Pennsylvania (see Map 15.3). Lee's triumph two months earlier at Chancellorsville over Joseph "Fighting Joe" Hooker had revived his confidence, even though the battle cost him his favorite commander, the incomparable Stonewall Jackson, accidentally shot in the dark by his own troops. Lee wanted to relieve Virginia of the burden of the fighting, and he felt bold enough to think that he could deliver a morale-crunching defeat to the Yankees on their home turf.

*The North ground out the victory, bloody battle by bloody battle. The balance tipped in the Union's favor in 1863, but if the Confederacy was beaten, Southerners clearly did not know it.*

In June, Lee's 75,000-man Army of Northern Virginia invaded Pennsylvania. On June 28, the Army of the Potomac, under its new commander, General George G. Meade, moved quickly to intercept it. Advanced units of both armies met at the small town of Gettysburg, and Union forces occupied the high ground. Three days of furious fighting, involving 165,000 soldiers, could not dislodge them from the ridges and hills. But Lee ached for a decisive victory, and on July 3 he ordered a major assault against the Union center on Cemetery Ridge. The open, rolling fields provided the dug-in Yankees with three-quarters of a mile of clear vision, and they raked the mile-wide line of Confederates with cannon and rifle fire. Time and again, the rebels closed ranks and raced on, until finally their momentum failed. Gettysburg cost Lee more than one-third of his army—28,000 casualties. "It's all my

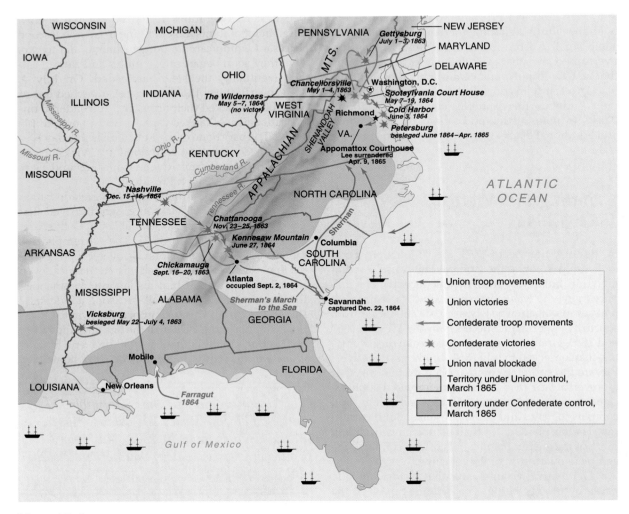

MAP 15.3
*The Civil War, 1863–1865*
*Ulysses S. Grant's victory at Vicksburg divided the Confederacy at the Mississippi River.*
*William T. Sherman's march from Chattanooga to Savannah divided it again. In northern Vir-*
*ginia, Robert E. Lee fought fiercely, but Grant's larger, better-supplied armies prevailed.*

fault," he said. In a drenching rain on the night of July 4, 1863, he marched his battered army back to Virginia.

The twin disasters at Vicksburg and Gettysburg proved to be the turning point of the war. The Confederacy could not replace the nearly 60,000 soldiers who were captured, wounded, or killed. Lee never launched another major offensive north of the Mason-Dixon line. But it is hindsight that permits us to see the pair of battles as decisive. At the time the Confederacy still controlled the heartland

of the South, and Lee, back on the defensive in Virginia, still had a vicious sting. War-weariness threatened to erode the North's will to win before Union armies destroyed the Confederacy's ability to go on.

## Grant Takes Command

In September 1863, Union General William Rose-crans placed his army in a dangerous situation in Chattanooga, Tennessee, where he had retreated after taking a whipping at the battle of Chicka-mauga (see Map 15.3). Rebels surrounded the dis-organized bluecoats and threatened to starve them into submission. Ulysses S. Grant, whom Lincoln had made commander of all Union forces between the Mississippi and the Appalachians, arrived in Chattanooga in October. Within weeks, he opened an effective supply line, broke the siege, and then (largely because troops disobeyed orders and charged wildly up Missionary Ridge) routed the Confederate army. The victory at Chattanooga had immense strategic value. It opened the door to Georgia. It also confirmed Lincoln's estimation of Grant. In March 1864, the president asked him to come east to become the general in chief of all Union armies.

In Washington, Grant implemented his grand strategy of a war of annihilation. He ordered a se-ries of simultaneous assaults from Virginia to Louisiana. Two actions proved more significant than the others. In one, General William T. Sherman, whom Grant appointed his successor to command the western armies, plunged southeast toward At-lanta. In the other, Grant, who took control of the Army of the Potomac, went head to head with Lee for almost four straight weeks in Virginia.

Grant and Lee met in early May 1864 at the Wilderness, a dense tangle of scrub oaks and small pines that proved to be Lee's ally, for it helped off-set the Yankees' numerical superiority. Often unable to see more than ten paces, the armies pounded away at each other until 18,000 Yankees and 11,000 rebels had fallen. But the savagery of the Wilderness did not compare with that at Spot-sylvania Court House a few days later. Frenzied men fought hand to hand for eighteen hours in the rain. One veteran remembered men "piled upon each other in some places four layers deep, ex-hibiting every ghastly phase of mutilation." Spot-sylvania cost Grant another 18,000 casualties and Lee 10,000. But the Yankee bulldog would not let go. Grant kept moving and caught Lee again at Cold Harbor, where he lost 13,000 additional troops to Lee's 5,000. (See the Historical Question on page 406.)

Twice as many Northerners as Southerners died in the four weeks of fighting in Virginia in the spring of 1864. Yet Grant did not consider himself defeated. Since Lee had only half the number of troops, he lost proportionally as many men as Grant. More-over, the campaign had carried Grant to the out-skirts of Petersburg, just south of the Confederate capital. Since most of the major railroad lines sup-

**GRANT AT COLD HARBOR**
*Seated next to his chief of staff, John A. Rawlins, at his Cold Harbor, Virginia, headquarters, Ulysses S. Grant plots his next move against Robert E. Lee. On June 3, 1864, Grant ordered frontal assaults against entrenched Confederate forces, resulting in enormous Union losses. "I am dis-gusted with the generalship displayed," young Brigadier General Emory Upton exclaimed. "Our men have, in many cases, been foolishly and wantonly slaughtered." Years later, Grant said that he regretted the assault at Cold Harbor, but in 1864 he kept pushing toward Richmond.* Chicago Historical Society.

# Why Did So Many Soldiers Die?

F ROM 1861 TO 1865, Americans killed Americans on a scale that had never before been seen. Not until the First World War, a half century later, would the world match (and surpass) the killing fields at Shiloh, Antietam, and Gettysburg. Why were the totals so appallingly large? Why did 260,000 rebel soldiers and 373,000 Union soldiers die in the Civil War?

The balance between the ability to kill and the ability to save lives had tipped disastrously toward death. The sheer size of the armies—some battles involved more than 200,000 soldiers—ensured that battlefields would turn red with blood. Moreover, armies fought with antiquated strategy. In the generals' eyes, the ideal soldier remained the veteran of Napoleonic warfare, a man trained to advance with his comrades in a compact, close-order formation. Theory also emphasized frontal assaults. In classrooms at West Point and on the high plains of Mexico in the 1840s, men who would one day be officers in rival armies learned that infantry advancing shoulder to shoulder, supported by artillery, carried the day.

But by the 1860s, modern technology had made such strategy obsolete. Weapons with rifled barrels were replacing old smoothbore muskets. Whereas muskets had an effective range of only about eighty yards, rifles propelled spinning bullets four times as far. The rifle's greater range and accuracy, along with cannons firing canisters filled with flesh-ripping, bone-breaking steel shot, made sitting ducks of charging infantry units and gave enormous advantage to entrenched defensive forces. As a result, battles took thousands of lives on a single afternoon. On July 2, 1862, the morning after the battle at Malvern Hill in eastern Virginia, a Union officer surveyed the scene: "Over five thousand dead and wounded men were on the ground . . . enough were alive and moving to give to the field a singular crawling effect."

Soldiers who littered the battlefields often lay for hours, sometimes days, without water or care of any kind. When the war began, no one anticipated casualty lists with thousands of names. Union and Confederate medical departments could not cope with skirmishes, much less large-scale battles. They had no ambulance corps to lift the wounded from the battlefields. They had no field hospitals to deliver them to. At first, the Quartermaster Department, which was responsible for constructing Union hospitals, answered demands that it do something with the retort "Men need guns, not beds." It took the shock of massive casualties to compel reform. Although a lack of resources meant that the South lagged behind the North, both North and South gradually organized effective ambulance corps, built hospitals, and hired trained surgeons and nurses.

Soldiers did not always count speedy transportation to a field hospital as a blessing, however. As one Union soldier said, "I had rather risk a battle than the Hospitals." Real danger lurked behind the lines. While the technology of killing had advanced to very high standards, medicine remained in the dark ages. Physicians had the reputation of butchers, and soldiers dreaded the operating table more than they did entrenched riflemen. Serious wounds to the leg or arm usually meant amputation, the best way doctors knew to save lives. After major battles, surgeons worked among piles of wounded men's limbs.

The wounded man's real enemy was not callous doctors, but medical ignorance. Physicians had almost no knowledge of the cause and transmission of disease or the use of antiseptics. Lacking knowledge of basic germ theory, they spread infection almost every time they operated. Doctors wore the same bloody smock for days and washed their hands and their scalpels and saws in buckets of dirty water. When they had difficulty threading their needles, they wet the thread with their own saliva. Soldiers often did not survive amputations, not because of the operation but because of the infection that inevitably followed. More than half of the Union soldiers whose legs were amputated

**THE DEAD OF ANTIETAM**
*In October 1862, Mathew
Brady opened an exhibition at
his New York gallery that
shocked the nation. Entitled
"The Dead of Antietam" and
consisting of ninety-five photographs, it presented the battlefield as the soldiers saw it.
This photograph depicts Confederate troops lined up for
burial. Among the thousands
of visitors to the exhibit was a
reporter for the* New York
Times, *who observed: "Mr.
Brady has done something to
bring to us the terrible reality
and earnestness of the war. If
he has not brought bodies and
laid them in our door-yards
and along [our] streets, he has
done something very like it."*
Library of Congress.

above the knee died. A Union doctor discovered in 1864 that bromine arrested gangrene, but the best most amputees could hope for was maggots, which ate dead flesh on the stump and thus inhibited the spread of infection. During the Civil War, nearly one wounded rebel soldier died for every five wounded and one in every six Yankees. A century later, in Vietnam, the proportion was one wounded American soldier in four hundred.

Soldiers who avoided battlefield wounds and hospital infections still faced disease. Killer diseases swept through crowded army camps, where latrines were often in dangerous proximity to water supplies. The principal killers were dysentery and typhoid, but pneumonia and malaria also cut down thousands of men. Doctors did what they could, but their treatments often only added to the misery. They prescribed doses of turpentine for patients with typhoid, fought respiratory problems with mustard plasters, and attacked intestinal disorders with blisters and sulfuric acid.

Dorothea Dix, Clara Barton, Juliet Ann Opie Hopkins, and thousands of other female nurses in the North and South improved the wounded men's odds and alleviated their misery. Civilian relief agencies, such as the U.S. Sanitary Commission and the Women's Relief Society of the Confederacy, promoted hygiene in army camps and made some headway. Nevertheless, disease killed approximately twice as many soldiers as did combat. Many who died of disease were prisoners of war. Approximately 30,000 Northerners died in Confederate prisons, and approximately 26,000 Southerners died in Union prisons. No northern prison, however, could equal the horror of Andersonville in southern Georgia. In August 1864, about 33,000 emaciated men lived in unspeakable conditions in a twenty-six-acre barren stockade with no shelter except what the prisoners were able to construct. More than 13,000 perished.

In the end, 633,000 northern and southern soldiers died, a staggering death toll.

plying Richmond ran through Petersburg, Lee had little choice but to defend the city. Grant abandoned the costly tactic of the frontal assault and began a siege that immobilized both armies and dragged on for nine months.

There was no pause in "Uncle Billy" Sherman's invasion of Georgia. Grant had instructed Sherman to "get into the interior of the enemy's country as far as you can, inflicting all the damage you can against their War resources." In early May, while Grant thrashed in the Wilderness, Sherman moved 100,000 men south against the 65,000 rebels in the rugged mountains of northern Georgia. Skillful maneuvering, constant skirmishing, and one pitched battle (Kennesaw Mountain) brought Sherman to Atlanta, which fell on September 1.

Sherman was only warming up. Intending to "make Georgia howl," he marched out of Atlanta on November 15 with 62,000 battle-hardened veterans, heading for Savannah, 285 miles away. Cutting a swath from 25 to 60 miles wide, federal troops, one veteran remembered, "destroyed all we could not eat, stole their niggers, burned their cotton & gins, spilled their sorghum, burned & twisted their R. Roads and raised Hell generally." Sherman's scorched-earth campaign aimed at destroying the will of the southern people. A few weeks earlier, General Philip Sheridan had tried as much in the Shenandoah Valley, complying with Grant's order to turn the valley into "a barren waste . . . so that crows flying over it for the balance of this season will have to carry their provender [food] with them." When Sherman's troops entered an undefended Savannah in the third week of December, the general telegraphed Lincoln that he had "a Christmas gift" for him.

## The Election of 1864

In the fall, white men in the Union states turned to the election of a president. Never before had a nation held general elections in the midst of war. "We can not have free government without elections," Lincoln explained, "and if the rebellion could force us to forgo, or postpone a national election, it might fairly claim to have already conquered and ruined us."

Lincoln's determination to hold elections is especially noteworthy because the Democratic Party smelled victory. With Sherman temporarily checked outside Atlanta and Grant bogged down in the siege of Petersburg, frustration had settled over the North. Rankled by inflation, the draft, the attack on

civil liberties, and the commitment to blacks, Northerners appeared ready for a change. Lincoln himself concluded in the gloomy summer of 1864, "It seems exceedingly probable that this administration will not be re-elected."

Democrats were badly divided, however. "Peace" Democrats insisted on an armistice, while "war" Democrats supported the conflict but opposed Republican means of fighting it. They tried to paper over the chasm by nominating a war candidate, General George McClellan, but adopting a peace platform that demanded that "immediate efforts be made for a cessation of hostilities." Republicans labeled the peace plank a conspiracy of "Copperheads" (after a deadly, easily concealed snake) to sell out the Union and claimed that it "virtually proposed to surrender the country to the rebels in arms against us."

Lincoln was no shoo-in for renomination, much less reelection. But frightened by the strength of the peace Democrats, the Republican Party stuck with Lincoln. In an effort to reach out to the largest number of voters, however, the Republicans made two changes. First, they chose a new name. As the Union Party, they made it easier for prowar Democrats to embrace Lincoln. Second, they chose a new vice presidential candidate. Dumping Hannibal Hamlin of Maine, the incumbent vice president, they turned to Andrew Johnson of Tennessee, the only southern senator to remain in Congress when his colleagues fled south in the winter of 1860–61. As a Southerner, a former slaveholder, and a former Democrat, Johnson personified the message that the party of Lincoln was broad enough to include any uncompromising Unionist.

Lincoln's pessimism about being reelected proved to be unfounded. The capture of Atlanta in September had turned the political tide in favor of the Republicans. Lincoln received 55 percent of the popular vote, but his electoral margin was a whopping 212 to McClellan's 21. The Republicans also stormed back in the congressional elections, gaining large margins over the Democrats in the Senate and the House. The Union Party bristled with factions, but they united for a resounding victory. The victory gave Lincoln a mandate to continue the war until slavery and the Confederacy were dead.

## The Confederacy Collapses

Jefferson Davis found little to celebrate as the new year of 1865 dawned in Richmond. Military disaster littered the Confederate landscape. With the destruction of John B. Hood's army at Nashville in November, the interior of the Confederacy lay in Yankee hands. Sherman's troops, resting momentarily in Savannah, eyed South Carolina hungrily. Only Lee's army remained, and Grant had it pinned down in Petersburg just a few miles from Richmond. Southerners took out their frustration and bitterness on their president. Kinder than most, Alexander Stephens, vice president of the Confederacy, likened Davis to "my poor old blind and deaf dog."

At the end, events came with a rush. On February 1, 1865, Sherman's troops stormed out of Savannah into South Carolina, the "cradle of the Confederacy." But before Sherman could push through North Carolina and arrive at the rear of Lee's army at Petersburg, where he expected to crush the Confederates between his hammer and Grant's anvil, Lee abandoned the city. Jefferson Davis fled Richmond, and the capital city fell a few days later. Grant pursued Lee for one hundred miles, until Lee surrendered on April 9, 1865, in a farmhouse near Appomattox Courthouse, Virginia. The beaten man arrived in an immaculate full-dress uniform, complete with sash and sword; the victor came in his usual mud-splattered private's outfit. Grant offered a generous peace. He allowed Lee's men to return home and to take their horses to help "put in a crop to carry themselves and their families through the next winter." With Lee gone, the remaining ragtag Confederate armies lost hope and gave up. After four years, the war was over.

The day after Lee's surrender, a brass band led a happy crowd of three thousand up to the White House, where they pleaded with Lincoln for a speech. He begged off and asked the band to strike up "Dixie." He knew that the rebels had claimed the tune as their own, he said, but it was one of his favorites, and now he was taking it back. The crowd roared its approval, and the band played "Dixie," following it with "Yankee Doodle." No one was more relieved than Lincoln that the war was over, but his celebration was restrained. He told his cabinet that his postwar burdens would weigh almost as heavily as those of wartime. But Lincoln had other things on his mind when he attended the theater on the evening of Good Friday, April 14, 1865. While he and his wife, Mary, enjoyed *Our American Cousin*, a British comedy, John Wilkes Booth, an actor with southern sympathies, slipped into the president's box and mortally wounded Lincoln with a single shot to his head. The man who had led the nation through the war would not lead it in its postwar search for a just peace.

**RUINS OF RICHMOND**
*A Union soldier and a small boy in a Union cap contemplate the silence and devastation of Richmond, the Confederacy's capital. On their way out of the city on the evening of April 2, 1865, Confederate demolition squads set fire to tobacco warehouses and ammunition dumps. Huge explosions tore holes in the city, and windswept fires destroyed much of what was left standing. As one Confederate observed, "The old war-scarred city seemed to prefer annihilation to conquest."*
Library of Congress.

## Conclusion: The Second American Revolution

The Civil War had a profound effect on the nation and its people. It laid waste to the South. Three-fourths of southern white men of military age served in the army, and at least half of them were captured, wounded, or killed or died of disease. The war destroyed two-fifths of the South's livestock, wrecked half of the farm machinery, and blackened dozens of cities and towns. And, as Frederick Douglass had predicted, it ended slavery, the linchpin of southern society and economy. The immediate impact of the war on the North was more paradoxical. Putting down the slaveholders' rebellion cost the North a heavy price: 373,000 lives. But rather than devastating the land, the war set the countryside and cities humming with business activity.

A transformed nation emerged from the crucible of war. Antebellum America was decentralized politically and loosely integrated economically. To bend the resources of the country to a Union victory, Congress enacted legislation that reshaped the nation's political and economic character. It adopted policies that established the sovereignty of the federal government and the dominance of industrial capitalism. Moreover, the common sacrifice of northern people to save the nation created an even more fierce national loyalty. The shift in power from South to North and the creation of a national government, a national economy, and a national spirit led one historian to call the American Civil War the "Second American Revolution."

Most revolutionary of all, the war ended slavery. Because that ancient labor and racial system was entangled in almost every aspect of southern life, slavery's uprooting would mean fundamental change. But the full meaning of abolition remained unclear in 1865. The task of determining the new economic, political, and social status of four million ex-slaves would be the principal task of Reconstruction.

## CHRONOLOGY

1861 **March 4.** Abraham Lincoln sworn in as sixteenth president of the United States.

**April 12–13.** Confederate forces attack Fort Sumter, South Carolina, in opening engagement of Civil War.

**April.** Dorothea Dix named superintendent of female nurses.

**April–May.** Four Upper South states secede and join Confederacy.

**July.** Union forces routed at Manassas, Virginia, in first major clash of war.

**August.** Congress approves First Confiscation Act, which allows seizure of any slave employed by Confederate military.

1862 **February.** Legal Tender Act creates first national currency, called "greenbacks."

**February.** Union forces in West under General Ulysses S. Grant capture Fort Henry and Fort Donelson and drive Confederates from Kentucky and most of Tennessee.

**April.** Battle of Shiloh in Tennessee results in huge casualties and ends Confederate bid to control Mississippi valley.

**April.** Confederate Congress passes first draft law in American history.

**May.** Homestead Act offers western land to those who would live and labor on it.

**May–July.** General George McClellan's Union forces defeated during peninsula campaign in Virginia.

**July.** Congress approves second Confiscation Act, freeing all slaves of rebel masters.

**July.** Congress passes Militia Act, authorizing enrollment of blacks in Union military.

1862  **September 17.** Battle of Antietam stops Lee's advance into Maryland, but Confederate forces escape to Virginia.

**September 22.** Lincoln announces preliminary emancipation proclamation.

**December.** Battle of Fredericksburg results in huge Union casualties.

1863  **January 1.** Emancipation Proclamation becomes law, freeing slaves in areas still in rebellion.

**February.** National Banking Act creates system of national banks.

**March.** Congress authorizes draft.

**July.** Vicksburg falls to Union forces under Grant, effectively cutting Confederacy in two along Mississippi River.

**July.** Battle of Gettysburg results in Confederate defeat and Lee's last offensive into North.

1864  **March.** Grant appointed general in chief of all Union forces.

**May–June.** Grant's forces engage Confederates in Virginia in bloodiest fighting of war, from Wilderness campaign to beginnings of siege of Petersburg.

**September.** Atlanta falls to Union forces under General William T. Sherman.

**November.** Lincoln reelected president.

**December.** Sherman occupies Savannah after scorched-earth campaign in Georgia.

1865  **April 9.** Lee surrenders to Grant at Appomattox Courthouse, Virginia, essentially ending Confederate resistance.

**April 14.** Lincoln shot by John Wilkes Booth at Ford's Theatre in Washington. He dies on April 15, succeeded by Vice President Andrew Johnson.

# SUGGESTED READINGS

Ira Berlin et al., *Free at Last: A Documentary History of Slavery, Freedom, and the Civil War* (1992). A stunning collection of testimony by ex-slaves about the meaning of freedom.

David W. Blight, *Frederick Douglass's Civil War: Keeping Faith in Jubilee* (1989). An eloquent depiction of Douglass's efforts on behalf of freedom.

Gabor S. Boritt, ed., *Why the Confederacy Lost* (1992); David H. Donald, ed., *Why the North Won the Civil War* (1961). Two collections of essays that probe the large issues of victory and defeat.

Catherine Clinton and Nina Silber, eds., *Divided Houses: Gender and the Civil War* (1992). Lively essays that explore gender issues in the North and South.

David Donald, *Lincoln* (1995). A superb biography of Lincoln.

Drew Gilpin Faust, *Mothers of Invention: Women of the Slaveholding South in the American Civil War* (1996); George C. Rable, *Civil Wars: Women and the Crisis of Southern Nationalism* (1989). Provocative analyses of southern women at war.

Joseph T. Glatthaar, *Forged in Battle: The Civil War Alliance of Black Soldiers and White Officers* (1990). A thoughtful exploration of the experience of black soldiers.

William S. McFeely, *Grant* (1981). A provocative interpretation of the Union general's personality and career.

James M. McPherson, *Battle Cry of Freedom: The Civil War Era* (1988). A sweeping survey of the war's coming, course, and consequences.

Stephen B. Oates, *A Woman of Valor: Clara Barton and the Civil War* (1994); Thomas J. Brown, *Dorothea Dix: New England Reformer* (1998). Fine biographies of the North's most famous nurses.

Philip S. Paludan, *"A People's Contest": The Union at War, 1861–1865* (1988). A comprehensive survey of the North at war.

James I. Robertson Jr., *Soldiers Blue and Gray* (1988). The war as experienced by the soldiers.

Emory M. Thomas, *The Confederate Nation, 1861–1865* (1979). The best history of the Confederacy.

### ONE-CENT PRIMER

*"The people are hungry and thirsty after knowledge,"* a former slave from South Carolina observed after the Civil War. Future African American leader Booker T. Washington remembered *"a whole race trying to go to school. Few were too young, and none too old, to make the attempt to learn."* Inexpensive elementary textbooks (this humble eight-page primer cost a penny) offered poor ex-slaves the basic elements of literacy—the letters of the alphabet and the sounds they make. For people who had been forbidden to learn to read and write as slaves, literacy symbolized freedom. It also meant that deeply religious people could experience the joy of reading the Bible. Literacy provided a crucial tool for negotiating the hostile world of the postwar South. Reading and writing permitted African Americans to understand labor agreements, sign contracts, and participate knowledgeably in politics.

The William Gladstone Collection.

# RECONSTRUCTION
## 1863–1877

# 16

WHEN THE WAR WAS OVER, swarms of northern journalists and government officials rushed to the South to see what four years of fighting had accomplished. Ugly stories of stiff-necked defiance toward Yankees and brutal violence toward ex-slaves had drifted northward. Andrew Johnson, Abraham Lincoln's successor in the White House, asked General Carl Schurz to undertake a special fact-finding tour to assess conditions in the ex-Confederate states. In July 1865, Schurz, a leading antislavery lecturer and Union general, arrived in Charleston, South Carolina, the "Queen City of the South."

Charleston greeted the visitor with an empty harbor, rotting wharves, and gutted buildings. The city looked, Schurz observed, as if it had been struck with "the sudden and irresistible force of a thunderbolt." Cattle grazed in its weed-filled streets. Schurz met former cotton kings and rice barons who could not afford to buy breakfast. Ex-slaves, now Union soldiers, patrolled the city's streets. Schools overflowed with African American children whom it was formerly considered a crime to educate. The Citadel, the state's military school, where once "the chivalric youth of South Carolina was educated for the task of perpetuating slavery by force of arms," now housed the Fifty-fourth Massachusetts Colored Regiment.

Some whites openly expressed their hatred for the new order. Schurz came across defiant young men still "in a swearing mood" who wanted to "fight the war over again." Planters had not changed their minds about slavery. "The nigger is free, to be sure," ex-slaveholders told Schurz repeatedly, "but he will not work unless compelled to work; we must make him work somehow." Women too, he discovered, remained as "vindictive and defiant as ever." Schurz witnessed one incident in a hotel. "A day or two ago a Union officer, yielding to an impulse of politeness, handed a dish of pickles to a Southern lady at the dinner-table," he said. "A look of unspeakable scorn and indignation met him. 'So you think,' said the lady, 'a Southern woman will take a dish of pickles from a hand that is dripping with the blood of her countrymen?'"

Two months in the South convinced Schurz that withdrawing federal troops and restoring self-government would be a fatal error. He called the Civil War a "revolution but half accomplished." Military victory had destroyed slavery, but it had not erased proslavery ideas. Left to themselves, ex-Confederates would "introduce some new system of forced labor, not perhaps exactly slavery in its old form but something similar to it." To defend themselves, blacks would need land of their own and voting rights, Schurz concluded. Until whites "cut loose from the past," he declared, "it will be a dangerous experiment to put Southern society upon its own legs."

As Schurz discovered, the end of the war did not mean the beginning of peace. Instead, the nation entered one of its most chaotic and conflicted eras—Reconstruction. It was not that the Civil War failed to resolve anything. Northern victory

**RUINS OF PINCKNEY HOUSE, CHARLESTON, SOUTH CAROLINA**
*Northerners had a special hatred for Charleston. According to one inhabitant, Northerners promised: "The rebellion commenced where Charleston is, and shall end, where Charleston was." A devastating fire and three years of Yankee bombardment had almost fulfilled the promise. But in 1865, other consequences of the war alarmed white Southerners even more than the physical destruction. South Carolina planter Henry Middleton told his sister in Philadelphia that no one could imagine "the utter topsy-turveying of all our institutions."*
Library of Congress.

had determined once and for all the fates of secession and slavery, but out of the war emerged two new divisive questions. First, what was the status of the defeated South within the Union? Would the eleven ex-Confederate states be quickly and forgivingly welcomed back, or would they be held at arm's length and required to reform before resuming their former places? Second, what would freedom mean for ex-slaves? Would they be left to make their place in the South on their own, or would the federal government guarantee full citizenship, free labor, and equality?

In one way or another, everyone agreed that the central issue was the place of African Americans in American society. North and South divided over the issue, but neither region spoke with a single voice. Still, a majority of southern whites rejected black rights. Southern stubbornness in turn helped northern Republicans to close ranks and shifted the party's center toward more radical definitions of black freedom. It was never simply a debate between whites, however. Blacks emerged from slavery with their own ideas, and they became active agents in the struggle to define freedom.

The political part of that struggle took place in the nation's capital and in the state legislatures and county seats of the South. But the struggle also engaged the economic and social consequences of emancipation. In masters' kitchens and in plantation fields, ex-slaves strove to leave slavery behind and to become free laborers and free people. Many whites, as Carl Schurz learned, resisted letting go of the Old South. Nevertheless, emancipation and the developments of Reconstruction had profound consequences for blacks and whites in the South and for the nation as a whole.

## Wartime Reconstruction

Reconstruction did not wait for the end of war. As the odds of a northern victory increased, thinking about reunification quickened. Immediately, a question arose: Who had authority to devise a plan of reconstruction? The Founders had not anticipated such a problem, and so the Constitution stood silent. Lincoln believed firmly that reconstruction was a matter of executive responsibility. Congress just as firmly asserted its jurisdiction. Fueling the argument about who had authority to set the terms of reconstruction were significant differences about the terms themselves. Lincoln's primary aim was the restoration of national unity, which he sought through a program of speedy, forgiving political reconciliation. Congress feared that the president's program amounted to restoring the old southern ruling class to power. It wanted greater assurances of white loyalty and greater guarantees of black rights.

In their eagerness to formulate a plan for political reunification, neither Lincoln nor Congress gave much attention to the South's land and labor problems. But war was rapidly eroding slavery and traditional plantation agriculture, and Yankee military commanders in the Union-occupied areas of the Confederacy had no choice but to oversee the emergence of a new labor system. With little guidance from Washington, northern officials felt their way along, bumping heads with both planters and freedmen.

## "To Bind Up the Nation's Wounds"

On March 4, 1865, President Abraham Lincoln delivered his second inaugural address. His words blazed with religious imagery as he surveyed the history of the long, deadly war and then looked ahead to peace. "With malice toward none; with charity for all; with firmness in the right, as God gives us to see the right," Lincoln said, "let us strive on to finish the work we are in; to bind up the nation's wounds . . . to do all which may achieve and cherish a just, and a lasting peace." Lincoln had contemplated reunion for nearly two years. Deep compassion for the enemy guided his thinking about peace. But kindness is not the key to understanding Lincoln's program. His reconstruction plan aimed primarily at shortening the war and ending slavery.

In his Proclamation of Amnesty and Reconstruction, issued in December 1863, when Union forces had finally gained the upper hand on the battlefield, Lincoln offered a full pardon to rebels willing to renounce secession and to accept the abolition of slavery. (Pardons were valuable because they restored all property, except slaves, and full politi-

cal rights.) His offer excluded several groups of Confederates, such as high-ranking civilian and military officers, but the plan called for no mass arrests, no trials for treason, and no executions. Instead, when only 10 percent of men who had been qualified voters in 1860 had taken an oath of allegiance, they could organize a new state government. His plan did not require that ex-rebels extend social or political rights to ex-slaves, nor did it anticipate a program of long-term federal assistance to freedmen. Clearly, the president sought to restore the broken Union, not to reform it.

*Lincoln believed firmly that reconstruction was a matter of executive responsibility. Congress just as firmly asserted its jurisdiction.*

Lincoln's easy terms enraged abolitionists like Wendell Phillips, who charged that the president "makes the negro's freedom a mere sham." He "is willing that the negro should be free but seeks nothing else for him," Phillips declared. Phillips and other northern radicals called instead for a thorough overhaul of southern society. Their ideas proved to be too drastic for most Republicans during the war years, but Congress agreed that Lincoln's plan was inadequate. In July 1864, Congress put forward a plan of its own.

As General William T. Sherman was marching on Atlanta, Congressman Henry Winter Davis of Maryland and Senator Benjamin Wade of Ohio jointly sponsored a bill that threw out Lincoln's "10 percent plan" and demanded that at least half of the voters in a conquered rebel state take the oath of allegiance before reconstruction could begin. Moreover, the Wade-Davis bill banned ex-Confederates from participating in the drafting of new state constitutions. Finally, the bill guaranteed the equality of freedmen before the law. Congress's reconstruction would be neither as quick nor as forgiving as Lincoln's. Still, the Wade-Davis bill angered radicals because it did not include a provision for black suffrage. When Lincoln exercised his right not to sign the bill and let it die instead, Wade and Davis published a manifesto charging the president with usurpation of power. They warned Lincoln to confine himself to "his executive duties—to obey and execute, not make the laws—to suppress by arms armed rebellion, and leave political organization to Congress."

Undeterred, Lincoln continued to nurture the formation of loyal state governments under his own plan. Four states—Louisiana, Arkansas, Tennessee, and Virginia—fulfilled the president's requirements, but Congress refused to seat representatives from the "Lincoln states." In his last public address in April 1865, Lincoln defended his plan but stressed his willingness to be flexible. For the first time he expressed publicly his endorsement of suffrage for southern blacks, at least "the very intelligent, and . . . those who serve our cause as soldiers." The announcement demonstrated that Lincoln's thinking about reconstruction was still evolving. Four days later, he was dead.

## Land and Labor

Of all the problems raised by emancipation, none proved more critical than the transition from slave to free labor. Slavery had been, at bottom, a labor system, and while Republicans agreed that free labor would replace forced labor, they disagreed about what free labor would mean in the South. As Yankee armies proceeded to invade and occupy the Confederacy during the war, hundreds of thousands of slaves became free workers. Moreover, Yankee occupation meant that Union armies controlled vast territories where legal title to land had become unclear. The wartime Confiscation Acts punished "traitors" by confiscating their property. What to do with federally occupied land and how to organize labor on it engaged former slaves, former slaveholders, Union military commanders, and federal government officials long before the war ended.

Up and down the Mississippi valley, occupying federal troops ended slavery, which had already begun to fall apart because of slaves' resistance, and announced a new labor code. It required planters to sign contracts with their laborers and to pay wages. The code also obligated employers to provide food, housing, and medical care. It outlawed whipping and other forms of physical punishment, but it reserved to the army the right to discipline blacks who refused to work. The code required black laborers to enter into contracts, work diligently, and remain subordinate and obedient. The military clearly had no intention of promoting a social or economic revolution. Instead, it sought to restore plantation agriculture with wage labor. The effort resulted in a hybrid system of "compulsory free labor" that satisfied no one. Depending on one's point of view, it either provided too little or too much of a break with the past.

Planters complained because the new system fell short of slavery. Ex-slaves could not be "transformed by proclamation," a Louisiana sugar planter warned. Yet under the new system, blacks "are expected to perform their new obligations without coercion, & without the fear of punishment which is essential to stimulate the idle and correct the vicious." Without the right to whip, he concluded, the new labor system did not have a chance.

African Americans found the new regime too reminiscent of slavery to be called "free labor." Of its many shortcomings, none disappointed ex-slaves more than the failure to provide them land of their own. "What's the use of being free if you don't own land enough to be buried in?" one man asked. Freedmen believed they had a moral right to land because they and their ancestors had worked it without compensation for more than two centuries. Moreover, several wartime developments seemed to indicate that the federal government planned to link black freedom and landownership.

In January 1865, General Sherman had set aside for black settlement part of the coast south of Charleston. He devised the plan to relieve himself of the burden of thousands of impoverished blacks who trailed desperately after his army. By June 1865, some 40,000 freedmen sat on 400,000 acres of "Sherman land." In addition, in March 1865, Congress established the Bureau of Refugees, Freedmen, and Abandoned Lands. The Freedmen's Bureau, as it was called, distributed food and clothing to destitute Southerners and eased the transition of blacks from slaves to free persons. Congress also authorized the agency to divide abandoned and confiscated land into 40-acre plots, to rent them to freedmen, and eventually to sell them "with such title as the United States can convey." By June 1865, the bureau had situated nearly 10,000 black families on a half million acres that had been abandoned by fleeing South Carolina and Georgia planters. Hundreds of thousands of other ex-slaves eagerly anticipated farms of their own.

Despite the flurry of activity, wartime reconstruction had settled nothing. Two years of controversy had failed to produce agreement about whether the president or Congress had the authority to devise and direct policy or what proper policy should be. Lincoln had organized several new state governments, but Congress had not readmitted a single "reconstructed" state into the Union. There were hints of a revolution in landholding, but the "compulsory free labor" system that emerged

**AN INDEPENDENT
BLACK CHURCH**
*Poor freedmen found that one
of the sweetest fruits of emancipation was the opportunity
to worship in churches of their
own. White observers characterized black worship as
nothing but "visions and
trances," but independent black
churches did more than permit
members to dance and shout if
they wanted. They also promoted black education, extended relief to freedmen who
could not provide for themselves, and engaged in Republican politics.*
South Carolina Historical Society.

on southern plantations suggested more continuity
with antebellum traditions. Clearly, the nation faced
dilemmas and difficulties almost as burdensome as
those of the war.

## The African American Quest for Autonomy

Although white politicians had difficulty agreeing,
ex-slaves never had any doubt about what they
wanted freedom to mean. They had only to contemplate what they had been denied as slaves. (See
Texts in Historical Context on page 418.) Slaves had
to remain on their plantations; freedom allowed
blacks to go wherever they pleased. Thus, in the first
heady weeks after emancipation, freedmen often
abandoned their plantations just to see what was on
the other side of the hill and to feel freedom under
their feet. Slaves had to be at work in the fields by
dawn; freedom permitted blacks to taste the forbidden pleasure of sleeping through a sunrise. Slaves
had to defer to whites; freedom saw them test the etiquette of racial subordination. "Lizzie's maid passed
me today when I was coming from church *without
speaking to me*," huffed one plantation mistress.

To whites, it looked like pure anarchy. Without
the discipline of slavery, they said, blacks had reverted to their natural condition: lazy, irresponsible,
and wild. Actually, former slaves were experimenting with freedom, in both trivial and profound
ways. But poor black people could not long afford
to roam the countryside, neglect work, and casually
provoke whites. Soon, most were back on plantations, at work in the fields and kitchens.

But other items on ex-slaves' agenda of freedom
endured. Freedmen did not easily give up their
quest for economic independence. In addition, slavery had deliberately kept blacks illiterate, and freedmen emerged from bondage eager to read and
write. Moreover, bondage had denied slaves secure
family lives and the restoration of their families became a persistent black aspiration. Although slave
marriages and family relations had existed only at
the master's whim, slaves had nevertheless managed to create deep, enduring family bonds. Still,
slave sales had often severed family ties. As a consequence, thousands of black men and women took
to the roads in 1865 to look for relations who had
been sold away. One northern newspaperman encountered a ragged freedman who had walked six
hundred miles to North Carolina, where he had

# The Meaning of Freedom

On New Year's Day 1863, President Abraham Lincoln issued the Emancipation Proclamation. It stated that "all persons held as slaves" within the states still in rebellion "are, and henceforward shall be, free." Although it did not in and of itself free any slaves, it transformed the character of the war. Despite often intolerable conditions, black people focused on the possibilities of freedom.

John Q. A. Dennis, formerly a slave in Maryland, wrote to Secretary of War Edwin M. Stanton to ask his help in reuniting his family.

### Document 1. Letter from John Q. A. Dennis to Edwin M. Stanton

Boston July 26th 1864

Dear Sir I am Glad that I have the Honour to Write you afew line I have been in troble for about four yars my Dear wife was taken from me Nov 19th 1859 and left me with three Children and I being a Slave At the time Could Not do Anny thing for the poor little Children for my master it was took me Carry me some forty mile from them So I Could Not do for them and the man that they live with half feed them and half Cloth them & beat them like dogs & when I was admitted to go to see them it use to brake my heart & Now I say agian I am Glad to have the honour to write to you to see if you Can Do Anny thing for me or for my poor little Children I was keap in Slavy untell last Novr 1863. then the Good lord sent the Cornel borne [William Birney?] Down their in Marland in worsester Co So as I have been recently freed I have but letle to live on but I am Striveing Dear Sir but what I went too know of you Sir is is it possible for me to go & take my Children from those men that keep them in Savery if it is possible will you pleas give me a permit from your hand then I think they would let them go . . .

Hon sir will you please excuse my Miserable writeing & answer me as soon as you can I want get the little Children out of Slavery, I being Criple would like to know of you also if I Cant be permited to rase a Shool Down there & on what turm I Could be admited to Do so No more At present Dear Hon Sir

Freedom also prompted ex-slaves to seek legal marriages, which under slavery had been impossible. On February 28, 1865, in Little Rock, Arkansas, A. B. Randall, the white chaplain of a black regiment, in a report to the adjutant general of the Union army, affirmed the importance of marriage to freed slaves and emphasized their conviction that emancipation was just the first step toward full freedom.

### Document 2. Report from Reverend A. B. Randall

Weddings, just now, are very popular, and abundant among the Colored People. They have just learned, of the Special Order No' 15. of Gen Thomas [Adjutant General Lorenzo Thomas] by which, they may not only be lawfully married, but have their Marriage Certificates, Recorded; in a book furnished by the Government. This is most desirable. . . . Those who were captured . . . at Ivy's Ford, on the 17th of January, by Col Brooks, had their Marriage Certificates, taken from them; and destroyed; and then were roundly cursed, for having such papers in their posession. I have married, during the month, at this Post; Twenty five couples; mostly, those, who have families; & have been living together for years. I try to dissuade single men, who are soldiers, from marrying, till their time of enlistment is out: as that course seems to me, to be most judicious.

The Colord People here, generally consider, this war not only; their exodus, from bondage; but the road, to Responsibility; Competency; and an honorable Citizenship—God grant that their hopes and expectations may be fully realized.

Early efforts at political reconstruction prompted petitions from former slaves demanding civil and political rights. In January 1865, black Tennesseans petitioned a convention of white unionists debating the reorganization of state government.

### Document 3. Petition "to the Union Convention of Tennessee Assembled in the Capitol at Nashville, January 9th, 1865"

We the undersigned petitioners, American citizens of African descent, natives and residents of Tennessee, and devoted friends of the great National cause, do most respectfully ask a patient hearing of your honorable body in regard to matters deeply affecting the future condition of our unfortunate and long suffering race.

First of all, however, we would say that words are too weak to tell how profoundly grateful we are to the Federal Government for the good work of freedom which it is gradually carrying forward; and for the Emancipation Proclamation which has set free all the slaves in some of the rebellious States, as well as many of the slaves in Tennessee. . . .

We claim freedom, as our natural right, and ask that in harmony and co-operation with the nation at large, you should cut up by the roots the system of slavery, which is not only a wrong to us, but the source of all the evil which at present afflicts the State. For slavery, corrupt itself, corrupted nearly all, also, around it, so that it has influenced nearly all the slave States to rebel against the Federal Government, in order to set up a government of pirates under which slavery might be perpetrated.

In the contest between the nation and slavery, our unfortunate people have sided, by instinct, with the former. We have little fortune to devote to the national cause, for a hard fate has hitherto forced us to live in poverty, but we do devote to its success, our hopes, our toils, our whole heart, our sacred honor, and our lives. We will work, pray, live, and, if need be, die for the Union, as cheerfully as ever a white patriot died for his country. The color of our skin does not lessen in the least degree, our love either for God or for the land of our birth. . . .

We know the burdens of citizenship, and are ready to bear them. We know the duties of the good citizen, and are ready to perform them cheerfully, and would ask to be put in a position in which we can discharge them more effectually. We do not ask for the privilege of citizenship, wishing to shun the obligations imposed by it. . . .

This is a democracy—a government of the people. It should aim to make every man, without regard to the color of his skin, the amount of his wealth, or the character of his religious faith, feel personally interested in its welfare. Every man who lives under the Government should feel that it is his property, his treasure, the bulwark and defence of himself and his family, his pearl of great price, which he must preserve, protect, and defend faithfully at all times, on all occasions, in every possible manner.

This is not a Democratic Government if a numerous, law-abiding, industrious, and useful class of citizens, born and bred on the soil, are to be treated as aliens and enemies, as an inferior degraded class, who must have no voice in the Government which they support, protect and defend, with all their heart, soul, mind, and body, both in peace and war. . . .

. . . The nation is fighting for its life, and cannot afford to be controlled by prejudice. Had prejudice prevailed instead of principle, not a single colored soldier would have been in the Union army to-day. But principle and justice triumphed, and now near 200,000 colored patriots stand under the folds of the national flag, and brave their breasts to the bullets of the rebels. As we are in the battlefield, so we swear before heaven, by all that is dear to men, to be at the ballot-box faithful and true to the Union.

The possibility that the negro suffrage proposition may shock popular prejudice at first sight, is not a conclusive argument against its wisdom and policy. No proposition ever met with more furious or general opposition than the one to enlist colored soldiers in the United States army. The opponents of the measure exclaimed on all hands that the negro was a coward; that he would not fight; that one white man, with a whip in his hand could put to flight a regiment of them; that the experiment would end in the utter rout and ruin of the Federal army. Yet the colored man has fought so well, on almost every occasion, that the rebel government is prevented, only by its fears and distrust of being able to force him to fight for slavery as well as he fights against it, from putting half a million of negroes into its ranks.

The Government has asked the colored man to fight for its preservation and gladly has he done it. It can afford to trust him with a vote as safely as it trusted him with a bayonet.

**Document 1.** Ira Berlin, Joseph P. Reidy, and Leslie S. Rowland, eds., *Freedom: A Documentary History of Emancipation, 1861–1867.* Ser. 1, vol. 1, *The Destruction of Slavery* (Cambridge University Press, 1985), 386.

**Document 2.** Ira Berlin, Joseph P. Reidy, and Leslie S. Rowland, eds., *Freedom: A Documentary History of Emancipation, 1861–1867.* Ser. 2, *The Black Military Experience* (Cambridge University Press, 1982), 712.

**Document 3.** Ibid., 811–16.

*heard* that his wife and children had been sold. Couples who emerged from slavery with their marriages intact often rushed to northern military chaplains to legalize their unions.

Another hunger that freedom permitted African Americans to satisfy was independent worship. Under slavery, blacks had often, like it or not, prayed with whites in biracial churches. Intent on religious independence, blacks greeted freedom with a mass exodus from white churches. Some joined the newly established southern branches of all-black northern churches, such as the African Methodist Episcopal Church. Others formed black versions of the major southern denominations, Baptists and Methodists. Slaves had viewed their tribulations through the lens of their deeply felt Christian faith, and freedmen comprehended the events of the Civil War and reconstruction as people of faith. It was not surprising that ex-slaves claimed Abraham Lincoln as their Moses.

## Presidential Reconstruction

Abraham Lincoln died on April 15, 1865, just hours after John Wilkes Booth had shot him at a Washington, D.C., theater. Chief Justice Salmon P. Chase immediately administered the oath of office to Vice President Andrew Johnson. Lincoln's assassination thrust the Tennessean into responsibility at a time of grave national crisis. Moreover, Congress had adjourned in March, which meant that legislators were away from Washington when Lincoln was killed. They would not reconvene until December. Throughout the summer and fall, therefore, the "accidental president" made critical decisions about the future of the South. Like Lincoln, Johnson believed that responsibility for restoring the Union lay with the president. With dizzying speed, he drew up and executed a plan of reconstruction.

Congress returned to the capital in December to find that, as far as the president and former Confederates were concerned, reconstruction was over. To most Republicans, Johnson's modest demands of ex-rebels made a mockery of the sacrifice of Union soldiers. In an 1863 speech dedicating the cemetery at Gettysburg, Lincoln had spoken of the "great task remaining before us . . . that we here highly resolve that these dead shall not have died in vain—that this nation, under God, shall have a new birth of freedom." Instead, Johnson had acted as midwife to the rebirth of the Old South. He had achieved po-

litical reunification at the cost of black liberty. To let his program stand, Republican legislators said, would mean that the North's dead had indeed died in vain.

### Johnson's Program of Reconciliation

Born in 1808 in Raleigh, North Carolina, Andrew Johnson was the son of poor, illiterate parents. Unable to afford to send her son to school, Johnson's widowed mother apprenticed him to a tailor. Self-educated and ambitious, the young man ran away before completing his indenture and headed for Tennessee. There he worked as a tailor, accumulated a fortune in land, acquired five slaves, and built a career in politics championing the South's common white people and assailing its "illegitimate, swaggering, bastard, scrub aristocracy." The only senator from a Confederate state to remain loyal to the Union, Johnson held no grudge against the South's rebel yeomen. He believed that they had been hoodwinked by slaveholding secessionists. Less than two weeks before he became president, he made it clear what he would do to the rascals if he ever had the chance: "I would arrest them—I would try them—I would convict them and I would hang them."

But Johnson was no friend of northern radicals. A Democrat all his life, Johnson occupied the White House only because the Republican Party in 1864 had needed to broaden its appeal to loyal, Union-supporting Democrats. As a Tennessee congressman and senator, Johnson had championed traditional Democratic causes, vigorously defending states' rights (but not secession) and opposing Republican efforts to expand the power of the federal government, especially in the economic realm. He had voted against almost every federal appropriation, including a bill to pave the streets of Washington.

Moreover, Johnson had been a steadfast defender of slavery. At a time when the nation faced its moment of truth regarding black Americans, the new president harbored unshakable racist convictions. Africans, he said, were "inferior to the white man in point of intellect—better calculated in physical structure to undergo drudgery and hardship." On the eve of his inauguration as vice president, he had reiterated his belief in a white man's government.

Johnson presented his plan of reconstruction as a continuation of Lincoln's plan, and in some ways it was. Like Lincoln, he stressed reconciliation between the Union and the defeated Confederacy and rapid restoration of civil government in the South. He offered to pardon most ex-rebels. Like Lincoln, Johnson excluded high-ranking ex-Confederates, but he also excluded all ex-rebels with property worth more than $20,000. The Tennessee tailor was apparently taking aim at his old enemy, the planter aristocrats. Wealthy individuals would have to apply directly to the president for pardons. Johnson recognized the state governments created by Lincoln and set out his own requirements for restoring the rebel states to the Union. All that the citizens of a state had to do was to renounce the right of secession, deny that the debts of the Confederacy were legal and binding, and ratify the Thirteenth Amendment abolishing slavery, which became part of the Constitution in December 1865. Johnson's plan ignored Lincoln's acceptance near the end of his life of some form of limited black voting.

---

*Like Lincoln, Johnson believed that responsibility for restoring the Union lay with the president. With dizzying speed, he drew up and executed a plan of reconstruction.*

---

Johnson's eagerness to normalize relations with southern states and his lack of sympathy for blacks also led him to instruct military and government officials to return to pardoned ex-Confederates all confiscated and abandoned land, even if it was in the hands of freedmen. Reformers were shocked. They had expected the president's vendetta against planters to mean the permanent confiscation of the South's plantations and the distribution of the land to loyal freedmen. Instead, his instructions canceled the promising beginnings made by General Sherman and the Freedmen's Bureau to settle blacks on land of their own. As one freedman observed, "things was hurt by Mr. Lincoln getting killed."

## Southern Resistance and Black Codes

In the summer of 1865, delegates across the South gathered to draw up the new state constitutions required by Johnson's plan of reconstruction. They revealed that while they had been defeated, they had not been subdued. Rather than take their medicine, they choked on even the president's mild require-

ments. Refusing to declare their secession ordinances null and void, the South Carolina and Georgia conventions merely "repudiated" their ordinances, preserving in principle their right to secede. In addition, every state convention wrangled over the precise wording of the constitutional amendment ending slavery. In the end, Mississippi rejected the Thirteenth Amendment outright, and Alabama rejected it in part. Despite these defiant acts, Johnson did not demand that Southerners comply with his lenient terms. By failing to draw a hard line, he rekindled southern resistance. White Southerners began to think that by standing up for themselves they—not victorious Northerners—would shape the transition from slavery to freedom. In the fall of 1865, newly elected southern legislators set out to reverse the "retreat into barbarism" that followed emancipation.

Under the mantle of protectors of the freedmen, state governments across the South adopted a series of laws known as the black codes. While emancipation had brought freedmen important rights that they had lacked as slaves—to own property, to make contracts, to marry legally, and to sue and be sued in court—the black codes made a travesty of freedom. They sought to keep blacks subordinate to whites by subjecting blacks to every sort of discrimination. Several states made it illegal for blacks to own a gun. Blacks were barred from jury duty. Not a single southern state granted any black—no matter how educated, wealthy, or refined—the right to vote.

At the core of the black codes, however, lay the matter of labor. Faced with the death of slavery and the disintegration of plantations, legislators sought to hustle freedmen back into traditional tasks. South Carolina attempted to limit blacks to either farmwork or domestic service by requiring them to pay annual taxes of $10 to $100 to work in any other occupation. Mississippi declared that blacks who did not possess written evidence of employment could be declared vagrants and be subject to fines or involuntary plantation labor. Most states allowed judges to bind black children—orphans and others whose parents they deemed unable to support them—to white employers. Under these so-called apprenticeship laws, courts bound out thousands of black children to planter "guardians." Legislators bent every effort to resuscitate the traditional plantation economy and resurrect as nearly as possible the old regime.

Johnson refused to intervene decisively. A staunch defender of states' rights, he believed that the citizens of every state—even those citizens who had attempted to destroy the Union—should be free to write their own constitutions and laws. Moreover, since he was as eager as other white Southerners to restore white supremacy and black subordination, the black codes did not offend him.

But Johnson also followed the path he believed offered him the greatest political return. A conservative Tennessee Democrat at the head of a northern Republican Party, he began to look southwards for political allies. Despite tough talk about punishing traitors, he issued more than 14,000 special pardons to wealthy or high-ranking ex-Confederates. By pardoning planters and Confederate officials, by acquiescing in the South's black codes, and by accepting the new southern governments even when they failed to satisfy his minimal demands, he won useful allies.

If Northerners had any doubts about the mood of the South, they evaporated in the elections of 1865. To represent them in Congress, white Southerners chose former Confederates, not loyal Unionists. Of the eighty senators and representatives they sent to Washington, fifteen had served in the Confederate army, ten of them as generals. Another sixteen had served in civil and judicial posts in the Confederacy. Nine others had served in the Confederate Congress. One—Alexander Stephens—had been vice president of the Confederacy. In December, this remarkable group arrived on the steps of the nation's Capitol to be seated in Congress. As one Georgian later remarked: "It looked as though Richmond had moved to Washington."

## Expansion of Black Rights and Federal Authority

Southerners had blundered monumentally. They had assumed that what Andrew Johnson was willing to accept, the northern public and Congress would accept as well. But southern intransigence compelled even moderate Republicans to conclude that ex-rebels were a "generation of vipers," still dangerous, still untrustworthy.

The black codes in particular soured moderate Republicans on the South. The codes became a symbol of southern intentions not to accept the verdict of the battlefields, but instead to "restore all of slavery but its name." Northerners were hardly saints when it came to racial justice, but black freedom had become a hallowed war aim. "We tell the white men of Mississippi," the *Chicago Tribune* roared, "that the

men of the North will convert the State of Mississippi into a frog pond before they will allow such laws to disgrace one foot of the soil in which the bones of our soldiers sleep and over which the flag of freedom waves." Moderates represented the mainstream of the Republican Party and wanted only assurance that slavery and treason were dead. They did not seek a revolution of the entire southern social order. They did not champion black equality or the confiscation of plantations or black voting, as did the Radicals, a minority faction within the Republican Party. In December 1865, however, when Congress convened in Washington, it became clear that events in the South had succeeded in forging unity (at least temporarily) among Republican factions. Exercising Congress's right to determine the qualifications of its members, the moderate majority and the Radical minority came together to refuse to seat the southern representatives. Rather than accept Johnson's claim that the "work of restoration" was done, Congress countered his executive power. Congressional Republicans enjoyed a three-to-one majority over the Democrats, and if they could agree on a program of reconstruction, they could easily pass legislation and even override presidential vetoes.

The moderates took the initiative. Senator Lyman Trumbull of Illinois declared that the president's policy of trusting southern whites proved that the ex-slave would "be tyrannized over, abused, and virtually reenslaved without some legislation by the nation for his protection." Early in 1866, the moderates produced two bills that strengthened the federal shield. The first, the Freedmen's Bureau bill, prolonged the life of the agency established by the previous Congress. Since the end of the war, it had distributed food, supervised labor contracts, and sponsored schools for freedmen. Arguing that the Constitution never contemplated a "system for the support of indigent persons," President Andrew Johnson vetoed the Freedmen's Bureau bill. Congress failed by only a narrow margin to override the president's veto.

Johnson's shocking veto galvanized nearly unanimous Republican support for the moderates' second measure, the Civil Rights Act. Designed to nullify the black codes, it affirmed the rights of blacks to enjoy "full and equal benefit of all laws and proceedings for the security of person and property as is enjoyed by white citizens." Modest on its surface, the act boldly required the end of legal discrimination in state laws and represented an extraordinary expansion of black rights and fed-

**THE LOST CAUSE**

*While politicians in Washington, D.C., debated the future of the South, white Southerners were coming to grips with their emotions and history. They began to refer to their failure to secede from the Union as the "Lost Cause." They enshrined the memory of certain former Confederates, especially Robert E. Lee. Lee's nobility and courage represented the white South's image of itself. This quilt from about 1870, with Lee stitched in the center, illustrates how common whites incorporated the symbols of the Lost Cause into their daily lives. The maker of the quilt, a woman whose name is unknown, also included miniature Confederate flags and memorial ribbons.*
Valentine Museum, Cook Collection.

eral authority. The president argued that the civil rights bill amounted to an "unconstitutional invasion of states' rights" and vetoed it. In essence, he denied that the federal government possessed authority to protect the civil rights of blacks.

Had Johnson's veto stood, reconstruction would have been over, and the president would have had the final word. But in April 1866, a thoroughly aroused Republican Party again pushed a civil rights bill through Congress and overrode another presidential veto. In July, it sustained another Freedmen's Bureau Act. For the first time in American history, Congress had overridden presidential

vetoes of major legislation. As a worried South Carolinian observed, Johnson had succeeded in uniting the Republicans and probably touched off "a fight this fall such as has never been seen."

# Congressional Reconstruction

By the summer of 1866, President Andrew Johnson and Congress had dropped their gloves and stood toe to toe in a bare-knuckled contest unprecedented in American history. Johnson had made it clear that he would not budge on either constitutional questions or policy. Moderate Republicans made a major effort to resolve the dilemma of reconstruction by amending the Constitution, but the obstinacy of Johnson and white Southerners pushed Republican moderates steadily closer to the Radicals and to acceptance of additional federal intervention in the South.

Congressional reconstruction evolved haltingly and unevenly, but through it all black suffrage acted like a powerful magnet that steadily drew discussion its way. In time, white men in Congress debated whether to give the ballot to black men. Outside of Congress, blacks raised their voices on behalf of color-blind voting rights, while women argued to make voting sex-blind as well as color-blind.

## The Fourteenth Amendment and Escalating Violence

In April 1866, Republican moderates introduced the Fourteenth Amendment to the Constitution, which both houses of Congress approved in June by the necessary two-thirds majority. The amendment then went to the states for ratification. Although it took two years to gather approval from the required three-fourths of the states, the Fourteenth Amendment had immediate consequences.

The most important provisions of this complex amendment made all native-born or naturalized persons American citizens and prohibited states from abridging the "privileges and immunities" of citizens, depriving them of "life, liberty, or property without due process of law," and denying them "equal protection of the laws." Lawyers have battled ever since about the meaning of this broad language, but by making blacks national citizens the amendment nullified the *Dred Scott* decision of 1857 and provided a national guarantee of equality before the law. In essence, it protected the rights of citizens against violation by their own state governments.

The Fourteenth Amendment also dealt with voting rights. Republicans revealed that while genuinely committed to black freedom, they were also alert to partisan advantage. Rather than explicitly granting the vote to blacks, as Radicals wanted, the amendment gave Congress the right to reduce the congressional representation of states that withheld suffrage from some of its adult male population. In other words, white Southerners could either allow their former slaves to vote or see their representation in Washington slashed.

The Republicans drafted the Fourteenth Amendment in such a way that they could not lose. If southern whites caved in and granted voting rights to freedmen, the Republican Party, entirely a northern party since its birth, would gain valuable black votes, establish a wing in the South, and secure its national power. But if whites refused, southern representation in Congress would plunge, and Republicans would still gain immunity from southern Democratic political power. The Fourteenth Amendment's voting provision included northern states, where whites were largely hostile to voting rights for black Northerners. But northern states could continue to withhold suffrage and not suffer in Washington, for their black populations were too small to count in figuring representation. Radicals labeled the Fourteenth Amendment's voting provision "hypocritical" and a "swindle," but they understood that it was the best they could get at the time.

---

*By the summer of 1866, President Andrew Johnson and Congress had dropped their gloves and stood toe to toe in a bare-knuckled contest unprecedented in American history.*

---

Tennessee approved the Fourteenth Amendment in July, and Congress promptly welcomed its representatives and senators back. Had Johnson counseled other southern states to ratify this relatively mild amendment and warned them that they faced the fury of an outraged Republican Party if they refused, they might have listened. Instead, Johnson advised Southerners to reject the Fourteenth Amendment and to rely on him to trounce the Republicans in the fall congressional elections.

Johnson had decided to make the Fourteenth Amendment the overriding issue of the 1866 congressional elections and to gather its white opponents into a new conservative party, the National Union Party. In August, his supporters met in Philadelphia, but the slim Republican turnout made it clear that rather than drawing disgruntled party members to him, Johnson had united nearly the entire Republican Party against him.

The president's strategy had already suffered a setback two weeks earlier when whites in several southern cities went on rampages against blacks. It was less an outbreak of violence than an escalation of the violence that had never ceased. In New Orleans, a mob assaulted delegates to a black suffrage convention, and thirty-four blacks died. In Memphis, white mobs hurtled through the black sections of town and killed at least forty-six people. The slaughter shocked Northerners and renewed skepticism about Johnson's claim that southern whites could be trusted.

In a last-ditch effort, Johnson took his case directly to the people. In August, he made an ill-fated "swing around the circle," which took him from Washington to Chicago and St. Louis and back to Washington. However, the president embarrassed himself and his office. When hostile crowds hurled insults, he gave as good as he got. It was Johnson at his worst—intemperate, crude, undignified. Even a friend agreed that he had "made an ass of himself." Johnson's reception on the campaign trail foretold the fate of the National Union movement in the elections. Rather than witnessing the birth of a new conservative party, the elections pitted traditional rivals: Democrats (who lined up with Johnson) against Republicans (who lined up against him). The result was an overwhelming Republican victory in which the party retained its three-to-one congressional majority.

Johnson had bet that Northerners would not support federal protection of black rights. He expected a racist backlash to defeat the Fourteenth Amendment and blast the Republican Party. But the cautious (and ingenious) amendment was not radical enough to drive Republican voters into Johnson's camp. Besides, the war was still fresh in northern minds. As one Republican explained, southern whites "with all their intelligence were traitors, the blacks with all their ignorance were loyal."

## Radical Reconstruction and Military Rule

The elections of 1866 should have taught southern whites the folly of relying on Andrew Johnson as a guide through the thicket of reconstruction. But when Johnson continued to urge Southerners toward rejection of the Fourteenth Amendment, one by one every southern state except Tennessee voted it down. "The last one of the sinful ten," thundered Representative James A. Garfield of Ohio, "has flung back into our teeth the magnanimous offer of a generous nation." In the void created by the South's rejection of the moderates' program, the Radicals seized the initiative.

Each act of defiance by southern whites had boosted the standing of the Radicals within the Republican Party. At the core was a small group of men who had cut their political teeth on the antebellum campaign against slavery, who had goaded Lincoln toward making the war a crusade for freedom, and who had carried into the postwar period the conviction that only federal power could protect the rights of the freedmen. Except for freedmen

themselves, no one did more to make freedom the "mighty moral question of the age." Men like Senator Charles Sumner, that pompous but sincere Massachusetts crusader, and Thaddeus Stevens, the caustic, cadaverous representative from Pennsylvania, did not speak with a single voice, but they united in calling for civil and political equality. They insisted on extending to ex-slaves the same opportunities that northern working people enjoyed under the free-labor system. The southern states were "like clay in the hands of the potter," Stevens declared in January 1867, and he called on Congress to begin reconstruction all over again.

In March 1867, after exhaustive debate, moderates joined the Radicals to overturn the Johnson state governments and initiate military rule of the South. The Military Reconstruction Act (and three subsequent acts) divided the ten unreconstructed

**BLACK POLITICS**
*The Reconstruction Act of 1867 revolutionized southern politics. It also galvanized the region's African American population. One black minister remembered, "Politics got in our midst and our revival or religious work for a while began to wane." While Congress enfranchised only black men, black women participated in the debates that sprang up everywhere. Political rights meant that freedmen had access to the power of the state to advance their interests, and women, as well as men, recognized the unprecedented opportunity.*
Library of Congress.

Confederate states into five military districts. Congress placed a Union general in charge of each district and instructed him to "suppress insurrection, disorder, and violence" and to begin political reform. After the military had completed voter registration, which would include black men and exclude all those barred by the Fourteenth Amendment from holding public office, voters would elect delegates to conventions that would draw up new state constitutions. Each constitution would guarantee black suffrage. When the voters of each state had approved the constitution and the first legislature had ratified the Fourteenth Amendment, the state could submit its work to Congress. If Congress approved, the state's senators and representatives could be seated and political reunification would be accomplished.

Radicals proclaimed the provision for black suffrage "a prodigious triumph." The doggedness of the Radicals and of African Americans, along with the pigheadedness of Johnson and the white South, had swept the Republican Party far beyond the timid suffrage provisions of the Fourteenth Amendment. Republicans finally agreed with Sumner that only the voting power of ex-slaves could bring about a permanent revolution in the South. Indeed, suffrage provided blacks with a powerful instrument of change and self-protection. When combined with the disfranchisement of thousands of ex-rebels, it promised to cripple any neo-Confederate resurgence and guarantee Republican governments in the South.

Despite its bold suffrage provision, the Military Reconstruction Act of 1867 disappointed those who advocated the confiscation and redistribution of southern plantations. No one in Washington was more distressed than Thaddeus Stevens. Unlike Sumner, who conceived of Reconstruction primarily in political terms, Stevens believed it was at bottom an economic problem. He agreed wholeheartedly with the ex-slave who said, "Give us our own land and we take care of ourselves, but without land, the old masters can hire us or starve us, as they please." But Johnson's offers of amnesty and pardon had reversed the small program of land transfer begun during the war. By early 1867, nearly all of the land had been returned to its ex-Confederate owners. Most Republicans believed that they had already provided blacks with the critical tools: equal legal rights and the ballot. If blacks were to get forty acres, they would have to gain it themselves.

Declaring that he would rather sever his right arm than sign such a formula for "anarchy and chaos," Andrew Johnson vetoed the Military Reconstruction Act. Congress overrode his veto the very same day, dramatizing the shift in power from the executive to the legislative branch of government. With the passage of the Reconstruction Acts of 1867, congressional reconstruction was virtually completed. Congress had left white folks owning most of the South's land, but in a radical departure it had given black men the ballot. More than any other provision, black suffrage justifies the term "radical reconstruction." In 1867, the nation began an unprecedented experiment in interracial democracy—at least in the South, for Congress's plan did not touch the North. Soon the former Confederate states would become the primary theater for political struggle. But before the spotlight swung away from Washington, the president and Congress had one more scene to play.

## Impeaching a President

Although Johnson had lost the support of the northern people and faced a hostile Republican majority in Congress, he had no intention of yielding control of reconstruction. As president, he was responsible for enforcing the laws that Congress enacted. As commander in chief, he oversaw the military rule of the South that Congress instituted. Yet in a dozen ways he sabotaged Congress's will and encouraged white belligerence and resistance. He issued a flood of pardons to undermine efforts at political and economic change. He waged war against the Freedmen's Bureau by removing officers who sympathized too fully with ex-slaves. And he replaced Union generals eager to enforce Congress's Reconstruction Acts with conservative men who were eager to defeat them. Johnson claimed that he was merely defending the "violated Constitution." At bottom, however, he subverted congressional reconstruction to protect southern whites from what he considered the horrors of "Negro domination."

When Congress learned that overriding Johnson's vetoes did not assure victory, it attempted to tie the president's hands. Congress required that all orders to field commanders pass through the General of the Army, Ulysses S. Grant, who Congress believed was sympathetic to southern freedmen, Unionists, and Republicans. It also enacted the Tenure of Office Act, which required the approval of the Senate for the removal of any government official who had been appointed with Senate consent. Republicans were seeking to protect Secretary of War Edwin M. Stanton, the lone cabinet officer who supported congressional policies. Some Republicans, however, believed that nothing less than removing Johnson from office could save reconstruction, and they initiated a crusade to impeach the president. According to the Constitution, the House of Representatives can impeach and the Senate can try any federal official for "Treason, Bribery, or other high Crimes and Misdemeanors."

As long as Johnson refrained from breaking a law, however, impeachment languished. Moderates interpreted "high Crimes and Misdemeanors" to mean violation of criminal statutes, and they did not believe that the president had committed an actual crime. Radicals argued that Johnson's abuse of

constitutional powers and his failure to fulfill constitutional obligations were impeachable offenses. But in August 1867, Johnson suspended Secretary of War Stanton from office. As required by the Tenure of Office Act, he requested the Senate to consent to dismissal. When the Senate balked, the president removed Stanton anyway. "Is the President crazy, or only drunk?" asked a dumbfounded Republican moderate. "I'm afraid his doings will make us all favor impeachment."

News of Johnson's open defiance of the law did indeed convince every Republican in the House to vote for a resolution impeaching the president. Chief Justice Salmon Chase presided over the Senate trial, which lasted from March until May 1868. Chase refused to allow Johnson's opponents to raise the broad issues of misuse of power, his "great crimes," and forced them to argue their case exclusively on the narrow legal grounds of Johnson's removal of Stanton. Johnson's lawyers argued that he had not committed a criminal offense, that the Tenure of Office Act was unconstitutional, and that in any case it did not apply to Stanton, who had been appointed by Lincoln. When the critical vote came, seven moderate Republicans broke with their party and joined the Democrats in voting "not guilty." With thirty-five in favor and nineteen opposed, the impeachment forces fell one vote short of the two-thirds needed to convict.

Republicans had put Johnson on trial because he threatened their efforts to remake the South. But some, including Chief Justice Chase, feared that impeachment for insufficient cause would permanently weaken the office of president. So Johnson survived, but he did not come through the ordeal unscathed. After his trial he called a truce, and for the remaining ten months of his term reconstruction proceeded unhindered by presidential interference.

**ANDREW JOHNSON, WITH ADDITIONS**
*This dignified portrait by Currier and Ives of President Andrew Johnson appeared in 1868, the year of his impeachment trial. The portrait was apparently amended by a disgruntled citizen. Johnson's vetoes of several reconstruction measures passed by Congress caused his opponents to charge him with arrogant monarchical behavior. Johnson preferred the unamended image—that of a plain and sturdy statesman.*
Museum of American Political Life.

## The Fifteenth Amendment and Women's Demands

In February 1869, Republicans passed their last major piece of reconstruction legislation: the Fifteenth Amendment to the Constitution. The amendment prohibited states from depriving any citizen of the right to vote because of "race, color, or previous condition of servitude." The Reconstruction Acts of 1867 had already required black suffrage in the South, but the Fifteenth Amendment extended black voting to the entire nation. Some Republicans felt morally obligated to do away with the double standard between North and South. Others believed that the freedman's ballot required the extra armor of a constitutional amendment to protect it from white counterattack. But partisan advantage also played an important role in the amendment's passage. Gains by northern Democrats in the 1868 elections worried Republicans, and black voters now represented the balance of power in several northern states. By giving ballots to northern blacks, Republicans could lessen their political vulnerability. As one Republican congressman observed, "party expediency and exact justice coincide for once."

Some Republicans, however, found the final wording of the Fifteenth Amendment "lame and halting." Rather than absolutely guaranteeing the right to vote, the amendment merely prohibited exclusion on grounds of race. The distinction would prove to be significant. In time, inventive white Southerners would devise tests of literacy and property and other apparently nonracial measures that would effectively disfranchise blacks and yet not violate the Fifteenth Amendment. But an amendment that guaranteed the right to vote courted defeat in the North. Rising antiforeign sentiment—against the Chinese in California and against European immigrants in the Northeast—caused states to resist giving up control of suffrage requirements. In March 1870, after three-fourths of the states had ratified it, the Fifteenth Amendment became part of the Constitution. Republicans generally breathed a sigh of relief, confident that black suffrage had been "the last great point that remained to be settled of the issues of the war."

But the Republican Party's reappraisal of suffrage had ignored completely the band of politicized and energized women who had emerged from the war demanding "the ballot for the two disenfranchised classes, negroes and women." Founding the Equal Rights Association in 1866, Susan B. Anthony and Elizabeth Cady Stanton lobbied for "a government by the people, and the whole people; for the people and the whole people." They felt betrayed when their old antislavery allies, who now occupied positions of national power, proved to be fickle and would not work for their goals. "It was the Negro's hour," Frederick Douglass later explained. The Republican Party had to avoid anything that might jeopardize black gains, Charles Sumner declared. He suggested that woman suffrage could be "the great question of the future."

It was not the first time women's expectations had been dashed. The Fourteenth Amendment had provided for punishment of any state that excluded voters on the basis of race but not on the basis of sex. It had also introduced the word *male* into the Constitution when it referred to a citizen's right to vote. Stanton had predicted that "if that word 'male'

**SUSAN B. ANTHONY**
*Like many outspoken suffragists, Anthony, depicted here around 1850, had begun her public career in the temperance and abolitionist movements. Her continuing passions for other causes—improving working conditions for labor, for example—caused some conservatives to oppose women's political rights because they equated the suffragist cause with radicalism in general. Women could not easily overcome such views, and the long struggle for suffrage eventually drew millions of women into public life.* Meserve-Kunhardt Collection.

be inserted, it will take us a century at least to get it out." The Fifteenth Amendment proved to be no less disappointing. Although women fought hard to include the word *sex*, the amendment denied states the right to forbid suffrage only on the basis of race. Stanton and Anthony condemned the Republicans' "negro first" strategy and concluded that woman "must not put her trust in man."

## The Struggle in the South

While Northerners believed they had discharged their responsibilities with the Reconstruction Acts and the amendments to the Constitution, Southerners knew that the battle had just begun. Black suffrage and large-scale rebel disfranchisement that came with congressional reconstruction had destroyed traditional southern politics and established the foundation for the rise of the Republican Party. Gathering together outsiders and outcasts from traditional society, the Republicans in the South won elections, wrote new state constitutions, and formed new state governments.

Challenging the established class for political control was dangerous business. Equally dangerous were the confrontations that took place on farms and plantations from Virginia to Texas. In the countryside, blacks sought to give practical, everyday meaning to their newly won legal and political equality. But ex-masters and other whites had their own ideas about the social and economic arrangements that should replace slavery. Freedom, then, remained contested territory, and Southerners fought pitched battles with each other to determine the boundaries of their postemancipation world.

## Freedmen, Yankees, and Yeomen

African Americans made up the majority of southern Republicans. Freedmen emerged from bondage illiterate and politically inexperienced, but they understood their own interests. They realized that without the ballot they were almost powerless, and they threw themselves into the suffrage campaign. Southern blacks gained voting rights in 1867, and within months virtually every eligible black man had registered to vote. Blacks (like whites) did not have identical political priorities, but almost all voted Republican, and they united in their desire for education and equal treatment before the laws.

*Black suffrage and large-scale rebel disfranchisement that came with congressional reconstruction had destroyed traditional southern politics and established the foundation for the rise of the Republican Party.*

Northern whites who decided to make the South their home after the war were a second element of the South's Republican Party. Conservative white Southerners called any northern migrant a "carpetbagger," a man so poor that he could pack all his earthly belongings in a single carpet-sided suitcase and swoop southward like a buzzard to "fatten on our misfortunes." Some Northerners who

moved south were scavengers, but most were restless, relatively well educated young men, often former Union officers and Freedmen's Bureau agents who looked upon the South as they did the West— as a promising place to make a living. Northerners in the southern Republican Party consistently supported programs that encouraged vigorous economic development along the lines of the northern free-labor model.

Southern whites made up the third element of the Republican Party in the South. Approximately one out of four white Southerners voted Republican. The other three cursed those who did. They condemned southern-born white Republicans as traitors to their region and their race and called them "scalawags," a term for runty horses and low-down, good-for-nothing rascals. Yeoman farmers in the piedmont accounted for the vast majority of white Republicans in the South. Many were Unionists who emerged from the war with bitter memories of Confederate persecution. Some small farmers also nursed long-standing grievances against planter domination and welcomed the Republican Party because it promised to end favoritism toward plantation interests. Yeomen usually supported initiatives for public schools and for expanding economic opportunity within a reinvigorated southern economy.

The Republican Party in the South, then, was made up of freedmen, Yankees, and yeomen—an improbable coalition. The mix of races, regions, and classes inevitably meant friction as each group maneuvered to define the party. Despite the stress and strain, reconstruction represents an extraordinary moment in American politics: Blacks and whites joined together to pursue political change. The Republican Party defended the political and civil equality of black Southerners and struggled to bring the South into the mainstream of American social and economic development.  Formally, of course, only men participated in politics—casting ballots and holding offices—but women also played parts in the political struggle. Women joined in parades and rallies, attended stump speeches, and even campaigned. In 1868, black maids in Yazoo, Mississippi, shocked their white employers when they showed up for work boldly wearing buttons depicting the Republican candidate for president: Ulysses S. Grant.

Reconstruction politics was not for cowards. Any political act, even wearing a political button, took courage. Congress had introduced hundreds of thousands of ex-slaves into the southern electorate against the will of the white majority. Then, according to one Democrat, the Republican Party herded them to the polls like "senseless cattle." Most whites in the South condemned the entire political process as illegitimate and felt justified in doing whatever it took to stamp out Republicanism. Violence against blacks—the "white terror"—took brutal institutional form in 1866 with the formation of the Ku Klux Klan, a social club of Confederate veterans that quickly developed into a paramilitary organization armed against Republicans. The Klan went on a rampage of whipping, hanging, shooting, burning, and throat-cutting to defeat reconstruction and restore white supremacy. Rapid demobilization of the Union army after the war left only twenty thousand troops to patrol the entire South, a vast territory. Without effective military protection, southern Republicans had to take care of themselves.

## Republican Rule

The Reconstruction Acts required southern states to draw up new constitutions before they could be readmitted to Congress. Beginning in the fall of 1867, states held elections for delegates to constitutional conventions. About 40 percent of the white electorate stayed home, either because they had been disfranchised or because they were boycotting politics. Republicans won three-fourths of the seats. About 15 percent of the Republican delegates were Northerners who had moved south, 25 percent were African Americans, and 60 percent were white Southerners. As a British visitor observed, the elections reflected "the mighty revolution that had taken place in America." But Democrats described the conventions as zoos of "baboons, monkeys, mules . . . and other jackasses." In fact, the gatherings brought together serious, purposeful men who hammered out the legal framework for a new order.

The reconstruction constitutions introduced extensive changes into southern life. In general, changes fell into two categories: those that reduced aristocratic privilege and increased democratic equality and those that expanded the state's responsibility for the general welfare. In the first category, the constitutions adopted universal male suffrage, abolished property qualifications for holding office, and made more offices elective and fewer appointive. In the second category, they enacted prison reform; made the state responsible for caring for orphans, the insane, and the deaf and mute;

**KU KLUX KLAN ROBE AND HOOD**
*The white robes that we associate with the Ku Klux Klan are a twentieth-century phenomenon. During reconstruction, Klansmen donned robes of various designs and colors. It is unlikely that the man who wore this robe about 1866—with its eye holes carefully trimmed with blue fabric—sewed it himself. Women did not participate in midnight raids, but mothers, wives, and daughters of Klansmen often shared their reactionary vision and did what they could to bring about the triumph of white supremacy.*
Chicago Historical Society, Hope B. McCormick Center. Worn by Joseph Boyce Stewart, Lincoln County, Tenn., c. 1866. Gift of W. G. Dithmer.

and aided debtors by exempting their homes from seizure.

These forward-looking constitutions provided blueprints for a New South. But they stopped short of the specific reforms advocated by particular groups within southern Republicanism. Despite the wishes of virtually every former slave, no southern constitution confiscated and redistributed land. And despite the prediction of Unionists that unless all former Confederates were banned from politics they would storm back and wreck reconstruction, no constitution disfranchised ex-rebels wholesale.

But Democrats were blind to the limits of the Republican program. In their eyes, they stared at wild revolution. According to Democrats, Republican victories initiated "black and tan" (ex-slave and mulatto) governments. But the claims of "Negro domination" had almost no validity. Four out of five Republican voters were black men, but more than four out of five Republican officeholders were white. Southerners sent fourteen black congressmen and two black senators to Washington, but only 6 percent of Southerners in Congress during Reconstruction were black. With the exception of South Carolina, where blacks briefly held a majority in one house of the legislature, no state experienced "Negro rule," despite black majorities in the populations of three states.

In almost every state, voters ratified the new constitutions and swept Republicans into power. After they ratified the Fourteenth Amendment, the former Confederate states were readmitted to Congress. Southern Republicans then turned to a staggering array of problems. Wartime destruction still littered the landscape. The South's share of the nation's wealth had fallen from 30 percent to only 12 percent. Manufacturing limped along at a fraction of prewar levels, agricultural production remained anemic, and the region's railroads had hardly advanced from the devastated condition in which Sherman had left them. Without the efforts of the Freedmen's Bureau, people would have starved. Moreover, reactionary violence and racial harassment dogged the steps of Southerners who sought reform. In this desperate context, Republicans struggled to breathe life into their new state governments.

Activity focused on three major areas. First, every state inaugurated a system of public education and began building schools and training teachers. Persistent underfunding meant too few schools, dilapidated facilities, and poorly trained teachers, but literacy rates rose sharply, nevertheless. Although public schools were racially segregated, education remained for many blacks a tangible, deeply satisfying benefit of freedom and Republican rule.

Second, states attacked racial discrimination and defended civil rights. Republicans especially resisted efforts by whites to establish separate facilities for blacks in public transportation. Texas replaced its law requiring segregation in its railroads with one that outlawed seating by race. Mississippi went further, levying fines of up to $1,000 and three years in jail for railroads, steamboats, hotels, and theaters that denied "full and equal rights" to all citizens. But passing color-blind laws was one thing; enforcing them was another. Segregation—the separation of blacks and whites in public places—developed at white insistence despite the law and became a feature of southern life long before the end of reconstruction.

Third, Republican governments launched ambitious programs of economic development. They envisioned a South of diversified agriculture, roaring factories, and booming towns. Republican legislatures chartered scores of banks and industrial companies, appropriated funds to fix ruined levees and to drain swamps, and went on a railroad-building binge, repairing old lines and adding some seven thousand miles of track. The mania for railroads and state-sponsored economic development fell far short of solving the South's economic troubles, however. Republican spending to stimulate economic growth meant rising taxes and enormous debt that drained funds from schools and other programs.

The southern Republicans' record, then, was mixed. To their credit, the biracial Republican coalition had taken up an ambitious agenda to change the South. Success would have been difficult under the best of circumstances. As it was, money was scarce. In addition, Democrats kept up a constant drumbeat of harassment, while factionalism threatened the party from within. Moreover, corruption infected Republican governments in the South. Public morality reached new lows everywhere in the nation after the Civil War, and the chaos and disruption of the postwar South proved fertile soil for bribery, fraud, and influence peddling. Despite all of its problems and shortcomings, however, the Republican Party made headway in its efforts to purge the South of aristocratic privilege and racist oppression.

## White Landlords, Black Sharecroppers

Reconstruction politics did not arise within a vacuum. Sharp dissatisfaction with conditions in the southern countryside politicized blacks and fueled political upheaval. Clashes occurred daily between ex-slaves who wished to take control of the conditions of their own labor and ex-masters who wanted to reinstitute old ways.

The system of agricultural labor that emerged in 1865 grew out of the labor program begun during the war by the federal military. When the war ended, supervision shifted to the Freedmen's Bureau, which renewed the army's campaign to restore production by binding black laborers and planters with wage contracts. Except for having to put down the whip and pay subsistence wages, planters were not required to offer many concessions to emancipation. Instead, they moved quickly to restore the antebellum world of work gangs, white overseers, field labor for black women and children, clustered cabins, minimal personal freedom, and even corporal punishment whenever they could get away with it.

Ex-slaves resisted every effort to roll back the clock. Land of their own would do much to end planters' involvement in their personal lives. They wanted, for example, to make their own decisions about whether women and children would labor in the fields. Indeed, within months after the war, black women (perhaps one-third of them) abandoned field labor and began working full time within their own households. Whites claimed that they were "acting the lady," but what whites meant was that black women were not acting like slaves. Instead, they behaved like free mothers and housewives, occupied with the same arduous domestic chores as poor white women. Moreover, hundreds of thousands of black children enrolled in school.

The freedmen's dream of landownership never came true. Congress and southern legislatures refused to confiscate the planters' land, and without political intervention, landownership proved to be beyond the reach of all but a small fraction of blacks. Without land, ex-slaves would have little choice but to work on plantations.

Although blacks were forced to return to the planters' fields, freedmen resisted efforts to restore slavelike conditions. By working fewer days and shorter hours, by boycotting annual contracts, by striking, and by abandoning the most reactionary employers, they sought to force concessions. A tug-of-war between white landlords and black laborers took place on thousands of farms and plantations and out of it emerged sharecropping, a new system of southern agriculture.

Sharecropping was a compromise that offered both ex-masters and ex-slaves something but satisfied neither. Under the new system, planters divided their cotton plantations into small farms of twenty-five to thirty acres that freedmen rented, paying with a share of each year's crop, usually half. Sharecropping gave blacks more freedom than labor gangs and released them from the day-to-day supervision of whites. Black families abandoned the old slave quarters and scattered over plantations, building separate cabins on the patches of land they tilled (Map 16.1). Black families now decided who would work, for how long, and how hard. Still, most blacks remained dependent on the white landlord, who retained the power to expel them at the end of each season. For planters, sharecropping offered a way to resume agricultural production, but it did not allow them to reinstitute the unified plantation system or to administer what they considered necessary discipline.

An experiment at first, sharecropping spread quickly throughout the cotton South. By 1870, the old gang system, direct white supervision, and clustered black living quarters were fading memories. As increasing numbers of white yeomen lost their land in the downward spiral of postwar southern agriculture, sharecropping ensnared small white farmers as well as black farmers.

## Reconstruction Collapses

By 1870, Northerners looked forward to putting "the southern problem" behind them. They had written guarantees of civil and political rights for blacks into the Constitution and enacted a program of political reunification that had restored ex-Confederate states to the Union. Now, after a decade of engagement with the public issues of war and reconstruction, they wanted to turn to their own affairs. Increasingly, practical business-minded men came to the forefront of the Republican Party, replacing the band of reformers and idealists who had been prominent in the 1860s. While northern resolve to defend black freedom withered, southern commitment to white supremacy intensified. Without northern protection, southern Republicans were no match for the Democrats' economic coercion, political corruption, and violence. One by one, Republican state governments fell. The election of 1876 both confirmed and completed the collapse of reconstruction.

### The Grant Regime: Cronies, Corruption, and Economic Collapse

Ulysses S. Grant was the obvious choice for the Republican Party's presidential nomination in 1868. When the Civil War ended, the general who led the

**M AP  16.1**

*A Southern Plantation in 1860 and 1881*

*The maps of the Barrow plantation in Georgia illustrate some of the ways that ex-slaves ex-pressed their freedom. Former slaves deserted the clustered living quarters behind the Big House, scattered over the plantation, built new family cabins, and farmed rented land. These ex-slaves also worked together to build a school and a church.*

Union forces to victory was easily the most popu-lar man in the nation, at least north of the Mason-Dixon line. Radicals preferred someone with a deeper moral commitment to black equality, but Grant supported congressional reconstruction and that was enough for the Republican convention. The Democrats chose Horatio Seymour, former gover-nor of New York. Their platform blasted congres-sional reconstruction as "a flagrant usurpation of power . . . unconstitutional, revolutionary, and void." Republicans answered by "waving the bloody shirt," that is, they reminded the voters that the Democrats were "the party of rebellion," the party that stubbornly resisted a just peace. During the campaign, the Ku Klux Klan erupted in another reign of terror, murdering hundreds of southern Re-publicans. Terrorist tactics cut into Grant's tally, but

he gained a narrow 300,000-vote margin in the pop-ular vote and a substantial victory (214 votes to 80) in the electoral college.

*While northern resolve to defend black freedom withered, southern commitment to white supremacy intensified.*

Grant understood that most Northerners had grown weary of reconstruction. Conservative business-minded Northerners had become con-vinced that recurrent federal intrusion was itself a major cause of instability. Eager to invest in the South and especially to resume the profitable

**GRANT AND SCANDAL**
*This anti-Grant cartoon by the nation's most celebrated political cartoonist, Thomas Nast, shows the president falling headfirst into the barrel of fraud and corruption that tainted his administration. During Grant's eight years in the White House, many in his administration failed him. Sometimes duped, sometimes merely loyal, Grant stubbornly defended wrongdoers, even to the point of perjuring himself to keep an aide out of jail.*
Library of Congress.

cotton trade, they sought order, not disruption. A growing number of northern Republican leaders began to question the wisdom of their party's alliance with the South's lower classes—its small farmers and sharecroppers. Grant's secretary of the interior, Jacob D. Cox of Ohio, proposed allying with the "thinking and influential native southerners . . . the intelligent, well-to-do, and controlling class."

The talents Grant had demonstrated on the battlefield—decisiveness, clarity, and resolution—deserted him in the White House. Unclear about his objectives, he grew tentative, unsure of himself, and bewildered. Able advisers might have helped, but Grant surrounded himself with fumbling kinfolk and old cronies from his army days. He also made a string of dubious appointments that led to a series of damaging scandals. Charges of corruption tainted his vice president, Schuyler Colfax, and brought down his secretary of war and secretary of

the navy as well as his private secretary. Grant's dogged loyalty to liars and cheats only compounded the damage. While never personally implicated in any scandal, Grant was aggravatingly naive and his administration filled with rot.

In 1872, disgusted anti-Grant Republicans bolted and launched a third party, the Liberal Republicans. The Liberals promised to create a government "which the best people of this country will be proud of." They condemned the Grant regime as a riot of vulgarity—crude graft, tasteless materialism, and blatant anti-intellectualism. To clean up the mess, they proposed ending the spoils system, by which victorious parties rewarded loyal workers with public office, and replacing it with a nonpartisan civil service commission that would oversee competitive examinations for appointment to office. Moreover, they demanded that the government remove federal troops from the South and restore "home rule." Democrats especially liked the southern policy of the Liberals, and the Democratic Party endorsed the Liberal presidential candidate, Horace Greeley, the longtime editor of the *New York Tribune*. Despite Grant's problems, however, the nation still felt enormous affection for the man who had saved the Union. In the 1872 election, voters gave him a resounding victory.

The Grant administration was caught up in a tangle of complicated problems, including a devastating economic depression that began in 1873. Railroads, which had fueled the postwar boom, led directly to the bust. A major Philadelphia bank, headed by Jay Cooke, had poured enormous sums into railroads, become overextended with debt, and gone under, initiating the panic of 1873. Like dominoes, other companies failed, and soon the nation sank into its most severe depression to that time. More than 18,000 businesses collapsed in two years, and more than one million workers lost their jobs. Desperate times arrived at the doorsteps of most working people. Industrial violence kept pace with economic hardship. The violence subsided as men and women returned to work, but only at the end of the decade did the depression lift. By then, southern Republican governments had fallen, and the experiment of reconstruction had ended.

## Northern Resolve Withers

Although Northerners wanted desperately to shift their attention to the new issues, the old ones would not go away. When southern Republicans pleaded for federal protection from Klan violence, Congress enacted three laws in 1870 and 1871 that were intended to break the back of white terrorism. The severest of the three, the Ku Klux Klan Act, made interference with voting rights a felony and authorized the use of the army to enforce it. Intrepid federal marshals arrested thousands of suspected Klansmen. While the government came close to destroying the Klan, it did not end terrorism against blacks. Congress also passed the Civil Rights Act of 1875, which boldly outlawed racial discrimination in transportation, public accommodations, and juries. But federal authorities did little to enforce the law, and segregated facilities remained the rule throughout the South.

In reality, the retreat from reconstruction had begun in 1868 with Grant's election. Grant genuinely wanted to see blacks' civil and political rights protected, but he felt uneasy about an open-ended commitment that seemed to ignore constitutional limitations on federal power. Like his predecessor, he distributed pardons liberally and encouraged the passage of a general amnesty. In May 1872, Congress obliged and restored the right of officeholding to all but three hundred ex-rebels. Radicals did what they could to stiffen the North's resolve, but by the early 1870s reform had lost its principal spokesmen to death or defeat at the polls. Many Republicans had washed their hands of reconstruction, concluding that the quest for black equality was mistaken or hopelessly naive. Those who bolted to the Liberal Republican Party, for example, welcomed the South's "best people" back to power. Traditional white leaders, it seemed to them, offered the best hope for honesty, order, and prosperity.

The North's abandonment of reconstruction rested on more than weariness, greed, and disillusionment. Underlying everything was unyielding racial prejudice. Emancipation failed to uproot racism in either the South or the North. During the war, Northerners had learned to accept black freedom, but deep-seated prejudice prevented many from equating freedom with equality. Even the actions that they took on behalf of blacks often served partisan political advantage. Whether they expressed it quietly or boisterously, Northerners generally supported Indiana senator Thomas A. Hendricks's declaration that "this is a white man's Government, made by the white man for the white man." Increasingly, when Radicals asked Northerners to remember reconstruction's victims, northern sympathy went out to white Southerners.

The U.S. Supreme Court also did its part to undermine reconstruction. From the first, Republicans had feared that the conservative Court would declare their southern policies unconstitutional. In the 1870s, a series of Court decisions significantly weakened the federal government's ability to protect black Southerners under the Fourteenth and Fifteenth Amendments. In the *Slaughterhouse* cases (1873), the Court distinguished between national and state citizenship and ruled that the Fourteenth Amendment protected only those rights that stemmed from the federal government. Since the Court decided that most rights derived from the states, it sharply curtailed the federal government's authority to protect black citizens. Even more devastating, the *United States v. Cruikshank* (1876) ruling said that the reconstruction amendments gave Congress power to legislate only against discrimination by states, not by individuals. The "suppression of ordinary crime," such as assault, remained a state responsibility. The Supreme Court did not declare reconstruction unconstitutional, but it gradually undermined its legal foundation.

The mood of the North found political expression in the election of 1874, when for the first time in eighteen years the Democrats gained control of the House of Representatives. Voters blamed the Grant administration for the economic hard times that had begun the previous year, but they also sent a message about reconstruction. As one Republican observed, the people had grown tired of the "negro question, with all its complications, and the reconstruction of the Southern States, with all its interminable embroilments."

Reconstruction had come apart in the North. Congress gradually abandoned it. President Grant grew increasingly unwilling to enforce it. The Supreme Court busily denied the constitutionality of significant parts of it. And the people sent unmistakable messages that they were tired of it. Rather than defend reconstruction from its southern enemies, Northerners steadily backed away from the challenge. After the early 1870s, southern blacks faced the forces of reaction largely on their own.

### White Supremacy Triumphs

Republican governments in the South attracted more bitterness and hatred than any other political regimes in American history. In the eyes of the majority of whites, each day of Republican rule produced fresh insults: Black militiamen patrolled town streets, black laborers negotiated contracts with former masters, black maids stood up to former mistresses, black voters cast ballots, and black legislators enacted laws. The northern retreat from reconstruction permitted southern Democrats to harness this white rage to politics. Taking the name "Redeemers," they promised to replace "bayonet rule" (federal troops continued to be stationed in the South) with "home rule" (white southern control). They branded Republican governments a carnival of extravagance, waste, and fraud and promised that honest, thrifty Democrats would supplant the irresponsible tax-and-spend Republicans. Above all, they swore to save civilization from a descent into African "barbarism" and "negro rule." As one Redeemer put it, "We must render this either a

**IS THIS A REPUBLICAN FORM OF GOVERNMENT?**
*This powerful 1876 drawing by Thomas Nast depicts the end of Reconstruction as the tragedy it was. As white supremacists in the South piled up more and more bodies, supporters of civil rights accused the Grant administration of failing to protect black Southerners and legitimately elected governments. They pointed specifically to the constitutional requirement that "[t]he United States shall guarantee to every State in this Union a Republican Form of Government, and shall protect each of them . . . against domestic violence" (Article IV, section 4).*
Library of Congress.

white man's government, or convert the land into a Negro man's cemetery."

By the early 1870s, Democrats understood that race was their most potent weapon. They adopted a two-pronged racial strategy to overthrow Republican governments. First, they sought to polarize the parties around color, and, second, they relentlessly intimidated black voters. They went about gathering all the South's white voters into the Democratic Party, leaving the Republicans to depend on blacks. The "straight-out" appeal to whites promised great advantage because whites made up a majority of the population in every southern state except Mississippi, South Carolina, and Louisiana.

Democrats employed several devices to dislodge whites from the Republican Party. First and foremost, they fanned the flames of racial prejudice. In South Carolina, a Democrat crowed that his party appealed to the "proud Caucasian race, whose sovereignty on earth God has proclaimed." Ostracism also proved effective. Local newspapers published the names of whites who kept company with blacks. So complete was the ostracism that one of its victims said, "No white man can live in the South in the future and act with any other than the Democratic party unless he is willing and prepared to live a life of social isolation."

---

*Republican governments in the South attracted more bitterness and hatred than any other political regimes in American history.*

---

In addition, Democrats exploited the small white farmer's severe economic plight by blaming it on Republican financial policy. Government spending soared during reconstruction, and small farmers saw their tax burden skyrocket. Farms in Mississippi were taxed at four times the prewar level. When cotton prices fell by nearly 50 percent in the 1870s, yeomen farmers found cash in short supply. To pay their taxes, one man observed, "people are selling every egg and chicken they can get." Those unable to pay lost their land. In 1871, Mississippi reported that one-seventh of the state's land—3.3 million acres—had been forfeited for the nonpayment of taxes. The small farmer's economic distress had a racial dimension. Because few freedmen succeeded in acquiring land, they rarely paid taxes. In Georgia in 1874, blacks made up 46 percent of the population but paid only 2 percent of the taxes. From the perspective of the small white farmer, Republican rule meant not only that he was paying more taxes but that he was paying them to aid blacks. Democrats asked whether it was not time for hard-pressed yeomen to join the white man's party.

If racial pride, social isolation, and Republican financial policies proved insufficient to drive

yeomen from the Republican Party, Democrats turned to terrorism. "Night riders" targeted scalawags as well as blacks for murder and assassination. By the early 1870s, then, only a fraction of southern whites any longer professed allegiance to the party of Lincoln.

The second prong of Democratic strategy—intimidation of black voters—proved equally devastating. Antiblack political violence escalated to unprecedented levels. In 1873 in Louisiana, a clash between black militiamen and gun-toting whites killed two white men and an estimated seventy black men. Half of the black men were slaughtered after they had surrendered. Although the federal government indicted more than one hundred white men, local juries failed to convict a single one of them.

Even before adopting the all-out white supremacist tactics of the 1870s, Democrats had already captured Virginia, Tennessee, and North Carolina. The new campaign brought fresh gains. The Redeemers regained Georgia in 1872, Texas in 1873, and Arkansas and Alabama in 1874. In 1875, Mississippi fell. By 1876, only three Republican state governments—in Florida, Louisiana, and South Carolina—survived (Map 16.2).

## An Election and a Compromise

The centennial year of 1876 witnessed one of the most tumultuous elections in American history. Its chaos and confusion provided a fitting conclusion to the experiment known as reconstruction. The election took place in November, but not until March 2 of the following year, at 4 A.M., did the nation know who would be inaugurated president on March 4. For four months the country suffered through a constitutional and political crisis that jeopardized the peaceful transfer of power from one administration to the next. Sixteen years after Lincoln's election, Americans feared that a presidential contest would again precipitate civil war.

The Democrats had nominated New York's reform governor, Samuel J. Tilden, who immediately targeted the corruption of the Grant administration and the despotism of Republican reconstruction. The Republicans put forward a reformer of their own, Rutherford B. Hayes, governor of Ohio. Privately, Hayes considered "bayonet rule" a mistake, but he concluded that waving the bloody shirt, as threadbare as it was, remained the Republicans' best political strategy. "It leads people away from 'hard times,' which is our deadliest foe," Hayes said lamely.

On election day, Tilden tallied 4,284,000 votes to Hayes's 4,036,000. Yet in the all-important electoral college, Tilden fell one vote short of the majority required for victory. However, the electoral votes of three states remained in doubt and thus were uncounted. Both Democrats and Republicans claimed the nineteen votes of South Carolina, Louisiana, and Florida, the only remaining Republican strongholds in the South. To win, Tilden needed only one of the contested votes. Hayes had to have all of them to take the election. The two parties traded charges of fraud and intimidation. To be sure, Republicans had stuffed some ballot boxes, but stepped-up violence by the Democrats had kept hundreds of thousands of southern Republicans from the polls.

Congress had to decide who had actually won the elections in the three southern states and thus who would be president. The Constitution provided little guidance. Moreover, Democrats controlled the House, and Republicans the Senate. To break the deadlock, Congress created a special electoral commission to arbitrate the disputed returns. An odd and cumbersome compromise, the commission was made up of five representatives (two Republicans, three Democrats), five senators (two Democrats,

three Republicans), and five justices of the Supreme Court (two Republicans, two Democrats, and one justice who was considered an independent). But before the commission could meet, the Illinois legislature elected the independent justice to the Senate, and his place was filled with a Republican. The commissioners all voted the straight party line, giving every state to the Republican Hayes and putting him over the top in electoral votes (Map 16.3).

Some outraged Democrats vowed to resist Hayes's victory. But the impasse was broken when negotiations behind the scenes between Hayes's lieutenants and some moderate southern Democrats resulted in an informal understanding, known as the Compromise of 1877. In exchange for a Democratic promise not to block Hayes's inauguration and to deal fairly with the freedmen, Hayes vowed not to use the army to uphold the remaining Republican regimes. The South would also gain substantial federal subsidies for internal improvements. Two days later, the nation celebrated Hayes's peaceful inauguration.

The Compromise of 1877 confirmed the conservatism that had been growing in the North for years. New priorities meant that Northerners no longer wanted to intervene in the South, and, even without a deal, Hayes would probably have withdrawn the troops. The last three Republican state governments fell quickly once Hayes abandoned them.

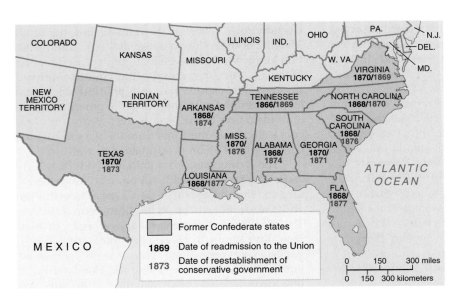

**MAP 16.2**
*The Reconstruction of the South*
*Myth has it that Republican rule of the former Confederacy was not only harsh but long. In most states, however, conservative southern whites stormed back into power in only a matter of a few months or a very few years. By the election of 1876, Republican governments could be found in only three states. And they soon fell.*

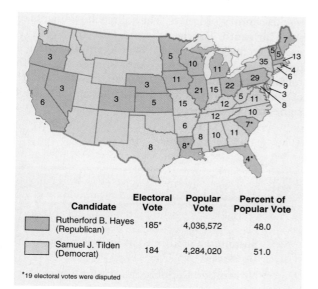

| Candidate | Electoral Vote | Popular Vote | Percent of Popular Vote |
|---|---|---|---|
| Rutherford B. Hayes (Republican) | 185* | 4,036,572 | 48.0 |
| Samuel J. Tilden (Democrat) | 184 | 4,284,020 | 51.0 |

*19 electoral votes were disputed

MAP 16.3
*The Election of 1876*

The nation's solution to this last crisis marked a return to the antebellum tradition of sectional compromise. As in previous crises, whites had found a way to bridge their differences and retain the peace, and again blacks had paid the price. In 1877, Republicans followed a path of expediency and gained the presidency. Southern Democrats got home rule and a free hand in racial matters. When reconstruction ended, black Southerners were not completely subordinated to whites, but their prospects in the New South looked bleak.

## Conclusion: "A Revolution but Half-Accomplished"

In 1865, when General Carl Schurz visited the South at President Andrew Johnson's behest, he discovered "a revolution but half-accomplished." Defeat had not prepared the South for an easy transition from slavery to free labor, from white racial despotism to equal justice, and from white political monopoly to biracial democracy. The old elite wanted to get "things back as near to slavery as possible," while ex-slaves and whites who had lacked power

in the slave regime were eager to exploit the revolutionary implications of defeat and emancipation.

Congress pushed the revolution along. Although it refused to provide an economic underpinning to black freedom, it required defeated Confederates to accept legal equality and share political power. But conservative whites fought ferociously to recover their power and privilege. When they regained control of politics, they used the power of the state, along with private violence, to wipe out many of the gains of reconstruction. So successful were the reactionaries that one observer concluded that the North had won the war but the South had won the peace.

But the Redeemer counterrevolution did not mean a return to slavery. Abolition destroyed the old plantation of slavery days, and ex-slaves gained the freedom not to be whipped or sold, to send their children to school, to worship in their own churches, and to work independently on their own rented farms. The lives of impoverished sharecroppers overflowed with hardships, but even sharecropping provided more autonomy and economic welfare than bondage had. It was limited freedom, to be sure, but it was not slavery.

Emancipation set in motion the most profound upheaval in the nation's history, and nothing whites could do could entirely erase its revolutionary effects. War destroyed the richest and largest slave society in the New World. It cost masters three billion dollars in lost property and destroyed the foundation of planter wealth. Abolition overturned the social and economic order that had dominated the region for nearly two centuries. Even today, some Southerners divide history into "before the war" and "after the war."

The Civil War and emancipation mark a watershed not just in the South's history but in that of the entire nation. War served as midwife for the birth of a modern nation-state, and for the first time sovereignty rested uncontested in the federal government. Moreover, the South returned to the Union, but as a junior partner. The victorious North now possessed the power to establish the nation's direction, and it set its compass toward the expansion of industrial capitalism. War laid the foundation for the power of big business and its captains in postwar America.

Still, the Civil War remained only a "half-accomplished" revolution. As such, reconstruction represents a tragedy of enormous proportions. The nation did not fulfill the promises that it seemed to hold out to black Americans at war's end. The revolution raced forward, halted, and then slipped back, coming to rest far short of equality and justice. The failure had enduring consequences. Almost a century after reconstruction, the nation would embark on what one observer called a "second reconstruction," another effort to fulfill nineteenth-century promises. The solid achievements of the Thirteenth, Fourteenth, and Fifteenth Amendments to the Constitution would provide a legal foundation for the renewed commitment. It is worth remembering, though, that it was only the failure of the first reconstruction that made a modern civil rights movement necessary.

## CHRONOLOGY

**1863**  **December.** Lincoln issues Proclamation of Amnesty and Reconstruction.

**1864**  **July.** Congress offers more stringent plan for reconstruction, Wade-Davis bill.

**1865**  **January.** General William T. Sherman sets aside land in South Carolina for black settlement.

**March 4.** Lincoln sworn in for second term as president of United States.

**March.** Congress establishes Freedmen's Bureau.

**April 14.** Lincoln shot, dies on April 15, succeeded by Vice President Andrew Johnson.

**Fall.** Southern legislatures enact discriminatory black codes.

**December.** Thirteenth Amendment abolishing slavery becomes part of U.S. Constitution.

**1866**  **April.** Congress approves Fourteenth Amendment making native-born blacks American citizens and guaranteeing all American citizens "equal protection of the laws." Amendment becomes part of Constitution in 1868.

**April.** Congress passes Civil Rights Act over President Johnson's veto.

**May.** Susan B. Anthony and Elizabeth Cady Stanton found Equal Rights Association to lobby for vote for women.

**July.** Congress extends Freedmen's Bureau over President Johnson's veto.

**Summer.** Ku Klux Klan founded in Tennessee.

**November.** Republicans triumph over Johnson in congressional elections.

**1867**  **March.** Congress passes Military Reconstruction Act imposing military rule on South and requiring states to guarantee vote to black men.

**1868**  **March–May.** Senate impeachment trial of President Johnson results in acquittal.

**November.** Ulysses S. Grant elected president of the United States.

**1869**  **February.** Congress approves Fifteenth Amendment prohibiting racial discrimination in voting rights. Amendment becomes part of Constitution in 1870.

**1871**  **April.** Congress enacts Ku Klux Klan Act in effort to end white terrorism in South.

**1872**  **November.** President Grant reelected.

**1873**  Economic depression sets in for remainder of decade.

**1874**  **November.** Elections return Democratic majority to House of Representatives.

**1875**  **February.** Civil Rights Act of 1875 outlaws racial discrimination, but federal authorities do little to enforce law.

**1877**  **March.** Special congressional committee awards disputed electoral votes to Republican Rutherford B. Hayes, making him president of United States; Hayes agrees to pull military out of South.

# SUGGESTED READINGS

Michael Les Benedict, *A Compromise of Principle: Congressional Republicans and Reconstruction* (1974). Explains the evolution of the reconstruction policies of Congress.

Michael Les Benedict, *The Impeachment of Andrew Johnson* (1973), and Hans L. Trefousse, *Impeachment of a President: Andrew Johnson, the Blacks, and Reconstruction* (1975). Investigations of the Johnson impeachment.

Ira Berlin, et al., eds., *Freedom: A Documentary History of Emancipation, 1861–1867* (1982–). Vividly documents the aspirations of ex-slaves.

Dan T. Carter, *When the War Was Over: The Failure of Self Reconstruction in the South, 1865–1867* (1985). Analyzes Johnson's conservative regimes in the South.

Eric Foner, *Reconstruction: America's Unfinished Revolution* (1988). A thoroughly researched, comprehensive interpretation that views the African American experience as central to the era.

Michael Perman, *Reunion Without Compromise: The South and Reconstruction, 1865–1868* (1973), and *The Road to Redemption: Southern Politics, 1869–1879* (1984). Analyses of the South's political response to reconstruction.

George C. Rable, *But There Was No Peace: The Role of Violence in the Politics of Reconstruction* (1984). Emphasizes the pervasiveness of political violence.

Brooks D. Simpson, *The Reconstruction Presidents* (1998). A lively examination of the reconstruction policies of Lincoln, Johnson, Grant, and Hayes.

C. Vann Woodward, *Reunion and Reaction: The Compromise of 1877 and the End of Reconstruction* (1951). The classic and still valuable analysis of the election of 1876 and its aftermath.

**KANSAS QUILT C. 1880S**

*This carefully hand-stitched quilt, made from pieces of leftover wool clothing and blankets, shows how a woman named Nancy Miller Grider responded creatively to the challenges of her life in Russell County, Kansas, in the 1880s. Historically, women have produced quilts as a visual language, to tell something about themselves by using materials at hand. The circular pattern in Grider's quilt may represent the spokes of a wheel—a fitting symbol not only of her own migration west but of the mass migrations taking place after the Civil War when restless Americans on the move peopled the West and fed the growth of the big cities.*

Collection of the Kentucky Quilt Project, photograph courtesy of the Kentucky Quilt Project, Inc., Louisville, Ky.

# AMERICANS ON THE MOVE: THE SETTLEMENT OF THE WEST AND THE RISE OF THE CITY

## 17

### 1860–1900

A MISSOURI HOMESTEADER REMEMBERED packing as the family pulled up stakes and headed west to Oklahoma:

> We were going to God's Country. Eighteen hundred and 90. . . . It was pretty hard to part with some of our things. We didn't have much but we had worked hard for everything we had. You had to work hard in that rocky country in Missouri. I was glad to be leaving it. We were going to God's Country. . . . We were going to a new land and get rich.

In the Dakotas an Oglala Sioux recalled moving with his family as a child:

> The snow was deep and it was very cold, and I remember sitting in another pony drag beside my father and mother, all wrapped up in fur. We were going away from where the soldiers were, and I do not know where we went, but it was west.

In the Midwest a young man turned his face to the city, leaving his hometown behind:

> He saw again in his mind's eye, as he tramped the road, a picture of the map on the wall of the railway station—the map with a picture of iron roads from all over the Middle West centering in a dark blotch in the corner. . . .
> "Chicago!" he said to himself.

And in Russia a young girl on her way to America bid good-bye to her village:

> I remember how the women crowded around mother . . . how, finally, the ringing of the signal bell set them all talking faster and louder than ever, in desperate efforts to give the last bits of advice, deliver the last messages, and, to their credit let it be said, to give the final, hearty, unfeigned good-bye kisses, hugs, and good wishes.

America in the nineteenth century witnessed a massive movement of peoples as men and women searched for jobs, land, and opportunity. Or, in the case of American Indians, they sought a place where they might live their traditional life in peace. In the last three decades of the century, this movement took many forms and went in many directions. The trek to the West continued apace as homesteaders, ranchers, and miners sought their fortunes. They in turn pushed Native Americans off the land and farther toward the sunset.

At the same time, the pull of the great industrial centers in the Northeast counterbalanced the westward migration. Farmers left the country to seek jobs in industrial centers like Chicago, New York, Pittsburgh, and Detroit. African Americans from the South began a migration to the northern cities, and Canadians crossed the border to work in the factories and mill towns of New England.

Fourteen million immigrants braved the Atlantic to come to America from Europe, creating the great migration that we think of as part of a worldwide westward movement. But the movement of peoples was by no means limited to one direction. Immigrants from Mexico and Latin America journeyed to "El Norte." Canadians headed south. Asians voyaged east across the Pacific to work on the "gold mountain" of California. It is not an exaggeration to say that the decades surrounding the turn of the twentieth century witnessed a migration unmatched in the history of the world.

By the end of the century, Americans on the move had peopled a continent and created the outlines of modern America. As industrial capitalism transformed the nation from a rural agrarian economy into an increasingly urban, industrial society, it changed life not just in the burgeoning cities but also on the plains of the Dakotas, in the mines of Colorado, and on the farms of Texas and California. Iron rails and a national market economy inextricably linked the country and the city. The settlement of the West and the rise of the city occurred simultaneously and witnessed many of the same economic, social, and political manifestations—the rise of big combinations, growing ethnic and racial tensions, and the exploitation of labor and natural resources. It makes more sense to look at the West not as separate and unique, but as an important part of a nationwide transformation that took place in the last three decades of the nineteenth century.

**RAILROAD LOCOMOTIVE**
*In the years following the Civil War, the locomotive replaced the covered wagon, enabling settlers to travel from Chicago or St. Louis to the West Coast in two days. By the 1890s, more than 72,000 miles of track stretched west of the Mississippi River. In this photograph, men and women hop aboard a locomotive to celebrate the completion of a section of track.*
Library of Congress.

# Western Land Fever

Americans by the hundreds of thousands packed up and moved, pinning their hopes and ambitions on the American West. In the three decades following 1870, this westward stream of migration swelled into a torrent, spilling across the prairies, moving on to the Pacific coast, and eventually flooding back onto the Great Plains. During this brief span of time, more land was settled than in all the previous history of the country. Between 1876 and 1900, eight new states entered the Union—Colorado, Montana, North and South Dakota, Washington, Idaho, Wyoming, and Utah—leaving only three territories—Oklahoma, New Mexico, and Arizona—in the continental United States.

*Americans by the hundreds of thousands packed up and moved, pinning their hopes and ambitions on the American West.*

Two factors stimulated the rapid settlement of the trans-Mississippi West. The Homestead Act of 1862 which promised 160 acres free to any citizen or prospective citizen, male or female, who settled on the land for five years. And railroads opened up new areas for settlement and actively recruited settlers. In the 1870s, the promise of land lured thousands west across the plains in covered wagons, a hard journey that took many months and cost many lives. With the completion of a transcontinental railroad system in the 1880s, settlers could choose from four competing rail lines and often made the trip in less than a week.

While the country was rich in land and resources, not all who wanted to own their own land were able to do so. A growing number of Americans found themselves dispossessed, forced to work for wages on land they would never own.

## Moving West: Farmers, Ranchers, and Speculators

Families who ventured west searching for "God's country" faced hardship, loneliness, and deprivation. Blizzards, tornadoes, grasshoppers, hailstorms, drought, prairie fires, accidental death, and disease were only a few of the catastrophes that could befall even the best farmer. Homesteaders on "free" land needed as much as a thousand dollars

for a house, a team of farm animals, a well, fencing, and seed. Poor farmers, called "sodbusters," did without even these basics, living in dugouts carved in the land and using muscle instead of machinery. The first years were critical. If the farm did not fare well, if the crop failed, the farmer faced a downward spiral into a mire of debt. Dependent on the weather, the bank, the railroad, and the market, the so-called independent farmer labored against heavy odds.

For women on the frontier, simple daily necessities like obtaining water and fuel meant backbreaking labor. Out on the plains, where water was scarce, women often had to trudge to the nearest creek or spring. "A yoke was made to place across the shoulders, so as to carry at each end a bucket of water," one daughter recollected, "and then water was brought a half mile from spring to house." Gathering fuel was another heavy chore. Without ready sources of coal or firewood, settlers on the prairies and plains turned to what substitutes they could scavenge. Anything that would burn—twigs, tufts of grass, old corncobs, sunflower stalks—was used for fuel. But by far the most prevalent fuel used for cooking and heating were "chips," which were chunks of dried cattle and buffalo dung found in abundance on the plains and grasslands.

Many settlers succeeded in building comfortable lives. But for others the opportunities of the West failed to materialize. Already by the 1870s, much of the best land had been taken, given to the railroads as land grants or to the states to finance education. Too often, the homesteaders found that only the least desirable tracts were left—poorer lands, far from markets, transportation, and society. Land speculators took the lion's share of the remaining land. "There is plenty of land for sale in California," one migrant complained in 1870, but "the majority of the available lands are held by speculators, at prices far beyond the reach of a poor man."

The railroads were by far the biggest winners in the scramble for western land. To encourage railroad building in the decades after the Civil War, the federal government and the states gave public lands to the railroads. Together the land grants totaled approximately 180 million acres—an area almost one-tenth the size of the United States (Map 17.1). Farmers who went west to homestead often ended up buying land from the railroads or from the speculators and land companies that quickly followed the railroads into the new territories. Of the two and a half million farms established on public lands between 1860 and 1900, homesteading accounted for

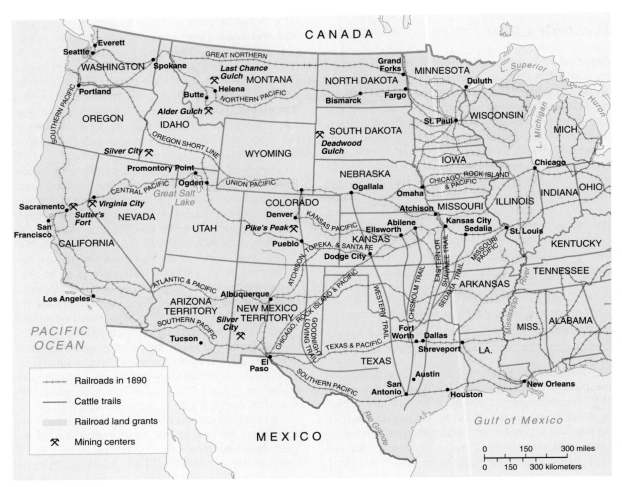

M A P 17.1
*Federal Land Grants to Railroads and the Development of the West, 1850–1900*
*Generous federal land grants meant that railroads could sell the desirable land next to the track*
*at a profit or hold it for speculation. Railroads received more than 180 million acres, an area*
*equal to the size of Texas. Note how the cattle trails connect with major railheads in Dodge City,*
*Abilene, and Kansas City and to mines in Montana, Nevada, Colorado, and New Mexico.*

only one in five; the vast majority of farmland sold for a profit.

As land for homesteading grew scarce on the prairie in the 1870s, farmers began to push farther westward, moving into western Kansas, Nebraska, and eastern Colorado—the land called the Great American Desert by settlers who had passed over it on their way to California and Oregon. Although many agricultural experts warned that the semiarid land (where less than twenty inches of rain fell annually) should be reserved for grazing, their words

of caution were drowned out by the extravagant claims of western promoters. "Rain follows the plow" became the slogan of western boosters, who insisted that cultivation would alter the climate of the region and bring more rainfall.

It would have been more accurate to say that drought followed the plow. Periodic droughts at roughly twenty-year intervals were a fact of life on the Great Plains. Plowed up, the dry topsoil blew away in the wind. A period of relatively good rainfall in the early 1880s encouraged settlement, but a protracted drought in the late 1880s and early 1890s sent starving farmers reeling back from the plains. Hundreds of thousands retreated from western Kansas and Nebraska, some in wagons carrying the slogan "In God we trusted, in Kansas we busted." A popular ballad bitterly summed up the plight of the worst off, those too poor to leave:

But here I am stuck and here I must stay
My money's all gone and I can't get away;
There's nothing will make a man hard and
    profane
Like starving to death on a government claim.

The fever for fertile land set off a series of spectacular land runs in Oklahoma. When the government opened two million acres in former Indian territory to settlement in 1889, thousands rushed to grab a piece. Federal troops kept order as the homesteaders massed on the border. On April 22 at noon, pistol shots signaled the opening, and they were off. "Along the line as far as the eye could reach, with a shout and a yell the swift riders shot out, then followed the light buggies or wagons and last the lumbering prairie schooners and freighters' wagons," a reporter wrote. "Above all a great cloud of dust hover[ed] like smoke over a battlefield." By the end of the day, hundreds of homesteaders had staked claims, and Oklahoma boasted two tent cities with more than 10,000 residents.

*The railroads were by far the biggest winners in the scramble for western land.*

In later years, other portions of Indian territory opened for settlement. In a frenzied land rush on the Cherokee strip in Oklahoma Territory in 1893, more than 100,000 homesteaders competed for 40,000 claims. Several settlers were killed in the stampede, and nervous men guarded their claims with rifles. As public lands grew smaller, the hunger for land grew fiercer.

## The Dispossessed: Tenants, Sharecroppers, and Migrants

Landownership, the symbol of the American dream in the nineteenth century, remained an elusive goal for many Americans—newly freed slaves, immigrants arriving from Europe and Asia, and Mexi-

cans on the Texas border. In the post–Civil War period, as agriculture became a big business tied to national and global markets, an increasing number of dispossessed laborers worked land that they would never own.

In the southern United States, the farmer labored under particularly heavy burdens. The Civil War wiped out much of the region's capital, which had been invested in slaves, and crippled the plantation economy. The newly freed slaves rarely managed to obtain land of their own. Instead, they soon found themselves reduced to propertyless farm laborers. "The colored folks stayed with the old boss man and farmed and worked on the plantations," a black Alabama sharecropper observed bitterly. "They were still slaves, but they were free slaves."

Tenancy and sharecropping became a way of life for poor blacks and whites alike. The tenant rented land; the sharecropper worked someone else's land for a share of the proceeds. Even those who owned their own land faced enormous difficulties. In the states of the old Confederacy, both money and credit were in short supply. In desperation, southern farmers turned for credit to country merchants, some of whom were ex-masters who opened stores on their plantations. Under an arrangement called crop lien, local merchants supplied goods to the farmers on credit; in return, the farmers put up their next year's crop as collateral. The merchants charged exorbitant interest, up to 60 percent, on the goods they sold—from seed to a slab of bacon. At "settling up time," after the landlord took half the farmer's yield, the merchant consulted the debt ledger. Invariably, the farmer's expenses exceeded the income from his half of the cotton crop, and the cropper went home empty-handed, only to begin the cycle all over again (Figure 17.1).

There was no escape. Indebtedness bound the sharecroppers to the landlords and the merchants by prohibiting them from moving or buying from another store. Even small farmers who owned their own land suffered under the crop lien system. After seven years, farmers who did not "pay out" lost their land. Across the South the merchant became known as the "furnishing man." Black farmers called him simply "the man." By the beginning of the twentieth century, a majority of white farmers had become landless sharecroppers, outnumbering even the freedpeople caught in the system.

In Texas, the coming of the railroads at the turn of the century led to the rise of a segregated farm

**FIGURE 17.1**
*Tenancy and the Crop Lien System*
*The crop lien system was designed to deal with the shortage of money and credit in the postreconstruction South. The local furnishing merchant provided seed and supplies to farmers who pledged their crop as collateral. A complex skein of relationships developed among merchant, landowner, and tenant farmer.*

society in which a growing number of Mexican wageworkers labored on huge spreads owned by Anglos or by European syndicates. As early as the 1860s, the large ranchers had begun to enclose the open range with barbed-wire fences. Fencing eliminated landless cattle and sheep ranchers, who had grazed their herds on the open range, and forced small-time landowners who could not afford to buy barbed wire or to sink wells to sell out for the best price they could get. After the heyday of cattle ranching ended in the late 1880s came the rise of cotton production in the southeastern regions of Texas. Ranchers turned their pastures into sharecroppers' plots and hired displaced cowboys, most of them Mexican, as seasonal laborers for as little as seventy-five cents a day. Within the space of ten years, ranch life in southern Texas gave way to a growing army of agricultural wageworkers.

In California, a pattern of land monopoly and large-scale farming fostered tenancy and migratory labor. By the 1870s, less than one percent of the population owned half of the state's available agricultural land. The rigid economics of large-scale commercial agriculture and the seasonal nature of the crops spawned a ragged army of migratory agricultural laborers. Derisively labeled "blanket men" or "bindle stiffs," these homeless and landless transients worked the fields in the growing season and wintered in the flophouses of San Francisco. Bonanza wheat farming in California in the 1870s and 1880s exhausted the land and was replaced, with the introduction of irrigation, by fruit and sugar beet farming. Most of the California farm laborers were Chinese immigrants until the enactment of Chinese exclusion in 1882 forced big growers to tap other groups, including Mexicans, Filipinos, and Japanese, for farm labor.

## The Changing Face of Rural America

In the late nineteenth century, America's population remained overwhelmingly rural. The 1870 census showed that nearly 80 percent of the nation's people lived on farms and in villages of less than eight thousand inhabitants. In 1900, the figure had dropped to 66 percent. But while the percentage of rural inhabitants fell, the number of farms grew—from 2 million in 1860 to over 5.7 million in 1900. Rapid growth in the West accounted for the rise in the number of farms, but not all the nation's farmers lived in the West. The rural population spread evenly across the country, with rural inhabitants outnumbering city dwellers even in industrial states like Pennsylvania and New York as late as 1880.

Like all aspects of American life, farm life changed rapidly in the last decades of the nineteenth century. With the rise of industrialization and the growth of big cities, many farmers gave up their farms and moved to towns and cities. Those who stayed behind increasingly adopted new technologies, making farming less a way of life and more a business venture. In the states of the old Confederacy, cotton remained king, and the region's emphasis on a cash-crop economy signaled a nationwide trend away from family farming and toward agribusiness.

## The Colonial Economy of the New South

In the decades following the Civil War, the South struggled to regain its economic footing. The region's economy, devastated by war and altered forever by the abolition of slavery, foundered at the same time the North experienced an unprecedented industrial boom. No wonder some Southerners called for a New South modeled on the industrial North. Henry Grady, the ebullient young editor of the *Atlanta Constitution,* used his paper's substantial influence (it boasted the largest circulation of any weekly in the country) to extol the virtues of a new industrial South. Part bully, part booster, Grady exhorted the South to use its natural advantages—cheap labor and abundant natural resources—to go head to head in competition with northern industry.

Grady's message fell on receptive ears. Many Southerners, men and women, black and white, joined the national migration from farm to city, leaving the old plantations to molder and decay. With the end of military rule in 1877, the southern Democrats who called themselves "Redeemers" regained political power in the southern states and enthusiastically embraced northern promoters who promised prosperity and profits. Northern capital rushed south in the waning years of the 1870s as the country recovered from the hard times precipitated by the panic of 1873.

The railroads came first, opening up the region for industrial development. Railroad mileage grew fourfold from 1865 to 1890 (see Map 17.1). So too did the number of cotton spindles soar as textile mill owners abandoned New England in search of the cheap labor, low taxes, and proximity to raw materials promised in the South. By 1900, the South had become the nation's leading producer of cloth, and more than 100,000 Southerners, many of them women and children, had traded agricultural labor for work in textile mills.

The extractive industries, mining and lumber, also experienced a boom in the New South, but with devastating results. Coal from Appalachia could now be transported by rail to fuel the blast furnaces

and factories of the nation. In the race to exploit the South's coal reserves, whole mountains were eaten up, often with catastrophic environmental and human costs. But investors in the North and abroad, not Southerners, reaped the lion's share of the plunder. The miners themselves violently protested their poor wages and dangerous working conditions in a series of strikes that gave one county in Kentucky the name Bloody Harlan. In the lumber industry, the demand for southern wood led to untrammeled expansion. Twenty years of milling resulted in what one contemporary forestry expert called "probably the most rapid and reckless destruction of forests known to history."

Of all its industries, the New South was proudest of its iron and steel industry, which grew up in the area surrounding Birmingham, Alabama. Soon the smokestack replaced the white-pillared plantation as the symbol of the South. Pennsylvania iron magnate Andrew Carnegie toured the region in 1889 and observed, "The South is Pennsylvania's most formidable industrial enemy." But as long as control of southern industry remained in the hands of northern investors, Pennsylvania had nothing to fear. Whatever the South's natural advantages, northern bankers and investors had no intention of letting the South beat the North at its own game. Elaborate mechanisms rigged the price of southern steel, inflating it, as one northern insider confessed, "for the purpose of protecting the Pittsburgh mills and in turn the Pittsburgh steel users."

---

*In practical terms, the industrialized New South proved an illusion. Instead of thriving, the South found itself reduced virtually to the status of an economic colony of the North.*

---

In only one industry did the South truly dominate—tobacco. Capitalizing on the invention of a machine for rolling cigarettes, the Duke family of Virginia eventually dominated the industry with their American Tobacco Company. The new popularity of cigarettes, which replaced chewing tobacco among America's growing urban population, provided a booming market for Duke's "ready-made" cigarettes. Soon the company was selling 400,000 cigarettes a day.

In practical terms, the industrialized New South proved an illusion. Instead of thriving, the South found itself reduced virtually to the status of an economic colony of the North. Just as today's colonial economies the world over feature cheap labor, extractive industries, and exported raw materials, so too did the New South. Similarly, the region experienced low wages, absentee ownership, and little control over policy or pricing—key determinants of colonial status.

Agriculture in the New South fared no better. Dependence on cotton increased rather than decreased in the postbellum period. Landlords and merchants alike demanded that sharecroppers grow cotton, which they considered an easily marketable cash crop. Before the end of the nineteenth century, the South was producing nearly three times as much cotton as it had before the Civil War. Unfortunately, the South's vastly increased production, combined now with millions of bales from Egypt and India, coincided with a slowdown in world demand. Cotton prices plummeted. Further, relentless cotton cultivation exhausted the soil and eroded the countryside. Although a few merchants and landowners managed to hold on and even profit, the majority of Southerners succumbed to the numbing poverty that settled over the rural South. Dissatisfaction with this state of affairs would fuel the Populist movement in the 1890s.

## From the Family Farm toward Agribusiness

The promise of cheap land lured many settlers west at the same time the growing cities acted as powerful magnets, particularly to young people, pulling them off the farm. In the 1870s and 1890s, crop failures and economic depression forced many farmers into foreclosure and off the land. By the 1890s, rural depopulation caused a growing chorus of alarm. "One by one, family by family, [the] inhabitants slip away in search of other homes," a New England writer lamented, observing "the young, the hopeful, the ambitious" left, while "the superannuated, the feeble, the dull" stayed. The farmer, who had once been the symbol of America, was increasingly ridiculed and caricatured. Derogatory terms like "hayseed" and "hick" entered the American vocabulary.

However much the image of the farmer suffered in the popular culture of the time, in the late nineteenth century farming itself was thriving as an agricultural revolution transformed American farm life. Scientific farming and mechanization enabled one farmer to do the work of several

hands. New plows and reapers halved the time and labor cost of production and made it possible to farm vast tracts of land. Industrialization and urbanization provided farmers with expanding markets for their produce, and railroads carried farmers' crops to markets thousands of miles away. The diversified family farm of the past began to give way to specialized, commercial farming. By the turn of the twentieth century, American agriculture had entered the era of what would come to be called "agribusiness"—farming as a big business.

*The new farmer existed in a web of dependence, not only on weather and credit but increasingly on a world market.*

Business became the order of the day. Instead of extolling the virtues of the self-sufficient farmer, farm journals, agricultural societies, and educators pushed farmers to act more like businessmen, to specialize and to consolidate. Together they helped to create a striking new image of what constituted successful farming. "Farming for business, not for a living—this is the motif of the New Farmer," announced one agricultural writer. The message was clear: The job of the up-to-date farmer was to produce money, not just crops.

As farming moved onto the prairies and plains, mechanization took command. Steel plows, reapers, mowers, harrows, seed drills, combines, and threshers replaced human muscle on the farm. Horse-drawn implements gave way to steam-powered machinery. By 1880, a new harvester could reap and shock twenty acres of wheat in a day, and a single combine could do the work of twenty men. Machines enabled farmers to vastly increase their acreage. Two men with one machine could cultivate 250 acres of wheat. Production soared. The agricultural revolution meant that Americans raised more than four times the corn, five times the hay, and seven times the wheat and oats as they had before the Civil War.

The new farmer existed in a web of dependence, not only on weather and credit but increasingly on a world market. American foodstuffs fed people as far away as England and Germany. Farmers exported 217 million bushels of wheat and 212 million bushels of corn by 1897. A fall in commodity prices meant that a farmer's entire crop went to pay off debts. In periods of depression, many heavily mortgaged farmers lost their land to creditors.

The protective tariff, endorsed by every Republican president from Abraham Lincoln to William Howard Taft, further hurt the farmer. The tariff, designed to protect "infant industries," prevented foreign competition and effectively raised the price of manufactured goods. Almost everything the farmer purchased, from plows and reapers to kerosene and calico, cost more because of the tariff. Habitual debtors, farmers also suffered from the government's tight monetary policy. The gold standard caused a steady deflation, which forced debtors to repay loans with money worth much more than the money they had originally borrowed. Or put in terms of labor, a farmer who had borrowed a thousand dollars in 1868 had to grow twice as much wheat in 1888 than he would have had to grow twenty years earlier to pay back his loan. Farmers also resented the profits made by bankers and mortgage lenders and by the owners of grain elevators, who often made more money storing the farmers' grain than the farmers made when they sold it. "By the time the World Gets their Liveing out of the Farmer as we have to Feed the World," a Texas cotton farmer complained in the 1890s, "we the Farmer has nothing Left but a Bear Hard Liveing."

Since the days of Thomas Jefferson, farming had been linked with the highest ideals of a democratic society. Now agrarianism itself had been transformed. The farmer was no longer the self-sufficient yeoman, but a businessman on the one hand or a dispossessed wage laborer on the other, both tied to a global market. And even as farm production soared, industrial production outstripped it. More and more farmers left the fields for the factories. Now that the future seemed to lie with the cities, was democracy itself at risk? This question would ignite a farmers' revolt in the 1880s and dominate political debate in the 1890s.

# The American West: A Clash of Cultures

In the movies, the American West is often portrayed in mythic terms as a picturesque landscape where strong-jawed heroes square off against villains. The good guys are always white, even their hats. Often the bad guys are red—Indians, the name Columbus mistakenly gave to Native Americans. In this masculine tableau the setting is so timeless that it is easy to forget that the action takes place at roughly the same time that waves of new immigrants sailed past the Statue of Liberty, engineers built the Brooklyn Bridge, and men like John D. Rockefeller consolidated their empires in emerging industrial America. The mythical West exists away from all of this, out of time.

Once the West is situated within its historical context, however, once it is seen as a particular place at a particular time, reality supersedes myth, and the West appears to be not so different from the rest of the country. The problems and issues facing the nation at the beginning of the twentieth century—the growing power of corporations, ethnic and racial animosity, the exploitation of labor and of natural resources—all played themselves out under western skies.

## The Peoples of the Great Plains and the Far West

"West" has always been a relative term. Until the gold rush of 1849 focused attention on California, the West for settlers lay beyond the Appalachians, east of the Mississippi in the lands drained by the Ohio River—a part of the country that we now call the Old Northwest. But by 1870, "West" increasingly referred to the land across the Mississippi, from the Great Plains to the Pacific Ocean.

The West of the late nineteenth century was a polyglot place, as much so as the big cities of the East. An illustrator on his way to the California gold fields deftly depicted the mix:

> The stranger as he ascends the mountains towards the mining towns . . . notices the contrast in the scenes around him to anything he ever saw before. Indians are met in groups. . . . Strings of Chinamen pass, and greet you in broken English. . . . Next comes a Negro, with a polite "good morning, sar" or Chileno, Mexican, or Kanaka.

The parade of peoples who came to the West included immigrants from Europe, Asia, and Canada, not to mention New Englanders, Mormons, African Americans, Mexicans, Latinos, and numerous Indian tribes removed by the government. The sheer number of races that came together

**COPPER MINE**
*This 1887 photograph of the Phelps-Dodge copper mining operation in Morenci, Arizona, indicates the development of western mining. In 1881, a westerner named William Church, who had bought out the original prospector, traveled to New York to persuade the giant Phelps-Dodge mining corporation to lend him $50,000 to develop a copper mine at Morenci. Phelps-Dodge agreed. Six years later Church sold out, leaving the corporation the sole owner of the mine. In a story told over and over again, mechanized mining replaced the prospector and his burro, and mining became a big business with western mines owned by large eastern conglomerates. Note the pollution attendant on copper mining evidenced by the slag heaps in the foreground.*
Courtesy of the Arizona Historical Society, Tucson, #26,720.

and mingled in the West produced a complex racism. One historian has noted, not entirely facetiously, that there were at least eight oppressed races in the West—Indians, Latinos, Chinese, Japanese, blacks, Mormons, strikers, and radicals. The Chinese suffered brutal treatment at the hands of employers and other laborers. Fearful of competition, workingmen rioted in the 1870s and fought to keep the Chinese out of the United States. Hispanic peoples, who had lived in Texas and the Southwest since Juan de Oñate led his pioneer settlers up the Rio Grande in 1598 and who had occupied the Pacific coast since San Diego was founded in 1769, overnight were reduced to a "minority" after the United States annexed Texas and took California in the Mexican War of the 1840s. African Americans who ventured out to the terri-

tories faced hostile settlers determined to keep the West "for whites only." And Native Americans, who once warred with one another, increasingly united to fight off white encroachment.

The Mormons, followers of Joseph Smith, the founder and prophet of the Church of Jesus Christ of Latter-Day Saints, fled west to avoid religious persecution. They believed that they had a divine right to the land, and their messianic militancy contributed to making them outcasts. Although they were not the only religious sect of this period to practice plural marriage, the Mormons' polygamy (taking more than one wife) became a convenient point of attack for those who hated and feared the group. After Smith was killed by an Illinois mob in 1844, Brigham Young led the flock, which numbered more than twenty thousand, over the Rockies to the valley of the Great Salt Lake in Utah. The Utah land that they settled was a virtual desert, but the Mormons quickly set to work irrigating it. Lacking foreign or eastern capital to back them, they relied on cooperation and communalism. The church established and controlled water supplies, stores, insurance companies, and later factories and mining smelters. By 1882, the Mormons had built a thriving city of more than 150,000 residents in Salt Lake City. Not until 1896, however, when the church discontinued the practice of polygamy, did Congress grant Utah statehood.

---

*One historian has noted, not entirely facetiously, that there were at least eight oppressed races in the West—Indians, Latinos, Chinese, Japanese, blacks, Mormons, strikers, and radicals.*

---

Prospectors and cowboys have a special place in the folklore of the West. Yet by the 1870s, both mining and cattle had become big business. The colorful prospector, with his pan and his burro, gave way to huge underground operations and quartz mines in which rock was crushed to extract gold and base metals. Corporate control replaced individual prospecting, and New York replaced San Francisco as the center of speculation in mining stock.

The story of mining in the West is a tale of one rush after another in lands rich with gold, silver, lead, zinc, and copper. Boomtown to ghost town in a matter of years was a pattern common in western mining, a pattern that left an ominous legacy of reckless exploitation. Labor as well as land was harshly treated. Miners in the West, like their counterparts in Kentucky, worked for low wages in dangerous conditions. In a scenario familiar in the East, desperate miners in Coeur d'Alene, Idaho, struck for union recognition in 1892, only to be put down by state troops.

Like mining, cattle ranching became a big business in the 1870s. On the range, the cowboy gave way to the cattle king. Cattle ranchers followed the railroads onto the plains, establishing in the years between 1865 and 1885 a cattle kingdom from Texas to Wyoming. By 1886, cattle overcrowded the range. Severe blizzards during the next two winters decimated the herds. "A whole generation of cowmen," wrote one chronicler, "went dead broke." Cattle

ranching, like mining, became largely a corporate business with distant boards of directors in the East and wage-earning workers on the range.

The cowboy, that symbol of American independence, became, like the miner, a wage laborer. Though the cowboy was more colorful than his eastern counterparts in the factory, his life was no easier. Many cowboys were African Americans and Mexicans, although western literature chose to ignore that fact and transformed the black cowboy Deadwood Dick into a white man. Like many other dissatisfied workers, cowboys organized labor unions in the 1880s and mounted strikes in both Texas and Wyoming.

The American West in the nineteenth century witnessed more than its share of bloodshed. Violence broke out between cattle ranchers and sheep ranchers, between ranchers and farmers, between strikers and bosses, between rival Indian groups, and between whites and those whom they judged "lesser breeds." At issue was who would control the vast resources of the emerging region. Each group claimed the public domain as its own, and each group was prepared to fight for it. In the ensuing struggle for preeminence, the biggest losers with the most broken promises were those with the best claim to the land, the Americans who had been living on it since before Columbus or Coronado or de Soto arrived.

## The Final Removal of the Indians

In the 1830s, President Andrew Jackson initiated the policy of Indian removal by pushing the Cherokee, Choctaw, Chickasaw, Creek, and Seminole tribes off their lands in the southern United States. Jackson's Indian removal forced thousands of men, women, and children to leave their homes in Georgia and Tennessee and walk hundreds of miles to lands across the Mississippi River. So many died of hunger, exhaustion, and disease along the way that the Cherokees called their path "the trail on which we cried." At the end of this trail of tears stood the Great Plains. Here, the government promised the Indians, they could remain "as long as grass shall grow."

But in the 1840s, the gold rush in California, the Mexican War, and Oregon land fever put an end to the promise. Settlers repeatedly trespassed onto Indian land and then were surprised when they encountered hostility. Indignantly, they demanded protection from the U.S. army. The result was thirty years of Indian wars that culminated in a final removal of the Indians.

The Indian wars on the plains lasted from 1861 until 1890. By the time they ended, only 250,000 Native Americans remained of the estimated 2.5 million who had lived on the continent when Columbus landed. To Americans filled with theories of racial superiority, the Indian constituted, in the words of a Colorado militia major, "an obstacle to civilization." Testifying before a congressional commission in 1864, the major concluded that they "should be exterminated." The federal government, acting through the army, adopted a different policy, succinctly summed up by General William T. Sherman: "Rather remove all to a safe place and then reduce them to a helpless condition." The government herded the Indians into ever dwindling reservations where the U.S. Bureau of Indian Affairs, a badly managed, weak agency, often acting through corrupt agents, supposedly ministered to their needs (Map 17.2).

On the plains, the Sioux, Cheyenne, Arapaho, Nez Perce, Comanche, Kiowa, Ute, Apache, and Navajo nations put up a determined resistance. The Indian wars involved violence and atrocities on both sides. (See the Historical Question on page 456.) In 1864 at Sand Creek, Colonel John M. Chivington, leader of the local Colorado militia, slaughtered an entire village of Cheyenne. An upright Methodist elder, Chivington watched as his men mutilated their hapless victims and later justified the killing of Indian children with the terse remark "Nits make lice." The city of Denver treated Chivington and his men as heroes, but after a congressional inquiry he was forced to resign his commission to avoid court-martial.

Two years later, the Cheyenne united with the Sioux and retaliated on the Bozeman Trail in Montana and Wyoming. Captain William Fetterman, who had boasted that with eighty men he could ride through the Sioux nation, was killed, along with all eighty-one of his troops. The Sioux's impressive victories led to a treaty in 1868, under which the government promised to give the Indians lands stretching from the Missouri River to the Black Hills in western South Dakota in return for their promise to stop fighting. The great chief Red Cloud led many of his people onto the new reservation. But several young chiefs, among them Crazy Horse of the Oglala band and Sitting Bull of the Hunkpapa, refused to go. Crazy Horse said that he wanted no part of the "piecemeal penning" of his people. Rene-

gade bands of Sioux continued to roam the plains, hunting buffalo.

The buffalo had a more dangerous enemy than the Indian—the railroad. To the Sioux and the Kiowa the buffalo constituted a way of life, the source of food, fuel, and shelter and a central part of religion and ritual. To the railroads the buffalo were a nuisance, at best a target for sport and a source of cheap meat for the workers. Buffalo hunters hired by the railroads decimated the great herds; sport hunters fired at random from railroad cars just for the thrill of it. In the heyday of buffalo hunting in the 1880s, hunters sold as many as fifty thousand hides at a time to tanneries in the East. In thirty years, more than sixty million animals were slaughtered. General Philip Sheridan applauded the hunters for "destroying the Indians' commissary." The army took credit for subduing the Indians, but their defeat came about more as a result of the decimation of the buffalo herds.

In 1876, rumors of gold in the Black Hills effectively nullified the government's promise to Red Cloud. Miners began pouring into the area, and the Northern Pacific Railroad made plans to build tracks. Lieutenant Colonel George Armstrong Custer fed the fever by trumpeting news of the first gold strikes. Under the leadership of Crazy Horse and Sitting Bull, the Sioux tribes massed to resist the incursion. In June, Custer led the two hundred men of the Seventh Cavalry into the largest group of Indians ever assembled in one place on the plains. At the Little Bighorn River in Montana Territory, four thousand Sioux warriors set upon them. No federal soldier lived to tell the story, but Crazy Horse, Sitting Bull, and others recounted the killing of Pahuska or Long Hair, as the Indians called the dashing Custer. Their victory was short-lived. In the next year, Crazy Horse was killed and Sitting Bull surrendered. Chief Joseph of the Nez Perce resisted removal and fled toward Canada. Just forty miles from freedom, federal troops caught up with his band. With his people cold and starving, the chief surrendered. His speech stands as an eloquent statement of the plight of the Indians:

I am tired of fighting. Our chiefs are killed. . . . It is cold and we have no blankets. The little children are freezing to death. My people, some of them, have run away to the hills, and have no blankets, no food; no one knows where they are—perhaps freezing to death. I want to have time to look for my children and see how many I can find. Maybe I shall find

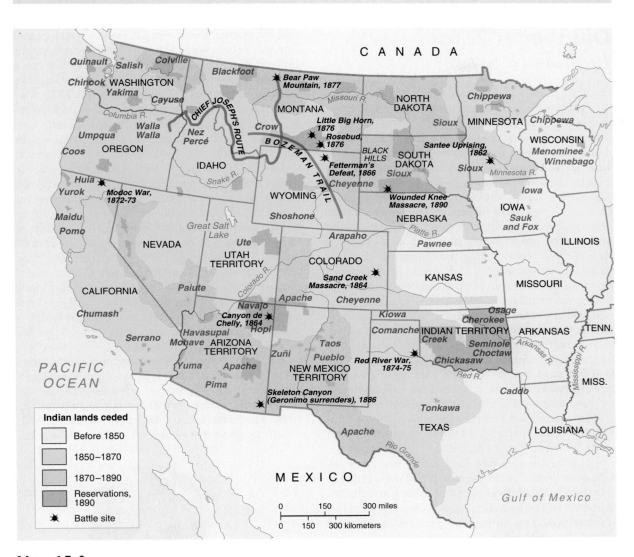

## MAP 17.2
### The Loss of Indian Lands, 1850–1890

*By 1890, western Indians were isolated on small, scattered reservations. Native Americans strug-gled to retain their land in major battles, from the Santee uprising in Minnesota in 1862 to the massacre at Wounded Knee, South Dakota, in 1890.*

them among the dead. Hear me, my chiefs, I am tired; my heart is sick and sad. From where the sun now stands, I will fight no more forever.

The policy of rounding up Indians and herding them onto reservations gained momentum. After Custer's Last Stand, as the battle in 1876 came to be called, policy toward the Indians toughened. Even the most philanthropic Americans seemed con-

vinced that the Indian way of life must go. Instead of remaining American Indians, they had to become Indian Americans. When Indians resisted, their children were taken off the reservations and sent to special schools to learn white ways—to play the piano, to farm, to act like white Americans.

In 1887, Congress passed the Dawes Act, breaking up the reservations and giving each Indian an allotment of land. The act effectively reduced Indian

# Did Whites Teach Indians to Scalp?

IN 1879, JUST THREE YEARS AFTER Custer and his troops were massacred at the Little Bighorn, Susette La Flesche, a member of the Omaha tribe, made a national tour to promote justice for Native Americans. Using her Indian name, Bright Eyes, La Flesche made a fascinating spokesperson for Indian rights. Her father, one of the best known of the Omaha chiefs, was of mixed blood, as was his wife. The La Flesche family embraced Christianity and advocated "progressive" Indian policy. Working closely with Presbyterian missionaries, they attacked the use of alcohol and urged Indians to take up farming. Susette grew up in the first frame house on the reservation in Nebraska. All the La Flesche children attended Presbyterian mission school at the Omaha agency. Later Susette and her sisters were sent to boarding school in New Jersey. Susette's sister Susan La Flesche Picotte became the first Indian woman to receive a medical degree, and her brother Francis became the first Indian anthropologist employed by the Smithsonian Institution. To Victorian society, the remarkable La Flesche family offered an inspiring example of the transition from "savagery" to civilization.

Susette La Flesche's East Coast tour was intended to publicize the plight of the Ponca Indians, who had lost their land in one of the many swindles perpetrated by the federal government. Boston audiences expecting an Indian "princess" dressed in deerskin encountered instead an educated young woman in a black velvet bonnet. But for all her modest demeanor, La Flesche did not hesitate in pointing out the routine barbarity of the U.S. army in its treatment of the Plains tribes. In Chicago, she was accosted by a reporter who chided her, pointing to the Indians' "barbarous . . . acts of atrocity upon captives and the bodies of the dead." La Flesche shot back, "Scalping, you mean, I suppose. Don't you know that the white man taught Indians that?" She insisted that "scalping was first practiced in New England on the Penobscot Indians." The General Court of the province of Massachusetts, she informed the reporter, "offered a bounty of forty pounds for every scalp of a male Indian brought in as evidence of his being killed, and for every scalp of a female or male Indian under twelve years, twenty pounds."

A hundred years later, La Flesche's charge that European colonists in New England had taught the Indians to scalp was well on its way to becoming accepted wisdom. Native American author Vine Deloria, in his widely read manifesto *Custer Died for Your Sins* (1969), echoed the belief that eighteenth-century European settlers with their bounty laws had introduced the practice of scalping among the eastern tribes.

Certainly scalping became synonymous with Indian barbarity. Europeans might draw and quarter, burn at the stake, and introduce the tortures of the rack, but Indian mutilation of the dead remained the quintessential symbol of "savagery." Not surprisingly, La Flesche's effort to rehabilitate the popular image of the Indian in 1879 and Deloria's similar effort a century later began by calling into question the Indian origin of scalping. If whites had taught Indians to scalp, who then was the "savage"? As scholars became more sympathetic to the dispossession of American Indians and sought to rehabilitate the stereotype of the "fiendish savage," the charge that scalping was a white invention gained wide acceptance. But was it factual? Had the European settlers, with their bounties on scalps, introduced the practice?

Historian James Axtell set out to find the answer. But what sources would provide "proof"? Axtell drew on the records of early explorers and

**SUSETTE LA FLESCHE**
*Susette La Flesche toured the country in 1879 using her Indian name, Bright Eyes, to publicize the plight of the Ponca Indians. It was La Flesche who alleged that whites had taught the Indians to scalp.*
Nebraska State Historical Society.

settlers and on the work of ethnohistorians, who study "primitive" peoples, and archaeologists. All of the evidence seemed to point in the opposite direction from Susette La Flesche's confident assertion. Among the earliest visitors to American shores, Jacques Cartier in 1535 described "skins of five men's heads, stretched on hoops, like parchment." The practice was widespread, noted by Cartier in the North and by Hernando de Soto's men in Florida and the Southeast. As Axtell carefully demonstrated, "the list of Europeans who found scalping among the eastern Indians in the earliest stages of contact could be extended almost indefinitely."

Furthermore, although Europeans practiced many barbarities during the sixteenth and seventeenth centuries, nowhere was there evidence that they ever scalped their victims. The European languages did not even have a word to describe the practice. Archaeological evidence, too, pointed away from La Flesche's claim. Pre-Columbian skulls collected by early anthropologists showed distinct evidence of scalping.

What role, then, did scalping play in Indian culture? According to ethnohistorians and their Indian subjects, the practice, while widespread, varied markedly from tribe to tribe. Often the scalp served as more than physical proof of valor. The Iroquois believed that after death the soul hovered by the body. To take the scalp, they believed, was to take the spiritual life of the enemy. However, the practice of scalping took on a different character during the French and Indian War when both sides offered their Indian allies bounties for scalps, sometimes as much as one hundred pounds (roughly two hundred dollars) for every scalp of an adult male. Soon the trading of scalps became part of the complex web that bound Indians and whites in colonial commerce. In Salem, Massachusetts, scalps that had been redeemed for bounties decorated the walls of the town courthouse until it was torn down in 1785.

By the nineteenth century, bounties had long been outlawed, and scalping existed among the Plains Indians in the context of tribal practice. Black Elk, an Oglala Sioux, recounted how he took his first scalp and proudly presented the trophy to his mother for her approval.

One final intriguing piece of the puzzle is the question of how Custer escaped scalping. Well known for his flowing locks, Custer, by all accounts, was not scalped after the battle, as were many of his men. Although no soldier lived to describe the battle scene, Indian accounts are unanimous in their assertion that Custer's body was not mutilated, except for one fingertip. Why did the Indians not take his scalp for a trophy? In large part the answer has changed as Custer's fortunes with historians and the public have waxed and waned. At the time of his death, when Custer was viewed as a brave martyr, writers conjectured that his Indian foes respected his bravery and refused to mutilate the man they called Pahuska, or Long Hair. As Custer's reputation sank to low ebb in the mid-twentieth century, writers became more skeptical. One author guessed that Custer, who was balding by 1879 and had cut his hair, was spared because from a warrior's point of view his scalp made a poor trophy.

lands from 138 million acres to a scant 48 million, making it, in the words of one critic, "a bill to despoil the Indians of their lands and to make them vagabonds on the face of the earth." The surplus land was then opened to white settlement, setting off the great land rushes in Oklahoma. Well-meaning philanthropists viewed the Dawes Act as a way to foster individualism among the Indians and to extend to them the rights of citizenship. The result of this legislation, however, was the further destruction of Indian culture.

## Indian Resistance

Faced with the extinction of their entire way of life and means of livelihood, different groups of Indians responded in different ways. Outright violent resistance was perhaps best embodied in the Apache Geronimo, while nonviolent resistance was exemplified in the Ghost Dance religion, a nonviolent movement that swept the Plains in the 1890s. Both met with the same brutal military repression.

The Apache tribes who roamed the Sonoran desert of southern Arizona and northern Mexico never combined as the Plains Indians had done so successfully at the Little Bighorn. Instead they operated in small raiding parties, perfecting a hit-and-run guerrilla warfare that deviled the army in the 1870s and 1880s. General George Crook, a skilled Indian fighter, combined a policy of dogged pursuit with judicious diplomacy. Convinced that white troops could not fight the Apache on their home ground, Crook relied on Indian scouts, recruiting nearly two hundred, to hunt down the Apaches.

**INDIANS**

*Sevara, identified as a Ute chieftain, poses with three generations of his family in this photograph. Pictures like this one depict a way of life that by the end of the nineteenth century was already becoming extinct. Only in posed photographs carefully crafted for public consumption did the proud history of Native Americans seem able to survive.*

From *Birth of a Century,* KEA Publishing Services, Ltd.

Eventually Crook was able to persuade most of the renegades to surrender. By 1882, the Apaches had settled on the San Carlos reservation.

Reservation life was particularly difficult for the nomadic Apache. Geronimo, a warrior chief, repeatedly led raiding parties of renegades off the reservation. They were fierce warriors who raided ranches, killing the ranchers and stealing their cattle and horses. In the spring of 1885, Geronimo went on a ten-month rampage, moving from his sanctuary in the Sierra Madre to raid and burn ranches and towns on both sides of the Mexican border. General Crook captured Geronimo in the fall, only to have him slip away with a small band on the way back to San Carlos. Chagrined, Crook resigned his post. General Nelson Miles, Crook's replacement, determined to put an end to Geronimo once and for all, adopted a policy of hunt and destroy.

There were only thirty-three Apaches still at large, thirteen of them women, but they eluded Miles's troops for more than five months. Throughout the blistering summer, the Indians, constantly on the move, kept one step ahead of the army. In the end this small band of Apaches fought two thousand soldiers to a stalemate. Caught between Mexican regulars and the American army, Geronimo agreed to march north with the soldiers and negotiate a settlement. "We have not slept for six months," Geronimo admitted, "and we are worn out." Geronimo met with Miles and negotiated a peace, but, as in the past, the Indians did not get what they were promised.

Less than three dozen Apaches had been hostile when General Miles induced them to surrender, yet the government gathered up nearly five hundred Apaches and sent them as prisoners to Florida, including former scouts who had helped track Geronimo. By 1889, more than a quarter of them had died, some by illness contracted in the damp, lowland climate and some by suicide. Their plight roused public opinion and eventually, in 1892, they were moved to Fort Sill in Oklahoma and later to New Mexico.

Geronimo lived to become something of a celebrity. He appeared at the St. Louis Exposition in 1904, where he sold pictures of himself for twenty-five cents apiece, and rode in President Theodore Roosevelt's inaugural parade in 1905. In a newspaper interview he confessed, "I want to go to my old home before I die. . . . Want to go back to the mountains again. I asked the Great White Father to allow

**GHOST DANCE DRESS**
*This deerskin dress was worn by an Arapaho woman during the ghost dance fervor of the 1880s in Oklahoma. Decorated with stars and eagles, it evoked powerful magic to protect its wearer.*
National Museum of the American Indian.

me to go back, but he said no." None of the Apaches were permitted to return to Arizona; when Geronimo died in 1909, he was buried in Oklahoma.

On the Plains many different tribes turned to a nonviolent form of resistance—a compelling new religion, the Ghost Dance. The Paiute shaman Wovoka, drawing on a cult that had developed in the 1870s, combined elements of Christianity and traditional Indian religion to found the Ghost Dance religion in 1889. Wovoka claimed that he had received a vision in which the Great Spirit spoke through him to all Indians, urging them to unite and promising that whites would be destroyed in an apocalypse. The Indian warriors slain in battle would return to life, and buffalo once again would roam the land unimpeded.

This religion of despair with its message of hope spread like wildfire over the plains. It was danced in Idaho, Montana, Utah, Wyoming, Colorado, Nebraska, Kansas, the Dakotas, and Oklahoma Territory by tribes as diverse as the Arapaho, Cheyenne, Pawnee, and Shoshone. Various tribes developed different forms of the dance, but all dances were held in a circle. Often dancers went into hypnotic trances. Some danced until they dropped from sheer physical exhaustion.

Ghost Dances were generally nonviolent, but among the Sioux, especially the Oglala, Blackfeet, and Hunkpapa, the dance took on a more militant flavor. Sioux disciples of the Ghost Dance religion taught that the wearing of white ghost shirts made Indians immune to the bullets of the soldiers. Their message frightened whites, who began to fear an uprising. "Indians are dancing in the snow and are wild and crazy," wrote the Bureau of Indian Affairs agent at the Pine Ridge reservation in South Dakota. Frantic, he pleaded for reinforcements. "We are at the mercy of these dancers. We need protection, and we need it now." President Benjamin Harrison dispatched several thousand federal troops to Sioux country to handle any outbreak.

In December 1889, when Sitting Bull sought permission to go to the Pine Ridge reservation to meet with Wovoka, the local Indian agent laid a trap for him, and Sitting Bull was shot. His people, fleeing the scene, were apprehended by the Seventh Cavalry, Custer's old regiment, near Wounded Knee Creek, South Dakota. As the Indians laid down their arms, a shot rang out and the army opened fire. In the ensuing melee, Indian warriors stormed the troops, killing more than thirty soldiers. But they were badly outgunned. Men, women, and children were mowed down in minutes by the army's brutally efficient Hotchkiss machine guns. More than two hundred Sioux lay dead or dying in the snow. Settler Jules Sandoz surveyed the scene the day after the massacre. "Here in ten minutes an entire community was as the buffalo that bleached on the plains," he wrote. "There was something loose in the world that hated joy and happiness as it hated brightness and color, reducing everything to drab agony and gray."

Although the massacre at Wounded Knee did not end the story of Native Americans, it did eliminate their way of life. The Indian population would gradually recover; the 1990 census showed 1.9 million Native Americans. But their culture sustained a crushing blow. In the words of the visionary Black Elk, "The nation's hoop is broken and scattered. There is no center any longer, and the sacred tree is dead."

## The West of the Imagination

Even as the Old West was dying, the myth of the West was being created. The dime novel, a precursor of today's paperback, capitalized on western heroes like Kit Carson, Wild Bill Hickok, Calamity Jane, and Deadwood Dick to entertain eastern readers seeking escapist fare. Published in the East and sometimes written by tenderfeet who had never ventured beyond the Hudson River, dime novels sold at a prodigious rate.

The prince of the dime novel heroes was Buffalo Bill, featured in more than two hundred titles. Born William F. Cody, the real-life Buffalo Bill had panned for gold, ridden for the Pony Express, scouted for the army, and earned his nickname hunting buffalo for the railroad. A masterful showman, he capitalized on his success and formed a touring Wild West Company in 1883. Part circus, part theater, the Wild West extravaganza featured exhibitions of riding, shooting, and roping and presented dramatic reenactments of great moments in western U.S. history. The star of the show was Annie Oakley, a crack shot who delighted the crowd by shooting a dime out of her husband's hand. The centerpiece of Buffalo Bill's Wild West Show was the reenactment of Custer's Last Stand, in which Indians in war paint and bonnets massacred the hapless Custer and his men. At the end, Buffalo Bill galloped in with a cloud of dust and dramatically mouthed the words "Too late!"

The Wild West that Buffalo Bill presented to the American people indiscriminately mixed the authentic with the romantic until reality itself was blurred in the popular mind. Cody had not arrived too late at the Little Bighorn. But some of the Indians in his troupe had been there and knew their parts firsthand. During the 1885 season, Sitting Bull, a veteran of the Little Bighorn, toured with Buffalo Bill. The rapid demise of the Wild West that Buffalo Bill enshrined in his show may perhaps best be comprehended if we juxtapose Cody with historian Frederick Jackson Turner. At the 1893 Columbian Exposition in Chicago, Turner addressed the American Historical Association on "The Significance of the Frontier in American History." Turner postulated that the frontier had vanished, that by 1890 American settlers had filled the map of the West so that no clear frontier line could be discerned. Later historians would take issue with Turner's thesis that what made America unique was some fixed, retreating frontier. But the sense of an old world

**BUFFALO BILL POSTER**
*Buffalo Bill Cody used colorful posters to publicize his Wild West Show during the 1880s and 1890s. One of his most popular features was the reenactment of Custer's Last Stand, which he performed for Queen Victoria in London and at the World Columbian Exposition in Chicago.*
Buffalo Bill Historical Center, Cody, Wyoming.

passing that Turner summed up in his speech was perhaps nowhere better demonstrated than across the Chicago fairground in the spectacle of Buffalo Bill's Wild West Show performing the "Battle of the Little Bighorn" to sellout crowds in the bleachers. The high drama of the struggle for the West by 1893 had become no more than a thrilling but harmless entertainment.

The West of the imagination, the West of Buffalo Bill, of artists Frederic Remington and Albert Bierstadt, of novelists Owen Wister and Zane Grey, shrouded the region in myth. Yet the historical reality was every bit as dramatic as the fictions it sparked: By the 1890s, the American West had been transformed. More than seven-tenths of the farmland west of the Mississippi River was owned by investors who neither farmed nor ranched the land

themselves. The shift from farming and ranching to agribusiness, not the disappearance of some magical frontier line, marked the end of an era in America. Far from being a mythic landscape out of place and time, the West was linked inextricably to the urban East by capital investment and iron rails that carried western goods to world markets.

## The Rise of the City

Although much of the nation remained heavily rural, the last decades of the nineteenth century witnessed an urban explosion. Cities and towns grew more than twice as rapidly as the total population, far outstripping rural growth. Patterns of global migration contributed to the ascendancy of urban America. In the port cities, immigrants from southern and eastern Europe lived in dense ghettos where the English language was rarely heard. The word *slum* entered the American vocabulary during these years and with it a growing concern over the gap between the rich and the poor, a gap only widened by the changing social geography of the cities.

## The Urban Explosion, a Global Migration

"We cannot all live in cities, yet nearly all seem determined to do so," New York editor Horace Greeley complained. The astonishing growth that occurred in the nation's cities between 1870 and 1900 came about not from the natural increase of the city population but from the internal and international movement of people.

The percentage of people living in towns and cities leaped from 20 percent in 1870 to 33 percent by 1900. Growth in the urban population actually divided about evenly between large and small cities. But the emergence of the modern metropolis marked the most dramatic demographic development of the period. The number of cities with more than 100,000 inhabitants jumped from eighteen in 1870 to thirty-eight by 1900. As the twentieth century began, the United States could boast three cities with more than a million inhabitants—New York, Chicago, and Philadelphia.

Railroad growth stimulated urban development. Cities like Reno, Butte, and Cheyenne sprang up along the tracks long before the surrounding countryside was settled. The transcontinental rail lines set off booms in Kansas City, Omaha, and Salt Lake City.

---

*The astonishing growth that occurred in the nation's cities between 1870 and 1900 came about not from the natural increase of the city population but from the internal and international movement of people.*

---

Urbanization went hand in hand with industrialization. As workers left the farm for the factory, the growth of the urban population fueled a constantly expanding market. In a process that economists call the multiplier effect, the growing market in turn stimulated greater and greater production, creating more jobs in an expanding spiral. The emergence of a mass consumer market enabled cities to become centers for wholesaling and retailing, not just manufacturing and industry. Chicago, with its mail order houses like Montgomery Ward and Sears, Roebuck, along with its great department stores, Marshall Field and Carson Pirie Scott, led the country as an urban marketing center.

The United States grew up in the country and moved to the city, or so it seemed by the twentieth century. Hundreds of thousands of farm boys and girls ran away to the city looking for jobs in the burgeoning industrial centers and hoping to make their fortunes. But for at least one group, the move to the city promised something more. African Americans came north looking not just for economic opportunity. Restrictive laws that segregated blacks, called Jim Crow laws, became common throughout the South in the decades following reconstruction. The South's efforts to segregate and subordinate African Americans gained federal endorsement when in 1896 the United States Supreme Court in the landmark case *Plessy v. Ferguson* upheld the legality of segregated facilities under the doctrine of "separate but equal." Intimidation and lynching, justified by white Southerners as necessary to "keep the Negro in his place," also became increasingly common throughout the South. "To die from the bite of frost is far more glorious than at the hands of a mob," proclaimed the *Defender*, Chicago's largest African American newspaper. As early as the 1890s, many blacks agreed. They moved North, settling for the most part in the growing cities. Racial discrimination and poverty limited blacks' options in the North, just as they had in the South. Yet by 1900, New York, Philadelphia, and Chicago contained the largest black communities in the nation. Although the greatest African American migration out of the South would occur during and after the end of World War I, the great exodus was already under way.

Rural migrants to the cities were by no means limited to American farmers and southern blacks. Worldwide in scope, the movement from rural areas to industrial centers attracted to the United States more than fourteen million Europeans in the waning decades of the nineteenth century. That migration came in two distinct waves that have been called the old and the new immigration. (See page A-46 in the Appendix.) Before 1880, the bulk of the new arrivals came from northern and western Europe, with the Germans, Irish, English, and Scandinavians making up approximately 85 percent of the newcomers.

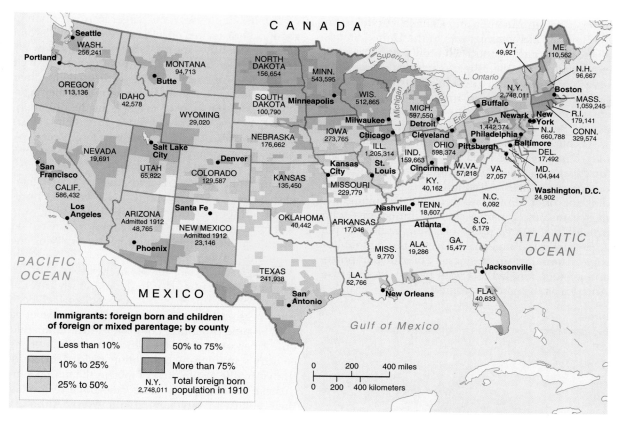

**MAP 17.3**
*The Impact of Immigration to 1910*
*Immigration flowed in all directions, as the map indicates—south from Canada, north from Mexico, east from Asia to the port cities Seattle and San Francisco, and west from Europe to ports in Boston and New York. By 1910, the immigrant population was spread throughout the country, with the notable exception of the southern states. In some areas—along the Canadian border and the Rio Grande and in the nation's burgeoning cities—the foreign born and their children totaled over 75 percent of the population.*

After 1880, the pattern shifted, with more and more immigrant ships carrying passengers from southern and eastern Europe. Italians, Hungarians, eastern European Jews, Turks, Armenians, and Poles, Russians, and other Slavic peoples accounted for more than 80 percent of all the immigrants by 1896. Alongside the tide of new European immigrants streamed Japanese coming east from Asia, French Canadians flowing south to work in New England's mill towns, and Mexicans and other Latin Americans heading north to settle in California and the Southwest (Map 17.3).

In sheer numbers, the new immigration was unprecedented. In 1888 alone, more than half a million Europeans came to America, 75 percent landing in New York City. The Statue of Liberty, a gift from the people of France erected in 1886, stood sentinel in the harbor. A young Jewish girl named Emma Lazarus penned the verse at Liberty's base:

> Give me your tired, your poor,
> Your huddled masses yearning to breathe free,
> The wretched refuse of your teeming shore,
> Send these, the homeless, tempest-tost to me,
> I lift my lamp beside the golden door!

## The New Immigrants and the Call for Immigration Restriction

The new wave of immigration at the turn of the century resulted from a number of factors. Improved economic conditions in western Europe, as well as immigration to Australia and Canada, cut down on the flow of "old" immigrants to the United States. At the same time, a protracted economic depression in southern Italy, the religious persecution of Jews in eastern Europe, and a general desire to avoid conscription into the Russian army led many in southern and eastern Europe to move to the United States. (See page A-46 in the Appendix.)

Economic factors in the United States also played a role. The need of America's industries for cheap, unskilled labor stimulated immigration during good times. Although the U.S. government did not offer direct inducements to immigrate, the steamship companies courted immigrants, who provided a highly profitable, self-loading cargo. Agents from the large lines traveled throughout Europe drumming up business. Colorful pamphlets and posters mingled fact with fantasy to advertise America as the land of promise.

**IMMIGRANTS**

*Dressed in the clothing of the old country (cap and collarless shirt, apron and shawl), this immigrant couple carries their meager possessions, bedding in his bundle, food and utensils in her basket, and two umbrellas tied together. Note how the man gazes confidently, almost defiantly, into the camera, while the woman, looking miserable, averts her eyes. What do their postures tell about whose decision it was to come to America and about their hopes and apprehensions?*
Wide World Photos, Inc.

Would-be immigrants eager for information about America relied on letters, advertisements, and word of mouth—sources that were not always dependable or truthful. Even photographs proved deceptive—American workers dressed in their Sunday best looked more prosperous than they actually were to the eyes of relatives in the old country, where only the very wealthy wore white collars or silk dresses. As one Italian immigrant recalled, "Everything emanating from America reached [Italy] as a distortion. . . . News was colored, success magnified, comforts and advantages exaggerated beyond all proportions." No wonder immigrants left for America believing "that if they were ever fortunate enough to reach America, they would fall into a pile of manure and get up brushing the diamonds out of their hair."

In at least one respect, life in the new world differed markedly from that in the old. In their countries of origin, most of the newcomers had been rural peasants, farmers, and villagers. In America they became urbanites, both out of inclination and out of necessity. By 1900, almost two-thirds of the country's immigrant population resided in cities, drawn by the availability of jobs in the nation's industrial centers at the same time poverty limited their ability to buy land in the West. Although nowhere did the foreign-born population outnumber the native-born population, taken together foreign immigrants and their American-born children did constitute a majority in many of the nation's largest cities. Fifty percent of Philadelphia's population was foreign-born or born of foreign parents, and the percentages were even higher in other cities: 66 percent in Boston, 75 percent in Chicago, and an amazing 80 percent in New York City.

Not all the newcomers came to stay. Perhaps eight million, mostly young men, worked for a year or a season and then returned to their homelands. American immigration officers referred to these young male immigrants as "birds of passage" because they followed a regular pattern of migration to and from the United States. By 1900, almost 75 percent of the new immigrants were single young men. Intent on making money as quickly as possible, they were willing to accept conditions that other workers regarded as intolerable. They showed little interest in labor unions and organized only when the dream of returning home faded, as it did for millions who ultimately remained in the United States.

Jews from eastern Europe most often came with their families and came to stay. In the 1880s, a wave of violent pogroms, or persecutions, in Rus-

**STUDIO PORTRAIT OF IMMIGRANTS**
*Studio portraits of immigrant families, like this one of a Russian Jewish family taken at the turn of the century, showed everyone dressed in their finest clothes—the men in starched shirts and collars, the women in silk dresses or lacy shirtwaists. Mailed back to relatives in Europe, these pictures provided a tantalizing but not always entirely accurate picture of the promise of America.*
Collection of Sharon Salinger.

sia and Poland led to the departure of more than a million Jews in the next two decades. They settled mostly in the port cities of the East. New York City's Lower East Side replicated the Jewish ghettos of eastern Europe, teeming with street peddlers and pushcarts.

To many Americans, the new immigrants from southern and eastern Europe seemed uneducated, backward, and outlandish in appearance—impossible to assimilate. "These people are not Americans," editorialized the popular journal *Public Opinion*, "they are the very scum and offal of Europe." Terence Powderly, head of the labor organization the Knights of Labor, complained that the newcomers "herded together like animals and lived like beasts."

Old-stock aristocrats such as Senator Henry Cabot Lodge of Massachusetts formed an unlikely alliance with organized labor to press for immigration restriction. A precedent for keeping out "undesirable" immigrants had been established in 1882, when labor agitation and racism in California led to passage of the Chinese Exclusion Act. On the East Coast, Lodge and his followers championed a literacy test, a device designed to limit immigration from Italy and eastern Europe by requiring immigrants to demonstrate the ability to read and write in their native language. Since the vast majority of Italian and Slavic peasants had no schooling, it was assumed that few would be able to pass the test. In

1906, Congress approved a literacy test for immigrants, but President Grover Cleveland promptly vetoed it. "It is said," the president reminded Congress, "that the quality of recent immigration is undesirable. The time is quite within recent memory when the same thing was said of immigrants, who, with their descendants, are now numbered among our best citizens." Cleveland's veto forestalled immigration restriction but did not stop the forces seeking to close the gates. They would continue to press for restriction until they achieved their goal in the 1920s.

## The Social Geography of the City

In the 1870s, Cleveland, Ohio, was a small city, in both population and geographical area. Oil magnate John D. Rockefeller could, and often did, walk from his large brick townhouse on Euclid Avenue to his office downtown. On his way he passed the small homes of his clerks and other middle-class families. Behind these homes ran miles of alleys crowded with the dwellings of Cleveland's working class. Farther out, on the shores of Lake Erie, close to the factories and foundries, clustered the shanties of the city's poorest laborers.

Within two decades, the Cleveland that Rockefeller knew no longer existed. With the coming of mass transit, the walking city was transformed. In its place emerged a central business district surrounded by concentric rings of residences graded by ethnicity and income. First the horsecar in the 1870s and then the electric streetcar in the 1880s made it possible to commute to work. City workers could enjoy single-family homes with lawns, gardens, and trees and still travel to work downtown for as little as five cents a day. By the early twentieth century, more than half of Cleveland's residents rode the streetcars to work. This pattern of development was repeated throughout the country as urban congestion and suburban sprawl forever altered the social geography of the city.

The city's poor, unable to afford even the few cents for trolley fare, crowded into the inner city or lived "back of the yards" near the factories where they worked. The term *slum* came into common use by the mid-nineteenth century, coinciding with the increased clustering of the poor in the least desirable areas of the city. This social segregation—rich and poor, ethnic and old-stock Americans—was one of the major social changes engendered by the rise of the industrial metropolis, and it occurred not only in Cleveland but in cities across the nation.

Race and ethnicity affected the way in which cities evolved. Newcomers to the burgeoning cities, whether Jews and Italians "just off the boat" or African Americans up from the South, sought out their kin and countryfolk and struggled to maintain their culture in distinct neighborhoods that often formed around the synagogue or church. Blacks typically experienced the greatest residential segregation, but every large city had its ethnic neighborhoods, its Little Italy, Chinatown, Bohemia Flats, or Germantown, where one could walk for blocks without hearing a word of English.

In 1890, a young police reporter named Jacob Riis took his notebook and his camera into the tenements of New York's Lower East Side; the result was the best-selling book *How the Other Half Lives*. Riis invited his audience into a Cherry Street tenement:

> Be careful please! The hall is dark and you might stumble over the children pitching pennies back there. . . . Close? Yes! What would you have? All the fresh air that ever enters these stairs comes from the hall door and is forever slamming, and from the windows of dark bedrooms that in turn receive from the stairs their sole supply of the elements God meant to be free, but man deals out with such niggardly hand. . . .
> Here is a door. Listen! That short hacking cough, that tiny, helpless wail—what do they mean? They mean that the soiled bow of white you saw on the door downstairs will have another story

to tell—Oh! a sadly familiar story—before the day is at an end. The child is dying with measles. With half a chance it might have lived; but it had none. That dark bedroom killed it.

As Riis discovered, poverty, crowding, dirt, and disease constituted the daily reality of New York's poor. Riis's book, like his photographs, presented a world of black and white. There were many layers to the population Riis labeled "the other half," distinctions furthered by ethnicity, religion, race, and gender. *How the Other Half Lives* must be read more as a call to action than as an accurate portrayal.

Jacob Riis's audience shivered at his revelations about the "other half." But middle-class Americans worried equally about the excesses of the wealthy and the class antagonism fueled by the growing chasm between the rich and the poor. Many people shared Riis's view that "the real danger to society comes not only from the tenements, but from the ill-spent wealth which reared them."

---

*Jacob Riis's audience shivered at his revelations about the "other half." But middle-class Americans worried equally about the excesses of the wealthy and the class antagonism fueled by the growing chasm between the rich and the poor.*

---

The excesses of newly minted millionaires in the decades following the Civil War were nowhere more visible than in the lifestyle of the Vanderbilts. In 1883, Alva Vanderbilt (Mrs. William K. Vanderbilt I) determined to gain admittance to old New York society, which had resisted the inclusion of the *nouveaux riches* (newly rich). She threw a costume party so lavish that no one could resist an invitation. Dressed as a Venetian princess, Alva Vanderbilt greeted her twelve hundred guests. But her sister-in-law capped the evening, appearing in costume as that miraculous new invention, the electric light, resplendent in a white satin evening dress studded with diamonds. Many costumes cost as much as $1,500 apiece, three times the average yearly wage of a worker. Vanderbilt's ball stands as a legend in the annals of social excess.

Such ostentatious displays of wealth became even more alarming when they were coupled with disdain for the general welfare of the people. When a reporter in 1882 asked William Vanderbilt whether he considered the public good in running his rail-roads, he shot back, "The public be damned." The fear that America had become a plutocracy—a society ruled by the rich—gained credence from the fact that the wealthiest one percent of the population owned more than half the real and personal property in the country (a century later, the top one percent controlled less than a quarter).

## City Life and City Images

In America, private enterprise built the cities. Boosters, builders, businessmen, planners, and politicians all had a hand in creating the modern city. With a few notable exceptions, such as Washington, D.C., there was no such thing as a comprehensive city plan. Cities simply mushroomed, formed by the dictates of private enterprise and the exigencies of local politics. With the rise of the city came the need for public facilities, transportation, and services that would tax the imaginations of America's architects and engineers and set the scene for the rough and tumble story of big-city politics and politicians.

### Big-City Government and the "Bosses"

The physical growth of the cities required the expansion of public services and the creation of entirely new facilities: streets, subways, elevated trains, bridges, docks, parks, sewers, and public utilities. There was work to be done and money to be made. The professional politician—the colorful big-city boss—became a phenomenon of nineteenth-century urban growth. Although corrupt and often criminal, the boss saw to the building of the city and provided needed social services for the new residents. Not even the big-city boss could be said to rule the unruly city. The governing of America's cities resembled more a tug-of-war than boss rule.

The most notorious of all the city bosses was William Marcy Tweed of New York. At midcentury, Boss Tweed's Democratic Party machine held sway. A machine was really no more than a political party organized on the grassroots level. It existed to win elections and reward its followers with jobs on the city's payroll. New York's citywide Democratic organization, Tammany Hall, consisted of an army of party functionaries. At the bottom were the district captains. In return for votes, they provided services for their constituents, everything from a scuttle of coal in the winter to housing for an evicted family.

**TAMMANY BANK**
*This cast-iron bank, a campaign novelty, is named after the New York City Democratic machine. It tells its political reform message graphically: When you put a penny into the politician's hand, he puts it in his pocket. Tammany Hall dominated city politics for more than a century, dispensing contracts and franchises worth millions of dollars. Some of those dollars invariably found their way into the pockets of Tammany politicians.*
Collection of Janice L. and David J. Frent.

At the top were the powerful ward bosses who distributed lucrative franchises for subways and streetcars. They formed a shadow government, more powerful than the city's elected officials. Tweed held the official title of alderman. But as a ward boss and chairman of the Tammany general committee, he wielded more power than the mayor. Through the use of bribery and graft, he held the Democratic Party together and ran the city.

The cost of Tweed's rule was staggering. The construction of New York City's courthouse, budgeted at $250,000, ended up costing the taxpayers $14 million. The inflated sum represented bribery, kickbacks, and the greasing of many palms. The excesses of the Tweed ring soon led to a clamor for reform and cries of "Throw the rascals out." Cartoonist Thomas Nast pilloried Tweed in the pages of *Harper's Weekly.* His cartoons, easily understood even by those who could not read, did the boss more harm than hundreds of outraged editorials.

Tweed fled to Europe in 1871 to avoid prosecution, but eventually he was tried and convicted and died in jail.

New York was not the only city to be charged with bossism and corruption. The British visitor James Bryce concluded in 1888, "There is no denying that the government of cities is the one conspicuous failure of the United States." More than 80 percent of the nation's thirty largest cities experienced some form of boss rule in the decades around the turn of the century.

Infighting among powerful ward bosses was more typical in municipal government than domination by one big-city boss. "Czar" Martin Lomasney in Boston and Chicago's "Bathhouse" John Coughlin and Michael "Hinky Dink" Kenna exemplified the breed. Their colorful nicknames signaled their distance from respectable society and hinted at unsavory connections with an underworld of crime and vice. The power they wielded belied the charge that any single boss enjoyed hegemony in the big cities.

Occasionally, a political strategist of more than ordinary skill emerged to become a bona fide boss. Less notorious but more powerful than Boss Tweed was Richard Croker of New York. Croker, who ruled Tammany Hall beginning in 1886, relied more on bureaucracy than boodle (bribery). He directed the distribution of lucrative construction contracts, he controlled franchises for street railways and public utilities, and he made sure these plums went to men who supported the party machine. Like Tweed, Croker held no elective office. As boss, he did not want to govern; he simply wanted to ensure that he and his supporters benefited from government. Unlike Tweed, who died in jail, Croker retired in 1901 to Wantage, his country estate in Ireland, a move that led one of his critics to quip, "New York's wastage is Croker's Wantage."

In the late nineteenth century, urban reformers and proponents of good government (derisively called "goo goos" by their rivals) challenged machine rule and sometimes succeeded in electing reform mayors. But the reformers rarely managed to stay in office for long. Their detractors called them "mornin' glories," observing that they "looked lovely in the mornin' and withered up in a short time." New York's William Strong is a fair example of the breed. A businessman, he won office in 1894 on the basis of his reputation for honesty and integrity. But Strong lacked the political skills needed to win reelection.

The bosses enjoyed continued success over the reformers for one main reason: the help the urban political machine handed out to the cities' immigrants and poor. In return for votes the machine provided legal aid, jobs, fuel, temporary shelter, and a host of small favors. The ability to combine philanthropy and politics was a hallmark of the urban boss. "What tells in holding your district is to go right down among the poor and help them in the different ways they need help," a Tammany ward boss observed. "It's philanthropy, but it's politics, too—mighty good politics." For the social services they received (and not because they were ignorant or undemocratic, as critics charged), the urban poor remained the bosses' staunchest allies.

*For all the color and flamboyance of the big-city boss, he was simply one of many actors in the drama of municipal government.*

Some reform mayors managed to achieve success and longevity. In cities where they sponsored public services and championed the working class, reformers proved as unbeatable as any boss. Hazen S. Pingree of Detroit exemplified the successful reform mayor. A businessman who went into politics in the 1890s, Pingree, like most good-government candidates, promised to root out dishonesty and inefficiency. He did, but he also tangled with business interests when he tried to lower streetcar fares and utility rates. When the depression of 1893 struck, Pingree emerged as a champion of the working class and the poor. He hired the unemployed to build schools, parks, and public baths. And he fought for and got public ownership of electric utilities. By providing needed services, he built a powerful political organization based on working-class support. Detroit's voters kept him in the mayor's office for four terms and then helped elect him governor twice.

While most good-government candidates harped on the Sunday closing of saloons and attacked vice and crime, Pingree demurred. "The most dangerous enemies to good government are not the saloons, the dives, the dens of iniquity and the criminals," but "the temptations which are offered to city officials when franchises are sought by wealthy corporations, or contracts are to be let for public works."

As Pingree shrewdly observed, not only the urban poor but the business class benefited from bossism and corruption. The boss could juggle tax assessments for property owners and provide lucrative franchises. Through the skillful orchestration of rewards, an astute political operator like Croker exerted powerful leverage and lined up support for his party from a broad range of constituents, from the urban poor to wealthy industrialists. When journalist Lincoln Steffens wrote *The Shame of the Cities* in 1904, a series of articles exposing city corruption, he found that business leaders who fastidiously refused to mingle socially with the bosses nevertheless struck deals with them. "He is a self-righteous fraud, this big businessman," Steffens concluded. "I found him buying boodlers [bribers] in St. Louis, defending grafters in Minneapolis, originating corruption in Pittsburgh, sharing with bosses in Philadelphia, deploring reform in Chicago, and beating good government with corruption funds in New York."

The complexity of big-city government, apparent in the levels of corruption Steffens uncovered, pointed to one conclusion: For all the color and flamboyance of the big-city boss, he was simply one of many actors in the drama of municipal government. The successful boss was not an autocratic ruler but a power broker. Old-stock aristocrats, new professionals, saloonkeepers, pushcart peddlers, and politicians all fought for their interests in the hurly-burly of city government. They didn't much like each other and they sometimes fought savagely. But they learned to live with one another. Compromise and accommodation—not boss rule—best characterized big-city government by the turn of the century.

## Building Cities of Stone and Steel

"A town that crawled now stands erect," boasted an ironworker. "And we whose backs were bent above the [open] hearths know how it got its spine." Technology transformed the urban landscape in the late nineteenth and early twentieth centuries. Where once wooden buildings had stood rooted in the mire of unpaved streets, new cities of stone and steel sprang up. The skyscrapers and mighty bridges dominated the imagination and the urban landscape at the turn of the century. Less imposing, but no less significant, were the paved streets, the parks and public libraries, and the subways and sewers. In the late nineteenth century, Americans rushed to embrace new technology, making their cities the most modern in the world.

The Brooklyn Bridge opened in May 1883 and was quickly proclaimed "one of the wonders of the world." The world's longest suspension bridge soared over the East River in a single mile-long span

connecting Brooklyn and Manhattan. Begun in 1869 during the days of Boss Tweed, the great bridge was the dream of John Roebling, who never lived to see it completed. His son, Washington Roebling, carried on the great work.

The building of the Brooklyn Bridge called forth heroic effort. It took fourteen years and cost the lives of twenty men. To sink the foundation deep into the riverbed, laborers tunneled down through the mud and debris, working in reinforced wooden boxes called caissons, which were open at the bottom and pressurized to keep the water from flooding in. When the men emerged after a hard day's work, they often came up too quickly and suffered from the crippling effects of "the bends," a painful,

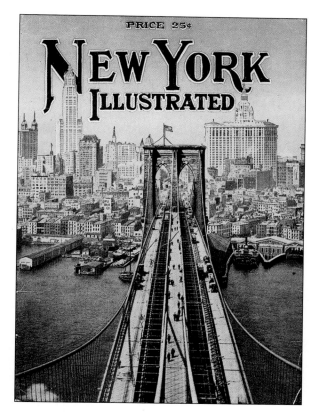

**BROOKLYN BRIDGE**
*Arching 130 feet above the East River, the Brooklyn Bridge has proven not only aesthetically pleasing but remarkably functional for more than a century. A raised walkway allows pedestrians to enjoy their view above the traffic. Roebling succeeded in his goal—to create "a great work of art" as well as "a successful specimen of advanced Bridge engineering."*
Picture Research Consultants & Archives.

debilitating condition caused by nitrogen bubbles forming in the blood. Washington Roebling himself fell victim to this disorder and ended up an invalid. He directed the completion of the bridge from his window in Brooklyn Heights through a telescope while his wife, Emily Warren Roebling, acted as site superintendent and general engineer of the project. When the bridge was dedicated in 1883, Roebling turned to his wife and said, "I want the world to know that you, too, are one of the Builders of the Bridge."

Skyscrapers as well as bridges changed the cityscape. Competition for space in Manhattan pushed the city up into the air even before the use of steel. The invention of Elisha Otis's elevator (called a "safety hoister") in the 1850s led to the construction of cast-iron buildings with elevators that carried passengers as high as ten stories. In 1890, the Pulitzer Building climbed to 349 feet, the tallest office building in the world. But until the advent of structural steel, no building in Manhattan topped the spire of Wall Street's Trinity Church.

Chicago, not New York, gave birth to the modern skyscraper. Rising from the ashes of the Great Fire of 1871, Chicago offered a generation of skilled architects and engineers the chance to experiment with new technologies. Commercial architecture reached an art form at the hands of a skilled group of architects who together constituted the "Chicago school." Men of genius such as Louis Sullivan and John Wellborn Root gave Chicago some of the world's finest commercial buildings. Employing the dictum "form follows function," they built startlingly modern structures. The massive commercial buildings, in Root's words, "carried out the ideas of modern business life, simplicity, breadth, dignity." A fitting symbol of modern America, the skyscraper expressed and exalted the domination of corporate power.

Alongside the skyscrapers rose new residential apartments for the rich and middle class. The "French flat" gained popularity in the 1880s as city dwellers overcame their distaste for multifamily housing (which carried the stigma of the tenement) and gave in to "flat fever." Fashionable new apartments, built for affluent tenants, boasted such modern luxuries as electricity, telephones, central heating, elevators, and modern plumbing. The convenience of apartment living appealed particularly to women. "Housekeeping isn't fun," cried one New York woman. "Give us flats!" In 1883 alone, more than one thousand new apartments went up in Chicago.

The flush toilets, bathtubs, and sinks in the new apartments would not have been possible without major improvements in city sewers and water mains. Under the direction of enlightened city engineers, municipalities expanded their sewers and devised ingenious ways to bring clean water to the urban population. Rudolph Herring earned the title Dean of Sanitary Engineering by planning the sewer systems for Philadelphia, New York City, Chicago, Los Angeles, Baltimore, Washington, D.C., Minneapolis, Montreal, Toronto, and Mexico City. By the 1890s, the residents of American cities demanded and received, at the twist of a faucet, water for their bathtubs, toilets, and even their lawn sprinklers. Those who could afford it enjoyed a standard of living that was the envy of European capitals.

Throughout the United States, municipal governments undertook public works on a scale unknown in European cities. They paved streets with asphalt, replaced gas lamps with electric lights, ran trolley tracks on the old horsecar lines, and dug underground to build subways and tore down the unsightly elevated tracks that had clogged the city streets. In San Francisco, Andrew Smith Hallidie mastered the city's hills, building a system of cable cars in 1873. Montgomery, Alabama, became the first city in the country to install a fully electrified streetcar system in 1886. Boston completed the nation's first subway system in 1897, and New York and Philadelphia soon followed.

To fight disease and dirt, cities enlisted an army of public health inspectors. Using the latest methods made possible by the discovery of the microbe in the 1870s, they battled cholera, smallpox, and diphtheria. In 1874–1875 alone, New York vaccinated more than 126,000 people against smallpox. Municipal health departments became common in all the nation's large cities.

Cities became not only healthier, but also more beautiful as planners created urban public parks. Much of the credit for America's public parks goes to one man—landscape architect Frederick Law Olmsted. Olmsted designed parks in cities from Atlanta, Brooklyn, and Hartford to Detroit, Chicago, and Louisville. The indefatigable Olmsted also laid out the grounds for the U.S. Capitol and planned an entire city, Riverside, Illinois. The Boston park system, a seven-mile ring of green that Olmsted called the city's "emerald necklace," was his most ambitious and successful project. But he is best remembered for the creation of New York's Central Park. He and his partner Calvert Vaux directed the planting of more than five million trees, shrubs, and vines to transform the eight hundred acres between 59th and 110th Streets into an oasis for urban dwellers. "We want a ground to which people may easily go after their day's work is done," he wrote, "where they may stroll for an hour, seeing, hearing, and feeling nothing of the bustle and jar of the streets."

---

*The enduring monuments of America's cities—the bridges, skyscrapers, apartments, parks, and libraries—stood as the undeniable achievements of the same system of municipal government that many reformers dismissed as boss-ridden, criminal, and corrupt.*

---

American cities did not overlook the mind in their efforts at improvement. They created a comprehensive free public school system that educated everyone from the children of urban professionals to the sons and daughters of immigrants. The exploding urban population strained the system and led to crowded and inadequate facilities, but no one was turned away. In 1899, more than 544,000 pupils attended school in New York's five boroughs. Schools in Boston, New York, Chicago, and Detroit as well as other cities and towns provided the only classrooms in the world where students could attend secondary school free of charge.

In addition to schools, the cities built libraries to educate their citizens. American cities in the late nineteenth century created the most extensive free public library system in the world. In 1895, the Boston Public Library opened its bronze doors under the inscription "Free to All." Designed in the style of a Renaissance palazzo, with more than 700,000 books on the shelves ready to be checked out, the library earned the description "a palace of the people." Across the United States, other cities participated in the public library movement. Cincinnati, Detroit, St. Louis, Chicago, and Cleveland sponsored libraries in the 1870s. And in New York, Philadelphia, and Buffalo, the city stepped in with support when private libraries faltered in the 1890s.

Despite the Boston Public Library's legend "Free to All," the poor did not share equally in the advantages of city life. The parks, the libraries, and even the subways and sewers benefited some city dwellers more than others. Few library cards were held by Boston's laborers, who worked six days a week and found the library closed on Sunday. And

in the 1890s, there was nothing central about New York's Central Park. It was a four-mile walk from the tenements of Hester Street to the park's entrance at 59th Street and Fifth Avenue. Cities spent more money on plumbing improvements for affluent apartment dwellers than on public baths and lodging houses for the down and out. Even the uniform subway fare, which enabled Boston and New York riders to travel anywhere in the system for five cents, worked to the advantage of the middle-class commuter and not the downtown poor. Then, as now, the comfortable majority and not the indigent minority reaped a disproportionate share of the benefits in the nation's big cities.

Any story of the American city, it seems, must be a tale of two cities—or, more correctly, given the great diversity, a tale of many cities within each metropolis. At the turn of the century a central paradox emerged: The enduring monuments of America's cities—the bridges, skyscrapers, apartments, parks, and libraries—stood as the undeniable achievements of the same system of municipal government that many reformers dismissed as boss-ridden, criminal, and corrupt.

## Conclusion: The City and the Country

By 1900, Americans on the move had populated a continent. Settlers had pushed into the trans-Mississippi West, forcing Native Americans onto reservations and establishing eight new states and three territories. At the same time a massive migration of peoples, global in its scope, touched off an urban explosion, filling the cities and in some cases doubling the urban population each decade. Mass migration transformed both rural and urban life. As settlers pushed out onto the plains agriculture became increasingly commercial, with bonanza farms totaling thousands of acres tilled by machine, not muscle. In urban America mass transportation and the development of the skyscraper transformed the cityscape at the same time that millions of new immigrants arrived on the shores.

Increasingly, the city and the country were two parts of a whole, tied together by rails of steel. A vast spiderweb of railway tracks linked the burgeoning cities to the orange groves of California, the cotton fields of Texas, and the cattle ranches of Montana—collapsing time and distance.

# CHRONOLOGY

**1860** 2.5 million farms established on public lands.

**1862** Homestead Act promises 160 acres of western land to anyone who settles on land for five years.

**1870** 80 percent of population lives in rural areas, according to U.S. census.

**1870s** Cattle ranching and mining become big business in West.

**1871** William Marcy Tweed's rule in New York ends in ignominy.

Fire ravages Chicago and leads to new boom in architectural innovation as city rebuilds.

**1873** Panic on Wall Street leads to nationwide economic depression.

**1876** George Armstrong Custer and cavalry force of two hundred killed by four thousand Indians near Little Bighorn River in Montana Territory.

Statehood granted to Colorado.

**1880–1890** Rural areas of New England and Midwest suffer depopulation.

**1880s** Immigration patterns shift as more people arrive from southern and eastern Europe.

Heyday of buffalo hunting in West leads to slaughter of sixty million animals.

**1882** Chinese Exclusion Act prohibits immigration of Chinese nationals to United States.

**1883** Buffalo Bill Cody begins to tour with his Wild West company.

Brooklyn Bridge opens over New York City's East River.

**1886** Statue of Liberty, a gift from France, dedicated in New York harbor.

Severe blizzards in Dakotas devastate cattle ranching.

Geronimo surrenders and is shipped to Florida as prisoner of war.

**1887** Congress passes Dawes Act, breaking up Indian lands.

Massive droughts defeat homesteaders on Great Plains.

**1889** Rise of Ghost Dance religion among Native Americans in West.

Sitting Bull killed by U.S. soldiers at Pine Ridge reservation.

Government opens two million acres of former Indian territory in Oklahoma to settlement.

Statehood granted to Montana, North Dakota, South Dakota, and Washington.

**1890** Last remnant of Sioux surrender, and army troops kill 200 Indians at Wounded Knee, South Dakota. Only 250,000 Indians remain from an estimated 2.5 million living when Christopher Columbus landed.

Jacob Riis's *How the Other Half Lives* documents harsh poverty in New York City tenements.

Statehood granted to Idaho and Wyoming.

**1890s** First wave of African American migration from South to North begins.

**1893** Panic on Wall Street touches off major economic depression.

Columbian Exposition opens in Chicago.

Frenzied land rush takes place on Cherokee strip in Oklahoma Territory.

**1895** Boston Public Library opens under slogan "Free to All."

**1896** Statehood granted to Utah.

**1900** Census finds that 66 percent of population live in rural areas, compared with 80 percent in 1870.

Three cities—New York, Chicago, and Philadelphia—top one million inhabitants.

# SUGGESTED READINGS

Edward L. Ayers, *The Promise of the New South: Life After Reconstruction* (1992). A comprehensive cultural, political, and social history of the region after the Civil War which emphasizes the role played by the railroad not only in the economy, but in the development of racial segregation.

John Bodnar, *The Transplanted: A History of Immigration in Urban America* (1985). Emphasizing the specificity rather than the normative nature of immigrant experience, Bodnar provides a look at the "new" immigrants of the late nineteenth century.

John B. Boles, *The South through Time* (1995). The most recent survey of the South incorporating the latest scholarship with particular attention to Indians, African Americans, and women.

William Cronon, *Nature's Metropolis: Chicago and the Great West* (1991). Convincingly demonstrates the interstices of city and country in the booming metropolis of Chicago. Cronon documents the widespread effects of the city on the surrounding ecological, cultural, and economic frontier.

David C. Hammack, *Power and Society: Greater New York at the Turn of the Century* (1982). A comprehensive history of New York City's transformation in the late nineteenth century from a mercantile center to a modern metropolis. Focuses on how many groups, from immigrants to elites, sought to shape the modern city.

Patricia Nelson Limerick, *The Legacy of Conquest: The Unbroken Past of the American West* (1987). Limerick's bold and provocative look at the West touched off a major revision in Western history. Limerick strongly argues that the history of the trans-Mississippi West is not so different from that of the rest of the country.

Nell Irvin Painter, *Standing at Armageddon: The United States, 1877–1919* (1987). Painter convincingly captures the feeling of apprehension that accompanied the major social, economic, and political developments in the period from the end of the Civil War to the end of World War I.

Roy Rosenzweig and Elizabeth Blackmar, *The Park and the People: A History of Central Park* (1992). A social history of New York's Central Park that shows the antagonism between the place of repose intended by Frederick Law Olmsted and the people's wish for a playground.

Lillian Schlissel, Byrd Gibbens, and Elizabeth Hampsten, *Far from Home: Families of the Westward Migration* (1989). Through documentary texts, provides the flavor of life in the West as it was experienced by women and families.

Jon C. Teaford, *Unheralded Triumph: City Government in America, 1870–1919* (1987). A reexamination of the achievements, as well as the corruption, associated with the rise of urban America. Teaford argues that the "bosses'" power has been exaggerated.

Richard White, *"It's Your Misfortune and None of My Own": A History of the American West* (1991). A lively and readable synthesis of Western history. Building on the work of Limerick and the "new Western history," White emphasizes the West's diversity and what makes it similar, as well as different, from the rest of America.

**CAMPAIGN LANTERN**

*Political parties gave out novelty items like this paper lantern from Republican Benjamin Harrison's 1888 presidential campaign. The log cabin, a staple political icon, celebrates the candidate's humble origins, while the reference to Tippecanoe highlights his relationship to President William Henry Harrison, his grandfather, the victor of the Battle of Tippecanoe in 1811. "Protection" in bold letters underscores the Republican Party's support for a tariff designed to protect the country's industries from foreign competition.*

Collection of Janice L. and David J. Frent.

# BUSINESS AND POLITICS IN THE GILDED AGE

## 18

### 1877–1895

THROUGHOUT THE WINTER OF 1894–95, in the midst of the worst depression the country had yet seen, President Grover Cleveland walked the floor of the White House, sleepless over the prospect that the United States might go bankrupt. The Treasury's gold reserves had dipped so low that unless gold could be purchased abroad, the unthinkable might happen—the U.S. Treasury might not be able to meet its obligations.

Cleveland, like many honest and upright men of his era, believed that the only sound money was gold. Although other forms of currency circulated, notably paper money like banknotes and greenbacks, the government's support of the gold standard meant that all currency could be redeemed for gold. A major Wall Street panic in 1893 precipitated financial uncertainty, and in its wake banks and individuals rushed to cash in their banknotes and demand gold.

In late January 1895, New York financiers John Pierpont Morgan and August Belmont suggested a plan whereby a private group of bankers would purchase gold abroad and supply it to the Treasury. Cleveland knew only too well that the scheme might give the financial community confidence, but it would bring a thunder of protest from people and politicians suspicious of the power the influential bankers wielded. He vacillated, hesitant to strike a deal.

Early in February 1895, J. P. Morgan traveled by private railway car to Washington to meet with the president. Cleveland, still brooding over his dilemma, refused to see Morgan. The great banker appeared unruffled by the snub. "I have come down to see the president," he told the crowd of reporters, "and I am going to stay here until I see him."

The next day, Cleveland summoned Morgan to the White House. When a phone call informed the president that only $9 million in gold remained in the New York branch of the Treasury, Morgan responded ominously that he knew of a $10 million debt outstanding. "What suggestion have you to make, Mr. Morgan?" Cleveland asked. To save the gold standard, the president had no choice but to turn to Morgan for help.

A storm of controversy erupted over the deal between Cleveland and Morgan. The press claimed that the president had lined his own pockets in the transaction and rumored that Morgan had made $8.9 million in profits. With the convenience of hindsight, it is difficult to see what all the fuss was about. The historical record has shown that Cleveland was an honest though stubborn man and that Morgan acted more from patriotism than for profit. His share, far from the millions his critics claimed, amounted to $295,652.

Yet the passions stirred by Cleveland's bond deal in 1895 cannot be dismissed lightly. If Morgan and Cleveland managed to salvage the gold standard, their

**J. P. MORGAN, PHOTOGRAPH BY EDWARD STEICHEN**
*Few photographs of J. P. Morgan exist. Morgan, who suffered from a skin condition that left him with a misshapen strawberry of a nose, rarely allowed his picture to be taken. But it was his eyes that people remembered—eyes so piercing that Edward Steichen, who took this photograph, observed that "meeting his gaze was a little like confronting the headlights of an express train."*
Courtesy of George Eastman House, reprinted with permission of Joanna T. Steichen.

action did not save the country. The winter of 1894–95 was one of the hardest in American history. People faced unemployment, cold, and hunger. Neither Cleveland nor Morgan acknowledged that their great faith in gold prolonged the depression, favored creditors over debtors, and caused immense hardship for millions of Americans.

Perhaps the real meaning of the crisis of 1895 had more to do with power than gold. Cleveland's actions made it clear that J. P. Morgan, and not the president, had it in his power to save the Treasury. How had such enormous power accrued to businessmen? And what did it mean for the future of American democracy? The increasing emphasis on money and moneymaking stimulated by industrial development also worried the writer Mark Twain, who coined the term "Gilded Age" to highlight the

crass materialism of the era. (See Texts in Historical Context on page 480.)

The rise of industrialism in the United States and the interplay of business and politics strike the key themes in the Gilded Age, the period from the 1870s to the 1890s. Bound closer by a network of railroads and telegraphs, with the fate of small towns and rural areas linked as never before to the fortunes of big cities, America in the late nineteenth century became united in fact as well as in name. Industrial development transformed the lives of all Americans, from factory workers to farmers. In the United States, the transition from a rural, agricultural economy to urban industrialism proved a deeply unsettling experience. The hopes and fears that industrialism inspired can be seen in the public's attitude toward the great business moguls of the day, men like Jay Gould, Andrew Carnegie, John D. Rockefeller, and J. P. Morgan. These larger-than-life figures dominated not only business but the popular imagination as the heroes and villains in the high drama of industrialization. At no other period in U.S. history would the industrial giants and the businesses they built (and sometimes wrecked) loom so large in American life.

## Old Industries Transformed, New Industries Born

In the years following the Civil War, the scale and scope of American industry expanded dramatically. Old industries became modern big businesses, while discovery and invention stimulated new industries such as oil and electric power. The rise of the railroad played the key role in the transformation of the American economy, creating a national market that enabled businesses to expand from a local to a nationwide scale. Needing more and better rails to carry freight, the railroad radically changed the iron industry by speeding the transition from iron to steel. The railroad had what economists call a multiplier effect, accelerating the pace of growth in many segments of the economy.

### The Railroads, America's First Big Business

In the decades following the Civil War, the United States built the greatest railroad network in the world and in the process created America's first big business. In 1869, America's first transcontinental railroad system was completed when the Union Pacific and Central Pacific tracks came together in Promontory Point, Utah, and a golden spike was driven to commemorate the occasion. Between 1870 and 1880, the amount of track laid in the country doubled, and it nearly doubled again in the following decade. By 1900, the country boasted over 193,000 miles of track, more than all of Europe and Russia combined (Map 18.1).

To understand how the railroads developed and came to dominate American life, there is no better study than the career of Jay Gould, a man who came to personify the Gilded Age. Jason "Jay" Gould bought his first railroad before he was twenty-five years old. It was only sixty-two miles long, in bad repair, and on the brink of failure. But within two years, he had sold it at a profit of

$130,000. Thus began the career of the man who would pioneer the development of America's railway system and become the era's most notorious speculator. Gould, the sickly, frail son of a farmer, decided early to run away to the city to make his fortune. Like many Americans in the 1850s, he saw the railroad as the key to the future.

Gould, by his own account, knew little about railroads and cared less about their operation. Nevertheless, he became a master of corporate expansion, the architect of the vast railway systems that developed in the 1870s. The secretive Gould operated like a shark in the stock market, looking for vulnerable railroads, buying enough of their stock to take control, and threatening to undercut his competitors until they bought him out at a high profit. The railroads that fell into his hands, like the

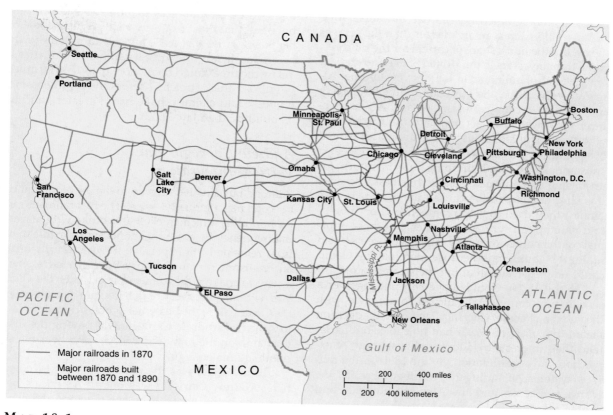

**M A P  18.1**
*Railroad Expansion, 1870–1890*
*Railroad mileage nearly quadrupled between 1870 and 1890, with the greatest growth coming in the trans-Mississippi West. New transcontinental lines—the Great Northern, the Northern Pacific, the Southern Pacific, and the Atlantic*

*and Pacific—were completed in the 1880s. Small feeder lines like the Oregon Short Line and the Atchison, Topeka, and Santa Fe fed into the great transcontinental systems, knitting the nation together.*

Erie, fared badly and often went bankrupt. But Gould's genius lay in cleverly buying and selling railroad stock, not in providing transportation.

Jay Gould's power and success underscored the haphazard development of the American railway system. To encourage railroad building, the federal and state governments provided the railroads with generous cash subsidies and grants of land. States and local communities clamored to offer inducements to railroad builders, knowing that towns and villages along the tracks would grow and flourish. Since the federal government held vast tracts of public land in the West, Congress did not hesitate to give it away to promote railroad building. The railroads not only received land for rights-of-way but were granted liberal sections on alternating sides of the track to do with as they pleased, most often to sell to the settlers who followed the railroads into the West. Over the years, the federal government alone granted the railroad builders a total of 180 million acres, an area larger than the state of Texas. But the lion's share of capital for the railroads came from investors in the United States and abroad.

Lack of planning soon led to overbuilding. Already by the 1870s, the railroads competed fiercely for business on the eastern seaboard. A manufacturer who needed to get goods to the market and who was fortunate enough to be in an area served by a number of competing railroads could get a substantially reduced shipping rate in return for promising the railroad steady business. Because this kind of competition caused the owners to lose money, they tried to set up agreements or "pools" to divide up territory and set rates. But these informal combinations invariably failed because they had no legal standing and because men like Jay Gould could not resist undercutting their competitors.

In the 1880s, Gould moved to put together a second transcontinental railroad to compete with the Union Pacific/Central Pacific. His decision meant that other railroads had no choice but to defend their interests by adopting his strategy of expansion and consolidation. By the 1890s, large railway systems, including the Southern Pacific, the Northern Pacific, and the Atchison, Topeka, and Santa Fe Railroads, dominated American rail travel.

Not all the early railroad builders were as unscrupulous as Gould. James J. Hill built the Great Northern and built it well. Without benefit of land grants or subsidies, Hill had to plan carefully and calculate which areas would best be served by the railroad in order to maximize returns to his investors. As a result, the Great Northern was one of the few major railroads able to weather the hard times of the 1890s. In contrast, speculators like Daniel Drew and James Fisk, Gould's partners at the Erie, could more accurately be described as wreckers than as builders. They ruined the Erie Railroad, gambling with its stock to line their own pockets. In the West, the Big Four railroad builders—Collis P. Huntington, Richard Crocker, Leland Stanford, and Mark Hopkins—became so powerful that critics charged that the Southern Pacific held California in the grip of an "octopus."

The public's alarm at the control wielded by the new railroads provided a barometer of attitudes toward big business itself. When Jay Gould died in 1892, the press described him as "the world's richest man," estimating his fortune at over $100 million. His competitor "Commodore" Cornelius Vanderbilt, who built the New York Central Railroad, judged Gould "the smartest man in America." But to the American public, who found in Gould a symbol of all that most troubled them about the rise of big business, he was, as he himself admitted shortly before his death, "the most hated man in America." Yet by the time Gould died, more than 150,000 miles of railroad track stretched across the continent and no one could claim to have had a greater hand in its building than Jay Gould.

## Andrew Carnegie and Vertical Integration

Railroad building led directly to the development of a second major industry—steel. The first railroads ran on iron rails, which cracked and broke with alarming frequency. Steel, stronger and more flexible than iron, remained too expensive for use in rails until an Englishman named Henry Bessemer developed a way to make steel from pig iron. After the Civil War, with the discovery of rich iron ore deposits near the Great Lakes, the Bessemer process came into use in America. Andrew Carnegie was among the first to champion the new "King Steel," and he came to dominate the emerging industry.

If Jay Gould was the man Americans loved to hate, Andrew Carnegie was one of America's heroes. The hatred toward the one man and the popularity of the other testified to the country's ambivalent reaction to industrialism. Carnegie, a Scots immigrant, landed in New York in 1848 at the age of twelve. He rose from a job cleaning bobbins in a textile factory at $1.20 a week to become one of the richest men in America. Before he died, he gave away more than $300 million of his fortune, most

**LET THEM HAVE IT ALL, AND BE DONE WITH IT!**

**RAILROAD TYCOONS**

*This political cartoon appeared in* Puck, *a magazine with a partisan Democratic bent. Here the railroad barons, notably Jay Gould and William Vanderbilt, are caricatured carving up the country with long knives. The power wielded by*

*these railroad tycoons worried many who feared that their machinations were detrimental to small business, farmers, and labor.*

Culver Pictures.

notably to public libraries. His generosity, combined with his own rise from poverty, gave him a positive image with the public. But he had another side— that of a shrewd businessman capable of making harsh demands on those who worked for him.

When Carnegie was still a teenager, his skill as a telegraph operator caught the attention of Tom Scott, superintendent of the Pennsylvania Railroad. Scott hired Carnegie, soon promoted him, and lent him the money for his first investments. A millionaire before he turned thirty, Carnegie struck out on his own to reshape the iron and steel industries. "My preference was always manufacturing," he wrote. "I wished to make something tangible." By applying the lessons of cost accounting and efficiency that he had learned from twelve years with

the Pennsylvania Railroad, Carnegie turned steel into the nation's first manufacturing big business.

In Braddock, on the outskirts of Pittsburgh, Pennsylvania, in 1872 he built the most up-to-date Bessemer steel plant in the world and began turning out steel at a furious rate. At that time, steelmakers were able to produce about seventy tons a week. Within two decades, Carnegie's blast furnaces poured out an incredible ten thousand tons a week. Using railroad accounting methods, he cut the cost of making rails in half, from $58 to $25 a ton. Carnegie's formula for success was simple: "Cut the prices, scoop the market, run the mills full; watch the costs and profits will take care of themselves." And they did. By 1900, Carnegie Steel earned $40 million in a single year.

# Mark Twain and
# The Gilded Age

*In 1874 Mark Twain (Samuel Langhorne Clemens) and Charles Dudley Warner published* The Gilded Age, *a novel that quickly became a runaway best-seller. Warner supplied the sentimental melodrama, while Twain "hurled in the facts." The result was uneven as fiction, but offered a savage satire of the speculative mania of the Grant era that ever after would be known as the* Gilded Age.

*In a typical passage Colonel Beriah Sellars, a prime example of the speculator/entrepreneur, spins castles in the air for the gullible Washington Hawkins, the novel's naive hero.*

"I intend to look out for you, Washington, my boy. I hunted up a place for you yesterday, but I am not referring to that, now—that is a mere livelihood— mere bread and butter; but when I say I mean to look out for you I mean something very different. I mean to put things in your way that will make a mere livelihood a trifling thing. I'll put you in the way to make more money than you'll ever know what to do with. You'll be right here where I can put my hand on you when anything turns up. I got some prodigious operations on foot; but I'm keeping quiet; mum's the word; your old hand don't go around powwowing and letting everybody see his k'yards and find out his little game. But all in good time, Washington, all in good time. You'll see. Now there's an operation in corn that looks well. Some New York men are trying to get me to go into it— buy up all the growing crops and just boss the market when they mature—ah I tell you it's a great thing. And it only costs a trifle; two millions or two

and a half will do it. I haven't exactly promised yet—there's no hurry—the more indifferent I seem, you know, the more anxious those fellows will get. . . .

"And then there is the hog speculation—that's bigger still. We've got quiet men at work," [he was very impressive here,] "mousing around, to get propositions out of all the farmers in the whole west and northwest for the hog crop, and other agents quietly getting propositions and terms out of all the manufactories—and don't you see, if we can get all the hogs and all the slaughter houses into our hands on the dead quiet—whew! It would take three ships to carry the money,—I've looked into the thing— calculated all the chances for and all the chances against and though I shake my head and hesitate and keep on thinking, apparently I've got my mind made up that if the thing can be done on a capital of six millions, that's a horse to put up money on! Why Washington—but what's the use of talking about it—any man can see that there's whole Atlantic oceans of cash in it, gulfs and bays thrown in. But there's a bigger thing than that, yet—a bigger——"

. . . Washington finally got his breath and said:

"Oh, it is perfectly wonderful! Why couldn't these things have happened in father's day? And I—it's of no use—they simply lie before my face and mock me. There is nothing for me but to stand helpless and see other people reap the astonishing harvest."

"Never mind Washington, don't you worry. I'll fix you. There's plenty of chances. How much money have you got?"

In the presence of so many millions, Washington could not keep from blushing when he had to confess that he had but eighteen dollars in the world."

"Well, all right—don't despair. Other people have been obliged to begin with less. I have a small idea that may develop into something for us both all in good time. . . . I've been experimenting (to pass away the time,) on a little preparation for curing sore eyes—a king of decoction nine-tenths water and the other tenth drugs that don't cost more than a dollar a barrel; . . . and before many weeks I wager the country will ring with the fame of Eschol Sellars' Infallible Imperial Oriental Optic Liniment and Salvation for Sore Eyes—the Medical Wonder of the Age!"

$10,000 each—$20,000; and there's $100,000 of the money gone, to begin with. Then, seven male lobbyists, at $3,000 each—$21,000; one female lobbyist, $3,000; a high moral Congressman or Senator here and there—the high moral ones cost more, because they give tone to a measure—say ten of these at $3,000 each, is $30,000; then a lot of small fry country members who won't vote for anything whatever without pay—say twenty at $500 apiece, is $10,000 altogether;  lot of jimcracks for Congressmen's wives and children—those go a long way—you can't spend too much money in that line—well, those things cost in a lump, say $10,000—along there somewhere;—and then comes your printed documents—your maps, your tinted engravings, your pamphlets, your illuminated show cards, your advertisements in a hundred and fifty papers at ever so much a line—because you've got to keep the papers all right or you are gone up, you know. Oh, my dear sir, printing bills are destruction itself. Ours, so far amount to—let me see—10; 52; 22; 13;—and then there's 11; 14; 33—well, never mind the details, the total in clean numbers foots up $118,254.42 thus far!"

**MARK TWAIN**

*Popular author Mark Twain (Samuel Langhorne Clemens) wrote acerbically about the excesses of the Gilded Age. No one knew the meretricious lure of the era better than Twain, who succumbed to a get-rich-quick scheme that left him virtually bankrupt.*

Beinecke Rare Book and Manuscript Library, Yale University.

---

*T*wain left no one unscathed—political hacks, Washington lobbyists, Wall Street financiers, small-town boosters, wildcat miners, and the "great putty-hearted public" that tolerated the plunder. In the following passage a savvy insider describes how an appropriation bill is put through Congress.

"Why the matter is simple enough. A Congressional appropriation costs money. Just reflect, for instance. A majority of the House committee, say $10,000 apiece—$40,000; a majority of the Senate Committee, the same each—say $40,000; a little extra to one or two chairmen of one or two such committees, say

*A child of his age, Twain knew intimately the allure of money and power and the giddy rise and fall of fortune. Succumbing without much struggle to the money fever, Twain plunged into a scheme worthy of Colonel Sellars. In 1887 Twain invested $30,000 in the Paige typesetting machine, an invention Twain thought would make him millions. A complicated device with more than eighteen thousand separate parts, the machine constantly demanded more tinkering. To "perfect" it Twain threw good money after bad, until by 1891 the "infernal machine" had eaten up over $190,000, draining Twain's account and depleting his wife's inheritance. By 1894 Twain faced bankruptcy. Only the help of Standard Oil millionaire Henry H. Rogers enabled him to begin his dogged climb out of debt.*

*Twain's indictment of his times in* The Gilded Age *was not the detached disdain of an observer. Rather, it was the bitter recognition of a man deeply mired in the gaudy, meretricious lure of the era he so aptly named.*

---

Mark Twain (Samuel L. Clemens) and Charles Dudley Warner, *The Gilded Age, A Tale of To-Day* (Hartford, Conn.: American Publishing Company, 1974), 84–87, 254–256.

To guarantee the lowest costs and the maximum output, Carnegie pioneered a system of business organization called *vertical integration*. All aspects of the business were under Carnegie's control. From the mining of iron ore to its transport on the Great Lakes to the production of crude steel and rails, vertical integration in steel meant, in the words of one observer, that "from the moment these crude stuffs were dug out of the earth until they flowed in a stream of liquid steel in the ladles, there was never a price, profit, or royalty paid to any outsider."

Andrew Carnegie dominated the steel industry for three decades, building Carnegie Steel into an industrial giant, the largest steel producer in the world. Carnegie's steel built the first skyscraper in America, formed the skeleton of the Washington Monument, supported the elevated trains in Chicago and New York, and provided the superstructure for the Brooklyn Bridge. By 1900, Andrew Carnegie had become the best-known manufacturer in the world and the age of iron had yielded to an age of steel.

## Standard Oil and the Trust

Edwin Drake's discovery of oil in Pennsylvania in 1859 sent thousands rushing to the oil fields in search of "black gold." In the days before the automobile and gasoline, crude oil was refined into lubricating oil for machinery and kerosene for lamps, a major source of lighting for nineteenth-century Americans in the age before electricity. The amount of capital needed to buy or build an oil refinery in the 1860s and 1870s remained relatively low, less than $25,000, or roughly what it cost to lay one mile of railroad track. Since investment cost was low, the story of the new petroleum industry was one of riotous competition among many small refineries. Ultimately, one company came to dominate oil refining through the use of a new organizational strategy called the trust. The company, Standard Oil, founded by John D. Rockefeller, eventually succeeded in controlling nine-tenths of the oil refining business.

*The trust was a form of horizontal integration, which differed markedly from Carnegie's vertical approach in steel. Instead of attempting to control all aspects of the oil business, from the well to the consumer, Rockefeller moved horizontally to control only the refining process.*

**ANDREW CARNEGIE**
*Andrew Carnegie, shown here in 1861, made a small fortune as a young man. In 1868, he totaled his assets. "Thirty three and an income of $50,000 per annum," he recorded. "Beyond this never earn—make no effort to increase fortune, but spend the surplus each year for benovelent [sic] purposes." Carnegie didn't stick to his plan. In 1872, he founded Carnegie Steel and went on to become one of the richest men in America, giving away an estimated $300 million to charitable causes before his death in 1919.*
Carnegie Library.

In 1865, John D. Rockefeller bought out his partner with borrowed money and took control of the largest oil refinery in Cleveland. Like a growing number of businessmen, Rockefeller abandoned partnership or single proprietorship to embrace the corporation as a business structure best suited to maximizing profit and minimizing personal liability. In 1870, he incorporated his oil business, founding the Standard Oil Company, the precursor of today's Exxon Corporation.

As the largest refiner in Cleveland, Standard Oil demanded rebates, or secret refunds, from the rail-

**MᶜCLURE'S MAGAZINE**

Christmas
1903

NINE SHORT STORIES
Pictures in Color

The Story of
Rockefeller

OPENING OF
THE SECOND PART OF
THE HISTORY
OF STANDARD OIL

By

Ida M. Tarbell

John La Farge on the Hundred
Greatest Pictures, and
Other Features

S. S. McCLURE CO., NEW YORK AND LONDON

**IDA TARBELL AND *MCCLURE'S***
*Ida Tarbell's* History of the Standard Oil Company *ran in McClure's Magazine for three years. Her revelations of the ruthless practices Rockefeller used to seize control of the oil industry convinced readers that it was time for economic and political reforms to curb the power of big business. She grew up in the Pennsylvania oil region and knew firsthand how Standard Oil forced out its competitors.*
Culver Pictures; Corbis-Bettmann.

roads. These rebates enabled Rockefeller to undercut his competitors. The railroads wanted his business so badly that they not only gave him the rebates on his shipping fares but also granted him a share of the rates paid by his competitors. Using this kind of leverage, Standard Oil pressured competing refiners to sell out or face ruin.

To gain legal standing for Standard Oil's secret deals, Rockefeller pioneered a new form of corporate structure—the trust. Several trustees held stock in the various refineries "in trust" for Standard's stockholders. The trust was a form of horizontal integration, which differed markedly from Carnegie's vertical approach in steel. Instead of attempting to control all aspects of the oil business, from the well to the consumer, Rockefeller moved horizontally to control only the refining process.

When the government threatened to outlaw the trust as a violation of free trade, Standard changed its tactics and in 1889 organized into a holding company. Holding companies operated in much the same way as trusts, but they were legal. Instead of competing companies entering into agreements to set prices and determine territories, the holding company simply combined competing companies under one central administration. New Jersey facilitated the development of the holding company by passing a law in 1889 that allowed corporations chartered in the state to hold stock in out-of-state ventures. Other businesses soon imitated Standard Oil's tactics. By the 1890s, New Jersey had become the home of a number of holding companies, the largest of which was Standard Oil.

As Standard Oil's empire grew, central control became essential. Rockefeller began to integrate vertically, even as Standard Oil expanded horizontally. Through centralized control, Standard Oil ended the independence of the refinery operators and closed inefficient plants. Next Rockefeller moved to control sources of crude oil and took charge of the transportation and marketing of petroleum products. By the 1890s, Standard Oil controlled a vast, vertically integrated organization that controlled more than 90 percent of the oil business.

John D. Rockefeller enjoyed unequaled business success. Before he died in 1937, at the age of ninety-eight, he had become the country's first billionaire. But despite his modest habits, his pious Baptist faith, and his many charitable gifts, he never shared in the public affection that Carnegie enjoyed.

Journalist Ida M. Tarbell, whose *History of the Standard Oil Company* ran for three years (1902–1905) in serial form in *McClure's Magazine,* largely shaped the public's harsh view of Rockefeller. She had grown up in the Pennsylvania oil region, and her father had owned one of the small refineries gobbled up by Standard Oil. Her devastatingly thorough history chronicled the methods Rockefeller had used to gain control of the oil industry. By the time she finished her story, Rockefeller slept with a loaded revolver by his bed in fear of would-be assassins. Standard Oil and the man who created it had become the symbol of heartless monopoly.

AN UNRESTRAINED DEMON.

**FEARS OF ELECTRICITY**
*Electricity was by no means a technology easy to sell, as this 1889 cartoon shows. Innocent pedestrians are electrocuted by the wires, a woman swoons, presumably as a result of the buzzing current, a horse and driver have collapsed, and a policeman runs for help. The skull in the wires attached to the electric lightbulb warns that this new technology is deadly. Both an urban sophisticate in a top hat and a cowboy in boots have succumbed to the deadly wires. Edison had to develop an entirely new system of marketing that relied on skilled engineers to sell electric light and power.*
The Granger Collection.

## Electricity and the Telephone

Although Americans frequently disliked industrial giants like Rockefeller, they admired inventors. At the turn of the century, Thomas Alva Edison and Alexander Graham Bell became folk heroes. But no matter how dramatic the inventors or the inventions themselves were, the new electric and telephone industries they pioneered soon eclipsed their inventors and fell under the control of the bankers and the industrialists.

Alexander Graham Bell, a Scot with a passion to find a way to teach the deaf to speak, instead developed a way to transmit voice over wires—the telephone. The emperor of Brazil, dumbfounded by the telephone on display at the Philadelphia Centennial Exposition in 1876, cried out, "My God, it talks!" American Bell, a company formed by the inventor in 1880, marketed the telephone under the skilled direction of a professional manager named Theodore N. Vail. Vail pioneered long lines, or long-distance telephone service, creating American Telephone and Telegraph (AT&T) to build the lines as a subsidiary of American Bell. In 1900, AT&T became the parent company of the system as a whole, controlling Western Electric, which manufactured and installed the equipment, and coordinating the Bell regional divisions. In practical terms, this complicated organizational structure meant that men and women could communicate not only locally in their cities but across the country. The telephone connected parties immediately and privately, contributing greatly to speed and efficiency in business.

Thomas Alva Edison embodied the old-fashioned virtues of Yankee ingenuity and rugged individualism that Americans most admired. A self-educated dynamo, he worked twenty hours a day in his laboratory in Menlo Park, New Jersey, vowing to turn out "a minor invention every ten days and a big thing every six months or so." He almost made good on his promise. At the height of his career, he averaged a patent every eleven days and invented such "big things" as the phonograph, the motion picture camera, and the electric lightbulb.

By 1900, electricity had become a part of American urban life. It powered trolley cars, subways, and factory machinery. It lighted homes, apartments, factories, and office buildings. Indeed, electricity became so prevalent in urban life that it symbolized the city, whose "bright lights" contrasted with a rural America, left largely in the dark. As late as the 1930s, only 10 percent of the nation's farms had electricity.

While Americans thrilled to the new electric cities, the day of the inventor quietly yielded to the heyday of the corporation. In 1892, J. P. Morgan consolidated the electric industry, selling Edison General Electric out from under its inventor and dropping Edison's name from the title. The new General Electric Company soon dominated the market.

# From Competition to Consolidation

Even as Rockefeller and Carnegie built their empires, the era of the industrial giant was coming to a close. Business increasingly developed into the anonymous corporate world of the twentieth century as the corporation became the dominant form of business organization and as corporate mergers restructured American industry.

Banks and financiers played a key role in this consolidation, so much so that the era of the individual entrepreneur yielded to a new era of finance capitalism—investment sponsored by banks and bankers. The great banker J. P. Morgan took the lead in reshaping American business at the turn of the twentieth century, consolidating several major industries, including the railroads and steel. During these years, a new social philosophy based on the theories of Charles Darwin helped to justify consolidation and to inhibit state or federal regulation of business. The Supreme Court, a bastion of conservatism during this period, further proscribed attempts to control business by consistently declaring unconstitutional legislation designed to regulate railroad rates and to outlaw trusts and monopolies.

## J. P. Morgan and Finance Capitalism

The great business leaders of the era loathed competition and sought whenever possible to substitute consolidation and central control. None had a greater passion for order, predictability, and profit than J. P. Morgan, the banker who became the architect of business consolidation (Figure 18.1). John Pierpont Morgan dominated the financial world of Wall Street. Aloof and silent, he looked down on the climbers and the speculators with a haughtiness that led his rivals to call him "Jupiter," after the Roman god. For three decades, Morgan dominated American banking and finance, exerting an influence so powerful that his critics charged that he controlled a vast "money trust."

**FIGURE 18.1**
*Merger Mania, 1890–1905*
*The depression that began with the Panic of 1893 fueled a "merger mania," as businesses consolidated and reorganized, often at the prompting of finance capitalists like J. P. Morgan. The number of mergers peaked in 1899 but continued into the first decade of the twentieth century.*

Morgan acted as a power broker in the reorganization of the railroads and the creation of industrial giants like General Electric and U.S. Steel. When the railroads fell on hard times in the 1890s, Morgan, with his passion for order and his access to capital, took them in hand. He eliminated competition by creating a "community of interest" among the managers, men he handpicked. Often, Morgan's partners sat on the boards of competing firms, forming interlocking directorates. By the time Morgan was finished, seven major groups controlled two-thirds of the nation's railroad mileage.

Banker control of the railroads rationalized, or coordinated, the industry. But peace came at a high price. Morgan heavily "watered" the stock of the railroads, issuing new stock lavishly to keep old investors happy and to guarantee huge profits. Morgan's firm made millions of dollars from commissions and from blocks of stock acquired through reorganization. The flagrant overcapitalization created by the watered stock hurt the railroads in the long run, saddling them with enormous debts. Equally harmful was the management style of the Morgan directors who ran the railroads. They were not railroad men. They looked at the railroads from a banker's viewpoint, "as a . . . set of books." Their

conservatism discouraged the continued technological and organizational innovation needed to run the railroads effectively.

In 1898, Morgan moved into the steel industry. The story of his acquisition of Carnegie Steel is the story of the passing of one age and the coming of a new one. The era of the individual entrepreneur was ending and in its place came the rise of the huge corporation. Carnegie represented the old order, Morgan the new. As he began to challenge Carnegie's control, Morgan supervised the mergers of several smaller steel companies, which soon began to integrate vertically by moving from the manufacture of finished goods into steel production. Carnegie, who for decades had controlled the production of crude steel, countered by creating a new plant for the manufacture of finished products such as tubing, nails, wire, and hoops. A pugnacious Carnegie cabled his partners in the summer of 1900: "Action essential: crisis has arrived . . . have no fear as to the result; victory certain."

The press trumpeted news of the impending fight between the feisty little Scot and the haughty Wall Street banker, but the "battle of the giants" in the end proved little more than the wily maneuvering of two businessmen so adept that even today it is difficult to say who won. The sixty-six-year-old Carnegie, for all his belligerence, yearned to retire to Skibo Castle, his home in Scotland, and may well have invited Morgan's bid for power, knowing only Morgan could command the capital to buy him out. Morgan, who disdained haggling, agreed to pay Carnegie's asking price, $480 million (the equivalent of $9.6 billion, in today's currency). Carnegie's personal share alone amounted to more than $250 million ($5 billion today). According to legend, when Carnegie later teased Morgan, saying that he should have asked $100 million more, Morgan replied: "You would have got it if you had."

*The era of the individual entrepreneur was ending and in its place came the rise of the huge corporation. Carnegie represented the old order, Morgan the new.*

Morgan quickly moved to pull together Carnegie's chief competitors to form a huge new steel corporation, United States Steel, known today as USX. Capitalized (some said grossly overcapitalized) at $1.4 billion, U.S. Steel was the largest corporation in the world. Yet for all its size, it did not hold a monopoly in the steel industry. Significant small competitors such as Bethlehem Steel remained independent, creating a competitive system called an oligopoly, in which several large combinations, not one alone, controlled production. Other industries, such as electricity and meatpacking, were also oligopolies. These businesses seldom competed by cutting prices, as older businesses had done. Instead, the smaller firms simply followed the lead of giants like U.S. Steel in setting prices and dividing the market so that each business held a comfortable share. Although oligopoly did not entirely eliminate competition, it did effectively blunt it.

When J. P. Morgan died in 1913, his estate totaled $68 million, not counting an estimated $50 million in art treasures. Andrew Carnegie, who gave away more than $300 million before his death six years later, is said to have quipped, "And to think he was not a rich man!" But Carnegie's gibe missed the mark. The quest for power, not wealth, characterized J. P. Morgan, and his power could best be measured not in the millions he owned, but in the billions he controlled. Morgan, even more than Carnegie or Rockefeller, left his stamp on twentieth-century America. When the country faced bankruptcy in 1895, it was Morgan to whom the president turned. And as the reorganizer of America's railroads and the creator of U.S. Steel, General Electric, and other large combinations, Morgan was the architect of twentieth-century American business.

## Social Darwinism and the Gospel of Wealth

John D. Rockefeller Jr., the son of the founder of Standard Oil, once told his Baptist Bible class that the Standard Oil Company, like the American Beauty rose, resulted from "pruning the early buds that grew up around it." The elimination of smaller, inefficient units was, he said, "merely the working out of a law of nature and a law of God."

The comparison of the business world to the natural world formed the backbone of a new theory of society based on the "law of evolution" formulated by British scientist Charles Darwin. In his monumental work *On the Origin of Species,* published in 1859, Darwin theorized that in the struggle for survival, the process of adaptation to environment triggered a natural selection process among species that led to evolutionary progress. In the late nineteenth century, Herbert Spencer in Britain and William Graham Sumner in the United States developed a theory called social Darwinism. Crudely applying Darwin's teachings to human society, they concluded that progress came about as a result of relentless competition in which the strong survived and the weak died out.

In social terms, the doctrine of "survival of the fittest" had profound significance, as Sumner, a professor of political economy at Yale University, made clear in his 1883 book *What Social Classes Owe to Each Other.* "The drunkard in the gutter is just where he

**THE HOMESTEAD STEEL MILL**
*The Homestead steel works outside of Pittsburgh, Pennsylvania, was just one of the mills J. P. Morgan purchased from Andrew Carnegie in 1900 for $480 million. Morgan's acquisition led to the creation of the country's first billion-dollar corporation, U.S. Steel, known today as USX.*
Hagley Museum and Library.

ought to be, according to the fitness and tendency of things," Sumner insisted. Any efforts by one class to aid another only tampered with the rigid laws of nature and slowed down evolution.

Social Darwinism's insistence that human interference hampered evolutionary progress acted as a strong curb to reform at the same time that it glorified great wealth. In an age when men like Rockefeller and Carnegie amassed hundreds of millions of dollars (billions in today's currency) while the average worker earned $500 a year (the equivalent of about $8,300 today), social Darwinism justified economic inequality.

Andrew Carnegie softened some of the harsher features of social Darwinism in his *Gospel of Wealth,* published in 1889. The millionaire, Carnegie insisted, acted as a "mere trustee and agent for his poorer brethren, bringing to their service his superior wisdom, experience, and ability to administer, doing for them better than they could or would do for themselves." Carnegie preached philanthropy and urged the rich to "live unostentatious lives" and "administer surplus wealth for the good of the people." But although his *Gospel of Wealth* earned much praise, it won few converts. Most millionaires followed J. P. Morgan's lead, amassing private treasures in his marble library rather than distributing his wealth as Carnegie counseled.

Social Darwinism and the *Gospel of Wealth* suited an age in which the baffling changes accompanying industrialization seemed to cry out for some rational explanation. According to social Darwinism, the success of huge industries and great industrialists was a sign of their superiority and therefore inevitable. Social Darwinism claimed that to interfere with natural law would only slow evolutionary progress. This inflexible "law" assuaged the individual's conscience and made it possible to neglect the poor in the name of "race progress." When the poor were different—new immigrants, poor blacks—as they so often were, social Darwinism smacked of racism. This ugly aspect was never far from social Darwinist ideology, which judged Anglo-Saxons superior to all other groups. Social Darwinism provided a perfect rationale for the status quo.

## Laissez-faire and the Courts

At first glance it seems ironic that William Graham Sumner, who so often sounded like an apologist for the rich, incurred the wrath of wealthy Yale alumni. But in 1890, they almost succeeded in getting him fired. The problem was that strict social Darwinists

like Sumner insisted absolutely that the government ought not to meddle in the economy, subscribing to a doctrine called laissez-faire (French for "let it alone"). In practice, Sumner opposed protective tariffs, which levied duties on imported goods to raise their prices so that they could not compete effectively with American products. His sharp attacks on the high tariffs angered Yale's alumni. While in theory laissez-faire constrained the government from playing an active role in business affairs, in practice businessmen fought for government favors—whether tariffs, land grants, or subsidies—that helped business. Only when it came to taxes or regulation were they quick to cry laissez-faire.

> In an age when men like Rockefeller and Carnegie amassed hundreds of millions of dollars while the average worker earned $500 a year, social Darwinism justified economic inequality.

Business found a strong ally in the U.S. Supreme Court. During the 1880s and 1890s, the Court increasingly reinterpreted the Constitution to protect business from taxation, regulation, labor organization, and antitrust legislation. In a series of landmark decisions, the Court used the Fourteenth Amendment, originally intended to protect freed slaves from state laws violating their rights, to protect corporations. The Fourteenth Amendment declares that no state can "deprive any person of life, liberty, or property, without due process of law." By defining corporations as "persons" under the law, the Court determined that legislation designed to regulate corporations deprived them of "due process." Using this reasoning, the Court struck down state laws regulating railroad rates, declared income tax unconstitutional, and judged labor unions a "conspiracy in restraint of trade."

In the face of the host of economic and social dislocations caused by industrialism, the Court insisted on elevating the rights of property over the rights of people. According to Justice Stephen J. Field, the Constitution "allows no impediments to the acquisition of property." Field, born to a wealthy family, spoke with the bias of the privileged class to whom property rights were sacrosanct. Imbued with this ideology, the Court refused to impede corporate consolidation and did nothing to curb the excesses of corporate capitalism.

# Party Politics in an Age of Enterprise

Writing of the late-nineteenth-century presidents, the novelist Thomas Wolfe observed, "Garfield, Arthur, Harrison, and Hayes, for me they were the lost Americans: Their gravely vacant and be-whiskered faces mixed, melted, swam together in the sea depths of a past intangible, immeasurable, and unknowable." Why do the great industrialists like Rockefeller, Morgan, and Carnegie jump vividly from the pages of the past while the presidents of that period remain so pallid?

The presidents from Rutherford B. Hayes (1877–1881) to William McKinley (1897–1900) are indeed forgotten men, largely because so little was expected of them. Until the 1890s, few Americans thought the president or the national government had any role in addressing the problems accompanying the industrial transformation of the nation. The dominant creed of laissez-faire, coupled with the dictates of social Darwinism, warned government to leave business alone: Intervention to soften even the harshest evils of industrialization would only slow evolutionary progress. This crippling view of the rights and responsibilities of the federal government in the economy and in society reduced it to something of a sideshow. The real action took place elsewhere—in party politics on the local and state levels and in the centers of business and industry.

## Politics and Culture

There is some irony when we observe that the voters of the day swarmed to the polls in record numbers to elect presidents who today seem so colorless. Voter turnout in the last three decades of the nineteenth century averaged a hefty 80 percent, compared with a turnout of 54 percent in the period from 1968–1996. Why were voters then so eager to cast their ballots?

The answer lies in the role politics played in the culture of the late nineteenth century. Political parties used state, local, and federal jobs to reward voters for their support. Many voters owed their livelihood to party bosses. Political affiliation also provided a sense of group identity for many participants proud of their loyalty to the Democrats or the Republicans. Moreover, politics constituted one of the chief forms of entertainment for voters and nonvoters alike in an age before mass recreation and

amusement. Political parties sponsored parades, rallies, speeches, picnics, torchlight processions, and Fourth of July fireworks, attracting millions of Americans. Outside the big cities, only religious revivals and traveling shows could compete.

*Until the 1890s, few Americans thought the president or the national government had any role in addressing the problems accompanying the industrial transformation of the nation. . . . The real action took place elsewhere—in party politics on the local and state levels and in the centers of business and industry.*

After the end of reconstruction, the old Confederate South voted Democratic in every election for the next seventy years. Opposing the "solid South" was the Republican Northeast, with nearly enough electoral votes to guarantee control of the presidency. To preserve Republican rule, the party had to carry key states such as Ohio, Indiana, and New York and had to prevent an alliance from developing between the agricultural South and the West. Republican politicians, like their Democratic rivals, encouraged sectional divisions by emotional appeals to the Civil War, a tactic known as "waving the bloody shirt." Strong Unionist states in the Midwest responded by voting consistently Republican. "Iowa will go Democratic," one observer joked, "when Hell goes Methodist."

Religion and ethnicity also played a significant role in politics. In the North, Protestants from the old-line denominations, particularly Presbyterians and Methodists, were drawn to the Republican Party, which championed a series of moral reforms such as temperance, the campaign against alcoholic beverages. The Democratic Party courted immigrants and attracted Catholic and Jewish voters by consistently opposing laws to close taverns and other businesses on Sunday and by charging that crusades against liquor only masked attacks on immigrant culture.

Electoral politics, like tobacco, remained exclusively a male pursuit. Women did not vote until the 1890s and then in only four western states: Wyoming (1890), Colorado (1893), and Utah and Idaho (1896). Elsewhere, they continued to fight for suffrage by campaigning for state referenda across the nation. And increasingly in the 1890s, politics became limited to white males only. Although black men gained the vote during reconstruction, the withdrawal of federal troops from the South in 1877 led to a massive deterioration in black voters' franchise.

The power of the two major parties remained about equally divided from the 1870s into the 1890s. Although the Republicans captured the White House in four out of five elections, they rarely controlled the Congress. The Democrats, noted more for their local appeal than for their national unity, for the most part dominated the U.S. House of Representatives.

During this period, senators were not directly elected by the voters but were selected by state legislatures. In an era noted for its tolerance of all but the most flagrant bribery and corruption, state legislatures frequently came under the influence of powerful business interests. In *Wealth Against Commonwealth* (1894), his book on the Standard Oil Company, journalist Henry Demarest Lloyd wrote, "The Standard has done everything with the Pennsylvania legislature except to refine it." Senators were often closely identified with business interests, as in the case of Nelson Aldrich, the powerful Republican from Rhode Island. Aldrich, whose daughter married John D. Rockefeller Jr., did not object to being called "the senator from Standard Oil."

## Corruption and Party Strife

The political corruption and party factionalism that characterized the administration of Ulysses S. Grant (1869–1877) continued to trouble the nation in the 1880s. The spoils system—the awarding of jobs for political purposes—remained the driving force of party politics. The concept of ethics in government, precluding private individuals from getting rich from public office, remained an issue raised only by a small band of reformers during this period. Most respectable Americans viewed politics as a sordid business; corruption at the ballot box and in public office came to be taken for granted.

President Rutherford B. Hayes, whose disputed election in 1876 marked the end of reconstruction in the South, proved to be a hardworking, well-informed executive who wanted peace, prosperity, and an end to party strife. Although he was ridiculed by the Democratic press as "Rutherfraud" and "His Fraudulency," Hayes was a figure of honesty and integrity who seemed well suited to his role as a national leader. But it was not an easy task. The Republican Party remained divided into fac-

tions led by strong party bosses who boasted that they could make or break a president.

The three Republican factions bore the colorful names Stalwarts, Half-Breeds, and Mugwumps. The Stalwarts remained loyal to Grant and consequently carried with them the taint of corruption from the scandals of his administration. Opposing them were the Half-Breeds, led by Senator James G. Blaine of Maine, who opposed the flagrant corruption of the Stalwarts but drew no fine distinction between public service and private gain and was himself tarnished by certain shady dealings in railroad bonds. Standing against both factions was a small but prominent group of liberal Republican reformers, mostly from Massachusetts and New York, whose critics later dubbed them Mugwumps. The name came from an Indian chief of the Algonquian but was used derisively by those who insisted that the Mugwumps straddled the fence on issues of party loyalty, "with their mug on one side and wump on the other." Often Mugwumps were men of influence like former abolitionist and Union general Carl Schurz and E. L. Goodkin, editor of the *Nation*. They were eager to reform government and put it in the hands of competent, honest men like themselves. In their pursuit of reform, they largely evaded the complex and divisive economic issues of the day and called instead for the purification of the government through civil service reforms designed to set standards for officeholders and put an end to the spoils system.

President Hayes, despite his virtues, soon managed to alienate his party. A realist, he used federal patronage to build Republican strength by selecting for government jobs, if not the best men, the best Republicans he could find. To the Stalwarts, who wanted more positions, his action constituted betrayal; to the Mugwumps, it smacked too much of the spoils system. Hayes soon found himself a man without a party and announced that he would not seek reelection in 1880.

The Republicans avoided choosing sides and selected a dark-horse candidate, Representative James A. Garfield from Ohio, as their presidential nominee. To appease the Stalwarts, though, they picked Chester A. Arthur of New York as the vice presidential candidate. The Democrats made an attempt to break down sectionalism and establish a national party by selecting as their presidential standard-bearer the old Union general Winfield Scott Hancock. But as one observer noted, "It is a peculiarly constituted party which sends rebel brigadiers to Congress because of their rebellion, and which nominated a Union General as its candidate for president because of his loyalty." Although the popular vote was close, Garfield won 214 electoral votes to Hancock's 155.

## Garfield's Assassination and Civil Service Reform

Government bureaucracy grew in the years following the Civil War until nearly 150,000 jobs existed on the federal payroll. The spoils system proved a poor way to select qualified individuals to serve as the clerks, civil engineers, and trained professionals needed in the new government posts. Politicians from the president down were tormented by a steady stream of office seekers. Critics soon called for civil service reform designed to mandate examinations and establish a merit system to screen applicants for government jobs. The struggle for civil service reform would come to a head with the assassination of President James Garfield.

"My God," President Garfield swore after only a few months in office, "what is there in this place that a man should ever want to get into it?" Garfield, like Hayes, faced the difficult task of remaining independent while pacifying the bosses and placating the reformers. To an indecisive man like Garfield, the presidency was a torment. Thousands of office seekers swarmed to the nation's capital, each clamoring for a place. In an era before presidents received Secret Service protection, the White House door stood open to all comers. Garfield took a fatalistic view. "Assassination," he told a friend, "can no more be guarded against than death by lightning, and it is best not to worry about either."

On July 2, 1881, less than four months after taking office, Garfield was shot in the back at a Washington, D.C., railroad station while catching a train. His assassin, Charles Guiteau, though clearly insane, was a disappointed office seeker who claimed to be motivated by political partisanship. He told the police officer who arrested him, "I did it; I will go to jail for it; Arthur is president, and I am a Stalwart." Garfield lingered on through the hot summer while the nation held a long deathbed vigil. He died on September 19, 1881.

The press almost universally condemned the Stalwarts, if not for inspiring Guiteau, then for creating the political climate that produced him. Attacks on the spoils system increased, as did a rising public demand for civil service reform. But though Garfield's death crystallized the desire for civil service reform, the debate was long and hard. Many

of those who opposed reform recognized that civil service had built-in class and ethnic biases. They knew that when Mugwumps spoke of government run by the "best men," they meant men of their own class. Just as Irish Americans were beginning to carve out a place for themselves in local and state politics, civil service threatened to turn government back over to an educated Yankee elite. At a time when few men had more than a grammar school education, office seekers did not relish the prospect of written civil service examinations. One opponent argued, "George Washington could not have passed examination for a clerkship," observing that "in his will written by his own hand, he spells clothes, cloathes."

The legislation that established civil service reform—the Pendleton Act—passed in 1883, after more than a year of congressional debate and compromise. Both parties claimed credit for the act, which established a permanent Civil Service Commission of three members, appointed by the president. Some 14,000 jobs were placed under a merit system that required examinations for office and made it impossible to remove jobholders for political reasons. Half of the postal jobs and most of the customhouse jobs, the lion's share of the spoils system's bounty, passed to the control of the Civil Service Commission. The new law sought to prohibit federal jobholders from contributing to political campaigns, thus drying up a major source of the party bosses' revenue. Soon business interests replaced officeholders as the nation's chief political contributors. Ironically, civil service reform thus gave business an even greater influence in political life than it already had.

"Chet Arthur, president of the United States! Good God!" incredulous men exclaimed on hearing of Garfield's death. Surely little in his background made Chester A. Arthur seem like a man suited for the highest office in the country. Only four years earlier, he had been dismissed from his position in the customhouse in New York because of his close association with corrupt politicians. But as president, he quickly dispelled the nation's fears and acted independently, signing the Pendleton Act, which his fellow Stalwarts had so long opposed. Arthur himself had little "faith in reform" but knew enough of politics not to stand in the path of public sentiment. Arthur surprised his critics by turning out to be a competent president, but his was a lackluster administration. The Republicans quickly looked to Blaine to bear the party standard in 1884.

## The Political Circus: The Campaign of 1884

With the downfall of the Stalwarts, James G. Blaine assumed leadership of the Republican Party and at long last captured the presidential nomination in 1884. A magnetic Irish American politician whose followers dubbed him the "Plumed Knight," Blaine inspired such devotion that his supporters were called Blainiacs. But to many reformers, Blaine personified corruption. Led by Carl Schurz, who insisted that the Plumed Knight "wallowed in spoils like a rhinoceros in an African pool," the Mugwumps bolted the party and embraced the Democratic presidential candidate, the stolid Grover Cleveland, reform governor of New York. The burly, beer-drinking Cleveland distinguished himself from an entire generation of politicians by the simple motto "A public office is a public trust." First as mayor of Buffalo and later as governor of New York, he built a solid reputation for honesty, economy, and administrative efficiency. He soon alienated the Tammany Hall political machine; but with reform in the air, the enemies he made only added to his appeal. The Democrats, who had not won the presidency since 1856, rushed to nominate him. As was expected, Cleveland received the enthusiastic endorsement of the Mugwumps, who announced that "the paramount issue this year is moral rather than political."

They would soon regret their words. The 1884 contest degenerated into nasty mudslinging. One disgusted journalist styled it "the vilest campaign ever waged." Grover Cleveland, whatever his reform virtues, made an easy target. In July, his hometown paper, the Buffalo *Telegraph,* dropped the bombshell that the bachelor candidate had fathered an illegitimate child in an affair with a widow named Maria Halpin. The crestfallen Mugwumps tried to argue the difference between public and private morality. But robbed of their moral righteousness, they lost much of their enthusiasm. "Now I fear it has resolved itself into a choice of two evils," one weary reformer confessed.

At public rallies, Blaine's partisans taunted Cleveland, chanting:

> Ma, ma, where's my pa?
> Going to the White House
> ha! ha! ha!

The stoic Cleveland accepted responsibility for the child, who may in fact have been fathered by Cleveland's partner, whose daughter Cleveland would

Bye, free trade baby!
Rock it, Grover, tenderly?
Bye, free trade baby,
We've smashed the cradle!
Good-by!

Ma, Ma, Where's My Pa.
Fired from the White House.
———HA, HA, HA!

**ANTI-CLEVELAND POSTER, 1888**
*In this early example of negative campaign advertising, Republicans pillory Democratic President Grover Cleveland as an advocate of free trade, along with his new wife. The cartoon dredges up the image of his illegitimate child, an issue that had proved such a scandal in the 1884 campaign. The bottom lines echo the earlier campaign ditty "Ma Ma, Where's My Pa?" In this election, the tariff became a potent issue, winning support from business and labor and helping to elect Republican Benjamin Harrison.* Collection of David J. and Janice L. Frent.

later marry. Silent but fuming, he waged his campaign in the traditional fashion by staying home. Blaine broke precedent by making a national tour. On a last-minute stop in New York, the exhausted candidate overlooked a remark by a local clergyman—and he may have lost the election as a result. The Reverend Samuel Burchard, while introducing Blaine, blasted the Democrats as the party of "Rum, Romanism, and Rebellion." An Associated Press correspondent hurriedly filed his story, crying, "If anything will elect Cleveland, these words will do it." By linking drinking and Catholicism, Burchard cast a slur on Irish Catholic voters, who had been counted on to desert the Democratic Party and support Blaine because of his Irish background.

With less than a week to go until the election, Blaine had no chance to recover from the negative publicity. He lost New York State by less than 1,200 votes and with it the election, although the vote was so close that the outcome remained uncertain for several days. In the final tally, the Democrats ended twenty-five years of Republican rule, defeating Blaine by a scant 30,000 votes nationwide, but winning 219 electoral votes to 182. Cleveland's followers had the last word:

> Hurrah for Maria! Hurrah for the kid!
> I voted for Cleveland,
> And Damned glad I did!

## Economic Issues and Party Realignment

Four years later, in the election of 1888, fickle voters would turn Cleveland out, electing Republican Benjamin Harrison, the grandson of President William Henry Harrison. Then, in the only instance in America's history when a president who had been defeated at the polls was returned to office, the voters brought Cleveland back in the election of 1892. What factors account for such a surprising turnaround? The strengths and weaknesses of the men themselves partially determined the outcome. The stubborn Cleveland, newly married to Frances Folsom in 1886, resented demands on his time and refused to campaign in 1888. Although he won more votes than Harrison, he lost the electoral college. Once in office, Harrison proved to be a cold and distant leader. His critics called him "the human iceberg."

But issues as well as personalities increasingly swayed the voters. The 1880s witnessed a remarkable political realignment as a new set of economic concerns replaced the Civil War rhetoric of carpetbaggers, rebels, and the bloody shirt. The tariff, federal regulation of the railroads and trusts, and the campaign for free silver restructured American politics.

### The Tariff and the Politics of Protection

The concept of a protective tariff to raise the price of imported goods and stimulate American industry dated back to Alexander Hamilton in the found-

ing days of the Republic. Congress enacted the first tariff following the War of 1812. The Republicans turned the tariff to political ends by enacting a measure in 1861 that rewarded their industrial supporters who wanted protection from foreign competition at the same time that it raised revenues for the Civil War. After the war, the Republicans continued to revise and enlarge the tariff at the prompting of northeastern industrialists. By the 1880s, the tariff posed a threat to prosperity. The huge surplus sat in the Treasury's vaults, depriving the country of money that might otherwise have been invested to create jobs and products, while the government argued about how (or even whether) to spend it.

To many Americans, particularly southern and midwestern farmers who sold their crops in a world market yet had to buy high-priced protected goods, the answer was simple: Reduce the tariff. Advocates of free trade and moderates agitated for tariff reform. But those who benefited from the tariff—industrialists like Andrew Carnegie who insisted that America's "infant industries" needed protection and westerners producing protected raw materials such as wool, hides, and lumber—firmly opposed lowering the tariff. Many workers, too, believed that the tariff protected American wage levels by giving American products a competitive edge over goods imported from other countries.

The Republican Party seized on the tariff issue to forge a new national alliance. Blaine shrewdly recognized its potent political uses. "Fold up the bloody shirt and lay it away," he advised a colleague in 1880. "It's of no use to us. You want to shift the main issue to protection." By encouraging an alliance among industrialists, labor, and western producers of raw materials, Blaine hoped to solidify the North and West against the solidly Democratic South.

Although his tactic failed in the election of 1884, it worked four years later. Cleveland, who straddled the tariff issue in the election of 1884, startled the nation in 1887 by calling for tariff reform. The Republicans countered by arguing that "tariff tinkering" would only unsettle prosperous industries, drive down wages, and shrink the farmers' home market. Benjamin Harrison, who supported the tariff, captured the White House in 1888, carrying all the northern and western states except Connecticut and New Jersey.

Back in office, the Republicans demonstrated their new commitment to economics over ideology by abandoning their support for freed slaves at the same time that they curried favor with the new industrialists. Senator Henry Cabot Lodge's Force

**"HE WON'T HAVE IT!" BY C. JAY TAYLOR**

*"He Won't Have It," this 1888 political cartoon announces, showing a stern Uncle Sam castigating James G. Blaine and steel magnate Andrew Carnegie. Republican Blaine's support of the protective tariff fed the profits of industrialists like Carnegie and, the cartoon implied, lined Blaine's pockets as well, with labor sharing little in the bargain. As the signs proclaim, the steel and sugar trusts cut wages and laid off workers. In fact, Republicans used the tariff issue effectively to recruit voters from the ranks of labor by arguing that protection kept American wages higher than if workers were forced to compete with goods produced cheaply abroad.*
The Granger Collection.

Bill, a federal election law to restore the vote to African Americans in the South, died in the same Republican Congress that passed the highest tariff in the nation's history in 1890. The new tariff sponsored by representative William McKinley of Ohio stirred a hornet's nest of protest. The American people had elected Harrison to preserve protection, not to enact a higher tariff. The McKinley tariff set about solving the vexing problem of too much revenue by raising duties so high that foreign producers no longer wanted to sell their goods to Americans.

Democrats condemned the McKinley tariff and labeled the Republican Congress that passed it the "Billion Dollar Congress" for its carnival of spending. The Fifty-first Congress earned its title by spending the nation's surplus on a series of "pork barrel" programs—legislation shamelessly designed to bring federal money to their constituents. In the congressional election of 1890, angry voters swept the hap-less Republicans, including tariff sponsor McKinley, out of office. Two years later, Harrison himself was defeated as Grover Cleveland, whose call for tariff revision had lost him the election in 1888, triumphantly returned to the White House vowing to lower the tariff. Such were the changes in the political winds whipped up by the tariff issue.

## The Railroads, the Trusts, and the Federal Government

American voters may have divided on the tariff, but increasingly they agreed on the need for federal regulation of the railroads and federal legislation against the trusts. As early as the 1870s, angry farmers had organized to attack the railroads. The Patrons of Husbandry, or the Grange, founded in 1867 as a social and educational organization for farmers, soon became an independent political movement. By electing Grangers to state office, farmers made it possible for several midwestern states to pass laws regulating the railroads. At first the Supreme Court ruled in favor of regulation (*Munn v. Illinois,* 1877). But in 1886, the Supreme Court reversed itself, ruling that because railroads crossed state boundaries, they fell outside state jurisdiction (*Wabash v. Illinois*). With more than three-fourths of railroads crossing state lines, the Supreme Court's decision effectively quashed railroad regulation.

Anger over the Supreme Court decision finally led to the passage of the first federal law to regulate the railroads, the Interstate Commerce Act, passed in 1887 during Cleveland's first administration. The act established the nation's first federal regulatory agency, the Interstate Commerce Commission (ICC). In its early years, the ICC was never strong enough or sure enough of what it should do to pose a serious threat to the railroads. It proved more important as a precedent than effective as a watchdog.

Concern over the growing power of the trusts led the federal government to pass the Sherman Antitrust Act in 1890. The law outlawed pools and trusts, ruling that businesses could no longer enter into agreements to restrict competition. It did nothing, however, to restrict huge holding companies like Standard Oil.

The Sherman Act proved to be a weak sword against the trusts. In the decade after its passage, the government successfully struck down only six trusts. However, the law was used four times against labor by outlawing unions as a "conspiracy in restraint of trade." In 1895, the Supreme Court dealt the law a crippling blow in the E. C. Knight case. The Court drastically narrowed the law by allowing the American Sugar Refining Company, which controlled 98 percent of the production of sugar, to continue its virtual monopoly on the grounds that *manufacture* did not constitute *trade.*

Both the Interstate Commerce Commission and the Sherman Antitrust Act testified to the nation's concern about the abuses of big business and to a growing willingness to use federal power to intervene on behalf of the public interest. Not until the twentieth century would more active presidents sharpen and use these weapons against the large corporations.

## The Fight for Free Silver

The silver issue stirred passions like no other issue of the day. On one side stood those who believed that gold constituted the only honest money. Many, but not all, were eastern creditors who did not wish to be paid in devalued dollars. On the opposite side stood a coalition of silver barons and poor farmers. The mining interests, who had seen the silver bonanza in the West drive down the price of silver, wanted the government to buy the metal and mint silver dollars to help jack up the price. Farmers from the West and South who had suffered economically during the 1870s and 1880s hoped that increasing the money supply with silver dollars would give them some relief.

Advocates of silver pointed out that until 1873 the country had enjoyed a system of bimetallism, with both silver and gold minted into coins. In that year, Congress had demonetized (stopped buying and minting) silver, an act advocates of bimetallism denounced as the "crime of '73." In 1878, Congress took steps to appease advocates of silver by passing the Bland-Allison Act over President Hayes's veto. The measure required the government to buy silver and issue silver certificates. The Bland-Allison Act helped mine owners, who now had a buyer for their ore, but it had little inflationary impact.

Pressures for inflation continued, but the silver advocates were unable to make any headway until 1890, when in return for their support of the McKinley tariff, Congress passed the Sherman Silver Purchase Act, increasing the amount of silver the government bought. Once again, the measure failed to produce the desired inflationary effect, and advocates began to call for "the free and unlimited coinage of silver," a plan whereby virtually all the silver that was mined would be minted into silver coins circulated at the rate of sixteen ounces of silver to one ounce of gold.

The silver issue crossed party lines, but the Democrats hoped to use it to achieve a union between western and southern voters. Unfortunately for them, Grover Cleveland, a conservative in money matters and a strong supporter of the gold standard, sat in the White House. Overlooking the crying need for depression relief, he called a special session of Congress in August 1893 and bullied the legislature into repealing the Sherman Silver Purchase Act. Repeal did not produce recovery or save the gold reserves. But it did divide the country, making the Mississippi River for a time as potent a political boundary as the Mason-Dixon line. Angry farmers warned Cleveland not to travel west of the river if he valued his life.

Their economic plight worsened after a panic on Wall Street in 1893 touched off a deep economic depression. In the winter of 1894–95, Cleveland aggravated the already highly charged political climate by his deal with J. P. Morgan to save the country's gold reserves. The Morgan bond sale underscored the government's ties to the great money men. By the 1890s, the United States faced a crisis. Agrarian discontent, labor unrest, depression, unemployment—problems that were not only economic but also social and political—cried out for solutions. In the grim darkness of the winter of 1894–95, men and women talked of revolution, some of them in fear and some of them in anger.

## Conclusion: The Gilded Age

Mark Twain, humorist, author, and one of the shrewdest critics of his era, called the period following reconstruction the "Gilded Age." He chose this title to ridicule the ugliness, crass materialism, and sham of a time when glitter on the outside masked what lay beneath. Twain's label has stood for more than a century as a fair representation of an age that spawned greed, corruption, and vulgarity on a grand scale, when speculator/industrialists like Jay Gould could build or wreck railways to turn paper profits and boasted openly of buying politicians who lined their pockets at the public's expense.

Nevertheless, the era was not without its share of solid achievements. In these years, America made the leap into the industrial age. Factories and mills poured out American goods in unprecedented numbers. Where dusty roads and cattle trails once sprawled across the continent, steel rails now bound together a nation. Cities grew from the ground into the sky. In New York City, the Brooklyn Bridge spanned the East River with steel and stone, more strikingly beautiful than all the showy mansions on Fifth Avenue. In the offices and boardrooms of business, men like Carnegie, Rockefeller, and Morgan consolidated American industry. By the end of the nineteenth century, the country had achieved industrial maturity. No other era in the nation's history witnessed such a transformation. It remained to be seen whether the nation could solve the social and economic problems accompanying industrialization and curb the vast power of the financiers and corporations.

## CHRONOLOGY

| | |
|---|---|
| **1869** | Completion of first transcontinental railroad. |
| **1870** | John D. Rockefeller incorporates Standard Oil Company in Cleveland. |
| **1872** | Andrew Carnegie builds largest Bessemer process steel plant near Pittsburgh. |
| **1873** | U.S. government decides to stop minting silver dollars. |
| | Panic on Wall Street leads to major economic depression. |
| **1874** | Pennsylvania Railroad capitalized at $400 million and employing 55,000; largest private enterprise in the world. |
| | Mark Twain and Charles Dudley Warner publish *The Gilded Age*, a novel satirizing the speculative mania of the age. |

| | |
|---|---|
| **1876** | Alexander Graham Bell demonstrates telephone at Philadelphia Centennial Exposition. |
| **1877** | Rutherford B. Hayes sworn in as president of United States after disputed election. |
| | U.S. Supreme Court upholds right of states to regulate railroads in *Munn v. Illinois*. |
| **1879** | Congress votes to resume gold standard. |
| | Thomas Alva Edison perfects filament for incandescent lightbulb. |
| **1880s** | Jay Gould becomes architect of a transcontinental railway system. |
| **1880** | Dark horse Republican candidate James A. Garfield elected president of United States. |

| | | | |
|---|---|---|---|
| 1881 | President Garfield assassinated; Vice President Chester A. Arthur becomes president. | 1889 | Standard Oil reorganizes into holding company. |
| 1882 | Standard Oil develops the trust. | 1890 | Congress passes McKinley tariff and Sherman Silver Purchase Act. |
| 1883 | Congress passes Pendleton Act establishing civil service reform. | | Congress passes Sherman Antitrust Act. |
| 1884 | Grover Cleveland wins presidency, first Democrat to serve since before Civil War. | 1892 | Grover Cleveland elected to second term as president. |
| 1886 | In *Wabash* case, U.S. Supreme Court reverses itself and disallows state regulation of railroads that cross state lines. | | J. P. Morgan consolidates electric industry, creating the General Electric Company. |
| 1887 | Congress passes Interstate Commerce Act, first federal law to regulate railroads. | 1893 | Panic devastates financial markets and touches off national depression. |
| | | 1895 | J. P. Morgan bails out U.S. Treasury and saves country's gold reserves. |
| 1888 | Benjamin Harrison elected president of United States. | 1901 | J. P. Morgan buys out Carnegie Steel and creates U.S. Steel, first billion dollar corporation in United States. |

# SUGGESTED READINGS

Sean Dennis Cashman, *America in the Gilded Age: From the Death of Lincoln to the Rise of Theodore Roosevelt* (3rd ed., 1993). A survey of the period's political landscape, with attention to social and economic currents.

Alfred D. Chandler Jr., *Scale and Scope: The Dynamics of Industrial Capitalism* (1990). An exploration of the development of modern industrial enterprise and the rise of managerial capitalism in a comparative framework, examining the United States, Great Britain, and Germany.

Ron Chernow, *The House of Morgan: An American Banking Dynasty and the Rise of Modern Finance* (1990). A multigenerational study of the Morgan bankers with emphasis on J. P., who brought banking and finance into the twentieth century.

Ron Chernow, *Titan, the Life of John D. Rockefeller, Sr.* (1998). Exhaustively researched and written in a lively, readable style, this recent biography explores the brilliance and rapacity of the founder of Standard Oil.

Alan Dawley, *Struggles for Justice: Social Responsibility and the Liberal State* (1991). An integrated synthesis of political, economic, and social history. In Part I, Dawley explores the tensions confronting the state and society from the 1890s to 1912.

Ellen Gruber Garvey, *The Adman in the Parlor: Magazines and the Gendering of American Culture, 1880s to 1910s* (1996). A look at magazines, the principal national mass medium at the turn of the twentieth century, and the interplay of advertising and fiction.

Carol Marvin, *When Old Technologies Were New* (1988). A fresh look at the impact of technologies we now take for granted and how they influenced American life.

Jean Strouse, *Morgan: American Financier* (1999). The best glimpse yet of the private person who was the most powerful man in the United States.

Alan Trachtenburg, *The Incorporation of America: Culture and Society in the Gilded Age* (1984). Business and culture get equal treatment in this survey of the period.

Joseph Frazier Wall, *Andrew Carnegie* (1970). A model biography, thoughtful and judicious, of the complicated man whose rags-to-riches life and cheerful beneficence made him an American icon.

**MINER'S SAFETY LAMP AND CANVAS CAP WITH OIL LAMP**

*This lamp and cap were used by coal miners in Pennsylvania in the mid to late nineteenth century. The oil-wick lamp, attached to the cap by a hook, was introduced by immigrant miners from Great Britain. The wick was soaked in oil stored inside the lamp and lit the miner's path with a smoky flame. Although these lamps were cheaper and burned longer than the candles they replaced, any open flame presented a serious danger: explosions and fires often resulted when flame came in contact with methane and other underground gases. Falling rock and cave-ins were also common occurrences, but the canvas hat offered little protection. Improvements in safety were implemented gradually. British inventors developed a lamp that enclosed the flame in steel netting to prevent reaction with gases. Because the flame grew higher when exposed to certain gases, the safety lamp (left) did double duty in lighting the miners' way and detecting dangerous gases. After World War I, cloth caps were replaced by hard hats with electric lights.*

Pennsylvania Historical and Museum Commission, Bureau of Historic Sites and Museums, Anthracite Museum Complex.

# AMERICA THROUGH THE EYES OF THE WORKERS

## 19

### 1870–1890

FOR TWO WEEKS DURING THE SUMMER of 1877, President Rutherford B. Hayes faced an insurrection that was greater than any since the Civil War. Hayes met daily with his cabinet to plan military strategy and sat up late into the night receiving reports from his generals. He dispatched federal troops to nine states, ordered warships to protect the nation's capital, and threatened to declare martial law. Not since the Confederates fired on Fort Sumter had the nation witnessed such an alarm. Who posed this threat to the Republic? Not former rebels or foreign armies, but American workers engaged in the first nationwide labor strike in the country's history.

Economic depression following the panic of 1873 had thrown as many as three million people out of work. Those who were lucky enough to keep their jobs watched as pay cuts eroded their wages until they could no longer feed their families. When the Baltimore and Ohio (B&O) Railroad announced a 10 percent wage reduction in the summer of 1877 at the same time it declared a 10 percent dividend to its stockholders, the brakemen in West Virginia, whose wages had already fallen from $70 to $30 a month, walked out on strike. One B&O worker described the hardship that had driven him to take such desperate action: "We eat our hard bread and tainted meat two days old on the sooty cars up the road, and when we come home, find our children gnawing bones and our wives complaining that they cannot even buy hominy and molasses for food."

The strike by brakemen in West Virginia touched off a nationwide uprising, known as the Great Railroad Strike, that spread rapidly to Pittsburgh and Chicago, St. Louis and San Francisco. Within a few days, nearly 100,000 railroad workers went out on strike. The spark of rebellion soon fired other workers to action. An estimated 500,000 joined the striking train workers. Violence erupted as the strikers clashed with state militia. President Hayes, after hesitating briefly, called up federal troops. In three weeks it was over. "The strikes have been put down by *force*," Hayes noted in his diary on August 5. "But now for the real remedy. Can't something be done by education of the strikers, by judicious control of the capitalists, by wise general policy to end or diminish the evil? The railroad strikers, as a rule, are good men, sober, intelligent, and industrious."

The uprising of the workers in 1877 underscored the tensions produced by rapid industrialization and pointed to many legitimate grievances on the part of labor. The explosion of industrial growth that occurred after the Civil War came about as a result of the labor of millions of men, women, and children who toiled

**PITTSBURGH AFTER THE GREAT RAILROAD STRIKE**
*The Great Railroad Strike of 1877 left two miles of downtown Pittsburgh a mass of twisted rails and rubble. When the militia fired on the crowds, angry workers fought back. More than forty people were shot, and damage to property amounted to two million dollars. The middle class, which had initially sympathized with strikers, grew fearful of the violence and destruction. The shift in public opinion helped the railroad owners put down the strike.*
Carnegie Library, Pittsburgh.

in workshops and factories, in sweatshops and mines, on the railroads and construction sites across America. Their stories provide a different perspective from that of the great industrialists and the politicians. Through their eyes it is possible to gauge how corporate capitalism transformed old work patterns and affected the social and cultural as well as the economic and political life of the United States.

## America's New Industrial Workers

America's industrial growth in the years following the Civil War brought about a massive redistribution of population as agricultural workers moved to the city and became recruits in the industrial labor force. Burgeoning industrial centers such as Pittsburgh, Chicago, New York, and Detroit acted like giant magnets, attracting workers from the countryside. The movement from the rural periphery to industrial centers was not just American in

scope. Farm boys and girls from western Pennsylvania who left for the mills of Pittsburgh were part of a global migration that included rural immigrants from Ireland, southern Italy, Russia, Japan, and China. As labor historian David Montgomery has pointed out, "the rural periphery of the nineteenth century industrial world became the primary source of supply for 'human machines.'"

## Workers from the Rural Periphery

By the 1870s, the world could be seen as divided into three interlocking geographic regions forming roughly concentric circles. At the center stood an industrial core bounded by Chicago and St. Louis in the west; Toronto, Glasgow, and Berlin in the north; Warsaw in the east; and Milan, Barcelona, Richmond, and Louisville in the south (Map 19.1).

Surrounding the industrial core and its urban outposts lay a vast agricultural domain encompassing Canada, much of Scandinavia, Russia and Poland, Hungary, Greece, Italy and Sicily, southern Spain, the defeated Confederate states and the Great

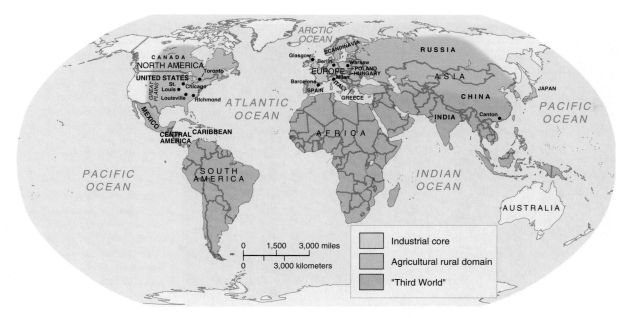

**M AP 19.1**
*Economic Regions of the World*
*The global nature of the world economy at the turn of the twentieth century is indicated by three interlocking geographic regions. At the center was the industrial core—Western Europe and the northeastern United States; the agricultural rural periphery (rural domain) supplied immigrant laborers to the industries in the core. Beyond these regions lay a "third world" tied economically to the industrial core by colonialism.*

Plains of America, central and northern Mexico, the hinterlands of Canton, China, and later the southern islands of Japan. Capitalist development in the late nineteenth century shattered traditional patterns of economic activity in this rural periphery. As old patterns broke down, the rural areas exported, along with other raw materials, new recruits for the industrial labor force.

Beyond this second circle lay an even larger "third world" including the Caribbean, Central and South America, the Middle East, Africa, India, and most of Asia. This area too became increasingly tied to the industrial core in the late nineteenth century, but its peoples largely stayed put. They worked on the plantations and railroads, in the mines and ports as part of a huge export network managed by foreign powers that staked out spheres of influence and colonies, often with gunboats and soldiers.

Beginning in the 1870s, railroad expansion and low steamship fares gave the world's peoples a newfound mobility that enabled industrialists to draw on a worldwide population for cheap labor. The Carnegie steel mills outside of Pittsburgh pro-

vide a good example. When Andrew Carnegie opened his first mill in 1872, his superintendent hired workers he called "buckwheats"—young American boys just off the farm. By the 1890s, however, Carnegie's workforce was liberally sprinkled with other rural boys—Hungarians and Slavs who had migrated to the United States, willing to work for low wages.

The ability to draw on cheap labor on a global scale helps explain why, in spite of the soaring demand for laborers after the Civil War, the wages of unskilled workers in the United States remained relatively stagnant. Their pay fell dramatically during the depressions of 1873–1878 and 1893–1896 and did not regain 1872 levels before the end of the century.

## Immigration, Ethnic Rivalry, and Racism

Ethnic diversity played a role in dividing skilled workers (those with a craft or specialized ability) from the unskilled (those who supplied muscle and brawn). As managers increasingly mechanized to

**"BREAKER BOYS"**
*Child labor in America's mines and mills was common at the turn of the century, despite state laws that attempted to restrict it. Here "breaker boys" in the 1890s take a rest from their twelve-hour day in the coal mines of Appalachia. Their unsmiling faces bear testimony to their hard and dangerous work. A committee investigating child labor found more than 10,000 children illegally employed in the Pennsylvania coal fields.*
Brown Brothers.

replace skilled craftsworkers with lower-paid, unskilled labor, they drew on immigrants from southern and eastern Europe. The skilled workers, most from northern or western Europe, found it easy to criticize the newcomers. As one Irish worker complained, "There should be a law . . . to keep all the I-talians from comin' in and takin' the bread out of the mouths of honest people."

The Irish worker's resentment of the new Italian immigrants brings into focus the importance of the ideology and practice of racism in the experience of America's immigrant laborers. Throughout the nineteenth century, ethnic and even religious differences were perceived as *racial* characteristics. Members of the educated elite as well as workers spoke of the Polish "race" or the Jewish "race" in uncomplimentary terms. Each wave of newcomers was perceived as being somehow inferior to the established residents. The Irish who judged the Italians so harshly had themselves been seen as a subhuman species just a generation before. Immigrants brought their own religious and racial prejudices to this country and also absorbed the popular prejudices of American culture. Social Darwinism, with

its strongly racist overtones, decreed that whites stood at the top of the evolutionary ladder. But who was "white"? The social construction of race is nowhere more apparent than in the testimony of an Irish dockworker, who boasted that he hired only "white men" to load cargo, a category that he insisted excluded "Poles and Italians."

Racism took its most blatant form in the treatment of African Americans and Asians. Like other migrants from the rural periphery, African American men in the South, former slaves and the children of slaves, found work as human machines. The labor gang system used in many industries was most extreme and brutal in the South, where private employers contracted prison labor, mostly African Americans jailed for such minor "crimes" as vagrancy. Shackled together by chains as they worked under the watchful eyes of armed guards, these workers formed the bottom rung on labor's ladder. A Georgia man who escaped the brutal chain gang system remarked, "Call it slavery, peonage, or what not, the truth is we lived in a hell on earth."

On the West Coast, Asian immigrants became the scapegoats of the changing economy. The Chinese and later the Japanese were vigorously attacked as the "tools of corporate interest" recruited by the bosses to undercut wages and threaten "white society." The labor movement played a key role in excluding Asians from American life. Labor unions practiced exclusionary policies against both Chinese and Japanese workers and championed the 1882 Chinese Exclusion Act, which prohibited the immigration of Chinese nationals to the United States.

## The Family Economy: Women and Children

Many working-class families, whether native-born or immigrant, lived in poverty or near poverty. Family economic survival depended on the contributions of all, regardless of sex or age. The paid and unpaid work of women and children became essential for family survival and economic advancement. In the mines and textile mills, child labor had been common since midcentury. As other industries mechanized in the 1880s and 1890s, they hired children, girls as well as boys, who often could tend machines as efficiently as adults yet received wages considerably lower.

Attempts to abolish child labor began before the Civil War. By 1863, seven states had passed laws limiting the hours of child workers to forty-eight a week, but often the laws were not strictly enforced. Most southern states refused to regulate child labor, and children continued to be widely employed in southern mills, some as young as six or seven years old. In the nation's mines, particularly in Appalachia, young boys were recruited to pick out the slate and waste from coal as it passed along chutes. Suspended on wooden boards over the moving coal, these breaker boys engaged in backbreaking, dangerous work. A boy who slipped into the coal had little chance of surviving without serious injury. When a child labor committee investigated conditions in Pennsylvania, it found that more than 10,000 children were illegally employed in the coal fields. Child labor increased decade by decade, with the percentage of children under fifteen engaged in paid labor not dropping until after World War I. The 1900 census showed that 1,750,178 children age ten to fifteen were employed, an increase of more than one million since 1870. Children from ten to fifteen years old constituted over 18 percent of the labor force and 7 percent of all nonagricultural workers.

Even children who did not work for wages contributed to the family economy by scavenging fire-

wood and coal. Gangs of children patrolled the railroad tracks, picking up the coal that fell from the coal cars that fueled the locomotives. Other children worked as street vendors, newsboys, and bootblacks. Although laws in many states mandated school attendance, harried truant officers found it hard to collar children whose parents insisted they work rather than go to school.

In the late nineteenth century, the number of women workers rose sharply, with their most common occupation changing slowly from domestic service to factory work and then to office work. The 1870 census listed 1.5 million women working in nonagricultural occupations. By 1890, more than 3.7 million women earned wages, although they were paid less than men (Figure 19.1).

Women's working patterns varied considerably according to race and ethnicity. White married women, even among the working class, rarely

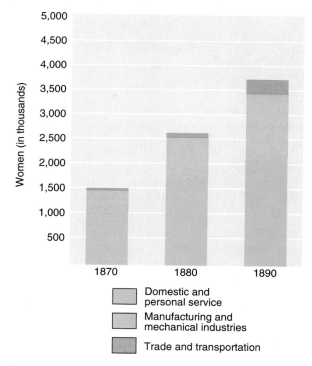

**FIGURE 19.1**
*Women and Work, 1870–1890*
*In 1870 close to 1.5 million women worked in nonagricultural occupations. By 1890 that number had more than doubled to 3.7 million. The total number of women workers rose sharply while the most common occupation changed from domestic work to industry and later to office work.*

**CHINESE RAILROAD WORKERS**
*Chinese workers like this section gang pictured at Promontory Point, Utah, in 1869 made up
more than 80 percent of the workforce that built America's first transcontinental railroad. Charles
Crocker of the Central Pacific hired them, reasoning that the race that built the Great Wall could
build his road across the treacherous Sierra Nevada. Besides, the Chinese workers were a bargain:
Crocker paid them $10 dollars a month less than he paid his Irish section gangs.*
Denver Public Library, Western History Collection, photo by J. B. Silvis.

worked outside the home. In 1890, only 3 percent
of white married women were employed. Nevertheless, many married women found ways to contribute to the family economy. Families often took
in boarders to supplement the family income. In
many Italian families, homework, such as artificial
flower making, allowed married women to contribute to the family economy without leaving their
homes. Black women, married and unmarried,
worked for wages outside their homes at a much
higher rate than white women. The 1890 census
showed that 25 percent of African American married women worked outside the home, often as domestics in the houses of white families.

## At Work

Throughout the nineteenth century, America's industrial workers toiled in a variety of settings.
Skilled craftsmen and artisans still worked in small
workshops or alone. But with the rise of corporate
capitalism, large factories, mills, and mines increasingly dotted the landscape. Sweatshops and
outwork, the contracting of piecework performed
in the home, provided a different work experience
from that of the factory operative (machine tender)
or the industrial worker. Pick and shovel labor,
whether on the railroads or in the building trades,

constituted another kind of work. The best way to get a sense of the diversity of workers and work-places is to look at several distinct types of industrial work: common labor, skilled work, factory work, sweatshop labor, and mining.

Common laborers formed the backbone of the American labor force throughout the nineteenth century. They built the railroads and subways, tunneled under the East River to anchor the Brooklyn Bridge, and helped to lay the foundation of industrial America. In her book *China Men,* Maxine Hong Kingston tells the story of Ah Goong, one of the *gam saan haak* (travelers to the gold mountain) who came to California in 1863 and went to work for the Central Pacific Railroad. For less than a dollar a day, Ah Goong hung in a basket on the cliffs above the American River, setting black powder in the crevices and firing the fuses to blast a path through the mountains. To earn an extra dollar, he sometimes risked his life to go back into the tunnel to investigate when the experimental explosive nitroglycerine had not exploded. Working in the dark tunnel, Ah Goong toiled on eight-hour shifts seven days a week. When the railroad tried to increase the shift to ten hours, Ah Goong and ten thousand of his fellow workers went on strike in 1867. They demanded the same wages paid to the white, mostly Irish gangs, who earned $40 a month compared with Ah Goong's $30. Construction superintendent Charles Crocker broke the strike, but in the end he raised the wages of the Chinese workers to $35 a month.

Life was cheap on the Central Pacific. Men died on the cliffs when they failed to scramble out of the way before the blast or when the ropes to the baskets broke. Men died in the tunnels when the nitroglycerine exploded without warning. Ah Goong was one of the lucky ones; he lived to see the Central Pacific reach Promontory Point, Utah, where it joined the Union Pacific to form the first transcontinental railroad in 1869. In the celebration that followed, orators basked in the accomplishment of the "greatest monument of human labor," never mentioning the Chinese workers whose prodigious labor had built the railroad.

At the opposite end of the economic ladder from common laborers were skilled craftsmen like iron puddler James J. Davis, a Welsh immigrant boy. Davis went into the iron mills in Sharon, Pennsylvania, at the age of eleven and won the title master puddler by sixteen. He later became a labor organizer and served in Congress and as secretary of labor in the 1920s. Iron puddlers were an elite among skilled craftsmen. Using brains along with brawn, they took the melted pig iron in the heat of the furnace and, with long poles, formed the cooling metal into two-hundred-pound balls, relying on eye and intuition to make each ball uniform. Davis compared the task to baking bread: "I am like some frantic baker in the inferno kneading a batch of iron bread for the devil's breakfast. My spoon weighs twenty-five pounds, my porridge is pasty iron, and the heat of my kitchen is so great that if my body was not hardened to it, the ordeal would drop me in my tracks."

*Common laborers built the railroads and subways, tunneled under the East River to anchor the Brooklyn Bridge, and helped to lay the foundation of industrial America.*

Possessing such a skill meant earning good wages, up to $7 a day, when there was work. But often no work could be found. Much industry and manufacturing in the nineteenth century remained seasonal; it was a rare worker who could count on year-round pay. In addition, two major depressions only twenty years apart, in 1873 and 1893, spelled unemployment and hardship for all workers, including Davis, who tramped the countryside looking for work in the 1890s. In an era before unemployment insurance, workers' compensation, or old-age pensions, even the best worker could not guarantee security for his family. "The fear of ending in the poor-house is one of the terrors that dog a man through life," Davis confessed.

In the iron industry, puddlers controlled the pace of work, the organization of the job, and the rate of pay. Such worker control posed a challenge to employers. As the century wore on, employers attempted to limit the workers' autonomy by replacing people with machinery, breaking down skilled work into ever smaller parts, and replacing skilled workers with unskilled operatives willing to work for less money. The textile mills provide a classic example of mechanized factory labor in the nineteenth century. Mary, a weaver at the mills in Fall River, Massachusetts, told her story to the *Independent* magazine in 1903. She had gone to work in the 1880s at the age of twelve and had begun weaving at fourteen. Mechanization of the looms had reduced the job of the weaver to watching for breaks in the thread. "At first the noise is fierce, and you have to breathe the cotton all the time, but you get used to it," Mary told her interviewer. "When the bobbin flies out and a girl gets hurt, you can't hear her shout—not if she just screams, you can't. She's got to wait, 'till you see her. . . . Lots of us is deaf," she confessed.

The majority of factory operatives in the mills were young, unmarried women like Mary who were paid by the piece rather than by the day or hour. Mary worked from six in the morning to six at night, six days a week, and took home about a dollar a day. The seasonal nature of the work also drove wages down. "Like as not your mill will 'shut down' three months," and "some weeks you only get two or three days' work, when they're curtailin'," Mary recounted. After twenty years of working in the mill, Mary's family had not been able to scrape together enough money to buy a house. "We saved some, but something always comes."

Mechanization transformed the garment industry as well. With the introduction of the foot-pedaled sewing machine in the 1850s and the use of mechanical cloth-cutting knives in the 1870s, independent tailors were replaced with sweatshop workers hired by contractors to sew together pieces of cloth into clothing. Working in sweatshops, small rooms hired for the season, or even the contractor's own tenement, women and children formed an important segment of garment workers.

Sadie Frowne, a sixteen-year-old Polish Jew, went to work in a Brooklyn sweatshop in the 1890s. In a room twenty feet long and fourteen feet wide containing fourteen machines, Frowne sewed for eleven hours a day. "The machines go like mad all day, because the faster you work the more money you get," she recalled. Paid by the piece, she earned about $4.50 a week and, by rigid economy, tried to save $2. As a young, single woman Sadie typified the woman wage earner in the late nineteenth century. The largest percentage of women worked in the needle trades, but factory work ranked a close second. In 1890, the average workingwoman had started to work at age fifteen and was now twenty-two, working twelve hours a day, six days a week, and earning less than $6 a week. Discriminated against in the marketplace, where they earned less than men, and largely ignored by the labor unions during this period, women generally worked only eight to ten years at most, until they married. These young workingwomen formed a unique subculture. Their youth, high spirits, and camaraderie made the hard, repetitive work they did bearable, and they relished the "cheap amusements" of the day—the dance halls, social clubs, and amusement parks.

The most hazardous work and the worst working conditions existed in metal and coal mining, along with extractive industries such as lumbering. To look closely at conditions in the mines, mills, and forests, in the words of one historian, is to enter a "chamber of horrors." Ross Moudy, a miner in Cripple Creek, Colorado, recounted the dangers he faced, first in a chlorination mill. For nine or ten hours a day, he worked for $1.50 to $2, breathing sulfur dioxide or chlorine fumes and working in dust so thick that "one cannot see an object two feet away." He soon quit and went to work in a Cripple Creek gold mine. There, according to Moudy, "dangers do not seem so great to a practiced miner, who is used to climbing hundreds of feet on . . . braces put about six feet apart . . . and then walking the same distance on a couple of poles sometimes not larger than fence rails, where a misstep would mean a long drop."

Miners died in explosions, cave-ins, and fires. New technology eliminated some dangers but often added others, for machinery could maim and kill. In the hard-rock mines of the West in the 1870s, accidents annually disabled one out of every thirty miners and killed one in eighty. Moudy's biggest worry was the carbon dioxide that often filled the tunnels because of poor ventilation. "Many times," he confessed, "I have been carried out unconscious and not able to work for two or three days after." Those who avoided accidents still breathed air so dangerous that respiratory diseases eventually disabled them. After a year on the job, Moudy joined the union "because I saw it would help me to keep in work and for protection in case of accident or sickness." The union provided good sick benefits and hired nurses, "so if one is alone and sick he is sure to be taken care of." Moudy acknowledged that there were some "hotheads" in the union, the militant Western Federation of Miners. But he insisted that most union men "believe the change will come about gradually and not by revolution."

A glimpse of the lives of this handful of American workers shows both the variety of work performed and the disparities among workers. Although real wages (pay measured in terms of buying power) rose 15 percent between 1873 and 1893, workers did not share equally in the improvement. African American men and women, for example, continued to be paid at a much lower rate than white men, as did immigrant laborers and white women. And the protracted depressions following the panics of 1873 and 1893 undercut many of labor's gains. What most distinguished American wages by 1900 from those in industrialized Europe was not simply the higher average wage but rather the striking differential between workers.

## Managers and White Collars

In the late nineteenth century, business expansion and consolidation led to a managerial revolution, creating a need for a new class of managers. As skilled workers saw their crafts replaced by mechanization, some moved into management positions. At the same time, new white-collar jobs in department stores and offices attracted a growing number of women workers.

### The New Managerial Class

"The middle class is becoming a salaried class," the *Independent* magazine observed in 1903, "and is rapidly losing the economic and moral independence of former days." As large business organizations consolidated and created national markets, they replaced what economist Adam Smith had called "the invisible hand" of market forces with the "visible hand" of salaried managers. The majority of these new middle managers were white men drawn from the 8 percent of the American population who held high school diplomas. And until late in the century, when engineering schools began to supply recruits, skilled workers trained on the job often moved from the shop floor to positions of considerable responsibility. The career of Captain William "Billy" Jones provides a glimpse of a skilled ironworker turned manager. Jones, the son of a Welsh immigrant, grew up in the heat of the blast furnaces, where he started working as an apprentice at the age of ten. During the Civil War, he served in the Union

**CLERICAL WORKER**

*A stenographer takes dictation in an 1890s office. Note that the apron, a symbol of feminine domesticity, has accompanied the woman into the workplace. In the 1880s, with the invention of the typewriter, many women were able to put their literacy skills to use for wages in the nation's offices.*

Brown Brothers.

army and earned the rank of captain, a title he used for the rest of his life. When Andrew Carnegie opened his steelworks on the outskirts of Pittsburgh in 1872, he hired Jones as his plant superintendent. By all accounts, Jones was the best steel man in the industry. He loved his work and drove himself and his men. "Good wages and good workmen" was his motto. Carnegie constantly tried to force down wages, but Jones fought for his men. In 1881, he succeeded in shortening the shift from twelve to eight hours a day by convincing Carnegie that good labor policy would reduce absenteeism and accidents. Jones himself demanded and received a "hell of a big salary." Carnegie paid him $25,000—the same salary as the president of the United States—a stupendous sum in 1881 and one that testified to the value the tightfisted Carnegie placed on his superintendent. Captain Jones did not have long to enjoy his newfound wealth. He died in 1889 when a blast furnace exploded, adding his name to the estimated 35,000 killed each year in industrial accidents.

## Office Work and Women "Typewriters"

As businesses became larger and more far-flung in the decades after the Civil War, the greater volume of correspondence and the need for more elaborate and exact records led to the hiring of more office workers. Mechanization soon transformed business as it had industry and manufacturing. The adding machine, the cash register, and the typewriter came into general use in the 1880s. Employers seeking literate workers soon turned to women. Educated men had many other career choices, while for women secretarial work constituted one of the few areas where they could put their literacy to use for wages.

Sylvie Thygeson was typical of the young women, particularly white, middle-class women, who went to work as secretaries. Thygeson grew up in an Illinois prairie town. When her father died in 1884, Thygeson, after graduating high school, went to work at the age of sixteen. After a brief stint as a country schoolteacher, she learned typing and stenography and found work as a secretary to help support her family. According to her account, she made "a fabulous sum of money." Nevertheless, she gave up her job after a few years when she met and married her husband.

Called "typewriters," women workers like Thygeson were quite literally identified as indistinguishable from the machines they operated. But far from seeing their work as dehumanizing, they viewed it with pride and relished the economic independence it afforded them. By the 1890s, secretarial work was the overwhelming choice of white, native-born women, who constituted over 90 percent of the female clerical force. Not only was it considered more genteel than factory work or domestic labor, office work meant more money for shorter hours. Boston's clerical workers made more than $6 a week in 1883, compared with less than $5 for women working in manufacturing. For Sylvie Thygeson and thousands of women like her, the office provided a welcome alternative to the limited options available to women workers.

## The Department Store

With the rise of industrial capitalism, a new consumer culture came to dominate American life, as men and women increasingly sought security, comfort, material well-being, and pleasure. Department stores became the symbol of this new consumer culture. Boasting ornate facades, large plate-glass display windows, marble and brass fixtures, and elegant skylights and galleries, department stores like Macy's in New York, Wanamaker's in Philadelphia, and Marshall Field in Chicago stood as monuments to the material promise of the era and the new culture of consumption.

**CONSUMER CULTURE**

*With the rise of consumer culture in urban America came huge new department and specialty stores. Johnson's Broadway store in New York advertised as "the largest millinery house in the world." In an era when no woman left her home without a hat, millinery stores sold the laces, flowers, ribbons, and feathers used to trim ladies' hats. The insatiable demand for fancy feathers led a group of prominent Boston women in 1896 to found the Massachusetts Audubon Society. Named for naturalist and painter John James Audubon, the group protested the indiscriminate slaughter of birds to provide feathers for the millinery trade.*
Library of Congress.

Within these palaces of consumption, the gender segregation that kept women's wages low in the office and the factory was also apparent. Male supervisors, called floorwalkers, commanded salaries from $10 to $16 per week at a time when the typical Macy's saleswoman received $5 to $6. In all stores, saleswomen were subject to harsh and arbitrary discipline. Sitting was forbidden, and conversation with other clerks led to instant dismissal. Fines for tardiness or gum chewing pared down already meager wages. Yet white-collar workers counted themselves a cut above factory workers, even when their pay envelopes were thinner and did not justify the sense of superiority.

## At Home and at Play

The growth of American industrial capitalism not only dramatically altered the workplace but indirectly transformed home and family life and gave rise to new forms of commercialized leisure. Industrialization redefined the very concepts of work and home. Increasingly, men went out to work for wages, while most white married women stayed home, either working in the home without pay— cleaning, cooking, and rearing children—or supervising paid domestic servants who did the housework. The growing separation of workplace and home led to a new ideology, one that sentimentalized the home and women's role in it.

### Domesticity and "Domestics"

The separation of the workplace and the home that marked the shift to industrial society in the early nineteenth century redefined the home as a "haven in the heartless world," presided over by a wife and mother who made the household her "separate sphere." The cultural ideology that dictated that woman's place was in the home has been called the "cult of domesticity," a phrase used to prescribe an ideal of womanhood that dominated the period from 1820 to the end of the nineteenth century.

In the decades after the Civil War, the typical middle-class dwelling in which women were to find their place became more embellished architecturally and its interiors more cluttered. Possession of such a home, indeed of any home at all, marked the gulf between the working poor and the middle class. Homeowners constituted only 36 percent of the housing population in 1900, compared with 66 percent today.

The cult of domesticity and the elaboration of the middle-class home in the nineteenth century led to a major change in patterns of hiring household help in the North. (The South continued to rely on black female labor, first slave and later free.) Domestic labor changed over the course of the nineteenth century from the "hired girl," who worked beside the housewife/employer, to the live-in servant, or "domestic." In American cities by 1870, from 15 to 30 percent of all households included live-in domestic servants, more than 90 percent of whom were women. As the cult of domesticity and growing consumerism raised the expectations of the urban middle and upper classes, domestics no longer "helped"; increasingly they carried the main burden of housework alone. Investigators found that domestic servants not only worked longer hours than any other women workers but also spent their "free" time on call. "She is liable to be rung up at all hours," one study reported. "Her very meals are not secure from interruption, and even her sleep is not sacred."

> *The growth of American industrial capitalism not only dramatically altered the workplace but indirectly transformed home and family life and gave rise to new forms of commercialized leisure.*

By the mid-nineteenth century, native-born women increasingly took up other work and left domestic service to immigrants. The maid was so often Irish that "Bridget" became a generic term for female domestics. Domestic servants by all accounts resented their lack of privacy and their limited opportunities for socializing. Furthermore, going into service carried a social stigma. As one young woman observed, "If a girl goes into the kitchen she is sneered at and called 'the Bridget,' but if she goes behind the counter she is escorted by gentlemen." No wonder domestic service was the occupation of last resort, a "hard and lonely life" in the words of one servant girl.

For women of the white middle class, domestics were a boon, freeing them from household drudgery and giving them more time to spend with their children or to pursue club work or reform. Thus, domestic service, while it supported the cult of domesticity, created for those women who could afford it opportunities that expanded their horizons outside the home and worked to subvert accepted notions of "woman's place."

## Mill Towns and Company Towns

In the mill towns and company towns across America, industrial capitalism redefined the concept of the home for the working class. Homestead, the Carnegie mill town outside of Pittsburgh, grew up haphazardly. By 1892, eight thousand people lived in Homestead, transforming what had been a rural village into a bustling mill town that belied its pastoral name. As the Carnegie steelworks expanded, they encroached on the residential area, pushing the homes out of the flatlands along the Monongahela River. Workers moved into the hills and ravines. In an area called the Hollow, shanties hung precariously on the hillsides. These small, boxlike dwellings—many no larger than two rooms—housed the unskilled laborers from the mills.

Elsewhere, particularly in New England and the South, the company itself planned and built the town. The Amoskeag textile mill in Manchester, New Hampshire, was a self-contained world laid out according to a master plan conceived in the 1830s. Such planned communities rested on the notion of benevolent corporate paternalism. Viewing the workers as the "corporation's children," Amoskeag's owners sought to socialize their increasingly immigrant workforce to the patterns of industrial work and to instill loyalty to the company, curb labor unrest, and prevent unionization.

Perhaps the most famous company town in the United States was built by sleeping car king George M. Pullman nine miles south of Chicago on the shores of Lake Calumet. In the wake of the Great Railroad Strike of 1877, Pullman determined to remove his plant and workers from the "snares of the great city." In 1880, Pullman purchased 4,300 acres of bare prairie, and on this isolated site he built his model town according to the principle on which he built the Pullman Palace cars that made his fortune—to be orderly, clean, and with the appearance of luxury. It was "to the employer's interest," he determined, "to see that his men are clean, contented, sober, educated, and happy."

When the first family moved in on January 1, 1881, the model town of Pullman boasted parks, artificial lakes, fountains, playgrounds, an auditorium, a library, a hotel, shops and markets, a men's club, and 1,800 units of housing. Noticeably absent was a saloon. One worker lamented that he frequently walked by and "looked at but dared not enter Pullman's hotel with its private bar." The worker's intimidation underscored a major flaw in Pullman's plan. In his eagerness to inculcate what

he referred to as the "habits of respectability," Pullman consulted his own wishes and tastes, never those of his workers.

Pullman's town offered housing that was clearly superior to that in neighboring towns. But workers paid for the eye appeal. Pullman intended the town to support itself and expected a 6 percent return on his investment. As a result, Pullman's rents ran 10 to 20 percent higher than working-class accommodations in nearby communities. And a family could not own its own home in Pullman. George Pullman refused to "sell an acre under any circumstances." As long as he controlled the town absolutely, he held the powerful whip of eviction over his employees and could quickly get rid of troublemakers. Although observers were at first dazzled by its beauty and order, it was not long before critics compared Pullman's model town to a "gilded cage" for workers. The economist Richard T. Ely went to the heart of what most concerned workers and critics alike when he concluded in 1884: "The idea of Pullman is un-American. . . . It is benevolent, well wishing feudalism, which desires the happiness of the people, but in such way as shall please the authorities."

The autocracy that many feared in Pullman was realized south of the Mason-Dixon line in the southern textile mill towns. "Practically speaking," a federal investigator observed, "the company owns everything and controls everything, and to a large extent controls everybody in the mill village." These largely nameless company towns, with their company-controlled stores, churches, schools, and houses, are a classic example of social control over workers. Paid in company currency, or scrip, workers had no choice but to patronize the company store, where high prices led to a mounting spiral of debt that reduced the workers to virtual captives of the company. By 1890, 92 percent of southern textile workers' families lived in company towns.

The mill towns and company towns of America provide only the most dramatic examples of the ways in which industrialization and the rise of corporate capitalism changed the landscape of the United States and altered traditional patterns of work and home life. After the Civil War, communities where men and women of different classes knew and dealt with one another personally became more and more rare. In the face of increasing business consolidation and impersonality, traditional ideas about equal competition in the marketplace and the relative independence of employers and employees lost much of their hold.

## Cheap Amusements

Growing class divisions manifested themselves in patterns of leisure as well as in work. The poor and working class took their leisure, when they had it, in the streets, the dance halls, the music houses, the ballparks, and the amusement arcades, which by the 1890s formed a familiar part of the landscape. Saloons played a central role in workers' lives, often serving informally as political headquarters, employment agencies, and union halls. But not all the working class thronged to the saloons. Recreation varied according to ethnicity, religion, gender, and age. For many new immigrants, social life revolved around the family; weddings, baptisms, birthdays, and bar mitzvahs constituted the chief celebrations. Generally, older-stock American men spent more time away from home in neighborhood clubs, saloons, and fraternal orders than did their immigrant counterparts. German beer gardens, for example, were designed for the whole family. But more often, men and women took their leisure separately, except during youth and courtship.

The growing anonymity of urban industrial society posed a challenge to traditional rituals of courtship. Adolescent working girls, immigrant and old stock, no longer met prospective husbands only through their families. Fleeing crowded tenements, the young sought each other's company in dance halls and other commercial retreats. Reformers worried that the dance halls served as a breeding ground for drunkenness and prostitution. In 1884, millionaire heiress Grace Dodge, determined to help young workingwomen find respectability, set up a Working Girl's Club in New York City. Members contributed twenty-five cents a month to rent and furnish a comfortable club room where young women could relax and entertain. Designed as an alternative to dance halls and amusement resorts, the Working Girl's Club sought to replicate patterns of middle-class courtship, where the young met under the watchful eye of older adults. By 1885, branches had sprung up in Brooklyn, Philadelphia, and Boston. But by far the majority of young workingwomen seemed to prefer the pleasure (and danger) of the dance halls.

Baseball became a national pastime in the 1870s—then, as now, one force in urban life that was capable of uniting a city across class lines. Cincinnati mounted the first professional team, the Red Stockings, in 1869. Teams proliferated in cities across the nation and Mark Twain hailed baseball as "the

**CONEY ISLAND**
*Coney Island became a pleasure resort in the 1870s, but at the turn of the century, with the development of elaborate amusement parks like Steeplechase, Luna, and Dreamland, Coney Island came into its own as the capital of commercialized leisure. This official guide highlighted the beach, the vaudeville hall, and the midway with its rides and its risqué harem dancers. In the foreground a barker gesticulates and a hawker urges a young man in a straw hat to buy souvenir photographs for his companion.*
Brooklyn Historical Society.

very symbol, the outward and visible expression, of the drive and push and rush and struggle of the raging, tearing, booming nineteenth century."

The increasing commercialization of entertainment in the late nineteenth century can best be seen at Coney Island. A two-mile stretch of beach that was close to Manhattan by trolley or steamship, Coney Island in the 1870s and 1880s attracted visitors to its beaches, boardwalk, and dance pavilions and penny arcades. In the 1890s, Coney Island was transformed into the site of some of the largest and most elaborate amusement parks in the country. Promoter George Tilyou built Steeplechase Park in 1897, advertising "10 hours of fun for 10 cents." By 1900, as many as half a million New Yorkers flocked to Coney Island on a weekend for fun. Other cities rushed to build their own playgrounds—Boston's Paragon Park and Revere Beach, Philadelphia's Willow Grove, Cleveland's Euclid Beach—but none rivaled Coney Island. The popularity of the amusement park signaled the rise of mass entertainment, making Coney Island the unofficial capital of a new mass culture.

## The Labor Movement

By the late nineteenth century, workers were losing control in the workplace. In the fierce competition to lower prices and cut costs, industrialists like Andrew Carnegie invested heavily in new machinery

that enabled them to replace skilled workers with unskilled workers. The erosion of skill and the redefinition of labor as machine tending left the worker with a growing sense of individual helplessness that served as a spur to collective action. Alone, the worker might be helpless in the face of the anonymous corporation, but together, workers could challenge the bosses and reassert their power in the workplace.

## The Great Railroad Strike of 1877

Labor flexed its muscle and showed its combined might with notable results during the summer of 1877 in the Great Railroad Strike. The strike, which began on the Baltimore and Ohio Railroad in West Virginia on July 16, quickly swept across the nation's rails until it involved 100,000 railroad workers (Map 19.2). The strikers, whose wages had been repeatedly cut, aroused a good deal of public sympathy, even among the militia sent to put

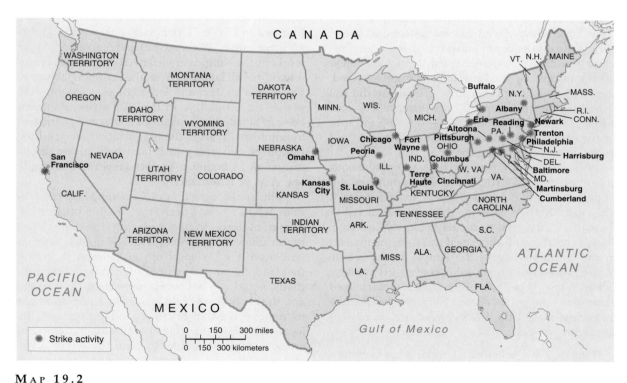

MAP 19.2
*The Great Railroad Strike of 1877*
*Starting in West Virginia and Pennsylvania, the Great Railroad Strike of 1877 spread as far north as Buffalo and as far west as San Francisco, bringing rail traffic to a standstill.*

them down. In Reading, Pennsylvania, militiamen refused to fire on the strikers, saying, "We may be militiamen, but we are workmen first." Rail traffic ground to a halt, and for a brief period the nation lay paralyzed by the strike.

Violence erupted as the strike spread. In Pittsburgh, striking Pennsylvania Railroad workers were joined in the streets by steel rollers, mechanics, the unemployed, and women and children who were determined to "make a common fight against the corporations." The militiamen recruited from Philadelphia arrogantly boasted that they would clean up the "workingmen's town." Opening fire on the crowd, they killed twenty people. Predictably, angry workers retaliated, and the resulting conflagration reduced an area of two miles along the track to smoldering rubble. Before the day ended, twenty more workers had been shot and the railroad had sustained property damage totaling $2 million.

Within the space of eight days, the governors of nine states, acting at the prompting of the railroad owners and managers, defined the strike as an "insurrection" and called for federal troops. President Rutherford B. Hayes (who, according to the New York World, owed his contested election in 1876 to the influence of Pennsylvania Railroad president Tom Scott) hesitated briefly and then called up the troops. By the time federal troops arrived, the violence had run its course. The army did not shoot a single striker in 1877. Its primary task consisted of acting as strikebreaker—opening rail traffic, protecting nonstriking "scab" train crews, and maintaining peace along the line.

Although the Great Strike was spontaneous and unorganized, it frightened the authorities and upper classes like nothing before in U.S. history. They quickly tried to blame the tiny radical Workingman's Party and predicted a bloody uprising. "Any hour the mob chooses it can destroy any city in the country—that is the simple truth," wrote future Secretary of State John Hay to his wealthy father-in-law. The New York Times editorialized about the "dangerous classes," and the Independent magazine offered the following advice on how to deal with "rioters":

> If the club of a policeman, knocking out the brains of the rioter, will answer, then well and good; but if it does not promptly meet the exigency, then bullets and bayonets, canister and grape . . . constitutes the one remedy and one duty of the hour.

Although large numbers of middle-class Americans had initially sympathized with the awful financial

conditions that led the workers to strike, they blamed the strikers for the violence and property damage that occurred.

In the end, the strikers, whose united action had raised the specter of revolution, won few concrete gains. On most railroads, wage cuts remained in force, and hundreds of strikers were fired and their names circulated on a blacklist to prevent them from ever being rehired. But the workers were far from demoralized. They had learned the power of concerted action and would use it in the future. As labor leader Samuel Gompers acknowledged fifty years later, "The railroad strike of 1877 was the tocsin [alarm bell] that sounded a ringing message of hope to us all."

## The Knights of Labor and the American Federation of Labor

The Knights of Labor, the first mass organization of America's working class, proved the chief beneficiary of labor's newfound consciousness. The Noble and Holy Order of the Knights of Labor had been founded in 1869 by Uriah Stephens, a Philadelphia garment cutter. A secret but peaceable society of workers, the Knights envisioned a "universal brotherhood" of all laborers, from the common laborer to the master craftsman. Although the Knights had played no active role in the 1877 strike, its membership swelled as a result of the growing interest in unionism. In 1878, the organization dropped the trappings of secrecy and launched an ambitious campaign to organize workers regardless of skill, sex, race, or nationality.

Under the direction of General Master Workman Terence V. Powderly, the Knights became the dominant force in labor during the 1880s. The union advocated a kind of workers' democracy that embraced a wide spectrum of reforms including free land, income tax, public ownership of the railroads, equal pay for work performed by women, and the abolition of child labor. The Knights sought to remove class distinctions and encouraged its local assemblies to welcome all comers, employees and employers alike. "I hate the word 'class' and would drive it from the English language if I could," Powderly stated. Only the "parasitic" members of society—gamblers, stockbrokers, lawyers, bankers, and liquor dealers—were denied membership.

In theory, the Knights of Labor opposed strikes. Powderly championed arbitration and preferred to use boycotts. But in practice, much of the organization's appeal came from the successful strike the Knights mounted in 1885 against three railroads controlled by Jay Gould. The Knights won a sweeping victory, including the revocation of a 15 percent pay cut. Despite the reservations of its leadership, the Knights of Labor was quickly becoming a militant labor organization that excited passionate support from working people.

The Knights of Labor was not without rivals. Other trade unionists disliked the broad reform goals of the Knights and sought to focus on workplace issues. Samuel Gompers, a cigar maker born in London of Dutch Jewish ancestry, promoted what he called "pure and simple" unionism. Gompers founded the Organized Trades and Labor Unions in 1881 and reorganized it in 1886 into the American Federation of Labor (AFL), which coordinated the activities of craft unions throughout the United States. His plan was simple: Organize skilled workers, those with the most bargaining power, and use strikes to gain immediate objectives such as higher pay and better working conditions. Gompers at first drew few converts. The AFL had only 138,000 members in 1886, compared with 730,000 for the Knights of Labor. But events soon brought down the Knights and enabled Gompers to take control of the labor movement.

## Haymarket and the Specter of Labor Radicalism

While the AFL and the Knights of Labor competed for members, radical socialists and anarchists offered competing visions of labor's true path. The radicals, many of whom were immigrants steeped in the tradition of European socialism, believed that reform was futile; they called for social revolution, in theory if not in practice. Anarchists also wanted revolutionary change but envisioned a smaller role for the state. Both groups, sensitive to criticism that they preferred revolution in theory to improvements here and now, rallied around the popular issue of the eight-hour day.

Since the 1840s, labor had sought to end the twelve-hour workday, which was standard in industry and manufacturing. By the mid-1880s, it seemed clear that labor shared too little in the new prosperity of the decade, and once again pressure mounted for the eight-hour day. The radicals seized on the popular issue and launched major rallies in cities across the nation. Supporters of the movement

**SAMUEL GOMPERS**
*Samuel Gompers, pictured here in 1895, founded the American Federation of Labor in 1886 and served as its president continuously (except for 1895) until his death in 1924. Unlike the Knights of Labor, who supported the Populist Party in the 1890s, the AFL advocated "pure and simple unionism." Gompers, convinced that workers could gain little from politics, organized only skilled workers and focused on bread-and-butter issues.*
The George Meany Memorial Archives.

set May 1, 1886, as the date for a nationwide general strike in support of the eight-hour day.

All factions of the nascent labor movement came together in Chicago on May Day, for what was billed as the largest demonstration in history in support of the eight-hour day. A group of radicals led by anarchist Albert Parsons, a *Mayflower* descendant, and August Spies, a German immigrant, spearheaded the eight-hour movement in Chicago. Chicago's Knights of Labor rallied to the cause even though Powderly and the union's leadership, worried by the increasing activism of the rank and file, refused to champion the movement for shorter hours.

Samuel Gompers was on hand, too, to rally the city's trade unionists, although he privately urged the AFL assemblies not to participate in a general strike. Gompers's skilled workers were labor's elite. Many still worked in small shops where negotiations between workers and employers took place in an environment tempered by personal relationships. In their Prince Albert coats and starched shirts, they stood in sharp contrast to the dispossessed strikers across town at Chicago's huge McCormick reaper works. There, strikers watched helplessly as the company brought in strikebreakers to take their jobs and marched them to work under the protection of the Chicago police and security guards supplied by the Pinkerton Detective Agency. Cyrus McCormick Jr., son of the inventor of the mechanical reaper, viewed labor organization as a threat to his power as well as to his profits; he was determined to smash the union.

On May Day, 45,000 workers paraded peacefully down Michigan Avenue in support of the eight-hour day, many singing the song that had become the movement's anthem:

> We mean to make things over;
> we're tired of toil for naught
> But bare enough to live on: never
> an hour for thought.
> We want to feel the sunshine; we
> want to smell the flowers;
> We're sure that God has willed it,
> and we mean to have eight hours.
> We're summoning our forces from
> shipyard, shop, and mill:
> Eight hours for work, eight hours for rest,
> eight hours for what we will!

Trouble came two days later, when strikers attacked scabs outside the McCormick works and police opened fire, killing or wounding six men. Angry radicals rushed out a circular urging workingmen to "arm yourselves and appear in full force" at a rally in Haymarket Square. At Haymarket on the evening of May 4, the turnout was disappointing. No more than 2,000 to 3,000 gathered in the drizzle to hear Spies, Parsons, and the other anarchist speakers. Mayor Carter Harrison, known as a friend of labor, mingled conspicuously in the crowd, pronounced the meeting peaceable, and went home to bed. A short time later, police captain John "Blackjack" Bonfield, who had made his reputation cracking skulls, marched his men into the crowd of fewer than 300 people and demanded that they disperse.

Suddenly, someone threw a bomb into the police ranks. After a moment of stunned silence, the police drew their revolvers. "Fire and kill all you can," shouted a police lieutenant. When the melee ended, seven policemen and an unknown number of civilians lay dead. An additional sixty policemen and thirty or forty civilians suffered injuries.

News of the "Haymarket riot" provoked a nationwide convulsion of fear, followed by blind rage directed at anarchists, labor unions, strikers, immigrants, and the working class in general. The hysteria ran deepest in Chicago. The police rounded up Spies and the other Haymarket speakers and jailed hundreds of radicals. Parsons, who had managed to escape capture, turned himself in to stand trial with his fellows.

The men were on trial for their ideas, not their actions. "Convict these men," cried State's Attorney Julius S. Grinnell, "make examples of them, hang them, and you save our institutions." Although the state could not link any of the defendants with the bomb throwing, the jury nevertheless found them all guilty. Four were executed, one committed suicide, and three received prison sentences. On the gallows, August Spies spoke for the Haymarket martyrs: "The time will come when our silence will be more powerful than the voices you throttle today."

In 1893, Governor John Peter Altgeld, after a thorough investigation, pardoned the three remaining Haymarket anarchists. He denounced the trial as a shameless travesty of justice and concluded that Captain Bonfield was "the man really responsible for the death of the police officers." The governor's action brought on a storm of protest and cost him his political career. But through the entire process, Altgeld never wavered. "If I decide they are innocent, I will pardon them," he promised, "even if I never hold office another day." He did, and he didn't.

The bomb blast at Haymarket had lasting repercussions. To commemorate the death of the Haymarket martyrs, labor would make May 1 an international celebration of the worker. But the Haymarket bomb, in the eyes of one observer, proved "a godsend to all enemies of the labor movement." It effectively scotched the eight-hour day and dealt a fatal blow to the Knights of Labor. With the labor movement everywhere under attack, many workers severed their radical connections, and many skilled workers turned to the American Federation of Labor. Under the leadership of Samuel Gompers, the AFL soon became the dominant voice of American labor. In the aftermath of Haymarket, Gompers urged workers to focus on concrete gains—higher wages, shorter hours—and use strikes and boycotts judiciously to win its demands. Gompers's narrow economic strategy made sense at the time and enabled one segment of the workforce—the skilled—to organize effectively and achieve tangible gains. But the majority of unskilled workers remained largely untouched by the AFL's brand of "pure and simple" trade unionism.

# Visions of a Better Life

Fear of social upheaval generated by the uprisings of workers in the 1870s and 1880s led to a search for social solutions. Liberal reformers, sympathetic to labor's plight but fearful of violence, sought schemes that would mitigate economic injustice without threatening bloodshed or class warfare. Two journalists, Henry George and Edward Bellamy, put forward visions of a better life that captured the imagination of their times. The utopian plans of George and Bellamy expressed both fears about the present and hopes for a better future.

## Henry George and the Single Tax

The Great Railroad Strike of 1877 inspired San Francisco journalist Henry George to write a book that soon became a classic of American political economy. George knew poverty firsthand and harbored a deep sympathy for the underdog. In this spirit, he published *Progress and Poverty* in 1879, dedicating it "to those who, seeing the vice and misery that spring from the unequal distribution of wealth and privilege, feel the possibility of a higher social state and would strive for its attainment." George explored the paradox central to American life: Why, in a land so rich, was there such inequality? (See the Historical Question on page 518.) He elaborated a theory that tied increasing inequality and growing monopoly to the scarcity of land caused by speculation (the practice of buying land and holding it until the price went up). Land speculators, he charged, contributed nothing to the economy yet made huge profits in "unearned increment." George championed a single tax on unimproved land. Once speculators could no longer turn large profits on the land they held, the way lay open to utopia. Land would become available for farming. Industrial workers would leave the factories for the farms. Wages would naturally increase, and the life of industrial laborers would become more secure. Government, and with it the political corruption of the Gilded Age, would virtually disappear. To underscore the urgent need for change, George ended his book with an apocalyptic vision of what would befall the United States if ac-

tion were not taken: disease, pauperism, and an atmosphere of "brooding revolution." His single tax offered a way out, an alternative to class warfare.

George's message found many ready adherents who made the single tax a rallying cry for reform. George moved east after the publication of *Progress and Poverty* and in 1886, in the aftermath of the Haymarket affair, ran for mayor of New York City on the United Labor Party ticket. A printer, a unionist, and a member of the Knights of Labor, George appealed to labor, which saw him as one of its own.

*Liberal reformers, sympathetic to labor's plight but fearful of violence, sought schemes that would mitigate economic injustice without threatening bloodshed or class warfare.*

At first, George's opponents dismissed him as a "humbug" and a "busybody" with no real chance. But when 34,000 laborers signed a petition endorsing him, Democrats and Republicans began to take him seriously. Samuel Gompers himself became the chair of George's city organization and headed the speakers' bureau. Staunch Republican liberals, fearful of class war, threw their support to the Democrats and tarred George as "an apostle of anarchy and destruction." In what George accurately described as "one of the fiercest contests that ever took place in this or any other city," he lost the election by 20,000 votes, despite strong working-class support. The Democratic candidate beat George, who in turn nosed out his Republican rival, a political newcomer named Theodore Roosevelt.

## Looking Backward from the Year 2000

While Henry George campaigned for mayor of New York and the country awaited the execution of the Haymarket anarchists, Edward Bellamy took up his pen to write a novel that ranks with Harriet Beecher Stowe's antislavery novel *Uncle Tom's Cabin* in terms of sales and influence. In 1888, Bellamy, a Massachusetts newspaper writer forced by tuberculosis to give up his editorial career, published *Looking Backward: 2000–1887*, a combination of utopian fantasy and genteel romance that spoke to the concerns of millions in the United States who were looking for a peaceful solution to the labor problem.

In *Looking Backward*, Bellamy's upper-crust hero, Julian West, falls asleep in Boston in 1887 and wakes in the year 2000 to find the world trans-

# From Rags to Riches: What Is "Making It" in America?

THE RAGS TO RICHES FABLES of novelists like Horatio Alger fueled the dreams of countless young people at the end of the nineteenth century. Alger's formulaic novels feature fatherless young men who through the right combination of "pluck and luck" move ahead in the world. Yet despite the myth, few Americans rose from rags to riches. Even Alger's heroes, like his popular Ragged Dick, more often traded rags for respectability.

Without exception, Alger's characters came from old stock and were not the new immigrants who poured through the "golden door" into the United States at the turn of the century. What were their chances of success? Literature written by the new immigrants themselves tells different stories. Abraham Cahan's *The Rise of David Levinsky* (1917) describes the experience of an eastern European Jewish immigrant who, as the title indicates, rises to gain material success. But while the theme of success is distinctively American, the treatment is not. The author laments that Levinsky's "rise" is paralleled by a spiritual loss. "I cannot escape from my old self," Levinsky confesses at the end of the novel. "David, the poor lad swinging over a Talmud volume at the Preacher's Synagogue, seems to have more in common with my inner identity than David Levinsky the well-known cloak manufacturer." Having sacrificed all to the material, Levinsky acknowledges, "At the height of my business success I feel that if I had my life to live over again I should never think of a business career."

Mike Gold tells a darker story of immigrant life in *Jews without Money* (1930), an autobiographical tale of the implacable economic forces that devastated Gold's fictional family and turned its young protagonist to communism. Gold's characters inhabit a world of grinding poverty and ignorance, a landscape so bleak that one character comes to doubt the existence of a benevolent God, asking plaintively, "Did God make bedbugs?" Determined to "write a truthful book of Poverty," Gold pledged, "I will mention bedbugs."

It wasn't a lack of cleanliness in our home. My mother was as clean as any German housewife; she slaved, she worked herself to the bone keeping us fresh and neat. The bedbugs were a torment to her. She doused the beds with kerosene, changed the sheets, sprayed the mattresses in an endless frantic war with the bedbugs. What was the use; nothing could help. It was Poverty; it was the Tenement.

Yet Gold's own success belied the grim economic determinism of his fiction. He made it out of the ghetto and into the world of literature and social activism.

Historians have been fascinated by the question of "making it" in America. Repeatedly they have attempted to measure economic and social mobility, from colonial times to the twentieth century. Looking at the lives of common folk, scholars have struggled to determine who made it and who didn't and why. Was America a land of boundless opportunity where the poor could rise? Or did the rich stay rich and the poor stay poor-to-middling, as pioneering studies of social mobility in the 1950s indicated?

By the 1960s, quantitative methods made possible by advances in computer technology promised to move history away from the "impressionistic," anecdotal evidence of fiction and memoirs and provide a statistical framework in which to measure success. But just what could historians measure with their new tools? Comparing Jewish and Italian immigrants in New York City at the turn of the century, one historian concluded that the Jews had done a better job of making it. By employing a table that categorized occupations, ranking them from professional, white-collar jobs to unskilled labor, the historian duly noted the movement from one category to another, concluding from his data that Jews moved more quickly into the white-collar class.

Studies of occupational mobility, however, contained major flaws. In a country where money has been and continues to be the common measure of success, historians' decision to use occupational categories and not income as the yardstick of mobility and success seemed to beg the question. Yet the choice was not surprising, given that census data, the staple of quantitative studies, provide information on occupation but not on income. Even occupational mobility proved difficult to measure accurately. For example, in the study cited, peddlers somewhat arbitrarily ranked at low white-collar sta-

**RAGS TO RICHES**

*Horatio Alger's novels like* Ragged Dick *(1868) invariably end with the young hero on the road to success. Contrast Alger's cheerful message with the bathos of the 1900 song "No One Cares for Me," in which the young newsboy in his rags replicates Alger's hero. But instead of getting ahead, his lot is portrayed as one of cruel neglect. Which portrait is more accurate? Historians for decades have wrestled with the question of social mobility and success.*

Picture Research Consultants & Archives; Culver Pictures.

tus because they were self-employed. Yet the push-cart peddler and the Italian street vendor could hardly be said to have enjoyed white-collar status in the larger society in which they moved. Students must look carefully at what historians are measuring, recognizing that occupational mobility may not equate with social mobility or economic success.

The larger question remains: What is "making it" in America and how best can it be measured—in dollars and cents, job satisfaction, occupational status, comparison with the lives of one's parents or neighbors? And what of the immigrants themselves? How did they define it? If becoming a brick-layer spelled success to the Italian immigrant and

his family, do studies of occupational mobility based on statisticians' categories and job rankings distort his lived reality? In dealing with the issue of "making it" in America, historians have increasingly come to recognize that each immigrant group had its own unique definition of success. Not all immigrants sought upward mobility, whether economic or occupational. Cultural factors, such as the value Italians placed on loyalty to the family, also played a key role. Ultimately, questions of success and mobility cannot easily be quantified, and they demand attention to the larger cultural context that shaped individual economic and occupational choices.

formed. No labor strife, no class antagonism, no extremes of poverty and wealth exist in the twenty-first century. Instead, the people are organized into an efficient industrial army in which all men and women between the ages of twenty-one and forty-five work for the same guaranteed annual income. In Bellamy's highly centralized state, the disharmony, corruption, and party strife of the Gilded Age have vanished, replaced by benevolent bureaucracy.

Bellamy's utopia comes complete with visions of technological marvels that were unheard of in the 1880s—the radio and moving sidewalks. But although the material conditions of the people have improved, Bellamy makes it clear that the new world came about from a spiritual and not a material transformation. The Religion of Solidarity, or "nationalism," transformed society, eliminating the destructive energies of both capitalist greed and proletarian envy and hatred. All society had to do was recognize and cooperate in the inevitable evolutionary process from competition to cooperation.

Julian himself experiences a conversion and, by the book's end, overcomes the smug selfishness that was the hallmark of his class. Looking back at his old life, he compares society in the late nineteenth century to "a prodigious coach which the masses of humanity were harnessed to and dragged toilsomely along a very hilly and sandy road." The driver of the coach is hunger, and his whips cut deep into the backs of the struggling team below. On top of the coach, "well up out of the dust," perch the passengers, who occasionally call down encouragement to the toilers below, "exhorting them to patience, and holding out hopes of possible compensation in another world for the hardness of their lot." Such inhumanity, Julian patiently explains to his twenty-first-century audience, could be explained by the conviction that "there was no other way in which Society could get along, except that the many pulled at the rope and the few rode." Besides, the riders suffer from the hallucination that "they [are] not exactly like their brothers and sisters" but are made "of finer clay." "This seems unaccountable," Julian confesses, "but, as I once rode this very coach and shared that very hallucination, I ought to be believed."

In the parable of the stagecoach, Bellamy offered a scathing critique of social Darwinism and a call to action. The book caused a sensation. Within three years, over a million copies had been sold, and enthusiastic readers launched 165 Bellamy Clubs devoted to discussing nationalism and implementing the social goals expressed in *Looking Backward*.

While neither George's single tax nor Bellamy's nationalist utopia produced the kind of mass movement for social change envisioned by the two authors, the enthusiastic response to both books indicated that many Americans feared social cataclysm and were ready to take action.

## Conclusion: The Workers' Own Struggle

The late nineteenth century witnessed many competing visions of a better life as Americans sought solutions to the problems attending urban industrialization and corporate capitalism. Henry George's single tax won supporters across the country and rallied New York's laborers to support him for mayor. Bellamy's nationalist utopia attracted followers drawn largely from the "sensible middle class." President Hayes called for "education" and a "wise judicious policy" to avoid labor upheavals like the Great Railroad Strike of 1877. American workers themselves had their own vision of what a better life might be—a life in which the independence eroded by industrialization could be countered by collective action, workers could regain some control of the workplace, and a shorter day and a higher wage promised escape from a brutal life of toil. Their vision and their willingness to fight for it made them active agents of social change, willing to risk their livelihood and sometimes even their very lives in the struggle.

Looking at the impact on his life occasioned by industrialization, a Massachusetts machinist declared in the 1890s:

> The workers of Massachusetts have always been law and order men. We loved our country and respected the laws. For the last five years the times have been growing worse every year, until we have been brought down so far that we have not much farther to go. What do the Mechanics of Massachusetts say to each other? I will tell you: "We must have a change. Any thing is better than this. We cannot be worse off, no matter what the change is."

Mounting anger and frustration would lead American workers and farmers to join forces in the 1890s and create a grassroots movement to fight for change under the banner of a new People's Party.

## CHRONOLOGY

**1869** Uriah Stephens founds Knights of Labor. Cincinnati mounts first professional baseball team, the Red Stockings.

**1870** Wage earners account for over half of those employed in 1870 census.

**1872** Andrew Carnegie opens his steelworks outside Pittsburgh and hires Captain William "Billy" Jones as superintendent.

**1877** Great Railroad Strike paralyzes nation.

**1878** Knights of Labor campaigns to organize workers regardless of skill, sex, or race.

**1879** H. George publishes *Progress and Poverty.*

**1880** George M. Pullman builds model town on 4,300 acres near Chicago.

**1881** Samuel Gompers founds Organized Trades and Labor Unions.

**1884** Grace Dodge organizes first Working Girl's Club in New York City.

**1886** Organized Trades and Labor Unions reorganized as the American Federation of Labor (AFL).

**May 1.** Massive rally in support of eight-hour workday takes place in Chicago.

**May 4.** Haymarket bombing in Chicago results in widening fear of anarchy and a blow to the labor movement.

Henry George campaigns for mayor of New York City on United Labor Party ticket and loses in close election.

**1888** E. Bellamy publishes *Looking Backward: 2000–1887.*

**1893** Governor John Peter Altgeld pardons three remaining Haymarket anarchists.

**1897** Steeplechase amusement park opens on Coney Island.

# SUGGESTED READINGS

Paul Avrich, *The Haymarket Tragedy* (1984). An exhaustive study of Haymarket and its aftermath. Avrich offers a convincing theory on who actually threw the bomb.

Susan Porter Benson, *Counter Cultures: Saleswomen, Managers, and Customers in American Department Stores, 1890–1940* (1986). A fascinating look at the development of consumer culture in America told in the context of the rise of the department store.

Faye E. Dudden, *Serving Women: Household Service in Nineteenth-Century America* (1983). From hired girl to domestic servant, an examination of the changing patterns of domestic service and a look at the lives of working girls and their female employers.

Warren Goldstein, *A Brief History of American Sports* (1993). The best comprehensive survey of the development of sport and its place in American culture.

Steven Mintz and Susan Kellogg, *Domestic Revolutions: A Social History of American Family Life* (1988). A sweeping survey that shows how industrial capitalism and urban life changed the American family.

David Montgomery, *The Fall of the House of Labor: The Workplace, the State, and American Labor Activism, 1865–1925* (1987). Labor history from the workers' perspective, with the focus on how industrial capitalism moved to deskill workers and wrest control of the workplace.

David Nasaw, *Going Out: The Rise and Fall of Public Amusements* (1993). An account of the rise of public amusements—theaters, concert saloons, vaudeville, dance halls, amusement parks—as uniquely urban phenomena, both public and commercial.

Nell Irvin Painter, *Standing at Armageddon: The United States, 1877–1919* (1987). A vivid picture of the social and political upheaval that marked the rise of industrial capitalism at the turn of the twentieth century and led so many to warn of coming cataclysm.

Kathy Peiss, *Cheap Amusements: Working Women and Leisure in Turn of the Century New York* (1986). A fascinating exploration of the lives of single workingwomen and their own unique culture.

Roy Rosenzweig, *Eight Hours for What We Will: Workers and Leisure in an Industrial City, 1870–1920* (1983). A comprehensive study of American working-class recreation that points to the interplay of class, ethnicity, and economics in shaping leisure culture in Worcester, Massachusetts.

**FARMERS ALLIANCE SONGBOOK**

*In the 1880s, the Farmers Alliance recruited followers in the South and Midwest at the rate of twenty thousand a month, using lecturers, camp meetings, and even songs to educate and organize. Copies of this Farmers Alliance songbook sold by the hundreds—testimony to the growing movement. In the cover picture, an Alliance farmer shakes the hand of a blacksmith, who bears a not coincidental resemblance to Abraham Lincoln. The handshake symbolizes the willingness of the alliance to make common cause with laborers of every stripe, a message reiterated in the four corners with images of school, farm, factory, and ship.*

East Carolina Manuscript Collection, J. Y. Joyner Library, East Carolina University, Greenville, N.C. Photo by Dewan Frentger.

# FIGHTING FOR CHANGE IN THE TURBULENT NINETIES

## 20

### 1890–1900

S T. LOUIS IN FEBRUARY 1892 played host to one of the most striking political gatherings of the century. Thousands of "mostly gray-haired, sunburned and roughly clothed men" assembled under a banner that proclaimed, "We do not ask for sympathy or pity. We ask for justice."

Exposition Music Hall presented a colorful spectacle. "The banners of the different states rose above the delegates throughout the hall, fluttering like the flags over an army encamped," wrote one reporter. Ignatius Donnelly, the crowd's favorite orator, attacked the money kings of Wall Street. Mary Elizabeth Lease, a veteran campaigner from Kansas known for exhorting farmers to "raise less corn and more hell," lent her powerful voice to the cause. Terence V. Powderly, head of the Knights of Labor, called on workers to join hands with farmers against the "nonproducing classes." And Frances Willard of the Woman's Christian Temperance Union argued against liquor and for woman suffrage. Between speeches the crowd sang songs like "All Hail the Power of Laboring Men" and "Justice for the Farmer."

In the course of the next few days, delegates hammered out a series of demands that were breathtaking in their scope. They tackled the tough questions of the day—the regulation of business, the need for banking and currency reform, the rights of labor, and the role of the federal government in guaranteeing democracy. The convention, noted a reporter, ended its work amid a din of cheers. "Cheer after cheer thundered and reverberated through the vast hall reaching the outside of the building where thousands who had been waiting the outcome, joined in the applause till for blocks in every direction the exultation made the din indescribable."

What was all the shouting about? People were building a new political party, the People's, or Populist, Party. Dissatisfied with the Democrats and Republicans, a broad coalition of groups came together in St. Louis to fight for change. They determined to reconvene in Omaha in July to nominate candidates for the upcoming presidential election.

The 1890s, one of the most turbulent decades in U.S. history, was marked by unrest, agitation, agrarian revolt, labor strikes, and a severe financial panic and depression. While the major parties continued to do business as usual, Americans flocked to organizations like the Knights of Labor, the Farmers Alliance, and the Woman's Christian Temperance Union and worked together to create new political alliances. The St. Louis gathering marked just one milestone on the road to a

**ON THE WAY TO A POPULIST MEETING IN KANSAS**
*Populism was more than a political movement; it was a culture unto itself. For farmers in sparsely settled regions, the movement provided reassurance that they were not alone, that others shared their problems, and that solutions could be found. When the Populists called a meeting, wagons came from miles around, as in this gathering in Dickinson County, Kansas. Men, women, and children were embraced by the Populist movement, which recognized that a strong economic and political movement could be a social force.*
Kansas State Historical Society, Topeka, Kansas.

new politics. The People's Party challenged laissez-faire by insisting that the federal government play a more active role to ensure greater economic equity in industrial America. This challenge to the status quo would culminate in 1896 in one of the most hotly contested presidential elections in the nation's history. At the close of this tumultuous decade, America entered the twentieth century after a war for expansion that helped to bring the country together even as it raised new questions about the direction in which the United States was heading.

## Militant Women

"Do everything," Frances Willard urged her followers in 1881. The new president of the Woman's Christian Temperance Union (WCTU) meant what she said. The path of the WCTU followed a trajectory that was common in the late nineteenth century. As women organized to deal with issues that touched

their homes and families, they moved almost inevitably into politics, lending a new urgency to the cause of woman suffrage (the vote for women). Women's activism and reform were by no means limited to the white middle class, as Ida B. Wells's antilynching campaign forcefully demonstrated.

### The Woman's Christian Temperance Union and Woman Suffrage

Frances Willard, the visionary leader of the WCTU, spoke for a group that was left almost entirely out of the electoral process—women. In 1881, only two territories, Utah and Wyoming, allowed women to vote. But lack of the franchise did not mean that women were apolitical. The WCTU demonstrates the breadth of women's political activity in the late nineteenth century.

The WCTU was created in 1874 following an unprecedented uprising in the Midwest known as the Woman's Crusade. During the winter of 1873–74, women, armed with Bibles and singing hymns, marched on taverns and saloons and refused to leave until the proprietors signed a pledge to quit selling liquor. The crusade spread like a prairie fire through small towns in Ohio, Indiana, Michigan, and Illinois and soon moved east into New York,

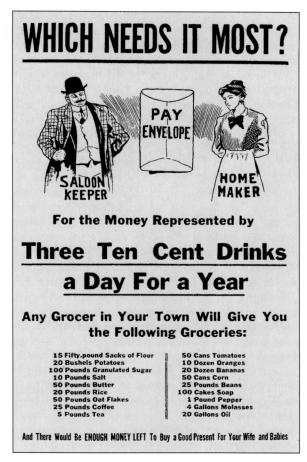

**WCTU FLYER**

*This Woman's Christian Temperance Union flyer shows the wife pitted against the saloon keeper for her husband's pay. The economic consequences to the family of a drinker were a serious matter. At a time when the average worker made only $500 a year, the money spent on alcohol meant less to eat for the family. As the poster indicates, thirty cents a day for a year paid for a substantial amount of family staples. Beer and liquor lobbyists worked hard not only to counter the WCTU but to fight woman suffrage because they feared when women got the vote they would enact prohibition.*

Culver Pictures.

New England, and Pennsylvania. Before it was over, more than 100,000 women marched in over 450 cities and towns. For the first time since the days of the antislavery movement, middle-class, respectable churchwomen took to the streets to demand change.

The women's tactics were new, but temperance (the movement to ban the sale of alcoholic beverages and eliminate drunkenness) dated back to the 1820s. Temperance was an especially explosive issue that divided communities, pitting middle class against working class, native-born against immigrant, Protestant against Catholic, and women against men. It had won significant victories in the 1850s when states, starting with Maine, passed laws to prohibit the sale of liquor (the laws became known as "Maine laws"). But by the late 1860s and 1870s, the liquor business was on the rise, with about one saloon for every fifty males over the age of fifteen. Willing to spend as much money as it took, the liquor interests mounted a powerful lobby to fight temperance while both the Democratic and Republican Parties avoided the divisive issue by leaving it up to counties and towns to decide whether to ban the sale of liquor.

*As women organized to deal with issues that touched their homes and families, they moved almost inevitably into politics, lending a new urgency to the cause of woman suffrage.*

After a decade of quiescence, the Woman's Crusade dramatically brought the issue of temperance back into the national spotlight with a new organization, the Woman's Christian Temperance Union. Composed entirely of women, the WCTU advocated total abstinence from alcohol. In its first five years, under the leadership of Annie Wittenmyer, the WCTU relied on education and persuasion to achieve its goal. When Frances Willard became president in 1879, she radically changed the direction of the organization. Under her leadership, the WCTU moved closer to the view that alcoholism was a disease and not a sin and that poverty could be as much a cause as a result of drink. Accordingly, social action replaced prayer as women's answer to the threat of drunkenness. Using "home protection" as her watchword, Willard capitalized on the cult of domesticity to move women into public life, arguing that they needed to attack the saloon to protect the home and family.

In its pursuit of temperance, the WCTU soon moved toward advocacy of woman suffrage, which Willard supported as early as 1875 and which the WCTU formally embraced in 1884 by calling for the "home protection ballot." By the 1890s, the WCTU's grassroots network of local unions had penetrated all but the most isolated rural areas of the country. Strong and rich, with over 150,000 dues-paying members, the WCTU was a force to be reckoned with.

Willard worked to create a broad reform coalition in the 1890s, embracing the Knights of Labor, the People's Party, and the Prohibition Party. Until her death in 1898, she led, if not a women's rights movement, then the first organized mass movement of women united around a women's issue. By 1900, women could claim a generation of experience in political action—speaking, lobbying, organizing, drafting legislation, and running private charitable institutions. As Willard observed, "All this work has tended more toward the liberation of women than it has toward the extinction of the saloon."

Unlike the WCTU, the organized movement for woman suffrage was small and relatively weak in the late nineteenth century. But militant suffragists, like the temperance women, fought aggressively for change. The women's rights movement that had begun at Seneca Falls in 1848 had split over the issue of the Fifteenth Amendment, which granted voting rights to African American men. Women's rights activists like Elizabeth Cady Stanton and Susan B. Anthony had wanted the amendment, ratified in 1870, to apply to women as well as to African Americans newly freed from slavery. But advocates of black suffrage such as Lucy Stone and Frederick Douglass urged women to wait, insisting that it was "the Negro's hour."

The split among women's rights activists produced two rival woman suffrage organizations. Stanton and Anthony formed the National Woman Suffrage Association (NWSA) in 1869, launching the first independent women's rights movement in the United States. The more conservative American Woman Suffrage Association formed the same year. Unlike the NWSA, this group included men as well as women and welcomed many members who believed that women should vote in local but not national elections.

In 1890, the two groups united under the rubric of the National American Woman Suffrage Association (NAWSA). Thanks to the WCTU's support of

the "home protection ballot," suffrage had become accepted as a means to an end even when it was not embraced as woman's natural right. The NAWSA honored Elizabeth Cady Stanton by electing her its first president, but Susan B. Anthony, who took the helm in 1892, emerged as the leading figure in the new united organization.

Although it would take almost three decades for all women to gain the vote with the ratification of the Nineteenth Amendment in 1920, the unification of the two woman suffrage groups in 1890 signaled a new era in women's fight for the vote. And Frances Willard's place on the platform in 1892 at the founding of the People's Party in St. Louis symbolized women's growing role in politics and reform.

## Ida B. Wells and the Antilynching Campaign

While most white women focused on reforms designed to counter the impact of urban industrialism in the North, black women followed a different path. The majority of African Americans were neither urban nor industrial. As late as 1890, more than 90 percent of the black population remained in the South, and those who migrated north found that discrimination blocked their employment in industry. As a result, African American women activists organized around issues that affected life in the rural South. Foremost among their activities was the antilynching campaign mounted by Ida B. Wells.

In 1892, after a white mob lynched a friend of Wells's whose only crime was that his grocery business competed too successfully against a white competitor, Wells concluded that lynching served "as an excuse to get rid of Negroes who were acquiring wealth and property and thus keep the race terrorized." Determined to do something, she began systematically to collect data on lynching. In the decade between 1882 and 1892, she discovered, lynching in the South increased by an overwhelming 200 percent, with more than 241 people killed. The increase testified to the retreat of the federal government following Reconstruction and to Southerners' determination to maintain white supremacy through terrorism and intimidation.

At the time Wells began her antilynching campaign, she had already earned a reputation as a militant activist for African American rights. Born a slave in Holly Springs, Mississippi, in 1862, Wells grew up during Reconstruction. Her parents were active in the struggle for Negro rights and provided their daughter with strong role models. Their deaths from yellow fever left Wells an orphan at the age of sixteen. She took over as head of the family, leaving Rust College to support her five siblings. Wells found work in the Memphis city schools and became an active member in the local African Methodist Episcopal church. She also joined a local lyceum, or literary group. It was there that she began her career as a journalist, writing for the lyceum's newspaper. In 1889, she became the co-owner of the *Free Speech and Headlight,* later shortened to *Free Speech.*

As the first salvo in her attack on lynching, Wells put to rest the "old threadbare lie that Negro men assault white women." As she pointed out, violations of black women by white men, which were much more frequent than black attacks on white women, went unnoticed and unpunished. Wells articulated lynching as a problem of race and gender, with the myth of black attacks on "white Southern womanhood" masking the reality that mob violence had more to do with economics and the shifting social structure of the South than with rape. She demonstrated in a sophisticated way how the southern patriarchal system, having lost its control over blacks with the end of slavery, used its control over women to circumscribe the liberty of black men.

Wells's strong stance immediately resulted in reprisal. While she was traveling in the North, her office was ransacked and her printing equipment destroyed. The warning that she would be killed on sight if she ever returned to Memphis only stiffened her resolve. As she wrote in her autobiography, *Crusade for Justice,* "Having lost my paper, had a price put on my life and been made an exile . . . , I felt that I owed it to myself and to my race to tell the whole truth now that I was where I could do so freely." Antilynching became a lifelong commitment that took Wells twice to Britain, where she placed lynching on the international agenda. As a reporter, first for the *New York Age* and later for the *Chicago Inter-Ocean,* she used every opportunity to hammer home her message.

Wells's activities mobilized other black women, including Victoria Earle Matthews and Maritcha Lyons, who were already engaged in social reform and self-improvement. They hosted a testimonial dinner for Wells in New York in 1892 that led to the organization of a black women's club, the Women's Loyal Union. The club became a spearhead for the creation of the National Association of Colored Women (NACW) in 1896. The organization's first

**IDA B. WELLS**

*Ida B. Wells led the movement to end lynching, traveling the country to raise people's consciousness about this heinous and illegal practice. In 1895, Wells married Ferdinand L. Barnett, a black attorney, editor, and founder of the* Chicago Conservator. *Shown here with Charles, the first of the couple's four children, Wells remained active in African American leadership, helping to found the National Association of Colored Women in 1896.*

Courtesy of University of Chicago, Department of Special Collections.

president, Mary Church Terrell of Washington, D.C., urged her followers to "promote the welfare of our race, along all the lines that tend to its development and advancement." Taking as their motto "Lifting As We Climb," the women of the NACW shouldered the double burden of self-improvement and social reform. They attacked myriad issues, including health care, housing, education, and the promotion of a positive image of the Negro race. In their efforts, African American club women enjoyed little help from white women's clubs. The General Federation of Women's Clubs remained largely segregated at the insistence of its southern constituency. The NACW played a critical role in Wells's antilynching campaign by lobbying for legislation that would make lynching a federal crime. Beginning in 1894 and continuing for decades after, antilynching bills were introduced in Congress only to be defeated by southern opposition.

Lynching did not end during Ida B. Wells's lifetime, nor did antilynching legislation gain passage in Congress; but Wells's forceful voice brought the issue to national prominence. At her funeral in 1931, black leader W. E. B. Du Bois eulogized Wells as the woman who "began the awakening of the conscience of the nation."

## The Farmers' Revolt

Farmers counted themselves among the most disaffected Americans in the country. Hard times in the 1880s and 1890s created a groundswell of agrarian revolt. Farm prices fell, decade after decade. Wheat that sold for a dollar a bushel in 1870 dropped to sixty cents in the 1890s. Cotton plummeted from fifteen cents to five cents a pound. Corn started at forty-five cents and fell to thirty cents a bushel by the 1890s. By 1894, in Kansas alone almost half the farms had fallen into the hands of the banks through foreclosure because poor farmers could not make enough money to pay their mortgages.

In the West, farmers rankled under a system in which railroads charged them exorbitant freight rates while granting discounts to large shippers. Also, the railroads' policy of charging higher rates for a short haul than for a long haul meant that large grain elevator companies could ship their wheat from Chicago to New York and across the ocean to England for less money than it cost a Dakota farmer to send a crop to mills in nearby Minneapolis. In the South, the lack of currency and credit had driven farmers to the stopgap credit system of the crop lien. The combined southern states actually had less money in circulation than did the state of Massachusetts.

During the depression of the 1890s, the human cost was staggering. "I Take my pen in hand to let you know that we are Starving to death," a Kansas farm woman wrote to the governor in 1894. Everywhere, the farmer seemed to be the victim of rules, such as the tariff, that worked to the advantage of big business. At the heart of the problem stood a banking system that was rooted in the gold standard and dominated by eastern commercial banks. In the face of their grievances, angry farmers across the United States raised a chorus of protest.

### The Farmers Alliance

Farm protest was not new. In the 1870s, farmers had supported the Grange and the Greenback Labor Party. But with the farmers' situation growing more desperate, the 1880s witnessed a spontaneous outbreak as farmers organized into alliances. The first group of farmers gathered at a Lampasas County farm in Texas and banded together into the Farmers Alliance to fight "landsharks and horse thieves." In frontier farmhouses in Texas, in log cabins in backwoods Arkansas, in the rural parishes of Louisiana, separate groups formed similar alliances for self-help.

*Farmers soon realized that the alliance cooperatives stood little chance of working unless fundamental changes were made in the American money and credit system.*

As the movement grew, the farmers consolidated into two regional alliances, the Northwestern Farmers Alliance, which included the old Granger states of the Midwest, and the more radical Southern Farmers Alliance, which began in Texas but soon spread into Georgia and united with groups in Louisiana and Arkansas. By 1887, the Southern Alliance had grown to more than 200,000 members, and by 1890 it counted more than three million. Determined to reach black farmers as well as whites, the Southern Alliance sponsored a separate National Colored Farmers Alliance that recruited more than a quarter of a million members.

At the same time, the Farmers Alliance broadened its base by reaching out to workers during the Great Southwestern Strike against Jay Gould's Texas and Pacific Railroad in 1886. The alliance insisted that the farmer, too, was a worker and that the labor question was a crucial issue for both the farmer and the wage laborer. The Southern Farmers Alliance issued a proclamation in support of the Knights of Labor, calling on farmers to boycott

Gould's railroad, and rushed food and supplies to the strikers.

At the heart of the alliance movement was a series of farmers' cooperatives. By "bulking" their cotton, that is, selling it together, farmers could negotiate a better price. And by setting up trade stores and exchanges, they sought to escape the grasp of the merchant/creditor. Soon alliances in a dozen states competed to pioneer new purchasing cooperatives. Through the cooperatives, the Farmers Alliance promised to change the way farmers lived. "We are going to get out of debt and be free and independent people once more," exulted one Georgia farmer. But the alliance failed in its attempt to replace the southern furnishing merchant with cooperative stores. Opposition by merchants, bankers, wholesalers, and manufacturers made it impossible for the cooperatives to get credit. The Texas exchange survived only one season. Farmers soon realized that the alliance cooperatives stood little chance of working unless fundamental changes were made in the American money and credit system.

As the cooperative movement died, a new culture of politics was born. What had begun as an organization for self-help moved toward direct political action. Texas farmers drafted a set of demands in 1886 and pressured political candidates to endorse them. These demands became the basis of a platform proposed by the Southern Alliance in 1890 calling for railroad regulation and control, laws against land speculation, and currency and credit reform. But it proved easier to get politicians to make promises than to persuade them to enact reform legislation. Confounded by the failure of the Democrats and Republicans to break with commercial interests and support the farmer, the alliance moved, often reluctantly, in the direction of a third party.

At its start in 1877, alliance leader C. W. Macune had insisted, "The Alliance is a strictly white man's nonpolitical, secret business association." But by 1892, after more than a decade of organization, education, and politicization, the alliance was none of those things. Although some southern leaders, like Macune, made it clear that they would never threaten the unity of the white vote in the South by leaving the Democratic Party, advocates of a third party carried the day at the convention of laborers, farmers, and common folk in St. Louis. There, the Farmers Alliance gave birth to the People's Party and launched the Populist movement.

## The Populist Movement

"There is something at the back of all this turmoil more than the failure of crops or the scarcity of ready cash," a journalist observed in 1892. Populism was more than a set of demands and a list of economic grievances. At its heart were the emotion and the promise of a religious revival. Wagon trains carrying ten thousand farmers gathered at camp meetings to listen to speeches by the angry prophets of the movement. Populism was a mass movement with its own political language and its own slogan: "The alliance is the people and the people are together."

The Populists mounted a critique of industrial society and a call for action. Convinced that the money and banking systems worked to the advantage of the few and not the many, they demanded economic democracy. To solve the farmers' credit problem, C. W. Macune hit on the ingenious idea of the subtreasury, a plan that would allow farmers to store nonperishable crops in government storehouses until the market was advantageous. At the same time, they would receive commodity credit from the federal government that would enable them to buy needed supplies and seed for the coming year's crops. The subtreasury became an article of faith in the South, where it promised to eliminate the crop lien system once and for all. Although Macune's idea would be enacted piecemeal in Progressive and New Deal legislation after the start of the twentieth century, at the time he proposed it in the 1890s it was dismissed by conservatives as farfetched and communistic.

*Populism was more than a set of demands and a list of economic grievances. At its heart were the emotion and the promise of a religious revival.*

For the western farmer, whose enemy was not the merchant but the mortgage, Populism promised land reform. The Populists called for a plan that would reclaim excessive lands granted or sold to railroads and foreign investors. The Populists' boldest proposal called for government ownership of the railroads and telegraphs to put an end to discriminatory rate practices. With the powerful railroads dominating politics and effectively nullifying the

Interstate Commerce Act of 1887, Populists did not shrink from advocating what their opponents called state socialism.

Money joined transportation and land as the third major thrust of the Populist movement. Farmers in all sections rallied to the cry for cheaper currency, endorsing platform planks calling for free silver and greenbacks. To show their support for labor, Populists supported the eight-hour day and an end to contract labor. And to empower the common people, their platform called for the direct election of senators and electoral reforms including the secret ballot and the right to initiate legislation, to recall elected officials, and to submit issues to the people via referendum. More than just a response to hard times, Populism presented an alternative vision of what America could become. As Henry Demarest Lloyd, an enthusiastic supporter of Populism, observed, "The People's Party is more than the organized discontent of the people. It is the organized aspiration of the people for a fuller, nobler, richer, kindlier life for every man, woman, and child in the ranks of humanity." It represented, in Lloyd's words, "an uprising of principle."

## The Labor Wars

While the farmers united to fight for change, industrial laborers fought their own battles in a series of bloody strikes so fiercely waged on both sides that one historian has called them the "labor wars." Across the nation, workers in the 1890s struggled to organize and to gain legitimacy for their right to bargain collectively and to have some say on the shop floor. Against them they found arrayed not only the power of the industrialists, but also the might of the state, the authority of the courts, and the influence of the press. The labor wars of the 1890s rarely ended successfully for the strikers, but they dramatized the willingness of workers to fight for their rights and forced the nation to confront the issue of industrial strife.

### The Homestead Lockout and Strike

At first glance it seemed ironic that Carnegie Steel's Homestead mill became the storm center of labor's fight for the right to unionize. Andrew Carnegie was unique among industrialists as a self-styled friend of labor. In 1886 he had written, "The right of the workingmen to combine and to form trades unions is no less sacred than the right of the manufacturer to enter into associations and conferences with his fellows." Yet six years later at Homestead, Carnegie set out to crush a union in one of labor's legendary confrontations.

As much as he cherished his liberal beliefs, Carnegie cherished his profits more. Labor unions had worked well for him during the years when he was building his empire. Labor strife at Homestead during the 1870s had enabled Carnegie to buy the plant from his competitors at cost and to take over the steel industry. And during the 1880s, strong national craft unions ensured that competing mills could not undercut his labor costs. But by the 1890s, Carnegie held nearly total control of the steelmaking business. Standing in his way was the Amalgamated Association of Iron and Steel Workers, one of the largest and richest of the craft unions that made up the American Federation of Labor.

In 1892, when the Amalgamated attempted to renew its contract at Carnegie's Homestead mill, its leaders were told that since "the vast majority of our employees are Non union, the Firm has decided that the minority must give place to the majority." While it was true that only eight hundred skilled workers belonged to the elite Amalgamated, the union had long enjoyed the support of the plant's three thousand nonunion workers. Slavs who did much of the unskilled work made common cause with the Welsh, Scots, and Irish who belonged to the union. Never before had the Amalgamated been denied a contract.

As the situation built toward a showdown, Carnegie sailed to Scotland in the spring. No doubt aware of his hypocrisy, he preferred not to be directly involved. He left Henry Clay Frick, the toughest antilabor man in the industry, in charge of the Homestead plant.

By summer a strike looked inevitable. Frick prepared for the showdown by erecting a fifteen-foot fence around the plant and topping it with barbed wire. With platforms for searchlights and holes for rifles, the fence gave the mill a distinctly military look. Workers aptly dubbed it "Fort Frick." To defend his fort Frick hired 316 mercenaries from the Pinkerton Detective Agency at the rate of five dollars per day, more than double the wage of the average Homestead worker.

On June 28, Frick locked the workers out of the mills. They immediately rallied to the support of the Amalgamated and declared a strike. Hugh O'Donnell, the young Irishman who led the union, vowed

**THE BATTLE AT THE HOMESTEAD STEEL MILL**
*This contemporary lithograph portrays scenes from the battle between workers and strikebreakers in July 1892: the workers attacking the barges, the cannonading of the barges, the surrender of the Pinkertons, the captives being led to prison, and, finally, the arrival of the militia and the soldiers in camp. The lithograph also shows (lower right) the revenge the strikers took on the hated "Pinks." Of the 316 Pinkertons, not one escaped injury as the angry crowd, armed with clubs, hoes, and brickbats, forced them to run a bloody gauntlet.*
Carnegie Library, Pittsburgh.

to prevent strikebreakers from entering the plant. On July 6 at four in the morning, a lookout spotted two barges moving up the Monongahela River in the fog. Frick was attempting to smuggle his Pinkertons into Homestead. Workers sounded the alarm, and within minutes a crowd of more than one thousand, hastily armed with rifles, hoes, and fence posts, rushed to the riverbank to meet the enemy. When the Pinkertons attempted to come ashore, gunfire broke out, and more than a dozen Pinkertons and some thirty strikers fell, killed or wounded. The Pinkertons retreated back onto the barges.

For twelve hours the strikers threw everything they had at the barges. Finally, the Pinkertons

hoisted a white flag and arranged with O'Donnell to surrender. With eight strikers dead or dying and scores wounded, the crowd, now numbering perhaps ten thousand, was in no mood for conciliation. As the hated "Pinks" came up the hill, they were forced to run a gauntlet of screaming, cursing men, women, and children. When a young guard dropped to his knees, weeping for mercy, a woman used her umbrella to poke out his eye. Only one Pinkerton had been killed in the siege on the barges, but in the grim rout that followed their surrender, three men died as a result of the beatings, and not one avoided injury.

The "battle of Fort Frick" ended in a dubious victory for the workers. They took control of the plant and elected a council to run the community. At first, public opinion favored their cause. Newspapers urged Frick to negotiate or submit to arbitration. A congressman castigated Carnegie for "skulking in his castle in Scotland," and the Populists, meeting in St. Louis, condemned the use of "hireling armies."

But the action of the strikers struck at the heart of the capitalist system, pitting the workers' right to their jobs against the rights of private property. Four days after the confrontation, the Pennsylvania governor, who sympathized with the workers, nonetheless yielded to pressure from Frick and ordered eight thousand National Guard troops into Homestead to protect Carnegie's mills. The strikers, thinking they had won the day, welcomed the troops with a brass band. But they soon understood the reality. The guard's ninety-five-day occupation not only protected Carnegie's property but also enabled Frick to reopen the mills using strikebreakers. "We have been deceived," one worker bitterly complained. "We have stood idly by and let the town be occupied by soldiers who come here, not as our protectors, but as the protectors of non-union men. . . . If we undertake to resist the seizure of our jobs, we will be shot down like dogs."

Then, in a misguided effort to ignite a general uprising, Alexander Berkman, a Russian immigrant and anarchist, attempted to assassinate Frick. Berkman's ally in his undertaking was the noted anarchist Emma Goldman, a Russian Jewish immigrant who had won a national reputation for her fiery speeches against capitalism and in favor of birth control. Berkman bungled his attempt. Frick, shot twice, survived and showed considerable courage, allowing doctors to remove the bullets from his neck but refusing to leave his desk until the day's work was completed. "I do not think that I shall die," Frick remarked coolly, "but whether I do or not, the Company will pursue the same policy and it will win."

After the assassination attempt, public opinion turned against the workers. Berkman was quickly tried and sentenced to prison. Although the Amalgamated and the AFL denounced his action, the incident linked anarchism and unionism, already associated in the public mind as a result of the Haymarket bombing in 1886. Hugh O'Donnell later wrote that "the bullet from Berkman's pistol, failing in its foul intent, went straight through the heart of the Homestead strike."

In the end, the workers' resistance was crushed. The strike collapsed after four and a half months.

The Homestead mill reopened in November and the men returned to work, except for the union leaders, who were blacklisted in every steel and iron mill in the country. In the drama and melodrama of events surrounding Homestead, the ideological and political significance of what occurred often remained obscured: The workers at Homestead had been taught a lesson. They would never again, in the words of the National Guard commander, "believe the works are their's [sic] quite as much as Carnegie's."

*The action of the Homestead strikers struck at the heart of the capitalist system, pitting the workers' right to their jobs against the rights of private property.*

With the owners firmly in charge, the mills reopened. The company slashed wages, reinstated the twelve-hour day, and eliminated five hundred jobs. The workers lapsed into a demoralized and hopeless state. It would take another forty-five years before steelworkers successfully unionized. In the meantime, Carnegie's production tripled, even in the midst of a depression. "Ashamed to tell you profits these days," Carnegie wrote a friend in 1899. And no wonder; Carnegie's profits had grown from $4 million in 1892 to $40 million in 1900.

## Eugene V. Debs and the Pullman Strike

A year after the Homestead lockout, a major panic and depression hit the nation. A stock market crash on Wall Street in the spring of 1893 led to bitter hard times. The ranks of the unemployed swelled to three million, almost half of the working population. "A fearful crisis is upon us," wrote a labor publication. "Countless thousands of our fellow men are unemployed; men, women and children are suffering the pangs of hunger." Nowhere were workers more demoralized than in the model town of Pullman on the outskirts of Chicago. George M. Pullman, who made his millions by building Pullman Palace cars and leasing them to the railroads, prided himself on his enlightened approach to labor. But in 1893, Pullman's workers saw their pay sliced five times between May and December, with cuts totaling at least 28 percent.

At the same time, Pullman refused to lower the rents in his model town, insisting that "the renting of the dwellings and the employment of workmen at Pullman are in no way tied together." When workers went to the bank to cash their checks, the rent was taken out. One worker found that he had only forty-seven cents to live on for two weeks. When the bank teller asked him whether he wanted to apply it to his back rent, he retorted, "If Mr. Pullman needs that forty-seven cents worse than I do, let him have it." In the meantime, Pullman continued to pay his stockholders an 8 percent dividend, and the company accumulated a $25 million surplus.

At the heart of the labor problems at Pullman was not only economic inequity but the company's attempt to control the work process, substituting piecework for day wages and undermining the skilled craftsworkers. The Pullman workers rebelled. During the spring of 1894, they flocked to the ranks of the American Railway Union (ARU), a new organization led by Eugene Victor Debs. The ARU, unlike the skilled craft unions of the AFL, pledged to organize all railway workers from the engineers down to the engine wipers.

George Pullman responded to his workers' grievances by firing three of the union's leaders the day after they led a delegation to protest wage cuts. Angry men and women walked off the job in disgust. What began as a spontaneous protest in May 1894 blossomed into a strike that involved more than 90 percent of Pullman's 3,300 workers. "We do not know what the outcome will be, and in fact we do not much care," one worker confessed. "We do know that we are working for less wages than will maintain ourselves and families in the necessaries of life, and on that proposition we refuse to work any longer." Pullman countered by shutting down the plant.

In June, the Pullman strikers appealed to the ARU to come to their aid. Debs sympathized with the strikers, but he hesitated to commit his fledgling union to a major strike in the midst of a depression. He pleaded with the workers to find another solution. When Pullman adamantly refused to arbitrate, the ARU membership, brushing aside Debs's call for caution, voted to boycott all Pullman cars. Beginning on June 29, switchmen refused to handle any train that carried Pullman cars.

The conflict escalated quickly. The General Managers Association (GMA), a combination of managers from twenty-four different railroads, acted in concert to quash the boycott. Determined

to kill the ARU, they recruited strikebreakers and fired all the protesting switchmen. Their tactics set off a chain reaction. Entire train crews walked off the job in a show of solidarity with the Pullman workers. In a matter of days the boycott/strike spread to more than fifteen railroads and affected twenty-seven states and territories. By July 2, rail lines from New York to California lay paralyzed. Even the GMA was forced to concede that the railroads had been "fought to a standstill."

The strike remained surprisingly peaceful. Mobs stopped trains carrying Pullman cars and forced their crews to uncouple the cars and leave them on the sidings. But no major riots broke out, and no serious damage was done to railroad property. Debs, in a whirlwind of activity, fired off telegrams to all parts of the country advising his followers to avoid violence, to use no force to stop trains, and to respect law and order. But the nation's newspapers, fed press releases by the GMA, distorted and misrepresented the strike. Across the country, papers ran headlines like "Wild Riot in Chicago" and "Mob Is in Control." Editors rushed to denounce "Dictator Debs."

---

*At the heart of the labor problems at Pullman was not only economic inequity but the company's attempt to control the work process, substituting piecework for day wages and undermining the skilled craftsworkers.*

---

In Washington, Attorney General Richard B. Olney, a lawyer with strong ties to the railroads, determined to put down the strike. When Illinois governor John Peter Altgeld refused to call out troops, Olney, acting in concert with the GMA, convinced President Grover Cleveland that federal troops should intervene to protect the mails. To further cripple the strike, two Chicago judges issued an injunction against the boycott so sweeping that it prohibited Debs from even speaking in public. The court in effect made the strike a crime punishable by jail sentence for contempt of court, a civil process that did not require trial by jury. Even the conservative *Chicago Tribune* judged the injunction "a menace to liberty . . . a weapon ever ready for the capitalist." Furious, Debs risked jail by refusing to honor it.

Olney's strategy worked. With the strikers violating a federal injunction and with the mails in jeopardy (the GMA made sure that Pullman cars were put on every mail train), Cleveland called out the army. On July 5, nearly eight thousand troops marched into Chicago. Violence immediately erupted. In one day, more than $340,000 worth of property was destroyed, twenty-five workers were shot, and more than sixty were wounded. In the face of bullets and bayonets, the strikers held firm. "Troops cannot move trains," Debs reminded the strikers, a fact that was borne out as the railroads remained paralyzed despite the military intervention. But if the army could not put down the strike, the injunction could and did. Debs was arrested and imprisoned for contempt of court. With its leader in jail, its headquarters raided and ransacked, and its members demoralized, the ARU was defeated along with the strike. Pullman reopened his factory, hiring new workers to replace many of the strikers and leaving sixteen hundred workers without jobs and without the means to relocate.

In the aftermath of the strike, a special commission investigated the events at Pullman, taking testimony from 107 witnesses, including workers and George M. Pullman himself. Stubborn and self-righteous, Pullman spoke for the business orthodoxy of his era, steadfastly affirming the right of business to safeguard its interests through confederacies like the General Managers Association and at the same time denying labor's right to organize. "If we were to receive these men as representatives of the union," he stated, "they could probably force us to pay any wages which they saw fit."

In his jail cell, Eugene Debs reviewed the events of the Pullman strike. With the courts and the army ready to come to the aid of property, labor had little recourse, Debs realized. Strikes seemed futile, and unions remained helpless; workers must take control of the state itself. Debs went into jail a trade unionist and came out six months later a socialist. After a brief flirtation with Populism, he would go on to form the Socialist Party in 1900 and run for president on its ticket five times.

## Depression Politics

The depression that began in the spring of 1893 and lasted for more than four years put nearly half of the labor force out of work. The country swarmed with people looking for jobs. They rode the rails,

slept in barns, begged for work, and, when they could not get work, begged for food.

The burden of feeding and sheltering the unemployed and their families fell to private charity, city government, and some of the stronger trade unions. The states and the federal government appropriated not a cent for aid. Following the harsh dictates of social Darwinism and laissez-faire, the majority of Americans believed that it was inappropriate for the government to intervene. But the scope of the depression made it impossible for local agencies to supply sufficient relief, and increasingly voices called on the federal government to take action. The American Federation of Labor declared that the "right to work is the right to life" and argued that "when the private employer cannot or will not give work, the municipality, state or nation must." Demands for government intervention mounted throughout the decade as poverty created its own politics.

## Coxey's "Army"

Masses of unemployed Americans marched to Washington, D.C., in the spring of 1894 to call attention to their plight and to urge Congress to take action. Jacob S. Coxey of Massilon, Ohio, led the most publicized contingent. Coxey, a wealthy manufacturer, had a plan to end unemployment. He proposed to put the jobless to work building badly needed roads. Coxey had been an ardent Greenbacker (he named his son Legal Tender), and he planned to finance his program of public works by an issue of paper currency (greenbacks) and no-interest bonds. His plan won the support of the AFL and the Populists.

*Like the Populist revolt, Coxey's army called into question the underlying values of the new industrial order and demonstrated how ordinary citizens turned to means outside the regular party system to influence politics in the 1890s.*

Starting out from Ohio with one hundred men, Coxey's "army" swelled as it marched east through the spring snows of the Alleghenies. In Home-

**COXEY'S ARMY**
*Coxey's army called itself a "petition in boots." Here a group of Coxeyites in coats, ties, and bowler hats march behind the American flag as women and children join the curious crowd that greets the marchers as they pass. These well-dressed marchers hardly seem like a menacing army. But many feared Coxey and his followers, and the military rhetoric of the press only fueled their fears. Coxey dramatized the plight of hundreds of thousands of workers left unemployed in the wake of the panic of 1893.*
Library of Congress.

stead, Coxey recruited several hundred from the ranks of those left unemployed by the lockout. Called by Coxey the "Commonweal of Christ," the army advanced to the tune of "Marching through Georgia":

> We are not tramps nor vagabonds,
>     that's shirking honest toil,
> But miners, clerks, skilled artisans,
>     and tillers of the soil
> Now forced to beg our brother worms
>     to give us leave to toil,
> While we are marching with Coxey.
>
> Hurrah! hurrah! for the unemployed's appeal
> Hurrah! hurrah! for the marching commonweal!

On May 1, Coxey's army arrived in Washington. Given permission to parade but forbidden to speak from the Capitol, Coxey defiantly marched his men onto the Capitol grounds. Police set upon the band, cracking heads and arresting Coxey and his lieutenants. Coxey went to jail for twenty days and was fined five dollars for "walking on the grass."

Coxey's army dramatized the plight of the unemployed and acted, in the words of one participant, as a "living, moving object lesson." Like the Populist revolt, Coxey's army called into question the underlying values of the new industrial order and demonstrated how ordinary citizens turned to means outside the regular party system to influence politics in the 1890s.

## The People's Party

"We meet in midst of a nation brought to the verge of moral, political, and material ruin," the Populists declared when they met in Omaha in July 1892 to nominate a national ticket. In the preamble to their platform, they cataloged their discontent:

> Corruption dominates the ballot-box, the legislatures, the Congress, and touches even the ermine of the bench. . . . The fruits of the toil of millions are boldly stolen to build up colossal fortunes for a few. . . . From the same prolific womb of governmental injustice we breed the two great classes—tramps and millionaires.

Ignatius Donnelly, author of the fiery preamble, spoke of a "vast conspiracy against mankind" and warned of "terrible social convulsions, the destruction of civilization." To answer this threat, he called on the Populists "to restore the government of the Republic to the hands of 'the plain people.'"

**CAMPAIGN RIBBONS**
*Political paraphernalia from the election of 1892 tells a good deal about each party's candidates and beliefs. The People's Party standard-bearer, General James B. Weaver, and his running mate are pictured under a banner promising "Homes for the Toilers, Equal Rights to All, Special Privileges to None." Populist issues are clearly spelled out—"Money, Land, and Transportation." The Populists' hope that these economic issues would replace sectional loyalties is evident in the symbolism of the blue Union and gray Confederate hands shaking. The beliefs of Democratic candidate Grover Cleveland are summed up in the phrase that became his motto, "Public Office Is a Public Trust." Republican Benjamin Harrison, who enjoyed the support of the business community, is aptly portrayed as sponsored by the Bankers and Brokers Republican Club.*
Collection of Janice L. and David J. Frent.

The Populists who arrived in Omaha on the Fourth of July nominated as their presidential candidate General James B. Weaver of Iowa, a former Union general who had headed the Greenback Labor ticket in 1880. They selected an ex-Confederate general as his running mate. The legacy of the Civil War cast its long shadow over Populist Party politics. Many southern Democrats could not bring themselves to break with the Democratic "party of the fathers" and stayed away from the convention. As befitted a party of principle, the longest ovation came not for the candidate but for the platform. When the chairman read the list of demands hammered out in St. Louis in February, the crowd went wild. To the eyes of one frightened eastern journalist, the enthusiasm evoked the spirit of the French Revolution.

Denouncing the Populists as "cranks, lunatics, and idiots," righteous editors dismissed them as "calamity howlers." Populist Lorenzo Lewelling of Kansas shot back: "They say that I am a 'calamity howler.' If that is so I want to continue to howl until those conditions are improved." And Mary Elizabeth Lease, accused of being a communist, responded unperturbed, "You may call me an anarchist, a socialist or a communist, I care not, but I hold to the theory that if one man has not enough to eat three times a day and another man has $25 million, that last man has something that belongs to the first."

The Populists garnered more than a million votes in the presidential election of 1892, a respectable showing for a new party. They won ten seats in Congress, three governorships, and, on the local level, put into office more than fifteen hundred county officials and state legislators. By working with the party out of power, usually the Democrats in the West and the Republicans in the South, they tipped the balance in the national election. This kind of fusion worked well in the West, where it took enough votes away from incumbent Republican President Benjamin Harrison to allow Democrat Grover Cleveland to return to the White House. But in the South the Populists made a disappointing showing. It was hard for southern Democrats recently converted to Populism to fuse with Republicans, especially to vote for a former Union general. The People's Party fared better in the 1894 congressional elections, when, unencumbered by a Yankee general, the Populists added half a million voters to their column.

More than their alliance with the Yankee North, it was the Populists' willingness to form common cause with black farmers that made them anathema in the South. Tom Watson of Georgia tackled the "Negro question" head on in 1892. Realizing that race prejudice obscured the common interests of black and white farmers, Watson openly courted African Americans, appearing on platforms with black speakers and promising "to wipe out the color line." When angry Georgia whites threatened to lynch a black Populist preacher, Watson rallied two thousand gun-toting Populists to the man's defense. The spectacle of white Georgians protecting a black man from lynching was symptomatic of the enormous changes Populism promised in the South.

## McKinley, Bryan, and the Election of 1896

As the election of 1896 approached, depression intensified the need for currency reform. Once again, cries for free silver (the coinage of silver in addition to gold) stirred rebellion in the ranks of both the Democratic and Republican Parties. When the Republicans nominated Ohio governor William McKinley on a platform pledging the preservation of the gold standard, western advocates of free silver walked out of the convention. Open rebellion also split the Democratic Party as vast segments in the West and South repudiated President Grover Cleveland because of his support for the gold standard. In South Carolina, Benjamin Tillman won his race for Congress by promising, "Send me to Washington and I'll stick my pitchfork into [Cleveland's] old ribs!"

The spirit of revolt animated the Democratic convention in Chicago in the summer of 1896. "Pitchfork" Ben Tillman set the tone by attacking the party's president, denouncing the Cleveland administration as "undemocratic and tyrannical." But the man of the hour was William Jennings Bryan of Nebraska, the thirty-six-year-old "boy orator from the Platte," who whipped the convention to a frenzy with his passionate call for free silver. In his keynote address, Bryan masterfully cataloged the grievances of farmers and laborers, closing his dramatic speech with the ringing exhortation "Do not crucify mankind upon a cross of gold." Pandemonium immediately broke loose as delegates stampeded to nominate Bryan, the youngest candidate ever to run for the presidency.

The juggernaut of free silver rolled out of Chicago and on to St. Louis, where the People's Party met a week after the Democrats adjourned.

Smelling victory, many western Populists urged the party to endorse Bryan. A note of warning came from Populists like Tom Watson, who denounced the Bryanites as opportunists and urged the Populists to steer clear of both major parties and stick to "the middle of the road." In the South, where Democrats had resorted to fraud and violence to steal elections from the Populists in 1892 and 1894, support for a Democratic ticket proved especially hard for Populists to swallow. Another obstacle in the path of fusion was Arthur M. Sewall, Bryan's running mate. A Maine railway director and bank president, Sewall had been placed on the ticket to appease conservative Democrats. But to the Populists, Sewall symbolized everything they opposed.

Populist delegates tried to remain true to their principles and their platform in St. Louis. They voted to support all the planks of the 1892 Omaha platform, added to it a call for public works projects for the unemployed, and narrowly defeated a plank for woman suffrage. Only deceit and trickery enabled the fusionists to carry the day. In an unorthodox turn of events, the convention selected the vice presidential candidate first. By nominating Tom Watson to replace Sewall, the party undercut opposition to fusing with the Democrats. Bryan quickly wired the chairman of the convention, protesting that he would not drop Sewall as his running mate or run on a Populist ticket with Watson. Mysteriously, his message never reached the convention floor. Watson's nomination paved the way for the selection of Bryan by a lopsided vote. The Populists did not know it, but their cheers for Bryan in St. Louis signaled not a chorus of victory, but the death knell of the People's Party.

Few contests in the nation's history have been as fiercely fought and as full of emotion as the presidential election of 1896. On one side stood Republican William McKinley, backed by the wealthy industrialist and party boss Marcus Alonzo Hanna. Hanna played on business fears of free silver to raise more than $4 million for the Republican war chest, double that of any previous campaign. On the other side, William Jennings Bryan, with few assets beyond his silver tongue, struggled to make up in energy and eloquence what his party lacked in campaign funds. He set a new style for presidential campaigning, crossing and recrossing the country in a whirlwind tour, traveling more than eighteen thousand miles, and delivering more than six hundred speeches in three months. According to his

own reckoning, he visited twenty-seven states and spoke to more than five million Americans.

As election day approached, the silver states of the Rocky Mountains lined up for Bryan. The Northeast stood solidly for McKinley. Much of the South, with the exception of the border states, came back to the Democratic fold, leaving Tom Watson to lament that in the politics of fusion, "we play Jonah while they play the whale." The Midwest was in the balance. Bryan intensified his campaign in Illinois, Michigan, Ohio, and Indiana. But midwestern farmers could smell economic recovery and were less receptive to the blandishments of free silver than were voters farther west. In the cities, Democrats charged the Republicans with mass intimidation. "Men, vote as you please," the head of Brooklyn's Steinway Piano Company reportedly announced on the eve of the election, "but if Bryan is elected tomorrow the whistle will not blow Wednesday morning."

*The Populists did not know it, but their cheers for Bryan in St. Louis signaled not a chorus of victory, but the death knell of the People's Party.*

Intimidation alone did not explain the failure of urban labor to rally to Bryan. Republicans repeatedly warned workers that if the Democrats won, the inflated silver dollar would be worth only fifty cents. However much farmers and laborers might insist that they were united as producers against the nonproducing bosses, it was equally true that inflation did not promise the boon to urban laborers that it did to western debtors.

On election day, four out of every five voters went to the polls in an unprecedented turnout. In the critical midwestern states, as many as 95 percent of the eligible voters cast their ballots. In the end, the election outcome hinged on as few as one hundred to one thousand votes in several key states. Although McKinley won twenty-three states to Bryan's twenty-two, the electoral vote showed a lopsided 271–176 (Map 20.1).

The biggest losers in 1896 turned out to be the Populists. On the national level, they polled less than 300,000 votes, over a million less than in 1894. In the clamor to support Bryan, Populists in the South drifted back to the Democratic Party. The People's Party was crushed, and with it died the agrarian revolt.

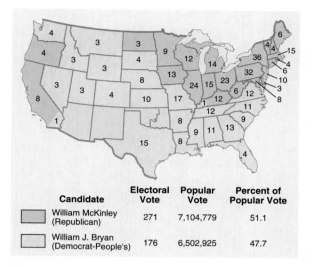

| Candidate | Electoral Vote | Popular Vote | Percent of Popular Vote |
|---|---|---|---|
| William McKinley (Republican) | 271 | 7,104,779 | 51.1 |
| William J. Bryan (Democrat-People's) | 176 | 6,502,925 | 47.7 |

**M A P   2 0 . 1**
*The Election of 1896*

---

But if Populism proved unsuccessful, it set the political agenda for the United States in the next decades, highlighting issues such as banking and currency reform, electoral reforms, and an enlarged role for the federal government in the economy. As the decade ended, the bugle call to arms drowned out the trumpet of reform as American expansionism spawned a "splendid little war" that whipped up patriotic fervor, uniting the country and announcing the emergence of the United States as a major world power.

# American Expansionism and the "White Man's Burden"

As the United States stood on the brink of the twentieth century, the European powers—Great Britain, France, Germany, Spain, and Belgium—as well as an increasingly powerful Japan competed for empires abroad, gobbling up what they liked to call the great "empty spaces" on the globe in Asia, Africa, Latin America, and the Pacific. Between 1870 and 1900, European nations gained control of more than 20 percent of the land and 10 percent of the earth's population. The United States, intent on conquering its own western frontier, had remained largely aloof from the scramble for colonies but not uninterested in the riches to be found abroad.

## The Monroe Doctrine and the Open Door Policy

American foreign policy at the dawn of the twentieth century rested on two pillars, one that dated back to President James Monroe in the 1820s and another recently developed under William McKinley. The first, the Monroe Doctrine, proclaimed the Western Hemisphere an American "sphere of influence" and warned European powers to keep their hands off or risk war. The second, the Open Door, dealt with Asia, an area coveted by American merchants since the 1840s, the heyday of the clipper ships and the China trade. In the 1890s, China, weakened by years of warfare, looked as if it might be partitioned into spheres of influence by England, Japan, Germany, France, and Russia. Concerned about American trade and the integrity of China, Secretary of State John Hay in 1899–1900 hastily wrote a series of notes calling for an "open door" policy that would ensure trade access to all and maintain the semblance of Chinese sovereignty. The notes—sent to Britain, Germany, and Russia and later to France, Japan, and Italy—were greeted with polite evasions. Nevertheless, Hay boldly announced in 1900 that the Open Door was international policy.

*American foreign policy reflected a curious paradox. Just as the United States wished to keep the Western Hemisphere closed to foreign influences, it wished to keep the Eastern Hemisphere open for its own purposes.*

American foreign policy reflected a curious paradox. Just as the United States wished to keep the Western Hemisphere (particularly Latin America and the Caribbean) closed to foreign influences, it wished to keep the Eastern Hemisphere (especially Asia) open for its own purposes. The twin pillars of U.S. foreign policy may not have been consistent, but they worked well to further the country's economic interests. By insisting on its Open Door policy in Asia, the United States largely avoided the problems of maintaining a far-flung colonial empire while at the same time exerting its economic power.

**THE OPEN DOOR**
*The trade advantage gained by the United States through the Open Door policy enunciated by Secretary of State John Hay in 1900 is portrayed graphically in this political cartoon. Uncle Sam stands prominently in the "open door" while representatives of the other great powers seek admittance to the "Flowery Kingdom" of China. Great Britain is symbolized by the stocky figure of John Bull; czarist Russia is portrayed by the bearded figure with the hat sporting the imperial double eagle. Other imperialist powers variously represented have yielded to Uncle Sam, who holds the golden key of "American Diplomacy" while the Chinese beam with pleasure. In fact, the Open Door policy promised only equal access for all powers to the China trade, not United States preeminence as the cartoon implies.*
Culver Pictures.

Throughout much of the last half of the nineteenth century, U.S. interest in foreign policy took a backseat to domestic developments. "Foreign relations," one historian has written, "were composed of incidents, not policies." One of these incidents occurred in 1889, when Germany threatened war with the United States. Eleven years after a treaty gave the United States the right to the harbor at the Pacific port of Pago Pago in the Samoan Islands, Germany, seeking dominance over the islands, sent

warships to support its honor and its claims. But before any fighting broke out, a great typhoon destroyed the German and American ships. Acceding to the will of nature, the potential combatants divided the islands amicably between themselves (Map 20.2).

Elsewhere, America's foreign adventures appeared little more than a sidelight to business development. In Hawaii, American sugar interests fomented a rebellion in 1893, toppling the increas-

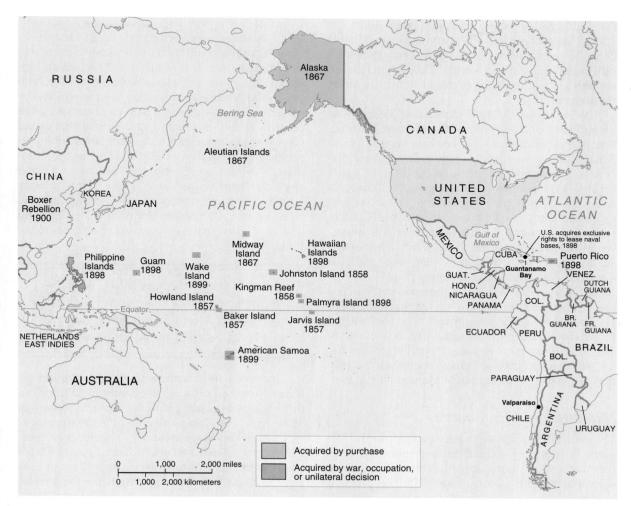

**MAP 20.2**
*U.S. Territorial Expansion through 1900*
*The United States extended its interests abroad with a series of territorial acquisitions. Alaska was purchased in 1867; the Philippines and other Spanish island possessions, including Puerto Rico and Guam, were won in the Spanish-American War of 1898. Although Cuba was granted independence, the Platt amendment kept the new nation firmly under U.S. control. For good measure, President McKinley annexed Hawaii. In the wake of the Spanish-American War, the United States woke up to find it held an empire extending halfway around the globe.*

ingly anti-American Queen Liliuokalani. They then proceeded to press President Cleveland to annex the islands, a move that would allow the planters to avoid overly high duties on sugar. When Cleveland learned that the Hawaiian population opposed annexation, he withdrew the proposal from Senate consideration.

Closer to home, the United States actively worked to buttress the Monroe Doctrine, with its assertion of American hegemony (domination) in the Western Hemisphere. In the 1880s, Republican Secretary of State James G. Blaine promoted hemispheric peace and trade through Pan-American cooperation at the same time that he used American troops to intervene in Latin American border disputes. In 1891, war with Chile almost erupted after two American sailors were killed and several were injured in a barroom brawl in Valparaíso. President Benjamin Harrison threatened war but backed down after Chile apologized. He was wise to do so, for Chile had a better equipped navy than the United States. Late in the century, the United States began to strengthen its navy, but its army remained little more than a token force of 25,000, barely large enough to handle disturbances at home, let alone fight abroad.

Nevertheless, in 1895 Americans risked war with Great Britain to enforce the Monroe Doctrine. When a border dispute arose between Venezuela and British Guiana over lands where gold had been discovered, President Cleveland asserted the U.S. prerogative to step in and mediate, reducing Venezuela to the role of mere onlooker. At first, Britain refused to accept the United States as mediator. Conflict seemed imminent. "Let the fight come if it must," wrote Theodore Roosevelt. "I don't care whether our sea coast cities are bombarded or not; we would take Canada." Cleveland, less bellicose than Roosevelt, wished only to see America's presence in the hemisphere respected and its solution for peace accepted. He was relieved when the British, who also wished to avoid war, accepted the terms of U.S. mediation. The Venezuelan crisis signaled the willingness of the United States to play an active role beyond its borders, especially to preserve the Monroe Doctrine.

## Markets and Missionaries

The depression of the 1890s provided a powerful impetus to American commercial expansion. As markets weakened at home, American businesses looked abroad for profits. Captain Alfred Thayer Mahan, leader of a growing group of American expansionists that included Henry Cabot Lodge, John Hay, and Theodore Roosevelt, prophesied as early as 1890, "Whether they will or not, Americans must now begin to look outward. The growing production of the country requires it." Exports of cloth, kerosene, flour, and steel already constituted a small but significant percentage of the profits of American business. And where American interests led, businessmen expected American power and influence to follow to protect their investments. Companies like Standard Oil actively sought to use the government as their agent, often putting foreign service employees on the payroll. "Our ambassadors and ministers and consuls," wrote John D. Rockefeller appreciatively, "have aided to push our way into new markets to the utmost corners of the world." Whether by "our" he meant the United States or Standard Oil remained ambiguous; in practice, the distinction was of little importance in late-nineteenth-century foreign policy.

However compelling the economic arguments about overseas markets proved, business interests alone did not account for the new expansionism that seized the nation during the 1890s. As Mahan confessed, "Even when material interests are the original exciting cause, it is the sentiment to which they give rise, the moral tone which emotion takes that constitutes the greater force." Much of that moral tone was set by American missionaries intent on spreading the gospel of Christianity to the "heathen." No area on the globe constituted a greater challenge than China. In 1858, the Tientsin treaty admitted foreign missionaries—Roman Catholics from France, Protestants from Britain, Germany, and the United States—to spread the gospel to the hinterlands.

*The moral tone of the age, set by social Darwinism with its emphasis on survival of the fittest and Anglo-Saxon racial superiority, proved ideally suited to imperialism.*

Increased missionary activity and Western enterprise touched off a series of antiforeign uprisings in China that culminated in the Boxer Rebellion of 1900–1901. The Chinese resented the interference of missionaries in village life and the preference and protection they afforded their Christian converts. Opposition to foreign missionaries took the form of antiforeign secret societies, most notably the Boxers, whose Chinese name translated literally into "Righteous Harmonious Fist." No simple pugilists, the Boxers believed that through ritual they could induce a trance that would make them invincible to Western weapons. Under the slogan "Uphold the Ch'ing Dynasty, Exterminate the Foreigners," they began to terrorize Chinese Christians and later missionaries in northern China. As they became bolder, they attacked railroads and telegraph lines, the twin symbols of Western imperialism. Their rampage eventually led to the massacre of some 2,000 Chinese converts and 250 missionaries and their families. In the end, 2,500 U.S. troops joined an allied force including British and German troops sent to save the besieged foreigners in Peking (now Beijing). The arrival of foreign troops chastened the imperial government, which adopted a tougher stance against the Boxers and a more accommodationist policy toward foreign missionaries.

In their fight against the Boxers, the missionaries saw no paradox in bringing Christianity to

**WOMEN MISSIONARIES IN CHINA**
*Methodist women missionaries in the Szechuan province of China relied on traditional means of transportation, in this case "back chairs." The independence enjoyed by women missionaries, who made up more than 60 percent of the foreign mission force by 1890, stood in marked contrast to the restrictions placed on young, unmarried women of their class at home.*
Courtesy of the Yale Divinity School Library.

China at gunpoint. "It is worth any cost in money, worth any cost in bloodshed," argued one bishop, "if we can make millions of Chinese true and intelligent Christians." Yet their work bore little fruit. By 1900, an estimated 100,000 converts existed in a total population of 400 million Chinese.

Patriotism, as much as missionary zeal and trade considerations, fueled American expansionism. The moral tone of the age, set by social Darwinism with its emphasis on survival of the fittest and Anglo-Saxon racial superiority, proved ideally suited to imperialism. Congregational minister Josiah Strong revealed this mix of racism and missionary zeal when he remarked, "It seems to me that God, with infinite wisdom and skill, is training the Anglo Saxon race for an hour sure to come in the world's future." British poet Rudyard Kipling expressed it in verse:

> Take up the white man's burden
>   Send forth the best ye breed—
> Go bind your sons to exile
>   To serve your captive's need;
> To wait, in heavy harness,
>   On fluttered folk and wild—
> Your new-caught sullen people,
>   Half devil and half child.

No one exemplified the new jingoism (extreme nationalism tinged with belligerency) more than Theodore Roosevelt, the rising young Republican from New York. Always more concerned with manliness than money, Roosevelt believed that nations and individuals needed the test of combat to maintain their virility. "This country needs a war," Roosevelt asserted in 1895. Power, not profits, motivated expansionists of Roosevelt's stripe. Intent on asserting the United States' place in the world of nations, they pressed for a more expansionist policy, judging imperialism "a fine expression of the American spirit."

## The United States on the World Stage

As the leading industrial nation in the world, the United States was destined to play a significant role in world politics. Yet not until the end of the century did the country take its place on the world stage by confronting and easily defeating a European power. On the surface, the Spanish-American War seemed a giant contradiction: A war begun as

# The Spanish-American War: Eyewitness Accounts

*The Spanish-American War received more eyewitness news coverage than any previous war in American history. Hearst's papers had fanned the flames of war and, once it started in earnest, reporters fed a public hungry for news about the conflict. In addition to daily newspapers, weekly illustrated papers like* Collier's, Leslie's, *and* Harper's *covered the war, using dispatches wired from the front and illustrations by some of the leading artists of the day.*

*The press shared the country's enthusiasm for battle. Richard Harding Davis, a star foreign correspondent, observed on the eve of the troops' departure from Tampa, "It was a most happy-go-lucky expedition, run with real American optimism and readiness to take big chances, and with the spirit of a people who recklessly trust that it will come out all right in the end. . . . As one of the generals on board said, 'This is God Almighty's war, and we are only His agents.'"*

*Men's letters home spoke of more mundane aspects of army life.*

### DOCUMENT 1. Rough Rider Arthur Fortunatus Cosby, Letter to a friend, June 1898

Personally I expected anything and I have no complaints to make, but a lot of the "boys" don't like it. Our food on board ship is the same; coffee, hardtack, with canned beef (that must have been cooked it is so stringy and tasteless), canned tomatoes and beans. These are travel rations and we have now had ten days of them with 5 days more on the road. We get the coffee hot, but the other things are usually cold unless an enterprising fellow will make a mess of the whole thing which he calls a stew.

We have all gone expert in "rustling" food, begging it, buying it from the ship's cook who is supposed not to sell, smuggling it in from shore etc. . . .

All the boys have lost flesh at the most astonishing rate. . . . Then too although our passage has been remarkably quiet many of the boys have been sea-sick. This with the confinement and heat to which they are not accustomed, and poor food has weakened them. I am very much afraid that we shan't do much.

*When the troops put ashore, General William Shafter attempted to hold the reporters on the ship until after the troops had landed. An irate Richard Harding Davis confronted the general, explaining that he was a "descriptive writer" and needed to be at the scene. Shafter retorted, "I do not care a damn what you are, I'll treat all of you alike." Davis managed to catch up to the troops and dispatch the following account of the landing.*

### DOCUMENT 2. Richard Harding Davis Reports on the Cuban Landing, June 1898

No one slept that night, for until two o'clock in the morning troops were still being disembarked in the surf, and two ships of war had their searchlights turned on the landingplace, and made Siboney as light as a ball-room. Back of the searchlights was an ocean white with moonlight, and on the shore red camp-fires, at which the half-drowned troops were drying their uniforms, and the Rough Riders, who had just marched in from Daiquiri, were cooking their coffee and bacon. . . .

It was one of the most weird and remarkable scenes of the war, probably of any war. An army was being landed on an enemy's coast at the dead of night, but with somewhat more of cheers and shrieks of laughter than rise from the bathers in the surf at Coney Island on a hot Sunday. . . . The men still to be landed from the "prison hulks," as they called the transports, were singing in chorus, the men already on shore were dancing naked around the camp-fires on the beach, or shouting with delight as they plunged into the first bath that had

Lawrence Goodwyn, *The Populist Moment: A Short History of the Agrarian Revolt in America* (1978). Explores the culture of politics in the Farmers Alliance and its move toward Populism.

Walter LaFeber, *The New Empire: An Interpretation of American Expansion, 1860–1898* (1963). Presents the background leading up to America's venture into colonialism in the Spanish-American War.

Albert A. Nofi, *The Spanish-American War: 1898* (1997). Detailed history of the war enlivened by sidebar stories and behind-the-scenes events.

Emily S. Rosenberg, *Spreading the American Dream: American Economic and Cultural Expansion, 1890–1945* (1982). Explores American imperialism from the standpoint of culture and economics.

Nick Salvatore, *Eugene V. Debs: Citizen and Socialist* (1982). A study of Debs as a home-grown radical, champion of labor, and perennial presidential candidate of the Socialist Party.

Carl Smith, *Urban Disorder and the Shape of Belief: The Great Chicago Fire, the Haymarket Bomb, and the Model Town of Pullman* (1995). Excellent treatment of Pullman and a provocative look at the events in Chicago at the turn of the twentieth century that helped make "urban" and "disorder" often synonymous.

Ian Tyrell, *Woman's World, Woman's Empire: The Woman's Christian Temperance Union in International Perspective, 1880–1930* (1991). The most recent history of the WCTU and its political impact.

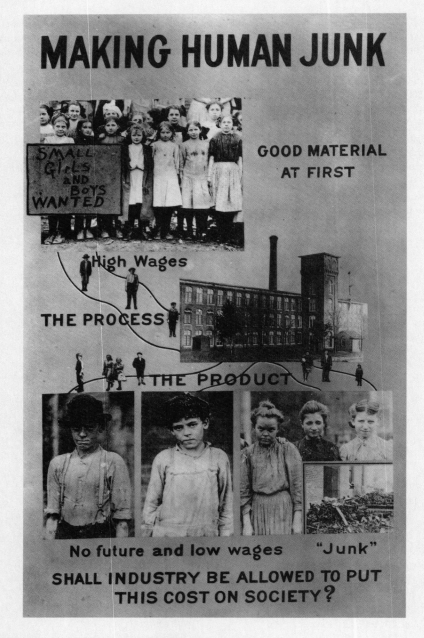

**PROGRESSIVE POSTER CONDEMNING CHILD LABOR**

*This poster attacks child labor, borrowing the convention of the business flow chart to portray graphically how industries employing children are "making human junk." Progressives' concern for the plight of poor children won them the label "the child savers." Although activists worked hard to enact federal legislation prohibiting child labor in 1916, the Supreme Court declared the law unconstitutional two years later on the grounds that Congress had no right to regulate manufacturing within states.*

Library of Congress.

# PROGRESSIVE REFORM FROM THE GRASS ROOTS TO THE WHITE HOUSE

## 1890–1916

I N THE SUMMER OF 1889, a young woman leased the upper floor of a dilapidated mansion on Chicago's West Side in the heart of a burgeoning immigrant population of Italians, Russian Jews, and Greeks. Watching the preparations at number 335, the neighbors scratched their heads, wondering why the well-dressed woman, who surely could afford a better house in a better neighborhood, chose to live on South Halsted Street. Yet the house built by Charles Hull precisely suited the needs of Jane Addams. In September, she and her college friend Ellen Gates Starr moved in. "Probably no young matron ever placed her own things in her own house with more pleasure," she wrote.

For Addams, personal action marked the first step in the search for solutions to the social problems fostered by urban industrialism. Her object was twofold: She wanted to help her immigrant neighbors and she wanted to offer an opportunity for educated women like herself to find meaningful work. As she later wrote in her autobiography, *Twenty Years at Hull-House* (1910), "I gradually became convinced that it would be a good thing to rent a house in a part of the city where many primitive and actual needs are found, in which young women who had been given over too exclusively to study might restore a balance of activity along traditional lines and learn of life from life itself." Addams's emphasis on the reciprocal relationship between the classes made Hull House different from other philanthropic enterprises. She wished to do things with, not just for, Chicago's poor.

By 1907, Hull House had expanded from one rented floor in the old brick mansion to some thirteen buildings that housed a remarkable variety of activities. The bathrooms in the basement had been converted into public baths; a coffee shop and restaurant sold take-out food to workingwomen too tired to cook after their long shifts; and a nursery and kindergarten provided care for neighborhood children. Hull House offered classes, lectures, art exhibits, musical instruction, and college extension courses. It boasted a gymnasium, a theater, a manual training workshop, a labor museum, and the first public playground in Chicago.

But Hull House was more than a group of buildings. From the first, it attracted an extraordinary set of inhabitants. Some stayed for decades, as did Julia Lathrop before she went to Washington, D.C., in 1912 to head the Children's Bureau. Others, like Gerard Swope, who later became president of the General Electric Company,

**JANE ADDAMS**
*Jane Addams was twenty-nine years old when she founded Hull House on Halsted Street in Chicago. Her desire to live among the poor and her insistence that settlement house work provide benefits for educated women like herself as well as for the poor neighborhood residents separated her from the charity workers who had come before her and marked the distance from philanthropy to progressive reform.*
University of Illinois at Chicago, the University Library,
Jane Addams Memorial Collection.

to city hall but to the state capitol and even further to Washington, D.C. A strong advocate of woman suffrage, she argued that city women needed the ballot, not the broom, to keep their neighborhoods clean.

Under Jane Addams's leadership, Hull House, the premier social settlement in the United States, became a "spearhead for reform," part of a broader movement that contemporaries called the progressive movement. The transition from personal action to political activism that Addams personified became one of the hallmarks of this reform period, which lasted for almost three decades, from the 1890s to World War I.

What motivated comfortable, middle-class women and men to launch one of the major movements for social and political reform in U.S. history? There is no one answer because there is no single progressive profile. The progressives were a diverse group with a variety of goals. A sense of Christian mission inspired some. Others, frightened by the political tensions of the 1890s, feared social upheaval unless conditions were improved. Progressives shared a growing concern about the power of wealthy individuals and corporations and a strong dislike of the trusts. But often they feared the new immigrants as well and sought to control and Americanize them. Along with moral fervor, a belief in expertise and scientific principles informed progressivism and made the cult of efficiency part and parcel of the movement. All of these elements—uplift and efficiency, social justice and social control—came together in the Progressive Era.

## Grassroots Progressivism

While reform flourished in many different settings across the country, the problems of urban America called forth the greatest efforts of the women and men who styled themselves progressives. In their zeal to "civilize the city," reformers founded settlement houses, professed a new Christian social gospel, and campaigned against vice and crime in the name of "social purity." Allying with the working class, they sought to better the lot of sweatshop garment workers and to end child labor. While their reform efforts often began on the local level, they just as often ended up being debated in state legislatures, in Congress, and in the Oval Office. From

came for only a short while. Most had jobs, paid room and board, and devoted time to research and reform. The people who lived at Hull House were among the first to investigate the problems of the city with scientific precision. Armed with statistics, they launched campaigns to improve housing, end child labor, fund playgrounds, mediate between labor and management, and lobby for protective legislation.

Addams quickly learned that it was impossible to deal with urban problems without becoming involved in political action. Her path led her not only

Hull House to the White House, progressivism became a major political force in the first decade of the twentieth century.

## Civilizing the City

Typically, progressives attacked the problems of the city on many fronts. The settlement house movement attempted to bridge the distance between the classes. The social gospel called for the churches to play a new role in social reformation. And the social purity movement campaigned to clean up vice, particularly prostitution.

The settlement house movement was imported from England in 1886 with the opening of the University Settlement House in New York City. Americans modified the settlement significantly, abandoning the strong religious overtones of the English movement. Settlement house workers quickly recognized that it would be divisive and counterproductive to promote Protestantism among their largely Catholic and Jewish neighbors. Another change from the English model was the substantial role of women, particularly college-educated women. Women formed the backbone of the settlement house movement and helped it to grow in the decades between 1891 and 1911 from six settlements to more than four hundred. Eager to use their knowledge, educated women found themselves blocked from medicine, law, and the clergy. Fewer than fifteen hundred women practiced law in 1900, and women constituted only 6 percent of the medical profession. College women like Jane Addams found settlements a way to use their talents in the service of society. In the process, they created the new profession of social work. Florence Kelley, Julia Lathrop, Alice Hamilton, and Grace and Edith Abbott are only a few of the best known of these influential settlement house residents.

For their part, the churches confronted the social problems raised in the cities by enunciating a new social gospel, one that saw its mission as not simply to reform individuals but to reform society. On the simplest level, the social gospel offered a powerful corrective to the gospel of wealth, with its belief that riches somehow signaled divine favor. Washington Gladden, a prominent social gospel minister, challenged that view when he urged Congregationalists to turn down a gift from John D. Rockefeller, arguing that it was "tainted money." In place of the gospel of wealth, the clergy urged their congregations to put Christ's teachings to work in their daily lives. In *Christianity and the Social Crisis* (1907),

Baptist minister William Rauschenbusch called for the church to play a new role in promoting social justice.

Ministers also played an active role in the social purity movement, the campaign to attack vice. The Reverend Charles Parkhurst shocked his New York congregation in the 1890s by donning a disguise and touring the city's brothels, asking at each dive, "Show me something worse." Progressives insisted that poverty bred prostitution and argued for higher wages. "Is it any wonder," asked the Chicago vice commission, "that a tempted girl who receives only six dollars per week working with her hands sells her body for twenty-five dollars per week when she learns there is a demand for it and men are willing to pay the price?"

---

*Women formed the backbone of the settlement house movement and helped it to grow in the decades between 1891 and 1911 from six settlements to more than four hundred. In the process, they created the new profession of social work.*

---

To end the "social evil," as reformers quite euphemistically called prostitution, the social purity movement brought together doctors who were concerned about the spread of venereal disease, ministers like Parkhurst who wished to stamp out sin, and women reformers who were determined to fight the double standard that made it acceptable for men to engage in premarital and extramarital sex but punished women who strayed. Together, they waged campaigns to close red-light districts in cities across the country and lobbied for the Mann Act, passed in 1910, which made it illegal to transport women across state lines for immoral purposes. Moreover, on the state level, they struck at venereal disease by securing legislation requiring a blood test for syphilis before marriage.

Attacks on alcohol went hand in hand with the push for social purity. The temperance campaign launched by the Woman's Christian Temperance Union (WCTU) heated up in the early twentieth century. The Anti-Saloon League, formed in 1895 under the leadership of Protestant clergy, campaigned for an end to the sale of liquor. Reformers pointed to the links connecting drink with prostitution, wife and child abuse, unemployment, and industrial accidents. The powerful liquor lobby

**WOMEN STRIKERS**

*The "uprising of twenty thousand" pitted garment workers against their employers in a strike*
*that lasted throughout the bitter winter of 1909–10. The strikers, primarily young women from*
*the Jewish and Italian immigrant communities, joined the International Ladies' Garment Workers*
*Union and showed that women could be unionized and mount an effective strike.*
Labor-Management Documentation Center, Cornell University.

fought back, spending liberally in elections to defeat not only prohibition but woman suffrage and, in the process, fueling the charge that liquor corrupted the political process.

An element of nativism (dislike of foreigners) ran through the move for prohibition. Progressives failed to see the important role the tavern played in many ethnic communities. They sought to enforce Sunday closings of taverns and other forms of social control to deny the working class access to alcohol. By 1912, seven states had outlawed the liquor traffic.

Progressives' efforts to civilize the city, whether by launching social settlements or campaigning against prostitution and alcohol, demonstrated their willingness to take action, their belief that environment, not heredity alone, determined human behavior, and their optimism that conditions could be corrected through government action without radically altering America's economy or institutions. All of these attitudes characterized the progressive movement.

## Progressives and the Working Class

Day-to-day contact with their neighbors made settlement house workers particularly sympathetic to labor unions. When Mary Kenney O'Sullivan told Jane Addams that her bookbinders' union met in a dirty, noisy saloon, Addams invited the union to meet at Hull House. And during the Pullman strike in 1894, Hull House residents organized strike relief and lent their prestige and financial resources. "Hull-House has been so unionized," grumbled one Chicago businessman, "that it has lost its usefulness and become a detriment and harm to the community." But to the working class, the support of middle-class reformers marked a significant gain.

Attempts to forge a cross-class alliance became institutionalized in 1903 with the creation of the Women's Trade Union League (WTUL). The WTUL brought together middle-class "allies" and women workers. Its goal was to organize workingwomen into unions under the auspices of the American Federation of Labor (AFL). However, the AFL provided little more than lip service to the organization of women workers. As one workingwoman confided, "The men think that the girls should not get as good work as the men and should not make half as much money as a man." When it came to women, the AFL's main concern seemed to be to protect men from female competition. Samuel Gompers, president of the AFL, endorsed the principle of equal pay for equal work, shrewdly observing that it would help male workers more than women, since many employers hired women precisely because they could be paid less. Given the AFL's attitude, it was not surprising that the money and leadership to organize women came largely from wealthy allies in the WTUL.

The league's most notable success came in 1909 in the "uprising of twenty thousand." In November hundreds of women employees of the Triangle Shirt-

**TRIANGLE SHIRTWAIST FACTORY FIRE**
*A grim newspaper photo shows the broken bodies of garment workers who jumped to their deaths when fire broke out in the Triangle Shirtwaist Factory on Saturday, March 25, 1911. Nearly five hundred women and girls worked in the firetrap and many were unable to escape because the doors had been locked to prevent employees from taking breaks. Firefighters rushed to the scene, but their ladders reached only to the sixth floor, leaving those on the seventh, eighth, and ninth floors with little choice but to jump.*
*The New York Herald,* March 26, 1911.

waist Company in New York City went on strike to protest low wages, dangerous and demeaning working conditions, and management's refusal to recognize their union, the International Ladies' Garment Workers Union (ILGWU). In support of the walkout, the ILGWU called for a general strike of all garment workers. An estimated twenty thousand workers, most of them teenage girls and many of them Jewish and Italian immigrants, went out on strike and stayed out through the winter, picketing in the bitter cold. More than six hundred were arrested, and many were sent to jail for "streetwalking," a move by the authorities to try to impugn the morals of the striking women. By the time the strike ended in February 1910, the workers had won some important demands in many shops. But they lost their bid to gain recognition for their union, the ILGWU. The solidarity shown by the women workers proved to be the strike's greatest achievement. As Clara Lemlich, one of the strike's leaders, exclaimed, "They used to say that you couldn't even organize women. They wouldn't come to union meetings. They were 'temporary' workers. Well we showed them!"

The WTUL made enormous contributions to the success of the strike. The league provided volunteers for the picket lines, posted more than $29,000 in bail, protested police brutality, organized almost overnight a massive parade of ten thousand strikers, took part in the arbitration conference, arranged mass meetings, appealed for funds, and generated publicity for the strike. Under the leadership of the WTUL, women from every class of society, from J. P. Morgan's daughter Anne to socialists on New York's Lower East Side, joined the strikers in a dramatic demonstration of cross-class alliance.

But for all its success, the uprising of the twenty thousand failed fundamentally to change conditions for women workers. In 1911, a little over a year after the shirtwaist makers' strike ended, fire alarms sounded at the Triangle factory. The ramshackle building, full of lint and combustible cloth, went up in flames in minutes. A WTUL member described the scene below on the street: "Two young girls whom I knew to be working in the vicinity came rushing toward me, tears were running from their eyes and they were white and shaking as they caught me by the arm. 'Oh,' shrieked one of them, 'they are jumping. Jumping from ten stories up! They are going through the air like bundles of clothes.'"

The terrified Triangle workers had little choice but to jump. One door was blocked by flames, and

the door to the fire escape had been locked to prevent the girls from sneaking out on breaks. Of 500 workers, 146 died and scores of others were injured. The owners of the Triangle firm were later tried for negligence, but they avoided conviction when authorities determined that the fire had been started by a careless smoker. The Triangle Shirtwaist Company reopened in another firetrap within a matter of weeks.

The Triangle fire tested severely the bonds of the cross-class alliance. Outrage and a sense of futility overwhelmed Rose Schneiderman, a leading WTUL organizer, who made a bitter speech at the memorial service for the dead Triangle workers. "I would be a traitor to those poor burned bodies if I came here to talk good fellowship," she told her audience. "We have tried you good people of the public and we have found you wanting. . . . I know from my experience it is up to the working people to save themselves . . . by a strong working class movement."

Increasingly, the WTUL turned its efforts to lobbying for protective legislation—laws that would limit hours and regulate working conditions. The principle of protective legislation won a major victory in 1908 when the U.S. Supreme Court, in *Muller v. Oregon,* reversed its previous rulings and upheld an Oregon law that limited the hours women could work to ten a day. A mass of sociological evidence put together by Florence Kelley of the National Consumers League and Josephine Goldmark of the WTUL and presented by Goldmark's brother-in-law, lawyer Louis Brandeis, demonstrated the ill effects of long hours on the health and safety of women. The "Brandeis brief" convinced the Court that long hours endangered women and therefore the entire race. The Court's ruling set a precedent, but one that separated the well-being of women workers from that of men by arguing that women's reproductive role justified special treatment. Later generations of women fighting for equality would question the effectiveness of this strategy and argue that it ultimately closed good jobs to women. But for the WTUL, protective legislation was greeted as a first stage in the attempt to ensure the safety not just of women but of all workers.

The National Consumers League, like the WTUL, fostered cross-class alliance. Formed in 1899 and led by Florence Kelley, the Consumers League urged middle-class women to boycott stores and exert pressure for decent wages and working conditions for women employees, primarily saleswomen. But like the WTUL, the Consumers League turned increasingly to protective legislation to achieve its goals in the first decade of the twentieth century. Frustrated by the reluctance of the private sector to respond to the need for reform, progressives turned to government at all levels. Critics would later charge that the progressives assumed too easily that government regulation could best solve social problems.

# Progressivism: Theory and Practice

Progressive reformers developed a theoretical basis for their activist approach by countering social Darwinism with a dynamic new reform Darwinism and by championing the uniquely American philosophy of pragmatism. The progressives emphasized action and experimentation. No longer was the universe seen as a massive, slow-moving machine, but as a system amenable to tinkering by human intelligence. An unchecked admiration for speed and efficiency also inspired enthusiasm for scientific management and a new cult of efficiency. These varied strands of progressive theory found practical application in state and local politics. Political progressivism originated at the local level and percolated upward to the state and national governments. The politicians who became premier progressives were generally the followers, not the leaders, in a movement that was already well advanced at the grassroots level.

## Reform Darwinism and Social Engineering

The active, interventionist approach of the progressives directly challenged social Darwinism, with its insistence that the world operated on the principle of survival of the fittest and that human beings were powerless in the face of the law of natural selection. Without abandoning the evolutionary framework of Darwinism, a new group of sociologists argued that evolution could be advanced more rapidly if men and women used their intellects to alter the environment. Dubbed "reform Darwinism," the new sociological theory condemned laissez-faire, insisting that the liberal state should play a more active role in solving social problems. Reform Darwinism pro-

vided a rationale for attacking social ills and became the ideological basis for progressive reform.

In their pursuit of reform, progressives were influenced by the work of two philosophers, William James and John Dewey, who argued for a new test for truth, insisting that there were no eternal verities and that the real worth of any idea was in its consequences. They called their pluralistic, relativistic philosophy "pragmatism." Dewey put his theories to the test in the classroom of his laboratory school at the University of Chicago. A pioneer in American education, he emphasized process rather than content and encouraged more child-centered schools where students learned by doing. By championing social experimentation, the American pragmatists provided an important impetus for progressive reform.

*Progressive reformers' emphasis on expertise inevitably fostered a kind of elitism. Whereas Populism had called for a greater voice for the masses, progressivism, for all its emphasis on social justice, insisted that experts be put in charge.*

Increased emphasis on means as well as ends marked progressive reform. Efficiency and expertise became watchwords in the progressive vocabulary. The journalist and critic Walter Lippmann, in *Drift and Mastery* (1914), a classic statement of the progressive agenda, called for skilled technocrats who would use scientific techniques to control social change, substituting mastery for aimless drift. Progressive reformers' emphasis on expertise inevitably fostered a kind of elitism. Whereas Populism had called for a greater voice for the masses, progressivism, for all its emphasis on social justice, insisted that experts be put in charge.

At its extreme, the application of expertise and social engineering took the form of scientific management, which alienated the working class while elevating productivity and efficiency above all. Frederick Winslow Taylor, who after a nervous breakdown left Harvard to become a machinist, pioneered "systematized shop management." Taylor was obsessed with making humans and machines produce more and faster. Earning a master of engineering degree in 1885, he went back to work at Midvale Steel in Pennsylvania. With his stopwatch he carefully timed workers and attempted to break their work down into its simplest components, one repetitious action after another, on the theory that productivity would increase if tasks were reduced to their simplest parts. When he died in 1915, stop-watch in hand, workers bitterly pointed to the speedup—pushing workers to produce more in less time and for less pay—as his legacy. But Taylor's many advocates included progressives like Louis Brandeis who applauded the increased productiv-ity and efficiency of Taylor's system.

The progressive reformers who championed scientific management and social engineering never faced the contradiction between the means they ad-vocated and the ends they desired. The central paradox of progressivism was its insistence that so-cial justice could be brought about by social engi-neering—that a just society could be achieved by applying scientific principles.

## Progressivism in Action: Cleveland and Wisconsin

Progressivism burst forth at every level in 1901, but nowhere more forcefully than in Cleveland, Ohio, where the voters elected Thomas Lofton Johnson mayor. Johnson, a self-made millionaire by the age of forty, turned his back on business and entered politics after reading Henry George's *Progress and Poverty* (1879). A Democrat and an advocate of free trade and Henry George's single tax, Johnson pledged during the campaign to reduce the street-car fare from five cents to three cents. His election touched off a seven-year war between advocates of the lower fare, who believed that workers paid a disproportionate share of their meager earnings for transportation, and the streetcar moguls, who ar-gued that they couldn't meet costs with the lower fare. When Johnson responded by building his own streetcar line, his foes tore up the tracks or blocked him with court injunctions and legal delays. At the prompting of his opponents, the Ohio legislature sought to limit Johnson's mayoral power by revok-ing the charters of every city in the state, replacing home rule with central control from the capital, Columbus.

During his tenure as mayor, Johnson fought for home rule and fair taxation even as he called for greater democracy through the use of the initiative, referendum, and recall—devices that allowed the voters to have a direct say in legislative and judi-

**THREE-CENT STREETCAR TOKEN**
*Tom Johnson, the reform mayor of Cleveland, Ohio, from 1901 to 1909, fought for a three-cent streetcar fare for more than seven years, winning the support of the work-ing class at the same time he angered the business inter-ests who ran the city's streetcars. To get his cheaper fare, Johnson finally instituted municipal ownership of the transit system. Johnson used a three-cent token in his re-election campaign in 1907.*
The Western Reserve Historical Society, Cleveland, Ohio.

cial matters. Frustrated in his attempt to bring the streetcar industry to heel, he successfully champi-oned municipal ownership of street railways and public utilities, a tactic that progressives called "gas and water socialism." The city bought the streetcar system and instituted the three-cent fare. Under Johnson's administration, Cleveland became, in the words of journalist Lincoln Steffens, the "best gov-erned city in America."

In Wisconsin, Robert M. La Follette, who as a young congressional representative had supported William McKinley, abandoned Republican conser-vatism and converted to the progressive cause early in the 1900s. An astute politician, La Follette capital-ized on the grassroots movement for reform to launch his long political career, first as governor (1901–1905) and later as senator (1906–1925). A grad-uate of the University of Wisconsin, La Follette brought scientists and professors into his administration and used the university, only a few blocks from the state house in Madison, as a resource in drafting legislation. As governor, he lowered railroad rates, raised railroad taxes, improved education, championed conservation, established factory regulation and workers' compensation, instituted the first direct primary in the country, and inaugurated the first state income tax. Under his leadership, Wisconsin earned the title "laboratory of democracy."

A fiery orator, "Fighting Bob" La Follette united his supporters around issues that transcended old party loyalties. This emphasis on reform rather than party loyalty became a characteristic of progressivism, which attracted followers from both major parties. Democrats like Tom Johnson and Republicans like Robert La Follette could lay equal claim to the label "progressive."

# Progressivism Finds a President: Theodore Roosevelt

On September 6, 1901, President William McKinley was shot and gravely wounded while attending the Pan American Exposition in Buffalo, New York. After lingering for a week, he died on September 14. When news of McKinley's assassination reached his friend and political mentor Marcus Alonzo Hanna, Hanna is said to have growled, "Now that damned cowboy is president." Hanna was speaking of Vice President Theodore Roosevelt, the colorful hero of San Juan Hill, who had indeed punched cattle in the Dakotas in the 1880s.

Roosevelt's status as a Spanish-American War hero had propelled him to the governorship of New York in 1898. A moderate reformer, he clashed with party bosses, who were happy to "kick him upstairs" to the vice presidency in 1900, where he added luster to the ticket and helped reelect McKinley to a second term. As vice president, party leaders reasoned, Roosevelt could do little harm. But one bullet proved the error of their logic. Overnight, Roosevelt was president, and Mark Hanna was not alone in his concern that the conservative politics of McKinley had died with him. An activist and a moralist, imbued with progressive spirit, Roosevelt would turn the White House into a "bully pulpit" and, in the process, shift the nation's center of power from Wall Street to Washington.

## The Square Deal

At the age of forty-two, Roosevelt was the youngest man ever to move into the White House. A patrician by birth and an activist by temperament, Roosevelt brought to the job enormous talent and energy. By the time he graduated from Harvard, he was already an accomplished naturalist, an enthusiastic historian, and a naval strategist. He could have picked from any of these promising careers. Instead, he chose politics, where his rise was nothing less than meteoric. He went from the New York state assembly at the age of twenty-three to the presidency in twenty years, with time out to be a cowboy in the Dakotas, police commissioner of New York City, and colonel of the Rough Riders.

The "absolutely vital question" facing the country, Roosevelt wrote to a friend in 1901, was "whether or not the government has the power to control the trusts." The Sherman Antitrust Act of 1890 had been badly weakened by a conservative Supreme Court and by attorneys general more willing to use it against unions than against monopolies. To determine if the law had any teeth left, Roosevelt, in one of his first acts as president, ordered his attorney general to begin a secret antitrust investigation of the Northern Securities Company.

*An activist and a moralist, imbued with progressive spirit, Roosevelt would turn the White House into a "bully pulpit" and, in the process, shift the nation's center of power from Wall Street to Washington.*

Roosevelt trained his sights on a good target. Northern Securities resulted from one of the most controversial mergers in American history. When Edward C. Harriman, who controlled the Union Pacific and the Southern Pacific Railroads, attempted to add the Northern Pacific to his holdings, James J. Hill of the Great Northern squared off against him. The result was a ruinous railroad war that precipitated a panic on Wall Street, bankrupting thousands of small investors. To bring peace, financier J. P. Morgan created the Northern Securities Company in 1901, combining under one management three competing railroads. This new giant monopolized railroad traffic in the Northwest. Small investors still smarting from their losses, farmers worried about freight rates, and the public in general saw in Northern Securities the symbol of corporate high-handedness.

In February 1902, Wall Street rocked with the news that the government had filed suit against Northern Securities. Roosevelt's thunderbolt put Wall Street on notice that the money men were dealing with a president who demanded to be treated as an equal and who was willing to use government as an instrument to control business. Perhaps sensing the new mood, the Supreme Court, in a significant turnaround, upheld the Sherman Act and called for the dissolution of Northern Securities in 1904.

"Hurrah for Teddy the Trustbuster," cheered the papers. Roosevelt went on to use the Sherman Act against forty-three trusts, including such giants as the American Tobacco Company, Du Pont, and Standard Oil. Always the moralist, he insisted on a "rule of reason." He would punish the "bad" trusts (those that broke the law) and leave the "good" ones alone. In practice, he preferred regulation to antitrust suits. In 1903, he pressured Congress to pass the Elkins Act, a law outlawing railroad rebates (money returned to a shipper to guarantee his business). And he created the new cabinet department of Commerce and Labor with a subsidiary Bureau of Corporations to act as a corporate watchdog.

In his handling of the anthracite coal strike in 1902 Roosevelt again demonstrated his willingness to assert the moral and political authority of the presidency, this time to mediate between labor and management. In May, more than fifty thousand coal miners in Pennsylvania went out on strike, demanding higher wages, shorter hours, and recognition of the United Mine Workers (UMW) union. "The miners don't suffer," scoffed George Baer, the operator's spokesman, "why they can't even speak English." Six eastern railroads owned over 70 percent of the anthracite mines. With the power of the railroads behind them, the mine owners refused to budge.

The strike dragged on through the summer and into the fall. Hoarding and profiteering drove the price of coal up from $2.50 to $6 a ton. Most homes were heated with coal, and, with winter approaching, near riots broke out in big cities. In the face of mounting tension, Roosevelt issued a personal invitation to representatives from both sides to meet in Washington in October. At the meeting, Baer and the mine owners refused to talk to the union representatives, insulting both the president and the attorney general. Angered by the "wooden-headed obstinacy and stupidity" of management, Roosevelt threatened to seize the mines and run them with federal troops. It was a powerful bluff that called into question not only the supremacy of private property but the rule of law. The specter of federal troops being used to operate the mines quickly brought management around. At the prompting of J. P. Morgan, the mine owners agreed to arbitration. In the end, the miners won a reduction in hours and a wage increase, but the owners succeeded in preventing formal recognition of the UMW.

Taken together, Roosevelt's actions in the Northern Securities case and the anthracite coal strike marked a dramatic departure from the tradition of William McKinley. Roosevelt demonstrated conclusively that government intended to act as a force independent of big business. Pleased with his role in the anthracite strike, Roosevelt announced that all he had tried to do was give labor and capital a "square deal."

The phrase became his slogan in the 1904 election campaign. To win the presidency in his own right, Roosevelt had to wrest control of the Republican Party from Mark Hanna, the only man who stood between him and the nomination. By the time Hanna died of typhoid fever in 1904, Roosevelt was the undisputed leader of the party.

In the presidential election of 1904, the Democrats abandoned William Jennings Bryan, their candidate in the previous two elections, to support Judge Alton B. Parker, a "safe" candidate who they hoped would win business votes away from Roosevelt. In the months before the election, the president prudently toned down his criticism of big business. Wealthy Republicans like J. P. Morgan, while privately branding Roosevelt a class traitor, remained loyal to the party and gave it their money and their votes. In November 1904, Roosevelt swept into office with the largest popular majority, 57.9 percent, any candidate had polled to that time.

## Roosevelt the Reformer

Roosevelt needed all the popularity and political savvy he could muster to guide his reform measures through Congress, which was controlled by a staunchly conservative Republican "old guard" in

**THEODORE ROOSEVELT**
*At forty-two, Theodore Roosevelt was the youngest president to occupy the White House. He brought to the office energy, intellect, and activism in equal measure, moving the presidency into the twentieth century. Described aptly as a "steam engine in trousers," Roosevelt enjoyed the presidency and worked tirelessly to make the office a "bully pulpit" from which he advocated an astounding series of reforms, from conservation to simplified spelling.*
Collection of the New-York Historical Society.

the Senate. Roosevelt's pet project remained railroad regulation. The Elkins Act prohibiting rebates had not worked. No one could stop big shippers from wringing concessions from the railroads. The Interstate Commerce Commission (ICC), created in 1887 to regulate the railroads, had been stripped of its powers by the Supreme Court. In the face of a widespread call for railroad reform, Roosevelt determined that the only solution lay in giving the ICC real power to set rates and prevent discriminatory practices. But business remained adamant in its opposition to federal rate setting. The right to determine the price of goods or services was an age-old prerogative of private enterprise and one that business had no intention of yielding to government.

To ensure passage of the Hepburn Railway Act, a bill increasing the power of the ICC, Roosevelt worked skillfully behind the scenes. Once again, he showed his power to bluff. By threatening to call for

tariff reform, a volatile issue that might split the party, he succeeded in getting a recalcitrant House of Representatives to pass the Hepburn Act. But the bill bogged down in the Senate, where Nelson Aldrich of Rhode Island, aptly dubbed "the senator from Standard Oil," attempted to amend it to death. To get the best bill possible, Roosevelt first worked with insurgent progressives and then, when they could not muster the needed votes, switched sides and succeeded in getting Aldrich and the Republican regulars to accept a compromise. In its final form, the Hepburn Act, passed in May 1906, gave the ICC power to set rates subject to court review. Committed progressives like La Follette judged the bill a defeat for reform. Die-hard conservatives branded it a "piece of populism." Both sides exaggerated. The bill left the courts too much power, and it failed to provide adequate means for the ICC to determine rates realistically, but its passage marked a landmark in the evolution of federal control of private industry. For the first time, a government commission had the power to investigate private business records and to set rates.

Passage of the Hepburn Act marked the high point of Roosevelt's presidency. In a serious political blunder, Roosevelt had announced on the eve of his election in 1904 that he would not run again. By 1906, his term was starting to run out, and his influence on Congress and his party was waning. Ironically, he had become a "lame duck" at the very moment when he was enjoying his greatest public popularity and when he wanted to press for more reform.

Always an apt reader of the public temper, Roosevelt witnessed a growing appetite for reform fed by the revelations of corporate and political wrongdoing that filled the papers and boosted the sales of popular periodicals. In October 1902, Lincoln Steffens's "Tweed Days in St. Louis" appeared in *McClure's Magazine,* the first part of a series entitled "The Shame of the Cities" (later published as a book). The next month, Ida Tarbell, a schoolteacher turned journalist, began her sharply critical series on Standard Oil in *McClure's.* Soon other journalists such as Ray Stannard Baker and Robert Hunter tried their hand at the new brand of investigative reporting. Their hard-hitting exposés swelled magazine circulation and touched off a public clamor for reform.

Roosevelt, who wielded publicity like a weapon in reform, counted many of these new journalists, notably Jacob Riis and Lincoln Steffens, as friends. But when David Graham Phillips attacked the Republican old guard in 1906 in a series of articles entitled "The Treason of the Senate," the character assassination of his fellow Republicans offended the president. Roosevelt warned journalists that they should not be like the allegorical character in *Pilgrim's Progress* who was so busy raking up muck that he took no notice of higher things. Roosevelt's criticism gave the American vocabulary a new word: *muckraker.* Journalists soon appropriated the term and turned it into a badge of honor.

Muckraking, as Roosevelt was keenly aware, had been of enormous help in securing progressive legislation. The passage of the Pure Food and Drug Act and the Meat Inspection Act were powerful examples. In 1905, the president had belatedly thrown his support behind legislation to outlaw misbranded and adulterated foods, drinks, and drugs. For years, Dr. Harvey Washington Wiley, chief

chemist in the Department of Agriculture, had agitated for a federal law requiring accurate labeling of foods and drugs. Mark Sullivan's exposés of patent medicines in the *Ladies' Home Journal* and Samuel Hopkins Adams's "Great American Fraud" series in *Collier's* kept the issue before the public. "Gullible America," Adams announced in 1905, "will swallow huge quantities of alcohol, an appalling amount of opiates and narcotics, a wide assortment of varied drugs . . . and far in excess of all other ingredients, undiluted fraud."

In the spring of 1906, the publicity generated by the muckrakers goaded Congress into action. With Roosevelt's backing, a pure food and drug bill passed the Senate and went to the House, where its opponents hoped to keep it locked up in committee. There it would have died, were it not for publication of Upton Sinclair's novel *The Jungle,* with its sensational account of the filthy conditions in the meatpacking industry. A massive public out-

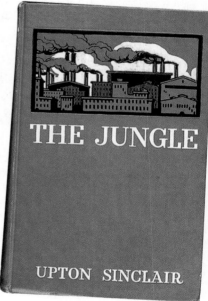

**THE JUNGLE**
*Novelist Upton Sinclair, a lifelong socialist, wrote* The Jungle *to expose the evils of capitalism. But readers were more horrified by the unsanitary conditions he described in the meatpacking industry, where Sinclair's hapless hero encountered rats, filth, and diseased animals processed into potted beef. It was rumored that after reading the book, President Theodore Roosevelt could no longer stomach sausage for breakfast. The president immediately ordered a thorough study of conditions in the meatpacking industry. The public outcry surrounding* The Jungle *contributed to the enactment of pure food and drug legislation and federal meat inspection. Sinclair ruefully remarked, "I aimed at the public's heart, but I hit them in the stomach."*
By permission of the Houghton Library, Harvard University.

**ROOSEVELT AND MUIR**
*In this famous photograph, Theodore Roosevelt poses at Glacier Peak in Yosemite National Park in 1903 with John Muir, naturalist and founder of the Sierra Club. Roosevelt's years as a rancher in the Dakotas made him the first president to have experienced firsthand the American West. As president, he acted vigorously to protect the beauty and resources of the West for posterity, using executive power to set aside more than a hundred million acres in government reserves and to create six national parks.*
Yosemite Museum/Leroy Radanovich.

cry led to the passage of a tough Pure Food and Drug Act and a bill mandating federal inspection of meat.

In the waning years of his administration, Roosevelt moved to the left, allying with the more progressive elements of the Republican Party. In speech after speech he attacked the "malefactors of great wealth." Styling himself a "radical," he claimed credit for leading the "ultra conservative" party of McKinley to a position of "progressive conservatism and conservative radicalism." His rhetoric led John D. Rockefeller to predict early in 1907 that Roosevelt's attacks on big business would precipitate a depression.

When a business panic developed in the fall of 1907, business interests quickly blamed the president. The panic of 1907 proved to be severe but short. Once again J. P. Morgan stepped in to avert disaster, switching funds from one bank to another to prop up weak institutions and keep them from

failing. For his services, he claimed the Tennessee Coal and Iron Company, an independent steel business that had long been coveted by his U.S. Steel. Morgan dispatched his lieutenants to Washington, where they told Roosevelt that the sale of the company would aid the economy "but little benefit" U.S. Steel. Roosevelt, willing to take the word of a gentleman, tacitly agreed not to institute antitrust proceedings against U.S. Steel. As Roosevelt later learned, Morgan and his men had been less than candid. The acquisition of Tennessee Coal and Iron for a price under market value greatly strengthened U.S. Steel and undercut the economy of the Southeast. The episode would come back to haunt Roosevelt, as it gave rise to the charge that he acted as a tool of the Morgan interests.

The charge of collusion between business and government underscored the extent to which business leaders like Morgan and his partner George W. Perkins found federal regulation preferable to unbridled competition or harsher state measures. During the Progressive Era, enlightened business leaders cooperated with government in the hope of avoiding antitrust prosecution. Roosevelt, convinced that regulation and not trust-busting was the best way to deal with big business, never acknowledged that for all his strong rhetoric, his regulatory policies fostered an alliance between business and government. As Roosevelt's actions in the panic of 1907 demonstrated, despite his harsh attacks on the "malefactors of great wealth," the president remained indebted to Morgan, who still functioned as the national bank and would continue to do so until the passage of the Federal Reserve Act six years later.

In at least one area, Roosevelt was well ahead of his time. Robert La Follette, who found much to criticize in Roosevelt's presidency, called his efforts in conservation of natural resources the progressive president's "greatest work." When Roosevelt took office, some 45 million acres of land remained as government reserves. He more than tripled that number to 150 million acres, buying land and creating national parks and wildlife preserves by executive order. To conserve natural resources, he fought not only western cattle barons, lumber kings, and mining interests but powerful leaders in Congress, including Speaker of the House Joseph Cannon, who was determined to spend "not one cent for scenery."

> *During the Progressive Era, enlightened business leaders cooperated with government in the hope of avoiding antitrust prosecution. Roosevelt, convinced that regulation and not trust-busting was the best way to deal with big business, never acknowledged that his regulatory policies fostered an alliance between business and government.*

Roosevelt had no sooner entered the White House than he launched his conservation campaign, naming the able Gifford Pinchot his chief forester. In one of their most effective ploys, they fought private utilities that were intent on gobbling up water-power sites and creating a monopoly of hydroelectric power. Pinchot protected 2,565 sites, often on the pretext that he planned to establish ranger sta-

tions on the lands. "Public rights come first and private interest second," Roosevelt insisted.

By 1907, Roosevelt had stepped on the toes of every major interest in the West. To curb the president, Congress added a rider to an appropriations bill that barred the creation of any new reserves in six western states. Roosevelt could not veto the bill, but he worked feverishly in the ten days before it became law to establish twenty-one new reserves and save 16 million acres for posterity. Today, six national parks, sixteen national monuments, and fifty-one wildlife refuges stand as witness to Roosevelt's substantial accomplishments as a conservationist.

## Roosevelt the Diplomat

Just as in domestic affairs, Roosevelt relied on executive power to effect a vigorous foreign policy, sometimes stretching his powers beyond legal limits in his pursuit of American interests. A man who relished military discipline and viewed life as a constant conflict for supremacy, Roosevelt believed that the "civilized nations" should police the world and hold the "backward" countries in line. In his relations with the great European powers, he relied on military strength and diplomacy, a combination he aptly described with the aphorism "Speak softly but carry a big stick."

In the Caribbean, Roosevelt jealously guarded the Monroe Doctrine's American sphere of influence. In 1902, he risked war to keep Germany from intervening in Venezuela when the country's dictator (whom Roosevelt dismissed as "a villainous little monkey") borrowed money in Europe and could not pay it back. Roosevelt issued an ultimatum to the kaiser, warning him to stay out of Latin American affairs or face war with the United States. The matter was eventually settled by arbitration.

Roosevelt's proprietary attitude toward the hemisphere became evident in the infamous case of the Panama Canal. A firm advocate of naval power and an astute naval strategist, Roosevelt had long been a supporter of a canal connecting the Caribbean and the Pacific. By enabling the navy to move quickly from the Atlantic to the Pacific, the canal would, in effect, double the nation's naval power. The United States began a joint venture with England to build a canal but in 1901 abandoned the partnership and moved forward alone. Two sites were possible, one in Nicaragua, which had the advantage of being at sea level, the other in Panama, where the rough and hilly terrain required a system of locks. In the end, the choice was made not by logic but by politics. Private investors who held rights to build in Panama lobbied Congress shamelessly until they won approval for the route.

The Panamanian isthmus (the narrow strip of land connecting North and South America) was at this time part of Colombia, so in 1902 Roosevelt began negotiations to gain access to the land. He offered the Colombian government $10 million and an annual rent of $250,000. When the government in Bogotá refused to accept the offer, Roosevelt became incensed at what he called the "homicidal corruptionists" in Colombia for trying to "blackmail" the United States. The result was an uprising in Panama in 1903 arranged by New York investors. The U.S. government aided and protected the "revolution" by placing the warship *Nashville* off the isthmus, and the State Department recognized the new government of Panama within twenty-four hours. The new Panamanian government promptly accepted the $10 million, and the building of the canal got under way (Map 21.1). Roosevelt later boasted that he "took Panama"; although most Americans applauded his action, the episode be-

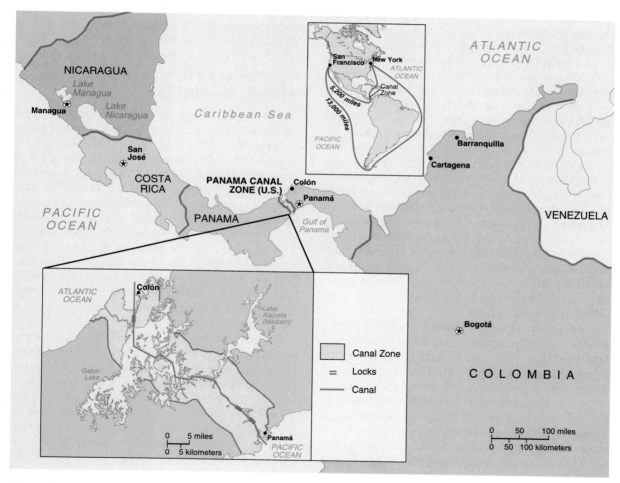

**M A P  21.1**
*The Panama Canal, 1914*
*The Panama Canal, completed in 1914, bisected the isthmus in a series of massive locks and dams. As Theodore Roosevelt had planned, the canal greatly strengthened the navy by allowing ships to move from the Atlantic to the Pacific in a matter of days.*

came a national disgrace. President Woodrow Wilson would later insist on paying the Colombian government $25 million.

In the wake of the Panama affair and the confrontation with Germany over Venezuela, Roosevelt announced what became known as the Roosevelt Corollary to the Monroe Doctrine. The United States would not intervene in Latin America as long as nations conducted their affairs with "decency." But Roosevelt warned that if any Latin American nation proved guilty of "brutal wrongdoing," as in the case of Venezuela's default on its debt to Germany, the United States would insist on stepping in. The Roosevelt Corollary in effect made the United States the policeman of the hemisphere and served notice to the European powers to keep out. Critics called Roosevelt's policy "gunboat diplomacy," and with good reason. In the administrations of Roosevelt and his successor, William Howard Taft, U.S. marines were frequently dispatched to the Caribbean to take over customhouses or otherwise show U.S. force. The legacy of gunboat diplomacy was a bitter anti-American sentiment that would last throughout the century.

In his relations with Europe, Roosevelt sought to establish the United States, fresh from its victory over Spain, as a rising force in world affairs. When tensions flared between France and Germany in Morocco in 1905, Roosevelt set up a conference in Algeciras, Spain, where he worked to maintain a balance of power to help neutralize German ambitions. His skillful mediation of the dispute gained him a reputation as an astute player on the world stage and demonstrated the United States' new presence in world affairs.

Roosevelt earned the Nobel Peace Prize in 1906 for his role in negotiating an end to the Russo-Japanese War, which had broken out when the Japanese invaded Chinese Manchuria, threatening Russia's sphere of influence in the area. Once again, Roosevelt sought to maintain a balance of power, in this case working to curb Japanese expansionism. Roosevelt admired the Japanese, judging them "the most dashing fighters in the world," but he did not want Japan to become too strong in Asia. He offered to mediate and presided over the peace conference at Portsmouth, New Hampshire. At the peace conference, he was able to prevent Japan from dominating Manchuria, but he had no qualms about granting the Japanese control of Korea, a sovereign country.

Roosevelt fumed when the United States' good relations with Japan were jeopardized in 1906 by discriminatory legislation in California calling for segregated public schools for "Orientals." Roosevelt smoothed over the incident by negotiating a "gentlemen's agreement" in 1907 whereby he would reverse the segregation order in exchange for voluntary restrictions on Japanese immigration to the United States. This informal arrangement allowed the Japanese to save face, while at the same time placating nativist sentiment in California. To counter Japan's growing bellicosity, Roosevelt immediately dispatched the Great White Fleet, the navy's most up-to-date battleships, on a "goodwill" mission around the world. This show of American force constituted a classic example of his dictum "Speak softly but carry a big stick."

## The Troubled Presidency of William Howard Taft

When Roosevelt retired from the presidency in 1909 at the age of fifty to go on safari and shoot big game in Africa, he turned the White House over to his handpicked successor, William Howard Taft. In the presidential election of 1908, Taft soundly defeated the perennial Democratic candidate, the "Great Commoner," William Jennings Bryan, but his popular majority was only half of Roosevelt's record in 1904. On the eve of his inauguration, Taft showed little enthusiasm about his triumph and little zest for the future. In fact, the presidency for Taft proved an ordeal to be endured. As a symptom of his discomfort in office, his weight ballooned from an already hefty 297 pounds to over 350 pounds.

A genial man with a talent for law, Taft had no experience in elective office and no feel for politics. He proved a perfect tool in the hands of Republicans who yearned for a return to the days of McKinley. Taft's greatest strength proved to be his greatest weakness. A lawyer by training and instinct, he believed that it was up to the courts, not the president, to arbitrate social issues. Roosevelt had carried presidential power to a new level, often castigating the judiciary and flouting the separation of powers. Taft the legalist found it difficult to condone such actions. Wary of the progressive insurgents in his own party and without Roosevelt to guide him, Taft relied increasingly on conservatives in the Republican Party. As a progressive senator

**WILLIAM HOWARD TAFT**

*William Howard Taft had little aptitude for politics. When Theodore Roosevelt tapped him as his successor in 1908, Taft had never held an elected office. A legalist by training and temperament, Taft moved congenially in the conservative circles of the Republican Party. His actions dismayed progressives and eventually led Roosevelt to challenge him for the presidency in 1912. The break with Roosevelt saddened and embittered Taft, who heartily disliked the presidency and was glad to leave it.*
Library of Congress.

lamented, "Taft is a ponderous and amiable man completely surrounded by men who know exactly what they want."

Taft's troubles began on the eve of his inaugural when he called a special session of Congress to deal with the tariff. Roosevelt had been too politically astute to tackle the troublesome tariff issue, even though he knew that rates needed to be lowered. Taft, with his stubborn courage, blundered into the fray. The House of Representatives passed a modest downward revision and, to make up for lost rev-

enue, imposed a small inheritance tax. Led by Senator Aldrich, the conservative Senate struck down the tax and added more than eight hundred crippling amendments to the tariff. The Payne-Aldrich bill that emerged actually raised the tariff. Taft, as if paralyzed, neither fought for changes nor vetoed the measure. On a tour of the Midwest in 1909, he was greeted with jeers when he claimed, "I think the Payne bill is the best bill that the Republican party ever passed." In the eyes of a growing number of critics, his praise of the tariff made him either a fool or a liar.

Taft's legalism got him into hot water in the controversy over conservation. He refused to endorse his predecessor's methods of bending the law to protect the wilderness. He undid Roosevelt's work to preserve water-power sites when he learned that they had been improperly designated as ranger stations. And when Gifford Pinchot publicly denounced Taft's secretary of the interior, Richard Ballinger, as a tool of western land-grabbers, Taft fired Pinchot, touching off a storm of controversy that damaged Taft and alienated Roosevelt.

Talk of substituting Roosevelt on the ticket in 1912 grew as Republican progressives became increasingly dissatisfied with Taft's policies. In June 1910, Roosevelt returned to New York, where he received a hero's welcome and attracted a stream of visitors and reporters seeking his advice and opinions. Hurt, Taft kept his distance. By late summer, Roosevelt had taken sides with the progressive insurgents in his party. "Taft is utterly hopeless as a leader," Roosevelt confided to his son as he set out on a speaking tour of the West. Reading the mood of the country, Roosevelt began to sound more and more like a candidate.

With the Republican Party divided, the Democrats swept the congressional elections of 1910. Branding the Payne-Aldrich tariff "the mother of trusts," they captured a majority in the House of Representatives and won several key governorships. The revitalized Democratic Party could look to new leaders, among them the progressive governor of New Jersey, Woodrow Wilson.

With a Democratic majority in the House and progressive Republicans holding the balance of power in the Senate, Congress enacted a number of key reforms, including legislation to regulate mine and railroad safety, to create a Children's Bureau in the Department of Labor, and to establish an eight-hour day for federal workers. Two significant constitutional amendments—the Sixteenth Amendment, which provided for a modest graduated income tax, and the Seventeenth Amendment, which called for the direct election of senators (who had formerly been chosen by their state legislatures)—went to the states, where they would later win ratification in 1913. While Congress rode the high tide of progressive reform, Taft indeed sat on the sidelines.

In foreign policy as well as in the domestic arena, Taft had a difficult time following in Roosevelt's footsteps. In the Caribbean he pursued a policy of "dollar diplomacy," championing commercial goals rather than the strategic aims that Roosevelt had advocated. He provoked anti-American feeling by attempting to force commercial treaties on Nicaragua and Honduras and by dispatching the U.S. marines to Nicaragua and Santo Domingo in 1912.

In Asia, Taft's foreign policy proved equally inept. He openly avowed his intent to promote in China "active intervention to secure for . . . our capitalists opportunity for profitable investment." Lacking Roosevelt's understanding of power politics, Taft naively believed that he could substitute "dollars for bullets." He never recognized that an aggressive commercial policy could not exist without military might. As a result, dollar diplomacy was doomed to failure. Even Taft was forced to recognize its limits when revolution broke out in Mexico in 1911. Under pressure to protect American investment, which amounted to more than $4 billion, he mobilized troops along the border. But in the end, he relied on diplomatic pressure to salvage American interests.

Always a legalist at heart, Taft hoped to encourage world peace through the use of a world court and arbitration. He unsuccessfully sponsored a series of arbitration treaties that Roosevelt, who prized national honor more than international law, vehemently opposed. By 1910, Roosevelt had become a vocal critic of Taft's foreign policy, which he dismissed as "maudlin folly."

The final breech between Taft and Roosevelt came in 1911, when Taft's attorney general filed an antitrust suit against U.S. Steel. In its brief against the steel giant, the government cited Roosevelt's agreement with the Morgan interests in the 1907 acquisition of Tennessee Coal and Iron by U.S. Steel. The incident greatly embarrassed Roosevelt by making it clear he either had been hoodwinked or had acted as a tool of Wall Street. Thoroughly enraged, Roosevelt lambasted Taft's "archaic" antitrust policy and began to hint that he might be persuaded to run for president again.

## The Election of 1912

In February 1912, Roosevelt announced, "My hat is in the ring." But for all his popularity, Roosevelt no longer controlled the party machinery. Taft, with uncharacteristic strength, refused to step aside. As he bitterly told a journalist, "Even a rat in a corner

**PASS PROSPERITY AROUND**

**BULL MOOSE POSTER**
*Accepting the nomination of the Progressive Party in 1912, Theodore Roosevelt exclaimed, "I feel as strong as a bull moose." Instantly the new party had a mascot and a nickname. The Bull Moose soon decorated party emblems, as in this poster where the animal is featured more prominently than Roosevelt or his vice presidential candidate, Hiram Johnson. The slogan "Pass Prosperity Around" may refer to the party's platform, which pledged to tax the great fortunes of the day by enacting the country's first graduated income tax.*
Collection of Janice L. and David J. Frent.

will fight." Roosevelt took advantage of newly passed primary election laws and ran in thirteen states, winning 278 delegates to Taft's 48. But at the Chicago convention, Taft's bosses refused to seat the Roosevelt delegates. Fistfights broke out on the convention floor as Taft won renomination on the first ballot. Crying robbery, Roosevelt's supporters bolted the party.

Seven weeks later, in the same Chicago auditorium, a hastily organized Progressive Party met to nominate Roosevelt. Few Republican officeholders joined the new party, but the advance guard of progressivism turned out in full force. Amid a thunder of applause, Jane Addams seconded Roosevelt's nomination. Full of reforming zeal, the delegates approved the most advanced platform since the Populists' in 1892. Planks called for woman suffrage, the direct election of senators, presidential primaries, conservation of natural resources, minimum wages for women, an end to child labor, workers' compensation, social security, and a federal income tax.

Roosevelt arrived in Chicago to accept the nomination and announced that he felt "as strong as a bull moose," giving the new party a nickname and a mascot. But for all the excitement and the cheering, the new Progressive Party was doomed, and the candidate knew it. The people may have supported the party, but the politicians, even insurgents like La Follette, stayed within the Republican fold. "I am under no illusion about it," Roosevelt confessed to a friend. "It is a forlorn hope." But he had gone too far to turn back. He led the Bull Moose Party into the fray, exhorting his followers in ringing biblical tones, "We shall not falter, we stand at Armageddon and do battle for the Lord."

The Democrats, delighted at the split in the Republican ranks, smelled victory for the first time since 1892. Their convention turned into a bitter fight for the nomination. After forty-six ballots, William Jennings Bryan threw his support to Woodrow Wilson, who became the party's nominee. Wilson's career in politics was nothing short of astounding. After only eighteen months in office as governor of New Jersey, the former professor and president of Princeton University found himself running for President of the United States.

Wilson ran on a platform designed to appeal to the diverse constituents of the Democratic Party. To the farmers, the platform promised a lower tariff and cheaper agricultural loans; to labor unions, it promised to limit the use of injunctions and anti-

trust laws against labor; and to small business owners, it vowed to return to competition through the breakup of the trusts. As if that were not enough, Wilson's vice presidential candidate, Thomas R. Marshall, went on record avowing, "What America needs is a good five-cent cigar."

Voters in 1912 could choose from three candidates, each of whom claimed to be a progressive. That the term could stretch to cover all three underscored some major disagreements in progressive thinking about the relation between business and government. Taft, for all his trust-busting, was generally conceded to be the candidate of the old guard. The real contest was between Roosevelt and Wilson and the two political philosophies summed up in their campaign slogans: "The New Nationalism" and "The New Freedom."

Roosevelt's New Nationalism enunciated his belief in federal planning and regulation. He accepted big business as inevitable but demanded that government supervise it and act as "a steward of the people." Roosevelt called for an increase in the power of the federal government, a decrease in the power of the courts, and an active role for the president. As political theorist Herbert Croly pointed out in his influential book, *The Promise of American Life* (1909), Roosevelt hoped to use the Hamiltonian means of a centralized federal government to further the Jeffersonian end of greater democracy.

> *Voters in 1912 could choose from three candidates, each of whom claimed to be a progressive.*

Wilson, schooled in the Democratic principles of limited government and states' rights, set a markedly different course with his New Freedom. Tutored in economics by *Muller v. Oregon* lawyer Louis Brandeis, who railed against the "curse of bigness," Wilson promised to use antitrust legislation to get rid of big corporations and to give small businesses and farmers better opportunities in the marketplace.

Wilson and Roosevelt fought it out, but in the end only the energy and emotional enthusiasm of the Bull Moosers obscured the inevitable outcome of a race in which the Republican vote was split while the Democrats remained united. No candidate could claim a majority in the three-way race. Wilson captured a bare 42 percent of the popular vote, polling fewer votes than Bryan had received when he lost to Taft in 1908. Roosevelt and his Bull Moose Progressive Party won 27 percent of the vote, an unprecedented amount for a new party. The incumbent Taft came in third with 23 percent. But in the electoral college, Wilson won a decisive 435, with 88 going to Roosevelt and only 8 to Taft. The real loser in 1912 was not Taft but the Bull Moose Party, which essentially collapsed after Roosevelt's defeat. It had always been, in the words of one particular observer, "a house divided against itself and already mortgaged."

## Woodrow Wilson and Progressivism at High Tide

Born in Virginia and raised in Georgia, Woodrow Wilson was the first Southerner to be elected president since James K. Polk in 1844 and only the second Democrat to occupy the White House since Reconstruction. Democrats who anticipated a wild celebration when Wilson took office soon had their hopes dashed. The son of a Presbyterian minister, Wilson was a teetotaler more given to Scripture than to celebration. He canceled the inaugural ball and called instead for a day of prayer.

This lean, ascetic man with an otherworldly gaze had come to politics by a strange route. A scholar and an academician, he had earned his doctorate at Johns Hopkins University and had taught at Bryn Mawr, Wesleyan, and Princeton, serving as president of the latter for eight years. In 1910, the New Jersey Democratic machine, looking for a respectable candidate, tapped him for governor. Once in office, he quickly cut his ties with the bosses and went over to the progressive camp. He was a man, as one observer conceded, whose "political convictions were never as fixed as his ambition."

Wilson brought to the White House a gift for oratory, a stern will, and a set of fixed beliefs. His tendency to turn differences of opinion into personal hatreds would impair his leadership and damage his presidency. Fortunately for Wilson, he came to power with a Democratic Congress ready to do his bidding. Before he was finished, Wilson would preside over progressivism at high tide and see enacted

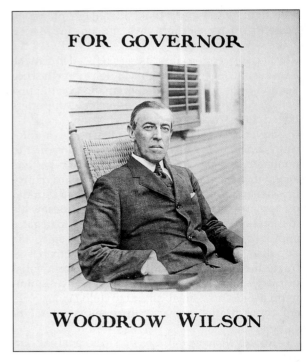

**FOR GOVERNOR**

**WOODROW WILSON**

**WOODROW WILSON**
*Woodrow Wilson's political career was meteoric, propelling him from the presidency of Princeton University to the presidency of the United States in three years. As governor of New Jersey from 1910 to 1912, Wilson turned his back on the Democratic machine that had backed him and made a reputation as a champion of progressive reform. Elected to the White House in 1912, he presided over the high tide of progressive reform.*
Collection of Janice L. and David J. Frent.

not only the platform of the Democratic Party but many of the humanitarian reforms championed by Roosevelt's Progressive Party as well.

## Banking Reform and the Trusts

In March 1913, Wilson became the first president since John Adams to go to Capitol Hill and speak directly to Congress, calling for tariff reform. "The object of the tariff," Wilson told Congress, "must be effective competition." Eager to topple the high tariff, the Democratic House of Representatives hastily passed the Underwood tariff, which lowered rates by 15 percent. To compensate for lost revenue, Congress approved a moderate income tax made possible by ratification of the Sixteenth Amendment a month earlier. In the Senate, lobbyists for industries quietly went to work to get the tariff raised, but Wilson rallied public opinion by attacking the "industrious and insidious lobby." Robert La Follette went further and demanded an investigation of the ties between business and the legislature. When senators for the first time had to disclose their finances, the public learned that more than a few were on the payrolls of big corporations. In the harsh glare of publicity, the Senate passed the Underwood tariff, which earned praise as "the most honest tariff since the Civil War."

Wilson turned his attention next to banking. The panic of 1907 had dramatically testified to the failure of the banking system. Once again, a president had had to turn to J. P. Morgan. But Morgan's legendary power was coming under close scrutiny. In 1913, Arsène Pujo, a Democratic senator from Louisiana, headed a committee to investigate the "money trust," calling J. P. Morgan himself to testify. The Pujo committee uncovered an alarming concentration of banking power. J. P. Morgan and Company and its affiliates held 341 directorships in 112 corporations, controlling assets of more than $22 billion. The sensational findings created a mandate for banking reform.

The Federal Reserve Act of 1913 was the most significant piece of domestic legislation in Wilson's presidency. It established a national banking system composed of twelve regional banks, privately controlled but regulated and supervised by a Federal Reserve Board appointed by the president. It gave the United States its first efficient banking and currency system and, at the same time, provided for a larger degree of government control over banking than had ever existed before. The new system made currency more elastic and credit adequate for the needs of business and agriculture. It did not, however, attempt to take control of the boom and bust cycles in the U.S. economy that would produce another major depression in the 1930s.

Flushed with success, Wilson tackled the trust issue. When Congress reconvened in January 1914, Wilson supported the Clayton bill to outlaw "unfair competition"—practices such as price discrimination and interlocking directorates (directors from one corporation sitting on the board of another). Despite a grandiose preamble which stated, "The labor of human beings is not a commodity or article of commerce," the Clayton Act did not succeed in improving labor's position. Although AFL President Samuel Gompers hailed the act as the "Magna Carta of labor," the conservative courts continued to issue injunctions and to use antitrust legislation against labor unions.

In the midst of the fight for the Clayton Act, Wilson, at the prompting of Louis Brandeis, threw his support behind the creation of the Federal Trade Commission (FTC), precisely the kind of federal regulatory agency that Roosevelt had advocated. The FTC, created in 1913, had not only wide investigatory powers but the authority to prosecute corporations for "unfair trade practices" and to enforce its judgments by issuing "cease and desist" orders. Along with the Clayton Act, Wilson's antitrust program worked to regulate rather than to break up big business.

*Before he was finished, Wilson would preside over progressivism at high tide and see enacted not only the platform of the Democratic Party but many of the humanitarian reforms championed by Roosevelt's Progressive Party as well.*

By the fall of 1914 Wilson had exhausted the stock of ideas that made up the New Freedom. He alarmed progressives by declaring that the progressive movement had fulfilled its mission and that the country needed "a time of healing." Having fought provisions in the Federal Reserve Act that would give bankers control, Wilson promptly named a banker, Paul Warburg, as the first chief of the Federal Reserve Board. Appointments to the new FTC also went to conservative businessmen. The progressive penchant for expertise helps explain Wilson's choices. Believing that experts in the field could best understand the complex issues at stake, Wilson appointed bankers to oversee the banks and businessmen to regulate business.

## Wilson, Reluctant Progressive

Progressives watched in dismay as Wilson repeatedly obstructed or obstinately refused to encourage further progressive reforms. He failed to support labor's demand for an end to injunctions. He twice threatened to veto legislation providing for farm credits on nonperishable crops. He refused to support child labor legislation or woman suffrage. Wilson justified his actions in the rhetoric of the New Freedom by claiming that his administration would condone "special privileges to none." Virtually the only progressive measure that passed was the Seaman's Bill in 1915, a long overdue measure to improve the working conditions of sailors.

In the face of Wilson's obstinacy, reform might have ended in 1913 had not politics intruded. In the congressional elections of 1914, the Republican Party, no longer split by Roosevelt's Bull Moose faction, won substantial gains. Democratic strategists, with their eyes on the 1916 presidential race, recognized that Wilson needed to pick up support in the Midwest and the West by capturing votes from former Bull Moose progressives.

Wilson responded belatedly to this political pressure by championing reform in 1916. In a sharp about-face, he cultivated union labor, farmers, and social reformers. To please labor, he appointed Louis Brandeis to the Supreme Court. To woo farmers, he threw his support behind legislation to obtain rural credits. And he won support from advanced progressives such as Jane Addams by supporting workers' compensation and the Keating-Owen child labor law. When a railroad strike threatened in the months before the election, Wilson virtually ordered Congress to establish an eight-hour day at ten-hour pay on the railroads. He had moved a long way from his position in 1912 to embrace many of the social reforms championed by Theodore Roosevelt. (See Texts in Historical Context on page 576.) As Wilson boasted, the Democrats had "opened their hearts to the demands of social justice" and had "come very near to carrying out the platform of the Progressive Party."

# The Limits of Reform

Progressivism was never a radical movement. Its goal remained the preservation of the existing system—by government intervention if necessary, but without uprooting any of the traditional American political, economic, or social institutions. As Theodore Roosevelt, the bellwether of the movement, insisted, "The only true conservative is the man who resolutely sets his face toward the future." Roosevelt was such a man, and progressivism was such a movement. Its basic conservatism can be seen by comparing it to more radical movements of the era and by looking at the groups progressive reform left behind.

## Radical Alternatives

The year 1900 witnessed the birth of the Social Democratic Party in America, later called simply the Socialist Party. Like the progressives, the socialists were middle class and native-born. They had broken with the older, more militant Socialist Labor Party precisely because of its dogmatic approach and immigrant constituency. The new group of socialists, men such as Upton Sinclair, Walter Lippmann, and John Reed, were eager to appeal to a broad mass of Americans.

*Progressivism was never a radical movement. Its goal remained the preservation of the existing system—by government intervention if necessary.*

The Socialist Party chose as its standard-bearer Eugene V. Debs, whose experience in the Pullman strike of 1894 convinced him that "there is no hope for the toiling masses of my countrymen, except by the pathways mapped out by Socialism." Debs's brand of socialism, which owed as much to the social gospel as to the theories of Karl Marx, advocated cooperation over competition and urged men and women to liberate themselves from "the barbarism of private ownership and wage slavery." He was described by his followers as "a poet, a saint, a sweetly strong man," Debs declared, "While there is a lower class I am of it, while there is a criminal class I am of it, while there is a soul in prison I am not free."

Roosevelt labeled Debs a "mere inciter to murder and preacher of applied anarchy." Debs, for his part, pointed to the conservatism that underlay Roosevelt's fiery rhetoric. In the 1912 election, Debs indicted both parties as "Tweedledee and Tweedledum," each dedicated to the preservation of capitalism and the continuation of the wage system. The Socialist Party alone, he argued, was the "revolutionary party of the working class." Debs would run for president five times, in every election (except 1916) from 1900 to 1920. His best showing came in 1912, when he polled 6 percent of the popular vote, capturing almost a million votes.

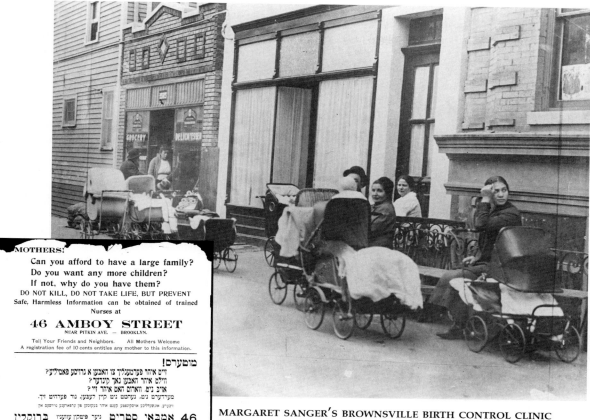

**MARGARET SANGER'S BROWNSVILLE BIRTH CONTROL CLINIC**
*Margaret Sanger opened the first birth control clinic in the United States in the Brownsville section of Brooklyn in 1916. During the nine days it operated before police shut it down, more than four hundred women visited the clinic. Here they are shown waiting patiently in line with their baby carriages. Sanger published her flyers in English, Yiddish, and Italian, and her clinic attracted immigrant women, proving that Italian Catholics and Russian Jews wanted birth control information as much as their middle- and upper-class Protestant counterparts did.*
Sophia Smith Collection.

Farther to the left of the socialists stood the Industrial Workers of the World (IWW), nicknamed the Wobblies. In 1905, Debs, along with Big Bill Haywood, created the IWW, "one big union" dedicated to organizing the most destitute segment of the workforce, the unskilled workers disdained by Samuel Gompers's AFL—western miners, migrant farmworkers, lumbermen, and immigrant textile workers. Haywood, a craggy-faced miner with one eye (he had lost the other in a childhood accident), was a charismatic leader and a proletarian intellectual. While Debs insisted that change could

come from ballots, not bullets, the IWW unhesitatingly advocated direct action, sabotage, and the general strike—tactics designed to trigger a workers' uprising.

In contrast to political radicals like Debs and Haywood, Margaret Sanger, a nurse and social activist, promoted birth control as a movement for radical change. Sanger, the daughter of a radical Irish father and a mother who died at fifty after bearing eleven children, coined the term *birth control* and launched a movement with broad social implications. She and her followers saw birth control

# The Issue of Child Labor

*B*y the early years of the twentieth century, as many as four million children between the ages of ten and fifteen toiled long hours at low pay. They could be found in the depths of coal mines, in the searing heat of glass factories, in canneries and textile mills, in cotton fields—wherever employers coveted small size and nimble fingers. Progressive reformers, often called the "child savers," attempted to curb exploitation of children under the age of fourteen in sweatshops, mines, and mills across America. But they ran into solid opposition not only from employers, who had a vested interest in the cheap labor children performed, but also from parents, who counted on the meager wages of their children. In rural America, no one had questioned parents' right to put children to hard tasks in the fields and on the farm. Similarly, immigrants from rural Italy, Germany, or Russia could see no harm in putting children to work in factories or sweatshops in America's industrial cities and viewed it as the parents' prerogative to command their children's wages. Progressives found themselves up against stiff opposition.

Not just immigrants but old-stock Americans relied on child labor, particularly in the South, where entire families of poor whites left the land to work side by side in the textile mills. On May 22, 1914, a South Carolina mill owner testified before the House of Representatives Committee on Labor on why child labor was necessary in the South.

### DOCUMENT 1. Lewis W. Parker, Testimony before the Congressional Committee on Labor, 1914

It is not possible for a man who has been working on a farm who is an adult—after the age of 21 years, for instance—to become a skilled employee in a cotton mill. His fingers are knotted and gnarled; he is slow in action, whereas activity is required in working in the cotton mills. Therefore, as a matter of necessity, the adult of the family had to come to the cotton mill as an unskilled employee, and it was the children of the family who became the skilled employees in the cotton mills. For that reason it was the children who had to support the families for the time being. I have seen instances in which a child of 12 years of age, working in the cotton mills, is earning one and one-half times as much as his father of 40 or 50 years of age.

*P*rogressives countered these arguments with poignant testimony about the plight of young workers and the failure of the states to enforce the law. At the same 1914 committee hearings, reformer Florence Kelley described her experiences investigating child labor practices in Illinois.

### DOCUMENT 2. Florence Kelley, Testimony before the Congressional Committee on Labor, 1914

. . . I was at one time chief inspector of factories and workshops in the State of Illinois. I found great numbers of children working at night—working illegally. The superintendent of a glass-bottle company told me himself that this occurred once when he was rushed with work: A widow had come to him bringing two little boys, one still in kilts [baby skirts worn by small boys] and one in knee breeches. She told him that their father had just been killed on the railroad, and that they were penniless; and she wanted the older little boy to go to work in the glassworks, where he would get 40 cents a day. The superintendent was pressed for boys, and said, "I won't take the bigger fellow alone, but if you will take the baby back home and put him into knee pants, and then bring them both back in trousers, I will take them both." She did so, and those two little fellows, aged 9 and 7 years, began their work on the night shift.

Despite heavy odds against them, progressives achieved victory in 1916 when the National Child Labor Committee finally convinced Congress and President Woodrow Wilson to enact the Keating-Owen bill forbidding the regular employment of children under sixteen. The child savers' victory proved short-lived, however. Powerful business interests and a Supreme Court sympathetic to their views took advantage of the waning fervor for reform and in 1918 in Hammer v. Dagenhart struck down the child labor law on the grounds that Congress could not regulate manufacturing within states. This decision made it legal for the chief plaintiff in the case, Roland Dagenhart, to continue having his young sons, ages thirteen and seven, work in a North Carolina cotton mill. It also protected the boys' "constitutional right" to continue to work at the mill, where they put in twelve-hour days and sometimes worked night shifts as well.

Ironically, one of the plaintiffs in the Dagenhart case had a very negative view of its outcome. In 1923, reporter Lowell Mellett tracked down Reuben Dagenhart, one of the boys in whose favor the Supreme Court had ruled six years earlier. In an article published in Labor in November 1923, Mellett recounted his meeting with Dagenhart.

### DOCUMENT 3. Lowell Mellett, Interview with Reuben Dagenhart, 1923

I found him at his home in Charlotte. He is about the size of the office boy—weighs 105 pounds, he told me. But he is a married man with a child. He is 20 years old.

"What benefit," I asked him, "did you get out of the suit which you won in the United States Supreme Court?"

"You mean the suit the Fidelity Manufacturing Company won? (It was the Fidelity Company for which the Dagenharts were working.) I don't see that I got any benefit. I guess I'd been alot better off if they hadn't won it. . . .

"Look at me! A hundred and five pounds, a grown man and no education. I may be mistaken, but I think the years I've put in in the cotton mills have stunted my growth. They kept me from getting

any schooling. I had to stop school after the third grade and now I need the education I didn't get."

"How was your growth stunted?"

"I don't know—the dust and the lint, maybe. But from 12 years old on, I was working 12 hours a day—from 6 in the morning till 7 at night, with time out for meals. And sometimes I worked nights besides. Lifting a hundred pounds and I only weighed 65 pounds myself."

He explained that he and his sister worked together, "on section," spinning. They each made about a dollar a day, though later he worked up to where he could make $2. His father made $15 a week and infant John, at the time the suit was brought, was making close to $1 a day.

"Just what did you and John get out of that suit, then?"

"Why, we got some automobile rides when them big lawyers from the North was down here. Oh, yes, and they brought both of us a coca-cola! That's all we got out of it."

"What did you tell the judge when you were in court?"

"Oh, John and me never was in court! Just Paw was there. John and me was just little kids in short pants. I guess we wouldn't have looked like much in court. We were working in the mill while the case was going on. But Paw went up to Washington."

Reuben hasn't been to school, but his mind has not been idle.

"It would have been a good thing for all the kids in this state if that law they passed had been kept. . . . I know one thing. I ain't going to let them put my kid sister in the mill. . . . She's only 15 and she's crippled and I bet I stop that!"

Despite the efforts of committed reformers, child labor persisted into the 1920s, immune from federal law and condoned by states reluctant to exercise their authority against the force of private money and growing public indifference.

---

Documents 1 and 2. *House of Representatives Hearings before the Committee on Labor* (1914), 93, 35–36.
Document 3. *Labor*, November 17, 1923.

not only as a sexual and medical reform but also as a means to alter social and political power relationships and to alleviate human misery.

Although birth control became a public issue only in the early twentieth century, the birthrate in the United States had been falling consistently throughout the nineteenth century, with the average number of children per family falling from 7 in 1800 to 3.6 by 1900. The desire for family limitation was widespread, and, in this sense, birth control was nothing new. But the open advocacy of contraception, the use of artificial means to prevent pregnancy, seemed to many people both new and shocking. Theodore Roosevelt fulminated against birth control as "race suicide," warning that the "white" population was declining while immigrants and "undesirables" continued to breed.

Convinced that women needed to be able to control their pregnancies but unsure of the best methods for doing so, Sanger traveled to Europe in 1913 to learn more about contraceptive techniques. On her return in 1914, she promoted birth control in her newspaper, *The Woman Rebel*. Purity laws passed in the 1870s made it illegal to distribute information on birth control or contraceptive devices, classing both as pornography. When the post office declared Sanger's publication obscene and brought charges against her, she responded defiantly by drafting a detailed pamphlet called "Family Limitation" and getting the IWW to distribute 100,000 copies. Facing arrest, she fled to Europe only to return in 1916 something of a national celebrity. In her absence, birth control had become linked with free speech and had been taken up as a liberal cause. Under public pressure, the government dropped charges against Sanger, who undertook a nationwide tour to publicize the birth control cause.

Sanger then turned to direct action, opening the nation's first birth control clinic in the Brownsville section of Brooklyn, New York. Located in the heart of a Jewish and Italian immigrant neighborhood, the clinic attracted 464 clients in the nine days it was open. On the tenth day, police shut down the clinic and put Sanger in jail. By then she had become a national figure, and the cause she championed had gained legitimacy, if not legality.

## Progressivism for White Men Only

The day before President Woodrow Wilson's inauguration in March 1913, more than five thousand demonstrators marched in Washington to demand the vote for women. A rowdy crowd on hand to celebrate the Democrats' triumph heckled the marchers, as did the police. "If my wife were where you are," a burly cop told one suffragist, "I'd break her head." But for all the marching, Wilson, who didn't believe that a "lady" should vote, pointedly ignored woman suffrage in his inaugural address the next day.

The march served as a reminder that the political gains of progressivism were not spread equally in the population. When the twentieth century dawned, women still could not vote in most states. Increasingly, however, woman suffrage had become an international movement. In Great Britain, Emmeline Pankhurst and her daughters Cristabel and Sylvia promoted a new, militant suffragism. They seized the spotlight in a series of marches, mass meetings, and acts of civil disobedience, which sometimes escalated into violence, riots, and arson.

The activism of the British suffragists sparked new action in the United States, where progress toward full suffrage had moved slowly. After a victory in Washington State in 1910, suffragists experienced a stinging defeat in California in 1911. Kansas, Oregon, and Arizona joined the suffrage column in 1912, evidence that suffragists were perfecting their lobbying techniques. Yet some suffragists, attracted to the flamboyance of the British movement, urged more direct action. Alice Paul, a Quaker social worker who had visited England and participated in suffrage activism there, returned to the United States in 1910 in time to plan the mass march on the eve of Wilson's inauguration and to lobby for a federal amendment to give women the vote. Paul's dramatic tactics alienated many in the National American Woman Suffrage Association (NAWSA). In 1916, she founded the militant National Woman's Party (NWP), which became the radical voice of the suffrage movement, advocating direct action and civil disobedience. Paul and her followers rejected the state-by-state strategy of the NAWSA and continued to press for a constitutional suffrage amendment, called by its supporters the Susan B. Anthony amendment.

The NAWSA, spurred by the actions of Paul and her followers, gained new direction when Carrie Chapman Catt became president in 1915. Catt revitalized the organization with a carefully crafted "winning plan" designed to achieve suffrage in six years. While Paul and her Woman's Party held a six-month vigil outside the White House with banners that read "Mr. Wilson, What Will You Do for

Woman Suffrage?" Catt led a centrally directed effort that worked on several levels. In states where women already voted, Catt lobbied for a federal amendment. Where state referenda could be won, she launched campaigns to maintain the suffrage momentum. Catt's strategy was to "keep so much 'suffrage noise' going all over the country that neither the enemy [n]or friends will discover where the real battle is." Catt's "winning plan" worked effectively, taking only four years instead of the six Catt had predicted.

World War I would provide the final impetus for woman suffrage. Paul and the NWP refused to work for the war and insisted that "democracy should begin at home." In contrast, Catt seized the mantle of patriotism, arguing that there was no conflict between fighting for suffrage and aiding the war effort. It would take several more years before the Nineteenth Amendment became part of the U.S. Constitution, but when it was ratified in August 1920, the victory belonged both to Catt and to Paul, for without the militancy of the Woman's Party, the NAWSA would not have seemed so moderate and respectable.

Women were not alone in being left out of progressive advances. It was one of the great ironies of progressivism that, as it was practiced south of the Mason-Dixon line, it preached disfranchisement of black voters as a "reform." During the bitter electoral fights that had pitted Populists against Democrats in the 1890s, the charge was often made that the party of white supremacy held its power only by the votes of the black belt. To guard against electoral fraud, where, it was alleged, African American votes were purchased by money or threats of coercion, southern progressives proposed to "reform" the electoral system by eliminating black voters. Southern states, beginning in 1890 with Mississippi, sought to curtail the African American vote through devices like the poll tax (a fee required to vote) and the literacy test. Not coincidentally, these measures also denied access to poor, illiterate whites likely to vote against the reigning Democrats and for the Populist Party. But the racist intention of southern voting legislation became clear when states resorted to such transparent ruses as the "grandfather clause," a legal device that allowed anyone to vote whose grandparent had cast a ballot, thus including virtually any southern white and excluding every black voter, whose grandparent had most likely been a slave.

The Progressive Era witnessed not only the systematic disfranchisement of black voters but the rise of "Jim Crow" laws to segregate public facilities. (The name "Jim Crow" derived from a character in a popular minstrel song.) The new railroads precipitated segregation in the South where it had rarely existed, at least on paper, before. Blacks were segregated in Jim Crow train coaches, even when they paid a first-class fare. Soon separate waiting rooms, separate bathrooms, and separate dining facilities sprang up across the South. In courtrooms in the state of Mississippi, blacks were even required to swear on a separate Bible.

*It was one of the great ironies of progressivism that, as it was practiced south of the Mason-Dixon line, it preached disfranchisement of black voters as a "reform."*

In the face of this growing repression, Booker T. Washington, the preeminent black leader of the day, urged caution and restraint. A former slave, Washington opened the Tuskegee Institute in Alabama in 1881 to teach vocational skills to African Americans. Washington emphasized education and economic progress for his race and urged African Americans to put aside issues of political and social equality. In an 1895 speech in Atlanta, which came to be known as the "Atlanta Compromise," he stated, "In all things that are purely social we can be as separate as the fingers, yet one as the hand in all things essential to mutual progress." Washington's accommodationist policy appealed to whites in all sections, who elevated "the wizard of Tuskegee" to the role of national spokesman for African Americans.

The year after Washington proclaimed the Atlanta Compromise, the Supreme Court upheld the legality of racial segregation, affirming in *Plessy v. Ferguson* (1896) the constitutionality of the doctrine of "separate but equal." Blacks could be segregated in separate facilities, from schools to rest rooms, as long as the facilities were "equal." In actuality, facilities rarely were equal. In the North, where the growing tide of new immigrants led to a clamor for restrictive legislation, support for African American rights found few advocates. Increasingly, the doctrine of "white supremacy" found support in all sections of the country.

When Theodore Roosevelt invited Booker T. Washington to dine at the White House in 1901, a storm of racist criticism erupted. One southern editor fumed that the White House "had been painted

DINNER GIVEN AT THE WHITE HOUSE BY PRESIDENT ROOSEVELT TO BOOKER T. WASHINGTON, OCTOBER 17th, 1901

**BOOKER T. WASHINGTON AND THEODORE ROOSEVELT DINE AT THE WHITE HOUSE**
*When Theodore Roosevelt invited Booker T. Washington to the White House in 1901, he stirred up a hornet's nest of controversy that continued into the election of 1904. Here in a Republican campaign piece, the meeting is portrayed positively, with Roosevelt and Washington pictured under a portrait of Abraham Lincoln, signaling the party's historic commitment to African Americans. Democrats portrayed the meeting in a very different light; their campaign buttons pictured Washington with darker skin and implied that Roosevelt favored "race mingling."*
Collection of Janice L. and David J. Frent.

black." But Roosevelt summoned Washington to talk politics and patronage, not African American rights. Busy tearing apart Mark Hanna's Republican machine and creating his own, Roosevelt wanted Washington's counsel in selecting black Republicans for party posts in the South. The president remained more interested in his own political fortunes than in those of African Americans.

When Woodrow Wilson came to power, he brought with him southern attitudes toward race and racial segregation. He allowed his postmaster general to segregate facilities, including drinking fountains and rest rooms, in the nation's capital. When critics attacked the policy, Wilson insisted that segregation was "in the interest of the Negro."

Faced with intolerance and open persecution, educated blacks in the North rebelled against the conservative leadership of Booker T. Washington. In *The Souls of Black Folk* (1903), Harvard graduate W. E. B. Du Bois attacked the "Tuskegee Machine," comparing Washington to a political boss and charging that he used his influence to silence his critics and reward his followers. Du Bois founded the Niagara movement in 1905, calling for universal suffrage, civil rights, and leadership by a black intellectual elite. In 1909, the Niagara movement helped found the National Association for the Advancement of Colored People (NAACP), a coalition of blacks and whites that sought legal and political rights for African Americans. Like many progressive reform coalitions, the NAACP contained a diverse group—social workers, socialists, and black intellectuals. In the decades that followed, the NAACP came to represent the future for African Americans, while Booker T. Washington, who died in 1915, represented the past.

## Conclusion: Progressivism in Perspective

The limitations of progressive reform should not obscure its very real achievements. The progressive movement brought significant gains as government moved away from laissez-faire and social Darwinism to embrace a more active role designed to bring about social justice and to achieve a better balance between business and government. Both Jane Addams and Theodore Roosevelt could lay equal claim to a movement that brought American politics into the twentieth century.

Progressivism contained many paradoxes. A diverse coalition of individuals and interests, the progressive movement began at the grass roots but left as its legacy a stronger presidency and unprecedented federal involvement in the economy and social welfare. A movement that believed in social justice, progressivism often promoted social control. And while progressives called for greater democracy, they worshiped experts and efficiency. But whatever its inconsistencies, progressivism attempted to deal with the problems posed by urban industrialism and, by increasing the power of the presidency and expanding the power of the government, helped to launch the liberal state of the twentieth century. War on a global scale would provide progressivism with yet another challenge even before it had completed its ambitious agenda.

## CHRONOLOGY

**1889**  Jane Addams opens Hull House in Chicago.

**1895**  Booker T. Washington enunciates "Atlanta Compromise," accepting segregation in return for economic opportunity.

Anti-Saloon League founded by Protestant clergy.

**1896**  U.S. Supreme Court upholds doctrine of "separate but equal" in *Plessy v. Ferguson.*

**1900**  Socialist Party founded with Eugene V. Debs as standard-bearer.

**1901**  Thomas Lofton Johnson elected mayor of Cleveland, Ohio.

Robert M. La Follette elected governor of Wisconsin.

Theodore Roosevelt succeeds to presidency following assassination of William McKinley.

Roosevelt brings labor and management to bargaining table in anthracite coal strike.

Roosevelt initiates investigation of Northern Securities Company for antitrust violations.

**1902**  Dispute between United States and Germany over Venezuelan debt ends in arbitration.

Lincoln Steffens's muckraking series "The Shame of the Cities" begins in *McClure's Magazine.*

U.S. government files antitrust law suit against Northern Securities Company.

**1903**  U.S.-backed uprising in Panama leads to Panamanian independence and U.S. begins construction of the Panama canal.

W. E. B. Du Bois challenges Booker T. Washington in *The Souls of Black Folk*.

Women's Trade Union League (WTUL) founded.

**1904**  Theodore Roosevelt wins presidential election in landslide.

**1905**  Industrial Workers of the World (IWW) founded by Big Bill Haywood.

**1906**  Pure Food and Drug Act and meat inspection legislation passed after publicity generated by Upton Sinclair's muckraking novel *The Jungle*.

Robert M. La Follette elected U.S. senator.

Congress passes Hepburn Act to regulate railroads and strengthen Interstate Commerce Commission.

Roosevelt receives Nobel Peace Prize for his role in mediating Russo-Japanese War.

**1907**  Panic on Wall Street. J. P. Morgan's U.S. Steel acquires Tennessee Coal and Iron Company.

Roosevelt dispatches navy's Great White Fleet on world cruise to display U.S. naval power.

Walter Rauschenbusch publishes *Christianity and the Social Crisis*.

**1908**  U.S. Supreme Court upholds Oregon state law limiting women's working hours to ten a day (*Muller v. Oregon*).

William Howard Taft elected president to succeed Theodore Roosevelt.

**1909**  "Uprising of twenty thousand" in New York City: shirtwaist makers' strike backed by WTUL.

National Association for the Advancement of Colored People (NAACP) formed.

President Taft defends Payne-Aldrich tariff.

**1911**  Triangle fire in New York City kills 146 workers.

**1912**  President Taft sends marines into Nicaragua and Santo Domingo.

Republican's nominate incumbent William Howard Taft.

Theodore Roosevelt runs for president on Progressive Bull Moose Party ticket.

Democrat Woodrow Wilson elected president, defeating Taft and Roosevelt.

**1913**  Federal Reserve Act provides twelve regional banks supervised by a Federal Reserve Board.

Wilson signs legislation establishing Federal Trade Commission (FTC).

**1914**  Congress passes Clayton Antitrust Act.

Walter Lippmann publishes *Drift and Mastery,* a statement of the progressive philosophy.

**1915**  Carrie Chapman Catt takes over leadership of national woman suffrage movement.

**1916**  Alice Paul launches National Woman's Party.

Margaret Sanger opens first birth control clinic in the Brownsville section of Brooklyn, New York.

Keating-Owen bill outlawing child labor passed.

**1918**  Supreme Court strikes down child labor law in *Hammer v. Dagenhart*.

# SUGGESTED READINGS

Ellen Chesler, *Woman of Valor: Margaret Sanger and the Birth Control Movement in America* (1993). A lively biography of the woman who founded the American birth control movement that is at once laudatory and critical.

Ellen Fitzpatrick, *Endless Crusade: Women, Social Scientists, and Progressive Reform* (1990). An exploration of the careers of four women who played decisive roles in early social reform.

Louis R. Harlan, *Booker T. Washington: The Wizard of Tuskegee, 1901–1915* (1983). The second in a two-volume biography, focusing on Washington's national role in the Progressive period.

Jack Temple Kirby, *Darkness at the Dawning: Race and Reform in the Progressive South* (1972). Examines the paradox of disfranchisement as a reform in the South.

Anthony Lukas, *Big Trouble: A Murder in a Small Western Town Sets Off a Struggle for the Soul of America* (1998). Recounting the trial of Big Bill Haywood for the murder of a former Idaho governor in 1905, Lukas examines the entire social, political, economic, and cultural context, from small-town baseball to hard rock mining.

Robyn Muncy, *Creating a Female Dominion in American Reform* (1991). Women's political activism from the Progressive era to the New Deal, focusing on the relationship between gender and welfare policy.

Kathryn Kish Sklar, *Florence Kelley and the Nation's Work: The Rise of Women's Political Culture, 1830–1900* (1995). Volume 1 of a prospective two-volume study exploring Kelley's life and demonstrating women's role in and merger of public and private themes that characterized reform.

David P. Thelen, *The New Citizenship: Origins of Progressivism in Wisconsin, 1885–1900* (1972). An examination of progressivism in the state that came to be called the "laboratory" of the progressive movement.

# WAR

Which Bird?

*As viewed by Life*

**LIFE MAGAZINE COVER**
*This 1914 magazine cover provides a vivid visual demonstration of the early tendency of the American press to support U.S. entry into World War I. The image makes no bones about the way a viewer should answer the question posed below it. The American eagle in the center, wings spread and screaming for action, dominates the picture and makes the dove holding an olive branch appear pathetically weak. Considering the stereotyped knife, gun, and bomb-wielding foreigners lurking in the background, the sailor has understandably turned toward the eagle for inspiration to fight against the enemies of democracy.*
Picture Research Archives and Consultants.

# THE UNITED STATES AND THE "GREAT WAR"

## 22

### 1914–1920

O N AUGUST 6, 1914, after more than forty years of peace, Europe exploded in war. When the news arrived in Washington, President Woodrow Wilson saw it as a repudiation of progressive ideals of social reform and international harmony that had seemed on the verge of realization. "What a pathetic thing," he lamented, "to have this come just as we were so full of hope!" Wilson's despair also reflected the unfolding of personal tragedy, for the buildup to war occurred as his beloved wife, Ellen, lay dying. The president received reports of belligerent nations mobilizing during his final vigil at her bedside, and when Ellen's death and the end of peace finally struck on the same day, Wilson was doubly devastated. According to the White House physician, he was a "man with his heart torn out."

Hardening himself to his grief and disillusionment, Wilson formulated a national policy regarding the war in Europe. He never had any doubt that the only virtuous course was absolute neutrality. Even though his sympathies lay with Great Britain and France, Wilson concluded that blame for the war did not lie entirely with Germany. Moreover, he believed that the United States had no vital stake in a European power struggle. Wilson agreed with the American ambassador in London, who declared, "Again and ever I thank heaven for the Atlantic Ocean." Wilson also had to consider that the United States was a nation of immigrants, millions of whom had only recently come from countries on both sides of the war. As Wilson told the German ambassador, "We definitely have to be neutral, since otherwise our mixed populations would wage war on each other."

There was another idealistic reason to stay out of the European struggle. As Wilson explained less than two weeks after the war started, the United States could offer "impartial mediation" and show the world the way to reconciliation and a healing peace. To make the most of this opportunity for service, Wilson told the American people, they must restrain their tendency to favor one side or the other and remain "impartial in thought as well as action."

Most Americans agreed with Wilson that the country should stay neutral, but they were less eager to use that neutrality to broker a peace. Essentially, the nation tried to distance itself from the conflict and just go about its business. But events were to prove that the Atlantic was no moat. Trade and travel webbed the modern world and eventually entangled the United States in the war's violence and the arguments advanced to justify it. Step by step Europe's troubles became America's, and the forces that undermined Europeans' self-confident belief in progress also ended America's Progressive Era. After nearly three years of trying to steer a neutral course, Woodrow Wilson went before Congress on April 2, 1917, to ask for a

**WOODROW WILSON**
*Passing by a cheering multitude, Wilson basks in his most cherished role as champion of heroic idealism. Erect, beaming, eyes on the horizon, he seems to be savoring a triumphal moment. Although he often struck this pose to inspire support for the war to end all wars, Wilson also endured moments of extreme suffering, beginning with the death of his wife and extending to the defeat of his hope for world democracy. Such vast swings between elation and despair characterized Wilson's ordeal during and after the war.*
Library of Congress.

declaration of war against Germany. America's participation would be a crusade to make the First World War the war to end all wars, Wilson vowed. And America's goodness and disinterestedness would ensure a just peace "to make the world safe for democracy."

The conflict in which America finally came to have a vital stake was rightly called the "Great War," for it engendered great destruction and dras-

tically altered the structure of international order. War stretched across continents, and nations measured their casualties in the millions. When peace arrived in 1919, both the victors and the vanquished were decimated and exhausted.

America's experience was exceptional. At home, war and prosperity went hand in hand. But America paid a price as citizens and the government cracked down on dissent and demanded conformity. "Over There," as Americans called the war theater in Europe, the nation lost 112,000 soldiers, but their performance on the battlefields affected the outcome of the war. In the peace negotiations that followed the armistice, Woodrow Wilson played a principal role, but the results did not confirm Wilson's impossible vision of himself as personal savior of the world. He had promised more than anyone could deliver, and the nation turned bitter and disillusioned.

In December 1919, Wilson's personal friend and chief foreign policy adviser, Colonel Edward House, summarized the nation's ordeal: "We came near doing a great thing in a great way, but Fate ordained otherwise and while something may still be done, it will be done in a small way and in a way full of humiliation for those who wished to see the United States lead in a new world movement."

## Woodrow Wilson and the World

Shortly after winning election to the presidency in 1912, Woodrow Wilson confided to a friend: "It would be an irony of fate if my administration had to deal chiefly with foreign affairs." Indeed, Wilson had based his life and career on local attachments. He had never shown an interest in venturing far from home and had traveled abroad only on brief vacations. As president of Princeton University and then governor of New Jersey, he had remained rooted in domestic concerns. During his campaign for the presidency, Wilson had argued passionately for domestic reform, referring only rarely to foreign affairs.

But Wilson could not avoid the world. The Wilsonian foreign policy that emerged in 1913–1914 reflected his conviction that the United States should set the example in international affairs by championing the principles of liberal democracy: individual liberty, the right of national self-determination, peaceful free trade, and political democracy. Support for these principles meant opposing imperialism, large armed forces, and trade barriers. Above all, it meant righteous behavior. "We dare not turn from the principle that morality and not expediency is the thing that must guide us," Wilson announced loftily.

## Taming the Americas

The rising tide of militarism, nationalism, and violence severely tested Wilson's principles. When he came to office, Wilson sought to distinguish his foreign policy from that of his Republican predecessors. To Wilson, Theodore Roosevelt's "big stick" smacked of the blantant use of military force, and William Howard Taft's "dollar diplomacy" appeared to be a similarly crude flexing of economic muscle. Seeking a morally superior alternative, Wilson appointed William Jennings Bryan as secretary of state. A pacifist on religious grounds, Bryan immediately turned his attention to making agreements with thirty nations for the peaceful settlement of disputes.

But Wilson and Bryan, like Roosevelt and Taft, also believed that the Monroe Doctrine gave the United States special rights and responsibilities in the Western Hemisphere. The Wilson administration had the dubious goal, then, of encouraging justice and democracy in the Western Hemisphere while protecting and expanding American investments there. Wilson thus accepted the 1912 occupation of Nicaragua by U.S. marines to thwart a radical revolution that threatened American property. In 1915, he sent marines into Haiti to quell lawlessness and to protect American interests and in 1916 followed a similar course in the Dominican Republic. So firm was Wilson's view of American dominance in the hemisphere that when the Central American court of justice issued a ruling against American presence as a violation of national sovereignty, he simply ignored it (Map 22.1).

Wilson's most serious and controversial involvement in Latin America came in Mexico. Just weeks before Wilson was elected, General Victoriano Huerta seized power by violent means. Most European nations promptly recognized Huerta as the new president, but Wilson balked, declaring that he would not support a "government of butchers." In April 1914, Huerta's refusal to apologize for briefly detaining American sailors in Tampico prompted Wilson to declare that it was time "to teach the South American republics to elect good men!" The president ordered eight hundred marines to seize the port of Veracruz and prevent the unloading of a large shipment of arms for Huerta, who was by then involved in a civil war of his own. After brief resistance, Huerta fled to Spain, and the United States welcomed a more compliant government.

*The Wilson administration had the dubious goal of encouraging justice and democracy in the Western Hemisphere while protecting and expanding American investments there.*

Wilson was not able to subdue Mexico that easily, however. A rebellion erupted among desperately poor farmers who believed that the new government, aided by American business interests, had betrayed the revolution's promise to help the common people. Their leader, Francisco "Pancho" Villa, had instilled in his followers a brutal willingness to strike back at their oppressors. In January 1916, a band of Villistas seized a trainload of gold from an American-owned mine deep within Mexico and killed the seventeen American engineers who were carrying it to Texas. Another Villista band crossed the border on March 9 for a predawn raid on Columbus, New Mexico, that cost several lives and left the town in flames. Wilson promptly dispatched twelve thousand troops led by General John J. Pershing, who years earlier had chased the Apache chief Geronimo through the same Mexican desert. The American cavalry never managed to catch Villa's raiders. In January 1917, Pershing finally led his weary troops back across the border, ending Wilson's heavy-handed intervention into Mexican affairs. The revolution raged on in Mexico until 1920, however, and ended in the death of about two million people, one out of every eight Mexicans. Well before then, American attention had shifted to the situation in Europe.

## The European Crisis

Early in the twentieth century, European leaders often proclaimed proudly that they had done away with war. But the many years of peace enjoyed by the great powers before 1914 masked profound tensions caused by nationalist desires and imperial rivalries. The consolidation of the German and Italian states into unified nations and the similar ambition of Russia to create a "Pan-Slavic" union initiated new rivalries throughout Europe. As the conviction spread that colonial possessions were a

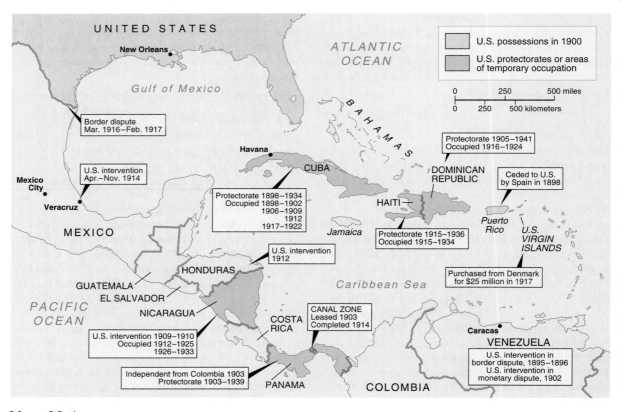

**MAP 22.1**

***U.S. Involvement in Latin America and the Caribbean, 1895–1941***

*Victory against Spain in 1898 made Puerto Rico an American possession and Cuba a protectorate. America also gained control over the Panama Canal and was quick to protect expanding economic interests with military force to make sure that stable, if not necessarily democratic, governments prevailed.*

mark of national greatness, competition expanded onto the world stage. In particular, Germany's efforts, under Kaiser Wilhelm II, to create an empire abroad, to build industrial muscle at home, and to challenge Britain's domination of the sea threatened the balance of power in Europe and stimulated competition among nations.

Within this explosive atmosphere, a complex web of military and diplomatic alliances grew. By 1914, Germany, Austria-Hungary, and Italy (the Triple Alliance) stood opposed to Great Britain, France, and Russia (the Triple Entente). In their effort to prevent war through a balance of power, the nations of Europe had actually magnified the possibility of conflict by creating national borders that

were in effect trip wires between two heavily armed power blocs.

The fatal sequence started in southeastern Europe, in the Balkans. On June 28, 1914, a Bosnian Serb terrorist demonstrated Serbia's persistent desire to extend its territory to the Adriatic Sea by killing Archduke Franz Ferdinand of Austria as he toured the Bosnian coastal city of Sarajevo, then part of the Austro-Hungarian Empire. Austria-Hungary, holding Serbia to account for the assassination, declared war on that nation on July 28. The alliance system then swung into action. Russia, determined to protect its Slavic kin, announced that it would back the Serbs. Germany, feeling compelled to support Austria-Hungary, then declared war on Russia and on France. In response, Great Britain, upholding its pact with France, declared war on Germany. The conflict became a world war when Japan, seeing an opportunity to rid itself of competition in China, joined the Allied cause against Germany.

Recognizing how terrible the situation had become for the civilization he had known, England's foreign secretary, Edward Grey, said: "The lamps are going out all over Europe. We shall not see them lit again in our lifetime." But with his usual grave dignity, Grey assured Parliament that Great Britain would rally to the cause of war when it "realizes what is at stake, what the real issues are." The next day, the German imperial chancellor, Theobald von Bethmann Hollweg, insisted that Germany had grown strong "in the works of peace" and that "only in defense of a just cause shall our sword fly from its scabbard." But beyond vague assertions from each side that aggression must be halted and honor upheld, little was done to define "just cause."

## The Ordeal of Neutrality

The concept of neutrality was fuzzy in international law, but the United States had traditionally insisted on the broadest possible definition. In the American view, "free ships made free goods," that is, neutral nations had the right to trade freely with all nations at war, to send their ships safely through the open seas, and to demand the safe passage of their citizens on the merchant and passenger ships of all belligerents. More was involved in upholding neutral rights than principle. The year before Europe went to war, the American economy had started to slide into a recession that threatened to rival the depression of the 1890s. American trade with Europe offered hope of ending hardship at home; a disruption of European trade would add greatly to the distress.

Great Britain was the first to step on America's neutral rights. Britain's powerful fleet controlled the seas, and it quickly set up a blockade against Germany. The United States vigorously protested British action, but Britain refused to give up its naval advantage. In the fall of 1914, the Wilson administration reluctantly accepted the British blockade, thus indicating the widespread sympathy for Britain within the State Department and beginning the fateful process of alienation from Germany. But the huge volume of war-related trade that sprang up between the United States and Britain was enough to pull the American economy out of its prewar slump. Between 1914 and the spring of 1917, exports to Britain escalated some 300 percent, while trade with Germany and its allies was reduced to the vanishing point.

Germany retaliated with a submarine blockade. This new form of combat by *Unterseebooten*, or

**"PANCHO" VILLA AND GENERAL PERSHING**
*Here in 1914 Mexican revolutionary Francisco "Pancho" Villa (center) and American general John J. Pershing (right) pose genially as allies in the struggle to overthrow the dictatorial ruler of Mexico, Victoriano Huerta. Soon afterward Villa and Pershing would be adversaries. After a raid by "Villistas" across the New Mexico border in 1915 to punish Americans for aiding Villa's revolutionary rivals, Pershing pursued Villa into Mexico.*
Corbis-Bettmann.

U-boats, posed a disturbing threat to the traditional rules of war. Unlike surface warships that could harmlessly confiscate freighters or prevent them from entering a war zone, submarines relied on surprising and sinking their quarry. And once they sank a ship, the tiny, cramped U-boats could not possibly pick up the survivors. To much of the world, submarine warfare violated notions of how a "civilized" nation should behave. Nevertheless, in February 1915, the German high command declared the waters around Britain a war zone and warned that any ship in the area would be subject to attack.

Woodrow Wilson responded harshly, declaring that the United States would regard the loss of an American ship or the loss of American lives on a belligerent ship as "a flagrant violation of neutral rights" and would hold Germany to "strict accountability." What "strict accountability" meant was still unclear when Wilson received the shocking news of the sinking of the British liner *Lusitania* off the coast of Ireland on May 7, 1915, with the loss of 1,198 lives, including 128 Americans.

American newspapers appeared with drawings of drowning women and children, and some called for war. Most Americans, however, did not want to break relations with Germany. Some pointed out that the German embassy had warned prospective passengers that the *Lusitania* carried millions of rounds of ammunition and so was a legitimate target. Bryan, speaking for the peace movement within the administration, said that a ship carrying war materiel "should not rely on passengers to protect

**SINKING OF THE LUSITANIA** *Military prowess and civilian tragedy came together with shocking effect in the sinking of the British passenger liner* Lusitania, *on May 7, 1915. Captain Walter Schwieger, commander of the German submarine U-20, who spotted the ship off the coast of Ireland, skillfully sank the great liner with a single torpedo. After watching the chaos that ensued in which more than 1,200 people lost their lives, he remembered the scene as the most awful one he had ever witnessed. For Americans, the fate of the* Lusitania *was crucial in turning public sentiment against Germany. This poster by Fred Spear captured the outrage felt at the loss of many women and almost 100 children. Nearly two years before America entered the war, posters like this urged Americans to enlist as preparation for the day when they must surely save civilization from German barbarism.*
UPI/Bettmann Archive; Library of Congress.

her from attack—it would be like putting women and children in front of an army." He argued that Wilson should instead warn American citizens using ships of belligerent countries that they traveled at their own risk.

Wilson sought a middle course that would retain his commitment to peace and neutrality without condoning German attacks on passenger ships. On May 10, he distanced himself from the interventionists by declaring that "there is such a thing as a man being too proud to fight," for which former president Theodore Roosevelt raged at him for being a "flub dub and mollycoddle" who should be too proud *not* to fight. But Wilson also rejected Bryan's position. Any further destruction of ships, Wilson warned, would be regarded as "deliberately unfriendly" and might lead the United States to break diplomatic relations with Germany. Wilson's insistence that Americans had the right to travel unharmed made Bryan realize that his pacifist hopes were doomed. When the secretary of state resigned, Wilson quickly replaced him with Robert Lansing, a veteran State Department officer and a strong advocate of the Allied cause.

For a while after the *Lusitania* crisis, the tension subsided. Germany, anxious not to provoke the United States, apologized for civilian deaths and offered an indemnity. After the sinking of the English steamer *Sussex* in 1916, at the cost of two more American lives, the German government quickly acted to head off war by promising no more submarine attacks without warning and without provisions for the safety of civilians. Observers hailed the pledge as a victory for Wilson's policy of careful negotiation between the poles of Bryan's pacifism and Roosevelt's bellicosity.

Wilson's efforts for peace served him well in his bid for reelection in 1916. Still, controversies over neutrality, intervention in Mexico, and the government's role in regulating the economy made Wilson's chances uncertain. Unlike the situation in 1912, Wilson faced a united Republican challenge after Theodore Roosevelt declined to run for the Progressive Party. Wilson's opponent was the able associate justice of the Supreme Court Charles Evans Hughes, former governor of New York. The Democratic Party ran Wilson under the slogan "He kept us out of war," but Wilson shied away from the claim, protesting that "they talk of me as though I were a god. Any little German lieutenant can push us into the war at any time by some calculated outrage." Wilson said nothing, however, when the Democrats argued that the Republican candidate was

more likely to lead the nation into war. Ultimately, Wilson's case for neutrality appealed to the majority in favor of peace. Wilson won, but by only 600,000 popular and 23 electoral votes, leaving in doubt whether he spoke for a unified nation in foreign policy.

## The United States Enters the War

In the end, the determination by the warring sides to achieve peace on their own terms scuttled any chance for a negotiated peace. The Germans refused to specify their war aims, and the Allies made mediation difficult by announcing aims that would have broken up the Austro-Hungarian Empire and required the Germans to pay damages for the war. In early January 1917, the German military high command persuaded the kaiser that the country could no longer afford to allow neutral shipping to reach Great Britain while the enemy blockade threatened to starve Germany. Germany would resume unrestricted submarine warfare at the end of the month and sink without warning any ship found in the waters off Great Britain. The German military understood that it risked war with the United States but gambled that Germany would achieve a quick military victory before the United States could bring its armed might to bear.

---

*In the end, the determination by the warring sides to achieve peace on their own terms scuttled any chance for a negotiated peace.*

---

Most of Wilson's advisers joined Theodore Roosevelt in demanding a declaration of war, but Wilson, still hoping for a peaceful way out, would only sever diplomatic relations with Germany. Then on February 25, 1917, British authorities informed Wilson of a secret telegram sent by the German foreign secretary, Arthur Zimmermann, to the German minister in Mexico. It promised that in the event of war between Germany and the United States, Germany would see that Mexico regained the territories in the Southwest it had lost in the Mexican War if Mexico would declare war against the United States. Wilson angrily responded to the Zimmermann telegram by asking Congress to approve a policy of "armed neutrality" that would allow merchant ships to fight back against any attackers.

In mid-March, German submarines sank five American vessels in the sea lanes to Britain. After agonizing over the probable consequences, the president prevailed on Congress to issue a declaration of war on April 6. No longer too proud to fight, Wilson accused Germany of "warfare against mankind." But he insisted that the destruction of Germany was not the U.S. goal. Instead, the United States fought to make the world "safe for democracy" and to "vindicate the principles of peace and justice" in which a reconstructed Germany would find a democratic place.

Wilson did not overlook the tragic difference between those lofty aims and the brutal means chosen to achieve them. He spoke despairingly to a friend just before his appearance before Congress: "Once lead this people into war, and they'll forget there ever was such a thing as tolerance. To fight you must be brutal and ruthless, and the spirit of ruthless brutality will infect Congress, the courts, the policeman on the beat, the man in the street."

## The Crusade for Democracy

Despite Wilson's misgivings, progressives hoped that war would improve the quality of American life as well as free Europe from its bondage to tyranny and militarism. The American Expeditionary Force (AEF) that eventually carried two million troops to Europe, by far the largest military venture the United States had ever undertaken on foreign soil, was trained to be morally straight and knowledgeable about the civilization it was to save. Progressive enthusiasm also powered the mobilization of industrial and agricultural production. Moreover, labor shortages caused by workers leaving the labor force for military service provided new opportunities in the booming wartime economy. Where once they had been excluded, African Americans and women found work and also gained new respect and recognition for their wartime endeavors.

To instill loyalty in a public whose ancestry was rooted in all the belligerent nations, Wilson supported indoctrination in the schools, set up a government agent to promote official propaganda, and sponsored parades, rallies, films, and other forms of patriotic expression. But with commitment to patriotism also went suppression of dissent. The government launched a harsh assault on civil liberties. In addition, mobs attacked those whom they considered disloyal. Increasingly, attachment to the war stressed emotion rather than reason, and, as Wilson predicted, the progressive ideal of rational progress and free expression suffered grievous loss as the nation undertook its crusade for democracy.

### The Call to Arms

When the United States entered the war in April 1917, the nation was woefully unprepared, even as it had become clear that the Allies could win only with massive and swift American involvement. War-weary Britain and France were virtually exhausted after almost three years of conflict. Hundreds of thousands of their soldiers had perished in the trenches; morale and food supplies were dangerously low. Russia was in turmoil: A democratic revolution had forced Tsar Nicholas II's abdication in March 1917, and eight months later the Bolshevik Revolution removed Russia from the war. To meet the demand for fighting men, food, and war materiel, the United States would have to mobilize not only an army but its economy as well.

On May 18, 1917, Wilson signed a sweeping Selective Service Act, authorizing a draft of all young men into the armed forces. Conscription soon transformed a tiny volunteer armed force of 80,000 men, spread thinly around the United States and in outposts from the Caribbean to China, into a vast army and navy. Although almost 350,000 inductees either failed to report or claimed conscientious objector status, the draft boards eventually inducted 2.8 million men into the armed services, substantially more than the 2 million who volunteered.

Eventually, almost half of the 4.8 million armed forces served in Europe. In the training camps that transformed raw recruits into fighting men, medical examinations, along with recently developed sociological and psychological techniques, took the measure of American youth. The shocking news that almost 30 percent of those drafted were rejected on physical grounds acted as a stimulus to the public health and physical education movements. Secretary of War Newton D. Baker, whose outlook had been shaped by reform crusades as mayor of Cleveland, created a Commission on Training Camp Activities staffed by YMCA workers and veterans of the settlement house and playground movements. They merged military training with games, singing, and college extension courses. The Military Draft Act of 1917 prohibited prostitution and alcohol near training camps. Never before had there been such armed encampments, which Baker described in full progressive fervor as "national universities—training schools to which the flower of American youth

**WORLD WAR I RECRUITING POSTER**
*Recruiting posters often appealed to young men's concerns about chivalry and manhood. One navy poster showed a uniform draped over a chair, with the words "It takes a man to fill it." In another, a provocative woman beckoned saying, "I want you . . . for the navy." In this poster, anxiety is the key. The fastidious appearance and somewhat languid pose of the worried civilian in his darkened interior contrasts with the bright, flag-filled outdoors of the marching troops. Of course, anyone with an ounce of spunk would go out and fall in line.*
Library of Congress.

is being sent" to fit them with an "invisible armor" of education, comradeship, and moral fitness.

Wilson's selection of General John J. Pershing to command the new American Expeditionary Force recognized the need for hard professionalism in the lead, not the sort of romantic patriotism that had given amateurs like Theodore Roosevelt the chance to command combat troops in the Spanish-American War. Pershing had graduated from West Point in the 1880s and then seen combat in the Indian wars on the plains and against the Spanish in Cuba. Pershing's impeccable military bearing and professional standing gave promise that he would carry out his duties in the cool, efficient way required of modern war on a vast scale.

When Pershing and the wide-eyed troops of the AEF marched through Paris on the Fourth of July 1917, just a week after the first troopship landed, a grateful populace showered them with flowers. At the statue of the hero who symbolized France's aid to the American Revolution, an officer stepped out and proclaimed in an inspired phrase that summed up the spirit of the occasion, "Lafayette, we are here!"

## The Progressive Stake in the War

The idea of the war as an agent of social improvement fanned the old zeal and earnestness of the progressive movement. In particular, the war captivated progressives who were believers in strong government and who had been lukewarm about Wilson's cautious New Freedom. The Wilson administration realized that Washington would have to assert greater control to mobilize the nation's resources and to avoid chaos. To oversee the transformation of the economy, the administration established a multitude of new federal war agencies to deal with specific war needs.

The War Industries Board (WIB), created to direct and stimulate industrial production, was fortunate in the choice of Bernard Baruch to head it. At once a wealthy southern gentleman, a Jewish Wall Street stockbroker, and a reform Democrat, Baruch could speak to many constituencies. Shrewdly bullying and wheedling scientists, industrialists, public administrators, and public relations experts into efficient teams, he oversaw production of everything from boots to bullets that made the American soldier the most fully equipped in the world. Only in the vital area of weaponry did the quality of American equipment lag behind that of the Europeans who had long fielded large armies.

Herbert Hoover, self-made millionaire engineer, headed the Food Administration. Sober and tireless, he led remarkably successful "Hooverizing" campaigns for "wheatless" Mondays, "meatless" Tuesdays, and other means of conserving resources. Guaranteed high prices for wheat and other staples, the American heartland not only supplied the needs of the American people and its armed forces but also became the breadbasket of

America's allies. Even the First Family, including Wilson's new wife, Edith Galt, did its part, with a White House "victory garden" and sheep munching the White House lawn in place of the gardeners, who had moved on to new work in the war effort.

---

*The idea of the war as an agent of social improvement fanned the old zeal and earnestness of the progressive movement.*

---

Washington soon bristled with hastily created agencies charged with managing the war effort. The Railroads' War Board directed railroad traffic, the Fuel Administration coordinated the coal industry and other fuel suppliers, the Shipping Board organized the merchant marine, and the National War Labor Policies Board resolved labor disputes. The administration gave progressives reason to believe that the new agencies would mediate between business and government and encourage harmony in the public interest. Buoyed by these developments, influential voices like those of philosopher-educator John Dewey and journalist-critic Walter Lippmann argued for public support of the war as a means of progressive reform at home and abroad. Industrial leaders were also cheered that, in achieving feats of production and efficiency, wartime agencies helped corporate profits triple.

To raise the $33 billion it cost to wage the war (more than the federal government's total expenses from 1789 to 1917) imaginative fundraising strategies were needed as well. Secretary of the Treasury William McAdoo, who happened to be Wilson's son-in-law, became the principal cheerleader for the purchase of war bonds, called Liberty Bonds.

Reformers also had cause to celebrate the effect of the war on the labor front. Full mobilization meant high prices for farmers and plentiful jobs in the new war industries. Aware that increased industrial production required peaceful labor relations and the avoidance of strikes, the National War Labor Policies Board and other agencies enacted the eight-hour day, a living minimum wage, and collective bargaining rights in industries that had long resisted them. Wages rose sharply during the war, and the American Federation of Labor saw its membership soar from 2.7 million to more than 5 million. After long insisting that health was a private matter, Congress bowed to the patriotic cause of providing death and disability insurance for the armed forces.

The war also provided a huge boost to the stalled moral crusade to ban alcohol. Before the war, prohibitionists had campaigned fervently for a constitutional amendment to ban the manufacture and sale of alcoholic beverages, and by 1917, nineteen states had gone dry. Liquor's opponents could now cite the war as a reason for national prohibition, which would make the cause of democracy powerful and pure. At the same time, shutting down the distilleries would save millions of bushels of grain that could feed the United States and its allies. Prohibitionists also claimed that closing breweries with German names like Schlitz, Pabst, and Anheuser-Busch would deal a blow to Kaiser Wilhelm and the German cause. Swept along by these arguments, Congress passed the Eighteenth Amendment, which banned the manufacture, transportation, and sale of alcohol, in December 1917; after swift ratification by all the states, the amendment went into effect on January 1, 1920.

## The Advance to Woman Suffrage

The war also presented new opportunities for women. More than twenty thousand women served with the armed forces, a large number of them as nurses in France. In the private sector, long-standing barriers against hiring women fell when millions of workingmen became soldiers and few new immigrant workers found safe passage across the Atlantic. The new Women's Bureau of the Department of Labor along with the Women's Trade Union League (WTUL) helped open jobs to women, often against the opposition of the major trade organization, the American Federation of Labor (AFL). For the first time, women in sizable numbers found work with the railroads and in defense plants as welders and heavy machine operators. Some gained entry to labor unions, whose members usually earned far higher wages than nonunion workers. "This is the women's age," exulted Margaret Dreier Robins, president of the WTUL. "At last . . . women are coming into the labor and festival of life on equal terms with men."

The war effort spurred women to victory in the political arena as well. Since the Seneca Falls convention of 1848, where women voiced their first formal demand for the ballot, the struggle for woman suffrage had inched forward. Using a state-by-state approach, suffragists had achieved success in Wyoming in 1890 and in several other western states in the following years, but elsewhere they met

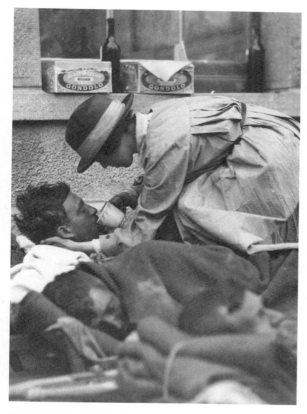

**WORLD WAR I RED CROSS WORKER**
*An American Red Cross worker gives water to a badly wounded British soldier on a French railway platform in May 1918. More than twenty thousand women served with the armed forces, many of them as nurses in France.*
National Archives.

House made the suffrage campaign impossible to ignore. Finally, Woodrow Wilson gave his support to suffrage. It would be wrong, he conceded, not to reward the "partnership of suffering and sacrifice" with a "partnership of privilege and right." In 1919, Congress passed the Nineteenth Amendment, granting women the vote, and by 1920 it had been ratified by the required two-thirds of the states. Looking back on the struggle, two suffrage leaders remarked: "How much time and patience, how much work, energy and aspiration, how much faith, how much hope, how much despair went into it."

## The "Great Migration" of African Americans

In 1900, thirty-five years after emancipation, African Americans had made little progress toward achieving full citizenship. Nine of every ten African Americans were Southerners, and disfranchisement, segregation, and violence dominated their lives. The majority of black men still toiled in agriculture, either mired in tenancy or working for wages of sixty cents a day. Black women worked in the homes of whites as domestics for two dollars or less a week. Racial violence descended on anyone whites considered "uppity." "If we own a good farm or horse, or cow, or bird-dog, or yoke of oxen," a black Mississippian observed in 1913, "we are harassed until we are bound to sell, give away, or run away, before we can have any peace in our lives."

The First World War provided African Americans with the opportunity to escape the South's cotton fields and kitchens. Blacks who were once welcome in the urban North only in personal service occupations now found work as unskilled and semiskilled industrial workers. Young black men, who made up the bulk of the migrants, found jobs in steel mills, shipyards, munitions plants, railroad yards, and mines. From 1915 to 1920, half a million blacks (approximately 10 percent of the South's black population) boarded trains bound for Philadelphia, Detroit, Cleveland, Chicago, St. Louis, and other industrial cities.

Blacks who joined the "great migration" were not just moving north. They were fleeing the South. Whole churches, almost entire communities, sometimes transplanted themselves to northern cities. By 1930, for example, Chicago claimed nearly forty thousand black Mississippians, almost as many as Jackson, Meridian, and Greenville combined. One

defeat. In New York, for example, suffragists waged a massive door-to-door referendum campaign in 1915 for an amendment to the state constitution, only to have the male electorate reject woman suffrage resoundingly. Two years later suffragists met a similar fate in Ohio (Map 22.2).

By linking their crusade for a constitutional amendment to wartime emphasis on national unity and by adopting increasingly militant tactics, the crusaders for woman suffrage finally triumphed. Women's wartime service as nurses, factory workers, and patriotic volunteers convinced many American men that women could shoulder public responsibilities. Militant suffragists, such as Alice Paul, the head of the new National Woman's Party, and women continuously picketing the White

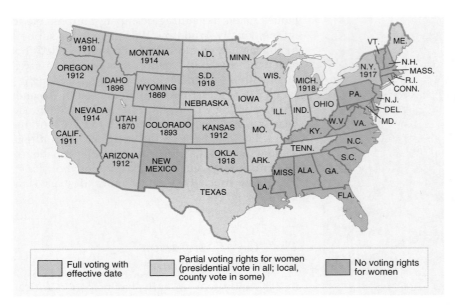

**MAP 22.2**
*Women's Voting Rights before the Nineteenth Amendment*
The long campaign for women's voting rights reversed the pioneer epic—rolling eastward from its first successes in the new democratic openness of the West toward the entrenched, male-dominated public life of the Northeast and South.

man, writing to a church congregation he'd left behind, announced proudly that he had recently been elevated to "first assistant to the head carpenter." "I should have been here twenty years ago. I just begin to feel like a man. It's a great deal of pleasure in knowing that you got some privileges. My children are going to the same school with the whites and I don't have to [h]umble to no one. I have registered—will vote the next election and there ain't any 'yes sir'—it's all yes and no and Sam and Bill."

But the North was not all milk and honey. Whites fearful of losing jobs and status lashed out against the latest immigrants. In 1918, the nation witnessed ninety-six lynchings of blacks, some of them veterans still wearing their military uniforms. Race riots ripped two dozen northern cities. One of the worst occurred on a hot July night in 1917 in East St. Louis, Illinois. A mob of whites invaded a section of the city crowded with blacks who had been recruited to help break a strike, killing at least thirty-nine people and leaving most of the black district in flames.

African Americans in the military also experienced racial violence. The most disastrous episode occurred in August 1917 when a group of armed black soldiers went to Houston, Texas, to avenge incidents of harassment by the police. In the clash that followed, thirteen whites, including several policemen, and one black soldier were killed. With vengeful swiftness that denied any appeal to the War Department, thirteen of the black soldiers were hanged and forty-one others sentenced to life imprison-

ment. Black leaders charged grimly that the incident demonstrated the tragic shortcomings of America's crusade for democracy. (See the Historical Question on page 598.)

## The Struggle over National Purpose

From the moment war broke out in Europe in 1914, Wilson's foreign policy had become a lightning rod for interventionists and noninterventionists alike. When Wilson finally did commit the nation to war, most peace advocates rallied around the flag. The Carnegie Endowment for International Peace, for example, issued a resolution that "the most effectual means of promoting peace is to prosecute the war against the Imperial German Government" and adopted new stationery with the heading "Peace through Victory."

As prewar peace societies converted from pacifism to patriotism, a handful of new groups took up the cause of peace. As early as 1914, a group of professional women, led by settlement house leader Jane Addams and economics professor Emily Greene Balch, convened to resist what Addams described as "the pathetic belief in the regenerative results of war." The Women's Peace Party that emerged in 1915 and its foreign affiliates in the Women's International League for Peace and Freedom (WILPF) led the struggle to persuade governments to negotiate peace and spare dissenters from harsh punishment. It was discouraging, unpopular work. Participants were routinely labeled cowards and traitors, their efforts crushed by the steamroller of war enthusiasm.

Wilson's major strategy for fending off criticism of the war was to stir up patriotism with fervent flag-waving. In 1917, the president created the Committee on Public Information (CPI) under the direction of George Creel, a progressive journalist who thumped for the war like a cheerleader at the big game. He sent "Four-Minute Men," a squad of 75,000 volunteers, around the country to give brief pep talks and distribute millions of press releases that described successes on the battlefields and in the factories. But information and education slid easily into propaganda. The CPI created a stream of posters, pamphlets, and cartoons that depicted brave American soldiers and sailors defending freedom and democracy against the evil Hun.

To help Creel's campaign, the film industry cranked out reels of melodrama about battle-line and home-front heroes and induced audiences to hiss at the German kaiser as "the Beast of Berlin." Colleges and universities churned out war propaganda in the guise of scholarship and added courses presenting the war as a culmination of the age-old struggle for civilization. When Professor James McKeen Cattell of Columbia made known his view that America should seek peace with Germany short of victory, university president Nicholas Murray Butler fired him. In a blunt summation of the campaign for patriotic conformity, Butler declared in his 1917 commencement address that "what had been folly is now treason."

A firestorm of anti-German passion swept the nation. Campaigns with the slogan "100% American" enlisted ordinary people to act as vigilantes sniffing out disloyalty and treason. German, the most widely taught foreign language in 1914, virtually disappeared from the high school and college curriculum. German-born Americans were ostracized, including Karl Muck, conductor of the Boston Symphony Orchestra, and the renowned violinist Fritz Kreisler, who were driven from the concert stage. The rabid attempt to punish the enemy reached its extreme with the lynching of Robert Prager in Collinsville, Illinois. In the atmosphere of mob rule, it was enough that Prager was German-born and had socialist leanings, even

**AFRICAN AMERICANS MIGRATE NORTH**

*These newcomers to a northern city in 1912 pose in their best dress on the threshold of a changed life. Several factors combined to prompt almost four and a half million African Americans to leave the South by midcentury. To the burden of racism was added the steady erosion of opportunities to make a living. In the 1920s, many rural blacks lost work when a boll weevil invasion reduced the cotton crop drastically. Subsequently, mechanization and government programs to support crop prices by reducing acreage drove many more people off the land.* Schomburg Center for Research in Black Culture, New York Public Library.

# What Did the War Mean to African Americans?

WHEN THE UNITED STATES ENTERED the First World War, some black leaders remembered the crucial role of African American soldiers in the Civil War. They rejoiced that military service would again offer blacks a chance to prove their worth. Robert Moton, president of the nation's foremost black college, Tuskegee Institute, recollected clearly when that thought had come to him. He was sitting in the midst of "dignified bankers [and] merchants" gathered in the Waldorf-Astoria Hotel in New York City to promote the sale of Liberty Bonds. At that moment of patriotic inclusion, Moton "could not but feel that my people by their contribution, their loyalty, and their spirit . . . realized fully that they are heirs of America, and that as such they must be sharers of her struggles as well as partakers of her glory."

More surprising was the support for the war voiced by W. E. B. Du Bois. Known for his bold dissent against the white power structure, Du Bois shocked many readers with his editorial in the NAACP's journal *Crisis*, urging blacks to "close ranks" and "forget our special grievances" until after a unified nation had won the war. The enemy of the moment, Du Bois insisted, was German "military despotism." Unchecked, that despotism "spells death to the aspirations of Negroes and all darker races for equality, freedom, and democracy."

Although critics bitterly assailed Du Bois for not demanding equal treatment for blacks who fought for their country, African Americans generally followed his advice and closed ranks. On the first day of registration for military service, more than 700,000 black men signed in at their draft boards. By war's end, 370,000 blacks had been inducted, some 31 percent of the total registered. The figure for whites was 26 percent.

During training, black recruits suffered the same prejudices that they had encountered in civilian life. Rigidly segregated, they were usually assigned to labor battalions. They faced crude abuse and miserable conditions. One base in Virginia that trained blacks as cargo handlers quartered troops in tents without floors or stoves and provided no changes of clothes, no blankets for the winter—not even facilities for bathing. Only several deaths from disease and exposure moved the authorities to make conditions barely tolerable.

When black soldiers began arriving in Europe, white commanders made a point of maintaining racial distinctions. A special report from the headquarters of the American commander, General John J. Pershing, advised the French that their failure to draw the color line threatened Franco-American relations. They should resist the urge, the report declared, to accept blacks as equals or to thank them for their efforts, for fear of "spoiling the Negroes."

Under such circumstances, German propagandists raised some painful questions. One leaflet distributed by the Germans to black troops reminded them that they lacked the rights that whites enjoyed and that they were segregated and were often lynched. "Why, then, fight the Germans," the leaflet asked, "only for the benefit of the Wall Street robbers and to protect the millions they have loaned to the British, French, and Italians?" Why, indeed?

Black soldiers hoped to prove a point. While they worked at first mainly as laborers and stevedores, before long they had their chance to fight. In February 1918, General Pershing received an urgent call from the French for help in the Meuse-Argonne sector. Reluctant to lose command over the white troops he valued the most, he sent black soldiers—the 369th, 370th, 371st, and 372nd Regiments of the 92nd Division—to the front, where they were integrated into units of the French army. In the 191 days spent in battle—longer than the time spent by any other American outfit—the 369th Regiment won the most medals of any American combat unit, more than one hundred Croix de Guerre alone, and had no prisoners taken. In June 1918, the French high command paid its highest respect by asking the Americans to send all the black troops they could spare.

When the battle-scarred survivors of the 92nd Division returned home, they marched proudly past cheering crowds in Manhattan and Chicago. Black spokesmen proclaimed a new era for black Americans. In May 1919, Du Bois argued that it was time for African Americans to collect what was due them. "We return from fighting," Du Bois declared. "We return fighting. Make way for Democracy. We saved it in France, and by the Great Jehovah, we will save it in the U.S.A., or know the reason why."

Reasons soon presented themselves. Segregation remained entrenched, and its defenders continued to hold power in Congress and in the White

**AFRICAN AMERICAN MACHINE GUN COMPANY**
*This company from the 370th Regiment of the Illinois National Guard, shown early in their training, exemplifies the proud determination of black soldiers to prove their worth in battle. Once in France, the 370th encountered resistance from American commanders reluctant to use combat-ready black troops for anything but hard labor behind the lines. When desperation in the face of a German offensive in the spring of 1918 gave them the chance to fight with French units, the 370th showed its mettle and received the Croix de Guerre. Adding to the irony of black soldiers having to gain respect as Americans by serving with the French was the fact that the first black soldier from Lincoln's state of Illinois to fall in battle was a private named Robert E. Lee.*
Picture Research Consultants and Archives.

House. Postwar recession left blacks worse off economically than before their wartime glory and also made them scapegoats for white resentments. Whites launched race riots against blacks in two dozen cities. The willingness of blacks to stand their ground showed a more determined self-esteem, but it also meant more suffering from escalating violence. Nor did the armed services permanently offer new opportunities. Until the late 1940s, after the next world war, the American military remained segregated and almost devoid of black officers. Discrimination extended even beyond the ultimate sacrifice. When the organizers of a trip to France for parents of soldiers lost in the First World War announced that the boat would be segregated, black mothers felt honor-bound to decline the offer to visit the cemeteries where their sons lay.

It took decades for the nation to recognize the sacrifice and heroism of black soldiers in France. As one critic observed about the 92nd Division, "the

example [they set] was so bright that most eyes closed against it." But in 1991, as the nation cheered American success in the Persian Gulf War, Americans began to see the light. A Defense Department investigating team, though insisting it had found no evidence of discrimination in the fact that none of the 127 Medals of Honor awarded during World War I had gone to blacks, declared that the time had come to correct an "administrative oversight." For leading a charge on September 28, 1918, up a German-held hill that cost him and 40 percent of his company their lives, Corporal Freddie Stowers would receive the Medal of Honor—until then the only one attained by an African American in the world wars. The slain soldier's elderly sister, who had survived seventy-three years to accept the award for her hero brother, could take solace that recognition came under the command of General Colin Powell, the first black chairman of the Joint Chiefs of Staff.

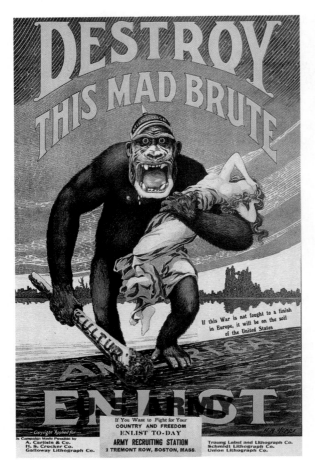

**PROPAGANDA POSTER**
*All the primal fears of rape, invasion, and violence at the hands of a monster wielding the weapon of "Kultur" are brought together in this 1916 scare poster. Germans so resented the dehumanizing portrait of themselves that in World War II, Nazi propagandists reproduced the poster with the warning that the poster had really been telling the American people to "destroy the German people."*
Library of Congress.

though he had not opposed American participation in the war. The defense lawyer for the drunken men who attacked Prager praised what he called a "patriotic murder." The local jury took only twenty-five minutes to acquit.

As hysteria increased, absurdity mingled with cruelty. In Montana, a school board barred a history text that had good things to say about medieval Germany. Menus across the nation changed German toast to French toast and sauerkraut to liberty cab-

bage. The fearful saw evidence of the enemy everywhere. One vigilant citizen claimed to see a periscope in the Great Lakes, and on the dunes of Cape Cod the fiancée of one of the war's leading critics was caught dancing and was held on suspicion of signaling to German submarines.

---

*A firestorm of anti-German passion swept the nation.*

---

The Wilson administration suppressed dissent with a zeal that contrasted ironically with its commitment to defend democracy. In the name of self-defense the Espionage Act (June 1917), the Trading with the Enemy Act (October 1917), and the Sedition Act (May 1918) gave the government sweeping powers to punish any opinion it considered "disloyal, profane, scurrilous, or abusive" of the American flag or uniform. Postmaster General Albert Burleson blocked mailing privileges for publications he personally considered disloyal; a number of independent-minded journals were forced to close down, including the leading literary magazine *Seven Arts*. Of the fifteen hundred individuals eventually charged with sedition, all but a dozen had merely spoken words the government found objectionable. One of them was Eugene V. Debs, the leader of the Socialist Party, who was convicted under the Espionage Act for speeches condemning the war as a capitalist plot and was sent to the Atlanta penitentiary.

The president also hoped that national commitment to the war would subdue partisan politics. He could not legitimately repress his Republican rivals, however, and they found many opportunities to use the war as a weapon against the Democrats. The trick was to oppose Wilson's conduct of the war but not the war itself. For example, Republicans outshouted Wilson on the nation's need to mobilize for war but then complained that Wilson's War Industries Board was a tyrannical agency that crushed free enterprise. Republican attacks appealed to widely diverse business, labor, and patriotic groups. With each month of the war, Republicans gathered power against the coalition of Democrats and progressives that had narrowly reelected Wilson in 1916.

Wilson erred when he attempted to make the off-year congressional elections of 1918 a referendum on his leadership. Instead, amidst criticism of the White House for playing politics with the war, Republicans gained a narrow majority in both the House and the Senate. The end of Democratic control of Congress not only suspended any possibility of further domestic reform but also meant that the United States would advance toward military victory with authority divided between a Democratic presidency and a Republican Congress.

## Over There

As the struggle over leadership and war aims unfolded at home, the American Expeditionary Force gathered strength in Europe. At the front, however, the AEF discovered a desperate situation. The three-year-old war had degenerated into a stalemate of armies dug defensively into miles of trenches across France. Soldiers huddled in the stinking mud, separated from the enemy by only a few hundred yards of "no-man's-land." When ordered "over the top," troops raced furiously toward the enemy's trenches, only to be entangled in barbed wire, enveloped in poison gas, and mowed down by machine guns. Only with tragic slowness did commanders realize the impasse of modern warfare. After three days of futile attempts to mount an assault at the Battle of the Somme in 1916, French and British forces lost 600,000 (dead and wounded), while German losses reached 500,000. At the end of the ghastly campaign, the French and British had advanced their trenches only a few miles across devastated land.

To General Pershing, the tactics of stalemate violated the lessons that Civil War veterans had given him at West Point and that he had put in practice in swift, mobile warfare on the plains and in Cuba. His commitment was to what has been termed the "American way of war"—heavy frontal pressure through weight of numbers combined with swift surprise attacks on the flanks of infantry and cavalry. Pershing thus refused to allow his fresh new army to merge with French and British units, despite the protests of the Allied commander in chief, General Ferdinand Foch. Pershing would save his soldiers for the moment when a series of lightning strikes might prove decisive.

In the best army fashion, then, American troops hurried to France, only to wait. They saw almost no combat in 1917, instead using most of their free time to see the sights. American officials did not object to some tourism; but they became flustered when French Premier Georges Clemenceau offered to supply American troops with licensed prostitutes.

Sightseeing ended abruptly in March 1918 when the Germans launched a massive offensive aimed at French ports on the Atlantic. After six thousand cannons let loose the heaviest barrage in history, a million German soldiers smashed a hole forty miles deep into the French and British lines west of the

**AVENUE OF THE ALLIES**
*Childe Hassam, the impressionist painter famous for his colorful portrayals of New York City, expressed his strong support of World War I through a series of paintings of flags draped along the "Avenue of the Allies" section of Fifth Avenue. This 1918 painting featuring French flags had great emotional impact on its viewers as American troops were fighting in France, helping to bring the war to a close. A French critic praised Hassam's uniquely American character: "No one had ever painted flags before; so now when one thinks of flags one thinks of Hassam's flag pictures. . . . He made the flags symbols of his heritage."*
Musée National de la Cooperation Franco-Americaine © photo RMN-Jean.

Somme River at a cost of a quarter of a million casualties on each side. Paris became gripped with the greatest terror of the war when shells fired eighty miles away by "Big Bertha" cannons began falling on the city. More than a thousand civilians died, and a mood of defeatism began to rise. Pershing, who had waited impatiently for months for a call to the front, visited Foch to ask for the "great honor" of becoming "engaged in the greatest battle in history." Foch agreed to Pershing's terms of a separate American command and in May assigned a combined army and marine force to the central sector.

Once committed, the Americans remained true to their way of war. At Cantigny and then at Château-Thierry, the fresh but green Americans checked the German advance with a series of dashing assaults (Map 22.3). Then they headed toward the forest stronghold of Belleau Wood. The American force, with the Fifth and Sixth Marine Regiments in the lead, made its way against streams of refugees and retreating Allied soldiers who cried that the Germans had won: "*La guerre est finie! (The war is over!)*" But when a French officer commanded the marines to turn and retreat with them, the American commander replied sharply, "Retreat, hell. We just got here." After charging through a wheat field against withering machine gun fire, the marines plunged into a hand-to-hand forest battle of stalking and ambush. Victory came hard. On the single day of June 6, 1918, the marine spearhead lost 1,087 men, more than had been killed in the previous 143 years of marine corps history. In praise of the enemy's spirit, a German report noted that "the Americans' nerves are not yet worn out." Indeed, it was German morale that was on the verge of cracking.

**MAP 22.3**
*The American Expeditionary Force, 1917–1918*
In the last year of the war, the American Expeditionary Force joined the French army on the western front to counterattack the final German offensive and pursue the retreating enemy until surrender.

In July 1918, the Allies launched a massive counteroffensive that would end the war. A quarter of a million American troops joined in the rout of German forces along the Marne River. In September, more than a million Americans joined the assault that threw the Germans back from positions along the Meuse River. American forces drove toward the town of Sedan, where the French had lost a war to Germany in 1870 and whose capture was thus of great symbolic importance. In early November, the Allies overran stubborn German resistance around Sedan and sent the survivors trudging northward. Soon after, a revolt against the German government sent Kaiser Wilhelm fleeing to Holland. On November 11, 1918, a delegation from the newly established German republic met with the French high command in a railroad car in Compiègne to sign an armistice that brought the fighting to an end.

The adventure of the AEF was brief, bloody, and victorious—just the right combination to fix vivid memories of a successful crusade. When Germany resumed unrestricted U-boat warfare in 1917, it had gambled that it could defeat Britain and France before the Americans could raise and train an army and ship it to France. The German military had miscalculated. Of the 2 million American troops in Europe, 1.3 million saw at least some action. Some 112,000 soldiers of the AEF perished, their deaths divided equally between wounds and disease. Another 230,000 Americans suffered casualties but survived, many of them with permanent physical and psychological disabilities. Only the Civil War, lasting for a much longer period, had been more costly in American lives. European nations suffered much greater losses, however: 2.2 million Germans, 1.9 million Russians, 1.4 million French, and 900,000 Britons. Where they had fought and died, the landscape was as blasted and barren as the moon.

# A Compromised Peace

Wilson decided to reaffirm his noble war aims by announcing his peace aims even before the end of hostilities was in sight. He hoped that America's allies would rally around his generous ideas. He soon discovered, however, that his plan for international democracy did not receive ready acceptance by European heads of state. The leaders of England, France, and Italy understood that Wilson's principles jeopardized their own postwar plans for

the acquisition of enemy territory, new colonial empires, and reparations. In his effort to draw public opinion to his side, Wilson also had to confront bitter political opposition at home.

## Wilson's Fourteen Points

On January 8, 1918, ten months before the armistice in Europe, President Wilson delivered a speech to Congress that summarized American war aims and revealed his vision of a liberal peace. In his famous list of "Fourteen Points," Wilson provided a blueprint for a new democratic world order. The first five points affirmed basic liberal ideals: "open covenants of peace, openly arrived at," that is, an end to secret treaties; freedom of the seas in war and peace; removal of economic barriers to free trade; reduction of weapons of war; and recognition of the rights of colonized peoples. The next eight points supported the right to self-determination of European peoples who had been dominated by Germany or its allies. Wilson's final point called for a "general association of nations"—a League of Nations—to provide "mutual guarantees of political independence and territorial integrity to great and small states alike." The insistence on a League of Nations reflected Wilson's lifelong dream of a "parliament of man." Only such an organization, he believed, could resolve and justify the war. Wilson concluded his speech by pledging that the United States would welcome Germany into the family of "peace-loving nations," if it would renounce its militarism and imperialism.

---

*In his famous list of "Fourteen Points," Wilson provided a blueprint for a new democratic world order.*

---

The Fourteen Points roused popular enthusiasm in the United States and every Allied country. Armed with such public support, Wilson felt confident that he could prevail against undemocratic forces at the peace table. During the final year of the war, he pressured the Allies to accept the Fourteen Points as the basis of the settlement. But he also conveyed his willingness, if necessary, to speak over the heads of government leaders directly to the people and so expand his role as spokesman for American citizens to the grand role of champion of all the world's people. The Allies had won the war; Wilson would win the peace.

## The Paris Peace Conference

Buoyed by his sense of mission, Wilson decided to attend the Paris peace conference in 1919 as head of the American delegation himself. The decision to leave the country at a time when his opponents were sharply contesting his leadership was risky enough; but his stubborn refusal to include prominent Republicans in the delegation proved foolhardy.

The peace venture began well. As Wilson's motorcade made its way from the port of Le Havre to Paris, huge crowds cheered the American president. After four terrible years of war, Europeans looked upon Wilson as someone who would create a safer, more decent world. When the peace conference convened at Louis XIV's palace at Versailles, however, Wilson encountered a very different reception. Rep-

resenting the Allies were the decidedly unidealistic David Lloyd George of Britain, Georges Clemenceau of France, and Vittorio Orlando of Italy. To them, Wilson was a naive and impractical man whose desire to reconcile former foes within a new international democratic order showed that he understood little about hard European realities. The Allies wanted to fasten blame for the war on Germany, totally disarm it, and make it pay so dearly that it would never threaten its neighbors again. The French, in particular, demanded retribution in the form of territory containing some of Germany's richest mineral resources.

Wilson was forced to make drastic compromises. In return for French moderation of territorial claims, Wilson agreed to support Article 231 of the peace treaty, assigning war guilt to Germany. Though saved from the permanent loss of Rhineland territory occupied by the French, Germany was outraged at being singled out as the instigator of the war and saddled with more than $33 billion in damages. Many Germans felt that their nation had been stabbed in the back. After agreeing to an armistice on the belief that peace terms would be based on Wilson's generous Fourteen Points, they faced hardship and humiliation instead.

Wilson had better success in establishing the principle of self-determination. On that basis the conference redrew the map of Europe. Portions of the Austro-Hungarian Empire were ceded to Italy, Poland, and Romania, and the remainder was reassembled into Austria, Hungary, Czechoslovakia, and Yugoslavia—independent republics with boundaries determined according to concentrations of ethnic groups. More arbitrarily, the Ottoman Empire was carved up into small mandates (including Palestine) under the control of France and Great Britain, partly to meet Allied concerns about stability in the Middle East and partly in accord with historical patterns of national sovereignty. Thus, with varying degrees of danger from ethnic and nationalist rivalries, each reconstructed nation faced the challenge of trying to make a new democratic government work (Map 22.4).

Wilson hoped that self-determination would also be the fate of Germany's colonies in Asia and Africa. But the Allies who had taken over the colonies during the war would go no further than allowing the League of Nations a mandate to administer them. Technically, the mandate system rejected imperialism. But is also denied self-determination to the former German colonies, even as the Allies retained their own colonial empires.

The cause of democratic equality suffered another setback when the peace conference refused to

**THE BIG FOUR**

*Cynics who sought a glimpse behind the flags and victory parades suspected that the world war had been orchestrated by leading politicians, bankers, and industrialists for their own advantage. This cartoon was typical of the view that deals struck behind closed doors made a mockery of Wilson's profession that "open covenants of peace, openly arrived at" would "make the world safe for democracy."*
Catherine LeRoy/AP, print courtesy Time Inc. Picture Collection.

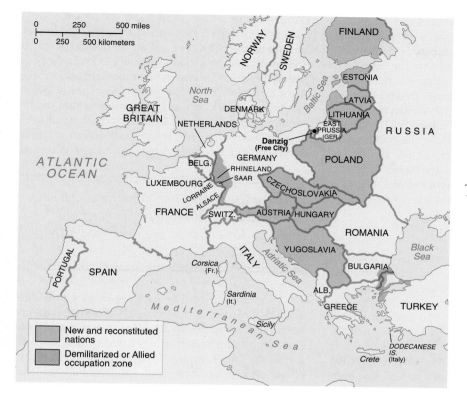

**MAP 22.4**
*Europe after World War I*
*The post–World War I settlement redrew boundaries to create new nations based on ethnic groupings. This left bitter peoples within defeated Germany and Russia who resolved to recover territory that the new arrangements took from their homelands.*

endorse Japan's proposal for a clause proclaiming the principle of racial equality. Wilson's belief in the superiority of whites, as well as his apprehension about how Americans would respond to such a declaration, led him to oppose the clause. To soothe hurt feelings, Wilson agreed to grant Japan a mandate over the Shantung Peninsula in northern China, which had formerly been controlled by Germany. The gesture mollified Japan's moderate leaders, but the military faction getting ready to take over the country used bitterness toward racist Western colonialism to build support for expanding Japanese power throughout Asia.

Revolutionary upheaval also affected the dream to make the world safe for democracy. Most important was the revolution in Russia in March 1917, after terrible defeats in the war, that forced Tsar Nicholas II to abdicate. Wilson, who was just then leading his country into war, greeted the Russian Revolution as confirmation that democracy would rise from the ashes of war's destruction. In reckless enthusiasm, Wilson declared that Russia had always been "democratic at heart." A very different reality soon emerged, however. Marxist radicals calling themselves Bolsheviks seized control of the nation in November 1917 and made their leader,

Vladimir Ilyich Lenin, ruler of the revolutionary state that came to be known as the Soviet Union. On December 15, 1917, Lenin concluded a separate peace with Germany. To make matters worse for Wilsonian idealists, Lenin insisted that the war was being fought not for democracy but to extend capitalist power. Outraged by what he considered the Bolsheviks' betrayal of the Russian Revolution and the war for democracy, Wilson reacted as he had to the Mexican revolution by refusing to recognize the new Russian government.

Respect for self-determination kept Wilson from agreeing with British leader Winston Churchill that "the Bolshevik infant should be strangled in its cradle" by direct military action. Nonetheless, in September 1918 the president did send fourteen thousand troops to Siberia to join British and French forces assisting a Russian army loyal to the tsar that was battling to overthrow Lenin and annul the Bolshevik Revolution. American opinion divided significantly. A few observers believed that the war had created possibilities for suffering millions to overthrow the tyrants who had oppressed them. Most Americans, however, saw the outcome as evidence that the cause of democracy had fallen short and left the world full of radical menace.

To many Europeans and Americans whose hopes had been stirred by Wilson's lofty aims, the Versailles treaty came as a bitter disappointment. Wilson's admirers were shocked that the president dealt in compromise, like any other politician. But without Wilson's presence, the treaty that was signed on June 28, 1919, would surely have been more vindictive. Wilson returned home in July 1919 consoled that, despite his many frustrations, he had gained what he most wanted—creation of the League of Nations. His hopes rested on the belief that the league could remedy the imperfections born of compromise and provide peace its strongest ally.

## The Fight for the Treaty

The tumultuous reception Wilson received when he arrived home persuaded him, probably correctly, that the American people supported the treaty. On July 10, 1919, the president submitted the treaty to the Senate, warning that failure to ratify it would "break the heart of the world." By then, news of the treaty's provisions had spread, and criticism was mounting, especially from Americans concerned that their countries of ethnic origin had not been given fair treatment. Even Wilson's liberal supporters worried that the president's concessions at Versailles had jeopardized the treaty's capacity to provide a generous plan for rebuilding Europe and to guarantee the peace.

Some of the most potent critics were found in the Senate, which would have to ratify the treaty. Bolstered by a slight Republican majority in Congress, a group of Republican "irreconcilables," which included such powerful isolationist senators as Hiram Johnson of California and William Borah of Idaho, condemned the treaty for entangling the United States in world affairs. A larger group of Republicans did not object to U.S. participation in world politics but feared that membership in the League of Nations would jeopardize the nation's independence in foreign affairs. No Republican, in any case, was eager to hand Wilson and the Democrats a foreign policy victory with the 1920 presidential election little more than a year away.

At the center of Republican opposition was Wilson's archenemy, Senator Henry Cabot Lodge of Massachusetts. Before Wilson had entered politics, Lodge, with his Ph.D. and historical publications, had become known as "the Scholar of the Senate." It rankled Lodge to be eclipsed by a rival of greater intellectual eminence who had also risen above him politically to become president. That injured pride tended to inflame Lodge's opposition to Wilson's Democratic reforms and to deepen Lodge's resentment at being left off the peace delegation. Lodge was no isolationist, however. Like his friend Theodore Roosevelt, who had died in January 1919, Lodge expected the United States' economic might and strong army and navy to propel the nation into a major role in world affairs. But Lodge insisted that membership in the League of Nations, which would require collective action to maintain peace, threatened the nation's freedom of choice in foreign relations.

> *To many Europeans and Americans whose hopes had been stirred by Wilson's lofty aims, the Versailles treaty came as a bitter disappointment.*

To undermine public support of Wilson, Lodge used his position as chairman of the Senate Foreign Relations Committee to air every sort of complaint. Out of the committee hearings came several amendments, or "reservations," that sought to limit the consequences of American membership in the league. For example, several reservations required approval of both the House and the Senate before the United States could participate in league-sponsored economic sanctions or military action. Eventually, it became clear that ratification of the treaty depended on acceptance of the Lodge reservations. Democratic senators, who overwhelmingly supported the treaty, urged Wilson to accept the reservations, arguing that they left the essentials of the treaty intact. Wilson, however, insisted that the reservations amounted to a "nullification" of the treaty. He expressed personal frustration as well. "*Lodge* reservations?" he thundered. "Never! I'll never consent to adopt any policy with which that impossible name is so prominently identified."

With the treaty about to be reported from the Foreign Relations Committee to the full Senate with reservations attached, Wilson decided to take his case directly to the people. On September 3, 1919, he set out by train on the most ambitious speaking tour ever undertaken by a president. Always uncomfortable with stump speaking and warned by his doctors that his health would not stand the strain, Wilson nevertheless became more eloquent, more forceful each week. But in Pueblo, Colorado, on September 25, just as his appeal seemed to be gaining momentum, Wilson collapsed and had to return to Washington. There he suffered a massive stroke that partially paralyzed him. From his bedroom, Wilson sent messages through his wife and cabinet instructing Democrats in the Senate to hold firm against any and all reservations. In the end, Wilson commanded enough loyalty to ensure a vote against the Lodge reservations. But when the treaty came up for a vote in the Senate in March 1920, the combined opposition of the Republican irreconcilables and Republican reservationists left Wilson six votes short of the two-thirds majority needed for passage.

The nations of Europe then went about organizing the league at Geneva, Switzerland, but the United States never became a member. Whether American membership could have prevented another war in Europe in 1939 is debatable, but America's failure to join certainly left the league a much weaker institution. Brought low by their feud, Woodrow Wilson and Henry Cabot Lodge both died in 1924, never seeing international order or security, never knowing the whirlwind that would eventually follow the failure to make the world safe for democracy.

## Postwar Change

The defeat of Wilson's idealistic hopes for international democracy was the crowning blow to progressives at home who had hoped that the war could serve as a vehicle for reform. The reaction against idealism included an urge to demobilize swiftly. In the process, servicemen, defense workers, and farmers lost their connection to national purpose and much of their economic security. The combination of displaced veterans returning home, a stalled economy, and leftover wartime patriotism looking for a new cause was so volatile that it could hardly fail to explode.

### Economic Hardship and Labor Upheaval

With the armistice came the need to convert the United States back to a peacetime economy. The impulse to end the wartime experiment in government-business cooperation, dismantle the federal agencies responsible for war production, and return to free enterprise proved irresistible to economic and political leaders. Deconversion of the economy and demobilization of the armed forces came swiftly and was largely unplanned. The government simply abandoned its wartime controls on the economy and almost overnight canceled millions of dollars in orders for war materiel. In a matter of months, more than three million soldiers were mustered out of the military with only sixty dollars and a one-

way ticket home. When war production ceased and veterans flooded the job market, unemployment rose sharply. At the same time, consumers went on a postwar spending spree, and inflation soared. In 1919, prices rose an astonishing 75 percent over pre-war levels, and in 1920, while inflation slowed, prices rose another 28 percent.

Labor had enjoyed a share of wartime prosperity, but most of the gains for workers evaporated in the postwar period. Business, freed from control and eager to restore the more favorable position it held before the war, turned against the eight-hour day and declared war on labor unions. Rather than sit back and watch inflation eat up their paychecks and bosses destroy their unions, workers fought back. The year 1919 witnessed nearly 3,600 strikes involving four million workers.

The most spectacular strike occurred in February 1919 in Seattle, where large numbers of metalworkers and shipbuilders had been put out of work by demobilization. When a coalition of the radical Industrial Workers of the World (IWW) and the moderate American Federation of Labor (AFL) called a general strike, the largest work stoppage in American history shut down the city for several days. Nationwide, elected officials and newspaper editorials echoed claims in the Seattle *Times* that the walkout was "a Bolshevik effort to start a revolution" engineered by "Seattle labor criminals." An effort to deport strike leaders failed because they were citizens, not aliens, but the suppression of the strike by Seattle's anti-union mayor, Ole Hanson, and widespread alarm about radicalism cost the AFL much of the support it had gained through the war and contributed to the destruction of the IWW soon afterward.

Labor strife climaxed in the grim steel strike of 1919. Steelworkers had serious grievances, but for decades the steel industry had succeeded in beating back all their efforts to unionize. In 1919, however, the AFL, still led by its founding father, Samuel Gompers, decided it was time to try again in the face of the industry's plan to revert to seven-day weeks, twelve-hour days, and weekly wages of about twenty dollars. Having loyally supported the government's war effort, the AFL expected federal support for unionization. When Gompers began to recruit union members, however, he learned that he faced the steel barons alone. When U.S. Steel and Bethlehem Steel refused to negotiate with the AFL, Gompers called for a strike; 350,000 workers in fifteen states walked out in September 1919.

The steel industry hired 30,000 strikebreakers (many of them African Americans) and turned public opinion against the strikers by portraying them as

### RETURNING VETERANS AND WORK

*After the triumphal parades passed by, attention turned to the question of what the heroes would do at home. This Department of Labor poster tries to convey a strong image of purposefulness and prosperity by framing a soldier in a victory arch in front of a booming industrial landscape. Under the circumstances, though, the soldier can best be regarded as a displaced person, teetering on a windowsill, dangerously high in the air. The U.S. Employment Service had little to offer veterans beyond posters such as this; and unions were unprepared to cope with the massive numbers of former soldiers who needed retraining. As workplace conditions deteriorated, the largest number of strikes in the nation's history broke out in 1919. The Chicago steel strikers in the photograph look very different from the returning soldier in the poster. Their fate was to lose the strike and return to harsh conditions. No record was kept of ex-servicemen, left to find their own way in the postwar world.*

Library of Congress; UPI/Bettmann Archive.

Bolsheviks bent on subverting the Republic. State and federal troops blocked union members from getting close to the steel mills to discourage scabs from crossing their picket line. In January 1920, after eighteen workers had been killed, the strike collapsed. That devastating defeat initiated a sharp decline in the fortunes of the labor movement, a trend that would continue for almost twenty years.

## The Red Scare

Response to labor strikes was one manifestation of a general fear of internal subversion that swept the nation in 1919. The "Red scare" of that time, which far outstripped the assault on civil liberties during the war, had homegrown causes in the postwar recession, labor unrest, and the difficulties of reintegrating millions of returning veterans. But unsettling events abroad also added to Americans' anxieties. Russian bolshevism became even more menacing in March 1919 when the new Soviet leaders created the Third International to foment revolution in capitalist countries. The chance of a Communist revolution in the United States was zero, but a flurry of isolated terrorist acts in 1919, most notably thirty-eight bombs mailed to prominent Americans, made it seem to edgy Americans that revolutionaries were at the door. Although the post office intercepted all but one of the bombs, fear, anger, and uncertainty about the motives of terrorists led swiftly to a hunt for scapegoats. In 1919 and 1920, Attorney General A. Mitchell Palmer led an assault on alleged conspirators. Targeting men and women who had broken no laws but who harbored what Palmer considered ideas that could lead to violence, the Justice Department unleashed a witch-hunt against the supposed enemies of America.

In January 1920, Palmer ordered a series of raids that netted six thousand alleged subversives. Though he did not find the plans for revolution and caches of weapons he had suspected, Palmer nevertheless ordered five hundred of the suspects deported. His order came in the midst of a campaign against the most notorious radical alien, Russian-born Emma Goldman. Before the war, Goldman's passionate support of labor strikes, women's rights, and birth control had made her a leading symbol of outspoken disrespect for mainstream opinion. Finally, after a stay in prison for attacking military conscription, she was ordered deported by the fervent young director of the Radical Division of the Justice Department, J. Edgar Hoover. In December 1919, as Goldman and 250 other unwanted alien radicals boarded a ship for exile in the Soviet Union, the unchastened

rebel turned on the gangplank to thumb her nose at a jeering crowd and disappeared onto the deck.

The effort to rid the country of alien radicals was matched by efforts to crush radicals entitled to remain. The climax was reached on Armistice Day, November 11, 1919, in Centralia, Washington. A rugged lumber town, Centralia contained one of only two IWW halls left in the state. Rumors circulated that the hall would be raided on the first anniversary of the end of the war. When a menacing crowd gathered in front of the hall, nervous IWW members fired into the crowd, killing three people. Three IWW members were arrested and later convicted of murder, but another, an ex-soldier, was carried off by a mob that castrated him and then, after hanging him from a bridge, riddled his body with bullets. A scattering of other law enforcement officials, taking to that style of vigilante patriotism, also staged raids to rid their cities and towns of "Reds."

*The chance of a Communist revolution in the United States was zero, but a flurry of isolated terrorist acts in 1919 made it seem to edgy Americans that revolutionaries were at the door.*

Public institutions joined the attack on civil liberties. Local libraries removed dissenting books. Schools and colleges fired unorthodox teachers. Police shut down radical newspapers. State legislatures refused to seat elected representatives who professed socialist ideas. In 1919, Congress removed its lone socialist representative, Victor Berger, on the grounds that he was a threat to national safety. That same year, the Supreme Court provided a formula for restricting free speech. In upholding the conviction of socialist Charles Schenck for publishing a pamphlet urging resistance to the draft during wartime (*Schenck v. United States*), Justice Oliver Wendell Holmes, writing for the Court, established a "clear and present danger" test. Such utterances as Schenck's during a time of national peril, Holmes wrote, were equivalent to shouting "Fire!" in a crowded theater. But the analogy was false. Schenck's pamphlet echoed faintly in the open air, not in a crowded theater, and had little power to provoke a public firmly opposed to its message.

In time, the "Red scare" lost credibility. The lack of any real radical menace became clear after newspaper headlines carried Attorney General Palmer's warning that radicals were planning to celebrate the Bolshevik Revolution with a nation-wide wave of violence on May 1, 1920. Officials responded by calling out state militia, fortifying public buildings and churches, mobilizing bomb squads, even putting machine gun nests at major city intersections. When May 1 came and went without a single disturbance, the public mood turned from fear to scorn, and Palmer, who had taken to calling himself the "Fighting Quaker," was jeered as the "Quaking Fighter."

## Conclusion: Troubled Crusade

At home and abroad, the First World War was a traumatic experience for the American people. Woodrow Wilson sought to keep the nation out of war, but when war arrived in 1917, he promised that American intervention would further the noble cause of worldwide democracy. Serving under idealistic banners, American soldiers and sailors encountered unprecedented horrors—submarines, poison gas, machine guns—and more than 100,000 died. Rather than redeem their sacrifice, the peace that followed the armistice tarnished it. Few found consolation in the fact that the war thrust the nation into a position of international preeminence. At home, war brought prosperity, but rather than permanently improve working conditions, advance public health, and spread educational opportunity as progressives had hoped, the war threatened to undermine the achievements of the previous two decades.

In 1920, a bruised and disillusioned society stumbled into a new decade. The era coming to an end had called on Americans to crusade and sacrifice. Now whoever could promise them peace, prosperity, and a good time would have the best chance to win their hearts.

## CHRONOLOGY

| | |
|---|---|
| **1914** | Attempting to impose democracy on Mexico, President Woodrow Wilson sends marines to occupy port of Veracruz. |
| | **August 6.** All-out conflict erupts when Germany declares war on Russia. |
| **1915** | German submarine sinks British liner *Lusitania,* with loss of almost 1,200 lives, including 128 Americans. |
| | Settlement House reformer Jane Addams helps form Women's Peace Party to seek peaceful resolution of war. |
| **1916** | General Pershing leads military expedition into Mexico in pursuit of rebel leader "Pancho" Villa. |
| **1917** | British authorities inform Wilson of Zimmermann telegram. |
| | **April 6.** Submarine attacks on American vessels convince Wilson to declare war on Germany. |
| | Wilson creates Committee on Public Information to promote U.S. war aims. |
| | Selective Service Act authorizes military draft that brings 2.8 million men into armed services. |

| | |
|---|---|
| | Espionage Act passed, limiting First Amendment rights. |
| | Resentment against blacks migrating northward in search of work ignites violent race riot in East St. Louis, Illinois. |
| | Armed action by black soldiers against racial discrimination in Houston results in execution of thirteen of the soldiers and life sentences for forty-one more. |
| | Bolshevik Revolution ends Russian participation in war. |
| **1918** | **January 8.** President Wilson outlines his fourteen-point plan for peace. |
| | **May–June.** American marines succeed in their first major combat with Germans at Cantigny and Château-Thierry. |
| | **November 11.** Armistice signed ending World War I. |
| **1918–1920** | American forces deployed in Russia to protect Allied supplies and ports from Germany and then to support White Russian efforts to undo Bolshevik Revolution. |

| 1919 | **January 18.** Paris peace conference begins, with President Wilson as head of U.S. delegation. | 1920 | **January 1.** Prohibition goes into effect, following ratification of Eighteenth Amendment. |

**1919**    **January 18.** Paris peace conference begins, with President Wilson as head of U.S. delegation.

**June 28.** Versailles peace treaty signed. Wilson undertakes speaking tour to rally support for ratification of Versailles treaty and League of Nations.

Postwar recession and ending of wartime support for labor unions lead to wave of strikes.

**1919–1920**    Attorney General A. Mitchell Palmer leads effort, known as Red scare, to rid country of anarchists and aliens.

**1920**    **January 1.** Prohibition goes into effect, following ratification of Eighteenth Amendment.

Organized labor suffers its greatest defeat by ending steel strike without settlement.

Senate votes against ratification of Versailles peace treaty.

**August 18.** Nineteenth Amendment, granting women the vote, ratified by states.

# SUGGESTED READINGS

David Brody, *Labor in Crisis: The Steel Strike of 1919* (1965). A brief yet incisive examination of the industrial situation after war's end, as shown by the most significant labor conflict of the era.

Edward M. Coffman, *The War to End All Wars: The American Military Experience in World War I* (1968). A comprehensive account of American participation from mobilization to victory.

John Milton Cooper Jr., *Pivotal Decades: The United States, 1900–1920* (1990). An insightful overview of the period by the biographer of its two most important presidents, Roosevelt and Wilson. Cooper discusses politics within their social context and explains how war ushered out the Progressive era.

Robert D. Cuff, *The War Industries Board: Business-Government Relations during World War I* (1973). A full account of industrial mobilization for war which does justice to both the political and the technological aspects.

John S. D. Eisenhower, *Intervention! The United States and the Mexican Revolution, 1913–1917* (1993). A vivid examination of how cultural and economic tensions affected both the relations between Mexico and the United States and the outcome of the Mexican Revolution.

Modris Eksteins, *Rites of Spring: The Great War and the Birth of the Modern Age* (1990). An exploration of the way cultural values and popular tastes influenced European society to accept war and then developed in distinctly new ways as a result of war. The book concludes by drawing a connection between that modernist transformation and the coming of the Second World War.

Paul Fussell, *The Great War and Modern Memory* (1975). A moving and compassionate study of the psychological aftermath of conflict as expressed in certain literary and artistic forms and symbols.

James Joll, *The Origins of the First World War* (1992). Admirably concise and detailed explanation of the steps leading up to war. Joll concentrates on national rivalries and the consequences of entangling alliances.

David Kennedy, *Over Here: The First World War and American Society* (1980). A study of how civilians and soldiers responded to the non-military challenges of war, and how wartime pressures affected values and mores.

Thomas Knock, *To End All Wars: Woodrow Wilson and the Quest for a New World Order* (1992). A shrewd and sensitive analysis of Wilson's international policy, told from a perspective sympathetic to Wilson's ideals.

Carole Marks, *Farewell—We're Good and Gone: The Great Black Migration* (1989). An account of the exodus from the South to northern cities by African Americans seeking wartime opportunities. Both origins and destinations are adequately examined.

John F. McClymer, *War and Welfare: Social Engineering in America, 1890–1925* (1980). A study that places the gearing up for war of material and human resources within long-range efforts to perfect society through efficient use of moral and scientific principles.

Paul L. Murphy, *World War I and the Origin of Civil Liberties in the United States* (1979). The story of action taken against subversive thought and action during the war and how these led to Constitutional principles guiding legal protection of First Amendment rights.

Bernard C. Nalty, *Strength for the Fight: A History of Black Americans in the Military* (1986). A survey of African American experience in the military from the Civil War through the Korean War, placing a brief telling of the World War I period within a usefully broad perspective.

**PANORAMIC HATBOX**

*Illustrated hatboxes, like the hats within them, were a favorite symbol of affluent style in the 1920s. This hatbox displays the extravagant round of life on Fifth Avenue, the most fashionable milieu of all. Americans looked to New York wit and sophistication as a guide to how to transform the nation into an urban society.*

Picture Research Consultants & Archives.

# FROM NEW ERA TO GREAT DEPRESSION

# 23

## 1920–1932

O N A GRAY CHRISTMAS MORNING IN 1922, Federal Prisoner #9653 began his last day at the Atlanta penitentiary. The frail old man glanced at the crucifix on his cell wall before exchanging his jailhouse fatigues for a cheap new suit the guard had brought. For Eugene Victor Debs, the leader and five-time presidential candidate of the Socialist Party, a long ordeal was over. President Warren Harding had granted him the pardon Woodrow Wilson had bitterly refused. After three long years in prison for opposition to World War I, Debs was at last a free man.

As he neared the main prison gate, Debs remembered, he heard behind him "what seemed a rumbling of the earth as if shaken by some violent explosion." Against every rule, the warden had allowed all 2,300 inmates out of their cells to cheer the departure of the man they had come to know as a sympathetic friend. Debs had an uncanny hold on the hopes and feelings of downtrodden people. One of them was his cell mate, Sam Moore, who recalled many years later how much Debs's compassionate character had meant to him. "As miserable as I was I would defy fate with all its cruelty as long as Debs held my hand, and I was the most miserably happiest man on earth when I knew he was going home Christmas."

Debs's first stop was the White House, where his benefactor, President Harding, curious to meet America's most famous political prisoner, had invited him for a visit. The genial Harding bounded from behind his desk to shake Debs's hand, exclaiming, "Well, I have heard so damned much about you, Mr. Debs, that I am now very glad to meet you personally."

At the end of his journey, in Terre Haute, Indiana, a crowd estimated at 25,000 met Debs at the station. They lifted the old warrior into the same horse-drawn wagon that had carried him back from his first imprisonment in 1895, when he had gone to jail for defying a federal injunction during the Pullman strike. When the parade arrived at the family home near the railroad tracks, Debs gave an impromptu speech from the porch, urging his cheering supporters to view his release as a step toward the ultimate victory of socialism and the working class.

It was a touching moment, but Debs's show of the old revolutionary fire would not be able to ignite a society very different from the one he envisioned. The Harding administration shrewdly realized that pardoning America's leading antiwar martyr, along with others who had opposed the war, would reduce tensions caused by wartime repression with little risk to its conservative policies. The public, bitterly disillusioned with the outcome of World War I, no longer thrilled to the Christian moralism and idealism that had fueled the crusades of socialists and progressives.

Although Debs's stature as a jailed martyr had won him 919,000 votes (the most ever for a Socialist candidate) when he ran for president from his cell in 1920, the Socialist Party itself was in drastic decline. By the time Debs left prison, Socialist membership had fallen to 120,000. Nearly broke, the party would soon have to sell its headquarters in Chicago and move into an attic.

## The New Era

The nation had turned a corner away from progressive reform into a spectacular burst of economic prosperity. Without a central focus on national crusades, once Wilson's leadership ended, the energy generated by the war flowed away from civic unity toward private economic enterprise and personal creativity. The rise of a freewheeling economy and the new sense of individual freedom caused Secretary of Commerce Herbert Hoover to declare that Americans had entered a "new era."

This newness developed in an uneasy tension with older ways that made the 1920s a time of contradiction and ambivalence. For the first time, according to the census of 1920, Americans lived in urban rather than rural areas, yet nostalgia idealized the farm and the small town. Although the nation prospered as a whole, the new wealth widened the gap between rich and poor. The more city life and cultural diversity flourished, the stronger pressures for conformity became. While millions admired the new, sophisticated style, millions of others condemned postwar society for its vulgar materialism. And the greatest outpouring of creative talent in the nation's history produced artists of all types who indicted the United States for being artistically barren.

The ambivalence of the 1920s finds expression in the competing myths and labels attached to the age. Some terms focus on the era's high-spirited energy: "Roaring Twenties," "Jazz Age," "Flaming Youth," "Age of the Flapper." Others echo the rising importance of money—"Dollar Decade," "Golden Twenties," "Prosperity Decade"—or reflect the sinister side of gangster profiteering—"Lawless Decade." Still other terms emphasize fragile dreams and loneliness: "Lost Generation," "Beautiful and the Damned." In contrast to these romantic images of the twenties, President Calvin Coolidge aptly characterized the situation for those who wielded power and prestige when he declared, "The business of America is business." For the hopes and fortunes of the era rose, and then crashed, according to the values and ideology of the business community.

## Postwar Politics and the Election of 1920

The economic chaos that accompanied the return to a peacetime economy was crucial in making Americans yearn for security rather than for more progressive adventures. As inflation soared, people on fixed salaries—many of them middle-class progressive supporters of Wilson—lost heart as inflation shrank their purchasing power. Organized labor, after its defeats in 1919, faced grim prospects. By the winter of 1920–21, the national unemployment rate hit 20 percent, the highest ever suffered up to that time. Farmers fared worst, as their bankruptcy rate increased tenfold and real farm income fell far below wartime levels.

*In tune with the national need for reassurance, the Republican Party chose handsome, gregarious Warren Gamaliel Harding, senator from Ohio, as its presidential candidate.*

President Woodrow Wilson, bedridden and partially paralyzed from his 1919 stroke, squandered his party's chances by refusing to allow anyone within his administration to construct a program for the postwar era. Instead, Wilson insisted that the 1920 election would be a "solemn referendum" on the League of Nations. The Democratic nominees for president, James M. Cox, three-time governor of Ohio, and for vice president, the New York aristocrat Franklin Delano Roosevelt, bearer of "Uncle Ted's" famous name, dutifully campaigned on Wilson's international ideals.

In tune with the national need for reassurance, the Republican Party chose handsome, gregarious Warren Gamaliel Harding, senator from Ohio, as its presidential candidate. Unlike so many others of his generation who left the countryside to make their fortunes in the city, Harding stayed home in Marion, Ohio, to edit a newspaper and enjoy the pleasures of small-town life. His subsequent rise in

**REPUBLICAN CAMPAIGN DECAL**
*Looking grimly dignified, these 1920 Republican candidates seek to persuade voters that they can put an end to radical and alien disruption and restore old-fashioned American values. Harding, the Washington insider from the traditional Republican strong-hold of Ohio, promises to get the country "back to normal"; his running mate, Calvin Coolidge, the Massachusetts governor who gained national fame by crushing the Boston police strike, appears as the exemplar of "law and order."* Collection of Janice L. and David J. Frent.

party politics was a tribute to his amiable ability to connect with grassroots sentiment, rather than to any political commitment. Harding vaguely opposed the progressive policies of economic regulation, agricultural subsidies, and graduated income taxes. Wanting to succeed in an atmosphere of goodwill, he developed an ability to land on the winning side of an argument without having to grapple with conscience or complexity. On the two most heated domestic issues of the day—woman suffrage and prohibition—Harding showed little knowledge or conviction. He remarked that he saw no good reason for the reforms, but eventually he voted for them in a nod to public opinion.

Harding struck upon the winning formula in one of his campaign speeches by declaring that "America's present need is not heroics, but healing; not nostrums [questionable remedies] but normalcy." But what was "normalcy"? Harding explained: "By 'normalcy' I don't mean the old order but a regular steady order of things. I mean normal procedure, the natural way, without excess." The urbane *New York Times* understood its appeal, observing, "Mr. Harding is not writing for the super-fine weighers of verbs and adjectives but for the men and women who see in his expressions their own ideas."

Eager to put the poisonous atmosphere of the Red scare and the labor strife of 1919 behind them, the voters responded by giving him the largest margin of victory any presidential candidate had ever received: 60.5 percent of the popular vote and 76 percent of the electoral vote (Map 23.1). On his coattails rode Republican majorities in both houses of Congress. In early March, the Hardings arrived at the White House and threw open the barred gates, which had been closed since the declaration of war in 1917. Their welcome to the public, who came by the thousands, lifted the national pall and signified a new era of easygoing good cheer.

In accord with his promise to have a government run by the best minds, Harding chose some men of stature for his cabinet. Charles Evans Hughes, former associate justice of the Supreme Court, became secretary of state; Herbert Hoover, the self-made millionaire and former head of the

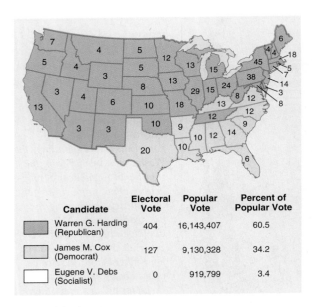

| Candidate | Electoral Vote | Popular Vote | Percent of Popular Vote |
|---|---|---|---|
| Warren G. Harding (Republican) | 404 | 16,143,407 | 60.5 |
| James M. Cox (Democrat) | 127 | 9,130,328 | 34.2 |
| Eugene V. Debs (Socialist) | 0 | 919,799 | 3.4 |

MAP 23.1
*The Election of 1920*

wartime Food Administration, was tapped for secretary of commerce; and the leading champion of scientific agriculture, Henry C. Wallace, took over as secretary of agriculture. But wealth also counted. Most significantly, Harding answered the call of conservatives to name Andrew Mellon, one of the richest men in America, secretary of the treasury. And then there was friendship. Loyally, Harding handed out jobs to acquaintances even though some of their qualifications were suspect. This curious combination of merit and cronyism made for a disjointed administration in which a few "best minds" debated national needs, while much lesser men looked for ways to advance their own interests.

## The "Noble Experiment" and Woman Suffrage

The shift from reform earnestness to normalcy showed in the public reaction to the last two great progressive achievements passed prior to Harding's inauguration—prohibition and woman suffrage. In January 1920, the Eighteenth Amendment prohibiting the sale of alcohol took effect. "The noble experiment," as admirers called it, succeeded in lowering the consumption of alcohol, at least in rural America, but it also led to widespread disregard for the law. The "speakeasy," a place where men (and,

increasingly, women) drank publicly, became a common feature of the urban landscape. There "bootleggers," so named a century before because they put bottles in their tall boots to sneak past the tax collectors, provided liquor from Canada or concocted in makeshift stills. Otherwise upright people discovered the thrill of breaking the law; and one dealer, trading on common knowledge that whiskey still flowed in the White House, distributed cards advertising himself as the "President's Bootlegger."

Eventually, serious criminals took over most of the liquor trade. Al Capone became the era's most notorious gang lord by establishing a bootlegging empire in Chicago that reputedly grossed more than $60 million in a single year. The gang-war slayings that marked the struggle for control of the lucrative market prompted public cynicism about the "noble experiment." Each year, support for the Eighteenth Amendment shrank, until in 1933 it was repealed.

The Nineteenth Amendment, fulfilling nearly a century of struggle to achieve political rights for women, finally provided the chance to answer the question How would women vote? The militant National Woman's Party, headed by Alice Paul, wanted women to form a progressive reform bloc and fight for an Equal Rights Amendment (ERA), which the party put before Congress in 1923. The more moderate League of Women Voters (LWV), formed out of the National American Woman Suffrage Association after it had achieved its goal, had the less partisan aim of educating the new electorate on the issues. Activists in both groups looked to woman suffrage, the greatest single change ever made in voting eligibility, to reshape the political landscape, starting with passage of protective legislation for women and children that had long been high on their reform agenda.

As with prohibition, however, reality did not bear out expectations. Male domination and lack of experience in voting, especially among recent immigrants and southerners, kept many women away from the polls or voting as their husbands instructed. Partly for that reason, in 1920 and 1924, for the first time in American history, less than a majority of eligible voters cast ballots in the presidential elections. Those women who did vote showed no unified commitment to the goals of suffrage leaders.

It took a while for the conservative politicians who had seized control of both major parties to realize that they need not fear any female voting bloc. Assuming that women would have considerable

**SATURDAY NIGHT**
*With a sly wink, the young dandy dips for movie money
while his date looks dubious about what will go on in the
dark of that dry night. With this title, Harry Ruby, the
popular songwriter, capitalizes on the expectation that resourceful Americans out for a good time will find ways
around the prohibition amendment's attempt to enforce
sober morality.*
Picture Research Consultants & Archives.

**WOMEN VOTING IN NEW YORK CITY**
*Sharply attired New York City officials look wearily re-
signed or bemused as one of them hands ballots to two
women voting for the first time in 1920. The contrast in
appearance and demeanor of the two groups facing each
other is strikingly reminiscent of photographs of apprehensive new immigrants applying for entry.*
UPI/Bettmann Archive.

political leverage, the new Congress passed the
Sheppard-Towner bill in 1921, providing federal
funds for maternal and infant health care. As the realization of the new voters' weak influence sank in,
however, and the protests of doctors against "socialist" interference intensified, Congress reduced
funds for the program and in 1928 eliminated it altogether. Those women who stuck with a progressive agenda were forced to work within a network
of private agencies and reform associations to continue to press the causes of birth control, protective
legislation for the workplace, legal equality for minorities, and the end of child labor. In doing so, they
laid the groundwork for the time when their efforts
would be supported by those in power.

## The United States Retreats
## from the World

Harding's desire for harmony equipped him well to
preside over the country's retreat from international
leadership. Only four months after his inauguration, he concluded peace treaties with Germany,
Austria, and Hungary that removed the United
States from supervision over their affairs. Harding's
most ambitious foreign policy initiative was the
Washington Disarmament Conference he convened
in 1921 to establish a global balance of naval power.
By gaining agreement on the proportional reduction
of naval might among the major powers—Britain,
France, Japan, Italy, and the United States—Harding

hoped to preserve peace without the bother of joining the League of Nations. A grateful citizenry breathed a sigh of relief that the threat of war seemed so easily removed at a conference noted for its international goodwill and optimism.

The campaign to limit immigration, however, was more troubling. By the time Harding took office, tensions about ethnic class differences and alien radicals had convinced the public that the time had come for drastic immigration restriction. Alongside the "100 percenters"—native-born Americans totally opposed to immigration on racist and patriotic grounds—stood union members, who feared immigrant competition for jobs, and traditionalists, who felt that the nation had completed its destined growth. In full accord, Harding made it one of his first acts to sign a quota law. The act limited the number of immigrants to no more than 357,000 per year and gave each European nation a quota, based on 3 percent of the number of people from that country listed in the U.S. census of 1910. The law effectively reversed the trend toward immigration from southern and eastern Europe, which by 1914 had amounted to 75 percent of the yearly total. Rejecting the old commitment to welcome millions of "huddled masses yearning to breathe free," the United States placed the nation's destiny in the hands of those whose northern European ancestors had gotten there first. Congress cut the quota in half in 1923 and followed up the next year by excluding Asians and shifting the census standard back from 1910 to 1890, before the great influx of southern and eastern Europeans.

Anti-foreign hysteria climaxed in the trial of two anarchist immigrants from Italy, Nicola Sacco and Bartolomeo Vanzetti. Arrested in 1920 for robbery and murder in South Braintree, Massachusetts, the men were sentenced to death by a judge who openly referred to them as "anarchist bastards." In response to doubts about the fairness of the verdict, the governor of Massachusetts named a review committee of establishment notables, including the presidents of Harvard and MIT. The panel found the trial judge guilty of a "grave breach of official decorum" but refused to recommend a motion for retrial.

For six years, critics who saw the verdict as an indication that the country was in the grip of a rich elite willing to exploit minorities and crush dissent tried vainly to save Sacco and Vanzetti from the electric chair. After the anarchists were finally executed on August 23, 1927, writer John Dos Passos

**AGITATING FOR SACCO AND VANZETTI**
*This image appeared in the anarchist journal that Bartolomeo Vanzetti's friend and fellow immigrant Aldino Felicani created to raise support for pardoning Sacco and Vanzetti. By writing in English under an Italian masthead, Felicani sought to make the two accused men symbols of both immigrant and working-class suffering. In the cartoon's dramatic version of events, capitalism's executioner, leaning on the electric chair like a sinister barber, summons working-class victims to their doom. In fact, deportation and mob violence were the typical weapons used against alien radicals and others deemed dangerously un-American.*
L'Agitazione, August 20, 1921.

summed up their despair in his novel *The Big Money*. Dos Passos describes the crowd of fifty thousand mourners who followed the coffins through the rain and then has a bystander lament the executions as a death blow to the idea of inclusive democracy. "All right," he announces with grim resignation, "all right, we are two nations."

## A Business Government

By screening out the world, the Harding administration could concentrate on prosperity at home. The American way, Harding declared, was to combine profit making and service to one's own community. Accordingly, he supported high tariffs to protect American businesses, price supports for agriculture, and the dismantling of wartime government control over industry in favor of unregulated private direction. Passage of the Fordney-McCumber tariff in 1922 raised duties on imports to unprecedented heights. Harding's policies to boost American enterprise made him a very popular president; but ultimately the small-town congeniality and trusting ways that had made his career possible did him in. The "Ohio gang"— wheeler-dealers, including some of his old friends— held forth at what became known as the "little green house on K Street," a hideaway where whiskey and poker mixed with business, some of it illegal. The affable Harding resisted admitting for as long as he could that certain of his friends were involved in law-breaking more serious than drinking bootlegged gin.

In the end, three of Harding's appointees would go to jail and others would be indicted. When Interior Secretary Albert Fall, the highest official caught up in the scandal, was convicted of accepting bribes of more than $400,000 for leasing oil reserves on public land in Teapot Dome, Wyoming, "Teapot Dome" entered the language permanently as a label for political corruption.

Harding set off on a trip to Alaska in the summer of 1923 to escape his troubles. Baffled about how to deal with "my God-damned friends," the president found no rest and his health continued to decline. On August 2, 1923, a shocked nation learned of Harding's sudden death at the age of fifty-eight from a stroke. Harding himself was not involved in any financial wrongdoing, but only his death saved him from the further embarrassment of trying to do a job that was too big for him.

Vice President Calvin Coolidge was vacationing at his family's farmhouse in Plymouth Notch, Vermont, when he was wakened during the night with the news of Harding's death. The family gathered in the parlor where, by the flickering light of an oil lamp, Coolidge's father, a justice of the peace, swore his son in as president. This rustic drama had the intended calming effect on a nation confronting scandal. Harding's successor basked in the public's acceptance of him as a savior, wisely steeped in old-fashioned Yankee morality.

A spare, solemn man—one critic thought he must have been "weaned on a pickle"—Coolidge had won national publicity in 1919 when as governor of Massachusetts he had called out the National Guard to maintain order during the Boston police strike. In 1920, the Republican convention chose him as a man of decisiveness to stand behind the more pliable Harding. The Coolidge administration differed from its discredited predecessor in its more formal and proper White House and close-mouthed presidential style. But these differences merely gave a different tone to the basic similarities in policies, particularly regarding business.

Coolidge, who once remarked, "The man who builds a factory builds a temple, the man who works there worships there," believed that government should restrict itself to being the servant of business. Coolidge rarely stirred in the White House and discouraged others in his administration from taking initiatives. His policy was to help businesses operate efficiently and profitably with a minimum of public restraint. With his approval, Secretary of the Treasury Andrew Mellon focused on reducing the role of government through tax cuts for corporations and wealthy individuals. Obligingly, Congress passed legislation that reduced its tax revenue by about half. The most active cabinet member, Secretary of Commerce Herbert Hoover, encouraged trade associations that would keep business honest and efficient through voluntary cooperation, rather than government regulation.

The Supreme Court supported the Coolidge approach. The Court had long opposed federal regulation of hours, wages, and working conditions, arguing frequently that such legislation was the proper concern of the states. In 1916, on those grounds, the Court had struck down the federal Child Labor Act. Early in the Coolidge years, the Court found ways to curtail state regulation even as it had previously used that remedy to disallow federal action. In 1923, the Court declared unconstitutional the District of Columbia's minimum-wage law for women, asserting that the law interfered with the freedom of employer and employee to make labor contracts. Soon afterward, the Court showed its partiality toward management by ruling against "closed shops" where only union members could be employed, while confirming the right of owners to form exclusive trade associations.

The election of 1924 ratified the defeat of progressive principles. To oppose Coolidge the Democrats nominated John W. Davis, a corporate lawyer whose conservative views differed little from Republican principles. In a last-gasp attempt to offer a reform alternative, the Progressive Party made Senator Robert La Follette of Wisconsin its presidential nominee. In the showdown, for which Republicans coined the slogan "Coolidge or Chaos," the mostly silent president managed to capture more votes than both his opponents put together, and conservative Republicans strengthened their majorities in both houses of Congress. Apathy was the real winner, however. The percentage of eligible voters who bothered to go to the polls was the lowest ever.

## Henry Ford and Assembly Line Progress

With politics in eclipse, the most admired American in the 1920s was Henry Ford, the mass production innovator who put America on wheels. Born in 1863 on a farm in Dearborn, Michigan, just outside Detroit, Ford soon rejected farmwork in favor of tinkering with machines. In 1893, he put together one of the first successful gasoline-driven carriages in the United States. Ten years later, with $28,000 from a few backers impressed by his mechanical skills, Ford gathered twelve workers in a 250-by-50-foot shed and created the Ford Motor Company.

Ford's timing and location could not have been better. The growing country had moved to its outer limits, leaving Americans, especially those west of the Mississippi, distant from neighbors and services. With fewer than ten people to a square mile, the Midwest needed machinery to help its farmers make a living and to escape isolation. Ford's Detroit was well situated to meet these needs. The mining and manufacture of key materials for the automobile and the tractor—steel, oil, glass, and rubber—were concentrated in nearby cities in Pennsylvania, Ohio, Indiana, and Illinois and were easily transported across the waterways of the Great Lakes and over the midwestern railroads (Map 23.2). So great was the automobile industry's demands for materials that by 1929 one American in four found employment directly or indirectly in the industry. "Give us our daily bread," one commentator quipped, was no longer addressed to the Almighty, but to Detroit. Henry Ford's reward was dominance over the market. Throughout the rapid expansion of the automotive industry, the Ford Motor Company remained the industry leader, peaking in 1925 when it outsold all its rivals combined.

The key to Ford's success in the factory was mass production. By installing a continuous conveyor belt, or assembly line, in his plant in 1913, Ford was able to produce a car every ninety-three minutes, in contrast to the fourteen hours it had taken before. Mass production enabled Ford to drop the price of his cars from $845 to less than $300. Soon the working class joined the wealthy on the roads. The Model T—homely and available only in black, but rugged and cheap—became a prime symbol of the New Era. Aided by the federal government's

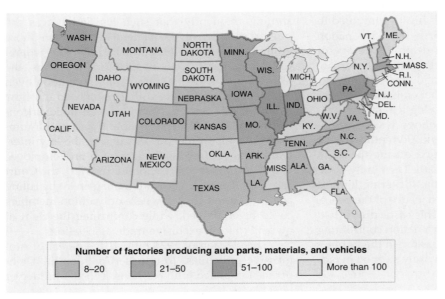

**Number of factories producing auto parts, materials, and vehicles**
8–20    21–50    51–100    More than 100

**MAP 23.2**
*Auto Manufacturing*
By the mid-1920s, the massive coal and steel industries of the Midwest had made the region the center of the new automobile industry. A major road-building program by the federal government carried the thousands of new cars produced each day to every corner of the country.

willingness to spend more on roads than on anything else, cars, trucks, and buses surged past the railroads by the end of the 1920s as the primary haulers of passengers and freight.

The automobile changed the face of America. Hundreds of small towns declined or died within the decade, largely because the automobile could connect people in rural communities with distant cities and thus bypass the small towns that had formerly provided services. The one-room schoolhouse and the crossroads church began to vanish from the landscape. At the same time, some larger towns prospered by catering to the new auto trade. "Guest cottages" were thrown up for auto tourists, and the word *motel* was coined to describe roadside accommodations. More prosperous towns paved and widened city streets, cutting down the trees on Main Street to make way for parking spaces.

Nobody entertained grander or more contradictory visions of the new America he had helped to create than Henry Ford himself. When Ford began his rise, progressive critics were vilifying the industrial giants of the nineteenth century as "robber barons" who lived in luxury while reducing their workers to wage slaves. Ford, however, was just a poor farm boy when the robber barons arose. By identifying himself with the common folk he wanted to work for him, Ford sought to claim his place as benefactor of striving Americans yearning to be free and mobile. Highly regimented automobile plants at the cutting edge of modern technology made Ford very wealthy during the 1920s. But Ford looked backward and moralized about the country's rural values. His pet project was to revive the past in Greenfield Village outside Detroit, where he relocated buildings from a bygone era, including his parents' farmhouse, to convey the rural simplicity of his childhood. With its exhibits of homespun family life and crafts, Greenfield Village contrasted poignantly with the roaring, racing Ford plant farther along the Detroit River at River Rouge. In the factory toiled the African American and immigrant workers left out of Ford's village idyll. Yet all would be well, Ford insisted, if Americans remained loyal to the virtues of an agrarian past and somehow managed to be modern and scientific at the same time.

With Ford's assembly line method in ascendancy, those interested in progress looked to science and technology for guidance. Scientific management, which Frederick Winslow Taylor had pioneered at the end of the nineteenth century at Mid-

vale Steel Company in Pennsylvania, reached its heyday during the 1920s. In an effort to become more streamlined and efficient, corporations established increasingly bureaucratic management structures. Specialized divisions sprang up—procurement, production, marketing, employee relations—each with its own team of professionally trained managers. It followed that, with approximately the same number of workers, industry produced almost twice as many goods. The result was vastly increased business profits and lower consumer prices, but only slightly higher wages for labor, since productivity was measured in part by how little had to be spent on the workforce. Moreover, as the assembly line became standard in almost every American factory, laborers lost many of the skills in which they had once taken pride.

To extend at least some of the benefits of scientific management to workers, industries developed paternalistic programs that came to be called "welfare capitalism." With the help of industrial psychologists and worker councils, businesses improved safety and sanitation inside factories and instituted paid vacations and contributory pension plans. In some places, company unions also gave workers a limited means of voicing grievances.

Belief in scientific management helped advance the cause of higher education and the professions: Corporations needed educated managers. By the end of the decade, enrollments in colleges and universities were more than three times those at the turn of the century. During the 1920s, graduate education expanded at an even faster rate. Funding agencies such as the Rockefeller Foundation, the John Simon Guggenheim Foundation, and the Social Science Research Council were established to support scientific research and channel it into useful applications. Private business kept pace by increasing the number of industrial research laboratories from around three hundred in 1920 to more than a thousand by the end of the decade.

Welfare service also underwent professional change, especially in the growing new field of social work. Trained social workers focused more on individual psychology and less on the social justice concerns of the settlement house founders. Understanding of human behavior became more precise, but also more detached and fragmented. The aim was to adjust clients to the new, highly organized, tensely hurried business civilization all around them, not to nurture an independent sense of community and identity.

City to Hollywood, California, where producers found open space and endless sunshine. Like Ford's River Rouge plant, Hollywood mass-produced enough pictures to satisfy Americans' growing appetite for vicarious experience. By 1929, as many people went to the movies in a single week as lived in the entire country.

In Hollywood, a new breed of industrial entrepreneur, the movie mogul, soon discovered the successful formula of combining opulence, sex, and adventure on the screen. Actors with exotic names like Pola Negri, Rudolph Valentino, and Vilma Banky portrayed the romance of foreign lands where passion was allegedly freer. For settings closer to home, "America's Sweetheart," Mary Pickford, and her real-life husband, Douglas Fairbanks, offered more wholesome adventure. Comedy made the closest connection with audiences, however, especially in calling sympathetic attention to the pitfalls and absurdity ordinary people faced. Most versatile of all the comics was Charlie Chaplin, whose famous character, the wistful tramp, showed an endearing inability to cope with the rules and complexities of modern life.

Moralists who worried that the screen images might subvert propriety soon pressed for government regulation. To head off censorship, in 1922 the Motion Picture Producers and Directors of America hired former Postmaster General Will Hays to monitor films for "decency and taste." Hays screened films and tried to balance the interests of public morality, creativity, and commerce without eliminating the raciness that made the movies so popular.

Like a magnet, the movie industry drew its leading figures from all points of the compass. Many studio owners and producers came from eastern European immigrant communities, while directors were often refugees from the stage or European film studios. Actors of color were still largely excluded (except when they were used for comic relief or as villains), but among the white majority, anyone who looked good on screen and could invent an elegant or rugged-sounding name could hope to become a star.

## Sports and Hero Worship

Americans also found heroes in sports. Baseball, professionalized since 1871, solidified its place as the national pastime in the 1920s. It remained essentially a game played by and for the working class, an outlet for raw energy and even a tinge of rebelliousness. In Babe Ruth, baseball had the most cherished free spirit of the time. An orphan who never really grew up, Ruth mixed his record-setting home runs with rowdy escapades, satisfying the view that sports offered a way to break out of the ordinariness of everyday life.

The public also fell in love with a young boxer from the grim mining districts of Colorado. As a teenager, Jack Dempsey had made his living hanging around saloons betting he could beat anyone in the house. When he took the heavyweight crown just after World War I, he was revered as America's equalizer, a stand-in for the average American who felt increasingly hemmed in by bureaucracy and machine-made culture.

*For the first time, youth in the 1920s became a social class distinct in itself. As the traditional bonds of community, religion, and family loosened, the young felt less pressure to imitate their elders and more freedom to develop their own culture.*

Football, an essentially college sport, held greater sway with the upper classes. The most celebrated coach, Knute Rockne of Notre Dame, was beloved for his advocacy of football as a parable of the good life of hard work and teamwork. Let the professors make learning as interesting as football, Rockne advised, and the problem of getting youth to learn would disappear. But in keeping with the times, football moved toward becoming a more public spectacle. The gridiron's greatest hero, Red Grange, a quiet, straitlaced son of the prairies, went on from the University of Illinois to apply both his skill and steady business sense to the development of a professional league.

The decade's hero worship reached its zenith in the celebration of Charles Lindbergh, a young pilot who had survived stunt flying and the equally risky pioneer air mail routes. On May 20, 1927, Lindbergh set out from Long Island in his specially built monoplane, *The Spirit of St. Louis,* to become the first person to fly nonstop across the Atlantic. Thirty-three hours later Lindbergh landed at the Paris airport, where he was greeted by a wildly cheering crowd. Newspapers tagged Lindbergh the "Lone Eagle"—the perfect hero for an age that celebrated individual accomplishment. "Charles Lindbergh is the heir of all that we like to think is best in America," one journalist proclaimed. "He is the stuff out of which have been made the pioneers that opened up the wilderness. His are the qualities which we, as a people, must nourish." Lindbergh realized, however, that technical and organizational complexity was fast reducing chances for solitary achievement. To make the point about a new sort of heroism, he entitled his book about the flight *We* and cautioned cheering crowds not to forget the wonderful engine that made it all possible. Lindbergh reassured Americans that possibilities for human achievement remained for those with just the right technological mastery.

## Women and Men of the Jazz Age

The first licensed radio station, KDKA in Pittsburgh, began broadcasting in 1920, and soon American airwaves buzzed with news, sermons, soap operas, sports, comedy, and, most of all, music. Americans isolated in the high plains laughed at the latest jokes from New York. For the first time, citizens were able to listen to the voices of political candidates without leaving home. Between 1922 and 1929, the number of radio stations increased from 30 to 606. In those seven short years, the number of homes with radios jumped from 60,000 to a staggering 10,250,000.

Radio added to the growth of popular music, especially jazz. Jazz, with its energetic style and its suggestion of youthful freedom and sexual openness, was the product of African American artists. But in the 1920s, although a radio broadcast might occasionally feature the ragged rhythms of the King Oliver Creole Jazz Band or the "walking bass" stride piano style of James P. Johnson, white audiences for the most part embraced a classically trained musician aptly named Paul Whiteman. Although Whiteman's "symphonic jazz," with its strict tempos and avoidance of improvisation, left most black jazz fans cold, it helped bring white audiences around to a form of music which had often been condemned as crude and low class.

For the first time, youth in the 1920s became a social class distinct in itself. As the traditional bonds of community, religion, and family loosened, the young felt less pressure to imitate their elders and more freedom to develop their own culture. An increasing number of college students helped the "rah-rah" style of college life become a fad, promoted in movies, songs, and advertisements. The

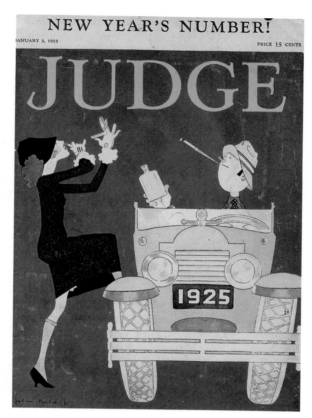

**HELD MAGAZINE COVER**
*Artist John Held lived and drew the extravagant life of the flaming youth of the Roaring Twenties. Raised in Mormon Utah, Held followed his artistic and journalistic skills to New York City and there found endless subjects to amuse himself. His caricatures of the Jazz Age came to typify it and made him a fortune. Like the high-living sorts he satirized, Held married and divorced a couple of times, dividing his time among his New York penthouse, Palm Beach cabana, and estate in Connecticut. Then, following the curve, he went broke in the Great Crash of 1929. Held gave up cartooning for landscape painting and sculpture and settled down on a small farm. Shown here is Held's inimitable style on the cover of the 1920s leading humor magazine: sporty convertible, the flapper, and Held's signature caricature of the round-headed, almost puppetlike young man.*
Culver Pictures.

collegiate set was the vanguard of the decade's "flaming youth."

Most stunning were the changes in the behavior of young women. In the 1920s, the typical urban woman shed up to twelve yards of clothing, "parked" her corset in the cloakroom (if she wore one at all), bared her knees, smoked cigarettes, drank in speakeasies, and generally played havoc with traditionally conservative notions of female behavior. The daring "flapper," as she was called, became the symbol of youthful revolt. As her contemporary and chronicler F. Scott Fitzgerald described her in his novel *This Side of Paradise* (1920), she was "lovely and expensive and about nineteen."

For all their spirit, rarely did the youth of the 1920s pose a threat to the status quo. For the most part, young people remained apathetic about social issues and eager to participate in the new consumer culture. "Flaming youth" rapidly cooled in office jobs and suburbs, and high-spirited flappers eventually settled down to become wives and mothers and employees. Yet even at home women's lives reflected the changes of the new era. The greater availability of birth control allowed married people to remain passionate and yet have fewer children to take care of. New home appliances also lightened the load, although most rural homes were beyond the reach of power lines and urban middle-class women who had appliances still spent many hours cooking, mending, and cleaning.

For women who worked outside the home, the changing economy of the 1920s offered wider, but still limited, opportunity. Many factory jobs, such as those in the booming automobile industry, and most management positions remained male domains. Women continued to become teachers and nurses, but even more found work as poorly paid secretaries, typists, file clerks, and salesclerks. By 1930, nearly eleven million women were employed, constituting 24 percent of the workforce, compared with 18 percent in 1900.

## Black Assertion and the Harlem Renaissance

Cheers for the black soldiers who marched up Broadway after the First World War soon faded, and grim days of race riots and hardship followed. Still, a sense of optimism remained strong among African Americans. In New York City, the key elements of hope and talent came together to form an exceptionally dynamic moment in black history. In the years before the war, black people in New York had moved uptown from their cramped confinement in Hell's Kitchen to the spacious heights of Harlem. A highly cosmopolitan population soon filled the new

**NOAH'S ARK**

*The Harlem Renaissance gained its principal visual expression at the hands of Kansas-born painter Aaron Douglas. When Douglas arrived in New York City in 1925, he quickly attracted the attention of W. E. B. Du Bois, who placed great importance on the arts as a carrier of the African American soul. At Du Bois's urging, Douglas sought ways of integrating the African cultural heritage with American experience. This depiction of an African Noah commanding the loading of the ark displays a technique that became closely associated with African American art: strong silhouetted figures awash in misty color, indicating a connection between Christian faith and the vital, colorful origins of black Americans in a distant, mythologized African past.*

Fisk University Art Galleries, Nashville, Tennessee.

area, including poor migrants from the South seeking economic opportunity and a more sophisticated wave of immigrants from the West Indies. Black artists and writers made Harlem a special place. There the "New Negro," as critic and historian Alain Locke put it in a book by that name, could rise from the ashes of a subjugated past and discover the race's true, creative identity.

That quest would prove more aggressive than it had been before the war. The military service of black troops raised their expectations of higher status in American society. Disillusioned with mainstream politics, many poor urban blacks turned for new leadership to a Jamaican visionary named Marcus Garvey. Garvey urged African Americans to rediscover the heritage of Africa and to take pride in their own culture and achievements. In 1917, Garvey launched the Universal Negro Improvement Association (UNIA) to help African Americans gain economic and political independence entirely outside of white society. Through their own shipping company, the Black Star Line, Garvey's followers aimed to finance their Back to Africa movement.

Garvey's message of the African "promised land" drew enthusiastic crowds in Harlem and brought delegates from many countries to the UNIA convention of 1920. Garvey knew how to inspire followers; but he was a naive businessman, unprepared for the rough opposition he encountered. Sharp operators sold bad ships to the Black Star Line, and the federal government pinned charges of illegal practices on Garvey and deported him to Jamaica in 1927. The issues Garvey raised about black identity, racial pride, and the search for equality persisted, however, and his legacy remained at the center of black nationalist thought.

Hope for the emergence of a "New Negro" was also roused by an artistic outpouring in the 1920s that came to be known as the Harlem Renaissance. The poet Langston Hughes summed up the movement's theme of self-respect in verse that shouted: "I am a Negro—and beautiful." In his music and writing, James Weldon Johnson focused on the rural southern culture that migrants brought into the streets of Harlem. In 1903, he had written the "Negro national anthem," "Lift Every Voice," and in 1927, in "God's Trombones," he expressed the wisdom and beauty of black folktales. Zora Neale Hurston, as an anthropology student at Barnard College, focused on black folktales. Her masterpiece, a novel called *Their Eyes Were Watching God* (1937), explores the complex passions of people within a self-governing southern black community of the rare sort she had known as a child in Florida. Langston Hughes, Claude McKay, and Countee Cullen added poetry as a way of conveying the vitality of life in Harlem amid the indifference and hostility of white America. Harlem painters, led by Aaron Douglas, sought to adapt African art, from which European modernist artists had begun taking inspiration, to the concept of the New Negro. In bold, colorful scenes Douglas combined biblical and African myths in ways that placed African Americans within a strong and unique tradition.

White patrons became an important means of support for the Harlem Renaissance. But for most whites, Harlem was an exotic dark continent just up the street where they could find a lively nightlife. The most famous spot was the Cotton Club, a gangster-owned outlet for bootleggers. The black performers hired to entertain the strictly white audience had to enter by the delivery doors and make careful preparations not to need the restrooms, which were for whites only. For all its vigor and optimism, the Harlem Renaissance existed as an isolated demonstration of achievement in a society not yet prepared to allow African American talent full opportunity to flourish.

## The Lost Generation

For many white writers and artists who felt alienated from a society they found crude and materialistic, Europe seemed the place to seek their renaissance. Young and mostly college-educated, these expatriates, as they came to be called, felt embittered by the war and renounced the progressives and patriots who had promoted it as a crusade. The poet Ezra Pound captured their view of what so many young men had died for:

> For an old bitch gone in the teeth,
> For a botched civilization.

In 1922, a young writer named Harold Stearns announced the secession of his generation through publication of a group of essays he had gathered under the ironic title *Civilization in the United States*. Relentlessly, the authors condemned the way sexual prudery and greed blighted virtually every aspect of the America they knew. Then, amid much public fanfare, Stearns and other alienated critics set sail for France, where they experienced an exhilarating sense of liberation. The American-born writer Gertrude Stein, long established in Paris, remarked famously, "They are the lost generation." Most of the expatriates, however, believed to the contrary that they had finally found themselves. The cost of living in Paris was low and the culture receptive to free expression. Far from the complications of home and steady work, the expatriates helped launch the most creative period in American art and literature in the twentieth century.

The novelist whose spare, clean style best exemplified the expatriate efforts to reduce art to a mirror of basic reality was Ernest Hemingway. Hemingway's experience in the war, where he was wounded, convinced him that the conventional world in which he was raised, with its Christian moralism and belief in progress, was bankrupt. His own stern personal code of honor dismissed creeds, ideologies, and patriotism as pious attempts to cover up the fact that life is a losing battle with death. Hemingway's ideal of macho courage, "grace under pressure," guided a lonely, doomed struggle with the inevitable (in his case, suicide). In his novel *The Sun Also Rises* (1926), Hemingway makes the point with harrowing directness. His main character, Jake Barnes, is impotent as the result of a war wound. Bereft of conventional beliefs, Barnes and his friends set out on an aimless journey through France and Spain, discovering little to sustain them except their own animal ability to appreciate sensual experience and endure suffering. Admirers of this exemplary work praised Hemingway's style because, in paring away unnecessary words, it seemed to express so perfectly a world stripped of illusions.

Writers who remained in America were often exiles in spirit who hoped that freedom from claims of duty and convention would help them explore the limits of creativity. Theater critic George Jean Nathan increased his fame when he proclaimed that "the great problems of the world—social, political, economic, and theological—do not concern me in the slightest." Within that atmosphere, novelist Sinclair Lewis in *Main Street* (1920) and *Babbitt* (1922) devastatingly satirized his native Midwest as a cultural wasteland. Humorists like James Thurber and Don Marquis created outlandish forms and characters to poke fun at taboos and inhibitions. And southern writers, led by William Faulkner, rallied against the South's reputation as a literary Sahara by exploring the dark undercurrents of that region's class and race heritage. But doubts about the new freedom surfaced as well. From the vantage of his own fame and wealth as chronicler of flaming youth, F. Scott Fitzgerald spoke with guilty brilliance in *This Side of Paradise* (1920) of a disillusioned generation "grown up to find all Gods dead, all wars fought, all faiths in man shaken."

# Rural America and Resistance to Change

Rural America and urban America had eyed each other warily since the nineteenth century. But suspicion turned to outright hostility in the 1920s when country people saw the center of American life shift from farm to city. The rapid growth of cities and suburbs cost rural America its dominance over the nation's political and cultural life. It also put economic distance between city and country. Between 1918 and 1921, the value of farmland and farm incomes fell by 30 to 50 percent. Only large-scale farmers were able to afford technological advances. Others were hard pressed even to hold on to the agrarian ideal of self-reliant individualism; by the

**THE LAW IS TOO SLOW**
*This stark depiction of a lynching by George Bellows in 1923 appeared just as the revived Ku Klux Klan was proclaiming itself the defender of traditional virtue in a sinful modern world. Bellows, an athlete as well as an artist, had gained fame as a realist and tough-minded radical before World War I and continued until his death in 1925 to spur social conscience even after doing so had gone out of fashion.*
The Art Institute of Chicago. All rights reserved, © 1996.

end of the decade, 40 percent of the nation's farmers had become landless and 90 percent of rural homes in 1930 had no indoor plumbing, gas, or electricity.

## The Rebirth of the Ku Klux Klan

Some of those who felt forsaken by the modern world channeled their desperation into a revived Ku Klux Klan that first appeared in 1915. Although the new Klan rose once again in the South, where its predecessor had been created to curb the rights of blacks during Reconstruction, it swiftly moved beyond the region. Imperial Grand Wizard Hiram Wesley Evans, a Texas dentist who styled himself as "the most average man in America," employed modern sales techniques to organize a network of klaverns (local societies) across the country. The nation, Evans argued, needed a thorough cleansing. He promised that Klansmen would stoutly defend family, morality, and traditional values against the threat posed by blacks, immigrants, radicals, Catholics, Jews, and foreigners.

Insecurity about their economic and social status underlay the Klansmen's sense of a world turning against them and fueled their appeal among small, independent merchants and farmers marginalized by corporate giants and large-scale farming. At its peak, the Klan attracted some three to four million members and by the mid-1920s it virtually controlled Indiana and influenced politics in Illinois, California, Oregon, Texas, Louisiana, Oklahoma, and Kansas.

Eventually, the intolerance and lawlessness that revived the Klan caused it to wither away. Immigration restrictions eased the worry about invading foreigners, and sensational wrongdoing by Klan leaders cost it the support of radical moralists. Grand Dragon David Stephenson of Indiana, for example, went to jail for the kidnap and rape of a woman who subsequently committed suicide. Yet the social grievances and economic problems of the countryside and small towns remained, ready to be ignited by later protest movements.

## The Scopes Trial

The clash between the old-time religion and the new spirit of science reached a dramatic climax in the Scopes trial in 1925. The confrontation occurred after several southern and border states passed legislation in the early 1920s against the teaching of Charles Darwin's theory of evolution in the public schools. Fundamentalist Protestants insisted that the Bible's creation story be taught as the literal truth. In answer to a clamor from scientists and civil liberties organizations for a challenge to the law, John Scopes, a young schoolteacher in Dayton, Tennessee, offered to test his state's ban on teaching evolution. When Scopes was brought to trial in the summer of 1925, Clarence Darrow, a brilliant defense lawyer from Chicago, volunteered to defend him. Darrow, an avowed agnostic, took on state's attorney William Jennings Bryan, the old war horse of the Democratic Party and symbol of rural America. Bryan, now aging and ill, styled himself as the defender of Christian opposition to the idea that humans had evolved from apes.

> *The Ku Klux Klan and the Scopes trial dramatized and inflamed divisions between city and country, intellectuals and the unlettered, the privileged and the outcasts, the scoffers and the faithful.*

The Scopes trial quickly degenerated into a media circus, despite the serious religious and philosophical issues it raised. The first trial to be covered live on radio, it attracted an avid nationwide audience. Reporters from big-city papers who converged on Dayton were largely hostile to Bryan, none more so than the cynical H. L. Mencken, who painted Bryan as a sort of Darwinian missing link ("a sweating anthropoid," a "gaping primate"). When, under relentless questioning by Darrow, Bryan declared on the witness stand that he did indeed believe the world was created in six days and that Jonah had lived in the belly of a whale, his humiliation in the eyes of most urban observers was complete. Although the Tennessee court upheld the law in defiance of modern intellectual consensus and punished Scopes with a $100 fine, Mencken had the last word in a merciless obituary for Bryan, who died just weeks after the trial ended. Portraying the "monkey trial" as a battle between the country and the city, Mencken flayed Bryan as a "charlatan, a mountebank, a zany without shame or dignity," motivated solely by "hatred of the city men who had laughed at him for so long."

As Mencken's acid prose indicated, Bryan's humiliation was not purely a victory of reason and science. It also reduced the esteem in which country people and their old values were held. The Ku Klux

Klan and the Scopes trial dramatized and inflamed divisions between city and country, intellectuals and the unlettered, the privileged and the outcasts, the scoffers and the faithful.

### Al Smith and the Election of 1928

Calvin Coolidge, who seemed a pillar of common sense and moral principle, added to the confusion by announcing in the summer of 1927 that he would not seek re-election. Who would now defuse the issues splitting the nation—prohibition, religious bigotry, and the clash between rural and urban values?

Republicans chose Herbert Hoover, the energetic secretary of commerce who appeared best able to continue Coolidge's pro-business programs and bring conservative southern Democrats over to the Republican side. The Democrats nominated Governor Alfred E. Smith of New York, the son of Irish Catholic immigrant parents who had grown up on the sidewalks of New York and epitomized working-class city values. Smith, an outspoken "wet" (an opponent of prohibition), actively championed repeal of the Eighteenth Amendment. Against these positions Republicans mobilized opposition from rural and urban conservatives. Smith's greatest vulnerability, however, was that he was the first Catholic to run for president. An editorial in the *Baptist and Commoner* was typical of many such appeals to Protestant believers in arguing that the election of Smith "would be granting the Pope the right to dictate to this government what it should do." There would be edicts from the White House claiming that "Protestants are now living in adultery because they were not married by a priest." Are you willing, the editorial asked in its punch line, to accept a president who would tell us "our offspring are bastards"? Smith's connections with the Tammany Hall political machine also cost him support among moralists; and radio broadcasts added further to Smith's problems in the countryside, where listeners associated his New York City accent with alien and unrespectable elements.

Hoover, who neatly combined the images of morality, efficiency, service, and prosperity, won the election by a landslide. He received 58 percent of the vote, taking all but eight states, and gained 444 electoral votes to Smith's 87. The Republicans managed to retain support of blacks in the South and at the same time wrenched five states loose from the formerly solid Democratic South. The only black cloud over the Republican victory, not much noted at the time, was the party's reduced support in the cities and among discontented farmers. The nation's largest cities voted Democratic in a striking reversal from 1924, indicating the rising strength of ethnic minorities, including Smith's fellow Catholics.

## From the New Era to the Great Crash

At his inauguration in 1929, Herbert Hoover told the American people, "We in America today are nearer to the final triumph over poverty than ever before in the history of any land. The poorhouse is vanishing from among us." The nation had not yet reached that goal, he acknowledged, "but, given a chance to go forward with the policies of the last eight years, we shall soon with the help of God be in sight of the day when poverty will be banished from this nation." Those words came back to haunt Hoover, for in eight short months the Roaring Twenties came to a crashing halt. The prosperity Hoover touted collapsed with the stock market, and the nation fell into the most serious economic depression of all time. Hoover and his reputation were among the first casualties, along with the reverence for business that had been the hallmark of the New Era.

### The Distorted Economy

In the spring of 1929, when Hoover moved into the White House, the United States basked in the sunshine of a fool's paradise. Although America had become the world's leading economy, the nation's leaders acted as though it were still a weak, developing country. American isolationism meant that European countries, devastated by the First World War, could not get the help they needed for full recovery. Rather than stepping in to help rebuild Europe's shattered economy, the Harding and Coolidge administrations demanded that European nations repay their war loans. In addition, the United States enacted tariffs that kept other nations from selling their goods to Americans. Foreign nations thus had less money to buy American goods, which were pouring out in record abundance. In a move that could work only in the short run, the United States propped up its export trade by extending credit to its foreign customers. Debt piled onto debt in an absurd pyramid. By the end of the decade, the United States accounted for 40 percent of the world's economic production and had acquired most of the world's gold in return for its exports.

Despite America's growing trade advantage abroad, prosperity at home rested on shaky foundations. Farmers continued to suffer from low prices and chronic indebtedness. Labor's wages rose slightly in the 1920s, but they failed to keep up with productivity and corporate profits. Nearly two-thirds of all American families lived on less than the $2,000 per year that was needed to "supply only basic necessities." By the end of the decade, the imbalance of wealth produced a serious problem in consumption. The rich, brilliantly portrayed in F. Scott Fitzgerald's *The Great Gatsby* (1925), gave the era much of its mythical glitter with their careless spending; but they could absorb only a tiny fraction of the nation's output. Ordinary folk, on whom the system ultimately depended, were unable to take up the slack. For a time the new device of installment buying—buying on credit—kept consumer demand up; by the end of the decade four out of five automobiles and two out of three radios were bought on credit. But personal indebtedness rose to an all-time high that could not be sustained.

Signs of economic trouble began to appear at mid-decade. A slowdown of new construction after 1925 indicated that the rate of business expansion had decreased. Faltering automobile sales signaled that, with nearly thirty million cars already on the road, demand had been met and producers would begin to cut back production and lay off workers. Banks followed suit. Between 1921 and 1928, as investment and loan possibilities faded, five thousand banks failed. Still, the boom went on. Confidence in fundamental soundness and eagerness to profit from it remained strong enough to conceal underlying flaws in the economy.

## The Great Crash of 1929

The most spectacular example of the credit binge of the 1920s occurred in the stock market—the nerve center and symbol of the boom. Even after the economy began weakening in the mid-1920s, a get-rich-quick spirit persisted on Wall Street. There, buying stocks on margin—that is, putting up only part of the money at the time of purchase—became rampant. Many got rich in paper profits; but those who bought on credit could finance their loans only if their stock increased in value. Thus, the stock market became dependent on continued expansion, which the naive believed could go on forever. (See the Historical Question on page 632.) They had strong incentives to think so. Between 1924 and 1929, the values of stocks listed on the New York Stock Exchange increased more than 400 percent. From that height, speculators could not even imagine that the market could fall and force them to meet their margin loans with cash they never had.

*Thus, the stock market became dependent on continued expansion, which the naive believed could go on forever.*

When stock purchased on margin rose to about 20 percent of the total by the summer of 1929, Hoover urged Richard Whitney, the head of the New York Stock Exchange, to tighten requirements. But Whitney, who later went to prison for embezzlement, gave only empty promises. Other representatives from prestigious banks and investment houses assured Hoover that all was well. Former President Coolidge stated tersely that at current prices, stocks were a bargain. The prudent Hoover, however, decided to sell some of his own stocks. In rejecting the optimistic advice of the boosters, Hoover took to a saying he kept repeating for the rest of his battle-scarred life: "The only trouble with capitalism is capitalists. They're too damned greedy."

Finally, in the fall of 1929, the market hesitated. Like rabbits sniffing danger, investors nervously began to sell their overvalued stock. The dip quickly became a rush, building to panic on October 24, the day that came to be known as Black Thursday. Brokers jammed the stock exchange and overflowed into the street. Stirred by the cries of "Sell! Sell!" just outside their windows, the giants of finance gathered in the offices of J. P. Morgan Jr., son of the nineteenth-century Wall Street lion, to plot ways of restoring confidence. They injected $100 million of their assets to bolster the market and issued brave declarations of faith. But more panic selling came on Black Tuesday, October 29, the day the market suffered the greatest drop in history.

It was once thought that the Great Crash *caused* the Great Depression. It did not. In 1929, the national and international economies were already riddled with severe problems. But the dramatic loss of 10 percent of Americans' total personal wealth

# Was Samuel Insull a Villain or a Victim?

HENRY FORD BECAME the most famous American of his time for his production-line success in putting America on wheels. But most of the rest of the technological marvels that transformed society during the 1920s—the bright lights on Main Street, the movie palaces, radios, phonographs, labor-saving appliances, and gadgets of all kinds—depended on the way Samuel Insull organized the mass production of electricity.

Born the son of a poor dairyman in England, Insull showed an aptitude for business from the time he left school at fourteen and hired on with an auction firm in London. His quickness with numbers attracted the attention of Thomas Edison's representative in England and led to Insull's coming to America in 1881 as the great inventor's private secretary. Impressed by his assistant's shrewd attention to detail, Edison rewarded Insull in 1893 by making him president of the Chicago Edison Company.

Within fifteen years, Insull had gained control of the electric industry in Chicago. From there his rise to vast wealth and international prominence was swift. He served as president of 11 companies and board chairman or member of 150 more. His Edison Commonwealth empire, which included six thousand power plants in thirty-nine states, manufactured more than 10 percent of the nation's power and sold to twenty million customers. Honors showered down on Insull, and he responded by becoming a patron of culture. In 1929, Insull made his grandest gesture by building Chicago a dazzling new opera house. To a proud city, Insull seemed the perfect model of success, a strong moral contrast to the notorious criminal wealth flaunted by Al Capone and other Chicago gangsters.

Insull had no doubt that he deserved Chicago's adulation. When one of his opera singers gushed that he was like another Napoleon, Insull reminded her that Napoleon was only a soldier. Yet, like Napoleon, Insull overreached himself. Much of his empire had been bought on credit through the use of investors' money. To cover his tracks, Insull used his accounting genius to construct a network of holding companies. As the dominant shareholder—usually with about 25 percent of the total stock—Insull could run the companies' boards of directors and thus decide how to use their entire assets. The higher Insull's pyramid of holding companies rose, the wider the gap became between Insull's actual cash assets and the paper value of his empire. By the end of the 1920s, Insull's inner circle, including his brother and his son, held assets with a market value of about $2.5 billion, for which they had invested only $100 million, most of it other people's money.

The stock market crash in October 1929 brought down Insull's paper empire. Besieged by debt and unable to borrow more money, Insull resorted to declaring bankruptcy for his holding companies. As more and more investors learned that they had lost everything in the bankruptcy maneuvers and the nation lurched into the depression, the conviction grew that Insull personified those whose fake prosperity had brought on the Great Crash. They laughed bitterly at cowboy comedian Will Rogers's definition of a holding company as "a thing where you hand an accomplice the goods while the policeman searches you." The Union League Club, a Chicago watering hole for conservative investors, expressed its contempt for Insull by papering its dining room with Insull's worthless stock certificates. But the bottom was not reached until October 1932, when a grand jury indicted Insull and his brother on charges of embezzlement, larceny, and use of the mails to defraud. *Who's Who* rendered its own verdict by dropping the former first citizen of Chicago from its roster.

Insull read about the indictment in Paris, where he had fled after signing over all his bankrupt assets. Yet even with a trail of ruined lives behind him and ample time to reflect on his career, Insull still could not understand why he had lost favor. "Why am I not more popular in the United States?" he asked. "What have I done that every banker and business magnate has not done in the course of business?" When extradition orders for income tax evasion arrived, Insull fled to Italy and then eastward

**SAMUEL INSULL**

*This May 1934* Time *magazine cover shows Samuel Insull hiding his face as he enters the courtroom to face criminal charges. The words underneath—"His hands rocked the cradle before they rocked the boat."—remind readers that Insull had a key role both in building up and in tearing down the country. Journalists and moralists were eager to use Insull, America's most famous fugitive from justice, as the main symbol in a morality tale of how ruthlessly greedy tycoons had brought on the Great Depression.*

through Athens until he was finally cornered in a dank jail cell in Istanbul, where he was being held as a vagrant.

The captive's return to depression-wracked America in the spring of 1934 had the usual melodramatic touches of courtroom drama and disgrace. Insull appeared on the cover of *Time* magazine in the typical fugitive pose, hat pulled down over his face as he was hustled up the courthouse steps, while all around the country pundits declaimed that he had betrayed the public trust.

In the end, however, the incredible complexity of the financial empire that led to Insull's ruin also saved him. With checks, bonds, and stock certificates moving swiftly from one Insull subsidiary to another, who could tell what belonged to whom at any particular moment? No sleuth could match Insull's ingenuity in devising what one headline called the "Insull Daze-Maze." Even the U.S. Senate Banking and Currency Committee, which was investigating the stock market collapse, was stymied. One expert witness, Owen D. Young, chief legal counsel of General Electric, confessed to "a feeling of complete helplessness when I began to examine the complicated structure of the Insull group. . . . It was impossible to get an accounting system that would not have misled even the officers themselves."

While the state attorney thrashed about for incriminating evidence, Insull pleaded his case directly to the jurors. Abandoning his pose as a Napoleonic commander of industry, Insull presented himself as just another seeker of the American dream who like other Americans, from office boys to tycoons, had been caught in a terrible historical accident. For hours, he told the jury of his struggle to overcome meager origins and his bewilderment now, as just a poor old man, over how disaster had befallen the era of prosperity. In his summation to the jury, Insull's lawyer drove the point home. "You have had a description here of an age in American history which we hope will never be repeated. I say that we are trying that age." The jury agreed and found the age guilty, but Insull innocent.

Free but unwilling to remain in America as a nobody, Insull returned to anonymity in Paris, where he died in 1938. According to the police report, Insull collapsed and died of a heart attack in the Paris subway with only about 85 cents of loose change on him. But that was not quite right. Insull had ample resources stashed away and always carried a considerable amount of cash. Someone else from humble origins and similarly committed to the advancement of self-interest must have found the body first. Then Samuel Insull, the artful dodger of American finance, had his own pocket picked, and the police never noticed.

and the fear of risking what was left acted as a great brake on economic activity. With the collapse of the stock market went the New Era's aggressive confidence in America's future as a land of perpetually expanding prosperity.

## Hoover and the Limits of Individualism

Hoover's first act in the aftermath of the crash was characteristic. He called a White House conference of business and labor leaders and urged them to join in a voluntary plan for recovery. The president asked businesses to forge ahead with their pre-crash investment plans, maintain production, and keep their workers on the job. He asked labor to accept the status quo and relinquish demands for improvements in wages, hours, or conditions. Within a few months, however, the bargain had fallen apart. As demand for their products declined, industrialists cut production, sliced wages, and laid off workers. Poorly paid or unemployed workers could not buy much, and decreased spending led to further cuts in production and further loss of jobs. Thus began the terrible spiral of economic decline.

Hoover did not just sit back and watch the depression cut its swath through American society. He worked long hours, wracked his brain for solutions, and, despite what people thought, felt the suffering of the American people. But his belief in rugged individualism—"a quality of the individual alone"— hobbled his ability to act. He resisted plans that called for government intervention in the economy but also disagreed with Secretary of the Treasury Andrew Mellon, who counseled that there was nothing the administration could do but let the depression run a painful course of eliminating those too weak to compete. Hoover countered that cooperation between a free people and a sympathetic government could fix the problems and set the nation back on course.

In early 1930, Hoover got Congress to authorize $420 million for public works projects to give the unemployed something useful to do and create more purchasing power. Congress also agreed to cut taxes by $140 million to stimulate investment. To deal with the problems of rural America, Congress in 1930 passed the Agricultural Marketing Act. It created the Farm Board, which used its budget of $500 million to buy up agricultural surpluses and thus, it was hoped, raise prices. Although the Farm Board bought

**BLACK FRIDAY**
*Edward Laning, a mural painter who lost his personal fortune in the stock market crash, gained a measure of revenge in this melodramatic version of panic on the Stock Exchange floor. The painting shows Stock Exchange president Richard Whitney standing firm in the center as prices and brokers collapse around him. A few years later, however, Whitney went to prison for stealing from other people's accounts to cover his own losses. Laning went on to fame for the murals he painted to adorn Ellis Island and the New York Public Library.*
Collection of John P. Axelrod.

one-third of the nation's wheat supply, conditions worsened. To help end the decline, Hoover joined conservatives in urging protective tariffs on agricultural goods. With his approval, the Hawley-Smoot tariff of 1930 established the highest rates in history.

All to little avail. With each year of Hoover's administration, conditions worsened. Tariffs did not end the suffering of farmers because foreign nations retaliated with increased tariffs of their own that further crippled American farmers' ability to sell abroad. Even more pressing was the plight of the unemployed. Hundreds of thousands of additional workers lost their jobs each month. By 1932, one-quarter of the American workforce—more than 12 million men and women—were unemployed. There was no federal relief, and state services and private charities were swamped. Cries grew louder for the federal government to give hurting people relief, but Hoover counseled fortitude and private charity instead. Comparing federal aid to the "dole" in England, which he thought was destroying the moral fiber of the chronically unemployed, Hoover called upon the Red Cross in 1931 to distribute agricultural surpluses to the hungry. In the face of dire unmet need, he relaxed his principles enough in 1932 to offer small federal loans, not gifts, to the states to help them in their relief efforts. But these concessions were no more than Band-Aids on deep wounds.

Hoover's response to hard-pressed industry was more generous. In keeping with his previous efforts to promote cooperation between business and government, Hoover sponsored the Reconstruction Finance Corporation (RFC), a federal agency empowered to lend government funds to endangered banks, insurance companies, and railroads. It was a "trickle-down" theory: Pump money into the economy at the top, and in the long run the people at the bottom would benefit. But in the long run, as the great English economist of the day John Maynard Keynes put it, we are all dead. In the short run, what critics of the RFC called a "millionaires' dole" trickled very little down to the poor.

# Life in the Depression

In 1930, the nation woke up to the realization that prosperity would not soon return. The trouble was too deep, the engine too cold to restart. Suffering and trial on a massive scale began, and a mood of cold despair settled over the land. Hollow-eyed men and women grew increasingly bewildered and angry in the face of cruel ambiguities. They saw unsellable agricultural surpluses in the countryside and knew that their children were going to bed hungry. They saw factories standing idle and knew that they and millions of others were willing to work. The gap between the American people and leaders who failed to resolve these contradictions widened as the depression deepened. By 1932, America's economic problems had become a dangerous social crisis.

## The Human Toll

Statistics provide a scaffolding for understanding the human dimension of the Great Depression. When Herbert Hoover took office in 1929, the American economy stood at its peak. When he left in 1933, it had reached its twentieth-century low. More than nine thousand banks had shut their doors, and depositors had lost more than $2.5 billion. In 1929, national income was $88 billion. By 1933, it had declined to $40 billion. In 1929, unemployment was 3.1 percent, one and a half million workers. By 1933, unemployment stood at 25 percent, twelve and a half million workers.

Jobless, homeless victims wandered in search of work, and the tramp, or hobo, became one of the most visible figures of the decade. Young men and women unable to land their first job made up about half of the million-strong army of hoboes. Riding the rails or hitchhiking, the vagabonds tended to move southward and westward, toward the sun and opportunities, they hoped, for seasonal agricultural work.

Other unemployed men and women, less hopeful or sick, huddled in doorways—human "junk," as one writer put it. Scavengers haunted alleys behind restaurants and picked over garbage dumps in search of food. In describing what he called the "American Earthquake," the writer Edmund Wilson told of an elderly woman who always took off her glasses to avoid seeing the maggots crawling over the garbage she ate. Starvation claimed its victims. Four New York City hospitals reported 95 deaths from hunger in 1931. But enervating, rampant malnutrition posed the greater threat. The Children's Bureau announced that one of five schoolchildren did not get enough to eat.

*Jobless, homeless victims wandered in search of work, and the tramp, or hobo, became one of the most visible figures of the decade.*

Rural poverty was most acute. Landless tenant farmers and sharecroppers, mainly in the South, came to symbolize the ways poverty crushed the human spirit. In 1930, eight and a half million people, three million of them black, lived in tenant and sharecropping families—amounting to one-quarter of the total southern population. Often illiterate, usually without cash incomes, they crowded into two- and three-room cabins lacking screens or even doors, without plumbing, electricity, running water, or sanitary wells. They subsisted—just barely—on salt pork, cornmeal, molasses, beans, peas, and whatever they could hunt or fish. All the diseases of dietary and vitamin deficiencies wracked them. When economist John Maynard Keynes was asked whether anything like this degradation had existed before, he replied, "Yes, it was called the Dark Ages and it lasted four hundred years."

To meet this human catastrophe, the nation was equipped with the most limited welfare system in the Western world. There was no federal assistance, only a patchwork of voluntary institutions and pinchpenny state and local agencies. For a family of four without any income, the best the city of Philadelphia could do was provide $5.50 per week. That was not enough to live on, but still comparatively generous. New York City, where the greatest number of welfare cases gathered, provided only $2.39 per week; and Detroit, devastated when the bottom fell out of the auto industry, allotted 60 cents a week before the city ran out of money altogether.

The deepening crisis roused old fears and caused some Americans to look for scapegoats. Among the most thoroughly scapegoated were Mexican Americans. During the relatively prosperous years of the 1920s, cheap agricultural labor from Mexico flowed legally across the United States border, welcomed by the large farmers. In the 1930s, however, public opinion turned on the newcomers, styling them as dangerous aliens who took jobs from Americans. Government officials, most prominently those in Los Angeles County, with support from the Department of Labor, targeted all Mexican residents for deportation, regardless of citizenship status. As many as half a million Mexicans and Mexican Americans were deported or fled to Mexico. Among them were children born in the United States, American citizens from the start who had never lived outside the country.

The depression deeply affected the American family. Young people postponed marriage; when they did marry, they produced so few children that demographers warned that, for the first time, the United States was on the verge of losing population. White women, who generally worked in low-paying service areas—as cooks, salesclerks, and secretaries—did not lose their jobs as often as men who worked in industry. Even as the resentment of unemployed men increased toward women workers, necessity drove women into the marketplace. Over-

all, some 25 percent more women were employed for wages in 1940 than in 1930.

As women left the home to replace their husbands as breadwinners, families experienced stress. After a decade of rising consumption, smaller incomes led to significant belt tightening. Working women became increasingly decisive and self-reliant at the same time idle men fell prey to guilt and loss of self-esteem. Yet, though family violence, alcoholism, and suicide escalated, the divorce rate went down. The desperately poor could not afford the legal expense; instead, in dramatically rising numbers, men resorted to desertion.

*Even as the resentment of unemployed men increased toward women workers, necessity drove women into the marketplace.*

As the economy sank, so did Hoover's reputation. Makeshift shantytowns that sprang up on the edges of America's cities were called "Hoovervilles." Newspapers used as cover by those sleeping on the streets were "Hoover blankets." An empty pocket turned inside out was a "Hoover flag," and jackrabbits caught for food were "Hoover hogs." Innumerable bitter jokes circulated about Hoover. One gibe asserted that Hoover was the world's greatest engineer: "In a little more than two years he has drained, ditched, and damned the United States." Another story told of Hoover's request of Andrew Mellon for a nickel to call up a friend. "Here's a dime," Mellon is said to have replied, "call up all your friends."

Hoover's effort to set an example did not help. To express his confidence in prosperity, he favored formal dress and manners in the White House and for dinner, with or without guests, he was attended by a retinue of valets and waiters. No one was starving, he calmly assured the American people from within that display of prosperity.

Not that his administration considered it the business of the federal government to investigate the truth of that assertion. Walter Gifford, president of the American Telephone and Telegraph Company, appointed by Hoover to coordinate private relief efforts, acknowledged to a Senate subcommittee that he had made no attempt to compile figures on how many people were out of work and on relief. Exasperated, Senator Robert La Follette asked if Gifford had any

**PRIVATE CAR**

*In the mid-1930s, LeConte Stewart, an artist who spent most of his life painting the landscapes of his native Utah, noticed a new sight. From his remote hillside above the Union Pacific railroad tracks, he witnessed a stream of tramps heading west. The sight of one young man jauntily braced in the doorway of a boxcar made Stewart think of the elegant private cars of millionaires that used to travel along those same tracks. Stewart entitled this painting* Private Car *and achieved fame for his beautifully ironic depiction of a new wave of pioneers fleeing trouble.*

Private Car *by LeConte Stewart. © The Church of Latter-Day Saints. Used by permission.*

impulse to know the facts. Gifford's response reflected how the nation's business leadership distanced itself from the problems of failure and poverty. "Well," said Gifford genially, "I will not say that I did not make any estimate for my own interest and amusement."

While the wealthy practiced denial, other Americans sought refuge from reality at the movies. Throughout the depression, between sixty and seventy-five million people (nearly two-thirds of the nation) managed to scrounge up enough dimes to fill the movie palaces every week. Box office successes typically blended nostalgia for the lost Golden Twenties with the hope that renewed prosperity lay just around the corner. The leading musicals in 1933, *Forty-Second Street* and *Gold Diggers,* each offered a variation on the old rags-to-riches story of the chorus girl who makes the most of her big break.

As conditions in the country worsened, filmmakers also turned to grittier material. Films such as King Vidor's *Our Daily Bread* (1932) and John Ford's *The Grapes of Wrath* (1940) expressed compassion for the down and out. Gangster films taught grim lessons about ill-gotten gains. Indeed, under the new production code of 1930, designed to protect public morals, all movies had to find some way to show that crime did not pay. *Public Enemy* (1931), the classic cautionary tale about the doom that awaits those who break the law found a particularly shocking way to do so when it ended with gangsters delivering the bullet-riddled body of a hoodlum to the doorstep of his saintly, long-suffering mother.

Despite Hollywood's efforts to keep Americans on the right side of the law, crime increased in the early 1930s. Away from the movie palaces, out in the countryside, the plight of people who had lost their farms to bank foreclosures cut so deep that the romantic idea took hold that bank robbers were only getting back what banks had stolen from the poor. Woody Guthrie, the populist folk singer from Oklahoma, captured the public's tolerance for outlaws in his widely admired tribute to a murderous bank robber with a choirboy face, "The Ballad of Pretty Boy Floyd":

> Yes, as through this world I ramble,
> I see lots of funny men,
> Some will rob you with a six-gun,
> Some will rob you with a pen.
> But as through your life you'll travel,
> Wherever you may roam,
> You won't never see an outlaw drive
> A family from their home.

## Working-Class Militancy

Although the nation's working people bore the brunt of the economic collapse, the labor movement, including the dominant American Federation of Labor (AFL), was slow to respond. Organized labor had been hobbled during the 1920s by courts issuing injunctions curtailing the right of unions to organize and strike. Early in the depression, William Green, head of the AFL, echoed Hoover when he argued that a dole would turn the worker into "a ward of the state." But by 1931, Green had turned militant. "I warn the people who are exploiting the workers," he shouted at the AFL's annual convention, "that they can drive them only so far before they will turn on them and destroy them. They are taking no account of the history of nations in which governments have been overturned. Revolutions grow out of the depths of hunger."

Like the labor leaders, the American people were slow to anger, then strong in protest. On the morning of March 7, 1932, several thousand unemployed autoworkers massed at the gates of Ford's River Rouge factory in Dearborn, Michigan, to demand work. Henry Ford sent out his private security forces, who told the demonstrators to disperse. The workers refused and began hurling rocks. The Ford army responded with tear gas and freezing water but quickly escalated to gunfire. When they stopped, four demonstrators were dead and dozens more wounded. An outraged public—forty thousand strong—turned out for the unemployed men's funerals. Editorials and protest rallies across the country denounced Ford's callous and brutal resort to violence.

Farmers, who desperately needed relief, mounted an uprising of their own soon afterward. When Congress refused to guarantee farm prices that would at least equal the cost of production, some three thousand farmers, led by the flamboyant Milo Reno, created the National Farmers' Holiday Association, so named because its members planned to force farmers to take a "holiday" from delivering produce to the public. Invoking the Boston Tea Party, Reno and his followers barricaded roads around Sioux City, Iowa, turned back farmers heading for market, and dumped thousands of gallons of milk in the ditches. Although the rebellion was short-lived and did not force a critical shortage of food, it raised general awareness of farm grievances. Farm militants had fuller material effect with what they called "penny sales." When farms defaulted on their mortgages and were put up for auction, neighbors packed the auctions and, after warning others not to bid, bought the foreclosed property for a few pennies and returned it to the bankrupt owners. Under this kind of pressure, some states suspended debts or reduced mortgages.

In the vast agricultural holdings of California, resistance combined farmer and labor tactics. When landowners cut their already substandard wages to laborers in what one critic aptly called "factories in the fields," more than fifty thousand farmworkers, most of them Mexicans, went on strike. Surveying the strife mounting nationwide, John Simpson, president of the National Farmers Union, observed in 1933 that "the biggest and finest crop of revolutions you ever saw is sprouting all over the country right now."

Hard times also revived the left in America. When the crash struck, Eugene Debs was dead and so, for all purposes, was the Socialist Party. But the Great Depression—the massive failure of Western capitalism—brought socialism back to life and the American Communist Party to its greatest size and influence in American history. Eventually, some

100,000 disillusioned Americans—workers, intellectuals, college students—joined the Communist Party in the belief that only an overthrow of the capitalist system could save the victims of depression. In 1931, the party, having increased membership in its National Miners Union from one hundred to twenty-five thousand, carried its convictions into Harlan County, Kentucky, to support a strike by harshly oppressed coal miners. Newspapers and newsreels riveted the attention of the public with their graphic portrayal of the violence unleashed by mine owners' thugs against the strikers. Eventually, the miners were beaten down, but the Communist Party emerged from the coal fields with a reputation as the most dedicated and fearless champions of the union cause.

---

*The Great Depression brought socialism back to life and the American Communist Party to its greatest size and influence in American history.*

---

The left also led the fight against racism. While both major parties hesitated to challenge the system of segregation in the South, the Socialist Party, led by moral reformer Norman Thomas, sought to break down the system of sharecropping that left many African Americans in poverty and virtual servitude. The Communist Party took action as well. When nine young black men in Scottsboro, Alabama, were arrested on trumped-up rape charges, a team of lawyers sent by the party managed to save the defendants from the electric chair. The party also opposed the efforts of Alabama plantation owners to evict their black tenants. Although Communists were unable to force much change on the deeply entrenched southern way of life, their efforts briefly attracted new recruits to the party. From only about fifty black members in 1930, party totals rose to ten thousand by the end of the decade before most of the converts returned to traditional reform movements rooted in constitutional rights and religious conviction.

The left often sparked action, but protests by workers and farmers occurred on a far greater scale. Breadlines, soup kitchens, foreclosures, unemployment, and cold despair drove patriotic men and women to question American capitalism. "I am as conservative as any man could be," a Wisconsin farmer explained, "but any economic system that has in its power to set me and my wife in the streets, at my age—what can I see but red?"

## Conclusion: The Era of Boom and Bust

The decade of the 1920s defies generalization. During those years living standards rose, economic opportunity increased, and an image of cultural and personal liberation prevailed. For many Americans at the time, however, none of the glamor had much meaning. Instead of plunging into speculation on Wall Street, seeking thrills at speakeasies, or escaping to Paris, the vast majority went ahead as before with the struggle to attain a decent existence.

After the crash swept away the aura of high living, different images emerged to fix the depression in memory: apple sellers on Broadway; empty apartment buildings alongside cardboard shantytowns; mountains of oranges rotting in the California sun while guards with shotguns chased away the hungry. Sometimes the image was of sullen apathy flaming into revolt: a line of unemployed men in New York City suddenly charging hiring agents and destitute farmers invading England, Arkansas, to loot the food stores at gunpoint.

Eugene Debs, the most beloved socialist and friend of the common man, took from his battles in and out of prison the lesson that human happiness is never found through a solitary search. "When I rise," he liked to say, "it will be *with* the ranks, and not *from* the ranks." In the depths of the depression, however, faith in any sort of rise waned as the laboring ranks receded into hardship. The businessmen who rallied round Herbert Hoover thus faced something more desperate, more radical, than the old call for working-class solidarity and progressive reform. On a night in June 1931 a man driving a large car on the outskirts of Gary, Indiana, got a taste of what that might be when a brick crashed through his windshield. "What's the big idea?" he shouted, as he slammed on his brakes. Out of the darkness came the reply: "All rich guys ought to be strung up." "Who are you?" the driver asked. "We're the fellows that'll do the stringing."

## CHRONOLOGY

**1920**  Eighteenth Amendment, prohibiting sale of liquor, goes into effect.

Nineteenth Amendment, granting women the vote, ratified.

Station KDKA in Pittsburgh begins first regular commercial radio broadcasts.

Marcus Garvey hosts Universal Negro Improvement Association conference in Harlem.

Republican Warren G. Harding elected president.

**1921**  Sheppard-Towner Act, providing infant health care, passes in Congress.

**1922**  Fordney-McCumber Act sets protective tariffs at record heights.

Principles of new business-minded era expressed in publication of Henry Ford's *My Life and Work* and Herbert Hoover's *American Individualism.*

About thirty artists and intellectuals renounce American society in *Civilization in the United States.*

New laws imposing quotas according to nationality end historical tradition of open immigration.

**1923**  Equal Rights Amendment introduced in Congress.

**August.** Harding dies in office, succeeded by Calvin Coolidge.

**1924**  Calvin Coolidge elected president.

**1925**  John Scopes convicted for violating Tennessee statute forbidding teaching of evolution.

Alain Locke expresses cultural aspirations of Harlem Renaissance in *The New Negro.*

**1926**  Ernest Hemingway's novel of expatriate Paris, *The Sun Also Rises,* published.

**1927**  Charles Lindbergh becomes America's most famous hero by flying alone across Atlantic.

Italian anarchist immigrants Sacco and Vanzetti executed.

**1928**  Herbert Hoover defeats Alfred E. Smith.

**1929**  Robert and Helen Lynd publish their study of an average American small city, *Middletown.*

**October 24.** Stock market collapses on Black Thursday.

**1931**  Nine black men arrested in Scottsboro case.

**1932**  Several thousand demonstrators at Ford plant protest unemployment; security forces fire on crowd, killing four.

Farmers' Holiday movement blocks roads and pours milk on ground to protest falling prices.

## SUGGESTED READINGS

Frederick Lewis Allen, *Only Yesterday: An Informal History of the Nineteen-Twenties* (1930). A readable, perceptive account of the decade by a journalist who lived through it. Allen makes up for his disappointment over the defeat of Progressivism by focusing on the absurdities and bad judgment that brought the New Era down.

William J. Barber, *From New Era to New Deal: Herbert Hoover, the Economists, and American Economic Policy, 1921–1933* (1985). An explanation by a socially focused economist of how the economy of the 1920s worked and why it was unable to withstand destabilizing forces. Barber shows how the situation reflected Hoover's thinking and anticipated New Deal reform.

Irving Bernstein, *The Lean Years: A History of the American Worker, 1920–1933* (1960). A sympathetic account by one experienced in the labor wars of how workers had a small share of prosperity in the 1920s but a full measure of hardship after the Crash. Bernstein is effective in relating the fate of organized labor with the lives of individuals.

David Burner, *Herbert Hoover: A Public Life* (1979). A balanced analysis of Hoover's involvement with public affairs over a long lifetime. Hoover's strengths and weaknesses are well explained, as is his rise and fall and rise again in public esteem.

Dan T. Carter, *Scottsboro: A Tragedy of the Modern South* (1969). A vivid account of a famous trial. Carter shows how southern justice during the era of segregation disadvantaged blacks, while also explaining the forces of reform that eventually won acquittal.

Malcolm Cowley, *Exile's Return* (1934; 1954). The classic memoir of a generation of rebellious artists who fled America for Paris in the 1920s. Cowley charts the curve from alienation during the New Era to return and recommitment as prosperity ended.

Ann Douglas, *Mongrel Manhattan in the 1920s* (1994). New York as the center of wealth, art, and glamour in the New Era emerges clearly in this rich account. Douglas makes a valuable new contribution by relating the Harlem Renaissance to the life of the city around it.

Nancy MacLean, *Behind the Mask of Chivalry: The Making of the Second Ku Klux Klan* (1994). An examination of the Klan that recognizes it as a moralizing protest against change as well as an outlaw hate group. MacLean helps us see both the socioeconomic and ideological roots of the revived Klan.

Lary May, *Screening out the Past: The Birth of Mass Culture and the Motion Picture Industry* (1980). A history of the movies that explains how they reflected and changed popular culture. May deals with film as a medium and with the social customs and institutions that grew up around it.

Michael Parrish, *Anxious Decades: America in Prosperity and Depression, 1920–1941* (1992). An overview that explains a wide range of events and the persons responsible for them. Although he is primarily a social and economic historian, Parrish includes perceptive insight into the highly creative imaginativeness of the time.

David P. Peeler, *Hope among Us Yet: Social Criticism and Social Solace in the Depression Years* (1987). An examination of attempts during the 1930s to explain and alleviate the effects of the depression on the outlook and morale of its victims. Peeler discusses the ways visual, literary, and critical modes came together to form new perspectives on the human condition.

Ted Vincent, *Mudville's Revenge: The Rise and Fall of American Sport* (1981). An energetic telling that is in keeping with the turbulence of the golden age of sport during the 1920s. Vincent's treatment of his cast of characters and events comes together in a mirror of social attitudes.

T. H. Watkins, *The Great Depression: America in the 1930s* (1993). A companion volume to the Blackside film documentary on the depression that offers both a panoramic view and vividly apt analyses of why things happened the way they did.

Reynold M. Wik, *Henry Ford and Grass-Roots America* (1972). The importance of Ford as both common-man sage and revolutionizer of industry are well blended in this account. Wik goes far in making Ford a symbol of his times.

William Young and David E. Kaiser, *Postmortem: New Evidence in the Case of Sacco and Vanzetti* (1985). Written in response to those disputing the condemned anarchists' claims of innocence, this book offers the most recent and effective evidence that Sacco and Vanzetti were framed.

**SOUVENIR SEWING NEEDLE BOOK**
*Borrowing the current popular tune "Happy Days Are Here Again" as the theme song for Roosevelt's 1932 campaign was an inspired act of wishful thinking in those dark days. By 1936, conditions had improved enough that this souvenir needle book could celebrate "Happiness Restored" a bit more realistically. The major places where economic recovery was to be created—farm, factory, and office—are shown operating in full swing on the cover of this little container that held sewing needles. But in accord with the New Deal emphasis on security at home, the figure of domestic happiness looms largest in the center under the arch of prosperity.*
Collection of Janice L. and David J. Frent.

# THE NEW DEAL ERA
## 1932–1939

I N JULY 1932, A RAGGED, DUSTY CONTINGENT of some fifteen thousand World War I veterans, calling themselves the Bonus Expeditionary Army, marched into Washington, D.C., to request the bonus for their military service that was supposed to be paid in 1945. Destitute, many of these petitioners thumbed rides to Washington or came in boxcars, shipped free by sympathetic railway workers. They first camped in unfinished federal buildings just three blocks from the Capitol and then overflowed onto the mud flats along the Anacostia River.

President Hoover, angered by these disturbers of the peace and raiders of the Treasury, urged Congress to vote against the bonus because its $2.4 billion cost was more than the government could afford. To strengthen their defense of a balanced budget, which they believed necessary to restore prosperity, Hoover and his supporters vilified the bonus marchers themselves. Despite an official study showing that 94 percent of the marchers had served in the armed forces, they claimed that many in the bonus army were not veterans at all. Compounding the slander were false reports, which Hoover repeated, that the march was a revolutionary menace because its leaders were Communists. In reality, most of the marchers believed in traditional values. They had come to Washington to regain their respectability, not to overthrow the government.

Refusing to confer with men whom he thought undeserving of such recognition, Hoover resorted to force. Army Chief of Staff Douglas MacArthur assured Hoover that the military would quickly get rid of the squatters and impress the public with the government's authority. Late in the afternoon of July 28, Hoover watched from the Oval Office as one thousand soldiers lobbed tear gas into the buildings occupied by the marchers. Then, in defiance of Hoover's orders to refrain from a direct attack, MacArthur commanded his troops to charge the nearby open-air encampment. In the rout that followed, several bonus marchers suffered bayonet wounds and one infant died of gas poisoning.

The following day, Franklin D. Roosevelt, Hoover's Democratic rival in the 1932 presidential campaign, read about the attack with "a feeling of horror." Were it up to him, Roosevelt declared, he would have taken coffee and doughnuts to the protesters and invited them to work on reforestation projects or to settle on vacant federal land where they could farm and regain their independence.

Roosevelt's instinctive response echoed the slogan he had announced when he accepted the Democratic nomination: "I pledge you, I pledge myself, to a new deal for the American people." Like Hoover, Roosevelt thought the bonus payment was too expensive, but, unlike Hoover, he declared repeatedly that if people desperately needed help, the government should find a way to give it.

Almost a year later—after Roosevelt had been elected president—a second group of about 3,000 veterans gathered in Washington to lobby for payment of the

*WASHINGTON BONUS MARCH*
*This watercolor is one of a series executed by twenty-four-year-old Lewis Rubenstein in 1932*
*after traveling as an observer with the bonus marchers. Here he depicts the march in its early*
*stages as a hopeful, somewhat theatrical adventure. The figure on the running board of the car,*
*megaphone in hand, seems almost like a cheerleader encouraging the team as it advances on its*
*goal—in this case the steps of the United States Capitol.*
Janet Marqusee Fine Arts Ltd.

bonus. Roosevelt arranged for the men to be fed and housed in military barracks at government expense while they petitioned Congress. Eleanor Roosevelt strode into their camp to express her concern and lead the men in singing favorite wartime songs. Franklin Roosevelt then received a delegation at the White House and genially recalled how they had all served together in the war and reassured them that, although he could not support the bonus, the government was prepared to rescue victims of the depression. In the end, 2,600 of the 3,000 marchers enrolled in the government's Civilian Conservation Corps, designed to put people to work conserving the nation's natural resources, rather than accepting government transportation home.

Roosevelt's deft response to the war veterans stood in stark contrast to Hoover's refusal even to meet with the first bonus marchers. As the Second Bonus Army prepared to break camp, a reporter overheard remarks that brought into focus part of the meaning of Roosevelt's reform program that he called the New Deal. One particular rain-soaked veteran asked, "What is this bird Roosevelt up to?" Another shrugged and replied, "All I know is he's a hooman bein'."

# Franklin D. Roosevelt: A Patrician in Government

The man elected president in 1932 was born into wealth and social prominence yet managed to establish an extraordinary relationship with the American people, especially the poor and dispossessed. The explanation of his success lay partly in the circumstances in which he held office. In his twelve-year reign, Roosevelt experienced two of the nation's greatest crises—the Great Depression and World War II. But simply presiding over economic catastrophe and war was no guarantee of popularity or greatness. Roosevelt's ability to convey sympathetic concern and to inspire the confidence to act against trouble as well as his political skills made him the dominant figure of his age.

## The Growth of a Politician

Born in 1882, the only child of a family with substantial inherited wealth, Franklin Delano Roosevelt grew up in a safe and secure environment that steeped him in the values of Christian service. He absorbed early a belief, which never left him, that the privileged had a duty to look after the poor and weak. At Groton Academy and Harvard University, his beliefs were fitted into an education designed to prepare him to take his place within the leadership reserved for his elite social class.

After a brief career as a reform member of the New York state legislature from 1910 to 1912 and as assistant secretary of the navy in Woodrow Wilson's administration, Roosevelt was nominated by the Democrats for the vice presidency in 1920. Despite Harding's landslide win, Roosevelt's spirited campaigning convinced many that he had a golden future in politics.

Fate, however, had a grim detour in store. In the summer of 1921, Roosevelt became paralyzed from the waist down, a victim of the polio virus. Despite battling the affliction with cheerful fortitude, Roosevelt would never again walk unassisted. But with the help of his devoted wife, Eleanor, and his tireless aide Louis Howe, he did regain his intense desire for an active political career. He became a student of public life and acquired an encyclopedic knowledge of local conditions and political activities. Getting to know people in their own setting had always been Roosevelt's personal and political style. Now, after the polio attack, he found ways to draw people to him through maps, letters, phone calls, receptions, dinner parties, cruises, and the Warm Springs, Georgia, polio sanitarium that he founded. No longer able to distract himself in physical activity, he concentrated on the art of political strategy.

Roosevelt's chance to return to political office came sooner than he expected. When New York Governor Al Smith announced his presidential candidacy in 1928, he convinced Roosevelt to run for his vacated position and so help Smith capture the state's electoral votes. The tactic did not work for Smith, who was defeated by Herbert Hoover, but Roosevelt managed a narrow upset victory. As the newly elected governor, he proposed a balanced program of conservation and scientific farming in the countryside combined with improved social services and working conditions in the cities.

Then the 1929 stock market crash forced him to take a different approach. His belief in government's prime role to respond to social need and in the idea that states could be laboratories for national policy allowed him to find democratic and humane ways of dealing with the crisis.

On that basis of compelling necessity, Roosevelt supported the largest state relief program in the nation's history. He played down any appearance of radical change by naming the initiative the Temporary Emergency Relief Act (TERA). Using words like *temporary* and *emergency* made it possible to reassure a fearful public that the new initiatives were set securely within the established traditions of democracy and capitalism.

Roosevelt's highly visible efforts to do something constructive gained him the gratitude of constituents and the attention of national politicians. In 1930, New Yorkers reelected him governor by a margin of 750,000 votes and assured his position as the Democratic Party's leading candidate in the 1932 presidential election.

In an address to the New York legislature in August, 1931, Roosevelt summed up his activist credo:

> The duty of the State toward the citizen is the duty of the servant to its master. . . . One of these duties of the State is that of caring for those of its citizens who find themselves the victims of such adverse circumstances as make them unable to obtain even the necessities for mere existence without the aid of others. . . . To these unfortunate citizens aid must be extended by governments, not as a matter of charity but as a matter of social duty. . . . [No one should go] unfed, unclothed, or unsheltered.

## The Election of 1932

Roosevelt announced his candidacy for the presidency in January 1932. The Roosevelt name, his radiant personal charm, his earlier service in Washington, and his stature as a vice presidential candidate had made him a national figure before the crash. Afterward, his smashing reelection and leading role among governors in combating the depression gave him stature as the most active champion of recovery. In all respects, Roosevelt's record compared favorably with Hoover's dismal image as a last-ditch defender of the old order.

To supply his campaign with fresh ideas, Roosevelt assembled a group of experts on national issues that a journalist dubbed the "Brains Trust." Led by a Columbia professor, Rexford Tugwell, and a lawyer and economist, Adolf Berle, the Brains Trust plied Roosevelt with passionate arguments in favor of government planning to introduce stability and fair play into the marketplace and a welfare state to aid the helpless and end poverty. Despite support from the Brains Trust and his own personal and political strengths, Roosevelt still had to overcome the old split in the Democratic Party between the rural South and the working-class cities. Moreover, he had to avoid alienating the party faithful, who often did not agree among themselves. He added the West to his eastern and southern base through support of direct cash subsidies to farmers and commitment to the West's interest in conservation of natural resources and water development.

Roosevelt needed all his impressive political skills to overcome his rivals within the Democratic Party. On the right, Al Smith, the party's 1928 presidential candidate, attacked him as a fomenter of class conflict, while progressives chided Roosevelt for his unwillingness to offer bold plans for redistributing wealth and regulating the economy, steps considered to be class warfare by Smith's faction of the party. At the end of the scramble for votes, Roosevelt narrowly won the nomination at the head of a peculiar new coalition. It lumped together his friends within the Democratic Party's eastern establishment, big-city machine bosses, old Wilsonian reformers, entrenched southerners—many of them deeply conservative and racist—along with angry farmers, labor unions, and urban ethnic communities. To give that unwieldy coalition any degree of coherence, Roosevelt realized that he needed to establish a personal, symbolic presence above the fray of political battle.

Roosevelt broke with the precedent that the nominee should stay at home during the party's convention and await word of the party's choice. Instead, he flew to the convention in Chicago to deliver his acceptance speech in person. The flight, he told the delegates, signified his intention to be bold and active. He proposed to lead the party in the direction "of liberal thought, of planned action, of enlightened international outlook, and of the greatest good to the greatest number of our citizens." Roosevelt expressed his twin allegiance to the New Freedom of Woodrow Wilson and the Square Deal of Theodore Roosevelt by forging the label for his own program: the New Deal.

> *Roosevelt realized that he needed to establish a personal, symbolic presence above the fray of political battle.*

Frustrated that his glib opponent tried out a variety of positions rather than committing to only one, President Hoover, the Republican nominee, attacked Roosevelt as a "chameleon on plaid" and decried the New Deal as un-American collectivism of the sort that Communists and fascists used to sub-

**ROOSEVELT CALLS FOR ACTION**
*Franklin Roosevelt charged toward the presidential nomination in 1932, stressing the need for government action against the depression. To dramatize his point, he broke with custom by traveling to the convention in Chicago to accept the nomination. Once at the podium to launch a "New Deal," Roosevelt spoke with animated force to establish a contrast with the stolid lecturing style of his opponent, Herbert Hoover. As this and all other authorized pictures demonstrate, Roosevelt insisted that his activist image never be undermined by any indication that he required leg braces and assistance to walk.*
Franklin D. Roosevelt Library.

due the masses. Hoover praised the tried-and-true virtues of self-reliance, rather than handouts and government controls. Many voters, however, heard Hoover's appeals for individual effort and sacrifice as coldhearted rhetoric that ignored their suffering. The president soon became the scapegoat for all ills, his very name a label for poverty. New York City's Parks Department officially designated as "Hoover Valley" a gully where derelicts huddled in Central Park. When home-run king Babe Ruth was criticized for requesting a salary higher than President Hoover's, the Babe shot back with indisputable accuracy, "So what? I had a better year."

On election day, Hoover went down to utter defeat. Roosevelt received 22.8 million votes, 57 percent of the total, to 15.8 million votes for Hoover. In the electoral college, Roosevelt's margin was even more lopsided, 472 to 59. Riding Roosevelt's political coattails, Democrats swept into control of Congress for the first time since 1916. Democrats ruled the Senate by a margin of 59 to 36 and dominated the House by 313 to 117. Although Roosevelt had barely secured the Democrats' nomination, he won an overwhelming victory at the head of a fragmented party that had not received a majority of the votes in a presidential election since Franklin Pierce won in 1852.

The electoral switch from a landslide for Hoover and the Republicans in the 1928 election to a landslide for Roosevelt and the Democrats in 1932 was the greatest change in voter choice in the nation's history (Map 24.1). It began what political analysts have termed the "Roosevelt Revolution"—a fundamental realignment of voter allegiance that linked farmers, industrial laborers, white-collar workers, African Americans, immigrants, women, and intellectuals to the New Deal. The concept that had prevailed since the Civil War of weak central government deferring to economic free enterprise had been repudiated by a public eager to place its faith in a man who promised drastic change.

## The First New Deal in Action

At noon on March 4, 1933, Americans anxiously gathered around their radios to hear a serene and confident new president declare that the "only thing we have to fear is fear itself" and then promise "di-rect, vigorous action." The first months of Roosevelt's administration, called "the Hundred Days," were a blur of action that carried out that promise. The most immediate task was to offer relief to the destitute, including the 25 percent of the workforce that was unemployed. Their plight pointed toward a second need: the recovery of business and farming so that jobs would be available to all workers. And that goal led to the third challenge: reform of the system to guard against any future economic collapse.

### The New Dealers

The New Deal was the only moment in American history when a president receptive to reforms took office in bad times rather than good. Roosevelt's reform heroes—Andrew Jackson, Theodore Roosevelt, and Woodrow Wilson—had the good fortune to serve during economic booms. Roosevelt confronted the more daunting task of reversing an economic depression without violating the nation's allegiance to democracy and capitalism. Great numbers of reformers hurried to Washington in the spring of 1933, drawn by the combination of public desperation and the chance to serve under a president receptive to new ideas. "As for those first New Deal days," Gardiner C. Means, an economic adviser, recalled, "much of the excitement came from improvisation. Nothing was fully set in the minds of the people there. They were open to fresh ideas. Always."

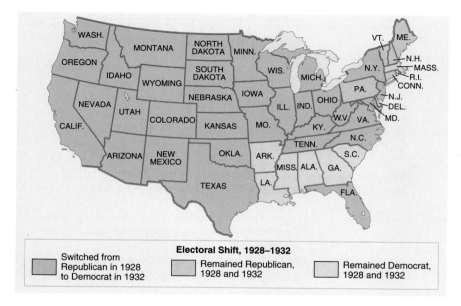

**MAP 24.1**
*Electoral Shift, 1928–1932*
Democratic victory in 1932 signaled the rise of a New Deal coalition within which women and minorities, many of them new voters, made the Democrats the majority party for the first time in the twentieth century.

**Electoral Shift, 1928–1932**

Switched from Republican in 1928 to Democrat in 1932

Remained Republican, 1928 and 1932

Remained Democrat, 1928 and 1932

In recognition of his sprawling party base, Roosevelt selected his cabinet and staff to represent important constituencies. He also chose advisers who would be loyal to him and who would be unlikely to become rivals for power. His vice president, John "Catcus Jack" Garner of Texas, was a source of pride to the Southwest and a shrewd negotiator with Congress. For secretary of state, Roosevelt chose an old Wilsonian southerner and advocate of free trade, Cordell Hull, and to head the treasury, Roosevelt called upon Will Woodin, a former industrialist and lifelong Republican who was nonetheless eager to carry out Roosevelt's experimental approach. In these appointments, Roosevelt made clear his intention to establish a friendly, cooperative relationship with businessmen and bankers yet, at the same time, to proceed openly to test ways of rescuing the economic system.

For the heads of the Labor and Agriculture Departments, whose constituencies were more fully the forgotten and the hard-pressed, Roosevelt turned to reformers. He chose Frances Perkins, the New York State labor commissioner during his governorship, to become the first female secretary of labor, much to the outrage of traditional labor leaders. Henry A. Wallace of Iowa, a voice for scientific experiment and government regulation of markets, was tapped to be secretary of agriculture.

For other, less central appointments Roosevelt rounded out a cabinet and a set of advisers that represented virtually all sections of the country, both major parties, the three major religions, and both sexes. Through it all, Roosevelt radiated good cheer and relished his task as the impresario of a great rescue operation and the restorer of public confidence. Roosevelt wore out his assistants, picking their brains, prodding them to find fresh solutions. To communicate with the public, he began his practice of frequent news conferences, which brought him face to face with the press thirty times during the Hundred Days and at least once a week thereafter. His wide grin and infectious optimism made him the personal symbol of recovery, the emblem of hope for millions.

## Banking and Finance Reform

The new administration first targeted the disaster engulfing America's banking system. By March 4, 1933, when Roosevelt was inaugurated, the nation's governors had suspended almost all banking operations within their states. That was a desperate action, but since 1930 more than five thousand banks with $3.4 billion in assets had gone under. On March 5, 1933, Roosevelt made good his inaugural pledge for "action now" by announcing a four-day "bank holiday" that converted emergency state action into federal policy. Three days later, Roosevelt sent Congress the Emergency Banking Act, which Congress passed in four hours (Table 24.1). Under the provisions of the bill, the secretary of the treasury could decide which banks were stable enough to reopen and could authorize the Reconstruction Finance

---

**TABLE 24.1**

MAJOR LEGISLATION OF THE NEW DEAL'S FIRST HUNDRED DAYS

| Name of Act | Date Passed | Basic Provisions |
|---|---|---|
| Emergency Banking Act | March 9, 1933 | Provided for reopening stable banks and authorizing RFC supply funds |
| Civilian Conservation Corps Act | March 31, 1933 | Provided jobs for unemployed youth |
| Agricultural Adjustment Act | May 12, 1933 | Provided funds to pay farmers for not growing surplus crops |
| Federal Emergency Relief Act | May 12, 1933 | Provided relief funds for the destitute |
| Tennessee Valley Authority Act | May 18, 1933 | Set up authority for development of electric power and conservation |
| National Industrial Recovery Act | June 16, 1933 | Specified cooperation among business, government, and labor in setting fair prices and working conditions |
| Glass-Steagall Banking Act | June 16, 1933 | Created Federal Deposit Insurance Corporation (FDIC) to insure bank deposits |

**LISTENING TO FDR'S FIRESIDE CHATS**
*Roosevelt's "fireside chat" radio talks enabled the president to address national problems in the intimate style of a family friend offering advice. In this photograph, one of the "common men" whom the New Deal would be expected to affect leans toward his radio in apparent recognition that he has much at stake in what is being said.*
Franklin D. Roosevelt Library.

Corporation (RFC) to supply funds for immediate circulation. Congress then created the Federal Deposit Insurance Corporation (FDIC) to insure bank customers against the loss of their deposits if their bank should fail.

The New Deal's more radical supporters were disappointed that Roosevelt did not nationalize the banks and make them a firm cornerstone for national planning. Instead, the private banking system was propped up with federal funds and subjected to federal regulation and oversight, and individual deposits were secured by the United States government. Within a few days, most of the nation's major banks had reopened their doors, and they remained solvent throughout the depression years.

On March 12, Roosevelt broadcast his first "fireside chat" to the nation, explaining why the banking legislation was needed and how it gave good reason for confidence. That radio talk, suggesting a cozy gathering of the nation at the family hearth to discuss how much spending money was left, was a masterstroke. Roosevelt, speaking in cheerful, simple, fatherly terms, came through as a friendly savior echoing his inaugural address with

his reassurance against fear. In the minds of a majority of Americans, the New Deal had established its competence and humaneness, and a glimmer of the nation's old optimism returned.

Turning to the stock market, whose scandals so vividly symbolized the 1920s, Roosevelt was eager to enact provisions that would end dubious practices such as the pyramiding of holding companies that created Samuel Insull's false fortune or profitable stock trading on the basis of insider information. At his insistence, Congress passed legislation in 1933 and 1934 that created the Securities and Exchange Commission (SEC) to license investment dealers, monitor all stock transactions, restrict margin buying, and require corporate officers to make full disclosures of their stock offerings and take responsibility for any claims they made about their companies.

Roosevelt named an abrasive and successful Wall Street trader, Joseph P. Kennedy, as chairman of the SEC. When critics opposed the choice of someone whose reputation had been clouded by shrewd stock manipulation, Roosevelt replied wickedly, "Set a thief to catch a thief." Kennedy proved to be tough enough to face down threats by brokers, some of them with things to hide, to boycott the exchange or even move it out of the country. Soon the SEC won praise for its effectiveness, and Wall Street regained respect within business circles.

## Relief and Conservation Programs

Having rescued the nation's financial structure, Roosevelt took on the plight of the unemployed, the landless, the disabled, and those who were too old or too young to work. The Federal Emergency Relief Administration (FERA) Act made good on the president's promise that he would not abandon Americans to hunger and homelessness. Soon, FERA supported from four to five million households each month and funded thousands of work projects for the unemployed. Dera Johnson, wife of an Alabama coal miner who had become too sick to work, expressed the hope underlying the program when she described the teaching job she had gotten through FERA: "That class was a lifesaver to my family. I taught it for a year, and his rest had improved Johnson so much that he went back to work." FERA also took the lead in providing vaccinations and immunizations for millions of unprotected poor people, helped build desperately needed flood protection systems, and supported literacy classes for the most ill-prepared citizens.

*Having rescued the financial structure, Roosevelt took on the plight of the unemployed, the landless, the disabled, and those who were too old or too young to work.*

Roosevelt's favorite work relief program was the Civilian Conservation Corps (CCC), which offered unemployed young men a chance to perform useful outdoor work and reflected Roosevelt's longstanding enthusiasm for conservation and his preference for the country over the city. Many of the recipients from the cities had good reason to agree with him. Blackie Gold remembered how as a child he had "to go out and beg for coal, buy bread that's two, three days old" in order to help support his large family. In 1937, when he was seventeen, Gold joined the CCC for thirty dollars a month. "I really enjoyed it," he remembered, adding appreciatively,

"I had three wonderful square meals a day." By the time the vigorous program ended in 1942, the CCC had enrolled three million young people and achieved significant results. The CCC erected dams to stop soil erosion and tame rivers, and it also planted more than two billion new trees to replenish forest preserves and check dust storms in the Southwest. CCC workers strung 83,000 miles of telephone wires, constructed 122,000 miles of minor roads and trails, and located 23,000 new water sources in the nation's wilderness. In the end, the CCC left a legacy of magnificent outdoor recreation areas, along with the roads and communication that made them accessible to millions of people.

The most spectacular accomplishment of the New Deal's conservation efforts was the Tennessee Valley Authority (TVA), established in 1933. The TVA was a regional organization designed to build hydroelectric power dams along the Tennessee River and to bring power and light to impoverished rural communities. The TVA planned to build model towns for power station workers and provide new homes for farmers who would benefit from electricity and flood control. At the same time, the TVA sponsored programs to encourage local crafts and other folkways (Map 24.2).

Following the Tennessee River across the state lines of Kentucky, Virginia, North Carolina, Tennessee, Georgia, Alabama, and Mississippi, the TVA set out to demonstrate that a partnership between the federal government and local residents could overcome traditional limitations of state boundaries and free enterprise to make efficient use of abundant resources and break an ancient cycle of poverty. The TVA became the most ambitious example of New Deal enthusiasm for planning. But hampered by bitter resistance from competing private power companies, the TVA never fully realized its utopian ends. It did, however, succeed in bringing electric power, flood protection, soil reclamation, and, therefore, sharply improved prosperity to the area it served.

## Agricultural Initiatives

Farmers in the 1930s sought to make up for low crop prices by increasing production, causing a self-defeating cycle of crop surpluses and still lower prices. At the same time, unemployment robbed consumers of the money to buy even low-priced farm products. In response to the crisis, a farm

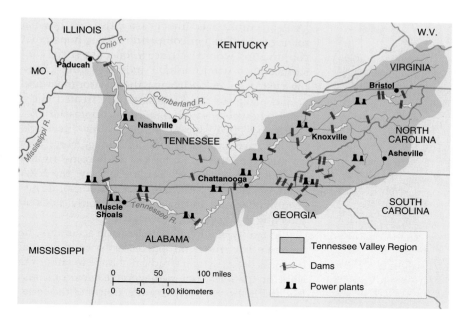

**MAP 24.2**
*The Tennessee Valley Authority*
*The New Deal created the Tennessee Valley Authority to modernize a vast impoverished region with hydroelectric power dams and, at the same time, to reclaim eroded lands and preserve old folkways.*

economist named M. L. Wilson devised the voluntary domestic allotment plan, which called for paying farmers to leave some of their land idle, thus reducing crop surpluses and boosting prices. In May, Congress enthusiastically incorporated Wilson's plan within the Agricultural Adjustment Act (AAA) and soon afterward passed companion legislation, the Farm Credit Act (FCA), to provide credit on mortgaged farm property to head off foreclosures that would drive debt-ridden farmers from their land.

The security provided by the AAA and FCA dampened the urge for farm revolts and nudged prices upward. Overall results were mixed, however. In the corn, hog, and wheat region of the Midwest, farmers came together democratically, and a reasonably equitable distribution of benefits followed. In the South, local control meant that sharecroppers and tenant farmers on cotton plantations were denied a decent share of the benefits, while large growers reaped huge subsidies for putting land out of production—and tenants out of work.

Nonetheless, the AAA and FCA guided agriculture toward prosperity. With almost all major crops limited, surpluses declined and gross farm income rose from $6.4 billion in 1932 to $8.5 billion in 1934. The trickle of 7,800 federal loans in 1932 rose to a flood of 287,881 in less than a year after the FCA was enacted in 1933. By the end of the decade, the federal government had financed 40 percent of farm

mortgage debt, and the shadow of foreclosure had receded from most farmers' doorsteps.

After putting both the TVA and AAA in place, the administration turned to fulfilling the old progressive dream that electricity and all its modern benefits be extended to rural America. When Roosevelt became president, about 90 percent of the country outside the cities and towns was without electricity. Power magnates like Samuel Insull saw little profit in sending expensive transmission lines into sparsely settled territory. In May 1935, the New Deal finally overcame the resistance of the private power industry and created the Rural Electrification Administration (REA). Encouraged by the successes of the AAA and TVA, the REA gave low-cost loans to farm cooperatives to bring power into their communities. By 1941, the REA succeeded in raising to 40 percent the number of farms with electricity. By 1950, nine out of every ten American farms were electrified. With the possible exception of the automobile, nothing did as much to improve the quality of rural life and close the gap between country and city.

## Industrial Recovery

The New Deal's National Recovery Administration (NRA), established in June 1933 under the National Industrial Recovery Act (NIRA), was a far less successful experiment than the agricultural programs.

**NRA QUILT**

*The Blue Eagle of the National Recovery Administration, fiercely clutching a machine gear and lightning bolts, symbolized the government's determination to bring American industry around to a coordinated plan for recovery. The attempt to balance the interests of producers, workers, and consumers proved too much for the Blue Eagle, however. Yet, as this backcountry quilt indicates, the Blue Eagle was sometimes able to carry the spirit of cooperation far from the centers of industrial turmoil.* Franklin D. Roosevelt Library.

The NRA's objective was to coordinate management, labor, and the federal government through a network of industrial codes that governed working conditions, prices, and trade practices. To deal with the contentious issue of worker rights, the NRA struck a bargain with business leaders to ease antitrust regulations in exchange for the right of labor to engage in collective bargaining. By the end of 1933, most industries were represented within the 541 NRA codes, and the Blue Eagle symbol displayed in store windows let the public know.

The stage seemed set for a major transformation of American industry, but opinions differed widely on the direction it would take. The New

Dealers emphasized the possibilities for rational management and fair competition. They hoped that coordination would produce a collective social conscience that would inhibit industry from cheating customers or destroying the environment and would make sure that workers were treated fairly. Critics, however, saw bureaucratic oppression. Because the NRA skirted antimonopoly laws and left industry subject to federal management, they claimed that the economy would become rigidly controlled from the top. Some even saw the NRA as an American version of Mussolini's corporate fascism in Italy, a means for controlling individuals by directing their economic lives.

In reality, neither prediction was accurate. The outcome was more an extension of conventional business practice than a radical change to either the right or the left. Poor management gave business leaders the opportunity to gain control of the code-writing mechanism, and they made sure the codes would first serve the interests of corporate profits rather than workers or the general welfare. By the mid-1930s, prospects for a rationally coordinated business system had faded.

*The magnitude and scope of the depression and the speed of the New Deal attack ensured that the Roosevelt administration would have failures as well as successes.*

The blizzard of new agencies and programs created in the Hundred Days succeeded in reversing the economic decline and restoring the nation's confidence, but it did not produce full recovery. The magnitude and scope of the depression and the speed of the New Deal attack ensured that the Roosevelt administration would have failures as well as successes. Inevitably, disappointment and resistance mounted.

## Challenges to the New Deal

After the early rush of excitement, a discontented minority began to challenge Roosevelt's initiatives. Businessmen expressed open hostility to the ways New Deal planning intruded on their affairs. Many conservatives insisted that New Deal changes had been too radical, undermined economic stability, and threatened American democratic values. On the left, critics faulted the administration for not having programs radical enough to meet the people's needs.

## Resistance to Business Reform

Since the New Deal sought economic recovery, New Dealers expected business leaders to come around eventually and welcome cooperative planning. But the administration was sorely disappointed. In the Tennessee valley, private power companies battled the TVA as "creeping socialism" and unfair competition. The NRA took even greater abuse. The alliance of the New Deal with urban labor and constant feuding between business representatives and NRA officials over the industry codes caused strain from the outset. Furthermore, business leaders never reconciled themselves to the administration's planning concept. One Republican senator derided the creator of the NRA as "Frankenstein" Roosevelt and declared that the Blue Eagle was really "the Soviet duck" in disguise.

Ironically, the business community kept up its criticism even though its situation improved more steadily during the depression than did that of most other social groups, including farmers and workers. The managerial elite remained mostly intact—despite some spectacular jailings, flights from prosecution, and suicides. So did the hierarchical corporate structure that had been developed during the boom years at the turn of the century. The greatest wounds business leaders suffered were to their confidence and pride. Fearful of government regulation, higher taxes, and union organization, they created stridently anti–New Deal public relations offices and—more ominously—sometimes deployed company spies to seek out disloyal workers. The rage of business leaders toward the New Deal fastened on Franklin Roosevelt as the source of their loss of public admiration and government favor.

By 1935, the two major business organizations—the National Association of Manufacturers and the Chamber of Commerce—had become openly anti–New Deal. But their critiques were mild compared with the all-out assault of the American Liberty League, founded in 1934 as the NRA came under bitter attack. Prominent members of the league had once been leaders in the Democratic Party, but now they decried the New Deal as a betrayer of basic constitutional guarantees of freedom and individualism. To them the AAA was a "trend toward fascist control of agriculture," relief programs marked "the end of democracy," and the

NRA was a plunge into the "quicksand of visionary experimentation." Although the league's membership never exceeded 125,000, its well-financed publicity campaign led the way in widening the rift between Roosevelt and the business class.

Planners and labor leaders who favored more worker control attacked the New Deal from the other direction. In their view, the NRA had stifled enterprise by permitting monopolistic practices. They pointed out that industrial trade associations twisted codes to suit their aims, thwarted competition, and engaged in price gouging. Labor leaders especially resented the willingness of the NRA to allow companies to form their own unions, while blocking the organization of genuine grassroots unions that permitted workers to bargain on terms they chose for themselves.

> *In its failure, the NRA demonstrated both historic American resistance to economic planning and the refusal of the business community to yield its autonomy unless forced to do so.*

In the midst of the cross fire, the Supreme Court in May 1935 declared that the NRA unconstitutionally conferred legislative power on an administrative agency and overstepped the limits of federal power to regulate interstate commerce. The agency lingered briefly, but its codes evaporated, and business leaders rejected most proposals for cooperation with government. In its failure, the NRA demonstrated both historic American resistance to economic planning and the refusal of the business community to yield its autonomy unless forced to do so.

## Reaction against the New Deal Farm Program

The AAA weathered its battering by champions of the old order better than the NRA, and so the majority of farmers were more content with the New Deal than businessmen were. Even though farmers were reluctant to abandon their practice of increasing production as a matter of pride and survival, the allotment checks for keeping land fallow and the higher prices for farm produce created loyalty among those with enough acreage to participate.

Protest stirred, however, among those with smaller farms who did not qualify for allotments.

**BLACK SHARECROPPERS**
*A painful, unintended consequence of the New Deal plan to maintain farm prices by reducing acreage in production was the eviction of tenant farmers when the land they worked was unused. Champions of the tenant farmers, most notably the Southern Farm Tenants Union, protested that federal crop subsidies should be shared between owners and those who usually worked the land. Often, however, sharecroppers like these were simply cast adrift, and lobbies for farm owners thwarted any governmental challenge. The sad state of tenant farmers continued until World War II provided opportunities for displaced tenants to escape to the cities.*
UPI/Bettmann Archives.

The Southern Farm Tenants Union argued passionately that the AAA was a device for enriching large farmers at the expense of smaller ones. By taking out of production the land on which tenants lived, owners could simultaneously qualify for government subsidies and be relieved of the need to provide for the dependent tenants. Already at the bottom of the economic ladder, tenant farmers and sharecroppers faced a grave situation. One black sharecropper explained why only seventy-five dollars a year from the plantation cotton subsidies made its way down to her: "De landlord think he ought to have *all* the acre p'duction checks, 'cause it his land." Bypassing the intention of New Deal programs was simple enough in her part of Arkansas because "de landlord is landlord, de politicians is landlord, de judge is landlord, de shurf [sheriff] is landlord, ever'body is landlord, en we ain' got nothin'!" Stories like this convinced critics that the New Deal was fostering just the sort of inequality and misery—among both whites and blacks—that it had set out to eliminate.

The AAA's most potent critics, however, were agricultural processors and distributors. They were unhappy that the AAA reduced the volume of production—the only source of their profits—while they were required to pay for the very program that disadvantaged them. In 1936, the Supreme Court agreed with their contention that they were the poor victims of an illegal attempt to tax one group (processors and distributors) to enrich another (farmers). Down but not out, the AAA rebounded from the Supreme Court ruling by redesigning its allotment provisions with legislation that focused more on conservation measures the Court found acceptable.

## Politics on the Fringes

The New Deal also faced challenges from a small but growing minority drawn to radical movements. Socialists and Communists accused the New Deal of mounting a feeble resistance to business elites or, worse, rescuing capitalism from its self-inflicted crisis. Among those drawn to the left were many intellectuals and artists, who decided it was time to use their talents to advance the cause of radical change. Socialist author Upton Sinclair became the most prominent of the intellectuals who went directly into politics when he ran for governor of California in 1934. Rousing wide public support for his EPIC (End Poverty in California) plan to put the unemployed to work in idle factories, Sinclair lost by a narrow margin only because fraudulent charges that he was a Communist caused Roosevelt to withdraw his support.

With that one exception, the left was never able to mount a serious electoral challenge to the New Deal. And for all the doctrinaire talk of violent overthrow of the government by the proletariat, there was no real chance of that happening after Roosevelt's election. With varying degrees of militancy, most Americans sought inclusion, not revolution, fundamental entitlements, not radical novelties. Accordingly, homespun populist agitators preaching old-style religion and harping on birthrights drew the biggest crowds looking for an alternative to the status quo.

The most formidable coalition of down-and-outers challenging the New Deal was led by a Catholic priest in Detroit named Charles Coughlin. Father Coughlin expressed his outrage at the depression in a series of radio broadcasts that drew a nationwide audience of forty million by 1930. The "Radio Priest" found villains in all the conventional places. He denounced Communists as traditional foes of the church and soon shifted to bankers and other "predatory capitalists," who, he increasingly insisted, were dominated by Jews. After first welcoming Roosevelt in 1932 as the nation's political savior, Coughlin soon turned against the administration for its failure to "drive the moneychangers from the temple." By the presidential election of 1936, Coughlin had converted his grassroots coalition into the Union Party and called on other dissidents to join him in mounting an election challenge to Roosevelt.

One of those who answered Father Coughlin's call was Dr. Francis Townsend, an elderly public health officer in Long Beach, California, angered that his retired patients existed in misery in the golden land. In late 1933, Townsend proposed the Old Age Revolving Pension, which would pay all persons over age sixty $200 a month on the condition that they spend the entire amount within thirty days and thereby stimulate the economy. Buoyed by 90 percent of all Long Beach voters who endorsed his petition to the federal government, Townsend organized pension clubs that attracted between 2 and 3.5 million paying members looking for security. His plan rebuffed by the major parties as impractical, Townsend merged his forces with Coughlin's Union Party in time for the 1936 election.

The most important of the rebellious populists came from another region ripe for protest. Huey Pierce Long, son of a backcountry farmer, had used his immense talents to become governor of Louisiana in 1928 and U.S. senator in 1932. Long reached out to the poor and dispossessed with brash rhetoric and country humor. With their support, he swept out of power a reactionary political machine that had kept Louisiana one of the poorest and most backward states. By delivering on his promises to build roads, schools, and hospitals and provide jobs, Long shone as a beacon of hope among the desperate during the early depression years. To his relatively well-to-do enemies, he was a menace ruthlessly gathering power into his own hands. (See the Historical Question on page 656.)

Populist unrest typified by Coughlin, Townsend, and Long stirred the New Deal administration to solidify its winning coalition. An early test came in the 1934 elections, normally a time when a seated president loses support. Roosevelt approached the elections as an opportunity to distance the New Deal from radical and crank causes on the right and left. In August, the president embarked on a national tour to support loyal Democratic candidates as champions of average people and traditional American values. An unusually high percentage of voters turned out to give New Dealers a landslide victory. Democrats increased their numbers in the House of Representatives from 310 to 319 out of 422; and in the Senate, the party gained 10 new seats to take a commanding two-thirds majority, the greatest margin ever achieved in that body.

## The Second New Deal and the Rise of the Welfare State

Though Roosevelt had been "all but crowned by the people," as one journalist put it, New Dealers found the outlook at mid-decade troubling. The First New Deal had halted the economic decline and restored hope; yet a glance at almost any economic index—employment, production, income—revealed how anemic the economy remained. The Hundred Days had spent itself, and major programs were faltering (AAA) or had been invalidated by the Supreme Court (NRA). With criticism of insufficient action intensifying on the right and the left, Roosevelt decided it was time for a departure.

# Huey Long:
# Demagogue or Champion
# of the Dispossessed?

FROM THE TIME HE WAS A SMALL CHILD, Huey P. Long was what one exasperated neighbor called a "pesterance." Defiant at school, artful at avoiding any disagreeable chores, ruthlessly driven to be the center of attention, Long got ahead through the shrewdness of his extraordinary intelligence and brash willingness to flout conventional rules. Though he spent only brief periods at the University of Oklahoma and Tulane University, he cajoled a judge to convene a special bar examination, which he passed easily at the age of twenty-one. Declaring that he came out of that examination "running for office," Long rose swiftly from election as state railroad commissioner in 1918 to governor ten years later. Along the way, he dazzled the public with rhetorical gifts never before approached in the state and argued successfully before the Supreme Court with a skill that archconservative Chief Justice William Howard Taft—not a man to be taken in by a small-town southern lawyer—judged to be as keen as any he had ever encountered.

Circumstances and temperament dictated the political stance Long took all his life. The populist tradition of Winn Parish, where he grew up, instilled a basic loyalty to poor, rural folk. The small population of blacks in the parish and a history of blacks and whites forming a common front against rich sawmill and plantation owners meant that there never had been much race baiting in Winn. The rest of the state was very different, however. There, blacks and whites divided evenly, and the state's leaders made white supremacy the cornerstone of their rule. Out of step with majority opinion on race, Long could only hope to advance his fortunes by appealing to class division—rich against poor, rural against urban, the humble against the elite.

Long decided to focus his reform program on a more equitable distribution of income and opportunity. At St. Martinsville, deep in swampy Cajun country, he asked, "Where are the schools that you have waited for your children to have, that have never come? Where are the roads and the highways that you sent your money to build . . . ? Where are the institutions to care for the sick and disabled?" When Long assumed the governorship, Louisiana had only 331 miles of paved roads outside the cities. It was also the most illiterate state in the country. In 1893, when Long was born, 45 percent of those above the age of ten could not read; by 1920, the rate of illiteracy was still 22 percent, including 38 percent of all blacks.

Long articulated the grievances and hopes of the poor people of Louisiana; he also behaved utterly ruthlessly. After overcoming an impeachment effort in 1929, Long moved to consolidate his power. "I used to try to get things done by saying 'please,'" he said. "That didn't work and now I'm a dynamiter. I dynamite 'em out of my path." By 1930, Long completely dominated the state. Journalists around the country routinely referred to him as "the dictator of Louisiana." He made no effort to hide his power. Once an angry opponent thrust a volume in his face and shouted, "Maybe you've heard of this book. It's the constitution of the state of Louisiana." Long shrugged and said, "I'm the constitution here now." He bullied and bribed the state legislature into a rubber-stamp body that passed a series of laws giving him the power to count ballots and thus determine the outcome of elections. He intimidated the courts and made them heel to his demands. Every state employee knew that his or her job depended on loyalty to the *Kingfish,* as Long liked to call himself.

His grasp on Louisiana firm, Long made his leap into the national limelight by winning election to the United States Senate in 1932. With none of the freshman senator's expected deference to senior members, Long introduced a sweeping "soak-the-rich" tax bill that would outlaw annual personal incomes of more than $1 million and inheritances of more than $5 million. Swift rejection by the Senate triggered his long-range strategy of becoming president by mobilizing the vast numbers of low-income Americans into a Share Our Wealth protest movement. Long's plan was to mount a presidential campaign in 1936 that would take enough votes from Roosevelt to tip the election to the Republican candidate. After four years of Republican failure to alleviate the depression with conservative policies, Long would sweep into the presidency in 1940, the savior of a suffering people.

**HUEY LONG**

*Huey Long's ability to adapt his captivating stump speech style to the radio made him the one rival politician who gave Roosevelt serious concern in the mid-1930s. Here Long is shown in 1932 campaigning in Arkansas in support of Hattie Carraway's bid for election to the United States Senate. Carraway, stigmatized as both a woman and a populist reformer, seemed a sure loser until Long crossed the border from Louisiana on her behalf. In a mere two weeks of speaking and pressing the flesh, Long brushed aside criticism that he was an interloper and boosted Carraway to victory as part of his crusade to share the wealth.*

UPI/Bettmann Archive.

---

The electoral showdown never came, however. On September 8, 1935, a young physician named Carl Austin Weiss, enraged by the dishonor Long had visited on his family by removing his father from the Louisiana bench and suggesting black ancestry, fatally shot Long in a corridor of the Louisiana State House and was immediately gunned down by Long's bodyguards. The long lines of worn and ragged people passing by Long's coffin in the capitol and the smaller number of better-dressed mourners at Weiss's funeral testified to the split in Louisiana along class lines. Some people at Weiss's funeral even proposed erecting a monument to Long's assassin.

Long always answered charges that he was a dictator, rather than a man of the people, by insisting that the polite ways of conventional democratic rules could never cure the nation's deepest ills. Only forceful means, he insisted, could finally break the hold of the privileged and extend opportunity to everyone. He could point to real achievements in Louisiana. As promised, he taxed the oil companies and utilities that had run Louisiana for decades and funneled the revenue into programs to benefit those who had been left out. While he built monuments to his own vanity, like the thirty-four-story state capitol with his profile in bronze on the elevator doors, Long addressed some of the state's real social needs. At one time, Louisiana's road-building program was the biggest in the nation, and by 1935 the state had ten times more paved roads than when Long became governor. He made Louisiana State University a major university. He greatly expanded the state's pitiful public health facilities. For children, he provided free schoolbooks and new schools. For adults, he started night schools that attacked illiteracy.

Critics labeled Long was a homegrown fascist. They called him "the Messiah of the Rednecks," disdainful both of Long and of those who turned to him. They compared him to Mussolini or Hitler and expressed relief that his life, and thus the damage he and the rabble who supported him could do, was cut short. The bitter controversy over Long related to vital American political issues. Roosevelt had recognized that the New Deal must reach out to the "forgotten man." Long reached farther to connect with dispossessed outsiders who had never even been noticed. He gave Americans the only chance they ever had, for better or worse, to vote for a candidate with a broad national following who offered sweeping change comparable to that of parties on the radical right and left in other countries.

After Long's death, the hopes of the underclass to share the wealth lapsed into silent neglect. Mostly, they voted for Roosevelt, when they voted at all, but remained largely alienated from the prevailing system. They did achieve connection in memory, however. In 1974, a Louisiana newspaper asked citizens to name the greatest governor in the history of the state. Much to the paper's editorial dismay, the overwhelming choice was Huey Long.

**SKETCH FOR A WPA MURAL**
*This sketch for a mural commissioned for Lenoir City, Tennessee, is typical of the Federal Arts Program's goal to memorialize significant moments of achievement in every region of the country. For rural folk, the sight of Rural Electrification Authority workers extending power lines was one of the more exciting symbols of the New Deal. When the REA came into existence in 1935, less than 10 percent of the nation outside the cities had electricity. By 1941, REA programs had increased that number to 40 percent; ten years later the figure had risen to 90 percent, and the gulf of silence and darkness between town and country was successfully bridged.*
Public Buildings Service, General Services Administration.

In 1935, New Dealers surged ahead with a flurry of new policies, called the Second Hundred Days or the Second New Deal, that moved away from central economic planning toward provision for the special needs of various social groups. The keystone of the emerging coalition was labor. Workers had felt overlooked in the 1920s, and Roosevelt reached out with both legislation and genuine concern and sympathy. Out of the welter of legislative and executive action that made up the Second New Deal emerged the first elements of an American welfare state. Reformers who recognized that individuals were more often victims of economic forces beyond their control now looked to government as the legitimate, even sole, power able to improve the nation's economic health and guard its citizens' well-being.

### Relief for the Unemployed

Like Hoover, Roosevelt lamented that the millions of Americans who were out of work suffered a devastating blow to "their self-respect, their self-confidence and courage and determination." Unlike Hoover, in May 1935 Roosevelt set up an independent agency, the Works Progress Administration (WPA), to put the unemployed to work for the public benefit. The WPA imposed few limits on the sort of work to be done but merely specified that the projects be useful, be undertaken in places where unemployment was high, and produce results that would bring revenues back to the Treasury as soon as possible. State and municipal agencies had the responsibility to propose what needed to be done.

*Out of the welter of legislative and executive action that made up the Second New Deal emerged the first elements of an American welfare state.*

By 1943, the WPA had generated jobs costing $10 billion that provided an average of a year's worth of work for each of the thirteen million unemployed put on the payroll. Construction amounted to about three-fourths of the total WPA projects, resulting in 572,000 miles of country roads, 40,000 buildings, 67,000 miles of city streets, 78,000 bridges, 8,000 parks, and 350 airports, along with a variety of smaller projects.

In a striking departure from the usual pick and shovel relief program, the WPA also allowed unemployed people in the arts to make use of their talents for public benefit. After all, Roosevelt pointed out in endorsing the idea, artists "have to live . . . and surely there must be some public place where paintings are wanted." At its peak, the WPA employed some six thousand artists, musicians, actors, journalists, Ph.D.'s, poets, and novelists. The roster included many unknowns but also towering figures such as novelist John Steinbeck and poet Conrad Aiken. WPA Theater brought sixty million people into its performances; and in the first fifteen months of the WPA Music Project, fifty million Americans heard concerts. The artist Robert Gwathmey recalled that the government imposed no restrictions: "You were a painter: Do your work. You

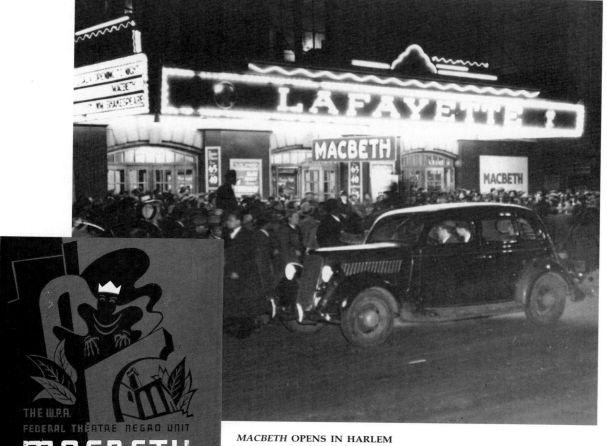

**MACBETH OPENS IN HARLEM**
*The New Deal Federal Theater Project, which began in 1935, had the good fortune of attracting as one of its directors a twenty-year-old genius named Orson Welles. Acting on news that Welles and an African American theater group had prepared a version of* Macbeth *set in Haiti, an opening night crowd in 1938 mobbed the Lafayette theater in Harlem. As one reviewer put it, the play was "a classic stunt" that ensured the director's reputation and indicated new directions for the American theater.*
Library of Congress.

were a sculptor: Do your work. . . . An artist could do anything he damn pleased." At a cost of only $23 million, paintings, sculptures, and prints came to grace America's courthouses, public buildings, and museums.

## Empowering Labor

In 1934, a series of local uprisings, mostly by unskilled workers who had no unions to join, set in motion a labor revolution. Striking workers in Toledo, Minneapolis, and San Francisco, asserting their right to picket their employers, encountered ferocious opposition by police and the National Guard. Bloody battles in the streets and on the docks made plain the determination of militant new labor leaders to break the dominance that industrial management had achieved over workers during the 1920s.

After the violence of 1934 subsided, labor leaders focused on the National Labor Relations Act (NLRA), a bill sponsored by Senator Robert Wagner of New York that would create federal supervision of labor disputes. Justly termed a Magna Carta for labor, the Wagner Act, as it came to be called, guaranteed workers the right to organize freely and created a National Labor Relations Board to oversee elections for union representation. If the majority of workers voted for a union, the union became the sole bargaining agent for the entire workplace, and employers were required to negotiate with the duly elected union leaders. Roosevelt was at first reluctant to have his NRA ideal of cooperative decision making replaced by adversarial collective bargaining. But he signed the Wagner Act into law in July 1935 as the best way available to protect the rights of workers and unions and attach them to the New Deal.

While the Wagner Act moved through Congress, unskilled workers, who had been largely unrepresented within organized labor, began to press for inclusion. Under the aggressive leadership of John L. Lewis, head of the United Mine Workers (UMW), and Sidney Hillman, head of the Amalgamated Clothing Workers, a coalition of unskilled workers gathered in 1935 to form the Committee for Industrial Organization (CIO; later the Congress of Industrial Organizations). By mobilizing unskilled workers the CIO greatly reduced the lordly power of industrialists and began to win significant concessions on wages and working conditions.

The achievements that flowed from the new militancy of labor and a sympathetic government were formidable. When Roosevelt took office in 1933, AFL membership stood at three million, down by half since the end of World War I. Once the Wagner Act took hold after 1935, unions expanded almost fivefold to fourteen million members by 1945. Thirty percent of the workforce was then unionized, the highest union representation ever reached. During the New Deal era, large numbers of unskilled assembly line workers, many of them African Americans or immigrants, flocked to unions whose membership at the start of the 1930s, and especially its leadership, had been skilled, native-born workers of northern European ancestry. A new left-wing militance had something to do with these expanding union memberships. The exceptional courage and organizing skill of Communists and other radicals in the CIO earned them leadership roles in the campaign to organize resistant workers in the automobile and steel industries.

The campaign by the United Auto Workers (UAW) to unionize workers at General Motors (GM) climaxed in January 1937 when workers occupied the main assembly plant in Flint, Michigan, in a "sit-down" strike that reduced the plant's production of 15,000 cars a week to a mere 150. In desperation, General Motors obtained injunctions against the sit-down. But neither Roosevelt nor Michigan Governor Frank Murphy would act. Although they did not approve of the strikers' illegal occupation of the plant, they were unwilling to end the strike by force. Stymied, General Motors signed an agreement that made the UAW the sole bargaining agent for all GM workers and prohibited the company from interfering with union activity. Having beaten the automobile industry's leading producer, the UAW expanded its campaign until, with the capitulation of Ford in 1941, the entire industry was unionized.

The CIO hoped to ride success in automobile plants to victory in the steel mills. But after unionizing the giant U.S. Steel Company, the CIO ran up against fanatic opposition from smaller steel firms, led by Bethlehem Steel's Tom Girdler. The climax came in May 1937, when a crowd of strikers gathered in a field outside Chicago to organize a picket line around Republic Steel. Without warning, police who had been sent there to keep order charged the crowd, firing their sidearms and wielding clubs, killing ten and injuring scores. The battered steelworkers then halted their organizing campaign. In steel and other major industries, such as the highly resistant southern textile mills, unions would have renewed success only after 1941, when the demands of military buildup gave unions greater bargaining power.

## Social Security and Tax Reform

Standing alongside the Wagner Act and the WPA as a major New Deal accomplishment in 1935 was the Social Security Act, designed to provide a supplementary income for aged and retired persons. Taking care of hard-hit elderly people during the depression became almost as desperate a necessity as providing relief to the unemployed. The population over age sixty-five had doubled between 1870 and 1930 at the same time that work for the elderly declined. Of the tiny minority who worked, only 15 percent had pension plans, and insolvent corporations and banks often could not come up with funds during the depression to pay the meager pensions they had promised. Just eighteen states provided elderly assistance, which usually amounted to about a dollar a day for impoverished individuals. With the aggressive agitation of Dr. Townsend, Father Coughlin, and Huey Long rumbling ominously in the background, Roosevelt became the first president to advocate protection for the elderly, describing it as "our plain duty to provide for that security upon which [the general] welfare depends." In 1935, he appointed Frances Perkins to chair a committee that readied the Social Security Act for his signature in August of that year.

The struggle for Social Security brought out class differences in their starkest form. Support for the measure came from a coalition of advocate groups for the elderly and the poor, traditional progressives, leftists, social workers, labor unions, and educators. Arrayed against them were economic conservatives, including the Liberty League, the National Association of Manufacturers, the Chamber of Commerce, and the American Medical Association. Enact the Social Security system, these conservatives and their representatives in the Republican Party warned, and the government will gain a whip hand over private property, initiative will be destroyed, and proud individuals will be reduced to spineless loafers.

Obvious need and the large New Deal majority in Congress carried the day. The Social Security program required that pensions for the elderly be funded by tax contributions from workers and their employers. It also created unemployment insurance, paid for by employers' contributions. In a bow to traditional local responsibility for public assistance, Social Security issued grants for the states to use to support dependent mothers and children, public health services, and the blind. As a result, the elderly began to rise out of the lowest economic status, and the attachment of ordinary workers to the New Deal became even stronger.

Opposition to Social Security struck New Dealers as evidence that the rich had learned little from the depression. Roosevelt had long felt contempt for the moneyed elite and looked for a way to redistribute wealth that would, in a single stroke, weaken conservative opposition, advance the cause of social equity, and defuse populist challenges on the fringe. In June 1935, as the Social Security Act was being debated, Roosevelt delivered a message to Congress outlining comprehensive tax reform. He urged a graduated tax on corporations, a similar tax on holding company dividends used to shelter corporate income, an inheritance tax, and an increase in maximum personal income taxes from 63 to 79 percent. These measures were designed to place the burden of paying for recovery programs and balancing the federal budget on the shoulders of those with the most money. In addition, Roosevelt argued that a more progressive tax structure would increase opportunity for the common people at the bottom of the economic ladder. Against charges that higher taxes on the rich would dampen their initiative, Roosevelt contended that the new measures would instead stimulate competition. If the idle rich were required to pay for their unfair advantages of monopolies and inherited fortunes, ordinary Americans in small, innovative enterprises would have a better chance to succeed.

Congress endorsed Roosevelt's basic taxation principle by enacting a slightly progressive tax on undistributed corporate profits. From there, with the Revenue Act of 1937, Roosevelt moved to close loopholes that he considered outrageous. Threatening to name names of the wealthy who were not paying their fair share of taxes, Roosevelt persuaded Congress to eliminate a number of tax shelters, including such relics from the New Era as deductions for company yachts and country estates.

## Broadening the New Deal Coalition

The largest groups that had been persistently excluded from economic and political benefits were women and African Americans. Their stories were strikingly parallel. Both received wages substantially lower than white men and owned only a tiny sliver of the nation's property. Though constitutionally entitled to vote since Reconstruction, most African Americans had been disfranchised by intimidation and legal subterfuge. Women, too, had the right to vote, but they were only starting to exercise their electoral power in numbers comparable to those of men.

Eleanor Roosevelt was determined to use her position as First Lady to increase the influence of women and minorities. At her urging, President Roosevelt allowed the Democratic National Committee to create a Women's Division in 1933 to define women's issues and to screen candidates for administration positions. Headed by Molly Dewson, a former leader in the suffrage movement and the National Consumers League, the Women's Division created a talent pool of eighty thousand women from which the New Deal hired an unprecedented number for government positions.

Most remarkable was the entry of women into executive positions that had always been considered for men only. Frances Perkins became the first woman cabinet officer; Ruth Bryan Owen the first woman to hold an ambassadorial post as envoy to Denmark; Florence Allen the first woman judge on a district court of appeals; and Nellie Tayloe Ross the first director of the U.S. Mint. Alongside these breakthroughs, women gained prominent positions within relief and welfare programs. Under the broad WPA umbrella, Ellen Woodward headed Women's and Professional Projects, Hallie Flanagan directed the Federal Theater Project, and Hilda Smith organized Workers' Education. Women also played key roles in the Division of Labor Standards,

**ELEANOR ROOSEVELT MEETING WOMEN REPORTERS**
*Even though the editorial opinion of newspaper owners was about 80 percent opposed to the president and his wife, both Franklin and Eleanor Roosevelt had close rapport with the working press. Making the point that women had something important to contribute to public affairs and that the First Lady could be more than simply a White House hostess, Eleanor Roosevelt wrote a daily column, "My Day," and held regular news conferences to which only women reporters were admitted. She used the occasions to reinvigorate the commitment women had begun in the Progressive Era to education, equal rights, decent working conditions, and child welfare.*
Stock Montage.

in the Children's Bureau, and in the administration of relief to the unemployed and destitute, both locally and in Washington.

These activities did not, however, result in equality between the sexes, either economically or politically. Indeed, the efforts women made within the New Deal were limited to improving conditions of children, the infirm, the unemployed, and others who lacked the ability to take care of themselves. Nonetheless, the experience of women in community organization and the design of welfare legislation established a foundation of skill and influence that buttressed future efforts to attain equal rights.

Eleanor Roosevelt also helped link the causes of gender and racial discrimination. One of her strongest allies among African American women was Mary McLeod Bethune, the founder of the Daytona Normal and Industrial Institute for Negro Women in Florida and a cofounder of the National Council on Negro Women in 1935. Bethune's accomplishments brought her to the attention of Eleanor Roosevelt and resulted in her appointment as the highest-ranking black official in the federal government as head of the Division of Negro Affairs in the National Youth Administration. Bethune used her position to guide a core group of black professionals and civil rights activists to posts within the New Deal. Nicknamed the "Black Cabinet," the group was the first sizable African American presence in the federal government. By mid-decade, their efforts helped open the way for inclusion of African Americans in New Deal relief programs to the point where about one-quarter of all blacks received some sort of federal assistance.

The conditions with which the Black Cabinet grappled were bleak in the extreme. At the outset of the New Deal, about half of urban blacks were out of work, twice the unemployment rate among whites. In the rural South, the black majority had slim prospects of making a living or even retaining their place on the land as owners or tenants. To struggle against such deepening misery proved dangerous. After years of decline, lynching increased during the depression, and a Georgia chain gang was the fate of radical black unionist Angelo Herndon for trying to organize black workers. Up north, a riot in Harlem, where the artistic Renaissance had once flourished, dramatized blacks' despair in 1935.

The New Deal response was cautious. Roosevelt believed that to enact ambitious New Deal reforms, he was obliged to appease powerful con-

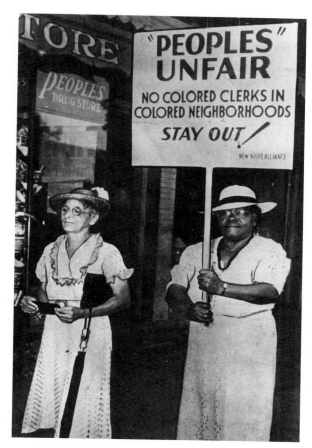

**MARY MCLEOD BETHUNE**
*At the urging of Eleanor Roosevelt, Mary McLeod Bethune, a southern educational and civil rights leader, became director of the National Youth Administration's Division of Negro Affairs. The first black woman to head a federal agency, Bethune used her federal position to promote social change. Here Bethune takes her mission to the streets to protest the Peoples Drug Store chain's discriminatory hiring practices in the nation's capital.*
Moorland Spingarn Research Center, Howard University.

servative, segregationist, southern Democrats. Reflecting these political pressures, the major New Deal programs for economic recovery, the NRA and AAA, failed in large measure to serve African Americans. Relief work gained through the WPA was also discriminatory. Only eleven of more than ten thousand WPA supervisors in the South were black.

Stymied administratively and legislatively, New Dealers turned to coalition building with blacks. During Roosevelt's first presidential campaign, black journalist Robert Vann called on African Americans to "turn Lincoln's picture to the wall. That debt has been paid in full." In 1934, black voters noticeably shifted from the Republican to the Democratic Party, helping elect New Deal Democrats in numerous congressional and gubernatorial races.

By the end of Roosevelt's second term, however, African Americans still suffered severe handicaps. Most of the thirteen million black workers toiled at low-paying menial jobs. Infant mortality was half again as great as for whites, and life expectancy twelve years shorter. Segregation in the South was unmoved; nor was the equal part of "separate but equal" much advanced. Black schools had less money and worse facilities than those of whites, and only 1 percent of black students earned college degrees. In southern states, where most blacks lived, there were no black police officers or judges and hardly any black lawyers, and lynching of blacks went unpunished. By mid-decade, little had happened to refute the grim witticism that, for African Americans, America was "the land of the tree and the home of the grave."

Hispanic Americans and Asian Americans had even fewer voters than women and blacks and consequently less political clout. Mexican Americans, already at the economic margins, saw their wages in California's fields plummet to not much more than a dime an hour. Even then they had to face a new challenge from other victims of the depression. When persistent drought raised huge dust storms and turned large areas of the plains into a "dust bowl," hundreds of thousands of ruined farmers— called "Okies" and "Arkies" because most of them came from Oklahoma and Arkansas—moved westward and competed with Mexican Americans for scarce agricultural work. In addition, local administration of many New Deal programs meant that the treatment of minorities rested in the hands of established white leadership. In the West, when Hispanics and Indians were permitted to join government work projects they often received lower pay than white Americans on government work projects, and less aid when out of a job.

Asian Americans fared no better. Asian immigrants were still excluded from U.S. citizenship and in many states were not permitted to own land. Although more than half of the Japanese American population by 1930 had been born in the United States, they were still liable to discrimination. Even college-educated Asian Americans worked at family shops, restaurants, and laundries. As one frustrated young man said: "I am a fruitstand worker.

**HISPANIC-AMERICAN ALLIANCE BANNER**
*Between 1910 and 1940, when refugees from the Mexican revolution poured across the American border, the Hispanic-American Alliance and other such organizations sought to protect Mexican American rights against nativist fears and hostility. In the years between the world wars, many alliance banners such as this one flew in opposition to the deportation of Mexican aliens, an attempt in 1926 to bar Mexican Americans from city jobs in Los Angeles, and the disproportionately high use of the death penalty against Mexicans convicted of crimes. Throughout these and other trials, the alliance steadfastly emphasized the desire of Mexican Americans to receive permanent status in the United States.*
The Oakland Museum.

I would much rather it were doctor or lawyer . . . but my aspirations [were] frustrated long ago by circumstances [and] I am only what I am, a professional carrot washer."

Native Americans, however, experienced a major change in their circumstances during the New Deal. Ever since the Dawes Act of 1887, the government had tried to solve the "Indian problem" by encouraging assimilation, that is, an end to a separate

Indian identity. Because of the commitment of John Collier, commissioner of Indian affairs, that policy was mostly reversed in the Indian Reorganization Act of 1934. The act restored to Native Americans the right to own land communally. Though the change brought little immediate benefit and Indians remained the poorest of Americans, it did provide a foundation for economic and cultural resurgence a generation later.

## The New Deal's Final Phase: From Victory to Deadlock

To speed up recovery, Roosevelt shifted the emphasis of the New Deal at mid-decade. Having failed to build a cooperative commonwealth out of all interest groups, Roosevelt decided in his second term to rely on the New Deal coalition to force reform on bitterly resisting business groups. Support for the New Deal in the farm states and in the big cities had grown vast, mainly because of the rise in the number of women and recent immigrants inspired by the New Deal to begin voting. Roosevelt even gained some unlikely allies on the left. Throughout Roosevelt's first term, socialists and Communists had denounced the slow pace of change and charged the New Deal with failing to serve the interests of the workers who produced the nation's wealth. But in 1935 the Soviet Union, worried about the threat of fascism in Europe, instructed Communists throughout the world to join hands in a "Popular Front" to advance the fortunes of the working class. With varying degrees of enthusiasm, radicals switched from opposition to the New Deal to support for its relief programs and encouragement of unions.

The president's business and conservative opponents reacted to the massing of New Deal force by intensifying their opposition to the welfare state. To Roosevelt, the situation seemed part of a central drama that had played out since the nation's beginning, pitting a Hamiltonian faction of wealth and privilege against the heirs of Jefferson who, like Roosevelt himself, favored shared wealth and equal opportunity.

### The Election of 1936

Roosevelt believed that the presidential election of 1936 would be a test of his ideals and leadership and of New Deal progressivism. Many to the right

and left of the New Deal also welcomed a national referendum. Opinion polls showed that Roosevelt's popularity had dipped. Between 8.5 and 12.5 million workers were still unemployed, and most farmers remained poor. Opposition leaders took that as an indication that the American people were poised to vote against a failed experiment. From the Republican standpoint, the New Deal was undermining the traditional values that had made the country strong. Radical opponents insisted that the New Deal had missed its opportunity to displace capitalism with a socialized economy.

Republicans turned to the Kansas heartland to select Governor Alfred Landon as their nominee for president. A moderate who had supported New Deal measures for conservation and farm relief and promised labor and independent unions a fair deal, Landon stressed standard Republican proposals to achieve a balanced budget through businesslike efficiency and to ease the perils of illness and old age with old-fashioned neighborliness instead of Social Security.

Roosevelt put his faith in the growing coalition of New Deal supporters, who he believed shared his conviction that the New Deal was the nation's liberator from a long period of privilege and wealth for a few and "economic slavery" for the rest. At the end of the campaign, Roosevelt struck a defiant pose before a thunderous crowd at Madison Square Garden. Assailing his "old enemies—monopoly, speculation, reckless banking, class antagonism"—he proclaimed, "Never before in all our history have these forces been so united against one candidate as they stand today. They are unanimous in their hate for me—and I welcome their hatred." When the crowd's roar subsided, Roosevelt concluded: "I should like to have it said of my first Administration that in it the forces of selfishness and of lust for power met their match. I should like to have it said of my second Administration that in it these forces met their master."

Roosevelt triumphed spectacularly. He received eleven million *more* votes than Landon. His 60.8 percent majority was the widest ever in a presidential race and won him every state except the Republican strongholds of Maine and Vermont. Congressional results were equally lopsided, with Democrats outnumbering Republicans by more than three to one in both houses. And in the states, Democrats won twenty-six of thirty-three gubernatorial races, including the one in Landon's Kansas.

Roosevelt's triumph was a testimony to the New Deal coalition. Northern blacks gave Roosevelt

76 percent of their votes, allowing him to wrench the key states of Illinois, Michigan, and New Jersey away from the Republicans. In the nineteen northern cities where more than half the population was composed of first- and second-generation immigrants, the crisis and Democratic encouragement had greatly increased voting participation. Overwhelmingly, the new voters tilted toward the New Deal. Democratic votes increased by 205 percent over their total in 1932, while Republicans gained only 29 percent. Roosevelt also managed to retain the support of every traditionally Democratic southern state, delaying Hoover's dream of bringing the South into the Republican Party.

## Court Packing

In the afterglow of his triumph, Roosevelt went on a cruise to ponder how to remove the remaining obstacles to New Deal reforms. He returned intent on targeting the Supreme Court. Ladened with conservatives left over from the discredited Republican era, the Court had invalidated eleven New Deal measures as unwarranted interference with free enterprise; in more than 140 years before 1932, the Court had nullified only sixty laws. At that moment, Social Security, the Wagner Act, the Securities and Exchange Commission, and other New Deal innovations were moving toward an ominous rendezvous with the Court. Roosevelt concluded that he must do something to make sure the Court's "horse and buggy" notions did not nullify the popular will and demolish the New Deal.

Despite indications that more than two-thirds of Americans believed the Supreme Court should be free from political interference, Roosevelt proposed that one new justice be added to the Court for each existing judge who had already served for ten years and was over the age of seventy. In effect, the proposed law would give the president the power to overwhelm the elderly, conservative Republican justices by naming up to six New Dealers to the bench.

A storm of public protest, egged on by conservatives, sank the Court bill in the Senate. Business spokesmen waxed indignant because Roosevelt's plan blatantly violated constitutional ideals and cleared the way, as the journalist Walter Lippmann claimed, "to establish the political framework for, and to destroy the safeguards against, a dictator." The implication that individuals over seventy had diminished mental capacity also affronted many veteran members of Congress who

were being asked to rule against justices their same age.

Although the Court reform plan failed, it apparently sounded the alarm for Supreme Court justices. After the furor abated, Chief Justice Charles Evans Hughes and fellow moderate Owen Roberts altered their views enough to keep the Court from invalidating the Wagner Act and Social Security. Then the most resistant of the elderly justices—the "four horsemen of reaction," as New Dealer and future Supreme Court Justice Felix Frankfurter called them—began to retire. After being unable to make any appointments to the Court during his first term, Roosevelt went on to name eight justices—more than any other president. His choice of liberals to fill the vacancies on the Court ultimately ensured safe passage of New Deal laws through the shoals of judicial review. But Roosevelt's error in proposing his court-packing scheme had handed conservatives a popular issue to use against the New Deal.

## Reaction and Recession

Republicans and southern Democrats rallied around their common conservatism to obstruct additional reform. Factors other than the court-packing fiasco also began to work against the extension of the New Deal. The progress made in reviving the economy and alleviating hardship tended to reduce the enthusiasm of many people for new efforts. Arguments over how to proceed and how far to go weakened consensus among reformers and, as the Court fight showed, sparked antagonisms between Congress and the White House. In a surprisingly short time, these impediments made Roosevelt's 1936 landslide begin to seem like a mirage.

*Despite indications that more than two-thirds of Americans believed the Supreme Court should be free from political interference, Roosevelt proposed that one new justice be added to the Court for each existing judge who had already served for ten years and was over the age of seventy.*

No action by New Deal opponents was more damaging than the administration's self-inflicted wounds. Soon after his second term began, Roosevelt accepted the view that the steady, though incomplete, economic recovery since 1933 had largely eliminated the depression crisis. He was persuaded that additional deficit spending designed to pump up the economy was no longer necessary. He also worried that inflation would reduce the value of savings and new investments the New Deal had tried to build up. Accordingly, he moved cautiously toward a balanced budget by cutting funds for relief projects.

Roosevelt's fiscal retrenchment soon backfired. Rather than preventing inflation, the reduction in deficit spending cooled down the economy too much. Roosevelt's anxiety about inflation had failed to take into full consideration how far the economy had to go before it would reach inflationary levels. Even at the high-water mark of recovery in the summer of 1937, unemployment remained at about 14 percent, some seven million people in all. In the next few months, national income and production slipped backward so steeply that almost two-thirds of the economic gains since 1933 were lost by June 1938. Farm prices dropped 20 percent, and unemployment rose by more than two million.

This economic downturn hurt the New Deal politically. Conservatives argued that the recession proved that New Deal measures were fundamentally wrong and had produced only an illusion of progress. They maintained that the New Deal's progressive tax policy helped cause the recession by funneling money away from productive investment. Herbert Hoover had been right after all, they claimed. The way to weather the recession was to spend less, save more, and wait for the laws of the free enterprise system to restore prosperity.

Many New Dealers believed instead that the recession showed there was no going back to the orthodoxies of free enterprise. They insisted that the crash and the depression had demonstrated the shortcomings of an unregulated economy. They demanded that the administration revive federal spending and redouble efforts to stimulate the economy. In 1938, Congress heeded Roosevelt's plea to enact a massive new program of spending to revitalize the economy.

The New Deal's methods received support from new economic ideas advanced by the brilliant British economist John Maynard Keynes. In his influential work *The General Theory of Employment, Interest, and Money* (1936), Keynes made a sophisticated, theoretical argument in favor of practices that New Deal relief agencies had developed in an ad hoc, commonsense way. A nation's economy, Keynes declared, could not automatically reach its full potential in the complex, interdependent modern world. The depression had painfully illustrated that economic activity could become stalled at a level far short of a society's true potential. When that happened, only government intervention could pump enough money into the system to revive production, boost consumption, and restore prosperity.

Roosevelt never had the inclination or the time to follow his economic advisers into the thicket of Keynesian theory. But the recession scare of 1938 taught him the Keynesian lesson that economic growth had to be carefully nurtured, not left to self-regulating market forces. Escape from the depression required a plan for large-scale spending to alleviate distress and stimulate economic growth.

## The Last of the New Deal Reforms

From the moment he entered office, Roosevelt had tinkered with the small and antiquated office of the presidency. He believed that the powers of the presidency were inadequate, especially during emergencies such as the depression. He also wanted more power over the federal bureaucracy. Arguing the need for "efficiency," Roosevelt submitted an ambitious plan of executive reorganization to Congress in 1937. The bill failed, but in September 1939 Congress passed the Administrative Reorganization Act, which gave Roosevelt part of what he desired and strengthened the office of the president. With a Democratic majority in Congress, a now friendly Supreme Court, and the revival of deficit spending, the newly empowered White House seemed to be in a good position to move ahead with a third New Deal.

The farm sector had strong claims on New Deal attention in the face of drought, declining prices, and an impoverished class of landless hired hands. In 1937, the Agriculture Department created the Farm Security Administration (FSA) to provide housing and loans to help tenant farmers become independent. For those who owned farms, the New Deal completed its efforts to establish a secure plateau of prosperity with the Agricultural Adjustment Act (AAA) of February 1938. The plan combined production quotas on five staple crops—cotton, tobacco, wheat, corn, and rice—with storage loans through its Commodity Credit Corporation to moderate price swings by regulating supply. The most prosperous farmers benefited most, but the act's Federal Surplus Commodities Corporation added an element of charity by issuing food stamps so that the poor could purchase surplus food. Through that

### NEW DEAL HOUSING GOALS

*The eradication of slum housing (top) such as this in Atlanta in 1936 came to be a prime test of overcoming the depression. In his inaugural address for his second term, Roosevelt focused on the need to rescue the one-third of the nation still "ill-housed, ill-clad, and ill-nourished." The most famous attempt to point the way was the greenbelt town program run by the Resettlement Administration of the Department of Agriculture to relocate people forced off the farms. The picture of Greendale, Wisconsin (bottom), taken in 1939, offers an idea of the uniform utopia the Roosevelt administration favored but was prevented from continuing by the shifting of resources to fight World War II.*

Library of Congress.

balance the AAA of 1938 brought stability to American agriculture and ample food to the table.

Advocates for the urban underclass also had modest luck gaining attention after decades of neglect. New York Senator Robert Wagner convinced Congress to pass the National Housing Act in September 1937. By 1941, some 160,000 residences had been made available at rates affordable for those below the poverty line. The project did not come close to meeting the need for affordable housing, but for the first time the federal government took an active role in providing decent urban housing.

---

*The last major piece of New Deal labor legislation, the Fair Labor Standards Act of June 1938, reiterated the original New Deal pledge to provide workers with a decent standard of living.*

---

The last major piece of New Deal labor legislation, the Fair Labor Standards Act of June 1938, reiterated the original New Deal pledge to provide workers with a decent standard of living. After unprecedented haggling and compromise that revealed the waning strength of the New Deal, Congress finally agreed to intervene in the long sacrosanct realm of worker contracts. The act set minimum-wage and maximum-hours standards and curbed the use of child labor. The minimum-wage level was modest—twenty-five cents an hour for a maximum of forty-four hours a week. And the act exempted merchant seamen, fishermen, domestic help, and farm laborers from these wage and hours standards in order to attract enough conservative votes to pass the act. Nevertheless, the new standards were an important step toward realization of the New Deal promise to work actively to eliminate poverty.

The final New Deal reform effort failed to make much headway against the hidebound system of racial segregation. Although Roosevelt was willing to denounce lynching as murder, he would not jeopardize his vital base of southern political support by designating antilynching bills as "must" legislation. In 1934 and 1935, Congress voted down attempts to make lynching a federal crime, and in 1938 the last antilynching bill of the decade died in a Senate filibuster. Laws to eliminate the poll tax—used to deny blacks the opportunity to vote—encountered the same overwhelming resistance. African Americans

received some meager benefit from employment opportunities in northern relief projects and federal agencies, but the New Deal refused to confront the injustice of racial segregation with the same vigor it had brought to bear on economic hardship.

By the end of 1938, the New Deal had run out of fresh ideas and into stiff opposition. As legislative initiative waned and programs played themselves out, the conservative tide rose. In the congressional elections of 1938, Republicans picked up seven seats in the Senate and eighty in the House, making them a power for the first time since 1932. New Dealers could claim unprecedented and resounding achievement since 1933 when Roosevelt entered the White House, but ten million unemployed five years later, about two-thirds as many as in 1932 under Hoover, were powerful reminders that the depression had not been whipped. In his annual message to Congress in January 1939, however, Roosevelt called a halt to the great reform movement of the Second New Deal. He spoke of preserving the progress already achieved, not of extending it. As conditions dictated a pause in domestic reform, the time had come to pay more attention to America's place in a dangerous world. Roosevelt would end the decade by pointing to the threat posed by fascist aggression proposing expenditures for defense surpassing those allocated for relief and economic revival.

## Conclusion: A New Departure

Looking on ruefully as the Bonus Army fled the capital in 1932, humorist Will Rogers remarked that the old soldiers could get any road out of Washington, but they couldn't get a sandwich out of Congress. Into that mood of defeat and discouragement Roosevelt brought an optimistic spirit of experimental action. An ever more inclusive majority agreed with the president that society should help those in need and that the federal government was an appropriate vehicle to deliver aid. In the process of fighting the depression, the Roosevelt administration vastly expanded the size and power of the federal government and changed the way the American people looked on Washington. It won major successes such as Social Security, labor's right to organize, and guarantees that prosperous farm prices would be maintained through controls on production and marketing.

To Hoover and many conservatives, New Deal planning appeared to be a dangerous form of socialism that threatened the foundations of democracy and capitalism. But as Frances Perkins said, Franklin Roosevelt took capitalism as much for granted as he did his family. Rather than attack capitalism, he boldly sought to save it. The daring innovation and persistent experimentation of the New Deal precluded radical and revolutionary transformation. Like his cousin Teddy, Franklin Roosevelt understood that things would have to change in order to remain the same. Both believed that a strengthened national government was necessary to curb the destructive tendencies of increasing complexity and material power. That shift of power to the center, they believed, provided the means necessary for preserving America's democratic tradition and giving individuals full opportunity. Reflecting their belief in a militant government, New Dealers repeatedly described their programs as a kind of warfare against the adversities of the 1930s. But in the next decade, with the depression only partly overcome, the Roosevelt administration would have to turn from the symbolic New Deal war at home to test its strength in a shooting war against the enemies of democracy abroad.

## CHRONOLOGY

**1932**    The Bonus Army marches on Washington.

**1933**    Franklin D. Roosevelt assumes presidency.
Roosevelt closes nation's banks for four-day "holiday" to allow time to stabilize banking system.
**March–June.** New Deal established through passage of reform legislation of the Hundred Days.
The Civil Works Administration (CWA) provides relief for unemployed.

**1934**    Securities and Exchange Commission licenses and regulates stock exchanges.
Upton Sinclair loses bid for governor of California and chance to enact his EPIC work relief program.
Wealthy conservatives of American Liberty League oppose New Deal.
"Radio Priest" Father Charles Coughlin begins National Union for Social Justice.
Dr. Francis Townsend devises Old Age Revolving Pension scheme to provide money to impoverished elderly.
Congress adopts Indian Reorganization Act.

**1935**    Louisiana Senator Huey Long assassinated.
As part of Second New Deal, legislation creates Works Progress Administration (WPA).

Committee for Industrial Organization (CIO) founded to provide union representation for unskilled workers.
Congress passes Wagner Act to guarantee workers the right to organize unions and bargain collectively.

**1936**    John Maynard Keynes publishes *The General Theory of Employment, Interest, and Money,* providing theoretical justification for government deficit financing.
Franklin Roosevelt reelected by landslide over Republican Alfred Landon.

**1937**    CIO stages successful sit-down strike at General Motors plant in Flint, Michigan.
Roosevelt's "court-packing" legislation defeated in Senate.

**1937–**    Economic recession slows recovery
**1938**    from depression.

**1938**    Second Agricultural Adjustment Act and Fair Labor Standards Act bring New Deal legislation to an end.
Congress rejects administration's anti-lynching bill.

**1939**    Administrative Reorganization Act enlarges scope and power of presidency.
African American contralto Marian Anderson gives concert at Lincoln Memorial.

# SUGGESTED READINGS

Alan Brinkley, *Voices of Protest* (1983). A concise and perceptive account of the radical opposition to the New Deal by Father Coughlin, Huey Long, and Francis Townsend. The history and motivations of both leaders and followers are explained in ways that help clarify the challenges the New Deal faced in trying to gain support from the common man.

William R. Brock, *Welfare, Democracy, and the New Deal* (1987). A probing study of the encounter between the New Deal and habitual American ways of governing and providing assistance to the needy. Brock succeeds in showing the limitations of welfare reform in an individualist society.

Lizabeth Cohen, *Making a New Deal: Industrial Workers in Chicago, 1919–1939* (1990). A story of how workers in a major city used their ethnic and community resources to weather the corporate welfare of the 1920s and then form organized alliances with New Deal reform. Cohen's focus on workers rather than unions illuminates links between social context and the workplace.

Blanche Wiessen Cook, *Eleanor Roosevelt*, 2 vols. (1992; 1997). An admiring life and times that explains Eleanor Roosevelt's character and the world from which she came, demonstrating her broad effect on social policy and on bringing women into political life.

David E. Hamilton, *From New Day to New Deal: American Farm Policy from Hoover to Roosevelt, 1928–1933* (1991). A comprehensive review of the state of American agriculture and contrasting approaches to its chronic problems. By showing how farm policy evolved toward a reformed consensus, Hamilton offers varying measures of credit and blame to both the Hoover and Roosevelt administrations.

Ellis Hawley, *The New Deal and the Problem of Monopoly: A Study in Economic Ambivalence* (1996). A complex but lucid study of the New Deal attempt to establish a prosperous relationship between government and industry. Hawley identifies chronic difficulties in regulation and cooperation that hampered plans for fashioning a regulatory system.

William E. Leuchtenburg, *Franklin D. Roosevelt and the New Deal, 1932–1940* (1963). Still the most engaging and sweeping one-volume account of the New Deal. Leuchtenburg employs a mastery of detail and anecdote to carry his sympathetic story along.

Jerre Mangione, *The Dream and the Deal* (1972). The chaotic story of the New Deal relief project for unemployed writers, as told by a participant. Mangione makes plain that this novel program increased general awareness of the nation's regions and peoples, just as it nurtured a new generation of writers.

Richard H. Pells, *Radical Visions and American Dreams: Culture and Social Thought in the Depression Years* (1973). A skillful meshing of the radical enthusiasms of the New Deal era with critical and artistic expression that either mirrored or sought to escape the realities of the time. Pells focuses his discussion on the struggle between New Deal reforms and more sweeping ideas of critics on the left.

Harvard Sitkoff, ed., *Fifty Years Later: The New Deal Evaluated* (1985). A collection of essays on key aspects of the New Deal. The authors cover domestic and foreign policy, as well as the cultural legacy of the New Deal.

Patricia Sullivan, *Days of Hope: Race and Democracy in the New Deal Era* (1996). A critical examination of the persistent conflict between racial thought and democracy. Sullivan helps explain how discrimination and hardship marred the attempt of African Americans to ally with the New Deal.

Geoffrey C. Ward, *A First-Class Temperament: The Emergence of Franklin Roosevelt* (1989). A massive biography of Roosevelt and his social and political milieu. Through his deployment of detail, Ward goes far in explaining the inner character of a man often described as an enigma.

Susan Ware, *Beyond Suffrage: Women in the New Deal* (1981). A useful compendium of information on the first significant involvement of women in national politics. Ware also indicates the importance of the newcomer coalition of women in preparing the way for another new coalition of African Americans.

Frank A. Warren, *Liberalism and Communism: The "Red Decade" Revisited* (1993). A thoughtful exploration of the opposing New Deal and radical spheres. In the process Warren indicates the limits of reform and the problem of determining what needed to change.

GOD BLESS AMERICA

**MEMENTO OF WAR**
*To mark the seriousness of going to war, servicemen and their families often mounted photos in special settings, such as this painted-on-glass frame. Symbols of God and country sum up patriotic devotion to a just cause. And in the midst of these ritualized sentiments, as if looking back through a window draped in his honor, an unknown sailor seems about to tell us something more.*
Private Collection.

# THE UNITED STATES AND THE SECOND WORLD WAR

## 25

### 1939–1945

EXCITED AND UNCERTAIN ABOUT WHAT TO EXPECT, a noisy crowd of eight thousand jostled into the America First rally in Des Moines, Iowa, on the evening of September 1, 1941. They came to hear Charles Lindbergh, the first person to fly solo across the Atlantic, the nation's most famous hero. Lindbergh was speaking against President Franklin Roosevelt's order that would allow American warships to "shoot on sight" any German vessel that interfered with American shipping to Great Britain. A shy, private man who had resisted every effort by the media to make him a celebrity, Lindbergh dreaded the event. Only a compelling sense of duty convinced him that he must suffer the spotlight again to take a stand against American involvement in another war.

Lindbergh's speech was sponsored by the America First Committee (AFC), organized in the fall of 1940 to keep the United States out of the war that had erupted in Europe the year before. The AFC's youthful organizers attracted a considerable following, including two draft-age future presidents, Gerald Ford and John Kennedy. But denunciation of America Firsters by supporters of the Allied struggle against Nazi aggression, led by the Roosevelt administration, was far more vociferous. Secretary of the Interior Harold Ickes labeled Lindbergh "America's No. 1 Nazi fellow traveler," and a year earlier Roosevelt had gone even further. "I am absolutely convinced," he told Secretary of the Treasury Henry Morgenthau, "that Lindbergh is a Nazi."

Yet the man who had flown the Atlantic alone still had such a strong hold on the American imagination that the crowd in Des Moines settled down immediately when he stepped onto the stage, straight and tall, still at thirty-nine the godlike young aviator. In his clear, earnest voice Lindbergh declared that war would needlessly take the lives of the nation's best young men and bleed precious resources. Bluntly, he declared that "the three most important groups who have been pressing this country toward war are the British, the Jewish, and the Roosevelt administration." Lindbergh received a standing ovation. Elsewhere, however, accusations mounted that Lindbergh was anti-Semitic, if not pro-Nazi, and even close associates backed away. In the few months left before the United States entered the war in December 1941, the "Lone Eagle" was alone again.

In 1940–1941, millions of other Americans shared Lindbergh's concerns about the threat of war, but few resisted involvement as hard or as long as he did. Nor

**CHARLES LINDBERGH**

*When he came home to a hero's welcome after his famous flight across the Atlantic, Charles Lindbergh told his countrymen that he hoped the feat would bring Europe and America together as friends. The outbreak of war in 1939 dashed that vision and led Lindbergh to join the isolationist America First Committee. He drew huge crowds when he spoke at rallies against intervention, such as the one shown here (left) at the Manhattan Center in April 1941. After America was attacked a few months later, Lindbergh's sense of duty shifted to all-out support of the war effort—including combat missions in the Pacific. Yet, even with victory, he never lost the sense that war meant something had gone terribly wrong with civilization.*
Wide World photos (left) and McGuire Air Force Base (right).

did many of them question the Allied cause. Torn between abhorrence of Nazism and a desire not to be drawn into another world war, the American people reluctantly endorsed Roosevelt's support for Britain's last-ditch defense against tyranny. Only when the nation was attacked did Americans throw themselves unreservedly into a struggle they were convinced was necessary to preserve democracy. With less emotion but deeper conviction than during World War I, Americans believed they were fighting a "good war."

The American experience in World War II was unique. No fighting occurred on American soil, yet the nation engaged in a total war that influenced every American and almost every aspect of American life. The war put Americans to work again and ended the depression. It ended the New Deal's drive for reform and the nation's isolationism. American soldiers and sailors, many of whom had never been beyond their hometowns, fought on distant continents and seas and came home changed. As one rifleman said of his experience abroad: "I went there a skinny, gaunt mama's boy, full of wonderment. I came back much more circumspect in my judgment of people. And of governments." Nearly four years of war also changed individuals and society at home. Women did "men's" work, minorities stepped out of their "places," and, as one woman remembered, people came out of the war "with more money than they'd had in years." But hundreds of thousands of families also lost fathers, husbands, and sons, wounds that would never heal. A victorious nation, grieving yet still optimistic, emerged from World War II the strongest industrial and military power in the world.

## Peacetime Dilemmas

With the Japanese invasion of Manchuria in 1931, the arms buildup and talk of the glories of war in fascist Italy, and the swearing in of Adolf Hitler as chancellor of Germany in 1933, the peace structure so hopefully put into place during the Versailles Peace Conference following World War I grew more precarious. As the tide of violent nationalism rose, the United States retreated even further behind its ocean shield, with New Dealers determined to concentrate on domestic policies first and not allow international complications to hinder the country's economic recovery. With few exceptions, American policy took on a peculiar polarity: In the face of crises, the nation's leaders took bold action at home but shrank from involvement abroad.

### FDR and Reluctant Isolation

Nowhere was the contrast between domestic boldness and international caution more evident than in the change in Franklin Delano Roosevelt's public position on foreign policy. As assistant secretary of the navy in the Wilson administration, Roosevelt urged American preparedness when World War I broke out in Europe and he welcomed U.S. entry into the fray. True to Wilson's vision that the United States should take the lead in making the world "safe for democracy," Roosevelt went against the isolationist tide in the 1920s by arguing for American membership in the League of Nations. When he reentered politics in 1928 to run for the governorship of the state of New York, he charged that the Republicans had undermined chances for a prosperous peace by setting high tariffs while also insisting that the exhausted Europeans pay off their loans and reparations.

The depression forced Roosevelt to retreat from his internationalism, persuaded that expending effort and money on foreign ventures was a risky diversion from domestic recovery. During his 1932 run for the presidency, Roosevelt sought to defuse charges that he was an international adventurer by pulling back from his endorsement of the League of Nations and reversing his position on forgiving European war debts.

Once in office, Roosevelt sought to join domestic economic recovery with a foreign policy that encouraged free trade and disarmament. He had always believed that peace, prosperity, and free trade were linked. "Foreign markets must be regained if America's producers are to rebuild a full and enduring domestic prosperity for our people," Roosevelt declared in 1935. The concept of an interdependent and open world led to the most successful initiative of his first year in office—recognition of the Soviet Union, which had been shunned as a revolutionary menace since the Bolshevik Revolution of 1917. After a careful survey of American public opinion convinced him of the nation's support on the issue, Roosevelt pressed forward with negotiations that resulted in formal recognition of the Soviet Union on November 17, 1933.

*New Dealers were determined to concentrate on domestic policies first and not allow international complications to hinder the country's economic recovery.*

Despite this bold initiative, Roosevelt was hemmed in by circumstances. Because the New Deal needed support from isolationists in Congress, Roosevelt could not offer to help the League of Nations or the World Court curb aggression. American endorsement of international cooperation could go no further than to express watery praise for the concept of collective security. America could only watch from the sidelines as the League of Nations gradually lost its ability to maintain peace. When rebuked for its invasion of Manchuria, Japan withdrew from the league and rejected limitations on its naval strength imposed after World War I. In the fall of 1933, the new Nazi chancellor of Germany, Adolf Hitler, further dimmed the league's prospects by condemning the organization as an obstacle to Germany's national aspirations and recalling Germany's representatives to the league. Shocked by the ominous turn of events, Roosevelt reassured Americans that support of the league's objectives would not go so far as to involve the United States in war. Under no circumstances, he declared, would the nation "use its armed forces for the settlement of any dispute anywhere."

## The Good Neighbor Policy

In his inaugural address in 1933, Franklin Roosevelt dedicated the United States to "the policy of the good neighbor" in foreign affairs. A few weeks later, he specifically applied the phrase to Latin America, signaling a shift from the arrogant insistence of previous administrations that they had the right to intervene in the internal affairs of Latin American nations. By offering a "helping hand" and enjoying "the cooperation of others," Roosevelt declared, the United States could engender "more order in this hemisphere and less dislike." In December 1933, Secretary of State Cordell Hull carried that message to the Inter-American Conference in Montevideo, Uruguay, where he signed a joint declaration asserting that no nation had the right to intervene in the internal or external affairs of another.

The United States' commitment to nonintervention was quickly put to the test. When Mexico nationalized American oil holdings and when revolution boiled over in Nicaragua, Guatemala, and Cuba, Roosevelt refrained from his cousin Theodore's easy resort to sending in the marines to defend the interests of American corporations. But nonintervention was a double-edged sword. While it honored the principle of national self-determination, it did not necessarily promote freedom. American business, emboldened by Roosevelt's policy, entered into lucrative arrangements with dictators like Anastasio Somoza in Nicaragua and Fulgencio Batista in Cuba that enabled those tyrants to become wealthy and powerful by exploiting and terrorizing the rest of the population.

Adoption of the "good neighbor policy," therefore, did not mean that Roosevelt had abandoned Woodrow Wilson's aim of achieving economic preeminence in the region. Roosevelt did not so much retreat from empire in Latin America as reject military force as the way to retain it. With Roosevelt's blessing, Hull engineered passage of the Reciprocal Trade Agreements Act of 1934. The act gave the president power to reduce the nation's high tariffs on a nation-by-nation basis with countries that would set the same tariff standards in return. By 1940, Hull's initiative persuaded twenty-two nations to sign treaties that set the pattern for most of America's foreign trade. Trade reciprocity had significant results, with American exports to Latin America doubling from 1933 to 1940. Trade reciprocity, however, did not prevent a widening of the gap between American economic power and that of the rest of the Western Hemisphere. Still, the seeds of friendship and solidarity planted in Latin America grew in importance as events in Europe and Asia eroded the hope for peace.

## The Price of Noninvolvement

Increasingly in the 1930s, international order broke down. Countries beset by economic hardship, ethnic rivalries, and historic grievances turned to aggressive nationalism as the way to end their troubles. Italian strongman Benito Mussolini set the pattern. Through harsh militarist means, Mussolini constructed an authoritarian state that created a semblance of order and efficiency. "War is to the man what maternity is to the woman," Mussolini proclaimed with a theatrical strut. "I do not believe in perpetual peace; not only do I not believe in it, but I find it depressing and a negation of all the fundamental virtues of man."

In Germany, Hitler was feverishly rearming his nation in open defiance of the Versailles treaty. British and French leaders had the power to compel German compliance, but they contented themselves with verbal protest. In 1935, Britain concluded a treaty with the Nazis that conceded to Germany equality in submarines and the right to build a surface fleet one-third the size of the British navy. Still, Hitler ranted against the Jews as the enemies of the Aryan master race and threatened action to avenge humiliating defeat in World War I. His statements about restoring territories with German inhabitants to the "Fatherland" became harder to ignore.

Political and economic tensions in the Far East also gave rise to a militant movement in Japan that resembled European fascism in the way it subordinated the economy to a ruling caste and sought national advantage through conquest. After absorbing Manchuria in 1932, Japan began a military campaign to take the five northern provinces of China. What they believed would be a mere skirmish became a long and vicious war when Chinese Nationalist leader Chiang Kai-shek rallied his troops and courageously resisted the Japanese invasion.

At first, alarm in the United States over escalating hostility abroad played into the hands of the isolationists. Disillusionment over the failure of

World War I to make the world safe for democracy convinced many Americans that the opponents of the war had been right all along. In 1933, a senatorial committee investigated the U.S. entry into the war. Chaired by Republican Gerald Nye of North Dakota, the committee concluded that the greed of American munitions makers, bankers, and financiers was responsible for dragging the country into war. Although it had little evidence, the Nye committee nevertheless convinced thousands of Americans that such a tragic mistake must never happen again.

The Nye committee's report and the rapidly deteriorating international situation prodded Congress into action. Between 1935 and 1937, legislators passed a series of neutrality acts designed to prevent the recurrence of the circumstances that they now believed had involved the country in World War I. One act forbade the extension of loans to nations at war. Another gave the president the power to warn Americans about traveling on ships of belligerent nations. A third prohibited arms sales to nations at war.

But by 1937, trade in nonmilitary goods had also become an issue. Some Americans argued that any trade, not just in munitions, could draw the nation into war and called for a total embargo of all American products to warring countries. Most members of Congress, however, recognized that a total trade ban would devastate the shaky American economy. Congress believed that it found a way out in the Neutrality Act of 1937, which allowed nonmilitary goods to continue to flow to nations at war *if* the foreign nations paid cash (thus avoiding American loans) and shipped the goods in their own vessels (thus avoiding the use of American ships in war zones). The so-called cash-and-carry policy seemed to promise that the United States could have both peace and prosperous foreign trade.

Emboldened by democracy's presumed lack of resolve to stand firm against pressure, Germany, Italy, and Japan went from one triumphant strike to the next. In March 1936, Nazi troops marched unopposed into the Rhineland on Germany's western border in blatant violation of the Treaty of Versailles, which had placed the area under French authority. One month later, Italian armies completed their conquest of Ethiopia. Aggression in the Far East reached its climax in December 1937 when Japanese troops captured Nanking and celebrated their triumph with a murderous rampage that cost the lives of 200,000 Chinese civilians.

These brutal events occurred alongside a tragic drama in Spain that demonstrated the threat of fascist power to democracy. In 1936, Spain erupted in a civil war between Loyalists, representing the existing republican government, and rebel fascists led by General Francisco Franco. In what became widely described as a rehearsal for the next world war, Germany and Italy sent troops and arms to Franco, and the Soviet Union, on a much smaller scale, came to the aid of the Loyalists. The American government and public opinion favored the Loyalists as the democratically elected government, but neither the United States nor European democracies offered assistance to either side. Neutrality meant that Loyalist forces were at a disadvantage against rebel forces amply supplied by fascist and Nazi nations that welcomed war. In an effort to make up for their nation's inaction, over three thousand Americans, many of them inspired by the Soviet Union's intervention, enlisted in the Lincoln Brigade to fight for the Loyalists with several thousand volunteers from other countries.

Increasingly convinced that the United States needed to play a stronger role in stopping aggression, Roosevelt spoke on October 5, 1937, in Chicago, the heartland of isolationist sentiment, in an attempt to persuade Americans that the government should be more assertive against aggression. "America hates war," he said. "America hopes for peace. Therefore, America actively engages in the search for peace."

The speech advocated no specific action, but it ignited a storm of protest. Peace groups unloosed a letter-writing campaign to newspapers and politicians. The *Chicago Tribune* charged that the president wanted to replace "Americanism" with "internationalism." Most ominously, leaders in Congress remained silent. Roosevelt, who already had his hands full with fighting the depression, pulled back. "It's a terrible thing," he remarked to an aide, "to look over your shoulder when you are trying to lead and find no one there."

## The Onset of War

By 1939, world events and Roosevelt's efforts to educate Americans to the dangers of isolationism were bringing about a profound change in attitude. When war finally came to America, the nation united to defeat the Axis powers.

## Nazi Aggression and War in Europe

Under the spell of neutrality, Americans watched helplessly as Adolf Hitler continued his campaign to dominate Europe. In the name of the Fatherland's "destiny" to unite all German peoples, Hitler in 1938 bullied Austria into accepting incorporation—"Anschluss"—into the Nazi Third Reich. He then turned his attention to the German-speaking Sudetenland, granted to Czechoslovakia by the Versailles treaty.

Although the Czechs were prepared to fight rather than surrender territory, the British and French wanted peace and sought to strike a deal with Hitler. British Prime Minister Neville Chamberlain went to confer with the German ruler in Munich, offering terms of "appeasement," as he called it, that would turn over the Sudetenland to Germany in exchange for leaving the rest of Czechoslovakia alone. On September 29, 1938, Hitler accepted the offer, solemnly promising that he would make no more territorial

MAP 25.1
*Axis Aggression through 1941*
*In a series of surprise military strikes, Hitler reclaimed German territories occupied by France after World War I, annexed Austria, and then launched World War II to extend German power over the "inferior" peoples across Germany's borders.*

claims in Europe. Chamberlain returned home convinced that he had obtained "peace in our time." In March 1939, Hitler marched the German army into weakened Czechoslovakia and took over the entire country without a shot being fired (Map 25.1).

Hardly pausing for breath, Hitler in April demanded that Poland return the German territory it had been awarded after World War I. Britain and France finally recognized that the policy of appeasement was a failure. They assured Poland that they would go to its aid if Hitler attacked. Hitler then offered Premier Joseph Stalin concessions to prevent the Soviet Union from joining Germany's adversaries in the West. Despite deep enmity between Nazi Germany and the Communist Soviet Union, the two powers shocked the world by signing a Nazi-Soviet treaty of nonaggression in August 1939.

Hitler's only worry then was that something would interfere with his lust for war. He fretted, "I am afraid some pig-dog will make a proposal for mediation as at Munich." To prevent any such interruption, he exhorted his generals to be as ruthless as possible. "Close your hearts to pity! Act brutally! . . . In starting and waging a war it is not Right that matters, but Victory." At dawn on September 1, 1939, fully in accord with Hitler's wishes and spirit, the German army crossed the Polish border. France and Britain kept their word by declaring war. The greatest conflict in history had begun.

## From Neutrality to the Arsenal of Democracy

When war erupted, Roosevelt issued an official proclamation of American neutrality. But unlike Woodrow Wilson, he did not ask Americans to be impartial in thought as well as deed, since he and the vast majority of Americans strongly favored Britain, France, and the Allied cause. Antifascist yet neutral, the nation debated what it should do short of war to aid the Allies.

Roosevelt's immediate objective was to persuade Congress to repeal the arms embargo mandated by the neutrality legislation. He believed that France and Britain could defeat Germany only if they had access to weapons. The president's request provoked frenzied debate across the nation. Charles Lindbergh said that the war was a European matter and that the United States should stay out of it. Senator William Borah of Idaho declared that Roosevelt's proposal was equivalent to taking sides and would drag the United States into war. But Congress finally consented to modify neutrality legislation and adopt a cash-and-carry policy for arms sales.

After Hitler's armies overran Poland, they paused; but the lull was shattered in the spring of 1940 by a series of Nazi hammer blows. In a lightning-fast attack called a "blitzkrieg," German dive-bombers and tanks smashed through Denmark, Norway, Belgium, and Holland and into northern France. The French made the fatal mistake of believing that they could hold out behind the Maginot Line, a massive concrete fortification that stretched from the Swiss border to the Ardennes forest on the edge of Belgium (see Map. 25.1). Reality struck in early summer when Mussolini's armies invaded France from the south, while Hitler's blitzkrieg flanked the Maginot Line in the north.

*At dawn on September 1, 1939, fully in accord with Hitler's wishes and spirit, the German army crossed the Polish border. France and Britain kept their word by declaring war. The greatest conflict in history had begun.*

British forces in the north were then trapped by the swift German advance and forced to retreat to the port of Dunkirk, from which they were narrowly rescued by a heroic sealift that used every boat able to make it across the Channel. Less than three weeks later, reeling from a German sweep southward, the French surrendered the largest army in the world and signed an armistice that placed three-fifths of the country under German control.

With the possibility of a German invasion across the Channel now looming, Parliament turned the appeaser Neville Chamberlain out of office and welcomed as prime minister the defiant Winston Churchill. Churchill had watched from the sidelines with mounting fury as Chamberlain kowtowed to Hitler. When the Germans attacked Britain itself, Churchill was ready with a vengeance to take over the last-ditch defense of the nation. His oratorical genius shone through the intensive German bombing campaign against English cities in the summer and fall of 1940. By the time the Royal Air Force won the Battle of Britain in November, ridding the skies of German bombers, Churchill had become the symbol of indomitable British resistance.

Roosevelt strove for a comparable role as leader and symbol by weaning the public away from the isolationist arguments. In the spring of 1940, the president prevailed on Kansas journalist William Allen White to form the Committee to Defend America by Aiding the Allies and mount a nationwide campaign to generate public support for Roosevelt's policy of providing all aid to the Allies short of war.

In the midst of this vital debate about American foreign policy, the presidential election of 1940 unfolded. Having decided to run for an unprecedented third term rather than step aside in the midst of crisis, Roosevelt looked forward to a campaign pitting the reformist, internationalist thrust of the New Deal against Republican isolationism and business conservatism. Instead he faced Wendell Willkie, a former Democrat who supported most of the New Deal domestic program and generally agreed with Roosevelt's foreign policy. Realizing that he trailed Roosevelt badly, Willkie veered from internationalism and attacked Roosevelt as a warmonger, forcing the president to declare, "Your boys are not going to be sent into any foreign wars." With mixed messages about opposing fascist aggression and staying out of war, Roosevelt claimed a comfortable victory. Although his margin was smaller than in 1936, he won easily, 27.3 million votes to 22.3 million votes and 449 electoral votes to 82.

The president interpreted his victory as a mandate to continue to support Britain in every way short of war. By then the British were in desperate straits; their treasury exhausted, they could no longer pay cash for weapons. To head off the catastrophic end of American aid, Roosevelt held a fireside chat with the American people on December 16, 1940, to explain that only the British stood between the United States and Nazi aggression. "We must be the great arsenal of democracy," he declared. As for how the British would pay, he offered the homey example of a man who lent his neighbor a garden hose when his house caught on fire. "I don't say to him . . . 'you have to pay me $15 for it.' I don't want $15—I want my garden hose back after the fire is over."

Buoyed by favorable public response, Congress approved the Lend-Lease Act in March, 1941, which allowed the British to obtain armaments from the United States so long as they returned them or their equivalent after the war was over. In reality, Lend-Lease was a charade to retain the semblance of neutrality. As one observer noted, "Lending war materiel is a little like lending chewing gum. You don't want it back." With Lend-Lease, the United States entered into full-fledged economic warfare against Germany. Moreover, since Britain could not sustain its shipping in the face of losses to German submarines, the United States would need inevitably to build and protect a vast merchant fleet. It was only a matter of time before an armed attack occurred of the sort that had precipitated World War I.

The predictable series of events began on June 11, 1941, when a German U-boat (submarine) sank the American freighter *Robin Moor* off the coast of Africa. Several months later, an American destroyer and a German submarine engaged in a firefight, Roosevelt issued a "shoot on sight" policy for American escort vessels, and by September 1941 an "undeclared war" was under way.

As danger in the Atlantic mounted, Hitler took a terrible gamble by launching a massive invasion of the Soviet Union on June 22, 1941. Until that violent rupture of the Nazi-Soviet pact, Americans generally thought no better of the Communists than they did of the Nazis. But the brutal facts of war called for drastic change. Churchill bluntly welcomed his old archenemy Joseph Stalin to the cause by stating that he would not hesitate to deal with the devil if Hitler invaded hell. Roosevelt stressed the importance of Russia's entrance in diverting German forces away from the hard-pressed British and quickly persuaded Congress to extend Lend-Lease to the Russians.

## War Comes to America

Despite the United States' primary concern with Europe, the expansion of the Japanese empire made the danger of war for America most immediate in Asia. The rising tide of Japanese imperialism clashed with U.S. aspirations and commitments, especially in China. America's China policy had been set in 1899 when Secretary of State John Hay issued the Open Door notes demanding that the United States have equal access to the rich markets of China and that China maintain its territorial integrity. But the island-bound Japanese also wanted raw material and markets and their weak neighbor China was the natural place to turn. The military invasion of Manchuria in 1931 proved to be the opening salvo of continuing Japanese aggression in China (Map 25.2). Each act of territorial conquest received a stern rebuke from the Roosevelt admin-

**MAP 25.2**

*Japanese Aggression through 1941*

*Beginning with the invasion of Manchuria in 1931, Japan sought to force its imperialist control over most of East Asia. Japanese aggression was driven by the need for raw materials for the country's expanding industries and by the military government's devotion to martial honor.*

istration, but toothless proclamations did little to deter the Japanese.

In 1940, Japan signed the Tripartite Pact, a defensive alliance with Germany and Italy. It also obtained from the Vichy government, the German puppet regime in France, the right to build airfields and station troops in northern Indochina. In 1941, U.S. naval intelligence cracked the Japanese code and learned that Tokyo had set its sights on the resource-rich Dutch East Indies. In response, the Roosevelt administration announced a complete trade embargo, which denied Japan access to essential oil and scrap iron. Roosevelt had given Japan a choice: Japan would either have to halt its aggression and restore relations and trade with the United States, or it would have to find new sources of vital supplies, most likely by seizing British, French, and Dutch possessions in the Far East.

Japanese nationalists were increasingly offended by the pressure against Japan's economic and territorial ambitions. In October 1941, a military clique headed by General Hideki Tojo seized control and persuaded other leaders, including Emperor Hirohito, who originally called the idea "harebrained," that swift destruction of American bases in the Pacific would leave Japan free to follow its destiny. Despite knowledge from decoded Japanese messages that an attack was imminent, the Roosevelt administration disastrously underestimated the reach of Japanese military power. Consequently, American forces were unprepared for the blow that struck the Pearl Harbor naval base in Hawaii on December 7, 1941. At dawn, a swarm of Japanese carrier-borne fighters, bombers, and torpedo planes found most of the American fleet at anchor and American planes neatly crowded together at Hickam Field. In two hours, the raiders sank or damaged all eight battleships of the fleet and disabled ten other ships. Three hundred and forty airplanes were wrecked and more than 3,500 Americans were killed or wounded.

**PEARL HARBOR, DECEMBER 7, 1941**
*A rescue fireboat is hopelessly dwarfed by the enormous catastrophe of the battleship* West Virginia *aflame and sinking at its mooring in Pearl Harbor. With the dramatic force of a vast seascape painting, this photograph was widely reproduced as a graphic indication of how great a crime the Japanese had committed.*
U.S. Army.

Though the raid scored a stunning tactical success, in the larger sense it was a colossal blunder. Overnight, disagreement in the United States about foreign policy ended, and Americans united in their commitment to war and desire for revenge. In his message to Congress declaring war, Roosevelt said:

> Yesterday, December 7, 1941—a date which will live in infamy—the United States of America was suddenly and deliberately attacked by naval and air forces of the Empire of Japan. . . . Always will we remember the character of the onslaught against us. No matter how long it may take us to overcome this premeditated invasion, the American people in their righteous might will win through to absolute victory.

Congress endorsed the message unanimously, except for Quaker pacifist Jeannette Rankin, who had also voted against U.S. entry into World War I. Although Hitler and Mussolini had not known about the Japanese attack in advance, Germany and Italy declared war against America on December 11.

# Fighting Back: 1941 – 1943

Never had the United States faced such a desperate military situation or so staggering a task as it did in 1941. Hitler and his armies had conquered most of Europe, and the Japanese military machine was slicing through the Pacific with amazing speed. From the beginning, American concern had centered on saving Britain and the Soviet Union from defeat so that the United States would not have to face Hitler alone. Roosevelt and his military commanders decided on a strategy that would concentrate on Germany first and then bring the nation's full armed might to bear on the Japanese. But before turning to Hitler, the United States and its allies would have to stop the Japanese advance through the Pacific. By 1943, the Allies had checked their enemies and were pushing them back. But the Allies could claim victory in neither Europe nor Asia. The "good war" would also be a long one.

## Turning the Tide in the Pacific

Following Pearl Harbor, Japan's leading military genius, Admiral Isoroku Yamamoto, ordered an all-out offensive in the Pacific on the belief that, if his forces did not win quickly, Japan would lose the war

to America's far greater manpower and resources. With lightning speed, the Japanese attacked American airfields in the Philippines and captured the American outposts of Guam and Wake Island. Singapore, the great British naval base in Malaya, surrendered in February 1942, and most of Burma had fallen by March. All that stood in the way of Japan's total domination of the southwestern Pacific was the Philippine Islands.

*Though the raid on Pearl Harbor scored a stunning tactical success, in the larger sense it was a colossal blunder. Overnight, disagreement in the United States about foreign policy ended, and Americans united in their commitment to war and desire for revenge.*

Under intense attack, General Douglas MacArthur, who commanded the Philippine defenses, retreated to fortifications on the Bataan Peninsula across the harbor from Manila. In March, MacArthur escaped to Australian command headquarters, leaving General Jonathan Wainwright to hold out as long as possible. When Wainwright surrendered the Corregidor fortress in May, Japanese soldiers marched the starved and ill survivors sixty-five miles to a concentration camp. Hundreds of Americans and as many as ten thousand Filipinos died en route. Of those who survived the Bataan Death March, sixteen thousand died within weeks from disease and mistreatment in the brutal prison camp. By summer 1942, the Japanese war machine had also conquered the oil-rich Dutch East Indies and was poised to strike at Australia and New Zealand (see Map 25.4).

The dark events that followed Pearl Harbor struck hard at American confidence. Jukeboxes may have been blaring "Goodbye, Mama, I'm Off to Yokohama," but the nation had learned that the soldiers of the Rising Sun were tough and fearless and prepared to fight to the death for honor and the emperor. At sea, the Japanese had larger, faster, heavier armored ships with bigger guns and more accurate torpedoes. And the four different kinds of airplanes that rained bombs and bullets on Pearl Harbor outperformed anything the Americans could send up against them.

The string of unbroken Japanese victories caused Americans at home to worry about their own safety. A false report that Japanese fighter planes had been spotted near Los Angeles set off an antiaircraft barrage and inspired the commander of West Coast defenses to announce that "death and destruction [from enemy planes] are likely to come at any moment." Antiaircraft guns sprouted up and down the Pacific coast. In Hawaii, still shaken from the attack on Pearl Harbor, one vigilant citizen advised the authorities that he had spotted a dog on the beach "barking in Morse code to Japanese subs offshore." Clearly, Americans needed some sort of success to take the edge off panic.

By spring of 1942, U.S. forces were ready to strike back with a mighty two-pronged offensive that the Americans hoped would stop and then reverse the Japanese advance. The plan called for an army led by General MacArthur to move north from Australia and recapture the Philippines, while forces under Admiral Chester W. Nimitz sailed west from Hawaii and retook the Japanese-held islands in the mid-Pacific. Both offensives scored immediate victories. On May 7, 1942, in the Coral Sea just north of Australia, an American fleet and carrier-based planes stopped the Japanese fleet that was sailing around the coast of New Guinea.

The Battle of the Coral Sea was a prelude to an even more significant encounter. Learning that the Japanese were sending an invasion force against Midway Island, an outpost guarding the Hawaiian Islands, Admiral Nimitz moved his carriers and cruisers into the Central Pacific. In a wild melee that raged from June 3 to June 6, American planes sank four Japanese carriers, a heavy cruiser, and two destroyers, while the American armada lost only one carrier and a destroyer. The Battle of the Coral Sea and the Battle of Midway marked the high tide of Japanese power in the Pacific.

### The Campaign in Europe

With the Japanese offensive in the Pacific halted, American attention focused on defeating Germany. In the dark months after Pearl Harbor, the war news from Europe was as depressing as that from the Pacific. While imperial Japanese forces were spreading through Asia, Hitler's army smashed deep into the Soviet Union and prepared for an invasion of Britain. The Germans attempted, as in World War I, to starve the British into submission by destroying their seaborne lifeline. Advances in technology made German U-boats so much more effective than in World War I that at first they sank American ships faster than new ones could be built. The toll eventually

reached 4,786 merchant ships, nearly double the number in World War I, and almost 200 warships. The human cost was 40,000 Allied seamen and almost as many Germans who perished in their 781 stricken U-boats.

The Allies had done little to prepare for another battle on the Atlantic. The British had not laid down mines to defend coastal waters nor armed merchant vessels. Because Americans did not institute blackouts until the spring of 1942, lights on shore illuminated merchant targets. Using only 6 U-boats, the Germans sank 82 ships off the American East Coast and more than 200 additional ships in the waters around Bermuda and the Caribbean islands.

Until 1943, the war in the Atlantic remained in doubt and the British Isles hung by a precarious thread. But the use of newly invented radar detectors and production of sufficient destroyer escorts for merchant vessels allowed the United States to move massive amounts of supplies to England and to the Soviet ports. The battle of the Atlantic had been won.

*While imperial Japanese forces were spreading through Asia, Hitler's army smashed deep into the Soviet Union and prepared for an invasion of Britain.*

The big question then was when and where to open a second front against the Nazis on the continent. Stalin, desperate to keep German divisions away from his bloody doorstep, strongly urged an immediate and massive invasion of France across the English Channel. But Churchill favored something smaller, perhaps a Mediterranean target such as Europe's "soft underbelly," the Balkans. Roosevelt worried about a plan that would merely "peck on the periphery," but ultimately he backed an invasion of North Africa as a first step. Since the United States' rapidly expanding military force was clearly the vital element in any western front, Roosevelt's wishes prevailed.

The strategy targeted the one area where the Allies were having some success against the Germans. In October 1942, at El-Alamein in Egypt, the British halted General Erwin Rommel's drive to capture the Suez Canal. A few weeks later, an American army landed in French Morocco under the supreme commander of American forces in Europe, General Dwight D. Eisenhower. General George Patton, the ablest U.S. tank commander, swiftly joined the British in pursuit of the German and Italian armies, and in May 1943 Allied armies closed the jaws of a gigantic vice on the last enemy troops in North Africa. The North African campaign cost Germany and Italy dearly—some 350,000 dead and captured—and reopened the Mediterranean to Allied shipping and Italy to invasion (see Map 25.3).

As the North African campaign unfolded, Roosevelt arrived at the Moroccan city of Casablanca in January 1943 to confer with his fellow Allied leaders, Winston Churchill and General Charles de Gaulle, the leader of the Free French government in exile. Stalin, preoccupied with the desperate defense of Stalingrad, was an absent but watchful partner. Pledged to rid the world of Germany and Italy's menace, the Allied leaders announced that they would insist on "unconditional surrender." Of equal importance was their judgment that more time was needed for the buildup of enough forces in England to launch a successful cross-channel invasion of France. A strike against Italy in the meantime, the Allies decided, would capitalize on success in North Africa, a decision that meant the Soviet Union would continue to absorb the brunt of the Nazi attack for another year.

On July 10, 1943, a combined American and British amphibious operation, the largest in history, landed 160,000 troops in Sicily. The badly equipped Italian defenders, many of whom had lost their will to fight in the disastrous North African campaign, quickly withdrew to the mainland. The Allies followed in September, and almost immediately the Italian government surrendered unconditionally. To halt the advance, the Germans rushed additional divisions into the country and seized Rome, at which point the military campaign in Italy became a war of liberation against German occupation.

Success came hard against the occupiers, who waited in sophisticated fortifications atop the mountainous Italian terrain. Not until June 1944, after a long and bloody campaign, did massive firepower finally breach the German lines and enable Allied forces to liberate Rome. From that time until the end of the war, the Allies struggled against German mountain defenses in northern Italy. The Italian campaign, which fell frustratingly below total victory, was the costliest of the war to the American infantry and did not satisfy an increasingly embittered Stalin's demand for a second front. It did, however, manage to fully embroil twenty-five German divisions that might otherwise have been used against either the Russians or a second front in France.

# The War at Home

World War II brought no physical destruction to the United States; no one starved, and no civilians lost their lives in the fighting. Still, World War II changed the nation. Inevitably, a war as vast and as long as World War II disrupted the traditional social patterns it sought to defend. Total war meant that millions of troops went to unheard of places to face unimagined dangers. Conversion of the economy to war purposes also drew millions of civilians away from their roots to seize opportunities they never had before in places where they never expected to live. Women welding in the shipyards in California, men building tanks in the factories of Detroit, and children everywhere stripping scarce tinfoil from empty cigarette packs—all felt the impact of the war and were changed by it.

## From Reform to Recovery

There is partial truth in the observation that Adolf Hitler was more responsible for ending the depression in the United States than was Franklin Roosevelt. In 1939, the federal budget was $9 billion; by 1945, at the end of total mobilization for war, it had grown to $100 billion. Within months after Pearl Harbor, unemployment, which in 1940 had stood at 14.6 percent of the nation's workforce, had virtually disappeared. Industrial cities boomed with orders for war materiel, enough not only to give work to urban workers but also to draw displaced farm laborers into the cities where they enjoyed a modest prosperity far beyond anything they had known.

There was no longer much talk about social reform, however. The New Deal had run its course; and, as Roosevelt offhandedly remarked, he had given up being "Dr. New Deal" in order to become "Dr. Win the War." In the spirit of winning the war at all costs, the Roosevelt administration oversaw a miracle of production. Called to Washington by a president they had mostly opposed, "dollar-a-year" businessmen (so called because they served without pay) headed the rapidly multiplying war production agencies. Despite confusion and chaos from the rapid conversion of the economy to war making, output was staggering. The United States produced 275,000 airplanes during the war and by 1945 was launching a new ship every twenty-four hours. The arsenal of democracy not only equipped its own gigantic armed forces but also supplied its allies in Europe and Asia with a large part of what they required. By 1942, American production equaled that of Germany, Italy, and Japan combined; by 1944, it doubled their production. From these prodigies came confirmation that the depression was over when business profit margins in 1943 soared well beyond those of 1929.

The nation's economic expansion was powered by the mobilization of its citizens. Draft boards registered 31 million men, of whom 10 million were inducted into service. In addition, more than 5 million men and women volunteered. When the war ended, 10,400,000 had served in the army, 3,900,000 in the navy, 600,000 in the marines, and 240,000 in the coast guard.

The war boom also accelerated the transformation of agriculture that the New Deal had begun. Family farms declined and tenant farmers virtually disappeared, many of them transplanted to urban centers of war production. Traditional patterns of rural black life underwent especially dramatic change. By 1950, the official census showed that only 115,000 African Americans remained on the land out of a total of 1,406,000 who had lived on farms when the war started. For the increasing proportion of large farms that remained, the task of feeding both Americans and Allies meant an increase of production by 25 percent each year of the war.

The war also restored prosperity to American workers. With more than 15 million adults in the military, new workers—the old, the young, and especially women—were brought into the labor force. The cost of living increased 30 percent from 1941 to 1945; but the rise in weekly earnings of workers employed in manufacturing was far ahead at 70 percent. Finding much to spend the new money on was another matter. Conversion of industrial plants to war purposes meant that automobiles, washing machines, refrigerators, and numerous other consumer items were no longer being manufactured. Many other civilian goods were rationed because they were hard to obtain from war zones or were needed in large quantities for the military: automobile tires, gasoline, shoes, meat.

## Political Crosscurrents

Inconveniences and dislocations notwithstanding, Americans on the home front rallied around the war effort in unprecedented unity. But the waning of New Deal reform and early reverses in the war made it difficult for the Roosevelt administration to hold its governing coalition together. Moreover, in the congressional elections of 1942, Democrats were denied considerable support from soldiers and defense workers who were unable to cast their usual Democratic votes because the war had taken them away from the hometowns where they were registered. Low voter turnout thus helped Republicans to gain forty-four seats in the House and nine in the Senate.

Republican opponents saw the war years as an opportunity to roll back New Deal reforms in favor of traditional American free enterprise. A conservative coalition of Republicans and southern Democrats succeeded in abolishing several New Deal agencies in 1942 and 1943, including the Work Projects Administration and the Civilian Conservation Corps. But the Democratic administration did not sit idly by while Republicans dismantled their work of the 1930s. By persuading states to ease residency requirements and Congress to guarantee absentee ballots for servicemen, they arranged to bring scattered members of the New Deal coalition back to the voting booth.

Franklin Roosevelt, though exhausted and gravely ill, nevertheless decided to run for an unprecedented fourth term rather than turn the uncompleted war effort over to a new leader. Convinced that many Americans had soured on liberal reform, Roosevelt replaced Vice President Henry Wallace, an outspoken progressive, with a more politically viable running mate, Senator Harry S. Truman of Missouri. A reliable party man from a border state, Truman seemed likely to satisfy urban Democratic leaders while not posing a threat to southerners who were nervous about challenges to segregation.

The Republicans, confident of a strong conservative upsurge, nominated the governor of New York, Thomas E. Dewey, who had made his reputation as a tough crime fighter. Roosevelt's failing health alarmed many observers and limited his ability to campaign. In the final reckoning, though, that weakness was outweighed by the unwillingness of the American people to change presidents at the height of a foreign war or to accept Dewey's recycling of Herbert Hoover's argument that the New Deal was a creeping socialist menace. At only 53.5 percent of the popular vote, Roosevelt's victory was his narrowest; but it virtually assured that he would remain commander in chief throughout the war, if he lived.

## Women, Family, and the War

During the depression, female workers were often accused of taking a husband's or father's job. A shortage of manpower during the war, however, reversed the trend, and millions of women found themselves being courted by the defense industry. Three-fourths of these women were married and nearly four million had children. Often they moved from traditional jobs as domestic servants, secretaries, and waitresses to better-paying industrial work that had generally been considered beyond their skills and endurance.

*During the depression, female workers were often accused of taking a husband's or father's job. A shortage of manpower during the war, however, reversed the trend, and millions of women found themselves being courted by the defense industry.*

The ambivalence of the women's situation, divided between home and factory, showed in the fact that the average age for marriage went down to just over twenty and the birthrate rose, while at the same time women increased their presence in industry, especially in war production. By 1944, some 18 million women had jobs, 50 percent more than in 1939. *Chicago Tribune* columnist Mike Royko remembered: "My sister became Rosie the Riveter. She put a bandanna on her head every day and went down to this organ company that had been converted to war work. . . . There was a sense of mission about it. Her husband was Over There." Along with the mission came an amazing rise in pay. A mountain woman remembered her first job after the depression at a munitions plant in Viola, Kentucky. "We made the fabulous sum of thirty-two dollars a week," she said. "To us it was just an absolute miracle. Before that, we made nothing." In the patriotic euphoria over a rise in women's weekly wages to an average of $31, it was understandable that few complained that men received $54 for comparable work.

Alongside women in the civilian workforce stood 350,000 women who joined the Nurse's Corps and the newly created military units the army WACs, navy Waves, coast guard Spars, and the Women's Marine Corps. Women also served as pilots in the WASPs (Women Air Service Pilots). While

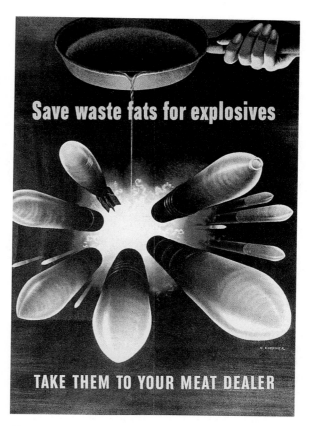

**Save waste fats for explosives**

**TAKE THEM TO YOUR MEAT DEALER**

**OWI PROPAGANDA POSTER**
*The Office of War Information mobilized art and propaganda in many ways to connect the home front with the battlefield. Though little fat actually went from the frying pan into the firing line, this poster is a visually startling example of attempts to remind people that even the simplest acts could contribute to the war effort.*
Library of Congress.

barred from combat duty, women worked at nearly every noncombat assignment.

Despite the war's dynamic social changes, most women remained in the home and worked only part-time or not at all. For them the experience was stressfully divided. The yearning in the midst of war for the peacetime joys of security and family, felt mutually by isolated women and fighting men, reinforced traditional attitudes. At the same time, the war also took a toll on families. The number of marriages and the birthrate rose, but so too did illegitimacy and divorce. In many cases children compensated for the absence of fathers by doing their part for the war effort. Girl and boy scouts, for example, sponsored scrap drives collecting iron, steel, brass, bronze, tin, and wastepaper; and older teenagers took jobs formerly reserved for adults. But new responsibilities and opportunities were countered by disruptive problems. Children in the workplace faced the same hardships that caused resistance to child labor in the first place. The absence of older men also meant that young people had less guidance than usual, and juvenile delinquency, especially among girls, increased accordingly. The yearning for war's end included a desire for stability at home as well as abroad.

## Prejudice and the War

Fighting against Nazism and its ideology of Aryan racial supremacy under the banner of democracy forced Americans to examine prejudice in their own society. African American leader W. E. B. Du Bois, who had welcomed World War I as a chance for black Americans to prove their worth, defined World War II as a "war for racial equality" and a struggle for "democracy not only for white folks but for yellow, brown, and black." Such aspirations squared perfectly with official proclamations of the war as a fight for democracy. In a letter to the Southern Negro Youth Congress, Roosevelt declared that blacks were in the war "not only to defend America but . . . to establish a universal freedom under which a new basis of security and prosperity can be established for all—regardless of station, race, or creed." The Pittsburgh *Courier,* a leading black newspaper, rejoiced that, though "war may be hell for some," it appeared ready to "open up the portals of heaven for us."

Others sought to enter those portals as well. More than 13,000 Chinese Americans and more than 25,000 Native Americans fought in the armed forces. Mexican Americans feared that for them the war would mean deportation; instead, more than 200,000 laborers were imported from Mexico to cultivate American crops in the federal government's *bracero* program. In addition 500,000 Mexican Americans served in the U.S. armed forces.

Crisis also stirred old prejudices, however, which sometimes flared into violence. In 1943, riots occurred in Los Angeles when hundreds of white servicemen, claiming they were punishing draft dodgers, chased and beat young Chicano men who dressed in distinctive broad-shouldered, peglegged "zoot" suits. Prejudice caused Japanese Americans to be confined in concentration camps

**FEMALE DEFENSE WORKER**
*The war effort brought persons and activities together in unlikely ways, leading to unexpected outcomes. In this photo, the Army magazine* Yank *sought to boost morale by presenting a defense worker as pinup girl. No one could know that the young propeller technician, nineteen-year-old Norma Jean Baker Dougherty, would later remake herself as the most glamorous of movie stars, Marilyn Monroe.*
David Conover Images © Norma Jean Enterprises, a division of 733548 Ontario Limited.

as possible subversive agents of their ancestral nation. Jews had to face the refusal of the government to admit more Jewish refugees because of vague fears that they might compete for scarce work or divert the war effort to their own purposes.

In an attempt to root old prejudicial patterns out of the war effort, black organizations sent a barrage of petitions to Congress and the White House demanding that the federal government require companies receiving defense contracts to integrate their workforces. A. Philip Randolph, head of the almost completely black Brotherhood of Sleeping Car Porters, promised that 100,000 marchers would descend on Washington if the president did not eliminate discrimination in defense industries. The president overcame his nervousness about offending old southern and union allies and issued Executive Order 8802, authorizing a Committee on Fair Employment Practices to investigate and prevent race discrimination in employment. Civil rights champions hailed the act as the first direct presidential intervention on behalf of black civil rights, and Randolph triumphantly called the march off.

Actual progress developed slowly, however. The five and a half million blacks who flooded into industrial cities during the 1940s, making African Americans a predominantly urban population for the first time, discovered that industry policies barred them from many skilled jobs. At least eighteen major unions, including such vital participants in the defense industry as the machinists, iron shipbuilders, and railway workers, had explicit bans against black membership.

*African American leader W. E. B. Du Bois, who had welcomed World War I as a chance for black Americans to prove their worth, defined World War II as a "war for racial equality" and a struggle for "democracy not only for white folks but for yellow, brown, and black."*

In time, however, severe labor shortages and government pressure opened up defense plants to African American workers. Black unemployment dropped by about 80 percent during the war, and the percentage of blacks in the defense industry doubled to a level almost equal to the percentage of blacks in the general population. Though equality of pay was still a distant hope, by the end of the war the average income of black families had risen to half that of white families.

With migration and progress went racial antagonism, which boiled over in the hot summer of 1943 when 242 racial outbreaks in forty-seven different cities far surpassed the 26 riots in the Red scare year of 1919. Worst of all were two days of mayhem in Detroit. Conflict between whites and blacks at a city park ignited a race war that saw whites smash their way with clubs through black neighborhoods and blacks retaliate by destroying and looting white-owned businesses. In the end, scores of persons suffered injury and thirty-four died, including twenty-five African Americans.

Out of the depths of violence came the stimulus for promising new strategies. The National Association for the Advancement of Colored People (NAACP) launched the "Double V" campaign—victory at home and abroad—and mounted legal challenges that would eventually outlaw segregation. In 1942, civil rights activists who wanted more direct confrontations founded a new organization, the Congress of Racial Equality (CORE), that organized picketing and sit-ins against Jim Crow restaurants and theaters and would achieve significant results after the war.

The military was no more free of discrimination than was the home front. Secretary of War Henry Stimson opposed any change in the segregation of blacks and whites into separate units and declared that the military effort should not serve as a "sociological laboratory." In 1942, Stimson fumed in his diary about what he deemed the absurdly presumptuous claims of black reformers: "What these foolish leaders of the colored race are seeking is at bottom social equality." Denied integrated armed forces, blacks joined anyway, and by the end of the

**DOUBLE V BUTTON**
*The Double V became African Americans' special version of the official "V for victory" symbol. Thousands of these buttons were worn as a reminder that both the Axis powers and racial discrimination should surrender unconditionally.*
Private Collection.

war nearly one million African American men and women had served. Segregated practices loosened as the war progressed. Blacks were trained as pilots for the first time, served on warships with white sailors, and saw extensive combat duty in the ground war in Europe and the Pacific. Yet military facilities remained segregated, and the Red Cross even segregated by race the blood it supplied to treat battlefield casualties. Perhaps nothing more poignantly captured the reality of wartime race relations than the moment when Lloyd Brown, a black soldier caught in the dusty heat of a Kansas summer day, gazed past the restaurant owner denying him entry and saw a row of German prisoners of war enjoying their lunch at the counter.

World War II did not witness a repetition of the hysteria and viciousness that had characterized the home front during World War I. With almost no dissent against the war, the government felt no need to engage in a high-powered propaganda campaign to limit civil liberties. Americans did worry about espionage, however. Walls were plastered with slogans such as "Loose lips sink ships" and "Enemy agents are always near; if you don't talk, they won't hear."

There was one major exception to the atmosphere of tolerance—the drastic violation of the rights of Japanese Americans, the only minority group to lose ground during the war. From the time of their first entry into the country in significant numbers in the 1890s, mainly to settle on the West Coast, the Japanese had encountered hostility as economic competitors and intruders in a "white man's country." Although they were law-abiding and successful in small businesses and farming, white prejudice prevailed in the first years of the twentieth century; steadily tightening limits on newcomers climaxed in 1924 in the declaration of the federal government that Japanese immigrants were "aliens ineligible to citizenship." In the 1930s, the *Los Angeles Times* led a new anti-Japanese campaign, arguing that Japanese Americans were still a threat because they would multiply endlessly and outcompete "real" Americans. Any recognition that the real role of most Japanese was to provide cheap food—exactly what white workers, managers, and homemakers should have hailed—was swallowed up in the storm of hatred that followed the attack on Pearl Harbor. (See Texts in Historical Context on page 692.)

Even though a military survey concluded that Japanese Americans posed no danger, President

Roosevelt on February 19, 1942, gave that racist premise the force of law in an executive order authorizing the roundup of all Americans of Japanese descent. Allowed little time to secure or sell their property, the victims lost most of their assets, their jobs, and their homes. Most were American citizens and not a single case of subversion or sabotage was ever uncovered. Still, Japanese Americans were sent to "relocation centers"—basically makeshift prison camps—in remote areas of the Southwest and Great Plains—penned in by barbed wire and armed guards for more than three years. Not until 1988 did Congress award modest reparations to Japanese Americans for their wartime losses.

War posed challenges for homosexual Americans in some ways comparable to those faced by other marginalized groups. The view that gays were a threat to good order and were apt to crack under stress had long dominated military thinking. In World War I, that prejudice began to harden into a system of exclusion; soon afterward the military tightened its psychological screening process and specified criminal proceedings against homosexual acts by those who slipped through the net. Stigmatized, gay Americans, like other disadvantaged minorities, found the war to be a special sort of transforming experience. Ironically, the very crisis that renewed prejudice also worked against enforcing it. The need to build a huge fighting force made those in charge less able, or willing, to discriminate closely against potential recruits. And because screening procedures had been set up with only men in mind, lesbians volunteering for the newly formed women's branches of service were rarely excluded.

Like other beleaguered minorities, gays sought to demonstrate their worth under fire. "I was superpatriotic," explained a combat veteran. "And being a homosexual, I had that constant compelling need to prove how virile I was." In the midst of life or death realities, as one gay survivor of the Iwo Jima campaign put it, "who in the hell is going to worry about this shit?"

When peace came, gay veterans tended to cluster in large cities where their sense of mutual interests and loyalty shaped their communities. Toughened by the military ordeal and angry that they had been part of a successful war against oppression while remaining oppressed themselves, veterans led the way in promoting the gay liberation movement. In 1950, a group of gay veterans formed the Mattachine Society to combat discrimination, and

**FBI SEARCHING JAPANESE AMERICAN HOME**
*When President Roosevelt informed military commanders that they might "from time to time" remove persons deemed dangerous, he had reason to suspect that virtually all Japanese Americans would be affected. An army "expert" on Asian culture had already advised the War Department that, "as you cannot . . . penetrate the Oriental thinking . . . the easiest course is to remove them all from the West Coast and place them . . . under guard." Intent on getting to the bottom of one Japanese American family's allegiance, an FBI agent in 1942 scrutinizes a picture album, while family members whose home has been invaded look on helplessly.*
Los Angeles Daily News Morgue, Department of Special Collections, University Research Library, UCLA.

five years later lesbians in San Francisco followed their example by founding the Daughters of Bilitis. These efforts provided the impetus for gay activism to join in the broad front of civil rights insurgency that arose in the 1960s.

## Refugees from the Holocaust

Throughout the 1930s, Spanish Loyalists fleeing Franco, opponents of Mussolini, and, most numerous, the targets of Hitler's maniacal racism clamored for asylum. As Hitler expanded his campaign to "purify" Germany, Jews, gypsies, religious dissenters, homosexuals, avant-garde artists, and others came under increasing pressure to flee or risk extermination. As American resolve against totali-

tarian oppression stiffened, a desperate contest arose between those who would rescue the victims of persecution and those who would bar the gate.

Roosevelt sympathized with the pleas for help, but only if action did not jeopardize his foreign policy or his hold on the electorate. After the German army took over Austria in March 1938, crowds of Jews besieged the American embassy in Vienna, seeking immigration visas. Roosevelt tried to raise the annual quota, which allowed only 1,400 Austrians into the country, but Congress, trying to keep out of war and mindful of polls showing that 82 percent of Americans were against admitting Jewish exiles, refused the request. Roosevelt then sought to persuade countries in Latin America and Africa to accept refugees. None would agree. In a

# Japanese Internment

*A* ngrily determined that the bombing of Pearl Harbor would not be followed by more sneak attacks, military and political leaders on the West Coast targeted persons of Japanese descent—alien and citizen alike—as potential saboteurs. Early in 1942, General John DeWitt, commander of the Western Defense Command, persuaded President Franklin Roosevelt to issue an executive order authorizing the removal of the Japanese living in the United States. Subsequently, some 110,000 Japanese Americans were confined to relocation camps in remote areas, surrounded by barbed wire and armed guards. DeWitt's recommendation expressed concern for military security within racist conceptions long used to curb Asian immigration.

## Document 1. Final Recommendations of the Commanding General, Western Defense Command and Fourth Army, Submitted to the Secretary of War

February 14, 1942

Memorandum for the Secretary of War.

Subject: Evacuation of Japanese and Other Subversive Persons from the Pacific Coast.

1. In presenting a recommendation for the evacuation of Japanese and other subversive persons from the Pacific Coast, the following facts have been considered:

    a. Mission of the Western Defense Command and Fourth Army.

      (1) Defense of the Pacific Coast of the Western Defense Command, as extended, against attacks by sea, land, or air;

      (2) Local protection of establishment and communications vital to the National Defense for which adequate defense cannot be provided by local civilian authorities.

    b. Brief Estimate of the Situation.

      (1) . . . The following are possible and probable enemy activities: . . .

        (a) Naval attack on shipping on coastal waters;

        (b) Naval attack on coastal cities and vital installations;

        (c) Air raids on vital installations, particularly within two hundred miles of the coast;

        (d) Sabotage of vital installations throughout the Western Defense Command.

Hostile Naval and air raids will be assisted by enemy agents signaling from the coastline and the vicinity thereof; and by supplying and otherwise assisting enemy vessels and by sabotage.

In the war in which we are now engaged racial affinities are severed by migration. The Japanese race is an enemy race and while many second and third generation Japanese born on United States soil, possessed of United States citizenship, have become "Americanized," the racial strains are undiluted. To conclude otherwise is to expect that children born of white parents on Japanese soil sever all racial affinity and become loyal Japanese subjects, ready to fight and, if necessary, to die for Japan in a war against the nation of their parents. . . .

It, therefore, follows that along the vital Pacific Coast over 112,000 potential enemies, of Japanese extraction, are at large today. There are indications that these are organized and ready for concerted action at a favorable opportunity. The very fact that no sabotage has taken place to date is a disturbing and confirming indication that such action will be taken. . . .

*I* mprisoned in bleak surroundings far from home, Japanese internees were prey to despair and bitterness. Looking back after forty years, Kazue Yamane recalled her confinement as a disturbing and baffling experience.

## Document 2. An Oral History of Life in the Japanese American Detention Camps

In April 1942, my husband and I and our two children left for camp, and my mother-in-law and father-in-law came about a month later. I wasn't afraid, but I kept asking in my mind, how could they? This is impossible. Even today I still think it was a nightmarish thing. I cannot reconcile myself to the fact that I had to go, that I was interned, that I was segregated, that I was taken away, even though it goes back forty years. . . .

I was separated from my husband; he went to the Santa Fe, New Mexico, camp. All our letters were censored; all our letters were cut in parts and all that. So we were not too sure what messages was getting through and not getting through, but I do know that I informed him many times of his mother's condition. He should have been allowed to come back to see her, because I thought she wouldn't live too long, but they never did allow him to come back, even for her funeral. They did not allow that. I learned that a lot of the messages didn't get to him; they were crossed out. I now have those letters with me.

In 1944 I was left with his parents and our kids. But I had no time to think of what was going to happen because my child was always sick and I had been quite sick. . . .

My son knew what was going on, and he too had many times asked me why . . . you know, why? why? Of course, I had no explanation why this was happening to us. . . .

*Forcibly removed from the tension between his life as a student at the University of California at Berkeley and his unassimilated family, Charles Kikuchi sought in his prison camp diary to make sense of the internment and to judge where it would lead.*

## Document 3. The Kikuchi Diary

*December 7, 1941, Berkeley, California*
Pearl Harbor. We are at war! Jesus Christ, the Japs bombed Hawaii and the entire fleet has been sunk. I just can't believe it. I don't know what in the hell is going to happen to us, but we will all be called into the Army right away.

. . . The next five years will determine the future of the Nisei [Japanese American citizens]. They are now at the crossroads. Will they be able to take it or will they go under? If we are ever going to prove our Americanism, this is the time. The Anti-Jap feeling is bound to rise to hysterical heights, and it is most likely that the Nisei will be included as Japs. I wanted to go to San Francisco tonight, but Pierre says I am crazy. He says it's best we stick on campus. In any event, we can't remain on the fence, and a positive approach must be taken if we are to have a place in fulfilling the Promise of America. I think the U.S. is in danger of going Fascist too, or maybe Socialist. . . .

I don't know what to think or do. Everybody is in a daze.

*April 30, 1942, Berkeley*
Today is the day that we are going to get kicked out of Berkeley. It certainly is degrading. . . .

I'm supposed to see my family at Tanforan as Jack told me to give the same family number. I wonder how it is going to be living with them as I haven't done this for years and years? I should have gone over to San Francisco and evacuated with them, but I had a last final to take. I understand that we are going to live in the horse stalls. I hope that the Army has the courtesy to remove the manure first. . . .

*July 14, 1942*
Marie, Ann, Mitch, Jimmy, Jack, and myself got into a long discussion about how much democracy meant to us as individuals. Mitch says that he would even go in the army and die for it, in spite of the fact that he knew he would be kept down. Marie said that although democracy was not perfect, it was the only system that offered any hope for a future, if we could fulfill its destinies. Jack was a little more skeptical. He even suggested that we [could] be in such grave danger that we would then realize that we were losing something. Where this point was he could not say. I said that this was what happened in France and they lost all. Jimmy suggested that the colored races of the world had reason to feel despair and mistrust the white man because of the past experiences. . . .

In reviewing the four months here, the chief value I got out of this forced evacuation was the strengthening of the family bonds. I never knew my family before this and this was the first chance that I have had to really get acquainted. . . .

**Document 1.** *Final Recommendations,* report by General John Lesesne DeWitt to the United States Secretary of War, February 14, 1942.

**Document 2.** John Tateishi, *And Justice for All.* Copyright © 1984 by John Tateishi. Reprinted by permission of Random House, Inc.

**Document 3.** John Modell, ed., *The Kikuchi Diary: Chronicle from an American Concentration Camp,* 43, 51, 183, 252. Copyright 1973 by the Board of Trustees of the University of Illinois. Used with the permission of University of Illinois Press.

last attempt before war broke out, friends of the refugees introduced legislation in Congress in 1939 that would grant asylum to 20,000 German refugee children, most of them Jewish. Anti-Semitism as well as isolationism were undoubtedly factors in the defeat of the bill, for the following year refugee English children who were not predominantly Jewish gained entry without delay.

In 1942, word leaked out that Hitler was implementing a "final solution": Jews and other "undesirables" were being sent to concentration camps in remote areas; old people, children, and others deemed too weak to work were gassed and cremated while the able-bodied were put to work until lack of food and harsh conditions killed them. Even then skeptical State Department officials stood firmly in the way. In all, up to the start of war, only 152,000 Jews managed to gain entry into the United States. The numbers dropped steadily to a mere 2,400 in 1944. Those trapped in Europe could only wait for rescue by Allied armies while their champions abroad vainly pleaded with the Allies to bomb the Nazi death camps and the railroad tracks leading to them to hamper the killing operation.

When Russian troops arrived at Auschwitz in Poland in February 1945, they found only a handful of emaciated prisoners, some too weak to survive their liberation. Skeletal corpses, some half burned, lay around them; nearby were ponds and pits filled with the ashes of those who had perished. The Russians discovered sheds filled with loot stripped from the dead—clothing, gold fillings, false teeth, even cloth made from human hair. At last, the truth about Nazi atrocities breached the wall of denial. But by then, it was too late; Nazi extermination had reached its final toll of 9 million victims.

## Military Victory: 1943–1945

By early 1943, the defensive phase of the war was over. Having halted the German and Japanese offenses in Europe and in Asia, the Allies faced the daunting task of driving the Axis back, retaking vast conquered areas, and finally defeating Germany and Japan on their home territory. The Allied alliance of the United States, Britain, and the Soviet Union suffered enormous conflict over opening a second front in Europe to relieve the Soviet Union from the brunt of Hitler's attack. By June 1944, when a true second front was launched, the Soviet Union had already broken German power in the east. Simultaneously

in the Pacific, the United States, fighting with Australia and New Zealand, unleashed its final victorious drive toward the Japanese mainland.

## From Normandy to Berlin

In November 1943, as the Italian campaign ground on at its cold, muddy pace, Churchill, Roosevelt, and Stalin held meetings in Teheran, the capital of Iran, and Cairo to plan the final assault on Hitler.

*By June 1944 the Soviet Union had already broken German power in the east. Simultaneously in the Pacific, the United States unleashed its final victorious drive toward the Japanese mainland.*

Stalin finally succeeded in getting Roosevelt and Churchill to commit to a great invasion of Europe in May 1944. The Allies had been gathering an enormous army and navy in Great Britain for nearly two years in anticipation of a return to France. General Dwight D. Eisenhower, with his great tact and organizing skills, became Supreme Commander of the Allied forces—American, British, and Free French—while General Sir Bernard Montgomery, the hero of victory in North Africa, took charge of the landing itself.

German forces, directed by the master tactician General Erwin Rommel, fortified the cliffs and mined the beaches of northwestern France. Yet, as Rommel realized more clearly than Hitler, the huge deployment of German armies in the east trying to contain the massive Soviet offensive in the spring of 1943 left Rommel without adequate troops to stop the 3 million Allied soldiers waiting in England. Even more of a handicap was Rommel's inability to control the air. On the eve of invasion, the Luftwaffe (German air force) had only 300 fighter planes to face 12,000 Allied aircraft poised for massive bombardment.

False radio signals, invented armies, and fake air sorties encouraged the Germans to expect an Allied invasion at the Pas de Calais area, where the English Channel is narrowest. The actual invasion took place miles to the south on the beaches of Normandy (Map 25.3). First came raging air and naval attacks, then the landing of paratroopers behind the German lines, and finally at 7:30 A.M. on June 6, 1944, referred to as "D Day," seaborne soldiers hit

**MAP 25.3**

*The European Theater of World War II, 1942–1945*

*Russian reversal of the German offensive by breaking the sieges of Stalingrad and Leningrad, combined with Allied landings in North Africa and Normandy, placed Germany in a closing vise of armies from all sides.*

the beaches. For a perilous few hours, rough seas and fortified machine guns stopped the assault in a chaos of overturned tanks, drowning men, and frantic attempts by those who made it ashore to find cover. But paratroopers coming up behind the Ger-man line and rangers scaling the cliffs to knock out enemy gun emplacements finally secured the beachhead. As General Omar N. Bradley observed, the Allies prevailed only by "guts, valor, and extreme bravery."

**D DAY LANDING**
*Amid a dense thicket of landing craft, men and equipment lucky enough to have made it through rough seas and enemy fire struggle onto the beach at Normandy on June 6, 1944, to open a second front in Europe. An intrepid photographer caught this brief moment of safe passage just before the troops advanced into withering enemy fire from the high cliffs beyond the beach.*
UPI/Bettmann Archive.

Within a week, Allied forces had broken out of the Normandy pocket and begun their massive sweep toward Germany. On August 25, the Allies liberated Paris from four years of Nazi occupation. Two months later, they made their first foray into Germany to capture the city of Aachen. Hitler then took a mad gamble as the giant pincers of the Allied and Soviet armies closed on German headquarters in Berlin. In December 1944, he ordered a counterattack through Belgium to recapture Antwerp and deny the Allies their major supply port. Massive German forces drove fifty-five miles into Allied lines in what was known as the Battle of the Bulge before being stopped at Bastogne. German losses of 82,000 men and hundreds of tanks proved disastrous. By committing so many of his reserves to the Bulge, Hitler left the remnant of his army, facing the Russians, close to collapse.

In February 1945, with the end in sight, Churchill, Stalin, and a seriously ill Roosevelt met secretly at the Russian Black Sea resort town of Yalta to discuss the structure of the postwar world. Talks centered on three major topics: rearranging the political map of Europe; creating a new international organization; and achieving victory over Japan. Although his stamina and mental alertness flickered, Roosevelt still managed to secure a major share of what he sought. The Soviets agreed to a declaration of self-determination for the countries their armies occupied in Eastern Europe. Chiang Kai-shek would receive Allied support as leader of China in the war against Japan. And the Soviet Union would have a say in the governance of Korea and Manchuria in exchange for entering the war against Japan after the defeat of Germany.

The "Big Three" also agreed on the creation of a new international organization, the United Nations. All countries would have a place in the organization's General Assembly, but the Security Council would ultimately wield decisive power. The

Security Council would be composed of temporary members and of permanent representatives from China, France, Great Britain, the Soviet Union, and the United States, each of which would retain the veto.

American response to the creation of the UN was startlingly different from the nation's refusal to join the League of Nations in 1919. Internationalism triumphed when Republican Senator Arthur Vandenberg of Michigan, who had long been a staunch isolationist, declared that it was his mission to "end the miserable notion that the Republican Party will return to its foxhole when the last shot in this war has been fired and will blindly let the world rot in its own anarchy." The Senate ratified the United Nations charter in July by a vote of eighty-nine to two.

Following the Yalta agreement, the Allies began the final assault on Hitler. While American forces pounded Germany from the west, the Soviets, having swept through Poland, arrived at the outskirts of Berlin in April 1945. Hitler, who had descended into his underground bunker on January 16, signaled the end of Nazism by committing suicide on April 30. On May 7, a provisional German government surrendered unconditionally.

Franklin Roosevelt did not live to witness the end of the Nazi horror. On April 12, while resting in Warm Springs, Georgia, the president suffered a fatal stroke. Americans grieved publicly for the man who had led them through more than twelve years of depression and world war. And they worried aloud about his successor, Vice President Harry S. Truman. Truman's colleagues in Congress generally

**YALTA CONFERENCE**
*In February 1945, President Roosevelt and British Prime Minister Winston Churchill met with Russian leader Joseph Stalin at the Black Sea resort of Yalta to plan the postwar reconstruction of Europe. Roosevelt, near the end of his life, and Churchill, soon to suffer reelection defeat, look weary next to the resolute "Man of Steel." Controversy would later arise over whether a stronger stand by the American and British leaders could have prevented the Soviet Union from imposing Communist rule on Eastern Europe.*
U.S. Army.

believed he would be little more than a caretaker, and Truman seemed to agree. When a reporter called him "Mr. President," he replied uneasily, "I wish you didn't have to call me that." To other reporters he pleaded, "Boys, if newspapermen pray, pray for me now." Truman soon showed himself to be tough-minded and a quick learner, however, with a knowledge of history deeper than that of almost any previous president. It soon became clear that he would not hesitate to make hard decisions.

## The Defeat of Japan

American victories at sea in early 1942 halted the Japanese advance in the Pacific. By mid-1942, the Americans had taken the offensive. Japan had intended to use its navy to shield a vast economic empire in China and Southeast Asia. Instead, it had to fend off revived and aroused Allied forces in the Pacific while also trying to quell renewed resistance on the Asian mainland. In China, the Japanese

**M A P  2 5 . 4**
*The Pacific Theater of World War II, 1941–1945*
*To drive the Japanese from their far-flung empire, the Allies launched two combined naval and military offensives—one to recapture the Philippines and then attack Japanese forces in China, the other to hop from island to island in the Central Pacific toward the Japanese mainland.*

armies had scored many victories but were unable to finish off Chiang Kai-shek. Japanese forces had advanced westward almost to India, but in 1943 British and American forces, along with Indian and Chinese troops, were preparing for a counterthrust through Burma and into China. The most decisive action, however, came in the Pacific, where the Allies moved slowly and painfully, island by island, toward the Japanese homeland (Map 25.4).

In August 1942, the island campaign began when the First Marine Division landed on Guadalcanal where the Japanese were constructing an airfield. For the next six months, a savage battle raged for control of the strategic area. Finally, during the night of February 7, 1943, Japanese forces withdrew after terrible losses on both sides that indicated just how costly the long march to Japan would be.

In mid-1943, American, Australian, and New Zealand forces launched new offensives that penetrated the outer perimeter of Japanese defenses. Bloody campaigns in New Guinea and the Solomon Islands gradually secured the South Pacific. In the Central Pacific, amphibious forces, borne by the greatest fleet in history, took the Gilbert and Marshall Islands, which served eventually as forward positions for launching the decisive air and ground assaults on the Japanese home islands.

As the Allied offensive pressed on, resistance grew fiercer from Japanese soldiers who had been instructed to stand firm to the death. The landing on Tarawa made plain their tenacity. Stymied by a tide that grounded their landing craft far from shore, the invading marines had to wade a half mile, waist-deep, through brutal enemy fire. Survivors of that barrage then faced fortified emplacements manned by well-armed troops who had no intention of retreating. Within three days, the marines had suffered one thousand dead and another two thousand wounded—all to take a barren coral island not three square miles. Only seventeen of the three thousand Japanese defenders were left alive to surrender. Thereafter island to island warfare took on an awful sameness of rooting the enemy out of bunkers and caves with explosives and flamethrowers.

Both land and sea war climaxed in the fall of 1944 with the invasion of the Philippines and the battle for Leyte Gulf. The greatest naval encounter in history cost the Japanese practically their entire fleet. Before the Philippines were retaken, Allied forces captured two vital island strongholds—Iwo Jima, 750 miles from Japan, and Okinawa, only 370 miles from Tokyo. To defend Okinawa and prevent

the American invaders from getting within close bombing range of their home islands, the Japanese called on thousands of suicide pilots, known as "kamikaze" ("divine wind"). Their mission was to crash bomb-laden planes into Allied ships and thus, it was hoped, make the landing forces turn back. The kamikaze made life harrowing for the American fleet but did not deter it. Rather, the suicide gesture destroyed the last vestige of the Japanese air force. By June 1945, the Japanese were virtually defenseless on sea and in the air.

## Atomic Warfare

Just as the island campaigns drew to an end, American scientists were completing work on a secret weapon. The race to develop an atomic bomb had begun in 1942 after refugee scientists warned that the Nazis were working to convert nuclear energy into a superbomb. The Roosevelt administration authorized the top-secret Manhattan Project to develop the bomb before the Germans did. In thirty-seven locations across the country, coordinated by leading theorists at Los Alamos, New Mexico, 100,000 persons worked at top speed to win the race.

Germany surrendered before it produced a bomb and before the United States was ready to test its own. But just before dawn on July 16, 1945, a test explosion lit up the sky in an isolated corner of the Alamogordo Air Base near Los Alamos. None of the project scientists had guessed that the force of the bomb would be equivalent to 20,000 tons of TNT. Nor was anyone prepared for a flash of multicolored light more brilliant than ever seen before or the vast fireball and mushroom-shaped cloud of dust and debris that rose eight miles into the upper atmosphere.

A small circle of scientists and officials, troubled by the power they had unleashed, proposed a public demonstration of the bomb's doomsday force to persuade Japan to surrender. With Japanese forces incapable of offensive action and Japan totally blockaded, test proponents argued that the United States could afford to wait until the point of the demonstration sank in. The Japanese government had already sent emissaries to see if a negotiated peace could be reached. The sticking point was that the Japanese wanted to retain their emperor, while the American government remained committed to unconditional surrender.

In the end, all reluctance to unleash the atomic monster on populated targets yielded to other

**HIROSHIMA BOMBING**
*This rare shot taken by a news photographer in Hiroshima immediately after the atomic bomb
exploded on August 6, 1945, suggests the shock and incomprehension that survivors would
describe as their first reaction. Three days later another atomic bomb devastated Nagasaki.*
U.N. photo.

urgent considerations. When President Truman
heard about the bomb test, he was involved in hard
bargaining with the Soviets in Potsdam, Germany,
about how to reorganize the postwar world. Clearly,
the bomb made it unnecessary to call on the Russian promise to hasten victory by declaring war on
Japan. Rather, a surprise use of the new super-
weapon might end the conflict before the Soviet
Union could attack the Japanese in Korea and
Manchuria. Perhaps, also, the bomb's devastation
would convince the Soviets that they could not
safely challenge American leadership after the war
ended.

A more basic motive was to save American lives.
As Truman pondered his options, Americans were
preparing for Operation Downfall—the invasion of

the Japanese home islands in the fall. Experience
with Japanese soldiers who fought to the death filled
American military and civilian leaders with dread.
Intelligence reports indicated that more than 2 million Japanese army troops were available for a last-
ditch defense of their homeland. Behind them were
28 million men, women, and boys of the civilian militia, armed with sharpened bamboo stakes, farm implements, and any other weapons they could muster.

Truman, who had been a commander of combat
troops on the ground in World War I, was keenly
sympathetic to the ordeal facing an invading army.
He saw no reason not to use a weapon of war, even
a terribly destructive one, if it would save American
lives. But first he issued an ultimatum that Japan
must surrender unconditionally or face utter ruin.

When the Japanese failed to respond by the deadline, Truman turned to his advisory committee's recommendation that, to shock the Japanese into surrender, the bomb be dropped without warning on cities that had not already been heavily damaged. On August 6, a single B-29, the *Enola Gay,* droned over Hiroshima and released one of the three operational atomic bombs the Americans possessed. As the plane banked sharply away, crew members could see behind them the mushroom cloud that signified the obliteration of the city and the death of 78,000 inhabitants. Three days later a second atomic bomb devastated Nagasaki with more than 100,000 deaths.

In the midst of ruin, a peace faction took control of the Japanese government from diehard military leaders, and with assurance that the emperor could retain his throne under Allied control, Japan surrendered on August 14. Whether allowing the Japanese to retain their emperor before using atomic bombs would have been enough to induce surrender can never be known. Emperor Hirohito's power to shift the Japanese spirit from war to peace became clear, however, when he informed his people in a radio broadcast—the first words that the public had ever heard the emperor utter—of his divine will that they cease fighting. Loyally, his subjects laid down their arms and stood quietly by as the giant battleship *Missouri* sailed into Tokyo harbor for the formal signing of surrender on September 2, 1945.

## Conclusion: Victory and Uncertainty

For Americans, the attack on Pearl Harbor was just the first shock of a war whose scope and violence was unprecedented. Never before had armies been flung across such vast stretches of the globe. And on the seas there were more battles, with more ships lost, than in all other modern wars combined. According to one estimate, the death toll reached 35 million, evenly divided between military and civilian losses. Some countries suffered much more than others. Approximately 400,000 Americans lost their lives in military service; the Soviet Union lost more in the battle of Stalingrad alone and eventually suffered nearly 20 million civilian and military deaths.

Out of war's carnage arose misgivings about human nature and the sort of world that would emerge from the ashes. The Holocaust exhibited cruelty beyond what many had imagined possible; and the devastating use of the atomic bomb added similar alarm over the destructive powers of science and technology. Charles Lindbergh, who had been vilified for questioning America's intervention, found much to reinforce his forebodings during his service in both theaters of war. Just days after Germany's surrender, an assignment to study German jet planes caused Lindbergh to pass through a liberated death camp at Nordhausen. Gaunt survivors and the furnaces designed to cremate them forced memories of the savage Pacific campaign back on Lindbergh: Japanese prisoners machine-gunned on an airstrip; others pushed out of transport planes supposed to take them to safe captivity; shin bones cut for letter openers. Committing atrocities, he realized at that moment, "is not a thing confined to any nation or to any people. . . . It is not the Germans alone, or the Japs, but the men of all nations to whom this war has brought shame and degradation."

Nevertheless, most Americans emerged from the conflict convinced that they had won the "good war." The Roosevelt administration had taken the lead in creating the United Nations during the war and had made it plain that America, as the most powerful nation on earth, would devote its resources to rebuilding worldwide political and economic stability. Although some economists expressed anxiety that the nation might return to depression after its giant war machine was dismantled, indications were strong that war had brought firm recovery. Unemployment was negligible and the gross national product had soared to four times what it had been when Roosevelt was elected president in 1932, while average family income had risen by half. The challenge to postwar success at home lay mainly in stabilizing the changes that had occurred during the war and reintegrating the millions of men and women who were returning from the fighting.

The postwar challenges abroad were grimmer. The United States and Western Europe soon found themselves at odds with the Communist Soviet Union and China. Efforts by Britain and France to maintain their colonial empires also violated democratic principles and met mounting resistance from national forces seeking liberation. Under these circumstances, the confidence bred of winning the "good war" began to give way to the anxious uncertainties of the "cold war."

## CHRONOLOGY

**1933** Adolf Hitler becomes chancellor of Germany.

United States recognizes Soviet Union.

**1935–1937** Congress seeks to shield America from world conflicts with neutrality acts.

**1936** Nazi Germany occupies Rhineland.

Mussolini's fascist Italian regime conquers Ethiopia.

Civil war breaks out in Spain.

**1937** Japanese troops capture Nanking.

Roosevelt delivers speech urging "quarantine" against aggressor nations.

**1938** Hitler annexes Austria.

British Prime Minister Chamberlain meets with Hitler in Munich and agrees to German seizure of Sudetenland in Czechoslovakia.

**1939** German troops occupy remainder of Czechoslovakia without resistance.

Nazi Germany and Soviet Union sign nonaggression pact.

**September 1.** Germany's attack on Poland begins World War II.

United States and Great Britain conclude cash-and-carry agreement.

**1940** **May–June.** British troops evacuated at Dunkirk.

**June.** German occupation of France begins.

Isolationists, including Charles Lindbergh, create America First Committee.

Roosevelt wins reelection against Wendell Willkie.

**1941** Lend-Lease Act enables Britain to obtain war materiel from United States on credit.

**June.** Germany invades Soviet Union.

**August.** Atlantic Charter devised by Roosevelt and Allies to guarantee human and international freedoms after war.

**December 7.** Japanese launch surprise attack on Pearl Harbor. United States declares war on Japan.

**1942** Japan captures Philippines.

Civil rights activists found Congress of Racial Equality (CORE).

U.S. navy scores its first major victories in Battle of Coral Sea and at Midway.

Roosevelt authorizes top-secret Manhattan Project.

**November.** U.S. forces invade North Africa.

Roosevelt authorizes internment of Japanese Americans.

**1943** Allied leaders agree that war will end only with unconditional surrender of Axis forces.

"Zoot suit" riots explode in Los Angeles.

U.S. forces invade Sicily.

**1944** **June 6.** Combined Allied army stages successful D Day landing at Normandy.

Roosevelt wins reelection against Thomas E. Dewey.

**1945** The Allies meet to plan reconstruction of Europe after defeat of Germany.

**April 12.** Franklin Roosevelt dies and Harry Truman becomes president.

Delegates from fifty nations, meeting in San Francisco, approve charter of United Nations.

**May 7.** Germany surrenders.

**August 6.** United States drops atomic bomb on Hiroshima.

**August 8.** United States drops atomic bomb on Nagasaki.

**August 14.** Japan surrenders, ending World War II.

# SUGGESTED READINGS

Michael Adams, *The Best War Ever* (1994). A succinct account of war aims and the sometimes contradictory ways in which the war was fought. Adams stresses psychological and moral strains imposed by the fierceness of combat.

Gar Alperovitz, *The Decision to Use the Atomic Bomb and the Architecture of an American Myth* (1995). A brief version of the author's case that the use of the atomic bomb on Japan was both unnecessary and an effort to intimidate the Soviet Union. This contention sparked an as yet unconcluded controversy over the moral and strategic meaning of atomic warfare.

Stephen Ambrose, *D-Day, June 6, 1944* (1994). A highly dramatic account of the landing on Normandy that sealed the fate of Nazi Germany. Ambrose honors the 50th anniversary of D Day with a full description of the feelings as well as the actions of those who made the invasion a success.

Allan Berube, *Coming Out under Fire: The History of Gay Men and Women in World War Two* (1990). A pioneering account of gays in the military. Berube concludes that gays and straights performed much the same in combat and that the experience stimulated the postwar gay-rights movement.

John Morton Blum, *V Was for Victory: Politics and American Culture during World War II* (1977). An examination of how the country organized for war and sought to justify it. Blum offers broad insight into government policies and the transformation of life on the home front.

Wayne Cole, *Roosevelt and the Isolationists, 1932–1945* (1983). The definitive account of the champions of neutrality and of intervention. Cole looks at the entire range of isolationists—from pacifists to appeasers of fascism—and gives a vivid sense of the difficulty of finding a sound moral choice between war and peace.

Robert Dallek, *Franklin D. Roosevelt and American Foreign Policy, 1932–1945* (1979). A thorough account of America's place in the world during the New Deal era. Dallek offers a generally approving analysis of Roosevelt's strategy, while acknowledging its drawbacks.

Paul Fussell, *Wartime* (1989). Remembrances by a combat veteran of horrors that belie the description of World War II as "the good war." Fussell is unsparing in his criticism of leadership and policies that made life unnecessarily bad for those doing the fighting.

Susan Hartmann, *The Home Front and Beyond: American Women in the 1940s* (1982). A highly informative description of the transformation in women's lives that occurred during the war and afterward. Hartmann explains why women could not return to prewar life, even though they were urged after the war to retire to the home.

Akira Iriye, *Power and Culture: The Japanese-American War, 1941–1945* (1982). By adding an analysis of Japanese motivations and strategies, Iriye rounds out a full account of the war. His treatment also sheds light on relations between the two countries before and after the war.

Joyce Milton, *Loss of Eden: A Biography of Charles and Anne Morrow Lindbergh* (1994). A joint biography focusing on the difficult fit between the Lindbergh's famous achievements and the unwanted attention of society. Milton explains how Charles Lindbergh's concern about bad social tendencies influenced his reluctance to embrace war.

William O'Neill, *A Democracy at War: America's Fight at Home and Abroad in World War II* (1993). A highly readable account linking the war and home fronts. O'Neill sees the efforts by women and minorities to improve their lot as a test of war aims and strategies.

Ronald Schaffer, *Wings of Judgment: American Bombing in World War II* (1988). A discussion of the concepts and effects of bombing during history's first great use of air power. Schaffer helps distinguish between the effectiveness of bombing against tactical targets and the strategic bombing attempt to destroy civilian morale.

William Tuttle, *Daddy's Gone to War: The Second World War in the Lives of America's Children* (1993). A child's-eye view of the war. Tuttle shows the confusion and dislocations affecting children as indicative of the overall stresses of war.

Gerhard Weinberg, *World at Arms: A Global History of World War II* (1994). A comprehensive history of the war in all sectors and phases. Weinberg provides meticulously detailed explanations of how the war unfolded and what its consequences were.

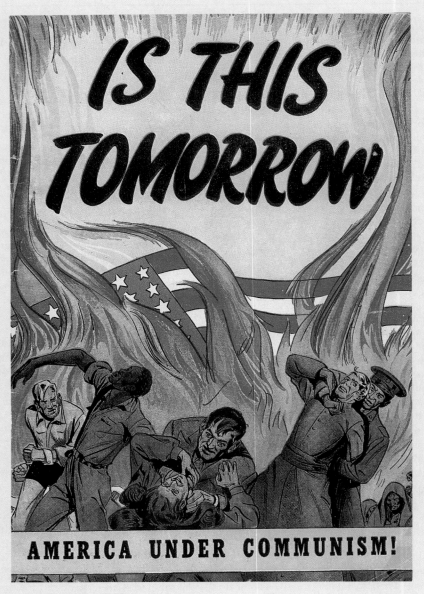

**COLD WAR COMIC BOOK**

*Americans barely had time to celebrate the Allied victory in World War II when they perceived another threat, that posed by the Soviet Union. Fear of communism dominated much of postwar American life and politics, even invading the realm of popular culture. Four million copies of this comic book, published by a religious organization in 1947, painted a terrifying picture of what would happen to Americans if the Soviets took over the country. Such takeover stories appeared in movies, cartoons, and magazines as well as in other comic books.*
Collection of Charles Christensen.

# COLD WAR POLITICS IN THE TRUMAN YEARS

## 26

### 1945–1953

O N NOVEMBER 5, 1946, President Harry S. Truman, his wife, and his daughter boarded the train back to Washington from Truman's hometown, Independence, Missouri, where they had gone to vote. In the congressional elections, Republicans had blasted Truman as incapable of dealing with economic problems and with the threat of communism. The president's approval rating with the public had sunk to a mere 32 percent. Many Democratic candidates avoided mentioning his name, hoping to stir voters with recordings of the late Franklin Roosevelt's voice. Playing poker with reporters on the train as the returns came in, Truman appeared unconcerned. But the results were devastating: The Republicans had captured both the House and the Senate by substantial majorities.

When Truman stepped off the train in Washington at the lowest point of his presidency, only one member of his administration showed up to greet him, Undersecretary of State Dean Acheson. Acheson's gesture signaled a developing relationship of central importance to the two men as well as to postwar history. The fifty-three-year-old Acheson shared most of Truman's political principles, but their backgrounds could not have differed more. Acheson had enjoyed a typical upper-class education at prep school, Yale University, where classmates voted him "wittiest" and the "spiciest" dresser, and Harvard Law School. After clerking at the Supreme Court, Acheson earned a comfortable living as a corporate lawyer. In contrast, Truman, the son of a Missouri farmer, had not attended college and had failed in a business venture before entering local politics in the 1920s.

Despite his wealth and privilege, Acheson supported most of the New Deal and staunchly defended organized labor. He spoke out against isolationism in the late 1930s, and in 1941 he accepted President Roosevelt's offer of a job at the State Department. Shortly after Truman became president, Acheson wrote his son about shortcomings in Truman's "judgment and wisdom that the limitations of his experience produce," but he also found the fledgling president a man who "will learn fast and will inspire confidence." In June 1947, Acheson left the State Department, but Truman lured him back to be secretary of state during the president's second term. Acheson appreciated Truman's willingness to make tough decisions and respected the man whose "ego never came between him and his job." Truman cherished Acheson's abiding loyalty. Relying on him as secretary of state until they both left office in January 1953, Truman called Acheson "my good right hand."

Truman needed all the help he could get. The "accidental" president lacked the charisma, experience, and political skills with which Roosevelt had transformed both foreign and domestic policy, won four presidential elections, and forged a Democratic Party coalition that dominated national politics. Initially criticized and abandoned by many Roosevelt loyalists, Truman faced a resurgent Republican Party as well as revolts from within his own party. Besides domestic problems left over from the New Deal—how to sustain economic growth and avoid another depression without the war to fuel the economy—Truman faced the necessity of redefining the nation's central foreign policy goals in a new international context.

**DEAN ACHESON**
*No individual had more to do with transforming America's role in the world after World War II than Dean Acheson, President Truman's closest foreign policy adviser. Acheson, seen here in 1945, criticized those who saw the cold war in black and white terms and communism as an evil that the United States could expel from the earth. Rather, he advocated that American leaders learn "to limit objectives, to get ourselves away from the search for the absolute, to find out what is within our powers."*
Library of Congress.

Dean Acheson was instrumental in forging that foreign policy. As early as 1946, Acheson became convinced that the Soviet Union posed the major threat to U.S. security. With other officials, he helped to shape a policy designed to contain and thwart Soviet power and influence wherever they threatened to spread. By 1947, a new term had been coined to describe the intense hostility and rivalry between the superpowers—the "cold war." The containment policy worked in Western Europe, but at home it produced a wave of anti-Communist hysteria that cost many Americans their jobs, and many more grew reluctant to express unpopular ideas or to criticize U.S. policies and institutions.

Although Acheson kept his job, as the preeminent foreign policy official and defender of a former colleague accused of being a Soviet spy, he too reaped abuse from Republicans for being "soft on communism." At the height of the anti-Communist hysteria, Acheson received so much hate mail that guards were posted at his house. Yet he kept a sense of humor. When cab drivers asked him, "Aren't you Dean Acheson?" he would reply, "Yes. Do I have to get out?"

## From the Grand Alliance to Containment

With victory over Japan in August 1945, Americans looked forward to the return of their loved ones, an absence of international crises, and the dismantling of the large military establishment. Officials and civilians alike expected the Allies, led by the United States and working within the United Nations, to cooperate in the management of international peace. Postwar realities quickly dashed these expectations. The wartime alliance forged by the United States, Great Britain, and the Soviet Union crumbled, and the United States began to develop the military and diplomatic means to contain the spread of Soviet power around the globe.

### Moving from Wartime Coalition to Cold War

"The guys who came out of World War II were idealistic," reported Harold Russell, a young paratrooper who lost his hands in a training accident. "We felt the day had come when the wars were all over." Public opinion polls revealed that most Americans shared the veterans' confidence in the promise of peace. But political leaders were less optimistic. Winston Churchill had always distrusted the Soviets; in a moment of frustration during the war, he had said that the only thing worse than fighting with allies was fighting without them. Once the Allies had overcome a common enemy, the prewar mistrust and antagonism between the Soviet Union and the West resurfaced over their very different plans for the postwar world.

*The wartime alliance forged by the United States, Great Britain, and the Soviet Union crumbled, and the United States began to develop the military and diplomatic means to contain the spread of Soviet power around the globe.*

Soviet suspicions of the United States grew during the war when the Allies resisted Soviet leader Joseph Stalin's repeated pleas to open a second front in Western Europe. The Soviet Union had made supreme wartime sacrifices, losing more than twenty million citizens and vast portions of its agricultural and industrial capacity. Now Stalin wanted to make Germany pay for the rebuilding of the Soviet economy, to eliminate future threats, and to expand Soviet influence in the world. Above all, Stalin wanted governments friendly to the Soviet Union on its borders in Eastern Europe, especially in Poland, through which Germany had attacked the Soviet Union twice within twenty-five years.

In contrast, enemy fire had never touched the land of the United States, and its 405,000 dead amounted to just 2 percent of the Soviet loss. With vastly expanded productive capacity, a monopoly on atomic weapons, and supreme confidence in American institutions, the United States emerged from the war as the most powerful nation on the planet in the unprecedented role of world leadership.

Worried about a return of the depression, U.S. officials believed that a healthy economy depended on conditions in the rest of the world. The United States needed access to raw materials, markets for its goods, and security for American investments abroad. These needs could be better met in countries with economic and political systems resem-

bling its own, not in countries whose governments might institute economic controls and interfere with the free flow of products and dollars. As Truman put it in 1947, "The American system can survive in America only if it becomes a world system." At the same time, Americans viewed their foreign policy not as a self-interested campaign to meet economic needs, but as an idealistic crusade to bring freedom, democracy, and capitalism to the rest of the world.

The man with ultimate responsibility for U.S. policy came to the White House with little international experience and strong anti-Communist sentiments. Truman hoped to maintain Soviet-American cooperation, but confident that America's nuclear monopoly gave him the upper hand, he demanded that the Soviet Union comply with U.S. plans for the postwar world and restrain its expansionist impulses.

Soviet and American interests clashed first in Eastern Europe. Stalin insisted that the Allies' wartime agreements gave him a free hand in the countries defeated or liberated by the Red Army, just as the United States was unilaterally reconstructing governments in Italy and Japan. In Poland and Bulgaria, countries bordering the Soviet Union, Stalin used harsh methods to install Communist governments. Elsewhere, the Soviets initially tolerated non-Communist governments in Hungary and Czechoslovakia. And under pressure from the West, in the spring of 1946 Stalin removed troops from Iran, the Soviet Union's neighbor to the southwest, opening the door for the United States to gain important oil concessions there.

To Stalin, U.S. policy seemed hypocritical in demanding democratic elections in Eastern Europe while supporting dictatorships friendly to U.S. interests in Cuba, Nicaragua, and other Latin American countries. The United States clung to its own sphere of influence while adamantly denying one to the Soviets. But the tough words of the Western allies were no match for the Soviet armies occupying Eastern Europe: The United States and Britain issued sharp protests but would not use military force against the puppet governments installed by Stalin.

In 1946, the wartime Allies contended over the future of Germany. American policymakers wanted to strip Germany of its military capacity, but they also knew that a rapid industrial revival in Germany would foster European economic recovery and thus America's own long-term prosperity. By

M A P  2 6 . 1
*The Division of Europe after World War II*
*The "iron curtain," a term coined by Winston Churchill to refer to the Soviet grip on Eastern
and central Europe, divided Europe for nearly fifty years. Communist governments controlled
every country along the Soviet Union's western border, except Finland, which remained neutral.*

contrast, the Soviet Union resolved to keep Germany militarily and economically weak and to exact heavy reparations that it could use to rebuild the Soviet economy. Unable to settle their differences, the Allies divided Germany. The Soviet Union installed a puppet Communist government in the eastern section, and in December 1946 Britain, France, and the United States unified their occupation zones and began the process that led to creation of the Federal Republic of Germany—West Germany—in 1949 (Map 26.1).

Soviet and Western leaders faced off with hostile words in 1946. In February, Stalin called his former allies a more serious threat than Nazi Germany. One month later, Truman traveled with Winston Churchill to Westminster College in Fulton, Missouri, where the former prime minister denounced Soviet suppression of the popular will in Eastern and central Europe. "From Stettin in the Baltic to Trieste in the Adriatic, an iron curtain has descended across the continent," Churchill said. Although Truman did not officially endorse Churchill's "iron curtain speech," his presence implied agreement with the call for the development of joint British-American strength to combat Soviet aggression.

In February 1946, career diplomat George F. Kennan wrote a memo that furnished a comprehensive rationale for hard-line foreign policy. Kennan, who had served in U.S. embassies in Eastern

Europe and Moscow, was convinced that optimistic assumptions about Soviet-American cooperation were "pipe dreams." He downplayed the influence of Communist ideology in Soviet policy but noted the Soviets' insecurity and their need to maintain authority at home. These circumstances, Kennan argued, made it impossible to negotiate with the Soviets, a conclusion shared by Secretary of State James F. Byrnes, Undersecretary Dean Acheson, and other key Truman advisers.

Kennan predicted that the Soviet Union would try to expand its influence worldwide but would retreat "in the face of superior force." Therefore, the United States should respond with "unalterable counterforce," making Russia "face frustration indefinitely," an approach that came to be called "containment," and which would eventually, Kennan predicted, end in "either the breakup or the gradual mellowing of Soviet power." His analysis marked a turning point in the development of the cold war, providing the argument and the framework for using U.S. power to check the spread of Soviet influence.

Administration officials promoting a more conciliatory policy found themselves out of work. Secretary of Commerce Henry A. Wallace, Truman's predecessor as vice president, urged greater understanding of Soviets' concerns about their nation's security. In a major speech in September 1946, Wallace maintained that "'getting tough' never brought anything real and lasting—whether for schoolyard bullies or businessmen or world powers." He insisted "that we have no more business in the political affairs of Eastern Europe than Russia has in the political affairs of Latin America." State Department officials were furious. When Wallace refused to be muzzled on foreign policy topics, Truman fired him days later.

## The Truman Doctrine and the Marshall Plan

In 1947, the United States moved from tough words to action, implementing the doctrine of containment that would guide foreign policy for the next four decades. It was not an easy transition; despite public approval of a verbal hard line, Americans wanted to keep their soldiers and tax dollars at home. In addition to selling containment to the public, Truman had to persuade a Republican-controlled Congress, which contained a strong isolationist element led by Ohio Senator Robert Taft.

Crises in two Mediterranean countries triggered the implementation of containment. In February 1947, Britain informed the United States that its crippled economy could no longer sustain military assistance to Greece and Turkey. Turkey was trying to resist Soviet pressures, and the monarchist government in Greece faced a challenge from internal leftists. Truman promptly decided to ask Congress for authority to send military and economic missions along with $400 million in aid to the two countries. At a private meeting that Truman called with congressional leaders, Michigan Senator Arthur Vandenberg, the Republican foreign policy leader and a recent convert from isolationism, warned that to get approval, Truman would have to "scare hell out of the country."

*The assumption that American security depended on rescuing any anti-Communist government from internal rebels or outside pressure became the cornerstone of U.S. foreign policy from 1947 until the end of the 1980s.*

Truman did just that. To Congress, he presented what would later be called the "domino theory," warning that if Greece fell to the rebels, "confusion and disorder might well spread throughout the entire Middle East . . . and would have a profound effect upon . . . Europe." Failure to step in "may endanger the peace of the world—and shall surely endanger the welfare of the nation." According to what came to be called the Truman Doctrine, it was not just Soviet military power that must be resisted. The United States must "support free peoples who are resisting attempted subjugation by armed minorities or by outside pressures." Congressional authorization of aid for Greece and Turkey did not entail formal acceptance of the Truman Doctrine. Yet the assumption that American security depended on rescuing any anti-Communist government from internal rebels or outside pressure became the cornerstone of U.S. foreign policy from 1947 until the end of the 1980s.

Aid to Greece and Turkey was a prelude to a much larger program for Europe. In May 1947, Dean Acheson described a war-ravaged Western Europe, with "factories destroyed, fields impoverished, transportation systems wrecked, populations scattered and on the borderline of starvation." American

**THE BERLIN AIRLIFT**
*These German children standing on the rubble of war wave to planes carrying food and other ne-*
*cessities to Berlin during the Soviet blockade in 1948. Truman and his advisers were "prepared to*
*use any means that may be necessary to stay in Berlin." To reduce the risk of war, the president*
*decided on an airlift rather than attempting to send ground convoys through Soviet lines.*
Corbis-Bettmann.

citizens were sending generous amounts of private aid, but Europe needed large-scale assistance. It was "a matter of national self-interest," Acheson argued, for the United States to provide aid. Only economic recovery could halt the growth of socialist and Communist parties in France and Italy and confine Soviet influence to Eastern Europe.

In March 1948, Congress approved the European Recovery Program—also called the Marshall Plan, after retired General George C. Marshall, then serving as secretary of state—and over the next five years the United States allocated $13 billion to restore the economies of Western Europe. A program of economic rather than military aid, the Marshall Plan helped the nations of Western Europe rebuild their war-ravaged economies and move toward a united European economy. It was also good business for the United States, because the European nations spent most of the dollars to buy American products carried on American ships. The economic

recovery of Europe expanded the realm of raw materials, markets, and investment opportunities available to American capitalists. And the Truman administration could point to another victory for containment, since every Western European government remained non-Communist.

While Congress debated the Marshall Plan, in February 1948 the Soviets staged a brutal coup against the elected government of Czechoslovakia and installed a Communist regime. Next Soviet leaders threatened Western access to Berlin. The former capital of Germany lay within Soviet-controlled East Germany, but all four Allies jointly occupied Berlin, dividing it into separate administrative units (see Map 26.1). As the Western Allies moved to organize West Germany as a separate nation, the Soviets retaliated by blocking roads and rail lines from West Germany to the Western-held sections of Berlin, cutting off food, fuel, and other essentials to two million inhabitants.

"We stay in Berlin, period," Truman insisted. Yet he wanted to avoid an armed confrontation with Soviet troops. So for fifteen months, U.S. and British pilots, landing a plane every eight minutes, airlifted 2.3 million tons of goods to sustain the West Berliners. Stalin hesitated to shoot down these cargo planes, and in 1949 he lifted the blockade. The city was formally divided into East Berlin, under Soviet control, and West Berlin, which became part of West Germany. For many Americans, the Berlin airlift confirmed the wisdom of containment: When challenged, the Russians backed down, as Kennan had predicted.

## Creating a National Security State

The new policy of containment quickly acquired a military capacity to back it up. During the Truman years, the United States fashioned a five-pronged defense strategy: (1) development of atomic weapons, (2) strengthening of traditional military power, (3) military alliances with other nations, (4) military and economic aid to friendly nations, and (5) an espionage network and secret means to subvert Communist expansion.

In September 1949, the United States lost its nuclear monopoly when officials confirmed that the Soviets had detonated an atomic bomb. Within months Truman approved development of an even deadlier weapon, a hydrogen bomb based on a thermonuclear explosion equivalent to five hundred atomic bombs. The "super bomb" passed its first test explosion in March 1954, but America's thermonuclear advantage was brief. In November 1955, the Soviet Union exploded its own hydrogen bomb.

From the 1950s through the 1980s, "deterrence" formed the basis of American nuclear strategy. To deter the Soviet Union from attacking, the United States had to maintain a more powerful nuclear force than the Soviets. Because the Russians pursued a similar policy, the superpowers became locked in an ever-escalating race for nuclear dominance. Albert Einstein, whose mathematical discoveries had laid the foundations for nuclear weapons, commented grimly on the enormous destructive force now possessed by the superpowers. The war that came after World War III, he said, would be fought with stones.

The United States also beefed up its conventional military power to deter Soviet threats that might not warrant nuclear retaliation, such as the Berlin blockade. To streamline defense planning, Congress passed the National Security Act in 1947, uniting the military branches under a single secretary of defense and creating the National Security Council (NSC) to advise the president. As the Berlin crisis simmered in 1948, Congress stepped up appropriations for the air force and enacted a peacetime draft. Urged on by military leaders, Congress also granted permanent status to the women's military branches, thereby allowing women to volunteer. With about 1.5 million men and women in uniform in 1950, the military strength of the United States had quadrupled since the 1930s.

Collective security, the third arm of postwar military strategy and the sharpest break from America's past, also developed during the Berlin showdown. In June 1948, the Senate approved the general principle of regional military alliances. One year later, the United States joined Canada and Western European nations in its first peacetime military alliance, the North Atlantic Treaty Organization (NATO), designed to counter the Soviet threat to Western Europe. For the first time in its history the United States pledged to go to war should one of its allies be attacked.

The fourth element of defense strategy involved foreign aid programs to strengthen friendly countries, such as the aid to Greece and Turkey in 1947. A much larger program was the $13 billion Marshall Plan that helped rebuild Western European economies. In addition, in 1949, Congress approved $1 billion of military aid to its NATO allies and began economic assistance to nations in other parts of the world.

> *To deter the Soviet Union from attacking, the United States had to maintain a more powerful nuclear force than the Soviets. Because the Russians pursued a similar policy, the superpowers became locked in an ever-escalating race for nuclear dominance.*

Finally, the United States began to develop its espionage capacities and the means to deter communism through secret activities. The National Security Act of 1947 created the Central Intelligence Agency (CIA) to gather information considered necessary to the national defense and to perform any "functions and duties related to intelligence affecting the national security" that the NSC might authorize. Eventually, CIA agents conducted secret operations that toppled legitimate foreign governments and violated the rights of U.S. citizens. In many respects, the CIA was virtually unaccountable to Congress or the public.

By 1950, the United States had abandoned age-old tenets of foreign policy. Isolationism and neutrality were replaced with a regional military alliance and economic and military efforts to control events far beyond its borders. Short of war, the United States could not stop the descent of the iron curtain, but it aggressively and successfully promoted economic recovery and a military shield for the rest of Europe.

## Superpower Rivalry around the Globe

Europe was not the only place where the Truman administration sought to implement containment. In Africa, Asia, and the Middle East, World War II furthered a tide of national liberation movements against war-weakened imperial powers. Between 1945 and 1960, forty countries containing more than one-quarter of the world's people won their independence. These nations came to be referred to collectively, along with Latin America, as the "third world," a term denoting countries outside the Western and Soviet orbits that had not developed industrial economies. Promoting the ideal of self-determination, the United States granted independence to its own dominion, the Philippines, in 1946; applauded the British withdrawal from India; and encouraged France to relinquish its empire in Indochina. At the same time, both the United States and the Soviet Union cultivated governments in these new nations that were friendly to their own interests and institutions.

Leaders of many liberation movements, impressed with the Russian Revolution and the rapid economic growth it had spawned, adopted socialist or Communist ideas, although they had few or no ties with the Soviet Union. But American leaders insisted on viewing these movements as a threatening extension of Soviet power. Seeking to hold communism at bay by fostering economic development and political stability, in 1949 the Truman administration initiated the Point IV program, providing modest amounts of technical aid to the third world. Most of the administration's efforts focused on Asia and the Middle East, the third world hot spots of the Truman years.

In Asia, civil war raged in China, where the Communists, led by Mao Zedong (Mao Tse-tung),

**CHIANG KAI-SHEK AND MAO ZEDONG**
*The leaders of the opposing sides in the Chinese civil war—the Communist Mao Zedong (on the right) and the Nationalist Chiang Kai-shek—met in Chungking in 1945 to discuss forming a coalition government after driving out the Japanese. These negotiations failed. After four years of conflict, in 1949 the Communists established the People's Republic of China under Mao, while Chiang and his supporters fled to the island of Taiwan.*
Jack Wilkes, *Life* Magazine © Time Inc.

fought the official Nationalist government under Chiang Kai-shek. The Communists gained support among the peasants for their valiant stand against the Japanese and their land reforms. In contrast, Chiang's corrupt government and poor management of the war against Japan alienated much of the population. The so-called China bloc, a lobby that included Republican members of Congress and religious groups and individuals with missionary ties to China, pressured the Truman administration not to "lose" China to the Communists. Truman and his advisers, however, believed that to divert resources from Europe to China would be not only unwise, but also futile, given the ineptness of Chiang's government. After an effort at negotiations between Chiang and Mao in 1946 failed, the United States limited its role to modest aid to the Nationalists.

In December 1949, Mao established the People's Republic of China (PRC), and the Nationalists fled to the island of Taiwan. Some administration officials urged accommodation with Communist China, but the outbreak of war in Korea in June 1950 foreclosed that option. The United States refused to recognize the existence of the PRC, blocked its admission to the United Nations, and continued to aid Chiang's government in Taiwan. Nothing less than a massive U.S. military commitment could have stopped the Chinese Communists, but some Americans blamed Truman and his advisers. Republicans cried that Truman and "the pro-Communists in the State Department" had "lost" China. Thus China became a political albatross for the Democrats, who resolved never again to be in a position where they could be accused of being soft on communism.

As it became clear that China would not be a stable capitalist ally in Asia, the administration reconsidered its plans for postwar Japan. Initially, the U.S. military occupation had aimed to prevent Japan from threatening peace again by reforming its government, purging Japanese militarists from official positions, and decentralizing its economy. But by 1948, U.S. policy had shifted to concentrate on economic recovery. The new goals were to rapidly reindustrialize and to secure Japanese access to markets and natural resources in Asia. After a sluggish start, the Japanese economy flourished. American soldiers remained on military bases in Japan, but the official occupation ended when the two nations signed a peace treaty and a mutual security pact in September 1951. As had been the case with West Germany, Japan sat squarely within the American orbit, ready to serve as an economic hub for Asia.

The one area where cold war considerations did not control American policy was Palestine. In 1943, then Senator Harry Truman spoke passionately about the Holocaust, asserting, "This is not a Jewish problem, it is an American problem—and we must . . . face it squarely and honorably." As president, he had the opportunity to make good on his words. Jews had been migrating to Palestine since the nineteenth century, and one result was tension and hostilities between Palestinian Arabs and Jews. After World War II, as hundreds of thousands of European Jews sought refuge in Palestine, fighting raged into brutal terrorism on both sides. Most of Truman's foreign policy experts saw American-

**SURVIVORS OF THE HOLOCAUST IN ISRAEL**
*These young women, refugees from Nazi persecution, are shown doing laundry at a center for new immigrants in Palestine in June 1946. The desperation of thousands of Jews who defied immigration restrictions to get to what they hoped would be a Jewish homeland in Palestine contributed to President Truman's decision to recognize Israel as an independent state in May 1948. Isaac Halevi Herzog, the chief rabbi of Israel, later told Truman, "God put you in your mother's womb so you would be the instrument to bring the rebirth of Israel after two thousand years."*
Wide World.

Arab friendship as a critical barrier against Soviet influence in the Middle East and a means to secure U.S. interests in Arabian oil. Uncharacteristically defying his advisers, the president was moved instead by the pressure exerted by Jewish organizations, by his moral commitment to Holocaust survivors, and by his interest in the American Jewish vote for the 1948 elections. When Jews in Palestine declared the independent state of Israel in May 1948, Truman quickly recognized the new country and made the defense of Israel the cornerstone of U.S./Middle East policy. Yet that region remained in turmoil for decades to come.

## Truman and the Fair Deal at Home

Referring to the Civil War general who coined the phrase "War is hell," Truman said in December 1945, "Sherman was wrong. I'm telling you I find peace is hell." Challenged by thorny problems abroad, Truman also had to deal with shortages, strikes, inflation, and other problems attending the reconversion of the economy to peacetime production. At the same time, he tried to expand New Deal reform, most notably into the areas of civil rights, housing, education, and health care. Yet obstacles abounded to Truman's domestic agenda, which came to be known as the Fair Deal, and Truman had to settle for consolidation of reforms that were already in place.

### Reconversion and the Postwar Economic Boom

Despite deprivations and inconveniences during World War II, most Americans had enjoyed a wartime standard of living that was higher than ever before. Economic experts as well as ordinary citizens worried about sustaining that standard in peacetime while providing jobs for millions of returning soldiers. Truman wasted no time unveiling his plan for converting the economy to peacetime production, asking Congress to enact a twenty-one-point program of economic controls and social and economic reforms. "Not even President Roosevelt ever asked for as much at one sitting," exploded Republican leader Joseph W. Martin Jr.

Congress approved only one of Truman's key proposals, enacting a watered-down version of full-employment legislation. The Employment Act of 1946 invested the federal government with responsibility "to promote maximum employment, production, and purchasing power," thereby formalizing what had been implicit in Roosevelt's actions to counter the depression—government's responsibility for maintaining a healthy economy. The law created a Council of Economic Advisers to assist the president in economic planning, but it authorized no new powers to translate the government's obligation into effective action.

Inflation turned out to be the most severe problem in the early postwar years. Unable to buy civilian goods during the war, in 1945 consumers had $30 billion of savings that they now itched to spend. But shortages of meat, automobiles, housing, and a host of other items persisted. Some six million people wanted new cars in 1946, but auto manufacturers could produce fewer than three million. Housing was so scarce that returning veterans lived in basements and garages. Until industry could convert fully to civilian production and make more goods available, consumer demand could only drive up prices. The consumer price index—an official measurement of the rate of inflation—shot up by 18 percent in 1946.

*Obstacles abounded to Truman's domestic agenda, which came to be known as the Fair Deal, and Truman had to settle for consolidation of reforms that were already in place.*

Labor relations were another thorn in Truman's side. Organized labor survived the war stronger than ever, its 14.5 million members making up 35 percent of the civilian workforce. Yet union members feared erosion of wartime gains. With wage controls in place throughout the war, the rising incomes enjoyed by working-class families had come largely from the availability of new, higher-paying jobs and the chance to work longer hours. The end of overtime meant a 30 percent cut in take-home pay for most workers.

Women who had flocked into wartime jobs also saw their earnings decline. Most of the women who remained in the workforce had to settle for lower-paying jobs in light industry or the service sector. (See the Historical Question on page 716.) Men replaced

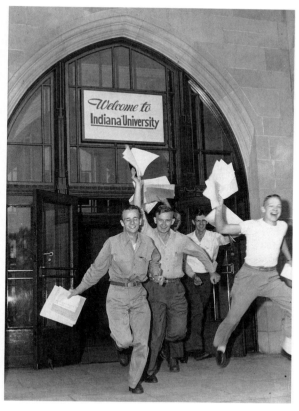

**VETERANS GO TO COLLEGE**
*So many World War II veterans wanted to use their
GI benefits for higher education that colleges were overwhelmed, and many had to turn away students. These
veterans, sprinting out of the building where they have
just registered, express their joy at having been admitted
to Indiana University in 1947.*
Indiana University Photographic Services.

steam to his mother in October 1945: "The Congress
[is] balking, labor has gone crazy, and management
isn't far from insane in selfishness." In May 1946,
after coal miners rejected government recommendations for a settlement and their strike threatened
the steel, auto, and railroad industries as well, Truman placed the mines under federal control. When
the massive wave of strikes subsided at the end of
1946, workers had won wage increases of about 20
percent, but the loss of overtime along with rising
prices left labor's purchasing power only slightly
higher than in 1942.

By 1947, the nation had survived the strains of
reconversion and avoided a postwar depression.
Wartime profits enabled businesses to invest in new
plants and equipment. Consumers used their billions of dollars in wartime savings to buy the
houses, cars, and appliances that lay beyond their
reach during the depression and war. Defense
spending and the $38 billion in grants and loans that
enabled war-torn countries to purchase American
goods also stimulated the economy. A soaring
birthrate, 25 percent higher in 1949 than in 1940, further sustained consumer demand.

The nation's gratitude to its returning warriors
also boosted the economy. Under the Servicemen's
Readjustment Act (the GI Bill), passed in 1944, 16 million veterans could claim unemployment compensation while they looked for jobs; low-interest loans
to purchase homes, farms, and small businesses; and
funds for job training and education. By 1948, some
1.3 million veterans had bought houses with government loans, and more than 7 million had received
government-subsidized job training and education.

Yet economic prosperity was not universal. The
real gains came during the war, and while wages and
salaries increased by 23 percent from 1945 to 1950,
prices went up by 36.2 percent. A recession in 1949
threw 7 percent of the labor force out of work; it
abated only when the Korean War sparked economic
recovery. Moreover, the one-third of all Americans
who lived in poverty failed to receive any significant
benefits from the return to peacetime production.

## Black Protest and the Politics of Civil Rights

"I spent four years in the army to free a bunch of
Frenchmen and Dutchmen," an African American
corporal declared, "and I'm hanged if I'm going to
let the Alabama version of the Germans kick me

tens of thousands of women in iron, steel, and other
heavy industries that paid relatively good wages.

Most unions defending labor's interests paid
scant attention to the problems of women workers.
More strikes took place in 1946 than at any other
time in U.S. history, disrupting production in virtually every major industry. Although most Americans approved of unions in principle, they became
fed up with labor stoppages, blamed unions for rising prices and shortages of consumer goods, and
wanted more government restrictions on organized
labor. Truman shared the public exasperation, although he spread the blame around when he let off

# What Happened to Rosie the Riveter?

ALTHOUGH STUDIES HAVE BEEN DONE of the postwar lives of World War II soldiers, we know much less about another group of "veterans," the women who helped fight the war on the domestic front. Statistics show that women's employment fell by more than two million between 1945 and 1947. But gross statistics do not reveal which women left the labor force and why, and they obscure the experiences of women who continued to work but in different jobs.

We do know what public officials and business and labor leaders expected of women who had taken up "men's" work during the war. With the shadow of the depression still hovering, Americans doubted that the economy could accommodate the six million new women workers along with millions of returning veterans once wartime production had ceased. A nearly universal response to anxieties about unemployment pushed a big part of the responsibility on women: Their wartime duty to produce the goods needed for victory was replaced with their postwar obligation to withdraw from the labor force.

The message that they should quit their jobs "for the sake of their homes as well as the labor situation" overwhelmed women. The company newspaper at Kaiser shipyards in the Pacific Northwest proclaimed in May 1945, "The Kitchen—Women's Big Post-War Goal." Putting words into the mouths of Kaiser's female employees, the article asserted, "Brothers, the tin hat and welder's torch will be yours! . . . The thing we want to do is take off these unfeminine garments and button ourselves into something starched and pretty." A General Electric ad predicted that women would welcome a return to "their old housekeeping routine" because GE intended to transform housework with new appliances. Some experts connected married women's employment to their obligations to help their husbands readjust to civilian life. A psychiatrist warned that women's economic independence might "raise problems in the future," urging women to realize that "reunion means relinquishing [independence]—to some extent at any rate."

Other evidence suggests that many women did not have to be told to give up their wartime jobs. Skyrocketing marriage and birthrates reveal the attraction of home and family life to people compelled to postpone marriage and childbearing during the depression and the war. Thanks to the accumulation of wartime savings, veterans' benefits, and favorable opportunities for men in the postwar economy, many families found it possible to rely on a single earner.

The double burdens of married women who took wartime jobs suggest another reason for women's voluntary withdrawal from the workforce. The wartime scarcity of goods had made housekeeping much more difficult, especially for women who typically worked forty-eight hours a week with one day off. Shopping became a problem because stores often sold out of goods early in the day, and few shops kept evening or Sunday hours. Washing machines, refrigerators, vacuum cleaners, and other appliances that might have lightened women's burdens were not produced at all during the war. Child care centers accommodated only about 10 percent of the children of employed mothers. Employed women with families to care for were simply worn out.

Yet surveys reported that 75 percent of women in wartime jobs wanted—and usually needed—to keep them. As two women employed at a Ford plant in Memphis put it, "Women didn't stop eating when the war stopped." Those who needed and wanted to remain in the workforce experienced the most wrenching changes. The vast majority were able to find jobs; in fact, women's workforce participation began growing again in 1947 and reached the wartime peak by 1950. But women lost the traditionally male, higher-paying jobs in durable goods industries (such as iron and steel and automobile and machinery production) and were pushed back into the lower-paying light manufacturing and service industries that had customarily welcomed them.

Statistics tell part of the story of this displacement. Women virtually disappeared from shipbuilding, and their share of jobs in the auto industry fell from 25 percent in 1944 to 10 percent in 1950. In the burgeoning Los Angeles aircraft industry, the proportion of women plunged from a wartime peak of 40 percent to 12 percent in 1948, rising to just 25

WOMEN'S POSTWAR FUTURE
*This photograph headed an article in the* New York Times Magazine *in June 1946. The article, written by the head of the Women's Bureau of the Department of Labor, discussed the needs of women workers, stressed their right to work and to equal pay, but also assumed that they would all but vanish from heavy manufacturing.*
Ellen Kaiper.

Sisters under the apron—Yesterday's war worker becomes today's housewife.

# What's Become of Rosie the Riveter?

percent in the 1950s. Even in light manufacturing, such as the electrical goods industry, where women had claimed one-third of the prewar jobs, women maintained their numbers but were bumped down to lower-paying work. During the war, women had narrowed the wage gap between men and women, but in 1950, women earned only 53 percent of what men did.

How women reacted to their displacement can be pieced together to some extent from what they were willing to say to reporters and oral history interviewers and what they wrote to government agencies and labor unions. "Women do not expect or want to hold jobs at the expense of returning soldiers," proclaimed a resolution passed by the Women's Trade Union League, expressing women's overwhelming support for veterans' claims to jobs based on seniority awarded for the years of their wartime service. According to Tina Hill, a black worker at North American Aircraft in Los Angeles, being laid off "didn't bother me much. I was just glad that the war was over . . . [and] my husband had a job." Nonetheless, after doing domestic work, when North American called her back, she recalled, "was I a happy soul!"

When management violated women's seniority rights by hiring nonveterans, some women protested bitterly. According to an automobile worker, "We have women laid off with seniority . . . and every day they hire in new men off the street. They hire men, they say, to do the heavy work. . . . During the war they didn't care what kind of work we did." When Ford laid off women with as many as twenty-seven years' seniority, 150 women picketed with signs that read, "The Hand That Rocks the Cradle Can Build Tractors, Too." A worker infuriated by her union's failure to protect women's seniority rights told a reporter, "We are making the bullets now, and we will give the [union executive] board members a blast that will blow them out of their shoes."

Protest from a minority of women workers could not save the jobs that "Rosies" had held during the war. Despite women's exemplary performance, most employers still saw women and men as different species fit for different roles and deserving of disparate rewards. Most labor unions paid lip service to representing all their members, but even the most progressive unions gave low priority to protecting women's seniority rights. In the absence of a feminist movement that could have given visibility and credibility to their claims for equal treatment, most Rosie the Riveters resigned themselves to "women's work."

around when I get home." Black soldiers and civilians alike resolved that the return to peace would not be a return to the racial injustices of prewar America. Their political clout had grown with the migration of two million African Americans to northern and western cities, where they could vote and make a difference. Even in the South, the proportion of blacks who cast ballots inched up from 2 percent to 12 percent in the 1940s. Pursuing civil rights through the courts and Congress, the National Association for the Advancement of Colored People (NAACP) counted half a million members.

> *Black soldiers and civilians alike resolved that the return to peace would not be a return to the racial injustices of prewar America.*

In the postwar years, individuals broke through the color barrier, achieving several "firsts" for their race. Jackie Robinson integrated major league baseball when he took over second base for the Brooklyn Dodgers in 1947. In 1950, Ralph J. Bunche won the Nobel Peace Prize for his contributions to the United Nations, and Gwendolyn Brooks earned the Pulitzer Prize for poetry.

However, in most respects, African Americans found that little had changed, especially in the South, where violence greeted their attempts to assert their rights. White men with guns turned back Medgar Evers (who would become a key civil rights leader in the 1960s) and four other veterans who were trying to vote in Mississippi. A mob lynched Isaac Nixon for voting in Georgia, and an all-white jury acquitted those accused of his murder. Governors, U.S. senators, and other southern politicians routinely intimidated potential voters with threats of economic retaliation and violence.

"My very stomach turned over when I learned that Negro soldiers just back from overseas were being dumped out of army trucks in Mississippi and beaten," wrote Truman, shaken by the violence and under pressure to act by civil rights leaders and liberals. Wrestling with the Democrat's need for northern black and liberal votes as well as white southern votes, Truman acted more boldly on civil rights than had any previous president. In 1946, he created a Committee on Civil Rights, asking Congress in February 1948 to enact the committee's recommendations. The first president to address the

NAACP, Truman announced that all Americans should have equal rights to housing, education, employment, and the ballot. But the president failed to follow up on his messages by having specific bills introduced in Congress. In the throes of the 1948 election campaign and under threat of civil disobedience by civil rights activists, Truman did issue an executive order to desegregate the armed services. But he allowed the order to go unimplemented until the need for military personnel during the Korean War forced the military's hand.

Although the gap loomed large between what Truman said about civil rights and what his administration accomplished, the desegregation of the military and the administration's support of civil

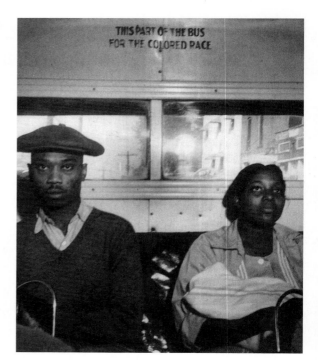

**SEGREGATION**
*Signs like this were a normal feature of life in the South from the late nineteenth century until the 1960s. State and local laws mandated segregation in every aspect of life, literally from the cradle to the grave. African Americans could not use white hospitals, cemeteries, schools, libraries, swimming pools, playgrounds, restrooms, or drinking fountains. They were relegated to balconies in movie theaters and kept apart from whites in all public meetings.*
Marion Palfi/Courtesy, Center for Creative Photography, University of Arizona.

rights cases in the Supreme Court kindled far-reaching changes. Breaking sharply with the past, Truman used his office to educate the public and set a moral agenda that would last into the next few decades.

## The Fair Deal Flounders

Republicans capitalized on the public frustrations with economic reconversion in the 1946 congressional elections. Portraying Truman as a little man in a job that was way over his head, they accused his administration of "confusion, corruption, and communism" and jeered, "To Err Is Truman." Capturing Congress for the first time in fourteen years, Republicans looked eagerly to the 1948 presidential campaign. Yet although many Republicans campaigned against New Deal "regimentation" and "radicalism" in 1946, their dominance of the 80th Congress failed to dismantle the reforms of the 1930s. Congress made budget cuts in some reform programs and, overriding Truman's veto, favored higher income groups with tax cuts. Its most serious attack on the New Deal was the Taft-Hartley Act, passed in 1947 over Truman's veto. Called a "slave labor" law and "Tuff-Heartless" by unions, Taft-Hartley imposed restrictions on the right to strike and on organizing workers. States could now pass "right to work" laws banning the practice of requiring all workers to join a union once a majority had voted for it. The law also compelled union leaders to swear that they were not Communists and to make annual financial reports. The New Deal principle of government protection for collective bargaining remained, but Taft-Hartley put the government more squarely between labor and management and between unions and individual workers.

As the 1948 elections approached, Thomas E. Dewey, the Republican nominee who had lost to Roosevelt in 1944, was sure that his time had come, and so was nearly everyone else. Truman faced not only a resurgent Republican Party but also two revolts from within his own party. On the left, Henry Wallace, pushed out of the cabinet for his foreign policy views, led a new Progressive Party. On the right, South Carolina Governor J. Strom Thurmond headed the States' Rights Party—the Dixiecrats—formed by southern Democrats opposed to the party's growing support for civil rights.

Virtually alone in believing he could win, Truman crisscrossed the country by train, answering

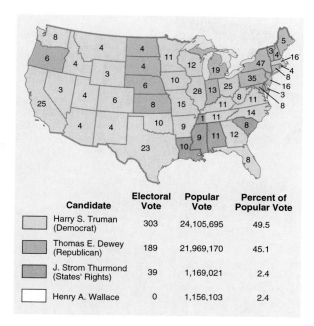

| Candidate | Electoral Vote | Popular Vote | Percent of Popular Vote |
|---|---|---|---|
| Harry S. Truman (Democrat) | 303 | 24,105,695 | 49.5 |
| Thomas E. Dewey (Republican) | 189 | 21,969,170 | 45.1 |
| J. Strom Thurmond (States' Rights) | 39 | 1,169,021 | 2.4 |
| Henry A. Wallace | 0 | 1,156,103 | 2.4 |

**MAP 26.2**
*The Election of 1948*

supporters' cries of "Give'em hell, Harry." So bleak were Truman's prospects that the overconfident Dewey ran a low-key campaign and on election night the *Chicago Tribune* printed its day-after-election issue with the banner headline DEWEY DEFEATS TRUMAN. But Truman took 303 electoral votes to Dewey's 189 (Map 26.2), as his party regained control of Congress. In addition to reflecting popular support for his foreign policy, Truman's unexpected victory attested to his skills as a campaigner and to the enduring popularity of New Deal reform.

Yet the victory of Truman and the Democrats did not result in enactment of his Fair Deal. Congress made modest improvements in Social Security and raised the minimum wage, but its only significant reform initiative was in housing. The Housing Act of 1949 furnished 350,000 units of government-constructed housing over the next fifteen years. Although it fell far short of actual need and many projects were poorly designed and cheaply built, the legislation represented a landmark commitment by the government to address the housing needs of the poor.

With southern Democrats often joining the Republicans on domestic issues, Congress rejected

### TRUMAN'S WHISTLE-STOP CAMPAIGN

*Harry Truman rallies a crowd from his campaign train at a stop in Bridgeport, Pennsylvania, in October 1948. His campaign theme song, "I'm Just Wild about Harry," was borrowed, with the words slightly changed, from the 1921 musical* Shuffle Along. *This was the last election in which the pollsters predicted the wrong winner. They stopped taking polls in mid-October, after which many voters apparently changed their minds. One commentator praised the American citizenry, who "couldn't be ticketed by the polls, knew its own mind and had picked the rather unlikely but courageous figure of Truman to carry on its banner."*
Photo: Truman Library; sheet music: Collection of Janice L. and David J. Frent.

Truman's civil rights measures; proposals for a federal health care program; federal aid to education; and a new agriculture program for small farmers and consumers. His efforts to revise immigration policy produced the McCarran-Walter Act of 1952, ending the outright ban on immigration and citizenship for Japanese and other Asians. But the law also authorized the government to bar suspected Communists and homosexuals and, to Truman's distress, maintained the discriminatory quota system established in the 1920s.

Although Truman blamed political opponents for defeating his Fair Deal, in fact Truman chose to devote much more energy to foreign policy than to his domestic proposals. Moreover, by late 1950, the Korean War embroiled Truman in controversy, diverted his attention from domestic affairs, and depleted his power as a legislative leader.

## The Domestic Chill: A Second Red Scare

Truman's domestic program also suffered from a wave of anti-Communist hysteria that weakened leftist and liberal forces. Both "red-baiting," the attempt to discredit individuals or ideas by associating them with Communists, and official retaliation against leftist critics of the government had flourished during the Red scare at the end of World War I. A second Red scare convulsed the United States after World War II, born of partisan political maneuvering, collapse of the Soviet-American alliance, setbacks in U.S. foreign policy, and disclosures of Soviet espionage.

Republicans jumped on cold war setbacks, such as the Communist triumph in China, to accuse the Democrats of fostering internal subversion. Wisconsin Republican Senator Joseph R. McCarthy, the leading anti-Communist, charged, "The Communists within our borders have been more responsible for the success of Communism abroad than Soviet Russia." Revelations of Soviet espionage and accusations made by former Communists furnished just enough credibility to such charges. For example, a number of ex-Communists, including Whittaker Chambers and Elizabeth Bentley, testified that they and others had provided secret documents to the Soviets. In 1950, a British physicist working on the atomic bomb project confessed that he was a spy and implicated several Americans, including a New York couple named Ethel and Julius Rosenberg. The Rosenbergs pleaded innocent but were convicted of conspiracy to commit espionage and executed in the electric chair in 1953.

At the peak of the hysteria, the U.S. Communist Party had only about twenty thousand members, some of them FBI agents. But many more Americans had once been members, had associated with other groups with Communist members, or had supported radical causes. Red-hunters cared little for such distinctions. For more than ten years following World War II, the House Un-American Activities Committee (HUAC), the Senate Internal Security Subcommittee (SISS), and a host of other official bodies ordered citizens to testify about their past and present political associations. If witnesses refused to testify, anti-Communists charged that silence was tantamount to confession, and these "unfriendly witnesses" suffered the loss of jobs and public ostracism.

The influence of Senator McCarthy was so great that "McCarthyism" became a term synonymous with the anti-Communist crusade, even though the hysteria ranged far beyond the senator. Attacking individuals recklessly, in 1950 McCarthy claimed to have a list of 205 "known Communists" working in the State Department. Even though many of his charges were absurd—such as his allegation that retired General George C. Marshall belonged to a Communist conspiracy—the press covered McCarthy avidly, and his photograph was featured on the covers of *Time* and *Newsweek*.

Not all Republicans joined McCarthyism, nor did the Republican Party have a monopoly on the politics of anticommunism. Under increasing pres-

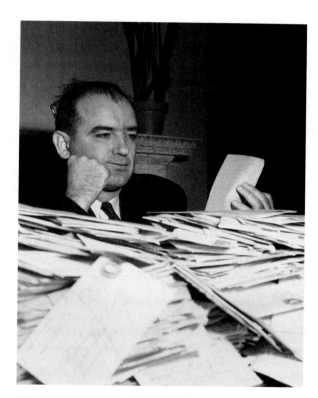

**SENATOR JOSEPH R. MCCARTHY**
*In March 1950, McCarthy reads letters responding to his claim to have a list of 205 Communists in the State Department. Although McCarthy made his reputation from anticommunism, he seized that issue more from the need to have a campaign platform in 1950 than from genuine concern grounded in real evidence. McCarthy loved politics from his high school days in Appleton, Wisconsin, and easily distorted the truth to promote his political ambitions. He died from alcoholism at the age of forty-eight, three years after the Senate condemned his conduct.*
Corbis-Bettmann.

sure from Republicans, in March 1947 Truman issued Executive Order 9835 requiring investigation of every federal employee. In effect, Truman's "loyalty program" violated the principles of American justice by allowing anonymous informers to make charges and then placing the burden of proof on the accused. The program extended into the mid-1950s, as more than two thousand civil service employees lost their jobs and another ten thousand resigned. Years later, Truman privately admitted that the loyalty program had been a mistake.

The Truman administration also went directly after the Communist Party, prosecuting its leaders under the Smith Act, passed in 1940, which made it a crime to "advocate the overthrow and destruction of the Government of the United States by force and violence." Although civil libertarians argued that prosecuting individuals for their ideas rather than their actions violated First Amendment rights to freedom of speech, press, and association, the Supreme Court ruled in 1951 (*Dennis v. United States*) that the Communist threat overrode the guarantees of the Constitution.

---

*Creating a climate of fear that stifled expression of dissenting ideas and removed unpopular causes from public contemplation, the anti-Communist crusade violated fundamental constitutional rights of freedom of speech and association.*

---

The internal cold war spread beyond the nation's capital. State and local governments undertook investigations, demanded loyalty oaths, fired individuals suspected of disloyalty, banned books from public libraries, and more. In addition, a 1950 Senate report claimed that homosexuals' "moral turpitude" and their susceptibility to blackmail made them unfit for government jobs. Purged from the civil service and drummed out of the military, gay men and women also suffered surveillance and harassment at the hands of the FBI, the post office, and local police forces. Rutgers, Harvard, Michigan, and other universities dismissed professors, and public school teachers lost their jobs in New York, Philadelphia, Los Angeles, and elsewhere. HUAC took on the movie industry in 1947, and when ten writers and directors refused to testify, they went to prison and later found themselves barred from

work in Hollywood, as did scores of others suspected of Communist associations. Because the Communist Party had helped organize unions and championed racial justice, labor and civil rights activists and organizations came under scrutiny.

McCarthyism brought personal distress to citizens who were innocent of breaking any law. Thousands of people found themselves humiliated and discredited, hounded from their jobs, some put behind prison bars. Creating a climate of fear that stifled expression of dissenting ideas and removed unpopular causes from public contemplation, the anti-Communist crusade violated fundamental constitutional rights of freedom of speech and association.

## The Cold War Becomes Hot: Korea

The cold war erupted into a shooting war in June 1950, when troops from Communist North Korea invaded South Korea. For the first time, Americans went into battle to implement containment. The United States, in concert with the United Nations, ultimately held the line in Korea, but at great cost in lives, dollars, and domestic unity.

### Korea and the Military Implementation of Containment

The war grew out of the artificial division of Korea after World War II. Having expelled the Japanese, who had controlled Korea since the Russo-Japanese War of 1904, the United States and the Soviet Union divided Korea at the thirty-eighth parallel into two occupation zones (Map 26.3). The Soviets supported the Korean Communist Party in the North, while the United States backed the Korean Democratic Party in the South. With Moscow and Washington unable to agree on a unification plan, in July 1948 the United Nations sponsored elections in South Korea. The American-favored candidate, Korean nationalist Syngman Rhee, who had spent most of his life in exile in the United States, was elected president, and the United States withdrew all but five hundred troops. In the fall of 1948, the Soviets established a People's Republic of North Korea and also withdrew their occupation forces.

Many U.S. officials doubted that Rhee's conservative, repressive government could sustain

**MAP 26.3**
*The Korean War, 1950–1953*
*After each side had plunged deep into its enemy's territory, the Korean War ended in 1953 with the dividing line between North and South Korea nearly the same as it had been before the war.*

On June 30, six days after learning of the attack, Truman decided to commit ground troops. Looking back on his presidency, Truman later regarded this decision as his most important one. The invasion had convinced him "beyond all doubt that Communism has passed beyond the use of subversion and will now use armed invasion and war." In addition, the U.S. representative to the UN persuaded the Security Council to sponsor a collective effort to repel the attack. Authorized by the Security Council to appoint a commander for the UN force, Truman named General Douglas MacArthur, hero of the American victory in the Pacific and head of the Allied postwar occupation in Japan.

> *Looking back on his presidency, Truman later regarded the commitment of ground troops in Korea as his most important decision.*

Sixteen nations, including many of the NATO allies, sent troops to Korea, but the United States contributed most of the personnel and weapons, deploying almost 1.8 million troops and essentially dictating military strategy. Yet Congress never declared war. Truman himself refused to call it a war, and "police action" became the official label. Some felt that fighting a war without an official declaration by Congress violated the spirit of the Constitution. The president's political opponents called it "Truman's war" when the military situation worsened.

The first American soldiers rushed to Korea unprepared and ill equipped. The North Koreans took the capital of Seoul and drove deep into the south between June and September, forcing UN troops to retreat south to Pusan. Then in September, MacArthur launched a bold counteroffensive, staging an amphibious landing at Inchon, 180 miles behind the North Korean lines. By mid-October, UN forces had pushed the North Koreans back to the thirty-eighth parallel. Now Truman had to decide whether to authorize an invasion of North Korea and seek to unify Korea under UN supervision.

## From Containment to Rollback to Containment

"Troops could not be expected . . . to march up to a surveyor's line and stop," remarked Dean Acheson, reflecting sentiment among the public and most government officials to transform the military

popular support. But to bolster Rhee's anticommunism, Truman decided to supply a small amount of economic and military aid to the Rhee government.

Skirmishes between North and South Korean troops had occurred since 1948, with both sides crossing the thirty-eighth parallel. In June 1950, however, ninety thousand North Koreans swept into South Korea. Truman's advisers immediately assumed that the Soviet Union, China, or both had instigated the attack. Revelations by former Soviet officials thirty years later indicated only that the Kremlin had acquiesced in North Korean plans.

**KOREA**
*During the winter of 1950–51, American soldiers in Korea faced bitter cold and bitter defeat as Chinese and North Korean troops pushed them back below the thirty-eighth parallel. Under the leadership of General Matthew Ridgway, American troops began to turn the tide again. When this photograph was taken, U.S. forces were close to regaining the thirty-eighth parallel in March 1951.*
Corbis-Bettmann.

objective from containment to elimination of the enemy and unification. With UN approval, on September 27, 1950, Truman ordered MacArthur to move beyond the thirty-eighth parallel if necessary to destroy North Korean forces. Concerned about possible intervention by China and the Soviet Union, Truman directed the general not to send UN troops close to the Chinese border. Yet MacArthur sent UN forces to within 40 miles of the Korean-Chinese border, whereupon more than 150,000 Chinese troops crossed the Yalu River into Korea. By December 1950, they had recaptured Seoul. It took three months of grueling battle for UN forces to work their way back to the thirty-eighth parallel. At that point, Truman decided to seek a negotiated settlement.

When the goal of the war reverted to containment, MacArthur vented his fury. A holding action against communism represented defeat. "There is no substitute for victory," he asserted. Truman and his advisers, however, resolved to avoid a wider war in Asia. According to General Omar Bradley,

chairman of the Joint Chiefs of Staff, MacArthur wanted to wage "the wrong war, at the wrong place, at the wrong time, with the wrong enemy."

MacArthur took his case public, in effect challenging the president's authority to make foreign policy and violating the principle of civilian control over the military. Fed up with MacArthur's insubordination, Truman relieved him of his command in April 1951. Three out of four Americans, however, sided with MacArthur rather than with Truman. "Quite an explosion . . . letters of abuse by the dozens," Truman recorded in his diary. The general came home to a hero's welcome. Millions saw his address to Congress on television, and more than seven million people turned out for his triumphant parade in New York City.

The adulation of MacArthur reflected Americans' frustrations with containment. Why should Americans die simply to preserve the status quo rather than wipe out the enemy once and for all? Siding with MacArthur enabled Americans to hold on to their belief that the United States was all-powerful and to pin the Korean stalemate on the government's ineptitude or willingness to shelter subversives.

Truman's success in "scaring the hell" out of the American people came back to haunt him. If communism was so threatening, so evil, why not stamp it out as MacArthur wanted? When Congress investigated MacArthur's firing, all of the top military leaders supported the president, yet he never recovered from the political fallout. Nor was Truman able to end the war. Cease-fire negotiations began in July 1951, but peace talks dragged on for two more years, while twelve thousand more U.S. soldiers died.

## Korea, Communism, and the 1952 Election

Popular discontent with "Truman's war" gave the Republicans a decided edge in the election battles of 1952. Their presidential candidate, General Dwight D. Eisenhower, enjoyed immense stature for his contributions to victory in World War II. Reared in modest circumstances in Abilene, Kansas, Eisenhower attended West Point and rose steadily through the army ranks. As supreme commander

in Europe, he won widespread praise for leading the Allied armies to victory over Germany.

Both Republicans and Democrats had courted Eisenhower for the presidency in 1948. Although he believed that civilian control over the military worked best when professional soldiers kept out of politics, the political situation gave him compelling reasons to run for the presidency in 1952. Eisenhower agreed with the broad scope of Democratic foreign policy, but he deplored the Democrats' efforts to solve domestic problems with new federal programs and large expenditures. He equally disliked the foreign policy views of the leading Republican presidential contender, Senator Robert A. Taft, who attacked containment and sought to cut defense spending. Eisenhower decided to run as much to stop Taft and the conservative wing of the party as to get the Democrats out of the White House.

Eisenhower defeated Taft for the nomination, but the old guard prevailed on the party platform. It damned containment as "negative, futile, and immoral" and charged the Truman administration with shielding "traitors to the Nation in high places." Eisenhower's choice of thirty-nine-year-old Senator Richard M. Nixon as his running mate

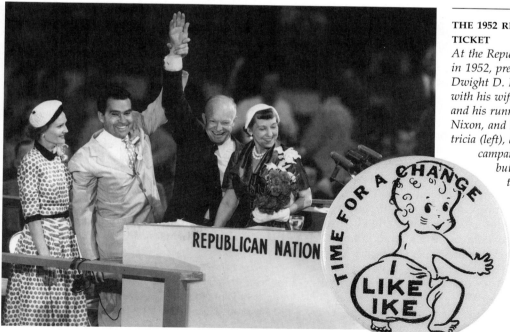

**THE 1952 REPUBLICAN TICKET**
*At the Republican convention in 1952, presidential nominee Dwight D. Eisenhower stands with his wife, Mamie (right), and his running mate, Richard Nixon, and Nixon's wife, Patricia (left), at the start of their campaign. The campaign button featured a theme common to candidates of the party currently out of power.*
Corbis-Bettmann; Collection of Janice L. and David J. Frent.

helped to appease the Republican right wing and ensured that anticommunism would be a major theme of the campaign.

From modest origins in southern California, Nixon had had to work his way through college and law school. After navy service and a brief law career, he helped the Republicans capture Congress in 1946, defeating a liberal incumbent for a seat in the House of Representatives. Nixon quickly made a name for himself as a member of the House Un-American Activities Committee. Accusing the Democrats of being soft on communism, Nixon found an issue to boost his career. In his 1950 bid for the Senate, he ran an effective smear campaign against Helen Gahagan Douglas, charging her with being "pink [Communist] right down to her underwear."

Having decided not to run for another term, Truman persuaded Adlai E. Stevenson, governor of Illinois, to seek the Democratic nomination. Witty and eloquent and a popular governor, acceptable to both liberals and southern Democrats, Stevenson easily won the nomination. Truman's unpopularity proved to be an unbearable burden, however, and Stevenson could not escape the domestic fallout from the Korean War.

---

*Adlai Stevenson easily won the nomination. Truman's unpopularity proved to be an unbearable burden, however, and Stevenson could not escape the domestic fallout from the Korean War.*

---

The Republican campaign faltered just once, when the last item of its "Korea, Communism, and Corruption" campaign came back to haunt the party. A newspaper reported that Nixon had accepted $18,000 from supporters in California. Although such gifts were common in politics at that time, Democrats jumped on Nixon, hoping to divert attention from the scandals that involved several figures in the Truman administration and the Democratic Party. As newspaper editorials called for Nixon to withdraw from the ticket, most of Eisenhower's advisers urged him to dump his running mate.

Nixon saved himself by exploiting the new medium of television. He made an emotional appeal to a national audience, disclosing his finances and documenting his modest standard of living. Conceding that the family pet Checkers could be considered an illegal gift, he vowed that he would not break his daughters' hearts by returning the cocker spaniel. The overwhelming popular response to the "Checkers speech" turned the tide for Nixon. Eisenhower embraced his running mate with the words "You're my boy!" Despite this endorsement, both men bore resentments about the incident and never achieved an easy or warm relationship.

With the issue of corruption neutralized, the Republicans harped on communism at home and failure to achieve victory in Korea. Less than two weeks before the election, Eisenhower made the dramatic announcement "I shall go to Korea," and voters registered their confidence in his ability to end the war. Cutting sharply into traditional Democratic territory, Eisenhower won several southern states and 55 percent of the popular vote. His coattails carried a narrow Republican majority to Congress.

## An Armistice and the War's Costs

Eisenhower made good on his pledge to end the Korean War. In July 1953, the two sides reached an armistice that left Korea divided just as it had been three years earlier. The war took the lives of 54,000 Americans and wounded more than 100,000. Total UN casualties included 118,515 killed, 264,591 wounded, and 92,987 captured, most of whom did not return alive.

Korean and civilian casualties were heavier still. More than 1.6 million North Koreans and Chinese were killed or wounded, and 3 million South Koreans died of war-related causes. The nature of the war and the unpopularity of the Rhee government made it difficult for soldiers to distinguish between friends and enemies, since civilian populations sometimes harbored North Korean agents. Consequently, as one journalist reported, the situation "forced upon our men in the field, acts and attitudes of the utmost savagery . . . the blotting out of villages where the enemy *might* be hiding, the shooting and shelling of refugees who *may* be North Koreans."

Viewing Korea as a test of its containment policy, the Truman administration judged the war a success. The United States had shown the world that it would help nations that were resisting communism. Moreover, both Truman and Eisenhower managed to contain what amounted to a world war—involving twenty nations on both sides—within a single country. And despite both presidents' threats to use nuclear bombs, they limited the Korean War to a conflict fought with conventional weapons.

In April 1950, two months before the Korean War began, the National Security Council had given Truman a top-secret report on the nation's military strength. NSC 68, as the document was called, warned that the survival of the nation and the world required a massive military buildup. Truman read the report but took no action on recommendations that would triple the current defense budget.

---

*Military spending shot up from $14 billion in 1950 to $50 billion in 1953. By 1953, defense spending claimed 60 percent of the federal budget, and the size of the armed forces had tripled.*

---

Nearly all of the military buildup called for in NSC 68 came about during the Korean War, vastly increasing U.S. capacity to act as a global power. Using the Korean crisis to expand American presence elsewhere, Truman got Congress to approve the rearming of West Germany and the commitment of troops to NATO. Military spending shot up from $14 billion in 1950 to $50 billion in 1953. By 1953, defense spending claimed 60 percent of the federal budget, and the size of the armed forces had tripled.

To General Matthew Ridgway, who succeeded MacArthur as commander of the UN forces, Korea taught the lesson that U.S. forces should never again fight a land war in Asia. Eisenhower concurred. Nevertheless, the Korean War induced the Truman administration to expand its role in Asia by increasing aid to the French, who were fighting to hang on to their colonial empire in Indochina. As marines retreated from a battle against Chinese soldiers in 1950, they sang, prophetically, "We're Harry's police force on call, / So put back your pack on, / The next step is Saigon, / Cheer up, me lads, bless 'em all."

# Conclusion: Meeting the Challenges of the Postwar World

Dean Acheson chose to title his memoir about the Truman years *Present at the Creation,* aptly capturing the magnitude of change that marked the aftermath of World War II. More than any development in the postwar world, the cold war defined American politics and society for years to come. Truman's decision to oppose communism throughout the world marked the most momentous foreign policy initiative in the nation's history. It transformed the federal government, shifting its attention from domestic to external affairs, greatly expanding its budget, and substantially increasing the power of the president. The nuclear arms race attending the cold war put the people of the world at risk, diverted resources that could have been used to improve living standards, and skewed the economy toward dependence on military projects. While Americans continued to debate who was responsible for the cold war and whether it could have been avoided, none could question its impact on American society or the world.

In sharp contrast to foreign policy, the domestic policies of the postwar years reflected continuity with the past. Preoccupied with foreign policy, Truman failed to mobilize support for his ambition to assist the disadvantaged with new initiatives in education, health, agriculture, and civil rights, but he successfully defended most New Deal reforms.

The anti-Communist hysteria that grew out of the cold war contributed to the domestic status quo by silencing the left, stifling debate, and narrowing the range of acceptable ideas. Partisan politics and the Truman administration's constant rhetoric about the Communist menace fueled McCarthyism, but the obsession with subversion also fed on popular frustrations over the failure of containment to produce clear-cut victories. Convulsing the nation in bitter disunity, McCarthyism reflected a loss of confidence in American power. It would be a major challenge of the next administration to restore that unity and confidence.

## CHRONOLOGY

**1945**    Harry Truman becomes president of United States upon death of Franklin D. Roosevelt.

Japan and Germany surrender to Allies, ending World War II.

**1946**    Severe labor unrest erupts throughout United States.

Truman creates Committee on Civil Rights.

United States grants independence to Philippines.

Congress passes Employment Act signifying government's responsibility for healthy economy.

Congressional elections result in Republican control of 80th Congress.

**1947**    George F. Kennan's article on policy of containment appears in *Foreign Affairs*.

National Security Act of 1947 unifies military services under secretary of defense and creates National Security Council (NSC) and Central Intelligence Agency (CIA).

Truman asks Congress for aid to Greece and Turkey to counter communism and announces Truman Doctrine.

Truman establishes Federal Employees Loyalty and Security Program to get rid of Communists and their sympathizers.

**1948**    Congress approves Marshall Plan, providing massive aid to stimulate European recovery.

Congress makes women permanent part of armed services.

Truman issues executive order to desegregate armed services.

United States recognizes state of Israel.

Truman defeats Thomas E. Dewey to win full term as president.

**1948–1949**    Soviets block access to West Berlin, setting off Berlin crisis and fifteen-month Western airlift.

**1949**    Communists under Mao Zedong win Chinese civil war and take over mainland China; Nationalists retreat to Taiwan.

NATO (North Atlantic Treaty Organization) organizes to counter Soviet threat to Western Europe.

Truman administration initiates Point IV technical aid program to third world nations.

Soviet Union explodes atomic bomb.

**1950**    Senator Joseph McCarthy begins campaign against alleged Communists in United States, giving his name to period of anti-Communist hysteria.

Truman approves development of hydrogen bomb.

United States sends troops to South Korea to repel North Korean assault.

**1951**    Truman relieves General MacArthur of command in Korea for insubordination.

United States ends postwar occupation of Japan; the two nations sign peace treaty and mutual security pact.

**1952**    Republican Dwight D. Eisenhower elected president of United States.

**1953**    Armistice signed in Korean War.

# SUGGESTED READINGS

Paul Boyer, *By the Bomb's Early Light: American Thought and Culture at the Dawn of the Atomic Age* (1994). An account of the impact of the atomic bomb on politics, society, and culture.

John Patrick Diggins, *The Proud Decades: America in War and Peace, 1941–1960* (1988). A wide-ranging survey of U.S. culture and politics.

John Egerton, *Speak Now against the Day: The Generation before the Civil Rights Movement in the South* (1994). Compelling stories of black and white Southerners who challenged racism in the generation before civil rights became a mass movement.

Alonzo L. Hamby, *Man of the People: A Life of Harry S. Truman* (1995). A lively and thorough biography presenting an overall positive assessment of Truman.

Melvyn Leffler, *A Preponderance of Power: National Security, the Truman Administration, and the Cold War* (1992). A comprehensive account of the early years of the cold war, culminating in the Korean War.

Thomas J. McCormick, *America's Half-Century: United States Foreign Policy in the Cold War* (1989). A cold war history from the perspective of U.S. efforts to create a global system of free trade.

Keith W. Olson, *The G.I. Bill, the Veterans, and the Colleges* (1974). A history of the program that profoundly shaped higher education in the United States.

David Oshinsky, *A Conspiracy So Immense: The World of Joe McCarthy* (1983). A biography of the man most closely associated with anticommunism in the postwar era.

Ellen Schrecker, *Many Are the Crimes: McCarthyism in America* (1998). A critical account of anticommunism from its origins in the 1930s to its long-term impact.

William Stueck, *The Korean War: An International History* (1995). A detailed history of the war as a conflict involving the major powers of the world.

Jules Tygiel, *Baseball's Great Experiment: Jackie Robinson and His Legacy* (1997). A biography that places Robinson in the context of baseball history and the civil rights movement.

Robert Zieger, *The CIO, 1935–1955* (1995). An account of the most dynamic element of organized labor in its period of growth.

**1954 CADILLAC**

*The automobile reflected both corporate and family prosperity in the 1950s. This car was man-*
*ufactured by General Motors, the biggest and richest corporation in the world and the first to*
*sell a billion dollars' worth of products. Costing about $5,000, the Cadillac was GM's top-line*
*car, one of the first purchases the McDonald brothers made when they struck it rich with their*
*hamburger stand in California. Even the cheaper models that average Americans could afford*
*featured the gas-guzzling size and space-age-inspired style of this Cadillac.*
Ron Kimball.

# THE POLITICS AND CULTURE OF ABUNDANCE

## 27

### 1952–1960

TRAILED BY REPORTERS AND PHOTOGRAPHERS, Vice President Richard M. Nixon led Soviet Premier Nikita Khrushchev through the American National Exhibition in Moscow in July 1959. The display of American consumer goods followed an exhibit of Soviet products in New York, part of a cultural exchange between the two superpowers that reflected a slight thaw in the cold war. Both Khrushchev and Nixon seized on the propaganda potential of their encounter, and as they made their way through the display their verbal sparring turned into a slugfest of words and gestures that reporters dubbed "the kitchen debate."

Showing off a new color television set, Nixon conceded that the Soviet Union "may be ahead of us . . . in the thrust of your rockets for . . . outer space," but he bragged that the United States outstripped the Soviets in consumer goods. "Any steelworker could buy this house," Nixon boasted, as they walked through a model of a six-room ranch-style house. Khrushchev responded that in the Soviet Union, "you are entitled to housing," whereas in the United States, "if you don't have a dollar," you are reduced to sleeping on the pavement.

While the two leaders inspected appliances in the model kitchen, Nixon declared, "These are designed to make things easier for our women." Khrushchev disparaged "the capitalist attitude toward women"; the Soviet Union appreciated women's contributions to the economy, he said, not their domesticity. Mocking American consumers' fondness for gadgetry, Khrushchev asked, "Don't you have a machine that puts food into the mouth and pushes it down?" When Nixon insisted, "Isn't it far better to be talking about washing machines than machines of war?" Khrushchev agreed. Yet he affirmed the persistence of cold war tensions when he later blustered, "We too are giants. You want to threaten—we will answer threats with threats."

The Eisenhower administration had in fact begun with threats to the Soviet Union. Republican campaigners vowed to roll back communism and liberate "enslaved" peoples under Soviet rule. In practice, however, Eisenhower settled for a containment policy that differed little from Truman's, though Eisenhower relied more on nuclear weapons and on secret actions of the CIA. Yet, as Nixon's visit to Moscow demonstrated, Eisenhower took advantage of changes in the government of the Soviet Union to reduce tensions in Soviet-American relations.

Continuity with the Truman administration also characterized domestic policy during Eisenhower's administration. A majority of Americans enjoyed prosperity under the immensely popular president and seemed content with his "moderate Republicanism." Cold war weapons production spurred the economy, and most Americans could afford the products on display in Moscow—homes, television sets, and other appliances that transformed their patterns of living and allowed them to settle into postwar marriage and family life that celebrated traditional gender roles.

African Americans mounted a strong challenge to tradition in the 1950s. Reacting against segregation and disfranchisement, they developed the institutions, leadership, strategies, and will to mount a civil rights movement of unprecedented size and power.

## Eisenhower and the Politics of the "Middle Way"

Moderation was the guiding principle of Eisenhower's domestic agenda and leadership style. His first State of the Union message pledged a "middle way between untrammeled freedom of the individual and the demands for the welfare of the whole Nation." His administration would "avoid government by bureaucracy as carefully as it avoids neglect of the helpless." Claiming that Democrats appealed to divisive class interests, Eisenhower presented himself as a leader above partisan politics and selfish interest groups who would govern by compromise and consensus. Called "Ike" by his friends and the public, the war hero remained popular throughout his presidency.

### The President and McCarthy

The new president attempted to distance himself from the anti-Communist controversy that had plagued the Truman administration. Eisenhower shared Senator Joseph McCarthy's goal of eliminating communism from American life, and though he deplored McCarthy's method, he made little effort to silence him. Recognizing McCarthy's popularity, Eisenhower feared that to denounce him would alienate powerful old guard Republicans in Congress. Even under a Republican administration, McCarthy continued his allegations of Communists in the government, including several of Eisenhower's appointees. Thousands of federal employees charged with disloyalty lost their jobs.

Eisenhower correctly predicted that McCarthy would ultimately destroy himself. With the conclu-

sion of the Korean War, popular frustrations over containment abated, and the anti-Communist hysteria subsided. McCarthy tightened his own noose in 1954 when he went after alleged Communists in the army. As he hurled reckless charges during weeks of televised committee hearings, public opinion turned against him. "Have you left no sense of decency?" demanded the army's lawyer, Joseph Welch. In December 1954, the Senate voted to condemn him. Eisenhower's inaction had allowed the senator to spread his poison longer than he might otherwise have done. Like Truman, Eisenhower lent the power of his office to the postwar Red scare and suppression of dissent.

## Moderate Republicanism and the "Hidden Hand"

For most of his two terms (1953–1961), Eisenhower presided over a divided government. In 1954, the Democrats regained control of Congress and maintained it for the rest of the decade. The "moderate Republicanism" of the Eisenhower years was shaped not just by Eisenhower's convictions but also by a Democratic majority in Congress that maintained the course charted by the New Deal and the Fair Deal.

*Eisenhower presented himself as a leader above partisan politics and selfish interest groups who would govern by compromise and consensus.*

Eisenhower claimed to be above interest-group politics, yet he turned for advice almost exclusively to business leaders and chose wealthy executives and attorneys for his cabinet. When he appointed Martin Durkin, president of the AFL plumbers union, as secretary of labor, a liberal journal quipped that Eisenhower had "picked a cabinet of eight millionaires and one plumber." The "plumber" lasted less than a year and was replaced by a retail executive. Eisenhower also maintained informal ties with a group of wealthy businessmen—his "gang"—from whom he sought advice and fellowship. Yet he remained firmly in charge, leading one scholar to characterize his administration as the "hidden-hand" presidency.

Eisenhower's choice of businessmen as advisers and friends also furthered his goal of unifying the Republican Party, which required winning over the conservative old guard Republicans, who opposed New Deal programs and containment. Eisenhower chose Richard Nixon for his running mate in 1952 in part because Nixon had close ties to the Republican right wing.

The president shared with the old guard a conviction that government was best left up to the states and economic decisions to private business, but he did expand the welfare state and involve the federal government in new projects. His "middle way" applied the brakes, but it did not reverse the growing federal responsibility for economic development and for the welfare of Americans who were unable to survive in the free market.

In 1954, Eisenhower signed legislation that provided higher Social Security benefits and extended coverage to some ten million workers and self-employed individuals. The Housing Act of 1954 continued the federal government's role in financing public housing. Whereas Truman had failed to win congressional approval for a new Department of Health, Education, and Welfare, Eisenhower succeeded. The second president to appoint a woman to his cabinet, Eisenhower named former WAC commander and Texas newspaper publisher Oveta Culp Hobby to head the new department. And when the spread of polio neared epidemic proportions in the 1950s, Eisenhower obtained funds from Congress to distribute a vaccine, even though conservatives preferred that states assume that responsibility.

Eisenhower's greatest domestic initiative was the Interstate Highway Act of 1956. Promoted as essential to the nation's cold war defense strategy and as a spur to economic growth, the law authorized construction of a national system of highways, with the federal government paying most of the costs through increased fuel and vehicle taxes. Millions of Americans would benefit from the greater ease of travel and improved transportation of goods, but the most direct and substantial gains went to the trucking, construction, and automobile industries, which had lobbied hard for the law. Unforeseen at the time, the monumental highway construction project eventually exacted severe costs in the form of air pollution, energy consumption, declining mass transportation, and the decay of central cities.

In other areas, Eisenhower restrained the federal government in favor of state governments and private enterprise. He achieved large tax cuts, for example, that favored business and the wealthy. Moreover, whereas Democrats sought to keep nuclear power in government hands, Eisenhower signed legislation authorizing the private manufacture and sale of nuclear power and directed the

Atomic Energy Commission (AEC) to provide materials and services to private utilities at cost. Ground was broken at Shippingport, Pennsylvania, for the first commercial nuclear power plant in the fall of 1954.

### The 1956 Election and the Second Term

With the nation at peace and the economy booming, Eisenhower easily defeated Adlai Stevenson in 1956. Eisenhower lost only seven states, trouncing Stevenson with 35.6 million to 26 million votes. But two years later, the Democrats all but wiped out the Republican Party, gaining a 64–34 majority in the Senate and a 282–135 advantage in the House. Though "Ike" captured voters' hearts, a majority of them remained wedded to the programs and policies of the Democrats.

In part because of the Democratic resurgence, Eisenhower's leadership faced more serious challenges in his second term. The economy plunged into a recession in late 1957, and unemployment rose to 7 percent. Eisenhower fought with Congress over the budget and vetoed a number of bills providing for expanded public works projects, a high level of price supports for farmers, and housing and urban development.

In the end, the first Republican administration after the New Deal left the size and functions of the federal government intact, as it tipped federal policy somewhat more in favor of corporate interests. Unparalleled prosperity graced the Eisenhower years, and inflation was confined to an annual average of 1.5 percent. The nation experienced two recessions in the 1950s, but the economy recovered without putting to a test the president's aversion to substantial federal intervention.

# Liberation Rhetoric and the Practice of Containment

Eisenhower wrote in 1951 that the nation's foreign policy should seek "for the United States to obtain certain raw materials to sustain its economy, and, when possible, to preserve profitable foreign markets for our surpluses." What distinguished Eisenhower's foreign policy from Truman's was its rhetoric, its means, and—after Stalin's death in 1953—its overtures toward accommodation with the Soviet Union.

Republican rhetoric, voiced most prominently by Secretary of State John Foster Dulles, deplored containment because it accepted the existing Soviet sphere of influence and control. Yet, despite promises to roll back Soviet power and liberate peoples under Communist rule, the Eisenhower administration carried out a policy of containment. It directed anticommunism at the margins of Communist power in Asia, the Middle East, and Latin America, not at its core in Europe. Eisenhower assigned nuclear weapons and secret operations larger roles in defense strategy. He avoided involvement in new wars and took steps to ease tensions between the superpowers.

### The "New Look" in Foreign Policy

To meet his goals of balancing the budget and cutting taxes, Eisenhower had to control military expenditures. Moreover, he feared that massive defense spending would threaten the internal economic strength of the nation. A state based on warfare could destroy the very society it was intended to protect. As he declared in 1953, "Every gun that is made, every warship launched, every rocket fired signifies, in the final sense, a theft from those who hunger and are not fed, those who are cold and not clothed."

---

*What distinguished Eisenhower's foreign policy from Truman's was its rhetoric, its means, and—after Stalin's death in 1953— its overtures toward accommodation with the Soviet Union.*

---

Thus, Eisenhower's defense strategy concentrated U.S. military strength in nuclear weapons. Instead of spending huge amounts for a large standing army, the United States would give friendly nations American weapons and back them up with an ominous nuclear arsenal. This was Eisenhower's "New Look" in foreign policy. Air power and nuclear weapons provided, in John Foster Dulles's words, "maximum deterrent at bearable cost" or, as Defense Secretary Charles Wilson put it, a "bigger bang for the buck." Dulles believed that America's willingness to "go to the brink" of war with its intimidating nuclear superiority would make the Soviets halt any efforts to extend the territory under their control.

Although the Soviets quickly developed nuclear weapons, the United States retained its superiority and deterrence capability. Nuclear bombs and missiles could not stop a Soviet attack, but they could inflict almost unimaginable destruction on the Soviet Union. The certainty of that "massive retaliation" was meant to deter the Soviets from launching an attack in the first place. Because the Soviet Union could respond similarly to an American first strike, this delicately balanced nuclear standoff became known as "mutually assured destruction," or MAD. Winston Churchill called it a "mutual balance of terror."

Nuclear weapons were useless, however, in rolling back the iron curtain, because they would destroy the very peoples that the administration promised to liberate. When an opportunity for liberation emerged in Hungary in 1956, such promises proved to be empty rhetoric. Unwilling to risk U.S. soldiers and a possible nuclear war, Eisenhower rebuffed the Hungarian Freedom Fighters' pleas for help, and Soviet troops suppressed the insurrection, killing thirty thousand Hungarians.

### Applying Containment to Vietnam

Accepting the status quo in Europe, the Eisenhower administration sought to contain communism in other parts of the world. The major challenge to that commitment came in Southeast Asia, where a nationalist coalition called the Vietminh, led by Ho Chi Minh, had declared the independence of Vietnam from France in 1945. When France fought to maintain its colony, Ho fought back, and the area plunged into war (see Map 29.2 in Chapter 29). Because Ho declared himself a Communist, the Truman administration had quietly begun to provide aid to the French.

Eisenhower viewed communism in Vietnam much as Truman had regarded it in Greece and Turkey. "You have a row of dominoes set up," Eisenhower said, and "you knock over the first one, and what will happen to the last one is the certainty that it will go over very quickly." The president warned that the fall of Southeast Asia to communism could well trigger the fall of Japan, Taiwan, and the Philippines. By 1954, the United States was contributing 75 percent of the cost of France's war. But the soldier-president also had a realistic view of American capabilities and interests. When in 1954 the French, trapped in their military base at Dien Bien Phu, asked for troops and airplanes from the United States, Eisenhower firmly said no. He would not commit U.S. troops to another ground war in Asia. Dien Bien Phu fell in May 1954 and with it the French colony of Vietnam.

Two months later in Geneva, France signed a truce. The Geneva accords drew a temporary line across the seventeenth parallel of Vietnam and prohibited either the Vietminh in the North or the puppet government that the French had set up in the South from joining a military alliance or permitting foreign bases on their soil. Within two years, the Vietnamese people were to vote in elections for a unified government. The United States promised to support free elections, but it did not sign the accords.

The French defeat in Vietnam did not cause Eisenhower to abandon containment in Asia. Instead, he tried to prop up the dominoes with a new alliance. In September 1954, the United States joined with Britain, France, Australia, New Zealand, Thailand, Pakistan, and the Philippines in the Southeast Asia Treaty Organization (SEATO), committed to the defense of Cambodia, Laos, and South Vietnam.

Seeking to make South Vietnam a bulwark against communism, the United States repeated most of the mistakes that had doomed the French. The ink was barely dry on the SEATO treaty when the United States began to send weapons and military advisers to South Vietnam. Knowing that the election mandated by the Geneva accords would result in a victory for Ho Chi Minh, the United States supported South Vietnamese Prime Minister Ngo Dinh Diem in his refusal to hold the election, in effect violating the Geneva agreement.

Between 1955 and 1961, the United States poured $1 billion into South Vietnam, 80 percent of which went to the South Vietnamese army (ARVN). Yet even with U.S. dollars, the ARVN proved to be grossly unprepared for the guerrilla warfare that began in the late 1950s. In 1959, Ho Chi Minh's government in Hanoi began sending military assistance to Vietminh rebels in the South, who stepped up their guerrilla attacks on the Diem government. The insurgents gained control over villages not only through sheer military power but also because peasants were outraged by Diem's repressive regime. Unable to reverse the growing opposition to Diem in the South and unwilling to abandon containment, Eisenhower passed the deteriorating situation on to his successor, John F. Kennedy, in 1961.

## Interventions in Latin America and the Middle East

While attempting to buttress friendly governments in Asia, the Eisenhower administration also worked to topple unfriendly ones in Latin America and the Middle East. Much more than Truman, Eisenhower relied on behind-the-scenes efforts and covert activities against such governments. Increasingly, the administration conducted foreign policy behind the back of Congress.

Taking extreme care not to leave a paper trail, Eisenhower authorized the Central Intelligence Agency (CIA), headed by Allen Dulles, the brother of the secretary of state, to eliminate a threat to U.S. interests in oil-rich Iran. In 1951, Iran's left-leaning prime minister, Mohammed Mossadegh, nationalized oil fields and refineries, thereby setting a precedent that threatened Western oil interests throughout the Middle East. Mossadegh also challenged the power of the shah, Mohammad Reza Pahlavi, Iran's hereditary leader, who favored foreign oil interests and the Iranian wealthy classes. Moreover, Mossadegh accepted support from the Iranian Communist Party.

With Eisenhower's approval, CIA agents bribed army officers and paid Iranians to demonstrate against Mossadegh's government. In August 1953, army officers took Mossadegh prisoner, and the shah's power was reestablished. Iran renegotiated oil concessions, giving U.S. companies a 40 percent share. Although the intervention worked in the short run, Americans in the 1970s and 1980s would feel the full fury of Iranian opposition to the repressive government that the United States had helped to reinstall.

Heady with the success in Iran, the Eisenhower administration soon turned to clandestine activities in Central America, where it perceived a Communist threat in Guatemala. As in Iran, the Guatemalan government was not Communist or Soviet-controlled, but it accepted support from the native Communist Party and threatened established economic interests. Authorized by Eisenhower, the CIA staged a coup in 1954, displacing the popularly elected government of Jacobo Arbenz with a military dictatorship. In both Guatemala and Iran, U.S. intervention thwarted the popular will, set up repressive dictatorships, and helped American corporations.

"We're going to take care of Castro just like we took care of Arbenz," promised a CIA agent when Cubans' desire for political and economic autonomy erupted in 1959. American companies had long controlled a large portion of Cuba's major resources, especially sugar and tobacco, and decisions made in Washington directly influenced the lives and livelihoods of the Cuban people. When an uprising led by Fidel Castro drove out dictator Fulgencio Batista, who had been supported by the United States, CIA director Dulles warned Eisenhower that "Communists and other extreme radicals appear to have penetrated the Castro movement." The United States denied Castro's requests for loans, and he turned for help to the Soviet Union and began to nationalize the property of U.S. companies. Eisenhower broke off diplomatic relations with Cuba and authorized the CIA to train Cuban exiles for an invasion. Time ran out on Eisenhower, and he bequeathed the Cuban situation, along with Vietnam, to the next administration.

In the Middle East, the Eisenhower administration turned from Truman's all-out support for Israel and attempted to foster friendships with Arab nations. But the smaller Arab nations preferred to seek aid from both the West and the Communist nations and rejected American insistence on complete loyalty to the United States. In 1955, Secretary of State Dulles began negotiating with Egypt about American support for building the Aswan Dam on the Nile River (see Map 30.1). But in 1956, Egypt's leader, Gamal Abdel Nasser, declared his intention to obtain arms from Communist Czechoslovakia, formed a military alliance with other Arab nations, and recognized the People's Republic of China.

Unwilling to tolerate such independence, Dulles called off the deal for the dam. On July 26, 1956, Nasser responded boldly by seizing the Suez Canal, then owned by Britain and France. Taking the canal advanced Nasser's prestige and power because it coincided with nationalist aspirations in the Arab world; and revenue from the canal could provide capital for constructing the dam. Britain and France immediately protested the canal seizure, but Eisenhower announced that the United States would not participate in military efforts to settle the Suez crisis. He recognized that the Egyptians had claimed their own territory, and he believed that Nasser "embodie[d] the emotional demands of the people . . . for independence."

Since the establishment of Israel in 1948, Egyptian and Israeli forces had engaged in skirmishes along their common border. When Egypt seized the Suez Canal, Israel attacked Egypt, with military support from France and Britain. Shocked and angered, Eisenhower cut off oil to Britain and France while calling on the United Nations to arrange a truce. Lacking U.S. support, the French and British soon pulled back, forcing Israel to retreat from territory it had captured in the Sinai Desert region of Egypt.

Although Eisenhower refused to intervene in the Suez crisis, he made clear that the United States

**FIDEL CASTRO TRIUMPHS IN CUBA**

*Castro came from a privileged family and attended law school at the University of Havana, but he spent his youth working for the overthrow of Cuban dictator Fulgencio Batista. After leading an assault on Batista's soldiers in 1953, he spent two years in prison and then slowly built up an army of guerrilla fighters. He is shown here during his triumphal entrance into Havana in January 1959.*
Corbis-Bettmann.

would actively combat communism in the Middle East. In March 1957, Congress passed a joint resolution approving economic and military aid to any Middle Eastern nation "requesting assistance against armed aggression from any country controlled by international communism." The president invoked this "Eisenhower Doctrine" to send aid to Jordan in 1957 and troops to Lebanon in 1958 to counter anti-Western pressures on those governments.

## The Nuclear Arms Race

A number of events encouraged Eisenhower to seek reduction of superpower tensions and accommodation with the Soviet Union. After Stalin's death in 1953, a more moderate leadership under Nikita Khrushchev emerged. The Soviet Union signed a peace treaty with Austria guaranteeing Austrian neutrality and removed its troops from that country. Like Eisenhower, Khrushchev worried about the domestic costs of the cold war and wanted to reduce defense spending and check the arms race.

Eisenhower and Khrushchev met in Geneva in 1955 at the first summit conference since the end of World War II. Though the summit produced no significant agreements, it nevertheless symbolized a lessening of tensions—as Eisenhower put it, "a new spirit of conciliation and cooperation." In 1959, Khrushchev visited the United States, and Nixon went to the Soviet Union. By 1960, the two sides were within reach of a ban on nuclear testing, and Khrushchev and Eisenhower agreed to meet again in Paris in May.

To avoid jeopardizing the summit, Eisenhower decided to cancel espionage flights over the Soviet Union, but his order came one day too late. On May 1, Soviet gunners shot down a U-2 spy plane over Soviet territory. Assuming that the pilot, Francis Gary Powers, had not survived, the State Department denied that U.S. planes had been deliberately violating Soviet air space. When the Soviets produced not only Powers but also the photos taken on his flight, they caught the United States in a lie. Eisenhower assumed responsibility but refused to apologize. He met with Khrushchev briefly in Paris, but the U-2 incident dashed all prospects for a nuclear arms agreement and aborted Eisenhower's planned visit to Moscow.

Eisenhower's "more bang for the buck" defense budget increased enormously the U.S. nuclear capacity. Between 1958 and 1960 alone, the stockpile of nuclear weapons tripled from six thousand to eighteen thousand. By the time Eisenhower left office in 1961, the United States had installed seventy-two intercontinental ballistic missiles (ICBMs) in the United States and Britain, was prepared to deploy additional missiles in Italy and Turkey, and had several hundred more under contract. The first Polaris submarine carrying nuclear missiles was launched in November 1960.

In August 1957, the Soviets test-fired their first intercontinental ballistic missile; two months later, they launched *Sputnik,* the first artificial satellite to circle the planet. *Sputnik* spread a sense of national humiliation that the United States lagged behind not only in missile development and space exploration but also in science, education, economic growth, and national resolve. When the United States tried to launch a response to *Sputnik,* its satellite exploded. Newspapers expressed the humiliation by calling it a "Stayputnik" or a "Flopnik." The United States finally launched its first satellite in January 1958.

---

*When the Soviets produced not only the pilot of the U-2 spy plane but also the photos taken on his flight, they caught the United States in a lie. The U-2 incident dashed all prospects for a nuclear arms agreement.*

---

Eisenhower insisted that the United States possessed nuclear superiority and took steps to diminish public panic. He established the National Aeronautics and Space Administration (NASA) in July 1958, approved a gigantic increase in the budget for space research and development, and signed the National Defense Education Act in 1958, providing loans and scholarships for students in math, foreign languages, and science.

Yet nuclear superiority did not guarantee security. Though the Soviet Union lagged behind the United States in military technology, it nonetheless possessed sufficient nuclear weapons to devastate the United States. American schoolchildren regularly dove under their desks during drills in preparation for a nuclear attack, and the Civil Defense Administration recommended that families construct home bomb shelters. Most American families did not build shelters, but they realized how precarious nuclear weapons had made their lives.

Just before he left office, Eisenhower emphasized another menace of the nuclear age: the growing influence of the "military-industrial complex"

**CHILDREN IN THE AGE OF NUCLEAR ANXIETY**
*As schools routinely held drills to prepare for possible Soviet attacks, children directly experienced the anxiety and insecurity of the 1950s nuclear arms race. The Soviet launching of* Sputnik *in 1957 intensified American fears and led to an even greater focus on civilian defense.*
Archive Photos.

in American government and life. To contain the defense budget, Eisenhower had struggled against persistent pressures from defense contractors who, in tandem with the military services, sought more dollars for newer, more powerful weapons systems. In his farewell address, he warned that the "conjunction of an immense military establishment and a large arms industry . . . exercised a total influence . . . in every city, every state house, every office of the federal government." The cold war had created a warfare state.

## Winners and Losers in an Economy of Abundance

Military spending helped to stimulate domestic prosperity. Economic productivity increased enormously in the 1950s, consumption of a multitude of new products became the order of the day, millions of Americans moved to the suburbs, and higher education became the norm for the middle class. Although every section of the nation enjoyed the new prosperity, the West and Southwest especially boomed in production, commerce, and population.

The nature of work changed, as farm labor continued to decline, white-collar employment overtook manufacturing jobs, and women's employment grew. These economic shifts disadvantaged some segments of the population, and some 40 million people—20 percent of all Americans—lived in poverty. Most Americans, however, enjoyed a higher standard of living, leading the economist John Kenneth Galbraith to call the United States "the affluent society."

## Technology Transforms Agriculture and Industry

Between 1940 and 1960, the output of American farms mushroomed, while the number of farmworkers declined by nearly one-third. Farmers achieved nearly miraculous agricultural productivity through greater crop specialization, more intensive use of fertilizers, and, above all, mechanization. Tractors, mechanical pickers, and other forms of machinery increasingly replaced human labor and animal power. The mechanical cotton picker alone replaced fifty people and reduced the cost of picking a bale of cotton from forty dollars to five dollars.

The decline of the family farm and the growth of large commercial farming, or "agribusiness," were both causes and consequences of mechanization. Larger farmers benefited handsomely from federal price support programs, and they more easily took advantage of technological improvements, while smaller producers lacked capital to invest in the machinery that was required to compete. Consequently, although the average farm size more than doubled between 1940 and 1964, the farm population declined from thirty million to thirteen million, and the number of farms decreased by more than 40 percent.

---

*Economic productivity increased enormously in the 1950s, consumption of a multitude of new products became the order of the day, millions of Americans moved to the suburbs, and higher education became the norm for the middle class.*

---

Many small farmers constituted a core of rural poverty that escaped the attention of those who celebrated the affluence of the 1950s. Southern sharecroppers fell victim to the transformation of agriculture, forced off the land when owners replaced them with machinery. Hundreds of thousands of African Americans joined an exodus to cities in the South, North, and West, where racial discrimination and a lack of jobs for which they could qualify mired them in urban poverty. A Mississippi woman whose family had worked on a plantation since slavery recalled that when her family heard that "it was going to be machines now that harvest the crops," most of her relatives went to Chicago. Worrying that "it might be worse up there," she faced an agonizing choice: "I'm afraid to leave and I'm afraid to stay, and whichever I do, I think it might be real bad for my boys and girls."

Although about one of every five Americans continued to live below the poverty line in 1960, economists claimed that some 60 percent of the population enjoyed middle-class incomes. Between 1950 and 1960, the gross national product (the value

of all goods and services produced during the year) as well as median family income grew by 25 percent in constant dollars. By the late 1950s, when the nation's population stood at 175 million, there were 74 million cars on the road. Four of every five families owned television sets and washing machines, and nearly all had refrigerators.

A number of forces spurred this unparalleled abundance. Even with Eisenhower's conservative fiscal policies, government spending reached $80 billion annually and stimulated the creation of jobs. A population explosion—from 140 million in 1945

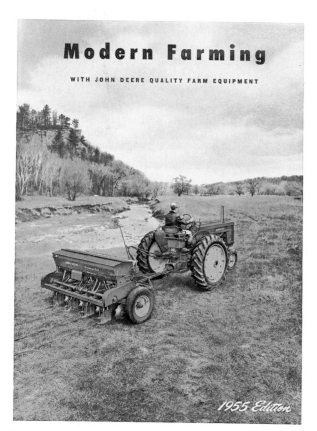

**MECHANIZING AGRICULTURE**
*This farm equipment ad reflects the growing application of technology to agriculture. Ever more elaborate machinery created a long-term trend in which family farms were overtaken by agribusiness. Giant farms employed the latest technology and thus reduced the need for human labor. Between 1945 and 1960, the nation's population living on farms shrank from 17.5 to 8.7 percent.*
John Deere Company.

to 176 million in 1960—expanded demand for products, and the rapidly growing youth population stimulated industries ranging from baby goods to records. Consumer borrowing also fueled the boom, as more and more people purchased houses, cars, and appliances on installment plans. The nation's dominance in the international economy meant that American producers found abundant markets for their products abroad and faced relatively little foreign competition in the domestic economy.

As in agriculture, technological innovation increased industrial production. In the automobile industry, for example, new technology cut the number of labor-hours needed to manufacture a car by one-half between 1945 and 1960. Technology also transformed such industries as electronics, chemicals, and air transportation and promoted the growth of newer industries, such as television and computers.

Labor unions enjoyed their greatest success during the 1950s as production workers saw their real earnings increase by 40 percent. The AFL-CIO merger in 1955 lessened jurisdictional conflicts and enabled labor to speak with one voice. Fringe benefits—pensions, health care, insurance, and paid vacations—became a staple of union contracts in most industries, though workers in the steel, automobile, and other heavy industries did much better than those in food processing, garment making, and other areas of light manufacturing.

The absolute number of union members continued to increase, but union membership as a percentage of the labor force peaked at 27.1 percent in 1957. Automation and other forces chipped away at jobs in heavy industry, where most union workers were concentrated. Technological advances reduced the number of workers in the steel, copper, and aluminum industries by 17 percent. Moreover, the economy as a whole was shifting from production (blue-collar) work to service (white-collar) occupations. Instead of manufacturing products, the typical worker now distributed goods, provided services, kept records, provided education, or peformed government work. Although unions made headway in some of these fields, most white-collar employees resisted unionization.

Female workers joined the workforce during the 1950s at a rate four times that of men. By the end of the decade, 35 percent of all women over age sixteen worked outside the home—twice as many as in 1940—and women held more than one-third of all jobs. Moreover, the largest increases in employment occurred for married women, who sought a second family paycheck to take advantage of the new commercial abundance. Women entered a sharply segregated workplace. The vast majority worked in clerical and service jobs, light manufacturing, domestic jobs, teaching, and nursing. Union organizers neglected most of these areas, and because they were female occupations, wages were relatively low. In 1960, the average female worker, employed full-time all year, earned just 60 percent of the average wage for a male worker. At the bottom of the employment ladder, black women earned, on average, 42 percent of what white men earned.

## Burgeoning Suburbs and Declining Cities

Although suburbs had existed since the nineteenth century, nothing symbolized the affluent society more than the move to the suburbs: Of the thirteen million new homes built in the 1950s, eleven million appeared in the suburbs, and more than one million Americans moved there every year. By 1960, one in every four Americans lived in the suburbs. And the suburbs were accessible to families with modest incomes. William J. Levitt pioneered construction of affordable housing with his 17,000-home development, called Levittown, on Long Island, New York. Modifying the assembly line process developed for automobiles by Henry Ford, Levitt planned nearly identical houses so that each construction worker could move from house to house and perform the same single operation in each, such as caulking windows or installing bathtubs. Individuals could purchase these mass-produced houses for just under $8,000 in 1949. Developments similar to Levittown, as well as more luxurious ones, quickly went up around metropolitan areas throughout the country.

While private industry built the suburbs, the government made home ownership possible by guaranteeing low-interest mortgages through the Federal Housing Administration and the Veterans Administration. A veteran could move into Levittown with payments of just $58 per month for twenty-five years. Thousands of interstate highway miles ran through urban areas, indirectly subsidizing suburban development. Without the automobile and the freeway, the suburban explosion would not have been possible.

Although the new suburbanites enjoyed the convenience and spaciousness of their new homes

**AN AFRICAN AMERICAN SUBURB**
*The pioneer of mass-produced suburban housing, William J. Levitt, reflected the racism that kept blacks out of suburbia when he said, "We can solve a housing problem, or we can try and solve a racial problem but we cannot combine the two." These African Americans developed their own suburb, a planned community for middle-class blacks in Richmond, California, which welcomed the first families in 1950.*
Courtesy Richmond Public Library.

and the social activities of their new neighborhoods, suburban culture was not without critics. Architecture critic Lewis Mumford blasted the suburbs as "a multitude of uniform, unidentifiable houses, lined up inflexibly, at uniform distances, on uniform roads, in a treeless communal wasteland, inhabited by people of the same class, the same income, the same age group." The growing suburbs did contribute to a more polarized society, especially along racial lines. Each Levittown homeowner signed a contract that "no dwelling shall be used or occupied by members of other than the Caucasian race." Although the Supreme Court declared such covenants unenforceable in 1948, suburban America remained almost exclusively white.

Blacks moved instead to cities in search of economic opportunity. In most cities, the number of black residents grew by 50 percent during the 1950s,

and Washington, D.C., became the first major city with a black majority. The newcomers came to cities that were already in decline, losing not only population but also commerce and industry to the suburbs. New manufacturing and wholesaling facilities began to ring central cities, and shoppers gradually chose suburban malls over downtown department stores. Many of the new jobs lay beyond the reach of the new black residents of the inner cities.

## The Democratization of Higher Education

The affluent postwar years spectacularly transformed higher education. Between 1940 and 1960, enrollments leaped from 1.5 million to 3.6 million, outstripping population growth. Whereas about

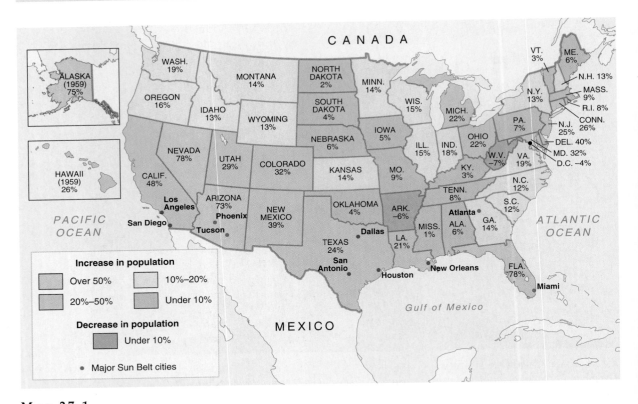

MAP 27.1
*The Rise of the Sun Belt, 1940–1980*
*The growth of defense industries, a nonunionized labor force, and the spread of air conditioning all helped spur economic development and population growth, which made the Sun Belt the fastest-growing region of the nation between 1940 and 1980.*

15 percent of college-age youths attended college in 1940, more than 40 percent did so by the mid-1960s. Higher education was no longer the domain of the privileged. Prosperity enabled many families to keep their children out of work and in school longer, and the federal government subsidized the education of more than 2 million World War II and Korean War veterans. The cold war also sent millions of federal dollars to universities for defense-related research. Total tax dollars spent for higher education more than doubled from 1950 to 1960, as state governments vastly expanded the number of four-year colleges and universities, and municipalities began to build two-year junior or community colleges.

The GI Bill made college possible for thousands of African Americans, the majority of whom attended black colleges. College enrollments of blacks surged from 37,000 in 1941 to 90,000 in 1961. Yet African Americans constituted only about 5 percent of all college students, less than half their percentage in the general population. Unlike their white counterparts, black men and women attended college in nearly equal numbers.

Initially, the democratization of higher education increased the gap in status between white men and women. The numbers of women college students grew, but their situation declined relative to that of men. In 1940, women constituted 40 percent of college graduating classes, but as veterans flocked to college campuses, women's proportion declined to just 25 percent in 1950. Even by 1960, women accounted for just 33 percent of college degrees.

## The Rise of the Sun Belt

The nation seemed to be tipped westward, quipped architect Frank Lloyd Wright: Everything not bolted down was sliding toward California. No region experienced the postwar economic and population boom more intensely than the West and Southwest. California's population more than doubled after World War II; by 1962, California overtook New York as the most populous state. A warm climate and a beautiful natural environment drew new residents to the West and Southwest, but no magnet proved stronger than the promise of economic opportunity.

As railroads had spurred western growth in the nineteenth century, the automobile and airplane helped generate the post–World War II surge, providing efficient transportation for both people and products. The aerospace industry boomed in Seattle–Tacoma, Los Angeles, Tucson, and Dallas–Fort Worth, and military bases helped underwrite prosperity in such cities as San Diego and San Antonio and throughout the so-called Sun Belt, which stretched from Florida to California (Map 27.1). The technology of air conditioning made possible industrial development in the Sun Belt and contributed to the population explosion there, cooling nearly eight million homes by 1960.

Although defense dollars benefited regions such as New England, with its electronics and research and development operations, the West captured the lion's share of cold war spending for research and production of bombers, missiles, other weapons, and satellites. In California alone, the federal government spent more than $100 billion for defense between 1945 and 1965. Nearly one of every three California workers held a defense-related job.

The high-technology basis of postwar economic development drew well-educated, highly skilled workers to the West. But the economic promise also attracted the poor. "We see opportunity all around us here. . . . We smell freedom here, and maybe soon we can taste it," commented a black mother in California. Between 1945 and 1960, more than one-third of the African Americans who left the South moved to the West.

The Mexican American, or Chicano, population also grew, especially in California and Texas. To supply California's vast agribusiness industry, the government continued the *bracero* program begun during World War II. Until the program ended in 1964, more than 100,000 Mexicans entered the United States each year to labor in the fields, and many of them stayed, legally or illegally. But while the government encouraged the use of Mexican labor, it responded to white Americans' opposition to permanent Mexican immigration, launching in 1954 a series of raids called "Operation Wetback."

**ROUNDING UP UNDOCUMENTED MIGRANTS**
*Not all Mexican Americans who wanted to work in the United States were accommodated by the* bracero *program. In 1953, Los Angeles police arrested these men who did not have legal documents and were hiding in a freight train. Americans used the crude term* wetback *to refer to illegal immigrants because many of them swam across the Rio Grande, on the border between the United States and Mexico.* Corbis-Bettmann.

Designed to ferret out and deport illegal immigrants, the operation made U.S. citizens of Mexican descent feel unwelcome and threatened them with incidents of mistaken identity.

Native Americans increased their numbers but also suffered under new government policies. In 1953, the Eisenhower administration introduced the policy called "termination," which aimed to end the special status of American Indians, eliminate their reservations, and do away with tribal sovereignty. Termination fit well with Eisenhower's preference for a limited federal government, but it proved devastating for Native Americans and was abandoned in the 1960s. Yet 170,000 Indians moved off their reservations, and, like most of the blacks who migrated from the South, they most typically exchanged rural poverty for urban poverty.

## The Culture of Abundance

With increased prosperity in the 1950s, more people married and the birthrate soared. Interest in religion quickened at the same time that Americans sought satisfaction in material possessions. Television entered the homes of most Americans, helping to promote a "consumer culture." Dominant values favored family life and traditional gender roles, consumption, conformity, and "belongingness." Undercurrents of rebellion, especially among youth, defied some of the dominant norms but did not disrupt greatly the complacency of the 1950s.

### The Revival of Domesticity and Religion

The entrance of married women into the workforce in unprecedented numbers coexisted with the dominant ideology that celebrated traditional family life and conventional gender roles. Even though more than one-third of mothers with school-age children left the home for work, the family ideal defined by popular culture and public figures persisted: a male breadwinner, a full-time homemaker, and three or four children living a safe, comfortable life in a new suburban home. Americans were eager to realize a traditional norm that had been disrupted by economic depression in the 1930s and war in the 1940s.

Writer and feminist Betty Friedan gave a name to the idealization of women's domestic roles in her book *The Feminine Mystique*, published in 1963.

Friedan claimed that advertisers, social scientists, educators, women's magazines, and public officials all encouraged women to seek their ultimate fulfillment in serving others through marriage and childrearing. According to the feminine mystique, biological differences fitted men and women for entirely different roles in life. The ideal woman kept a spotless house, cooked creative meals, raised her children to be good citizens, served her husband's career, and provided him emotional and sexual satisfaction. In 1956, *Life* magazine had declared, "Of all the accomplishments of the American woman, the one she brings off with the most spectacular success is having babies."

Although the glorification of domesticity clashed with married women's increasing participation in the labor force, the lives of many Americans did in fact embody the family ideal. Postwar prosperity enabled more people to rush to the altar and to have more children. In 1960, some 68 percent of all adults were married, the largest percentage in the twentieth century. After declining for a century, the birthrate soared after 1945, reaching a peak in 1957 with 4.3 million births and producing the "baby boom" generation (Figure 27.1).

The norms for childrearing were more demanding than ever before. Magnifying the importance of maternal attention in the child's daily development, Dr. Benjamin Spock's best-selling *Common Sense Book of Baby and Child Care* (1946) advocated a permissive approach in place of the more traditional emphasis on strictness and rigid schedules. Such an approach required that mothers devote their full time to childrearing. Experts in the 1950s also urged fathers to cultivate family "togetherness" and spend more time with their children.

*The entrance of married women into the workforce in unprecedented numbers coexisted with the dominant ideology that celebrated traditional family life and conventional gender roles.*

Along with a renewed emphasis on family life, the 1950s witnessed a surge of interest in religion. By 1960, about 63 percent of Americans belonged to churches and synagogues, up from 50 percent in 1940. Polls reported that 95 percent of all Americans professed a belief in God and 90 percent prayed. Evangelism took on new life, most notably in the nationwide crusades of Baptist minister Billy

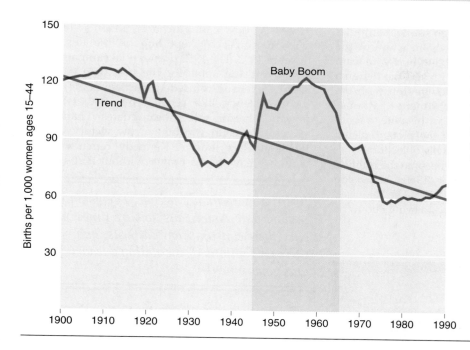

**FIGURE 27.1**
*U.S. Birthrate, 1900–1990*
*Notice the long-term trend of decline in birthrate over the twentieth century. What helps to account for the unusual plunge in the 1930s and the steep but temporary ascent in the 1950s?*

Graham, whose passionate and powerful oratory moved mass audiences to accept Christ. President-elect Eisenhower expressed the enthusiasm of the religious revival when he proclaimed in 1952 that "our government makes no sense unless it is founded on a deeply felt religious faith—and I don't care what it is!" Although religious conflict did not disappear, greater cooperation was evident in ecumenical movements such as the World Council of Churches, organized in 1948. Congress linked religion more closely to the state by adding "under God" to the pledge of allegiance in 1954 and by requiring in 1955 that "In God We Trust" be printed on all currency. Eisenhower's pastor attributed the renewed interest in religion to economic progress, which "provided the leisure, the energy, and the means for a level of human and spiritual values never before reached." Others suggested that Americans sought reassurance and peace of mind from cold war anxieties and the threat of nuclear annihilation.

Social critics questioned the depth of the religious revival, attributing the growth in church membership to a desire for conformity and a social outlet. One commentator, for example, noted that 53 percent of Americans could not name any book of the New Testament. The popularity of the Reverend Norman Vincent Peale, whose best-selling book *The Power of Positive Thinking* emphasized how

to be successful and happy, suggested to critics the superficiality of Americans' attachment to religion.

## Television Transforms Culture and Politics

In 1950, fewer than 10 percent of American homes boasted a television set, but by 1960 about 87 percent of all households owned one. On the average, Americans spent more than five hours each day in front of the screen, another respite from the anxieties of the cold war.

Television kept people at home more but did not necessarily enhance family relationships. When parents and children focused their attention on the TV screen, their conversation was limited. The new medium altered eating habits when, in 1954, the frozen dinner, a complete meal in an easily portable tray, enabled families to spend the dinner hour in front of the TV set. Noticing that the heaviest water consumption took place on the hour and the half hour, civil engineers in Toledo, Ohio, recognized that television regulated even trips to the bathroom.

Especially popular were situation comedies, which projected the family ideal and the feminine mystique into millions of homes. On TV, women with families did not work outside the home and ostensibly deferred to their husbands, though they often got the upper hand through subtle manipulation. In the most popular television show of the early 1950s, *I Love Lucy,* the husband-and-wife team of Lucille Ball and Desi Arnaz played the fictional couple Lucy and Ricky Ricardo. In step with the trends, they moved from an apartment to a house in suburbia. Ricky refused to allow his wife to work outside the home, and many of the plots depicted Lucy's zany attempts to thwart his objections.

Although TV news did not become the public's main source of news until the 1960s, television began to affect politics in the 1950s. The televised Army-McCarthy hearings helped to bring about the

**THE MADE-FOR-TV FAMILY**
*This scene is from the popular television sitcom* Father Knows Best, *which ran from 1954 to 1963 and which, along with other shows such as* Ozzie and Harriet *and* Leave It to Beaver, *idealized white family life. In these shows, no one got divorced or gravely ill, no one took drugs or seriously misbehaved, fathers held white-collar jobs, mothers did not work outside the home, and husbands and wives slept in twin beds.*
Culver Pictures/Rob Huntley, Lightstream/Picture Research Consultants, Inc.

senator's downfall. Richard Nixon's televised "Checkers speech" kept him on the Republican ticket in 1952. The 1952 presidential campaign used TV advertising spots for the first time, although Adlai Stevenson refused to participate in "selling the presidency like cereal." By 1960, television played a major role in candidates' chances for success. Reflecting on his narrow victory in 1960, President-elect John F. Kennedy remarked, "We wouldn't have had a prayer without that gadget."

*In little more than a decade, television came to dominate Americans' leisure time, influence their consumption patterns, and shape their perceptions of the nation's leadership and government.*

Unlike government-financed television in Europe, private enterprise paid for American TV through advertising, and advertisers did not hesitate to interfere with shows that might jeopardize the sale of their products. On the *Camel News Caravan,* for example, the sponsor, producer of Camel cigarettes, insisted that any film clips showing "No Smoking" signs be cut. Television became the major vehicle for selling the products of an affluent society; the soap manufacturer Procter and Gamble, for example, spent more than 90 percent of its advertising budget on TV.

In 1961, Newton Minow, chairman of the Federal Communications Commission, called television a "vast wasteland." While acknowledging some of TV's great achievements, particularly documentaries and drama, Minow depicted television programming as "a procession of game shows, . . . formula comedies about totally unbelievable families, blood and thunder, mayhem, violence, sadism, murder . . . and cartoons." But viewers kept tuning in. In little more than a decade, television came to dominate Americans' leisure time, influence their consumption patterns, and shape their perceptions of the nation's leadership and government.

## Countercurrents

Signals of unrest and dissent underlay the complacency of the 1950s. Some intellectuals took exception to the politics of consensus and to the materialism and conformity celebrated in popular culture. In *The Lonely Crowd* (1950), sociologist David Riesman expressed dismay at a shift from the "inner-directed" to the "other-directed" individual. In contrast to the independent thinking that had been at the heart of the American character in the past, Riesman found a regrettable eagerness to adapt to external standards of behavior and belief.

Other critics shared Riesman's distaste for the importance of "belonging" and the fear of seeming different. In his popular book *The Organization Man* (1956), William H. Whyte Jr. saw the villain as the modern corporation, whose employees had to tailor their behavior and ideas to get along with the group. According to Whyte, these "organization men" sacrificed risk taking and independence in favor of dull conformity.

Less direct challenges to mainstream culture's standards appeared in the everyday behavior of large numbers of Americans, especially youth. "Roll over Beethoven and tell Tchaikovsky the news!" belted out Chuck Berry in his hit record. White teenagers lionized Elvis Presley, who shocked their elders with his tight pants, hip-rolling gestures, and sensuous music, a blend of country and western and black rhythm and blues. "Before there was Elvis . . . I started going crazy for 'race music,'" recalled a white man of his teenage years. "It had a beat. I loved it. . . . That got me into trouble with my parents and the schools." This man's experience illustrates African Americans' contributions to rock-and-roll music as well as the rebellion expressed by white youths' attraction to black music.

Just as rock and roll's sexual suggestiveness violated norms of middle-class respectability, the sexual behavior of many Americans departed from the family ideal of the 1950s. Two books published by Alfred Kinsey and other researchers at Indiana University, *Sexual Behavior in the Human Male* (1948) and *Sexual Behavior in the Human Female* (1953), uncovered a surprising range of sexual conduct. In a survey of eighteen thousand individuals, Kinsey found that 85 percent of the men and 50 percent of the women had had sex before marriage; 50 percent of the husbands and 25 percent of the wives had engaged in extramarital sex; and one-third of the men and one-seventh of the women reported homosexual experience. Although Kinsey's sampling procedures cast doubt on his ability to generalize across the population, the books became best-sellers. They also drew a firestorm of outrage. Evangelist Billy Graham protested "the damage this book will do to the already deteriorating morals of America," and the Rockefeller Foundation stopped funding Kinsey's work. Critics objected most to Kinsey's refusal to make moral judgments about his findings.

The most extreme rebellion against conventionality came from the self-proclaimed Beat generation, a small group of literary figures based in New York City's Greenwich Village and in San Fran-

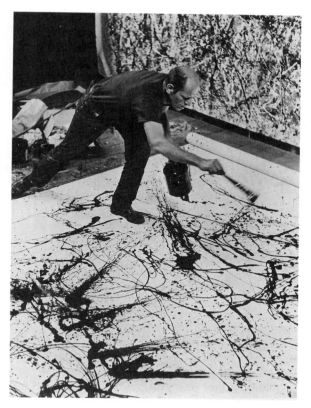

**JACKSON POLLOCK**

*The leading artist in the post–World War II revolution in painting, Jackson Pollock illustrates his technique of pouring and splattering paint onto the canvas. He worked with the canvas on the floor because, he said, "I feel nearer, more a part of the painting. . . . I can walk around it, work from the four sides and be literally 'in' the painting."*

Jackson Pollock, 1950 photograph by Hans Namuth © 1991 Hans Namuth Estate. Courtesy, Center for Creative Photography, Tucson.

cisco. Rejecting nearly everything in mainstream culture—patriotism, consumerism, technology, conventional family life, discipline—they favored spontaneity and absolute personal freedom, which included drug consumption and freewheeling sex. In his landmark poem *Howl* (1956), Allen Ginsberg inveighed against "Robot apartments! invisible suburbs! skeleton treasuries! blind capitals! demonic industries! . . . monstrous bombs!" and denounced the social forces that "frightened me out of my natural ecstasy!" Another leading member of the Beat generation, Jack Kerouac, wrote the best-selling novel *On the Road* (1957). The Beats' rebelliousness would provide a model for a much larger movement of youthful dissidents in the 1960s.

Developments in the visual arts also showed the 1950s to be more than a decade of bland conventionality. An artistic revolution that flowered in New York City redirected approaches to painting throughout the Western art world. Known as "action painting," "abstract expressionism," or the "New York school," this movement rejected the idea that painting should represent recognizable forms. Jackson Pollock and other abstract expressionists poured, dripped, and threw paint on canvases or substituted sticks and other implements for brushes. Their work emphasized energy and spontaneity, and it so captivated the art world that New York replaced Paris as its center.

# Emergence of a Civil Rights Movement

African Americans conducted the most dramatic challenge to the status quo of the 1950s as they sought to break the chains that had replaced the bonds of slavery. Every southern state mandated rigid segregation in public settings ranging from hospitals and schools to drinking fountains and rest rooms. Southern voting laws and practices disfranchised the vast majority of African Americans; employment discrimination kept them at the bottom of the economic ladder.

Although black protest was as old as American racism, in the 1950s that protest developed into a grassroots movement that attracted national attention and the support of white liberals. The Supreme Court initiated significant institutional reforms, but blacks themselves directed the most important changes. Ordinary African Americans in substantial numbers sought their own liberation, building a movement that would transform race relations in the United States.

## A Sympathetic Court and a Reluctant President

Between 1940 and 1960, more than three million African Americans moved out of the South into areas where they could vote and exert pressure on white politicians. In the South itself, African Americans controlled resources that were essential to a mass movement. The very system of segregation kept black talents within the African American community and encouraged the development of

black churches and colleges which developed leadership skills and provided a mass base and organizational network.

The legal strategy of the major civil rights organization, the National Association for the Advancement of Colored People (NAACP), reached its crowning achievement with the Supreme Court decision in *Brown v. Board of Education* in 1954. NAACP lawyers, led by Thurgood Marshall, who would later be appointed to the Supreme Court, urged the Court to overturn the fifty-eight-year-old precedent established in *Plessy v. Ferguson* (1896), which had enshrined "separate but equal" as the law of the land. A unanimous court, headed by Chief Justice Earl Warren, declared, "Separate educational facilities are inherently unequal" and thus violated the Fourteenth Amendment. In 1955, after waiting a year to deal with implementation, the Court called for desegregation "with all deliberate speed" but established no deadline.

Ultimate responsibility for enforcement of *Brown* lay with President Eisenhower, but he refused to endorse the decision or to urge the South to comply. Eisenhower's inaction fortified southern officials' determined resistance to school desegregation and contributed to the gravest constitutional crisis since the Civil War. The crisis came in Little Rock, Arkansas, in September 1957. Local officials dutifully prepared for the integration of Central High School, but on the first day of school, Governor Orval Faubus sent National Guard troops to block the enrollment of nine black students, claiming that their presence would cause public disorder.

*Although black protest was as old as American racism, in the 1950s that protest developed into a grassroots movement that attracted national attention and the support of white liberals.*

After nearly three weeks, Faubus agreed to allow the black students to enter, but he withdrew the National Guard, leaving the nine students to face an angry mob of whites. As television cameras transmitted the ugly scene across the nation, Eisenhower was forced into action. He sent in one thousand regular army troops and took federal control of the Arkansas National Guard. In this first federal military intervention in the South since Reconstruction, Eisenhower stated clearly that he acted

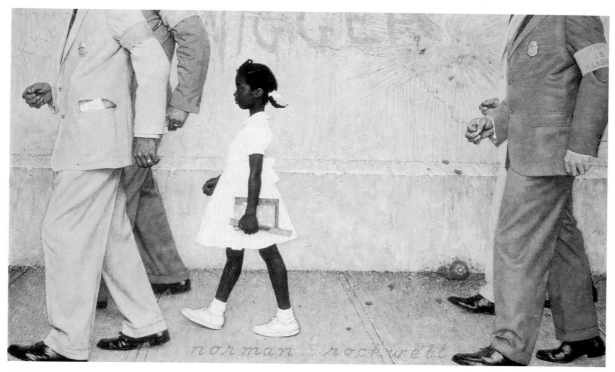

**SCHOOL INTEGRATION**

*In 1964, the popular artist Norman Rockwell painted* The Problem We All Live With, *based on the experience of Ruby Bridges during the 1962 integration of the New Orleans public schools. He hoped through this painting to get people to realize what America was doing to its children. How do the composition of the scene and the characteristics of the people indicate Rockwell's intentions?*

Norman Rockwell Family Trust and Curtis Archives.

not to achieve integration, but to enforce the law. Escorted by paratroopers, the black students stayed in school, and Eisenhower withdrew the army in November. Other southern cities avoided integration by closing public schools and using tax dollars to support private, white-only schools. In 1961—nearly seven years after the Supreme Court had outlawed segregation—only 6.4 percent of southern black students attended integrated schools. (See Texts in Historical Context on page 750.)

Eisenhower did order the integration of public facilities in Washington, D.C., and at military bases, and he supported the first federal civil rights legislation since Reconstruction, the Civil Rights Acts of 1957 and 1960. Although they established federal bodies to focus on civil rights, the laws represented only marginal progress toward the enfranchisement of blacks. In fact, baseball star Jackie Robinson spoke for many African Americans when he wired

Eisenhower, "We disagree that half a loaf is better than none. Have waited this long for bill with meaning—can wait a little longer."

Forceful and decisive in foreign affairs, Eisenhower saw no moral imperative in civil rights and moved in that arena only with the greatest reluctance. He appointed the first black professional to the White House staff, but E. Frederick Morrow confided to his diary, "I feel ridiculous . . . trying to defend the administration's record on civil rights." Morrow later remembered Eisenhower as "a great, gentle, and noble man . . . but neither intellectually nor emotionally disposed to combat segregation."

## Montgomery and Mass Protest

What set the civil rights movement of the 1950s and 1960s apart from earlier protests were the great numbers of people involved, blacks' willingness to

# *The* **Brown** *Decision*

*T*he Brown *decision along with a second Supreme Court ruling in 1955 about implementing desegregation outraged many southern whites. In 1956, more than one hundred members of Congress signed a manifesto pledging resistance to the decision.*

*I*n 1954, Chief Justice Earl Warren delivered the unanimous opinion of the Supreme Court in Brown v. Board of Education of Topeka, *declaring racial segregation in public education unconstitutional and explaining why.*

### DOCUMENT 1. *Brown v. Board of Education of Topeka,* **May 1954**

In these days, it is doubtful that any child may reasonably be expected to succeed in life if he is denied the opportunity of an education. Such an opportunity, if the state has undertaken to provide it, is a right that must be made available to all on equal terms. . . .

We come then to the question presented: Does segregation of children in public schools solely on the basis of race, even though the physical facilities and other "tangible" factors may be equal, deprive the children of the minority group of equal educational opportunities? We believe that it does. . . .

In *McLaurin* [a 1950 case], the Court, in requiring that a Negro admitted to a white graduate school be treated like all other students, again resorted to intangible considerations: " . . . his ability to study, to engage in discussions and exchange views with other students, and, in general, to learn his profession." Such considerations apply with added force to children in grade and high schools. To separate them from others of similar age and qualifications solely because of their race generates a feeling of inferiority as to their status in the community that may affect their hearts and minds in a way unlikely ever to be undone.

We conclude that in the field of public education the doctrine of "separate but equal" has no place. Separate educational facilities are inherently unequal. . . .

### DOCUMENT 2. **Southern Manifesto on Integration, March 1956**

We regard the decision of the Supreme Court in the school cases as a clear abuse of judicial power. It climaxes a trend in the Federal judiciary undertaking to legislate . . . and to encroach upon the reserved rights of the states and the people.

The original Constitution does not mention education. Neither does the Fourteenth Amendment nor any amendment. . . . The Supreme Court of the United States, with no legal basis for such action, undertook to exercise their naked judicial power and substituted their personal political and social ideas for the established law of the land.

This unwarranted exercise of power by the court, contrary to the Constitution, is creating chaos and confusion in the states principally affected. It is destroying the amicable relations between the white and negro races that have been created through ninety years of patient effort by the good people of both races. It has planted hatred and suspicion where there has been heretofore friendship and understanding. . . .

We pledge ourselves to use all lawful means to bring about a reversal of this decision which is contrary to the Constitution and to prevent the use of force in its implementation.

*I*n the face of white hostility, black children carried the burden of implementing the Brown *decision. The following accounts by black students reflect varied experiences, but even those who entered white schools fairly easily found obstacles to their full participation in school activities. Nonetheless, they cherished the new opportunities, favoring integration for reasons different from those given by the Supreme Court.*

## DOCUMENT 3. A High School Girl in the Deep South, May 1966

The first day a news reporter rode the bus with us. All around us were state troopers. In front of them were federal marshals. When we got to town there were lines of people and cars all along the road. A man without a badge or anything got on the bus and started beating up the newspaper reporter. . . . He was crying and bleeding. When we got to the school the students were all around looking through the windows. The mayor said we couldn't come there because the school was already filled to capacity [and] if six of us came in it would be a fire hazard. He told us to turn around and go back. We turned around and the students started yelling and clapping. When we went back [after obtaining a court order] there were no students there at all. There were only two teachers left so they had to bring a couple of teachers from other places. [The white students did not return, so the six black students finished the year by themselves.] The shocking thing was during the graduation ceremonies. All six of the students got together to make a speech. After we finished, I looked around and saw three teachers crying. The principal had tears in his eyes and he got up to make a little speech about us. He said at first he didn't think he would enjoy being around us. You could see in his face that he was really touched. We said something like we really enjoyed school together and that we were glad they stuck it out and all that kind of stuff.

## DOCUMENT 4. A High School Boy in Oak Ridge, Tennessee, 1957

I like it a whole lot better than the colored school. You have a chance to learn more and you have more sports. I play forward or guard on the basketball team, only I don't get to participate in all games. Some teams don't mind my playing. Some teams object not because of the fellows on the team, but because of the people in their community. Mostly it's the fans or the board of education that decides against me. . . . The same situation occurs in baseball. I'm catcher, but the first game I didn't get to participate in. A farm club of the major league wrote the coach that they were interested in seeing me play so maybe I'll get to play the next time.

## DOCUMENT 5. A High School Girl in the Deep South, May 1966

I chose to go because I felt that I could get a better education here. I knew that the [black] school that I was then attending wasn't giving me exactly what I should have had. As far as the Science Department was concerned, it just didn't have the chemicals we needed and I just decided to change. When I went over the students there weren't very friendly and when I graduated they still weren't. They didn't want us there and they made that plain, but we went there anyway and we stuck it out. The lessons there were harder, lots harder, but I studied and I managed to pass all my subjects.

## DOCUMENT 6. A High School Girl in Louisville, Kentucky, 1957

I'm accepted now as an individual rather than as a person belonging to the Negro race. People say to me, "I'm glad I met you because if I met someone else I might not have liked them." I don't think it's fair, this individual acceptance. I feel like I was some ambassador from some foreign country.

I couldn't go out for any extracurricular activities. Cheerleading, band, drum majorettes, the people who are members of these organizations, they go to camps in the summer which are segregated. Well, what can you do? It just leaves me out. It's not the school, it's the community.

**Document 1.** *Brown,* 347 U.S. 483 (1954).

**Document 2.** "Southern Manifesto on Integration" (1956).

**Document 3.** *In Their Own Words: A Student Appraisal of What Happened after School Desegregation* (Washington, D.C.: Department of Health, Education, and Welfare, Office of Education, 1966), 17–18.

**Document 4.** Dorothy Sterling, *Tender Warriors* (New York: Hill and Wang, 1958), 83.

**Document 5.** *In Their Own Words: A Student Appraisal of What Happened after School Desegregation* (Washington, D.C.: Department of Health, Education, and Welfare, Office of Education, 1966), 44.

**Document 6.** Dorothy Sterling, *Tender Warriors* (New York: Hill and Wang, 1958), 83.

confront white institutions directly, and the use of nonviolence and passive resistance to bring about change. The Congress of Racial Equality (CORE) and other groups had experimented with these tactics in the 1940s, but the first sustained protest to claim national attention occurred in Montgomery, Alabama, in 1955 and 1956.

On December 1, 1955, Montgomery police arrested a black woman, Rosa Parks, for violating a local segregation ordinance by refusing to give up her seat on a city bus to a white man. Parks had long been active in the local NAACP, and this was not the first time that she had rebelled against segregation. Her arrest galvanized Montgomery civil rights leaders who had been considering a challenge to segregation. On December 5, they founded the Montgomery Improvement Association (MIA) to organize and maintain a bus boycott among the African American community. The MIA ran an alternative transportation system, marshaled more than 90 percent of the black community to sustain the year-long boycott, and mounted a legal challenge that persuaded the Supreme Court to strike down the bus segregation ordinance in November 1956.

Elected to head the MIA was Martin Luther King Jr., a newcomer to Montgomery and pastor at the Dexter Avenue Baptist Church in Montgomery. Only twenty-six years old, King rose to the chal-

lenge of the boycott. Day after day, Montgomery blacks gathered at their churches to plan strategy and receive instructions and inspiration. A captivating speaker, King summoned their courage and inspired commitment by linking racial justice to the redeeming power of Christian love. He promised, "If you will protest courageously and yet with dignity and Christian love . . . historians will have to pause and say, 'There lived a great people—a black people—who injected a new meaning and dignity into the veins of civilization.' This is our challenge and our overwhelming responsibility."

Montgomery blacks summoned their courage and determination in abundance. They walked miles to get to work, contributed their meager financial resources, and stood up with dignity and discipline to legal, economic, and physical intimidation. They demonstrated that even without the ballot, they could struggle successfully against oppression.

In January 1957, black clergy from across the South met to coordinate local protests against segregation and to secure the ballot for blacks. They founded the Southern Christian Leadership Conference (SCLC) and chose King to head it. Although ministers dominated the SCLC, its success owed much to Ella Baker, a seasoned activist who came from New York to set up and run its office.

**MONTGOMERY CIVIL RIGHTS LEADERS**
*During the Montgomery, Alabama, bus boycott of 1955–1956, local white officials harassed African Americans with arrests and lawsuits. Here Rosa Parks, catalyst of the boycott and one of ninety-two defendants, ascends the steps of the Montgomery County courthouse in March 1956. She is accompanied by E. D. Nixon, a forceful civil rights leader and her longtime friend and associate in the Montgomery NAACP.* Wide World.

**MARTIN LUTHER KING JR. IN MONTGOMERY**
*During the Montgomery bus boycott, Martin Luther King Jr. preaches at the First Baptist Church, the congregation of Ralph D. Abernathy, the man who would become King's close associate in the crusades to come. The crucial role that black churches played in the black freedom struggle was not lost on white racists, who bombed First Baptist and three other black churches in Montgomery during the boycott.*
Dan Weiner, courtesy Sandra Weiner.

King's face on the cover of *Time* magazine in February 1957 marked his rapid rise to national and international fame. He crisscrossed the nation and the world, speaking to large audiences, raising funds, and meeting with other activists. In June 1958, Eisenhower extended his first invitation to black leaders, and King and three others met with the president. Meanwhile, in the late 1950s, the SCLC, NAACP, and CORE developed centers in several southern cities, paving the way for a mass movement that would revolutionize the racial system of the South.

## Conclusion: Assessing the "Ike Age"

At the American exhibition in Moscow in 1959, the combination of consumer goods that Nixon proudly displayed to Khrushchev and the cold war competition that crackled through their conversation reflected two dominant themes of the 1950s: the prosperity of the U.S. economy and the superpowers' success in keeping cold war competition within the bounds of peace. The tremendous economic growth of the 1950s and rising standard of living for most

Americans depended in part on cold war spending; one of every ten American jobs depended directly on defense spending.

The Eisenhower administration curbed domestic programs and favored big business, but it maintained the basic foundations of the welfare state. Eisenhower's insistence on moderation, consensus, and a limited federal role meant that he did not rally the nation behind efforts to promote racial justice and that he launched no major programs to deal with social problems such as urban poverty, health care, and public education.

In global affairs, Eisenhower demonstrated restraint and a recognition of the limits of U.S. power. In the name of deterrence, he promoted development of more destructive atomic weapons, but he resisted pressures for even larger defense budgets. Even though the United States and the Soviet Union made no substantive progress in solving cold war issues, Eisenhower began negotiations and helped to lessen tensions between the superpowers. Eisenhower took from Truman the assumption that the United States must fight communism everywhere and passed it on to the next administration. He sympathized with national liberation movements, but when movements in Iran, Guatemala, and Vietnam seemed too radical, too friendly to communism, or too inimical to American economic interests, he tried to undermine them, often with secret operations.

Thus, although Eisenhower presided over eight years of peace and prosperity, his foreign policy inspired anti-Americanism, established dangerous precedents for the expansion of executive power, and forged commitments that future generations would deem unwise. As Eisenhower's successors took on the struggle against communism and grappled with domestic problems he had avoided, the tranquility and consensus of the 1950s would give way to the turbulence and conflict of the 1960s.

## CHRONOLOGY

**1952** Dwight D. Eisenhower elected president of United States.

*I Love Lucy* becomes number one television show.

**1953** Government begins policy of termination of special status of American Indians and relocates thousands off reservations.

CIA engineers coup against government of Mohammed Mossadegh in Iran.

Julius and Ethel Rosenberg executed for passing atomic secrets to Soviet Union.

**1954** CIA stages coup against government of Jacobo Arbenz in Guatemala.

Eisenhower administration begins aid program to government of South Vietnam.

Government launches Operation Wetback, series of raids designed to seek out and deport illegal immigrants.

Ground broken in Pennsylvania for first commercial nuclear power plant.

U.S. Supreme Court declares segregation in public schools unconstitutional in *Brown v. Board of Education.*

United States organizes Southeast Asia Treaty Organization (SEATO) in wake of French defeat in Vietnam.

**1955** Eisenhower and Khrushchev meet in Geneva for first superpower summit since end of World War II.

**1955–1956** Montgomery, Alabama, bus boycott by African Americans focuses national attention on civil rights.

**1956** Interstate Highway Act involves federal government in road-building activities previously done by state and local governments.

Eisenhower reelected by landslide to second term.

Allen Ginsberg publishes poem *Howl,* expressing rebelliousness of Beat generation.

**1957** Southern Christian Leadership Conference (SCLC) organizes and elects Martin Luther King Jr. its president.

Soviets launch *Sputnik,* first satellite to orbit Earth.

Labor union membership peaks at 27.1 percent of labor force.

**1958** United States and Soviet Union suspend nuclear testing in atmosphere.

**1958–1960** U.S. nuclear weapons stockpile triples in size.

**1960** Soviets shoot down U.S. U-2 spy plane, causing rift in U.S.-Soviet relations.

Women represent one-third of labor force; 35 percent of women work outside the home.

One-quarter of Americans live in suburbs.

# SUGGESTED READINGS

Stephen E. Ambrose, *Eisenhower,* vol. 2, *The President* (1984). A generally admiring account of Eisenhower's eight years in office.

Erik Barnouw, *Tube of Plenty: The Evolution of American Television* (2nd rev. ed., 1990). The classic account of the development of TV.

Taylor Branch, *Parting the Waters: America in the King Years, 1954–63* (1988). The most thorough treatment of Martin Luther King Jr. and early civil rights activism.

Robert Ellwood, *The Fifties Spiritual Marketplace: American Religion in a Decade of Conflict* (1997). A survey of diverse and competing forms of religion and spirituality in the 1950s.

Peter Guralnick, *Last Train to Memphis: The Rise of Elvis Presley* (1994), and *Careless Love: The Unmaking of Elvis Presley* (1999). A sensitive two-volume biography that assesses Presley's human failings as well as his drive to encompass various American musical forms.

David Halberstam, *The Fifties* (1993). Lively chapters on Korea, civil rights, fast food, motels and other new industries, birth control, and other key political, economic, social, and cultural developments of the 1950s.

Kenneth T. Jackson, *Crabgrass Frontier: The Suburbanization of the United States* (1985). The classic history of American suburbs.

James Howard Jones, *Alfred C. Kinsey: A Public/Private Life* (1998). An engaging, definitive biography of the sex researcher.

Karal Ann Marling, *As Seen on TV: The Visual Culture of Everyday Life in the 1950s* (1994). Fascinating essays on popular culture in the 1950s.

Joanne Meyerowitz, ed., *Not June Cleaver: Women and Gender in Postwar America, 1945–1960* (1994). A collection of essays describing the variety of women's roles and experiences.

Aldon D. Morris, *The Origins of the Civil Rights Movement: Black Communities Organizing for Change* (1984). A keen analysis and account of the various roots of the black freedom struggle.

Chester J. Pach Jr. and Elmo Richardson, *The Presidency of Dwight D. Eisenhower* (rev. ed., 1991). The most recent survey of the Eisenhower administration.

**"COUNTRY JOE" MCDONALD'S GUITAR**
Music was an omnipresent element of protest movements in the 1960s. Civil rights demonstrators sang, "We Shall Overcome," antiwar rallies featured folk singers, and hippies turned on to acid rock. The guitar was the central musical instrument for each kind of music: traditional African American, folk, and rock. This wooden acoustic guitar belonged to "Country Joe" McDonald, who started his band, Country Joe and the Fish, at a draft protest in Oakland in 1965. The band was one of many that originated in the San Francisco Bay area, but its popularity soon spread across the country.
The Oakland Museum of California.

# A DECADE OF REBELLION AND REFORM

# 28

## 1960–1968

I N THE SUMMER OF 1960, Tom Hayden went to Los Angeles to cover the Democratic National Convention for the University of Michigan *Daily*. The twenty-year-old white college student heard presidential candidate John F. Kennedy declare, "We stand on the edge of a New Frontier . . . of unfulfilled hopes and threats." The speech, Hayden reported, "stirred me deeply," but his encounter with Martin Luther King Jr. inspired him even more. Eight years later, when the Democrats met in Chicago, both Kennedy and King had been murdered. Hayden and thousands of other protesters were there in open rebellion against much of what the Democrats and the government stood for. Hayden's political journey through the 1960s—the fading of his initial hopes into anger and frustration—mirrored a more general shift among Americans from optimism and consensus to disillusionment and divisiveness.

While Kennedy issued a vague challenge to Americans to attack unsolved problems with idealistic service, King called for personal sacrifice. "Ultimately, you have to take a stand with your life," he told Hayden. In 1961, Hayden went south to work with black activists. There he joined a civil rights movement that shook the national conscience, raised hopes for the possibility of change, and provided a model of protest that inspired other marginalized groups.

The prosperity of the 1960s contributed to the popular belief that the federal government should advance social welfare. The two Democratic presidents favored an activist government and pursued a vigorous attack on social and economic problems. After John F. Kennedy was assassinated in November 1963, Lyndon B. Johnson launched the Great Society—a multitude of programs aimed at promoting general economic growth, improving the conditions of racial minorities and the poor, and reforming education, health care, urban development, and the environment. Pushing this transformation in domestic policy was the black freedom struggle, which took on new form and urgency in 1960 when African Americans in massive numbers began to apply the tactics of civil disobedience in demonstrations throughout the South. The protesters endured brutality, saw their homes and churches burned, and sometimes lost their lives, but by the end of the decade, law had caught up with the American ideal of equality.

Yet it did not catch up fast enough. Although the Supreme Court issued path-breaking decisions strengthening civil rights, the law had no effect on the deplorable economic conditions of African Americans. By 1966, a minority of African American activists demanded black power; the movement splintered and white support sharply declined. Yet the black freedom struggle stimulated a multitude of new social movements. Other racial and ethnic minorities, students, and women benefited from the visibility of the civil rights movement as well as from its ideas, tactics, and policy precedents.

Tom Hayden went from civil rights activism to student organizing to protest against U.S. involvement in Vietnam. He and other student radicals who formed what came to be called the New Left scorned the Great Society for failing to strike at the roots of America's unjust political and economic system. Conservatives cried that the Great Society went too far and expressed outrage at the wholesale challenge to American values and institutions mounted by blacks, students, and others. A decade that began with idealism and promise ended in disillusionment and polarization.

## Kennedy and the New Frontier

In his New Frontier speech that stirred Tom Hayden at the Democratic convention in 1960, John F. Kennedy promised to confront "unsolved problems of peace and war, unconquered pockets of ignorance and prejudice, unanswered questions of poverty and surplus." Once in office, Kennedy instituted an aggressive foreign policy, but not until his final months did massive grassroots pressures spur him to launch a substantial assault on the problems of racism and poverty. Before these efforts reached fruition, an assassin ended his life.

### The Style and Promise of the New Frontier

John F. Kennedy grew up in privilege, the son of an Irish Catholic businessman who served in Franklin D. Roosevelt's administration and nourished political ambitions for his sons. Helped by a distinguished World War II navy record, Kennedy won election to the House of Representatives in 1946 and the Senate in 1952. The Massachusetts senator set his sights on the White House for 1960, using his family's fortunes to build a superb political machine directed by his brother Robert.

With his overwhelming financial advantage, handsome appearance, and dynamic style, Kennedy triumphed in a series of state primaries. A critical

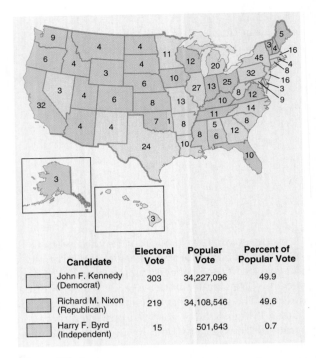

| Candidate | Electoral Vote | Popular Vote | Percent of Popular Vote |
|---|---|---|---|
| John F. Kennedy (Democrat) | 303 | 34,227,096 | 49.9 |
| Richard M. Nixon (Republican) | 219 | 34,108,546 | 49.6 |
| Harry F. Byrd (Independent) | 15 | 501,643 | 0.7 |

MAP 28.1
*The Election of 1960*

victory in West Virginia over Hubert H. Humphrey, the liberal senator from Minnesota, eliminated the question of his Catholicism, an issue that had doomed Al Smith's candidacy in 1928. After winning the nomination at the Democratic convention, Kennedy stunned nearly everyone by choosing Lyndon B. Johnson of Texas as his running mate. Although ticket balancing was a time-honored tradition, liberals detested the choice of a man whom they viewed as a typical southern conservative. The party platform, however, embodied liberal priorities, including the strongest civil rights plank the Democrats had ever endorsed.

The Republicans nominated Vice President Richard M. Nixon, who campaigned on his experience in the Eisenhower White House. While Kennedy promised to make the country stronger in the cold war, expand the welfare state, and increase the rate of economic growth, Nixon was stuck with defending the policies of the Eisenhower administration. The two candidates actually differed little, however, on defense and foreign policy questions.

Kennedy won the excruciatingly close election, helped in part by black voters. Nixon won 52 percent of the white vote, but the black preference for Kennedy gave him a 120,000-vote margin. In addition, Lyndon Johnson captured most of the South for the Democrats; and a third Eisenhower recession, which pushed unemployment above 6 percent in 1960, also contributed to the incumbent party's defeat (Map 28.1). Kennedy benefited as well from the first televised debates between presidential candidates, coming across as cool, experienced, handsome, and in command of the issues. Television also helped to increase interest in the campaign, which produced a 64 percent voter turnout, the highest in the twentieth century.

The Kennedy administration projected an aura of dynamism, idealism, and glamour. The nation warmed to images of a youthful president playing touch football, sailing with his chic and cultured wife, Jacqueline, and playing in the executive office with his young children. The Kennedys transformed the White House into a national showcase of culture and the arts, inviting prominent writers, artists, and musicians to visit and perform.

In his inaugural address, Kennedy called on all Americans to serve the common good. Declaring that a "new generation" was assuming leadership, he asked Americans to cast off the complacency and self-indulgence of the 1950s, to "ask not what your country can do for you—ask what you can do for your country." Kennedy described the cold war in a tone of crisis, emphasizing America's "role of defending freedom in its hour of maximum danger." He insisted, "If a free society cannot help the many who are poor, it cannot save the few who are rich"; yet his address gave domestic problems short shrift and delineated no specific programs. Still, his idealism inspired many, especially the young, to replace self-interest with service to a larger cause.

## The Substance of the New Frontier at Home

Commenting on John F. Kennedy's actions on civil rights, Martin Luther King Jr. described the president as "committed but . . . feeling his way," a char-

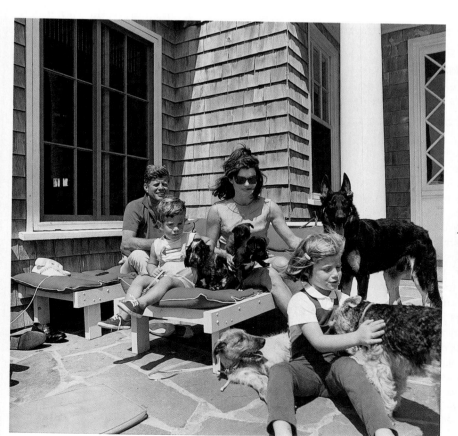

**THE KENNEDY FAMILY**
*John F. Kennedy's youthful good looks, glamorous background, and attractive family added to his appeal and continue to fascinate many Americans decades after his death. Here he relaxes with his wife, Jacqueline, and their children, Caroline and John, at their vacation home in Hyannisport on Cape Cod. This photograph was taken in August 1963, a few months before Kennedy's assassination.*
John F. Kennedy Library.

acterization that applied to Kennedy's domestic achievements in general. A number of factors account for the large gap between what Kennedy promised and what he was actually able to achieve. Despite the fact that his party controlled Congress, conservative southern Democrats combined with Republicans to block racial reform. Kennedy displayed much more zeal for foreign policy than for pursuing social justice and consigned domestic reform to a back burner.

Kennedy did win support for a two-billion-dollar slum clearance and urban renewal program; the Area Redevelopment Act of 1961, which gave incentives to businesses to locate in depressed areas; and the Manpower Development and Training Act of 1962, which provided training for the unemployed. But two key items on the Democratic agenda since the Truman administration, federal aid to education and health care for the elderly, got nowhere. Referring to a book Kennedy had published, *Profiles in Courage,* liberals jokingly expressed their dissatisfaction with his leadership by asking that he show "less profile and more courage."

*Kennedy displayed much more zeal for foreign policy than for pursuing social justice and consigned domestic reform to a back burner.*

Two initiatives of the Kennedy administration relating to women's rights received relatively little attention but had important ramifications. Although Kennedy had no particular interest in women's rights, in 1961 he heeded the advice of Esther Peterson, head of the Women's Bureau in the Department of Labor, to strengthen his support among women by appointing a President's Commission on the Status of Women. Chaired by Eleanor Roosevelt and composed of leaders from the government and private organizations, the commission reported its findings in October 1963, eight months after Betty Friedan had attacked sex discrimination in *The Feminine Mystique.* The commission report, *American Women,* identified widespread discrimination against women and recommended remedies. Spawning counterparts at the state level, the president's commission created networks of women aware of sex discrimination and eager for action.

The president's commission highlighted an area of discrimination that women's organizations and labor unions had been seeking to eliminate for two decades, the age-old custom of paying women less than men for doing the same work. They achieved their goal when Kennedy signed the Equal Pay Act in June 1963. Thereafter, wage disparities based solely on gender became illegal, and within a few years women began to win wage increases and back pay worth millions of dollars.

Kennedy believed that economic growth could solve most social problems, that increased production provided the best means to eradicate poverty and to make the nation more competitive with the Soviet Union. Key economic advisers argued that infusing money into the economy by reducing taxes would increase demand, boost production, and decrease unemployment. To that end, Kennedy asked Congress to pass an enormous tax cut in 1963. This use of fiscal policy to stimulate the economy even when there was no recession gained the name "the new economics."

Kennedy did not live to see approval of his bill. Passed in February 1964, the law contributed to the greatest economic boom since World War II. Unemployment dropped to 4.1 percent, and the gross national product shot up by 7 to 9 percent annually between 1964 and 1966. Some critics of the tax cut disputed its economic impact, pointing out that the surge was already under way. Conservatives warned that cutting taxes would result in a budget deficit and spark inflation. Liberals maintained that economic growth alone would not eliminate poverty, arguing instead for increased spending on social programs. Poverty had gained the Senate's attention in 1960, when a subcommittee reported "a growing and intense problem," the poverty of eight million older Americans, whose "declining years are without dignity." That same year Kennedy came face to face with the rural poor of Appalachia when he asked for their votes. In 1962, he read *The Other America,* Michael Harrington's devastating account of the hopelessness and wretched conditions endured by more than one in every five Americans.

The summer of 1963 marked a turning point in Kennedy's attitude toward domestic reform. In addition to asking aides to plan an attack on poverty, he issued a dramatic call for passage of a comprehensive civil rights bill. Whether he could have achieved these breakthroughs in domestic policy was left unanswered by his assassination on November 22, 1963.

**JOHN F. KENNEDY'S FUNERAL**
*For the few days following November 22, 1963, normal life stopped in the United States. Schools and businesses were closed, while tens of thousands of Americans traveled to Washington, D.C., to file past Kennedy's coffin in the rotunda of the Capitol. The relatively new medium of television unified the nation, as it allowed millions of viewers to experience every moment of that long, terrible weekend, culminating in the funeral procession, shown here. The president's widow, Jacqueline Kennedy, is escorted in the procession by the president's brothers Robert (left) and Edward.*
© Henri Dauman NYC.

## Assassination of a President

The murder of the president in Dallas, Texas, seared the consciousness of Americans as had no other event since the end of World War II. Within minutes of the shooting, radio and television broadcast the unfolding horror to the nation. Millions watched the return of *Air Force One* to Washington bearing the president's coffin, his widow in her blood-stained suit, and the new president, Lyndon Baines Johnson, who had taken the oath of office aboard the jet.

Stunned Americans struggled to determine what had happened and why. Soon after the shooting of Kennedy in a motorcade, police arrested Lee Harvey Oswald, and concluded that he had fired the shots from a nearby building. Two days later, as a television audience watched Oswald being transferred from one jail to another, a local nightclub operator, Jack Ruby, killed him. Suspicions arose that Ruby had killed Oswald to cover up a conspiracy.

Some people believed there had been a plot among ultraconservative Texans who hated Kennedy. Others suspected a Communist plot. To get at the truth and calm public fears, President Johnson appointed a commission headed by Chief Justice Earl Warren, which concluded in September 1964 that both Oswald and Ruby had acted alone. Several experts pointed to errors and omissions in the report, and later investigations both supported and contested the lone-killer explanation. As with Lincoln's assassination, the controversy persisted for decades.

Debate also continued over how to assess Kennedy's domestic record. It had been unremarkable in his first two years, but his initiatives on taxes, civil rights, and poverty in 1963 suggested an important turning point. Whether Kennedy could have persuaded Congress to enact his proposals cannot be known. In the words of journalist James Reston, "What was killed was not only the president but the promise. . . . He never reached his meridian: We saw him only as a rising sun."

## Johnson and the Great Society

Within six months of becoming president, Lyndon Johnson had found a theme for his administration. In May 1964, he announced the goal of a "Great Society, [which] rests on abundance and liberty for all. It demands an end to poverty and racial injustice." In pursuing that Great Society, Johnson got Congress to pass three civil rights acts and other legislation mandating an antipoverty program, education subsidies, medical care for the aged and poor, a massive housing program, consumer protection, pollution control, environmental preservation, and more. The legislation of the 1960s constituted a remarkable record of reform yet fell short of achieving the Great Society.

### Fulfilling the Kennedy Promise

Lyndon Johnson assumed the presidency with a wealth of political experience. A self-made man from the poor Texas hill country, he won election to the House of Representatives in 1937 and to the Senate in 1948. By 1955, he had secured the top post of Senate majority leader, which he used brilliantly to forge a Democratic consensus on the Civil Rights Acts of 1957 and 1960 and other liberal programs.

Johnson's coarse wit, excessive vanity, intense ambition, and Texas accent put off many who were accustomed to the sophisticated Kennedy style. But Johnson excelled behind the scenes where he could entice, cajole, or threaten legislators into support of his objectives. The famous "Johnson treatment" became legendary. In his ability to achieve his overriding goal of consensus—and in the means to which he was willing to resort—he had few peers in American history.

Mobilizing emotions aroused by the assassination, he asked Congress to act so that "John Fitzgerald Kennedy did not live or die in vain." By trimming the federal budget and promising government frugality, he won over fiscal conservatives and signed Kennedy's tax cut bill in February 1964.

Still more revolutionary was the Civil Rights Act of 1964, which banned discrimination in public accommodations, education, and employment. The president applied the Johnson treatment in full force to line up enough Republicans and southern Democrats to ensure passage. In July 1964, Johnson signed the strongest civil rights measure since Reconstruction.

Antipoverty legislation followed fast on the heels of the Civil Rights Act. In his first State of the Union message, Johnson called for "an unconditional war on poverty," and in August he signed the Economic Opportunity Act of 1964. The law authorized ten programs to be administered by a newly created Office of Economic Opportunity, allocating $800 million for the first year (about 1 percent of the federal budget). Many provisions were targeted at youth—from Head Start, a preschool program for poor children, to work-study grants for college students and job training programs for youth (the Job Corps). There were also loans to businesses willing

**THE "JOHNSON TREATMENT"**
*Abe Fortas was a distinguished lawyer who had argued one of the major criminal rights cases, Gideon v. Wainwright (1963), before the Supreme Court and who was a close friend and adviser to President Lyndon Johnson. When Johnson asked him to serve on the Supreme Court, he was reluctant to leave his lucrative law practice, and Johnson had to use his famous persuasive powers to secure his assent. This photograph of the president and Fortas taken in July 1965 illustrates how Johnson used his body as well as his voice to bend people to his will.*
Yoichi R. Okamoto/LBJ Library Collection.

to hire the long-term unemployed; aid to small farmers and rural businesses; and the Volunteers in Service to America (VISTA) program, which funded modest subsidies for volunteers working with the disadvantaged. A legal services program that provided lawyers for the poor resulted in lawsuits that enforced impoverished Americans' rights to welfare programs.

The most novel and controversial part of the law, the Community Action Program (CAP), required "maximum feasible participation" of poor people themselves in coordinating poverty programs. Unlike other aspects of the poverty program, this provision offered potential challenges to the system itself. Poor people began to organize community action programs to take control of their neighborhoods and to reform welfare agencies, school boards, police departments, housing authorities, and other agencies. Within months, mayors complained that activists were using federal funds to attack local governments and to "foster class struggle." Seeking to avoid conflict with mayors, Johnson directed federal poverty officials to back off from insistence on genuine representation for the poor. Although the CAP failed to live up to its promise, for the first time people who were routinely excluded from participating in government gained a voice, an incentive to act on their own behalf, and the opportunity to develop leadership skills.

## Completing the Great Society Agenda

Having steered the nation through the assassination trauma and established his capacity for national leadership, Johnson projected stability and security. With the economy booming, only a minority of voters proved willing to risk a change as dramatic as that promised by his Republican opponent in the 1964 election. Arizona Senator Barry M. Goldwater represented the right wing of U.S. politics, attacking the entire framework of the welfare state and suggesting the use of nuclear weapons if necessary to crush communism in Vietnam. Although Goldwater captured five states in the Deep South, Johnson accomplished a record-breaking landslide of 61 percent of the popular vote. On his coattails came resounding Democratic majorities in the House (295–140) and Senate (68–32).

Using a hunting analogy to stress his determination to make the most of his mandate, Johnson told his aides, "I want to see a whole bunch of coonskins on the wall." In the sheer amount and breadth of new legislation, Johnson succeeded extraordinarily, and public opinion polls gave impressively high

marks to both the president and Congress. Reporters called the legislation of the 89th Congress (1965–1966) "unprecedented" and "a political miracle."

The Economic Opportunity Act of 1964 had been just the opening shot in the War on Poverty. Congress increased the program's funding in 1965 to $2 billion and initiated two new assaults on poverty. The Appalachian Regional Development Act and the Public Works and Economic Development Act targeted depressed regions that the general economic boom had bypassed. These programs—like the tax cut of 1964—sought to help the poor indirectly by stimulating economic growth and providing jobs through road building and other public works projects.

*Johnson got Congress to pass three civil rights acts and other legislation mandating an antipoverty program, education subsidies, medical care for the aged and poor, a massive housing program, consumer protection, pollution control, environmental preservation, and more.*

A second approach promised to equip the poor with the training and skills necessary to find jobs. The largest assault on poverty through education was the Elementary and Secondary Education Act of 1965. Ever since establishing the land-grant college system in the nineteenth century, the federal government had funded education, but only for a specific purpose, such as science education in the National Defense Education Act of 1957. The 1965 legislation provided general aid, allocating funds to public school districts based on the number of poor children they educated and providing equipment and supplies to private and parochial schools to be used for poor children.

Other antipoverty efforts included a food stamp program that replaced the distribution of surplus commodities. Rent supplements also allowed some poor families more options, enabling them to avoid public housing projects, which often were massive high-rise buildings that afforded a poor environment for children. With the Model Cities Act, Congress authorized more than $1 billion to improve conditions in the nation's slums.

With the Higher Education Act of 1965, Congress vastly expanded federal assistance to colleges and universities, providing funds for buildings, programs, scholarships, and low-interest loans for students. In 1966, Congress renewed its commitment to education, appropriating nearly $4 billion for higher education for the next three years and $6.1 billion for a two-year extension of the elementary and secondary education program.

Congress also greatly increased the federal government's responsibility for health care. Trimming down the plan for universal care that Truman had proposed, Johnson focused his proposal on the elderly, who constituted a large portion of the nation's poor. Congress responded with the Medicare program, which provided the elderly with universal compulsory hospital insurance financed largely through Social Security taxes and a voluntary insurance program for other medical expenses funded by the government and individual contributions. The Medicaid program provided a system of federal grants to supplement state programs paying for medical care for poor people below the age of sixty-five.

In response to the growing force of the civil rights movement, Johnson persuaded Congress to pass the Voting Rights Act of 1965, which banned literacy tests and authorized federal intervention to enable African Americans to register and vote. (See the Historical Question on page 766.) The Immigration and Nationality Act of 1965 did away with the fifty-year-old quotas based on national origins, thereby ending discrimination against immigrants from areas outside northern and western Europe. It did, however, maintain caps on the number of immigrants and for the first time placed limits on immigration from the Western Hemisphere.

The benefits of the Great Society reached well beyond the poverty-stricken. Pressures from a growing consumer movement led by liberal activist Ralph Nader and others produced legislation to make automobiles safer and to raise standards for the food, drug, and cosmetics industries. In 1965, Johnson became the first president to send Congress a special message on the environment, obtaining measures to control water and air pollution and to preserve the natural beauty of the American landscape. The National Arts and Humanities Act of 1965 created programs to support artists, musicians, writers, and scholars and to bring their work to public audiences.

The flood of reform legislation dwindled to a trickle after 1966, when midterm elections reduced the Democrats' huge majorities in Congress. Even though a sizable majority of the poor were whites, the public tended to associate antipoverty programs with African Americans. The appearance of buttons reading "I fight poverty—I work" indicated a growing backlash against the disadvantaged. The Viet-

nam War dealt the largest blow to domestic reform. Growing opposition to the war diverted the president's attention from domestic affairs and put his entire leadership in jeopardy. Even more damaging was the war's cost, which rose to more than $2 billion a month by 1966, increased the federal deficit, and exerted inflationary pressures on the economy.

*The Vietnam War dealt the largest blow to domestic reform. Growing opposition to the war diverted the president's attention from domestic affairs and put his entire leadership in jeopardy.*

Against these odds, Johnson pried one more civil rights law out of Congress in 1968, which banned discrimination in housing, and he also secured a new housing program. The National Housing Act of 1968 authorized both an enormous increase in construction of low-income housing—1.7 million units over three years—and, by leaving construction and ownership in private hands, a new way of providing it. Poor people could purchase houses with low-interest loans guaranteed by the government, and developers could obtain low-interest loans to build housing for the needy.

## Assessing the War on Poverty

Measured by statistics, the reduction in poverty in the 1960s was significant. The number of impoverished Americans fell from forty million in 1959 to twenty-five million in 1968, from 22 percent of the population to around 13 percent (Figure 28.1). A growing number of people located the causes of poverty in economic and social circumstances rather than in individuals' shortcomings, and they assumed a national responsibility for alleviating it. Especially through the Community Action Programs, poor people themselves gained more control of their circumstances and a sense of their right to a fairer share of America's bounty.

Certain groups fared much better than others, however. Large numbers of the aged and members of male-headed families rose out of poverty, while the plight of female-headed families actually worsened. Although African American family income grew from 54 percent of white family income to 61 percent, whites escaped poverty at a faster rate than blacks, who constituted one-third of the poor population at the end of the decade. Moreover, despite the large increases in direct subsidies for food stamps, housing, medical care, and Aid to Families with Dependent Children (AFDC), a program launched by the New Deal, no significant redistribution of income resulted. The poorest 20 percent of the population received 5.1 percent of total national income in 1964 and 5.4 percent in 1974.

Conservatives charged that the Great Society programs discouraged initiative by giving the poor "handouts." Critics on the left claimed that the emphasis on training and education placed the responsibility for poverty on the poor themselves rather than on the economic system. Most job training programs prepared graduates for low-level occupations and could not guarantee jobs. Surveys in 1966 and 1967, for example, found 28 percent of Job Corps graduates unemployed six months after finishing their training.

Who reaped the greatest benefits from Great Society programs? Critics pointed out that most of the funds for Appalachia and other depressed areas built highways and thus helped the construction industry. Real estate developers, investors, and moderate-income families reaped the lion's share of benefits from the mortgage subsidies under the National Housing Act of 1968. Noting that in slum clearance programs, commercial development and high-income housing often displaced poor families, blacks called urban renewal "Negro removal." Physicians' fees and hospital costs soared after enactment of Medicare and Medicaid. Other beneficiaries of the Great Society programs were middle-class professionals who staffed the growing bureaucracy that ran the programs.

Some critics of the War on Poverty suggested that the solution to poverty lay in a major redistribution of income, through raising taxes and using those funds in the public sector to create jobs, overhaul social welfare systems, and rebuild slums. The Johnson administration programs did invest more heavily in the public sector, but funds for the poverty programs came from increasing revenues generated by economic growth, not from new taxes on the rich or middle class. Determined to promote consensus and avoid conflict, Johnson would not take from the advantaged to provide for the poor. Economic prosperity allowed spending for the poor to rise and significantly improved the lives of millions, but that spending never approached the amounts necessary to declare a victory in the war on poverty.

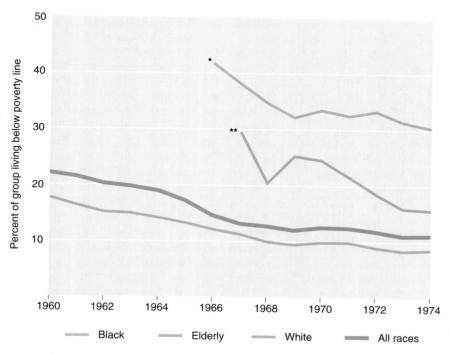

FIGURE 28.1
*Poverty in the U.S., 1960–1974*
*The short-term effects of economic growth and the Great Society's attack on poverty are seen here. Which groups experienced the sharpest decline in poverty and what might account for the differences?*

*Statistics on blacks for years 1960–1965 not available.
**Statistics on the elderly for years 1960–1966 not available.

# What Difference Did Black Voting Rights Make?

BORN TO POOR BLACK SHARECROPPERS in the Mississippi Delta, Unita Blackwell hearkened in church one Sunday in 1964 when an SNCC worker talked about voter registration. The very next day she went to the courthouse where, predictably, officials refused her application. Undeterred, she succeeded on the third try, threw herself into activism as an SNCC organizer, and saw her share of jail cells. In fact, she and her husband planned their protest activities so that only one would risk arrest and the other would remain free to care for their child. A founder of the Mississippi Freedom Democratic Party, which was established to challenge the all-white state organization, Blackwell saw the challenge compromised away at the 1964 Democratic National Convention. But four years later, she participated in the national convention with Mississippi's reconfigured biracial delegation. Subsequently, she served as vice chair of the state Democratic Party and on the Democratic National Committee. When her small town of Mayersville incorporated in 1976, Blackwell won election as its first mayor and the first black female mayor in Mississippi.

Blackwell's career is but one measure of the transformations generated by African Americans' struggle for the most basic right of citizenship. Their determination to register to vote and the resulting resistance and violence of southern whites created a crisis that the federal government could not ignore. Its response, the Voting Rights Act of 1965 and subsequent extensions, suspended the literacy tests that had been used to disqualify blacks but not whites and brought electoral operations in most southern states under federal supervision. The law required the Justice Department to approve in advance any changes in state procedures that might disadvantage black voters, and it empowered the attorney general to send federal agents to observe registration and election processes and even to register voters in areas of continued white resistance.

"Legislation is not self-implementing," noted NAACP leader Roy Wilkins. "There is work to be done." As was the case with its passage, implementation of the Voting Rights Act depended on the efforts of African Americans themselves. More than two hundred voter registration drives between 1966 and 1968 paid off in dramatic increases in the numbers of blacks registered. Throughout the South, the proportion of African Americans on voter rolls jumped from 43 percent in 1964 to 62 percent in 1968. In Mississippi, the percentage leaped from just 6.7 in 1964 to 68 percent in 1968.

African Americans also gained political offices in unprecedented numbers. Fewer than two dozen blacks held elective office in the South in 1964. In 1970, they claimed almost 500 elected government posts, and two years later the number reached nearly 1,200. Just seven years after whites bludgeoned civil rights activists during the Selma voting drive, black candidates won half of the 10 seats on Selma's city council. With the victories of Barbara Jordan from Houston, Texas, and Andrew Young from Atlanta, Georgia, in 1972, the former Confederacy sent its first African Americans to the House of Representatives since Reconstruction. Black electoral success was not limited to the South. Across the nation, African Americans held 1,500 elected positions in 1970, and by 1990 that number exceeded 7,000. The greatest progress came at the local level. The number of black mayors grew sixfold to more than 300 in the 1990s; the number of black city council members vaulted from 552 in 1970 to nearly 3,000 in 1989. The total of black representatives in Congress inched up from 10 in 1970 to 25 in 1990 and then soared to 38 in the 1992 elections.

Electoral success translated into tangible benefits. When black officials took office, their constituents saw improvements in public facilities, police protection, roads, trash collection, and other basic services. Referring to Unita Blackwell's accomplishments as mayor, a Mayersville resident noted, "She brought in the water tower. Mostly it was pumps then. . . . Sewage, too. There wasn't nothing but those little old outdoor houses." Another constituent pointed to "old folks' houses. And paved streets. I grew up here when they wasn't paved." Black local officials also awarded more government jobs to African Americans and contracts to minority businesses. Elected mayor of Atlanta in

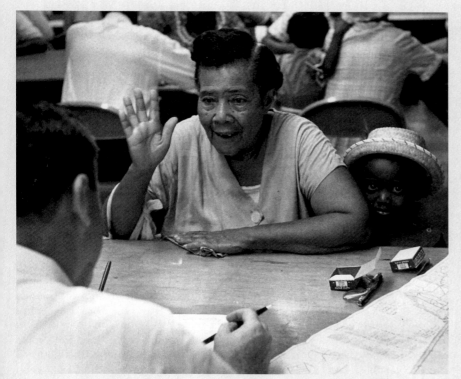

1973, Maynard Jackson appointed a black police chief and increased blacks' share of city jobs from 42 percent to 51 percent.

Most black officials had far less power than Jackson, but even when they were outnumbered by whites, they could at least introduce issues of concern to blacks that whites had ignored, and they gained access to information about behind-the-scenes government. An African American serving on a city council in Florida pointed out that "no matter what happened," his white colleagues "knew I was listening to everything that went on." Activist Fannie Lou Hamer noted the psychological benefits of electoral progress. When blacks had no political voice, she recalled, "some white folks would drive past your house in a pickup truck with guns hanging up on the back and give you hate stares. . . . Those same people now call me Mrs. Hamer."

Yet political power did not readily guarantee African Americans economic equality or even material security. Their minority status in the population and residential dispersion, combined with many whites' disinclination to vote for blacks, meant that even by the 1990s, African Americans occupied fewer than 2 percent of all elected positions in the nation. As African Americans looked to increase their political force and shape policy to meet their needs, they recognized that they would have to revive grassroots activism and seek coalitions with nonblacks. In addition they considered a number of electoral strategies to solidify black and minority strength in a majoritarian system: reducing the number of at-large elections, which dilute minorities' power, and increasing the number of single-member district systems; monitoring electoral redistricting to ensure as many black-majority districts as possible; and proportionate or cumulative voting.

Despite the limited reach of black enfranchisement, most experts nonetheless view the voting rights revolution as the most successful of all civil rights initiatives. As Unita Blackwell put it, "We didn't have nothing, and we changed the whole world with nothing. We changed a whole outlook."

# The Second Reconstruction

Unlike many of the Great Society reforms, which failed to live up to their promise and provoked widespread criticism, the civil rights movement effected a revolution in the legal status of African Americans and won widespread acceptance. The first Reconstruction in the aftermath of the Civil War had ended slavery and written racial equality into the Constitution; the second Reconstruction a century later made the guarantee of equal status under the law a reality. That accomplishment depended heavily on the courage and determination of black people themselves. In the words of Sheyann Webb, one of the thousands of marchers in the Selma, Alabama, campaign for voting rights, "We were just people, ordinary people, and we did it."

## The Flowering of the Black Freedom Struggle

The Montgomery bus boycott in the mid-1950s had given national visibility to the plight of southern blacks, produced a national leader in Martin Luther King Jr., and demonstrated the effectiveness of mass mobilization. Nevertheless, the boycott remained in a way a passive action—Montgomery blacks avoided riding the buses. In the 1960s, the form of protest underwent a major change, mobilizing blacks into direct and personal confrontation with the people and institutions that segregated and discriminated against them: lunch counters, department stores, public parks and libraries, buses and depots, and voting registrars.

Direct action as a mass movement began in February 1960, when four African American freshmen at North Carolina A&T College in Greensboro sat at the whites-only Woolworth's lunch counter and asked for service. Within days, hundreds of young people joined their demonstration. By the end of February, blacks had launched sit-ins in thirty-one cities in eight southern states. In April, Ella Baker, executive secretary of the Southern Christian Leadership Conference (SCLC), got activists together from college campuses, and they founded the Student Nonviolent Coordinating Committee (SNCC, pronounced "snick"), creating a decentralized, nonhierarchical structure that encouraged the development of leadership and decision making at the grassroots level. SNCC embraced civil disobedience and nonviolence; directly confronting the agents of oppression, students would stand up for their rights, but they would not practice self-defense against their enemies. At SNCC's founding conference, minister James Lawson defined a strategy for blacks that he believed could change the hearts of their oppressors: "We affirm . . . nonviolence as a foundation of our purpose, the presupposition of our faith, and the manner of our action."

When students returned to the field, their optimism and commitment to nonviolence met severe testing. Although some cities quietly accommodated to student demands, usually authorities and local citizens reacted with violence. Hostile whites poured food over demonstrators, burned them with cigarettes, called them "nigger," and pelted them with rocks. Local police went after protesters with clubs, fire hoses, and tear gas; they arrested more than 3,600 civil rights demonstrators in the year following the Greensboro sit-in.

In 1961, the Congress of Racial Equality (CORE) organized Freedom Rides to integrate interstate transportation. On May 4, six whites and seven blacks boarded two buses in Washington, D.C., for a thirteen-day ride to New Orleans. The riders crossed the color line without harm in Virginia and North Carolina, but in Alabama, white hoodlums bombed a bus and beat the riders with baseball bats. When the brutality turned some Freedom Riders back, SNCC members rushed in to take their places. After a huge mob attacked the Freedom Riders in Montgomery, Attorney General Robert Kennedy dispatched federal marshals to restore order. But when the buses reached Jackson, Mississippi, the Freedom Riders were promptly arrested, and several hundred spent part of the summer in Mississippi jails.

*Unlike many of the Great Society reforms, which failed to live up to their promise and provoked widespread criticism, the civil rights movement effected a revolution in the legal status of African Americans and won widespread acceptance.*

Encouraged in part by Kennedy administration officials who viewed voting rights as less controversial than civil disobedience (and more likely to benefit the Democratic Party), SNCC and other groups began a Voter Education Project in the summer of 1961. Yet as activists sought to register black voters in the Deep South, they too met violence. Whites bombed black churches, threw tenant farmers out of their homes, and beat and jailed activists.

**LUNCH COUNTER SIT-IN**
*John Salter Jr., a professor at Tougaloo College, and students Joan Trumpauer and Anne Moody take part in a 1963 sit-in at the Woolworth's lunch counter in Jackson, Mississippi. Shortly before this photograph was taken, whites had thrown two students to the floor and police had arrested one student. Salter was spattered with mustard and ketchup. Moody would publish a popular book in 1968 about her experiences in the black freedom struggle,* Coming of Age in Mississippi.
State Historical Society of Wisconsin.

Plantation worker Fannie Lou Hamer lost her job and home when she attempted to register to vote in Mississippi in 1962. She continued her efforts, and one year later police arrested and battered her so savagely that she hid her face from her family. In June 1963, a white man gunned down Mississippi NAACP leader Medgar Evers in front of his house in Jackson.

Television brought home to the entire world the brutality of southern resistance to racial equality in May 1963, when Martin Luther King Jr. and the SCLC launched a campaign in Birmingham, Alabama. As blacks massed in demonstrations, the city's police chief, Eugene "Bull" Connor, responded with police dogs, electric cattle prods, and high-pressure hoses. Hundreds of demonstrators, including school-age children, went to jail, and firebombs exploded at King's motel and his brother's house. Four months later, a bomb killed four black children attending Sunday school in Birmingham.

The largest demonstration took place in Washington, D.C., in August 1963. Sponsored by the major civil rights organizations, the march drew 250,000 blacks and whites to the nation's capital. King put his indelible stamp on the day. Moved by the intense emotions of the crowd, King departed from his formal speech, using all the passion and skills that made him the greatest orator of his day. His words came from the Bible, Negro spirituals, and the nation's patriotic anthems. "I have a dream," he repeated again and again, spelling out a future when "the sons of former slaves and the sons of former slave owners will be able to sit down together at the table of brotherhood." With the crowd roaring in support, he imagined the day "when all of God's children . . . will be able to join hands and sing . . . 'Free at last, free at last; thank God Almighty, we are free at last.'"

Media and public response to the March on Washington was overwhelmingly positive, but the buoyant euphoria of that day quickly faded as activists returned to continued violence in the South. In 1964, the Mississippi Freedom Summer Project mobilized more than one thousand northern college students, who paid their own expenses to conduct voter education classes and help blacks register to vote in Mississippi. Resistance was fierce. By the end of the summer, only twelve hundred new voters had been placed on the rolls, several people had been killed, eighty had been beaten, more than a thousand had been arrested, and thirty-five black churches had been burned.

Still the movement persisted. In January 1965, the SCLC and SNCC launched a voting drive in Selma, Alabama, against brutal opposition from local authorities. In March, Alabama troopers used such fierce force to turn back a fifty-mile march from Selma to the state capitol in Montgomery that the incident earned the name "Bloody Sunday." After several days, President Johnson called up the Alabama National Guard to protect the marchers. Before the Selma campaign was over, whites had shot or beaten to death three demonstrators. On Bloody Sunday, John Lewis, chairman of the SNCC, was beaten and hospitalized but managed to make the final march to the capitol. Looking back on that demonstration, he recalled it as one of the most meaningful events in his life: "In October of that year the Voting Rights bill was passed and we all felt we'd had a part in it."

## The Response in Washington

Civil rights leaders would have to wear sneakers, Lyndon Johnson said, if they were going to keep up with him. But both Kennedy and Johnson acted more in response to events created by the black freedom struggle than on their own initiative. Both presidents moved when events in the South gave them little choice. Kennedy sent federal marshals to Montgomery to protect the Freedom Riders; in 1962, he dispatched federal troops to enable James H. Meredith, a black air force veteran, to enroll in the all-white University of Mississippi; and he called up the Alabama National Guard during the Birmingham demonstrations in May 1963. But to activists pleading for more federal protection, Kennedy replied that law enforcement was a local matter. Well aware of the political costs of deploying federal force, the president and attorney general made it clear that they intervened to enforce the law, not to support the demonstrators.

In June 1963, Kennedy finally made good on his promise to seek civil rights legislation. In a nationally televised speech, he called civil rights "a moral issue . . . as old as the scriptures and . . . as clear as the American Constitution" and specifically supported voting rights and equal access to public schools and accommodations. Johnson took up Kennedy's commitment with zeal, and a number of factors assisted his efforts. Television captured the dignity and courage of African Americans and the brutal repression of southern officials. The growing public support for civil rights, the "Johnson treat-

**BIRMINGHAM DEMONSTRATORS**
*In April 1963, Martin Luther King Jr. and the Southern Christian Leadership Conference (SCLC) initiated a campaign to integrate Birmingham, Alabama, known as the most segregated city in the nation. City officials filled the jails with demonstrators, including King himself, and nine hundred children, like these young people being attacked with powerful hoses. One police officer remarked to a colleague, "Ten or fifteen years from now, we will look back on all this and we will say, 'How stupid can you be?' " Photographs like this one evoked outrage throughout the country.* Charles Moore/Black Star.

**THE MARCH
ON WASHINGTON**
*More than a quarter of a million
Americans, including fifty
thousand whites, gathered on
the Mall in the nation's capital
on August 28, 1963, to pressure
the government to support
African Americans' civil
rights. After Martin Luther
King Jr. gave his "I have a
dream" speech, Malcom X said
to march organizer Bayard
Rustin, "You know this dream
of King's is going to be a
nightmare before it's over."*
James P. Blair/National Geographic
Society Image Collection.

ment," and the president's ability to turn the measure into a memorial to the martyred Kennedy all produced the Civil Rights Act of 1964.

Passed in July 1964, the law guaranteed access for all Americans to public accommodations, public education, employment, and voting, thus sounding the death knell for the South's system of segregation and discrimination. Title VII of the measure, which banned discrimination in employment, also attacked racial inequality outside the South. In addition, Title VII outlawed sex discrimination in employment. (This provision came from a conservative southern opponent of civil rights, who hoped that including the sex provision would defeat the entire bill.) Because Title VII applied to wages, hiring, and promotion, it represented a giant step toward equal employment opportunity for women as well as racial minorities.

Within months of passage of the Civil Rights Act of 1964, Johnson ordered his aides to draft a new law, one that would remove "every remaining obstacle to the right and the opportunity to vote." In a televised speech before Congress, Johnson insisted, "Should we defeat every enemy, should we double our wealth and conquer the stars" without achieving racial equality, "we will have failed as a people and as a nation." The Voting Rights Act, which empowered the federal government to act directly and immediately to enable African Americans to register and vote, was signed by Johnson in August 1965. A major transformation began in southern politics.

Johnson also used his presidential authority in September 1965 to issue Executive Order 11246, which not only banned discrimination by employers holding government contracts (affecting about one-third of the labor force) but also required them to take affirmative action to ensure equal opportunity. Extended to cover women in 1967, the affirmative action program provoked more controversy than any of the civil rights measures. Calling it "reverse discrimination," many people thought—incorrectly—that affirmative action required absolute quotas for hiring minorities and women or employing unqualified candidates. In fact, the order required employers not just to stop discriminating but to act forcefully to bring their labor force into line with the available pool of qualified candidates. Within a few years, affirmative action came to be seen as a good employment practice by most large businesses.

Johnson's final effort to reconcile the actuality of race relations with the nation's vision of itself was the Civil Rights Act of 1968. That measure banned racial discrimination in housing—the most controversial provision—and in jury selection, and it empowered the federal government to intervene to protect civil rights workers from violence.

The three civil rights measures of the 1960s formed the most important legal gains for African Americans since Reconstruction. Yet the progress failed to match the rising aspirations of African Americans or to satisfy the needs of blacks that antidiscrimination measures alone could not address.

## Black Nationalism and the End of the Civil Rights Coalition

By 1966, the black freedom struggle encompassed racial oppression throughout the nation and broadened its goals from integration and legal equality to the elimination of poverty and miserable living conditions for millions of African Americans. In addition, many black activists had given up on white allies and the tactics of nonviolence. In part the new emphases resulted from the very success of civil rights legislation, as one layer of oppression receded only to reveal others more subtle but just as pervasive. Equal access to public facilities and institutions did little to improve the material conditions of blacks. How valuable was the freedom to patronize a restaurant if African Americans could not afford the price of a meal?

Black rage at oppressive conditions and impatience with legal changes erupted in a wave of riots that ignited cities in the North, Midwest, and West every summer from 1964 to 1968. The Watts district of Los Angeles in 1965, Newark and Detroit in 1967, and the nation's capital in 1968 saw the most destruction and violence, but hundreds of eruptions occurred across the country, usually sparked by an incident between white police and local blacks. In Detroit, rioters swept through fourteen square miles of the black ghetto; the result was 43 deaths, 7,000 arrests, 1,300 destroyed buildings, and 2,700 shops looted. "Our nation is moving toward two societies, one black, one white—separate and unequal," warned an investigating commission appointed by the president in 1967, but little was done to ameliorate the basic conditions from which riots sprang.

King himself realized that racism reached beyond the South, and in 1965 the SCLC mounted a drive for better jobs, schools, and housing in Chicago. King also pressed the government for more adequate funding of the antipoverty program and initiated plans for a Poor People's March to the nation's capital in 1968. Yet even as his goals changed, King stressed the principle of nonviolence and attempted to work with white supporters and government officials. For this he came increasingly under criticism from activists in CORE and SNCC.

In the North, a powerful voice rose to challenge the dominant ethos of the civil rights movement. Malcolm Little had grown up in poverty, first in Nebraska and then in Michigan. In prison at the age of twenty-one for attempted burglary, he educated himself and converted to the Nation of Islam. The Nation, whose adherents are called Black Muslims,

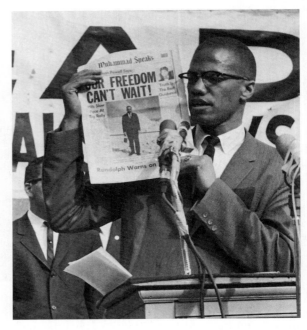

**MALCOLM X**
*Malcolm X addresses a Black Muslim rally in New York City in July 1963. The name of the newspaper he displays refers to the organization's leader, Elijah Muhammad, who had headed the Nation of Islam since 1934. In 1964, Malcolm broke with the leader. He did not abandon black nationalism and continued to urge radical change, but he no longer equated whites with the devil. "The white man is not inherently evil," he said, "but America's racist society influences him to act evilly."*
Wide World.

drew on a long African American tradition of nationalism and separatism. Released from jail in 1952, Malcolm Little changed his name to Malcolm X, to symbolize the African identity stripped from his ancestors, and went to work for the Nation of Islam. He attracted a large following, especially in urban ghettos, calling for separation from the "corrupt [white] society," black pride and autonomy, and self-defense against white violence. In 1964, Malcolm broke from the Black Muslims, began to cultivate a wider constituency, and expressed an openness to working with whites. At a Harlem rally in February 1965, three members of the Nation of Islam shot and killed him. Yet his ideas outlived his death and began to resonate in CORE and SNCC.

At a rally in Greenwood, Mississippi, in June 1966, SNCC chairman Stokely Carmichael gave that new approach a name. "We want black power," he shouted again and again. "Black power" quickly became the rallying cry in SNCC and CORE. Though embraced by only a minority of African Americans, the black power movement claimed the bulk of national attention in the late 1960s.

Carmichael and other activists issued no single systematic definition of black power. Calling integration "a subterfuge for the maintenance of white supremacy," Carmichael insisted on separation from whites, because assimilation implied the superiority of white institutions and values. African Americans were encouraged to develop independent businesses, control their own schools and other institutions, and form all-black political organizations, such as the Black Panther Party, founded in Oakland, California, in 1966. The phrase "Black is beautiful" emphasized the authenticity and worth of African American culture and racial pride.

To black power advocates, nonviolence only brought more beatings and killings. Malcolm X had said, "If someone puts a hand on you, send him to the cemetery." Carmichael agreed: "Black people should and must fight back." The press paid an inordinate amount of attention to black radicals, and the black power movement contributed to a severe white backlash. Although the urban riots erupted spontaneously, triggered by specific incidents, horrified whites blamed them on black power militants. By 1966, a full 85 percent of the white population thought that blacks were pressing for too much too quickly; two years earlier, only 34 percent had thought so.

King agreed with black power advocates about the need for "a radical reconstruction of society" but clung to nonviolence and integration as the means to this end. In March 1968, the thirty-nine-year-old leader took his movement to Memphis to support a strike of municipal garbage workers. There, on April 4, King was shot and killed. James Earl Ray, an escaped white convict, was arrested and confessed to the murder but later denied that he had killed King and insisted that he was a scapegoat for a wider conspiracy.

Black power advocates receded from national visibility by the end of the decade. Never able to command substantial support in the African American community, which revered King and his philosophy, black militants were harassed by the FBI, jailed, and sometimes killed by the police, whom they also sometimes killed. Black nationalism's emphasis on racial pride and culture and its critique of American institutions, however, resonated broadly and helped to shape the protest of other groups.

## Demands for Power to the People

With its incontrovertible moral claims, the civil rights movement helped to make protest respectable, and its ability to capture national attention and move the federal government suggested possibilities for other groups with grievances. College students, opponents of the war in Vietnam, women, Native Americans, Mexican Americans, and other minority groups drew on the black freedom struggle for inspiration and models of protest. These groups engaged in direct-action protests, expressed their own cultural nationalism, and challenged dominant institutions and values.

### Native American Protest

Protest was not new to the group with the oldest grievances, but Native American activism took on fresh militancy and goals in the 1960s. The cry "red power" reflected the influence of black radicalism on Native Americans who rejected the goal of assimilation. As one Indian put it, the civil rights struggle led by King "was within the System, and the System had nothing to do with Indians." Rather, American Indians sought tribal sovereignty and just treatment as independent nations.

*College students, opponents of the war in Vietnam, women, Native Americans, Mexican Americans, and other minority groups drew on the black freedom struggle for inspiration and models of protest.*

Native Americans demonstrated and occupied land and public buildings, claiming rights to natural resources and territory that they had owned collectively before European settlement. A new, more militant generation participated in these demonstrations through the National Indian Youth Council, founded in 1961. In the most dramatic action, Indians seized Alcatraz Island in San Francisco Bay in 1969 and used it as a cultural and educational center until the federal government ran them out in 1971.

Two Chippewa, Dennis Banks and George Mitchell, founded the American Indian Movement (AIM) in 1968 in Minneapolis to deal with problems in cities, where about 300,000 Indians lived. AIM focused on Native Americans who had been en-

**THE AMERICAN INDIAN MOVEMENT**
*Dennis Banks (right), a Chippewa who served in the U.S. air force, was a founder and leader of the American Indian Movement (AIM). Russell Means, a Sioux born on the Pine Ridge reservation, joined AIM in 1969. In 1973 Banks and Means led an occupation of Wounded Knee, a part of the Pine Ridge reservation where the army had massacred the Sioux in 1890. The two-month stand by two hundred occupiers, during which the Indians and federal agents exchanged gunfire that killed two Indians, produced no substantive reforms but called attention to the plight of Native Americans.* Wide World.

couraged or forced by the relocation and termination programs of the 1950s to migrate to urban areas, where they found unemployment, poverty, and alienation from their traditions. AIM sought to protect Indians from police harassment, secure antipoverty program funds for Indian-controlled organizations, and establish "survival schools" to teach the history and values of Indian culture. The appeal of AIM quickly spread beyond urban areas. AIM members "had a new look about them, not that hangdog reservation look I was used to," Mary Crow Dog wrote, and their visit to her reservation in South Dakota "loosened a sort of earthquake inside me."

Native American protest gained attention from the Bureau of Indian Affairs, legislation to meet educational and health needs of Indians, and government decisions recognizing Indian rights to ancestral lands. Taos Indians, for example, regained land in New Mexico, and the government paid the Sioux more than $100 million for lands that were taken in gold rush days in the nineteenth century. Native Americans recovered a measure of identity and pride, greater respect for and protection of their culture, and, in the words of President Johnson's special message to Congress in 1968, a recognition of "the right of the First Americans to remain Indians while exercising their rights as Americans."

## Hispanic American Struggles for Justice

The fastest-growing minority group in the 1960s was Hispanic Americans, people of Mexican, Puerto Rican, Caribbean, and other Spanish-speaking origins. Hispanics of Puerto Rican and Caribbean descent tended to live in urban areas on the East Coast. But more than half of the Hispanic population of the United States—some six million Mexican Americans—lived in California, Texas, Arizona, New Mexico, and Colorado. In addition, thousands of immigrants illegally crossed the unguarded two-thousand-mile border between Mexico and the United States in search of economic opportunity.

Throughout the twentieth century, Mexican Americans had formed organizations to push for political power and economic rights. But, like African Americans and Native Americans in the 1960s, young Hispanics increasingly rejected traditional politics in favor of direct action. One symbol of this generational challenge was the adoption of the name "Chicano" (from the Spanish word for Mexican, *mejicano*) by young Mexican American activists. Chicano activism drew national attention to California, where migrant workers endured wretched living and working conditions. In 1963, César Chávez organized the United Farm Workers Association (UFW) to improve conditions for Chicanos through union representation. UFW marches and strikes gained widespread support, and a national boycott of California grapes helped the UFW to win union recognition and a wage increase in 1970.

Chicanos mobilized elsewhere to end discrimination in employment and education, win their share of antipoverty funds, and combat police brutality. Spreading through the Southwest in 1968, a series of strikes, called "Blow Outs," registered high school students' protest against racism in the public schools. The separatist and nationalist strains of Chicano protest were evident in La Raza Unida (the United Race), a third party founded by José Angel Gutierrez in Texas and based on cultural pride and brotherhood.

Mexican Americans gradually won greater representation in government and more effective enforcement of antidiscrimination legislation. With blacks and Native Americans, they continued to be overrepresented among the poor but gained a sense of their potential power and respect for their culture.

## Student Rebellion and the New Left

The civil rights movement exerted direct and immediate influence on white activists who launched student protests, the antiwar movement, and the new feminist movement. Their confrontation with violent racism in the South and their disillusionment with the federal government radicalized and sensitized them to injustice. Tom Hayden's first meeting with SNCC activists in the fall of 1960 "was a key turning point, the moment my political identity began to take shape," he recalled. He became involved with Students for a Democratic Society (SDS), a small group of whites formed in 1960 from the remains of an older socialist-oriented student organization. In 1962, he met with about sixty other students in Port Huron, Michigan, and helped define the purpose and structure of SDS, which soon became the organizational focus of white student protest in the 1960s.

The Port Huron Statement articulated SDS's principles. "We are people of this generation, bred in at least modest comfort, housed now in universities, looking uncomfortably at the world we inherit," the statement began. The idealistic students criticized the complacency of their elders, the remoteness of decision makers from the will of the people, and the powerlessness and alienation that people experienced in a society run by impersonal bureaucratic institutions. SDS aimed to mobilize a new social movement, called the New Left, with

civil rights, peace, and universal economic security as its major targets. It remained small until 1965, but other forms of student activism soon followed.

The first large-scale white student protest arose in the free speech movement at the University of California, Berkeley, in the fall of 1964, when university officials banned student organizations from recruiting support for civil rights and other causes. Led by white activists who had worked in the South, the students claimed the right to freedom of expression and political action. They occupied the administration building, and more than seven hundred were arrested before the California Board of Regents overturned the new restrictions.

*Idealistic students criticized the complacency of their elders, the remoteness of decision makers from the will of the people, and the powerlessness and alienation that people experienced in a society run by impersonal bureaucratic institutions.*

Hundreds of student rebellions followed on campuses of various sizes and affiliations. Opposition to the Vietnam War activated the largest number of students, who rallied and occupied buildings in protest against universities' activities linked to the war. But they also demanded curricular reforms, more financial aid for minority and poor students, independence from paternalistic rules, the freedom to hear controversial speakers on campus, and a larger voice in campus decision making.

## The Counterculture

Growing up alongside the New Left and student movements and often overlapping them was a cultural rebellion known as the counterculture, which drew on the ideas and behavior of the Beats of the 1950s and focused on personal rather than political and institutional change.

Cultural radicals, or "hippies," as they were called, rejected mainstream norms that valued the work ethic, material possessions, rationality, order, and sexual control and embraced "Do your own thing" as their motto. Hippies stood out with their long hair and wildly colorful, often ragged clothing. The Haight-Ashbury district of San Francisco harbored the most widely known hippy community, but thousands of cultural radicals established communes in cities or on farms, where they renounced private property and shared everything, often including sex partners. Seeking heightened perceptions and freedom from all inhibitions, they replaced the alcohol, nicotine, and tranquilizers of their elders with illegal drugs such as marijuana and the hallucinogen LSD (lysergic acid diethylamide).

Rock music played a central role in both the counterculture and the political left. English groups such as the Beatles and the Rolling Stones and homegrown products including Bob Dylan, Janis Joplin, the Jefferson Airplane, and Jerry Garcia's Grateful Dead took American youth by storm. The 1960s music often carried insurgent political and social messages. "Eve of Destruction," a top hit of 1965, despaired of the violence around the world and the threat of nuclear annihilation and reminded young men, "You're old enough to kill but not for votin'." Other popular songs derided authority, touted the thrills of drugs, celebrated sexual freedom, and called for peace, love, and revolution.

Although cultural rebels remained a small minority, many elements of the counterculture—from rock music to jeans and long hair—filtered into the mainstream. Sexual relations outside marriage and tolerant attitudes about sexual morality spawned what came to be called a "sexual revolution." Self-fulfillment became a dominant concern of many Americans, and questioning of government and other authority became much more widespread. The hippies faded away in the early 1970s, but their counterculture continued to influence American society.

### Beginnings of a Feminist Movement

Both the civil rights struggle and the New Left served as inspiration and models for a new women's movement. The ban against sex discrimination in the Civil Rights Act of 1964 and the extension of affirmative action to women reflected feminists' efforts to "piggyback" onto civil rights measures. The new laws raised women's expectations, and feminists grew impatient when the government moved slowly against sex discrimination in employment. Deciding that they needed a "civil rights organization for women," Betty Friedan and others founded the National Organization for Women (NOW) in 1966.

Simultaneously a more radical feminism formed. From the civil rights movement and the New Left, women grasped a contradiction between the ideal of equality and the actual status of women.

Two white women, Mary King and Casey Hayden (then married to Tom Hayden), raised the issue in SNCC in 1964, and in 1965 they began circulating their ideas to other women active in the New Left. King and Hayden pointed out that, like blacks, women "seem[ed] to be caught up in a common-law caste system . . . forcing them to work around or outside hierarchical structures of power which may exclude them." Women, they contended, were also exploited and subordinated in personal relations. The 1965 memo struck a responsive chord among white activist women but elicited indifference or ridicule from most male radicals. Consequently, feminists created an independent women's liberation movement.

By the end of the 1960s, radical white women had established women's liberation groups in cities across the nation. They translated black pride into pride of womanhood, and they implemented the "participatory democracy" of SDS in their activities. Staging marches, sit-ins, and other demonstrations, they began to gain public attention, especially when one hundred women picketed the Miss America beauty pageant in 1968, protesting against being forced "to compete for male approval [and] enslaved by ludicrous 'beauty' standards." Activism by radicals and more moderate feminists surged into a mass movement that dramatically changed public policy and popular attitudes in the 1970s.

## The Judicial Revolution

For more than a decade, beginning with the *Brown* school desegregation decision in 1954, the Supreme Court under Chief Justice Earl Warren (presiding from 1953 to 1969) spearheaded another form of change. In expanding the Constitution's promise of equality and protection of individual rights, the Court shifted power from the states to the judicial branch of the federal government. The Warren Court interpreted the Constitution to place less emphasis on restricting injustices by government and more on requiring the government to act to prevent injustice and discrimination.

### Civil Rights and Criminal Justice

In articulating the rights of disadvantaged groups and accused criminals, Supreme Court decisions in the 1950s and 1960s jettisoned judicial tradition and often moved ahead of public opinion. Following the pathbreaking *Brown* decision, the Warren Court ruled against all-white public facilities and struck down educational plans devised by southern states to avoid integration. The Court also upheld the constitutional rights of African Americans to freedom of assembly and freedom of speech, thereby enabling the black freedom struggle to continue sit-ins, mass marches, and other civil disobedience tactics that proved critical to its success.

*The Warren Court interpreted the Constitution to place less emphasis on restricting injustices by government and more on requiring the government to act to prevent injustice and discrimination.*

Chief Justice Warren considered *Baker v. Carr* (1963) his most important decision. The case grew out of a complaint that Tennessee electoral districts were so inequitably drawn that sparsely populated rural districts had far more representatives in the state legislature than did densely populated metropolitan areas. Grounding its decisions on the Fourteenth Amendment guarantee of "equal protection of the laws," in *Baker* and companion cases the Court established the principle of "one person, one vote" for both houses of state legislatures and for the House of Representatives. Requiring most states to redraw electoral districts, the rulings helped to make state legislatures more responsive to metropolitan interests and problems.

The egalitarian thrust of the Warren Court also touched the criminal justice system. Between 1957 and 1967, the Court overturned a series of convictions on the grounds that the accused individuals had been deprived of "life, liberty, or property, without due process of law" and thus had been denied their rights under the Fourteenth Amendment. Furthermore, the Court interpreted that amendment to require that states as well as the federal government abide by the Bill of Rights. These rulings dramatically reformed law enforcement practices and the treatment of individuals accused of crime. In *Gideon v. Wainright* (1963), the Court ruled that states must provide lawyers to people accused of serious crime who cannot afford to pay lawyers themselves. In *Escobedo v. Illinois* (1964), the justices extended the right to counsel to the period when suspects are being questioned by police officers. Two years later,

in *Miranda v. Arizona,* the Court issued guidelines requiring officers to inform suspects that they may remain silent, that anything they say can be used against them, and that they are entitled to a lawyer. And it overturned convictions resulting from evidence obtained by unlawful arrest, by electronic surveillance, and by entering property without a search warrant.

Critics accused the Supreme Court of letting criminals go free by overturning convictions and obstructing law enforcement. Liberals, however, argued that these rulings promoted equal treatment in the criminal justice system: The wealthy always had access to legal counsel, and practiced criminals were well aware of their right to remain silent. The beneficiaries of the decisions were the poor, the ignorant, and the weak as well as the general population whose right to privacy was strengthened by the Court's stricter guidelines for admissible evidence.

## Dissent and Religious Issues

The Warren Court also strengthened protections for people suspected of being Communists or subversives, setting limits, for example, on government officials who investigated and prosecuted them. Like the criminal justice cases, these rulings guaranteed the rights of people on the margins of American society and reaped their share of criticism.

The Warren Court's decisions on prayer and Bible reading in the public schools provoked even greater outrage. In *Abington School District v. Schempp* (1963), the Court overturned a Pennsylvania law requiring Bible reading and recitation of the Lord's Prayer in the schools as a violation of the First Amendment principle of separation of church and state. Later decisions ruled out prayer in public schools even if students were not required to participate. An outraged Alabama legislator fumed, "They put Negroes in the schools and now they've driven God out." The Court's supporters, however, declared that the religion cases protected the rights of non-Christians and atheists.

Two or three justices who believed that the Court was overstepping its authority often issued sharp dissents. Outside the Court, opponents worked to pass laws or constitutional amendments that would upset despised decisions, legal experts pleaded for the Court to exercise judicial restraint, and billboards demanded, "Impeach Earl Warren." Nonetheless, the Court's major decisions withstood Warren's retirement in 1969 and the test of time.

## Conclusion: Achievements and Limitations of 1960s Liberalism

Surveying the record of the Johnson administration, Senate majority leader Mike Mansfield concluded that the president "has done more than FDR ever did, or ever thought of doing." Yet opposition to his leadership grew so strong by 1968 that Johnson abandoned hopes for reelection. As his liberal vision lay in ruins, he asked, "How was it possible that all these people could be so ungrateful to me after I have given them so much?"

The egomania reflected in that question was but one of several factors that contributed to Johnson's demise and the waning of Democratic liberalism. Inadequately planned and funded, many of the antipoverty programs ended up benefiting industry and the nonpoor as much as or more than the impoverished. Because Johnson refused to ask for sacrifices from prosperous Americans, the Great Society never approached the redistribution of wealth and resources that would have been necessary for the elimination of poverty.

Black aspirations exceeded white Americans' commitment to genuine equality. It was easy for northerners to be sympathetic when the civil rights movement focused on crude and blatant forms of racism in the South. But when it attacked the subtler forms of racism that existed throughout the nation and sought equality in fact as well as in rights, the black freedom struggle confronted a powerful backlash.

Most surprising was the opposition from the left. Radicalized by the black freedom struggle, a small but vocal minority of whites and blacks emphasized the shortcomings of the Great Society and questioned whether real reform could be achieved within the framework of traditional American institutions and values. Young radicals like Tom Hayden engaged in direct confrontations with the government and universities that, together with racial conflict, escalated into political discord and social disorder not seen since the union wars of the 1930s.

The war in Vietnam polarized American society as much as did the question of race or the behavior of young people. Johnson's conduct of the war undermined faith in his leadership. The war starved the Great Society, devouring revenues that might have been used for social reform and eclipsing the substantial progress that had actually been achieved.

## CHRONOLOGY

**1960**   African American college students in Greensboro, North Carolina, stage sit-in at whites-only lunch counter.

John F. Kennedy elected president of United States.

Student Nonviolent Coordinating Committee (SNCC) established to mobilize young people for direct action for civil rights.

Students for a Democratic Society (SDS) founded.

**1961**   Congress of Racial Equality (CORE) sponsors Freedom Rides to desegregate interstate transportation in South.

President Kennedy establishes President's Commission on the Status of Women.

**1963**   *Baker v. Carr* mandates electoral redistricting to enforce "one-person, one-vote" principle.

Betty Friedan's best-selling book *The Feminine Mystique* published.

Equal Pay Act makes wage disparities based solely on gender illegal.

Mississippi NAACP leader Medgar Evers assassinated in Jackson.

March on Washington becomes largest civil rights demonstration in U.S. history.

President's Commission on the Status of Women issues report detailing widespread discrimination against women.

| 1963 | President Kennedy assassinated in Dallas, Texas; Vice President Lyndon B. Johnson becomes president. | | Selma-to-Montgomery march for voting rights; Johnson orders federal protection for marchers after they are attacked. |

1963    President Kennedy assassinated in Dallas, Texas; Vice President Lyndon B. Johnson becomes president.

César Chávez founds United Farm Workers Association (UFW).

1964    Congress enacts Civil Rights Act of 1964, the strongest such measure since Reconstruction.

Economic Opportunity Act passed.

Free speech movement, first large-scale white student protest of 1960s, organized at University of California, Berkeley.

Malcolm X breaks from Nation of Islam and attracts wide following.

President Johnson elected to full term in landslide over Republican Senator Barry Goldwater.

Tax cut bill proposed by Kennedy administration passed.

1965    Malcolm X assassinated in New York City.

Selma-to-Montgomery march for voting rights; Johnson orders federal protection for marchers after they are attacked.

Congress passes Voting Rights Act.

1965–1966    89th Congress passes most of Johnson's Great Society domestic programs, including antipoverty measures, public works acts, aid to education, and Medicare-Medicaid.

1966    Black Panther Party founded, advocating African American economic and political autonomy.

In *Miranda v. Arizona,* Supreme Court requires police to inform suspects of their rights.

National Organization for Women (NOW) founded.

1968    American Indian Movement (AIM) founded.

# SUGGESTED READINGS

Terry H. Anderson, *The Movement and the Sixties* (1995). A lively narrative that captures the varieties of protest movements and their occurrence in all parts of the nation.

Taylor Branch, *Pillar of Fire: America in the King Years, 1963–65* (1998). The second volume of a comprehensive treatment of King's life and times.

Robert Dallek, *Flawed Giant: Lyndon B. Johnson, 1960–1973* (1998). An engrossing biography that analyzes Johnson's character and impact on history.

Michael Eric Dyson, *Making Malcolm: The Myth and Meaning of Malcolm X* (1995). Essays on Malcolm X's life as well as his continuing influence in American society and culture.

Sara Evans, *Personal Liberation: The Roots of Women's Liberation in the Civil Rights Movement and the New Left* (1978). A fascinating account of the origins of the radical wing of feminism.

Juan Gómez-Quiñones, *Chicano Politics: Reality and Promise, 1940–1990* (1990). A comprehensive history of the changing goals and nature of Mexican American activism.

Michael B. Katz, *The Undeserving Poor: From the War on Poverty to the War on Welfare* (1989). A very readable critique of how the United States has dealt with poverty since the 1950s.

Steven F. Lawson, *Running for Freedom: Civil Rights and Black Politics in America since 1941* (1991). An examination of how African Americans changed politics and government, focusing on the years since 1960.

Charles Payne, *I've Got the Light of Freedom: The Organizing Tradition and the Mississippi Freedom Struggle* (1995). A narrative of the black freedom struggle from the bottom up that highlights the work of grassroots men and women.

Gerald Posner, *Case Closed: Lee Harvey Oswald and the Assassination of JFK* (1993). A careful analysis that discredits conspiracy theories about the assassination.

Bernard Schwartz, ed., *The Warren Court: A Retrospective* (1996). A collection of essays that examine the justices, their decisions, and the legacy of the Warren Court.

**FATIGUE HAT WITH BUTTONS**

*The button on this fatigue hat of a veteran who had served two tours of duty evinces veterans' response to the many Americans who just wanted to forget the war that the United States had failed to win. Because their war was so different from other American wars, Vietnam veterans often came home to hostility or indifference. The POW-MIA pin refers to prisoners of war and those missing in action.*

Nancy Gewitz/Antique Textile Resource/Picture Resource Consultants, Inc.

# VIETNAM AND THE LIMITS OF POWER

## 29

### 1961–1975

As charles anderson's plane prepared to land, the pilot announced, "Gentlemen, we'll be touching down in Da Nang, Vietnam, in about ten minutes. . . . Fasten your seat belts, please. On behalf of the entire crew and staff, I'd like to say we've enjoyed having you with us . . . and we hope to see all of you again next year on your way home. Goodbye and good luck." Like most soldiers after 1966, Charles Anderson went to war on a commercial jetliner, complete with stewardesses (as they were called then) in miniskirts.

Military personnel traveling to battle as if they were businessmen or tourists only hints of the differences between the Vietnam War and America's previous wars. Marine infantry officer Philip Caputo landed at Da Nang in March 1965 confident that the enemy "would be quickly beaten and that we were doing something altogether noble and good." But in just a few months, "what had begun as an adventurous expedition had turned into an exhausting, indecisive war of attrition in which we fought for no other cause than our own survival."

Another soldier discovered even more quickly that "something was wrong." Wondering why the bus taking him from the air base to the compound had wire mesh over the windows, he was told, "It's the gooks man. . . . The gooks will throw grenades through the windows." Soldiers in Vietnam initially used the racist word *gook* to refer to the enemy—the North Vietnamese or their supporters in the South— but it quickly became a term used for any Vietnamese. "From one day to the next, you could see for yourself changes coming over guys on our side—decent fellows, who wouldn't dream of calling an Oriental a 'gook' back home," reported one American. The problem was that in this civil war, "they couldn't tell who was their friend and who wasn't. Day after day, out on patrol we'd come to . . . a shabby village, and the elders would welcome us and the children come running with smiles on their faces, waiting for the candy we'd give them. But . . . just as we were leaving the village behind, the enemy would open up on us, and there was bitterness among us that the villagers hadn't given us warning."

Americans' horrifying and bewildering experiences in Vietnam grew out of cold war commitments made in the 1940s and 1950s by Presidents Harry S. Truman and Dwight D. Eisenhower. John F. Kennedy wholeheartedly took on those commitments, promising more innovative, flexible, and vigorous efforts to thwart communism. In the most memorable words of his 1960 inaugural address, he declared, "Let every nation know, whether it wishes us well or ill, that we shall pay any price, bear any burden, meet any hardship, support any friend, oppose any foe to assure the survival and the success of liberty."

543,000 at peak strength in 1968 and to more than 3 million total throughout the war's duration. Yet not only did this massive intervention fail to defeat North Vietnam, but it added a new burden to the costs of fighting the cold war—intense discord among the people at home. The Vietnam War cost President Johnson another term in office and contributed to the political demise of his Republican successor, Richard M. Nixon. Some Americans lauded the U.S. goal in Vietnam and damned only the nation's unwillingness to pursue it effectively. Others believed that preserving a non-Communist South Vietnam was neither in the best interests of the United States nor within its capacity or moral right to achieve.

But none could deny the war's enormous costs. "The promises of the Great Society have been shot down on the battlefield of Vietnam," said Martin Luther King Jr. In addition to derailing domestic reform, the Vietnam War inflicted a heavy cost in American lives and dollars, kindled internal conflict and disorder, and led to the violation of the rights of antiwar protesters. With the exception of the African American freedom struggle, no post–World War II event affected Americans so intensely.

## New Frontiers in Foreign Policy

John F. Kennedy moved quickly to fulfill his campaign promises of a more aggressive, more flexible foreign policy. He embraced the goal of containment, and with his like-minded secretary of defense, Robert S. McNamara, he expanded the nation's ability to wage nuclear, conventional, or guerrilla warfare. To ensure United States superiority over the Soviet Union in every domain, Kennedy accelerated the nation's space exploration program and inaugurated new moralistic programs to promote economic development, political stability, and friendly governments in the third world.

In his unflinching determination to halt communism, Kennedy took the United States to the brink of nuclear war during the 1962 Cuban missile crisis. Less dramatically, but no less tenaciously, Kennedy stepped up American contributions of arms, aid, and personnel to save the government of South Vietnam from Communist insurgents.

**FIGHTING THE CLIMATE AND GEOGRAPHY**
*Steamy tropical conditions and an inhospitable terrain were among the nonhuman enemies U.S. troops faced in Vietnam. Soldiers like these men making their way through rice paddies in 1968 were soaked for weeks on end. Veteran Philip Caputo wrote about "being pounded numb by ceaseless rain" during the monsoon; "at night we squatted in muddy holes, picked off the leeches that sucked on our veins."*
C. Simon Pietri/Sygma.

The conflict in Vietnam became the foremost test of what the United States would or could do to "assure the survival and the success of liberty." Kennedy sent increasing amounts of American arms and personnel to help sustain the South Vietnamese government, and Lyndon B. Johnson dramatically escalated that commitment. By 1965, the civil war in Vietnam had become America's war.

The Americanization of the war increased the number of U.S. military personnel in Vietnam to

## Meeting the "Hour of Maximum Danger"

Kennedy and other Democrats criticized the Eisenhower administration for relying too heavily on nuclear weapons, thereby denying the nation a "flexible response" to Communist expansion. They also charged that Eisenhower's desire to limit defense spending had allowed the United States to fall behind even in nuclear capability. In January 1961, Kennedy warned that the nation faced a grave peril: "Each day the crises multiply. . . . Each day we draw nearer the hour of maximum danger."

Although the president exaggerated the actual threat to national security, several developments in 1961 heightened the sense of crisis and provided rationalization for a military buildup. In a speech made shortly before Kennedy's inauguration, Soviet Premier Nikita Khrushchev had encouraged

"wars of national liberation," thereby aligning the Soviet Union with independence (usually anti-Western) movements in the third world. Fidel Castro's revolution had already moved Cuba—just ninety miles from the United States—into the Soviet orbit; and under Eisenhower, the CIA had been planning an invasion by anti-Castro exiles. Kennedy ordered the invasion to proceed even though his military advisers gave it only a "fair" chance of success. To do otherwise, the president felt, would create an appearance of weakness.

On April 17, 1961, about 1,300 anti-Castro exiles, who had been trained and armed by the CIA, landed at the Bay of Pigs on the south shore of Cuba (Map 29.1). Contrary to the anticipation of the planners, no popular uprising materialized to support the anti-Castro brigade, which quickly fell to Castro's forces. The disaster was humiliating for Kennedy and the United States, posing a stark

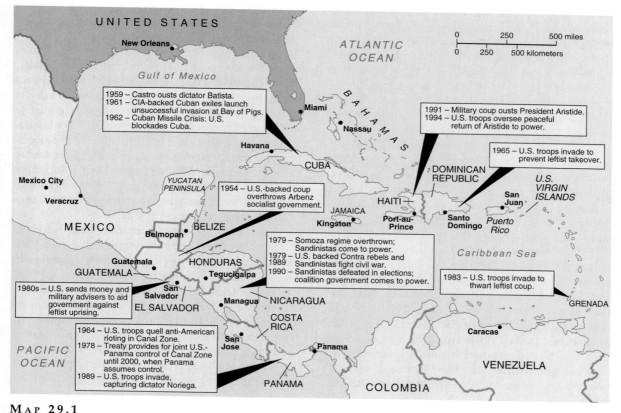

**M A P  2 9 . 1**

***U.S. Involvement in Latin America and the Caribbean, 1954–1996***
*During the cold war, the United States frequently intervened in Central American and Caribbean countries to suppress Communist or leftist movements.*

contrast to Kennedy's inaugural promise of a new, more effective foreign policy. The attempted armed interference in the affairs of another nation compromised the moral authority of the United States, evoked memories of Yankee imperialism among Latin American nations, and pushed Cuba even more tightly into the Soviet camp.

Shortly before the Bay of Pigs invasion, the United States had suffered a psychological blow when a Soviet astronaut became the first human to orbit the earth. In May 1961, Kennedy called for a huge new commitment to the space race. His goal: an American on the moon within six to eight years. Congress authorized the Apollo program and substantially boosted appropriations for space exploration. In 1962, John H. Glenn orbited the earth, less than a year behind the Soviets. And in 1969, the United States surpassed the Soviet Union when two Americans, Neil A. Armstrong and Edwin E. ("Buzz") Aldrin Jr., became the first humans to set foot on the moon.

In June 1961, Kennedy met Khrushchev in Vienna, Austria. Contrary to Kennedy's expectations, Khrushchev was belligerent and threatening and shook the president's confidence. To journalist James Reston, the shocked president reported, "He just beat [the] hell out of me. . . . If he thinks I'm inexperienced and have no guts . . . we won't get anywhere with him." Khrushchev demanded an agreement recognizing the existence of two Germanys; otherwise, he warned, the Soviets would sign a separate treaty with East Germany, a move that would threaten American occupation rights in and access to West Berlin, which lay some one hundred miles within East Germany. Kennedy held his ground. Returning home, he ordered more troops to Europe and a large increase in military forces.

The massive exodus of East Germans into West Berlin caused the Communists a major embarrassment. To stop this flow, on August 13, 1961, East Germany erected a wall between East and West Berlin, stunning the world. With the Berlin Wall stemming the tide of East German migration, Khrushchev backed off from his threats. Not until 1972 did the superpowers settle the issue when they recognized East and West Germany as separate nations and guaranteed Western access to West Berlin.

Kennedy used the Berlin crisis to add $3.2 billion to the defense budget, to mobilize the reserves and National Guard, and to expand the military by 300,000 troops. This buildup in conventional forces met Kennedy's demand for "a wider choice than humiliation or all-out nuclear action" by providing a "flexible response" strategy.

## New Approaches to the Third World

Kennedy administration officials sought fresh approaches to the wave of nationalism and revolutionary movements that had convulsed the world since the end of World War II. Much more than his predecessors, the president publicly supported third world democratic and nationalist aspirations. By helping to fulfill hopes for independence and democracy, he asserted, the United States could win the hearts and minds of people in the developing nations. To that end, Kennedy created the Alliance for Progress, promising $20 billion in aid for Latin America over the next decade. Like the Marshall Plan, the Alliance for Progress was designed to thwart communism and hold nations within the American sphere by fostering economic development. Likewise, the new Agency for International Development (AID) reversed the emphasis in foreign assistance from military to economic aid.

With an idea borrowed from Senator Hubert H. Humphrey, Kennedy launched his most dramatic third world initiative, establishment of the Peace Corps in 1961. Peace Corps volunteers studied a country's language and culture before going to work directly with its people, opening schools, providing basic health care, and assisting with agriculture and nutrition projects. Some seven thousand of them by the end of Kennedy's presidency and more than sixty thousand by the mid-1970s fanned out around the globe, serving two-year stints in villages in Latin America, Africa, and Asia.

Kennedy's foreign aid initiatives fell far short of their objectives. Though almost universally welcomed, Peace Corps projects numbered too few to make a dent in the poverty and suffering in third world countries. By 1969, the United States had provided only half of the $20 billion promised to the Alliance for Progress, and economic progress in Latin America was compromised by the lack of meaningful reforms and a soaring birthrate.

Kennedy also reverted to direct, military means to bring political stability to the third world. Although his speeches supported popular movements seeking independence and better living conditions, he drew the line at uprisings that appeared to have Communist connections or goals. Kennedy clung to the basic tenet of the cold war: that communism was

**PEACE CORPS VOLUNTEERS IN BOLIVIA**
*The majority of Peace Corps volunteers worked on educational projects in developing countries. Others helped to increase food production, build public works, and curb diseases, as did these volunteers vaccinating a young Bolivian girl. President John F. Kennedy saw the Peace Corps volunteers, with their dedication to freedom, "overcoming the efforts of Mr. Khrushchev's missionaries who are dedicated to undermining that freedom." In the course of their missions, however, some volunteers came to question the single-minded focus of U.S. policy on anticommunism.*
David S. Boyer © National Geographic Society.

a monolithic force and had to be contained, no matter what form it took. To that end, he promoted counterinsurgency forces to put down insurrections that smacked of communism (see Map 29.1). The showcase of the administration's counterinsurgency strategy was an elite corps from the four military branches that was trained to wage guerrilla warfare. Called "special forces," the corps had been established under Eisenhower to aid groups that were sympathetic to the United States and opposed

to Communist-leaning national liberation movements. Kennedy rapidly expanded the special forces, authorized their new name, the Green Berets (after their official headgear), and equipped them with the latest technology.

## The Arms Race and the Nuclear Brink

The final piece of the Kennedy-McNamara defense strategy was to gain even greater nuclear superiority over the Soviet Union. This drive for nuclear dominance increased the number of U.S. nuclear weapons based in Europe from 2,500 to 7,200 and multiplied fivefold the supply of intercontinental ballistic missiles (ICBMs). To the Soviets, this nuclear buildup suggested that the United States wanted not just superiority, but the capacity to launch a first strike, wiping out the Soviet missile sites before the Soviets could respond. The Kremlin therefore stepped up its own ICBM program, and the most intense arms race ever ensued.

In October 1962, the superpowers came perilously close to using those weapons of terror. In the summer of 1962, Khrushchev decided to install nuclear missiles in Cuba, and on October 16 the CIA gave Kennedy photographs taken from U-2 spy planes that showed launching sites under construction in Cuba for missiles that had ranges of 1,000 and 2,200 miles. The ensuing thirteen-day Cuban missile crisis brought the world closer to nuclear annihilation than ever before or since.

Working with a small group of top advisers meeting secretly and daily, Kennedy managed the crisis. On October 22, he told a television audience that he had placed the military on full alert and was imposing a "strict quarantine on all offensive military equipment" headed from the Soviet Union to Cuba. The U.S. navy would stop, search, and turn back any Soviet vessel suspected of carrying offensive missiles to Cuba. (Only later did the United States find out that offensive missiles were already in Cuba.) Kennedy warned Khrushchev that any attack launched from Cuba would trigger a full nuclear attack against the Soviet Union.

To Kennedy, projecting the appearance of toughness was paramount. According to his speechwriter, Theodore Sorensen, although the missiles did not "alter the strategic balance in fact . . . that balance would have been substantially altered in appearance; and in matters of national will and world leadership such appearances contribute to reality." But if Kennedy was willing to risk nuclear war for appearances, he also exercised considerable caution. He refused advice from the military to bomb the missile sites and instead ordered the quarantine to allow time for negotiations. On October 24, Russian ships carrying nuclear warheads suddenly stopped or turned back. Kennedy matched Khrushchev's restraint. When one ship crossed the blockade line, he ordered the navy to follow it rather than attempt to stop it. "We don't want to push him [Khrushchev] to a precipitous action," he said.

While Americans experienced the most fearful days of the cold war, Kennedy and Khrushchev exchanged offers and counteroffers. Finally, the Soviets removed the missiles and pledged not to introduce new offensive weapons into Cuba. The United States promised not to invade the island. Secretly, Kennedy also agreed to remove U.S. missiles based in Turkey and aimed at the Soviet Union, a decision that he had made months before but had not implemented.

---

*The thirteen-day Cuban missile crisis brought the world closer to nuclear annihilation than ever before or since.*

---

Even with the face-saving no-invasion promise from the United States, Khrushchev, in miscalculating Kennedy's resolution, lost badly. The Soviets lost ground in their contest with China for the allegiance of third world countries, and Khrushchev himself was so weakened that opponents deposed him two years later. Kennedy emerged triumphant. The image of an inexperienced president fumbling the Bay of Pigs invasion and being bullied by Khrushchev in Vienna gave way to that of a brilliant leader combining firmness with restraint, bearing the United States through its "hour of maximum danger."

Having proved his toughness, Kennedy could afford to be conciliatory. After the Cuban missile crisis, he acted to prevent future confrontations. He and Khrushchev agreed to install a special telephone "hot line" to speed top-level communication in moments of crisis. In a major speech at American University in June 1963, Kennedy called for a reexamination of cold war assumptions. Acknowledging that the superpowers could not quickly resolve all their differences, Kennedy stressed what they had in common: "We all inhabit this small planet. We all breathe the same air. We all cherish our children's future and we are all mortal."

Kennedy also called for an end to "a vicious cycle" in which "new weapons beget counterweapons." Two months later, the United States, the Soviet Union, and Great Britain signed a limited test ban treaty. Because France and China refused to sign, the agreement failed to stop the proliferation of nuclear weapons, and it did not apply to underground testing. Nonetheless, the limited test ban reduced the threat of radioactive fallout from nuclear testing, and it raised hopes for superpower accord on other issues.

## Venturing into a Quagmire in Vietnam

The new approach to the cold war that Kennedy outlined at American University did not mean abandoning efforts to save South Vietnam from communism. Kennedy had criticized the idea of "a Pax Americana enforced on the world by American weapons of war," but he increased the flow of those weapons into South Vietnam. His early foreign policy setbacks suggested the need to make a strong stand somewhere. "There are just so many concessions that one can make to the Communists in one year and survive politically," he remarked privately. Kennedy also remembered the political blows to the Democratic Party when China was "lost" in 1949.

Kennedy's strong anticommunism, his interpretation of "the lessons of history," and his commitment to an activist foreign policy prepared him to take a stand in Vietnam. The new counterinsurgency program provided the means. Kennedy's key military adviser, General Maxwell Taylor, thought that Vietnam would be a good testing ground for the Green Berets. Author of the "flexible response" strategy, Taylor believed that holding firm in Vietnam would show the Soviets that wars of national liberation were "costly, dangerous, and doomed to failure."

Two major problems, however, undercut Taylor's analysis. First, the South Vietnamese insurgents—called Vietcong, short for Vietnam Cong-san ("Vietnamese Communists"), by the Americans—were a genuine indigenous force whose initiative came from within, not from the Soviet Union or China. Even Ho Chi Minh's Communist government in North Vietnam did not begin to supply weapons or soldiers to the rebels in the South until 1959, after the rebels had initiated guerrilla activities against the South Vietnamese government on their own. The second problem lay in the South Vietnamese government and army (the Armed Forces of the Republic of Vietnam, or ARVN), which proved to be ineffective vehicles for the American goal of containing communism. Ngo Dinh Diem, South Vietnamese premier from 1954 to 1963, chose self-serving military leaders merely for their personal loyalty. The government's corruption and repression of opponents alienated growing numbers of South Vietnamese civilians, not just the Communists.

Intervention by North Vietnam made matters worse. In 1960, the Hanoi government established the National Liberation Front (NLF), composed of South Vietnamese rebels but directed by the North. The NLF recruited most of its forces from among the South Vietnamese and fought largely with American weapons captured from ARVN. In addition, Hanoi constructed a network of infiltration routes (called the "Ho Chi Minh Trail") in neighboring Laos through which it sent people and supplies to help liberate the South (see Map 29.2). Violence escalated between 1960 and 1963, bringing the Saigon government close to collapse.

When Kennedy took office, more than $1 billion of aid and about 700 military advisers from the U.S. had failed to stabilize South Vietnam. He resisted pressure from some advisers for an all-out effort, but in spring 1961, he began to escalate the American commitment. Within two years, military aid doubled, and 9,000 Americans served in Vietnam as military advisers, their activities occasionally going beyond training and advice to actual combat.

---

*Kennedy's strong anticommunism, his interpretation of "the lessons of history," and his commitment to an activist foreign policy prepared him to take a stand in Vietnam.*

---

Administration officials assumed that the latest military technology and sheer power could stem the Communist tide in South Vietnam. Yet that power and technology were ill suited to a guerrilla-type war and harmed the very people they were intended to save. Military personnel had trouble distinguishing the Vietcong and their supporters from innocent civilians. Thousands of peasants were uprooted from their land and resettled in new "strategic hamlets," supposedly out of the reach of the Communists. Those left in the countryside fell victim to bombs containing the highly flammable substance napalm dropped by South Vietnamese forces. In January 1962, U.S. planes began to spray herbicides to wipe out the Vietcong's jungle hideouts and destroy their food supply.

South Vietnamese military leaders effected a coup on November 2, 1963, brutally executing Premier Diem and his brother Ngo Dinh Nhu, head of the secret police. The killings shocked Kennedy, but in the three weeks he had left to live, he gave no indication of any change in policy. In a speech he planned to deliver on the day he was assassinated, Kennedy intended to call Americans to their responsibilities as "the watchmen on the walls of world freedom." Referring specifically to Southeast Asia, his undelivered speech warned, "We dare not weary of the task."

# Lyndon Johnson's War against Communism

The cold war assumptions that shaped Kennedy's foreign policy underlay the new president's approach to Southeast Asia and Latin America as well. Lyndon Johnson followed the basic outlines of Kennedy's policy, retained his key advisers, and continued the massive buildup of nuclear weapons and conventional and counterinsurgency forces that had begun in the early 1960s. In 1965, when the South Vietnamese government approached collapse, Johnson made the fateful decision to order U.S. troops into combat and initiate sustained bombing of the North. That same year, closer to home, Johnson sent U.S. marines to the Dominican Republic to crush a leftist rebellion.

## Toward an All-Out Commitment in Vietnam

During his first year as president, Lyndon Johnson expanded secret raids on North Vietnam, boosted military and economic aid to the South Vietnamese, and increased the number of American advisers to 23,000. In August 1964, Johnson seized an opportunity to increase the pressure on North Vietnam. American ships routinely engaged in espionage in the Gulf of Tonkin off the coast of North Vietnam, and on August 4, 1964, two U.S. destroyers reported that North Vietnamese gunboats had fired on them (Map 29.2). Despite uncertainty about whether the attacks had actually occurred, Johnson ordered air strikes on North Vietnamese torpedo bases and oil storage facilities. He also used the occasion to ask Congress for authority to take "all necessary measures to repel any armed attacks against the forces of the United States and to prevent further aggression." His portrayal of the situation was at best misleading, for he revealed neither the uncertainty about the attacks nor that the United States itself had engaged in provocative actions. Congress supported Johnson's plan by passing the Gulf of Tonkin Resolution on August 7, 1964, with just two senators voting no.

*In 1965, when the South Vietnamese government approached collapse, Johnson made the fateful decision to order U.S. troops into combat and initiate sustained bombing of the North.*

Johnson's tough stance just two months before the 1964 elections helped counter charges of his opponent, Barry Goldwater, that he was "soft on communism." Yet Johnson also presented himself as the peace candidate. When Goldwater proposed massive bombing of North Vietnam, Johnson asserted that bombing would expand the war and send American forces into battle. Again and again he insisted, "We seek no wider war."

Within months, however, Johnson did widen the war. He rejected peace overtures from North Vietnam, which insisted on American withdrawal and establishment of a coalition government in South Vietnam as steps toward ultimate unification of the country. McNamara and most advisers urged Johnson to begin a bombing campaign against the North, and in February 1965 Johnson initiated Operation Rolling Thunder, a strategy that involved the gradual intensified bombing of North Vietnam.

Less than a month later, two battalions of marines landed near Da Nang, South Vietnam, the first U.S. combat troops to serve in Vietnam. In July, Johnson shifted U.S. troops from defensive to offensive operations and authorized the dispatch of fifty thousand more soldiers, ordering aides to

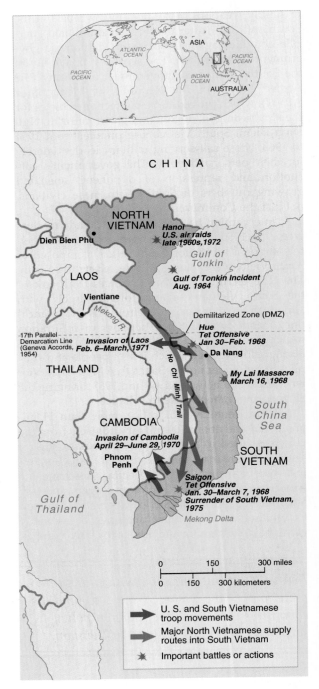

**Map 29.2**
*The Vietnam War, 1964–1975*
*The United States sent more than two million soldiers to Vietnam and spent more than $150 billion on the longest war in American history; but it was unable to prevent the unification of Vietnam under a Communist government.*

"minimize any appearance of sudden changes of policy." Yet those decisions marked a critical turning point. Now it was genuinely America's war.

## Preventing Another Castro in Latin America

Closer to home Johnson faced perpetual problems in Latin America, despite the efforts of the Alliance for Progress. Thirteen times during the 1960s, military coups replaced Latin American governments, and local insurgencies grew apace (see Map 29.1). The administration's response to such turmoil varied from case to case but centered on the determination to prevent any more Castro-type revolutions.

In 1964, riots erupted in the Panama Canal Zone, which the United States had made a territory early in the century. Instigated by Panamanian nationalists, the riots resulted in the deaths of four U.S. soldiers and more than twenty Panamanians. Johnson authorized U.S. troops to quell the disturbance, but he also initiated negotiations with Panamanian leaders. These talks dragged on until 1978, ultimately providing for Panama to assume full authority over the canal and for neutrality of the Canal Zone territory by the year 2000.

In 1965, Johnson's Latin American policy generated a new surge of anti-Americanism and cries of "Yankee imperialism." In 1961, voters in the Dominican Republic ousted a long-standing dictator and elected a constitutional government headed by Juan Bosch. But in 1963, a military coup overthrew Bosch, and two years later his supporters rallied in an uprising against the military government. When the revolt was just four days old, Johnson ordered marines to the island and eventually sent more than twenty thousand soldiers to take control. The administration said the intervention was necessary because the Boschist rebels included Communists. A special U.S. ambassador arranged a truce between the opposing sides and installed an interim government. When Dominican elections in 1966 established a constitutional government under a moderate rightist, it appeared that Johnson's policy had worked.

Yet this first outright show of Yankee force in Latin America in forty years damaged the administration at home and abroad. It quickly became clear that Communists had played no significant role in the revolt, and U.S. intervention kept the reform-oriented Boschists from returning to power. Moreover, the president had acted without the consent

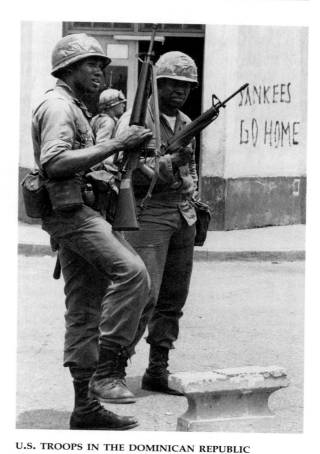

**U.S. TROOPS IN THE DOMINICAN REPUBLIC**
*These United States paratroopers were among the twenty thousand troops sent to the Dominican Republic in April and May 1965. The American invasion helped restore peace, but it also kept the popularly elected government of Juan Bosch from regaining office. Dominicans expressed their outrage in anti-American slogans that greeted troops throughout the capital, Santo Domingo. Bosch himself said, "This was a democratic revolution smashed by the leading democracy in the world."*
Corbis-Bettmann.

of the Dominicans or the Organization of American States (OAS), to which the United States had pledged to respect national sovereignty in Latin America.

Johnson believed that demonstrating strength in the Caribbean would help convince the North Vietnamese that the United States was determined to resist communism. The apparent success in the Dominican Republic no doubt encouraged the president to press on in Vietnam.

## The Americanized War

From Operation Rolling Thunder in 1965 to early 1968, the United States gradually escalated attacks against the North Vietnamese and their Vietcong allies, with the goal of breaking the will of the North Vietnamese while avoiding intervention by the Chinese. Johnson crudely explained the strategy to reporters as one of "seduction," from which the United States might ease off, rather than one of "rape," which might provoke China to respond as it had done in Korea.

Over the course of the war, U.S. pilots dropped 3.2 million tons of explosives, more than the United States had launched in all of World War II. (See the Historical Question on page 792.) The intensive bombing claimed monthly death tolls of more than two thousand North Vietnamese civilians and soldiers but failed to dampen the North's commitment. The Hanoi government dispersed and concealed industrial and military facilities, taught its citizens how to protect themselves, and relied on human labor to rebuild transportation routes. Both the Soviet Union and China helped North Vietnam replace what the bombing destroyed, supplying an estimated $2 billion worth of materials between 1965 and 1968.

The United States relied even more heavily on airpower in the South, raining down more than twice the tonnage of bombs dropped on North Vietnam. Military officials calculated progress not in territory seized, as they had in previous wars, but in "body counts" and "kill ratios," the number of enemies killed in relation to the cost in American and ARVN lives. General William Westmoreland's strategy of attrition was designed to search out and kill the Vietcong and North Vietnamese regular army, but in reality American soldiers did not always take care to distinguish between military combatants and civilians. Lieutenant Philip Caputo reported that the operating rule was "If it's dead and Vietnamese, it's VC [Vietcong]."

In contrast to World War II, when the average soldier was twenty-six years old, teenagers fought the Vietnam War. Until the Twenty-sixth Amendment reduced the voting age from twenty-one to eighteen in 1971, most soldiers, whose average age was nineteen, could not even vote for the officials who sent them to Vietnam. World War II had distributed the fighting among men of various economic levels, but Vietnam was the war of the poor and working class, who constituted about 80 percent of the troops. More privileged youth found it easier to avoid the draft, usually through college deferments. In the early years of the war, African Americans constituted 31 percent of all combat troops, often choosing the military over their meager opportunities in the civilian economy. Death rates among black soldiers were disproportionately high until 1966, when the military adjusted assignments of personnel to produce a more racially balanced distribution of sacrifice.

*World War II had distributed the fighting among men of various economic levels, but Vietnam was the war of the poor and working class, who constituted about 80 percent of the troops.*

American troops faced extremely difficult conditions. Soldiers fought in thick jungles and swamps filled with leeches, in oppressive heat, rain, and humidity. For most combat troops, Philip Caputo wrote, the war meant "weeks of expectant waiting and, at random intervals, of conducting vicious manhunts through jungles and swamps where snipers harassed us constantly and booby traps cut us down one by one." The U.S. military inflicted great losses on the enemy, estimated at more than 200,000 by the end of 1967. Yet the United States could claim no more than a stalemate.

After a series of coups and short-lived regimes, in 1965 the South Vietnamese government settled into a period of stability, if only in terms of personnel. Air Marshal Nguyen Cao Ky became prime minister, and General Nguyen Van Thieu took over as commander in chief of the military. But the Thieu-Ky government failed to rally popular support. Graft and corruption continued to flourish. In the intensified fighting and inability to distinguish friend from foe, thousands of South Vietnamese civilians were killed and wounded, their farms and villages bombed and burned. By 1968, five million people, nearly 30 percent of the population, had become refugees. Huge infusions of American dollars and goods produced rampant inflation, more opportunities for graft, the demise of local industries, and an increased dependence on foreign aid.

Johnson's Americanization of the war resulted from cautiously made decisions that flowed logically from the commitments of three presidents before him. All the same, 1965 marked a critical turn-

**HELICOPTERS IN VIETNAM**
*This helicopter has just delivered soldiers on a mission near the Ho Chi Minh Trail in April 1968. Because the enemy in Vietnam was widely dispersed, the helicopter became a key implement of war and an example of American reliance on technology. The United States used helicopters to evacuate wounded or to drop napalm and defoliants. The helicopter's mobility enabled efficient placement of troops, and as gunships they combined built-in weapons with the fire of soldiers on board.*
Philip Jones Griffith/Magnum Photos, Inc.

ing point: the rationale for involvement in the war shifted from the need to contain communism in Southeast Asia to the need to prove to the world the will and ability of the United States to make good on its commitments.

## A Nation Polarized

Domestic opposition to the war grew rapidly after 1965, and the United States entered into a period of internal conflict and violence unparalleled since the Civil War. Television brought the carnage of Vietnam into American homes day after day, making it the first "living room war." Torn between his domestic critics and the military's clamor for more troops, the president announced in March 1968 restrictions on the bombing, a new effort at negotiations, and his decision not to pursue reelection.

Throughout 1968, demonstrations, violence, and assassinations convulsed the nation. Vietnam took center stage in the election, and voters narrowly favored the Republican candidate, former Vice President Richard Nixon, who promised to "bring Americans together again" and to achieve "peace with honor."

### The Widening War at Home

Before 1965, American actions in Vietnam evoked little domestic criticism. But Johnson's authorization of Operation Rolling Thunder sparked a mass movement against the war. In April 1965, Students

# Why Couldn't the United States Bomb Its Way to Victory in Vietnam?

WORLD WAR II DEMONSTRATED the critical importance of airpower in modern war. According to the official U.S. study of strategic bombing during World War II, "No nation can long survive the free exploitation of air weapons over its homeland." In the Vietnam War, U.S. planes delivered even more explosives than they had in World War II. Why, then, did strategic bombing not bring victory in Vietnam?

"Our airpower did not fail us; it was the decision makers," asserted Admiral U. S. Grant Sharp, World War II veteran and commander in chief of the Pacific Command during the Vietnam War. Military officials welcomed President Johnson's order to begin bombing North Vietnam in February 1965 as a means to destroy the North's capacity and will to support the Communist insurgents in South Vietnam. But they chafed at Johnson's strategy of gradual escalation and the restrictions he imposed on Operation Rolling Thunder, the three-and-a-half-year bombing campaign. Military officials believed that the United States should have begun Operation Rolling Thunder with all-out massive bombing and continued until the devastation brought North Vietnam to its knees. Instead, they charged, civilian decision makers compelled the military to fight with one hand tied behind its back. Their arguments echoed General Douglas MacArthur's criticism of Truman's policy during the Korean War—though they did not repeat MacArthur's insubordination.

Unlike military officials, who could single-mindedly focus on defeating the enemy, the president balanced political considerations against military objectives and found compelling reasons to limit the application of airpower. Recalling the Korean War, Johnson noted that "China is there on the [North Vietnamese] border with 700 million men," and he studiously avoided action that might provoke intervention by the Chinese, who now possessed nuclear weapons. Johnson's strategy also aimed to keep the Soviet Union out of the war, to avoid inflaming antiwar sentiment at home, and to avert international criticism of the United States.

Consequently, the president would not permit bombing of areas where high civilian casualties might result and areas near the Chinese border. He banned strikes on airfields and missile sites that were under construction and thus likely to contain Chinese or Soviet advisers, and he refused to mine North Vietnam's harbors, through which Soviet ships imported goods to North Vietnam. But Johnson did escalate the pressure, increasing the intensity of the bombing fourfold by 1968. In all, Operation Rolling Thunder rained 643,000 tons of bombs on North Vietnam between 1965 and 1968.

Military leaders agreed with Johnson's desire to spare civilians. The Joint Chiefs of Staff never proposed, for example, strikes against a system of dikes and dams that could have disrupted food production and flooded Hanoi under twenty feet of water. Rather, they focused on destroying North Vietnam's industry and transportation system. Noncombatant casualties in North Vietnam contrasted sharply with those in World War II, when Anglo-American bombing of Dresden, Germany, alone took more than 35,000 civilian lives and the firebombing of Japan caused 330,000 civilian deaths. In three and a half years, Operation Rolling Thunder's bombing claimed an estimated 52,000 civilian lives.

The relatively low level of economic development in North Vietnam and the North Vietnamese government's ability to mobilize its citizens counteracted the military superiority of the United States. Sheer man-, woman-, and child-power compensated for the demolition of transportation sources, industry sites, and electric power plants. When bombs struck a rail line, civilians rushed with bicycles to unload a train's cargo, carry it beyond the break, and load it onto a second train. Three hundred thousand full-time workers and 200,000 farmers labored in their spare time to keep the Ho Chi Minh Trail usable in spite of heavy bombing. When bridges were destroyed, the North Vietnamese resorted to ferries and pontoons made from bamboo, and they rebuilt bridges slightly underwater to make them harder to detect from the air. They dispersed oil storage facilities and production centers throughout the countryside, and when bombs knocked out electric power plants, the Vietnamese turned to more than two thousand portable generators and used oil lamps and candles in their homes.

North Vietnam's needs were relatively small, and officials found ample means to meet them. In 1967, North Vietnam had only about 55,000 soldiers in South Vietnam, and because they waged a guerrilla war with only sporadic fighting, the insurgents in the South did not require huge amounts of supplies. What U.S. bombs destroyed, the North Vietnamese replaced with Chinese and Soviet imports. In 1967 alone, China provided 600,000 tons of rice, and it supplied small arms and ammunition, vehicles, and other goods throughout the war. Competing with China for influence in North Vietnam and favor in the third world, the Soviets contributed tanks, fighter planes, surface-to-air missiles, and other sophisticated weapons. Foreign aid substantially curtailed the effect of Operation Rolling Thunder, and the Soviet-installed modern defense systems made the bombing more difficult and dangerous for U.S. pilots.

In July 1969, Seventh Air Force commander General William W. Momyer commented on Operation Rolling Thunder to the retiring air force chief of staff, "We had the force, skill, and intelligence, but our civilian betters wouldn't turn us loose." Johnson refused to turn the military loose because in addition to the goal he shared with the military—breaking Hanoi's ability to support insurgency in the South—he also wanted to keep China and the Soviet Union—and nuclear weapons—out of the war and to contain domestic and international criticism of U.S. policy. Whether a more devastating air war would have provoked Chinese or Soviet intervention can never be known, of course.

Nor can we know whether all-out bombing of the North could have guaranteed an independent non-Communist government in the South. We do know that Johnson's military advisers imposed their own restraints, never recommending the wholesale attacks on civilians that took place in World War II. Short of decimating the civilian population, it is questionable whether more intense bombing could have completely halted North Vietnamese support for the Vietcong, given the nature of the North Vietnamese economy, the determination and ingenuity of its people, and the plentiful assistance from China and the Soviet Union. Whether the strategic bombing that worked so well in a world war against major industrial powers could be effective in a third world guerrilla war remained in doubt after the Vietnam War.

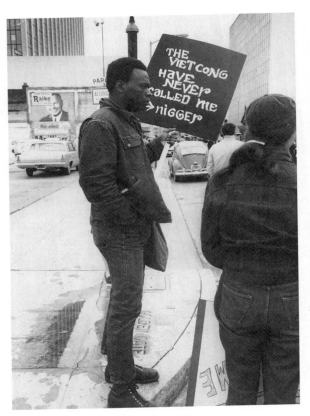

**AFRICAN AMERICAN ANTIWAR PROTEST**
*The first expression of African American opposition to the war in Vietnam occurred in Mississippi in July 1965 when a group of civil rights workers called for draft resistance. Blacks should not fight for freedom in Vietnam "until all the Negro People are free in Mississippi," they said, nor should they "risk our lives and kill other Colored People in Santo Domingo and Viet Nam." This protester on the West Coast in April 1967 expresses similar sentiments.*
Robert LeBeck/Black Star.

for a Democratic Society (SDS) launched the first major protest, recruiting twenty thousand people for a rally in Washington, D.C. SDS chapters sprang up on more than three hundred college campuses across the country. Thousands of young people also joined campus protests against Reserve Officers Training Corps (ROTC) programs, recruiters from the CIA, companies that manufactured war materials, and university departments that conducted research for the Defense Department. A new draft policy in 1967, which ended deferments for postgraduate education, gave male students a greater

stake in seeing the war end. In the spring of 1968, as many as one million college and high school students participated in a nationwide strike.

Antiwar sentiment also entered society's mainstream. The *New York Times* began to question the administration's policy as early as 1965, and by 1968 media critics included the *Wall Street Journal*, *Life* magazine, and popular TV journalist Walter Cronkite. Clergy, businesspeople, scientists, and physicians formed their own groups to pressure Johnson to stop the bombing and start negotiations. Though most of organized labor supported the president, some unions and their leaders joined the peace movement. Increasing numbers of prominent Democratic senators, including J. William Fulbright, George McGovern, and majority leader Mike Mansfield, urged Johnson to negotiate and not use force.

Opposition to the war took diverse forms: letter-writing campaigns to officials; teach-ins on college campuses; mass marches in major cities; student strikes; withholding of federal taxes; draft card burnings; civil disobedience against military centers and manufacturers of war materials; and attempts to stop trains carrying troops. Although the peace movement never claimed a majority of the population, it brought the war to the center of media attention and severely limited the administration's options. The twenty-year-old consensus about cold war foreign policy had broken down.

Many young men would not fight in the war. The World Boxing Association stripped Muhammad Ali, heavyweight champion of the world, of his title when he refused to serve in what he called a "white man's war." More than 170,000 men who opposed the war on moral grounds became conscientious objectors and performed nonmilitary duties at home or in Vietnam. About 60,000 young men fled the country to escape the draft, and more than 200,000 were accused of failing to register or other draft offenses.

Opponents of the war held far from unanimous views. Some condemned the war on moral grounds, challenging the right of the United States to interfere in the affairs of another country and stressing the suffering imposed on the Vietnamese people. Their goal was total withdrawal. But as American intervention escalated with no tangible results, many concluded that the war could not be won or that the cost in lives, dollars, and the sacrifice of domestic reform would be too great to bear. Not demanding withdrawal, they wanted Johnson to stop bombing North Vietnam and seek a negotiated settlement.

The antiwar movement outraged millions of Americans who supported the war. Some members of the older generation who had fought against Hitler could not understand a younger generation who failed to stand behind the government. Most repellent to many Americans were antiwar leaders like Tom Hayden, who went to North Vietnam and praised its people, and other peace advocates who expressed support for the enemy. "How can Americans take sides against their own young men sent to Vietnam to fight and perhaps die?" asked supporters of government policy.

While working-class people expressed doubts about the war as often as other Americans, they were especially conscious of the class dimensions of both the war and the public opposition to it. A firefighter whose son had died in Vietnam said bitterly,

"It's people like us who give up our sons for the country. The businesspeople, they run the country and make money from it. The college types . . . go to Washington and tell the government what to do. . . . But their sons don't end up in the swamps over there, in Vietnam."

In his domestic economic policies, Johnson tried to avoid actions that would focus attention on the war's burdens. He avoided price and wage controls, which had been employed in other wars to control inflation, and he did not call for a tax increase until the end of 1967. Congress agreed to a 10 percent surcharge on federal income taxes in June 1968, only after Johnson pledged to reduce domestic spending. Johnson's Great Society programs suffered, but the surcharge failed to reverse the inflationary surge.

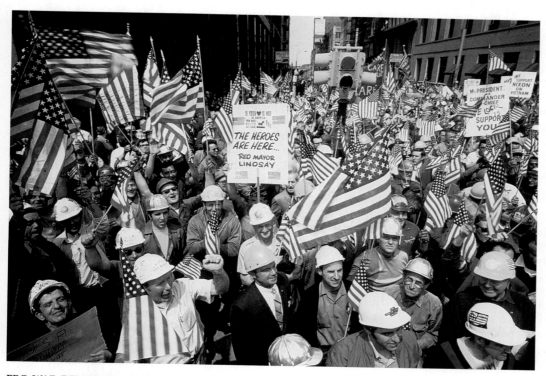

**PRO-WAR DEMONSTRATORS**

*Supporters as well as opponents of the war in Vietnam took to the streets, as these New Yorkers did in support of the U.S. invasion of Cambodia in May 1970. Construction workers—called "hard hats"—and other union members marched with American flags and posters supporting President Nixon's policies and blasting New York Mayor John Lindsay for his antiwar position. Following the demonstration, supportive union leaders presented Nixon with an honorary hard hat.*

Paul Fusco/Magnum Photos, Inc.

Johnson reacted harshly to antiwar sentiment. He agonized over casualty reports and felt personally wounded when protesters chanted outside the White House, "Hey, hey, LBJ, how many kids have you killed today?" In addition to undertaking a public relations campaign that cast the war's progress in a deceptively optimistic light, Johnson tried to discredit opponents by labeling them "nervous Nellies" or Communists.

*Domestic opposition to the war grew rapidly after 1965, and the United States entered into a period of internal conflict and violence unparalleled since the Civil War.*

The administration also employed direct means to silence critics. On Johnson's orders, the CIA spied on peace advocates, compiling secret files on more than seven thousand citizens. Law enforcement officials indicted not just draft resisters but also those like Dr. Benjamin Spock, the famous baby care expert, who counseled them. Without the president's specific authorization, the FBI infiltrated the peace movement and disrupted its work. However, even the resort to illegal measures failed to subdue the opposition.

## 1968: *Year of Upheaval*

Although the majority of Americans remained detached from the peace movement and many opposed it vigorously, by late 1967 public impatience and frustration had intensified. Among those dissatisfied, the "hawks" charged that the United States was fighting with one hand tied behind its back and wanted to apply more power against North Vietnam. The "doves" wanted deescalation or withdrawal. Most Americans were torn between their weariness of the war and their worry about abandoning the American commitment. As one woman said to a pollster, "I want to get out but I don't want to give up."

Grave doubts about the war penetrated the administration itself in 1967. Secretary of Defense McNamara, a principal architect of U.S. involvement, now doubted that the war was winnable. Ho Chi Minh, he believed, "won't quit no matter how much bombing we do." McNamara also feared for the image of the United States, "the world's greatest superpower killing or seriously injuring 1,000

noncombatants a week, while trying to pound a tiny, backward nation into submission on an issue whose merits are hotly disputed." McNamara kept those views to himself until thirty years later, but in early 1968 he left the administration to head the World Bank.

The critical turning point for Johnson came with the Tet Offensive, which began on January 30, 1968. Just a few weeks after General Westmoreland had reported that "the enemy has been driven away from the population centers [and] has been compelled to disperse," the North Vietnamese and Vietcong attacked key cities and every major American base in South Vietnam. The enemy even invaded the grounds of the U.S. embassy in Saigon, killing two Americans and holding the compound for six hours.

The Tet Offensive, named for its occurrence during the Vietnamese lunar new year celebration, Tet, was the biggest surprise of the war—and not simply because it violated a truce that both sides had generally observed during the holiday. Tet displayed the enemy's vitality and refusal to let the presence of half a million American soldiers deter it from launching a daring offensive. Militarily, the Vietcong and North Vietnamese suffered a defeat, losing more than 30,000 men, ten times the casualty rate of ARVN and U.S. forces. Psychologically, however, the Tet Offensive was a devastating blow to the United States.

Tet highlighted the credibility gap between official statements and the actual progress of the war and epitomized for more and more Americans the war's brutality and senselessness. The Tet Offensive created one million more South Vietnamese refugees along with widespread destruction. Referring to a village that he had helped to defend, a U.S. army official said, "We had to destroy the town to save it."

In the aftermath of the Tet Offensive, Johnson considered a request from Westmoreland for 200,000 more troops. He conferred with both his civilian advisers in the Department of Defense and an unofficial group of foreign policy experts, dubbed the "Wise Men," who had played key roles in designing cold war policies since World War II. Dean Acheson, secretary of state under Truman, summarized their conclusion: "We can no longer do the job we set out to do in the time we have left and we must begin to take steps to disengage."

On March 31, 1968, Lyndon Johnson, addressing the nation on television, announced that the United States would reduce its bombing of North

Vietnam and that he was prepared to begin peace talks with North Vietnam. Then he stunned his audience by concluding, "I shall not seek, and I will not accept, the nomination of my party for another term as your president."

Johnson's decision marked the end of the gradual escalation that had begun in 1965. It began a shift from "Americanization" to "Vietnamization" of the war. The United States, however, did not abandon the goal of a non-Communist South Vietnam; it simply hoped to reach that goal by relying more heavily on the South Vietnamese. In that sense, Johnson's announcement represented a return to pre-1965 policy.

Negotiations began in Paris in May 1968. But the United States would not agree to recognition of the NLF, a coalition government, and American withdrawal. The North Vietnamese would agree to nothing less. Although the talks continued, so did the fighting.

Meanwhile, violence escalated at home. Two months after the murder of Martin Luther King Jr. and the riots that erupted in its wake, another assassination stunned the nation. In the race for the Democratic presidential nomination, Senator Robert F. Kennedy, the late president's brother, had just celebrated his triumph in the California primary when he was shot in the head by a Palestinian Arab refugee, who was outraged by Kennedy's recent statement of support for Israel. Kennedy died twenty-six hours later, on June 6.

The spring of 1968 also saw campus violence intensify in some two hundred protests in the first half of the year. The bloodiest occurred at Columbia University, where students took over five buildings, demanding that the university stop uprooting African Americans in the neighboring community, do more to meet the needs of black students, stop sponsoring research for the Department of Defense, and grant amnesty to past and current student demonstrators. When negotiations failed, university officials called in the New York City police, who cleared the buildings, sent more than one hundred demonstrators to the hospital, and arrested more than seven hundred students. An ensuing student strike brought the academic year to a premature end.

In August, protesters battled the police in Chicago, where the Democratic Party convened to nominate its presidential ticket. Several thousand demonstrators came to Chicago, some to show their support for Eugene McCarthy's peace candidacy, others mobilized by the Youth International Party (Yippies), a splinter group of SDS. Its leaders, Abbie Hoffman and Jerry Rubin, urged students to demonstrate their hatred of the establishment by creating chaos and disorder in the backyard of the Democratic convention and provoking the police to violence.

Chicago's mayor and leading Democrat, Richard J. Daley, forbade demonstrators from holding rallies or marches, instituted a curfew, and mobilized thousands of police. When on August 25 police ordered demonstrators in Lincoln Park to disperse, only to be met with taunts and jeers, they attacked the protesters with tear gas and clubs. Street battles continued for three days, culminating in what an official commission later termed a "police riot" on the night of August 28. Taunted by the crowd, the police attacked with mace and nightsticks, clubbing not only those who had wanted to provoke violence, but also reporters, peaceful demonstrators, convention delegates, and bystanders.

The bloodshed in the streets had little effect on the outcome of the convention. Peace Democrats lost the presidential nomination, as Vice President Hubert H. Humphrey trounced Eugene McCarthy by nearly three to one. McCarthy's refusal to share the podium with Humphrey as the convention ended provided a stark illustration of the bitter split within the party.

In contrast, the Republican convention produced little controversy and nominated former Vice President Richard Nixon on the first ballot. For his running mate, Nixon chose Maryland Governor Spiro T. Agnew, hoping to gather southern support while not alienating northern and western voters. For the first time in nearly fifty years, a strong third party entered the electoral scene. Former Alabama Governor George C. Wallace, who had gained national attention for his segregationist stance, ran on the ticket of the American Independent Party. Gaining his strongest support from the Deep South, Wallace also appealed to Americans nationwide who were alarmed and disgusted by the changes that were sweeping their society and frustrated by the nation's inability to work its will in Vietnam.

Few differences separated the two major party candidates on the central issue of Vietnam. Nixon seized the advantage, criticizing the incumbent party for "four years in Vietnam with no end in sight." He promised to "bring an honorable end" to the war but did not indicate how he would do it. Attacking the Great Society for "pouring billions of dollars into programs that have failed" and appealing to "the forgotten Americans, the non-shouters, the non-demonstrators," Nixon more guardedly played on the resentments that fueled the Wallace campaign.

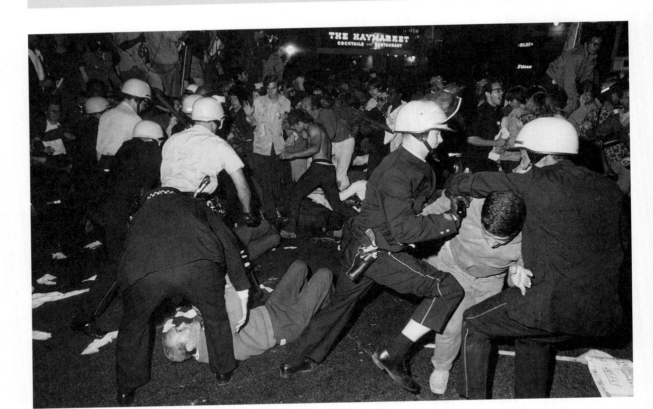

**PROTEST IN THE STREETS**

*The worst violence surrounding the 1968 Democratic National Convention in Chicago came on August 28 when protesters attempted to march to the convention site. Near the Hilton Hotel, where most of the delegates stayed, some three thousand protesters came up against a line of police. Taunted by cries of "Gestapo pigs" and pelted with rocks and bottles, the police attacked the demonstrators, as well as reporters, hotel guests, and bystanders, with nightsticks and mace, driving a crowd through the plate-glass window of the Hilton's cocktail lounge. What other police confrontation in Chicago does the name of the bar in the background recall?*
Corbis-Bettmann.

Humphrey had strong reservations about U.S. policy in Vietnam, yet as vice president he wanted to avoid a break with Johnson. At the end of October, Johnson boosted Humphrey's campaign when he announced a halt to the bombing of North Vietnam. By election eve, Nixon and Humphrey were in a neck-and-neck race.

With nearly ten million votes (13 percent of the total), the American Independent Party produced the strongest third-party finish since 1924. Nixon squeaked by Humphrey by just half a million votes, prevailing more strongly in the electoral college, with 301 votes to Humphrey's 191 and Wallace's 46. The Democrats lost a few seats in Congress but kept control of both the House and the Senate.

The 1968 elections revealed deep cracks in the coalition that had, with the exception of the Eisenhower years, kept the Democrats in power for thirty years. Opposition to the Democrats' policies on race moved most of the South behind Nixon or Wallace, breaking a century of Democratic Party ascendancy in that region. Although union leaders rallied strongly behind Humphrey, large numbers of blue-collar workers voted for Wallace or Nixon. Voters blamed the Democratic Party for its civil rights policies, the Great Society reforms, inflation, antiwar protesters, campus rebels, changing sexual mores, urban riots, and America's impotence in Vietnam. These resentments continued to simmer, later to be mobilized into a resurging right in American politics.

# Nixon's Failed Search for Peace with Honor

"I'm not going to end up like LBJ, holed up in the White House afraid to show my face on the street," the new president asserted. "I'm going to stop that war. Fast." Yet Nixon was no more willing than Johnson had been to allow South Vietnam to fall to the Communists and no more able to find a way to prevent it. Instead, the Nixon administration further polarized the nation and outdid its predecessor in deceiving Congress and the public and in harassing dissenters.

Unable to marshal support at home or to defeat the enemy abroad, in January 1973 the administration concluded a truce that ended the direct involvement of the United States. Far from achieving "peace with honor," the United States accepted conditions that led to total victory for the North Vietnamese in April 1975. By then, public disclosure of the illegal means Nixon had applied to silence his critics and defeat the political opposition at home had driven the president from office.

## Vietnamization and Negotiations

Nixon's most important adviser was not his secretary of state but his assistant for national security, Henry A. Kissinger, a German-born refugee from Hitler's Holocaust and a Harvard professor of international relations. Nixon and Kissinger embraced the overriding goal of the three preceding administrations: a non-Communist South Vietnam. By 1969, however, that goal had become almost incidental to the larger objective of maintaining American credibility. According to Kissinger, regardless of the wisdom of the initial intervention, "the commitment of five hundred thousand Americans has settled the importance of Vietnam. For what is involved now is confidence in American promises."

From 1969 to 1972, Nixon and Kissinger pursued a four-pronged approach. First, they tried to strengthen the South Vietnamese military and government. Second, to disarm the antiwar movement at home, Nixon gradually withdrew U.S. soldiers from combat, replacing them with South Vietnamese soldiers and American technology and bombs. Third, Nixon and Kissinger negotiated with both North Vietnam and the Soviet Union. Fourth, they applied enormous firepower in an effort to get Hanoi to accept American terms at the bargaining table.

As part of the Vietnamization of the war, ARVN forces grew to more than one million, supported with the latest American equipment, improved training, and increased pay scales and benefits. The South Vietnamese air force became the fourth largest in the world. U.S. advisers and funds also promoted land reform, village elections, and the building of schools, hospitals, and transportation facilities. Despite these improvements, whether South Vietnam could stand on its own remained doubtful.

*Nixon was no more willing than Johnson had been to allow South Vietnam to fall to the Communists and no more able to find a way to prevent it.*

The other side of Vietnamization was the withdrawal of U.S. forces. From a peak of 543,000 in June 1968, the number of GIs decreased to 140,000 by the end of 1971. Decreasing draft calls and casualties helped undercut the antiwar movement, yet more than 20,000 Americans perished in Vietnam during the last four years of the war.

Nixon and Kissinger also endeavored to capitalize on Soviet interest in expanded trade and arms reductions by linking U.S. goals in Vietnam with Soviet concerns elsewhere. However, their breakthroughs in summit diplomacy with the Soviet Union and China (discussed in Chapter 30) failed to change the course of the war. Little that the Soviet Union or China could or would do deterred the Communist leaders in Vietnam from pursuing their twenty-year-old goal of unification and national independence.

Nor did intensification of force achieve its objective. Kissinger believed that a "fourth-rate power like North Vietnam" had to have a "breaking point," but the hundreds of thousands of tons of bombs delivered by U.S. pilots failed to find it. Fierce application of American power bought time, but little else. (See the Historical Question on page 792.)

## Nixon's War

In the spring of 1969, Nixon began a fierce air war in Cambodia, carefully hiding it from Congress and the public for more than a year. Designed to knock out North Vietnamese sanctuaries in Cambodia, from which the enemy launched attacks on South

Vietnam, the campaign dropped more than 100,000 tons of bombs but succeeded only in sending the North Vietnamese to other hiding places. To support a new, pro-Western Cambodian government installed through a military coup in 1970 and "to show the enemy that we were still serious about our commitment in Vietnam," in April 1970 Nixon ordered a joint U.S.-ARVN invasion of Cambodia (see Map 29.2).

With that order, the president made Vietnam "Nixon's war" and provoked outrage at home. Nixon concluded a belligerent speech announcing his move by emphasizing the importance of U.S. credibility: "If when the chips are down, the world's most powerful nation acts like a pitiful helpless giant, the forces of totalitarianism and anarchy will threaten free nations . . . throughout the world."

"This will make the students puke," a cabinet member said about Nixon's speech. They did more. A protest in Washington drew upward of 100,000 people, and students demonstrated and boycotted classes on hundreds of campuses. At Kent State University in Ohio, where protesters had burned an ROTC building, the governor called out National Guard troops. At a peaceful rally on May 4, 1970, nervous troops fired at students, killing four and wounding ten others. "They're starting to treat their own children like they treat us," commented a black woman in Harlem. In a confrontation at Jackson State College in Mississippi on May 14, police shot into a dormitory, killing two black students.

Furious at the secret bombing and invasion of Cambodia, legislators attempted to curb the president. The Senate voted to terminate the Gulf of Tonkin Resolution and to cut off funds for the Cambodian operation. The House of Representatives refused to go along, but Congress was clearly becoming an obstacle to the Nixon administration's plans. By the end of June, Nixon pulled out all U.S. soldiers from Cambodia. But the following year, the United States supported an ARVN invasion of Laos.

The Cambodian invasion failed to break the will of the North Vietnamese, but it set in motion a terrible tragedy for the Cambodian people. The North Vietnamese moved farther into Cambodia and increased their support of the Khmer Rouge, Communist insurgents attempting to overthrow the U.S.-supported government of Lon Nol. A brutal civil war lasted until 1975, when the Khmer Rouge triumphed and imposed a savage rule that took millions of Cambodian lives.

In 1971, Vietnam veterans themselves became a visible part of the peace movement, the first men in U.S. history to oppose a war in which they had

**KENT STATE**
*Mary Ann Vecchio, who was not a student but happened to be at Kent State University in Ohio on May 4, 1970, expresses grief and horror just after National Guardsmen's bullets killed Jeff Miller and three other Kent State students. Shock and outrage spread across the United States. After the Kent State killings, about one and a half million students boycotted classes; one of every five campuses shut down for at least a day, and some closed for the rest of the academic year.*
John Filo.

fought. Veterans held a public investigation of "war crimes" in Vietnam, rallied in front of the Capitol, and cast away their war medals. In May 1971, veterans numbered among 40,000 protesters who engaged in civil disobedience in an effort to shut down Washington. Officials made more than 12,000 arrests, which courts later ruled violations of protesters' rights.

After the spring of 1971, there were fewer massive antiwar demonstrations, but vehement protest continued. Public attention focused on the court-martial of Lieutenant William Calley, which began in November 1970 and resulted in his conviction. During the trial, Americans learned that Calley's company had massacred more than two hundred civilians in the hamlet of My Lai in March 1968. Among those murdered were children and women, an atrocity that the military had covered up for more than a year.

Administration policy suffered another blow in June 1971 with publication of the *Pentagon Papers,* a secret, critical government study of U.S. policy in Vietnam. While working as an aide to Henry Kissinger, Daniel Ellsberg, who had previously served as a civilian adviser in Vietnam, came across the documents. Convinced that the war was futile and frustrated in his attempts to persuade officials of his view, Ellsberg copied the papers and gave them to the *New York Times.* Administration efforts to prevent publication of the papers were defeated by the Supreme Court as a violation of freedom of the press. The *Pentagon Papers* spurred disillusionment with the war by casting doubts on the government's credibility. Seventy-one percent of respondents to a public opinion poll in 1971 considered it a mistake to have sent American troops to Vietnam; 58 percent believed the war to be immoral.

## The Peace Accords and the Fall of Saigon

In 1972, Nixon and Kissinger continued to pursue a combined strategy of military force and negotiation. In March, responding to a strong North Vietnamese offensive, the United States resumed sustained bombing of the North, mined Haiphong and other harbors for the first time, and announced a naval blockade. With peace talks stalled in December 1972, Nixon ordered the most devastating bombing of North Vietnam yet: In twelve days, U.S. planes dropped more bombs than they had in all of 1969–1971. On January 27, 1973, representatives of

the United States, North Vietnam, the South Vietnamese government, and the Vietcong (now called the People's Revolutionary Government) signed a formal accord in Paris.

The agreement required removal of all U.S. troops and military advisers but allowed North Vietnamese forces to remain in place. Both sides agreed to return prisoners of war, including hundreds of Americans, some of whom had been held since the mid-1960s. The Thieu government continued in power, and the peace treaty allowed the United States a face-saving withdrawal, but it was doubtful that South Vietnam would remain non-Communist for long.

In 1975, North Vietnam launched a new offensive in South Vietnam, achieving victory in just five months. As South Vietnam neared collapse, Congress approved funds to evacuate Americans and to serve "humanitarian" purposes but refused to authorize any more military aid. On May 1, 1975, Vietcong troops occupied Saigon and renamed it Ho Chi Minh City to honor the Communist leader, who had not lived to see his goal of Vietnamese unification and independence realized.

Confusion, humiliation, and tragedy marked the departure of the last Americans in Vietnam. The United States got its own citizens out, along with 150,000 South Vietnamese allies. But it lacked sufficient aircraft, ships, and time to evacuate all those who wanted to leave. U.S. marines beat back desperate Vietnamese trying to escape through the U.S. embassy. Some South Vietnamese troops, frightened and angry at being left behind, fired on departing Americans.

## The Legacy of Defeat

It took Nixon four years to end the war. During that time, twenty thousand more Americans lost their lives, the conflict expanded into Cambodia and Laos, Southeast Asia endured massive bombing campaigns, and the Vietnam War became genuinely bipartisan. Although increasing numbers of legislators criticized the war, Congress never denied the funds to fight it.

Only after the peace accords did the legislative branch stiffen its constitutional authority over the making of war. In November 1973, Congress enacted the War Powers Act over Nixon's veto. The law required the president to report to Congress within forty-eight hours of deploying military forces in places where hostilities existed or were likely to occur. If Congress failed to endorse the president's action within sixty days, the troops would have to be withdrawn.

Defeat in Vietnam did not become a subject of partisan political debate. Most Americans wanted simply to forget the war. Moreover, the dire predictions of three presidents did not materialize. The Communist victory in South Vietnam did not set the dominoes cascading. Although Vietnam, Laos, and Cambodia all fell within the Communist camp in the spring of 1975, Thailand, Burma, Malaysia, and the rest of Southeast Asia did not. When China and Vietnam soon reverted to their historical relationship of hostility, the myth of a monolithic Communist power overrunning Asia evaporated.

Veterans and those who lost loved ones to the war could not so easily put the war behind them. The nation had always honored its soldiers' sacrifices, but three unique elements of the Vietnam War denied veterans the traditional homecoming: its lack of strong support at home, its character as a guerrilla war, and its ultimate failure. As one veteran remarked, "The left hated us for killing, and the right hated us for not killing enough."

---

*Three unique elements of the Vietnam War denied veterans the traditional homecoming: its lack of strong support at home, its character as a guerrilla war, and its ultimate failure.*

---

Because the Vietnam War was in large part a civil, guerrilla war, combat was especially brutal. The terrors of conventional warfare were multiplied, and so were the opportunities and motivations to commit atrocities. To demonstrate the immorality of the war, peace advocates stressed the atrocities, to which the media also gave substantial coverage in the war's later stages. This emphasis on the cruelties contributed to an image of the Vietnam War veteran as dehumanized and violent and thus deserving of public hostility or indifference.

Veterans expressed two kinds of reactions to the defeat. Many regarded the commitment as an honorable one and castigated the government for betraying them and their dead comrades by not letting them win the war. Others, sometimes expressing shame or guilt, blamed the government for sacrificing its youth in an immoral or useless war. The soldiers themselves best expressed the sense of the war's futility in the slang term they

used in referring to a comrade's death: He was "wasted."

No parades or other heroes' welcomes greeted the returning soldiers. Most came home to public neglect, while some faced harassment from antiwar activists who did not distinguish the war from the warriors. A veteran remembered the "feelings of rejection and scorn that a bunch of depressed and confused young men experienced when they returned home from doing what their country told them to do." Government benefits were less generous to Vietnam War veterans than they had been to World War II and Korean War soldiers. The 11,500 women who had served in Vietnam felt even more isolated and ignored by the government, the public, and veterans' groups.

The Veterans Administration (VA) estimated that nearly one-sixth of the three million veterans suffered from posttraumatic stress disorder, with its symptoms of fear, recurring nightmares, feelings of guilt and shame, violence, drug and alcohol abuse, and suicidal tendencies. More than fifteen years after the war's end, veterans remained on long waiting lists for treatment.

In the late 1970s, a larger proportion of those who had served in Vietnam than in the general population began to display a set of symptoms: They bore deformed children and fell ill themselves with cancer, severe skin disorders, and other ailments. Veterans claimed a link between these illnesses and Agent Orange, an herbicide that contained the deadly poison dioxin, which the military had sprayed by the millions of gallons over Vietnam. Scientists disagreed about the chemical's effects on veterans, and not until 1991 did Congress enact legislation extending benefits to veterans with diseases linked to Agent Orange.

Reversal of the government's position on Agent Orange coincided with a shift in the climate surrounding Vietnam War veterans. "It wasn't until the early 1980s," one veteran observed, "that it became 'all right' to be a combat veteran." The Vietnam War began to enter the realm of popular culture with novels, TV shows, and hit movies depicting a broad range of military experience—from soldiers reduced to brutality to men and women serving with courage and integrity.

The incorporation of the Vietnam War into the collective experience was symbolized most dramatically in the Vietnam Veterans Memorial, unveiled in Washington, D.C., in November 1982. The black, V-shaped wall inscribed with the names of 58,000 men and women lost to the war became the

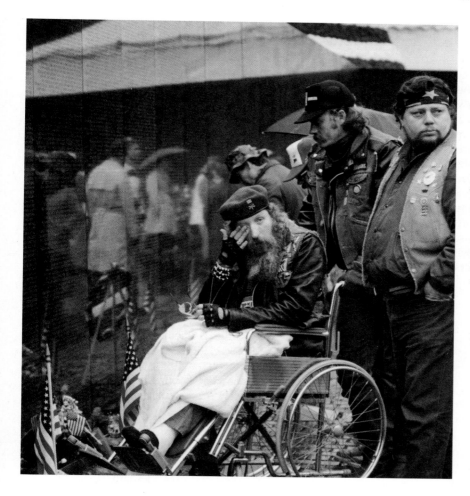

**THE VIETNAM VETERANS MEMORIAL**
*These Vietnam veterans honor their dead comrades at the memorial in the nation's capital. Many veterans found a healing moment in standing before the wall. As one explained at the memorial's dedication in 1982, they came "to find the names of those we lost in the war, as if by tracing the letters cut into the granite we could find what was left of ourselves."*

Peter Marbottom/Magnum Photos, Inc.

second most visited site in the capital, evoking emotional responses from visitors, many of whom adorned it with flowers, flags, messages, and mementos. In an article describing its dedication, a Vietnam combat veteran spoke to and for his former comrades: "Welcome home. The war is over."

## Conclusion: The Limits of American Power

Vietnam was America's longest war. The United States spent $150 billion and sent more than 3 million of its young men and women to Southeast Asia. Fifty-eight thousand never returned, and 300,000 suffered serious injury. The war shattered consensus at home and contributed to the most severe internal disorder in a century. It increased presiden-

tial power at the expense of congressional authority and public accountability and led to the downfall of two presidents. Defeat in Vietnam did not make the United States the "pitiful helpless giant" predicted by Nixon, but it did suggest the relative decline of U.S. power and the impossibility of containment on a global scale.

One of the constraints on U.S. power was the tenacity of revolutionary movements that were determined to achieve national independence. U.S. officials badly underestimated the sacrifices that the North Vietnamese and Vietcong were willing to make for the goal of national liberation. Policymakers overestimated the effectiveness of American technological superiority, and they failed to realize how easily the United States could be perceived as a colonial intruder, no more welcome than the French had been.

A second constraint on Eisenhower, Kennedy, Johnson, and Nixon was their resolve to avoid a major confrontation with the Soviet Union or China.

Johnson, who conducted the largest escalation of the war, especially needed to be cautious to avoid provoking direct intervention by the Communist superpowers. After China exploded its first atomic bomb in 1964, the potential heightened for the Vietnam conflict to escalate into worldwide disaster.

Third, in Vietnam the United States faced the problem of containment by means of an extremely weak ally. The South Vietnamese government never won the support of its people, and the intense devastation and suffering the war brought to the civilian population only made things worse. Short of taking over the South Vietnamese government and military, the United States could do little to strengthen South Vietnam's ability to resist communism.

Finally, domestic opposition to the war constrained the options of Johnson and Nixon. From its origin in 1965, the antiwar movement grew to include significant portions of mainstream America by 1968. As the war dragged on, with increasing American casualties and growing evidence of the damage being inflicted on the Vietnamese, more and more civilians wearied of the conflict. Even some who had fought the war joined the movement, including Philip Caputo, who sent his campaign ribbons and a bitter letter of protest to the White House.

By 1968, distinguished experts who had fashioned and implemented the containment policy recognized that erosion of support for the war made its continuation untenable. Yet the United States fought on for five more years before Nixon and Kissinger bowed to the resolution of the enemy and the limitations of U.S. power.

## CHRONOLOGY

**1961**   CIA-backed Cuban exiles launch unsuccessful invasion of Cuba at Bay of Pigs.

Berlin Wall erected, dividing East and West Berlin.

Kennedy administration increases military aid and military advisers in South Vietnam.

Kennedy administration creates Alliance for Progress and Peace Corps.

**1962**   Cuban missile crisis results in Soviet removal of missiles in Cuba.

**1963**   Limited nuclear test-ban treaty signed by United States and Soviet Union.

South Vietnamese military overthrows President Ngo Dinh Diem.

Lyndon Johnson assumes presidency after Kennedy's assassination; wins election in 1964.

**1964**   U.S. troops quell anti-American rioting in Panama Canal Zone.

President Johnson uses Gulf of Tonkin incident to get congressional resolution of support for escalating the war.

**1965**   First major protest demonstration in Washington, D.C., against Vietnam War attracts 20,000 people.

Johnson administration initiates Operation Rolling Thunder, intensified bombing of North Vietnam.

Johnson orders increase in number of U.S. troops in Vietnam; peak is 543,000 in 1968.

U.S. troops invade Dominican Republic to prevent leftist government from taking power.

**1968**   Hundreds of thousands of Americans demonstrate against war.

Vietnamese Communists' Tet Offensive leads Johnson administration to reverse its policy in Vietnam and seek negotiated settlement.

In wake of Tet Offensive, President Johnson decides not to seek second term.

Richard Nixon elected president.

**1969**   Nixon orders secret bombing of Cambodia.

| **1970** | Nixon orders joint U.S.–South Vietnamese invasion of Cambodia. | **1973** | Paris accords between United States, North and South Vietnam, and Vietcong bring formal end to U.S. role in Vietnam. |

**1970**  Nixon orders joint U.S.–South Vietnamese invasion of Cambodia.

Student protests leave four killed at Kent State and two at Jackson State.

Trial of Lieutenant William Calley for massacre of Vietnamese civilians at My Lai.

**1971**  *New York Times* publishes *Pentagon Papers,* a secret, critical government study of U.S. policy in Vietnam.

**1973**  Paris accords between United States, North and South Vietnam, and Vietcong bring formal end to U.S. role in Vietnam.

Congress enacts War Powers Act, limiting president's ability to send Americans to war without congressional consent.

**1975**  North Vietnam launches final offensive and takes over all of South Vietnam, ending war in Vietnam.

# SUGGESTED READINGS

Philip Caputo, *A Rumor of War* (1977). A gripping account of an infantry officer's experiences in Vietnam in 1965 and 1966.

Dan T. Carter, *The Politics of Race: George Wallace, the Origins of the New Conservatism, and the Transformation of American Politics* (1995). A fascinating biography of the man who led the third-party challenge in the 1968 election.

Charles DeBenedetti, with Charles Chatfield, *An American Ordeal: The Antiwar Movement of the Vietnam Era* (1990). A comprehensive account of antiwar protest.

David Donovan, *Once a Warrior King: Memories of an Officer in Vietnam* (1985). An unusually reflective memoir about the Vietnamization period of the war by a lieutenant sent to Mekong Delta in 1969.

George C. Herring, *America's Longest War: The United States and Vietnam, 1950–1975* (3rd ed., 1996). A relatively brief, balanced survey of the U.S. experience in Vietnam.

Elizabeth Cobbs Hoffman, *All You Need Is Love: The Peace Corps and the Spirit of the 1960s* (1998). An engaging account of the policy behind the Peace Corps, its impact, and the experiences of the volunteers.

Harry Maurer, *Strange Ground: Americans in Vietnam, 1945–1975, an Oral History* (1998). A substantial collection of first-person accounts, including government officials, civilians, pilots, medics, and soldiers.

Walter A. McDougall, *The Heavens and the Earth: A Political History of the Space Age* (reprint, 1997). A Pulitzer Prize–winning history of the space race.

Robert S. McNamara, *In Retrospect: The Tragedy and Lessons of Vietnam* (1995). The Secretary of Defense under Kennedy and Johnson provides an insider's account of how and why the United States undertook the defense of South Vietnam and explains why the policy was wrong.

David Rudenstine, *The Day the Presses Stopped: A History of the* Pentagon Papers *Case* (1996). A definitive account of the fight between the Nixon administration and the press over publication of the secret government study of the Vietnam War.

Amy Swerdlow, *Women Strike for Peace: Traditional Motherhood and Radical Politics in the 1960s* (1993). A fascinating account of one element of the peace movement.

Irwin Unger and Debi Unger, *Turning Point: 1968* (1988). A lively narrative and argument that 1968 was a pivotal year in foreign policy, politics, and social movements.

Mark J. White, *Missiles in Cuba: Kennedy, Khrushchev, Castro, and the 1962 Crisis* (1997). A thoughtful analysis of the causes and effects of the crisis as well as a narrative of the thirteen days.

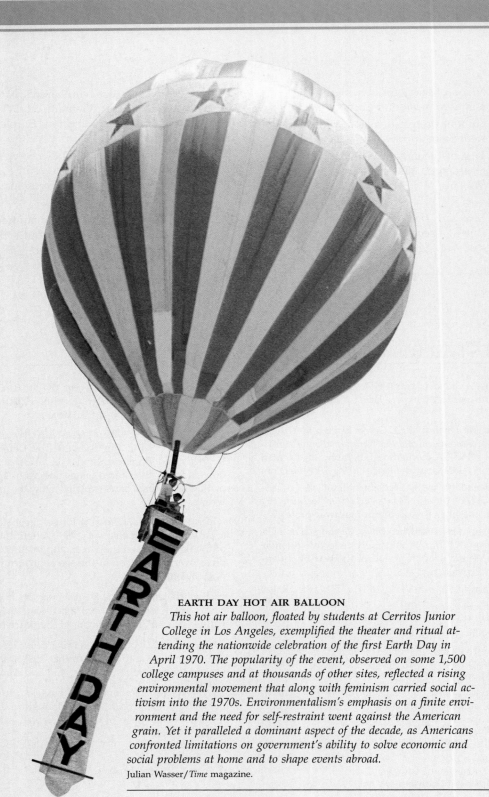

**EARTH DAY HOT AIR BALLOON**

This hot air balloon, floated by students at Cerritos Junior College in Los Angeles, exemplified the theater and ritual attending the nationwide celebration of the first Earth Day in April 1970. The popularity of the event, observed on some 1,500 college campuses and at thousands of other sites, reflected a rising environmental movement that along with feminism carried social activism into the 1970s. Environmentalism's emphasis on a finite environment and the need for self-restraint went against the American grain. Yet it paralleled a dominant aspect of the decade, as Americans confronted limitations on government's ability to solve economic and social problems at home and to shape events abroad.

Julian Wasser/*Time* magazine.

# THE DECLINE OF TRUST AND CONFIDENCE

## 1968–1980

# 30

O N THE EVENING OF JULY 25, 1974, Representative Barbara Jordan gazed solemnly into the television cameras. Not since the 1954 McCarthy hearings on charges of alleged Communists in the army had the activities of a congressional committee so riveted Americans to their TV screens. In a deep, commanding voice, Jordan said, "I am not going to sit here and be an idle spectator to the diminution, the subversion, the destruction of the Constitution." Thus began Jordan's argument for the impeachment of Richard M. Nixon, president of the United States.

That an African American woman from the South could influence the fate of the presidency marked the impact of the civil rights struggles of the preceding decade. Born in 1936, Jordan grew up in an all-black neighborhood in Houston, Texas, living with her grandparents, parents, and two sisters in a two-bedroom house. Her father's income as a warehouse clerk and part-time minister provided a modest standard of living but few extras. Instilled with discipline and ambition by her parents, Jordan attended a segregated high school and then went to the all-black Texas Southern University. Riding at the back of the bus, drinking out of water fountains marked "colored," and attending segregated, underfunded schools were routine for Jordan and her friends in the 1950s.

In high school and college, Jordan discovered and honed her skills as an orator and debater. After earning her degree from Boston University in 1960, she returned home to practice law. Local Democrats recognized her remarkable speaking skills, sent her out campaigning, and supported her candidacy for the Texas House of Representatives in 1962 and 1964. Running in countywide at-large elections, she lost both times to white candidates.

But the U.S. Supreme Court's "one person, one vote" decisions in the 1960s forced Texas to reapportion its legislative districts and opened political doors for Jordan. In 1966, she won election to the Texas Senate from her district, now heavily populated by African Americans, Chicanos, and white labor unionists, and became one of the first two African Americans to serve as Texas senators since 1882. In 1972, voters sent her to the U.S. House of Representatives, where she was appointed to the House Judiciary Committee.

Jordan's argument for impeachment reflected lifelong habits of painstaking research and careful deliberation, as she measured the illegal activities of President

**BARBARA JORDAN**
*After gaining national attention for her role in the Nixon impeachment hearings, Barbara Jordan served in the House of Representatives until she retired in 1978. The representative from Texas supported women's rights as well as civil rights; here she addresses the government-sponsored National Women's Conference in Dallas, Texas, in 1977.*
Owen Franken/Sygma.

zens' faith in government, and voter turnout reached only 52.3 percent in 1980. A fragmented congressional leadership—attempting to curb excessive presidential power yet feeling its own power drawn away from its traditional party centers—confronted critical challenges. Shifting relations between the superpowers and new shock waves in the Middle East threatened Western access to oil; at home, a sluggish economy, declining productivity, and rising unemployment replaced the rapid economic growth of the 1960s.

The right wing became a more vocal minority, and some 1960s reforms, including civil rights, suffered setbacks. Yet a few African Americans, such as Barbara Jordan, slowly edged into the margins of the power structure, and key elements of the Great Society actually expanded. A reconstituted Supreme Court under Chief Justice Warren Burger maintained most of the Warren Court's protections of individual rights. Two social movements that had begun late in the 1960s—environmentalism and feminism—achieved their greatest strength during the decade.

Yet a more prevalent pessimism took hold as a majority of Americans saw their standard of living slip and the global position of their nation decline. The heady optimism of the post–World War II era, badly shaken by defeat in Vietnam, shattered with the economic crises and foreign policy setbacks of the 1970s. Limitations rather than possibilities characterized both the popular mood and the state of the nation.

Nixon against historical and legal standards. If Nixon's offenses did not add up to impeachment, Jordan concluded, "then perhaps that eighteenth-century Constitution should be abandoned to a twentieth-century paper shredder." The next day, billboards sprang up in Houston reading, "Thank you, Barbara Jordan, for explaining the Constitution to us."

Before the House could act on impeachment, Nixon resigned the presidency in disgrace. His successor, Gerald R. Ford, occupied the Oval Office for little more than two years, defeated by Jimmy Carter in the 1976 election. After a single term, Carter too was voted out of office.

This rapid turnover in the presidency reflected in part a widespread loss of trust and confidence in government in the 1970s. Public opinion polls reported a drop from 56 percent to 29 percent in citi-

## Politics and the Persistence of Reform

Richard Nixon took his victory in 1968 as evidence that most Americans were fed up with social protest and government efforts to expand individual rights and opportunities. He continued to appeal to those frustrations, and the pace of reform slackened considerably during his administration. Yet Nixon had won the Republican nomination as a centrist. Like Eisenhower, he did not try to turn the clock back a decade, nor did his presidency bring reform efforts to a screeching halt.

The Democrats maintained a congressional majority, and the government faced pressures from popular movements that survived the 1960s—civil rights, women's rights, and environmentalism.

## Nixon's "Southern Strategy" and Race Relations

Nixon's 1968 campaign had exploited antipathy to black protest and new civil rights policies to woo white southerners away from the Democratic Party. This "southern strategy" won Nixon the electoral votes of the Upper South, yet George Wallace ran strongly in the South and made inroads into traditional white voting blocs in northern and western cities. The prospect of another Wallace campaign in 1972 encouraged Republicans to write off the black vote and appeal to whites who thought racial progress had gone far enough. Thus the president's public rhetoric and policies sought to slow the momentum of racial change and reap the political benefits of the white backlash.

*Richard Nixon took his victory in 1968 as evidence that most Americans were fed up with social protest and government efforts to expand individual rights and opportunities.*

Yet the Nixon administration had to answer to the courts and Congress. In 1968, fourteen years after the *Brown* decision, school desegregation had barely touched the South: Two-thirds of African American children did not have a single white schoolmate. Nixon wanted a freedom-of-choice approach that forbade discrimination but did not use federal power to compel integration. Nonetheless, when the Supreme Court overruled efforts by the Justice Department to delay court-ordered desegregation, in 1969 the administration agreed to enforce the law. By the time Nixon left office, fewer than one in ten black children attended totally segregated schools in the South.

In fact, school segregation was more extreme in northern and western cities, where segregated residential patterns left half of all African American children attending virtually all-black schools. By 1971, busing students from white to black neighborhoods and vice versa to achieve desegregation had become one of the most inflammatory civil rights issues. That year, in *Swann v. Charlotte-Mecklenburg Board of Education,* the Supreme Court ruled unanimously that busing was an appropriate remedy to overcome segregation previously sanctioned by the city. Subsequently, federal courts approved busing plans in cities that had not officially maintained segregated schools but that had residential patterns resulting in de facto segregation.

Busing for racial integration provoked outrage. When busing began at the formerly all-white South Boston High School in 1974, virtually all of the white students boycotted classes while angry whites threw rocks at black students. The whites most affected came from working-class families, who remained in cities abandoned by more affluent whites and who felt overlooked in favor of minorities and the poor. Moreover, white children rode buses to predominantly black schools where overcrowding and deficient facilities often meant inferior education. African Americans themselves were divided over the desirability of busing children across district lines.

Nixon failed to persuade Congress to end court-ordered busing, but after he had appointed four new justices, the Supreme Court moved in the president's direction in 1974. In a five-to-four decision concerning the Detroit public schools (*Milliken v. Bradley*), the Court imposed strict limits on the use of busing to achieve racial balance.

Despite Nixon's conservative rhetoric and practice, his administration did take some steps against discrimination, requiring contractors and unions to employ more minority workers on federally funded construction projects and raising the number of government contracts and loans awarded to minority businesses. Congress took the initiative in other areas, in 1970 extending the Voting Rights Act of 1965 by five years. In March 1972, Congress strengthened the Civil Rights Act of 1964 by enlarging the jurisdiction and authority of the Equal Employment Opportunity Commission, the act's enforcement agency.

Nixon believed that the Supreme Court under Chief Justice Earl Warren had been "unprecedentedly politically active . . . too often using their interpretation of the law to remake American society according to their own social, political, and ideological precepts." Through his judicial appointments, Nixon planned both to reverse the Court's direction and to implement his "southern strategy." When Warren resigned in June 1969, Nixon replaced him with Warren E. Burger, a federal appeals court judge, who was seen as a more conservative strict constructionist. When Nixon tried to appoint two conservative southern judges, however, the Senate forced him to settle on more moderate candidates. The Burger Court proved more sympathetic to the president's agenda, narrowing somewhat the protections of individual rights that the Warren Court had established. Yet it continued to uphold social reform, expanding the rights of welfare recipients and issuing decisions that favored victims of race and sex discrimination.

The Burger Court's approach to affirmative action reflected the middle ground it occupied. In *Regents of the University of California v. Bakke* (1978), the sharply divided justices ruled in favor of a white man who had been denied admission to a University of California medical school even though his test scores were higher than those of some minority applicants who were admitted. Yet the Court sanctioned affirmative action programs to attack the results of past discrimination as long as strict quotas or racial classifications were not involved.

## The New Feminism

On August 26, 1970, fifty years after women won the right to vote, tens of thousands of women took to the streets. In nationwide protests, called Women Strike for Peace and Equality, they carried signs reading "Sisterhood Is Powerful," "Don't Cook Dinner—Starve a Rat Today," and "Don't Iron While the Strike Is Hot." Some of the banners proclaimed, "The Women of Vietnam Are Our Sisters," and others demanded racial justice. But this time, women placed their own liberation at the forefront.

---

*Feminist activism produced the most sweeping changes in laws and policies concerning women since the Nineteenth Amendment in 1920 guaranteed women's right to vote.*

---

Organized largely by chapters of the National Organization for Women (NOW), the strike reflected the diverse strands that constituted the new feminism of the 1970s: radical women in jeans and conservatively dressed former suffragists, peace activists and politicians, and a sprinkling of women of color. The strike centered on NOW's three main demands: equality for women in employment and education; child care centers throughout the nation; and women's control over reproduction, including the right to abortion.

Feminism in the 1970s spawned hundreds of new organizations, radical changes in how women perceived themselves and their interests, and revolutionary changes in women's status under the law. Women's liberation, the radical wing of feminism, erupted from women's experiences in the civil rights and antiwar movements of the 1960s. Representing feminism's mainstream was NOW, founded in 1966, an outgrowth of the work of President Kennedy's Commission on the Status of Women.

Although NOW elected a black president, Aileen Hernandez, in 1970, white middle-class women in the political mainstream provided most of the national leadership and much of the constituency for the new feminism. They were criticized for their frequent indifference to the concerns of women who were unlike themselves, yet support for feminism was exceedingly multifaceted. Most African American women worked through their own groups such as the older National Council of Negro Women and the National Black Feminist Organization, founded in 1973. Similarly, in the early 1970s American Indian women and Mexican American women founded national organizations, and Asian American women formed their own local movements. Blue-collar women organized the National Coalition of Labor Union Women in 1974, and clerical workers founded Nine-to-Five. Lesbians established collectives throughout the country as well as their own caucuses in organizations such as NOW. Women formed a host of other groups that focused on single issues such as health, abortion rights, education, and violence against women.

Common threads underlay the great diversity of organizations, issues, and activities. Above all, feminism represented the belief that women were barred from, unequally treated in, or poorly served by the male-dominated public arena, encompassing politics, medicine, law enforcement, education, and religion. Feminists challenged traditional norms that identified women primarily as wives and mothers or sex objects, and they sought equality in both the private and public spheres.

The women's movement was an effect rather than a cause of women's rising employment, but feminism lifted female aspirations and helped lower barriers to jobs historically monopolized by men. Women made some inroads into skilled crafts and management positions. During the 1970s, their share of law degrees shot up from 5.4 percent to nearly 30 percent, and their proportion of medical degrees from 8.4 percent to 23 percent. In political

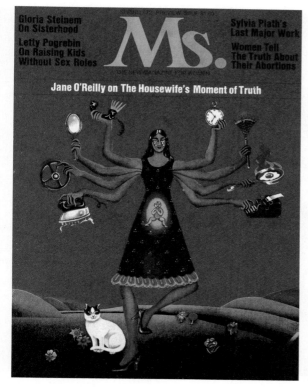

**MS. MAGAZINE**
*In 1972, Gloria Steinem and other journalists and writers
published the premier issue of the first mass-circulation
magazine to be controlled for and by women. Ms.: The
New Magazine for Women ignored the recipes and
fashion tips of typical women's magazines. It featured literature by women writers and articles on a broad range of
feminist issues. What concerns are suggested by the cover
of this premier issue?*
Courtesy, Lang Communications.

officeholding their gains came very slowly. Yet by
the late 1980s, women served as mayors in ten large
cities and held 15 percent of municipal offices and
state legislative seats.

Feminist activism produced the most sweeping
changes in laws and policies concerning women
since the Nineteenth Amendment in 1920 guaranteed women's right to vote. In 1972, Congress
passed Title IX of the Education Amendments Act,
banning sex discrimination in all aspects of education, such as admissions, athletics, and faculty hiring. Congress also outlawed sex discrimination in
granting credit in 1974, opened the military acade-

mies to women in 1976, and prohibited discrimination against pregnant workers in 1978.

At the state and local levels, radical feminists
spoke out about rape and won new state laws that
forced more humane and just treatment of rape victims by police departments and the legal system.
Groups of women set up shelters to provide safety
for battered women and their children. Nearly
every state passed laws affording greater protection
for victims of domestic violence and more effective
prosecution of offenders. Feminists pressured state
legislatures to end restrictions on abortion, and
many testified publicly about their own illegal abortions. In 1973, the Supreme Court issued the landmark *Roe v. Wade* decision, ruling that the Constitution protects the right to abortion and that states
cannot prohibit abortion in the early stages of pregnancy. However, later decisions allowed state governments to impose restrictions on that right. Most
states, for example, refused to pay for the procedure
under Medicaid and other government-financed
health programs, making it especially hard for poor
women to obtain abortions.

The Court also struck down laws that treated
men and women differently, such as those granting
Social Security and welfare benefits, workers' compensation, and access to military programs. Although the Court refused to adopt the same strict
standard for laws differentiating on the basis of sex
as it did for those involving race, these and other
rulings overturned centuries of law based on
women's dependency as daughters, wives, and
mothers.

Public opinion polls registered majorities in
favor of most feminist goals, yet by the mid-1970s
feminism faced a strong countermovement. Its
leader, Phyllis Schlafly, had built her political career
in the right-wing politics of fervent anticommunism
and opposition to big government and social welfare programs. In the 1970s, Schlafly and other conservatives broadened their program to include a defense of conventional sex roles and the traditional
family.

Antifeminism achieved its greatest victory in
blocking ratification of an Equal Rights Amendment
(ERA) to the Constitution that would outlaw any
differential treatment of men and women under all
state and federal laws. Initially proposed by a small
band of feminists in 1923, the ERA rode through
Congress in 1972 on the wave of the new feminism.
Most states rushed to ratify the amendment; yet by
1973, Schlafly and other conservative politicians, as

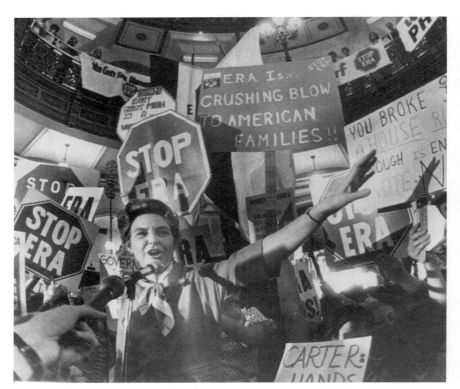

**PHYLLIS SCHLAFLY**
*As one of the few nonsouthern states that rejected ratification of the proposed Equal Rights Amendment, Illinois was the scene of feverish activity by supporters and opponents. Here STOP ERA leader Phyllis Schlafly rallies her followers in the rotunda of the Illinois capitol in Springfield in June 1978. STOP ERA women handed legislators apple pies bearing the words "For the sake of the family please vote no."*
Corbis-Bettmann.

well as a host of women at the grassroots level who feared a breakdown of traditional gender roles, had begun to organize massive resistance. When the time limit on ratification ran out in 1982, only thirty-five states had ratified the amendment, three short of the necessary three-fourths majority.

Opposition to the right to abortion was also intense. Many Americans believed that human life begins with conception, and they equated abortion with murder. The Catholic Church and other religious organizations provided institutional support for their protest. Right-wing politicians and their supporters constituted another segment of the right-to-life movement. Like opponents of the ERA, the right-to-life movement mobilized thousands of women who believed that abortion devalued motherhood and saw feminism as a threat to their traditional roles.

Feminists faced a host of other challenges as the 1970s ended. For example, despite the inroads women made into male-dominated occupations, most women still worked in traditionally female jobs with low pay scales. Moreover, employed women continued to bear primary responsibility for the care of their homes and families, thereby work-ing a "double day." As the number of female-headed families grew from 10 percent to 20 percent of all families between 1970 and 1990, the situation of employed mothers became even more critical.

## A Movement to Save the Environment

In April 1970, millions of Americans observed the first Earth Day to register their concern over the ravaging effects of industrial development on the environment. In Wisconsin, students distributed flyers on recycling, and a group of Detroit women picketed a steel plant that discharged industrial waste into a river. Girl scouts cleaned garbage from the Potomac River, Berkeley citizens attended an environmental teach-in, and African Americans in St. Louis dramatized the effects of poisons in lead paint.

Inheriting their concern for the natural world from the decades-old conservation movement, the new environmentalists had a far broader agenda. Even more important than preserving portions of the natural world for aesthetic and recreational purposes was protecting human beings, wildlife, and plants from the devastating side effects of industrial development and economic growth—polluted air and water and the spread of deadly chemicals. Older conservation organizations like the Sierra Club and the Wilderness Society expanded the scope of their concerns, and a host of new organizations arose. In 1971, environmentalists founded Greenpeace, which protested nuclear testing around the world and campaigned to save whales, other ocean animals, and tropical rain forests. Even more militant was Earth First!, created in 1980 and committed to direct action and sabotage of projects injurious to the environment.

Although President Nixon asserted that the nation must begin "reclaiming the purity of its air, its waters, our living environment," he generally favored economic growth over environmental considerations. He vetoed anti–water pollution bills and, against objections from environmentalists, pushed Congress to authorize construction of a 789-mile-long pipeline to carry oil across Alaska. Yet in other respects the Nixon administration proved a friend—or at least not an enemy—of the environmental movement. In 1970, Nixon established the Environmental Protection Agency (EPA), charged with enforcing clean air and water policies and regulating pesticides. He also signed the Occupational Safety and Health Act (OSHA), which safeguarded workers against workplace accidents and disease.

The strongest measure supported by the Nixon administration was the Clean Air Act of 1970, which

**EARTH DAY**
*Because of its association with nature and the earth, green was the color of the environmental movement, and environmentalists called themselves "greens." These activists leave no doubt about their affiliation at an Earth Day celebration in New York City in April 1970. The button, a takeoff on the antiwar slogan "Give Peace a Chance," reflects the continuing impact of the antiwar movement.*
Dennis Stock/Magnum Photos, Inc.; button: private collection.

set national standards for air quality and restricted factory and automobile emissions. Twenty years after enactment, no major city met the new standards, but even with lenient enforcement, the Clean Air Act cut the amount of air pollutants by one-third, despite population and economic growth.

---

*Inheriting their concern for the natural world from the decades-old conservation movement, the new environmentalists had a far broader agenda: protecting human beings, wildlife, and plants from the devastating side effects of industrial development and economic growth.*

---

Warning of radiation leakage, the potential for accidents, and the hazards of nuclear wastes, environmentalists also targeted nuclear power plants, which by 1977 produced about 11 percent of the country's electricity. The perils of nuclear energy came into dramatic focus in March 1979, when an accident occurred at the Three Mile Island nuclear facility in Pennsylvania. Technicians worked for days to prevent a meltdown of the reactor core, while thousands of people near the plant fled their homes and the threat of fatal radiation. The great expense of building nuclear plants and popular opposition stalled further development of the nuclear power industry; but antinuclear activism endured as a part of the environmental movement.

## Domestic and Foreign Initiatives of the Nixon Era

Not all of the reforms of the 1970s originated outside the White House. While Richard Nixon's public rhetoric appealed to Americans unhappy with the expanding federal programs of the 1960s, in practice his administration pursued a domestic agenda that sometimes bore marks of the very government activism that the president decried in his speeches. Growing out of political expediency, a Democratic Congress representing a broad spectrum of political positions, the president's eye on his place in history, and serious economic problems,

Nixon's domestic policies sustained many of the reforms of the 1960s and even expanded the government's role.

Nixon's foreign policy also diverged from Republican orthodoxy, most markedly by seeking accommodation with the Soviet Union and China. Yet at the same time, in Vietnam, the Middle East, and Latin America, the administration pursued policies straight out of the cold war book of unrelenting opposition to communism.

### Extending the Welfare State

Richard Nixon's second inaugural address in 1973 encapsulated his objections to much of Lyndon Johnson's Great Society: "In trusting too much to government, we have asked more of it than it can deliver. . . . Government must learn to take less from people so people can do more for themselves." Nixon's words appealed to "middle America," which resented government's apparent disregard for its interests while favoring individuals who they felt lacked the discipline and willingness to help themselves. Congress resisted many of Nixon's attacks on antipoverty programs, refusing, for example, to eliminate the Office of Economic Opportunity. Key programs such as Medicare and Medicaid, Head Start, Legal Services, and job training remained intact. At the same time, Nixon blocked congressional initiatives such as the child care bill passed by Congress in 1971, objecting both to the program's $2 billion cost and to its "family-weakening implications."

More significant than the Nixon administration's battle against federal programs was its extension of government assistance to the disadvantaged. The federal budget for social services exceeded defense spending for the first time since World War II. Social Security benefits increased, now required to rise with the cost of living. Subsidies for low-income housing shot up from less than $1 million in 1969 to nearly $3 billion in 1973. A new program provided $1 billion in so-called Pell grants (named for the congressman who sponsored the law) for low-income students to attend college. And in response to growing public attention to undernourishment and concern that the Democrats would capitalize on that issue, Nixon proposed a huge expansion of the food stamp program; the number of recipients grew from 2.5 to 15 million between 1969 and 1974.

## The New Federalism and New Federal Activism

Nixon called his domestic agenda the New Federalism, expressing traditional Republican distaste for federal control and preference for state and local autonomy and responsibility. To this end, he made revenue sharing, the transfer of federal funds to state and local governments, a cornerstone of his domestic program. Enacted in October 1972, the revenue sharing law gave states and localities considerable discretion in spending decisions and strengthened their financial foundations. The law transferred more than $5 billion of federal funds annually to state and local governments. The administration also consolidated funding for existing programs into broad block grants. Although still targeted for specific purposes such as community development or job training, block grants allowed local governments greater discretion in their use. General revenue sharing and block grants represented only a small step toward the decentralization of government power.

Indeed, the expansion of federal controls in other areas overshadowed the New Federalism. Despite Nixon's aversion to a growing federal bureaucracy, certain problems eluded solution at the state level or posed economic or political threats that were too great to risk inaction. Thus, in addition to approving new environmental controls, Nixon expanded the government's role in dealing with energy shortages, inflation, and unemployment.

Throughout the post–World War II economic boom, the nation's abundant oil deposits along with access to cheap supplies of Middle Eastern oil had encouraged the building of large cars, suburban housing developments, and glass-enclosed skyscrapers with no concern for fuel efficiency. The traditional American assumption that energy resources were boundless and the resulting wasteful practices meant that by the 1970s the United States, with just 6 percent of the world's population, consumed one-third of its fuel resources.

In the fall of 1973, the United States faced its first energy crisis when Arab nations, furious at the Nixon administration's support of Israel during the Yom Kippur War, cut off oil shipments to the United States. Nations that did not join the embargo raised prices nearly tenfold. As supplies of oil fell in the winter of 1973–74, long lines formed at gas stations, where prices had nearly doubled, many homes were cold, and some schools had to close. In response, Nixon signed legislation authorizing temporary emergency powers to allocate petroleum and establishing a national 55-mile-per-hour speed limit to save gasoline. By the spring of 1974, the energy crisis had eased, thanks largely to these and other measures, voluntary conservation, a relatively mild winter, and cessation of the Arab oil embargo. But the United States had yet to come to grips with its seemingly unquenchable demand for fuel and its dependence on foreign oil.

Soaring energy prices contributed to the second serious economic problem: a rising cost of living. By 1969, the inflation rate had risen to 7 percent, an enormous increase to Americans used to rates of about 2 percent. By 1970, unemployment had joined inflation as a serious problem. This unprecedented combination of a stagnant economy and inflation soon received the name "stagflation."

Domestic troubles were compounded by the decline of American dominance in the international economy. Having fully recovered from World War II, the economies of Japan and Western Europe grew faster than the economy of the United States. Foreign cars, electronic equipment, and other products competed favorably with American goods throughout the world. In 1971, for the first time in decades, the United States imported more than it exported. Because the amount of dollars in foreign hands exceeded U.S. gold reserves, the nation could no longer back up its currency with gold.

Political considerations helped to shape the president's response to these economic problems, a response that diverged from conventional Republican doctrine. With an eye to the 1972 election, Nixon announced a "New Economic Policy" in August 1971. He abandoned the convertibility of dollars into gold, devalued the dollar to make American goods cheaper in foreign markets and thus increase exports, and imposed a 10 percent surcharge on most imports. Nixon also froze wages and prices, thus enabling the government to stimulate the economy without fueling more inflation.

In the short run, these policies worked. Exports surged ahead of imports, inflation subsided, unemployment fell below 5 percent, and Nixon was resoundingly reelected in 1972. Yet the New Economic Policy treated the economy only superficially. The lifting of price and wage controls in 1973, the Arab oil embargo, and rising food prices sent the consumer price index soaring to 11 percent by 1974. Unemployment also crept back up, and Nixon's successor inherited the most severe economic crisis since the depression of the 1930s.

## New Opportunities and Dangers in a Multipolar World

New approaches to China and the Soviet Union formed the keystone of Nixon's foreign policy, and his most important innovation was to deflate ideology as the driving force. As his chief foreign policy adviser, Henry Kissinger, put it in 1969, "We will judge other countries, including Communist countries, . . . on the basis of their actions and not on the basis of their domestic ideology." Nixon and Kissinger moved to exploit the deterioration in Soviet-Chinese relations that had begun in the early 1960s and had escalated into military clashes along their common border in 1969. If these two nations balanced and checked each other's power, the threat of either of them to the United States would lessen.

U.S. overtures through intermediaries set the stage for Nixon's most dramatic act as president. In February 1972, he became the nation's first president to set foot on Chinese soil—an astonishing act by a man who had climbed the political ladder as an all-out anti-Communist. Indeed, it was Nixon's irreproachable anti-Communist credentials that enabled him to conduct this shift in U.S.-Chinese relations with no significant objections at home. As he remarked to Chinese leader Mao Zedong, "Those on the right can do what those on the left only talk about." Although neither side expected immediate results from Nixon's largely symbolic act, his visit brought U.S. policy more into conformity with the actual world and paved the way for formal diplomatic relations by the end of the decade.

As Nixon and Kissinger hoped, the warming of U.S.-Chinese relations increased Soviet responsiveness to the Nixon-Kissinger strategy of détente, the term given to efforts to ease conflict with the Soviet Union. In pursuing détente, Nixon and Kissinger did not abandon the principle of containment but instead concentrated on issues of common concern to the two superpowers, such as arms control, trade, and stability in Europe. Containment would be achieved not only by military threat but also by ensuring that Russia and China had stakes in a stable international order and would therefore refrain from precipitating crises.

In May 1972, three months after his trip to China, Nixon met with Soviet leaders in Moscow, coming away with several agreements regarding trade and cooperation in science and space. Most significantly, Soviet and U.S. leaders signed arms

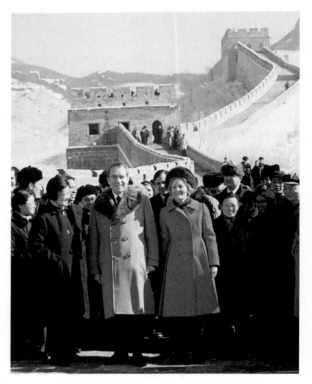

**NIXON IN CHINA**
*"This was the week that changed the world," proclaimed President Richard M. Nixon in February 1972, emphasizing the dramatic turnaround in relations with America's former enemy the People's Republic of China. The Great Wall of China forms the setting for this photograph of Nixon and his wife, Pat.*
Nixon Presidential Materials Project.

limitation treaties that, although not preventing research and development, limited antiballistic missile systems (ABMs) to two each and made the first advance in curbing offensive weapons.

In his second inaugural address in January 1973, Nixon said, "The time has passed when America will make every other nation's conflict our own . . . or presume to tell the people of other nations how to manage their own affairs." Yet even while minimizing ideology in dealing with China and the Soviet Union, in Vietnam and elsewhere Nixon and Kissinger continued to equate the ideology of Marxism with a threat to U.S. interests and actively resisted social revolutions.

The Nixon administration found that threat in Salvador Allende, a self-proclaimed Marxist who was elected president of Chile in 1970. Nixon announced that the United States "accepted that decision," yet the CIA made plans for a military coup to overthrow Allende, and the United States exerted political and economic pressure to destabilize the Allende government. In 1973, the Chilean military engineered a coup, killed Allende, and established a dictatorship under General Augusto Pinochet.

The Nixon administration moved closer to repressive governments in other parts of the world. In the Middle East, the United States found in the harsh Iranian regime a stable anti-Communist ally—one with enormous petroleum reserves. In 1972, the Nixon administration began secretly to provide massive amounts of arms to the shah of Iran, cementing a relationship that would ignite a new crisis for the United States when the shah was overthrown in 1979.

*While minimizing ideology in dealing with China and the Soviet Union, in Vietnam and elsewhere Nixon and Kissinger continued to equate the ideology of Marxism with a threat to U.S. interests and actively resisted social revolutions.*

Like its predecessors, the Nixon administration pursued a delicate balance between defending Israel's security and seeking the goodwill of Arab nations that were strategically and economically important to the United States. Conflict between Israel and the Arab nations had escalated into all-out war (the Six Day War) in 1967, when Israel won a stunning victory over Egyptian, Syrian, and Jordanian forces and took control of territory that amounted to twice the original size of Israel (Map 30.1). That decisive victory did not quell Middle Eastern turmoil. Instead, Palestinian refugees stepped up guerrilla attacks against the Israelis, and the Soviet Union expanded military aid to Arab countries, which refused to recognize Israel's right to exist. Israel would not withdraw from the territories occupied during the Six Day War, and no solution could be found for the Palestinian refugees who had been displaced by the creation of Israel in the late 1940s.

In October 1973, on Yom Kippur, the holiest day in the Jewish calendar, Egypt and Syria surprised Israel with a full-scale attack. When the Nixon administration sided with Israel, the Arab nations imposed an oil embargo. After Israel repulsed the attack, Kissinger assumed the role of mediator

between the two sides. Unable to resolve the underlying conflicts, he achieved some limited disengagements between Israeli forces and their enemies. As a result, the Arab nations lifted the oil embargo, and Soviet influence in the area declined as U.S. credibility among Arabs increased.

# Constitutional Crisis and Restoration

In the 1972 presidential election, Richard Nixon turned his narrow victory of 1968 into a massive landslide, and his approval ratings in the polls neared 70 percent. Less than two years later, Nixon abandoned the presidency in disgrace. His abuse of presidential power and efforts to cover up crimes that had been committed by subordinates betrayed the public trust and forced the first presidential resignation in history.

Nixon's handpicked successor, Gerald Ford, brought to the White House a reputation for decency and openness that helped to restore confidence in the presidency. Ford maintained the basic policy directions set by the Nixon administration, but he faced economic problems even more severe. In 1976, Ford lost the presidency to Democrat Jimmy Carter.

## From Triumph to Disgrace: Watergate

Nixon's most spectacular foreign policy initiatives, détente with the Soviet Union and the opening of relations with China, heightened his prospects for reelection in 1972. Although the war in Vietnam continued, antiwar protests diminished with the decrease in American ground forces and casualties. Nixon's New Economic Policy had temporarily checked both inflation and unemployment, and his attacks on busing and antiwar protesters had solidified his support on the right. At their convention in Miami Beach in August 1972, the Republicans resoundingly renominated Nixon and his vice president, Spiro Agnew.

A large field of contenders vied for the Democratic nomination, including New York Representative Shirley Chisholm, the first African American politician to make a serious bid for the presidency. Senator George S. McGovern of South Dakota chalked up primary victories in key states, while on the right, Governor George Wallace of Alabama won a series of southern primaries as well as those in Michigan and Maryland. Wallace's

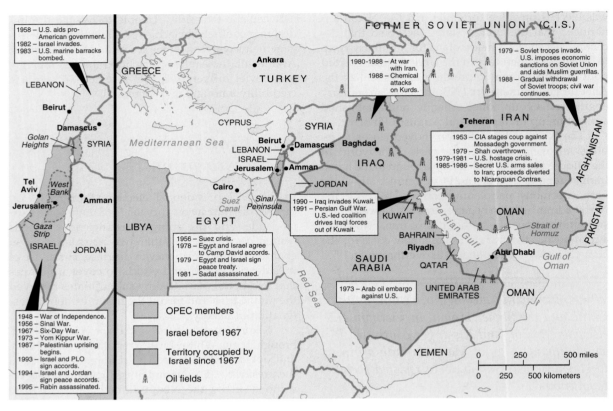

1958 – U.S. aids pro-American government.
1982 – Israel invades.
1983 – U.S. marine barracks bombed.

1980-1988 – At war with Iran.
1988 – Chemical attacks on Kurds.

1979 – Soviet troops invade. U.S. imposes economic sanctions on Soviet Union and aids Muslim guerrillas.
1988 – Gradual withdrawal of Soviet troops; civil war continues.

1953 – CIA stages coup against Mossadegh government.
1979 – Shah overthrown.
1979-1981 – U.S. hostage crisis.
1985-1986 – Secret U.S. arms sales to Iran; proceeds diverted to Nicaraguan Contras.

1990 – Iraq invades Kuwait.
1991 – Persian Gulf War. U.S.-led coalition drives Iraqi forces out of Kuwait.

1956 – Suez crisis.
1978 – Egypt and Israel agree to Camp David accords.
1979 – Egypt and Israel sign peace treaty.
1981 – Sadat assassinated.

1973 – Arab oil embargo against U.S.

1948 – War of Independence.
1956 – Sinai War.
1967 – Six-Day War.
1973 – Yom Kippur War.
1987 – Palestinian uprising begins.
1993 – Israel and PLO sign accords.
1994 – Israel and Jordan sign peace accords.
1995 – Rabin assassinated.

☐ OPEC members
☐ Israel before 1967
☐ Territory occupied by Israel since 1967
⚒ Oil fields

0   250   500 miles
0   250   500 kilometers

MAP 30.1
*The Middle East, 1948–1995*
*U.S. determination to preserve access to the rich oil reserves of the Middle East and its commitment to the security of Israel were the fundamental—and sometimes conflicting—principles of U.S. foreign policy in that region.*

campaign was cut short, however, when a deranged man shot him, leaving him paralyzed below the waist.

McGovern then won the nomination easily, but his campaign struggled from the outset. When the press reported that his running mate had undergone psychiatric treatment for nervous exhaustion and depression during the 1960s, McGovern at first refused to bow to prejudice concerning mental illness. But when he changed his mind and replaced his running mate, he lost the public's confidence in his judgment, decisiveness, and sincerity. In addition, Republicans portrayed McGovern as an extremist on the left, and he alienated more conservative, traditional Democrats with his call for immediate withdrawal from Vietnam and his pledge to cut $30 billion from the Pentagon's budget.

Nixon received 60.7 percent of the popular vote, carrying every state except Massachusetts in a landslide victory second only to that of Johnson in 1964. Although the Democrats maintained control of the House, the Senate, and thirty-one governorships, Nixon won a majority of votes among southerners, Catholics, urbanites, and blue-collar workers, all traditionally strong supporters of the Democratic Party. The president had little time to savor his triumph, however, as a series of revelations began to emerge about crimes and misdemeanors that had been committed to ensure the victory.

During the early morning hours of June 17, 1972, five men working for Nixon's reelection campaign crept into Democratic Party headquarters in the Watergate apartment and office complex, just a mile from the White House. Intending to repair a bugging device installed in an earlier break-in, they were discovered and arrested on the scene. In their effort to cover up the connection between those arrested and administration officials, Nixon and his aides set in motion the most serious constitutional crisis since the Civil War, which reporters dubbed "Watergate."

As the events of Watergate unfolded over the next two years, Americans learned that Nixon and his associates had engaged in a host of other abuses, such as accepting illegal campaign contributions, using "dirty tricks" to sabotage Democratic candidates, and unlawfully attempting to silence critics of the Vietnam War. Nixon was not the first president to lie to the public or to misuse presidential power. Every president since Roosevelt had enlarged the powers of the presidency, justifying his actions as necessary to protect national security in actual war or cold war. This expansion of executive powers, often called the growth of the "imperial presidency," weakened some of the traditional checks and balances on the executive branch and opened the door to abuses.

Certain of Nixon's personality traits—self-righteousness, insecurity, suspiciousness, and a tendency to see opposition to his policies as a conspiracy against him—all encouraged him to employ the vast powers of the executive against his enemies. Moreover, Nixon's relationships with most of his closest aides rested on political calculations rather than on trust and loyalty. These men tried above all to protect themselves, and few would confront him with the truth and the opportunity to save his presidency.

Watergate began when White House adviser Charles Colson established a secret unit nicknamed the "plumbers" to stop the kind of "leaks" that had led to publication of the *Pentagon Papers* in 1971. Former CIA agent E. Howard Hunt and former FBI employee G. Gordon Liddy led the plumbers, some of whom soon turned to projects to disrupt the Democratic presidential nomination process and discredit potential candidates. They worked for the Committee to Re-elect the President (CRP), a group that was independent of the Republican Party and directed by Nixon's former attorney general John Mitchell. The CRP funneled illegal campaign contributions into Nixon's campaign, and in 1972 CRP officials authorized the Watergate break-in to bug Democratic Party headquarters.

Although the Nixon administration immediately denied any connection with the break-in, in early 1973 Hunt, Liddy, and the five alleged burglars either pleaded guilty or were convicted of theft

and illegal electronic surveillance. One man broke ranks, charging perjury and administration involvement in the break-in. Faced with a grand jury investigation, a Senate inquiry, and press reports implicating Mitchell and presidential aides John W. Dean, John Ehrlichman, and H. R. Haldeman, Nixon decided to act.

In a television address at the end of April 1973, Nixon accepted official responsibility for Watergate but denied any personal knowledge of the break-in or of a cover-up. He also announced the resignations of Dean, Ehrlichman, Haldeman, and Attorney General Richard Kleindienst. In May, he authorized the appointment of an independent special prosecutor, Archibald Cox, to conduct an investigation.

Meanwhile, sensational revelations exploded in the Senate investigating committee, headed by Democrat Samuel J. Ervin of North Carolina. John Dean described White House projects to harass "enemies" through income tax audits and other illegal means and asserted that the president had long known of efforts to cover up the Watergate burglary. The most damaging blow struck when a White House aide disclosed that all conversations in the Oval Office in the White House were taped. Both Cox and the Ervin committee immediately asked for tapes related to Watergate. When Nixon refused to give them up, citing executive privilege and separation of powers, Cox and Ervin took their case to federal district court.

In the midst of the battle for the tapes, more damaging disclosures revealed Nixon's misuse of federal funds and tax evasion. In August 1973, Vice President Agnew was compelled to resign after an investigation revealed that he had taken bribes as governor of Maryland. Although Nixon's choice of House minority leader Gerald Ford of Michigan to succeed Agnew won widespread approval, the vice president's resignation further tarnished the administration.

Nixon continued to hold on to the tapes. On October 19, 1973, he ordered special prosecutor Cox to cease his efforts to get them. When Cox refused, Nixon ordered Attorney General Elliot Richardson to fire Cox. Richardson instead resigned, as did William D. Ruckelshaus, second in line at the Justice Department. Finally, the solicitor general, Robert Bork, agreed to carry out the president's order. The press called the series of dismissals and resignations the "Saturday night massacre," and 250,000 telegrams condemning Nixon's action flooded the White House. Nixon appointed a new special prosecutor but failed to quell demands that he resign and serious talk about impeachment in Congress. The president's support in public opinion polls plummeted to 27 percent.

In February 1974, the House of Representatives voted to begin an impeachment investigation. In April, Nixon began to release transcripts of the tapes that he himself had edited. As the public read passages sprinkled with "expletive deleted," the House Republican leader abandoned his support of the president, calling the transcripts a "deplorable, shabby, disgusting, and immoral performance by all." The transcripts included Nixon's orders to Mitchell and Dean in March 1973: "I don't give a shit what happens. I want you all to stonewall it, let them plead the Fifth Amendment, cover up or anything else, if it'll save it—save the plan."

---

*Nixon's abuse of presidential power and his efforts to cover up crimes that had been committed by subordinates betrayed the public trust and forced the first presidential resignation in history.*

---

In July 1974, the House Judiciary Committee began debate over specific charges for impeachment: (1) obstruction of justice, (2) abuse of power, (3) contempt of Congress, (4) unconstitutional waging of war by the secret bombing of Cambodia, and (5) tax evasion and the selling of political favors. While the last two counts failed to get a majority, the committee voted to take the first three charges to the House, where a vote of impeachment seemed certain.

On July 24, a unanimous Supreme Court ordered Nixon to hand over the remaining tapes. Transcripts of new tapes released August 5 sealed his fate, revealing that just six days after the break-in Nixon and Haldeman had discussed manipulating the CIA to hinder the FBI's investigation of the burglary. This evidence was sufficient to persuade even Nixon's staunchest supporters.

On August 8, 1974, Nixon announced his resignation to a national television audience. Acknowledging that he had made some incorrect judgments, he insisted that he had always tried to do what was best for the nation. The next morning, Nixon ended a rambling, emotional farewell to his staff with some advice: "Always give your best, never get discouraged, never get petty; always remember, others may hate you, but those who hate you don't win unless you hate them, and then you destroy yourself." Had he but practiced that advice, he might have saved his presidency.

## The Ford Interregnum

Gerald Ford, who had represented Michigan in the House of Representatives since 1948, had built a reputation as a conservative party loyalist who treated opponents with openness and cordiality. Not a brilliant thinker, Ford was known for his integrity, humility, and dedication to the responsibilities of public office. Most of official Washington and the American public looked favorably on his succession as president.

Upon taking office, Ford announced, "Our long nightmare is over," but he shocked many Americans one month later when he ended the particular nightmare of the former president. On September 8, 1974, Ford granted Nixon a pardon "for all offenses against the United States which he . . . has committed or may have committed or taken part in" during his presidency. In its universality and its promulgation even before any charges were filed, it was the most extravagant presidential pardon ever issued, and it saved Nixon from nearly certain indictment and trial. It also provoked a tremendous outcry from Congress and the public. (See the Historical Question on page 822.) Capitalizing on the revulsion over Watergate and the pardon, Democrats made impressive gains in the congressional elections in November.

Congress took steps to guard against abuses revealed in the Watergate investigations. The Federal Election Campaign Act of 1974, for example, established public financing of presidential campaigns. Special committees in the House and Senate discovered a host of illegal FBI and CIA activities stretching back to the 1950s. Both agencies had harassed and discredited political dissenters, and the CIA had also made plans to assassinate Fidel Castro and other foreign leaders. In response to these revelations, Ford established new controls on covert operations and Congress created permanent committees to oversee the intelligence agencies. Yet these measures did little to diminish the public cynicism and lack of trust in government that had been developing since the Johnson years and that reflected disgust with Democrats as well as Republicans.

Both unemployment and inflation intensified in 1974 and 1975. Lacking Nixon's flexibility and boldness, Ford reverted to traditional Republican policy, proposing to fight inflation by tightening the money supply and to balance the federal budget by cutting spending and increasing taxes. Although Ford curtailed some federal programs, the Democratic Congress ultimately prevailed with a tax cut and a $4 billion public works program. Unemployment and inflation abated somewhat, but underlying weaknesses in the U.S. economy remained: a low rate of growth, higher than normal unemployment, a deficit in foreign trade, and high energy prices tied to dependence on oil from abroad.

Keeping Henry Kissinger as secretary of state, Ford pursued foreign policy goals set by Nixon but failed to sustain widespread support of détente. Members of both parties worried that Soviet strength was overtaking that of the United States, and some Democrats charged that détente ignored Soviet violations of human rights.

Although negotiations continued, the superpowers achieved no further agreements to limit strategic arms. President Ford's most notable international agreement took place in 1975 in Helsinki, Finland, where he, Soviet leader Leonid Brezhnev, and European leaders formally recognized the existing post–World War II boundaries in Europe. In signing the Helsinki accords, the United States accepted the Soviets' domination over their satellite countries in Eastern Europe—a condition to which it had objected so bitterly thirty years earlier as the cold war began.

Opposition to détente fueled a major challenge from the Republican right to Ford's nomination for a full term in 1976. His leading opponent in the primaries, former California Governor Ronald Reagan, charged that Nixon and Ford had allowed the United States to become "number two in a world where it is dangerous—if not fatal—to be second best." Attacking Ford from the right on domestic issues as well, Reagan came close to capturing the nomination. But in an attempt to unify the party, Ford bowed to conservative Republicans on key platform planks that criticized his own foreign policy and selected conservative Senator Robert Dole of Kansas as his running mate.

On the Democratic side, former Georgia Governor James Earl (Jimmy) Carter Jr. began his campaign early in 1975. A graduate of the U.S. Naval Academy, Carter spent seven years in the navy and then ran the family peanut farming business. In 1962, he won election to the Georgia state senate, where he served for four years; he was elected governor in 1970. Highly intelligent and well prepared on the issues, the soft-spoken Carter stressed his small-town roots, deep religious commitment, unpretentiousness, and distance from the popularly suspect national government. "I will never tell a lie to the American people," Carter promised, stressing his campaign theme of morality in government.

Winning the Democratic nomination on the first ballot, Carter sought to unify the party by selecting liberal Senator Walter F. Mondale of Minnesota as his running mate and by accepting a platform that affirmed broad goals compatible with traditional Democratic principles. His nomination nonetheless represented a decided rightward turn in the party, reflected in Carter's campaign promises to eliminate the budget deficit and reduce federal controls and regulations on business.

Carter benefited from the Watergate backlash, the economic problems that plagued the Ford administration, the damage that the Reagan challenge had done to Ford, and his own ability to attract votes from the traditional Democratic coalition of blacks, southerners, organized labor, and ethnic groups. Yet his victory over Ford was narrow. Democrats retained substantial margins in the House and Senate, but Carter received just 50.1 percent of the popular vote to Ford's 48 percent.

## The "Outsider" Presidency of Jimmy Carter

In his campaign autobiography, *Why Not the Best?*, Jimmy Carter (the name he used even when signing state documents) advocated a government that was "competent" as well as "honest, decent, open, fair, and compassionate." Carter was extremely well informed, hardworking, and seemingly uninterested in personal or political aggrandizement. Yet while he refrained from abusing the power of his position, he seemed unable to wield his legitimate authority effectively and failed to win a second term.

The disastrous final year of Carter's presidency overshadowed some significant accomplishments of his administration, most notably in environmental and energy policies. In foreign affairs, Carter obtained ratification of treaties ending U.S. control over the Panama Canal—the most blatant symbol of Yankee imperialism—and, following up on Nixon's initiatives, he established normal diplomatic relations with China. His most brilliant achievement was securing a peace treaty between Israel and Egypt.

# Was Ford Right in Pardoning Nixon?

I N NOVEMBER 1973, during Gerald R. Ford's confirmation hearings for the vice presidency, a senator asked Ford whether he believed that a new president could stop criminal proceedings against the president he replaced. Ford replied, "I do not think the public would stand for it." Yet less than a year later, Ford did exactly that when he gave a blanket pardon to Richard M. Nixon just one month after Nixon had resigned the presidency to escape impeachment.

After returning from church on Sunday morning, September 8, 1974, President Ford called reporters to the White House, where he read a statement and signed a proclamation granting Nixon a "full, free, and absolute pardon" for all crimes that he "committed or may have committed or taken part in" while president. When Ford called congressional leaders just before announcing the pardon, the Democratic Speaker of the House, Tip O'Neill, had said, "You're crazy." And so thought a large segment of the public. White House switchboards lit up immediately, with opinion running strongly against the pardon. Ford's approval rating in public opinion polls plunged by twenty percentage points.

There were immediate charges that Ford had made a deal to pardon Nixon. Certainly, some of Nixon's aides—and no doubt Nixon himself—had given thought to a pardon even before he resigned. J. Fred Buzhardt, one of Nixon's lawyers, drafted a pardon in Ford's name while Nixon was still president. When Nixon's chief of staff, Alexander Haig, met with Ford to brief him on the release of tapes that would probably lead to Nixon's resignation, Haig outlined various strategies, one of which was that Nixon could be pardoned even before any indictment had taken place. When Ford reported the conversation to his own advisers, they insisted that he call Haig and tell him that nothing he had discussed with Haig should figure in Nixon's decision about whether to resign. Scholars have found no evidence of a deal, and Ford steadfastly denied any such thing. Nonetheless, Haig impressed on Ford the notion that a president had the power to issue a pardon even without an indictment.

If there was no deal, why did Ford pardon Nixon? First of all, the question of a possible pardon hovered over the White House throughout Ford's first weeks in office. Some of Nixon's aides whom Ford had kept on—including Haig, Henry Kissinger, and special counsel Leonard Garment—lobbied the new president to pardon their former boss. In addition, staff members at Nixon's home in San Clemente sent reports emphasizing the former president's serious health problems. The press hammered administration officials about a possible pardon, and reporters opened Ford's first televised press conference by asking whether Nixon should have immunity from prosecution. Ford later remarked, "I thought they had wasted my time," distracting him and the nation from important issues concerning the economy and foreign policy.

In the pardon proclamation and the statement accompanying it, Ford gave a number of reasons for his decision. He said that the "serious allegations and accusations hang[ing] like a sword" over the former president threatened his health. He insisted that "Nixon and his loved ones have suffered enough, and will continue to suffer no matter what I do." The president also suggested that pretrial publicity and lengthy delays would prevent Nixon from getting a fair trial and "equal justice." Ford questioned whether having "already paid the unprecedented penalty of relinquishing the highest office in the United States," Nixon should be exposed "to further punishment and degradation."

Although moved by compassion for Nixon, Ford insisted that "it is not the ultimate fate of Richard Nixon that most concerns me." Most of all, he said, the pardon was necessary to get rid of Watergate, the "ugly passions" that it aroused,

**GERALD FORD'S MOMENTOUS DECISION**

*On September 8, 1974, President Gerald Ford granted former President Richard Nixon a "full, free, and absolute pardon" for whatever crimes he may have committed in the Watergate affair. The pardon enabled Nixon to build a post-Watergate career as elder statesman, while it clouded the remainder of Ford's presidency and contributed to his defeat at the polls in 1976.*

© 1974 Time Inc. Reprinted by permission.

and the "polarization" that it engendered. During the debate over the proposed Constitution, Alexander Hamilton had envisioned the pardon provision being used at "critical moments, when a well-timed offer of pardon . . . may restore the tranquility of the commonwealth." Ford did not refer to the Founders, but he declared it his duty "to shut and seal this book" to ensure "domestic tranquility."

In the long run, the pardon probably furthered Ford's goal of getting the political establishment to put Watergate behind it and focus on what Ford considered the real issues confronting the nation. In the short run, however, it reopened the wounds, because many people believed that the pardon violated the principle that all Americans are equal under the law. Upon learning that Ford was going to issue the pardon, his press secretary, Jerald F. ter-Horst, submitted his resignation. It was "ethically wrong," he said, to "put just one man above the law," especially when all of Nixon's aides "were left to run the gauntlet of our judicial system."

TerHorst lamented that "Ford could throw away the new national mood of trust . . . without getting in return a signed confession." Adding fuel to the firestorm of protest was Nixon's response to the pardon. He failed to acknowledge guilt or express contrition for the abuses of power and obstruction of justice that were charged against him in the articles of impeachment and supported by the tapes. In Nixon's statement, which had been negotiated by Ford and Nixon's aides before the pardon was issued, he expressed only "regret" that he had made "mistakes and misjudgments" and acknowledged merely that he was "wrong in not acting more decisively and more forthrightly in dealing with Watergate."

Although we cannot measure the degree to which the pardon turned voters against the president and the Republican Party, Ford did pay a political price for it. Two months after the pardon, Republicans lost an exceedingly high number of seats in the congressional elections, and the pardon undoubtedly played a role in Ford's painfully close defeat for reelection in 1976. For Nixon, the pardon meant a new political life. His ability over the next two decades to rebuild his image into that of an elder statesman rested in large part on having gained a pardon without having to admit that he had broken the law, violated his oath of office, and betrayed his constituents' trust.

## Retreat from Liberalism

Jimmy Carter promised "to help the poor and aged, to improve education, and to provide jobs" but at the same time "not to waste money." He wanted a humane government that would help those in need, but one that also was efficiently managed and prudent in its spending. When these two aims conflicted, especially when inflation threatened economic stability, Carter's commitment to reform took second place. Liberal Democrats accused him of deserting the Democratic reform tradition that stretched back to Franklin Roosevelt.

As president, Carter stressed his status as an "outsider" to the deals, bargaining, and inefficiency that characterized national politics. Believing that congressional action was unduly shaped by powerful special interests and legislators' concerns for the next election, Carter saw his job as countering those special interests by acting as the trustee of all the people. His outsider status, while helping him into office, left him without strong ties to party insiders or prominent legislators. Moreover, his desire to propose comprehensive solutions to problems went against the congressional tendency to take a piecemeal, incremental approach. Legislators complained of inadequate consultation and Carter's tendency to flood them with a mass of unprioritized proposals.

Even a president without these shortcomings might not have done much better than Carter, as Congress itself weakened the ability of its party

**PRESIDENT CARTER'S INAUGURAL DAY**
*After his inauguration in January 1977, Jimmy Carter eschewed the customary presidential limousine and instead walked with his family down Pennsylvania Avenue from the Capitol to the White House. He wanted to emphasize his opposition to some of the trappings of office that separated the government from the people. Ordering cabinet heads to drive their own cars, he said, "Government officials can't be sensitive to your problems if we are living like royalty here."*
Jimmy Carter Presidential Library.

leaders to deliver a united front. While it flexed its muscles in response to Watergate and the abuse of presidential power, Congress reduced the power of its own committee chairs, weakened party control over legislators, and decentralized the decision-making process. In addition, because primary elections rather than party conventions now controlled the nominating process, candidates depended less on party support and more on campaign funds from interest groups.

For his White House staff, Carter relied heavily on associates from Georgia—who, like him, lacked experience in national politics—but his cabinet appointments included several men from the Kennedy and Johnson administrations. Rosalynn Carter, the president's wife, played a larger role in affairs of state than any First Lady since Eleanor Roosevelt. Carter involved other women in policy-making, including three at cabinet-level rank, far surpassing his predecessors in appointing women and members of minority groups to federal judgeships and high government positions. He also won congressional approval for the creation of two new departments, the Department of Education and the Department of Energy.

Carter took office confident that he could solve the unusually formidable problems that had eluded the Nixon and Ford administrations—unemployment, inflation, a slow rate of economic growth, and energy shortages. New tax cuts and federal spending seemed at first to succeed, as unemployment fell from near 8 percent in late 1976 to below 6 percent in 1978. But rising inflation soon impelled Carter to curtail federal spending and the Federal Reserve Board to increase interest rates and tighten the money supply. These policies not only failed to halt inflation, which surpassed 13 percent in 1980, but also contributed to rising unemployment, reversing the progress that had been made in Carter's first two years.

The administration achieved little progress on issues traditionally central to the Democratic Party. Carter's commitment to holding down the federal budget frustrated Democratic legislators pushing for comprehensive welfare reform and a national health insurance program. To ensure solvency in the Social Security system, Carter and Congress agreed to increase employer and employee contributions, but these measures also increased the tax burden of lower- and middle-income Americans.

Carter did win approval for several proposals that favored the wealthy and business. A sharp cut in the capital gains tax benefited high-income indi-

viduals. When the Chrysler Corporation approached bankruptcy in 1979, Congress responded with $1.5 billion worth of loan guarantees to ensure the survival of the tenth largest corporation in the country. The government also reduced controls in several industries, deregulating airlines in 1978 and the banking, trucking, and railroad industries in 1980.

---

*The disastrous final year of Carter's presidency overshadowed some significant accomplishments. His most brilliant achievement was securing a peace treaty between Israel and Egypt.*

---

Designating the energy issue "the moral equivalent of war," Carter fought for a comprehensive energy program. But his goal to limit consumption and to reduce U.S. dependence on foreign oil fell victim to his uneasy relationship with Congress and to competing demands among energy producers and consumers. In 1979, declines in oil production abroad created the most severe energy shortage yet. Hundreds of cars lined up at gas stations, and motorists' tempers rose even higher when prices at the pumps began to reflect enormous price hikes by the Organization of Petroleum Exporting Countries (OPEC). Congress eventually authorized programs to stimulate alternative fuel sources at the same time that it reduced controls on oil and gas and imposed a windfall profits tax on producers to redistribute some of the profits that would accrue with deregulation. Still falling short of Carter's initial proposal, the energy measures represented the nation's first comprehensive efforts to limit consumption and decrease its dependency on foreign oil.

## Idealism and Human Rights in Carter's Foreign Policy

Moral principles, Jimmy Carter promised, would guide his approach to foreign policy. His predecessors' obsession with protecting and expanding U.S. power by any means, Carter believed, had violated the nation's principles of freedom and human dignity. Carter promised to reverse the cynical support of dictators, secret diplomacy, interference in the internal affairs of other countries, and excessive reliance on military solutions.

Led by the president, U.S. officials took every opportunity to focus attention on governments that

**AN ACTIVE FIRST LADY**
*Rosalynn Carter was the most active First Lady in public affairs since Eleanor Roosevelt. Various members of Congress and diplomats criticized President Jimmy Carter for sending her on an official mission to Latin America to emphasize his administration's commitment to human rights and democracy there. Though critics said Latin American leaders wouldn't take her seriously, the seven-country visit in June 1977 proved successful. Here she meets with President Carlos Andrés Pérez of Venezuela.*
Walter Bennett/Sygma.

denied their citizens basic political and civil rights or freedom of religion and expression. The administration also applied economic pressure against a number of countries, including Argentina, Chile, and El Salvador, and the white minority governments of Rhodesia and South Africa, which blatantly violated the rights of their black majorities.

Yet the administration implemented the human rights policy with glaring inconsistencies. Establishing formal diplomatic relations with the People's Republic of China in 1979 took priority over attempts to secure democratic rights for the Chinese people. In dealing with staunch, anti-Communist allies, Carter sacrificed human rights to strategic and security considerations. The administration invoked no sanctions against Iran, South Korea, and the Philip-

pines, even though official oppression was obvious in those countries. Cold war considerations vied with concern for human rights in the administration's approach to Nicaragua, which had been ruled since 1936 by the corrupt and viciously oppressive Somoza regime. The administration complained about the Nicaraguan dictatorship's excesses and invoked some economic sanctions, but when civil war erupted there, its greatest concern was to contain Communist influence in the anti-Somoza movement. Officials were particularly uneasy about the Sandinistas, a leading element in the opposition with ties to Cuba. Nonetheless, when the Somoza regime fell in 1979 and Sandinista leader Daniel Ortega assumed power, the United States extended recognition and economic aid to the new government.

**THE CAMP DAVID ACCORDS**
*President Jimmy Carter oversees the meeting of Egyptian President Anwar Sadat, left, and Israeli Prime Minister Menachem Begin at Camp David, Maryland, in September 1978. Carter's passionate commitment to promoting peace helped produce the first easing of hostility between Arabs and Israelis in thirty years.*
Corbis-Bettmann.

The president took on heavy political burdens in applying moral principles to relations with Panama. Carter sped up the negotiations over control of the Panama Canal that the Johnson administration had begun. In 1977, the United States and Panama completed two treaties, one providing for joint control of the canal until the end of the century and the second defining U.S. rights after Panama assumed control. Although Carter viewed the treaties as recompense for the blatant use of U.S. power in obtaining the canal in 1903, angry opponents insisted on maintaining control of this vital waterway. Only after the administration undertook a massive campaign to rally support did the Senate ratify the treaties by the narrowest margins.

In applying his moral authority to peace in the Middle East, Carter achieved his most brilliant victory. He seized on the courage of Egyptian President Anwar Sadat, the first Arab leader to risk his political future by talking directly with Israeli officials. When initial discussions between Sadat and Israeli Prime Minister Menachem Begin faltered, Carter invited them to the presidential retreat at Camp David, Maryland, in September 1978. Carter studied all the issues down to the smallest details and then spent thirteen days at Camp David mediating between Begin and Sadat until they concluded a tentative agreement known popularly as the Camp David accords.

When subsequent negotiations bogged down, Carter flew to Jerusalem and Cairo and applied his tenacious diplomacy once more, obtaining a treaty that Begin and Sadat signed on the White House lawn in March 1979. In that pact, Egypt recognized Israel, and Israel agreed to gradual withdrawal from the Sinai Peninsula, territory that it had seized in the 1967 war (see Map 30.1). Although the issues of Palestinian self-determination in other Israeli-occupied territories (the West Bank and Gaza) and the plight of Palestinian refugees remained unresolved, the first real steps toward peace in the Middle East had been taken.

## Foreign Policy in Disarray

Carter's last two years as president saw both a shift in policies and severe setbacks to his original goals. Relations between the United States and the Soviet Union deteriorated, and the administration began a sizable military buildup.

**AMERICAN HOSTAGES IN IRAN**
*Iranian militants display one of the hostages they took when they occupied the American embassy
in Teheran on November 4, 1979. Until the hostages were released in January 1981, Americans
regularly watched TV images of the American captives being paraded before angry Iranian
crowds. The bound, blindfolded hostages served as humiliating symbols of the limitations of
American power.*
Ph. Ledru/Sygma.

Carter had initially approached the Soviet
Union with an air of accommodation and reassurance, while never ceasing to speak out about Soviet
suppression of Jews and dissidents. He set Secretary of State Cyrus Vance to work on a new agreement to replace the Strategic Arms Limitation Treaty
(SALT I), which was due to expire in 1977, and canceled production of the neutron bomb and the new
B-1 bomber. Two years of negotiations with the
Soviet Union produced a SALT II treaty in 1979, but
by then Carter had accepted his national security
adviser Zbigniew Brzezinski's warnings about the
need to counter a Soviet military buildup. The president authorized development of new intermediate-range missiles to be deployed in Western Europe
as well as an enormous new missile system (known
as MX) to be built in the United States. But even
this new emphasis on military strength did not
defuse criticism of SALT II and arms control, opposition that had grown with Carter's cancellation
of the B-1.

With Senate ratification of SALT II unlikely,
Carter withdrew the treaty in December 1979,
shortly after the Soviet Union invaded its neighbor
Afghanistan, whose recently installed pro-Soviet
government was threatened by Muslim opposition.

Asserting that the invasion "could pose the greatest threat to peace since the Second World War," Carter imposed economic sanctions on the Soviet Union, canceled U.S. participation in the 1980 Olympic Games in Moscow, and persuaded Congress to approve legislation requiring all nineteen-year-old men to register for the draft.

The president claimed that Soviet actions posed a threat to oil supplies from the Middle East and announced his own "Carter Doctrine," stating that the United States would intervene with any means necessary should an outside force try to gain control of the Persian Gulf. Finally, Carter called for hefty increases in defense spending over the next five years. Events in Iran fueled this reversion to a hard-line, militaristic approach. All the U.S. arms and support had not enabled the shah to suppress growing opposition to his regime. Iranian dissidents still resented the CIA's role in the overthrow of the Mossadegh government in 1953, and they deplored the Westernization of their country that accompanied the shah's rule as well as his savage attempts to silence opposition. In Teheran on New Year's Eve 1977, Carter toasted the shah's "great leadership," but fourteen months later a revolution forced the shah to abandon his throne and country. By March 1979, Ayatollah Ruholla Khomeini and other Shiite Islamic fundamentalists who were intensely hostile to the United States controlled the Iranian government.

When Carter permitted the shah to enter the United States for medical treatment, anti-American demonstrations escalated in Teheran. On November 4, 1979, a crowd broke into the U.S. embassy and held more than sixty Americans captive, demanding that the United States return the shah for trial. When Khomeini supported the captors and refused to negotiate, Carter froze Iranian assets in U.S. banks and placed an embargo on Iranian oil. For the next year, the hostage crisis dominated the news and absorbed vast amounts of the administration's time and energy.

After every attempt to negotiate was frustrated, in April 1980 Carter authorized force to rescue the hostages. But the operation failed, and eight Americans died when a U.S. plane and helicopter collided during the aborted evacuation. Failure of the rescue mission further embarrassed the president, and the hostage crisis burdened Carter's campaign for reelection. Continuing efforts to reach an agreement with Iran finally produced release of the hostages on the day Carter left office.

## Conclusion: The Loss of American Ascendancy

"What the people want is simple. They want an America as good as its promise." Barbara Jordan's words at Harvard University's commencement in June 1977 recognized the decline of public confidence and trust in government in the 1970s, a disillusionment caused in part by Watergate and other revelations of deception and corruption among public officials. Presidents Ford and Carter restored morality to the White House, but both were deficient in political skills. The 1970s saw continuation of key domestic reforms of the 1960s as well as new legislation in response to movements for women's rights and environmental protection. Yet the government seemed unable to deal with the gravest economic problems since the Great Depression—a low rate of economic growth, inflation combined with unemployment, and an increasing trade deficit.

Nor could Americans take much comfort in their country's relationships with the rest of the world. They applauded Carter's success in inching the Middle East slightly toward stability, but the Israeli-Egyptian accord failed to resolve the larger Middle East problems that affected Americans directly by disrupting energy supplies. And even though the Panama Canal treaties moved the United States toward more equitable relations with Latin American countries, they provoked strong opposition.

Normalization of relations with the People's Republic of China won widespread support, but critics of strategic arms limitation and Soviet-American détente gained the upper hand. This opposition, combined with the Soviet invasion of Afghanistan, nullified the thaw in Soviet-American relations begun under Nixon and Kissinger. By 1980, the hostile tone of the United States toward the Soviet Union and the growing emphasis on military expansion resembled the early years of the cold war. Four years after the fall of South Vietnam, another humiliation rocked the nation when Iran erupted in a burst of anti-Americanism and the United States proved unable to rescue its citizens who were held hostage there.

Americans' feeling of impotence in the face of the hostage crisis reflected a decline in U.S. power, but it was a relative descent from an artificially high base. The global ascendancy of the United States existed only as long as it took for other countries to recover from the ravages of World War II. The growing power of the Soviet Union and China set limits on the ability of the United States to intervene throughout the world without risking superpower confrontation. And the rise of nationalism in the third world posed further constraints on American power.

The recovery of Europe and Japan challenged U.S. economic supremacy and contributed to the domestic problems that plagued each administration in the 1970s, particularly the loss of foreign and domestic markets; the decline in electronics, steel, automobile, and other major industries; and the accompanying rising unemployment and sluggish economy. Whether and how the United States could regain its economic and political power provided the script for the 1980 elections.

## CHRONOLOGY

**1968** Richard Nixon elected president of United States.

**1969** Warren E. Burger appointed chief justice of United States by Nixon.

**1970** Earth Day demonstrations held to support environmental goals.

Congress passes Occupational Safety and Health Act.

Environmental Protection Agency established by Nixon.

Native American Women's Association founded.

Women Strike for Peace and Equality demonstrations take place nationwide.

**1971** First national Mexican American women's conference held.

In *Swann,* Supreme Court upholds legality of busing to achieve integration.

Nixon announces abandonment of gold standard in his New Economic Policy.

Nixon vetoes comprehensive child care bill.

**1972** Congress passes federal revenue sharing laws.

Congress passes Title IX of Education Amendments Act, banning sex discrimination in education.

*Ms.* magazine founded by Gloria Steinem and other feminists.

Nixon becomes first U.S. president to visit China.

Nixon visits Moscow to sign arms limitation treaties with Soviets.

Nixon campaign aides apprehended breaking into Democratic Party headquarters in Watergate apartment complex in Washington, D.C.

Richard Nixon reelected president in landslide.

**1973** Arab oil embargo in retaliation for U.S. support of Israel creates energy crisis in United States.

National Black Feminist Organization founded.

Senate Watergate hearings reveal widespread abuses of power in Nixon administration.

In *Roe v. Wade,* Supreme Court rules that abortion is constitutionally protected.

**1974** Nixon resigns as president in face of certain impeachment by House of Representatives over his role in Watergate affair; Gerald Ford becomes president of United States.

Ford pardons Nixon of any crimes he may have committed while president.

Supreme Court imposes some limitations on use of busing to achieve racial integration in schools.

**1976** Jimmy Carter elected president of United States.

| 1978 | Carter helps negotiate peace agreement between Israel and Egypt (Camp David accords).<br><br>In *Bakke,* Supreme Court rules against racial quotas and "reverse" discrimination.<br><br>Congress passes law banning discrimination against pregnant women. | 1979 | **November 4.** Beginning of hostage crisis in Iran. |
| --- | --- | --- | --- |
| | | 1979–1980 | Congress enacts measures to conserve energy and increase its production. |
| | | 1980 | **April.** Attempt to free U.S. hostages in Iran fails. |

# SUGGESTED READINGS

Peter N. Carroll, *It Seemed Like Nothing Happened: America in the 1970s* (1982). A lively account of major developments of the 1970s.

Gary M. Fink and Hugh Davis Graham, eds., *The Carter Presidency: Policy Choices in the Post–New Deal Era* (1998). A collection of essays on key issues addressed by the Carter administration.

Faye D. Ginsburg, *Contested Lives: The Abortion Debate in an American Community* (1998). A close look at the abortion issue, set in historical context.

Joan Hoff, *Nixon Reconsidered* (1994). A comprehensive history of Nixon's presidency emphasizing the importance of his domestic policies.

Stanley I. Kutler, ed., *Abuse of Power: The New Nixon Tapes* (1997). Transcripts of about two hundred hours of the Watergate tapes.

J. Anthony Lukas, *Common Ground: A Turbulent Decade in the Lives of Three American Families* (1986). A riveting account of race relations in Boston that culminates with the school busing crisis.

Donald G. Mathews and Jane Sherron De Hart, *Sex, Gender, and the Politics of ERA* (1990). A detailed history and analysis of the ERA ratification struggle that explores the experiences, worldviews, and emotions of feminists and antifeminists.

Keith I. Nelson, *The Making of Détente: Soviet-American Relations in the Shadow of Vietnam* (1995). A historical narrative analyzing the conditions on both sides that made possible the easing of U.S.-Soviet tensions in the first half of the 1970s.

Philip Shabecoff, *A Fierce Green Fire: The American Environmental Movement* (1993). A lively history of conservation throughout U.S. history with particular attention to the environmentalism of the 1970s and beyond.

Gaddis Smith, *Morality, Reason and Power: American Diplomacy in the Carter Years* (1986). A critical analysis of the Carter administration's foreign policy.

**WALL STREET VIDEO**

*The popular 1987 movie* Wall Street *captured elements of the economy and society that led some observers to talk about the "money culture" and call the 1980s the decade of "greed." Wealth accumulation and lavish consumption were more visible than usual. One indication of the prosperity enjoyed by some was the growing presence of technology in the home, including computers, microwave ovens, compact disc players, and, especially, videocassette recorders. As the number of households with VCRs jumped from 1 million in 1980 to nearly 70 million in 1990, more and more people saw movies like* Wall Street *by renting videotapes for home viewing.*

# CONSERVATIVE RESURGENCE AND A NEW WORLD ORDER

# 31

## 1980–1991

"FRANKLIN DELANO REAGAN," headlined the *New York Times* editorial on Ronald Wilson Reagan's acceptance speech at the Republican convention in 1980. The presidential nominee had repeatedly quoted Roosevelt, all the while promising to reduce drastically the federal government's role in American life. Once in the White House, Reagan promptly rehung a portrait of President Calvin Coolidge—that staunch Republican believer in the virtues of big business—but he continued to grasp the mantle of Roosevelt even as his policies formed the antithesis of New Deal liberalism.

Reagan's invocation of Franklin Roosevelt made good politics, bolstering his appeal to traditional Democrats. It also served to reconcile Reagan's own history—he had once been an active Democrat and ardent Roosevelt supporter—with his present conservative Republicanism. He pulled off his identification with Roosevelt by quoting selectively and by emphasizing Roosevelt's early advocacy of government retrenchment and frugality. Reagan genuinely admired Roosevelt's dynamism and his confidence in the nation's ability to rise to new challenges. He intended to exercise that same spirited leadership and to restore the United States to a global role as powerful as the one it held at the time of Roosevelt's death. He also aimed for a revolution in domestic policy as striking as Roosevelt's in extent, though not in kind, and a new national political alignment that would be as impressive as Roosevelt's New Deal coalition.

The frequent appeal by the most conservative president since Calvin Coolidge to the example of Franklin Roosevelt was not the only contradiction of the Reagan presidency. Reagan promised fiscal stringency and a balanced budget but left the largest government debt in the nation's history. He limited the role of the federal government through tax cuts and deregulation of business, but federal spending increased and the federal bureaucracy expanded during his eight years as president. Although Reagan voiced the most hawkish rhetoric since the days of John Foster Dulles and promoted the largest peacetime military buildup in U.S. history, when he left office the United States and the Soviet Union had moved closer together than at any time since World War II.

Unlike the era of Roosevelt, which had focused on the disadvantaged, the spotlight of the 1980s turned on the affluent. The inflation and unemployment that had bedeviled presidents in the 1970s receded, and the economy entered its longest boom in the nation's history. Better-off Americans enjoyed the greatest benefits.

of U.S. foreign policy for forty-five years, Bush heralded a "new world order." Freed from having to worry about the Soviet Union's response to U.S. intervention, Bush responded quickly to a new crisis in the Middle East. When Iraq invaded Kuwait in 1990, the United States led an international coalition that expelled the invaders.

## The Rising Tide of Conservatism

Ronald Reagan's landslide election to the presidency in 1980 marked the most important turning point in politics since Franklin D. Roosevelt's victory in 1932. Eisenhower and Nixon had campaigned as middle-of-the-road Republicans, but Reagan's victory established conservatism's dominance in the Republican Party. Since the 1930s, the Democratic Party had defined the major issues; in the 1980s, the Republicans assumed that initiative, while the Democrats moved toward the right in their search for an effective response.

An extraordinarily adept politician, Reagan appealed to a wide spectrum of conservative groups and sentiments: free-market conservatives, militant anti-Communists, fundamentalist Christians, and white working-class Democrats disenchanted with the Great Society. Above all, the high inflation and unemployment rates in the last years of the Carter administration enabled Reagan to win votes from people who suffered economically but who otherwise would not have supported a conservative. Although Reagan promoted a huge military buildup, superpower conflict was confined to public rhetoric and the bargaining table. On the periphery of the cold war, however, the nation pursued a more activist role, intervening in the Middle East and the Caribbean. On the domestic front, the Reagan administration left its most important mark on economic policies: victory over inflation, continued deregulation of industry, a moratorium on social spending, enormous tax cuts, and a staggering budget deficit.

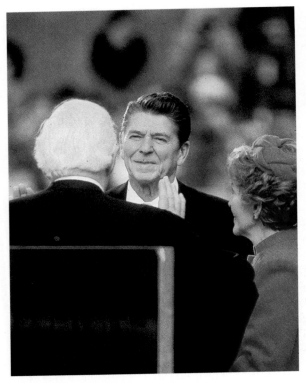

**THE REAGAN PRESIDENCY BEGINS**
*Ronald Reagan, one of the most popular presidents of the twentieth century, takes the oath of office in 1981 from Chief Justice Warren Burger. His wife, Nancy, looks on.*
Dick Halstead/*Time.*

Resembling the 1920s rather than the 1930s in economic terms, the Reagan era saw wealth redistributed upward while prosperity bypassed large segments of the population.

Reagan's successor, George Bush, deviated only slightly from Reagan's antigovernment philosophy. Aside from new laws dealing with civil rights, including those of disabled Americans, and environmental protection, domestic policy changed little from the Reagan years. With the president and Congress caught in gridlock, the economy slid into a recession in 1990.

In contrast to the domestic arena, massive changes swept through the world, surprising even the most astute foreign policy observers. Eastern Europe broke free of Communist control in 1989, and the Soviet Union disintegrated in 1991. With the end of the cold war, which had been the obsession

## The Election of 1980

The oldest candidate ever nominated for the presidency, Ronald Reagan was born in 1911 to a staunchly Democratic father. After attending a small religious college, Reagan worked as a sportscaster before becoming a movie actor and, later, president of the Screen Actors Guild. When the Red scare reached Hollywood, Reagan worked energetically to rid the movie industry of alleged Communists and sympathizers. His conservatism grew over the next decade, and by 1964 he was campaigning for Barry Goldwater, his shift to conservatism complete.

---

*Since the 1930s, the Democratic Party had defined the major issues; in the 1980s, the Republicans assumed that initiative, while the Democrats moved toward the right in their search for an effective response.*

---

Reagan's own political career took off when he was elected to the first of two terms as governor of California in 1966. Although he ran a conservative campaign, as governor he displayed considerable flexibility, approving a major tax increase, a strong measure to control water pollution, and a liberal abortion bill. Displaying similar flexibility in his 1980 presidential campaign, he softened his earlier attacks on the Panama Canal treaties and Social Security and chose as his running mate George Bush, a representative of the Republican center.

The poor state of the economy and the country's declining international stature provided ample weapons for Reagan's campaign. He kept reminding voters of the "misery index"—the combined rates of unemployment and inflation—and asked, "Are you better off now than you were four years ago?" Reagan also capitalized on the Iranian hostage crisis, accusing Jimmy Carter of weakening U.S. military strength and losing the confidence of the nation's allies and the respect of its enemies. He insisted that more effective leadership and a determination to "take government off the backs of the people" would restore Americans' morale and other nations' respect.

Having lost confidence in Carter, a narrow majority of voters responded to Reagan's upbeat message. Fifty-one percent of the electorate voted for Reagan, while 41 percent favored Carter, and 7 percent independent candidate John R. Anderson. The Republicans also picked up thirty-three new seats in the House and won control of the Senate.

## Reagan and the Spectrum of Conservatism

With the election of 1980, conservatism gained greater ascendancy in American political culture than at any time since the 1920s. Reagan clearly benefited from a lingering backlash against the upheavals associated with the 1960s—the civil rights revolution, the reforms of the Johnson era, the antiwar movement, feminism, the new sexual permissiveness, and the liberalism of the Supreme Court. Much of Reagan's support came from religious conservatives with an avid interest in social issues, who constituted a relatively new phenomenon known as the New Right. During the 1970s, evangelical Christianity claimed thousands of new adherents, abandoned the customary political neutrality of fundamentalist religion, and made adept use of new methods for mobilizing support, notably sophisticated mass-mailing techniques and the "electronic ministry." Evangelical ministers such as Jim Bakker and Pat Robertson preached to huge television audiences. Attacking feminism, abortion, homosexuality, and pornography, they called for restoration of old-fashioned "family values." They wanted prayer back in and sex education out of the schools.

Conservatives created or revitalized a raft of political organizations and journals. The religious right sought a Christian voice in government through the Moral Majority, founded by minister Jerry Falwell in 1979, and then through the Christian Coalition, which Pat Robertson created in 1989. Within a few years, the Christian Coalition claimed 1.6 million members and control of the Republican Party in more than a dozen states. The instruments of more traditional conservatives—those who advocated limited government at home and militant anticommunism abroad—likewise flourished. These included publications such as the *National Review,* edited by William F. Buckley Jr., and think tanks such as the American Enterprise Institute and the Heritage Foundation, which supported experts who developed and publicized new policy approaches.

Reagan embraced the full spectrum of conservatism, avowing agreement with the New Right on abortion, school prayer, and other social and moral issues. Yet he was careful not to alienate the more traditional conservatives, avoiding policy changes based on the moral stance of the New Right. Reagan promoted the conservative agenda most by strengthening the nation's anti-Communist posture and reducing government restraints on free enterprise.

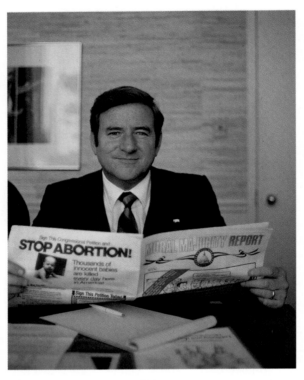

**EVANGELIST JERRY FALWELL**
*One of the most popular televangelists, Baptist minister Jerry Falwell of Lynchburg, Virginia, holds up the newsletter of the Moral Majority, the organization he founded in 1979. Established to promote "pro-God, pro-family policies in government," the Moral Majority and other groups of conservative Christians in the 1980s began to play a significant role in the Republican Party.*
Eve Arnold/Magnum Photos, Inc.

"In the present crisis," Reagan argued, "government is not the solution to our problem, government *is* the problem." Excessive government regulation and burdensome taxation crippled productivity, he claimed, while unbridled government spending was "mortgaging our future . . . for the temporary convenience of the present."

Reagan also pledged to restore the nation's global power. Using the most bellicose rhetoric since the early years of the cold war, Reagan called the Soviet Union an "evil empire" whose leaders "reserve unto themselves the right to commit any crime, to lie, to cheat." The United States, he insisted, must vastly increase its military might and demonstrate its resolve to confront communism anywhere in the world.

## Militarization and Interventions Abroad

Reagan moved quickly to accelerate the arms buildup that Carter had begun, overseeing plans for new bombers and missiles, an enhanced nuclear force in Europe, an expanded navy, and a rapid-deployment force. Congress approved most of these programs, and military expenditures shot up by one-third in the first half of the 1980s. Throughout Reagan's presidency, defense spending averaged $216 billion a year, higher even than in the Vietnam era.

One justification for the arms buildup was that the United States must negotiate with the Soviets from a position of strength. Its unintended effect was to provoke an outburst of calls to halt the arms race. A rally demanding a freeze on nuclear weapons at current levels drew 700,000 people in New York City in 1982. Hundreds of thousands of Europeans demonstrated across the continent, stimulated by fears of new U.S. missiles that were scheduled for deployment in NATO countries in 1983.

Reagan startled many of his own advisers in March 1983 by announcing plans for research on a Strategic Defense Initiative (SDI). Immediately dubbed "Star Wars" by its critics, who doubted its feasibility, the project envisioned deploying lasers in space to destroy enemy missiles before they could reach their targets. Reagan conceded that developing an SDI could be seen as "fostering an aggressive policy," since it would allow the United States to fire first and not fear retaliation. The Soviets reacted angrily because SDI development violated the 1972 treaty restricting antiballistic missile systems and would require the Soviets to invest huge sums in their own Star Wars technology. For several years, Reagan's attachment to SDI impeded superpower agreement on strategic arms control.

The U.S. military buildup placed the Soviets on the defensive, but it did not guarantee American dominance in the world. Although Iran released the American hostages the day of Reagan's inauguration, terrorism continued to plague the United States. In October 1983 in Lebanon, an Islamic extremist drove a bomb-filled truck into a marine barracks, killing 241 Americans. Faced with other incidents of murder, kidnapping, and hijacking by various Middle Eastern extremist groups, Reagan refused to negotiate. To bargain with terrorists, he insisted, would only encourage more assaults, and he pledged never to do so.

Closer to home, the U.S. military flexed its muscles. Just two days after the Lebanon disaster, U.S. troops invaded Grenada, a small British

Commonwealth island nation in the Caribbean, in response to a coup by left-wing forces. Ostensibly undertaken to protect U.S. medical students on the island, the intervention reflected administration fears that Grenada would fall into the Cuban-Soviet orbit.

Elsewhere, the United States sought to contain leftist movements privately and less aggressively. In Asia, Afghan rebels fighting to dislodge the Soviet-backed government received U.S. aid. In the African nation of Angola, the United States armed rebel forces against the Soviet- and Cuban-backed government. Siding with the racist South African government in the Angolan crisis did not trouble the president. But in 1985, Congress forced the administration to apply economic sanctions against South Africa by overriding Reagan's veto of a sanctions bill.

Left-wing movements in Central America created the most alarm among administration officials. These movements, Reagan charged, threatened to "destabilize the entire region from the Panama Canal to Mexico." When a leftist uprising occurred in El Salvador, the United States sent money and military advisers to prop up the government, even though it had committed murderous human rights violations and opposed social reform. In neighboring Nicaragua, Reagan aimed to unseat the Sandinistas, who had overthrown the repressive Somoza dictatorship and assumed power in 1979. The Reagan administration threw itself into efforts to undercut the Nicaraguan government by aiding the Contras, a coalition of armed opposition to the Sandinistas that included many individuals from the ousted regime. Deliberately overriding congressional refusal to authorize military aid and violating the will of a public that feared being drawn into another Vietnam, the administration secretly used economic pressure to destabilize the Sandinista government and provided weapons and training to the Contras. Through legal and illegal means, the Reagan administration helped sustain the Contra opposition and wreck the Nicaraguan economy, thereby undermining support for the government. After nine years of civil war, Daniel Ortega, the Sandinista president, agreed to a political settlement engineered by the leaders of the five Central American states. When elections were held in 1990, a coalition of all the opposition groups defeated the Sandinistas, and Ortega stepped aside.

## Unleashing Free Enterprise

Reagan's plan to reduce taxes came from a few conservative economists who argued that tax cuts were compatible with reduction of the federal budget deficit that had been growing since the 1960s and that such cuts would actually increase federal revenues. This theory of "supply-side economics" emphasized boosting production, or supply, which would in turn raise demand. In this view, high taxes had discouraged investment and weakened the economy; lower taxes would enable businesses to expand and would encourage individuals to work harder because they would keep more of their earnings. Tax reduction would increase the production of goods and services so dramatically that, even with lower rates, more revenue would flow to the federal government.

Although supply-side economics contradicted traditional Republican economic doctrine, which stressed a balanced budget, it fit perfectly with Reagan's emphasis on optimism and possibilities. In sharp contrast to Carter's talk of limitations and sacrifice, Reagan's agenda appeared to be pain-free. To allay worries about the budget deficit and sell his tax cut, Reagan promised to cut federal expenditures, a position fully compatible with his antigovernment views.

In the summer of 1981, Congress passed the Economic Recovery Tax Act, the largest tax reduction in history. Individual income taxes were cut, the lowest rate falling from 14 to 11 percent and the highest from 70 to 50 percent. Corporations also received tax breaks, and taxes on capital gains, gifts, and inheritances dropped. In contrast, Social Security contributions and other taxes that affected Americans across the board increased during the 1980s. The net effect was to make the entire tax structure more regressive—that is, affluent Americans saved far more on their tax bills than did the average taxpayer, and the distribution of wealth was further skewed in favor of the rich.

"Hack, chop, crunch!" was how *Time* magazine characterized the administration's efforts to free private enterprise from government restraints. Carter had confined deregulation to particular industries such as finance and transportation while increasing regulation in areas such as health, safety, equal employment opportunity, and environmental protection. The Reagan administration, by contrast, pursued across-the-board deregulation. Reagan presided over the most lax enforcement of the Sherman Antitrust Act—the law designed to reduce monopoly and promote competition—since its early history in the 1890s. In a decade of unprecedented business mergers and takeovers, the government opposed not a single one. The Reagan administration also loosened restraints on business imposed by employee health and safety measures and helped to weaken organized labor. When 13,000 members of the Professional Air Traffic Controllers Organization (PATCO) went on strike in 1981, Reagan fired them and destroyed their union.

Blaming environmental laws for the nation's sluggish economic growth, Reagan targeted them too for deregulation. His first secretary of the interior, James Watt, declared, "We will mine more, drill more, cut more timber," and released federal lands to private exploitation, while the head of the Environmental Protection Agency eased enforcement of air and water pollution measures. Popular support for environmental protection blocked complete realization of the administration's deregulatory goals. Congress overrode vetoes of clean water legislation and a bill to promote cleanup of hazardous waste sites (the Superfund).

Deregulation of the banking industry, supported by Democrats and Republicans alike, created a crisis in the savings and loan industry and, ultimately, a burden for taxpayers. When deregulatory laws lifted interest rate ceilings and permitted savings and loan institutions (S&Ls) to lend money more freely, some S&Ls extended enormous loans to real estate developers and invested in other high-yield but risky ventures. With lax federal oversight, S&L owners reaped lavish profits during the early 1980s, and their depositors enjoyed high interest rates. But when real estate values began to plunge in the mid-1980s, especially in California and the Southwest, hundreds of S&Ls went bankrupt. After Congress voted to bail out the S&L industry in 1989, the burden of the largest financial scandal in American history fell on American taxpayers, few of whom had profited from deregulation.

The S&L crisis deepened the federal budget deficit, which soared during the 1980s despite Reagan's pledge to pare federal spending. The administration achieved some savings in the Social Security and Aid to Families with Dependent Children programs. But these programs were not gutted; the Reagan program represented an attack on the Great Society rather than the New Deal. Congress agreed to cut food stamps (14 percent), job training (39 percent), aid to low-income students (16 percent), and health services (33 percent). Hundreds of thousands of people lost eligibility or some benefits. Those with incomes just around the poverty line took the hardest hits.

Even these cuts occupied too small a share of the total budget to make significant inroads in the deficit, and they were counterbalanced by increases in defense spending. After a recession in 1981–1982, the economy entered an unprecedented period of growth, but the budget deficit soared from $74 billion when Carter left office to a high of $220 billion in 1986. By then, interest on the national debt consumed one-seventh of all federal expenditures.

The problem of inflation was eliminated, but it took the severest recession since the 1930s to squeeze inflation out of the U.S. economy. Beginning in 1981, unemployment rose sharply, approaching 11 percent late in 1982. Record numbers of banks and businesses closed, and twelve million workers could not find jobs. The threat of unemployment further undermined organized labor, forcing unions to make concessions that management insisted were necessary for industry's survival. The economy recovered in 1983, and the number of jobs increased substantially, although unemployment never fell below 5 percent.

## Liberalism on the Defensive

The recession hurt Republicans in the 1982 congressional elections, but by 1984 the economy was booming, with inflation and unemployment at their lowest points in a decade. Reagan delivered a humiliating defeat to the Democratic ticket in his 1984 reelection, although the Democrats retained control of the House of Representatives and picked up two Senate seats.

Liberal movements survived the Reagan triumph, but their accomplishments during the 1980s were largely defensive. Civil rights advocates fought off administration attacks in the courts, and, when that failed, they managed to find some help in Congress. Feminists gained White House support on a few issues and looked to the states and to electoral politics to advance other items on their agenda. The gay rights movement acquired members and visibility, making small inroads against discrimination against homosexuals. Yet liberal movements lost a critical ally as President Reagan filled the federal judiciary with conservative appointments.

### The "Teflon President"

Even a less optimistic candidate than Reagan would have approached the 1984 election with confidence. No serious international crises loomed, and the economy was booming. Since the easing of the 1981–1982 recession, public opinion stood strongly in the president's favor.

Political observers marveled at Reagan's popularity. He was liked even by Americans who opposed his policies and even when he made glaring mistakes. At one meeting, he failed to recognize his own secretary of housing and urban development, calling him "Mr. Mayor." On another occasion he proclaimed that vegetation caused 90 percent of all air pollution. He made so many misstatements that aides tried to keep him away from reporters. When Reagan did need to appear in public, one aide reported, "Every moment . . . was scheduled, every word was scripted, every place where Reagan was expected to stand was chalked with toe marks."

---

*Liberal movements survived the Reagan triumph, but their accomplishments during the 1980s were largely defensive.*

---

Democratic Representative Patricia Schroeder tagged Reagan the "Teflon President" because none of his administration's mistakes, or even his own errors and falsehoods, seemed to stick to him. Reagan gave his own explanation when asked in 1980 what people saw in him: "I think, maybe, they see themselves and that I'm one of them?" he replied. His confidence and easygoing sense of humor were a large part of his appeal, and he had the ability to ignore or recast darker aspects of the nation's past and to present a version of history that Americans could feel good about. He also gained public sympathy after being shot by a would-be assassin in March 1981. Just before surgery for removal of a bullet in his chest, Reagan joked to physicians, "I hope you're Republicans."

Reagan's popularity and the prospering economy posed a formidable challenge for the Democrats. Among several candidates for the 1984 presidential nomination was the Reverend Jesse Jackson, who had fought civil rights battles with Martin Luther King Jr. and whose campaign stressed the needs of the disadvantaged. Walter F. Mondale, vice president under Carter, won the Democratic nomination and electrified the Democratic National Convention by naming as his running mate New York Representative Geraldine A. Ferraro, the first woman nominated on a major party ticket.

The Mondale-Ferraro campaign emphasized the hardships suffered by the unemployed, the poor, and victims of discrimination under the Reagan presidency. Attacking the budget deficit, Mondale charged that Reagan knew that taxes would

have to be raised. Reagan simply turned that challenge around: Democrats, he claimed, "see an America where every day is April 15th [the due date for income tax returns] . . . we see an America where every day is the Fourth of July." The Democrats, he insisted, stressed America's limits and failures; he emphasized success and possibility.

Voters responded to the president's vision and to the economic comeback. With 59 percent of the

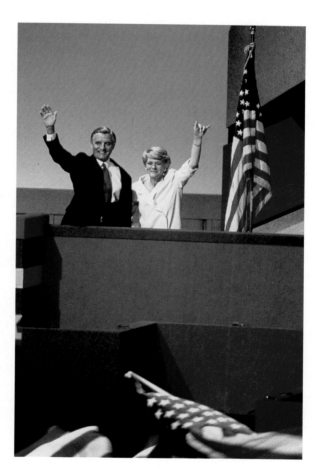

**THE DEMOCRATIC TICKET, 1984**
*Responding in part to feminist pressure, presidential nominee Walter F. Mondale electrified the Democratic Party convention when he announced his choice of Geraldine Ferraro for his running mate. An Italian American Catholic mother of three, Ferraro represented Queens, New York, in the House of Representatives. Although Reagan's landslide swept away Mondale and Ferraro, her candidacy was an important breakthrough for women in politics.*
Randy Taylor/Sygma.

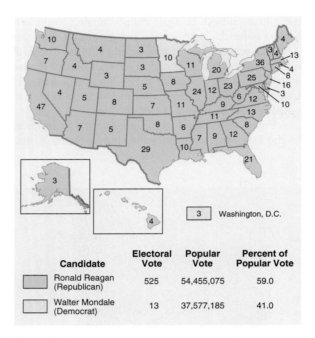

| Candidate | Electoral Vote | Popular Vote | Percent of Popular Vote |
|---|---|---|---|
| Ronald Reagan (Republican) | 525 | 54,455,075 | 59.0 |
| Walter Mondale (Democrat) | 13 | 37,577,185 | 41.0 |

MAP 31.1
*The Election of 1984*

vote, Reagan's landslide victory ranked close to those of Roosevelt in 1936, Johnson in 1964, and Nixon in 1972 (Map 31.1). But what the president would do with his mandate was not clear, for he had said little about policy goals. The Democrats, for their part, pondered what it would take to stem the exodus of longtime loyalists—particularly southern white males—to the Republican Party. Stung by Republican charges that the Democratic Party was captive to "special interests" such as labor, women, and minorities, some Democratic leaders urged that the party shift more toward the right.

## Continued Struggles over Rights

In keeping with its antigovernment philosophy, the Reagan administration tried to reverse federal protections of civil rights, particularly those of African Americans, women, and homosexuals. It broke sharply with the national commitment to equal opportunity undertaken in the 1960s, working to overturn busing and affirmative action agreements, even those that had been entered into voluntarily by school districts and employers. Although the Supreme Court upheld an Internal Revenue Service

policy that denied tax-exempt status to segregationist private schools, the Justice Department persuaded the Court to severely weaken Title IX of the Education Amendments Act of 1972, a crucial law promoting equal opportunity in education. In *Grove City College v. Bell* (1984), the Court ruled that an institution could practice discrimination in one of its programs, such as athletics, and still receive federal funds for scholarships and other programs that did not discriminate.

*Grove City* allowed the Justice Department to abandon dozens of civil rights cases against schools and colleges. It also galvanized a coalition of civil rights organizations and groups representing women, the aged and disabled, and their allies. In 1988, Congress passed the Civil Rights Restoration Act of 1988, which reversed the administration's victory in *Grove City* and—going even further—banned any organization that practiced discrimination on the basis of race, color, national origin, sex, handicap, or age from receiving government funds.

Congress also renewed and strengthened the Voting Rights Act over administration objections. Although Congress and the courts partially deflected the administration's drive to shrink the government's support for civil rights, critics claimed that the administration established a national climate that made it no longer unfashionable to express prejudice and thus contributed to new outbreaks of racial violence in the late 1980s.

Women also suffered from the administration's efforts to weaken antidiscrimination enforcement. For the first time in its history, the Republican Party took an explicitly antifeminist tone, opposing both the Equal Rights Amendment (ERA) and a woman's right to abortion, key goals of women's rights activists. In this hostile political environment, the women's movement shifted its strategies and goals. Defense of abortion rights, antidiscrimination measures, and affirmative action remained high priorities. But activists increased their attention to women's economic and family problems, which eluded the grasp of antidiscrimination policies. This new agenda recognized the needs of less advantaged women and acknowledged the disproportionate representation of women and children among the poor, a development that some termed "the feminization of poverty."

The Reagan administration had its own concerns about women, specifically about the "gender gap"—women's tendency throughout the 1980s to vote for liberal and Democratic candidates in larger numbers than men did. Reagan appointed three women

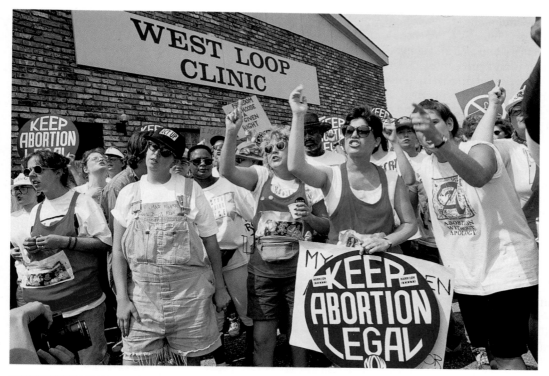

**CONFRONTATIONS OVER ABORTION**
*Failing to win a constitutional amendment banning abortion, in the late 1970s and 1980s some groups in the right-to-life movement adopted more militant tactics, picketing abortion clinics, yelling at patients and employees, and trying to block entrances into clinics. In response, prochoice activists defended clinic access and the right to abortion, as shown here.*
Paul S. Howell/Gamma Liaison.

to cabinet posts and the first woman, Sandra Day O'Connor, to the Supreme Court. But these "showcase" actions accompanied a general decline in the number of women and minorities in high-level positions. And with higher poverty rates than men, women suffered most from budget cuts in social programs.

Feminists found some common ground with the Reagan administration, however, in two measures that addressed women's economic distress. The Child Support Enforcement Amendments helped single and divorced mothers by facilitating collection of court-ordered child support payments from absent parents. The Retirement Equity Act of 1984 benefited divorced and older women by strengthening their claims to their husbands' pensions and enabling women to qualify more easily for private pensions. Feminists fought successfully to retain women's right to have an abortion, but

they hit a stone wall in their efforts to strengthen day care services, aid displaced homemakers, and promote pay equity—that is, equal pay for traditionally female jobs that were comparable in worth to jobs performed primarily by men.

*Women also suffered from the Reagan administration's efforts to weaken antidiscrimination enforcement. And with higher poverty rates than men, women suffered most from budget cuts in social programs.*

Like other pressure groups, the women's movement pursued locally what it failed to achieve at the federal level. The pay equity movement took hold in several states, and many states strengthened their laws against rape. States also increased funding for domestic violence programs and stepped up efforts to protect victims and prosecute abusers.

Using sophisticated fundraising and election-eering techniques, feminists helped move more women into political office. By the end of the 1980s, women had made their marks as governors of Kentucky, Vermont, and Nebraska; and women served as mayors of several large cities, including Jane Byrne of Chicago and Dianne Feinstein of San Francisco. Women won three U.S. Senate races, and their share of congressional seats inched up to 5.6 percent from 2.8 percent in 1971. By the end of the decade, women claimed 17.2 percent of seats in state legislatures.

Gay men and lesbians also accomplished small gains by 1990. Although an American organization for homosexual rights had existed as early as 1924, not until the 1980s did a national mass movement play a significant role in U.S. politics. The contemporary movement emerged out of the social upheaval of the 1960s, its beginnings symbolized by the Stonewall riot of 1969, when gay men and lesbians fought back against a police raid on a gay bar in New York City's Greenwich Village. Influenced by the black freedom struggle, the New Left, the counterculture, and feminism, gays and lesbians began to claim equal rights for homosexuals and to express pride in their sexual identities.

Although the Supreme Court in 1986 upheld the right of states to enforce sodomy laws, most states repealed their laws against homosexuality by the end of the decade. The federal government lifted its ban against homosexuals in all areas except the military and intelligence agencies. Beginning with the election of Elaine Noble to the Massachusetts legislature in 1974, several openly gay politicians won election and reelection to offices from mayor to member of Congress. The Democrats began to include gay rights planks in their party platforms.

The acquired immune deficiency syndrome (AIDS) epidemic further mobilized the gay and lesbian rights movement in the 1980s, because at first male homosexuals accounted for the majority of AIDS cases. As the disease swept through communities of gay men in New York, San Francisco, and elsewhere, gay men and lesbians organized for public education about AIDS and public funding for its treatment and prevention.

The gay and lesbian rights movement helped thousands of homosexuals experience the relief of

**THE AIDS CRISIS**
*American pop artist Keith Haring made this AIDS awareness drawing before the disease killed him in 1990, citing the "growing burden that each of us carries as the AIDS crisis continues to escalate around the world." During the 1990s, scientists made important advances in treatment, but the disease continued to elude a vaccine or a cure.*
© The Estate of Keith Haring.

being able to live openly. By "coming out" in great numbers, they helped to make homosexuality more visible and somewhat more accepted in the larger population. Activists organized gay rights and gay pride marches throughout the country, and the movement began to win local victories, gaining for lesbians and gay men some protections against discrimination. (See Texts in Historical Context on page 844.)

Yet these piecemeal victories left most gay men and lesbians still vulnerable to intolerance. The New Right targeted gays and lesbians as symbols of national immorality and succeeded in overturning some homosexual rights measures. Protections against discrimination for gay men and lesbians lagged far behind the civil rights guarantees that racial minorities and women had achieved.

## The Conservative Shift in the Federal Courts

Since the 1950s, proponents of reform had grown accustomed to counting on the federal judiciary as a powerful ally in their struggles for minority rights and social justice. Yet in the 1980s, liberals saw their allies slipping away as conservative justices increasingly populated the Supreme Court and the lower federal courts.

With the opportunity to appoint half of the 761 federal court judges and three new Supreme Court justices, President Reagan carefully selected candidates who had strongly conservative views and would help reverse the liberal direction taken by the Supreme Court since Earl Warren's tenure in the 1950s and 1960s. The Supreme Court did not execute an abrupt about-face: It upheld important affirmative action and antidiscrimination policies and ruled that sexual harassment in the workplace constituted sex discrimination. But with Reagan's appointees, the tide began to turn in favor of the doctrine of strict construction—that is, strict interpretation of the original aims of the Constitution's authors, an approach that limits judicial power to protect individual rights.

After appointing the moderate conservative Sandra Day O'Connor in 1981, Reagan strengthened the strict constructionists by elevating William J. Rehnquist, a Nixon appointee, to chief justice when Warren Burger retired in 1986. His next nominee, Antonin Scalia, tipped the balance further to the right. In 1987, a diverse coalition of civil rights advocates, trade unionists, feminists, environmentalists, and senior citizens pressured the Senate to reject the nomination of Robert H. Bork, a passionate strict constructionist. But Reagan's next choice, Anthony M. Kennedy, gave conservatives a slim majority on the Supreme Court (Reagan's three appointees plus Rehnquist and Byron White).

The full impact of Reagan's appointments continued after he left office. The Court allowed states to impose restrictions that limited access to abortion for poor and uneducated women and those living in rural areas. Other rulings weakened protections against employment discrimination and whittled away at legal safeguards around the death sentence.

# Disasters and Triumphs of the 1980s

In Reagan's second term (1985–1989), the costs of the administration's economic achievements became starkly clear. The federal budget deficit worsened, the nation continued to decline in global economic competitiveness, and corporations and individuals went further into debt. During his first term Reagan had achieved his counterrevolution in domestic affairs; subsequently Congress took control of the domestic agenda, reaching accord with the administration on major changes in the tax and welfare systems and enacting, over presidential objections, reforms in such areas as civil rights and the environment.

In foreign policy, the Iran-Contra affair with its revelations of illegal activities seriously damaged the president's credibility and leadership. Yet Reagan also responded favorably to new initiatives from the Soviet Union and presided over the most impressive improvement in superpower relations since the shattering of the World War II alliance.

## The Debt-Based Economy

The gross national product increased by 25 percent during the Reagan years, and inflation remained in check. But along with this growth, evidence of deep economic flaws mounted. The steel, automobile, and electronics industries suffered in competition with those of such countries as Germany and Japan; Americans bought more and more Toyotas and Hondas and fewer Fords and Chevrolets. With Americans purchasing more foreign-made goods than domestic producers sold abroad, the nation's trade deficit (the difference between imports and exports) soared to $126 billion in 1988.

*In Reagan's second term (1985–1989), the costs of the administration's economic achievements became starkly clear.*

International competition forced the collapse of some older companies, while others moved factories (and jobs) abroad to be closer to foreign markets or to benefit from the low wage standards of countries such as Mexico and Korea. The growth of

# Protecting Gay and Lesbian Rights

*Since the 1970s, the gay and lesbian rights movement has worked for passage of laws and ordinances to protect homosexuals from discrimination. In 1982, Wisconsin became the first state to ban discrimination on the basis of sexual orientation, following the lead of several cities that passed gay rights ordinances in the 1970s. By the mid-1990s, nine states and more than eighty cities had such legislation on the books. These measures ignited controversy that continued to surround the issue through the 1990s.*

*In 1974, the city council of Minneapolis amended its civil rights ordinance to cover discrimination based on sexual preference. The law provided a rationale for banning discrimination and, unlike some laws focusing exclusively on employment, encompassed a broad range of activities.*

## Document 1. Ordinance of the City of Minneapolis, 1974

It is determined that discriminatory practices based on race, color, creed, religion, national origin, sex or affectional or sexual preference, with respect to employment, labor union membership, housing accommodations, property rights, education, public accommodations, and public services, or any of them, tend to create and intensify conditions of poverty, ill health, unrest, civil disobedience, lawlessness, and vice and adversely affect the public health, safety, order, convenience, and general welfare; such discriminatory practices threaten the rights, privileges and opportunities of all inhabitants of the city and such rights, privileges and opportunities are hereby to be declared civil rights, and the adoption of this Chapter is deemed to be an exercise of the policy power of the City to protect such rights.

*Paul Moore, Episcopal bishop of New York, made a religious argument for gay rights in his letter to the editor of the* New York Times.

## Document 2. Letter to the Editor from Paul Moore, November 23, 1981

I quote our diocesan resolution: "Whereas this Convention, without making any judgment on the morality of homosexuality, agrees that homosexuals are entitled to full civil rights. Now therefore be it resolved this Convention supports laws guaranteeing homosexuals all civil rights guaranteed to other citizens."

The Bible stands for justice and compassion for all of God's children. To deny civil rights to anyone for something he or she cannot help is against the clear commandment of justice and love, which is the message of the word of God.

As a New Yorker I find it incredible that this great city, populated by more gay persons than any other city in the world, still denies them basic human rights. They make an enormous contribution to the commercial, artistic, and religious life of our city.

*The following statement from the Roman Catholic Church reflects the views of many religious groups that take positions against gay rights.*

## Document 3. Vatican Congregation for the Doctrine of the Faith, August 6, 1992

"Sexual orientation" does not constitute a quality comparable to race, ethnic background, etc., in respect to nondiscrimination. Unlike these, homosexual orientation is an objective disorder and evokes moral concern.

There are areas in which it is not unjust discrimination to take sexual orientation into account, for example, in the placement of children for adoption or foster care, in employment of teachers or athletic coaches, and in military recruitment.

*Although the U.S. Congress has never enacted legislation banning discrimination on the basis of sexual orientation, it has considered a number of bills for that purpose. Charles Cochrane Jr., an army veteran and police sergeant, testified on behalf of such a bill in 1982.*

## DOCUMENT 4. Testimony of Charles Cochrane Jr. before the House Subcommittee on Employment Opportunities of the Committee on Education and Labor, January 27, 1982

I am very proud of being a New York City policeman. And I am equally proud of being gay. I have always been gay.

I have been out of the closet for 4 years. November 6 was my anniversary. It took me 34 years to muster enough courage to declare myself openly.

We gays are loathed by some, pitied by others, and misunderstood by most. We are not cruel, wicked, cursed, sick, or possessed by demons. We are artists, business people, police officers, and clergymen. We are scientists, truck drivers, politicians; we work in every field. We are loving human beings who are in some ways different. . . .

During the early years of my association with the New York City Police Department a great deal of energy did go into guarding and concealing my innermost feelings. I believed that I would be subjected to ridicule and harassment were my colleagues to learn of my sexual orientation. Happily, when I actually began to integrate the various aspects of my total self, those who knew me did not reject me.

Then what need is there for such legislation as H.R. 1454? The crying need of others, still trapped in their closets, who must be protected, who must be reassured that honesty about themselves and their lives will not cost them their homes or their jobs. . . .

The bill before you will not act as a proselytizing agent in matters of sexual orientation or preference. It will not include affirmative action provisions. Passage of this bill will protect the inherent human rights of all people of the United States, while in no way diminishing the rights of those who do not see the need for such legislation. Finally, it will signify, quite clearly, recognition and compassion for a group which is often maligned without justification.

*Carl Horowitz, a policy analyst at a conservative think tank, the Heritage Foundation, expresses arguments of those opposed to measures banning discrimination against homosexuals.*

## DOCUMENT 5. Carl F. Horowitz, "Homosexuality's Legal Revolution," May 1991

Homosexual activists have all but completed their campaign to persuade the nation's educational establishment that homosexuality is normal "alternative" behavior, and thus any adverse reaction to it is akin to a phobia, such as fear of heights, or an ethnic prejudice, such as anti-Semitism.

The movement now stands on the verge of fully realizing its use of law to . . . intimidate heterosexuals uncomfortable about coming into contact with it. . . .

The movement seeks to win sinecures through the state, and over any objections by "homophobic" opposition. With a cloud of a heavy fine or even a jail sentence hanging over a mortgage lender, a rental agent, or a job interviewer who might be discomforted by them, homosexuals under these laws can win employment, credit, housing, and other economic entitlements. Heterosexuals would have no right to discriminate against homosexuals, but apparently, not vice versa. . . .

These laws will create market bottlenecks. Heterosexuals and even "closeted" homosexuals will be at a competitive disadvantage for jobs and housing. . . .

The new legalism will increase heterosexual anger—and even violence—toward homosexuals.

**Document 1.** Norman Dorsen and Aryeh Neier, eds., *The Rights of Gay People: The Basic ACLU Guide to a Gay Person's Rights* (New York: E. P. Dutton, 1992), 251.

**Document 2.** Paul Moore, letter to the editor, *New York Times,* December 8, 1981.

**Document 3.** Vatican Congregation for the Doctrine of the Faith, *Origins,* August 6, 1992.

**Document 4.** Hearing on H.R. 1454, House Subcommittee on Employment Opportunities of the Committee on Education and Labor, 97th Cong., 2nd sess., 1982, 54–56.

**Document 5.** Carl F. Horowitz, "Homosexuality's Legal Revolution," *Freeman,* May 1991.

service industries created new jobs at home, but former blue-collar workers who were forced to make the shift found their wages substantially lower. When David Ramos was laid off in 1982 from his $12.75-an-hour-job in a steel plant, his wages fell to just $5 an hour as a security guard, and his family of six was forced to rely on food stamps. Overall, the number of full-time workers earning wages below the poverty level ($12,195 for a family of four in 1990) rose sharply from 12 to 18 percent of all workers in the 1980s.

Labor unions wanted higher tariffs to protect American producers from foreign competition, a point made by Detroit autoworkers who took sledgehammers to a Japanese-produced car. Committed to free trade and opposed to tariffs, the Reagan administration sought to make other countries more receptive to U.S. exports and resisted extreme measures to keep out foreign products. The trade gap necessitated a vast increase in borrowing, and the largest creditor nation became the largest debtor nation in just one decade. Foreign investors from Japan, Western Europe, and the Middle East purchased American stocks and bonds, real estate, and corporations. Time-honored companies such as Firestone, Brooks Brothers, Sohio, 20th Century-Fox, and Capitol Records passed into foreign ownership. Local communities welcomed infusions of foreign capital, and several states went to great lengths to encourage Japanese companies to establish automobile plants within their boundaries.

Foreign investment in the U.S. economy helped compensate for a decline in domestic investment in the 1980s. Instead of putting their tax savings into new business enterprise or machinery that would boost productivity and create new jobs, as supply-siders had promised, entrepreneurs used them to take over other companies or to support lavish lifestyles. As savings and investment declined, indebtedness soared among rich and poor alike, and household debt, especially credit card spending, surpassed $3 trillion.

The federal government made its own contribution to national indebtedness with an annual deficit that reached $220 billion in 1986. By the time Reagan left office, the deficit had fallen to $160 billion, but prospects for further reduction were poor. With the accumulating annual budget deficits, in eight years the government had increased the national debt from $834 billion to $2.3 trillion (Figure 31.1).

The most important domestic initiative of Reagan's second term was the Tax Reform Act of 1986,

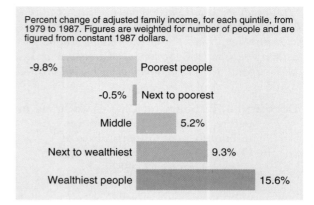

Percent change of adjusted family income, for each quintile, from 1979 to 1987. Figures are weighted for number of people and are figured from constant 1987 dollars.

-9.8% Poorest people
-0.5% Next to poorest
Middle 5.2%
Next to wealthiest 9.3%
Wealthiest people 15.6%

FIGURE 31.1
*The Growth of Inequality: Changes in Family Income, 1979–1987*
*For most of the post–World War II period, income increased for all groups on the economic ladder; but after 1979, income of the poorest families actually declined, while it grew substantially for the richest 20 percent of the population.*

Copyright © 1989 by The New York Times Co. Reprinted by Permission.

which included both tax cuts and tax reforms. The maximum tax rate on individual incomes fell from 50 percent to 28 percent and on businesses from 48 percent to 34 percent, and millions of low-income people escaped income taxes altogether. To compensate for these cuts, Congress raised the capital gains tax and reduced deductions and loopholes that favored corporations and the wealthy.

## The Initiative Shifts to Congress and the States

Having largely achieved his goal of getting the government off the back of free enterprise, Reagan was not about to reverse that trend with new programs. While his rhetoric continued to preach the aims of social conservatives, issues such as abortion were too politically charged to risk an all-out presidential effort. Moreover, disclosures of fraud and corruption among more than one hundred senior officials crippled Reagan's domestic leadership. Beset by internal conflicts, the administration also faced a more independent Congress after the Democrats recaptured the Senate in 1986.

In addition to defeating Bork's nomination, Congress overrode presidential vetoes of environmental protection legislation and highway and mass-transit programs and forced compromises with the executive branch on other issues. In 1987, Reagan reluctantly signed bills to aid the homeless. And in 1988, the two branches hammered out a $2.7 billion antidrug law, which included treatment programs for drug users and more severe penalties for dealers, including the death penalty for certain drug traffickers. Reforms of the welfare system in the Family Support Act of 1988 somewhat improved impoverished families' access to benefits while they sought to end welfare dependency by compelling single parents with children over the age of three to get jobs or to enroll in a job-training program. Even the law's sponsors considered the five-year appropriation of $3.34 billion inadequate for the training and education that would be required to escape poverty. Efforts to alleviate poverty were held hostage—like many other initiatives—to the federal deficit. The revival of Democratic strength in Congress tempered the president's efforts to minimize federal activity, but advocates of new programs were stymied by the lack of resources to fund them.

In trying to compensate for the paralyzing effect of the deficit on federal action, for the first time in decades state legislatures became more innovative than Washington. "Our federal politics are gridlocked, and governors have become the ones who have to have the courage to put their necks out," said a spokesperson for state governors. States passed bills to block corporate takeovers, raise the minimum wage, establish parental leave policies, require equal pay for jobs of equal worth in state and local governments, improve food labeling, protect the environment, and promote foreign trade.

## The Iran-Contra Scandal

In the Iran-Contra Scandal—the most serious revelations of executive branch misconduct since Watergate—administration officials engaged in secret and illegal activities, destroyed evidence of their undertakings, and lied to Congress. President Reagan himself escaped criminal charges. But evidence that he had said one thing and done another and failed to exercise control over his staff tarnished his administration.

The Iran-Contra affair began in 1985 as a scheme invented by heads of the National Security Council (NSC), NSC aide marine Lieutenant Colonel Oliver North, and CIA Director William Casey. They arranged to sell arms to Iran, which

was then at war with neighboring Iraq; in exchange Iranians would exert pressure on Muslim terrorists to release seven American hostages who were being held in Lebanon. Funds from the arms sales were then channeled through Swiss bank accounts to aid the Nicaraguan Contras in their efforts to overthrow that country's leftist government. Over the objections of Secretary of State George Shultz and Defense Secretary Caspar Weinberger, Reagan approved the arms sales. He and his cabinet secretaries subsequently disclaimed knowledge of the diversion of funds to the Contras.

*In the Iran-Contra scandal, administration officials engaged in secret and illegal activities, destroyed evidence of their undertakings, and lied to Congress.*

When news of the affair surfaced in November 1986, the administration faced a number of serious charges. First, the president who had consistently pledged never to bargain with terrorists was now revealed to have allowed his aides to do so, violating the United States' stated neutrality in the Iran-Iraq war. Even worse, the administration had defied Congress's express ban on military aid for the Contras. Although North and others destroyed incriminating documents, enough evidence remained to demonstrate the culpability of seven individuals. Brought to trial by an independent prosecutor appointed by Reagan, all pleaded guilty or were convicted of lying to Congress and destroying evidence. North's felony conviction was later overturned on a technicality, and President George Bush pardoned six officials in December 1992.

In public statements Reagan appeared as a detached, fumbling leader who could not remember key events. The independent prosecutor's final report, issued in 1994, found no evidence that Reagan had broken the law but concluded that both Reagan and Vice President Bush had known about the diversion of funds to the Contras and that Reagan had "knowingly participated or at least acquiesced" in covering up the scandal.

The Iran-Contra affair left the Reagan administration in disarray. Reagan ended his term with relatively high approval ratings, but his image as a confident leader was tarnished. More ominous for the nation, the scandal revealed that, despite all the efforts begun during the Nixon years to make the executive branch accountable to Congress and the public, it retained abundant capacity to conduct a secret foreign policy outside the law.

### A Thaw in Soviet-American Relations

Reagan weathered the Iran-Contra storm in part because a momentous thaw developed in the cold war. His own flexibility contributed to the Soviet-American accord, but it would not have happened without the innovative Soviet head of state who recognized that his country's domestic problems demanded a relaxation of cold war antagonism.

Mikhail Gorbachev assumed power in 1985 determined to revitalize the Soviet economy by introducing elements of free enterprise. He proclaimed a new era of *glasnost* (greater freedom of expression), eventually allowing such challenges to Communist rule as new political parties and contested elections. While Gorbachev was recognizing that cuts in the enormous military budget were key to economic revival, Reagan was facing congressional resistance to funding the arms race and popular support for arms reductions. When Gorbachev took the initiative, Reagan was ready to respond.

A positive personal chemistry developed between Reagan and Gorbachev, who met four times between 1985 and 1988. Negotiations stalemated when Reagan refused to stop research and development on Star Wars, but eventually Gorbachev gave up that demand. By December 1987, the superpowers had completed an intermediate-range nuclear weapons (INF) agreement, which eliminated all short- and medium-range missiles from Europe and provided for on-site inspection for the first time. In Africa, the Soviet Union, Cuba, and the United States agreed on a political settlement for the civil war in Angola. Although the Soviet Union had seized the initiative, Reagan could justifiably claim a share of the credit for what he called "a satisfying new closeness with the Soviet Union"—a détente that far surpassed what Nixon and Kissinger had accomplished.

# American Society in the "Decade of Greed"

"More prosperous, more secure and happier than it was eight years ago." So Ronald Reagan described the nation as he left the presidency in January 1989.

And so it was for a majority of Americans, especially those who were better off to begin with. Great fortunes were made during the 1980s, and making money and displaying wealth were celebrated in popular culture. At the same time, however, the population became more polarized along class lines as increasing homelessness and growing poverty reversed the post–World War II trend toward greater economic equality. New immigration made the nation more culturally diverse, but African Americans, Hispanic Americans, and other minority groups fell disproportionately among those passed over by the surge of prosperity.

### The Money Culture

Not since the Gilded Age of the 1890s had wealth been so extravagantly displayed, and not since the 1920s had American culture so venerated free enterprise and the entrepreneur. Books by businesspeople climbed onto best-seller lists. The press described lavish parties costing millions of dollars. Popular magazines featured articles entitled "High Life Afloat: Superduper Yachts" and "They're Like Us, Except They're Rich." Evidence of immense fortunes and conspicuous consumption ranged from multimillion-dollar Manhattan apartments to special area codes for coastal waters to accommodate the proliferation of yachts. Fascination with wealth and consumption drew vast audiences to prime-time TV serials such as *Dallas* and *Dynasty*. College students told poll takers that their primary ambition was to make money. Even fundamentalist ministers enjoyed homes with swimming pools and travel on private jets, though none lived as extravagantly as TV evangelist Jim Bakker, whose doghouses were air-conditioned.

Most Americans profited from the economic boom of the 1980s, but those already well off enjoyed the greatest gains. Family income for the richest one-fifth of the population increased by 11.1 percent between 1979 and 1987. The number of millionaires doubled during the decade, and the number of billionaires grew from thirteen to fifty-one. Greater concentration of wealth in fewer hands had been developing since the 1970s, but Reagan's tax and spending policies intensified the trend.

Participating conspicuously in the affluence of the 1980s were some members of the baby boom generation known popularly as "yuppies," short for "young urban professionals." These mostly white, well-educated young men and women tended to live in urban condominiums and to pursue fast-track careers; in their leisure time, they consumed lavishly—

**HOMELESSNESS**
*The increased presence of homeless people in cities across the nation challenged the view of the 1980s as a decade of prosperity. Hundreds of homeless people could be found on the sidewalks of the nation's capital every night. In November 1987, during the first snow of the season, a homeless man sleeps in Lafayette Square across from the White House.*
Corbis-Bettmann.

fancy sports cars, gourmet food, travel, electronic gadgets, and health clubs. Though constituting just a minority of their generation, they established consumption standards that many others tried to emulate.

> *Great fortunes were made during the 1980s. At the same time, however, American society became more polarized along class lines as increasing homelessness and growing poverty reversed the post–World War II trend toward greater economic equality.*

Most of those newly wealthy in the 1980s achieved success from moving assets around rather than from producing goods. There were notable exceptions, such as Steven Jobs, who invented the Apple computer in his garage, and Liz Claiborne, who in thirteen years turned a $250,000 investment into a billion-dollar fashion enterprise. But many others got rich—or richer—by manipulating debt and restructuring corporations through corporate mergers and takeovers. Large fortunes were made by "corporate raiders" who generated the capital to take over a corporation by issuing junk bonds, so called because they were high-risk and high-yield. Once in control, the raiders reaped huge profits by selling off some of the corporation's valuable divisions. All too often the result was to line the financiers' pockets and leave the corporation deeply in debt.

"To say these guys are entrepreneurs is like saying Jesse James was an entrepreneur," opined Texas businessman Ross Perot, who defined entrepreneurship as making things rather than making money. Most financial entrepreneurs operated within the law, but occasionally greed led to criminal convictions. Junk bonds pioneer Michael Milken took home well over $50 million a year. But he and others landed in jail for using insider information to maximize their financial manipulations.

## The Other Side of the 1980s

Even yuppies and financiers could see that the economic boom passed many Americans by. Affluent urbanites walked past numerous men and women sleeping in subway stations, on grates over steam vents, and on park benches near the White House. Experts debated the total number of homeless Americans—estimates ranged from 350,000 upwards—but no one doubted that homelessness had increased. Women and children constituted the fastest-growing population without shelter: One-fourth of the homeless were families with children. Those without homes included the victims of long-term unemployment, erosion of welfare benefits, and slum clearance as well as individuals suffering from mental illness, drug abuse, and alcoholism.

Reagan insisted that a booming economy would benefit everyone. Average personal income did rise during his tenure, but the trend of income polarization that had begun in the 1970s sharpened in the 1980s, in part because of the new tax policies. The rich got richer, a portion of the middle class did well, and the poor got poorer. Personal income shot up sharply for the wealthiest 20 percent of Americans while it fell for the poorest by 9.8 percent between 1979 and 1987.

Poverty statistics, too, revealed a reversal of the trend toward greater equality. Between 1980 and 1988, poor people increased from 11.7 to 13.5 percent of total U.S. population—the highest poverty rate in the industrialized world. A relatively low poverty rate among the elderly testified to the lasting success of New Deal and Great Society programs, especially Social Security and Medicare. Less fortunate were large segments of other groups that the economic boom had bypassed: racial minorities, female-headed families, and children. One child in every five lived in a household with income below the official poverty line.

Many Americans struggled not to lose ground. The decline in manufacturing jobs and weakening of organized labor eroded the position of blue-collar men with only high school educations. A second income was needed to stave off economic decline. By 1990, nearly 60 percent of married women with young children worked outside the home. Yet even with the growth of two-income families, fewer young families could purchase their first home. The average $10,000 per year disparity between male and female earnings made things even harder for the nearly 20 percent of families that were headed by women. One mother of two, divorced from an abusive husband, reported, "Jobs just don't pay good money." She supplemented her paycheck by selling her blood and accepting help from her church.

**THE NEW IMMIGRATION**
*Among Asian immigrants in the 1980s, the largest number came from Southeast Asia, where the Vietnam War and its aftermath created hundreds of thousands of refugees. Most of these refugees had little money and found adjustment difficult. Many like these Laotian Hmong immigrants in Providence, Rhode Island, came from rural, premodern societies.*
Ira Wyman/Sygma.

## Minorities' Struggles and Successes

Five million new immigrants sought to realize the American dream in the 1980s, surpassing the totals for every decade in the twentieth century but the first and exhibiting a striking difference in country of origin. While 85 percent of the previous immigrants had come from Europe, almost half of the recent arrivals were Asians, and nearly 40 percent migrated from Latin America and the Caribbean.

The racial composition of the new immigration revived the century-old wariness of the native-born toward recent arrivals. Pressure for more restrictive policies stemmed from beliefs (generally unfounded) that immigrants took jobs from the native-born, fears that immigrants would erode the dominant culture and language, and concern about population pressures on the environment. Americans expressed particular concern about immigrants who entered the country illegally. Primarily Latin Americans fleeing civil war and economic deprivation, they were estimated to number at least three million. To stem this tide, Congress passed the Immigration Reform and Control Act of 1986, which penalized employers who hired undocumented aliens but also granted amnesty to illegal immigrants who could prove residence before 1982. Some two million people took advantage of this provision (Figure 31.2).

Differential fertility rates in combination with migration patterns increased the racial and ethnic diversity in American society. While total population increased by around 9 percent in the 1980s, the black population grew by 13 percent, the Hispanic population by 39 percent, and the Asian American population by nearly 50 percent. By 2010, the Census Bureau projected, people of color would account for nearly 30 percent of the nation's residents. Yet minorities remained on the lower rungs of the economic ladder, and their situation worsened with the upward flow of wealth. Median income for white families surpassed $32,000 in 1988, in contrast to $18,000 for African Americans and $20,300 for His-

panic Americans. Poverty afflicted one in three African Americans and 28 percent of all Hispanic Americans.

The general sharpening of class differences in the 1980s also affected minorities. African Americans were barely present among the very rich, but substantial numbers improved their economic position, enlarging the black middle class. The most prosperous African Americans were members of families in which both parents had jobs; their median income reached 82 percent of that of comparable whites. But women headed half of all black families, and their income averaged less than one-third that of the typical American family.

The media hailed Asian Americans as "America's Super Minority" but failed to note vast differences among Asian Americans or their overall economic disadvantage. Median family income for Asian Americans surpassed that of whites, but only because Asian families had more wage earners. Although 39 percent of Asian Americans had completed college, in contrast to 22 percent of whites, they lagged behind whites in per capita income. Poor Chinese American women employed in the New York garment industry endured wages, hours,

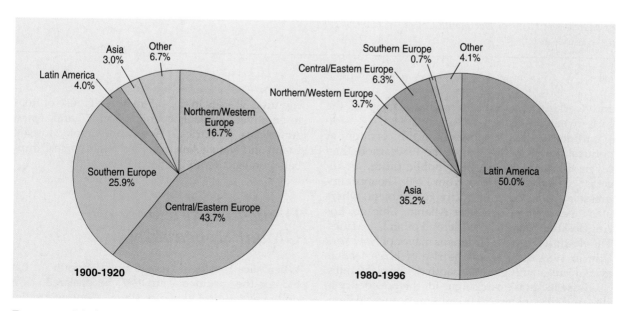

FIGURE 31.2
*The Changing Profile of Immigration, 1900–1920 and 1980–1996*
*The United States received its largest number of immigrants during the opening and closing decades of the twentieth century, but the cultures and countries of origin of the new arrivals shifted dramatically between the two periods.*

**A NEW VOICE IN POLITICS**
*Jesse Jackson was among the civil rights activists who turned to electoral politics. A Baptist minister
and dynamic speaker, Jackson mounted campaigns for the Democratic presidential nomination in
1984 and 1988, appealing to what he called a "Rainbow Coalition" of disadvantaged groups. Here
he addresses students at Dartmouth College in January 1984.*
Ira Wyman/Sygma.

and working conditions resembling those of the early-twentieth-century sweatshops.

Minorities edged slowly into the corridors of political power. At the end of the 1980s, more than seven thousand blacks held public office, an increase of nearly 50 percent from 1980. The most impressive gains occurred in city government, where black mayors presided over Atlanta, Chicago, Los Angeles, Philadelphia, Seattle, and other large cities. The election of David Dinkins as mayor of New York City in 1989 epitomized the rise of black leaders even in cities with predominantly white electorates.

Jesse Jackson's campaigns for the presidency in 1984 and 1988 inspired African Americans and demonstrated that many whites were willing to support a minority candidate. In 1989, Democrat L. Douglas Wilder of Virginia became the first black governor since Reconstruction, joining the only Hispanic governor, Republican Bob Martinez of Florida. In the 1992 elections, African Americans

captured 38 seats in the 435-member House of Representatives, while Hispanics won 17 and Asian Americans 5. African American Carol Moseley Braun and Native American Ben Nighthorse Campbell won election to the Senate.

## Domestic Stalemate and Global Upheaval

When Vice President George Bush announced his bid for the presidency in 1987, he declared, "We don't need radical new directions." Generally satisfied with the agenda set by Ronald Reagan, Bush proposed few domestic initiatives. In foreign policy Bush tended to react to events rather than to try to shape them. He sent American troops to overthrow the corrupt dictator of Panama, and he launched a full-scale war when Iraq threatened Middle Eastern stability by invading Kuwait in 1990. But the United States stood detached from the most momentous world events, as one by one the Eastern European bloc nations threw out their Communist rulers, and finally the Soviet Union itself disintegrated in 1991.

## Gridlock in Government

George Bush's campaign for the presidency in 1988 capped a long career in politics and government. The son of a wealthy New England senator, George Herbert Walker Bush grew up in a privileged milieu that put a premium on public service. After fighting in World War II, he earned a Yale degree and then settled in Texas to make his own way in the oil industry and politics.

Bush represented Texas in Congress during the 1960s and later represented the United States in China and headed the CIA during the Nixon-Ford years. When Ronald Reagan achieved a commanding lead in the 1980 primaries, Bush put his own aspirations on hold and accepted second place on the Republican ticket. In 1988, he won the Republican nomination only after bruising battles in the primaries.

The Democratic race was even more crowded. Jesse Jackson, whose Rainbow Coalition campaign centered on the needs of blacks and other minorities, women, working-class families, and the poor, won several state primaries, gathering seven million votes, almost one-third of them from white voters. In the end, however, his race, lack of experience in public office, and position on the left wing of the Democratic Party proved to be insuperable obstacles. Michael Dukakis, governor of Massachusetts, won the nomination.

"The Trivial Pursuit of the Presidency," the subtitle of one account of the 1988 campaign, expressed the general view of political commentators. Neither candidate presented a clear set of specific goals, and the campaign was unprecedentedly issueless and vitriolic. Half of the eligible voters stayed home on election day, indicating the electorate's general disgust with the campaign. Fifty-four percent of those who did vote were satisfied with the Republican record on peace and prosperity, but the Democrats gained seats in the House and Senate.

President Bush saw himself primarily as steward and guardian of the Reagan legacy. He promised "a kinder, gentler nation" and was more inclined than Reagan to approve government activity in the private sphere. But his most famous campaign pledge was "Read my lips: No new taxes." Boxed in by the budget deficit and his adamant refusal to seek new tax revenues, Bush opposed most proposals requiring additional federal funds.

He approved environmental protection legislation, the costs of which would be borne by industry and consumers. The Clean Air Act of 1990 was the strongest, most comprehensive environmental law in history, requiring power plants to cut sulphur dioxide emissions by more than half by the year 2000 and oil companies to develop cleaner-burning gasoline. Some forty million disabled Americans reaped the benefits of other regulatory legislation. Reflecting the growing power of the disability rights movement, the 1991 Americans with Disabilities Act banned job discrimination against the handicapped and required that private businesses, public accommodations, and transportation be made accessible to the disabled.

"If you're looking for George Bush's domestic program, and many people are, this is it: the veto pen," charged Democratic House majority leader Richard Gephardt in 1991. Bush blocked Congress thirty-six times, vetoing bills that lifted abortion restrictions, extended unemployment benefits, raised taxes, mandated family and medical leave for workers, and reformed campaign financing. By the end of his term, press reports were filled with the words *stalemate, gridlock,* and *divided government.*

The deadlock between president and Congress crippled the government's ability to deal with the budget deficit and the economic downswing that began in 1990. In June 1990, the worsening budget situation forced Bush to concede the fantasy of his "no new taxes" pledge, despite considerable Republican outrage. The next year's deficit was projected at a minimum of $160 billion, far above the $64 billion set by a law passed in 1985. Failure to meet the target would trigger automatic cuts of 25 percent in military spending and 37 percent in most domestic programs.

The administration and Congress hammered out a compromise that limited spending, increased taxes modestly for high-income Americans, and raised taxes on gasoline, cigarettes, alcoholic beverages, and luxury items. Although the budget agreement brought in new revenues and Congress stuck to the spending limits, three years later the deficit was even higher, boosted by rising costs in entitlement programs such as Social Security and Medicare-Medicaid as well as by spending on unforeseen emergencies of war and natural disasters.

Failure to control the deficit also resulted from an economic downswing that began in 1990. With

**M A P  3 1 . 2**
*Events in Eastern Europe, 1989–1992*
*The overthrow of Communist governments throughout Eastern and Central Europe and the splinter-
ing of the Soviet Union into more than a dozen separate nations were the most momentous changes
in the world since World War II.*

higher unemployment and a drop in the economy's growth rate, federal revenues declined. Although the recession ended in 1991, the economy grew at a snail's pace. General Motors, Time Warner, Xerox, and other major corporations announced permanent reductions in their workforces. With unemployment surpassing 7 percent, economists characterized the sluggish economy as "jobless recovery" from the recession.

The president's greatest opportunity to influence policy in a lasting way came through Supreme Court appointments. Bush's first nominee, federal appeals judge David Souter, won easy confirmation by the Senate. But in 1991, when Bush had to replace Justice Thurgood Marshall, the only African American on the Court, he set off a national controversy

by nominating Clarence Thomas, a conservative black appeals judge. Thomas had opposed affirmative action and busing as head of the Equal Employment Opportunity Commission under Reagan. Charging that Thomas would not protect minority rights, the NAACP and other civil rights organizations fought the nomination. In spite of this opposition and Thomas's low rating by the American Bar Association, confirmation seemed certain until the media reported charges that Thomas had sexually harassed Anita Hill, a law professor, when she worked for him in the early 1980s. The Senate Judiciary Committee held three days of nationally televised hearings to investigate the charges. Thomas angrily and steadfastly denied the alleged incidents, and Hill's testimony failed to sway the Senate, which voted fifty-two to forty-eight to confirm him.

The hearings sensitized the public to sexual harassment and gave the women's movement a boost. Many women, including a dozen congresswomen, expressed outrage at the shabby treatment that Hill received from senators who tried to discredit her. Feminists complained that men "still don't get it" and began preparing to put more women into office in the 1992 elections.

## Toward a New World Order

"All the action is in Moscow and Berlin, not here," complained a former Reagan aide, referring to the Bush administration's distance from events unfolding in Europe. Bush built on the Reagan-Gorbachev relationship to achieve another breakthrough in arms reductions in June 1990, a strategic arms reduction treaty (START) that actually eliminated existing nuclear weapons—about 30 percent of each superpower's nuclear arsenal. But the president articulated no additional goals, instead responding cautiously to initiatives produced by Gorbachev and European leaders.

The forces of change that Gorbachev had helped to unleash in the Soviet Union spread in 1989 to Eastern Europe, where popular uprisings demanded an end to state repression, official corruption, and economic bureaucracies that failed to deliver an acceptable standard of living. Communist governments fell like dominoes, in most cases with little bloodshed (Map 31.2). In the first multiparty elections since World War II, non-Communist governments took office in Czechoslovakia, East

**FALL OF THE BERLIN WALL**
*After 1961, the Berlin Wall symbolized the cold war and the iron grip of communism over Eastern Europe and the Soviet Union; more than four hundred easterners were killed trying to flee. After Communist authorities opened the wall on November 9, 1989, permitting free travel between east and west, Berliners from both sides gathered at the wall to celebrate.*
Eric Bouvet/Gamma Liaison.

Germany, Hungary, Poland, and Yugoslavia. The most dramatic moment came when East Germany opened its border with West Germany. On November 12, 1989, ecstatic Germans danced on the Berlin Wall, using whatever was at hand to begin demolishing that dominant symbol of the cold war.

> *The most dramatic moment in the collapse of the postwar order came when East Germany opened its border with West Germany. On November 12, 1989, ecstatic Germans danced on the Berlin Wall, using whatever was at hand to begin demolishing that dominant symbol of the cold war.*

West German Chancellor Helmut Kohl called for a united Germany immediately after the fall of the Berlin Wall, and with United States and Soviet support, unification of East and West Germany sped to completion in 1990. Germany would become a member of NATO, and though U.S. military forces would remain in Europe, the commanding role of the United States had been eclipsed. The same was true of its economic clout: Western Europe, including a unified Germany, would become a united economy in 1992. The destiny of Europe, to which the United States and the Soviet Union had held the key for forty-five years, now lay in European hands.

The Bush administration's approach to Panamanian dictator General Manuel Noriega was much less cautious than its response to European developments. Although Noriega had long sold the CIA information about Communist activities in Cuba and Central America, he also passed information to Castro in Cuba while amassing a fortune through dealing in illegal drugs, torturing and killing his domestic opposition. In 1988, a Miami grand jury indicted Noriega for drug trafficking, and in December 1989 President Bush ordered 25,000 troops into Panama to capture the dictator. The invasion forces quickly overcame Noriega's troops, at the cost of 23 American lives and hundreds of Panamanian lives, many of them civilians. This resort to military intervention revived the image of "Yankee imperialism," a stark contrast to the principles of self-determination and nonintervention that held sway in Eastern Europe.

The administration deployed much greater force and it acted with allies when Iraq's army invaded and quickly took over the small, oil-rich country of Kuwait in August 1990. Struggling with an enormous debt from the ten-year war against Iran, Iraqi President Saddam Hussein desperately needed revenues, and control of Kuwaiti oil would give him powerful leverage over prices. Within days of invading Kuwait, Iraqi troops moved toward the Saudi Arabian border, threatening the world's largest oil reserves.

In reacting to the invasion, President Bush invoked principles of national self-determination and international law, but oil primarily determined the U.S. response. With the consent of Saudi Arabia, Bush ordered Operation Desert Shield, a massive mobilization of land, air, and naval forces to counter the Iraqi threat. At the same time, the administration began to assemble an international coalition—ultimately involving European nations, Egypt, Syria, and other Arab states—to repel Iraqi aggression.

Reflecting the end of superpower conflict in the Middle East, the Soviet Union and the United States issued a joint condemnation of Iraq, and the Soviets cut off arms to Iraq. The United Nations instituted economic sanctions, and most of the world joined an embargo on oil from Iraq and Kuwait. In November, the United Nations authorized the use of force against Iraq if it did not withdraw from Kuwait by January 15, 1991. Meanwhile, Bush asked Congress for authorization to use military force against Iraq, and after three days of solemn debate, Congress approved what amounted to a declaration of war. Unlike Johnson in Vietnam, Bush would go to war with clear congressional authorization.

On January 17, 1991, Operation Desert Shield became Operation Desert Storm, when the U.S.-led coalition, including 400,000 American soldiers, began a forty-day air war against Iraq. Bombs and missiles smashed not only military targets but also power plants, oil refineries, and transportation networks. Having severely crippled Iraq through air bombardment, the coalition launched an all-out ground assault against Iraqi troops on February 23. Allied forces quickly routed the Iraqi soldiers, and within one hundred hours Hussein announced that he would withdraw from Kuwait.

"By God, we've kicked the Vietnam syndrome once and for all," President Bush said on March 1. Most Americans found no moral ambiguity in the Persian Gulf War and took pride in the display of military competence. The war's costs were relatively cheap: Germany and Japan (who sent no

**THE GULF WAR**
*These soldiers from the 24th Infantry arrived in Saudi Arabia in August 1990 as part of the U.S.-led effort to drive Iraq out of Kuwait. For the first time women served in combat-support positions with more than 33,000 stationed throughout the Gulf; 11 died and 2 were held as prisoners of war. Among their duties, women piloted planes and helicopters, directed artillery, and fought fires.*
Corbis-Bettmann.

After the Gulf War, the Bush administration stood on the sidelines as the world continued to remake itself. By the end of 1991, changes initiated by Gorbachev had brought about his own demise. Inspired by the liberation of Eastern Europe, Soviet republics sought their own independence, while the Soviet Union's efforts at economic change brought widespread destitution. According to one Muscovite, "Gorbachev knew how to bring us freedom but he did not know how to make sausage." In December 1991, Boris Yeltsin, president of the Russian Republic, announced that Russia and 11 other republics had joined a new Commonwealth of Independent States. The three Baltic republics—Estonia, Latvia, and Lithuania—and Georgia became independent. With nothing left to govern, Gorbachev resigned.

The United States officially recognized Russia, but the breakup of the Soviet Union seemed as ominous as its existence had once appeared. "During the cold war, the threat was deliberate Soviet attack," declared Democratic Representative Les Aspin. "Now the bigger threat seems to be chaos in a nation with 30,000 nuclear weapons." Russia and the three other republics possessing nuclear weapons—Ukraine, Belarus, and Kazakhstan—pledged to implement START, and Congress provided $400 million to help these nations store or destroy their nuclear weapons; but that process would take years to complete. Meanwhile, the Russian economy deteriorated further, causing widespread destitution and despair, and Yeltsin maintained a precarious hold on the government.

troops) and other coalition allies paid a substantial part of the bill, while 146 U.S. servicemen and -women were killed in action, and 124 died outside of combat. The United States stood at the apex of global leadership, steering a massive coalition in which, for the first time, Arab nations fought beside their former colonial rulers.

Yet victory did not bring stability to the Middle East. Israel, which had endured Iraqi missile attacks, was more secure, but the Israeli-Palestinian conflict continued to simmer. Despite military losses, Saddam Hussein remained in power and turned the remains of his war machine on Iraqi Kurds and Shiite Muslims, whom the United States had encouraged to rebel.

## Conclusion: Watersheds at Home and Abroad

The president who had invoked the words of Franklin D. Roosevelt led the United States in an explicit turn away from the assumptions that had shaped domestic policy since the New Deal. Republican presidents Eisenhower and Nixon had attempted to curb the role of the federal government, but no president before Ronald Reagan had applied the brakes so sharply to liberal reform or enjoyed such widespread popular support for those efforts.

The Reagan-Bush counterrevolution appealed to Americans whose real incomes declined in the 1970s as their tax bills increased and who resented government programs for poor and minority groups. Reagan cultivated these sentiments by winning enormous tax reductions and by portraying civil rights initiatives as favoritism. The tax cuts, combined with hefty increases in defense spending, created a federal deficit crisis that justified cuts in social welfare programs and made new federal initiatives unthinkable. Many Americans continued to look favorably on specific federal programs at the end of the Reagan-Bush years, but public sentiment about the government in general had undergone a U-turn from the Roosevelt era. To a large segment of the population, not only was the federal government ineffective at solving national problems, but government intervention often made things worse.

If Reagan and Bush could take credit for managing domestic change, the roots of global change were much more complex. Reagan and Bush claimed that their massive arms buildup had accounted for the worldwide fall of communism, but others pointed to the internal weaknesses of the Soviet economic system and the courageous risk-taking of Mikhail Gorbachev. None could deny, however, that between 1988 and 1992 the world had experienced the most cataclysmic changes since the 1940s.

Containment of communism had shaped the American economy and politics for nearly fifty years and formed the linchpin of U.S. foreign policy. Its sudden collapse left the nation without a global strategy. When Iraq invaded Kuwait, the Bush administration's decisive response demonstrated that the end of the cold war did not mean a diminution of U.S. leadership in world affairs. However, the country's leaders had yet to articulate what overarching vision would replace anticommunism as the major foreign policy goal and define the American purpose in the world.

By 1992, domestic problems seemed most urgent: the decline of industrial production and loss of good jobs, business instability and dependence on foreign investment, a worsening budget deficit, the end of the American dream for much of the middle class, and increasing poverty and growing economic disparity between the rich and poor and between whites and people of color. While public officials and the media trumpeted U.S. victory in the cold war, the nation had yet to come to grips with the economic casualties of that struggle. How the United States dealt with one part of the Reagan-Bush legacy—the economic problems—would depend on the strength and depth of the other part of that legacy—the turn against government as the guarantor of social and economic well-being.

## CHRONOLOGY

**1980**  Ronald Reagan elected president of United States, defeating incumbent Jimmy Carter.

**1981**  Researchers identify cause of AIDS epidemic as virus.

Would-be assassin wounds Reagan in Washington, D.C.

Congress passes Economic Recovery Tax Act advocated by Reagan, largest tax cut in U.S. history.

Reagan appoints Sandra Day O'Connor first female justice to U.S. Supreme Court.

**1982**  Congress extends Voting Rights Act over Reagan administration's objections.

Banking industry deregulated.

United States invades Grenada and topples its Marxist government.

**1983**  U.S. involvement in Lebanon terminated after bombing of marine barracks and deaths of 241 U.S. troops.

Reagan announces plans for Strategic Defense Initiative ("Star Wars").

**1984**  Democrats nominate Walter F. Mondale for president and Geraldine Ferraro for vice president.

Ronald Reagan reelected president.

U.S. Supreme Court rules that schools can continue to receive federal funds even if they practice discrimination in some programs (*Grove City College v. Bell*).

| | | | |
|---|---|---|---|
| **1986** | Iran-Contra scandal shakes Reagan administration. | **1989** | Communism collapses in Eastern Europe; and Berlin Wall falls. |
| **1987** | Soviet leader Mikhail Gorbachev visits Washington to sign INF agreement. | | United States invades Panama and ousts dictator Manuel Noriega, who is jailed in United States. |
| | Senate defeats nomination of Robert H. Bork to U.S. Supreme Court. | **1990** | Bush and Congress agree to tax increase because of mounting federal deficit. |
| **1988** | Reverend Jesse Jackson mounts strong campaign for Democratic presidential nomination. | **1991** | Bush's nominee Clarence Thomas becomes second African American to sit on U.S. Supreme Court. |
| | Democrats nominate Michael Dukakis for president and Lloyd Bentsen for vice president. | | United States commits more than 400,000 troops to oust Iraqi army from Kuwait in Persian Gulf War. |
| | Vice President George Bush elected forty-first president of United States. | | Congress passes Americans with Disabilities Act |

# SUGGESTED READINGS

Rick Atkinson, *Crusade: The Untold Story of the Persian Gulf War* (1994). An absorbing account of the forty-two-day Gulf War by a reporter who was there.

Thomas Carothers, *In the Name of Democracy: U.S. Policy toward Latin America in the Reagan Years* (1991). A critical account of American efforts to promote democracy in Latin America during the 1980s.

John D'Emilio, *Making Trouble: Essays on Gay History, Politics, and the University* (1992). Articles about homosexuals and the struggle for gay rights since World War II.

Kathryn Marie Dudley, *The End of the Line: Lost Jobs, New Lives in Postindustrial America* (1994). A detailed study of the human impact when Chrysler closed its plant in Kenosha, Wisconsin, in 1988.

Andrew Hacker, *Two Nations: Black and White, Separate, Hostile, Unequal* (1992). A sociologist's assessment of race relations at the end of the twentieth century.

Robert L. Hutchings, *American Diplomacy and the End of the Cold War: An Insider's Account of U.S. Policy in Europe, 1989–1992* (1997). An account of the Bush administration's response to the breakdown of communism in Eastern Europe.

Christopher Jencks, *The Homeless* (1994). An analysis of the numbers and causes of homelessness in the 1980s and 1990s.

William C. Martin, *With God on Our Side: The Rise of the Religious Right in America* (1996). A history of the people, organizations, and issues associated with the religious wing of conservatism.

Herbert S. Parmet, *George Bush: The Life of a Lone Star Yankee* (1997). A comprehensive biography stressing the pull between the New England culture and values from which Bush came and the Texas culture and values into which he moved.

William E. Pemberton, *Exit with Honor: The Life and Presidency of Ronald Reagan* (1997). A concise, balanced biography.

David M. Reimers, *Still the Golden Door: The Third World Comes to America* (1992). An account of the new immigration and American immigration policy since World War II.

Daniel Wirls, *Buildup: The Politics of Defense in the Reagan Era* (1992). A history of defense policy, including Star Wars, from the perspective of domestic politics.

**STATUE OF PRESIDENT
AS SAXOPHONIST**

*To boost his 1992 presidential
campaign, Bill Clinton went on the Arsenio
Hall television talk show, donned sunglasses, and
played the saxophone. Clinton's appearances on Hall's
show as well as on the cable network MTV were efforts to appeal to younger voters.
The instrument became Clinton's symbol, and after his victory saxophone pins were the
hottest selling inaugural items. Bill Potts of Denver, Colorado, made this carving and
presented it to the president in 1993.*

National Archives.

# THE SEARCH FOR A POPULAR CENTER

# 32

## 1992 to the Present

I N 1992, THE DEMOCRATIC PARTY concluded its nominating convention in accord with tradition, as the candidates, their families, and supporters celebrated on a massive podium above the cheering delegates. This year, however, the candidates represented something new. William Jefferson "Bill" Clinton and Albert Gore were both in their mid-forties, the first baby boomers to run on a major party ticket, the first candidates not to have experienced World War II. The music, too, symbolized a new era. Instead of "Happy Days Are Here Again," the Democratic theme song since the 1930s, the band blared Fleetwood Mac's rock music. "Don't stop thinking about tomorrow," the lyrics sang. "Yesterday's gone."

Clinton and Gore embodied change, and a majority of the voters agreed upon the need for significant changes in the way federal government operated. Yet no consensus existed about what kinds of changes should occur. Some Americans believed that the federal government had grown too large and powerful and worried about the growing federal debt. Yet most opposed higher taxes and did not want to give up the government benefits they enjoyed. As businesses tried to trim budgets and become more competitive, victims of corporate restructuring worried about finding new jobs. Access to good health care and reducing crime constituted other major concerns, but those goals depended on more federal spending or intrusion than most Americans seemed willing to accept.

Clinton wanted to restore confidence in government as a force for good, but he did not want to alienate antigovernment voters by proposing new large federal programs. Moreover, he inherited a national debt that had grown from less than $1 trillion in 1981 to $4.4 trillion in 1993—and the interest on that debt consumed one-fifth of the federal budget. Just as Clinton was short on cash for using government in positive ways, he was also short on political capital, for the Republicans controlled Congress all but his first two years in office.

Further, the cold war had ended. That conflict had given Americans a sense of national purpose and had encouraged domestic reform to strengthen the nation at home in order to combat communism abroad. After the cold war, no clear standards emerged to determine where and under what conditions the United States should act beyond its borders.

Clinton's personal qualities also complicated his presidency. Very smart, dedicated, and hardworking, he often displayed disorganization, indecisiveness, and recklessness in his personal life. From the beginning, he was subject to a series of allegations and scandals, which culminated in his impeachment trial during his second term in 1999. Yet Clinton continued to receive support from a majority of Americans, in part because they identified him with the buoyant economy that

**CLINTON AND GORE ON TOUR**
*The gregarious Bill Clinton excelled at political campaigning. During the 1992 presidential election campaign he, his wife Hillary, and running mate Al Gore and his wife Tipper went out on several bus tours as a way of demonstrating the Democrats' connection to ordinary people. Not far from this campaign stop in Sylvester, Georgia, the bus caravan passed by a handmade sign that read "Bubbas for Clinton/Gore."*
Copyright © Ira Wyman.

characterized the 1990s. Clinton's record included some reforms that used federal authority to solve national problems, but overall his administration solidified the retreat of the Democratic Party from the liberalism of the 1960s.

## The Promise of Change

Bill Clinton ran as a moderate, but he came to the White House with ambitious plans to spur economic growth, reform the health care system, improve public education, reduce taxes on the middle class, and more. Although he made good on many of his promises, he effected incremental rather than sweeping change. Halfway through his first term, Clinton remarked, "Most everybody is for change in general and then against it in particular."

### The 1992 Election

In March 1991, with victory in the Gulf War and an approval rating of 88 percent, President Bush's chances for reelection in 1992 looked golden, and the most prominent Democrats opted out of the presidential race. That, however, did not deter Bill Clinton, who at age forty-five had served as governor of Arkansas for twelve years. After winning the nomination, Clinton rejected traditional ticket balancing and chose fellow southerner Senator Albert

Gore Jr. for his running mate. Only forty-four, Gore had represented Tennessee in the U.S. House and Senate for a total of sixteen years. The youthfulness of the Democratic ticket reinforced Clinton's campaign theme of change.

Like Jimmy Carter in 1976 and Michael Dukakis in 1988, Clinton and Gore presented themselves as "new Democrats." Both belonged to the Democratic Leadership Council, which Clinton had helped found in 1985 to rid the party of its liberal image. Clinton deliberately distanced himself from the Reverend Jesse Jackson and his Rainbow Coalition and appealed to voters who believed that some Americans were getting a free ride at their expense. "We're going to put an end to welfare as we know it," Clinton claimed. Disavowing the "tax and spend" label that Republicans pinned on his party, Clinton promised a tax cut for the middle class. Portraying President Bush as a do-nothing official even while unemployment neared 8 percent, Clinton promised to reinvigorate government and the economy.

The popularity of a third candidate revealed Americans' frustrations with government and thirst for change. In announcing his candidacy for president on the popular talk show *Larry King Live*, self-made Texas billionaire H. Ross Perot set the tone of his unconventional campaign. He used television extensively but gave no press conferences, and he chose an inexperienced running mate. But he had plenty of money and attracted a sizable grassroots movement with his down-to-earth personality and appeals to voters' disgust with Washington politics and politicians. Perot's candidacy hurt Bush more than it hurt Clinton, and it established the federal budget deficit as a key campaign issue.

> *Although casting two-thirds of their votes against Bush demonstrated a mandate for change, voters formed no majority around a particular direction that change should take.*

Americans reversed the thirty-year decline in voter turnout as 55 percent of those eligible went to the polls. They gave Clinton 43 percent of their votes, Bush 38 percent, and Perot 19 percent—the strongest third-party finish since Theodore Roosevelt's Progressive Party candidacy in 1912. Although casting two-thirds of their votes against Bush demonstrated a mandate for change, voters formed no majority around a particular direction that change should take.

The Democrats barely maintained their majority in Congress, but the presence of women and minorities jumped significantly. In the House of Representatives, the number of seats held by women increased from twenty-eight to forty-seven. African Americans gained twelve seats in the House, bringing their total to thirty-eight, while the number of Hispanic representatives increased from ten to seventeen. This diversification of Congress continued through the 1990s.

In keeping with his promise to put together a cabinet "that looked like America," president-elect Clinton selected the most diverse group of department heads ever assembled. Of twenty-three key appointments, he named six women, three African Americans, and two Latinos. Janet Reno became the first female attorney general (in his second term, Clinton would appoint the first female secretary of state, Madeleine K. Albright).

Clinton's judicial appointments had a similar cast. Of his first 129 appointments to federal courts, nearly one-third were women, 31 were black, and 11 were Hispanic. In June 1993, he appointed the second woman to the Supreme Court, Ruth Bader Ginsburg, a self-identified feminist who had won key women's rights rulings from the Supreme Court before President Carter made her a federal appeals court judge in 1980.

## The Politics of Incrementalism

Upon taking office in 1993, Clinton quickly used his executive powers to reverse policies of Presidents Reagan and Bush. He issued executive orders that eased restrictions on abortion counseling and paved the way for import of the French abortion pill, RU-486. But vehement opposition from military leaders, enlisted men, and key legislators forced Clinton to back away from his campaign promise to lift the ban on homosexuals in the military. In June 1993, Clinton announced a compromise,

**GAYS IN THE MILITARY**
*When Chairman of the Joint Chiefs of Staff Colin Powell spoke at Harvard University's commencement in June 1993, gay rights advocates protested the government's ban on homosexuals in the military. Many found it ironic that General Powell, an African American who had been helped by the military's ban on racial discrimination, did not support President Clinton's effort to end discrimination against gays in military service.*
Wide World.

dubbed the "don't ask, don't tell" policy. It forbade officials from asking military personnel about their sexuality, but those who said they were gay or engaged in homosexual behavior could be dismissed. What began as an effort to promote tolerance ended in a 67 percent jump in discharges of homosexuals.

More successfully, Clinton signed several bills that Republicans had blocked during the previous twelve years, including gun control legislation, a $30 billion anticrime program, and the Family and Medical Leave Act, which enabled workers in larger companies to take time off for childbirth, adoption, care for aging parents, or family medical emergencies. Measures to increase the minimum wage, make voter registration easier, improve college students' access to federal loans, and establish Americorps, a program enabling students to pay for their education with community service, won approval. And, most significantly, Clinton pushed through a substantial increase in the earned income tax credit for low wage earners that would lift all families with a full-time worker above the poverty line.

"The economy, stupid." During the presidential campaign, this prominent sign at Clinton's headquarters reminded staffers to keep the focus on what they thought mattered most to voters. By the election, the economy had already begun to rebound, and the economic recovery and boom that followed helped boost Clinton's popularity through the 1990s. Economic expansion, along with budget cuts, tax increases, and declining unemployment, reduced the federal budget deficit by about half between 1992 and 1996. The seemingly inexorable trend of increasing government debt had turned around.

Clinton stumbled badly, however, over an ambitious health care reform plan, which had two key objectives: to help the 39 million Americans without health insurance by providing universal coverage and to curb the steeply rising costs of medical care—an objective necessary for continued progress on deficit reduction. Under the direction of First Lady Hillary Rodham Clinton, the administration presented a highly complex bill that much of the health care industry charged would mean higher taxes and government interference in health care decisions. Although the bill failed, private industry made strides in curtailing costs, at patients' expense, some argued; and Congress enacted piecemeal reform by enabling workers who changed jobs to retain health insurance and by establishing a new health care program for 5 million uninsured children. Yet the number of Americans without health insurance climbed to 44 million by 1999.

# The Battle for Center Ground

If some of President Clinton's initiatives sustained the traditional Democratic emphasis on using government to help the disadvantaged, his presidency in general moved the party to the right. Echoing Ronald Reagan, Clinton averred in his 1996 State of the Union address, "The era of big government is over." He took a number of Republican issues, such as welfare reform and downsizing government, and made them his own. This ability to undercut the Republicans and capture the middle ground of the electorate, along with the nation's economic successes, enabled Clinton to survive a series of scandals and an impeachment trial.

## The 1996 Election

Voters swept away the Democratic majorities in both houses of Congress in 1994, expressing their disgust with congressional infighting and their disillusionment with the president. Clinton's character and leadership had been tarnished by scandals surrounding his and his wife's financial dealings in an Arkansas real estate development called Whitewater and by charges that Clinton sexually harassed a state employee when he was governor.

Led by Representative Newt Gingrich of Georgia, Republicans considered the 1994 elections a mandate for their "contract with America," a conservative platform that included drastic contraction of the federal government, deep tax cuts, constitutional amendments to ban abortions, and term limits on members of Congress. Although Gingrich succeeded in moving the debate to the right, vetoes by Clinton and opposition from Democrats and more moderate Republicans stymied most of the contract pledges.

Far from Washington, a more extreme antigovernment movement emerged in the form of grassroots armed militias claiming patriotism and the need to defend themselves from government tyranny. Anticipating government repression, they stockpiled, according to one militia leader, "the four Bs: Bibles, bullets, beans, and bandages" and embraced a variety of sentiments, including opposition to taxes and the United Nations, anti-Semitism, and white supremacy. Their ranks grew after gun control legislation passed and after government agents stormed the headquarters of an armed religious cult in Waco, Texas, resulting in more than eighty deaths. On the second anniversary of that event, April 19, 1995, in the worst terrorist attack in the nation's history, a bomb leveled a federal building in Oklahoma City, taking 169 lives. Authorities quickly arrested two militia members, who were tried and convicted in 1997.

Clinton's reassuring handling of the Oklahoma City bombing helped restore his presidential stature. Looking toward the 1996 election, Clinton used his real and threatened veto power against what he labeled "extreme" Republican measures. Forcing the shaping of legislation along more moderate lines, he himself moved toward the center. For example, he firmly opposed deep cuts in education, environment, and welfare programs, but he cooperated with Republicans on a plan to balance the budget in seven years.

*Clinton's determination to cast himself as a centrist was nowhere more apparent than in his handling of welfare reform.*

Clinton's determination to cast himself as a centrist was nowhere more apparent than in his handling of welfare reform. Since Lyndon Johnson's war on poverty in the 1960s, public sentiment had shifted. Instead of blaming poverty on a shortage of adequate jobs, poor education, and other circumstances beyond an individual's control, more people were inclined to blame the poor themselves and government welfare, which they charged kept people in cycles of dependency. Nearly everyone considered work better than welfare but disagreed about whether the nation's economy could provide sufficient jobs at decent wages and how much government assistance poor people needed in the transition from welfare to work. Most estimates showed that it cost less to support a family on welfare than to provide the job training, child care, and other supports necessary for that transition.

Clinton allowed the Republicans to take the initiative in welfare reform, though he vetoed two measures and thereby forced a less punitive bill, which he signed as the 1996 election approached. The Personal Responsibility and Work Opportunity Reconciliation Act abolished Aid to Families with Dependent Children (AFDC) and with it society's pledge to provide a minimum level of subsistence for all its children. In place of AFDC, the law authorized grants to the states, with the requirement to limit welfare payments to two years whether the recipient could find a job or not. The law set a lifetime limit of aid at five years, barred legal immi-

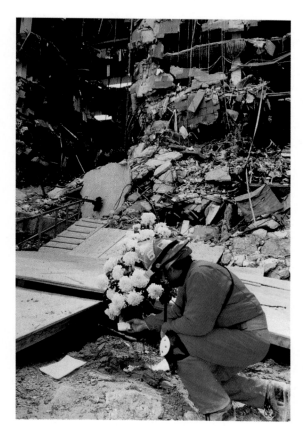

**OKLAHOMA CITY BOMBING**
*A worker at the site of the Oklahoma City bombing reads a card attached to flowers left at the devastated building. Many Americans initially assumed that foreign terrorists placed the bomb and were shocked to learn that American citizens were responsible for this violent act. The dead included nineteen children at the day care center that was housed in the federal building.*
Black Star.

grants who had not become citizens from food stamps and other benefits, and allowed states to stop Medicaid to legal immigrants.

A "moment of shame," cried Marian Wright Edelman, president of the Children's Defense Fund, when Clinton signed the bill. State and local officials across the country scrambled to understand the law and how to implement it. "We certainly endorse the overall direction toward work," a Minnesota official said, while expressing grave concern about how the law would operate. "A child could very well have to go to foster care," predicted a Louisiana social worker.

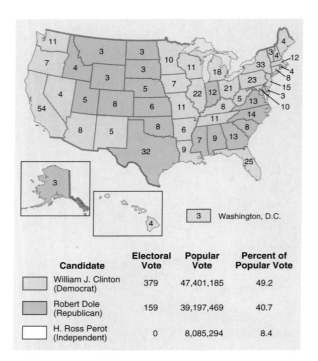

| Candidate | Electoral Vote | Popular Vote | Percent of Popular Vote |
|---|---|---|---|
| William J. Clinton (Democrat) | 379 | 47,401,185 | 49.2 |
| Robert Dole (Republican) | 159 | 39,197,469 | 40.7 |
| H. Ross Perot (Independent) | 0 | 8,085,294 | 8.4 |

**MAP 32.1**
*The Election of 1996*

Clinton claimed that the new law meant that "welfare will no longer be a political issue," and his signature on it meant that the Republicans could not use the welfare issue against him. In the 1996 election campaign, the president ran as a moderate who would save the country from extremist Republicans. In fact, the Republican Party also moved to the center, passing over a field of conservatives to nominate Kansan Robert Dole, a World War II hero as well as a former Senate majority leader who had served in Washington for more than two decades.

Whether out of satisfaction with a favorable economy or boredom with the candidates, about half of all voters stayed home. Fifty percent of those who voted chose Clinton, while 41 percent favored Dole, and 9 percent Perot, who ran again as a third-party candidate (Map 32.1). The largest gender gap to date appeared in the election: Women awarded 54 percent of their votes to Clinton and 38 percent to Dole, while men split their votes between the two candidates nearly evenly. Although Clinton won re-election with room to spare, voters sent a Republican majority back to Congress.

## Impeaching the President

Clinton's move to the right did not endear him to Republicans, and legislative strife and stalemate occupied much of his second term. One notable exception occurred in 1997, when the president and Congress managed to agree on the largest tax cut since 1981, which lowered levies on estates and capital gains and provided tax credits for families with children and for higher education. At the same time, they approved budget cuts and a plan designed to balance the federal budget by 2002. Thanks to a booming economy, that goal was reached in September 1998 when the government ended the fiscal year with a $70 billion surplus, the first since 1969.

Yet by 1998 Clinton and Republicans in Congress were embroiled in bitter hostility, manifested most dramatically in an effort to impeach the president. Early in the first Clinton administration, charges of illegalities relating to firings of White House staff, political use of FBI records, and the Clintons' involvement in the Whitewater real estate deal in Arkansas led to an official investigation by an independent prosecutor. Kenneth W. Starr, who took over the probe in 1994, won convictions of some Clinton associates related to Whitewater, but he could pin no illegalities on the President or the First Lady. Clinton also faced a charge of sexual harassment in a lawsuit filed in 1994 by Paula Corbin Jones, who asserted that in 1991 when he was governor of Arkansas and she worked for the state, he had made unwanted sexual advances. A federal court threw out Jones's suit in April 1998, but Clinton's relationships with other women continued to threaten his presidency.

In January 1998, independent prosecutor Starr began to investigate the most inflammatory charge—that Clinton had had sexual relations with a twenty-one-year-old White House intern, Monica S. Lewinsky, and then had tried to cover up the affair by lying about it to a federal grand jury. Clinton first vehemently denied the charge but subsequently bowed to the mounting evidence against him. In September, Starr took his case for impeachment to the House of Representatives, and in December 1998 the House voted, along mostly party lines and by margins of 228–206 and 221–212, to impeach the president on two counts, perjury and obstruction of justice. Clinton became the second president—after Andrew Johnson, in 1868—to be impeached by the House and tried by the Senate.

Most Americans believed that the president had lied and had acted recklessly and inappropriately with Lewinsky, yet they continued to express approval of his presidency and to oppose impeachment. Some saw Starr as a fanatic invading individuals' privacy; and most people clearly separated what they considered the president's private actions from his public duties. One man said, "Let him get a divorce from his wife. Don't take him out of office and disrupt the country." Those favoring impeachment insisted that the president must not be above the law, that he must set a high moral standard for the nation, and that lying to a grand jury was a serious offense even if it was about a private matter.

---

*Clinton became the second president—after Andrew Johnson, in 1868—to be impeached by the House and tried by the Senate.*

---

The Senate conducted the impeachment trial with much less partisanship than that displayed in the House. A number of senators believed that Clinton had committed perjury and obstruction of justice but did not find those actions to constitute the high crimes and misdemeanors required by the Constitution for removal of a president. With a two-thirds majority needed for that result, the Senate voted 45–55 (with 10 Republicans supporting the president) on the perjury count and 50–50 (with 5 Republicans joining the Democrats) on the obstruc-

tion of justice count. A majority of senators seemed to agree with Clinton's advocate, former Democratic Senator Dale Bumpers of Arkansas, who called the president's behavior "indefensible, outrageous, unforgivable, shameless," but insufficient to warrant his removal from office.

## Foreign Policy in a Post–Cold War World

The charges against President Clinton consumed large amounts of his attention and made even more difficult his responsibility for foreign policy. After the fall of communism, he inherited from the Bush administration the task of defining a clear and consistent role for the nation in a post–cold war world of some 190 nations. U.S. officials continued to wrestle with the problems of how to promote global economic prosperity and security from nuclear peril. A new challenge, now that communism was not the defining issue, was to determine which situations required the use of American diplomatic and military power.

### Deploying American Power

Guided largely by humanitarian concern, in December 1992 President Bush had attached U.S. forces to a United Nations operation in the small

**The Hangman**

HOW DOES HE DO IT?

**CLINTON'S IMPEACHMENT**
*This cartoon expresses the consternation of congressional Republicans when President Clinton's public approval ratings remained high despite revelations about his liaison with Monica Lewinsky that led to the House impeachment vote. Many Americans, although not condoning the president's behavior, separated what they considered his private actions from his public duties and criticized prosecuter Kenneth Starr and the Republicans for not doing the same.*

African country of Somalia, where famine and civil war raged. In summer 1993, Clinton allowed the humanitarian mission to turn into "nation building," an effort to restore national stability. Eighteen U.S. soldiers were killed in the process, and an outcry at home suggested that most Americans were not prepared to sacrifice lives when they perceived no vital interests at stake.

As a consequence, the Clinton administration moved slowly in deciding to risk U.S. troops in Haiti, where the United States had maintained a military presence from 1915 to 1934. After American withdrawal, Haitians suffered under harsh dictatorships until the country's first free election in December 1990, when the Reverend Jean-Bertrand Aristide won the presidency. Nine months later, a military coup overthrew the government.

Thousands of Haitians tried to escape the poverty and violence of the military dictatorship, many of them building flimsy boats and heading for Florida. With anti-immigrant sentiment already high in Florida and in the nation, Clinton was pressed hard to stop the refugee flow. (See the Historical Question on page 870.) At the same time, the Black Congressional Caucus and others insisted that the nation had a moral responsibility to end the suffering and restore democracy in Haiti.

After winning UN authorization, in September 1994 Clinton dispatched twenty thousand troops but also sent a last-minute mission, led by former President Jimmy Carter, to negotiate. Hours before the U.S. invasion was to begin, the negotiating team reached an agreement under which the military leaders promised to step down and restore Aristide as president. Initially a huge success, U.S. Haitian policy would continue to be tested until the Aristide government met the grave challenges of economic and political reconstruction.

But the area of the world that posed the greatest challenge to post–cold war diplomacy was the former Yugoslavia. After the Communists were swept out in 1989, Yugoslavia splintered into the three states of Serbia, Croatia, and Bosnia and then fell into a brutal civil war. The Serbs' ruthless aggression against the Bosnian Muslims horrified much of the world, and people remembered how an event in Sarajevo had sparked World War I. For several years, the United States joined with its European allies in NATO and the United Nations in peace efforts, but both the United States and the European nations studiously avoided direct intervention.

As the terror, rape, and torture in Bosnia worsened, American leaders worried about the image of the most powerful nation unwilling to use its power to stop the violence. In November 1995, the United States brought the leaders of Serbia, Croatia, and Bosnia to Dayton, Ohio, where they hammered out a peace treaty. President Clinton then agreed to send twenty thousand American troops to Bosnia as part of a NATO peacekeeping mission, and the peace held. But in 1998, new fighting broke out within Serbia, in its southern province of Kosovo. There ethnic Albanians, who constituted 90 percent of the population, fought for independence, and the Serbian army brutally retaliated, driving one-third of Kosovo's people from their homes.

*The area of the world that posed the greatest challenge to post–cold war diplomacy was the former Yugoslavia.*

President Clinton seemed less hesitant to deploy American power when he could send missiles rather than men and women; and he also proved willing to act without international support or United Nations sanction. In August 1998, bombs exploded in U.S. embassies in Kenya and Tanzania, killing 12 Americans and more than 250 Africans. Thirteen days later, Clinton ordered missile attacks on sites in Afghanistan suspected to be terrorist training camps and on a factory in Sudan alleged to produce chemical weapons. These facilities, Clinton asserted, were controlled by Osama bin Laden, a Saudi-born millionaire who financed an Islamic-extremist terrorist network and who officials believed directed the embassy bombings. Some U.S. experts challenged Clinton's claim, and critics charged that the bombings were intended to distract the public from the intensifying heat of impeachment.

A few months later, in December 1998, Clinton launched Desert Fox, a series of air strikes against Iraq. At the end of the Gulf War in 1991, President Saddam Hussein had agreed to eliminate Iraq's chemical, germ, and nuclear weapons of mass destruction and to allow inspections by United Nations officials. But he resisted compliance with the agreement, and when Iraq tried to block inspection officials late in 1998, the United States launched missile attacks on military installations. Whereas Bush had acted in the Gulf War with the support of an international force

**MADELEINE ALBRIGHT**
*This cartoon drawing of Madeleine Albright, the first woman to hold the position of secretary of state, appeared in* Time *magazine on March 1, 1999. It highlights her advocacy of the use of American force as a foreign policy tool, evidenced later that month when she promoted military intervention to stop Serbian leader Slobodan Milosevic's "ethnic cleansing" in the former Yugoslavia. Albright grew up in Czechoslovakia, fleeing first when the Nazis invaded her country and then immigrating to the United States after the Communists took control.*
Courtesy of Edward Sorel.

that included Arab states, Clinton acted in the face of Arab opposition and without authorization from the United Nations.

Using its diplomatic rather than its military power, the Clinton administration assisted with breakthroughs in the Israeli-Palestinian conflict. At a ceremony on the White House lawn in September 1993, Yasir Arafat, head of the Palestine Liberation Organization, and Yitzhak Rabin, Israeli prime minister, recognized the other's existence for the first time and agreed to Israeli withdrawal and self-government for Palestinians in the Gaza Strip and

Jericho. Less than a year later, in July 1994, Clinton presided over another turning point as Rabin and King Hussein of Jordan signed a declaration of peace. Although these constituted momentous steps, actually implementing the accords would prove very difficult indeed.

The president played an even more crucial role in persuading Irish and British officials in the spring of 1998 to take the first steps toward resolving the centuries-old conflict between Catholics and Protestants in Ireland. The Good Friday Agreement provided for the end of British rule in Northern Ireland, power sharing between Protestants and the Catholic minority living there, and closer relations between Northern Ireland and the largely Catholic Republic of Ireland to its south.

## Global Economics and Nuclear Weapons

With the cold war no longer monopolizing the foreign-policy agenda, global economic issues assumed a much larger place. Building on progress made in the Reagan and Bush administrations, Clinton sought easing of restrictions on international trade. In November 1993, Congress approved the North American Free Trade Agreement (NAFTA), a pact eliminating all tariffs and trade barriers among the United States, Canada, and Mexico. With 360 million people and a $6 billion economy, the NAFTA trio constituted the largest trading bloc in the world.

A year later, the Senate moved again to eliminate trade barriers by ratifying the General Agreement on Tariffs and Trade (GATT), signed by more than one hundred nations. GATT established a World Trade Organization to enforce provisions of the treaty, which included substantial tariff reductions and elimination of quotas on imports. Debates over NAFTA and GATT reflected two visions of the place of the United States in the world economy. Their supporters envisioned American prosperity flowing from the greater export opportunities that would come with freer trade. Opponents tied the nation's economic health to nurturing its established industries, thereby keeping its traditional jobs at home, and maintaining labor and environmental standards. That side prevailed in 1997 when Congress refused to renew the authority possessed by previous presidents to negotiate trade agreements.

# Still a Promised Land?

"THE UNITED STATES IS OUR LAND. . . . We intend to maintain it so. The day of unalloyed welcome to all peoples, the day of indiscriminate acceptance of all races, has definitely ended." So spoke Washington Senator Albert Johnson in 1924, just after Congress severely limited immigration with passage of the National Origins Act, which Johnson had sponsored. Thereafter immigration, which had forcefully shaped American society since its beginning, ebbed for several decades as the restrictive law combined with the Great Depression and World War II to discourage potential newcomers. In fact, during the worst years of the depression, more people left than migrated to the United States. Yet the immigration question had not been settled at last. By the 1980s, large numbers of immigrants once more entered the United States, reigniting old debates about whether Americans should share their promise of political freedom and economic opportunity with people from other lands.

What reopened the door to immigration after World War II? Economic considerations always loomed large in prompting migration to the United States and in determining how welcome immigrants would be: The twenty-five-year economic boom that followed World War II exerted a positive force on both ends. In fact, until 1964 the U.S. government actively encouraged the temporary migration of Mexicans by continuing the so-called *bracero* program that was begun during World War II to fill a shortage of agricultural workers. Hundreds of thousands of Mexicans established social networks in the United States and grew accustomed to crossing the border for jobs, even when the jobs were backbreaking and low-paying by U.S. standards. When the *bracero* program ended, many Mexicans continued to come north for work whether they could obtain legal authorization or not.

In addition to a prosperous economy, a growing tolerance toward people of different races and ethnic groups in the decades following World War II contributed to the increase in immigration. Like the key civil rights laws passed around the same time, the Immigration Act of 1965 reflected a more broad-minded climate of opinion based on the belief that people should be treated as human beings rather than as members of a particular group. The new immigration law ended the national quotas that were so insulting to non–Western European groups. It made possible a tremendous rise in the volume of immigration and facilitated a huge increase in newcomers from Asia and Latin America.

The new immigration law set an annual ceiling of 270,000, but the actual volume was much higher. Besides those who came illegally, hundreds of thousands of people fell into special categories that gained them legal admission above and beyond the ceiling. In 1986, for example, the United States admitted 335,000 immigrants over the ceiling: About two-thirds of these were children, spouses, or parents of U.S. citizens, and the rest were political refugees and asylum seekers. Migration chains were thus established by which, once newcomers became citizens, their sisters, brothers, and adult children received special preference, while even closer relatives gained entry without regard to the limit.

The new waves of immigration also grew directly from U.S. foreign policy after World War II. The cold war spread U.S. military and other personnel throughout the world, enabling foreigners to learn about the United States and make personal contacts with Americans. Once the cold war identified communism as an unmitigated evil, the United States could hardly refuse asylum to its enemy's victims. In the twenty-five years following Fidel Castro's revolution in 1959, for example, more than 800,000 Cubans fled to the United States. The Vietnam War and its aftermath brought more than 600,000 Vietnamese, Laotians, and Cambodians to the United States in the decade following 1974.

Not all refugees entered the United States so easily, for American refugee policy bore a distinct anti-Communist bias. Haitians, Salvadorans, and others fleeing right-wing dictatorships were frequently turned back or, having reached the United States, were denied asylum and deported. "Why let Poles stay but not Salvadorans?" demanded one advocate for these refugees, pointing out the more favorable treatment given to immigrants from Communist countries.

Even though U.S. policy failed to accommodate all who wanted to immigrate, by the 1980s immigration was once more a major force in American society. During that decade the six million legal and an estimated two million undocumented immigrants accounted for more than one-third of total population growth. Seventy-five percent of the immigrants settled in just seven states, with California, New York, Texas, and Florida receiving the most. After the 1990 census, California won five additional seats in the House of Representatives solely on the basis of immigrant additions to the population. A 1983 *Time* magazine article called Los Angeles "the new Ellis Island" because of its large Asian and Hispanic populations. A decade later, one-third of Los Angeles area residents were foreign-born.

The higher volume of immigration, its third world sources, and the economy's recession combined to reactivate nativist sentiment in the 1980s. Increasingly, Americans saw immigrants as taking jobs from the native-born and acting as a drain on schools, health care, police, and other services; and Congress sought to reduce illegal immigration with the Immigration Reform and Control Act of 1986. In the 1990s, anti-immigrant sentiment grew especially strong in California, then reeling from an economic slump owing to the downsizing of defense production. That state took in more than one-third of the nation's immigrants in the 1980s and an estimated one-half of the undocumented ones. Congress reflected national anti-immigrant feelings when it restricted health care, food stamps, and other benefits to immigrants as part of its transformation of welfare policy in 1996.

Greatest hostility focused on immigrants who entered without legal documentation, a phenomenon that the 1986 law penalizing employers of such people had not significantly curtailed. Some states, including California, Florida, and New Jersey, filed lawsuits charging the federal government with failure to stop the flow of illegal immigration and suing for the costs it added to state budgets.

Economic and political crises elsewhere and the continuing appeal of the United States meant that high levels of immigration—legal and illegal—persisted into the 1990s, as did the debate about how open U.S. policy should be. Even as anti-immigrant sentiment increased, however, the United States remained, as sociologist Nathan Glazer put it, a "permanently unfinished country."

**TRAGEDY IN KOSOVO**
*In the spring of 1999, NATO launched a bombing attack on Serbian military and government targets when President Slobodan Milosevic refused to agree to a peace settlement between Serbia and ethnic Albanians living in the Serb province of Kosovo. Instead Milosevic had Serb troops step up attacks on the Kosovars, forcing nearly 600,000, or one-third, of the 1.8 million Kosovo Albanians from their homes and into neighboring Albania, Macedonia, and Montenegro. This man pushes his grandmother to an Albanian border crossing.*
Wide World Photos.

"The post–cold war world is decidedly not postnuclear," said Clinton's first secretary of defense. Perhaps the biggest threat to American security lay in the proliferation of governments in possession of nuclear weapons. The breakdown of the Soviet Union meant that four countries with nuclear weapons—Russia, Ukraine, Belarus, and Kazakhstan—now stood in place of one, in addition to the United States, Britain, France, China, India, Israel, Pakistan, and possibly North Korea, still under a Communist dictatorship. In 1996, the world took a small step back from the nuclear brink when the leaders of the nuclear powers signed a comprehensive test ban treaty. Yet India and Pakistan, hostile neighbors, refused to sign the pact, and both exploded atomic devices in May 1998, increasing the nuclear risk in South Asia.

The future of Russia involved both economic and nuclear issues. In the post–cold war world, U.S. leaders promoted economic stability and political democracy in its former enemy, in no small part because Russia continued to possess large amounts of nuclear weapons. Yet despite Russia's rush to embrace capitalism, the United States continued to spend heavily—within the limits of arms reduction agreements—on defense in the 1990s. Not only was the nuclear balance tipped in favor of the United States, but in 1999, it posed what Russians could

construe as a further threat when it admitted the Czech Republic, Hungary, and Poland to NATO after rebuffing Russian efforts to join.

At the same time the United States committed far fewer resources to stabilization of the former Communist countries than it had to the nations it defeated in World War II. Even a severe economic crisis that swept through Asia in 1998 and further crippled the Russian economy did not call forth the systematic and sustained response that the United States had made to the rise of communism.

> *"The post–cold war world is decidedly not postnuclear," said Clinton's first secretary of defense. Perhaps the biggest threat to American security lay in the proliferation of governments in possession of nuclear weapons.*

The Clinton administration's foreign policy would be known for brief interventions—both verbal and violent—in trouble spots and for an overall withdrawal from the focused and intense international activity that had characterized the cold war era.

## Conclusion: Entering the New Millennium

As it enters the twenty-first century, the United States remains deeply embedded in the global economy as products and people cross international borders with ever greater frequency. U.S. officials continue to monitor developments across the globe and try through diplomacy to promote order and democracy, expand economic opportunities for American business, reduce population growth, and curtail environmental destruction. But, in contrast to their counterparts at the end of the nineteenth century, Americans displayed little taste for foreign adventures as the twentieth century closed. Nor did a majority want to see their tax dollars used for international purposes.

Instead, most Americans saw the main challenge as coming from within, and that challenge involved issues of economic justice, violence, and diversity that had engaged the nation for much of its history. Poverty and income inequality accompanied the economic boom of the 1990s: A growing chasm between the educated and the unskilled, a rising income gap between the rich and the poor, and a poverty rate of 20 percent among children threatened the American promise of opportunity and security. Although crime rates fell in the 1990s, the persistent poverty in urban ghettos contributed to a stream of violence that undermined Americans' physical security. As the United States became even more heterogeneous, American identity and how much the American promise should extend to diverse groups such as new immigrants, racial minorities, and homosexuals remained contested ground.

How to respond to the challenges of economic justice, physical security, and diversity often involved the question of the appropriate role of government. With a population derived to a great extent from people fleeing overweening governments, Americans had for more than two centuries debated what the government could or should do and what was best to leave to private enterprise, families, churches, and other voluntary institutions. Far more than other democracies, the United States had taken the path of private rather than public obligation, individual rather than collective solutions. In the twentieth century especially, Americans had entrusted the federal government with significantly greater powers and responsibilities. But as the century wound down, the debate continued as citizens struggled over both how to define and how to approach fulfillment of the American promise for the next century.

## CHRONOLOGY

**1992**  Bill Clinton elected forty-second president of the United States.

**1993**  Janet Reno appointed first female attorney general in U.S. history.

Ruth Bader Ginsburg appointed second woman to U.S. Supreme Court.

Clinton announces "don't ask, don't tell" policy for gays in military.

Israeli Prime Minister Yitzhak Rabin and PLO leader Yasir Arafat sign peace accords.

Gun control and anticrime bills passed.

Eighteen U.S. soldiers are killed in Somalia.

Congress approves North American Free Trade Agreement (NAFTA).

Clinton signs Family and Medical Leave Act, enabling many workers to take time off for childbirth, adoption, or family medical emergencies.

**1994**  U.S. troops oversee peaceful return of Haitian President Aristide to power.

Senate ratifies General Agreement on Tariffs and Trade (GATT).

**1994**  Republicans recapture both House and Senate in congressional elections.

Representative Newt Gingrich declares 1994 elections a mandate for Republicans' conservative "contract with America."

**1995**  **April 19.** Bomb destroys federal building in Oklahoma City, claiming 169 lives; two militia members convicted in 1997.

U.S. leaders broker peace accords among Serbia, Croatia, and Bosnia in Dayton, Ohio, temporarily ending civil war in former Yugoslavia.

**1996**  Clinton signs Personal Responsibility and Work Opportunity Reconciliation Act, ending the federal welfare program begun in 1930s.

Clinton reelected president.

Leaders of nuclear powers sign comprehensive test ban treaty at United Nations.

**1997**  Clinton signs largest tax cut since 1981.

**1998**  U.S. bombs alleged terrorist sites in Afghanistan and Sudan.

Federal budget shows surplus for first time since 1969.

U.S. bombs Iraq for failure to comply with its 1991 agreement to destroy its weapons of mass destruction.

House of Representatives votes to impeach President Clinton for perjury and obstruction of justice.

**1999**  Senate fails to approve articles of impeachment.

# SUGGESTED READINGS

Elizabeth Drew, *Whatever It Takes: The Real Struggle for Political Power in America* (1998). An account of the 1996 election that focuses on interest groups and campaign finance and examines closely three House races as well as the presidential election.

Jennifer L. Hochschild, *Facing Up to the American Dream: Race, Class, and the Soul of the Nation* (1995). An examination of attitudes and perspectives of blacks and whites on the status of African Americans in the late twentieth century.

William Hyland, *Clinton's World* (1999). A comprehensive survey of Clinton's foreign policy.

David G. Lawrence, *The Collapse of the Democratic Presidential Majority: Realignment, Dealignment, and Electoral Change from Franklin Roosevelt to Bill Clinton* (1996). An analysis of elections and party politics since World War II.

David Maraniss, *First in His Class: A Biography of Bill Clinton* (1995). A lively narrative and exploration of what shaped Clinton's political skills and his flaws.

Michael Meeropol, *Surrender: How the Clinton Administration Completed the Reagan Revolution* (1998). A critical study of Clinton's economic and social policies.

David M. Reimers, *Unwelcome Strangers: American Identity and the Turn against Immigration* (1998). A definitive history and analysis of anti-immigration attitudes, including contemporary debates.

James M. Scott, ed., *After the End: Making U.S. Foreign Policy in the Post–Cold War World* (1988). Essays on foreign policy since 1991 that explore a wide range of topics, including NAFTA and policies toward China, Russia, and other countries.

Eleanor C. Sloan, *Bosnia and the New Collective Security* (1998). A brief history and analysis of peace-keeping efforts in the former Yugoslavia.

Martin Walker, *The President We Deserve: Bill Clinton, His Rise, Falls, and Comebacks* (1996). A balanced political biography from a British perspective, which links Clinton's development to major forces of his times.

# THE DECLARATION OF INDEPENDENCE

*In Congress, July 4, 1776,*

THE UNANIMOUS DECLARATION OF THE
THIRTEEN UNITED STATES OF AMERICA

When in the course of human events, it becomes necessary for one people to dissolve the political bands which have connected them with another, and to assume, among the powers of the earth, the separate and equal station to which the laws of nature and of nature's God entitle them, a decent respect to the opinions of mankind requires that they should declare the causes which impel them to the separation.

We hold these truths to be self-evident, that all men are created equal; that they are endowed by their Creator with certain unalienable rights; that among these, are life, liberty, and the pursuit of happiness. That, to secure these rights, governments are instituted among men, deriving their just powers from the consent of the governed; that, whenever any form of government becomes destructive of these ends, it is the right of the people to alter or to abolish it, and to institute a new government, laying its foundation on such principles, and organizing its powers in such form, as to them shall seem most likely to effect their safety and happiness. Prudence, indeed, will dictate that governments long established, should not be changed for light and transient causes; and, accordingly, all experience hath shown, that mankind are more disposed to suffer, while evils are sufferable, than to right themselves by abolishing the forms to which they are accustomed. But, when a long train of abuses and usurpations, pursuing invariably the same object, evinces a design to reduce them under absolute despotism, it is their right, it is their duty, to throw off such government and to provide new guards for their future security. Such has been the patient sufferance of these colonies, and such is now the necessity which constrains them to alter their former systems of government. The history of the present King of Great Britain is a history of repeated injuries and usurpations, all having, in direct object, the establishment of an absolute tyranny over these States. To prove this, let facts be submitted to a candid world:

He has refused his assent to laws the most wholesome and necessary for the public good.

He has forbidden his governors to pass laws of immediate and pressing importance, unless suspended in their operation till his assent should be obtained; and, when so suspended, he has utterly neglected to attend to them.

He has refused to pass other laws for the accommodation of large districts of people, unless those people would relinquish the right of representation in the legislature; a right inestimable to them, and formidable to tyrants only.

He has called together legislative bodies at places unusual, uncomfortable, and distant from the depository of their public records, for the sole purpose of fatiguing them into compliance with his measures.

He has dissolved representative houses repeatedly for opposing, with manly firmness, his invasions on the rights of the people.

He has refused, for a long time after such dissolutions, to cause others to be elected; whereby the legislative powers, incapable of annihilation, have returned to the people at large for their exercise; the state remaining in the mean-time exposed to all the danger of invasion from without, and convulsions within.

He has endeavoured to prevent the population of these States; for that purpose, obstructing the laws for naturalization of foreigners, refusing to pass others to encourage their migration hither, and raising the conditions of new appropriations of lands.

He has obstructed the administration of justice, by refusing his assent to laws for establishing judiciary powers.

He has made judges dependent on his will alone, for the tenure of their offices, and the amount and payment of their salaries.

He has erected a multitude of new offices, and sent hither swarms of officers to harass our people, and eat out their substance.

He has kept among us, in times of peace, standing armies, without the consent of our legislature.

He has affected to render the military independent of, and superior to, the civil power.

He has combined, with others, to subject us to a jurisdiction foreign to our Constitution, and unacknowledged by our laws; giving his assent to their acts of pretended legislation:

For quartering large bodies of armed troops among us:

For protecting them by a mock trial, from punishment, for any murders which they should commit on the inhabitants of these States:

For cutting off our trade with all parts of the world:

For imposing taxes on us without our consent:

For depriving us, in many cases, of the benefit of trial by jury:

For transporting us beyond seas to be tried for pretended offences:

For abolishing the free system of English laws in a neighboring province, establishing therein an arbitrary government, and enlarging its boundaries, so as to render it at once an example and fit instrument for introducing the same absolute rule into these colonies:

For taking away our charters, abolishing our most valuable laws, and altering, fundamentally, the powers of our governments:

For suspending our own legislatures, and declaring themselves invested with power to legislate for us in all cases whatsoever.

He has abdicated government here, by declaring us out of his protection, and waging war against us.

He has plundered our seas, ravaged our coasts, burnt our towns, and destroyed the lives of our people.

He is, at this time, transporting large armies of foreign mercenaries to complete the works of death, desolation, and tyranny, already begun, with circumstances of cruelty and perfidy scarcely paralleled in the most barbarous ages, and totally unworthy the head of a civilized nation.

He has constrained our fellow citizens, taken captive on the high seas, to bear arms against their country, to become the executioners of their friends, and brethren, or to fall themselves by their hands.

He has excited domestic insurrections amongst us, and has endeavored to bring on the inhabitants of our frontiers, the merciless Indian savages, whose known rule of warfare is an undistinguished destruction of all ages, sexes, and conditions.

In every stage of these oppressions, we have petitioned for redress; in the most humble terms; our repeated petitions have been answered only by repeated injury. A prince, whose character is thus marked by every act which may define a tyrant, is unfit to be the ruler of a free people.

Nor have we been wanting in attention to our British brethren. We have warned them, from time to time, of attempts made by their legislature to extend an unwarrantable jurisdiction over us. We have reminded them of the circumstances of our emigration and settlement here. We have appealed to their native justice and magnanimity, and we have conjured them, by the ties of our common kindred, to disavow these usurpations, which would inevitably interrupt our connections and correspondence. They, too, have been deaf to the voice of justice and consanguinity. We must, therefore, acquiesce in the necessity which denounces our separation, and hold them as we hold the rest of mankind, enemies in war, in peace, friends.

We, therefore, the representatives of the United States of America, in general Congress assembled, appealing to the Supreme Judge of the world for the rectitude of our intentions, do, in the name, and by authority of the good people of these colonies, solemnly publish and declare, that these united colonies are, and of right ought to be, free and independent states: that they are absolved from all allegiance to the British Crown, and that all political connection between them and the state of Great Britain is, and ought to be, totally dissolved; and that, as free and independent states, they have full power to levy war, conclude peace, contract alliances, establish commerce, and to do all other acts and things which independent states may of right do. And, for the support of this declaration, with a firm reliance on the protection of Divine Providence, we mutually pledge to each other our lives, our fortunes, and our sacred honor.

The foregoing Declaration was, by order of Congress, engrossed, and signed by the following members:

## JOHN HANCOCK

**New Hampshire**
Josiah Bartlett
William Whipple
Matthew Thornton

**Massachusetts Bay**
Samuel Adams
John Adams
Robert Treat Paine
Elbridge Gerry

**New York**
William Floyd
Phillip Livingston
Francis Lewis
Lewis Morris

**New Jersey**
Richard Stockton
John Witherspoon
Francis Hopkinson
John Hart
Abraham Clark

**Rhode Island**
Stephen Hopkins
William Ellery

**Connecticut**
Roger Sherman
Samuel Huntington
William Williams
Oliver Wolcott

**Delaware**
Caesar Rodney
George Read
Thomas M'Kean

**Pennsylvania**
Robert Morris
Benjamin Rush
Benjamin Franklin
John Morton
George Clymer
James Smith
George Taylor
James Wilson
George Ross

**North Carolina**
William Hooper
Joseph Hewes
John Penn

**Maryland**
Samuel Chase
William Paca
Thomas Stone
Charles Carroll,
 of Carrollton

**Virginia**
George Wythe
Richard Henry Lee
Thomas Jefferson
Benjamin Harrison
Thomas Nelson, Jr.
Francis Lightfoot Lee
Carter Braxton

**South Carolina**
Edward Rutledge
Thomas Heyward, Jr.
Thomas Lynch, Jr.
Arthur Middleton

**Georgia**
Button Gwinnett
Lyman Hall
George Walton

*Resolved,* That copies of the Declaration be sent to the several assemblies, conventions, and committees, or councils of safety, and to the several commanding officers of the continental troops; that it be proclaimed in each of the United States, at the head of the army.

# THE CONSTITUTION OF THE UNITED STATES*

## Preamble

We the people of the United States, in order to form a more perfect union, establish justice, insure domestic tranquility, provide for the common defense, promote the general welfare, and secure the blessings of liberty to ourselves and our posterity, do ordain and establish this Constitution for the United States of America.

## Article I

**Section 1**  All legislative powers herein granted shall be vested in a Congress of the United States, which shall consist of a Senate and a House of Representatives.

**Section 2**  The House of Representatives shall be composed of members chosen every second year by the people of the several States, and the electors in each

---

*Passages no longer in effect are in italic type.

State shall have the qualifications requisite for electors of the most numerous branch of the State Legislature.

No person shall be a Representative who shall not have attained to the age of twenty-five years, and been seven years a citizen of the United States, and who shall not, when elected, be an inhabitant of that State in which he shall be chosen.

Representatives and direct taxes shall be apportioned among the several States which may be included within this Union, according to their respective numbers, *which shall be determined by adding to the whole number of free persons, including those bound to service for a term of years and excluding Indians not taxed, three-fifths of all other persons.* The actual enumeration shall be made within three years after the first meeting of the Congress of the United States, and within every subsequent term of ten years, in such manner as they shall by law direct. The number of Representatives shall not exceed one for every thirty thousand, but each State shall have at least one Representative; *and until such enumeration shall be made, the State of New Hampshire shall be entitled to choose three, Massachusetts eight, Rhode Island and Providence Plantations one, Connecticut five, New York six, New Jersey four, Pennsylvania eight, Delaware one, Maryland six, Virginia ten, North Carolina five, South Carolina five, and Georgia three.*

When vacancies happen in the representation from any State, the Executive authority thereof shall issue writs of election to fill such vacancies.

The House of Representatives shall choose their Speaker and other officers; and shall have the sole power of impeachment.

**Section 3**  The Senate of the United States shall be composed of two Senators from each State, *chosen by the legislature thereof*, for six years; and each Senator shall have one vote.

*Immediately after they shall be assembled in consequence of the first election, they shall be divided as equally as may be into three classes. The seats of the Senators of the first class shall be vacated at the expiration of the second year, of the second class at the expiration of the fourth year, and of the third class at the expiration of the sixth year*, so that one-third may be chosen every second year; *and if vacancies happen by resignation or otherwise, during the recess of the legislature of any State, the Executive thereof may make temporary appointments until the next meeting of the legislature, which shall then fill such vacancies.*

No person shall be a Senator who shall not have attained to the age of thirty years, and been nine years a citizen of the United States, and who shall not, when elected, be an inhabitant of that State for which he shall be chosen.

The Vice-President of the United States shall be President of the Senate, but shall have no vote, unless they be equally divided.

The Senate shall choose their other officers, and also a President *pro tempore*, in the absence of the Vice-President, or when he shall exercise the office of President of the United States.

The Senate shall have the sole power to try all impeachments. When sitting for that purpose, they shall be on oath or affirmation. When the President of the United States is tried, the Chief Justice shall preside: and no person shall be convicted without the concurrence of two-thirds of the members present.

Judgment in cases of impeachment shall not extend further than to removal from the office, and disqualification to hold and enjoy any office of honor, trust or profit under the United States: but the party convicted shall nevertheless be liable and subject to indictment, trial, judgment and punishment, according to law.

**Section 4**  The times, places and manner of holding elections for Senators and Representatives shall be pre-scribed in each State by the legislature thereof; but the Congress may at any time by law make or alter such regulations, except as to the places of choosing Senators.

The Congress shall assemble at least once in every year, and such meeting *shall be on the first Monday in December, unless they shall by law appoint a different day.*

**Section 5**  Each house shall be the judge of the elections, returns and qualifications of its own members, and a majority of each shall constitute a quorum to do business; but a smaller number may adjourn from day to day, and may be authorized to compel the attendance of absent members, in such manner, and under such penalties, as each house may provide.

Each house may determine the rules of its proceedings, punish its members for disorderly behavior, and with the concurrence of two-thirds, expel a member.

Each house shall keep a journal of its proceedings, and from time to time publish the same, excepting such parts as may in their judgment require secrecy; and the yeas and nays of the members of either house on any question shall, at the desire of one-fifth of those present, be entered on the journal.

Neither house, during the session of Congress, shall, without the consent of the other, adjourn for more than three days, nor to any other place than that in which the two houses shall be sitting.

**Section 6**  The Senators and Representatives shall receive a compensation for their services, to be ascertained by law and paid out of the treasury of the United States. They shall in all cases except treason, felony and breach of the peace, be privileged from arrest during their attendance at the session of their respective houses, and in going to and returning from the same; and for any speech or debate in either house, they shall not be questioned in any other place.

No Senator or Representative shall, during the time for which he was elected, be appointed to any civil office under the authority of the United States, which shall have been created, or the emoluments whereof shall have been increased, during such time; and no person holding any office under the United States shall be a member of either house during his continuance in office.

**Section 7**  All bills for raising revenue shall originate in the House of Representatives; but the Senate may propose or concur with amendments as on other bills.

Every bill which shall have passed the House of Representatives and the Senate, shall, before it become a law, be presented to the President of the United States; if he approve he shall sign it, but if not he shall return it with objections to that house in which it shall have originated, who shall enter the objections at large on their journal, and proceed to reconsider it. If after such reconsideration two-thirds of that house shall agree to pass the bill, it shall be sent, together with the objections, to the other house, by which it shall likewise be reconsidered, and, if approved by two-thirds of that house, it shall become a law. But in all such cases the votes of both houses shall be determined by yeas and nays, and the names of the persons voting for and against the bill shall be entered on the journal of each house respectively. If any bill shall not be returned by the President within ten days (Sundays excepted) after it shall have been presented to him, the same shall be a law, in like manner as if he had signed it, unless the Congress by their adjournment prevent its return, in which case it shall not be a law.

Every order, resolution, or vote to which the concurrence of the Senate and House of Representatives may be necessary (except on a question of adjournment) shall be presented to the President of the United States; and before the same shall take effect, shall be approved by him, or being disapproved by him, shall be repassed by two-thirds of the Senate and House of Representatives, according to the rules and limitations prescribed in the case of a bill.

*Section 8*   The Congress shall have power

To lay and collect taxes, duties, imposts, and excises, to pay the debts and provide for the common defense and general welfare of the United States; but all duties, imposts and excises shall be uniform throughout the United States;

To borrow money on the credit of the United States;

To regulate commerce with foreign nations, and among the several States, and with the Indian tribes;

To establish an uniform rule of naturalization, and uniform laws on the subject of bankruptcies throughout the United States;

To coin money, regulate the value thereof, and of foreign coin, and fix the standard of weights and measures;

To provide for the punishment of counterfeiting the securities and current coin of the United States;

To establish post offices and post roads;

To promote the progress of science and useful arts by securing for limited times to authors and inventors the exclusive right to their respective writings and discoveries;

To constitute tribunals inferior to the Supreme Court;

To define and punish piracies and felonies committed on the high seas and offences against the law of nations;

To declare war, grant letters of marque and reprisal, and make rules concerning captures on land and water;

To raise and support armies, but no appropriation of money to that use shall be for a longer term than two years;

To provide and maintain a navy;

To make rules for the government and regulation of the land and naval forces;

To provide for calling forth the militia to execute the laws of the Union, suppress insurrections and repel invasions;

To provide for organizing, arming, and disciplining the militia, and for governing such part of them as may be employed in the service of the United States, reserving to the States respectively the appointment of the officers, and the authority of training the militia according to the discipline prescribed by Congress;

To exercise exclusive legislation in all cases whatsoever, over such district (not exceeding ten miles square) as may, by cession of particular States, and the acceptance of Congress, become the seat of the government of the United States, and to exercise like authority over all places purchased by the consent of the legislature of the State, in which the same shall be, for erection of forts, magazines, arsenals, dock-yards, and other needful buildings;—and

To make all laws which shall be necessary and proper for carrying into execution the foregoing powers, and all other powers vested by this Constitution in the government of the United States, or in any department or officer thereof.

*Section 9*   *The migration or importation of such persons as any of the States now existing shall think proper to admit shall not be prohibited by the Congress prior to the year one thousand eight hundred and eight; but a tax or duty may be imposed on such importation, not exceeding ten dollars for each person.*

The privilege of the writ of habeas corpus shall not be suspended, unless when in cases of rebellion or invasion the public safety may require it.

No bill of attainder or ex post facto law shall be passed.

No capitation, or other direct, tax shall be laid, unless in proportion to the census or enumeration herein before directed to be taken.

No tax or duty shall be laid on articles exported from any State.

No preference shall be given by any regulation of commerce or revenue to the ports of one State over those of another; nor shall vessels bound to, or from, one State be obliged to enter, clear, or pay duties in another.

No money shall be drawn from the treasury, but in consequence of appropriations made by law; and a regular statement and account of the receipts and expenditures of all public money shall be published from time to time.

No title of nobility shall be granted by the United States: and no person holding any office of profit or trust under them, shall, without the consent of the Congress, accept of any present, emolument, office, or title, of any kind whatever, from any king, prince, or foreign state.

**Section 10**  No State shall enter into any treaty, alliance, or confederation; grant letters of marque and reprisal; coin money; emit bills of credit; make anything but gold and silver coin a tender in payment of debts; pass any bill of attainder, ex post facto law, or law impairing the obligation of contracts, or grant any title of nobility.

No State shall, without the consent of Congress, lay any imposts or duties on imports or exports, except what may be absolutely necessary for executing its inspection laws: and the net produce of all duties and imposts, laid by any State on imports or exports, shall be for the use of the treasury of the United States; and all such laws shall be subject to the revision and control of the Congress.

No State shall, without the consent of Congress, lay any duty of tonnage, keep troops, or ships of war in time of peace, enter into any agreement or compact with another State, or with a foreign power, or engage in war, unless actually invaded, or in such imminent danger as will not admit of delay.

## Article II

**Section 1**  The executive power shall be vested in a President of the United States of America. He shall hold his office during the term of four years, and, together with the Vice-President, chosen for the same term, be elected as follows:

Each State shall appoint, in such manner as the legislature thereof may direct, a number of electors, equal to the whole number of Senators and Representatives to which the State may be entitled in the Congress; but no Senator or Representative, or person holding an office of trust or profit under the United States, shall be appointed an elector.

*The electors shall meet in their respective States, and vote by ballot for two persons, of whom one at least shall not be an inhabitant of the same State with themselves. And they shall make a list of all the persons voted for, and of the number of votes for each; which list they shall sign and certify, and transmit sealed to the seat of government of the United States, directed to the President of the Senate. The President of the Senate shall, in the presence of the Senate and House of Representatives, open all the certificates, and the votes shall then be counted. The person having the greatest number of votes shall be the President, if such number be a majority of the whole number of electors appointed; and if there be more than one who have such majority, and have*

*an equal number of votes, then the House of Representatives shall immediately choose by ballot one of them for President; and if no person have a majority, then from the five highest on the list said house shall in like manner choose the President. But in choosing the President the votes shall be taken by States, the representation from each State having one vote; a quorum for this purpose shall consist of a member or members from two-thirds of the States, and a majority of all the States shall be necessary to a choice. In every case, after the choice of the President, the person having the greatest number of votes of the electors shall be the Vice-President. But if there should remain two or more who have equal votes, the Senate shall choose from them by ballot the Vice-President.*

The Congress may determine the time of choosing the electors, and the day on which they shall give their votes; which day shall be the same throughout the United States.

No person except a natural-born citizen, *or a citizen of the United States at the time of the adoption of this Constitution,* shall be eligible to the office of President; neither shall any person be eligible to that office who shall not have attained to the age of thirty-five years, and been fourteen years a resident within the United States.

In cases of the removal of the President from office or of his death, resignation, or inability to discharge the powers and duties of the said office, the same shall devolve on the Vice-President, and the Congress may by law provide for the case of removal, death, resignation, or inability, both of the President and Vice-President, declaring what officer shall then act as President, and such officer shall act accordingly, until the disability be removed, or a President shall be elected.

The President shall, at stated times, receive for his services a compensation, which shall neither be increased nor diminished during the period for which he shall have been elected, and he shall not receive within that period any other emolument from the United States, or any of them.

Before he enter on the execution of his office, he shall take the following oath or affirmation:—"I do solemnly swear (or affirm) that I will faithfully execute the office of the President of the United States, and will to the best of my ability preserve, protect and defend the Constitution of the United States."

**Section 2**  The President shall be commander in chief of the army and navy of the United States, and of the militia of the several States, when called into the actual service of the United States; he may require the opinion, in writing, of the principal officer in each of the executive departments, upon any subject relating to the duties of their respective offices, and he shall have power to grant reprieves and pardons for offenses against the United States, except in cases of impeachment.

He shall have power, by and with the advice and consent of the Senate, to make treaties, provided two-thirds of the Senators present concur; and he shall nominate, and by and with the advice and consent of the Senate, shall appoint ambassadors, other public ministers and consuls, judges of the Supreme Court, and all other officers of the United States, whose appointments are not herein otherwise provided for, and which shall be established by law: but Congress may by law vest the appointment of such inferior officers, as they think proper, in the President alone, in the courts of law, or in the heads of departments.

The President shall have power to fill up all vacancies that may happen during the recess of the Senate, by granting commissions which shall expire at the end of their next session.

**Section 3**   He shall from time to time give to the Congress information of the state of the Union, and recommend to their consideration such measures as he shall judge necessary and expedient; he may, on extraordinary occasions, convene both houses, or either of them, and in case of disagreement between them, with respect to the time of adjournment, he may adjourn them to such time as he shall think proper; he shall receive ambassadors and other public ministers; he shall take care that the laws be faithfully executed, and shall commission all the officers of the United States.

**Section 4**   The President, Vice-President and all civil officers of the United States shall be removed from office on impeachment for, and on conviction of, treason, bribery, or other high crimes and misdemeanors.

## Article III

**Section 1**   The judicial power of the United States shall be vested in one Supreme Court, and in such inferior courts as the Congress may from time to time ordain and establish. The judges, both of the Supreme and inferior courts, shall hold their offices during good behavior, and shall, at stated times, receive for their services a compensation which shall not be diminished during their continuance in office.

**Section 2**   The judicial power shall extend to all cases, in law and equity, arising under this Constitution, the laws of the United States, and treaties made, or which shall be made, under their authority;—to all cases affecting ambassadors, other public ministers and consuls;—to all cases of admiralty and maritime jurisdiction;—to controversies to which the United States shall be a party;—to controversies between two or more States;—*between a State and citizens of another State;*—between citizens of different States;—between citizens of the same State claiming lands under grants

of different States, and between a State, or the citizens thereof, and foreign states, citizens or subjects.

In all cases affecting ambassadors, other public ministers and consuls, and those in which a State shall be party, the Supreme Court shall have original jurisdiction. In all the other cases before mentioned, the Supreme Court shall have appellate jurisdiction, both as to law and fact, with such exceptions, and under such regulations, as the Congress shall make.

The trial of all crimes, except in cases of impeachment, shall be by jury; and such trial shall be held in the State where said crimes shall have been committed; but when not committed within any State, the trial shall be at such place or places as the Congress may by Law have directed.

**Section 3**   Treason against the United States shall consist only in levying war against them, or in adhering to their enemies, giving them aid and comfort. No person shall be convicted of treason unless on the testimony of two witnesses to the same overt act, or on confession in open court.

The Congress shall have power to declare the punishment of treason, but no attainder of treason shall work corruption of blood, or forfeiture except during the life of the person attainted.

## Article IV

**Section 1**   Full faith and credit shall be given in each State to the public acts, records, and judicial proceedings of every other State. And the Congress may by general laws prescribe the manner in which such acts, records, and proceedings shall be proved, and the effect thereof.

**Section 2**   The citizens of each State shall be entitled to all privileges and immunities of citizens in the several States.

A person charged in any State with treason, felony, or other crime, who shall flee from justice, and be found in another State, shall on demand of the executive authority of the State from which he fled, be delivered up, to be removed to the State having jurisdiction of the crime.

*No Person held to service or labor in one State, under the laws thereof, escaping into another, shall, in consequence of any law or regulation therein, be discharged from such service or labor, but shall be delivered up on claim of the party to whom such service or labor may be due.*

**Section 3**   New States may be admitted by the Congress into this Union; but no new State shall be formed or erected within the jurisdiction of any other State; nor any State be formed by the junction of two or more States, or parts of States, without the consent of the legislatures of the States concerned as well as of the Congress.

The Congress shall have power to dispose of and make all needful rules and regulations respecting the territory or other property belonging to the United States; and nothing in this Constitution shall be so construed as to prejudice any claims of the United States, or of any particular State.

*Section 4*  The United States shall guarantee to every State in this Union a republican form of government, and shall protect each of them against invasion; and on application of the legislature, or of the executive (when the legislature cannot be convened), against domestic violence.

## Article V

The Congress, whenever two-thirds of both houses shall deem it necessary, shall propose amendments to this Constitution, or, on the application of the legislatures of two-thirds of the several States, shall call a convention for proposing amendments, which, in either case, shall be valid to all intents and purposes, as part of this Constitution, when ratified by the legislatures of three-fourths of the several States, or by conventions in three-fourths thereof, as the one or the other mode of ratification may be proposed by the Congress; provided *that no amendments which may be made prior to the year one thousand eight hundred and eight shall in any manner affect the first and fourth clauses in the ninth section of the first article*; and that no State, without its consent, shall be deprived of its equal suffrage in the Senate.

## Article VI

All debts contracted and engagements entered into, before the adoption of this Constitution, shall be as valid against the United States under this Constitution, as under the Confederation.

This Constitution, and the laws of the United States which shall be made in pursuance thereof; and all treaties made, or which shall be made, under the authority of the United States, shall be the supreme law of the land; and the judges in every State shall be bound thereby, anything in the Constitution or laws of any State to the contrary notwithstanding.

The Senators and Representatives before mentioned, and the members of the several State legislatures, and all executive and judicial officers, both of the United States and of the several States, shall be bound by oath or affirmation to support this Constitution; but no religious test shall ever be required as a qualification to any office or public trust under the United States.

## Article VII

The ratification of the conventions of nine States shall be sufficient for the establishment of this Constitution between the States so ratifying the same.

Done in convention by the unanimous consent of the States present, the seventeenth day of September in the year of our Lord one thousand seven hundred and eighty-seven and of the Independence of the United States of America the twelfth. In witness whereof we have hereunto subscribed our names.

**GEORGE WASHINGTON**
PRESIDENT AND DEPUTY FROM VIRGINIA

**New Hampshire**
John Langdon
Nicholas Gilman

**Massachusetts**
Nathaniel Gorham
Rufus King

**Connecticut**
William Samuel
  Johnson
Roger Sherman

**New York**
Alexander Hamilton

**New Jersey**
William Livingston
David Brearley
William Paterson
Jonathan Dayton

**Pennsylvania**
Benjamin Franklin
Thomas Mifflin
Robert Morris
George Clymer
Thomas FitzSimons
Jared Ingersoll
James Wilson
Gouverneur Morris

**Delaware**
George Read
Gunning Bedford, Jr.
John Dickinson
Richard Bassett
Jacob Broom

**Maryland**
James McHenry
Daniel of
  St. Thomas Jenifer
Daniel Carroll

**Virginia**
John Blair
James Madison, Jr.

**North Carolina**
William Blount
Richard Dobbs
  Spaight
Hugh Williamson

**South Carolina**
John Rutledge
Charles Cotesworth
  Pinckney
Charles Pinckney
Pierce Butler

**Georgia**
William Few
Abraham Baldwin

# AMENDMENTS TO THE CONSTITUTION WITH ANNOTATIONS
## (Including the six unratified amendments)

In their effort to gain Antifederalists' support for the Constitution, Federalists frequently pointed to the inclusion of Article 5, which provides an orderly method of amending the Constitution. In contrast, the Articles of Confederation, which were universally recognized as seriously flawed, offered no means of amendment. For their part, Antifederalists argued that the amendment process was so "intricate" that one might as easily roll "sixes an hundred times in succession" as change the Constitution.

The system for amendment laid out in the Constitution requires that two-thirds of both houses of Congress agree to a proposed amendment, which must then be ratified by three-quarters of the legislatures of the states. Alternatively, an amendment may be proposed by a convention called by the legislatures of two-thirds of the states. Since 1789, members of Congress have proposed thousands of amendments. Besides the seventeen amendments added since 1789, only the six "unratified" ones included here were approved by two-thirds of both houses and sent to the states for ratification.

Among the many amendments that never made it out of Congress have been proposals to declare dueling, divorce, and interracial marriage unconstitutional as well as proposals to establish a national university, to acknowledge the sovereignty of Jesus Christ, and to prohibit any person from possessing wealth in excess of ten million dollars.[1]

Among the issues facing Americans today that might lead to constitutional amendment are efforts to balance the federal budget, to limit the number of terms elected officials may serve, to limit access to or prohibit abortion, to establish English as the official language of the United States, and to prohibit flag burning. None of these proposed amendments has yet garnered enough support in Congress to be sent to the states for ratification.

Although the first ten amendments to the Constitution are commonly known as the Bill of Rights, only Amendments 1–8 actually provide guarantees of individual rights. Amendments 9 and 10 deal with the structure of power within the constitutional system. The Bill of Rights was promised to appease Antifederalists who refused to ratify the Constitution without guarantees of

individual liberties and limitations to federal power. After studying more than two hundred amendments recommended by the ratifying conventions of the states, Federalist James Madison presented a list of seventeen to Congress, which used Madison's list as the foundation for the twelve amendments that were sent to the states for ratification. Ten of the twelve were adopted in 1791. The first on the list of twelve, known as the Reapportionment Amendment, was never adopted (see p. A-12). The second proposed amendment was adopted in 1992 as Amendment 27 (see p. A-21).

## Amendment I

Congress shall make no law respecting an establishment of religion, or prohibiting the free exercise thereof; or abridging the freedom of speech, or of the press; or the right of the people peaceably to assemble, and to petition the government for a redress of grievances.

◆ ◆ ◆

*The First Amendment is a potent symbol for many Americans. Most are well aware of their rights to free speech, freedom of the press, and freedom of religion and their rights to assemble and to petition, even if they cannot cite the exact words of this amendment.*

*The First Amendment guarantee of freedom of religion has two clauses: the "free exercise clause," which allows individuals to practice or not practice any religion, and the "establishment clause," which prevents the federal government from discriminating against or favoring any particular religion. This clause was designed to create what Thomas Jefferson referred to as "a wall of separation between church and state." In the 1960s, the Supreme Court ruled that the First Amendment prohibits prayer (see Engel v. Vitale, p. A-35) and Bible reading in public schools.*

*Although the rights to free speech and freedom of the press are established in the First Amendment, it was not until the twentieth century that the Supreme Court began to explore the full meaning of these guarantees. In 1919, the Court ruled in Schenck v. United States (see p. A-34) that the government could suppress free expression only where it could cite a "clear and present danger." In a decision that continues to raise controversies, the Court ruled in 1990, in Texas v. Johnson, that flag burning is a form of symbolic speech protected by the First Amendment.*

---

[1] Richard B. Bernstein, *Amending America* (New York: Times Books, 1993), 177–81.

## Amendment II

A well-regulated militia being necessary to the security of a free State, the right of the people to keep and bear arms shall not be infringed.

*Fear of a standing army under the control of a hostile government made the Second Amendment an important part of the Bill of Rights. Advocates of gun ownership claim that the amendment prevents the government from regulating firearms. Proponents of gun control argue that the amendment is designed only to protect the right of the states to maintain militia units.*

*In 1939, the Supreme Court ruled in* United States v. Miller *that the Second Amendment did not protect the right of an individual to own a sawed-off shotgun, which it argued was not ordinary militia equipment. Since then, the Supreme Court has refused to hear Second Amendment cases, while lower courts have upheld firearms regulations. Several justices currently on the bench seem to favor a narrow interpretation of the Second Amendment, which would allow gun control legislation. The controversy over the impact of the Second Amendment on gun owners and gun control legislation will certainly continue.*

## Amendment III

No soldier shall, in time of peace, be quartered in any house without the consent of the owner, nor in time of war, but in a manner to be prescribed by law.

*The Third Amendment was extremely important to the framers of the Constitution, but today it is nearly forgotten. American colonists were especially outraged that they were forced to quarter British troops in the years before and during the American Revolution. The philosophy of the Third Amendment has been viewed by some justices and scholars as the foundation of the modern constitutional right to privacy. One example of this can be found in Justice William O. Douglas's opinion in* Griswold v. Connecticut *(see p. A-36).*

## Amendment IV

The right of the people to be secure in their persons, houses, papers, and effects, against unreasonable searches and seizures, shall not be violated, and no warrants shall issue but upon probable cause, supported by oath or affirmation, and particularly describing the place to be searched, and the persons or things to be seized.

*In the years before the Revolution, the houses, barns, stores, and warehouses of American colonists were ransacked by British authorities under "writs of assistance" or general warrants. The British, thus empowered, searched for seditious material or smuggled goods that could then be used as evidence against colonists who were charged with a crime only after the items were found.*

*The first part of the Fourth Amendment protects citizens from "unreasonable" searches and seizures. The Supreme Court has interpreted this protection as well as the words* search and seizure *in different ways at different times. At one time, the Court did not recognize electronic eavesdropping as a form of search and seizure, though it does today. At times, an "unreasonable" search has been almost any search carried out without a warrant, but in the two decades before 1969 the Court sometimes sanctioned warrantless searches that it considered reasonable based on "the total atmosphere of the case."*

*The second part of the Fourth Amendment defines the procedure for issuing a search warrant and states the requirement of "probable cause," which is generally viewed as evidence indicating that a suspect has committed an offense.*

*The Fourth Amendment has been controversial because the Court has sometimes excluded evidence that has been seized in violation of constitutional standards. The justification is that excluding such evidence deters violations of the amendment, but doing so may allow a guilty person to escape punishment.*

## Amendment V

No person shall be held to answer for a capital, or otherwise infamous crime, unless on a presentment or indictment of a grand jury, except in cases arising in the land or naval forces, or in the militia, when in actual service in time of war or public danger; nor shall any person be subject for the same offence to be twice put in jeopardy of life or limb; nor shall be compelled in any criminal case to be a witness against himself, nor be deprived of life, liberty, or property, without due process of law; nor shall private property be taken for public use without just compensation.

*The Fifth Amendment protects people against government authority in the prosecution of criminal offenses. It prohibits the state, first, from charging a person with a serious crime without a grand jury hearing to decide whether there is sufficient evidence to support the charge and, second, from charging a person with the same crime twice. The best-known aspect of the Fifth Amendment is that it*

prevents a person from being "compelled . . . to be a wit-ness against himself." The last clause, the "takings clause," limits the power of the government to seize property.

Although invoking the Fifth Amendment is popularly viewed as a confession of guilt, a person may be innocent yet still fear prosecution. For example, during the Red-baiting era of the late 1940s and 1950s, many people who had participated in legal activities that were associated with the Communist Party claimed the Fifth Amendment privilege rather than testify before the House Un-American Activities Committee because the mood of the times cast those activities in a negative light. Since "taking the Fifth" was viewed as an admission of guilt, those people often lost their jobs or became unemployable. (See Chapter 26.) Nonetheless, the right to protect oneself against self-incrimination plays an important role in guarding against the collective power of the state.

## Amendment VI

In all criminal prosecutions, the accused shall enjoy the right to a speedy and public trial, by an impartial jury of the State and district wherein the crime shall have been committed, which district shall have been previously ascertained by law, and to be informed of the nature and cause of the accusation; to be confronted with the witnesses against him; to have compulsory process for obtaining witnesses in his favor, and to have the assistance of counsel for his defence.

◆ ◆ ◆

The original Constitution put few limits on the govern-ment's power to investigate, prosecute, and punish crime. This process was of great concern to the early Americans, however, and of the twenty-eight rights specified in the first eight amendments, fifteen have to do with it. Seven rights are specified in the Sixth Amendment. These include the right to a speedy trial, a public trial, a jury trial, a notice of accusation, confrontation by opposing witnesses, testimony by favorable witnesses, and the assistance of counsel.

Although this amendment originally guaranteed these rights only in cases involving the federal government, the adoption of the Fourteenth Amendment began a process of applying the protections of the Bill of Rights to the states through court cases such as Gideon v. Wainwright (see p. A-35).

## Amendment VII

In suits at common law, where the value in controversy shall exceed twenty dollars, the right of trial by jury shall be preserved, and no fact tried by a jury shall be otherwise reexamined in any court of the United States, than according to the rules of the common law.

◆ ◆ ◆

This amendment guarantees people the same right to a trial by jury as was guaranteed by English common law in 1791. Under common law, in civil trials (those involv-ing money damages) the role of the judge was to settle questions of law and that of the jury was to settle ques-tions of fact. The amendment does not specify the size of the jury or its role in a trial, however. The Supreme Court has generally held that those issues be determined by En-glish common law of 1791, which stated that a jury con-sists of twelve people, that a trial must be conducted be-fore a judge who instructs the jury on the law and advises it on facts, and that a verdict must be unanimous.

## Amendment VIII

Excessive bail shall not be required, nor excessive fines imposed, nor cruel and unusual punishments inflicted.

◆ ◆ ◆

The language used to guarantee the three rights in this amendment was inspired by the English Bill of Rights of 1689. The Supreme Court has not had a lot to say about "excessive fines." In recent years it has agreed that despite the provision against "excessive bail," persons who are be-lieved to be dangerous to others can be held without bail even before they have been convicted.

Although opponents of the death penalty have not succeeded in using the Eighth Amendment to achieve the end of capital punishment, the clause regarding "cruel and unusual punishments" has been used to prohibit capi-tal punishment in certain cases (see Furman v. Georgia, p. A-36) and to require improved conditions in prisons.

## Amendment IX

The enumeration in the Constitution, of certain rights, shall not be construed to deny or disparage others re-tained by the people.

◆ ◆ ◆

Some Federalists feared that inclusion of the Bill of Rights in the Constitution would allow later generations of inter-preters to claim that the people had surrendered any rights not specifically enumerated there. To guard against this, Madison added language that became the Ninth Amend-ment. Interest in this heretofore largely ignored amend-ment revived in 1965 when it was used in a concurring opinion in Griswold v. Connecticut (see p. A-36). While Justice William O. Douglas called on the Third Amend-ment to support the right to privacy in deciding that case, Justice Arthur Goldberg, in the concurring opinion, argued that the right to privacy regarding contraception was an unenumerated right that was protected by the Ninth Amendment.

In 1980, the Court ruled that the right of the press to attend a public trial was protected by the Ninth Amendment. While some scholars argue that modern judges cannot identify the unenumerated rights that the framers were trying to protect, others argue that the Ninth Amendment should be read as providing a constitutional "presumption of liberty" that allows people to act in any way that does not violate the rights of others.

## Amendment X

The powers not delegated to the United States by the Constitution, nor prohibited by it to the States, are reserved to the States respectively, or to the people.

*The Antifederalists were especially eager to see a "reserved powers clause" explicitly guaranteeing the states control over their internal affairs. Not surprisingly, the Tenth Amendment has been a frequent battleground in the struggle over states' rights and federal supremacy. Prior to the Civil War, the Democratic Republican Party and Jacksonian Democrats invoked the Tenth Amendment to prohibit the federal government from making decisions about whether people in individual states could own slaves. The Tenth Amendment was virtually suspended during Reconstruction following the Civil War. In 1883, however, the Supreme Court declared the Civil Rights Act of 1875 unconstitutional on the grounds that it violated the Tenth Amendment. Business interests also called on the amendment to block efforts at federal regulation.*

*The Court was inconsistent over the next several decades as it attempted to resolve the tension between the restrictions of the Tenth Amendment and the powers the Constitution granted to Congress to regulate interstate commerce and levy taxes. The Court upheld the Pure Food and Drug Act (1906), the Meat Inspection Acts (1906 and 1907), and the White Slave Traffic Act (1910), all of which affected the states, but struck down an act prohibiting interstate shipment of goods produced through child labor. Between 1934 and 1935, a number of New Deal programs created by Franklin D. Roosevelt were declared unconstitutional on the grounds that they violated the Tenth Amendment. (See Chapter 24.) As Roosevelt appointees changed the composition of the Court, the Tenth Amendment was declared to have no substantive meaning. Generally, the amendment is held to protect the rights of states to regulate internal matters such as local government, education, commerce, labor, and business, as well as matters involving families such as marriage, divorce, and inheritance within the state.*

## Unratified Amendment

**Reapportionment Amendment (proposed by Congress September 25, 1789, along with the Bill of Rights)**

After the first enumeration required by the first article of the Constitution, there shall be one Representative for every thirty thousand, until the number shall amount to one hundred, after which the proportion shall be so regulated by Congress, that there shall be not less than one hundred Representatives, nor less than one Representative for every forty thousand persons, until the number of Representatives shall amount to two hundred; after which the proportion shall be so regulated by Congress, that there shall not be less than two hundred Representatives, nor more than one Representative for every fifty thousand persons.

*If the Reapportionment Amendment had passed and remained in effect, the House of Representatives today would have more than 5,000 members rather than 435.*

## Amendment XI
### [Adopted 1798]

The judicial power of the United States shall not be construed to extend to any suit in law or equity, commenced or prosecuted against one of the United States by citizens of another State, or by citizens or subjects of any foreign state.

*In 1793, the Supreme Court ruled in favor of Alexander Chisholm, executor of the estate of a deceased South Carolina merchant. Chisholm was suing the state of Georgia because the merchant had never been paid for provisions he had supplied during the Revolution. Many regarded this Court decision as an error that violated the intent of the Constitution.*

*Antifederalists had long feared a federal court system with the power to overrule a state court. When the Constitution was being drafted, Federalists had assured worried Antifederalists that section 2 of Article 3, which allows federal courts to hear cases "between a State and citizens of another State," did not mean that the federal courts were authorized to hear suits against a state by citizens of another state or a foreign country. Antifederalists and many other Americans feared a powerful federal court system because they worried that it would become like the British courts of this period, which were accountable only to the monarch. Furthermore, Chisholm v. Georgia prompted a series of suits against state governments by creditors and suppliers who had made loans during the war.*

*In addition, state legislators and Congress feared that the shaky economies of the new states, as well as the country as a whole, would be destroyed, especially if Loyalists who had fled to other countries sought reimbursement for land and property that had been seized. The day after the Supreme Court announced its decision, a resolution proposing the Eleventh Amendment, which overturned the decision in* Chisholm v. Georgia, *was introduced in the U.S. Senate.*

## Amendment XII
### [Adopted 1804]

The electors shall meet in their respective States, and vote by ballot for President and Vice-President, one of whom, at least, shall not be an inhabitant of the same State with themselves; they shall name in their ballots the person voted for as President, and in distinct ballots the person voted for as Vice-President, and they shall make distinct lists of all persons voted for as President, and of all persons voted for as Vice-President, and of the number of votes for each, which lists they shall sign and certify, and transmit sealed to the seat of government of the United States, directed to the President of the Senate;—the President of the Senate shall, in the presence of the Senate and House of Representatives, open all the certificates and the votes shall then be counted;—the person having the greatest number of votes for President shall be the President, if such number be a majority of the whole number of electors appointed; and if no person have such majority, then from the persons having the highest numbers not exceeding three on the list of those voted for as President, the House of Representatives shall choose immediately, by ballot, the President. But in choosing the President, the votes shall be taken by States, the representation from each State having one vote; a quorum for this purpose shall consist of a member or members from two-thirds of the States, and a majority of all the States shall be necessary to a choice. And if the House of Representatives shall not choose a President whenever the right of choice shall devolve upon them, before *the fourth day of March* next following, then the Vice-President shall act as President, as in the case of the death or other constitutional disability of the President.

The person having the greatest number of votes as Vice-President shall be the Vice-President, if such number be a majority of the whole number of electors appointed; and if no person have a majority, then from the two highest numbers on the list the Senate shall choose the Vice-President; a quorum for the purpose shall consist of two-thirds of the whole number of Senators, and a majority of the whole number shall be necessary to a choice. But no person constitutionally ineligible to the office of President shall be eligible to that of Vice-President of the United States.

*The framers of the Constitution disliked political parties and assumed that none would ever form. Under the original system, electors chosen by the states would each vote for two candidates. The candidate who won the most votes would become president, while the person who won the second-highest number of votes would become vice president. Rivalries between Federalists and Antifederalists led to the formation of political parties, however, even before George Washington had left office. Though Washington was elected unanimously in 1789 and 1792, the elections of 1796 and 1800 were procedural disasters because of party maneuvering (see Chapters 9 and 10). In 1796, Federalist John Adams was chosen as president, and his great rival, the Antifederalist Thomas Jefferson (whose party was called the Republican Party), became his vice president. In 1800, all the electors cast their two votes as one of two party blocs. Jefferson and his fellow Republican nominee, Aaron Burr, were tied with seventy-three votes each. The contest went to the House of Representatives, which finally elected Jefferson after thirty-six ballots. The Twelfth Amendment prevents these problems by requiring electors to vote separately for the president and vice president.*

## Unratified Amendment
### Titles of Nobility Amendment (proposed by Congress May 1, 1810)

If any citizen of the United States shall accept, claim, receive or retain any title of nobility or honor or shall, without the consent of Congress, accept and retain any present, pension, office or emolument of any kind whatever, from any emperor, king, prince or foreign power, such person shall cease to be a citizen of the United States, and shall be incapable of holding any office of trust or profit under them, or either of them.

*This amendment would have extended Article 1, section 9, clause 8 of the Constitution, which prevents the awarding of titles by the United States and the acceptance of such awards from foreign powers without congressional consent. Historians speculate that general nervousness about the power of the Emperor Napoleon, who was at that time extending France's empire throughout Europe, may have prompted the proposal. Though it fell one vote short of ratification, Congress and the American people thought the proposal had been ratified and it was included in many nineteenth-century editions of the Constitution.*

## The Civil War and Reconstruction Amendments (Thirteenth, Fourteenth, and Fifteenth Amendments)

In the four months between the election of Abraham Lincoln and his inauguration, more than two hundred proposed constitutional amendments were presented to Congress as part of a desperate attempt to hold the rapidly dissolving Union together. Most of these were efforts to appease the southern states by protecting the right to own slaves or by disfranchising African Americans through constitutional amendment. None were able to win the votes required from Congress to send them to the states. The relatively innocuous Corwin Amendment seemed to be the only hope for preserving the Union by amending the Constitution.

The northern victors in the Civil War tried to restructure the Constitution just as the war had restructured the nation. Yet they were often divided in their goals. Some wanted to end slavery; others hoped for social and economic equality regardless of race; others hoped that extending the power of the ballot box to former slaves would help create a new political order. The debates over the Thirteenth, Fourteenth, and Fifteenth Amendments were bitter. Few of those who fought for these changes were satisfied with the amendments themselves; fewer still were satisfied with their interpretation. Although the amendments put an end to the legal status of slavery, it took nearly a hundred years after the amendments' passage before most of the descendants of former slaves could begin to experience the economic, social, and political equality the amendments had been intended to provide.

## Unratified Amendment
### Corwin Amendment (proposed by Congress March 2, 1861)

No amendment shall be made to the Constitution which will authorize or give to Congress the power to abolish or interfere, within any State, with the domestic institutions thereof, including that of persons held to labor or service by the laws of said State.

*Following the election of Abraham Lincoln, Congress scrambled to try to prevent the secession of the slaveholding states. House member Thomas Corwin of Ohio proposed the "unamendable" amendment in the hope that by protecting slavery where it existed, Congress would keep the southern states in the Union. Lincoln indicated his support for the proposed amendment in his first inaugural address. Only Ohio and Maryland ratified the Corwin Amendment before it was forgotten.*

## Amendment XIII
[Adopted 1865]

**Section 1**  Neither slavery nor involuntary servitude, except as a punishment for crime whereof the party shall have been duly convicted, shall exist within the United States, or any place subject to their jurisdiction.

**Section 2**  Congress shall have power to enforce this article by appropriate legislation.

*Although President Lincoln had abolished slavery in the Confederacy with the Emancipation Proclamation of 1863, abolitionists wanted to rid the entire country of slavery. The Thirteenth Amendment did this in a clear and straightforward manner. In February 1865, when the proposal was approved by the House, the gallery of the House was newly opened to black Americans who had a chance at last to see their government at work. Passage of the proposal was greeted by wild cheers from the gallery as well as tears on the House floor, where congressional representatives openly embraced one another.*

*The problem of ratification remained, however. The Union position was that the Confederate states were part of the country of thirty-six states. Therefore, twenty-seven states were needed to ratify the amendment. When Kentucky and Delaware rejected it, backers realized that without approval from at least four former Confederate states, the amendment would fail. Lincoln's successor, President Andrew Johnson, made ratification of the Thirteenth Amendment a condition for southern states to rejoin the Union. Under those terms, all the former Confederate states except Mississippi accepted the Thirteenth Amendment, and by the end of 1865 the amendment had become part of the Constitution and slavery had been prohibited in the United States.*

## Amendment XIV
[Adopted 1868]

**Section 1**  All persons born or naturalized in the United States, and subject to the jurisdiction thereof, are citizens of the United States and of the State wherein they reside. No State shall make or enforce any law which shall abridge the privileges or immunities of citizens of the United States; nor shall any State deprive any person of life, liberty, or property, without due process of law; nor deny to any person within its jurisdiction the equal protection of the laws.

**Section 2**  Representatives shall be appointed among the several States according to their respective numbers, counting the whole number of persons in each

State, excluding Indians not taxed. But when the right to vote at any election for the choice of Electors for President and Vice-President of the United States, Representatives in Congress, the executive and judicial officers of a State, or the members of the legislature thereof, is denied to any of the male inhabitants of such State, being twenty-one years of age and citizens of the United States, or in any way abridged, except for participation in rebellion, or other crime, the basis of representation therein shall be reduced in the proportion which the number of such male citizens shall bear to the whole number of male citizens twenty-one years of age in such State.

**Section 3**   No person shall be a Senator or Representative in Congress, or Elector of President and Vice-President, or hold any office, civil or military, under the United States, or under any State, who, having previously taken an oath, as a member of Congress, or as an officer of the United States, or as a member of any State legislature, or as an executive or judicial officer of any State, to support the Constitution of the United States, shall have engaged in insurrection or rebellion against the same, or given aid or comfort to the enemies thereof. Congress may, by a vote of two-thirds of each house, remove such disability.

**Section 4**   The validity of the public debt of the United States, authorized by law, including debts incurred for payment of pensions and bounties for services in suppressing insurrection or rebellion, shall not be questioned. But neither the United States nor any State shall assume or pay any debt or obligation incurred in aid of insurrection or rebellion against the United States, or any claim for the loss or emancipation of any slave; but all such debts, obligations, and claims shall be held illegal and void.

**Section 5**   The Congress shall have power to enforce, by appropriate legislation, the provisions of this article.

◆ ◆ ◆

*Without Lincoln's leadership in the reconstruction of the nation following the Civil War, it soon became clear that the Thirteenth Amendment needed additional constitutional support. Less than a year after Lincoln's assassination, Andrew Johnson was ready to bring the former Confederate states back into the Union with few changes in their governments or politics. Anxious Republicans drafted the Fourteenth Amendment to prevent that from happening. The most important provisions of this complex amendment made all native-born or naturalized persons American citizens and prohibited states from abridging the "privileges or immunities" of citizens; depriving them of "life, liberty, or*

*property, without due process of law"; and denying them "equal protection of the laws." In essence, it made all ex-slaves citizens and protected the rights of all citizens against violation by their own state governments.*

*As occurred in the case of the Thirteenth Amendment, former Confederate states were forced to ratify the amendment as a condition of representation in the House and the Senate. The intentions of the Fourteenth Amendment, and how those intentions should be enforced, have been the most debated point of constitutional history. The terms* due process *and* equal protection *have been especially troublesome. Was the amendment designed to outlaw racial segregation? Or was the goal simply to prevent the leaders of the rebellious South from gaining political power?*

*The framers of the Fourteenth Amendment hoped Article 2 would produce black voters who would increase the power of the Republican Party. The federal government, however, never used its power to punish states for denying blacks their right to vote. Although the Fourteenth Amendment had an immediate impact in giving black Americans citizenship, it did nothing to protect blacks from the vengeance of whites once Reconstruction ended. In the late nineteenth and early twentieth centuries, section 1 of the Fourteenth Amendment was often used to protect business interests and strike down laws protecting workers on the grounds that the rights of "persons," that is, corporations, were protected by "due process." More recently, the Fourteenth Amendment has been used to justify school desegregation and affirmative action programs, as well as to dismantle such programs.*

## Amendment XV
### [Adopted 1870]

**Section 1**   The right of citizens of the United States to vote shall not be denied or abridged by the United States or by any State on account of race, color, or previous condition of servitude.

**Section 2**   The Congress shall have power to enforce this article by appropriate legislation.

◆ ◆ ◆

*The Fifteenth Amendment was the last major piece of Reconstruction legislation. While earlier Reconstruction acts had already required black suffrage in the South, the Fifteenth Amendment extended black voting rights to the entire nation. Some Republicans felt morally obligated to do away with the double standard between North and South since many northern states had stubbornly refused to enfranchise blacks. Others believed that the freedman's ballot required the extra protection of a constitutional amendment to shield it from white counterattack. But partisan advantage also played an important role in the amendment's passage, since Republicans hoped that by giving the ballot to northern blacks, they could lessen their political vulnerability.*

*Many women's rights advocates had fought for the amendment. They had felt betrayed by the inclusion of the word* male *in section 2 of the Fourteenth Amendment and were further angered when the proposed Fifteenth Amendment failed to prohibit denial of the right to vote on the grounds of sex as well as "race, color, or previous condition of servitude." In this amendment, for the first time, the federal government claimed the power to regulate the franchise, or vote. It was also the first time the Constitution placed limits on the power of the states to regulate access to the franchise. Although ratified in 1870, however, the amendment was not enforced until the twentieth century.*

## The Progressive Amendments (Sixteenth–Nineteenth Amendments)

No amendments were added to the Constitution between the Civil War and the Progressive Era. America was changing, however, in fundamental ways. The rapid industrialization of the United States after the Civil War led to many social and economic problems. Hundreds of amendments were proposed, but none received enough support in Congress to be sent to the states. Some scholars believe that regional differences and rivalries were so strong during this period that it was almost impossible to gain a consensus on a constitutional amendment. During the Progressive Era, however, the Constitution was amended four times in seven years.

## Amendment XVI
### [Adopted 1913]

The Congress shall have power to lay and collect taxes on incomes, from whatever source derived, without apportionment among the several States, and without regard to any census or enumeration.

◆ ◆ ◆

*Until passage of the Sixteenth Amendment, most of the money used to run the federal government came from customs duties and taxes on specific items, such as liquor. During the Civil War, the federal government taxed incomes as an emergency measure. Pressure to enact an income tax came from those who were concerned about the growing gap between rich and poor in the United States. The Populist Party began campaigning for a graduated income tax in 1892, and support continued to grow. By 1909, thirty-three proposed income tax amendments had been presented in Congress, but lobbying by corporate and other special interests had defeated them all. In June 1909,*

*the growing pressure for an income tax, which had been endorsed by Presidents Roosevelt and Taft, finally pushed an amendment through the Senate. The required thirty-six states had ratified the amendment by February 1913.*

## Amendment XVII
### [Adopted 1913]

**Section 1** The Senate of the United States shall be composed of two Senators from each State, elected by the people thereof, for six years; and each Senator shall have one vote. The electors in each State shall have the qualifications requisite for electors of [voters for] the most numerous branch of the State legislatures.

**Section 2** When vacancies happen in the representation of any State in the Senate, the executive authority of such State shall issue writs of election to fill such vacancies: Provided, that the Legislature of any State may empower the executive thereof to make temporary appointments until the people fill the vacancies by election as the Legislature may direct.

**Section 3** This amendment shall not be so construed as to affect the election or term of any Senator chosen before it becomes valid as part of the Constitution.

◆ ◆ ◆

*The framers of the Constitution saw the members of the House as the representatives of the people and the members of the Senate as the representatives of the states. Originally senators were to be chosen by the state legislators. According to reform advocates, however, the growth of private industry and transportation conglomerates during the Gilded Age had created a network of corruption in which wealth and power were exchanged for influence and votes in the Senate. Senator Nelson Aldrich, who represented Rhode Island in the late nineteenth and early twentieth centuries, for example, was known as "the senator from Standard Oil" because of his open support of special business interests.*

*Efforts to amend the Constitution to allow direct election of senators had begun in 1826, but since any proposal had to be approved by the Senate, reform seemed impossible. Progressives tried to gain influence in the Senate by instituting party caucuses and primary elections, which gave citizens the chance to express their choice of a senator who could then be officially elected by the state legislature. By 1910, fourteen of the country's thirty senators received popular votes through a state primary before the state legislature made its selection. Despairing of getting a proposal through the Senate, supporters of a direct-election amendment had begun in 1893 to seek a convention of representatives from two-thirds of the states to propose an amendment that could then be ratified. By 1905, thirty-one of forty-five states had endorsed such an amendment. Finally, in 1911, despite extraordinary opposition, a proposed amendment passed the Senate; by 1913, it had been ratified.*

## Amendment XVIII
### [Adopted 1919; Repealed 1933 by Amendment XXI]

**Section 1**  After one year from the ratification of this article the manufacture, sale, or transportation of intoxicating liquors within, the importation thereof into, or the exportation thereof from the United States and all territory subject to the jurisdiction thereof, for beverage purposes, is hereby prohibited.

**Section 2**  The Congress and the several States shall have concurrent power to enforce this article by appropriate legislation.

**Section 3**  This article shall be inoperative unless it shall have been ratified as an amendment to the Constitution by the legislatures of the several States, as provided by the Constitution, within seven years from the date of the submission thereof to the States by the Congress.

◆ ◆ ◆

*The Prohibition Party, formed in 1869, began calling for a constitutional amendment to outlaw alcoholic beverages in 1872. A prohibition amendment was first proposed in the Senate in 1876 and was revived eighteen times before 1913. Between 1913 and 1919, another thirty-nine attempts were made to prohibit liquor in the United States through a constitutional amendment. Prohibition became a key element of the Progressive agenda as reformers linked alcohol and drunkenness to numerous social problems, including the corruption of immigrant voters. While opponents of such an amendment argued that it was undemocratic, supporters claimed that their efforts had widespread public support. The admission of twelve "dry" western states to the Union in the early twentieth century and the spirit of sacrifice during World War I laid the groundwork for passage and ratification of the Eighteenth Amendment in 1919. Opponents added a time limit to the amendment in the hope that they could thus block ratification, but this effort failed. (See also Amendment XXI.)*

## Amendment XIX
### [Adopted 1920]

**Section 1**  The right of citizens of the United States to vote shall not be denied or abridged by the United States or by any State on account of sex.

**Section 2**  Congress shall have the power to enforce this article by appropriate legislation.

◆ ◆ ◆

*Advocates of women's rights tried and failed to link woman suffrage to the Fourteenth and Fifteenth Amendments. Nonetheless, the effort for woman suffrage continued. Between 1878 and 1912, at least one and sometimes as many as four proposed amendments were introduced in Congress each year to grant women the right to vote. While over time women won very limited voting rights in some states, at both the state and federal levels opposition to an amendment for woman suffrage remained very strong. President Woodrow Wilson and other officials felt that the federal government should not interfere with the power of the states in this matter. Others worried that granting suffrage to women would encourage ethnic minorities to exercise their own right to vote. And many were concerned that giving women the vote would result in their abandoning traditional gender roles. In 1919, following a protracted and often bitter campaign of protest in which women went on hunger strikes and chained themselves to fences, an amendment was introduced with the backing of President Wilson. It narrowly passed the Senate (after efforts to limit the suffrage to white women failed) and was adopted in 1920 after Tennessee became the thirty-sixth state to ratify it.*

## Unratified Amendment
### Child Labor Amendment (proposed by Congress June 2, 1924)

**Section 1**  The Congress shall have power to limit, regulate, and prohibit the labor of persons under eighteen years of age.

**Section 2**  The power of the several States is unimpaired by this article except that the operation of State laws shall be suspended to the extent necessary to give effect to legislation enacted by Congress.

◆ ◆ ◆

*Throughout the late nineteenth and early twentieth centuries, alarm over the condition of child workers grew. Opponents of child labor argued that children worked in dangerous and unhealthy conditions, that they took jobs from adult workers, that they depressed wages in certain industries, and that states that allowed child labor had an economic advantage over those that did not. Defenders of child labor claimed that children provided needed income in many families, that working at a young age developed character, and that the effort to prohibit the practice constituted an invasion of family privacy.*

*In 1916, Congress passed a law that made it illegal to sell goods made by children through interstate commerce. The Supreme Court, however, ruled that the law violated the limits on the power of Congress to regulate interstate commerce. Congress then tried to penalize industries that used child labor by taxing such goods. This measure was also thrown out by the courts. In response, reformers set out to amend the Constitution. The proposed amendment was ratified by twenty-eight states, but by 1925, thirteen states had rejected it. Passage of the Fair Labor Standards Act in 1938, which was upheld by the Supreme Court in 1941, made the amendment irrelevant.*

## Amendment XX
### [Adopted 1933]

**Section 1**   The terms of the President and Vice President shall end at noon on the 20th day of January, and the terms of Senators and Representatives at noon on the 3rd day of January, of the years in which such terms would have ended if this article had not been ratified; and the terms of their successors shall then begin.

**Section 2**   The Congress shall assemble at least once in every year, and such meeting shall begin at noon on the 3d day of January, unless they shall by law appoint a different day.

**Section 3**   If, at the time fixed for the beginning of the term of the President, the President-elect shall have died, the Vice-President-elect shall become President. If a President shall not have been chosen before the time fixed for the beginning of his term, or if the President-elect shall have failed to qualify, then the Vice-President-elect shall act as President until a President shall have qualified; and the Congress may by law provide for the case wherein neither a President-elect nor a Vice-President-elect shall have qualified, declaring who shall then act as President, or the manner in which one who is to act shall be selected, and such person shall act accordingly until a President or Vice-President shall have qualified.

**Section 4**   The Congress may by law provide for the case of the death of any of the persons from whom the House of Representatives may choose a President whenever the right of choice shall have devolved upon them, and for the case of the death of any of the persons from whom the Senate may choose a Vice-President whenever the right of choice shall have devolved upon them.

**Section 5**   Sections 1 and 2 shall take effect on the 15th day of October following the ratification of this article.

**Section 6**   This article shall be inoperative unless it shall have been ratified as an amendment to the Constitution by the Legislatures of three-fourths of the several States within seven years from the date of its submission.

*Until 1933, presidents took office on March 4. Since elections are held in early November and electoral votes are counted in mid-December, this meant that more than three months passed between the time a new president was elected and when he took office. Moving the inauguration to January shortened the transition period and allowed Congress to begin its term closer to the time of the president's inauguration. Although this seems like a minor change, an amendment was required because the Constitution specifies terms of office. This amendment also deals with questions of succession in the event that a president- or vice president-elect dies before assuming office. Section 3 also clarifies a method for resolving a deadlock in the electoral college.*

## Amendment XXI
### [Adopted 1933]

**Section 1**   The eighteenth article of amendment to the Constitution of the United States is hereby repealed.

**Section 2**   The transportation or importation into any State, Territory, or Possession of the United States for delivery or use therein of intoxicating liquors, in violation of the laws thereof, is hereby prohibited.

**Section 3**   This article shall be inoperative unless it shall have been ratified as an amendment to the Constitution by conventions in the several States, as provided in the Constitution, within seven years from the date of the submission thereof to the States by the Congress.

*Widespread violation of the Volstead Act, the law enacted to enforce prohibition, made the United States a nation of lawbreakers. Prohibition caused more problems than it solved by encouraging crime, bribery, and corruption. Further, a coalition of liquor and beer manufacturers, personal liberty advocates, and constitutional scholars joined forces to challenge the amendment. By 1929, thirty proposed repeal amendments had been introduced in Congress, and the Democratic Party made repeal part of its platform in the 1932 presidential campaign. The Twenty-First Amendment was proposed in February 1933 and ratified less than a year later. The failure of the effort to enforce prohibition through a constitutional amendment has often been cited by opponents to subsequent efforts to shape public virtue and private morality.*

## Amendment XXII
*[Adopted 1951]*

**Section 1**   No person shall be elected to the office of the President more than twice, and no person who has held the office of President, or acted as President, for more than two years of a term to which some other person was elected President shall be elected to the office of President more than once. But this article shall not apply to any person holding the office of President when this Article was proposed by the Congress, and shall not prevent any person who may be holding the office of President, or acting as President, during the term within which this Article becomes operative from holding the office of President or acting as President during the remainder of such term.

**Section 2**   This article shall be inoperative unless it shall have been ratified as an amendment to the Constitution by the legislatures of three-fourths of the several States within seven years from the date of its submission to the States by the Congress.

◆ ◆ ◆

*George Washington's refusal to seek a third term of office set a precedent that stood until 1912, when former President Theodore Roosevelt sought, without success, another term as an independent candidate. Democrat Franklin Roosevelt was the only president to seek and win a fourth term, though he did so amid great controversy. Roosevelt died in April 1945, a few months after the beginning of his fourth term. In 1946, Republicans won control of the House and the Senate, and early in 1947 a proposal for an amendment to limit future presidents to two four-year terms was offered to the states for ratification. Democratic critics of the Twenty-Second Amendment charged that it was a partisan posthumous jab at Roosevelt.*

*Since the Twenty-Second Amendment was adopted, however, the only presidents who might have been able to seek a third term, had it not existed, were Republicans Dwight Eisenhower and Ronald Reagan. Since 1826, Congress has entertained 160 proposed amendments to limit the president to one six-year term. Such amendments have been backed by fifteen presidents, including Gerald Ford and Jimmy Carter.*

## Amendment XXIII
*[Adopted 1961]*

**Section 1**   The District constituting the seat of Government of the United States shall appoint in such manner as the Congress may direct: A number of electors of President and Vice-President equal to the whole number of Senators and Representatives in Congress to which the District would be entitled if it were a State, but in no event more than the least populous State; they shall be in addition to those appointed by the States, but they shall be considered for the purposes of the election of President and Vice-President, to be electors appointed by a State; and they shall meet in the District and perform such duties as provided by the twelfth article of amendment.

**Section 2**   The Congress shall have the power to enforce this article by appropriate legislation.

◆ ◆ ◆

*When Washington, D.C., was established as a federal district, no one expected that a significant number of people would make it their permanent and primary residence. A proposal to allow citizens of the district to vote in presidential elections was approved by Congress in June 1960 and was ratified on March 29, 1961.*

## Amendment XXIV
*[Adopted 1964]*

**Section 1**   The right of citizens of the United States to vote in any primary or other election for President or Vice-President, for electors for President or Vice-President, or for Senator or Representative in Congress, shall not be denied or abridged by the United States or any State by reason of failure to pay any poll tax or other tax.

**Section 2**   The Congress shall have the power to enforce this article by appropriate legislation.

◆ ◆ ◆

*In the colonial and Revolutionary eras, financial independence was seen as necessary to political independence, and the poll tax was used as a requirement for voting. By the twentieth century, however, the poll tax was used mostly to bar poor people, especially southern blacks, from voting. While conservatives complained that the amendment interfered with states' rights, liberals thought that the amendment did not go far enough because it barred the poll tax only in national elections and not in state or local elections. The amendment was ratified in 1964, however, and two years later, the Supreme Court ruled that poll taxes in state and local elections also violated the equal protection clause of the Fourteenth Amendment.*

## Amendment XXV
*[Adopted 1967]*

**Section 1**   In case of the removal of the President from office or of his death or resignation, the Vice-President shall become President.

**Section 2**  Whenever there is a vacancy in the office of the Vice-President, the President shall nominate a Vice-President who shall take office upon confirmation by a majority vote of both Houses of Congress.

**Section 3**  Whenever the President transmits to the President pro tempore of the Senate and the Speaker of the House of Representatives his written declaration that he is unable to discharge the powers and duties of his office, and until he transmits to them a written declaration to the contrary, such powers and duties shall be discharged by the Vice-President as Acting President.

**Section 4**  Whenever the Vice-President and a majority of either the principal officers of the executive departments or of such other body as Congress may by law provide, transmit to the President pro tempore of the Senate and the Speaker of the House of Representatives their written declaration that the President is unable to discharge the powers and duties of his office, the Vice-President shall immediately assume the powers and duties of the office as Acting President.

Thereafter, when the President transmits to the President pro tempore of the Senate and the Speaker of the House of Representatives his written declaration that no inability exists, he shall resume the powers and duties of his office unless the Vice-President and a majority of either the principal officers of the executive department[s] or of such other body as Congress may by law provide, transmit within four days to the President pro tempore of the Senate and the Speaker of the House of Representatives their written declaration that the President is unable to discharge the powers and duties of his office. Thereupon Congress shall decide the issue, assembling within forty-eight hours for that purpose if not in session. If the Congress, within twenty-one days after receipt of the latter written declaration, or, if Congress is not in session, within twenty-one days after Congress is required to assemble, determines by two-thirds vote of both Houses that the President is unable to discharge the powers and duties of his office, the Vice-President shall continue to discharge the same as Acting President; otherwise, the President shall resume the powers and duties of his office.

◆ ◆ ◆

*The framers of the Constitution established the office of vice president because someone was needed to preside over the Senate. The first president to die in office was William Henry Harrison, in 1841. Vice President John Tyler had himself sworn in as president, setting a precedent that was followed when seven later presidents died in office. The assassination of President James A. Garfield in 1881*

*posed a new problem, however. After he was shot, the president was incapacitated for two months before he died; he was unable to lead the country, while his vice president, Chester A. Arthur, was unable to assume leadership. Efforts to resolve questions of succession in the event of a presidential disability thus began with the death of Garfield.*

*In 1963, the assassination of President John F. Kennedy galvanized Congress to action. Vice President Lyndon Johnson was a chain smoker with a history of heart trouble. According to the 1947 Presidential Succession Act, the two men who stood in line to succeed him were the seventy-two-year-old Speaker of the House and the eighty-six-year-old president of the Senate. There were serious concerns that any of these men might become incapacitated while serving as chief executive. The first time the Twenty-Fifth Amendment was used, however, was not in the case of presidential death or illness, but during the Watergate crisis. When Vice President Spiro T. Agnew was forced to resign following allegations of bribery and tax violations, President Richard M. Nixon appointed House Minority Leader Gerald R. Ford vice president. Ford became president following Nixon's resignation eight months later and named Nelson A. Rockefeller as his vice president. Thus, for more than two years, the two highest offices in the country were held by people who had not been elected to them.*

## Amendment XXVI
### [Adopted 1971]

**Section 1**  The right of citizens of the United States, who are eighteen years of age or older, to vote shall not be denied or abridged by the United States or by any State on account of age.

**Section 2**  The Congress shall have power to enforce this article by appropriate legislation.

◆ ◆ ◆

*Efforts to lower the voting age from twenty-one to eighteen began during World War II. Recognizing that those who were old enough to fight a war should have some say in the government policies that involved them in the war, Presidents Eisenhower, Johnson, and Nixon endorsed the idea. In 1970, the combined pressure of the antiwar movement and the demographic pressure of the baby boom generation led to a Voting Rights Act lowering the voting age in federal, state, and local elections.*

*In Oregon v. Mitchell (1970), the state of Oregon challenged the right of Congress to determine the age at which people could vote in state or local elections. The Supreme Court agreed with Oregon. Since the Voting Rights Act was ruled unconstitutional, the Constitution had to be amended to allow passage of a law that would lower the voting age. The amendment was ratified in a little more than three months, making it the most rapidly ratified amendment in U.S. history.*

## Unratified Amendment

**Equal Rights Amendment (proposed by Congress March 22, 1972; seven-year deadline for ratification extended June 30, 1982)**

**Section 1**   Equality of rights under the law shall not be denied or abridged by the United States or by any State on account of sex.

**Section 2**   The Congress shall have the power to enforce, by appropriate legislation, the provisions of this article.

**Section 3**   This amendment shall take effect two years after the date of ratification.

◆ ◆ ◆

*In 1923, soon after women had won the right to vote, Alice Paul, a leading activist in the woman suffrage movement, proposed an amendment requiring equal treatment of men and women. Opponents of the proposal argued that such an amendment would invalidate laws that protected women and would make women subject to the military draft. After the 1964 Civil Rights Act was adopted, protective workplace legislation was removed anyway.*

*The renewal of the women's movement, as a byproduct of the civil rights and antiwar movements, led to a revival of the Equal Rights Amendment (ERA) in Congress. Disagreements over language held up congressional passage of the proposed amendment, but on March 22, 1972, the Senate approved the ERA by a vote of eightyfour to eight, and it was sent to the states. Six states ratified the amendment within two days, and by the middle of 1973 the amendment seemed well on its way to adoption, with thirty of the needed thirty-eight states having ratified it. In the mid-1970s, however, a powerful "Stop ERA" campaign developed. The campaign portrayed the ERA as a threat to "family values" and traditional relationships between men and women. Although thirty-five states ultimately ratified the ERA, five of those state legislatures voted to rescind ratification, and the amendment was never adopted.*

## Unratified Amendment

**D.C. Statehood Amendment (proposed by Congress August 22, 1978)**

**Section 1**   For purposes of representation in the Congress, election of the President and Vice President, and article V of this Constitution, the District constituting

the seat of government of the United States shall be treated as though it were a State.

**Section 2**   The exercise of the rights and powers conferred under this article shall be by the people of the District constituting the seat of government, and as shall be provided by Congress.

**Section 3**   The twenty-third article of amendment to the Constitution of the United States is hereby repealed.

**Section 4**   This article shall be inoperative, unless it shall have been ratified as an amendment to the Constitution by the legislatures of three-fourths of the several states within seven years from the date of its submission.

◆ ◆ ◆

*The 1961 ratification of the Twenty-Third Amendment, giving residents of the District of Columbia the right to vote for a president and vice president, inspired an effort to give residents of the district full voting rights. In 1966, President Lyndon Johnson appointed a mayor and city council; in 1971, D.C. residents were allowed to name a nonvoting delegate to the House; and in 1981, residents were allowed to elect the mayor and city council. Congress retained the right to overrule laws that might affect commuters, the height of federal buildings, and selection of judges and prosecutors. The district's nonvoting delegate to Congress, Walter Fauntroy, lobbied fiercely for a congressional amendment granting statehood to the district. In 1978, a proposed amendment was approved and sent to the states. A number of states quickly ratified the amendment, but, like the ERA, the D.C. Statehood Amendment ran into trouble. Opponents argued that section 2 created a separate category of "nominal" statehood. They argued that the federal district should be eliminated and that the territory should be reabsorbed into the state of Maryland. Although these theoretical arguments were strong, some scholars believe that racist attitudes toward the predominantly black population of the city was also a factor leading to the defeat of the amendment.*

## Amendment XXVII
### [Adopted 1992]

No law, varying the compensation for the services of the Senators and Representatives, shall take effect, until an election of Representatives shall have intervened.

◆ ◆ ◆

*While the Twenty-Sixth Amendment was the most rapidly ratified amendment in U.S. history, the Twenty-Seventh*

*Amendment had the longest journey to ratification. First proposed by James Madison in 1789 as part of the package that included the Bill of Rights, this amendment had been ratified by only six states by 1791. In 1873, however, it was ratified by Ohio to protest a massive retroactive salary increase by the federal government. Unlike later proposed amendments, this one came with no time limit on ratification. In the early 1980s, Gregory D. Watson, a University of Texas economics major, discovered the "lost" amendment and began a single-handed campaign to get state legislators to introduce it for ratification. In 1983, it was accepted by Maine. In 1984, it passed the Colorado legislature. Ratifications trickled in slowly until May 1992, when Michigan and New Jersey became the thirty-eighth and thirty-ninth states, respectively, to ratify. This amendment prevents members of Congress from raising their own salaries without giving voters a chance to vote them out of office before they can benefit from the raises.*

# U.S. POLITICS AND GOVERNMENT

## PRESIDENTIAL ELECTIONS

| Year | Candidates | Parties | Popular Vote | Percentage of Popular Vote | Electoral Vote | Percentage of Voter Participation |
|------|-----------|---------|-------------|---------------------------|---------------|----------------------------------|
| 1789 | **GEORGE WASHINGTON (Va.)*** | | | | 69 | |
| | John Adams | | | | 34 | |
| | Others | | | | 35 | |
| 1792 | **GEORGE WASHINGTON (Va.)** | | | | 132 | |
| | John Adams | | | | 77 | |
| | George Clinton | | | | 50 | |
| | Others | | | | 5 | |
| 1796 | **JOHN ADAMS (Mass.)** | Federalist | | | 71 | |
| | Thomas Jefferson | Democratic-Republican | | | 68 | |
| | Thomas Pinckney | Federalist | | | 59 | |
| | Aaron Burr | Dem.-Rep. | | | 30 | |
| | Others | | | | 48 | |
| 1800 | **THOMAS JEFFERSON (Va.)** | Dem.-Rep. | | | 73 | |
| | Aaron Burr | Dem.-Rep. | | | 73 | |
| | John Adams | Federalist | | | 65 | |
| | C. C. Pinckney | Federalist | | | 64 | |
| | John Jay | Federalist | | | 1 | |
| 1804 | **THOMAS JEFFERSON (Va.)** | Dem.-Rep. | | | 162 | |
| | C. C. Pinckney | Federalist | | | 14 | |
| 1808 | **JAMES MADISON (Va.)** | Dem.-Rep. | | | 122 | |
| | C. C. Pinckney | Federalist | | | 47 | |
| | George Clinton | Dem.-Rep. | | | 6 | |
| 1812 | **JAMES MADISON (Va.)** | Dem.-Rep. | | | 128 | |
| | De Witt Clinton | Federalist | | | 89 | |
| 1816 | **JAMES MONROE (Va.)** | Dem.-Rep. | | | 183 | |
| | Rufus King | Federalist | | | 34 | |
| 1820 | **JAMES MONROE (Va.)** | Dem.-Rep. | | | 231 | |
| | John Quincy Adams | Dem.-Rep. | | | 1 | |
| 1824 | **JOHN Q. ADAMS (Mass.)** | Dem.-Rep. | 108,740 | 30.5 | 84 | 26.9 |
| | Andrew Jackson | Dem.-Rep. | 153,544 | 43.1 | 99 | |
| | William H. Crawford | Dem.-Rep. | 46,618 | 13.1 | 41 | |
| | Henry Clay | Dem.-Rep. | 47,136 | 13.2 | 37 | |
| 1828 | **ANDREW JACKSON (Tenn.)** | Democratic | 647,286 | 56.0 | 178 | 57.6 |
| | John Quincy Adams | National Republican | 508,064 | 44.0 | 83 | |

*State of residence when elected president.

| Year | Candidates | Parties | Popular Vote | Percentage of Popular Vote | Electoral Vote | Percentage of Voter Participation |
|------|-----------|---------|-------------|---------------------------|---------------|-----------------------------------|
| 1832 | **ANDREW JACKSON (Tenn.)** | Democratic | 687,502 | 55.0 | 219 | 55.4 |
| | Henry Clay | National Republican | 530,189 | 42.4 | 49 | |
| | John Floyd | Independent | | | 11 | |
| | William Wirt | Anti-Mason | 33,108 | 2.6 | 7 | |
| 1836 | **MARTIN VAN BUREN (N.Y.)** | Democratic | 765,483 | 50.9 | 170 | 57.8 |
| | W. H. Harrison | Whig | | | 73 | |
| | Hugh L. White | Whig | 739,795 | 49.1 | 26 | |
| | Daniel Webster | Whig | | | 14 | |
| | W. P. Magnum | Independent | | | 11 | |
| 1840 | **WILLIAM H. HARRISON (Ohio)** | Whig | 1,274,624 | 53.1 | 234 | 80.2 |
| | Martin Van Buren | Democratic | 1,127,781 | 46.9 | 60 | |
| | J. G. Birney | Liberty | 7,069 | | — | |
| 1844 | **JAMES K. POLK (Tenn.)** | Democratic | 1,338,464 | 49.6 | 170 | 78.9 |
| | Henry Clay | Whig | 1,300,097 | 48.1 | 105 | |
| | J. G. Birney | Liberty | 62,300 | 2.3 | — | |
| 1848 | **ZACHARY TAYLOR (La.)** | Whig | 1,360,967 | 47.4 | 163 | 72.7 |
| | Lewis Cass | Democratic | 1,222,342 | 42.5 | 127 | |
| | Martin Van Buren | Free-Soil | 291,263 | 10.1 | — | |
| 1852 | **FRANKLIN PIERCE (N.H.)** | Democratic | 1,601,117 | 50.9 | 254 | 69.6 |
| | Winfield Scott | Whig | 1,385,453 | 44.1 | 42 | |
| | John P. Hale | Free-Soil | 155,825 | 5.0 | — | |
| 1856 | **JAMES BUCHANAN (Pa.)** | Democratic | 1,832,995 | 45.3 | 174 | 78.9 |
| | John C. Frémont | Republican | 1,339,932 | 33.1 | 114 | |
| | Millard Fillmore | American | 871,731 | 21.6 | 8 | |
| 1860 | **ABRAHAM LINCOLN (Ill.)** | Republican | 1,865,593 | 39.8 | 180 | 81.2 |
| | Stephen A. Douglas | Democratic | 1,382,713 | 29.5 | 12 | |
| | John C. Breckinridge | Democratic | 848,356 | 18.1 | 72 | |
| | John Bell | Union | 592,906 | 12.6 | 39 | |
| 1864 | **ABRAHAM LINCOLN (Ill.)** | Republican | 2,206,938 | 55.0 | 212 | 73.8 |
| | George B. McClellan | Democratic | 1,803,787 | 45.0 | 21 | |
| 1868 | **ULYSSES S. GRANT (Ill.)** | Republican | 3,012,833 | 52.7 | 214 | 78.1 |
| | Horatio Seymour | Democratic | 2,703,249 | 47.3 | 80 | |
| 1872 | **ULYSSES S. GRANT (Ill.)** | Republican | 3,597,132 | 55.6 | 286 | 71.3 |
| | Horace Greeley | Democratic; Liberal Republican | 2,834,125 | 43.9 | 66 | |
| 1876 | **RUTHERFORD B. HAYES (Ohio)** | Republican | 4,036,572 | 48.0 | 185 | 81.8 |
| | Samuel J. Tilden | Democratic | 4,284,020 | 51.0 | 184 | |
| 1880 | **JAMES A. GARFIELD (Ohio)** | Republican | 4,454,416 | 48.5 | 214 | 79.4 |
| | Winfield S. Hancock | Democratic | 4,444,952 | 48.1 | 155 | |
| 1884 | **GROVER CLEVELAND (N.Y.)** | Democratic | 4,879,507 | 48.5 | 219 | 77.5 |
| | James G. Blaine | Republican | 4,850,293 | 48.2 | 182 | |
| 1888 | **BENJAMIN HARRISON (Ind.)** | Republican | 5,439,853 | 47.9 | 233 | 79.3 |
| | Grover Cleveland | Democratic | 5,540,309 | 48.6 | 168 | |
| 1892 | **GROVER CLEVELAND (N.Y.)** | Democratic | 5,555,426 | 46.1 | 277 | 74.7 |
| | Benjamin Harrison | Republican | 5,182,690 | 43.0 | 145 | |
| | James B. Weaver | People's | 1,029,846 | 8.5 | 22 | |

| Year | Candidates | Parties | Popular Vote | Percentage of Popular Vote | Electoral Vote | Percentage of Voter Participation |
|---|---|---|---|---|---|---|
| 1896 | **WILLIAM McKINLEY (Ohio)** | Republican | 7,104,779 | 51.1 | 271 | 79.3 |
| | William J. Bryan | Democratic-People's | 6,502,925 | 47.7 | 176 | |
| 1900 | **WILLIAM McKINLEY (Ohio)** | Republican | 7,207,923 | 51.7 | 292 | 73.2 |
| | William J. Bryan | Dem.-Populist | 6,358,133 | 45.5 | 155 | |
| 1904 | **THEODORE ROOSEVELT (N.Y.)** | Republican | 7,623,486 | 57.9 | 336 | 65.2 |
| | Alton B. Parker | Democratic | 5,077,911 | 37.6 | 140 | |
| | Eugene V. Debs | Socialist | 402,283 | 3.0 | — | |
| 1908 | **WILLIAM H. TAFT (Ohio)** | Republican | 7,678,908 | 51.6 | 321 | 65.4 |
| | William J. Bryan | Democratic | 6,409,104 | 43.1 | 162 | |
| | Eugene V. Debs | Socialist | 420,793 | 2.8 | — | |
| 1912 | **WOODROW WILSON (N.J.)** | Democratic | 6,293,454 | 41.9 | 435 | 58.8 |
| | Theodore Roosevelt | Progressive | 4,119,538 | 27.4 | 88 | |
| | William H. Taft | Republican | 3,484,980 | 23.2 | 8 | |
| | Eugene V. Debs | Socialist | 900,672 | 6.1 | — | |
| 1916 | **WOODROW WILSON (N.J.)** | Democratic | 9,129,606 | 49.4 | 277 | 61.6 |
| | Charles E. Hughes | Republican | 8,538,221 | 46.2 | 254 | |
| | A. L. Benson | Socialist | 585,113 | 3.2 | — | |
| 1920 | **WARREN G. HARDING (Ohio)** | Republican | 16,143,407 | 60.5 | 404 | 49.2 |
| | James M. Cox | Democratic | 9,130,328 | 34.2 | 127 | |
| | Eugene V. Debs | Socialist | 919,799 | 3.4 | — | |
| 1924 | **CALVIN COOLIDGE (Mass.)** | Republican | 15,725,016 | 54.0 | 382 | 48.9 |
| | John W. Davis | Democratic | 8,386,503 | 28.8 | 136 | |
| | Robert M. LaFollette | Progressive | 4,822,856 | 16.6 | 13 | |
| 1928 | **HERBERT HOOVER (Calif.)** | Republican | 21,391,381 | 58.2 | 444 | 56.9 |
| | Alfred E. Smith | Democratic | 15,016,443 | 40.9 | 87 | |
| | Norman Thomas | Socialist | 267,835 | 0.7 | — | |
| 1932 | **FRANKLIN D. ROOSEVELT (N.Y.)** | Democratic | 22,809,638 | 57.4 | 472 | 56.9 |
| | Herbert Hoover | Republican | 15,758,901 | 39.7 | 59 | |
| | Norman Thomas | Socialist | 881,951 | 2.2 | — | |
| 1936 | **FRANKLIN D. ROOSEVELT (N.Y.)** | Democratic | 27,751,597 | 60.8 | 523 | 61.0 |
| | Alfred M. Landon | Republican | 16,679,583 | 36.5 | 8 | |
| | William Lemke | Union | 882,479 | 1.9 | — | |
| 1940 | **FRANKLIN D. ROOSEVELT (N.Y.)** | Democratic | 27,244,160 | 54.8 | 449 | 62.5 |
| | Wendell Willkie | Republican | 22,305,198 | 44.8 | 82 | |
| 1944 | **FRANKLIN D. ROOSEVELT (N.Y.)** | Democratic | 25,602,504 | 53.5 | 432 | 55.9 |
| | Thomas E. Dewey | Republican | 22,006,285 | 46.0 | 99 | |
| 1948 | **HARRY S. TRUMAN (Mo.)** | Democratic | 24,105,695 | 49.5 | 303 | 53.0 |
| | Thomas E. Dewey | Republican | 21,969,170 | 45.1 | 189 | |
| | J. Strom Thurmond | State-Rights Democratic | 1,169,021 | 2.4 | 38 | |
| | Henry A. Wallace | Progressive | 1,156,103 | 2.4 | — | |
| 1952 | **DWIGHT D. EISENHOWER (N.Y.)** | Republican | 33,936,252 | 55.1 | 442 | 63.3 |
| | Adlai Stevenson | Democratic | 27,314,992 | 44.4 | 89 | |
| 1956 | **DWIGHT D. EISENHOWER (N.Y.)** | Republican | 35,575,420 | 57.6 | 457 | 60.6 |
| | Adlai Stevenson | Democratic | 26,033,066 | 42.1 | 73 | |
| | Other | — | — | — | 1 | |

| Year | Candidates | Parties | Popular Vote | Percentage of Popular Vote | Electoral Vote | Percentage of Voter Participation |
|------|-----------|---------|-------------|----------------------------|----------------|------------------------------------|
| 1960 | **JOHN F. KENNEDY (Mass.)** | Democratic | 34,227,096 | 49.9 | 303 | 62.8 |
|      | Richard M. Nixon | Republican | 34,108,546 | 49.6 | 219 | |
|      | Other | — | — | | 15 | |
| 1964 | **LYNDON B. JOHNSON (Tex.)** | Democratic | 43,126,506 | 61.1 | 486 | 61.7 |
|      | Barry M. Goldwater | Republican | 27,176,799 | 38.5 | 52 | |
| 1968 | **RICHARD M. NIXON (N.Y.)** | Republican | 31,770,237 | 43.4 | 301 | 60.6 |
|      | Hubert H. Humphrey | Democratic | 31,270,533 | 42.7 | 191 | |
|      | George Wallace | American Indep. | 9,906,141 | 13.5 | 46 | |
| 1972 | **RICHARD M. NIXON (N.Y.)** | Republican | 47,169,911 | 60.7 | 520 | 55.2 |
|      | George S. McGovern | Democratic | 29,170,383 | 37.5 | 17 | |
|      | Other | — | — | | 1 | |
| 1976 | **JIMMY CARTER (Ga.)** | Democratic | 40,828,587 | 50.0 | 297 | 53.5 |
|      | Gerald R. Ford | Republican | 39,147,613 | 47.9 | 241 | |
|      | Other | — | 1,575,459 | 2.1 | — | |
| 1980 | **RONALD REAGAN (Calif.)** | Republican | 43,901,812 | 50.7 | 489 | 52.6 |
|      | Jimmy Carter | Democratic | 35,483,820 | 41.0 | 49 | |
|      | John B. Anderson | Independent | 5,719,722 | 6.6 | — | |
|      | Ed Clark | Libertarian | 921,188 | 1.1 | — | |
| 1984 | **RONALD REAGAN (Calif.)** | Republican | 54,455,075 | 59.0 | 525 | 53.3 |
|      | Walter Mondale | Democratic | 37,577,185 | 41.0 | 13 | |
| 1988 | **GEORGE BUSH (Texas)** | Republican | 47,946,422 | 54.0 | 426 | 50.2 |
|      | Michael S. Dukakis | Democratic | 41,016,429 | 46.0 | 112 | |
| 1992 | **WILLIAM J. CLINTON (Ark.)** | Democratic | 44,908,254 | 42.3 | 370 | 55.2 |
|      | George Bush | Republican | 39,102,282 | 37.4 | 168 | |
|      | H. Ross Perot | Independent | 19,721,433 | 18.9 | — | |
| 1996 | **WILLIAM J. CLINTON (Ark.)** | Democratic | 47,401,185 | 49.2 | 379 | 49.0 |
|      | Robert Dole | Republican | 39,197,469 | 40.7 | 159 | |
|      | H. Ross Perot | Independent | 8,085,294 | 8.4 | — | |

# PRESIDENTS, VICE PRESIDENTS, AND SECRETARIES OF STATE

## The Washington Administration (1789–1797)

| | | |
|---|---|---|
| Vice President | John Adams | 1789–1797 |
| Secretary of State | Thomas Jefferson | 1789–1793 |
| | Edmund Randolph | 1794–1795 |
| | Timothy Pickering | 1795–1797 |

## The John Adams Administration (1797–1801)

| | | |
|---|---|---|
| Vice President | Thomas Jefferson | 1797–1801 |
| Secretary of State | Timothy Pickering | 1797–1800 |
| | John Marshall | 1800–1801 |

## The Jefferson Administration (1801–1809)

| | | |
|---|---|---|
| Vice President | Aaron Burr | 1801–1805 |
| | George Clinton | 1805–1809 |
| Secretary of State | James Madison | 1801–1809 |

## The Madison Administration (1809–1817)

| | | |
|---|---|---|
| Vice President | George Clinton | 1809–1813 |
| | Elbridge Gerry | 1813–1817 |
| Secretary of State | Robert Smith | 1809–1811 |
| | James Monroe | 1811–1817 |

## The Monroe Administration (1817–1825)

| | | |
|---|---|---|
| Vice President | Daniel Tompkins | 1817–1825 |
| Secretary of State | John Quincy Adams | 1817–1825 |

## The John Quincy Adams Administration (1825–1829)

| | | |
|---|---|---|
| Vice President | John C. Calhoun | 1825–1829 |
| Secretary of State | Henry Clay | 1825–1829 |

## The Jackson Administration (1829–1837)

| | | |
|---|---|---|
| Vice President | John C. Calhoun | 1829–1833 |
| | Martin Van Buren | 1833–1837 |
| Secretary of State | Martin Van Buren | 1829–1831 |
| | Edward Livingston | 1831–1833 |
| | Louis McLane | 1833–1834 |
| | John Forsyth | 1834–1837 |

## The Van Buren Administration (1837–1841)

| | | |
|---|---|---|
| Vice President | Richard M. Johnson | 1837–1841 |
| Secretary of State | John Forsyth | 1837–1841 |

## The William Harrison Administration (1841)

| | | |
|---|---|---|
| Vice President | John Tyler | 1841 |
| Secretary of State | Daniel Webster | 1841 |

## The Tyler Administration (1841–1845)

| | | |
|---|---|---|
| Vice President | None | |
| Secretary of State | Daniel Webster | 1841–1843 |
| | Hugh S. Legaré | 1843 |
| | Abel P. Upshur | 1843–1844 |
| | John C. Calhoun | 1844–1845 |

## The Polk Administration (1845–1849)

| | | |
|---|---|---|
| Vice President | George M. Dallas | 1845–1849 |
| Secretary of State | James Buchanan | 1845–1849 |

## The Taylor Administration (1849–1850)

| | | |
|---|---|---|
| Vice President | Millard Fillmore | 1849–1850 |
| Secretary of State | John M. Clayton | 1849–1850 |

### The Fillmore Administration (1850–1853)

| | | |
|---|---|---|
| Vice President | None | |
| Secretary of State | Daniel Webster | 1850–1852 |
| | Edward Everett | 1852–1853 |

### The Pierce Administration (1853–1857)

| | | |
|---|---|---|
| Vice President | William R. King | 1853–1857 |
| Secretary of State | William L. Marcy | 1853–1857 |

### The Buchanan Administration (1857–1861)

| | | |
|---|---|---|
| Vice President | John C. Breckinridge | 1857–1861 |
| Secretary of State | Lewis Cass | 1857–1860 |
| | Jeremiah S. Black | 1860–1861 |

### The Lincoln Administration (1861–1865)

| | | |
|---|---|---|
| Vice President | Hannibal Hamlin | 1861–1865 |
| | Andrew Johnson | 1865 |
| Secretary of State | William H. Seward | 1861–1865 |

### The Andrew Johnson Administration (1865–1869)

| | | |
|---|---|---|
| Vice President | None | |
| Secretary of State | William H. Seward | 1865–1869 |

### The Grant Administration (1869–1877)

| | | |
|---|---|---|
| Vice President | Schuyler Colfax | 1869–1873 |
| | Henry Wilson | 1873–1877 |
| Secretary of State | Elihu B. Washburne | 1869 |
| | Hamilton Fish | 1869–1877 |

### The Hayes Administration (1877–1881)

| | | |
|---|---|---|
| Vice President | William A. Wheeler | 1877–1881 |
| Secretary of State | William M. Evarts | 1877–1881 |

### The Garfield Administration (1881)

| | | |
|---|---|---|
| Vice President | Chester A. Arthur | 1881 |
| Secretary of State | James G. Blaine | 1881 |

### The Arthur Administration (1881–1885)

| | | |
|---|---|---|
| Vice President | None | |
| Secretary of State | F. T. Frelinghuysen | 1881–1885 |

### The Cleveland Administration (1885–1889)

| | | |
|---|---|---|
| Vice President | Thomas A. Hendricks | 1885–1889 |
| Secretary of State | Thomas F. Bayard | 1885–1889 |

### The Benjamin Harrison Administration (1889–1893)

| | | |
|---|---|---|
| Vice President | Levi P. Morton | 1889–1893 |
| Secretary of State | James G. Blaine | 1889–1892 |
| | John W. Foster | 1892–1893 |

### The Cleveland Administration (1893–1897)

| | | |
|---|---|---|
| Vice President | Adlai E. Stevenson | 1893–1897 |
| Secretary of State | Walter Q. Gresham | 1893–1895 |
| | Richard Olney | 1895–1897 |

### The McKinley Administration (1897–1901)

| | | |
|---|---|---|
| Vice President | Garret A. Hobart | 1897–1901 |
| | Theodore Roosevelt | 1901 |
| Secretary of State | John Sherman | 1897–1898 |
| | William R. Day | 1898 |
| | John Hay | 1898–1901 |

### The Theodore Roosevelt Administration (1901–1909)

| | | |
|---|---|---|
| Vice President | Charles Fairbanks | 1905–1909 |
| Secretary of State | John Hay | 1901–1905 |
| | Elihu Root | 1905–1909 |
| | Robert Bacon | 1909 |

## The Taft Administration (1909–1913)

| | | |
|---|---|---|
| Vice President | James S. Sherman | 1909–1913 |
| Secretary of State | Philander C. Knox | 1909–1913 |

## The Wilson Administration (1913–1921)

| | | |
|---|---|---|
| Vice President | Thomas R. Marshall | 1913–1921 |
| Secretary of State | William J. Bryan | 1913–1915 |
| | Robert Lansing | 1915–1920 |
| | Bainbridge Colby | 1920–1921 |

## The Harding Administration (1921–1923)

| | | |
|---|---|---|
| Vice President | Calvin Coolidge | 1921–1923 |
| Secretary of State | Charles E. Hughes | 1921–1923 |

## The Coolidge Administration (1923–1929)

| | | |
|---|---|---|
| Vice President | Charles G. Dawes | 1925–1929 |
| Secretary of State | Charles E. Hughes | 1923–1925 |
| | Frank B. Kellogg | 1925–1929 |

## The Hoover Administration (1929–1933)

| | | |
|---|---|---|
| Vice President | Charles Curtis | 1929–1933 |
| Secretary of State | Henry L. Stimson | 1929–1933 |

## The Franklin D. Roosevelt Administration (1933–1945)

| | | |
|---|---|---|
| Vice President | John Nance Garner | 1933–1941 |
| | Henry A. Wallace | 1941–1945 |
| | Harry S. Truman | 1945 |
| Secretary of State | Cordell Hull | 1933–1944 |
| | Edward R. Stettinius Jr. | 1944–1945 |

## The Truman Administration (1945–1953)

| | | |
|---|---|---|
| Vice President | Alben W. Barkley | 1949–1953 |
| Secretary of State | Edward R. Stettinius Jr. | 1945 |
| | James F. Byrnes | 1945–1947 |
| | George C. Marshall | 1947–1949 |
| | Dean G. Acheson | 1949–1953 |

## The Eisenhower Administration (1953–1961)

| | | |
|---|---|---|
| Vice President | Richard M. Nixon | 1953–1961 |
| Secretary of State | John Foster Dulles | 1953–1959 |
| | Christian A. Herter | 1959–1961 |

## The Kennedy Administration (1961–1963)

| | | |
|---|---|---|
| Vice President | Lyndon B. Johnson | 1961–1963 |
| Secretary of State | Dean Rusk | 1961–1963 |

## The Lyndon Johnson Administration (1963–1969)

| | | |
|---|---|---|
| Vice President | Hubert H. Humphrey | 1965–1969 |
| Secretary of State | Dean Rusk | 1963–1969 |

## The Nixon Administration (1969–1974)

| | | |
|---|---|---|
| Vice President | Spiro T. Agnew | 1969–1973 |
| | Gerald R. Ford | 1973–1974 |
| Secretary of State | William P. Rogers | 1969–1973 |
| | Henry A. Kissinger | 1973–1974 |

## The Ford Administration (1974–1977)

| | | |
|---|---|---|
| Vice President | Nelson A. Rockefeller | 1974–1977 |
| Secretary of State | Henry A. Kissinger | 1974–1977 |

### The Carter Administration (1977–1981)

| Vice President | Walter F. Mondale | 1977–1981 |
| Secretary of State | Cyrus R. Vance | 1977–1980 |
|  | Edmund Muskie | 1980–1981 |

### The Reagan Administration (1981–1989)

| Vice President | George W. Bush | 1981–1989 |
| Secretary of State | Alexander M. Haig | 1981–1982 |
|  | George P. Shultz | 1982–1989 |

### The Bush Administration (1989–1993)

| Vice President | J. Danforth Quayle | 1989–1993 |
| Secretary of State | James A. Baker III | 1989–1992 |
|  | Lawrence S. Eagleburger | 1992–1993 |

### The Clinton Administration (1993–2000)

| Vice President | Albert Gore | 1993–2000 |
| Secretary of State | Warren M. Christopher | 1993–1997 |
|  | Madeleine K. Albright | 1997–2000 |

# ADMISSION OF STATES TO THE UNION

| State | Date of Admission | State | Date of Admission |
| --- | --- | --- | --- |
| Delaware | December 7, 1787 | Michigan | January 16, 1837 |
| Pennsylvania | December 12, 1787 | Florida | March 3, 1845 |
| New Jersey | December 18, 1787 | Texas | December 29, 1845 |
| Georgia | January 2, 1788 | Iowa | December 28, 1846 |
| Connecticut | January 9, 1788 | Wisconsin | May 29, 1848 |
| Massachusetts | February 6, 1788 | California | September 9, 1850 |
| Maryland | April 28, 1788 | Minnesota | May 11, 1858 |
| South Carolina | May 23, 1788 | Oregon | February 14, 1859 |
| New Hampshire | June 21, 1788 | Kansas | January 29, 1861 |
| Virginia | June 25, 1788 | West Virginia | June 19, 1863 |
| New York | July 26, 1788 | Nevada | October 31, 1864 |
| North Carolina | November 21, 1789 | Nebraska | March 1, 1867 |
| Rhode Island | May 29, 1790 | Colorado | August 1, 1876 |
| Vermont | March 4, 1791 | North Dakota | November 2, 1889 |
| Kentucky | June 1, 1792 | South Dakota | November 2, 1889 |
| Tennessee | June 1, 1796 | Montana | November 8, 1889 |
| Ohio | March 1, 1803 | Washington | November 11, 1889 |
| Louisiana | April 30, 1812 | Idaho | July 3, 1890 |
| Indiana | December 11, 1816 | Wyoming | July 10, 1890 |
| Mississippi | December 10, 1817 | Utah | January 4, 1896 |
| Illinois | December 3, 1818 | Oklahoma | November 16, 1907 |
| Alabama | December 14, 1819 | New Mexico | January 6, 1912 |
| Maine | March 15, 1820 | Arizona | February 14, 1912 |
| Missouri | August 10, 1821 | Alaska | January 3, 1959 |
| Arkansas | June 15, 1836 | Hawaii | August 21, 1959 |

# SUPREME COURT JUSTICES

| Name | Service | Appointed by |
|------|---------|--------------|
| **John Jay*** | 1789–1795 | Washington |
| James Wilson | 1789–1798 | Washington |
| John Blair | 1789–1796 | Washington |
| John Rutledge | 1790–1791 | Washington |
| William Cushing | 1790–1810 | Washington |
| James Iredell | 1790–1799 | Washington |
| Thomas Johnson | 1791–1793 | Washington |
| William Paterson | 1793–1806 | Washington |
| **John Rutledge†** | 1795 | Washington |
| Samuel Chase | 1796–1811 | Washington |
| **Oliver Ellsworth** | 1796–1799 | Washington |
| Bushrod Washington | 1798–1829 | J. Adams |
| Alfred Moore | 1799–1804 | J. Adams |
| **John Marshall** | 1801–1835 | J. Adams |
| William Johnson | 1804–1834 | Jefferson |
| Henry B. Livingston | 1806–1823 | Jefferson |
| Thomas Todd | 1807–1826 | Jefferson |
| Gabriel Duval | 1811–1836 | Madison |
| Joseph Story | 1811–1845 | Madison |
| Smith Thompson | 1823–1843 | Monroe |
| Robert Trimble | 1826–1828 | J. Q. Adams |
| John McLean | 1829–1861 | Jackson |
| Henry Baldwin | 1830–1844 | Jackson |
| James M. Wayne | 1835–1867 | Jackson |
| **Roger B. Taney** | 1836–1864 | Jackson |
| Philip P. Barbour | 1836–1841 | Jackson |
| John Catron | 1837–1865 | Van Buren |
| John McKinley | 1837–1852 | Van Buren |
| Peter V. Daniel | 1841–1860 | Van Buren |
| Samuel Nelson | 1845–1872 | Tyler |
| Levi Woodbury | 1845–1851 | Polk |
| Robert C. Grier | 1846–1870 | Polk |
| Benjamin R. Curtis | 1851–1857 | Fillmore |
| John A. Campbell | 1853–1861 | Pierce |
| Nathan Clifford | 1858–1881 | Buchanan |
| Noah H. Swayne | 1862–1881 | Lincoln |
| Samuel F. Miller | 1862–1890 | Lincoln |

*Chief Justices appear in bold type.
†Acting Chief Justice; Senate refused to confirm appointment.

| Name | Service | Appointed by |
|------|---------|--------------|
| David Davis | 1862–1877 | Lincoln |
| Stephen J. Field | 1863–1897 | Lincoln |
| **Salmon P. Chase** | 1864–1873 | Lincoln |
| William Strong | 1870–1880 | Grant |
| Joseph P. Bradley | 1870–1892 | Grant |
| Ward Hunt | 1873–1882 | Grant |
| **Morrison R. Waite** | 1874–1888 | Grant |
| John M. Harlan | 1877–1911 | Hayes |
| William B. Woods | 1880–1887 | Hayes |
| Stanley Matthews | 1881–1889 | Garfield |
| Horace Gray | 1882–1902 | Arthur |
| Samuel Blatchford | 1882–1893 | Arthur |
| Lucious Q. C. Lamar | 1888–1893 | Cleveland |
| **Melville W. Fuller** | 1888–1910 | Cleveland |
| David J. Brewer | 1889–1910 | B. Harrison |
| Henry B. Brown | 1890–1906 | B. Harrison |
| George Shiras | 1892–1903 | B. Harrison |
| Howell E. Jackson | 1893–1895 | B. Harrison |
| Edward D. White | 1894–1910 | Cleveland |
| Rufus W. Peckham | 1896–1909 | Cleveland |
| Joseph McKenna | 1898–1925 | McKinley |
| Oliver W. Holmes | 1902–1932 | T. Roosevelt |
| William R. Day | 1903–1922 | T. Roosevelt |
| William H. Moody | 1906–1910 | T. Roosevelt |
| Horace H. Lurton | 1910–1914 | Taft |
| Charles E. Hughes | 1910–1916 | Taft |
| Willis Van Devanter | 1910–1937 | Taft |
| Joseph R. Lamar | 1911–1916 | Taft |
| **Edward D. White** | 1910–1921 | Taft |
| Mahlon Pitney | 1912–1922 | Taft |
| James C. McReynolds | 1914–1941 | Wilson |
| Louis D. Brandeis | 1916–1939 | Wilson |
| John H. Clarke | 1916–1922 | Wilson |
| **William H. Taft** | 1921–1930 | Harding |
| George Sutherland | 1922–1938 | Harding |

| Name | Service | Appointed by |
|------|---------|--------------|
| Pierce Butler | 1923–1939 | Harding |
| Edward T. Sanford | 1923–1930 | Harding |
| Harlan F. Stone | 1925–1941 | Coolidge |
| **Charles E. Hughes** | 1930–1941 | Hoover |
| Owen J. Roberts | 1930–1945 | Hoover |
| Benjamin N. Cardozo | 1932–1938 | Hoover |
| Hugo L. Black | 1937–1971 | F. Roosevelt |
| Stanley F. Reed | 1938–1957 | F. Roosevelt |
| Felix Frankfurter | 1939–1962 | F. Roosevelt |
| William O. Douglas | 1939–1975 | F. Roosevelt |
| Frank Murphy | 1940–1949 | F. Roosevelt |
| **Harlan F. Stone** | 1941–1946 | F. Roosevelt |
| James F. Byrnes | 1941–1942 | F. Roosevelt |
| Robert H. Jackson | 1941–1954 | F. Roosevelt |
| Wiley B. Rutledge | 1943–1949 | F. Roosevelt |
| Harold H. Burton | 1945–1958 | Truman |
| **Frederick M. Vinson** | 1946–1953 | Truman |
| Tom C. Clark | 1949–1967 | Truman |
| Sherman Minton | 1949–1956 | Truman |
| **Earl Warren** | 1953–1969 | Eisenhower |
| John Marshall Harlan | 1955–1971 | Eisenhower |
| William J. Brennan Jr. | 1956–1990 | Eisenhower |
| Charles E. Whittaker | 1957–1962 | Eisenhower |

| Name | Service | Appointed by |
|------|---------|--------------|
| Potter Stewart | 1958–1981 | Eisenhower |
| Byron R. White | 1962–1993 | Kennedy |
| Arthur J. Goldberg | 1962–1965 | Kennedy |
| Abe Fortas | 1965–1969 | L. Johnson |
| Thurgood Marshall | 1967–1991 | L. Johnson |
| **Warren E. Burger** | 1969–1986 | Nixon |
| Harry A. Blackmun | 1970–1994 | Nixon |
| Lewis F. Powell Jr. | 1972–1988 | Nixon |
| William H. Rehnquist | 1972–1986 | Nixon |
| John Paul Stevens | 1975– | Ford |
| Sandra Day O'Connor | 1981– | Reagan |
| **William H. Rehnquist** | 1986– | Reagan |
| Antonin Scalia | 1986– | Reagan |
| Anthony M. Kennedy | 1988– | Reagan |
| David H. Souter | 1990– | Bush |
| Clarence Thomas | 1991– | Bush |
| Ruth Bader Ginsburg | 1993– | Clinton |
| Stephen Breyer | 1994– | Clinton |

# SIGNIFICANT SUPREME COURT CASES

## Marbury v. Madison (1803)

This case established the right of the Supreme Court to review the constitutionality of laws. The decision involved judicial appointments made during the last hours of the administration of President John Adams. Some commissions, including that of William Marbury, had not yet been delivered when President Thomas Jefferson took office. Infuriated by the last-minute nature of Adams's Federalist appointments, Jefferson refused to send the undelivered commissions out, and Marbury decided to sue. The Supreme Court, presided over by John Marshall, a Federalist who had assisted Adams in the judicial appointments, ruled that although Marbury's commission was valid and the new president should have delivered it, the Court could not compel him to do so. The Court based its reasoning on a finding that the grounds of Marbury's suit, resting in the Judiciary Act of 1789, were in conflict with the Constitution.

For the first time, the Court had overturned a national law on the grounds that it was unconstitutional. John Marshall had quietly established the concept of judicial review: The Supreme Court had given itself the authority to nullify acts of the other branches of the federal government. Although the Constitution provides for judicial review, the Court had not exercised this power before and did not use it again until 1857. It seems likely that if the Court had waited until 1857 to use this power, it would have been difficult to establish.

## McCulloch v. Maryland (1819)

In 1816, Congress authorized the creation of a national bank. To protect its own banks from competition with a branch of the national bank in Baltimore, the state legislature of Maryland placed a tax of 2 percent on all notes issued by any bank operating in Maryland that was not chartered by the state. McCulloch, cashier of the Baltimore branch of the Bank of the United States, was convicted for refusing to pay the tax. Under the leadership of Chief Justice John Marshall, the Court ruled that the federal government had the power to establish a bank, even though that specific authority was not mentioned in the Constitution.

Marshall maintained that the authority could be reasonably implied from Article 1, section 8, which gives Congress the power to make all laws that are necessary and proper to execute the enumerated powers.

Marshall also held that Maryland could not tax the national bank because in a conflict between federal and state laws, the federal law must take precedence. Thus he established the principles of implied powers and federal supremacy, both of which set a precedent for subsequent expansion of federal power at the expense of the states.

## Scott v. Sanford (1857)

Dred Scott was a slave who sued for his own and his family's freedom on the grounds, that, with his master, he had traveled to and lived in free territory that did not allow slavery. When his case reached the Supreme Court, the justices saw an opportunity to settle once and for all the vexing question of slavery in the territories. The Court's decision in this case proved that it enjoyed no special immunity from the sectional and partisan passions of the time. Five of the nine justices were from the South and seven were Democrats.

Chief Justice Roger B. Taney hated Republicans and detested racial equality; his decision reflects those prejudices. He wrote an opinion not only declaring that Scott was still a slave but also claiming that the Constitution denied citizenship or rights to blacks, that Congress had no right to exclude slavery from the territories, and that the Missouri Compromise was unconstitutional. While southern Democrats gloated over this seven-to-two decision, sectional tensions were further inflamed and the young Republican Party's claim that a hostile "slave power" was conspiring to destroy northern liberties was given further credence. The decision brought the nation closer to civil war and is generally regarded as the worst decision ever rendered by the Supreme Court.

## Butchers' Benevolent Association of New Orleans v. Crescent City Livestock Landing and Slaughterhouse Co. (1873)

The *Slaughterhouse* cases, as the cases docketed under the *Butchers'* title were known, were the first legal test of the Fourteenth Amendment. To cut down on cases of cholera believed to be caused by contaminated water, the state of Louisiana prohibited the slaughter of livestock in New Orleans except in one slaughterhouse, effectively giving that slaughterhouse a monopoly. Other New Orleans butchers claimed that the state had deprived them of their occupation without due process of law, thus violating the Fourteenth Amendment.

In a five-to-four decision, the Court upheld the Louisiana law, declaring that the Fourteenth Amendment protected only the rights of federal citizenship, like voting in federal elections and interstate travel. The federal government thus was not obliged to protect basic civil rights from violation by state governments. This decison would have significant implications for African Americans and their struggle for civil rights in the twentieth century.

## United States v. E. C. Knight Co. (1895)

Also known as the *Sugar Trust* case, this was among the first cases to reveal the weakness of the Sherman Antitrust Act in the hands of a pro-business Supreme Court. In 1895, American Sugar Refining Company purchased four other sugar producers, including the E. C. Knight Company, and thus took control of more than 98 percent of the sugar refining in the United States. In an effort to limit monopoly, the government brought suit against all five of the companies for violating the Sherman Antitrust Act, which outlawed trusts and other business combinations in restraint of trade. The Court dismissed the suit, however, arguing that the law applied only to commerce and not to manufacturing, defining the latter as a local concern and not part of the interstate commerce that the government could regulate.

## Plessy v. Ferguson (1896)

African American Homer Plessy challenged a Louisiana law that required segregation on trains passing through the state. After ensuring that the railroad and the conductor knew that he was of mixed race (Plessy appeared to be white but under the racial code of Louisiana was classified as "colored" because he was one-eighth black), he refused to move to the "colored only" section of the coach. The Court ruled against Plessy by a vote of seven to one, declaring that "separate but equal" facilities were permissible according to section 1 of the Fourteenth Amendment, which calls upon the states to provide "equal protection of the laws" to anyone within their jurisdiction. Although the case was viewed as relatively insignificant at the time, it cast a long shadow over several decades.

Initially, the decision was viewed as a victory for segregationists, but in the 1930s and 1940s civil rights advocates referred to the doctrine of "separate but equal" in their efforts to end segregation. They argued that segregated institutions and accommodations were often *not* equal to those available to whites, and finally succeeded in overturning *Plessy* in *Brown v. Board of Education* in 1954 (see p. A-35).

## Lochner v. New York (1905)

In this case, the Court ruled against a New York state law that prohibited employees from working in bakeries more than ten hours a day or sixty hours a week. The purpose of the law was to protect the health of workers, but the Court ruled that it was unconstitutional because it violated "freedom of contract" implicitly protected by the due process clause of the Fourteenth Amendment. Most of the justices believed strongly in a laissez-faire economic system that favored survival of the fittest. They felt that government protection of workers interfered with this system. In a dissenting opinion, Justice Oliver Wendell Holmes accused the majority of distorting the Constitution and of deciding the case on "an economic theory which a large part of the country does not entertain."

## Muller v. Oregon (1908)

In 1905, Curt Muller, owner of a Portland, Oregon, laundry, demanded that one of his employees, Mrs. Elmer Gotcher, work more than the ten hours allowed as a maximum workday for women under Oregon law. Muller argued that the law violated his "freedom of contract" as established in prior Supreme Court decisions.

Progressive lawyer Louis D. Brandeis defended the Oregon law by arguing that a state could be justified in abridging freedom of contract when the health, safety, and welfare of workers was at issue. His innovative strategy drew on ninety-five pages of excerpts from factory and medical reports to substantiate his argument that there was a direct connection between long hours and the health of women and thus the health of the nation. In a unanimous decision, the Court upheld the Oregon law, but later generations of women fighting for equality would question the strategy of arguing that women's reproductive role entitled them to special treatment.

## Schenck v. United States (1919)

During World War I, Charles Schenck and other members of the Socialist Party printed and mailed out flyers urging young men who were subject to the draft to oppose the war in Europe. In upholding the conviction of Schenck for publishing a pamphlet urging draft resistance, Justice Oliver Wendell Holmes established the "clear and present danger" test for freedom of speech. Such utterances as Schenck's during a time of national peril, Holmes wrote, could be considered the equivalent of shouting "Fire!" in a crowded theater. Congress had the right to protect the public against such an incitement to panic, the Court ruled in a unanimous decision. But the analogy was a false one. Schenck's pamphlet had little power to provoke a public firmly opposed to its message. Although Holmes later modified his position to state that the danger must relate to an immediate evil and a specific action, the "clear and present danger" test laid the groundwork for those who later sought to limit First Amendment freedoms.

## Schechter Poultry Corp. v. United States (1935)

During the Great Depression, the National Industrial Recovery Act (NIRA), which was passed under President Franklin D. Roosevelt, established fair competition codes that were designed to help businesses. The Schechter brothers of New York City, who sold chickens, were convicted of violating the codes. The Supreme Court ruled that the NIRA unconstitutionally conferred legislative power on an administrative agency and overstepped the limits of federal power to regulate interstate commerce. The decision was a significant blow to the New Deal recovery program, demonstrating both historic American resistance to economic planning and the refusal of the business community to yield its autonomy unless it was forced to do so.

## Brown v. Board of Education (1954)

In 1950, the families of eight Topeka, Kansas, children sued the Topeka Board of Education. The children were blacks who lived within walking distance of a whites-only school. The segregated school system required them to take a time-consuming, inconvenient, and dangerous route to get to a black school, and their parents argued that there was no reason their children should not be allowed to attend the nearest school. By the time the case reached the Supreme Court, it had been joined with similar cases regarding segregated schools in other states and the District of Columbia. A team of lawyers from the National Association for the Advancement of Colored People (NAACP), led by Thurgood Marshall (who would later be appointed to the Supreme Court), urged the Court to overturn the fifty-eight-year-old precedent established in *Plessy v. Ferguson*, which had enshrined "separate but equal" as the law of the land. A unanimous Court, led by Chief Justice Earl Warren, declared that "separate educa-

tional facilities are inherently unequal" and thus violate the Fourteenth Amendment. In 1955, the Court called for desegregation "with all deliberate speed" but established no deadline.

## Roth v. United States (1957)

In 1957, New Yorker Samuel Roth was convicted of sending obscene materials through the mail in a case that ultimately reached the Supreme Court. With a six-to-three vote, the Court reaffirmed the historical view that obscenity is not protected by the First Amendment. Yet it broke new ground by declaring that a work could be judged obscene only if, "taken as a whole," it appealed to the "prurient interest" of "the average person."

Prior to this case, work could be judged obscene if portions were thought able to "deprave and corrupt" the most susceptible part of an audience (such as children). Thus, serious works of literature such as Theodore Dreiser's *An American Tragedy*, which was banned in Boston when first published, had received no protection. Although this decision continued to pose problems of definition, it did help to protect most works that attempt to convey ideas, even if those ideas have to do with sex, from the threat of obscenity laws.

## Engel v. Vitale (1962)

In 1959, five parents with ten children in the New Hyde Park, New York, school system sued the school board. The parents argued that the so-called Regents' Prayer that public school students in New York recited at the start of every school day violated the doctrine of separation of church and state outlined in the First Amendment. In 1962, the Supreme Court voted six to one in favor of banning the Regents' Prayer.

The decision threw the religious community into an uproar. Many religious leaders expressed dismay and even shock; others welcomed the decision. Several efforts to introduce an amendment allowing school prayer have failed. Subsequent Supreme Court decisions have banned reading of the Bible in public schools. The Court has also declared mandatory flag saluting to be an infringement of religious and personal freedoms.

## Gideon v. Wainwright (1963)

When Clarence Earl Gideon was tried for breaking into a poolroom, the state of Florida rejected his demand for a court-appointed lawyer as guaranteed by the Sixth Amendment. In 1963, the Court upheld his demand in a unanimous decision that established the obligation of states to provide attorneys for indigent defendants in felony cases. Prior to this decision, the right to an attorney had applied only to federal cases, not state cases. In its ruling in *Gideon v. Wainwright*, the Supreme Court applied the Sixth through the Fourteenth Amendments to the states. In 1972, the Supreme Court extended the right to legal representation to all cases, not just felony cases, in its decision in *Argersinger v. Hamlin*.

## Griswold v. Connecticut (1965)

With a vote of seven to two, the Supreme Court reversed an "uncommonly silly law" (in the words of Justice Potter Stewart) that made it a crime for anyone in the state of Connecticut to use any drug, article, or instrument to prevent conception. *Griswold* became a landmark case because here, for the first time, the Court explicitly invested with full constitutional status "fundamental personal rights," such as the right to privacy, that were not expressly enumerated in the Bill of Rights. The majority opinion in the case held that the law infringed on the constitutionally protected right to privacy of married persons.

Although the Court had previously recognized fundamental rights not expressly enumerated in the Bill of Rights (such as the right to procreate in *Skinner v. Oklahoma* in 1942), *Griswold* was the first time the Court had justified, at length, the practice of investing such unenumerated rights with full constitutional status. Writing for the majority, Justice William O. Douglas explained that the First, Third, Fourth, Fifth, and Ninth Amendments imply "zones of privacy" that are the foundation for the general right to privacy affirmed in this case.

## Miranda v. Arizona (1966)

In 1966, the Supreme Court, by a vote of five to four, upheld the case of Ernesto Miranda, who appealed a murder conviction on the grounds that police had gotten him to confess without giving him access to an attorney. The *Miranda* case was the culmination of the Court's efforts to find a meaningful way of determining whether police had used due process in extracting confessions from people accused of crimes. The *Miranda* decision upholds the Fifth Amendment protection against self-incrimination outside the courtroom and requires that suspects be given what came to be known as the "Miranda warning," which advises them of their right to remain silent and warns them that anything they say might be used against them in a court of law. Suspects must also be told that they have a right to counsel.

## New York Times Co. v. United States (1971)

With a six-to-three vote, the Court upheld the right of the *New York Times* and the *Washington Post* to print materials from the so-called *Pentagon Papers*, a secret government study of U.S. policy in Vietnam, leaked by dissident Pentagon official Daniel Ellsberg. Since the papers revealed deception and secrecy in the conduct of the Vietnam War, the Nixon administration had quickly obtained a court injunction against their further publication, claiming that suppression was in the interests of national security. The Supreme Court's decision overturning the injunction strengthened the First Amendment protection of freedom of the press.

## Furman v. Georgia (1972)

In this case, the Supreme Court ruled five to four that the death penalty for murder or rape violated the cruel and unusual punishment clause of the Eighth Amendment because the manner in which the death penalty was meted out was irregular, "arbitrary," and "cruel." In response, most states enacted new statutes that allow the death penalty to be imposed only after a postconviction hearing at which evidence must be presented to show that "aggravating" or "mitigating" circumstances were factors in the crime. If the postconviction hearing hands down a death sentence, the case is automatically reviewed by an appellate court.

In 1976, the Court ruled in *Gregg v. Georgia* that these statutes were not unconstitutional. In 1977, the Court ruled in *Coker v. Georgia* that the death penalty for rape was "disproportionate and excessive," thus allowing the death penalty only in murder cases. Between 1977 and 1991, some 150 people were executed in the United States. Public opinion polls indicate that about 70 percent of Americans favor the death penalty for murder. Capital punishment continues to generate controversy, however, as opponents argue that there is no evidence that the death penalty deters crime and that its use reflects racial and economic bias.

## Roe v. Wade (1973)

In 1973, the Court found, by a vote of seven to two, that state laws restricting access to abortion violated a woman's right to privacy guaranteed by the due process clause of the Fourteenth Amendment. The decision was based on the cases of two women living in Texas and Georgia, both states with stringent anti-abortion laws. Upholding the individual rights of both women and physicians, the Court ruled that the Constitution protects the right to abortion and that states cannot prohibit abortions in the early stages of pregnancy.

The decision stimulated great debate among legal scholars as well as the public. Critics argued that since abortion was never addressed in the Constitution, the Court could not claim that legislation violated fundamental values of the Constitution. They also argued that since abortion was a medical procedure with an acknowledged impact on a fetus, it was inappropriate to invoke the kind of "privacy" argument that was used in *Griswold v. Connecticut* (see p. A-36), which was about contraception. Defenders suggested that the case should be argued as a case of gender discrimination, which did violate the equal protection clause of the Fourteenth Amendment. Others said that the right to privacy in sexual matters was indeed a fundamental right.

## Regents of the University of California v. Bakke (1978)

When Allan Bakke, a white man, was not accepted by the University of California Medical School at Davis, he filed a lawsuit alleging that the admissions program, which set up different standards for test scores and grades for members of certain minority groups, violated the Civil Rights Act of 1964, which outlawed racial or ethnic preferences in programs supported by federal funds. Bakke further argued that the university's practice of setting aside spaces for minority applicants denied him equal protection as guaranteed by the Fourteenth Amendment. In a five-to-four decision, the Court ordered that Bakke be admitted to the medical school, yet it sanctioned affirmative action programs to attack the results of past discrimination as long as strict quotas or racial classifications were not involved.

## Webster v. Reproductive Health Services (1989)

By a vote of five to four, the Court upheld several restrictions on the availability of abortions as imposed by Missouri state law. It upheld restrictions on the use of state property, including public hospitals, for abortions. It also upheld a provision requiring physicians to perform tests to determine the viability of a fetus that a doctor judged to be twenty weeks of age or older. Although the justices did not go so far as to overturn the decision in *Roe v. Wade* (see p. A-36), the ruling galvanized interest groups on both sides of the abortion issue. Opponents of abortion pressured state legislatures to place greater restrictions on abortions; those who favored availability of abortion tried to mobilize public action by presenting the decision as a major threat to the right to choose abortion.

## Cipollone v. Liggett (1992)

In a seven-to-two decision, the Court ruled in favor of the family of Rose Cipollone, a woman who died of lung cancer after smoking for forty-two years. The Court rejected arguments that health warnings on cigarette packages protected tobacco manufacturers from personal injury suits filed by smokers who contract cancer and other serious illnesses.

## Miller v. Johnson (1995)

In a five-to-four decision, the Supreme Court ruled that voting districts created to increase the voting power of racial minorities were unconstitutional. The decision threatens dozens of congressional, state, and local voting districts that were drawn to give minorities more representation as had been required by the Justice Department under the Voting Rights Act. If states are required to redraw voting districts, the number of black members of Congress could be sharply reduced.

## Romer v. Evans (1996)

In a six-to-three decision, the Court struck down a Colorado amendment that forbade local governments from banning discrimination against homosexuals. Writing for the majority, Justice Anthony Kennedy said that forbidding communities from taking action to protect the rights of homosexuals and not of other groups unlawfully deprived gays and lesbians of opportunities that were available to others. Kennedy based the decision on the guarantee of equal protection under the law as provided by the Fourteenth Amendment.

# THE AMERICAN ECONOMY

These four "snapshots" of the U.S. economy show significant changes over the past century and a half. In 1849, the agricultural sector was by far the largest contributor to the economy. By the turn of the century, with advances in technology and an abundance of cheap labor and raw materials, the country had experienced remarkable industrial expansion and the manufacturing industries dominated. By 1950, the service sector had increased significantly, fueled by the consumerism of the 1920s and the post–World War II years, and the economy was becoming more diversified. Note that by 1990, government's share in the economy was more than 10 percent and activity in both the trade and manufacturing sectors had declined, partly as a result of competition from Western Europe and Asia.

## *Main Sectors of the U.S. Economy: 1849, 1899, 1950, 1990*

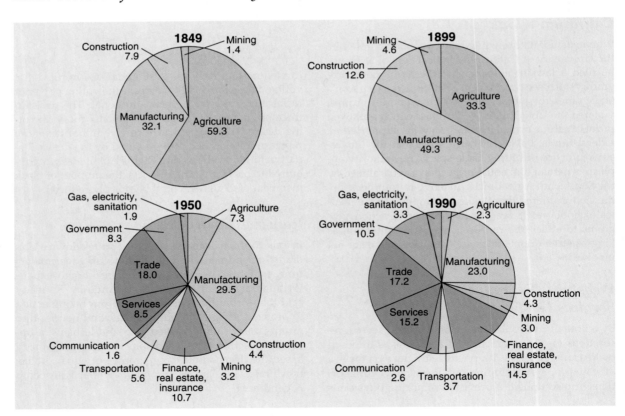

*Source: Historical Statistics of the U.S., Colonial Times to 1970 (1975) and Statistical Abstract of the U.S., 1996 (1996).*

## Federal Spending and the Economy, 1790–1995

| Year | Gross National Product (in billions) | Foreign Trade (in millions) Exports | Imports | Federal Budget (in billions) | Federal Surplus/Deficit (in billions) | Federal Debt (in billions) |
|------|------|------|------|------|------|------|
| 1790 | NA | 20 | 23 | 0.004 | 0.00015 | 0.076 |
| 1800 | NA | 71 | 91 | 0.011 | 0.0006 | 0.083 |
| 1810 | NA | 67 | 85 | 0.008 | 0.0012 | 0.053 |
| 1820 | NA | 70 | 74 | 0.018 | −0.0004 | 0.091 |
| 1830 | NA | 74 | 71 | 0.015 | 0.100 | 0.049 |
| 1840 | NA | 132 | 107 | 0.024 | −0.005 | 0.004 |
| 1850 | NA | 152 | 178 | 0.040 | 0.004 | 0.064 |
| 1860 | NA | 400 | 362 | 0.063 | −0.01 | 0.065 |
| 1870 | 7.4 | 451 | 462 | 0.310 | 0.10 | 2.4 |
| 1880 | 11.2 | 853 | 761 | 0.268 | 0.07 | 2.1 |
| 1890 | 13.1 | 910 | 823 | 0.318 | 0.09 | 1.2 |
| 1900 | 18.7 | 1,499 | 930 | 0.521 | 0.05 | 1.2 |
| 1910 | 35.3 | 1,919 | 1,646 | 0.694 | −0.02 | 1.1 |
| 1920 | 91.5 | 8,664 | 5,784 | 6.357 | 0.3 | 24.3 |
| 1930 | 90.4 | 4,013 | 3,500 | 3.320 | 0.7 | 16.3 |
| 1940 | 99.7 | 4,030 | 7,433 | 9.6 | −2.7 | 43.0 |
| 1950 | 284.8 | 10,816 | 9,125 | 43.1 | −2.2 | 257.4 |
| 1960 | 503.7 | 19,600 | 15,046 | 92.2 | 0.3 | 286.3 |
| 1970 | 977.1 | 42,700 | 40,189 | 195.6 | −2.8 | 371.0 |
| 1980 | 2,631.7 | 220,600 | 244,871 | 590.9 | −73.8 | 907.7 |
| 1990 | 5,524.5 | 393,600 | 495,300 | 1,252.15 | −221.1 | 3,233.3 |
| 1995 | 7,237.5 | 583,900 | 743,400 | 1,519.1 | −163.9 | 4,921.0 |

Source: Historical Statistics of the U.S., Colonial Times to 1970 (1975) and Statistical Abstract of the U.S., 1996 (1996).

# A DEMOGRAPHIC PROFILE OF THE UNITED STATES AND ITS PEOPLE

## POPULATION

FROM AN ESTIMATED 4,600 WHITE INHABITANTS IN 1630, the country's population grew to a total of just under 250 million in 1990. It is important to note that the U.S. census, first conducted in 1790 and the source of these figures, counted blacks, both free and slave, but did not include American Indians until 1860. The years 1790 to 1900 saw the most rapid population growth, with an average increase of 25 to 35 percent per decade. In addition to "natural" growth—birthrate exceeding death rate—immigration was also a factor in that rise, especially between 1840 and 1860, 1880 and 1890, and 1900 and 1910 (see table on page A-45). The twentieth century witnessed slower growth, partly a result of 1920s immigration restrictions and a decline in the birthrate, especially during the Depression era and the 1960s and 1970s. The U.S. population is expected to reach almost 300 million by the year 2010.

A DEMOGRAPHIC PROFILE OF THE UNITED STATES AND ITS PEOPLE

## Population Growth, 1630–2000

| Year | Population | Percent Increase |
|------|-----------|------------------|
| 1630 | 4,600 | — |
| 1640 | 26,600 | 473.3 |
| 1650 | 50,400 | 89.1 |
| 1660 | 75,100 | 49.0 |
| 1670 | 111,900 | 49.1 |
| 1680 | 151,500 | 35.4 |
| 1690 | 210,400 | 38.9 |
| 1700 | 250,900 | 19.3 |
| 1710 | 331,700 | 32.2 |
| 1720 | 466,200 | 40.5 |
| 1730 | 629,400 | 35.0 |
| 1740 | 905,600 | 43.9 |
| 1750 | 1,170,800 | 30.0 |
| 1760 | 1,593,600 | 36.1 |
| 1770 | 2,148,100 | 34.8 |
| 1780 | 2,780,400 | 29.4 |
| 1790 | 3,929,214 | 41.3 |
| 1800 | 5,308,483 | 35.1 |
| 1810 | 7,239,881 | 36.4 |
| 1820 | 9,638,453 | 33.1 |
| 1830 | 12,866,020 | 33.5 |
| 1840 | 17,069,453 | 32.7 |
| 1850 | 23,191,876 | 35.9 |
| 1860 | 31,443,321 | 35.6 |
| 1870 | 39,818,449 | 26.6 |
| 1880 | 50,155,783 | 26.0 |
| 1890 | 62,947,714 | 25.5 |
| 1900 | 75,994,575 | 20.7 |
| 1910 | 91,972,266 | 21.0 |
| 1920 | 105,710,620 | 14.9 |
| 1930 | 122,775,046 | 16.1 |
| 1940 | 131,669,275 | 7.2 |
| 1950 | 150,697,361 | 14.5 |
| 1960 | 179,323,175 | 19.0 |
| 1970 | 203,302,031 | 13.4 |
| 1980 | 226,542,199 | 11.4 |
| 1990 | 248,718,301 | 9.8 |
| 2000 | 274,634,000* | 11.0 |

*Projected

Source: Historical Statistics of the U.S. (1960), Historical Statistics of the U.S., Colonial Times to 1970 (1975), and Statistical Abstract of the U.S., 1996 (1996).

# VITAL STATISTICS

WITH SOME MINOR FLUCTUATIONS, the birthrate has been on a downward trend throughout the past century and a half, dipping especially low during the 1930s Depression years, when many economically hard-hit Americans postponed having children. A major exception to this decline was the steep but temporary rise nicknamed the "baby boom," which occurred during the relatively affluent post–World War II period. Improvements in health care and lifestyles have contributed to a decline in the death rate over the past century, which in turn has increased life expectancy figures. Over time, as people lived longer and the birthrate declined, the median age of Americans has increased from approximately seventeen in 1820 to thirty-three in 1990 and continues to rise.

### *Birthrate, 1820–2000*

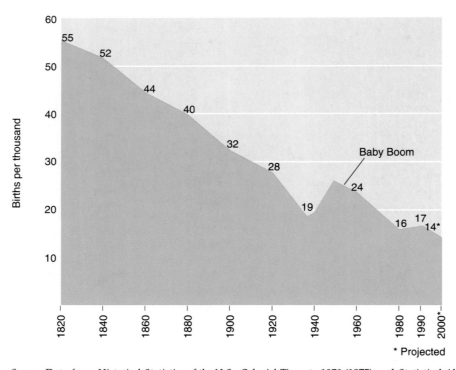

\* Projected

*Source:* Data from *Historical Statistics of the U.S., Colonial Times to 1970* (1975) and *Statistical Abstract of the U.S., 1996* (1996).

## *Death Rate, 1900–2000*

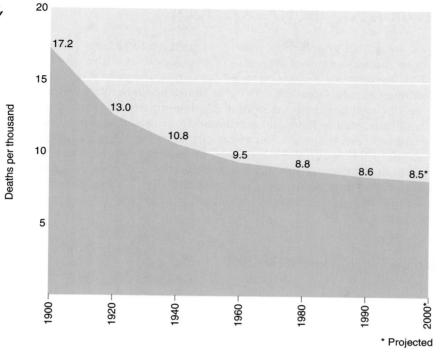

Source:    *Historical Statistics of the U.S., Colonial Times to 1970 (1975) and
Statistical Abstract of the U.S., 1996 (1996).*

## *Life Expectancy, 1900–2000*

Source:    *Historical Statistics of the U.S., Colonial Times to 1970 (1975) and
Statistical Abstract of the U.S., 1996 (1996).*

# MIGRATION AND IMMIGRATION

We tend to associate internal migration with movement westward, yet equally significant has been the movement of the nation's population from the country to the city. In 1790, the first U.S. census recorded that approximately 95 percent of the population lived in rural areas. By 1990, that figure had fallen to less than 25 percent. The decline of the agricultural way of life, late-nineteenth-century industrialization, and immigration have all contributed to increased urbanization. A more recent trend has been the migration, especially since the 1970s, of people to the Sun Belt states of the South and West, lured by factors as various as economic opportunities in the defense and high-tech industries and good weather. This migration has swelled the size of cities like Houston, Dallas, Tucson, Phoenix, and San Diego, all of which in recent years ranked among the top ten most populous U.S. cities.

## *Rural and Urban Population, 1750–2000*

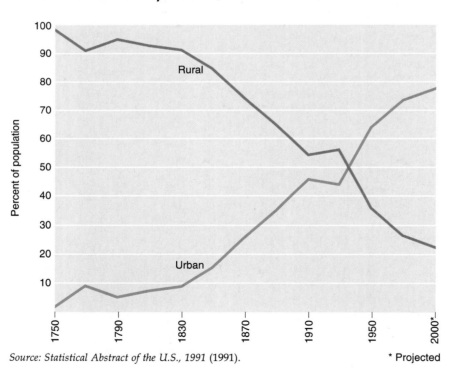

Source: *Statistical Abstract of the U.S., 1991* (1991).　　　　　　* Projected

A DEMOGRAPHIC PROFILE OF THE UNITED STATES AND ITS PEOPLE

THE QUANTITY AND CHARACTER OF IMMIGRATION to the United States has varied greatly over time. During the first major influx, between 1840 and 1860, newcomers hailed primarily from northern and western Europe. From 1880 to 1915, when rates soared even more dramatically, the profile changed, with 80 percent of the "new immigration" coming from central, eastern, and southern Europe. Following World War I, strict quotas reduced the flow considerably. Note also the significant falloff during the years of the Great Depression and World War II. The sources of immigration during the last half century have changed significantly, with the majority of people coming from Latin America, the Caribbean, and Asia. The latest surge during the 1980s brought more immigrants to the United States than in any decade except 1901–1910.

## Rates of Immigration, 1820–1994

| Year | Number | Percent of Total Population |
|------|--------|-----------------------------|
| 1821–1830 | 151,824 | 1.6 |
| 1831–1840 | 599,125 | 4.6 |
| 1841–1850 | 1,713,521 | 10.0 |
| 1851–1860 | 2,598,214 | 11.2 |
| 1861–1870 | 2,314,824 | 7.4 |
| 1871–1880 | 2,812,191 | 7.1 |
| 1881–1890 | 5,246,613 | 10.5 |
| 1891–1900 | 3,687,546 | 5.8 |
| 1901–1910 | 8,795,386 | 11.6 |
| 1911–1920 | 5,735,811 | 6.2 |
| 1921–1930 | 4,107,209 | 3.9 |
| 1931–1940 | 528,431 | 0.4 |
| 1941–1950 | 1,035,039 | 0.7 |
| 1951–1960 | 2,515,479 | 1.6 |
| 1961–1970 | 3,321,677 | 1.8 |
| 1971–1980 | 4,493,300 | 2.2 |
| 1981–1990 | 7,338,100 | 3.0 |
| 1991 | 1,827,167 | 7.2 |
| 1992 | 973,977 | 3.8 |
| 1993 | 904,292 | 3.5 |
| 1994 | 804,416 | 3.0 |

*Source: Historical Statistics of the U.S., Colonial Times to 1970 (1975), Statistical Abstract of the U.S., 1996 (1996).*

## *Major Trends in Immigration, 1820–1990*

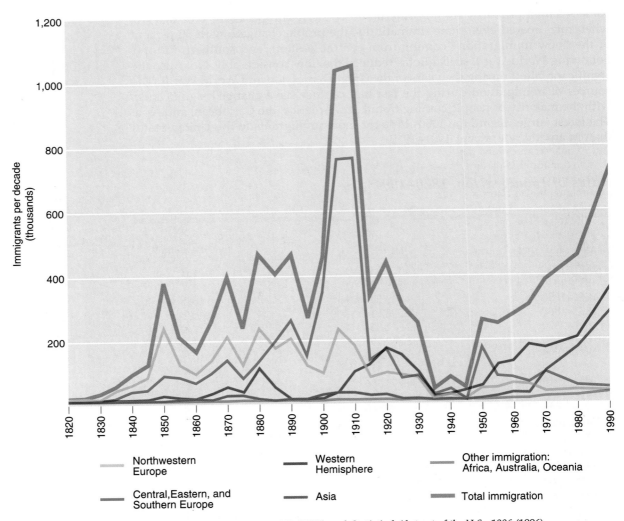

Source: *Historical Statistics of the U.S., Colonial Times to 1970* (1975) and *Statistical Abstract of the U.S., 1996* (1996).

# Appendix III. Research Resources in U.S. History

While doing research in history, you will use the library to track down primary and secondary sources and to answer questions that arise as you learn more about your topic. This appendix suggests helpful indexes, references, periodicals, and sources of primary documents. It also offers an overview of electronic resources available through the Internet. The materials listed here are not carried at all libraries, but they will give you an idea of the range of sources available. Remember, too, that librarians are an extremely helpful resource. They can direct you to useful materials throughout your research process.

## Bibliographies and Indexes

*American Historical Association Guide to Historical Literature.* 3rd ed. New York: Oxford University Press, 1995. Offers 27,000 citations to important historical literature, arranged in forty-eight sections covering theory, international history, and regional history. An indispensable guide recently updated to include current trends in historical research.

*American History and Life.* Santa Barbara: ABC-Clio, 1964–. Covers publications of all sorts on U.S. and Canadian history and culture in a chronological/regional format, with abstracts and alphabetical indexes. Available in computerized format. The most complete ongoing bibliography for American history.

Freidel, Frank Burt. *Harvard Guide to American History.* Cambridge: Harvard University Press, Belknap Press, 1974. Provides citations to books and articles on American history published before 1970. The first volume is arranged topically, the second chronologically. Though it does not cover current scholarship, it is a classic and remains useful for tracing older publications.

Prucha, Francis Paul. *Handbook for Research in American History: A Guide to Bibliographies and Other Reference Works.* 2nd rev. ed. Lincoln: University of Nebraska Press, 1994. Introduces a variety of research tools, including electronic ones. A good source to consult when planning an in-depth research project.

## General Overviews

*Dictionary of American Biography.* New York: Scribner's, 1928–1937, with supplements. Gives substantial biographies of prominent Americans in history.

*Dictionary of American History.* New York: Scribner's, 1976. An encyclopedia of terms, places, and concepts in U.S. history; other more specialized sets include the *Encyclopedia of North American Colonies* and the *Encyclopedia of the Confederacy.*

*Dictionary of Concepts in History.* New York: Greenwood, 1986. Contains essays defining concepts in historiography and describing how the concepts were formed; excellent bibliographies.

*Encyclopedia of American Social History.* New York: Scribner's, 1993. Surveys topics such as religion, class, gender, race, popular culture, regionalism, and everyday life from pre-Columbian to modern times.

*Encyclopedia of the United States in the Twentieth Century.* New York: Scribner's, 1996. An ambitious overview of American cultural, social, and intellectual history in broad articles arranged topically. Each article is followed by a thorough and very useful bibliography for further research.

## Specialized Information

*Black Women in America: An Historical Encyclopedia.* Brooklyn: Carlson, 1993. A scholarly compilation of biographical and topical articles that constitute a definitive history of African American women.

Carruth, Gordon. *The Encyclopedia of American Facts and Dates.* 9th ed. New York: HarperCollins, 1993. Covers American history chronologically from 986 to the present, offering information on treaties, battles, explorations, popular culture, philosophy, literature, and so on, mixing significant events with telling trivia. Tables allow for reviewing a year from a variety of angles. A thorough index helps pinpoint specific facts in time.

Cook, Chris. *Dictionary of Historical Terms.* 2nd ed. New York: Peter Bendrick, 1990. Covers a wide variety of terms—events, places, institutions, and topics—in history for all periods and places in a remarkably small package. A good place for quick identification of terms in the field.

*Dictionary of Afro-American Slavery.* New York: Greenwood, 1985. Surveys important people, events, and topics, with useful bibliographies; similar works include *Dictionary of the Vietnam War, Historical Dictionary of the New Deal*, and *Historical Dictionary of the Progressive Era.*

Knappman-Frost, Elizabeth. *The ABC-Clio Companion to Women's Progress in America.* Santa Barbara: ABC-Clio, 1994. Covers American women who were notable for their time as well as topics and organizations that have been significant in women's quest for equality. Each article is brief; there are a chronology and a bibliography at the back of the book.

United States. Bureau of the Census. *Historical Statistics of the United States, Colonial Times to 1970.* Washington, D.C.: Government Printing Office, 1975. Offers vital statistics, economic figures, and social data for the United States. An index at the back helps locate tables by subject. For statistics since 1970, consult the annual *Statistical Abstract of the United States.*

## Primary Resources

There are many routes to finding contemporary material for historical research. You may search your library catalog using the name of a prominent historical figure as an author; you may also find anthologies covering particular themes or periods in history. Consider also the following special materials for your research.

### The Press

*American Periodical Series, 1741–1900.* Ann Arbor: University Microfilms, 1946–1979. Microfilm collection of periodicals from the colonial period to the turn of the century. An index identifies periodicals that focused on particular topics.

*Herstory Microfilm Collection.* Berkeley: Women's History Research Center, 1973. A microfilm collection of alternative feminist periodicals published between 1960 and 1980. Offers an interesting documentary history of the women's movement.

*New York Times.* New York: New York Times, 1851–. Many libraries have this newspaper on microfilm going back to its beginning in 1851. An index is available to locate specific dates and pages of news stories; it also provides detailed chronologies of events as they were reported in the news.

*Readers' Guide to Periodical Literature.* New York: Wilson, 1900–. This index to popular magazines started in 1900; an earlier index, *Poole's Index to Periodical Literature*, covers 1802–1906, though it does not provide such thorough indexing.

## Diaries, Pamphlets, Books

*The American Culture Series.* Ann Arbor: University Microfilms, 1941–1974. A microfilm set, with a useful index, featuring books and pamphlets published between 1493 and 1875.

*American Women's Diaries.* New Canaan: Readex, 1984–. A collection of reproductions of women's diaries. There are different series for different regions of the country.

*The March of America Facsimile Series.* Ann Arbor: University Microfilms, 1966. A collection of more than ninety facsimiles of travel accounts to the New World published in English or English translation from the fifteenth through the nineteenth century.

*Women in America from Colonial Times to the Twentieth Century.* New York: Arno, 1974. A collection of reprints of dozens of books written by women describing women's lives and experiences in their own words.

## Government Documents

*Congressional Record.* Washington, D.C.: Government Printing Office, 1874–. Covers daily debates and proceedings of Congress. Earlier series were called *Debates and Proceedings in the Congress of the United States* and *The Congressional Globe.*

*Foreign Relations of the United States.* Washington, D.C.: Department of State, 1861–. A collection of documents from 1861, including diplomatic papers, correspondence, and memoranda, that provides a documentary record of U.S. foreign policy.

*Public Papers of the Presidents.* Washington, D.C.: Office of the Federal Register, 1957–. Includes major documents issued by the executive branch from the Hoover administration to the present.

*Serial Set.* Washington, D.C.: Government Printing Office, 1789–1969. A huge collection of congressional documents, available in many libraries on microfiche, with a useful index.

## Local History Collections

State and county historical societies often house a wealth of historical documents; consider their resources when planning your research—you may find yourself working with material that no one else has analyzed before.

# Internet Resources

The Internet has been a useful place for scholars to communicate and publish information in recent years. Electronic discussion lists, electronic journals, and primary texts are among the resources available for historians. The following sources are good places to find historical information. You can also search the World Wide Web using any of a number of search engines. However, bear in mind that there is no board of editors screening Internet sites for accuracy or usefulness, and the search engines generally rely on free-text searches rather than subject headings. Be critical of all of your sources, particularly those found on the Internet. Note that when this book went to press, the sites listed below were active and maintained.

*American Memory: Historical Collection from the National Digital Library Program.* <http://rs6.loc.gov/amhome .html> An Internet site that features digitized primary source materials from the Library of Congress, among them African American pamphlets, Civil War photographs, documents from the Continental Congress and the Constitutional Convention of 1774–1790, materials on woman suffrage, and oral histories.

*Decisions of the U.S. Supreme Court.* <http://supct.law .cornell.edu/supct> This database can be used to search for information on various Supreme Court cases. Although the site primarily covers cases that occurred after 1990, there is information on some earlier historic cases. The justices' opinions, as originally written, are also included.

*Directory of Scholarly and Professional Electronic Conferences.* <http://n2h2.com/KOVAKS> A good place to find out what electronic conversations are going on in a scholarly discipline. Includes a good search facility and instructions on how to connect to e-mail discussion lists, newsgroups, and interactive chat sites with academic content. Once identified, these conferences are good places to raise questions, find out what controversies are currently stirring the profession, and even find out about grants and jobs.

*Douglass Archives of American Public Address.* <http://douglass.speech.nwu.edu> An electronic archive of American speeches and documents by a variety of people from Jane Addams to Jonathan Edwards to Theodore Roosevelt.

*Historical Text Archive.* <http://www.msstate.edu /Archives/History> A Web interface for the oldest and largest Internet site for historical documents. Includes sections on Native American, African American, and U.S. history, in which can be found texts of the Declaration of Independence, the U.S. Constitu-

tion, the Constitution of Iroquois Nations, World War II surrender documents, photograph collections, and a great deal more. These can be used online or saved as files.

*History Links from Yahoo!* <http://www.yahoo.com /Humanities/History> A categorically arranged and frequently updated site list for all types of history. Some of the sources are more useful than others, but this can be a helpful gateway to some good information.

*Index of Civil War Information.* <http://www.cwc.lsu .edu/cwc/civlink.htm> Compiled by the United States Civil War Center, this index lists everything from diaries to historic battlefields to reenactments.

*Index of Native American Resources on the Internet.* <http:// www.hanksville.org/NAresources> A vast index of Native American resources organized by category. Within the history category, links are organized under subcategories: oral history, written history, geographical areas, timelines, and photographs and photographic archives. A central place to come in the search for information on Native American history.

*Index of Resources for Historians.* <http://www.ukans .edu/history> A vast list of more than 1,700 links to sites of interest to historians, arranged alphabetically by general topic. Some links are to sources for general reference information, but most are on historical topics. A good place to start an exploration of Internet resources.

*Internet Archive of Texts and Documents.* <http://history .hanover.edu/texts.html> As stated on its home page, the purpose of this site is to make primary sources available to students and faculty. Arranged chronologically, geographically, and by subject, the site lists speeches, reports, and other primary-document links. It also includes some secondary sources on each subject.

*Internet Resources for Students of Afro-American History.* <http://www.libraries.rutgers.edu/rulib/socsci/hist /afrores.htm> A good place to begin research on topics in African American history. The site is indexed and linked to a wide variety of sources, including primary documents, text collections, and archival sources on African American history. Individual documents such as slave narratives and petitions, the Fugitive Slave Acts, and speeches by W. E. B. Du Bois, Booker T. Washington, and Martin Luther King Jr. are categorized by century.

*The Martin Luther King Jr. Papers Project.* <http://www .stanford.edu/group/King> Organized by Stanford University, this site gives information about Martin Luther King Jr. and offers some of his writings.

*NativeWeb.* <http://www.nativeweb.org> One of the best-organized and most-accessible sites available on

Native American issues, *NativeWeb* combines an events calendar and message board with history, statistics, a list of news sources, archives, new and updated related sites each week, and documents. The text is indexed and can be searched by subject, nation, and geographic region.

*Perry-Castañeda Library Map Collection.* <http://www.lib.utexas.edu/Libs/PCL/Map_collection/Map_collection.html> The University of Texas at Austin library has put over seven hundred United States maps on the Web for viewing by students and professors alike.

*Smithsonian Institution.* <http://www.si.edu> Organized by subject, such as military history or Hispanic/Latino American resources, this site offers selected links to sites hosted by Smithsonian Institution museums and organizations. Content includes graphics of museum pieces and relevant textual information, book suggestions, maps, and links.

*United States History Index.* <http://www.ukans.edu/~usa> Maintained by a history professor and arranged by subject, such as women's history, labor history, and agricultural history, this index provides links to a variety of other sites. Although the list is extensive, it does not include a synopsis of each site, which makes finding specific information a time-consuming process.

*United States History Resources by Period.* <http://www.cms.ccsd.k12.co.us/SONY/Intrecs/byperiod.htm> This list of links to a variety of history sites is arranged chronologically and updated periodically.

*United States Holocaust Memorial Museum.* <http://www.ushmm.org/learn.htm> This site contains information about the Holocaust Museum in Washington, D.C., in particular and the Holocaust in general, and it lists links to related sites.

*Women's History Resources.* <http://www.mcps.k12.md.us/curriculum/socialstd/Women_Bookmarks.html> An extensive listing of women's history sources available on the Internet. The site indexes resources on subjects as diverse as woman suffrage, women in the workplace, and celebrated women writers. Some of the links are to equally-vast indexes, providing an overwhelming wealth of information.

# INDEX

final phase of, 665–670
first, 647–652
labor and, 658–660
legislation of, **648(t)**
Reagan and, 833, 838, 857
second, **655–665,** 669
Supreme Court and, 666
Truman and, 706, 727
women in, **661–663,** 662(i)
World War II and, 675, 680, 685
New England. *See also* Pilgrims;
Puritanism; *specific states*
in 1950s, 743
agriculture in, 16
black population in, 109
British strategy and, 169, 170(m),
176, 178
church membership in, 124
compared with Chesapeake Bay
colony, 82, 83, 94
Dominion of, 98, 99
economy of, 89
eighteenth-century, **106–109**
Embargo Act of 1807 and, 241, 243
immigrants from, 451
immigration to, 444, 463
mill towns in, 511
opposition to Louisiana Purchase,
239–240, 240(i)
opposition to War of 1812, 244, 245,
247
population in, 106, 109
religion in, 65, **82–91,** 204
Sabbath laws in, 204
scalping in, 456
in seventeenth century, 84(m)
taxes and, 220, 278
towns in, 83, 84(m)
war with Indians in, 97–98
witchcraft in, **92**
Woman's Crusade in, 525
New England Anti-Slavery Society,
274
New England Emigrant Aid
Company, 368
New Era (1920s), **614–622**
automobile industry and, 620
end of, 630, 634
New Deal and, 661
social change in, 622–628
New Federalism, 815
Newfoundland, 32, 47
New France, 126
New Freedom (Wilson campaign
slogan), 571, 593, 646
New Guinea, 684, 699
New Hampshire, 81, 107, 191, 220,
261
Democratic Party in, 281
ratification of Constitution, 203,
206, 211

New Haven (Connecticut)
nonconsumption in, 144
town plan of, 87(m)
New Jersey, 77, **95,** 125, 149, 375
Articles of Confederation and, 189
Continental army in, 176, 178
Continental Congress and, 187
FDR and, 666
holding companies in, 483–484
indictment of Burr, 237
loyalists in, 169, 173(m), 174
as proprietary colony, 91, 94
ratification of Constitution, 203
in Revolutionary War, 170(m), 171
voting rights in, 213–214, 248
New Jersey Plan, **201**
New Jerusalem, 249
New Left (1960s), 758, 775, 776, 842
New Mexico, 45, 337, 355
ancient Americans in, 2(i), 3, 6, 13
becomes territory, 357
Gadsden Purchase and, 361
Indian land in, 774
Indian reservations in, 459
Mexican War and, 341, 342, 345
popular sovereignty and, 357, 362,
367
railroads and, 446(i)
as territory, 445
New Netherland, 91, 94. *See also* New
York
New Orleans (Louisiana), 134, 233,
239, 260, 294, 308, 392, 424
New Orleans, Battle of (1814), **246,
246(m),** 247, 254
Newport (Rhode Island), 138, 169,
177, 195
Jewish community in, 205(i)
New Right (1980s), 835, 842
New South. *See* South: New
New Spain, 126
in sixteenth century, 39(m), 41, 42
mixed races in, 43(i)
*vs.* English colonies, 74, 99
Newspapers. *See also* Journalism
antislavery, 381
elections and, 258
FDR and, 662(i)
labor movement and, 532, 533,
534(i)
*New York Times,* 794, 801
partisan, 265
penny press, 269–270
political parties and, 229, 230, 265,
281, 437
public culture and, 258, 371(i)
Republican, 229, 230
Spanish-American War (1898) and,
544, 545, 546–547
strikes and, 639
Newton, Sir Isaac (1642–1727), 124

New World, 2–7, 18, 22, 26, **30–33,** 41
Europe and, **45–47,** 48
slave societies in, 289
New York Central Railroad, 478
New York City, 464, 470, 471, 496,
601(i), 612(i), 630
architecture of, 470
boss rule in, 467–468
British capture of, 169
British strategy and, 169, 174, 178,
180, 181
Civil War riots in, 402
as commercial city, 96, 261
Continental Congress in, 189, 218
film industry in, 623
French navy and, 177
in Great Depression, 636
Harlem Renaissance in, 626
import tax and, 195
independence and, 166–167
leisure activities in, 512–513
loyalists in, 173
punishment of slaves (1741) in, 112
reaction to Sugar Act of 1764, 138
in Revolutionary War, 178, 181
settlement houses in, 555
Stamp Act (1765) and, 140
transportation to and from, 216(m),
259, 259(m), 260
Washington's inaugural in, 210(i),
211
New York Female Moral Reform
Society, 273
New York State, 77, 103, 462, 489, 490
Antifederalism in, 206, 207
Articles of Confederation and, 200
British strategy and, 169, 170(m)
Cleveland, Grover, and, 492
Continental Congress and, 161, 164
FDR as governor of, 645
immigration to, 444, 463, 463(m),
500
mining industry and, 453
population of, 89(f)
population of (1900), 462
as proprietary colony, 91, 94
ratification of Constitution, 202–
203, 207
religion in, 99, 123, 204, 271
Revolutionary War debt of, 220
Roosevelt, Theodore, and, 561
uprisings in, 99
upstate, 81
Woman's Crusade in, 525
woman suffrage in, 595
New York Suspending Act (1765), 143
New Zealand, 683, 694, 699
Nez Perce Indians, 454
Ngo Dinh Diem (1901–1963), 735, 787
Ngo Dinh Nhu, 787
Nguyen Cao Ky, 790